Psychology and National Health Insurance

A Sourcebook

Edited by Charles A. Kiesler
        Nicholas A. Cummings
        Gary R. VandenBos

American Psychological Association, Inc.

368.42
P97

**Library of Congress Cataloging in
Publication Data**

Main entry under title:

Psychology and national health insurance.

Bibliography: p. 637
Includes index.
1. Insurance, Mental health—United States—
Addresses, essays, lectures. 2. Insurance, Health—
United States—Addresses, essays, lectures.
3. Mental health services—United States—Addresses,
essays, lectures. 4. Psychology—United States—
Addresses, essays, lectures.
I. Kiesler, Charles A. II. Cummings, Nicholas A.
III. VandenBos, Gary R. [DNLM: 1. Psychology—
Collected works. 2. National health insurance,
United States—Collected works. 3. Psychology,
Clinical—Collected works. 4. Community mental
health services—United States—Collected works.
5. Insurance, Psychiatric—United States—
Collected works. W275 AA1 P98]
HD7102.6.U5P76   368.4'2   79-19251

ISBN 0-912704-13-6 (clothbound)
ISBN 0-912704-11-X (paperbound)

Published by the American Psychological Association, Inc.
1200 Seventeenth Street, N.W., Washington, D.C. 20036
Copyright © 1979 by the American Psychological Association.
All rights reserved.

Contents

v

3
Current Legal and Legislative Status of Professional Psychology

4
Experience with Systems of Delivery of Services

7
Issues in Professional Training

Prologue

Scientific and professional psychologists have recently become increasingly aware of and engaged in issues related to public systems of delivery of mental health services. Partly stimulated by the historical maturation of psychology as a science and profession, partly resulting from a perceived need to broaden our collective search for research and training funds, and partly reflecting an increasing desire to demonstrate the public usefulness of psychology, psychologists' interests have converged on national health insurance.

Whatever the ultimate design of national health insurance, it will probably rank as the most important social program of our time. Specifically with regard to mental health benefits included under national health insurance, psychologists are interested in the scientific underpinnings of mental health treatment, its evaluation and cost-effectiveness, and social responsibility to the consumer of such services. Recent work in these various areas of interest has burgeoned. This edited collection, for example, includes almost exclusively work published since 1975.

No systematic effort has previously been made to bring the potential contribution of psychology before the public or the broad psychology community. All three of us, in our testimony before Congress and in interaction with heads of relevant federal and state agencies, have felt the need for an easily available collection that could adequately represent the range and rapid development of work in psychology. Although this collection was conceived for this limited purpose, it seemed worthwhile to share it with others as well.

This book attempts to deal with critical issues while they are still being discussed and before final national decisions are made. The various aspects of national health insurance—scientific, professional, social responsibility, and training—will become, in our opinion, controversial and critical issues for psychology in the coming decade or two. This book should be of interest to a substantial proportion of psychologists, since it deals with evaluative, scientific, and consumer issues in addition to areas of professional concern. We hope that the volume can be a teaching aid as well.

The book is divided into eleven sections, each with a short introduction. Our intent was to sample the flavor of the national discussion and include divergent points of view where controversy existed, to stimulate psychologists into some consideration of the emerging issues in this critical field, and to provide nonpsychologists and other decision makers with some sense of what psychology has to offer. We have made little effort to edit the individual contributions, although in several places they have been updated. Some of the issues are controversial, but we felt the reader's critical purpose could be better served by fuller, albeit fewer, reports.

In the long process of collecting the material and preparing this volume, we were aided by numerous people. We are indebted to the individuals whose work appears here, and we appreciate their timely response to our requests. It is because of the scientific and professional efforts of these and other psychologists that this volume is both needed and possible. We further appreciate the assistance of those who read and offered comments on the drafts of material newly written for this book: Gary Gottfredson, Walter Batchelor, Chris Pino, and Jan Woodring. Finally, we wish to acknowledge those Central Office staff who assisted in the development of the manuscript—John Estes, Carla Waltz, Jennifer Fransen, and Mark Stover—and in the final production of this volume—Brenda Bryant, Anita DeVivo, and Shelley Hammond.

We find the question of systems of mental health care delivery both intellectually fascinating and of great importance to psychologists and the nation. In the spirit of stimulating interest in this area we offer the present volume.

Charles A. Kiesler
Nicholas A. Cummings
Gary R. VandenBos

June 1979

1

National Voices

Psychology is relatively young as a science and a profession, being only about 100 years old. Psychology in general and clinical psychology in particular have experienced astronomical growth in the last 30 years, and much of it can be attributed to events related to World War II and its aftermath. Areas of applied psychology, particularly those related to physical health care, have shown an even more recent spurt in growth. Because of this rapid development, psychology faces problems related to identity and public knowledge that take on special relevance as national health insurance is considered.

The public has the most up-to-date conceptualization of professional psychology through its use of psychological services. Approximately 3 million patients receive 19 million hours of psychological services annually (see Gottfredson & Dyer in Section 2 of this book). In light of the possible advent of national health insurance, it is important that up-to-date information on the amount and range of services provided by psychologists be readily accessible. This information is needed to insure that the role of psychologists within a national health insurance plan is based on fact, not outdated perceptions of the profession. It is particularly necessary that such current information be available to government officials, who are often more familiar with medical practice than mental health practice and are often unaware that professional psychologists are fully trained, autonomous health care providers.

The articles in this section concern the status and contribution of psychology to health and mental health and psychology's possible contributions to national health insurance. In the first paper, Nicholas Cummings traces the development of third-party payment for health services in reviewing the growth of professional psychology and its struggle to establish autonomy, identity, and direction. Next, Patrick DeLeon considers the implication of national health policy on the future of professional psychology as well as on the range and quality of services available to the public. He notes how bias, lack of accurate knowledge, and short-run political pressures can result in legislation damaging to the goal of high-quality, comprehensive national health care. He calls for organized psychology to expand its involvement in policy issues on behalf of the public interest so as to maintain a broadly defined, high-quality, accessible health care system responsive to the needs and wishes of consumers. In the third article, Herbert Rie illustrates how many of the current efforts to secure third-party reimbursement and professional autonomy are similar to earlier professional efforts to secure academic freedom and research support. Such concern over apparently parochial issues is a phase of professional growth not unrelated to the public interest.

Charles Kiesler addresses three articles to a range of issues relevant to the training, status, and orientation of psychologists. The first paper describes the diversity and breadth of the science of psychology and notes the wide range of research topics that psychologists are actively investigating. There are other types of psychologists than health service providers, and they make contributions to research, education, and administration. Kiesler underscores the fact that all psychologists receive training in research as part of their professional education, a fact illustrating psychology's strong empirical orientation. In addition, he notes that clear standards exist for identifying health service providers in psychology, such as the criteria developed by the Council for the National Register of Health Service Providers in Psychology.

Kiesler's second paper includes the American Psychological Association's position statement on national health care, a summary of the recognition of psychology as of that date, and some information on the potential cost savings of the use of psychological services. He notes the Association's support for individual freedom of choice among practitioners, equal access to dignified and confidential health care services, including prevention services as well as treatment, consumer participation in the evaluation of services, increased research into the causes of mental and behavioral problems, and continuing rigorous evaluation of the quality, effectiveness, and availability of health care services.

The third Kiesler paper consists of testimony briefly stating five principles on the subject of national health insurance to the Secretary of the Department of Health, Education, and Welfare. The thrust of these principles is that mental health benefits need to be included in a cost-efficient, accessible, and public-oriented manner and that evaluation/accountability mechanisms should be an integral component of any national health insurance program, with measures geared toward prospectively articulated national outcome goals and consumer participation in the planning and evaluation of national health insurance.

Nicholas Cummings was one of the first researchers to conduct cost/benefit research concerning psychological services within a total health care system. The second Cummings reprint included in this section is testimony to the U.S. Senate regarding Medicare reform. Presenting a brief review of 20 years of health-services research conducted at Kaiser-Permanente, Cummings argues for the inclusion of mental health as an integral component of Medicare and national health insurance programming because the availability of mental health services dramatically reduces subsequent use of surgical, in-hospital, and diagnostic laboratory services. NIMH recently reviewed 17 replications of the original Follette and Cummings research and found that 16 of them supported the original findings.

All of the "national voices" to this point have been those of psychologists. National health care policy, however, covers a very large area, and psychology (and mental health) represents only a small part. The primary source of policy development is still the executive branch of government, although the roles of both the legislative and judicial branches have increased in recent years. Moreover, the executive branch influence is often indirect, determined by factors such as how an area of analysis is defined or how options sections of reports to Congress are prepared. The final two reports in this section provide a sample of the perspective of the federal government's mental health sector on mental health benefits within national health insurance.

The first is an NIMH report on the utilization and cost of mental health services that is noteworthy because it illustrates both the best and the worst in policy analysis. In its attempt to gather data from which to guide policy, the report is praiseworthy. NIMH reports, for example, that the average number of outpatient mental health visits among over 400 federally funded community mental health centers was 5.3 sessions in 1973, and it views this rate of utilization as relatively low. It accurately notes that the rate has been stable over the years and basically consistent with utilization rates among government programs, insurance plans, and health maintenance organizations (HMOs). It also acknowledges that the absolute number of patient care episodes has increased, as has the population, and notes the trend toward increased emphasis on outpatient care (although inpatient care still dominates in terms of costs). However, a bias toward psychiatry and a lack of meaningful analysis of central assumptions are also evident in the report. The "remedicalization" of mental health services is apparent in the use of such terms as *medical mental health services* and in the noncritical acceptance of the value of nonspecific, nonmonitored "mental health services" of variable quality provided by general-practice physicians. The fact that NIMH must assume a simple extension of data from psychiatrists to psychologists results from its regular failure to collect (or support the collection of) data on psychologists and/or to collect it in a manner meaningfully related to policy issues and comparable to the data on psychiatrists.

The second of the government-prepared reports is a summary of the recommendations of the President's Commission on Mental Health.

These statements of direction and goals represent core recommendations that will influence developments in mental health for the next decade. Numerous summaries of the Commission's recommendations have been published, but many have a selective bias emphasizing the author's interests and downplaying the disliked or nonvalued aspects. We have chosen to reprint the complete recommendations of the Commission, as they are brief and the thrust of their intent clear. The degree of shared perspective between the President's Commission on Mental Health and the profession of psychology will become apparent throughout the remainder of this volume.

Mental Health and National Health Insurance: A Case History of the Struggle for Professional Autonomy

Nicholas A. Cummings

The article traces the history of the struggle to gain professional and insurance-carrier recognition for psychology. Psychology's future under various national health insurance plans being considered by Congress, NIMH, and private organizations is examined, and several models of mental health service delivery are analyzed.

Paradoxically, the nation that was first to put a man on the moon may be the last major Western power to enact a universal, government-sponsored health system. The reasons for this are varied and complex, and only the highlights can be touched on in an overview. But placing the issue of mental health coverage within the overall perspective of the general issue of national health care is essential to its understanding. Psychology is a relatively recent arrival to the debate on national health insurance. Beginning with a trickle of dedicated interest nearly 20 years ago, the American Psychological Association (APA) now expends a significant portion of its total resources on matters relating to the issue of national health insurance. The way in which the APA became deeply involved in the matter is essentially a case study of one profession's struggle for professional autonomy and recognition.

General History

A universal, government-sponsored health system has been under discussion in the United States for several decades, but not until recently has a majority conceded that national health insurance is imminent and perhaps even overdue. The concept has its modern roots in the latter half of the 19th century, but the present overview begins with the economically depressed years of the 1930s when the possible provision of health services by the government to its citizens was a concept that began to intrigue proponents of the New Deal. The idea was then termed socialized medicine. It was only one of many ideological proposals proffered within the first two Roosevelt administrations, but it was the one that organized medicine was to attack openly and vigorously during the next three decades. Whether or not Congress would have enacted a comprehensive, government-sponsored health system during those years had not a rigorous battle been waged against it by the American Medical Association (AMA) can be left only to conjecture. But the AMA campaign resulted in a negative connotation to the term *socialized medicine*—a phrase that has all but disappeared from the American vocabulary. However, the concept, replaced in the lexicon by the current term of *national health insurance*, received new life in the blizzard of social legislation that characterized the Great Society of the Johnson administration.

In the mid-1960s Congress amended the appropriate 30-year-old Social Security Act to give a sizable portion of citizens, principally the elderly and the poor, a new kind of federally financed health care in the form of two new programs. These programs, Medicare and Medicaid (Titles 18 and 19) of the Social Security Act, were stridently opposed by the AMA. Following defeat in the legislative arena, AMA acquired, almost immediately, a more realistic and enlightened posture under the slogan, "don't oppose, but propose." Accepting federal and state intervention as inevitable, organized medicine now strives to guarantee medicine's control, or at least its preeminence, in whatever legislation is enacted. The strong resistance to outside interference can be at least partially justified by professional and scientific considerations. However, medicine's strident opposition to incursions from government, and more recently from consumer advocates, has its roots in the manner in which medicine began to flourish in the United States.

American medicine grew from a small entrepreneurial system relying heavily upon the apprenticeship model to a giant industry incongruously retaining much of its horse-and-buggy philosophy in the face of modern medical technology and runaway health costs. The image of the benevolent country doctor making calls by horse and buggy is the one that organized medicine would like to maintain in the minds of the public. To a surprising extent it has been successful; television's Marcus Welby is that benevolent country doctor, updated by present and futuristic science and technology and the elimination of house calls. Within the giant health care industry, the small-business individualism of the nation's physicians was safeguarded by an extensive system of medical-practices acts designed to prevent medical practice from falling into the employ or control of nonmedical forces. Small-business individualism, however, had the inadvertent effect of encouraging 19th-century entrepreneurialism. In order to care for the poor, the rich were "soaked." This medical Robin Hoodism never really worked from its inception. It had to be supplemented by a system of private charities which, in turn, had to be supplemented by county hospitals and clinics. This situation resulted in a two-tiered system of health care in which those who had the means visited the private practitioner, while the indigent were relegated to charity or county hospitals and clinics. Even within the private sector two levels of fees emerged, one for the middle class and the other for the carriage trade, with the middle class not infrequently and ignominiously falling into the charity tier in the face of catastrophic illness that could wipe out a

family's entire resources. The incomes of private-practicing physicians were maintained at a high level, while the hospitals balanced their budgets by including the training model within the two-tiered system. Thus, interns and residents struggled to get by on poverty-level salaries. In the public, or charity, sector, care could be excellent for patients in teaching hospitals who were fortunate enough to have an exotic illness considered helpful in the training of physicians. Those suffering from illnesses having little or no teaching value, no matter how serious, were often subjected to overextended stays and overcrowded conditions in substandard settings. The two-tiered system of medicine has survived a series of challenges, not the least of which has been the development of health insurance, and it is with us today in a form perhaps even more pervasive than ever.

The birth of the private health insurance industry was characterized throughout the thirties and forties more by exclusions, limitations, coinsurances, and deductions than by benefits. Encouraged by organized medicine as an acceptable alternative to socialized medicine, the health insurance industry grew in coverage and extensiveness to the point where most working Americans now have some kind of health insurance.

During this same era, various health care schemes have gradually been adopted so that an uncoordinated nonsystem of national health care somewhat like a giant patchwork quilt has evolved. Much of this has been accomplished by successive redefinitions of the concept of "medically needy" beyond the original eligibility of the indigent. Thus, a partial, unplanned national health care system is being created from the welfare model, which is gradually and inadvertently being turned into an unworkable nonmodel characterized by inefficiency and duplication and threatening to survive as an establishment within whatever national health insurance structure is eventually adopted. Interestingly, often those social planners who most decry the waste, duplication, and inefficiency of our current system of private–public care are those who become the most vigorous proponents of the next patch on the quilt.

The first large-scale thrust to promote national health insurance was made in the early

1960s by the labor unions, principally the United Auto Workers (UAW) under the leadership of the late Walter Reuther. Calling together prominent proponents from a widely representative segment of our society, Reuther established the Committee of 100 whose sole purpose was to promote the concept of a universal health care system in the United States. Today this effort is continued by the Committee for National Health Insurance, directed by Max Fine. Although it would be difficult to assess the direct impact of this group, there is virtually no question that the UAW conception of a national health insurance system has emerged in several Congressional bills, particularly those introduced by Senator Edward Kennedy and Representative Martha Griffiths.

National Health Insurance Versus National Health Care

Although national health insurance and national health care are often used interchangeably, it is important to point out that they are essentially two distinct national health schemes. *National health insurance* conceives of health services delivered within a variety of public and private institutions and financed by the Social Security system or by a method similar to the Social Security system (i.e., employer/employee contributions). Within *national health care,* on the other hand, the government would own all of the delivery systems in a manner similar to Veterans Administration medical service delivery. Some leadership within the Department of Health, Education, and Welfare and organized labor share a distrust of the private sector and favor national health care. The opposite is true within the majority of the Congress and certainly within the health insurance industry, which inherently resists government interference.

The last several years have seen over three dozen national health bills introduced into Congress, each reflecting the views of sponsors at several points along the continuum from national health insurance to national health care. Table 1 presents a sample of these bills to illustrate some of the similarities and differences. At one extreme, the UAW approach proposes complete health care provided under total government auspices. At the other extreme, the insurance-industry-sponsored bills suggest a system of delivery with minimum disturbance of the private sector. Predictably, most bills reflect an amalgam of these two disparate views.

How the APA Became Involved

The struggle to alert the American Psychological Association to the potential impact and implications of an inevitable national health system has spanned two decades and has literally reshaped the face of American psychology. Often bitter, sometimes comical, but always colorful, the movement to involve the APA in national health insurance advocacy demonstrates the dedication of a handful of early activists.

In the late 1950s, through a mechanism he called the National Clinical Liaison Committee, Leonard Small of New York began to circulate a mimeographed sheet warning clinical psychologists that it would not be long before most, if not all, psychotherapy in the United States would be financed by third-party payment. He argued that if psychology were not recognized as a primary mental health provider by insurance carriers and the government, who would comprise the third-party payers, the profession of psychology would suffer economic extinction. One of the first to heed Small's exhortation was Rogers Wright. Wright has spent his professional lifetime insisting that only organized psychology operating within an advocacy stance can assure the autonomy of the science and profession of psychology. He attracted a small number of activists who operated totally outside the APA governance structure for years but who began to be listened to by the state psychological associations, particularly in New York and California. Their objective was to energize the APA.

The first concession to these clinicians' demands came in 1963 when the APA sponsored the Ad hoc Committee on Insurance and Related Social Developments (AHCIRSD, which was acronymed a-curse-ed). The name derived from the conviction held at the time on the part of APA's Board of Professional Affairs that the subject of insurance was neither respectable enough for a standing committee nor important enough to occupy an ad hoc committee's entire

Table 1: *A Comparison of Major National Health Insurance Bills in the 94th Congress (as of June 1975). Prepared by the Committee for National Health Insurance.*

Legislative Proposal	Principal Congressional Sponsors & Endorsements	Concept	Coverage
Health Security Act S.3 HR 21	Representative Corman (D-Calif.) Senator Kennedy (D-Mass.) Committee for National Health Insurance AFL-CIO Church Groups Senior Citizens Consumer Groups Health Professionals	Universal, federalized comprehensive health insurance plan with provisions for reorganization of the health care system and development of health resources.	Covers all U.S. residents. Medicare repealed; Medicaid retained in part to cover services beyond benefits provided.
National Health Care Services, Financing & Reorganization Act HR 1	Representative Ullman (D-Ore.) American Hospital Association	Federally approved comprehensive private health insurance through (1) a plan requiring employers to provide private health insurance for employees, (2) a plan for individuals, (3) federally contracted coverage for the poor, the medically needy and the aged. Promotes non-profit Health Care Corporations (HCC).	Available to all U.S. residents except federal employees. Employers must provide plan for employees; self-employed covered through private purchase; the poor, medically needy and aged by federal government; those eligible, under unemployment compensation. Medicare replaced; Medicaid federalized, covers services beyond benefits provided.
The National Health Care Act of 1975 HR 5990 S 1438	Representative Burleson (D-Texas) Senator McIntyre (D-N.H.) Health Insurance Industry of America	A voluntary approach based on federal income tax incentives for employees and employers to encourage purchase of a minimum package of approved private health insurance, through (1) employer or (2) individual (private) plans, and (3) grants to states to buy insurance for the poor and the uninsurable through a state insurance pool (state plan). Includes minimal provisions to improve health care delivery.	Voluntary for all U.S. residents. Medicare continued; Medicaid covers services beyond benefits provided. Consumer could refuse to purchase. Non-citizen residents would not be eligible.
Comprehensive Health Care Insurance Act of 1975 HR 6222	Representative Fulton (D-Tenn.) Representative Duncan (R-Tenn.) American Medical Association	Mandates employers to offer qualified private health insurance to employees and families. Federal cash subsidies or tax credits to employers if program increases total payroll costs by 3% or more. Federal assistance via tax credits for non-employed and self-employed.	Voluntary acceptance of coverage by employees, non-employed and self-employed. Medicare population eligible for benefits equal to those for the general population. Health Insurance for the unemployed.
Long-Ribicoff (as introduced in the 93rd Congress)	Senator Long (D-La.) Senator Ribicoff (D-Conn.)	Three-part federal program providing (1) catastrophic coverage for all, (2) a medical assistance plan with basic benefits for the poor and medically needy, and (3) voluntary program for certification of private insurance to cover basic benefits.	Catastrophic coverage: all U.S. residents covered by Social Security. Medical assistance plan: all persons now receiving Medicaid plus others meeting certain income limits, varying according to family size, who are considered medically needy. Medicare continued; Medicaid federalized.

Benefit Structure	Financing
Benefits cover the entire range of personal health care services including prevention and early detection of disease without coinsurance, deductibles or waiting period. Some limitations on adult dental care, psychiatric care, long-term nursing home care and drugs. Grants to develop social care services to aid chronically ill, aged and other homebound patients.	50% from general tax revenue and 50% from a 3½% tax on employer payroll, a 1% tax on the first $21,150 a year in wages and a 2½% tax on the first $21,150 a year of self employment income and non-earned income all to be administered through a Health Security Trust Fund.
Phased in over 5-year period, with limits and/or copayments on: hospital in- and outpatient services; skilled nursing facility and nursing home care; services of physicians and other health professionals; medical appliances; outpatient prescription drugs; laboratory and x-ray services; home health services; in- and outpatient mental health services; and ambulance services. (Reduced limits for inpatient mental health, alcoholism, and drug abuse services for Health Care corporation [HCC] registrants.) Outpatient health maintenance services, such as periodic health evaluations; well-baby care; and vision and dental services through age 12—all without limits or copayments. Catastrophic coverage after out-of-pocket expenditures reach specified levels, related to family size and income.	Employer (minimum of 75%) and employee premium payments for purchase of private insurance, federal premium subsidy for low income workers. Self-employed pay own premiums at group rates. Low wage employers and self employed eligible for tax credits. Federal subsidies for full or partial purchase of private insurance from general tax revenues for the poor and medically needy, enrollee contributions based on income and family size, with lowest group paying nothing. Medicare, with part A and B merged, financed through present payroll tax and general federal revenues. 10% federal subsidy for HCC registrants. Deductibles and coinsurance for most services.
To be phased-in in two stages with maximum deductible of $100 and coinsurance of 20% with a maximum annual out-of-pocket expense per family per year of $1,000 with exceptions of mental health and dental benefits. In 1977 benefits would include unlimited hospital inpatient and outpatient physical and psychiatric care; physicians' services; 20 outpatient mental health visits; prescription drugs and contraceptive devices; 180 days of skilled nursing and 270 days home health care; certain oral surgery; well-child care. In 1985 coverage for very specific dental care, physical and speech therapy, eyeglasses and periodic physical examinations would be covered.	Complex provisions for purchase of private insurance based on three categories of beneficiaries: (1) employees, (2) individuals, and (3) state health care plans for the poor and near poor. A beneficiary can fall into one of 27 categories. Employer-plan: shared premiums for purchase of private policies; low income employee contributions limited according to wage level. Individual plan: enrollee pays full premium. Federal income tax deduction for employers and enrollees equal to full cost of premium payments for approved insurance; no tax deductions for unapproved plans. State plans: enrollee premium contributions based on income and family size; balance paid with state and federal general revenues through a state insurance pool. Federal share ranges from 70% to 90%.
Inpatient and outpatient hospital care services, 100 days in skilled nursing facility, diagnostic, therapeutic and preventive medical services, home health services, dental care for children 2 through 6, and emergency dental services and oral surgery for all. 20% coinsurance for all services with limits based on family income and ceilings of not more than $1,500 per individual and $2,000 per family.	Premium payments of at least 65% by employers and the rest by employees if they chose to participate. Federal assistance to employers whose payroll costs increased more than 3% because of the program, ranging from 80% of the excessive increase during the first year to 40% in the fifth year. Federal assistance in the form of tax credits for health care insurance for non-employed and self-employed individuals and their families. Amount of federal assistance scaled according to tax liability.
Catastrophic plan: all medical bills after out-of-pocket expenses reach $2,000 per family; all hospital costs over 60 days per person; additional copayments limited to $1,000 per family. Medical assistance plan: Hospital, skilled nursing, and intermediate facility care; home health services; physicians services; x-ray and laboratory medical appliances; prenatal and well-baby care; family planning; periodic screening, diagnosis and treatment to age 18; inpatient mental health care in community health centers. Copayments of $3 for each of first 10 visits to doctor per family. Certified private plans must provide coverage for pre-catastrophic costs with limits on cost sharing.	Catastrophic: .3% increase in Social Security payroll taxes on employees and employers. Medical assistance plan: general federal revenues with state contributions.

Legislative Proposal	Principal Congressional Sponsors & Endorsements	Cost Control Reimbursement of Providers	Quality Control
Health Security Act S.3 HR 21	Representative Corman (D-Calif.) Senator Kennedy (D-Mass.) Committee for National Health Insurance AFL-CIO Church Groups Senior Citizens Consumer Groups Health Professionals	Operates on annual national budget, regional budget, prospective budgets for hospitals and other institutions, negotiated budgets for prepaid group practices and negotiated payments to physicians in solo practice charging on a fee-for-service basis. Providers barred from making additional charges to individuals for services performed within the system.	Establishes quality control commission and national standards for participating professional and institutional providers. Regulation of major surgery and certain other specialist services; national licensure standards and requirements for continuing education.
National Health Care Services, Financing & Reorganization Act HR 1	Representative Ullman (D-Ore.) American Hospital Association	Payment to institutional providers and HCCs on prospectively approved budgets; to physicians on basis of reasonable charges. Both require State Health Commission (SHC) approval, under federal guidelines.	Department of Health sets standards of quality and establishes regulations for all providers with Medicare standards as minimum; SHCs implement regulations and monitor providers. All providers and HCCs must have systems of peer and utilization review.
The National Health Care Act of 1975 HR 5990 S 1438	Representative Burleson (D-Texas) Senator McIntyre (D-N.H.) Health Insurance Industry of America	Payments to institutions based on prospectively approved rates, by category of institution. State commission approves budgets and charge schedules on basis of reasonable charges, subject to HEW review. HMOs paid on per capita basis. Physicians paid on reasonable charges not exceeding customary and prevailing rates.	Except for meeting Medicare standards and regulations to be established for HMOs, no provision for quality control.
Comprehensive Health Care Insurance Act of 1975 HR 6222	Representative Fulton (D-Tenn.) Representative Duncan (R-Tenn.) American Medical Association	NONE	Amendments to PSROs to make them more responsive to Medical Societies.
Long-Ribicoff (as introduced in the 93rd Congress)	Senator Long (D-La.) Senator Ribicoff (D-Conn.)	Same as under Medicare. Payments must be accepted as payment in full under medical assistance program.	Same as under Medicare, including Professional Standards Review Organizations (PSROs).

Health Delivery and Resources	Administration
Health Resources Development Fund established for improving delivery and increasing resources with emphasis on development of various forms of prepaid group practice plans. Provisions for encouraging more efficient organization of existing health manpower, and of training and retraining of health professionals.	Publicly administered program in Department of HEW, five-member, full-time Health Security Board appointed by the President. Ten HEW regions, 200 sub-regions. Advisory councils at all levels with majority of members representing consumers.
Federal funds for development and operation of SHCs. Emphasis on formation of HCCs and outpatient care facilities, with incentives through payment mechanisms, federal grants and loans. Requires establishment of SHCs and HCCs. Funds for development of paramedical personnel. SHCs responsible for all state health planning, certification of need, licensure and approval of provider operations. National Health Services Advisory Council to study need for establishment of federal trust fund for resources development.	Establishes a Cabinet-level Department of Health to set standards for and coordinate all federal health programs. National Health Services Advisory Council at federal level, with consumer representation, reviews all regulations. State Health Commissions (SHCs) implement federal standards and regulate all providers and insurance carriers at state level, including approval of carrier rates and provider charges. Non-profit private or governmental HCCs to coordinate delivery of health services with designated geographic areas. Coverage provided through approved private insurance carriers; federal government contracts with private carriers for subsidized coverage.
Emphasis on creation of outpatient care centers through grants, loans, and loan guarantees. Loans and grants for health manpower development, with priority to shortage areas. Option to join HMOs to be available under all plans. Provisions to strengthen health planning, with increased funds and authority to state and local planning agencies. Presidential Health Policy Board set up to advise on planning and conduct research.	For the private plans, state insurance departments approve policies and monitor financial operations of private carriers. Treasury Department rules on tax status of plan. For state plans, HEW sets standards for operation of plans; state insurance departments supervise the operations. Thus, state insurance departments become the administrators.
Establishes Office of Rural Health within HEW to award grants, contracts, loans and loan guarantees for projects pertaining to rural health care delivery. Otherwise, no changes in present system.	A 15-member Health Insurance Advisory Board consisting of the Secretary of HEW, the Commissioner of Internal Revenue, six M.D.s, 1 D.O., 1 D.D.S., and the remaining five appointed by the President from the general public to prescribe regulations and federal standards for States' Insurance Departments and review effectiveness of the programs.
Same as Medicare; provides for HMO option.	Through Social Security Administration. HEW Secretary certifies private plans in voluntary program, based on adequacy of coverage, conditions of eligibility, and availability. Insurers not offering certified policies ineligible to serve as Medicare carriers or intermediaries.

attention. The Committee's chair, Milton Theaman, not only had the task of persuading insurance companies to recognize the services of psychologists but also had to constantly defend the activities of AHCIRSD as a legitimate APA endeavor. The demand by clinical psychologists for parity with psychiatrists tended to be viewed as an attempt to line the pockets of private practitioners, and it was difficult to keep the critics focused on the major issue of the professional autonomy of psychologists. If psychology were ever to provide alternative delivery modalities to the medical model it first had to achieve recognition and independence.

During its five years of existence AHCIRSD did, against overwhelming odds, persuade a handful of insurance carriers (representing an almost infinitesimal percentage of the insured) to recognize psychologists. This very modest achievement was offset by the success in persuading the APA to establish, in 1968, the standing Committee on Health Insurance (COHI). The first COHI chair, Nicholas Cummings, who had also served on AHCIRSD, immediately abandoned the previous strategy and devised the so-called freedom-of-choice legislation which by 1978 amended the insurance codes of 29 states. This amendment provided that any health insurance that reimburses for the services of a psychiatrist must also reimburse for those of a qualified psychologist. Thus the consumer was granted, for the first time, the freedom to choose between the two professions. Predictably, as with licensure or certification for psychologists, most or all states will eventually adopt such freedom-of-choice insurance legislation. The legislative struggle for recognition could stop here were it not for the implications of national health insurance. Should a redefinition under national health insurance exclude psychologists as independent providers (as was originally the case in Medicare and Medicaid), the successes won by this freedom-of-choice legislation would become irrelevant.

Indeed, it was the exclusion of psychologists as providers under Medicare and Medicaid that prompted professional psychologists to renew their efforts to move the APA into a legislative advocacy role in the early 1970s. Professionals, finding the APA unresponsive, were motivated to create the Council for the Advancement of the Psychological Professions and Sciences (CAPPS). The founding of CAPPS makes an interesting study in social process. Vowing not to emerge until there was a national advocacy structure, Wright (who was to serve for four years as the CAPPS president), Cummings, and Ernest Lawrence sequestered themselves on a Friday afternoon. By Saturday they had devised a structure for CAPPS and were contacting leading professional psychologists across the country with the goal of obtaining at least 500 persons to serve as the Board of Governors and to underwrite CAPPS by contributing $100 each. That same Sunday CAPPS was enthusiastically launched.

From its inception, professional psychologists flocked to CAPPS and made it an effective, self-sustained advocacy organization. The demise of CAPPS stemmed from its unfortunate embroilment in APA internal politics, for it was still the goal of the clinical activists to move the APA into the arena of advocacy. This goal was realized with the creation of CAPPS's successor, the Association for the Advancement of Psychology (AAP), which represents not only professional psychology, as did its predecessor, but also scientific and academic psychology. Federal cuts in research and training funds and other untoward events during this time convinced all facets of psychology of the need for advocacy on the federal level. By 1977 it became apparent that the legislative office previously maintained by APA (and which had been eliminated with the formation of AAP) had to be reestablished. Through this legislative office, not only does the APA contribute to AAP, but it also provides the guidance, leadership, direction, and position papers that only organized psychology, speaking thoughtfully and with careful deliberation, can provide.

Simultaneously, and under the leadership of many of the same professional-psychologist activists, two other forces were operating to further change the face of American psychology: the professional school movement and the politicization of the APA. The establishment in 1968 of the first two of the four campuses of the California School of Professional Psychology led the profession of psychology to see how it could have significant control in the training of its own future practitioners. Once the imagination of professionals was captured, events moved quickly. The Vail Conference on Levels and Patterns of Training occurred within five years. Within 10 years, 28 professional schools, conceived as semiautonomous units of a university campus, were either operative or about to become so.

The political transformation of the APA had its roots in the late 1950s under the thrust of the New York State Psychological Association and its skillful executive officer Allen Williams. Later, this group being eclipsed by the more strident voices in California and, to a lesser extent, New Jersey, the activists became embroiled in bitter quarrels with three successive APA executive officers. These activists did succeed, however, in achieving a greater professional balance within the Council of Representatives only to witness that body's new attention to professional issues relegated to low priority by an academician-dominated Board of Directors. In 1972 a formal political structure was launched called the Committee of Concerned Psychologists (CCP) whose avowed aim was to capture the APA presidency and to elect professional-oriented members to the Board of Directors in relative proportion to the number of professional psychologists within the APA. The inordinate success of CCP is attested to by the fact that three out of the last four individuals elected as presidents were clinicians and that a balanced Board of Directors has been achieved that no longer ignores the importance of national health insurance to the future autonomy of the profession. By 1978 social psychologists and finally academicians had also formed their own political coalitions, and the APA was thoroughly politicized.

At the present time the APA expends a significant portion of its resources and energy toward involvement in issues pertaining to national health insurance. This does not mean mere attention to guild issues at the expense of the consumer and the public welfare. There are three major groups of psychologists who have a substantial interest in national health insurance. Professional psychologists see it as an opportunity to deliver services and to develop their subfield of psychology. Other psychologists are concerned that our role in national health insurance be socially responsible and that it emphasize the needs of the consumer of such services. Scientific psychologists are concerned about a tough-minded approach to evaluation of national health insurance outcomes and evaluation of social programs in general. These three groups of psychologists have quite different views of national health insurance and the potential role of psychology in its development and implementation.

These three sets of beliefs and approaches logically imply a specific range of general outcomes. First, they imply that the APA should support national health insurance with specific constraints. One aspect of these constraints should be a tough-minded approach to evaluation and specific accounting of how the money is spent. Such a system of evaluation should provide feedback for future decisions about services. In 1976 the APA Board of Directors sponsored an ad hoc task force to develop such mechanisms of accountability and evaluation for both legislation and regulation within national health insurance.

Second, the program should be oriented toward social concerns and the problems of the individual as perceived by the individual. National health insurance should regularly solicit systematic consumer input regarding the nature and progress of the program. The planning of the delivery of services should be done in a socially responsible manner.

Finally, psychologists should actively work toward a concept of the experimenting society, in which science helps society to ask the right questions and to gather information that allows thoughtful decisions. The APA hopes to provide the core ingredients to focus various contingencies within psychology on the important professional and societal issue of providing useful services to society.

Systems of Mental Health Care

The two-tiered structure and patchwork nature of general health care delivery accurately reflect the manner in which mental health care is dispensed within the medical model. Psychologists aped psychiatric practice and rode the crest of the tremendous "overnight" demand for individual psychotherapy that swept the United States following World War II. Americans who could afford private fees were assured of care in well-appointed offices, while the care of the poor was relegated to the states (rather than the counties, as was the case with general medical care). As the state hospitals grew beyond all predicted proportions, they experienced difficulty in attracting qualified professionals away from the equally burgeoning but more lucrative and socially prestigious area of private practice. With the increase in third-party payment, the efforts of psychologists were directed toward changing the system that denied them parity with psychiatrists. This battle was aided by the shortage of psychiatrists in the face of what appeared to be an ever-growing public demand for psychotherapeutic services. However, not until recently have psychologists shown definite signs of shifting from demanding to be allowed into an outmoded system to proposing alternate delivery modalities based upon empirical research and clinical experience.

Modern clinical psychology was not born in the university but in the military during World War II. Quick, decisive, short-term psychotherapeutic intervention as close to the combat situation as possible was needed. Faced with a relatively tiny pool of trained psychiatrists, the military was forced to resort to the transforming of young physicians and clinically naive psychologists into "90-day psychiatrists and clinical psychologists." In this way the military gave birth to the new breed of clinical psychologist, and the Veterans Administration (VA) gave them their first home. In the VA there was an early recognition of clinical psychology, and although the control of mental health in the VA remained and continues to remain with medicine, professional psychologists have flourished there on as large a scale as anywhere, with the probable exception of private practice.

Originally the VA was intended as part of the two-tiered system in which care could be accorded needy veterans with service-connected disabilities or illnesses. Through a series of Congressional acts, eligibility has been extended beyond service connection and beyond original need. With the eventual extension of care to dependents of veterans, there are now 40 to 50 million Americans potentially eligible for VA care. If such a concept were to be implemented, the VA would become the largest patch on the quilt. Such a prediction is not so farfetched. One out of every 20 physicians currently practicing in the United States is employed by the VA. Should the proponents of national health care (as opposed to national health insurance) have their way in Washington, the VA would be the only viable government-owned health establishment able to undertake delivery of care. The VA has much to commend it, but the stretching of one of the nation's largest and most unwieldy bureaucracies to cover the health needs of all Americans is not likely to produce the best possible universal health delivery system.

Whereas VA psychologists have essentially fought their own internal struggle for recognition within their system, the private practitioner implored the help of the APA as soon as rules governing third-party payment threatened to encroach on the professional psychologist's autonomy. The demands on the APA by the private practitioner were in direct proportion to the severity of the threat. The government-employed psychologist who is not accorded recognition as an autonomous provider still has a job, albeit not exactly as desired. On the other hand, under a universal health care system, any profession not recognized as a provider will soon vanish into economic extinction. When the insurance industry began to offer mental health coverage 10 years ago in response to growing consumer demands, the same timidity that once characterized health coverage in general surfaced again in the area of mental health coverage, resulting in the numerous exclusions and limitations that now plague most benefits packages.

Demands by psychologists for parity with psychiatrists evoked responses that psychology had not yet identified its own journeyman-level health provider, and, indeed, psychology had not yet clearly declared itself to be a health profession. The publishing of the *National Register for Health Service Providers in Psychology* answered these challenges, but continued insurance-industry resistance reflected the fear that psychologists would push benefits beyond insurable "medical" definitions. Basically, insurance carriers respond to what has been axiomatic in the insurance industry: Adding a new profession as a provider increases costs. Finally, medically dominated plans, such as those offered by Blue Cross and Blue Shield, suffer from medicine's determination to maintain its pre-eminence.

Although psychologists have achieved considerable success in their fight for inclusion, the present accommodation is threatened by the possibility that psychologists will not be included as independent providers within national health insurance despite the report of the President's Commission on Mental Health, which respects the autonomy of the four major mental health professions: psychiatry, psychology, psychiatric social work, and psychiatric nursing. Lending credence to this threat are the documented practices of Medicare and Medicaid that accord psychologists spotty and limited participation primarily as providers in public or semipublic agencies.

With the spawning of a nationwide system of community mental health centers (CMHC) beginning with the Kennedy and Johnson administrations, an appropriate de-emphasis of long-term state hospitalization and a dismantling of our gargantuan state hospitals have taken place. The interplay among the CMHCs, the state hospitals, and Medicaid has been many-faceted. As the community model gained momentum, there was a shift of focus away from the state to the community level, but this also brought a shift from the back ward to the street. Many of the chronically emotionally disturbed now line the park benches instead of the back wards, and Medicaid provides for their health care. Not only have medical costs for these persons escalated inordinately, but the cost of providing outpatient psychotherapy can account for as much as 15% of a multibillion dollar expenditure. There is a growing uneasiness, as these chronic patients fill the streets and parks, that the more costly approach may have only slightly, if at all, bettered the situation.

The National Institute of Mental Health (NIMH) proposes that the CMHCs become the mainstay mental health delivery system under national health insurance. This is not surprising inasmuch as NIMH spawned the CMHC movement. Recently NIMH has been accused of wanting to slow down enactment of national health insurance until it can be assured of the survival of the centers it created. The Congress seems to have retrenched from the original overly ambitious Kennedy plan for developing a center in every community in the United States. And the CMHCs have come under attack, one criticism of them being their inordinate costs. Although CMHCs have a meaningful role, especially in underserved areas where even inordinate costs can be justified, most authorities would not regard their preemption of mental health delivery under national health insurance as desirable.

Responding to increasing mental health costs, CHAMPUS (the Civilian Health and Medical Program of the Uniformed Services) provided grants to psychology and psychiatry to seek methods of controlling costs. Rising to the challenge, psychology, through the auspices of the APA, has defined proper, customary, and effective practice and has provided methods of controlling it, thus taking a unique leadership position in innovating cost-therapeutically-effective techniques.

Probably the most unique and totally innovative mode of health care delivery to emerge within recent decades is the Health Maintenance Organization (HMO). Under the traditional system of third-party payment, the practitioner is reimbursed for services rendered, while under the HMO model a group of practitioners are given a monthly capitation, or a relatively small fee each month for every subscriber insured regardless of whether they seek services or not. Services are then provided the subscribers at no further cost to either the patient or the third-party payer (insurance carrier). Whereas in the traditional system the provider is compensated for services rendered to sick persons, under the HMO model the practitioner succeeds by keeping the insured healthy.

The prototype for the HMO model is the Kaiser-Permanente Health System, which began under the direction of Henry J. Kaiser as a service to his shipyard employees during World War II. Following the war it offered health coverage to the public and spread from the San Francisco Bay Area to Portland, Oregon, Southern California, Hawaii, Cleveland, and Denver. Several years ago HMO legislation was passed by the Congress, and Washington began to encourage the development of this concept. In addition to providing development, or start-up, monies, these laws have boosted HMOs by requiring employers who offer their employees insurance benefits to offer them the additional choice of one HMO along with the traditional choices.

To qualify as a Health Maintenance Organization a group must file a complicated application to the Department of Health, Education, and Welfare and comply with a maze of regulations. Kaiser-Permanente, as the prototype, regarded these criteria as destructive to the very concept they were designed to promote. Not until a series of waivers from these regulations were obtained did Kaiser-Permanente agree to qualify as an HMO under the law. In the meantime, there have been a number of scandals and bankruptcies among HMOs. Kaiser-Permanente, however, flourishes as the original system that almost alone continues to make the HMO concept work successfully, at least on the large scale of several million insureds.

The HMO model has become the prototype image to many individuals of what national health insurance might be like. Historically, however, organized, private-sector medicine opposed the Kaiser-Permanente plan in its early years and regarded it as "encroaching socialized medicine." In the Northern California Region of Kaiser-Permanente, the first of the series of semiautonomous regions of that health system, psychologists have flourished as the mainstay system of mental health delivery. It is here that the field research on the effects of psychotherapy, within a comprehensive health system, was conducted over a period of 18 years.

While learning from the successful experiences of Kaiser-Permanente, it is also possible to learn valuable lessons from unsuccessful experiences. Although labor unions provide the bulk of the millions of Kaiser Health Plan subscribers, Kaiser-Permanente has carefully avoided becoming directly and overly dependent upon any one segment of subscribers. The bitter consequences of such dependence were dramatically demonstrated with the demise of the excellent mental health system sponsored entirely by the Retail Clerks Los Angeles local. This system, which employed a wide variety of successful techniques including outreach, suddenly collapsed when an overly zealous union leadership mandated to the professionals involved that various forms of intervention be supplanted by mega-vitamin therapy and other questionable forms of treatment. Similarly, the UAW's attempt to create a showcase health service in Detroit resulted in near disaster. In that system, mental health services by professionals were mostly superseded by the utilization of co-workers, particularly shop stewards, trained as paraprofessionals. It was found that automobile workers failed to avail themselves of these services, *but the investigators missed the implication of this resistance.* The often-cited contention that blue-collar workers will not utilize mental health services when they are made available is a misinterpretation of the Detroit experience. The study really demonstrated that workers will not utilize shop stewards and fellow workers functioning as mental health counselors. When mental health services provided by professionals with full confidentiality are made available, blue-collar workers do utilize such services.

An interesting experiment that has avoided some of these pitfalls is the Group Health Cooperative of Puget Sound (in the state of Washington), where a subscription to the health plan is literally a share of ownership in the health system. Certainly this demonstration of shared control between professionals and consumers can yield a great deal of information, both good and bad, and suggests directions for future health plans.

Psychology, because of its research base and its concern for human welfare, is in a unique position to evaluate existing health systems, to formulate directions for innovative systems, and to provide continuing development and reevaluation of both systems and modes of practice that will define cost-therapeutic effectiveness. To do so, psychology must continue to insist upon its rightful autonomy, it must free itself from outmoded medical concepts, and it must persist in its concern for the consumer.

Nicholas A. Cummings is currently President, American Psychological Association; Director, Mental Research Institute, Palo Alto, California; and Clinical Director, Biodyne Institute.

Implications of National Health Policies for Professional Psychology

Patrick H. DeLeon

The future of professional psychology is intimately connected with the current debate on the federal government's ultimate role in our nation's health programs. The enactment of national health insurance will cause our public policy leaders to focus more intensely upon efforts to insure quality control and cost containment. Whether psychology will retain its professional autonomy will ultimately be determined by whether individual psychologists become actively involved in this public policy debate.

The future of psychology, especially clinical psychology, as a profession will be shaped by decisions being made in the federal government about the national health care systems. Many would argue that psychology is not an integral part of health care, that psychology should seek to divorce itself from the health-sickness model. However, such a position ignores both the considerable body of evidence that most physical-medical complaints have psychological components, as well as the practical consideration that the federal government supports programs and services under a medical model. Psychologists are providing services labeled *health services,* and the federal government is increasingly involved in determining the form and manner of delivery.

The current public policy debate will ultimately shape the course of our nation's health programs for at least the next 10 years. The United States is the last of the industrialized nations not to have enacted a comprehensive national health insurance program, and a sizable minority of our health experts would seriously question whether we have even developed a national health policy. There is almost daily debate on the pros and cons of enacting a "comprehensive" versus a "catastrophic" bill or of the necessity of totally eliminating the private health insurance industry versus the advantages of preserving the integrity of our free enterprise—profit-oriented economy. The debate, be it noted, is not whether there should *be* national health insurance but what *kind* of national health insurance should be enacted. The real argument focuses upon what benefits will be provided, whose services will be reimbursed, and how the program will ultimately be funded.

This is indeed a most exciting time in Washington but, with all candor, one that is also rather frightening and sobering, particularly when one realizes the extent to which our profession tends to talk only to itself and the extent to which we are truly naive about the importance of actively participating in the public policy arena. At our conventions and in our journals, we pride ourselves on our learned presentations and scholarly research. Unfortunately, very few decision makers ever hear what we have to say. We cite impressive statistics indicating that with certain populations over a 5-year period, one psychotherapy session alone can reduce medical use by 60%. We give ourselves credit for developing such innovative treatment approaches as crisis intervention teams, but we do not spend the time and the effort necessary to convey effectively the importance of these developments to our public leaders, to those who will ultimately decide whether these discoveries will be incorporated into the mainstream of our health delivery systems.

Reprinted from *Professional Psychology,* 1977, 8, 263–268.

Let us provide a concrete example. The Social Security Administration recently promulgated formal rules and regulations for Medicaid reimbursement requiring that all inpatient mental health services provided to those under the age of 21 be under the direction of a physician. It was noted that they had received approximately 81 comments on their draft regulations; 81 individuals or organizations had taken the time to express their views. Where was psychology? If members of our own profession are not concerned about being required to be supervised by another profession, be assured that very few public policy makers will speak out on our behalf.

Another example, which is perhaps even more prophetic, is the extent to which psychology receives training support from the federal government. The ultimate future of any profession will primarily be determined by the extent to which its training institutions are able to train new graduates and incorporate relevant technological and theoretical advances into their educational curricula. We have heard numerous discussions about how well trained our graduates are and about how selective our graduate schools can afford to be. Yet when we review the actual training budget for the National Institute of Mental Health (NIMH), it immediately becomes obvious that not everyone agrees that our contribution to society is really that unique. In recent years, NIMH released approximately $15 million for psychology training programs and, at the same time, $30 million for psychiatry training programs. Unfortunately, these figures reflect the current view of society on how to allocate very limited health manpower resources. Once again, the basic issue is our role in public policy formation—if our profession does not feel that a higher proportion of these training funds should be allocated to training psychologists, who else will?

In a recent *American Psychologist* article Charles Kiesler stated, "The national image of psychologists is not very realistic. . . . The current perception of psychology and psychologists is so removed from the truth that there is little danger of an unscientific oversell" (p. 400). In my view, our Executive Officer is a master of understatement.

Within the next 3–5 years, it seems certain that the Congress of the United States will enact a comprehensive national health insurance program. Regardless of the type of program that is finally decided upon, comprehensive mental health benefits will be provided for as long as they are an integral part of an organized health care system, such as a community mental health center or a health maintenance organization. It is conceivable that an organized group of psychologists could qualify for federal reimbursement, although this possibility is highly unlikely. It is beyond belief, however, that the traditional office-based, solo practitioner, with his/her individualized fee-for-service reimbursement schedule, will survive under national health insurance.

The central issue for psychology in the current debate on national health insurance is not whether one particular type of service will be included from the beginning, or phased in on an incremental basis, but the necessity of realizing that such a comprehensive program will entail a major reorganization of our nation's health priorities and resources. High quality health services will become the absolute right of every American, and for the first time in our nation's history, the federal government will undertake the responsibility of orchestrating our educational and service delivery components to insure that this mandate is fulfilled. Organized psychology will either become an integral segment of our nation's health system or it will be systematically excluded, with its current services being provided by the other health disciplines, such as nursing or psychiatry. Unfortunately, it would be an understatement to say that the leaders of our profession have just begun to appreciate the practical significance of this development. It would be reasonable to predict that our nation will eventually set a limit on its annual expenditures for health care and thereby establish a procedure under which all health care providers will, in essence, be on salary to the federal government.

From the tenor of the current debate, it is quite clear that our public policy decision makers will soon have to come to grips with the ever-recurring issues of accountability and quality of care. A recent oversight hearing held by the House of Representatives reported that in 1975 alone, the number of deaths from unnecessary surgery approximated 11,900. Such data bits, with which congressional committees are becoming more and more familiar, are forcing an increased governmental role in insuring quality care. Unfortunately, however, quality care is steadily becoming defined as that directly and personally supervised by a physician. Whereas our profession is constantly looking within itself for specific and experimentally reproducible measures of competency, our public policy makers, and this also increasingly includes the judiciary, are more concerned with such procedural and easily recognizable criteria as, Was a physician in charge? Did the practitioner possess a doctorate degree? Does the profession possess national standards of licensure, including a continuing education requirement? and so on. These opposing views of how to insure accountability and quality services reflect fundamental differences. Most psychologists are not aware of this, however, and naively assume that their viewpoint will ultimately prevail.

Since 1972 several minor pieces of health legislation have been eneacted into public law that have, for all practical purposes, established the mechanism by which the federal government will eventually be able to insist that as a condition for reimbursement, all health services will be directly supervised by physicians. The Professional Standards Review Organization legislation, PL 92-603, charges organized groups of physicians with the responsibility of reviewing the quality of medical care provided by their peers and, in so doing, of establishing local norms of care for both inpatient and outpatient treatment. At the present time, these physician organizations are responsible for "overseeing" the care provided to only Medicare and Medicaid patients. However, with the federal government presently paying approximately 40% of our nation's total health costs, the extension of this mechanism to cover all medical services is but the next logical step. Of direct interest to psychology is the fact that the law does not even mention nonphysician providers, whereas it clearly mandates physician review of *all* health care providers. In the accompanying committee report, professional standards review organizations are authorized to "retain and consult with other types of health care practitioners . . . to assist in reviewing services which their fellow practitioners provide" (p. 265). However, physicians are also encouraged to "participate in the review of services ordered by physicians but rendered by other health care practitioners. For example, physical therapists may be utilized in the review of physical therapy services, but physicians should determine whether the services should have been ordered" (p. 265). Thus, the ultimate responsibility for the patient's health care is clearly to reside with the physician.

The National Health Planning and Resources Development Act, PL 93-641, was signed into law in January 1975. The thrust behind this legislation was to strengthen our nation's health planning efforts. Accordingly, it provides for establishing a network of health systems agencies that are responsible for areawide planning and development. Among their many responsibilities, these agencies are also to review the proposed distribution of any federal funds in their area and the need for existing institutional health services, presumably including community mental health centers. Unfortunately for psychology, throughout the text of this legislation, there is again the clearly expressed notion that all health services will be provided under the direction of a physician.

Further, even a cursory review of the various national health insurance proposals, regardless of the philosophical or economic constituency whose interests they reflect, quickly indicates that there is very little enthusiasm for treating the nonphysician health care provider as an independent and autonomous professional. Practically every bill incorporates the language of our Medicare legislation, and under this act, psychological services are reimbursable only if they are under the direct supervision of a physician. Accordingly, approximately 2 years ago, Senator Inouye introduced Senate bill 123, which would effectively remove the supervision requirement. There is also an effort currently under way by the Social Security Administration in conducting a 2-year pilot evaluation in Colorado of the provisions of this bill for psychologists as independent providers of health services. Unfortunately, however, unless during this same time period our profession can develop sufficiently greater grass-roots support for our independent inclusion, it is probable that regardless of the results of the Colorado study, we will not be included as independent practitioners under Medicare. That the study was commissioned at all is some indication that as a profession we are becoming politically viable; however, it is doubtful that any knowledgeable expert really expects that this study will provide any additional information.

Finally within the past year or so there has been a marked attempt to consolidate and simplify a number of the all-too-often-conflicting rules and regulations promulgated by the various federal health programs, such as Medicaid, Medicare, and the Civilian Health and Medical Program of the Uniformed Services (CHAMPUS). The Department of Defense, in its CHAMPUS program, has recently expended considerable effort in developing an active peer review mechanism for its mental health services, which is quite similar to the basic professional standards review organization model. Special attention is also being given to a number of problems that on the surface do not seem especially relevant to psychology but which in the long run will have a definite impact on our profession. More specifically, the current geographical and specialty maldistribution of physician health services and the expectation that by 1990 30% of our physician health manpower may be foreign medical graduates are of concern; and the latter prospect has led to a number of legislative and administrative proposals that would in sum drastically increase the number of American medical school graduates, require national minimum standards for licensure (including a continuing education requirement for all health service providers), and shift the current training emphasis away from specialty development to an increasing reliance on developing family physicians and the use of physician extenders and nurse practitioners. From this frame of reference, it would be highly consistent to classify the clinical psychologist as essentially a high-paid specialist, like the surgeon, who should be relocated to a teaching or research role and his/her current clinical duties absorbed by the more generally trained family physicians and nurse practitioners. In fact, there are definite indications that NIMH is currently considering allocating a significant proportion of its future training budget to provide these latter personnel with special training in the mental health area.

From the foregoing comments, then, it seems clear that we need to make determined efforts to secure our position as health service providers through appropriate legislative and educational efforts as a concerted force of concerned professionals, and to mobilize our teaching and research colleagues to bring the scientific and research base that has been accumulated to focus upon the question of psychology as a health profession.

Reference

Kiesler, C. A. Report of the Executive Officer: 1975. *American Psychologist*, 1976, *31*, 393–401.

At the time of original publication of this article, *Patrick H. DeLeon* was a member of the APA Board of Professional Affairs, a Consulting Editor to *Professional Psychology*, and Legislative Assistant to U.S. Senator Daniel K. Inouye.

Psychology, Mental Health, and the Public Interest

Professional associations have increasingly offered the practitioner the career and status supports that academic settings have offered their faculties. Where tenure supports academic freedom, guarantees of third-party reimbursement support professional freedom. Both obviously establish financial security. Despite the seemingly self-serving quest of the practitioner for professional autonomy, he or she has functioned no more according to the principle of self-interest than has the academician who has accepted and supported the precept to "publish or perish." If the major constraints on the functioning of both groups were significantly altered, mental health problems might be addressed more coherently and collaboratively. This would require renunciation of the unequivocal commitment to publishing, on the one hand, and realization of genuine professional autonomy, on the other. Substantive issues might then more often replace concerns with status.

In recent years, the Ohio Psychological Association has been heavily involved in efforts to confirm the competence, the status, and the autonomy of psychologists as providers of mental health services. These activities were necessary and, to date, have been reasonably successful. I realize that this assertion, about both the necessity and the success of our endeavors, is viewed with skepticism by some of our colleagues who disdain to participate in the affairs of the association. Concern with legislation, negotiations with insurance firms and governmental agencies, and workshops for the aspiring practitioner have seemed to them much too undignified, much too public, possibly irrelevant, and not at all scholarly. And they are not altogether wrong, unless of course dignity is construed to mean avoidance of debate and controversy, excessive public activity is construed to mean any step beyond the cloistered campus, relevance is gauged by unimaginatively narrow criteria, and scholarship is confused with pedantry. To forestall the rapid attrition, at this point, in my intended audience—which is no more the campus scholar than the practitioner, as will become evident—I hasten to identify myself as a regular university faculty member and researcher, as well as a clinical psychologist. I have had these professional identities throughout my career.

I would remind my campus colleagues, who are sometimes critical of the association's interests and emphases, that their professional careers have, in some respects, been privileged. I do not refer to their relatively flexible schedules, their holidays, their long summers; their considerable opportunity for self-determination, or any of their other prerogatives, for these are bought, by many, at the considerable cost of countless hours devoted to their students and of frantic evenings, weekends, and summers committed to the endless task of preparation of manuscripts. Rather, I refer to the institutional supports that serve, both figuratively and literally, to establish and protect their status and their careers. From the physical boundaries of the typical campus, to the libraries and computer centers, to the hierarchy of professional rank, and perhaps most critically to the system of tenure, the faculty is ensconced in the protective skirts of alma mater.

Psychologists in other settings, who have characteristically lacked these forms of protection, of mutual support, and of confirmation of

Reprinted from *American Psychologist*, 1977, *32*, 1–4.

their professional identities, have sought them through membership in professional associations. Their utilization of these associations to represent them in status conflicts with other professions, institutions, or agencies is not substantially different from the faculty member's reliance on, and support of, the system of professorial rank and utilization of the AAUP (the American Association of University Professors) when his or her status is threatened. The activity of our association in establishing greater predictability of reimbursement for psychological services is not, in effect, vastly different from the adamant support for the tenure system by university faculty, which grants them reasonable and reassuring predictability of financial security. If the tenure system is defended on the grounds that, most fundamentally, it is a guarantee of academic freedom, one can as legitimately argue that the guarantee of third-party reimbursement for psychological services is as great a guarantee of freedom from arbitrary, inappropriate, or capricious control of a psychologist's legitimate professional functions. While these parallels may be suggestive of common basic needs, they may yet do little to convince the academician that support of the practitioner's efforts and of the professional association is in his or her own best interest. I shall return to that issue in a moment.

First, it is worth noting that academicians and practitioners have obviously functioned in rather different arenas. The former derive support from well-established traditions and systems which they share with scholars from many other fields. Their arena is relatively private, and their claims to status go largely unchallenged. The latter—the practitioners—seek support in the context of emerging but incomplete legal and social definition, and through formative if rapidly developing systems that are shared with no other profession. Their arena is relatively public, and their claims to status have been challenged frequently.

These differences enable the academicians to appear nearly devoid of self-interest, to accept—though they may not seek or claim—the vaunted image of scholars and scientists, and generally to remain sanguine about their condition. These differences require of the practitioners an insistent repetition of the legitimacy of their professional functions and of their claims to the rewards that typically accrue to a professional role. With stridency sometimes tuned to the magnitude of the obstacles, practitioners may *appear* to function primarily on the principle of self-interest—and perhaps to be derogated for it by their campus colleagues.

Yet, in both instances, I have considered these diverse expressions of presumably similar aims only from the perspective of self-interest and of immutable social and professional conditions. I should like to consider whether the balance between public interest and apparent, if not actual, self-interest might be altered if changes occurred in the professional and social conditions under which each has tended to function.

What might ensue, for example, if the "publish or perish" condition of faculty life ceased to obtain? Suppose that that determinant of faculty behavior were dismissed as an archaic remnant from the days when a university "department" was little more than a single professor with a retinue of assistants who were sustained intellectually by the products of their own investigations; when curricula were homemade, so to speak; and when a rather select group of scholars was virtually compelled to function creatively on the frontiers of discovery.

If "productivity" were not the hallmark of academic excellence, would short, easily completed studies be quite as common? Would samples so often be recruited from among the most readily available source? Would the variables studied remain as relatively circumscribed, the conditions as relatively contrived, and the findings as relatively limited in their applicability as is currently the case? Or is it possible that research might more often be directed toward the exploration of genuine human problems? Might it be possible to take the time to accumulate a relevant sample that is not readily available and that might even require attention after the data are in hand? Might not the graduate dissertation serve as a model of future research rather than as an isolated illustration of conditions that the applied psychologist may never encounter again? Might not the scientist find value in discourse with the practitioner because the practitioner's observations would yield fruitful hypotheses? And might the practitioner not find value in discourse with the scientist because the scientist's efforts would more often yield data, as well as research methodologies, that are relevant to his or her interests?

The conditions under which the academicians function are not of their own making and may not be amenable to change solely through their efforts. But they are conditions that they have accepted and supported and, despite appearances, they are conditions of self-interest.

The context in which psychologists in mental health fields have functioned has similarly not been of their making. However, where the academician could further his or her career by acceptance of the imposed conditions, the practitioner has been able to further his or her career only by opposing and changing the imposed conditions. And while these conditions have, in some respects, been the inadvertent products of traditions and practices evolving slowly from times when no applied psychology existed, rather than the consequence of a calculated conspiracy, they have nevertheless had the effect of thwarting the natural development of psychological practice.

What might ensue, for example, if the clinical psychologist were in all respects able to function as a fully autonomous mental health practitioner, consistent with his training, his competence, and indeed, his increasingly more precise legal definition? The constraints that still preclude this state of affairs are not as clearly defined as the "publish or perish" precept of faculty life and require specification.

Were the practitioner's status to change as envisioned, a variety of current practices, beliefs, traditions, myths, and irrational fears would require change.

Most obviously, the inclination to view extreme deviations in human adaptation—or psychopathology—as disease entities and hence as "medical" problems must finally be shed. This is neither a new nor a radical idea nor is it foreign to everyday practice, It is only at the policy levels, when acknowledgment of the realities of daily practice might require changes in prerogatives, in status, or in control, that the idea continues to meet resistance.

Implicit in this change is the elimination of the tendency to transform a client into a "patient" by the fact of hospitalization. After all, the overwhelming majority of individuals with psychological problems suffer no medical disorder and may require protection, not aseptic isolation and physiological monitoring. Desirable continuity of care could be maintained—in or out of residential settings—with medical evaluation and medication obtained by means of consultation request when these are necessary, without change of responsibility for the primary care of the individual. After all, that is precisely what happens to individuals admitted to hospitals with a primary medical problem for whom the physician chooses to seek a psychological consultation.

Implicit in this change is the transformation of institutions we now call hospitals into genuinely protective residences for those who need them regardless of their medical status. They would not need to be defined as "medical" institutions to be staffed exclusively by physicians on threat of loss of accreditation.

Implicit in this change is the final elimination of all vestiges of a hierarchic relationship between medicine and psychology and specifically between psychiatry and psychology. This would further imply the elimination of the transparent fiction that "psychotherapy" prefixed by the term *medical* and performed by a physician is somehow different from "psychotherapy" prefixed by the term *psychological* and performed by a psychologist. It is the height of irony that psychologists as well as psychiatrists have taught psychotherapy to students in both fields and that nonphysicians have been among the most prominent theorists, teachers, and practitioners of psychotherapy, notably Bruno Bettelheim, Ernst Kris, Rudolf Ekstein, Carl Rogers, Rollo May, Austin DesLauriers, Fritz Redl, Melanie Klein, Anna Freud, the more recent behavior therapists, and countless others.

Implicit in this change is the recognition and acknowledgment that the 5–7 years of postgraduate education and training of clinical psychologists does indeed qualify them as experts in psychopathology if a physician so qualifies after 3–4 years of a psychiatric residency.

Implicit in this change is the acknowledgment that psychologists are at least as committed to their clients as are their medical colleagues and are surely no more likely to ignore their medical problems than are physicians to ignore their patients' psychological problems, and perhaps less so. It should go without saying, though it seems to bear constant repetition, that psychologists have no interest in treating medical problems any more than the majority of physicians have any substantial interest in treatment psychological problems. A physician's interest—typically that of a psychiatrist—in psychological problems does not, of course, render such problems medical by arrogation. Nor indeed does the demonstrable effect of medication upon some forms of behavioral aberration redefine such aberration as medical. The significant effects of innumerable drugs upon *normal* behavior should long ago have disabused anyone of reliance on that criterion. The interest of physicians in psychological problems does not, as is sometimes claimed, warrant the interposition of a physician between a client, or a prospective client, and a psychologist any more than it would warrant the demand of an attorney, a clergyman, or a teacher that their interventions be mediated by a physician because the human problems they confront might possibly be the consequence of medical disorder.

Finally, implicit in this change is a significant restructuring of insurance programs to protect the public against the expense of psychodiagnostic and psychotherapeutic procedures when a qualified mental health professional is consulted. So long as protection is available only in the form of policies designated as "medical and surgical," psychologists either find that their services are not reimbursable—which may seem logical but is essentially irrational—or that they must seek compensation through medical policies—which may seem illogical but is eminently rational under present conditions.

What is obviously needed is a more generic form of insurance more appropriately designated "mental health" or something equally suitable. And while great strides have been made by legislatures, in Ohio and elsewhere, toward this more rational provision of professional services, through licensure and "freedom of choice" laws, consideration of the public need for protection against the expense of mental health problems is now essential.

If these various conditions were altered as I have proposed, is it possible that practitioners, no longer beleaguered, could relinquish the role of activist, which has proven so repugnant to their academic brethren? Is it possible that their quest for rational autonomy, perceived unjustly sometimes as self-seeking competitiveness, could then be foresaken for efforts that are more immediately and more obviously in the public interest? Is it possible, with status confirmed, that they could devote more effort toward a critical appraisal of their clinical endeavors, and indeed lead the several mental health professions in the direction of systematic appraisal of their impact on human welfare? Is it possible that practitioners—and the other mental health professionals with them—would less often incline addictively to each new part-technique, each catchword and slogan, each new enthusiasm, and less often adopt a posture of certainty on faith, hope, or conviction when they should have awaited the results of evaluative research? Is is possible, in fact, that these new practitioners would have the freedom to apply the research skills that are uniquely theirs among the mental health professionals and that they would find themselves engaged in a more coherent search for demonstrable solutions to human problems mutually with their academic colleagues?

If the skeptics detect in all this nothing but a circuitous enticement to join our association, I offer them a good-humored welcome. I would welcome them, however, not to serve those whom they would join nor primarily to serve themselves, but rather to a collaboration among all interested elements of society in the development of a more systematic, coherent, and rational program of mental health.

At the least, such a program would demand the displacement of special professional interests by a more general concern with public interest; a closer relation between psychological research and human problems; a critical stance toward clinical practice and a renunciation of techniques that are recommended only by routine and habit; circumspection about and systematic appraisal of any new or innovative practice; continuity of care and access to qualified professionals of one's own choice; uniform protection against the expense of mental health problems; evaluative research as an integral part of all grant-supported service programs; and significant, continuing governmental support for applied research, not as a luxury to be appended to direct care programs, but as the only promise of developing demonstrably successful modes of intervention. We must preclude the recurrence of the present appalling situation of Ohio, wherein no new research funds for mental health were allocated for the current fiscal year. All funds were withdrawn from such efforts in favor of patient care—an admittedly overwhelming need from which only imaginative research can hope to rescue us.

It is to this multifaceted task that we would call our colleagues both within and without our profession, that we would call health support systems and other associations, that we would call legislators and governmental agencies and departments, and it is to this substantial task—in the interest of both psychology and the public—that this association is committed.

At the time of original publication of this article, *Herbert E. Rie* taught at Ohio State University. The article was originally a presidential address, presented at the meeting of the Ohio Psychological Association, Perrysburg, Ohio, October 24, 1975. It has previously appeared in the *Ohio Psychologist*.

The Status of Psychology as a Profession and a Science

Charles A. Kiesler

This article describes the various subfields within psychology, emphasizing the continuous interaction between scientific and professional psychology. The similarities and differences in the perspectives of psychiatry and psychology are discussed, and it is argued that cooperation and communication between the two fields are essential to the public interest. The Liaison Group for Mental Health is described as one vehicle for achieving this.

The theme of this series is the role of the psychiatrist, the psychologist, and the behavioral scientist in the medical school in the year 2000. I'm not very skilled at making predictions for 25 years from now, but certainly the future of psychology and psychiatry rests with people like ourselves. Specifically, what we all do in the next one to three years will go a long way in determining what the next 25 years will look like. How we work together to handle our relationships with Congress and the White House in the next year or two, how we facilitate accurate pictures of mental health and its associated sciences, how well we know the talents and skills of our colleagues, how well we relate to science in a spirit of inquiry and self-criticism, and perhaps most of all, how well we relate to one another will probably have a greater impact on the role of psychology, psychiatry, and the behavioral sciences in the medical school than almost any other combination of variables.

For all the confusion in the public's mind about the difference between a psychiatrist and a psychologist, I find there to be a good deal of confusion in our own minds about what a psychiatrist is and what a psychologist is. A psychiatrist knows what a psychiatrist is but is less knowledgeable about what a psychologist is, and the reverse is true as well. I would like to talk a little today about my own field—psychology— its training and what it has to contribute to

science and to the delivery of services. I'd like to move from that to some problems between the fields of psychiatry and psychology and attempt to analyze those issues as a function of a difference in perspective. As a social psychologist, I think we could expect sizable differences between our fields, based simply on training and the perspective of our day-to-day environment. I'd like to talk also about some current cooperative efforts between psychiatry and psychology, and some prospects for the future. Some people these days have rather tender feelings on these issues, so I'll assure you in advance that there is no real desire to be parochial and no real intent to offend anyone by slighting various subfields.

Let's start with the organization of psychology. The American Psychological Association is, and has been for some time, a large and very rapidly growing organization, but few people realize how recent some of the growth is in both size and science. Although there is some dispute about specific dates, it has been about 100 years since the establishment of the first psychology laboratory. It has been 85 years since the establishment of the American Psychological Association in 1892. That sounds like a long history, but in the first 50 years of the APA's existence, there were approximately 3,000 cumulative members; that is, 3,000 people had belonged to the APA at one time or another someone actually submitted a list of those 3,000

From T. A. Williams and J. H. Johnson (eds.), *Mental Health in the 21st Century*. Lexington, Massachusetts: Lexington Books, in press.

the other day for publication in the *American Psychologist*. I was fascinated by the list, but publication space was too tight to accommodate it.

This year, there are almost 4,000 new members in the APA, more new members this year than there were total members over the first 50 years. This is rather typical, as you know if you enjoy the history of science. It varies a little bit from science to science, but approximately 85% of all scientists who ever lived are currently alive. That is the state of the burgeoning nature of science, and it is certainly true in psychology as well. In the last four years, for example, we have had more new members in the APA than the total membership of the American Sociological Association, one of our sister organizations with whom we work quite closely. So the APA is a giant compared to the other social and behavioral sciences, and it is a giant compared to other national psychology organizations. We have 45,000 members. The next largest national organization in the world is Great Britain's, which has about 8,000 members. I interact with British psychologists quite often and, in some respects, their problems with their 8,000 are quite similar to the problems our organization faced when we had 8,000 members.

There is an issue of size that itself produces problems for organizations of people. We all sometimes forget that we are not unique in our set of problems. I think that many of our young people, and obviously many people outside psychology, are not really attuned to how much scientific psychology, and more particularly, professional psychology, is a recent phenomenon since the second World War. You may know the recent history of psychiatry since the second World War and the different national events that had an impact on psychiatry; many of them had a similar impact on psychology. These events included the establishment of the National Institute of Mental Health and, more important to psychology, the National Science Foundation, a significant source of research funds, and the establishment of internships in the Veterans Administration. We now have about 700 of the latter, a significant group of trainees to interact with.

A great many psychologists worked full time on research during the second World War. I had dinner with a group of very distinguished speakers at our convention last August and my wife asked what they had been doing during the second World War. It turned out to be a fascinating question. Those people, distinguished and now in their 60s, were almost all involved in research in the second World War. There were exceptions, like Don Campbell, who was a naval officer on the firing line, and others who were bomber pilots and things of that nature. However, a substantial proportion had been involved in research, such as Skinner and his direction of missiles by pigeons—an idea, parenthetically, that worked but was never acceptable to the military. The others studied such problems as interaction patterns on the battlefield, psychological variables underlying survival in battle and among prisoners of war, and even training of espionage agents, which never worked very well either, partly because the failures never came back so one could never quite tell what the sources of errors in prediction were.

In my interactions with psychiatrists, I have found that one difference in their perspective about psychology is due to their considerable interaction with professional psychologists and substantially less interaction, either personally or professionally, with scientific psychologists. If you really want to understand psychology in some personal sense—feeling comfortable with your knowledge of the field and the commitments of psychologists—you really have to have some understanding of scientific psychology. Dr. Michael Pallak of APA prepared a little document about scientific psychologists that I will use here because I think the numbers are important. I apologize for overwhelming you with statistics, but I think they give some flavor of the importance and breadth of scientific psychology.

The science of psychology encompasses inquiry into learning, perception, physiology, development, personality, adjustment, achievement, attitudes, abilities, and motivation, as well as the diagnosis and treatment of mental health problems. Because the diversity and breadth of the science of psychology is not well understood, an outline of the content and recent accomplishments for a sample of the subfields of psychology might be helpful.

Scientists identifying themselves as experimental psychologists, of which there are about 2,600, are primarily engaged in basic research on problems of perception, learning, cognition, human performance, memory, and related issues. Recent contributions of psychologists working in this area include development of improved procedures with psychophysical scaling of stimuli and measurement of meaning, including work in the area commonly known as multidimensional scaling. Similarly, other researchers have made advances in the mathematical modeling of human learning and in simulations of natural language. There are about 800 physiological psychologists in the country engaged in searching for the engram of learning, in psychopharmacological research concerning the action of various chemicals ranging from psychogenics to anesthetics, and in research on neurosynapses and their relation to behavior. Physiological psychologists interested in motivational behavior—a traditional topic in physiological psychology—examine the relation of the endocrine, hypothalamic, and limbic substrates of behavior as they relate to the learning experience. More generally, these scientists are concerned with the fundamental problems of brain mechanisms underlying reward and reinforcement and how these operate to influence behavior. Other topics of interest to physiological psychologists include the biological bases of emotion, sensation, perception, learning, and memory.

There are about 1,300 developmental psychologists in the country. They conduct research concerning the behavior of infants, the effects of aging, peer and family relations, child-rearing environments, and individual differences in behavior. Recent interest in social ecology has led to increased attention to the enduring environments in which children develop. The effects on child development of maternal employment, neighborhood characteristics, and the qualities of physical settings have been of continuing interest. We will come back to some of these areas because they interact in different ways with our mutual concerns. Developmental psychologists are also engaged in research on socialization, the effects of hormones on the development of sex differences, and so forth. The results of a large proportion of developmental research have direct implications for the everyday lives of people. Research on child-to-caretaker ratios, cognitive processes, and adult-child relations has implications for day-care programs and parent education.

In the last few years, increased attention to life span development has led to a more integrated view of the quality of life and the normal life course for people of all ages. If you attend to textbooks in developmental psychology, you will have noted that the current trend is to concentrate not just on the child but across the life span. Indeed, the term *life span* in psychology appears in the titles of several new books. The interplay between developmental psychology and other research areas is substantial. For example, recent approaches to traditional areas of learning have suggested interesting species-specific behavioral relationships. A variety of notions borrowed from ecological and ethological areas, such as dominance hierarchies and species-specific communication, have influenced other research on peer groups, nonverbal communication, and maternal attachments.

I am a social psychologist; there are over 6,000 more of them in this country. We are group psychologists and we obviously have a large group. A friend of mine once defined social psychologists as those who like to go to a lot of cocktail parties. Behaviorally, there is some truth to that, but there is also a burgeoning science of social psychology that cuts across other areas and is a point of contact with many other areas, scientific and applied. This field encompasses both laboratory experimentation and, increasingly, a variety of techniques in natural settings. Social psychologists are interested in such topical areas as marital conflict resolution, educational intervention, jury decision making, and the design of social environments. Much of the basic theoretical work in social psychology has employed the frameworks of attribution theory, information processing, and decision-making models, and I will use them in analyzing some differences between psychiatrists and psychologists later. A major research emphasis, both basic and applied, concerns attitude development, attitude change, and the conditions under which individuals may act on their attitudes and beliefs. Other social psychological research is related to equity theory and the effect of the balance between perceived personal costs and personal gains on decisions and performance. Other research areas touched on include philanthropy and helping behavior and the conditions under which it occurs, hostility toward victims, romantic choices, and negative reactions to a benefactor. Some of these you may have heard of through the auspices of Senator Proxmire, because they have recently interested him. An interest in group dynamics persists among social psychologists who continue research on bargaining, negotiations, and mixed-motive gains. Some interest is currently focused on the effects of crowding and violations of perceived personal space.

Increasingly, social psychology has emerged with a broader, more environmentally oriented psychological approach, in which a variety of social problems are viewed in a more interdisciplinary context. The APA's Task Force on Environment and Behavior, established two years ago, now has a constituency of over 1,000 psychologists. This interest area is very heavily represented in your department of psychology here. Increasing numbers of psychologists are making career commitments in this area. These people are concerned with studies of cognitive, perceptual, and information processing and aspects of one's relations to one's environment. They have focused on cultural differences in reactions to space and the development of environmental cognitions and perception. They are interested in policy-related issues such as land use, leisure and recreation, and perceptions of urban environments. Research oriented toward social problems deals with such issues as housing for the elderly, institutional design, living arrangements, and the design of homes and communities.

Psychologists have increasingly turned their attention to issues of energy use, pollution, social impact assessment, and environmental attitudes. A lot of research is going on right now, for example, on the use of energy, that is, investigating psychological mechanisms determining the individual's use of energy. After all, a good deal of the energy used in the home and industry depends upon the behavior involved in turning a switch on or off, leaving a machine going or not going, or checking or not checking a gauge. Michael Pallak—a colleague of mine who is now at APA—has done some research with some very simple psychological mechanisms taken from the laboratory. With the cooperation of the power company, he found a 20% decrease in the use of electricity and gas over a six-month period after a simple one-time psychological treatment. These behavioral variables can have a potentially strong impact on issues of national interest.

There are over 2,000 psychologists who identify themselves as vocational, industrial, organizational, and engineering psychologists. These psychologists are concerned with human and organizational performance, work productivity, satisfaction, adjustment, safety, and the quality of the working environment, as well as the measurement of human competencies, job characteristics, job talents, and job redesign. Important advances in vocational psychology have been made by researchers who have mapped out the dimensions of work attributes, leading to unified systems for describing job components. Recent advances have been made in such areas as vocational adjustment and productivity, staffing designs in systems, and human factors in the engineering of work machine systems, and these advances have resulted in more efficient and safe work environments.

Scientists in clinical psychology, the number of which I am not absolutely certain (probably around 10,000 or 12,000), have made advances on areas related to aggression, phobic reactions, adjustment, stress, and psychosomatic disorders. Psychological researchers have worked on causal behavioral relationships for a variety of physical ailments including asthma, dermatosis, duodenal ulcer, colitis, hypertension, heart disease, arthritis, obesity, and chronic depression. A recent review of the literature of resistance to cancer has shown that personality variables are important in both onset and prognosis of cancer patients (APA Task Force on Health Research, 1976).

There are probably 20,000 psychologists in the country who identify themselves primarily as scientists. The reason I have gone through this lengthy introduction is that, in my experience at least, in departments of psychiatry there is much more experience with the professional psychologists than with the scientists. In relating to this field that you are working with in a collegial way, you should have a good intuitive sense of our scientific knowledge, goals, and commitments.

On the professional side, it's often useful to describe psychology in terms of its current legislative and legal status. In this context, there have been some perceived problems between psychiatrists and psychologists that I think it would be useful to talk about. I am glad that I'm speaking early in the day because we have the rest of the day to exchange points of view. When I mentioned to a colleague that I was going to bring some of these issues up, she said, "They'll hang you." I really don't think that's true.

I'm going to mention a few things from a pamphlet that APA's committee on health insurance prepared. It is a pamphlet designed to describe professional psychology and was made up a year ago but never published. The pamphlet outlines a large number of facts, but I am going to mention only about one out of six to give you some intuitive understanding of professional psychology, what its status is today, and therefore what its potential form of interaction is for the future.

For example, psychologists are involved in the CHAMPUS program, which I'm sure most of you are familiar with—the Civilian Health and Medical Program of the Uniformed Services. Psychologists are legally independent practitioners within that program. They are also legally recognized in the program of CHAMPVA, which is the program for dependents of totally disabled veterans included within the Rehabilitation Act of 1973. Public Law 93-363 of 1974 established parity between clinical psychologists and other providers of mental health services for about 8½ million federal workers nationwide. Related to this, my professional colleagues think that it is important to note that 26 states now have freedom-of-choice legislation, allowing the patient to choose to obtain services from a psychologist. In the HMO Development Act of 1973, clinical psychologists are enumerated. I think it is important to emphasize the clinical part throughout my description of professional psychology be-

cause in none of these cases are we talking about all psychologists. We are talking about half or fewer.

In the Department of Labor's regulations of 1974, the Comprehensive Manpower Program defined psychological services within health care to be reimbursable if they are necessary for work. Currently, a wide variety of health care bills and national health insurance bills include psychologists. It is important to emphasize the sheer variety of such bills going from practically nothing financially to practically everything financially, from practically no one reimbursable to practically everyone reimbursable. Perhaps that variety is not of critical importance, but I do want to come back to it when I discuss a quite different perspective, that of the consumer of services.

There are licensing or certification laws governing psychologists in every state of the union and the District of Columbia. The minimum standard of training from our point of view is a PhD in psychology. Most state licensing laws require a PhD and two years of postdoctoral, supervised experience. I think there is some confusion among others about the implications of both those points. Not every licensed psychologist is a PhD. I don't think there is a state law that does not have a grandfather clause in it, licensing MA psychologists who were in practice at the time the law was passed. Some of those MA psychologists in the states that were the early passers, in the 1950s, are pretty old now, but some laws are much more recent. That is an issue for psychology that one should not underrate.

Psychologists and psychiatrists differ considerably in their orientation toward full-time practice. Of all the psychologists in the country, there are only about 3,000 in full-time private practice. It is not a private-practice field. I don't think it will ever be a private-practice field. In relating to some of my colleagues in psychiatry, it has become obvious that they feel psychologists are much more interested in private practice than is empirically the case.

All Class A medical schools have psychologists on their faculty. There are about 1,300 psychologists spread out in medical schools around the country. In fact, that number is probably considerably out of date. We have recently established a *National Register of Health Service Providers in Psychology*. It is independent of APA and also includes a grandfather clause. Of the first year's entries, about 15% were MAs. That number will go down as the PhD restriction goes into place. We are talking not about a broadly defined group of professional psychologists but specifically about clinical and counseling psychologists. Our definition of professional psychology in terms of our standards of practice includes four fields—clinical, counseling, industrial-organizational, and school—and those are really quite different fields. Psychiatry's interaction is typically with the clinician but often with the counseling psychologist.

My intent in this description has been to give you a very brief overview of what the status of professional psychology is nationally, legislatively, and legally, and where, at least implicitly, areas of concern are according to our Committee on Health Insurance.

Some of the legal and legislative details have been discussed by psychiatrists. I do read the letters-to-the-editor column in the *Psychiatric News* and know that some people perceive that there are difficulties between the fields of psychology and psychiatry, now and for the future. That is true; there are. One needs to add, however, the perspective created by the fact that the relationships between psychology and psychiatry have waxed and waned over the years. The first interprofessional committee to study the problems of the relationship of psychiatry and psychology was formed in 1946. Things subsequently became better; if you trace a content analysis of letters to the editor over the years, I'm sure you would see a cyclical pattern. Currently, some of those issues are very hot. We do have another ad hoc group currently meeting. The Executive Director, the President, and the President-elect of each organization have been meeting every three or four months to talk about some of the current interprofessional stresses and, perhaps more importantly, to talk about collaboration for the future.

There are some real differences in the training and history of psychologists and psychiatrists that lead to a substantial difference in perspective. This difference in perspective and its sources in training are worth discussing.

There is probably much more variation within psychology than there is between psychology and psychiatry, but there are still differences between psychology and psychiatry that are of potential interest and related to the kinds of issues discussed between the fields. The psychiatrist's training is standard medical training with an internship, followed by three or four years of psychiatric residency. The psychologist's training is typically within the department of psychology. Nationally, for the clinical psychologist, the average length of time to complete the doctorate exceeds six years. The doctorate for clinical psychology includes a year of internship. The minimal formal program is less time-consuming than that, but most people typically seek out other professional training experiences, such as in the Veterans Administration (beyond the internship), and that elongates the training.

I think an important ingredient within the field of psychology is that the professional people and the scientific people take courses together a good deal of the time. They are involved in similar sets of enterprises: working on the master's thesis and on the doctoral dissertation (which is typically a full-time year's experience). Scientists and professionals also take courses in statistics together, of which some departments have as many as five semesters required of all graduate students. These are advanced statistics; entering students are expected to have had a course or two in their undergraduate work. Some departments require courses in computers of all students regardless of their specialty. The requirements actually vary a great deal from department to department, but there are some national regularities.

The key here, partly, is that psychology has largely developed through the years as a science, going back to the beginning of the century. Its organization and its journals have been dominated by the scientists through those years. The graduate departments have been similarly influenced. Philosophers of science often refer to psychology as one of the most sophisticated sciences, meaning that we pay a good deal of overt, explicit attention to the methods we use and the assumptions we make. In a sense, we are a very self-conscious science. Sometimes we spend time discussing how good a science it is when we should be back in the laboratory practicing it.

Practice and treatment of patients is a much more recent phenomenon within psychology. It is much more a part of our national organization, our journals, our department, and our training now than last year, the year before, or 10 years ago. There have been some scrapes and bruises within psychology on just those kinds of issues. In looking at some of the documents within psychiatry, I think that it would be fair to say that, at least in comparison to psychology, psychiatry's development has been related much more to service delivery than to science, both in training and in actual work. A recent report from the American Psychiatric Association says, for example, that in the late 1940s there were no more than 20 psychiatrists involved in full-time research in this country. That is an incredibly small number. That report, incidentally, which is sponsored by your APA and which was written by your association of chairpersons, is really an excellent document. It speaks strongly for psychiatry and raises all kinds of sympathetic feelings in me about the need to cooperate and coordinate on a variety of issues.

I too think that we need more research psychiatrists. Your own surveys have shown, for example, that given all the time of psychiatrists in the country and computing what percentage of time they spend on various activities, only about 4% of total psychiatrists' time is spent in research. The majority of time is spent in practice. In psychology, it is probably, if anything, the other way around. My own guess is that in psychology it must be about 30% full-time equivalent in research, compared to the 4% figure for psychiatry. Research is a substantial focus of our field. The difference in background and orientation between psychiatrists and psychologists can lead to quite different perspectives.

In social psychology we have a theory called attribution theory. It deals with the meanings people attach to the events in their worlds, the motivations they assign to others for their actions, and so on. The attribution term refers to the attribution of motive and meaning to objects or people. One of the findings of attribution theorists that is quite applicable to this discussion is the salience of immediate behavior. That is, we overly depend on our own behavior and events in the immediate environment in attaching meaning to the world around us. For example, a friend of mine, Dr. Daniel Batson at the University of Kansas, did research on welfare workers and their reactions to people who came in for welfare benefits. He hypothesized that welfare workers would begin their jobs with some real sympathy for those on welfare and some sense that it was really the system that was at fault. However, welfare workers have little power to change the system, and the system, largely because of its intractability, becomes a constant in their perceptual environment. The welfare applicants and their problems become the salient feature of the setting and increasingly an attributional object. Over time, Batson reasoned, welfare workers would attribute the problem to the person rather than to the system. He charted people's perceptions of their clients in the welfare office over a period of time and found just that. In the beginning welfare workers were very concerned about a system that would produce people on welfare and a life environment that led people to be on welfare by not offering valuable life alternatives. As time went by, welfare workers more and more perceived that the problem was in the individual, that he or she didn't want to work or wasn't trying hard enough. The meaning attached to significant events depends on what else is salient in one's life space.

We can extrapolate from such attributional ideas to perceptions between psychologists and psychiatrists. I'm going to exaggerate here to make a point, so I'm going to pull the fields a little farther apart than is legitimate. I think that psychiatrists tend to be trained more in specific mental disorders than are psychologists. Psychologists tend to be more broadly trained in human behavior than are psychiatrists. It may be a valid statement to say that psychiatrists, for example, are less interested in poor social learning and its causes than they are in schizophrenia and its causes, and the reverse may be true of the clinical psychologists. It is illustrative of some of the differences in focus between them. I didn't say it was good. I said it was illustrative. Psychiatrists clearly see more people in need of hospitalization than do psychologists. They tend to think that hospitalization is more generally necessary than do psychologists. If you ask just that question—What proportion of people who come to psychiatrists and psychologists should be hospitalized?—I'm sure you would get a quite significant difference between the responses of psychiatrists and psychologists. I was discussing with a distinguished psychiatrist alternative ways to handle national problems in systems of delivery of mental health services. It is a fascinating intellectual issue and one that deserves as much time as we can give it. He kept bringing up the issue of hospitalization and inpatient treatment. Finally I said, "Look at the figures. We're talking about a total of 220 million people. By your own estimates, 50% to 70% of the people who go to nonpsychiatric MDs have mental rather than physical health problems. That is a huge number of people, but how many of them can require hospitalization?" His answer startled me. He said, "More than we can handle." And that was probably true.

That is quite illustrative of how differently we sometimes approach a problem. I was thinking of a systems analysis of the whole problem—a pet bias of mine. He was thinking about the problems he sees every day that he is not staffed, equipped, or funded to handle. In any national system those problems would be exaggerated, and quite naturally they were most salient to him. I found that very impactful on my subsequent interactions with him, and it changed the texture of our conversation.

Psychiatrists are exceptionally well-trained in somatic components, and recent changes in recommended training are going to make them even better trained in somatic aspects of mental health. I think they tend to see more serious somatic problems in their practice, possibly through a process of self-selection and selective referral. As a result, those cases become a very salient part of their practice. Phenomenologically, the individual psychiatrist should thus judge the somatic component as being more central and critical than a psychologist would perceive or judge it to be across all cases.

Between the two fields, psychologists are probably more self-consciously scientific. They are very oriented toward a careful step-by-step evaluation of what they are doing. Sometimes

that is productive, and sometimes it is not so productive. I think you can see and predict some of the problems that would crop up between the fields and between individuals in the fields by simply analyzing some of those differences.

In talking to individual psychiatrists, a theme that constantly comes through is the tremendous concern for responsibility for the patient. And they usually add the adjective to make it "legal responsibility." They are probably talking more about inpatients, hospitalized patients, and patients who more often have a very strong and important somatic component to their problems. Of course they would be concerned. When psychologists discuss their role with hospitalized patients, they are much more likely to be talking about specific behavioral regimens, which need some constant attention. The psychologist must be concerned with the total life environment of the patient for a while, develop a set of behavioral orders, and watch to see that certain things get done. When psychiatrists and psychologists deliberate inpatient treatment, you can see them metaphorically passing in the night because they can have quite different things in mind. Psychologists are more concerned with changing the patient's overt behavior and emotional states. They tend to talk more about arousal states that can themselves be changed or can be misattributed. Patient treatment, as a term, can have quite different connotations for the two groups.

Psychologists and psychiatrists also differ substantively in their approach to service review. I think it is fair to say that psychiatrists have built their review system on the traditional medical one. The traditional medical one is a retrospective review system based on the assumption that there are accepted and traditional standards and methods of practice. Psychiatrists' orientation is to weed out some small percentage of people and/or practices not meeting those standards. I have no argument with this; it is perfectly plausible. But psychologists' ideas about standards of review are much more likely to be either concurrent or prospective. A psychologist dwells less on whether the method is traditionally accepted and more on whether the method works. In this view, the professional should state in advance of treatment what the patient's problem is, what treatment is recommended, and what specifically is predicted to be the outcome of the treatment. It is rather scientific and evaluative, but psychologists see this as a review. It is more of a review of a system of treatment than it is a review of an individual practitioner. When discussing the ideal Professional Standards Review Organization (PSRO), conversations between a psychiatrist and a psychologist can become quite animated because they are really talking about qualitatively different types of review.

Nationally there is a societal press to set some of these problems aside, or at least to set them in perspective. I am concerned about what the President and his administration really feel about the interplay between mental health and science. I have not seen any overt push for science from the President. I am worried about whether the President feels any great effort should go into studying human behavior and trying to find out more about it, or whether he thinks we already know enough to help everybody and should just get going. Stated in its extreme form, the situation exemplifies the difference between a spirit of inquiry and a spirit of action. There has been some considerable floundering in mental health policy in Washington. There is a Task Force on National Health Insurance within the Department of Health, Education, and Welfare, which, for a long time, had one person on it. All the other members were delayed presidential appointees at a time when we should have been talking about this important and complicated issue and getting things moving. There has been some conflict on policy and mental health policy between the White House and the Department of Health, Education, and Welfare, provoking the usual Washington rumors about who is going to last how long.

There have also been some recent collaborative efforts between psychology and psychiatry. One significant event was the recent congressional action to increase research funds for NIMH. Dr. Melvin Sabshin, Medical Director for the American Psychiatric Association, and I went to the Liaison Group for Mental Health, of which I was chairperson this year and Dr. Sabshin was chairperson last year. It includes 17 or 18 organizations of psychiatrists, psychologists, behavioral scientists, social workers, nurses, state mental health program directors, child psychiatrists, and the like. The group hammered out a joint statement on the NIMH budget—a lovely letter to write, representing 200,000 professionals in the field of mental health. That is the kind of letter that has an impact on congresspersons, and I think this one did. The separate organizations, of course, expressed their own statements in support of the need for further research funds. Although our efforts to educate Congress were only part of the process, the eventual outcome was the first real dollar increase in research funding for NIMH in five years. Every year before that, President Nixon had slashed that budget. Congress had restored some, but not all, of the eliminated funds. Every year the budget had gone down. In this case, it was a $13 million increase in basic research funds and, in fact, $27 million more than President Ford had recommended. The Health, Education, and Welfare budget was vetoed, and the veto was overridden the very next day.

A sidelight of the cooperative educational effort was that research became the number one priority of the Mental Health Association, the citizen's association. I thought that was a beautiful step forward for our scientists and professionals, to get together with our concerned citizens to discuss a common orientation to national needs. Psychology and psychiatry have also cooperated on recent problems regarding the Forward Plan for Health, in particular on a plan to eliminate disciplinary funding in professional training. We did raise this issue within NIMH and within the National Advisory Mental Health Council. Eventually, disciplinary professional funding for the four disciplines was put back into the budget, at more than a 90% level.

In the Liaison Group for Mental Health, we have taken what I think is a very positive step. It was a matter of concern to a number of people in Washington that the disciplines apparently could not agree on any approach to national health insurance. In the Liaison Group we tried to develop among those 17 or 18 groups (including the disciplines) a joint statement on national health insurance. Over the course of six or eight months we did come out with a statement. It was a statement that was voted out unanimously. We also went to considerable effort to state that the individuals who worked on this statement did not represent their organizations in any sense, and indeed the statement does not fit very well with some of the organizations. It is studiously ambiguous on several points; in essence, it finesses some issues where there is little agreement. On the other hand, it was an important step to state what we do agree on. Some organizations, such as the American Psychological Association, have formally adopted the statement as acceptable. Others, such as the American Medical Association, have disavowed it. It was a preliminary and somewhat controversial step but an important one nonetheless. There are strong agreement and strong collective commitments among us. There are also points of substantive disagreement that should be extensively discussed.

We need to build on and capitalize the differences between psychiatrists and psychologists. I think we need more of both. I think we need more of these two approaches, if you accept my categorization of them being somewhat different. Both are committed to human welfare and service to the national community. Both fields share the cyclical pitfalls in funding for research, training, and service. There hasn't been an instance of one field's funds being cut without the other's being cut. The funding for science, for example, in psychology has been squeezed tremendously in the last few years. In fiscal year 1972, psychology received 2.5% of the total federal funds for basic research in this country. Four years later, in fiscal 1976, our basic research funding decreased to 1.5%, whereas 11.5% of total doctoral scientists are psychologists. Dollars, inflation, and the like held constant, we were effectively cut in science funding relative to other sources. The recent report from the group of chairpersons of psychiatry departments describes a similar phenomenon in cuts of basic research funding for psychiatry, particularly in the area of career development. Funding for disciplinary training for psychology is being squeezed in both the science and professional areas. Psychiatry and psychology are cut at similar times. Actually, they tend to cut one field one year and the other the next year, and you have to go out of your way to collaborate and cooperate. I think we have to stay together on basic issues of planning and funding for science and professional training.

To some extent, psychology and psychiatry have failed to educate the public sufficiently as to their true worth to society. The media's emphasis on fads in both fields and the lack of sympathy for a basic need to fund research and professional training are partly our fault for not putting a sufficient amount of time, education, and money into the education of the public.

Psychology and psychiatry have come from quite different traditions. They have quite different strengths and weaknesses. I don't feel we should make them more alike but rather that we should carefully build bridges between the two fields and nurture their respective strengths. We need some mutually tolerant colleagueship, some collective action toward mutually acceptable goals, and some concerted action in educating the public regarding our ability to deliver services and to accumulate new knowledge. We need some acceptance of our own mutual commitment to public service, human welfare, and science. It is my firm belief that the roles of psychology, psychiatry, and the behavioral sciences in the medical school of the year 2000 depend on our ability to develop an overriding and superordinate sense of collective purpose among our fields.

Reference

American Psychological Association Task Force on Health Research. Contributions of psychology to health research: Patterns, problems, and potential. *American Psychologist*, 1976, *31*, 263–274.

Charles A. Kiesler is Executive Officer of the American Psychological Association. This article was an invited address in the John and Andrea Nielson Distinguished Lecture Series in Psychiatry at the University of Utah, presented in April 1977.

National Health Insurance Testimony to the House of Representatives, November 14, 1975

Charles A. Kiesler

This article summarizes APA's position on national health care and argues that coverage should be based on an individual's impairment rather than on a specific treatment modality. Psychology's pioneering of and advocacy for individualized treatment plans with measurable goals and outcomes, as a means of insuring accountability, is underscored.

Mr. Chairman, members of the Health Subcommittee of the Committee on Ways and Means, I am Charles A. Kiesler, Ph.D., a psychologist and Executive Officer of the American Psychological Association. I am accompanied here today by Herbert Dorken, Ph.D., a psychologist with the Langley Porter Neuropsychiatric Institute at the University of California system in San Francisco and currently chair of the APA's Committee on Health Insurance; and Clarence Martin, Executive Director and General Counsel of our sister organization, the Association for the Advancement of Psychology.

Mr. Chairman, the Board of Directors of the American Psychological Association adopted in July 1971 a position statement on National Health Care. These principles remain valid and I would like to take this opportunity to restate them. "1. All persons should have equal access to all health services, regardless of the ability to pay or of other circumstances such as geographical location. 2. The health care system should protect the individual's rights in regard to human dignity, privacy, and confidentiality. 3. Funding of the sytem should provide for each of the following: (a) direct services for both prevention and treatment of physical and mental illness; (b) a full range of health manpower, including necessary training and upgrading of health care personnel at all levels; (c) research into the causes of illness and its treatment; (d) public education and other population-oriented programs of prevention. 4. The health care system should permit the individual freedom of choice among the full range of health services and providers of these services. 5. Consumers, as well as providers of health services, should have an opportunity to participate in the development of the health care system. 6. Redress for grievances resulting from the providing of personal health services should be available from review bodies which include both consumers and health professionals. 7. The quality and availability of health services should be evaluated continuously by both consumers and health professionals. Research into the efficiency and effectiveness of the system should be conducted both internally and under independent auspices. 8. The system of health care should be responsive to the findings of review bodies, to the results of research, and to emergence of new concepts of service."

Since the adoption of those principles, much has happened in the field of health which reinforces the need for a national health system. Total federal expenditures for personal health services have increased 86 percent to an estimated $28.6 billion for fiscal 1975. The nation is now spending 8.3 percent of the total value of the goods and services it produces for health care. Our national health statistics, however, remain poor in comparison with other industrial nations. The members of this Committee and its predecessor committees in past Congresses have heard testimony on scores of health care bills.

From *The Clinical Psychologist*, 1976, *30*, 18–21. Copyright 1976 by the Division of Clinical Psychology of the American Psychological Association. Reprinted by permission.

The problems raised by these bills are many and the solutions offered by the hundreds of witnesses are often conflicting, seemingly irreconcilable or just down right too expensive. No one at this moment knows what an ideal health system will look like. We can probably reach a consensus, however, on what that ideal system should achieve. It should achieve a long productive life, minimal illness and disability, effective treatment of unavoidable trauma and disease, rapid restoration of optimal functioning following disability, humane treatment, equitable access to quality care; *and* at a cost that permits the realization individually and governmentally of other desirable social and personal goals.

I would like, Mr. Chairman, to address myself to several items which I hope go to specific concerns of this Committee, the interest of the public and the potential contribution of American psychology. The Committee must be concerned not only with the need for a service but with the cost. Health benefits must be paid for and we must all be concerned with cost both as taxpayers and as responsible citizens.

There is ample reason to urge that mental health problems be a major concern of national health programming. Mental health problems are debilitating and often seriously impair or prevent employment. They can and do lead to physical illness. They place inordinate demands on the time of medical practitioners not equipped by training to cope with them. Data indicate that psychological disorders are frequently the factors precipitating a visit to a physician. Reasonable mental health benefits, provided by qualified, experienced mental health practitioners including psychiatrists and psychologists will reduce the per capita cost of health care. The availability and provision of mental health services have been shown through research to reduce dramatically the extent of subsequent use of surgical, in-hospital and diagnostic laboratory services. From the available data it appears that there are in the United States somewhere between 8 million and 10 million persons presently utilizing mental health services. It is further estimated that an additional unmet need exists for 11 to 16 million individuals. Even if the incidences of need remain constant and increases only proportionate to population increases are projected, an additional

number will come in need each year. Kramer's data does show that patient care episodes increased from .63% of the population in 1946 to 1.03% in 1955, 1.2% in 1963 and 1.99% in 1971. Utilization of mental hospitals during this period declined from 61% in 1955 to 25% of the reported episodes in 1971. Outpatient clinics and community health centers accounted for 61% of the episodes.

An increase in total episodes as well as greater utilization of outpatient treatment argue the necessity of a health policy which not only covers mental treatment in hospitals and other institutional settings, but in outpatient facilities and private office settings as well. We strongly support the concept that defined mental health impairment, clearly delineated, should be included under National Health Insurance. We recognize also that it would be inappropriate and clearly impractical to try to include all human ills, mental or physical, under National Health Insurance. Limitations of treatment methods and utilization review of accepted treatments are necessary and proper in a NHI scheme.

Recent developments in the treatment of mental health problems have focused on the concept of individualized treatment plans for every patient. The individualized treatment plans include the nature of the problem, the goals for treatment, and the steps or procedures to be taken to meet those goals. It is no longer acceptable to simply state that a patient is under treatment. Every patient should have an individualized written treatment plan based on an assessment plan derived from diagnostic procedures developed along proven psychological principles. One of the great advantages of such a treatment plan is that it provides careful monitoring of the effectiveness of the treatment provided to each patient. It also provides for very careful control of the kind and amount of treatment provided. Individualized treatment plans are now required for meeting accreditation standards and have been required by court action.

Psychologists have pioneered in the development of specific treatment plans. The psychologist's basic orientation in the behavioral sciences with a special focus on mental health has encouraged psychologists to carefully monitor their treatment approaches. Psychologists were involved in setting up behavior or measurable objectives to treatment plans for some time. This very special orientation of the psychologist in the treatment of mental health problems permits not only careful monitoring of the treatment approaches but also effective evaluation of the outcomes of those approaches. With individualized written treatment plans which include objectives it is possible to determine to what extent the treatment plans are succeeding. Rather than maintaining a treatment approach which would not lead to changes, this system of individualized treatment plans permits the changing of treatment strategies to meet individualized patient needs. It also tends to maximize the treatment given by any therapist for any patient. This procedure has now been incorporated in the Standards for Providers of Psychological Services adopted by the American Psychological Association.

Limitations of Treatment

One of the significant concerns raised in any discussion of National Health Insurance coverage for mental health services involves the possibility of coverages for a range of treatment approaches some of which may not be standard or acceptable treatment methods. There have been in the mental health field innovative treatment approaches, some of which are clearly in the experimental stage and many of which may never achieve acceptance by the majority of the profession and would therefore never become acceptable standard procedures of the profession. It is critical that any National Health Insurance plan provide adequate coverage for the treatment procedures which have become acceptable, reasonable treatment methods meeting the standards of practice and ethics of the profession.

There are several controls and restrictions in this regard which should be pointed out. The training programs for clinical and counseling psychologists which exist in the major universities and hospitals throughout the country receive approval or accreditation by the American Psychological Association after careful review of all components of those programs.

The accreditation process by the American Psychological Association assures a very significant degree of control over the nature and quality of training programs for the future health service providers in psychology. The accreditation system provides reasonable and acceptable standards for insuring that the training of health service providers in psychology includes the standard and well-founded psychological principles and techniques which have proven useful in the mental health field.

Another aspect of the profession's concern with reasonable acceptable treatment procedures are the established Standards for Providers of Psychological Services, the Code of Ethics and Professional Conduct, and other professionally designated control systems.

Psychology's peer review programs now in effect in all 50 states provide perhaps the most significant control in this area. Peer review organizations have already proven extremely useful in providing the appropriate checks and balances to treatment approaches by mental health professionals. Given the current organization in all the states and the early successes of the peer review system, it is anticipated that the peer review experiences will provide an efficient and reasonable method of monitoring treatment approaches as well as insuring the best service available to every individual patient.

Focus of Treatment

The focus of the mental health coverage should be on the impairment of the individual rather than on any specific treatment approach. That is, coverages should be identified by the nature of impairment with the specific treatment plan to be determined by the individualized problem and treatment plan. One of the great problems in the mental health field is that some individuals will identify almost anything as being a reasonable psychological or mental health problem and therefore the cost projections become astronomical. This is clearly a distortion. The most accepted epidemiological estimates of the incidence of mental health problems in this country range around 10 to 20%. This is the percentage of individuals identified as being impaired in some fashion in their coping and requiring some kind of treatment. The population at risk then, for mental health insurance reaches a maximum of approximately 20%. Moreover, many of the problems which may be identified as mental health problems have in the past and continue to be seen by the general medical practice field. That is, there are existing mental health services which are being provided by health programs not necessarily identified as mental health. A large portion of a pediatrician's work for example, consists of dealing with a range of developmental, behavioral, and other mental health problems of the infant.

The recent experience of insurance firms in the coverage of mental health problems provides good data for delineating those services which should be reimbursable. It has become very obvious that it is possible to identify those services which should be reimbursable and to eliminate those which should not be reimbursable. The great concern of unlimited coverage for a range of human condition problems has been solved and control methods exist. We will cite specific examples under the cost and utilization material later in this testimony.

Who Treats Mental Illness

The number of psychologists and psychiatrists providing health services are about evenly divided. Most providers in both professions function in multiple delivery systems as well as in teaching, hospital and outpatient services. Psychologists are better distributed geographically than psychiatrists and there is a consistent trend towards recognition of psychologists as primary health providers in private insurance contracts and state and federal programs.

Estimates of total professional manpower in health delivery services by psychologists and psychiatrists have been estimated by DHEW as 28,332 physicians specializing in Psychiatry or Neurology (1972) and 26,927 psychologists (1970) in health providing services of some kind on a part or full time basis.

An American Psychological Association study in 1972 reported the following findings for psychologists in health delivery settings: 36% identified themselves as clinical psychologists;

19% were employed in hospital settings; 6% in medical schools, and 15% in clinics; 8% of the clinical psychologists were engaged in research and 13% were engaged in management or administration. Only 2% were foreign trained.

Psychologists practice in nearly all health care settings, with frequency of practice being approximately equally distributed among private practice, outpatient clinic, and hospital based practice. In hospitals, psychologists may be on the professional staff or the affiliated staff or on the hospital salary payroll. Psychologists are part of most Health Maintenance Organizations, and are involved in most Community Mental Health Centers, sometimes as program directors. They less commonly practice in Foundations for Medical Care, although they are included in such Foundations in several states. In California, recent legislation provides that in Health Maintenance Organizations offering mental health services, the staff shall include both psychologist and psychiatrist and the consumer shall have personal choice and direct access to either provider.

Psychologists are on the staffs of all accredited Medical Schools in the United States, and will typically have clinical as well as teaching and research responsibilities in such facilities.

Fee or funding arrangements for psychological services are quite varied, being rather evenly divided between fee-for-service charges and indirect charges included under hospital costs or similar organized health settings. The fee-for-service billing by the psychologist is the most common practice for licensed psychologists functioning as independent professionals, and is probably the least expensive to the consumer in the long run, because it does not include capital cost, overhead and other indirect expenses of an intermediary institution or professional referral.

Recognition of psychologists as independent qualified mental health service providers has recently been reflected by HEW spokesmen: *"The tradition that all service must be provided by a physician or under his guidance is now giving way to practical reality. As an example of this trend, as of January 1, 1975, all government employees' insurance plans will permit payments to psychologists, without requiring a physician's supervision. This more practical attitude should be encouraged by all of us."*

A number of other federal and state programs recognize psychologists as primary health providers. The Rehabilitation Act of 1973— Public Law 93-112—recognizes psychologists who are licensed/certified according to State statute, along with physicians, for diagnostic and restorative services to beneficiaries. CHAMPUS recognizes the autonomous practice of clinical psychology in its nationwide health benefits program which covers dependents of military personnel, retired military personnel, and other beneficiaries. CHAMPVA is a program for disabled veterans which recognizes psychologists as autonomous practitioners. Community Mental Health Centers regulations provide that psychologists may serve as program directors. Veterans Administration provides that directors of VA mental hygiene clinics may be qualified psychologists or other mental health professionals who will be responsible for the formation and general supervision of administrative activities inherent in the professional programs of the clinic. Veterans Administration regulations provide that psychologists and other health professionals licensed/certified by the State may provide services on a fee basis to outpatient through VA clinics. The Work Incentive Program (WIN) accepts professional evaluations by licensed/certified psychologists as well as physicians, as to evidence of determinable mental impairment. Work Injuries Compensation of Federal Employees coverage has been broadened so that the definitions of "physician" and "medical, surgical and hospital services and supplies" include clinical psychologists. (Public Law 93-416). The Social Security Bureau of Disability Insurance accepts the reports of psychologists without physician referral or endorsement as evidence of disability for social security benefits. Health Maintenance Organization legislation (Public Law 93-222) includes clinical psychologists among providers of services.

Department of Defense includes psychologists in its policy which provides that "any qualified health professional may command or exercise administrative direction of a military health care facility . . . without regard to the officer's basic health profession."

Some major health-insurance carriers have recognized the disadvantages of mandatory medical referral/supervision and have voluntarily included psychologists as autonomous providers of services in many of their contracts. These firms include, but are not limited to Aetna, Guardian, Liberty Mutual, Massachusetts Mutual, Occidental, Prudential, Travelers, and Teachers Insurance and Annuity Association (TIAA).

At this writing twenty-three states and the District of Columbia have enacted legislation requiring private major medical health insurance plans to make direct payments to psychologists in the same manner as payments are made to physicians without prior referral or supervision in plans providing mental health coverage.

Fifteen states give this kind of independent provider recognition to psychologists under their state Medicaid plans. The geographical distribution of psychology's service providers does not differ significantly by region from the 1970 population census: *"Psychologist service providers are distributed throughout the United States in approximately the same way that the total population of consumers of psychological services are distributed. Geographic maldistribution, at least regionally, apparently does not apply to psychologists."* An in depth study of geographical distribution in one state is the 1974 *Ohio* study by James T. Webb, Ph.D., *Ohio Psychologist,* (July 1974), XX, 4, 5–12, copies of which were submitted to this committee by us on April 15, 1975 and September 26, 1975.

Utilization and Cost

At the present time, it has been estimated that in the United States we are spending around $3 billion a year for the diagnosis and treatment of mental conditions. The cost of undiagnosed, untreated conditions has been estimated at $24 billion annually, including $10 billion in lost wages, $2 billion in lost taxes, $2 billion in the transfer of spendable income and $10 billion in improper diagnosis and ineffective treatment. The cost of untreated mental conditions is eight times the cost of direct services.

William Follette, chief psychiatrist, and Nicholas A. Cummings, chief psychologist, both of the Kaiser Foundation Hospital and the Permanente Medical Group of San Francisco, California, have recently completed a study, yet unpublished, on utilization of psychological services in the Kaiser experience. (Editor's note: See Cummings, Medicare Reform, Section I.)

Review of the literature shows that mental conditions can reduce efficiency on the job by 20%, tend to increase absenteeism significantly, result in the higher use of medical benefits and spuriously inflate the cost of health insurance contracts provided by employers. It has also been found that mental conditions result in under-employment and, with appropriate intervention and treatment, individuals with mental conditions can be rehabilitated into productive lives in which their incomes produce new tax money, off-setting the cost of treatment and reducing their burden to welfare rolls and state hospital systems.

When comparing the cost of treatment for mental conditions, it becomes evident that psychological therapy is the treatment of choice in the large majority of cases, with drug therapy running a second choice and hospitalization a third. However, the utilization of mental health services currently measured by dollar costs is just the reverse. Hospitalization tends to be over-utilized and could be reduced by one-third. Medication, where prescribed, may be used ineffectively and frequently avoids getting down to the basic problem, which can be uncovered through psychotherapy. Psychotherapy, though a costly procedure, is an insurable benefit and, in the final analysis, appears to be a most effective way of intervening into mental behavioral conditions.

Failure to diagnose and treat mental conditions put an undue burden on the delivery of other health services. There is general agreement that about 60% of the patients going to family doctors' offices for physical symptoms have a psychological problem which is either a primary problem or aggravates the physical conditions or interferes with effective treatment regimens.

Studies also indicate that high users of medical services are frequently emotionally disturbed, often suffering from mental depression. Other studies indicate that if appropriate recognition of mental conditions is made, medical utilization by these individuals can be reduced by as much as one-third, offsetting the cost of mental diagnosis and treatment. Studies further reveal that the general practice physician himself frequently does not recognize mental conditions, and, if he does, he may not know how to treat or how to refer the patient for appropriate help. "*In one of the few studies in an industrial setting (Kennecott Copper, Utah), access to mental health and counseling services showed a before and after reduction of hospital and medical-surgical costs (55%) and absenteeism (52%) for the treated employee. A comparable control group showed no favorable change over time.*"

Other sets of data indicate that with appropriate treatment, people with mental conditions, including the mentally retarded, can become gainfully employed, increase their incomes, improve their job efficiency, reduce sick time and absenteeism from the job. The cost of direct services for mental conditions can be offset by new tax monies on increased earnings to these individuals.

The cost of training the necessary manpower, the making of manpower available to various segments of the population, and the cost of needed research must be borne in mind in calculating the cost of services. However, comparing the cost of mental health manpower with the cost of training physician specialists reveals that it is cheaper to train mental health specialists and have them deal with the mental conditions at the earliest entry point into the health system. Reliance upon the primary physician as a referral source for mental conditions is not only a costly, but an inefficient way to get people into treatment.

Costs of mental health benefits under various insurance programs have been surveyed by a number of sources.

As the single largest group health plan in the United States, as well as a plan with virtually unlimited mental disorder insurance, the experience of the Civilian Health and Medical Plan of the Uniformed Services should be of particular interest.

Dorken's study of the CHAMPUS experience in those 10 states which constitute the concentrated use of CHAMPUS in FY 1973 reveals a great deal of information relatable to National Health Insurance. The benefits available under CHAMPUS in 1973 for mental disorder were almost unlimited. In the 10 states studied, the insured population under CHAMPUS consisted of 3.26 million individuals. Mental disorder utilization of the benefits consisted of 1.87% of the insured. Total cost per user averaged $1,138 (government cost $929) in the year. On a per capita basis these extensive mental health services were at an annual cost of $19.82 (CHAMPUS cost $16.15 or on a monthly basis, $1.35) per capita. The total mental health services absorbed 12.8% of the total health benefit funds before any adjustment for the savings they afforded from the decrease in utilization of physical health benefits, such as have been demonstrated in every program tracing the adjusted cost of mental health benefits. Of the unadjusted 12.8%, 58% was expended for hospital services, 30.5% for outpatient visits (all procedures, all professions). Of the outpatient visits, 46% were to psychiatrists, 23% psychologists, 10% social workers, 2% attending physicians, and the 19% balance distributed among all other therapists and clinics.

The unadjusted percentage of the total health benefit funds utilized by CHAMPUS is nearly twice as high as most plans report. This is probably due to two factors, the nearly unlimited extent of the benefits and the special make-up of the patient population.

The 1974 hearings before the Senate Post Office and Civil Service Committee on the 1973 Federal Employees Health Benefit Act found Blue Cross and Aetna reporting much lower figures. Policies under these two plans provide coverage for about 80% of the insured under FEHBA. Aetna reported a mental disorder utilization experience of 1.2% and the Blues reported 1.1%. Mental disorder cost for Blue Shield-Blue Cross represented an unadjusted 7.3% of total claims and have for several years remained in the 7% range. The plans cover over 5 million beneficiaries and based on the 1972 utilization rates for mental health services, 65% of which were utilized by hospitalized in-patients, show a cost of $11.92 per covered person (or less than one dollar a month). In 1971 Aetna cost allocated 8.6% to mental

disorder coverage; and in 1972, with psychologists recognized directly, without physician referral, the cost dropped to 8.5%.

Clearly, there is variance in utilization among age groups, sex, type of employment, socio-economic level, and type of insurance coverage available. Such variance notwithstanding, the growing body of reports, make it evident that meaningful mental health benefits are well within feasible fiscal limits. Indeed, there is some evidence, particularly from service in organized settings that the provision of mental health services can reduce other health plan utilization. These findings speak clearly to the need for comprehensive health benefits with continuity of care and incentives to community based alternatives to hospital care.

Spiro (Am. J. Pub. Health, 1975, 65, 139–43) compared fee service to cost financing in a union program and found that over the four-year period only 2.73% of the population at risk used mental health benefits. Utilization never exceeded 1.3% per year. Cost remained well under 50 cents per month per capita. "The removal of restrictive deductibles and early co-insurance produced none of the predicted dire effects." Hospitalization was found to be substantially higher in fee service clients. Removing barriers to hospitalization while placing restrictions on outpatient care, is a good way to run program costs up.

Scheidmandel summarized considerable utilization experience (Psychiatric Annals, 1974, 4, 58–74). She notes that all the group practice plans have much lower rates of hospital admissions and days of care than do fee service plans. Of plans reporting office visits, these ranged from an average of 4 to 15 per patient. Less than 10% of patients had more than 20 visits to a psychiatrist in a year.

Cohen and Hunter (Am. J. Orthopsychiatry, 1972, 42, 146–53) compared a fee service indemnity coverage to a community mental health center (CMHC) for retail clerk union groups in Los Angeles over a seven year period intended to provide saturation level services. Different patterns of utilization were apparent. Inpatient services accounted for 33% of costs in the Merged Trust Indemnity Plan, 8% at the center though overall utilization was higher 1.6% vs. 5.6%. The greater utilization through the center yielded higher costs but a lower cost per user, $345 vs. $245. It is concluded that hospitalization can only be avoided when community services are available in meaningful quantity unless the community is to become a dumping ground for hospitalized patients.

Mendel (American Psychiatric Association Convention, 1973) reported on prepaid experience with 6,000 welfare patients in Southern California. Utilization averaged 5.8% of the population with only one case hospitalized. The psychiatric care cost 41 cents per member per month. The importance of this study is that it contradicts the conventional wisdom that the indigent population is a higher risk for coverage than the employed. Substantial evidence indicates that utilization of mental health benefits do not produce an unwarranted demand for services that will financially endanger a health insurance program. The utilization of mental health benefits reduces medical and surgical utilization of the program and early availability of mental health treatment in outpatient facilities reduces the utilization of high cost institutional care.

Quality of Service

Psychologists are licensed or certified by statute in 47 states and the District of Columbia. The three states without statutes (Missouri, Vermont, and South Dakota) presently have legislation pending.

The standard for licensing developed by the American Psychological Association consists of a doctoral degree, a comprehensive written and oral standard examination, as well as supervised experience.

The Council for the National Register of Health Service Providers in Psychology was established at the request of the Board of Directors of the American Psychological Association to the American Board of Professional Psychology. The National Register of Health Service Providers in Psychology, a voluntary listing, is designed to identify psychologists who are licensed or certified to practice in their states *and* who are *health service providers.* Though only recently published, the Register has already

been adapted by Blue Cross-Blue Shield for its governmentwide federal employee plan.

Certification or licensure of psychologists under state law is not by specialty designation per se, no more than are physicians, dentists or lawyers licensed by specialty practice under their applicable state laws. The Register is designed to complement such statutes by identifying those licensed/certified psychologists who are health service providers.

The Council for the National Register has developed a very careful review process to assure that psychologists who are included in the Register will have had the minimum training and experience in the health services field. Specifically, to be included in the Register, the psychologists must have a *doctorate degree from an accredited university* (except for a few who have many years of practice and have been licensed at other academic levels) and must be *licensed or certified by the Boards of Examiners of Psychology* at the independent practice level in their states or the District of Columbia, and have a *minimum of two years of supervised health service experience.*

The Council for the National Register was established in recognition of the need for the development of a system by which various governmental, health services, other organizations, and individual consumers can identify psychologists who meet the *standards of practice in their states and who have training and experience in the health services field.* The National Register, working closely with the statutory State Boards of Examiners of Psychologists throughout the country and with other public and professional organizations identify psychologists who maintain the standards of their profession through state licensing and certification, and who are trained and experienced in the delivery of health services.

The first *National Register of Health Service Providers in Psychology* was published in July of 1975. This Register identifies psychologists throughout the country who meet the above-mentioned standards, assures the public, government agencies, and others that the persons included meet the criteria established by the Council for the National Register, based on the professional Standards of the American Psychological Association. The Register and supplement list approximately 7,500 licensed psychologists who meet the criteria of health service provider.

There are other safeguards within the profession of psychology to insure responsible professional service.

For twenty years the American Psychological Association with its affiliated state organizations has operated a system enforcing its Code of Ethical Conduct.

Organized psychology is developing a system of Professional Standards Review Committees at the Federal PSRO system, to review the quality, cost, and appropriateness of service beyond the strictures of ethical conduct. This system is currently operational in all fifty states and the District of Columbia, and even at this early stage in its development, it is obvious that it is very effective in identifying and controlling excessive cost, over-utilization and questionable practices. It has also proved helpful in verifying the utility of conventional and innovative therapeutic techniques.

Psychology believes that peer review is an absolute necessity in the continuing development of mental health services as well as in insuring economical and responsible treatment for those who seek mental health services today. We view the government's PSRO system with great hope and believe that if properly developed, PSRO will be a mechanism for determining more effective and appropriate treatment procedures in an area of health service where many questions remain unanswered. Psychologists do not believe that a great deal can be accomplished for the future under a peer review system and a mental health delivery system which retards the effectiveness of an open relationship between the professions working in the mental health area. By assuring access to the different disciplines in mental health, thereby imposing on them the responsibility of working together to find better ways of treating emotional and mental disorders, through PSRO, the Congress will have established the groundwork for rapid future progress in mental health. By failing to adequately recognize the interdisciplinary nature of mental health service, the Congress will have not so much damaged the profession of psychology as it will have damaged the opportunities for better service to the public in the future.

Charles A. Kiesler is Executive Officer of the American Psychological Association.

This testimony was developed in collaboration with Ralph Nemir and Clarence Martin, with the input and comments of Jack Donahue, Al Wellner, Herbert Dörken, and Mona Marie Olean, as well as the production assistance of the staff of the Association for the Advancement of Psychology.

Testimony of the American Psychological Association at the National Health Insurance Hearing, October 4, 1977

Charles A. Kiesler

This testimony states that national health insurance should include mental health benefits, psychologists as independent providers of mental health care, freedom for consumers to choose among health care providers and modes of service delivery, formulation of national health goals developed through public participation and open to change, and strong evaluation measures and accountability controls.

Mr. Secretary, thank you for this opportunity to give our views on national health insurance. I am Charles Kiesler, a psychologist and Executive Officer of the American Psychological Association.

I will present five brief statements on how psychologists view national health insurance and how we would hope to guide you in your deliberations.

Our first point: *Mental health benefits should be included in national health insurance on a cost-efficient basis.* By this I mean that mental health benefits should clearly be included in the insurance package for outpatient and inpatient care; but I also mean that those mental health services to be covered must be delivered in a manner that is effective for the client, equitable to all social and economic groups, and cost-efficient to the taxpayer. Simply put, we do not support insurance coverage for mental health care that is delivered in any other way. We firmly believe that psychological services can stand the tests of peer review, empirical testing, and cost-effectiveness evaluation. Allow me to give you a few examples.

In a study that has now gone on for over 15 years at a large health maintenance organization (HMO) in California, it was found that fully 60% of all patients coming to see a physician were suffering from problems that were emotional and not physical in origin. The researchers found that when patients are sys-

tematically referred for psychotherapy there is a dramatic reduction in utilization of medical services immediately and continuing over an 8-year period. In 85% of the cases, the individual was seen by a psychotherapist for 15 sessions or less. The conclusions of the researchers are that short-term therapy can not only pay for itself in reduced medical costs, it can actually save money for the HMO while assuring good patient care. They also suggest that if appropriate psychological services are not covered in national health insurance, the system could become swamped by those people with emotional problems who take them to a physician for medical treatment.

In another long-term study, an industrial company started a program of psychotherapy and systematic referral for their workers who abused alcohol. The results of the program in financial terms were very positive—they estimated a return of almost $6 for every $1 invested. In human terms the program meant significant reductions in job absenteeism and in the use of hospital, medical, and surgical services.

These two examples of psychological services delivered in a cost-efficient and effective way are not used to suggest that the main purpose of mental health benefits in national health insurance will be to reduce the costs of medical care. Millions of people have mental and emotional disorders, with symptoms that range in severity between a mild problem to total disability. They deserve to be treated for these disorders, but the questions of right to treatment and funding for that treatment through the specific mechanism of national health insurance should be considered separately. The separation point is our requirement for cost-efficiency, equity, and effectiveness.

The President's Commission on Mental Health, which has acknowledged its debt to you, Mr. Secretary, for your support, has outlined in its preliminary report the scope of mental health problems in our nation, some of the issues of financing, access to service, and insufficiency of support for our mental health system, and some of the problems in attempting to view mental health as something that can be differentiated from physical, social, and environmental factors. We echo those findings and suggest to you that the appropriate inclusion of mental health benefits on a cost-efficient basis in national health insurance will be a major step in improving the total health of our nation.

Our second point: *Psychologists should be included as independent providers of mental health care in national health insurance.* As a clinical profession, the practicing psychologist has had more years of education and training in the theory and practice of mental health care than any other health discipline. As a science-based profession, we are open to new ideas and have been in the forefront of support for peer review, formal evaluation of the outcome of therapy, interdisciplinary cooperation, strict and public standards for excellence, and accountability to the public for the services we provide.

The care that psychologists give, as well as the techniques of care that we have pioneered, have been shown to be effective, affordable, and appropriate. We are recognized directly in such major federal programs as CHAMPUS, the Federal Employees Health Benefits Plan, the community mental health centers program, and the HMO program. We expect to be included as independent providers of mental health care in national health insurance. To exclude psychologists will mean to deny the public access to one-half of the fully trained doctoral-level mental health service providers. Past experience in health insurance programs including CHAMPUS, Aetna, and Blue Cross has shown

that the inclusion of psychologists in a rational, controllable mental health benefits package is a positive step in promoting cost-efficient care and improved health status.

Our third point: *The consumers of health care must be assured of their right to choose among providers of care and modes of service delivery.* The structure of national health insurance must be such that there are specific details of coverage that are applicable across a broad range of service delivery options. The consumer of health care, and not the administrator of the health insurance program, should make the decision about which of a range of health professionals will provide care and through what mode of practice it will be delivered. Thus, coverage should be flexible enough to include the modes of private practice, HMOs, community mental health centers, and future innovations in delivery systems. We feel that a healthy spirit of competition among modes of delivery will only benefit the consumer.

Our fourth point: *Explicit national goals should be formulated to guide national health insurance. They should be created after open public participation and should be open to reconsideration and change.*

A major purpose of national health insurance must be to improve the quality, equity, and cost-efficiency of personal health services. It follows, then, that the program should be guided by national goals that reflect the needs and priorities of the citizens who receive those services. Open public discussion should provide the basis for these national goals, and public participation should be used to keep them flexible and responsive to needed change.

The goals should focus on the *outcomes* of service delivery. We can suggest such goals as these: reduce the needless use of medical care, increase the awareness of personal nutrition, reverse the rise of alcoholism, and provide adequate care for the mentally disabled in their own communities.

Through creation of national goals and through examination of our progress toward reaching them, we can evaluate the success of national health insurance. Through a reimbursement schedule that is created to achieve these outcome goals, we will have a clear direction for national health insurance. Through valid public participation in the creation and periodic reexamination of these national goals, we will provide relevance and public support for national health insurance.

Our final point: *Strong evaluation measures and accountability controls must be made an integral part of the national health insurance program.* The investment of time, energy, and dollars required for a comprehensive national health insurance package must not be wasted through inefficiency, ineffectiveness, or insufficiency of effort. To prevent this, we see three programs—valid data collection, strong evaluation measures, and realistic accountability controls—as vital parts of that package. These administrative and professional measures will allow us, (a) to have a clear idea of what our program outputs are, (b) to analyze that output in comparison to national goals and in comparison to our general goals of equity, effectiveness, and cost-efficiency, and (c) to make reasonable demands of our institutions and providers of health care that the services they provide be of benefit to the individual and the society.

We support peer review, but we emphasize that to be truly cost-effective, this review should be performed periodically through the course of treatment—not simply after that treatment has been completed. We support program evaluation but emphasize that this must be an integral, visible part of the national health insurance organization. Program evaluation should be explicitly tied to program change. We support research projects into the effects of alternative reimbursement procedures, where the outcome of that research is measured against its probable effect on achieving our national goals.

To summarize our viewpoint: We feel strongly that mental health services can be delivered in an effective, equitable, and cost-efficient way tailored to public national goals. The national health insurance proposal should take into account both specific national goals and the cost to human welfare in not achieving these goals. It is the net benefit, or cost, of this program to society for which we will all be held accountable. Thank you very much.

Charles A. Kiesler is Executive Officer of the American Psychological Association.

Medicare Reform: Testimony to the U.S. Senate

Nicholas A. Cummings

Medicare and national health insurance must provide mental health benefits because many physical symptoms defy organic explanation. A review of the Kaiser-Permanente Health Plan of Northern California and subsequent research shows that no comprehensive prepaid plan can survive economically without psychotherapy coverage and that a reduction in medical benefits paid to patients receiving psychological services is generally found.

I would like, Mr. Chairman, to address myself to several items which I hope go to specific concerns of this Committee, the interest of the public and the potential contribution of American psychology to the health delivery system in the United States. The Committee must be concerned not only with the need for a service but with the cost. Health benefits must be paid for and we must all be concerned with cost both as taxpayers and as responsible citizens.

There is ample reason to urge that mental health be a major concern of Medicare and NHI programming. The psychological aspects of disability, injury, illness, chronic disease, death, and dying—quite apart from mental disorder are widely recognized by the medical practitioner. In fact, Alex Kelley, M.D., when he testified on National Health Insurance last November before the Subcommittee on Health, House Committee on Ways and Means, took special note of the Kaiser Health Plan data, namely, ". . . that 68% of its doctor visits made by 36% of its 1.3 million members, were for complaints for which no organic cause could be found." (The data is reported in the *New England Journal of Medicine*.)

The Kaiser Health Plan to which Dr. Kelley refers is the Kaiser-Permanente Health Plan which I serve as Chief Clinical Psychologist, Kaiser-Permanente Center (Northern California) San Francisco. With my colleague William T. Follette, M.D., Chief of Psychiatry at the same institution, I have co-authored a number of studies which I believe will be of value to this Committee. The availability and provision of mental health services have been shown through research to reduce dramatically the extent of subsequent use of surgical, in hospital, and diagnostic laboratory services.

The Kaiser-Permanente Health Plan on the West Coast flourished in the post-World War II era because it provided comprehensive treatment at low subscriber rates for all ills without the exclusions, limitations, co-insurance and other troublesome features common to health plans at that time. Kaiser-Permanente, as the forerunner to the modern Health Maintenance Organization (HMO), soon found to its dismay that once a health system makes it simple and free for the patient to see a physician, an alarming inundation of medical clinics by seemingly physically healthy persons occurred. The opposite has always been relatively true in private practice where the doctor's fee is somewhat of a deterrent to overutilization of services. Furthermore, since the financial base at Kaiser-Permanente is one of capitation (subscription), and neither the physician nor the Health Plan derive an additional fee for seeing the patient, rather than becoming wealthy from imagined physical ills, Kaiser recognized early that the system could be bankrupted by what we regard as abuse by the hypochondriac. Early in its history, Kaiser-Permanente added psychotherapy to its list of services; first on a courtesy reduced fee of five dollars per visit and eventually as a prepaid benefit. This additional service was motivated not so much by an initial conviction of the efficacy of psychotherapy, but by the urgent need to get the so-called hypochondriac out of the doctor's office. Out of his initial perception began sixteen years of extensive research, leading to the conclusion that no comprehensive prepaid health system can survive without providing a psychotherapy benefit.

The conclusion from these studies is that in an HMO-type of health plan, patients in emotional distress, finding an unsympathetic or uncomprehending ear when they attempt to discuss their distress with their physician, quickly begin to translate their problems into physical symptoms for which they receive a great deal of attention in the form of X-rays, laboratory tests, prescriptions and return visits to the physician. The question then remained whether these patients would demonstrate a subsequently different utilization of health plan services, given psychotherapy as the treatment of choice for their emotional ills.

In the first of a series of investigations into the relationship between psychological services and medical utilization in a prepaid health plan setting, we (Follette and Cummings, 1967) compared the number and type of medical services sought before and after the intervention of psychotherapy in a large group of randomly selected patients. The outpatient and the inpatient medical utilization for the year prior to the initial interview in the Department of Psychotherapy as well as for the five years following were studied for three groups of psychotherapy patients (*one* interview only; brief therapy and *long-term* therapy) and a control group of matched patients demonstrating similar criteria of distress but not, in the six years under study, seen in psychotherapy. Their findings indicated that: (1) persons in emotional distress were significantly higher users of both inpatient and outpatient medical facilities as compared to the Health Plan average; (2) there were significant declines in medical utilization in those emotionally distressed individuals who received psychotherapy as compared to a control

group of matched emotionally distressed Health Plan members who were not accorded psychotherapy; (3) declines in medical utilization remained constant during the five years following the termination of psychotherapy; (4) the most significant declines occurred in the second year after the initial interview, and those patients receiving one session only or brief psychotherapy (two to eight sessions) did not require additional psychotherapy to maintain the lower level of utilization for five years; (5) patients seen two years or more in regular psychotherapy demonstrated no overall decline in total outpatient utilization inasmuch as psychotherapy visits tended to supplant medical visits. However, there was significant decline in inpatient utilization in this long-term therapy group from an initial hospitalization rate several times that of Health Plan average, to a level comparable to that of general adult Health Plan population.

In a subsequent study we (Cummings and Follette, 1968) found that intensive efforts to increase the number of referrals to psychotherapy, by computerized psychological screening with early detection and alerting of the attending physicians, did not increase significantly the number of patients seeking psychotherapy.

The authors concluded that in a prepaid health plan setting already maximally employing educative techniques to both patients and physicians, and already providing a range of prepaid psychological services, the number of Health Plan subscribers seeking psychotherapy reached an optimal level and remained fairly constant thereafter.

In summarizing sixteen years of prepayment experience we (Cummings and Follette, 1975) *demonstrate that there is no basis for the fear that an increased demand for psychotherapy will financially endanger the system,* for it is not the number of referrals received that will drive costs up, but the manner in which psychotherapy services are delivered that determines optimal cost-therapeutic effectiveness. The find that one session only, with no repeat psychological visits, could reduce medical utilization by 60% over the following five years, was surprising and totally unexpected. Equally surprising was the 75% reduction in medical utilization over a five year period in those patients initially receiving two to eight psychotherapy sessions (brief therapy).

The data offers no conclusive reason as to how and why this early, brief psychotherapeutic intervention resulted in a persistent reduction in medical utilization throughout the following half decade. We have speculated that the results obtained demonstrate a psychotherapeutic effect, inasmuch as the clinical procedure was to offer early and incisive intervention into the patient's crisis problem, get beneath the manifest symptoms to his/her real concerns, and offer a understanding and therapy within the very first session itself. Such a hypothesis would suggest that a patient's understanding or appreciation of the problem and its relationship to his/her symptoms would result in a diminution of the somaticizing of emotions, and a consequent reduction in medical visits. This is in keeping with the experiences of providing psychotherapy under national health care in Great Britain (Balint, 1957). Perhaps a less satisfactory, but an equally plausible hypothesis would hold that the patient attained no mastery over his/her problems and that subsequent to the psychological visit he/she found ways other than visiting the doctor to express emotional distress.

In a further present study we sought (in an eighth year telephone follow-up), to determine whether the results described previously were a therapeutic effect, or the consequence of extraneous factors, or a deleterious effect. It was hypothesized that if better understanding of the problem had occurred in the psychotherapeutic sessions, the patient would recall the actual problem rather than the presenting symptom, and would have both lost the presenting symptom and coped more effectively with the real problem.

The results suggest the reduction in medical utilization was the consequence of resolving the emotional distress that was being reflected in symptoms and doctor's visits. The model patient in this eighth year follow-up may be described as follows:

"She/he denies ever having consulted a physician for the symptoms for which she/he had been originally referred. Rather, the actual problem discussed with the psychotherapist is recalled as the reason for the 'psychiatric' visit, and although the problem is resolved, this reso-lution is attributed to the patient's own efforts and no credit is given the psychotherapist". This reaffirms the contention that the reduction in medical utilization reflected the diminution in the emotional distress which had been expressed in symptoms which were presented to the doctor.

The findings suggest that the expectations of the therapist influence the outcome of psychotherapy, for if the first interview is merely "evaluation" or "intake", not much of therapeutic value is likely to occur in the first interview. If the therapist's attitude is that no real help is forthcoming from less than prolonged "intensive" psychotherapy, she/he may be right (for his/her own patients). Malan (1963), in his classic study of brief psychotherapy, was able to honestly examine the prejudices of his group of psychiatrists about brief therapy: the kinds of benefit possible, the kinds of patients who could utilize it, the permanency of the results, and so forth. He concluded that traditional attitudes about very brief therapy were mostly in the nature of unjustified prejudices. It would appear that therapeutic effects of brief therapy which can be labelled "transference cure", "flight into health", "intellectualization", and other derogatory terms can often be long-lasting and result in a major change in the person's symptoms relationships and even life style. Many of the patients in this study would undoubtedly be called "poorly motivated for treatment" or "drop-outs from therapy" in many psychotherapy clinics.

The Kaiser-Permanente studies have been replicated in a variety of prepaid settings with similar findings. Recently Karon and VandenBos (1975) reported in a study of hospitalized schizophrenic patients that despite the expense of psychotherapy, there were savings of 22% to 36% in total treatment costs because of the shorter hospitalization of patients receiving psychotherapy as compared to patients who received medication and no psychotherapy.

The growing body of evidence reflects the rightful place of psychotherapy in any health delivery system, and suggests that the health model is the present entree for the psychologist into the health delivery system. Inclusion of psychologists as health service providers in medicare as well as national health care will conclude a difficult decade-and-a-half struggle for recognition on the part of the dedicated professional leadership of psychology. But this will occur not only because there is a need for psychotherapy within any comprehensive health delivery system, but also because psychologists are beginning to recognize the contribution of psychotherapy in the health setting.

No one at this moment knows what an ideal health system will look like. We can probably reach a consensus, however, on what that ideal system should achieve. It should achieve a long productive life, minimal illness and disability, effective treatment of unavoidable trauma and disease, rapid restoration of optimal functioning following disability, humane treatment, equitable access to quality care; *and* at a cost that permits the realization individually and governmentally of other desirable social and personal goals.

Summary

It is my contention, Mr. Chairman, a contention supported by substantial research data, that an efficient and economical health delivery system whether it be under Medicare or National Health Insurance can only be developed by making available a psychotherapy benefit similar to that provided under the Kaiser Plan.

We can, as a nation, invest more monies on direct mental health services and, at the same time, obtain significant savings in tax monies, prevent loss of money to employers and employees alike while promoting human welfare! Diagnosis and treatment can be made available to all citizens for a reasonably low cost, and the costs of treatment will be offset by substantial reductions in the costs of other health services.

References

Balint, Michael. *The Doctor, His Patient and the Illness.* New York. International Universities Press, 1957.

Balint, Michael, and Balint, Enid. *Psychotherapeutic Techniques in Medicine.* London, Tavistock Publications Limited, 1961.

Cummings, N. A., Kahn, B. I., and Sparkman, B. *Psychotherapy and Medical Utilization.* As cited in Greenfield, Margaret: *Providing for Mental Illness.* Berkeley, California, Berkeley Institute of Governmental Studies. University of California, 1964.

Cummings, N. A., and Follette, W. T. *Psychiatric Services and Medical Utilization in a Prepaid Health Plan Setting:* Part II. *Medical Care,* 5:25, 1967.

Cummings, N. A., and Follette, W. T. *Brief Psychotherapy and Medical Utilization: An Eight Year Follow-Up.* In Dorken, H. and Associates: *The Professional Psychologist Today: New Developments in Law, Health Insurance and Health Practice.* San Francisco, Jossey Bass (in press. 1975).

Follette, W., and Cummings, N. A. *Psychiatric Services and Medical Utilization in a Prepaid Health Plan Setting. Medical Care,* 5:25, 1967.

Karon, B. P., and VandenBos, G. R. *Treatment Costs of Psychotherapy Versus Medication for Schizophrenics. Professional Psychology,* 6:3, 1975.

Malan, D. H. *A Study of Brief Psychotherapy.* Springfield, Ill. Charles C. Thomas, 1963.

Nicholas A. Cummings presented this testimony on behalf of the Association for the Advancement of Psychology. The author wishes to express his appreciation to the entire staff of the AAP for their collaboration in the development and production of this testimony.

Utilization and Cost
of Mental Health Services

National Institute of Mental Health

More persons are receiving mental health services now than ever before. Long-term inpatient care is decreasing in favor of outpatient care, but inpatient care still consumes over two thirds of the mental health dollar. Outpatient care is the most frequent and least expensive, and utilization rates tend to average between 1% and 2% of those covered.

Introduction

Quantitative assessments of the need for, and feasibility of, a national health insurance mental health benefit must depend heavily on the available mental health services utilization and cost data. Although a wide range of mental health services exist in the traditional psychiatric, general medical, human services, and active lay public sectors, it will be necessary to focus this discussion on those settings which are likely to be eligible for a mental health insurance benefit.

This chapter will contain the highlights of available data which pertain both to current levels and to recent trends in the utilization of what may be termed "medical mental health services." Covered by this definition are the specialized mental health settings which are annually surveyed through the NIMH national reporting program including the inpatient, out-patient, and day treatment services of the following: State and County Mental Hospitals, Veterans and other public mental hospitals, private mental hospitals, psychiatric services in general hospitals, community mental health centers, free-standing outpatient psychiatric clinics, residential treatment centers for emotionally disturbed children, and other multi-service facilities. In addition, available data on the services provided by office-based private

practicing psychiatrists and psychologists will be presented to complete our profile of the specialized mental health services sector.

Finally, the contribution of the general medical sector to both identifying and treating individuals with mental disorders will be presented. Although the mental health services contribution of this sector has often been ignored in the U.S., those countries which have experienced national health insurance or a national health service have found that a substantial amount of these services are provided in the primary medical care sector, which the World Health Organization has called "the keystone of community psychiatry" (World Health Organization, 1973).

Specialized Mental Health Services

The sources of utilization data which report on the above defined specialized mental health service settings, differ considerably in both the methodology used to obtain data and in the content of the available data. These sources include the NIMH national reporting program; the National Ambulatory Medical Care Survey, a national survey of the Joint Information Service of the American Psychiatric Association

From National Institute of Mental Health, *Draft Report: The Financing, Utilization, and Quality of Mental Health Care in the United States*. Rockville, Md.: Office of Program Development and Analysis, National Institute of Mental Health, April 1976.

and the National Association for Mental Health; the Manpower Survey of the American Psychological Association; and the Monroe County, N.Y. Psychiatric Case Register. These multiple sources and others are used in a complementary fashion to fill in as many gaps as possible in the picture of U.S. mental health services utilization.

Inpatient Services Utilization

The inpatient treatment of psychiatric disorders was once the dominant mode of psychiatric care in this country. It remains as an essential form of care for severe psychiatric disorders and as the most costly form of psychiatric treatment. Hence, information on the current rates and manner in which this form of service is utilized are essential to national health insurance deliberations.

The National Institute of Mental Health reporting program found that there were 1,718,000 patient care episodes in all reporting inpatient facilities during 1973. By utilizing a conversion factor of 0.86 patients/episode/year derived from a psychiatric case register, it is possible to estimate that 1,477,000 persons or 0.70% of the population utilized a psychiatric inpatient service during 1973. The distribution of episodes by type of facility is included in Table 1.

The average length of stay varied considerably by type of psychiatric facility, as shown in Figure 1, for inpatient facilities during 1970-71. These data demonstrate that long term psychiatric hospitalization is far from being the modal practice of these facilities. The median lengths of stay for public non-federal general hospitals, private and voluntary general hospitals, private mental hospitals, and V. A.

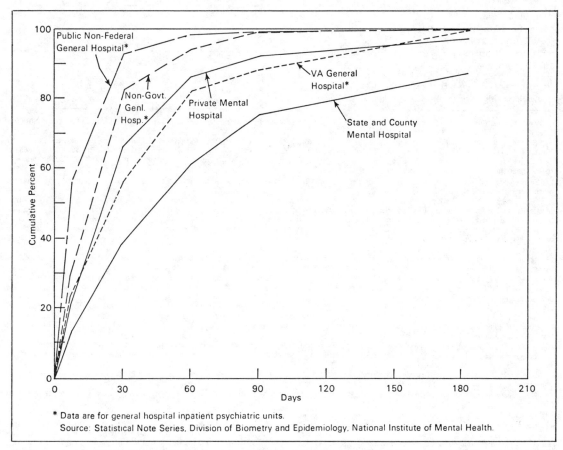

Figure 1: *Cumulative Percent of Patients Released Within Specified Time Periods By Type of Psychiatric Facility, United States, 1970–1971.*

Table 1: *Utilization of Specialized Mental Health Services by Modality and Locus of Care, United States, 1973*

Modality and Locus of Care and Percent of U.S. Population Served	Patient Care Episodes[a] (000s)	Persons Receiving Services[b]	
		Number (000s)	Percent
Inpatient treatment facilities—total	1,718	1,477	30.3
State and county mental hospitals	652		
Private mental hospitals and residential treatment centers	152		
General hospitals with psychiatric units	475		
VA hospitals	208		
Community mental health centers	192		
Other multi-service facilities	39		
Day treatment, all facilities—total	186	173	3.6
Outpatient treatment facilties—total, except private office practice	3,571	3,321	68.2
State and county mental hospitals	339		
Private mental hospitals and residential treatment centers	86		
General hospitals with outpatient psychiatric services	489		
VA hospitals	144		
Community mental health centers	983		
Freestanding and other outpatient facilities	1,530		
Total except private office practice	5,475	4,435[c]	91.1[c]
Outpatient treatment—private office			
Psychiatrists[d]	20,798 (visits)	495	10.2
Psychologists[e]	3,760 (visits)	145	3.0
Total all facilities:[f]			
Unadjusted (not unduplicated)[g]		5,075	
Adjusted (unduplicated)[h]		4,870	100
1973 population of U.S. (in 000s)		209,851	
Percent of population receiving specialized mental health services		2.3%	

[a] Source of data on episodes: Provisional Data on Patient Care Episodes in Mental Health Facilities—1973, Mental Health Statistical Note No. 127, Division of Biometry and Epidemiology, NIMH, 1976.

[b] Patient care episodes converted to number of persons by factors based on data from the Maryland Psychiatric Case Register, as reported by Bahn, A. K. et al: Services Received by Maryland Residents in Facilities Directed by a Psychiatrist. Public Health Reports 80: 405–416, 1965. Conversion factors (ratio of persons/episode): for inpatient care episodes, 0.86; for day treatment and outpatient care episodes, 0.93; for total episodes (inpatient + day treatment + outpatient), 0.81.

[c] Sum of persons receiving inpatient, day treatment and outpatient services exceeds the unduplicated total because some persons were seen in more than one treatment setting.

[d] Includes only office-based psychiatrists. Estimates based on data from following sources: (a) Number of visits from the National Ambulatory Medical Care Survey (NAMCS) 1973 Summary, United States, May 1973–April 1974. Vital and Health Statistics Series 13, No. 21, 1975; (b) Number of patients based on a weighted average of 42 visits/patient/year from Marmor, Judd, et al., *Psychiatrists and Their Patients—A National Study of Private Office Practice*, the Joint Information Service of the American Psychiatric Association and the National Association for Mental Health, Washington, D.C., 1975.

[e] Includes only self-employed clinical and counseling psychologists. Estimates from, or based on, the following sources: (a) American Psychological Association, unpublished data, 1974 Manpower Survey; (b) Visit and patient data are based on an estimate of 40 visits/ psychologist/week for 47 weeks, and an average of 26 visits/patient/year (the same as for non-analytic psychiatrists—see Marmor, J.—Noted).

[f] This total includes only specialized mental health professionals or facilities. Additional facilities providing mental health services, not covered here, include the following: prison hospitals (5,000 persons); nursing homes (462,000 persons); general medical care physicians, neighborhood health centers, and Indian Health Service (5,243,000 persons); Office of Education-supported school programs for emotionally disturbed children (100,000 persons); rehabilitation facilities (96,000 persons); halfway house facilities (62,000 persons); campus mental health facilities (535,000 persons); special military base clinics (50,000 persons); general hospitals without separate psychiatric units, military hospitals, and PHS hospitals (442,000 persons). The total number of patients served (assuming the above persons are unduplicated across facilities) would be 11,865 or 5.7% of the U.S. population.

Additional facilities providing mental health services for which data on persons served are not available include general hospital-based medical clinics and emergency rooms, independent specialized alcohol and drug abuse programs, independent practice social workers, and human service agencies (e.g., family service centers).

Although it is impossible to determine the number of patients using multiple facilities, these estimates are generally conservative and may be considered to be reasonable estimates of the number of persons receiving mental health services for the 1973 calendar year.

[g] Not adjusted for duplication of persons receiving services from both psychiatrists or psychologists in private office practice and other treatment facilities.

[h] Adjusted for duplication of persons treated in both private office practice and other settings. Unpublished data from the Monroe County Psychiatric Case Register for 1971 indicated that about 32% of patients treated by psychiatrists in office-based practice were also treated in other facilities. (Source: see Sharfstein, S. S., Taube, C. A. and Goldberg, I. D.: Private Psychiatry and Accountability: A Response to the APA Task Force Report on Private Practice, AM J Psychiatry 132:43–47 January 1975.) Assuming a similar duplication for patients of private practicing psychologists, and ignoring possible overlap among the estimated total 640,000 patients treated by private psychiatrists and psychologists, the 5,075,000 unadjusted total would be reduced by 205,000 (=0.32 × 640,000) yielding the estimated unduplicated total of 4,870,000. Sum of percents treated in private office practices and in other facilities exceeds 100% due to duplication of persons (205,000) treated in both private office practice and other treatment settings.

general hospitals, range from 7 days to 24 days. Even State and county hospitals, which have a median stay of 44 days, discharge over 75% of their patients within 3 months and over 85% by the end of 6 months. Hence, even the generally regarded "long term care" of the State and county mental hospitals is within the length of stay range of many acute nonpsychiatric medical illnesses.

Although longitudinal patient cohort data is unavailable on a national basis, the existence of a psychiatric case register in Monroe County, New York has made collection of this type of data possible. The Monroe County Psychiatric Case Register, which has been in existence since 1960, and which contains a record of almost all persons coming under care for psychiatric services in the county (including psychiatrists in private office practice), affords an opportunity to study the long term patterns of care received by the population residing in the county.

While Monroe county is not necessarily representative of the United States as a whole with respect to utilization of mental health services, the register data do provide an indication of the long range expectation of utilization of services in mental health settings by a patient cohort. In an analysis of these data now underway, all county residents who were reported for the first time ever to the register during the year ending June 30, 1962, were each "traced" for 10 full years to determine the amount and kinds of services that that patient cohort received over the 10-year period ending June 30, 1972 (Goldberg, 1976). Of particular interest here is the cumulated number of days of inpatient care that this cohort experienced over the decade of follow-up. The results of this analysis, which are summarized below, are also presented in Table 2.

In all, 4,474 persons were reported to the register for the first time during the year ending June 30, 1962. Of this total cohort, 1,876 (42%) had at least one inpatient episode (in Monroe County) over the 10 years following the initial contact, and they experienced an average of 332 days of inpatient care per person in this 10-year period. The corresponding average for the entire cohort (4,474) that came under care in 1962 was 139 inpatient days per person.

As one might anticipate, the utilization of inpatient services was largely concentrated in the years immediately following the initial psychiatric contact. For example, the entire cohort experienced a total of close to 2 million inpatient days in the 10-year period almost half (48%) of which were accumulated within the first three years.

The above data provide a picture of both the current and the long term utilization of in-

Table 2: *Psychiatric Care Experience of 1962 Cohort of New Psychiatric Patients Traced for One and Ten Years, and Similar 1972 Cohort Traced for One Year, Monroe County, New York*

Number of Patients and Type of Care	1962 Cohort Traced for:		1972 Cohort Traced for 1 year
	10 years	1 year	
Patient Cohort:[a]			
Total	4,474	4,474	7,319
With one or more inpatient episodes during period traced	1,876	1,551	1,300
With one or more outpatient episodes during period traced	4,028	3,950	6,934
Average days of care per person in total cohort:			
Inpatient days	139	30	8
Outpatient days[b]	298 (296)	74	81 (80)
Inpatient or outpatient days (total)	437 (430)	104	89 (88)
Average days of inpatient care per person with one or more inpatient episodes during period traced	332	86	47
Average days of outpatient care per person with one or more outpatient episodes during period traced	331 (329)	84	85

Source: Monroe County Psychiatric Case Register

Note: Figures in parentheses reflect average "calendar" days under care, i.e., exclude overlapping days for persons under care of more than one facility at the same time. Parentheses not shown where average "calendar" days and average "facility" days are the same.

[a] Persons reported to Monroe County Register for first time ever.

[b] Duration of each outpatient episode counted as interval between first and last visit.

patient mental health services in the U.S. and in the uniquely monitored Monroe County population. Elsewhere below, additional information is presented on trends and costs of inpatient care.

Outpatient Services Utilization

As noted earlier in this chapter, the primary modality of patient care in mental health facilities has shifted from inpatient to that of outpatient psychiatric care. In 1973, there were 3,571,000 outpatient care episodes reported to NIMH which represented an estimated 3,321,000 individual patients (Table 1). By utilizing data from the Joint Information Service of the American Psychiatric Association and the National Association for Mental Health, the National Ambulatory Medical Care Survey, and the American Psychological Association Manpower Data System, it was possible to estimate that self-employed, private, office-based psychiatrists, and Ph.D. psychologists treated an additional 495,000 and 145,000 individuals respectively in 1973, about two thirds of whom are not seen in other psychiatric settings[1] (Table 1). Thus, the estimated 3,756,000 individuals seen on an outpatient basis during 1973 would constitute approximately 1.8% of the total U.S. population for that year.

The average number of outpatient visits per patient (per episode of care or per year) is an important parameter of outpatient utilization statistics—similar in use to length of stay data which enhances the value of inpatient statistics. Except for community mental health centers, national data on the number of visits per episode for outpatient mental health services are not readily available from the NIMH reporting program. In 1973, there was an average of 5.3 visits per outpatient episode in the 400 reporting federally-funded community mental health centers (NIMH, 1975).

Additional visit data on outpatient mental health facilities are available for Connecticut in 1973 and are presented in Figure 2. These data show a distribution of median number of visits per patient terminated during the year for four types of outpatient clinics. Excluding termina-

tions from State alcohol and drug abuse clinics, the median number of visits in general hospital outpatient clinics, child guidance and community clinics, and State hospital outpatient clinics range from 5 to 8 visits per patient terminated in these settings.

In addition to visits as an index of utilization of outpatient services, the duration of outpatient care episodes (i.e., the interval between first and last visits) provides a useful descriptive measure of utilization. The Monroe County data for the 1962 cohort of new patients described earlier, provide a picture of long term utilization. Of the 4,474 persons in the total 1962 cohort, 4,028 (90%) had at least one outpatient episode of care over a 10-year period, with a 10-year average duration of 331 days per person. For the entire cohort who came under psychiatric care in 1962 (4,474), the corresponding average was 298 days per person (Table 2). Of the total outpatient days accumulated in the 10-year period, 49% were accounted for within the first three years following initial psychiatric contact.

The private office-based practice of psychiatry and psychology is considerably different, in terms of the average number of visits per patient per year, than the other above-mentioned outpatient care settings. For example, the Joint Information Service of the American Psychiatric Association and the National Association for Mental Health revealed that psychoanalysts had an average of 139 visits per patient per year for analytic patients, whereas non-analysts had an average of 26 visits per patient per year (Marmor, n.d.).

By utilizing the National Ambulatory Medical Care Survey data of 20,798,000 psychiatric visits and a weighted average of the visits per patient per year for 10,395 full and part-time office based psychiatrists, it was determined that these psychiatrists saw on the average only 48 different individual patients per year. (DeLozier, 1975; Regier & Goldberg, 1976). Although no direct data are available on the practice of office-based psychology, it was assumed that the approximately 2,000 self-employed clinical and counselling psychologists included saw an average of 26 visits per patient per year (the same average as non-analytic psychiatrists) which would result in an average of

---

[1] It is not known how many of the remaining one-third were seen in other *outpatient* settings.

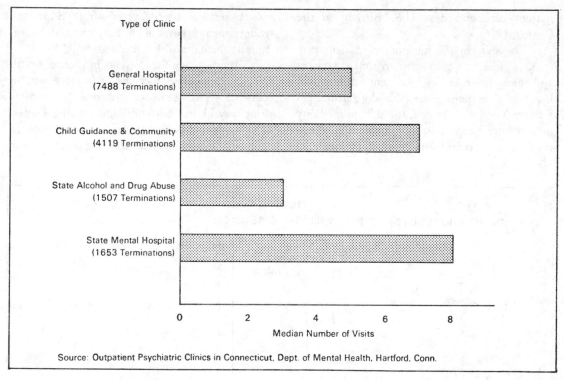

Figure 2: *Median Number of Visits per Patient Terminated, by Type of Clinic, Connecticut 1973.*

72 individual patients per psychologist per year (American Psychological Association, 1976). It is recognized that the statistics quoted here for private practice are extremely conservative in terms of the total volume of services and the total number of patients treated. These estimates would be enlarged considerably if there was an accurate way of estimating the contribution of those psychiatrists and psychologists who are principally employed in non-office-based settings, but who devote a substantial portion of time to the private, fee-for-service practice of their professions. The total volume of outpatient mental health services are also reduced by the unaccounted services provided by other mental health disciplines such as independent practice social workers.

Ideally, one would wish to combine a complete accounting of all persons utilizing outpatient mental health services with data on the intensity (visits per person per year) and duration of outpatient episodes in order to arrive at a more complete profile of outpatient utilization, however, these analyses await further advances in survey and mental health services research technology.

Trends in Utilization of Inpatient and Outpatient Care

In addition to noting the current overall utilization of service levels, it is important to be cognizant of significant trends that have occurred in mental health services utilization during the past few years. For example, significant shifts have occurred in the quantity of patient care episodes, the modality of services, the average length of services, and the locale in which services are delivered.

Figures 3 and 4 demonstrate that over the 19-year period 1955–1973, there was a threefold increase in the number of patient care episodes from 1.7 million to 5.5 million. There is further evidence that population shifts in the next decade will result in a relative increase of the population in those age ranges most at risk for requiring mental health services, with a consequent acceleration of the rate of increase in patient care episodes (U.S. Bureau of the Census, 1976).

The shift in the modality of patient care from inpatient to outpatient treatment services and the addition of day treatment services during this time period are also documented in Figures 3 and 4. Likewise, the shift in modality to a greater proportion of outpatient care has resulted in a corresponding shift of locale at which services are delivered—from State and county mental hospitals to outpatient and community mental health center settings.

Another significant trend in mental health services utilization has been the movement of patients age 65 and over with mental disorders from psychiatric hospitals into nursing homes. The extent of this transition is illustrated in Figure 5 which indicates that the proportion of

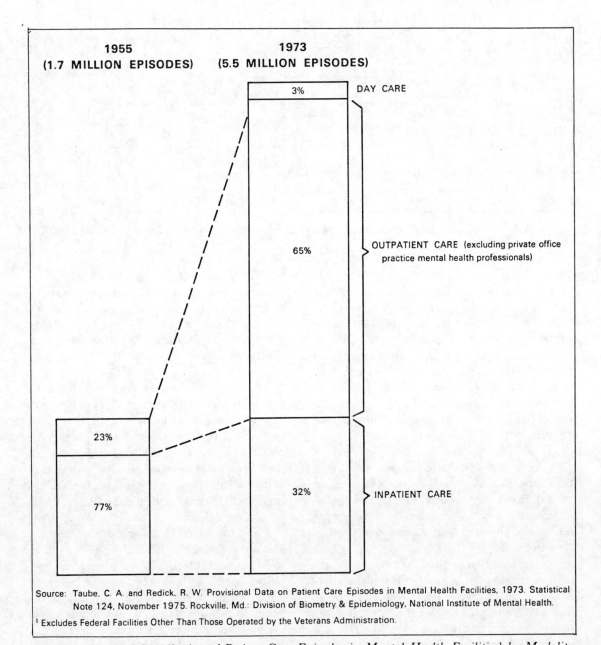

Source: Taube, C. A. and Redick, R. W. Provisional Data on Patient Care Episodes in Mental Health Facilities, 1973. Statistical Note 124, November 1975. Rockville, Md.: Division of Biometry & Epidemiology, National Institute of Mental Health.

[1] Excludes Federal Facilities Other Than Those Operated by the Veterans Administration.

Figure 3: *Percent Distribution of Patient Care Episodes in Mental Health Facilities[1] by Modality United States, 1955 and 1973.*

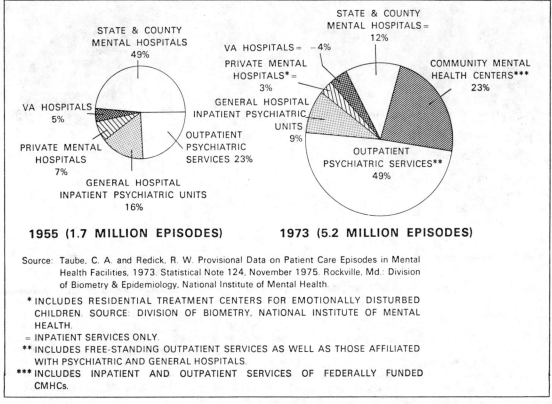

STATE & COUNTY
MENTAL HOSPITALS
49%

VA HOSPITALS
5%

PRIVATE MENTAL
HOSPITALS
7%

GENERAL HOSPITAL
INPATIENT PSYCHIATRIC UNITS
16%

OUTPATIENT
PSYCHIATRIC
SERVICES 23%

STATE & COUNTY
MENTAL HOSPITALS =
12%

VA HOSPITALS = −4%

PRIVATE MENTAL
HOSPITALS* =
3%

GENERAL HOSPITAL
INPATIENT PSYCHIATRIC
UNITS
9%

COMMUNITY MENTAL
HEALTH CENTERS***
23%

OUTPATIENT
PSYCHIATRIC SERVICES**
49%

1955 (1.7 MILLION EPISODES)   **1973 (5.2 MILLION EPISODES)**

Source: Taube, C. A. and Redick, R. W. Provisional Data on Patient Care Episodes in Mental
Health Facilities, 1973. Statistical Note 124, November 1975. Rockville, Md.: Division
of Biometry & Epidemiology, National Institute of Mental Health.

* INCLUDES RESIDENTIAL TREATMENT CENTERS FOR EMOTIONALLY DISTURBED
CHILDREN. SOURCE: DIVISION OF BIOMETRY, NATIONAL INSTITUTE OF MENTAL
HEALTH.
= INPATIENT SERVICES ONLY.
** INCLUDES FREE-STANDING OUTPATIENT SERVICES AS WELL AS THOSE AFFILIATED
WITH PSYCHIATRIC AND GENERAL HOSPITALS.
*** INCLUDES INPATIENT AND OUTPATIENT SERVICES OF FEDERALLY FUNDED
CMHCs.

Figure 4: *Percent Distributions of Inpatient and Outpatient Care Episodes in Mental Health Facilities, by Type of Facility: United States, 1955 and 1973.*

elderly patients with mental disorders in nursing homes compared to psychiatric hospitals has changed from a 53%/47% ratio in 1963 to a 75%/25% ratio in 1969.

As dramatic as the increase in the number of patient care episodes, has been the decrease in average length of stay for those admitted to psychiatric hospitals. This trend can be inferred from Figure 6 which shows the decline of resident patients in State and county mental hospitals and a corresponding increase in number of admissions from 1950 through 1974. Unfortunately, summary national data on actual length of stay trends are not readily available from the NIMH National Reporting program.

Further and more detailed confirmation of the trends in patient care episodes mentioned above for the U.S. are found in studies of actual persons receiving psychiatric services as recorded by the Monroe County Psychiatric Case Register. Among the resident population of Monroe County, New York, the number of persons who received psychiatric services (in in-

patient or outpatient facilities or from psychiatrists in private office practice) rose steadily from a level of 18.4 per 1,000 population in 1962 to 25.1 per 1,000 in 1971—a rise of 36% over this period of years (Figure 7). This rise in utilization is due to the increasing rate of persons receiving only outpatient services—the rate of persons who had at least one inpatient episode during the year fell to a level of 7.8 per 1,000 population in 1971 from a rate of 8.6 in 1962 and 8.9 in 1967.

The actual decrease in average length of stay for patients receiving inpatient psychiatric services in Monroe County is shown in Figure 8 for the same 10-year period. Including patient episodes continuing from the previous year, individuals receiving inpatient services were institutionalized on the average for a total of 182 days during 1962 compared with a corresponding total of 138 days in 1971, representing a decline of about 25% over this period. When episodes of persons already under care at the start of the year are excluded, persons admitted for

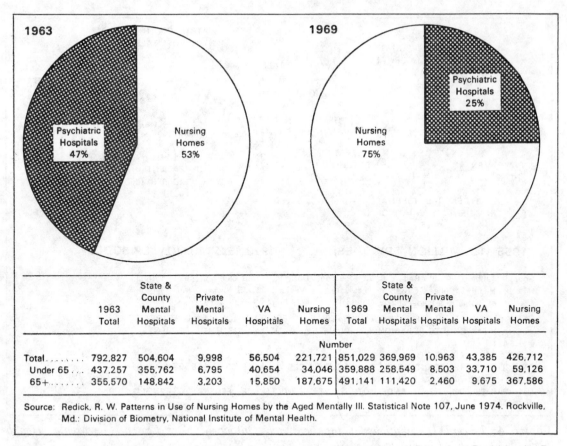

	1963 Total	State & County Mental Hospitals	Private Mental Hospitals	VA Hospitals	Nursing Homes	1969 Total	State & County Mental Hospitals	Private Mental Hospitals	VA Hospitals	Nursing Homes
				Number						
Total.........	792,827	504,604	9,998	56,504	221,721	851,029	369,969	10,963	43,385	426,712
Under 65 ...	437,257	355,762	6,795	40,654	34,046	359,888	258,549	8,503	33,710	59,126
65+........	355,570	148,842	3,203	15,850	187,675	491,141	111,420	2,460	9,675	367,586

Source: Redick, R. W. Patterns in Use of Nursing Homes by the Aged Mentally Ill. Statistical Note 107, June 1974. Rockville, Md.: Division of Biometry, National Institute of Mental Health.

Figure 5: *Number and Percent Distribution of Patients With Mental Disorders Resident in Psychiatric Hospitals and Nursing Homes, United States, 1963 and 1969.*

inpatient care during the year were hospitalized on the average for a total of 61 days during 1962 compared with only 44 days in 1971—a 28% decline.

Additional information on trends in duration of care is provided by a comparison of the Monroe County 1962 cohort mentioned earlier with a similar cohort for 1972, traced for one full year (Table 2). In contrast to the inpatient length of stay trends, Table 2 demonstrates that the average duration of outpatient care for both the 1962 and 1972 cohorts has remained relatively constant over the first year following an initial psychiatric contact. More specifically, there was an average of approximately 85 days of outpatient care per person for those with one or more outpatient episodes during the first year of recorded psychiatric treatment.

In summary, one can reasonably expect that there will continue to be increases in the total number of individuals utilizing mental health services, a decrease in the relative use of inpatient treatment, a decrease in mental hospital average length of stay, an increase in use of outpatient treatment modalities and facilities, and a continuing use of nursing homes for care of the elderly with mental disorders. However, new treatment technologies, changes in the organization of mental health services delivery, and new economic forces such as national health insurance will inevitably affect some or all of these trends.

General Medical Mental Health Services

It is difficult to overestimate the importance of the general medical sector in the provision of mental health services under a national health insurance program. Just as the treatment of viral upper respiratory conditions does not require the services of a specialist in pulmonary medicine, so the treatment of many mild and selected severe psychiatric disorders does not require the services of a mental health specialist. Indeed, the full responsibility for treatment of all psychiatric disorders could not possibly be borne by mental health professionals in this or any other country reporting to the World Health Organization (World Health Organization, 1973).

The magnitude of the prevalence of psychiatric disorders as detected by physicians in general medical practice settings may be summarized for adult patients age 15 and over. Approximately 5% of all patients who visit general medical physicians are undoubtedly affected by primary psychiatric disorders which must be dealt with by such physicians as the most urgent condition of these patients requiring treatment. This minimal figure has been found in studies of visits to office-based physicians in the National Ambulatory Medical Care Survey and in

multiple unduplicated patient cohort studies in various general medical care settings (Fink, 1969; Kessel, 1960; Leopold, Goldberg, David, & Schein, 1971; Locke, Finucane, & Hassler, 1967; Regier & Goldberg, 1976).

In studies where primary care physicians are either trained or sensitized to look for the presence of psychiatric disorders in their patients, it is found that 10% of patients may readily be identified as having a classifiable (ICDA Section V) mental disorder. An additional 5% of patients in these settings are found to have emotional or psychiatric-associated conditions which are not readily classifiable by the International Classification of Diseases. Hence, approximately 15% of patients in general medical settings may be diagnosed as having a psychiatric or emotional disorder (Shepherd, Cooper, Brown, & Kalton, 1966; Locke, 1966; Locke & Gardner, 1969). Specialized medical settings such as hospital-based general medical clinics and hospital emergency rooms are found to have significantly higher rates of psychiatric

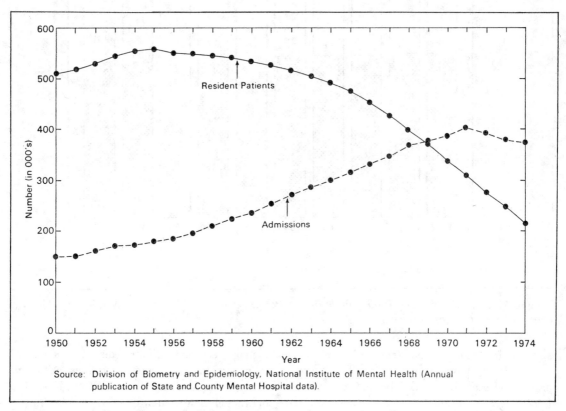

Source: Division of Biometry and Epidemiology, National Institute of Mental Health (Annual publication of State and County Mental Hospital data).

Figure 6: *Number of Resident Patients at end of Year and Total Admissions, State and County Mental Hospitals, United States 1950–1974.*

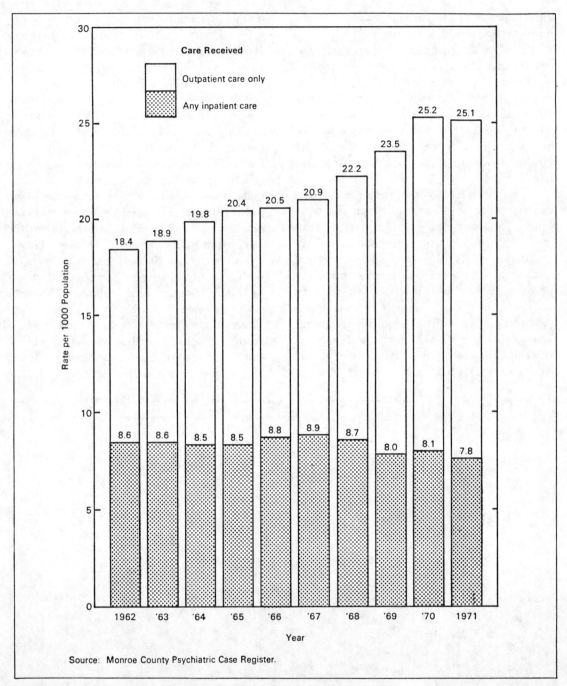

Figure 7: *Annual Rate per 1000 Population of Persons Receiving Psychiatric Services by Locus of Care, Monroe County, New York, 1962–1971.*

disorder in their patients (e.g., 22% in one study), than those reported for office-based practices (Rosen, Locke, Goldberg, & Babigian, 1972; Nigro, 1970).

The above referenced studies also contain a considerable amount of information on the management of psychiatric disorders identified in general medical practice settings. Although two of these studies indicated that at least 20% of the patients identified with psychiatric disorders received no specific treatment (Fink, 1969; Shepherd et al., 1966) upwards of 2/3 of

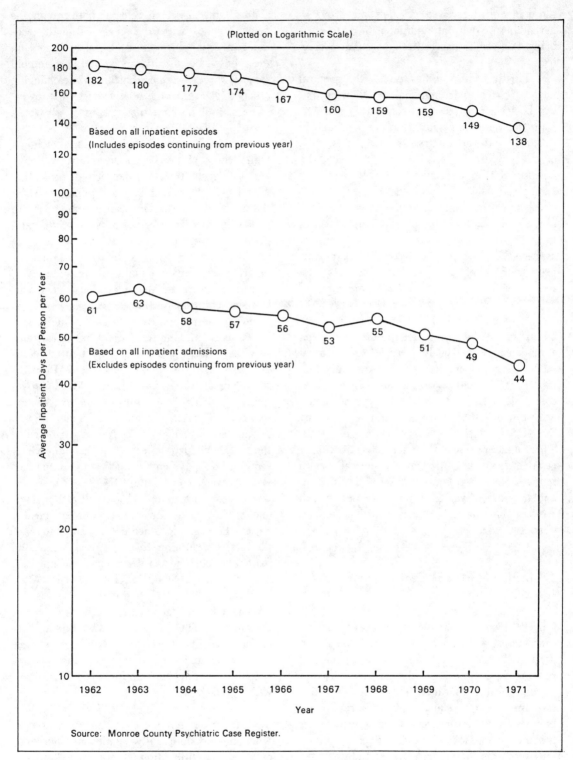

Figure 8: *Average Number of Inpatient Days per Hospitalized Person per Year, Monroe County, New York, 1962–1971.*
(Plotted on Logarithmic Scale)

those identified received psychotropic drugs or psychotherapy with an additional 0.7% to 2.9% being referred for specialized psychiatric services.

Finally, the significance of the general medical sector under national health insurance can be seen from recently acquired data on the Canadian national health insurance program. In that proto-typical country, as much as 30–40% of all psychiatric services are rendered by nonpsychiatric physicians. In Ontario, for example, 31% of all psychiatric services are provided by general practitioners who receive 28% of the total amount paid for psychiatric services in the province. Psychiatrists, who incidentally average 500 patients per psychiatrist per year, provide 64% of all psychiatric services and receive 68% of the total amount paid for psychiatric services in this province (Reed, 1975).

It should be noted that additional analyses of utilization data presented in the section on specialized mental health services and general medical services are included in Appendix I of this report. Variations in utilization by age, sex, color, diagnosis of patients, and type of facility are presented there from the data compiled by the NIMH national reporting program staff. These data are essential for the determination of relative risks of utilization of mental health services for sub-groups within the population, and thus are of value for public health, health services planning and actuarial health economics purposes.

Utilization of Mental Health Services by Insured Populations

Once the mental health services utilization characteristics of the U.S. population have been described, one is next faced with the problem of relating these statistics to the possible effects of national health insurance. The difficulty of this task may be appreciated when one recognizes that no health insurance plan currently covers the full range of mental health services including long-term inpatient services. In addition, the actual utilization of mental health services may be seen as the result of a complex interaction between the presence of a mental illness, cultural factors, demographic factors, economic factors, and physician referral patterns on the demand side, with the organizational, technological, manpower, and efficiency factors on the supply side. Ideally, one would wish to hold some of these variables constant while changing others to determine the relative effect that lowering economic barriers through insurance would have on utilization characteristics.

Although natural experiments allowing a high degree of precision are rarely available, we will next turn to the actual utilization experience of several insured populations. It should be noted that insurance companies are primarily concerned with units of service and percent of benefits devoted to specific types of services, rather than with the number of separate individuals actually treated. However, there are several notable exceptions which will be reviewed in this section.

The most complete data on the number of individuals utilizing outpatient mental health services are provided by the United Auto Workers Blue Cross-Blue Shield Plan of Michigan. In 1973, 2.4% of the 2.4 million participants utilized an outpatient psychiatric service. The relatively high percentage of this population utilizing services can be attributed to the reverse deductible feature of this plan which requires no copayment for the first five outpatient visits (Stevenson & Taaffe, 1974).

In contrast to the UAW utilization data, one study of the Federal Employees Health Benefit Program documented that only 0.63% of the total high option enrollees received an outpatient benefit and 0.13% received an inpatient benefit in the U.S. during 1973 (Reed, 1975). Although substantial regional variations occurred, with a particularly high rate in the Washington, D.C. area of 1.17% utilizing outpatient benefits, the lower FEHB utilization rate can be attributed to a $100 deductible that effectively eliminates counting the low utilizers which are, however, readily tabulated in the UAW plan.[2]

Health maintenance organizations represent another potentially significant source of data on the utilization of specialized mental

---

[2] A more recent unpublished study done by the Chief Actuary of the Civil Service Commission estimates the over-all Blue-Cross/Blue-Shield FEP mental utilization at 1.1% and the Washington, D.C. area utilization at 1.6%.

health services by insured populations. The same problems of incomplete coverage for all mental health services exist (particular for chronic conditions) as is true of indemnity type plans, but the utilization experience of these integrated health care settings which operate under specific benefit restrictions, can be gauged. Several HMOs limit the eligibility for psychiatric treatment services to those who have acute psychiatric conditions amenable to brief therapeutic intervention. The Health Insurance Plan of Greater New York and Group Health Association of Washington, D.C., which utilize these criteria, have found a utilization rate of 1.1% of the adult population, respectively (Fink, 1969; Locke, Krantz, & Kramer, 1966). The Kaiser Foundation Health Plan in Portland, Oregon, which uses a patient cost-sharing plan for mental health services, found that utilization of these services by all enrollees was 1.1% per year. Marked variations exist for the Kaiser Foundation sponsored group plans in southern California. Outpatient mental health service utilization rates range from a low of 1.0% by retail clerks local #899 to a high of 5.6% by another retail clerks local #770 which utilized a family-oriented mental health development center locus of treatment in contrast to the usual indemnity payment to private psychiatrists (Hunter, 1970).

The utilization figures noted above are by no means exhaustive, and the wide variations in utilization rates, which are due in part to varying benefit structures, require further analysis. A document is available from HEW which offers a more complete review of mental health services in health maintenance organizations (U.S. Dept. of HEW, 1970).

Cost of Mental Health Services

In 1974, national health expenditures totalled $104.2 billion which represented 7.7% of the gross national product. Of this total, an estimated $14.5 billion, or 14 percent, was expended for direct care of the mentally ill (Figure 9). Additional data on the indirect cost of mental illness are also presented in Figure 9 which result in an estimated total cost of mental illness of $36.8 billion for 1974. Slightly over half of the total expenditure for direct care of the mentally ill was concentrated in two types of facilities, mainly, nursing homes (29%) and State, county and other public mental hospitals (23%). General hospital psychiatric services accounted for another 12% of expenditures and private practice psychiatrists accounted for 9%. Each of the other categories of service accounted for 5% or less of the direct, mental health care expenditures (Figure 10). More detailed discussions of the cost of mental illness are available from NIMH publications including those referenced in Figures 9 and 10 (National Institute of Mental Health, 1975).

It is also of interest, with regard to national health insurance, to determine the long range costs which psychiatric patients may incur. Ten-year hospitalization cost estimates from the previously mentioned longitudinal analysis of a 1962 Monroe County patient cohort are now available. These data relate to the configuration of psychiatric services in Monroe County during the 1962–72 decade and exclude care received outside the county. Thus, at today's cost (estimated at $45 per patient day for State and VA hospitals, and $150 per day for general hospitals and CMHC facilities in Monroe County), the ten-year dollar amount for inpatient care required by this cohort averaged approximately $7,000 per person. If the Monroe County utilization experience could be applied to a community with a weighted cost of $100 per hospital day, accumulated ten-year inpatient costs would average almost $14,000 per person coming under psychiatric care (Goldberg, 1976).

The past decade has seen a dramatic decrease in mental hospitals' average length of stay, and an accompanying increase in the relative use of outpatient treatment modalities. However, relatively little information is available to document the effects of these changes on the welfare of patients and on the welfare of their families and communities. A national health insurance program could be expected to accelerate demands for information on treatment appropriateness and effectiveness. Public health-minded mental health professionals must ask the inevitable cost-benefit questions. The determination of who should appropriately treat what kind of mental disorder, with what therapeutic modality, with what level of effectiveness, and at

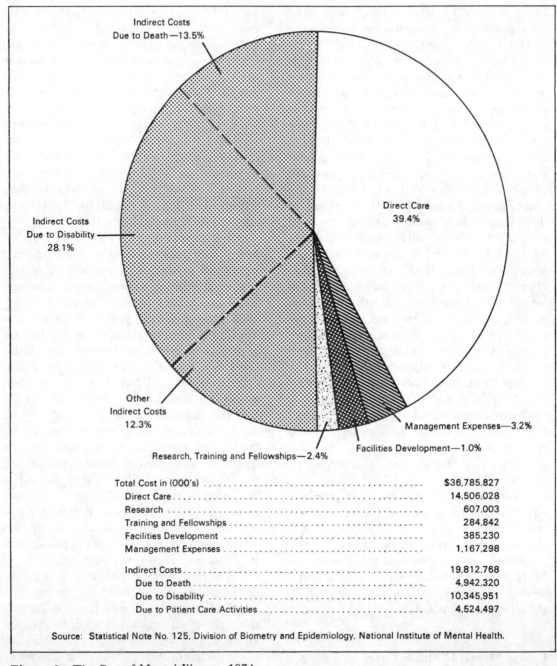

Indirect Costs
Due to Death—13.5%

Indirect Costs
Due to Disability
28.1%

Direct Care
39.4%

Other
Indirect Costs
12.3%

Management Expenses—3.2%

Facilities Development—1.0%

Research, Training and Fellowships—2.4%

Total Cost in (000's)	$36,785,827
Direct Care	14,506,028
Research	607,003
Training and Fellowships	284,842
Facilities Development	385,230
Management Expenses	1,167,298
Indirect Costs	19,812,768
Due to Death	4,942,320
Due to Disability	10,345,951
Due to Patient Care Activities	4,524,497

Source: Statistical Note No. 125, Division of Biometry and Epidemiology, National Institute of Mental Health.

Figure 9: *The Cost of Mental Illness—1974.*

what socially acceptable costs is one that our society should make on the basis of heretofore unavailable research data. It is doubtful that market mechanisms, professional codes, or political policies can substitute for these vitally needed research data.

Future Research Priorities

Future research on the public mental health implications of national health insurance should be directed toward the three areas of epidemiology, needs assessment, and the utilization (including

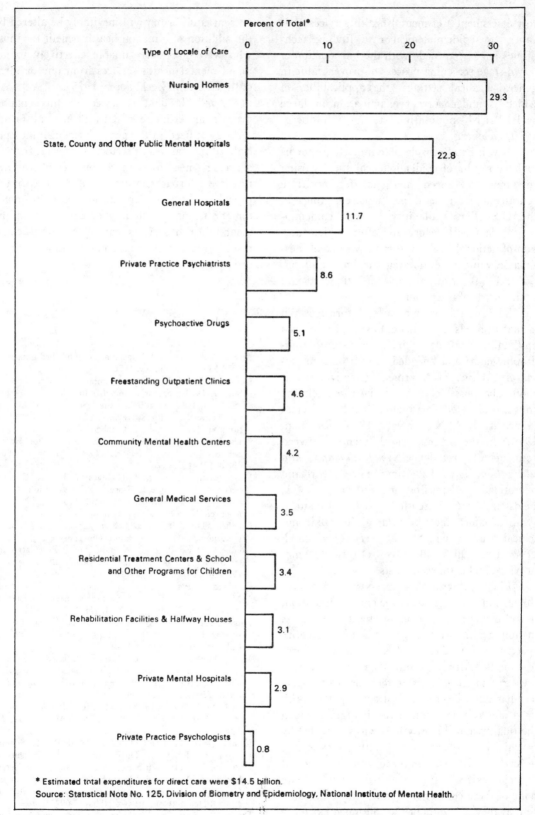

Percent of Total*

Type of Locale of Care

Nursing Homes — 29.3

State, County and Other Public Mental Hospitals — 22.8

General Hospitals — 11.7

Private Practice Psychiatrists — 8.6

Psychoactive Drugs — 5.1

Freestanding Outpatient Clinics — 4.6

Community Mental Health Centers — 4.2

General Medical Services — 3.5

Residential Treatment Centers & School and Other Programs for Children — 3.4

Rehabilitation Facilities & Halfway Houses — 3.1

Private Mental Hospitals — 2.9

Private Practice Psychologists — 0.8

* Estimated total expenditures for direct care were $14.5 billion.

Source: Statistical Note No. 125, Division of Biometry and Epidemiology, National Institute of Mental Health.

Figure 10: *Percent Distribution of Expenditures for Direct Care of the Mentally Ill by Type or Locale of Care, United States, 1974.*

cost assessments) of mental health services. Advances in epidemiological case finding techniques have been made with the introduction of a two-stage screening process of proven value in general medical settings—the applicability of which is under current examination in large scale British population studies (Goldberg, 1970; Goldberg, 1972).

It will be of considerable importance for us to have results of epidemiological studies using the most advanced methods, for multiple representative, general health care settings in the U.S. The availability of such epidemiological data both before and after implementation of national health insurance will be of inestimable value in evaluating the impact of national health insurance on the public mental health needs of the nation.

The second major area for future research is that of needs assessment. Based on improved epidemiological data, base-line socio-demographic data, and knowledge from outcome research studies of treatment effectiveness, it should be possible to make more explicit the concept of need for mental health services (Warheit, Bell, & Schwab, 1975; Richman, 1966). In the process, the differences between concepts of *prevalence, need, demand, and utilization,* should become more clear and operational (Jeffers, Boganno, & Bartlett, 1971; Feldstein, 1966; Rosenthal, 1968). Ultimately, synthetic efforts must be made to link epidemiological studies with health services research utilization studies and the cost-of-service studies provided by health economists.

Finally, if we are to express our concern for the mental health needs of the entire population, it will be necessary for our studies to encompass mental health services provided by the entire spectrum of medical and social services professionals. Although our current "pluralistic" system of delivering mental health services has often been described as a "patchwork" or "non-system," an equilibrium between the quality and quantity of services provided by psychiatrists, other mental health professionals, other physicians, and non-medical social agencies exists. As with any dynamic system, none of these components or sectors could function as they are without the continued existence and stable functioning of the others. Hence, the

present equilibrium will inevitably be altered by the addition of a mental health benefit for those who were previously unable effectively to demand mental health services from one or more of these sectors (Zeckhauser, 1975).

Available data reviewed in this chapter provide an estimate of current mental health services utilized in the general medical and specialized mental health sectors. However, there is a pressing need for a more comprehensive U.S. research effort to characterize and measure the prevalence of psychiatric disorders and to monitor the changes both in morbidity and in the mental health services equilibrium that could result from a future national health insurance program.

References

American Psychological Association, unpublished data from 1974 Manpower Survey, 1976.

DeLozier, James E. National Ambulatory Medical Care Survey, 1973 Summary, United States, May 1973-April 1974. Vital and Health Statistics: Series 13, Data from the National Health Survey; No. 21, DHEW Publication; No. (HRA) 76-1772, October 1975.

Feldstein, Paul J. "Research on the Demand for Health Services." *Milbank Memorial Fund Quarterly,* 1966, 43(3), 128–165.

Fink, Raymond S., et al. Changes in Family Doctors' Services for Emotional Disorders After Addition of Psychiatric Treatment to a Prepaid Practice Program. *Medical Care* 1969, 7, 209–224.

Goldberg, David P. *The Detection of Psychiatric Illness by Questionnaire.* London: Oxford University Press, 1972.

Goldberg, David P., et al. A Standardized Psychiatric Interview for Use in Community Surveys. *British Journal of Prev. Soc. Med.,* 1970, 24, 18–23.

Goldberg, Irving D. Analysis of unpublished data from Monroe County Psychiatric Case Register, Division of Biometry and Epidemiology, NIMH, 1976.

Hunter, Harold R. The Use of Mental Health Services By Insured Populations. (Doctoral dissertation, University of California, Los Angeles, 1970).

Jeffers, James R., Boganno, Mario F., & Bartlett, John C. On the Demand Versus the Need for Medical Services and the Concept of "Shortage". *American Journal of Public Health,* 1971, 61(1), 45–63.

Kessel, Neal. Psychiatric Morbidity in a London General Practice. *British Journal of Prev. Soc. Med.,* 1960, 14, 16–22.

Leopold, Robert L., Goldberg, David P., & Schein, Lawrence. Emotional Disturbance Among Patients of Private Non-Psychiatric Physicians in an Urban Neighborhood. Unpublished Report of a study sponsored by the Center for Epidemiologic studies, National Institute of Mental Health (Contract No. HSM-42-69-79), 1971.

Locke, Ben Z. Patients, Psychiatric Problems and Non-Psychiatrist Physicians in a Pre-Paid Group Practice

Program. *American Journal of Psychiatry,* 1966, 123(2), 207–210.

Locke, Ben Z., Finucane, Daniel L., & Hassler, Ferdinand. Emotionally Disturbed Patients Under Care of Private Non-Psychiatric Physician Care. Psychiatric Research Report No. 22, American Psychiatric Association, 1967, 23–248.

Locke, Ben Z., & Gardner, Elmer P. Psychiatric Disorders Among the Patients of General Practitioners and Internists. Public Health Reports, 1969, 84(2), 167–173.

Locke, Ben Z., Krantz, Goldie, & Kramer, Morton. Psychiatric Need and Demand in a Pre-Paid Group Practice Program. *American Journal of Public Health,* 56, 1966, June, 895–904.

Marmor, J., et al. *Psychiatrists and Their Patients, A National Study of Private Office Practice,* The Joint Information Service, Washington, D.C.

National Institute of Mental Health. The Cost of Mental Illness—1971, Report Series on Mental Health Statistics, Series B, No. 7, DHEW Publication Number (ADM) 76-265, 1975.

National Institute of Mental Health, Division of Biometry and Epidemiology. Provisional data on federally-funded Community Mental Health Centers 1973–74. Survey and Reports Branch, Division of Biometry and Epidemiology, NIMH, April 1975.

Nigro, Samuel A. "A Psychiatrist's Experiences in General Practice in a Hospital Emergency Room" *Journal of the American Medical Association,* 1970, *214,* 1657–1660.

Richman, A. Assessing the Need for Psychiatric Care: A Review of the Validity of Epidemiologic Surveys. *Canadian Psychiatric Association Journal,* 1966, *11,* 179–188.

Reed, Louis S. *Coverage and Utilization of Care for Mental Condition Under Health Insurance—Various Studies, 1973–1974,* American Psychiatric Association, 1975.

Regier, Darrel A. and Goldberg, Irving D. Analysis by NIMH Division of Biometry and Epidemiology of unpublished data from the NCHS National Ambulatory Medical Care Survey of office-based physicians (May 1973–April 1974), 1976.

Rosen, Beatrice M., Locke, Ben Z., Goldberg, Irving D., & Babigian, Haroutun M. Identification of Emotional Disturbance in Patients Seen in General Medical Clinics. *Hospital and Community Psychiatry,* 1972, *23,* 364–370.

Rosenthal, Gerald. The Operating Structure of the Medical Care System—an Overview. Federal Programs for the Development of Human Resources, Vol. 2, 1968.

Shepherd, Michael, Cooper, Brian, Brown, Alexander C., & Kalton, Graham. *Psychiatric Illness in General Practice,* London; Oxford University Press, 1966.

Stevenson, William E., & Taaffe, Gordon. Final Report, Preparation of Statistical Tables for Psychiatric Care Under Pre-Paid Health Insurance, for Contract Number ADM-42-74-75 (MH). Unpublished data. Blue Cross–Blue Shield of Michigan, December, 1974.

U.S. Bureau of the Census, *Current Population Reports,* Series P-25, No. 601, Table 8 (Series 2 Projections), 1976.

U.S. Department of Health, Education and Welfare. Inclusion of Mental Health Services in Health Maintenance and Related Organizations—A Review of Supplemental Benefits. Bureau of Community Health Services, Health Services Administration, DHEW Publication Number (HSA) 75-13019, 1974.

Warheit, G. J., Bell, R. A., & Schwab, J. J. Planning for Change: Needs Assessment Approaches. Unpublished manual made possible by NIH-MH-Grant 159-00-05 S-1, 1975.

World Health Organization. Psychiatry and Primary Medical Care. Report on a working group convened by the regional office for Europe of the World Health Organization, Lysebu, Oslo, 10–13 April, 1973, regional office for Europe, World Health Organization, Copenhagen, 1973.

Zeckhauser, R. J. A Framework for Assessing the Efficiency of Mental Health Care Delivery. Final Report on NIMH Contract No. ADM-42-74-57 (OP) March 30, 1975.

Summary of the Recommendations to the President

President's Commission on Mental Health

The specific recommendations of the President's Commission on Mental Health are summarized. These include encouraging naturally occurring support systems, developing a more responsive service system, recommendations for health insurance for the future, suggesting new directions in training mental health personnel, recommendations for protecting basic rights, strong support for expanding the base of knowledge, a strategy for prevention, and recommended efforts for improving public understanding.

In February of 1977, President Jimmy Carter established a Presidential Commission to study the issues facing the mental health field and to provide him with recommendations for initiatives to improve the availability and quality of mental health care in the United States. This action reflected the clear interest and commitment of himself and the First Lady, Rosalynn Carter. Over four hundred professionals and other concerned individuals participated directly in the work of the Commission. Thousands of others participated indirectly through public and written testimony and various special studies and analyses.

An enormous range of issues and topics was reviewed and discussed by the Commission and its task panels. The recommendations are equally broad. The following are the actual recommendations of the President's Commission on Mental Health. As in the PCMH Report, they are listed under the following categories: Community Supports, Responsive Service System, Insurance for the Future, New Directions for Personnel, Protecting Basic Rights, Expanding the Base of Knowledge, Strategy for Prevention, and Improving Public Understanding. These recommendations will provide the basis for future developments in mental health for the next decade.

The President's Commission on Mental Health recommends:

Community Supports

- A major effort be developed in the area of personal and community supports which will:
  (a) recognize and strengthen the natural networks to which people belong and on which they depend;
  (b) identify the potential social support that formal institutions within communities can provide;
  (c) improve the linkages between community support networks and formal mental health services; and
  (d) initiate research to increase our knowledge of informal and formal community support systems and networks.

The effort we recommend should be developed and located within the National Institute of Mental Health and could include the following types of activities:
  (a) coordination of existing Department of Health, Education, and Welfare programs for community support systems with the National Institute of Mental Health for the purpose of pooling information and technical assistance as requested by the community;
  (b) exchanges of information among lay

From President's Commission on Mental Health, *Report to the President From the President's Commission on Mental Health* (vol. 4). Washington, D.C.: U.S. Government Printing Office, 1978.

community groups and mental health professionals about model, ongoing community support programs;

(c) development, through grants and contracts, of demonstration programs with an evaluation component that can identify effective ways to establish linkages between community mental health services and community support systems; and

(d) development of research initiatives on the efficacy of social networks as adjuncts to mental health service delivery systems, and on the effects of informal and formal community support systems on the utilization of health and mental health services.

- Among the activities which should be developed at the State and local level are:

(a) the inclusion within the Health Systems Agency plan and the State Health Plan of material which takes into account the role of community support systems;

(b) the examination by community mental health service programs of their own program plans in terms of their complementing or supplementing local natural helping networks, with particular attention to the needs of families and to the social and cultural factors of the communities they serve;

(c) the involvement of community people in this process of needs assessment and ongoing program evaluation;

(d) the development of inservice training activities in community mental health service programs about the support systems indigenous to their community; and

(e) the participation in these programs of caregivers from the support systems so that mental health professionals and community caregivers can learn from each other.

A Responsive Service System

- A new Federal grant program for community mental health service to:

(a) encourage the creation of necessary services where none exist;

(b) supplement existing services where they are inadequate; and

(c) increase the flexibility of communities in planning a comprehensive network of services.

- Priority in the new grant program be given to:

(a) unserved and underserved areas;

(b) services for children, adolescents, and the elderly;

(c) specialized services for racial and ethnic minority populations; and

(d) services for people with chronic mental illness.

- An appropriation of at least $75 million in the first year and $100 million for each of the next two years.

- The National Institute of Mental Health fund approved applications in those areas identified as unserved or underserved.

- Limited Federal funding for certain services which centers now provide on a non-reimbursable basis.

  Special Federal funding for community mental health centers which have reached, or are reaching, the end of their eight-year Federal funding period.

- Greater flexibility in delineating catchment area boundaries.

  The Secretary of Health, Education, and Welfare encourage a waiver of catchment area population requirements where it would best serve the needs of natural communities and those requiring services.

- Encouragement of cross catchment area program sharing.

  The Department of Health, Education, and Welfare propose any necessary legislation to facilitate cross catchment area planning and delivery of high cost and/or specialized services.

- Allowing greater variation in governance and advisory board arrangements so that they properly reflect local circumstances.

  The National Institute of Mental Health seek changes in current legislation to permit differences in board and governance arrangements so they may properly reflect existing local circumstances.

- Assistance for the members of mental health advisory/governance boards in dealing with problems related to the planning and delivery of mental health care.

The National Institute of Mental Health strengthen its capacity to respond to requests for information and technical assistance for the members of mental health advisory/governance boards to deal with problems related to the planning and delivery of mental health care.

- Mental health service programs should:
  (a) actively involve ethnic and racial minorities in planning and developing services;
  (b) provide culturally relevant services and staff them with bilingual, bicultural personnel; and
  (c) contract with minority community-based organizations for delivery of services.
- The Department of Health, Education, and Welfare require that Health Systems Agencies perform biannually a culturally relevant assessment of mental health needs. Special attention should be given to ascertaining the needs of children, adolescents, and the elderly.
- Reviews for grant continuation direct careful attention to whether the applicant has demonstrated a significant effort toward meeting the special needs of high-risk populations.
- The Department of Health, Education, and Welfare, in consultation with State and local governments, develop a national plan for:
  (a) the continued phasing down and where appropriate closing of large State mental hospitals;
  (b) upgrading service quality in those State hospitals that remain; and
  (c) allocating increased resources for the development of comprehensive, integrated systems of care which include community-based services and the remaining smaller State hospitals.

The working alliance must be strengthened between the health and mental health systems. As initial steps, the Commission recommends:

Funding by the Department of Health, Education, and Welfare of a limited number of research projects to assess integrated general health care and mental health care services.

Requiring community mental health centers and community mental health service programs, where appropriate, to establish cooperative working arrangements with health care settings.

These arrangements should allow for:
  (a) mental health personnel to provide direct care and treatment in the health care setting to patients with emotional disorders whose problems exceed the skills of non-psychiatric health care practitioners;
  (b) consultation directed toward altering behavioral patterns that increase the risk of physical illness;
  (c) collaborative treatment with non-psychiatric health care practitioners for those patients with combined physical and mental illness; and
  (d) training non-psychiatric physicians and other health care personnel to enhance their skills in the treatment of patients with relatively mild emotional disorders.

Relevant Federal agencies review the feasibility of providing priority in hiring at Veterans' administration hospitals and other Federal installations for former employees of State mental hospitals, and review the feasibility of amending Federal personnel laws to permit the option of payment into State pension funds for State workers who are hired by the Federal government.

- Each State health plan describe the approach the State intends to take or is taking to meet the goals of the national plan.
- The Department of Health, Education, and Welfare develop a model for performance contracts in order that national goals for

phasing down State hospitals, upgrading the quality of care in those that remain, and improving aftercare services can be achieved in a mutually agreed upon manner.

- The Department of Health, Education, and Welfare seek authorization for an appropriations of up to 50 million new dollars for each of the next five years to assist in reaching the goals agreed to in these performance contracts.
- State mental health authorities develop a case management system for each geographic service area within the State.

  State mental health authorities, in consultation with local authorities, designate an agency in each geographic service area to assume responsibility for assisting the chronically mentally ill of that area.

  The agency assigned this responsibility employ trained case managers, either directly or by contract with another agency. The development of linkages with community support systems should be a recognized function of both the agency and the case manager.

- A new class of Intermediate Care Facilities-Mental Health (ICF-MH) be created within the Medicaid program and linked with local organized systems of mental health care.
- Based upon adequate documentation, Health Systems Agencies endorse the issuance of certificates of need for the allocation of a limited number of psychiatric beds in communities prior to the reduction of State hospital beds.
- The Department of Housing and Urban Development promulgate proposed regulations making rental assistance available to persons living in group homes.
- In the allocation of public housing, equal opportunity should be given to people with chronic mental illness discharged from institutions or at risk of hospitalization.
- The basic Supplemental Security Income benefit be increased to meet the needs of those persons who require specialized residential programs in the community.
- If a person "lives in the household of another," the Supplemental Security Income benefit should not be reduced.

- The budget ceiling of Title XX of the Social Security Act be raised for the purpose of allocating funds so people inappropriately placed in medical facilities can be transferred to residences in the community.
- Professional Standards Review Organizations make provision for multidisciplinary peer review of mental health care provided in multidisciplinary mental health settings.
- The Department of Health, Education, and Welfare combine into a single survey the inspections required of an institution for receipt of Medicare, Medicaid, and categorical health and mental health grants.
- The National Institute of Mental Health allocate to a selected number of programs an award of 10 percent in excess of their grant for the purpose of developing and assessing techniques to evaluate mental health service delivery.
- The Administrator of the Alcohol, Drug Abuse, and Mental Health Administration take the necessary steps to consolidate the information and data-gathering requirements of the National Institute of Mental Health, the National Institute on Drug Abuse, and the National Institute on Alcohol Abuse and Alcoholism into a single reporting system.
- Changes in existing statutes, regulations, and policies to facilitate:
- (a) coordinated health and mental health planning at the local and State level;

  Inclusion in the Health Systems Agency plan of a mental health component developed by local and regional mental health authorities with assistance of representative ethnic, professional, and consumer citizen advisory groups.

  Delegation by the health planning authority to the State Mental Health Authority of the responsibility for aggregating mental health plans and preparing the mental health component of the State Health Plan. Funds for such activities must be provided to the State Mental Health Authority.

  Designation of monies for mental health planning in the budget of each Health Systems Agency.

- (b) increased participation in the general

health planning process by citizens knowledgeable about, and representative of, the interests of mental health, alcoholism, and drug misuse; and

Reservation of at least two places on the National Health Planning Council for representatives of mental health interests.

A guarantee of 25% representation for mental health interests on the boards of Health Systems Agencies and on the State Health Coordinating Council.

A requirement that State Mental Health Advisory Boards review and comment upon the mental health component of the State Health Plan. This report of the State Mental Health Advisory Board would be submitted to the State Health Coordinating Council.

(c) provision for the resolution of differences in planning goals between the health care and mental health care sectors.

The State Health Plan be subject to the approval of the governor, with provision made for the resolution of differences between the State Health Coordinating Council and the Mental Health Advisory Board prior to submission of such plans to the Secretary of the Department of Health, Education, and Welfare.

• Changes in planning guidelines to ensure that the needs of the mentally disabled for education, housing, vocational rehabilitation, and social services are adequately met.

Guidelines for the preparation of the State Comprehensive Mental Health Services Plan be amended to require the inclusion and publication of health, social service, housing, rehabilitation, and education components in the plan.

Insurance for the Future

• Any national health insurance program and all existing private health insurance programs and public programs financing mental health care, such as Medicare and Medicaid, be governed by the following guidelines:
(a) *Benefits.* A reasonable array of emergency, outpatient, and inpatient care should be covered, including partial hospitalization and 24-hour residential treatment for children and adolescents, sufficient to permit treatment of mental disorders in the most appropriate and least restrictive setting.
(b) *Reimbursement.* Reimbursement should be provided for those mental health services involving the direct care of the patient and for care rendered to others where it is integral to the patient's treatment.
In the case of care provided in organized settings or systems of care, reimbursement should be made to the system rather than to the practitioner providing the care. All covered services must be rendered by, or be under the direct clinical supervision of, a physician, psychologist, social worker, or nurse with an earned doctorate or master's degree and with appropriate clinical competence as established by State licensure or certification by a national body.
Direct reimbursement should be made to independent qualified mental health practitioners as defined by national health insurance legislation. This issue should be re-examined under existing legislation.
Adequate provision for controlling costs and peer review should exist.
(c) *Cost Sharing.* There should be minimal patient-borne cost sharing for emergency care. In all other instances, patient-borne cost sharing, through copayments and deductibles for evaluation, diagnosis, and short-term therapy, should be no greater than that for a comparable course of physical illness.
(d) *Freedom of Choice.* The consumer should have a choice of provider and provider systems, and procedures should be developed to ensure that individuals have the necessary knowledge and information to make an effective choice.
• Amending current Medicare legislation so that:
(a) community mental health centers and other organized systems of community

mental health care be given provider status;

(b) the allowable reimbursement for the outpatient treatment of mental conditions be increased to at least $750 in any calendar year;

(c) the beneficiary coinsurance be reduced from 50% to 20% to conform to Medicare coinsurance requirements for physical illness;

(d) coverage for inpatient care of psychiatric disorders in acute care settings be extended so it is equivalent to that provided for physical illness; and

(e) two days of partial hospitalization be allowed for each day of inpatient care.

- The Secretary of Health, Education, and Welfare take those steps necessary to assure that:

(a) States have effective systems to prevent discrimination on the basis of diagnosis;

(b) mental health services be made available within Medicaid child health programs;

(c) State Medicaid plans offer a reasonable amount of ambulatory mental health services; and

(d) State Medicaid reimbursement policies not limit the availability of mental health services.

- The Secretary of Health, Education, and Welfare develop legislative proposals to amend Medicaid to:

(a) establish national minimum eligibility standards based on income and assets rather than on categorical requirements so that everyone who satisfied the definition of financial need would be eligible for assistance;

(b) establish national minimum mental health benefits to be included in every Medicaid State Plan; and

(c) remove provisions that allow for any discrimination in the allocation of services on the basis of age.

- States be encouraged to require that private health insurers offer an outpatient mental health benefit with low or no copayment for initial visits and extend coverage to family members whose treatment is vital to the care of the individual receiving benefits under the plan.

- The Secretary of Health, Education, and Welfare propose legislation to encourage employers to include mental health coverage for emergency, outpatient, partial hospitalization, and inpatient services in the health insurance plans offered their employees.

- The Department of Health, Education, and Welfare conduct a study of mental health costs, focused on those States which have enacted some form of mandatory mental health benefits for private health insurance plans.

- The Department of Health, Education, and Welfare explore the feasibility of creating a new system to meet the costs of chronic mental disability, either as an extension or modification of the Supplemental Security Income program or as a new federally financed income support system.

New Directions for Personnel

- Federal support for students in the core mental health professions be in the form of loans or scholarships which can be repaid by a period of service in designated geographic areas or facilities where there is a shortage of personnel.

- Grants and contracts to educational institutions for the training of mental health specialists be awarded only to programs specifically aimed at meeting major service delivery priorities or the needs of underserved populations.

> The National Institute of Mental Health establish a limited number of postgraduate teaching fellowships designed to improve the training capacity of facilities in underserved areas and increase the number of educators with special skill and competence in the problems encountered in working in rural areas and public facilities.

- The Health Professions Educational Assistance Act be amended to:

(a) designate psychiatry as a medical shortage specialty and require medical schools to set aside a certain proportion of their residency positions for this discipline; and

(b) permit those medical students who have an obligation to serve in the National Health Service Corps to defer such service until completion of psychiatric and/or child psychiatric residency training.

- The Department of Health, Education, and Welfare:
  (a) at the high school level, develop special projects to interest minority high school students in mental health careers and augment them by a program of summer and part-time internships which provide work opportunities in mental health facilities and programs;
  (b) at the college level, develop a program to provide scholarship support in the social, behavioral, and biomedical sciences to outstanding juniors and seniors interested in graduate training in the mental health professions. Stipends for summer jobs in mental health settings should also be provided;
  (c) at the graduate level, expand the minority fellowship program funded by the National Institute of Mental Health and administered by various professional associations to include trainees in psychiatry, psychology, psychiatric social work, and psychiatric nursing who are planning clinical, administrative, or academic careers; and
  (d) at the faculty level, develop a fellowship program to enable faculty of academic institutions engaged primarily in educating minority students to complete their doctoral work or to receive postdoctoral training.
- The Department of Health, Education, and Welfare fund efforts designed to increase the number of mental health professionals trained to work with children, adolescents, and the elderly with the provisions that:
  (a) programs include training in supervision, administration, and consultation as well as in diagnosis and treatment;
  (b) a reasonable amount of faculty supervised training be given in such facilities as schools, hospitals, clinics, nursing homes, and senior citizen programs; and
  (c) students receiving scholarship or loan support be required to repay them by service in publicly funded facilities or other shortage areas.

The Department of Health, Education, and Welfare fund a number of centers on the mental health of the elderly where graduate and postgraduate students in all major professions can be trained.

- The Department of Health, Education, and Welfare provide funding for education in mental health principles, psychiatric evaluation, and treatment to primary health care givers and students, particularly physicians and nurses, preparing for work in primary health care.
- The Department of Health, Education, and Welfare:
  (a) provide funding for selective projects designed to enhance the capability of personnel in mental health, health, social service, and community support systems to work more closely together; and
  (b) facilitate joint funding where an educational institution proposes to meet more than one target problem in a single special training program.
- The National Institute of Mental Health provide funding to special projects designed to develop programs in mental health administration, case management, and primary prevention.
- The National Institute of Mental Health, through grants and contracts, fund the development of culturally relevant training materials and model continuing education programs for both mental health professionals and paraprofessionals.
- The National Institute of Mental Health provide funds for developing and testing culturally relevant model curricula related to the nature and function of human service and community support systems for mental health specialists, paraprofessionals, and such community caregivers as primary care practitioners, clergy, and educators.
- The National Institute of Mental Health accelerate its efforts to develop guidelines defining the various levels of paraprofessionals, specifying the activities they should perform, and the supervision they need.

- The National Institute of Mental Health develop a comprehensive mental health personnel information system.
- The National Institute of Mental Health, through contracts and grants, undertake studies to:
  (a) describe the services required by people with different types of mental or emotional problems;
  (b) develop models of function and qualifications for the staffing of mental health facilities and the provision of these services; and
  (c) identify the ways in which the efficient utilization of personnel is impeded and suggest corrections.
- Funding for clinical and service manpower and training programs of the National Institute of Mental Health be increased to $85 million in fiscal year 1980, and in subsequent years be adjusted annually for inflation.
- The National Institute of Mental Health have the authority, for a period of no more than five years, to award distress grants for graduate professional education when it can be shown that a loss of current Federal funds would measurably alter the number of graduates or the quality of training.

Protecting Basic Rights

- The establishment of advocacy systems for the representation of mentally disabled individuals. In adversary or judicial settings we recognize the importance of counsel to represent not only the mentally disabled client (or those acting in his or her behalf) but also the State or provider against which a claim is made.

  Increased activities by the Legal Services Corporation to represent mentally handicapped persons more adequately and effectively.

- All Federal agencies enforce existing laws and regulations which prohibit discrimination against mentally disabled persons and seek to equalize opportunities for such individuals.
- All Federal agencies review their statutes, regulations, and programs for instances of discrimination against mentally handicapped persons.
- The Department of Health, Education, and Welfare vigorously implement the requirements of the Education for All Handicapped Children Act and formulate regulations to assist school districts to provide for the mental health needs of children and youth.
- Each State review its civil commitment and guardianship laws and revise them, if necessary, to incorporate increased procedural protections.

  Model legislation incorporate increased procedural protections including, but not limited to:
  (a) initial screening of potential commitment cases by mental health agencies;
  (b) a prompt commitment hearing preceded by adequate notice to interested parties;
  (c) the right to retained or assigned counsel;
  (d) the right to a retained or assigned independent mental health evaluator;
  (e) a transcript of the proceedings;
  (f) application of the principle of the least restrictive alternative;
  (g) a relatively stringent standard of proof (for example: "clear and convincing evidence");
  (h) durational limits on confinement (with the ability of a court to specify a period of confinement, short of the statutory maximum); and
  (i) the right to expedited appeal.

- State guardianship laws provide for a system of limited guardianship in which rights are removed, and supervision is provided, for only those activities in which a person has demonstrated an incapacity to act competently.

  Procedural protections in guardianship laws should include but not be limited to:
  (a) written and oral notice;
  (b) the right to be present at proceedings;
  (c) appointment of counsel;
  (d) a "clear and convincing evidence" standard as the burden of proof;

(e) a comprehensive evaluation of functional abilities conducted by trained personnel; and

(f) a judicial hearing that employs those procedural standards used in civil actions in the courts of any given State.

● Each State review its mental health laws and revise them, if necessary, to ensure that they provide for:

(a) a right to treatment/right to habilitation and to protection from harm for involuntarily confined mental patients and developmentally disabled individuals;

(b) a right to treatment in the least restrictive setting;

(c) a right to refuse treatment, with careful attention to the circumstances and procedures under which the right may be qualified; and

(d) a right to due process when community placement is being considered.

● Each State have a "Bill of Rights" for all mentally disabled persons, wherever they reside.

Such a bill of rights should include at least seven basic components:

(a) a statement that all mentally handicapped persons are entitled to the specified rights;

(b) a statement that rights cannot be abridged solely because of a person's handicap or because a person is being treated (whether voluntarily or involuntarily);

(c) a declaration of the right to treatment, the right to refuse treatment, the right to dignity, privacy, and confidentiality of personal records, the right to a humane physical and psychological environment, and the right to the least restrictive alternative setting for treatment;

(d) a statement of other, enumerated, fundamental rights which may not be abridged or limited;

(e) a statement of other specified rights which may be altered or limited only under specific, limited circumstances;

(f) an enforcement provision; and

(g) a statement that handicapped persons retain the right to enforce their rights through habeas corpus and all other common law or statutory remedies.

● All recipients of Federal funds to provide mental health services be required to adhere to certain basic principles of confidentiality, and that other institutions and facilities be encouraged to follow this practice.

● Mentally disabled persons in detention or correctional institutions should have access to appropriate mental health services on a voluntary basis and such access should not be connected with release considerations.

Each State should enact a prison-hospital transfer law with procedures to protect those prisoners who become patients.

Expanding the Base of Knowledge

● Priority be given to rebuilding our mental health research capacity over the next ten years and to investing an amount of money that is commensurate with the level of the problems associated with mental health, alcoholism, and drug abuse.

● The National Institute of Mental Health research budget be increased by $30 million to a level of $165.4 million in fiscal year 1980.

● The National Institute on Alcohol Abuse and Alcoholism research budget be increased by $9 million to a level of $30.2 million in fiscal year 1980.

● The National Institute on Drug Abuse research budget be increased by $9 million to a level of $55 million in fiscal year 1980.

● The Administrator of the Alcohol, Drug Abuse, and Mental Health Administration develop guidelines for providing Federal incentives to stimulate increased State support of research activities in mental health and related areas.

● Veterans' Administration funds allocated to mental health research be increased to a level which more closely matches the amount of mental health services it provides.

● A review of the current manner in which the Federal government supports and trains re search manpower, and a sensible increase over the next decade in that support to enhance our ability to train needed research personnel.

- The National Institute of Mental Health research training budget be increased by $6.3 million to a level of $25 million in fiscal year 1980.
- A central data retrieval system which can be used for research management be created within the Alcohol, Drug Abuse, and Mental Health Administration, and a central system for cataloging mental health research conducted throughout the Federal government also be developed.
- Attention be given by the Alcohol, Drug Abuse, and Mental Health Administration to measures for increasing the flow of knowledge from investigator to investigator, and from researchers to practitioners and the public.
- Immediate efforts to gather reliable data (including socioeconomic and demographic data) on the incidence of mental health problems and the utilization of mental health services. Particular attention should be paid to population groups within our society known to have special needs, such as children, adolescents, the aging women, and racial and ethnic minorities.
- Increased research efforts designed to produce greater understanding of the needs and problems of people who are underserved or inappropriately served or who are at high risk for mental disorders.
- Expanded research on the ways mental health services are delivered and the policies affecting these services.
- Research directed toward understanding major mental illnesses, mental retardation, and basic psychological, sociological, biological, and developmental processes receive greater support and increased priority.
- An entity be created to replace the National Commission for the Protection of Human Subjects of Biomedical and Behavioral Research. This entity should use a broad-based approach in evaluating policies developed by the current Commission and should address those questions still unanswered that relate to the protection of research subjects.

A Strategy for Prevention

- Comprehensive prenatal and early infant care be available to all women, with special consideration given to school-age pregnant women and other high-risk groups.
- A periodic, comprehensive, developmental assessment be available to all children, with consent of parents and with maximal parental involvement in all stages of the process.
- The Secretary of Health, Education, and Welfare review existing Federal programs that pertain to health and mental health services for infants and children and design a coordinated national plan to make available comprehensive services for all children.
- Increases in the number of Project Headstart and developmental daycare programs, so that within a reasonable period of time all children needing these and similar programs can have them available. Special attention should be paid to ensuring the inclusion of additional handicapped, rural, and migrant children. Such programs should be culturally acceptable to parents and the communities.

  Design a flexible program that supports a variety of child care arrangements, with adequate provision for evaluation.

  The Department of Health, Education, and Welfare support programs to recruit and train caretakers at all educational levels and from a wide variety of age, ethnic, and socio-cultural groups.

- When children are candidates for out-of-home placement, there should be prior evaluation of the child and of the need for such placement. Family counseling and support should be made available.
- A Center for Prevention be established in the National Institute of Mental Health.
- Primary prevention be the major priority of this Center.
- $10 million be allocated during the first year with a funding level of no less than 10% of the National Institute of Mental Health budget within ten years, to support epidemiological, biomedical, behavioral, and clinical research aimed at prevention; to assess and evaluate existing programs of prevention; to

replicate effective preventive programs, including those related to community support systems; and to engage in other appropriate activities.

Improving Public Understanding

• Research be conducted to design instruments that measure public attitudes toward people with various types and degrees of mental illness and toward mental health services and facilities. These instruments should measure attitudes related to the actual behavior of people being surveyed. They should be used to identify and develop public education programs and other techniques as well as to assess the effectiveness of current public service announcements in creating a climate of community undertaking and acceptance of mental patients and the facilities and services they need.

• A Collaborative Media Resources Center be established which would be operated by a consortium of mental health professional associations and voluntary groups and which would include the participation of patients or former patients. Information developed by the proposed Center should take into account cultural and linguistic differences in the population.

• The Department of Health, Education, and Welfare establish a task force, composed of members from the public and private sectors and including former patients from various segments of society, to propose and stimulate new approaches for reducing discrimination against the mentally disabled and the mentally retarded and toward increasing public understanding in these areas.

2

Characteristics of Providers

The National Institute of Mental Health was established in the late 1940s. One of its major commitments was the development of a mental health training system to meet a critical shortage of qualified mental health service personnel. The Veterans Administration, at the same time, was also providing training and internships to increase the number of mental health professionals. This policy has been successful, as today there are substantial numbers of individuals in each of the core mental health disciplines who provide mental health services and function as educators, researchers, planners, and administrators.

Recently, as general health care costs have skyrocketed, the federal policy of increasing the supply of health professionals has been questioned. In December of 1977, Gerald Klerman, the Administrator of the Alcohol, Drug Abuse, and Mental Health Administration (ADAMHA) formed a task force to identify the major policy issues affecting mental health personnel needs and to develop recommendations for future policies and programs. This task force (ADAMHA, 1978) concluded that "the available methods for projecting manpower requirements are not adequate to determine with any degree of certainty that there *is or is not* a national *shortage (or surplus)* of any category of mental health personnel, including psychiatrists." Nonetheless, the task force believed there had been a sufficient increase in the number of mental health professionals to warrant a redirection in federal mental health human resources policy. They recommended that federal training funds be targeted toward improving geographic distribution (increasing the number of providers in rural areas as well as low-income urban areas), improving accessibility to services (for the poor, the young, the elderly, and minorities), and improving utilization, productivity, and effectiveness. It was also recommended that efforts be made to increase the numbers of women and minority persons trained in the mental health fields.

This recommended reshaping of the mental health training system was done in the absence of meaningful data. In fact, one of the most valid observations of the task force concerned the inadequacy of the present human resources data base. The task force recommended improving the federal mental health human resources information systems, collaborative efforts with other federal health human resources data systems, funding the development and/or improvement of state mental health human resources systems, and coordination of definitions and efforts so as to make the various data compatible and complementary. While some data exist concerning the geographic distribution of mental health professionals, they are incomplete and difficult to compare. Data on professionals specifically trained to serve particular populations such as children, adolescents, the elderly, criminal offenders, or the poor are essentially guesses. Virtually no data exist on the geographic distribution of such specialists.

Psychology in general, and professional psychology in particular, has had continuing difficulty in getting relevant federal agencies to collect data on psychologists. In some cases data are not collected at all. In other situations, data on doctoral-level psychologists are grouped in the same category with data on program aides who happen to have bachelor's degrees in psychology. The federal government simply does not support the collection of data on this major mental health profession to an even remotely adequate extent.

Nonetheless, data do exist on the location and activities of psychologists. The articles presented in this section provide such data on health service providers in psychology. The information comes from a variety of sources: periodic surveys of APA members, a survey of all licensed or certified psychologists in the United States, an analysis of APA membership, and an independently conducted survey. No one survey is perfect. Each study samples a slightly different population of psychologists. However, the samples are carefully defined, thus facilitating comparisons between studies and permitting some fairly reasonable specification of the overall population of health service providers in psychology.

In the first article, Gottfredson and Dyer present the most recent data regarding employment setting, professional activities, and service provisions available from the American Psychological Association. This survey, conducted in late 1976, covers psychologists who were members of APA. Based on a stratified sample of over 7,300 APA members, Gottfredson and Dyer estimate that 56% of APA-member psychologists provide some health services. The data show that there were approximately 23,000 doctoral-level (APA-member) psychologist providers at that time. Based on similar surveys and estimates by the American Psychiatric Association, the number of doctoral-level health service provider psychologists and the number of practicing psychiatrists appear to be equal. The magnitude of the services provided by doctoral-level APA-member psychologists is also striking: over 19 million hours of service per year. The best estimate suggests that between 2.8 and 3.4 million patients/clients are seen by psychologist practitioners each year.

Gottfredson and Dyer estimate that 20.7% of psychologist providers are in full-time private practice, whereas Arnhoff and Kumbar (1973) of the American Psychiatric Association estimate that 35% of all psychiatrists derive their professional income primarily from private practice. The Marmor (1975) data suggest that over 60% of psychiatrists are in private practice. Fifty-two percent of those psychologists reporting any independent services for a fee provided 10 or fewer hours of such service per week. There is a strong acceptance of public service positions by psychologists. The majority of psychologist providers are employed full time in public agencies and provide additional services on an independent fee-for-service basis part time.

The 1977 survey reported by Mills, Wellner, and VandenBos in the second article was the first survey of all licensed or certified psychologists in the United States. An unduplicated roster of 25,510 licensed/certified psychologists was developed. While not all psychologists are health service providers, the figures revealed that 22,588 psychologists are trained and licensed/certified as health service providers. Only about 19,000 of these reported being currently active in the provision of services. Mills, Wellner, and VandenBos found that 24.8% of those actively involved in the provision of psychological services were in full-time private practice (this works out to 20.7% of those trained, licensed, and eligible to provide such services).

Dörken and Webb surveyed the practices of psychologists. Their survey covered all licensed/certified psychologists in 10 states (42% of the population of the United States). They found that psychology is a low-mobility profession: 51% of licensed psychologists received their doctoral degree in the state in which they worked. Over 98% of psychologists were U.S.-trained. Twenty-eight percent of the patients of psychologists were referred by nonpsychiatric physicians; this figure is highly similar to the percentage of patients of psychiatrists who are referred by general-practice physicians. Primary care provider physicians refer to psychologists; psychiatrists rarely make such referrals. Dörken and Webb's data also show that psychologists frequently refer patients to general-practice physicians for various conditions.

In the fourth article of this section, Dörken notes psychology's potential for meeting the unmet national mental health needs. He contrasts the training standards of psychology, psychiatry, and social work and concludes that the standards for training in psychology are better and more uniform than those of the other two professions.

In the final article, Richards and Gottfredson explore the relationship between the characteristics of cities and states and the geographic distribution of psychologists, psychiatrists, clinical social workers, and school guidance personnel. They find that the same distribution pattern exists for all groups and conclude that there is no evidence to support claims that any of these professions is better distributed to provide service to poor, minority, or rural patients. The tendency is for such professionals to be more numerous in larger states characterized by greater affluence and greater emphasis on education. In many ways this is not surprising. Such densely populated states are more likely to have large governmental mental health systems as well as many nonprofit agencies, more and larger universities, more comprehensive mental health benefits in government programs and private insurance plans, and a "consumer" population more likely to see mental health services as helpful and nonstigmatizing. As such, so-called "maldistribution" reflects consumer preferences and system-based inadequacies, not simply characteristics of providers.

References

Alcohol, Drug Abuse, and Mental Health Administration. *Report of the Manpower Policy Analysis Task Force*. Washington, D.C.: U.S. Department of Health, Education, and Welfare, Public Health Service, Alcohol, Drug Abuse, and Mental Health Administration, 1978.

Arnhoff, F. N., & Kumbar, A. H. *The nation's psychiatrists—1970 survey*. Washington, D.C.: American Psychiatric Association, 1973.

Marmor, J., Scheidemandel, P. L., & Kanno, C. K. *Psychiatrists and their patients*. Washington, D.C.: American Psychiatric Association, 1975.

Health Service Providers in Psychology

Gary D. Gottfredson and Sharon E. Dyer

Information about health service providers in psychology based on a stratified random sample of over 7,300 APA members shows that about 56% report providing some health services. A detailed examination of the characteristics of these health service providers implies that 81% of the doctoral-level providers are licensed and that the extent of licensure varies markedly according to the primary setting in which services are provided—90% of private practitioners, in contrast with 64% of those providing services in public mental hospitals, are licensed. Other details of employment settings, as well as time spent in research, service, and other activities, ethnicity, gender, age, salaries, and fees are summarized in 33 tables. Taken together, evidence suggests that doctoral psychologists provide about one third of a million hours of services each week and that the number of people who receive services from a doctoral psychologist in a year is on the order of 2–4 million, with over half of the services provided in private practice.

Information about psychology's human resources for providing health services is essential for policy and planning purposes. Knowledge about the number of providers, their training, experience, and credentials, and the nature and extent of the services they provide supplies not only valuable indexes of the availability of service providers but also a baseline for assessing the impact of national programs on health personnel. One such large-scale program with potential influence on patterns of service delivery is national health insurance (NHI), and information on health service providers is especially timely in this context. Similarly, information about the numbers and service-provision patterns of psychologists has implications for a national training policy. For the past several years, the federal role in the training of mental health specialists has been uncertain, and better information about the work of health providers in psychology can help guide policy.

One recent large-scale effort to provide needed information about health service providers in psychology is the series of reports by the Council for the National Register of Health Service Providers in Psychology (Mills & Wellner, Note 1, Note 2, Note 3, Note 4; Wellner & Mills, Note 5, Note 6, Note 7). This research focused on the 1976 pool of licensed or certified psychologists and offers valuable insight into the work of licensed psychologists providing health services, especially those in private practice. Other information about psychologists providing health services is dated or fragmentary (Albee, 1959; Boneau & Cuca, 1974; Clark, 1957; Dörken & Whiting, 1976; Jones, 1966, 1969; Kling & Davis, 1977; Peck, 1969; Cuca, Note 8; Whiting, Note 9) or is limited to the early posttraining employment of psychologists (Dyer, Note 10; Schneider, Note 11). More comprehensive information is needed about the extent of licensure among health service psychologists and the kind and extent of services provided by psychologists working in a variety of settings.

The present report broadens the range of available information by presenting a basic description of service providers who are members of the American Psychological Association (APA) in terms of their training, licensure, ethnicity, specialty fields, nature of services provided, geographical location, fees and income, and sources of training support. Among the specific research questions addressed in this report are the following:

Reprinted from *American Psychologist*, 1978, *33*, 314–338.

1. How many APA members now provide health services?
2. How many hours of services are provided?
3. How many people receive these health services?
4. Where do psychologists render health services?
5. What proportion of psychologists providing health services is licensed?
6. How are health service providers in psychology distributed geographically?
7. How much do psychologists charge for their services?
8. What proportion of health services is delivered via private practice versus other service settings?

Method

A questionnaire was sent to a stratified random sample of the U.S.-resident APA membership in late November 1976. In January 1977, a second questionnaire was mailed to nonrespondents to the first mailing. In all, 10,002 persons were included in the sample, and 7,373 questionnaires were returned, for an overall response rate of 74%. Finally, to help assess the potential effects of nonresponse on the results, a postcard was mailed to the 2,351 nonrespondents for whom we had valid addresses (i.e., when questionnaires returned by the post office indicated that an address was insufficient, that address was dropped from the postcard mailing). A total of 40% of these nonrespondents provided limited information about their status by returning this postcard.

We anticipated that the data collected in this survey would have many uses, including the examination of the characteristics of minorities, women, master's-degree holders, and young members of the Association. For this reason, women, persons who became members in 1976, and associate members were oversampled; all known minority-group members were included in the sample.

Results presented in this report are estimates that weight an individual's responses by the inverse probability of his or her selection for inclusion in the sample. This procedure produces estimates of the values that would have been obtained had a census of U.S.-resident APA members been conducted. Naturally, there

Table 1: *Approximate Standard Errors of Percentages for Weighted Totals of Various Sizes*

Weighted total	Percentage						
	5 or 95	10 or 90	15 or 85	20 or 80	30 or 70	40 or 60	50
50	6	8	10	11	13	14	14
100	4	6	7	8	9	10	10
200	3	4	5	6	6	7	7
300	2	3	4	5	5	6	6
400	2	3	4	4	4	5	5
500	2	3	3	4	4	4	4
1,000	1	2	2	2	3	3	3
2,000	1	1	2	2	2	2	2
4,000	1	1	1	1	1	2	2
6,000	<1	1	1	1	1	1	1
8,000	—	1	1	1	1	1	1
10,000	—	1	1	1	1	1	1
12,000	—	<1	1	1	1	1	1
14,000	—	—	1	1	1	1	1
16,000	—	—	<1	1	1	1	1
18,000	—	—	—	1	1	1	1

is no way to correct for the potentially biasing effects of nonresponse to the questionnaire. Because of rounding error in the weighting procedure used, the weighted totals shown in the tables sometimes differ slightly from the sums of row or column weighted *ns*.

Table 1 shows approximate standard errors of percentages to aid in interpreting the results. These are conservative estimates (i.e., they are slightly larger than the actual standard errors) for two reasons: (a) They assume no increase in precision associated with differences in population proportions across strata, and (b) they do not assume an increase in precision associated with sampling without replacement from a finite population. Readers can construct rough 95% confidence intervals for proportions by doubling the appropriate standard error from Table 1.

Tables generally show results separately by degree level (doctoral, master's, other postbaccalaureate degree, and no postbaccalaureate degree). In this report, a "doctoral" degree equals PhD, EdD, PsyD, or DSc; "master's" degree equals MA, MS, MEd, or MSW; "other postbaccalaureate" degree equals MD, JD, LLB, or other postbaccalaurate degrees not included in the above lists. Only the doctoral and master's groups are large enough to allow reliable estimates of proportions. Although the results for the other groups are often shown for completeness, the extremely small sample sizes make interpretation of the results difficult. Consequently, only the results for doctoral and master's service providers are described in the text.

Results

The results are organized in five sections. The first section describes psychologists providing health services in terms of gender, degree level, licensure or certification, field of specialization, age, ethnicity, and inclusion in the *National Register of Health Service Providers in Psychology*. The second section describes work settings and geographic locations. The third section describes work activities and the kinds of services provided. The fourth section describes the extent of services, and the fifth describes the fees and incomes of the service providers.

Characteristics of Service Providers

About 56% of the responding APA members provided health services. If we assume that nonrespondents resemble respondents to the survey, roughly 22,980 APA members were health service providers in late 1976.[1] The results in the following tables are based on the responses of those psychologists who indicated that they provided "psychotherapy, counseling, assessment, or other *health services*."

Most psychologists[2] providing health services held a doctoral degree (81%), and most of the rest (17%) held a master's degree. Table 2 shows further details of the composition of providers by degree level and gender. Over three fourths of the doctoral-level and 55% of the master's-level service providers were men.

---

[1] This estimate is obtained by multiplying the weighted number of providers (16,943) by the inverse of the response rate. An examination of the results of the postcard survey of psychologists who did not respond to the full survey lends credence to this estimate. Of full-survey nonrespondents returning the postcard ($n = 929$), 68.7% reported that they were health service providers.

[2] For simplicity, the word *psychologist* is often used in this report to stand for APA member psychologist. Naturally, not all psychologists are APA members. Boneau and Cuca (1974) estimated that 90% of doctoral psychologists are APA members.

Table 2: *Degree Level and Gender of Health Service Providers*

	Postbaccalaureate degree (%)				Total (%)
Gender	None	Other	Master's	Doctoral	
Male	66.9	59.9	55.4	76.1	72.3
Female	33.1	40.1	44.6	23.9	27.7
Weighted n	47	342	2,820	13,734	16,943

Note. Each entry represents a percentage of the weighted n for each respective column.

Table 3 shows that health service psychologists were generally young, with a median age of 42.0 for men and of 41.4 for women doctoral-level providers. Modal ages are even lower: 30–34 years for both men and women doctoral workers.

Table 3: *Age of Health Service Providers by Gender and Degree Level*

	Postbaccalaureate degree (%)			
Years of age	None	Other	Master's	Doctoral
Men				
24 or younger	.0	.0	.1	.0
25–29	10.8	12.5	18.9	3.5
30–34	11.0	12.9	23.4	20.3
35–39	7.4	8.8	10.4	19.1
40–44	.0	12.4	12.2	14.4
45–49	63.4	15.2	7.7	15.8
50–54	.0	16.0	13.1	13.8
55–59	7.4	10.7	8.5	6.9
60–64	.0	7.5	2.9	4.0
65–69	.0	.0	1.5	1.3
70 or older	.0	1.6	.1	.1
No response	.0	2.3	1.2	.7
Weighted n	31	205	1,563	10,445
Women				
24 or younger	.0	.0	.2	.0
25–29	15.4	5.2	13.3	7.3
30–34	13.4	12.3	14.3	21.8
35–39	.0	7.1	10.3	15.9
40–44	.0	13.4	10.9	12.8
45–49	12.9	15.8	12.1	12.9
50–54	24.7	14.4	17.4	11.7
55–59	.0	16.5	10.6	7.4
60–64	8.9	7.4	4.9	4.7
65–69	24.7	4.8	2.5	2.2
70 or older	.0	1.0	2.6	.7
No response	.0	2.0	.9	2.5
Weighted n	16	137	1,257	3.288

Note. Each entry represents a percentage of the weighted n for each respective column.

Table 4: *Ethnic Identification of Health Service Providers by Degree*

Ethnicity	Postbaccalaureate degree (%)			
	None	Other	Master's	Doctoral
White	97.7	91.8	94.5	95.0
Black	.0	1.9	1.5	.9
Spanish-speaking/ surnamed	2.0	.7	.5	.4
Asian	.0	.6	.4	.7
Native American	.0	.0	.3	.1
Other citizen	.0	.3	.8	1.1
Noncitizen	.0	1.0	.8	.9
No response	.0	3.7	1.2	.9
Weighted *n*	47	342	2,820	13,734

Note. Each entry represents a percentage of the weighted *n* for each respective column.

As Table 4 shows, about 95% of both master's- and doctoral-level workers were white. Black psychologists constituted 1.5% of service providers with master's degrees and only .9% of those with doctoral degrees. Spanish-speaking or Spanish-surnamed providers were also rare: .5% of those with master's degrees and .4% of the doctoral workers. Fewer than 1% of psychologists providing services were not U.S. citizens.

Clinical psychology was the most common specialty of psychologists providing health serv-

Table 5: *Major Field of Specialization for Health Service Providers by Degree*

Field	Postbaccalaureate degree (%)			
	None	Other	Master's	Doctoral
Clinical	42.6	22.2	40.8	62.4
Counseling	2.1	19.9	13.2	13.4
School	12.8	36.3	23.6	5.1
Educational	.0	2.6	2.4	2.4
Community	4.3	.3	2.9	1.9
Developmental	.0	.0	1.0	1.8
Pediatric	.0	.0	.7	1.4
Industrial/ organizational	.0	.6	2.2	1.1
Rehabilitation	.0	2.0	2.3	.7
Professional	2.1	.0	.6	.8
Experimental	.0	.0	.1	.8
Humanistic	.0	.0	.5	.7
All other	2.1	12.0	8.9	4.7
Unknown	34.0	4.1	.7	2.6
Weighted *n*	47	342	2,820	13,734

Note. Each entry represents a percentage of the weighted *n* for each respective column. All specialties with fewer than 100 people are included in the "all other" category.

Table 6: *Degree Level of Health Service Providers by Licensure or Certification Status*

Licensed/ certified	Postbaccalaureate degree (%)				
	None	Other	Master's	Doctoral	Weighted *n*
	Row percentage[a]				
Yes	.0	1.1	9.2	89.7	12,393
No	.3	4.9	38.4	56.4	4,262
No response	9.9	1.0	15.1	74.1	287
	Column percentage[b]				
Yes	9.9	38.5	40.4	81.0	12,393
No	29.7	60.7	58.1	17.5	4,262
No response	60.4	.8	1.5	1.6	287
Weighted *n*	47	342	2,820	13,734	16,943

[a] Each entry represents a percentage of the weighted *n* for each respective row.
[b] Each entry represents a percentage of the weighted *n* for each respective column.

ices (see Table 5). Over three fifths of the doctoral-level workers and two fifths of the master's-level workers indicated that clinical psychology was their major field of specialization. Counseling psychology was the specialty area of about 13% of both master's- and doctoral-level workers. School psychology was the specialty of 24% of the master's-level but of only 5% of the doctoral-level service providers. Other specialties accounted for smaller percentages of service providers.

Information about the licensure or certification status of the health service providers is shown in Table 6.[3] Roughly 90% of licensed and 56% of unlicensed service providers have a doctoral degree. About 81% of doctoral-level providers and about 40% of master's-level providers are licensed.

The *National Register of Health Service Providers in Psychology* (Council for the National Register, 1976) is a voluntary register of health service providers. These providers are screened to ensure that their credentials and ex-

[3] As of 1976, 49 states and the District of Columbia had licensing laws for the independent practice of psychology. In most states the doctoral degree is required, with some master's-level workers licensed under "grandfather" provisions. In general, laws exempt from licensing requirements psychologists who work in state-operated or Veterans Administration hospitals, community mental health centers, and universities. All 50 states and the District of Columbia now have psychology licensing laws.

Table 7: *Health Service Providers Listed in the National Register of Health Service Providers*

Listed in National Register	Postbaccalaureate degree (%)			
	None	Other	Master's	Doctoral
Yes	18.7	16.7	14.1	40.8
No	55.1	40.4	46.4	39.8
Don't know	24.2	39.4	33.1	16.4
No response	2.1	3.5	6.5	2.9
Weighted *n*	47	342	2,820	13,734

Note. Each entry represents a percentage of the weighted *n* for each respective column.

perience accord with the *Register*'s standards for inclusion: licensure, a doctoral degree or eligibility under a "grandfather" provision, and 2 years of supervised experience in health services. About 41% of the doctoral-level and 14% of the master's-level providers reported that they were listed in the *Register*. (See Table 7.)

Practice Locations of Service Providers

Two kinds of information about the work settings of service providers were requested. Providers were asked about their principal employment settings and about the primary settings in which they provided health services. The distinction is that a psychologist may provide health services primarily in a setting different from that in which he or she is principally employed. For example, a university faculty member may work part-time at a private practice. Table 8 shows the primary employment settings by degree level. About 21% of the doctoral-level providers are primarily employed in independent or group private practice. The next most frequent employment settings are university psychology departments (10%) and community mental health centers (CMHCs) or mental health centers (10%).

Table 9 summarizes the information about primary settings in which psychologists provide health services. Over two fifths of the doctoral-level workers provided services primarily in an organized setting (a CMHC, hospital, school, or counseling center). Although 15% of doctoral providers worked primarily in one of several types of hospitals, CMHCs were their single

Table 8: *Employment Settings of Health Service Providers by Degree Level—1976*

Employment setting	Postbaccalaureate degree (%)			
	None	Other	Master's	Doctoral
University				
Psychology department	3.0	7.6	2.6	10.5
Education department	.0	5.2	.8	3.2
Other department	.0	.0	.3	1.4
Administration	.0	1.5	.4	1.5
Counseling center	.0	2.2	2.4	4.6
Other	.0	.0	.7	.4
Four-year college				
Psychology department	.0	.3	1.1	3.8
Education department	.0	.0	.0	.3
Other department	.0	.0	.0	.3
Administration	.0	.0	.0	.4
Counseling center	.0	1.4	.8	.7
Other	.0	.0	.0	.1
Junior college	.0	2.5	2.9	2.0
Medical school				
Psychiatry department	.0	1.1	.8	3.5
Other department	.0	1.4	.4	1.1
Professional school	.0	.0	.0	.9
Other education	5.1	33.5	22.7	5.2
General hospital	.0	2.2	1.9	5.6
Mental hospital	9.8	6.1	7.6	8.1
Independent or group psychological practice	23.4	11.6	9.9	20.7
Medical/psychological group practice	.0	.3	.9	1.9
Outpatient clinic	29.9	2.8	4.8	3.3
Community mental health center or mental health center	9.5	7.6	14.5	10.3
Counseling and guidance center	2.1	5.0	3.4	1.3
Special health services	.0	2.8	7.2	2.6
Other human service setting	.0	2.5	6.1	2.7
Consulting firm	4.9	.7	1.1	.8
Industrial/management psychology practice	.0	.0	.1	.3
Independent research organization	.0	.0	.1	.1
Business or industry (other)	.0	.7	1.7	.1
Criminal justice system	4.9	.7	2.6	1.0
Military service (other)	.0	.0	.0	.1
Government civil service (other)	4.9	.3	.5	1.1
Other noneducational and nonservice	2.4	.0	.2	.0
No response	.0	.0	1.4	.2
Weighted *n*	47	342	2,820	13,734

Note. Each entry represents a percentage of the weighted *n* for each respective column.

Table 9: *Primary Settings for Service Provision by Degree—1976 Health Service Providers*

Setting	Postbaccalaureate degree (%)			
	None	Other	Master's	Doctoral
Individual private practice	26.2	25.8	13.3	34.2
Group private practice	2.1	.0	3.5	7.4
Health maintenance organization	.0	1.0	.4	.4
Community mental health center or clinic	41.8	6.0	19.4	13.0
Private general hospital	.0	.4	1.2	2.4
Public general hospital	.0	5.1	2.0	5.2
Private mental hospital	.0	1.1	1.5	1.8
Public mental hospital	9.8	3.5	5.7	5.3
University counseling center	3.0	4.4	3.3	7.6
Nonuniversity counseling center	2.1	4.3	3.5	2.4
School	5.1	40.7	28.1	6.1
Criminal justice system	4.9	1.4	2.8	1.7
Industrial organization	.0	.0	1.7	.4
Military organization	.0	.7	.2	.9
Other	4.9	4.5	11.9	9.0
No response	.0	1.1	1.5	2.3
Weighted *n*	47	342	2,820	13,734

Note. Each entry represents a percentage of the weighted *n* for each respective column.

most frequently reported organized setting (13%). In contrast, fewer master's-level health service providers worked in individual (13%) or group (4%) private practice. The largest primary setting for these workers was schools (28%), followed by CMHCs (19%).

The primary settings of licensed psychologists contrast with those of unlicensed psychologists (see Table 10). Whereas 38% of licensed psychologists provided services primarily in individual private practice, only 9% of unlicensed psychologists did so. Similarly, 8% of licensed and only 3% of unlicensed psychologists provided services primarily in group private practice. Relatively more unlicensed than licensed psychologists provided services primarily in organized settings, many of which currently carry exemptions from state licensure requirements.

Table 11 organizes the data about licensure and primary service setting in a different manner, showing that the extent of licensure varies widely across service settings. Relatively few practitioners in health maintenance organiza-

tions (44%), nonuniversity counseling centers (49%), school systems (56%), military organizations (57%), or public mental health hospitals (64%) were licensed, in contrast to high proportions of providers in individual (90%) or group (89%) private practice and private general hospitals (81%).

Table 12 shows information about the geographic location of psychologists by showing the numbers of providers per 100,000 state population. Excluding the District of Columbia, the number of doctoral-level health service psychologists ranged from .36 times the national average (Louisiana) to 1.73 times the national average (New York). Put another way, New York has 4.8 times as many doctoral-level health service psychologists relative to state population as does Louisiana. Master's-level individuals providing health services range from zero (North Dakota) to 2.41 times the national average (Vermont), again excluding the District of Columbia. Psychologists were concentrated in the District of Columbia, as is usual when the District is treated as a state in this kind of analysis.

Table 10: *Primary Service Setting by Licensure/Certification Status*

Service setting	Licensed or certified (%)		
	Yes	No	No response
Individual private practice	37.8	8.6	43.6
Group private practice	8.0	2.6	3.5
Health maintenance organization	.3	.9	.3
Community mental health center	12.8	17.5	13.5
Private general hospital	2.4	1.6	.0
Public general hospital	4.7	4.8	.0
Private mental hospital	1.8	1.8	.9
Public mental hospital	4.7	7.4	4.0
University counseling center	6.2	8.8	4.7
Nonuniversity counseling center	1.8	5.2	3.1
School system	8.0	18.0	6.4
Criminal justice system	1.5	2.9	1.0
Industrial organization setting	.5	.9	.3
Military organization	.6	1.3	.0
Other	7.0	15.7	17.0
Unknown	2.2	2.0	1.7
Weighted *n*	12,393	4,262	287

Note. Each entry represents a percentage of the weighted *n* for each respective column.

Table 11: *Primary Service Setting by Licensure/Certification Status*

| | Licensed or certified (%) | | | |
Service setting	Yes	No	No response	Row total
Individual private practice	90.5	7.1	2.4	5,176
Group private practice	89.0	10.2	.9	1,108
Health maintenance organization	44.5	54.2	1.3	74
Community mental health center	66.9	31.5	1.6	2,370
Private general hospital	80.7	19.3	.0	362
Public general hospital	73.7	26.3	.0	782
Private mental hospital	73.4	25.7	.8	297
Public mental hospital	64.2	34.6	1.3	906
University counseling center	66.6	32.3	1.2	1.157
Nonuniversity counseling center	49.0	49.0	2.0	449
School system	55.7	43.2	1.0	1,770
Criminal justice system	59.2	39.9	.9	314
Industrial organization setting	62.3	36.7	1.0	101
Military organization	56.8	43.2	.0	132
Other	54.7	42.2	3.1	1,584
Unknown	75.1	23.6	1.4	361
Weighted *n*	12,393	4,262	287	16,943

Note. Each entry represents a percentage of the weighted *n* for each respective row.

Work Activities and Types of Services Provided

Respondents were asked to provide detailed information about the way they spend their work time. In particular, they were asked to indicate the percentage of time spent during a typical work-week in each of the following categories of activity:

1. *Research* includes basic or applied research in any field of psychology.
2. *Human service* includes direct clinical services, counseling or guidance services, consultation, assessment, and supervision of human services activities.
3. *Other applied psychology* includes program evaluation, personnel selection or assessment, systems or equipment design or evaluation, organizational consultation, analysis, or training.
4. *Educational activities* includes teaching, student or intern supervision, curriculum development, and student or educational evaluation.
5. *Management and administration* of an organization or program includes policy or program development or review, personnel administration, recruiting, and budgeting.
6. *Other activities* includes any activity that cannot be reasonably assigned to one of the above categories.

Tables 13-18 show the mean percentage[4] of time spent in each of these six activities according to the principal employment setting of the respondent (doctoral-level providers only). As would be expected, these health providers report spending a large portion of their time in service activities, 49% overall. The fraction of work time spent on services varies widely for different employment settings. Percentages of time spent in this activity range from 4% for the small number of respondents working principally in nonpsychology or education departments in 4-year colleges, to 83% for those working principally in medical/psychological group practice. Independent practitioners (79%) and practitioners in medical/psychological group settings (83%) spend larger fractions of their time providing services than do other groups. Psychologists in counseling and guidance centers that are not associated with an academic setting also spend large percentages of their time in the delivery of services (64%). Around 50% of the time of those principally employed in organized settings such as hospitals or CMHCs is spent in service provision.

Service providers as a whole report spending roughly 6% of their time in research, 49% in services, 4% in other applications of psychology, 18% in educational activities, 11% in management or administration, and 1% in other activities. Note that the standard deviations are often quite large, implying that there is sub-

---

[4] Respondents were asked to use a grid to report the percentage of time they spent in each activity. Many respondents reported percentages in some of the categories and left others blank. When this occurred, the blank values were assumed to be equal to 0%. The sum of the percentages for the total sample across all six activities equals 90%.

Table 12: *APA Member Psychologists Providing Health Services per 100,000 State Population*

State	Master's	Doctoral	Total[a]	State	Master's	Doctoral	Total[a]
Alabama	.39	3.35	3.79	Montana	2.01	8.42	10.96
Alaska	1.42	4.83	6.25	Nebraska	1.23	6.66	7.89
Arizona	1.03	10.75	12.10	Nevada	.68	7.43	8.11
Arkansas	.66	3.97	4.58	New Hampshire	1.34	7.21	8.56
California	1.27	8.76	10.30	New Jersey	2.47	6.48	9.21
Colorado	1.18	7.46	8.92	New Mexico	.52	3.84	4.27
Connecticut	1.29	8.30	10.21	New York	2.47	11.16	13.92
Delaware	1.38	3.45	4.84	North Carolina	.50	5.36	5.87
District of Columbia	3.77	26.82	33.66	North Dakota	.00	5.20	5.20
Florida	.73	6.22	7.02	Ohio	1.31	5.40	6.74
Georgia	.35	4.45	4.89	Oklahoma	.37	3.43	3.87
Hawaii	.12	8.55	8.67	Oregon	.26	6.95	7.26
Idaho	.73	6.71	7.32	Pennsylvania	2.35	5.63	8.09
Illinois	1.88	4.98	6.90	Rhode Island	1.19	5.93	7.44
Indiana	.79	3.46	4.39	South Carolina	.57	5.78	6.42
Iowa	1.32	4.98	6.69	South Dakota	.15	9.08	9.22
Kansas	1.50	5.87	7.37	Tennessee	.64	5.28	5.97
Kentucky	.91	3.09	4.00	Texas	.94	5.14	6.25
Louisiana	.45	2.32	3.11	Utah	.91	6.14	7.05
Maine	1.04	5.19	6.42	Vermont	3.18	5.73	11.46
Maryland	1.37	7.76	9.22	Virginia	1.35	6.00	7.59
Massachusetts	1.60	9.75	11.77	Washington	.65	8.01	8.78
Michigan	1.49	5.57	7.31	West Virginia	1.22	3.49	4.88
Minnesota	1.68	5.40	7.18	Wisconsin	1.41	5.71	7.18
Mississippi	.38	2.39	2.86	Wyoming	.27	4.28	4.81
Missouri	.92	3.04	4.87	U.S. total[b]	1.32	6.44	7.95

[a] Includes "other" and "no postbaccalaureate" degrees.
[b] Includes 467 people with unknown states.

stantial variability in the amount of time spent in any given activity, even for workers employed in similar settings. Also note that many of the distributions are markedly skewed.

To gain insight into the kinds of services provided by workers with different levels of training, respondents were asked to specify which of several services best characterized the primary personal services they render. Table 19 shows that individual therapy was designated by about 39% of master's-level and 60% of doctoral-level providers. Assessment and evaluation characterized the services of 36% of the master's- and 16% of the doctoral-level workers. No other category of service constitutes a primary activity for more than 7% of the master's- or doctoral-level respondents.

Extent of Services Provided

This section presents information about the hours spent providing services, the numbers of clients seen, and the number of client visits.

Table 20 shows that the modal time spent providing services was 11–20 hours per week for master's-level workers and 1–10 hours per week for doctoral workers. The mean time spent by doctoral-level workers in the provision of services each week was 21.4 hours ($SD = 13.5$). The corresponding mean for master's-level workers was 22.4 hours ($SD = 12.4$). The results imply that doctoral-level members of the APA spent over 270,000 hours providing health services each week. If we assume that nonrespondents resemble respondents, about 366,000 hours (270,037/.7373) are spent by doctoral-level members in the provision of services each week.

More detailed information on the extent of services is provided in Table 21, which shows the reported hours of services by primary setting of service provision. About 30% of doctoral-level psychologists who provide services primarily in independent private practice did so for 10 or fewer hours per week; over half of these independent practitioners provided services half-time or less (i.e., 20 or fewer hours per week). Although there is some variability across settings,

Table 13: *Mean Percentage of Time Spent in Research by Doctoral Health Service Providers by Principal Employment Setting*

Employment setting	$\bar{X}$	SD	Weighted n
University			
Psychology department	14.2	15.3	1,438
Education department	7.0	9.0	438
Other academic department	14.4	16.8	188
Management or administrative office	6.7	9.6	204
Student counseling or services center	5.0	10.0	616
Other	15.2	24.2	53
Four-year college			
Psychology department	4.9	8.3	516
Education department	4.5	6.5	39
Other academic department	23.5	22.2	42
Management or administrative office	1.8	2.4	52
Student counseling or services center	2.0	3.7	95
Other	.0	.0	14
Junior or community college	1.4	2.2	274
Medical school			
Psychiatry department	19.9	20.5	454
Other department	11.8	10.0	147
Free-standing professional school	13.3	17.1	118
Other educational setting	2.1	7.5	717
Human service settings			
General hospital	5.4	7.8	767
Mental or psychiatric hospital	6.5	12.3	1,119
Independent or group psychological practice	1.7	4.3	2,843
Medical/psychological group practice	1.8	2.4	264
Outpatient clinic	3.3	5.0	460
Community mental health center or mental health center	2.8	8.4	1,413
Counseling and guidance center (not school or college)	2.9	4.4	172
Special health services	3.4	6.3	355
Other human service setting	3.2	6.4	371
Consulting firm	2.9	5.8	105
Industrial/management psychology practice	9.5	7.3	41
Independent research organization	63.6	36.4	21
Other business or industry	10.7	15.6	14
Criminal justice system	3.6	4.0	143
Government civil service (other)	9.3	22.0	147
Military service (other)	4.3	1.8	18
Other noneducational or nonhuman service	.0	.0	4
No response	.6	1.6	23
Total	5.8	11.5	13,685

Note. Persons (.4%) failing to provide information about their work activities are excluded from the table.

Table 14: *Mean Percentage of Time Spent in Services by Doctoral Health Service Providers by Principal Employment Setting*

Employment setting	$\bar{X}$	SD	Weighted n
University			
Psychology department	16.6	15.3	1,438
Education department	13.7	14.9	438
Other academic department	10.4	12.8	188
Management or administrative office	26.8	26.5	204
Student counseling or services center	54.4	23.7	616
Other	35.6	32.3	53
Four-year college			
Psychology department	17.0	15.4	516
Education department	14.5	9.8	39
Other academic department	3.5	3.6	42
Management or administrative office	5.8	7.7	52
Student counseling or services center	56.1	18.2	95
Other	40.8	18.4	14
Junior or community college	35.7	26.1	274
Medical school			
Psychiatry department	28.3	17.4	454
Other department	29.5	16.4	147
Free-standing professional school	26.3	19.4	118
Other educational setting	60.6	27.5	717
Human service settings			
General hospital	50.9	24.5	767
Mental or psychiatric hospital	48.0	28.4	1,119
Independent or group psychological practice	79.0	19.2	2,843
Medical/psychological group practice	83.2	15.5	264
Outpatient clinic	62.1	19.6	460
Community mental health center or mental health center	52.0	28.1	1,413
Counseling and guidance center (not school or college)	64.0	22.7	172
Special health services	46.6	32.0	355
Other human service setting	53.1	26.8	371
Consulting firm	39.8	29.3	105
Industrial/management psychology practice	12.9	10.3	41
Independent research organization	5.0	5.0	21
Other business or industry	14.9	10.2	14
Criminal justice system	34.0	21.6	143
Government civil service (other)	22.7	32.1	147
Military service (other)	18.2	32.8	18
Other noneducational or nonhuman service	28.1	21.6	4
No response	74.9	24.4	23
Total	48.7	31.9	13,685

Note. Persons (.4%) failing to provide information about their work activities are excluded from the table.

Table 15: *Mean Percentage of Time Spent in Other Applications by Doctoral Health Service Providers by Principal Employment Setting*

Employment setting	$\bar{X}$	SD	Weighted n
University			
Psychology department	2.2	3.9	1,438
Education department	1.9	3.4	438
Other academic department	1.4	2.6	188
Management or administrative office	3.5	5.8	204
Student counseling or services center	6.3	13.4	616
Other	2.7	4.6	53
Four-year college			
Psychology department	1.6	3.5	516
Education department	.8	1.9	39
Other academic department	.0	.0	42
Management or administrative office	4.5	15.8	52
Student counseling or services center	3.0	3.4	95
Other	.5	1.5	14
Junior or community college	6.9	19.2	274
Medical school			
Psychiatry department	3.1	6.2	454
Other department	2.8	5.1	147
Free-standing professional school	2.6	4.8	118
Other educational setting	6.4	10.6	717
Human service settings			
General hospital	5.4	10.7	767
Mental or psychiatric hospital	6.5	9.2	1,119
Independent or group psychological practice	2.7	7.7	2,843
Medical/psychological group practice	1.8	4.0	264
Outpatient clinic	3.0	6.5	460
Community mental health center or mental health center	4.6	7.5	1,413
Counseling and guidance center (not school or college)	1.8	4.3	172
Special health services	6.4	10.7	355
Other human service setting	5.6	9.8	371
Consulting firm	35.3	24.0	105
Industrial/management psychology practice	25.5	42.9	41
Independent research organization	.9	2.0	21
Other business or industry	21.3	17.8	14
Criminal justice system	12.6	17.5	143
Government civil service (other)	11.7	21.1	147
Military service (other)	22.8	10.4	18
Other noneducational or nonhuman service	1.2	2.5	4
No response	.6	1.6	23
Total	4.4	10.0	13,685

Note. Persons (.4%) failing to provide information about their work activities are excluded from the table.

Table 16: *Mean Percentage of Time Spent in Education by Doctoral Health Service Providers by Principal Employment Setting*

Employment setting	$\bar{X}$	SD	Weighted n
University			
Psychology department	48.6	20.2	1,438
Education department	57.2	20.3	438
Other academic department	45.6	24.9	188
Management or administrative office	14.8	16.8	204
Student counseling or services center	12.5	12.5	616
Other	33.1	28.8	53
Four-year college			
Psychology department	61.7	19.4	516
Education department	64.9	17.3	39
Other academic department	60.2	24.9	42
Management or administrative office	6.2	8.3	52
Student counseling or services center	16.3	13.7	95
Other	40.6	13.8	14
Junior or community college	43.4	32.1	274
Medical school			
Psychiatry department	24.8	15.0	454
Other department	22.9	16.8	147
Free-standing professional school	34.3	17.8	118
Other educational setting	10.7	13.4	717
Human service settings			
General hospital	13.1	12.3	767
Mental or psychiatric hospital	8.6	10.7	1,119
Independent or group psychological practice	5.2	8.5	2,843
Medical/psychological group practice	3.3	4.8	264
Outpatient clinic	8.2	10.2	460
Community mental health center or mental health center	7.0	8.7	1,413
Counseling and guidance center (not school or college)	10.2	11.3	172
Special health services	4.6	6.7	355
Other human service setting	9.3	12.4	371
Consulting firm	4.6	9.7	105
Industrial/management psychology practice	9.5	10.9	41
Independent research organization	.6	1.7	21
Other business or industry	3.4	2.4	14
Criminal justice system	8.1	7.6	143
Government civil service (other)	6.4	10.0	147
Military service (other)	10.6	7.0	18
Other noneducational or nonhuman service	4.9	7.0	4
No response	15.6	18.7	23
Total	18.5	23.1	13,685

Note. Persons (.4%) failing to provide information about their work activities are excluded from the table.

Table 17: *Mean Percentage of Time Spent in Management or Administration by Doctoral Health Service Providers by Principal Employment Setting*

Employment setting	$\overline{X}$	SD	Weighted n
University			
Psychology department	7.3	13.1	1,438
Education department	6.6	14.7	438
Other academic department	8.3	11.0	188
Management or administrative office	34.0	30.2	204
Student counseling or services center	10.5	14.8	616
Other	2.8	4.9	53
Four-year college			
Psychology department	5.2	10.6	516
Education department	3.4	6.4	39
Other academic department	1.4	4.4	42
Management or administrative office	47.5	33.3	52
Student counseling or services center	10.7	12.5	95
Other	5.0	.0	14
Junior or community college	7.7	16.4	274
Medical school			
Psychiatry department	8.4	9.3	454
Other department	11.9	12.6	147
Free-standing professional school	7.2	13.7	118
Other educational setting	10.5	18.8	717
Human service settings			
General hospital	13.6	17.3	767
Mental or psychiatric hospital	17.2	21.1	1,119
Independent or group psychological practice	2.3	6.0	2,843
Medical/psychological group practice	2.2	6.7	264
Outpatient clinic	10.3	14.9	460
Community mental health center or mental health center	21.1	23.4	1,413
Counseling and guidance center (not school or college)	8.4	13.9	172
Special health services	27.4	31.8	355
Other human service setting	16.6	23.0	371
Consulting firm	4.0	8.3	105
Industrial/management psychology practice	21.0	26.1	41
Independent research organization	16.7	31.1	21
Other business or industry	32.8	27.2	14
Criminal justice system	25.0	21.1	143
Government civil service (other)	23.6	30.7	147
Military service (other)	3.7	9.1	18
Other noneducational or nonhuman service	27.5	40.3	4
No response	.0	.0	23
Total	10.9	18.4	13,685

Note. Persons (.4%) failing to provide information about their work activities are excluded from the table.

Table 18: *Mean Percentage of Time Spent in Other Activities by Doctoral Health Service Providers by Principal Employment Setting*

Employment setting	$\overline{X}$	SD	Weighted n
University			
Psychology department	1.0	2.6	1,438
Education department	.9	2.1	438
Other academic department	3.9	9.6	188
Management or administrative office	1.1	2.3	204
Student counseling or services center	.8	2.1	616
Other	.5	1.5	53
Four-year college			
Psychology department	1.8	4.1	516
Education department	1.3	2.2	39
Other academic department	.0	.0	42
Management or administrative office	2.5	2.5	52
Student counseling or services center	1.2	3.3	95
Other	.0	.0	14
Junior or community college	1.0	3.0	274
Medical school			
Psychiatry department	1.4	4.5	454
Other department	2.1	4.5	147
Free-standing professional school	.0	.5	118
Other educational setting	1.2	3.8	717
Human service settings			
General hospital	1.3	4.2	767
Mental or psychiatric hospital	1.5	5.0	1,119
Independent or group psychological practice	1.4	7.8	2,843
Medical/psychological group practice	.6	1.8	264
Outpatient clinic	1.5	4.2	460
Community mental health center or mental health center	.9	3.7	1,413
Counseling and guidance center (not school or college)	.3	1.2	172
Special health services	.6	5.3	355
Other human service setting	1.5	3.7	371
Consulting firm	.0	.0	105
Industrial/management psychology practice	1.6	2.4	41
Independent research organization	.9	2.0	21
Other business or industry	1.8	6.6	14
Criminal justice system	4.7	13.4	143
Government civil service (other)	6.1	12.1	147
Military service (other)	18.4	10.6	18
Other noneducational or nonhuman service	22.0	25.9	4
No response	.0	.0	23
Total	1.3	5.4	13,685

Note. Persons (.4%) failing to provide information about their work activities are excluded from the table.

Table 19: *Primary Type of Personal Service by Degree Level—1976 Health Service Providers*

Type of service	Postbaccalaureate degree (%)			
	None	Other	Master's	Doctoral
Individual therapy	38.3	33.7	38.9	59.5
Group therapy	32.4	2.6	4.8	5.6
Marital or conjoint therapy	.0	10.0	1.4	3.1
Family therapy	.0	1.8	4.5	5.1
Assessment/evaluation	21.4	36.5	36.0	16.4
Consultation	3.0	9.2	6.4	5.1
Other	.0	4.4	5.2	2.0
No response	4.9	1.8	2.7	3.3
Weighted *n*	47	342	2,820	13,734

Note. Each entry represents a percentage of the weighted *n* for each respective column.

doctoral psychologists in general usually provide services for fewer than 30 hours per week.

Information about the number of hours spent in the independent provision of services for a fee is of use in characterizing the nature of typical private practices for psychologists. Table 22 shows that the independent provision of services for a fee was usually a part-time enterprise and that many doctoral service providers (30%) did not engage in any independent practice. The typical provider reported 10 or fewer hours of private practice per week. At the doctoral level, about 52% *of those reporting any independent services for a fee* (i.e., excluding nonrespondents or those reporting no time spent providing serv-

Table 20: *Hours per Week Spent in Health Service Provision by Degree Level*

Hours per week	Postbaccalaureate degree (%)			
	None	Other	Master's	Doctoral
None	4.9	.0	.2	.4
1–10	22.6	20.8	22.0	28.4
11–20	15.9	32.4	27.0	24.9
21–30	43.9	19.0	26.5	22.5
31–40	9.8	17.8	14.9	14.7
41–50	.0	6.6	3.4	4.9
51–60	.0	.3	1.5	1.9
61–70	.0	.0	.0	.0
71–80	.0	.0	.0	.0
Unknown	3.0	3.0	4.5	2.1
Weighted *n*	47	342	2,820	13,734

Note. Each entry represents a percentage of the weighted *n* for each respective column.

ices for a fee) provided 10 or fewer hours per week. Only 30% of the doctoral-level providers with any independent practice reported 21 or more hours each week in the provision of services for a fee.

Other information about the extent of services relates to the numbers of clients seen. Table 23 organizes responses to the following question: "About how many client visits occur in a typical week? (Count a group visit as equal to the number of people in the group.)" Over half of both master's- and doctoral-level workers reported 20 or fewer such visits per week. Almost no providers reported more than 80. The mean number of visits was 27.0 (*SD* = 55.0) for master's-level and 24.4 (*SD* = 28.5) for doctoral-level service providers.

Fees and Income

Table 24 summarizes information on the usual hourly fee charged individual clients by those psychologists who provide services for a fee. Usual fees varied greatly; about 15% of doctoral providers typically charged $45 or more and 24% charged $29 or less. The median hourly fee was $36.4 (semi-interquartile range = $6.2) for doctoral workers and $28.8 (semi-interquartile range = $7.0) for master's-level workers.

Table 25 shows that most fee-for-service providers adjust their fees according to the client's ability to pay. When nonrespondents are excluded, about 79% of doctoral providers and 72% of master's providers adjust their fees.

Information about the income of service providers is summarized in Table 26. The median *total earned income* for doctoral-level providers was about $27,400 (semi-interquartile range = $6,800), and for master's-level workers it was about $18,300 (semi-interquartile range = $5,400). In other words, the median total annual income of doctoral-level providers was about $9,000 higher than that of master's-level providers.

Independent practitioners are of special interest, and Table 27 shows information about the distribution of total earned incomes for psychologists providing services primarily via independent private practice versus those primarily providing services in other settings. Because of the small numbers involved, comparable results

Table 21: *Hours per Week Spent Providing Services by Primary Service Setting and Degree Level of Provider*

Primary service setting	None	1–10	11–20	21–30	31–40	41–50	51–60	61–70	71–80	No response	Weighted n
Doctoral level[a] (%)											
Individual private practice	.3	30.7	22.2	17.9	18.8	7.3	2.1	.1	.0	.7	4,701
Group private practice	.0	21.0	16.5	22.9	26.1	8.4	4.9	.0	.0	.2	1,010
Health maintenance organization	.0	30.2	33.2	12.8	22.0	.0	.0	.0	.0	1.7	59
Community mental health center	.1	24.1	31.3	28.1	10.6	2.3	1.6	.1	.0	1.8	1,784
Private general hospital	.0	20.1	39.0	25.3	8.5	5.1	.0	.0	.0	1.9	328
Public general hospital	.0	17.7	33.0	30.0	14.9	4.2	.0	.0	.0	.3	709
Private mental hospital	.0	17.3	19.6	34.6	18.9	9.6	.0	.0	.0	.0	252
Public mental hospital	.0	29.7	24.2	29.1	10.3	4.2	.7	.0	.0	1.8	727
University counseling center	.0	33.8	27.0	29.4	8.4	.9	.0	.0	.0	.5	1,047
Nonuniversity counseling center	.3	23.6	29.6	23.8	14.9	.0	3.9	.0	.0	3.9	334
School system	.2	23.7	22.2	30.0	13.5	4.5	3.4	.0	.1	2.5	836
Criminal justice system	.4	31.6	40.7	19.7	1.4	5.7	.4	.0	.0	.0	227
Industrial organization	.0	69.3	6.0	.0	24.8	.0	.0	.0	.0	.0	52
Military organization	.0	26.5	27.4	20.9	19.9	4.4	.9	.0	.0	.0	123
Other	3.0	44.7	25.6	14.8	7.5	2.3	1.5	.0	.0	.6	1,231
No response	.3	10.2	10.9	8.4	12.2	4.1	4.1	.0	.0	49.7	314
Master's level[b] (%)											
Individual private practice	.0	24.7	27.6	21.8	16.4	3.8	4.4	.0	.0	1.4	374
Group private practice	.0	16.1	41.5	15.3	15.3	8.1	2.4	.0	.0	1.4	97
Health maintenance organization	.0	20.6	38.6	40.8	.0	.0	.0	.0	.0	.0	12
Community mental health center	.0	15.6	22.1	32.6	18.9	5.7	.9	.0	.0	4.3	546
Private general hospital	.0	17.6	37.0	28.0	3.0	14.4	.0	.0	.0	.0	33
Public general hospital	.0	2.5	41.1	31.8	17.8	4.3	.0	.0	2.5	.0	56
Private mental hospital	.0	47.5	30.3	19.7	2.4	.0	.0	.0	.0	.0	41
Public mental hospital	.0	24.6	25.4	31.5	11.8	2.9	.0	.0	.0	3.8	162
University counseling center	1.1	29.2	28.4	31.4	5.2	.0	.0	.0	.0	4.6	94
Nonuniversity counseling center	.0	10.5	27.9	25.0	11.0	6.7	3.4	.0	.0	15.5	99
School system	.4	21.3	27.6	28.9	15.0	1.8	1.1	.0	.0	3.9	792
Criminal justice system	.0	24.3	24.5	24.4	18.2	2.9	4.2	.0	.0	1.4	79
Industrial organization	.0	74.2	16.3	4.7	4.7	.0	.0	.0	.0	.0	49
Military organization	.0	14.7	.0	85.3	.0	.0	.0	.0	.0	.0	7
Other	.6	28.1	29.0	20.2	16.2	2.5	.7	.0	.0	2.6	335
No response	.0	.0	14.0	5.9	9.0	.0	2.7	.0	.0	68.4	43

Note. Each entry represents a percentage of the weighted n for each respective row.
[a] $n = 13,734$.
[b] $n = 2,816$.

for "other" and "no postbaccalaureate" degree categories are not shown in order to ensure confidentiality. Independent practitioners make substantially more than other practitioners. The median total income for doctoral-level workers primarily in independent practice was about $6,000 higher than that for other doctoral-level workers. Master's-level workers in private practice made about $3,000 more than other master's-level practitioners. Also of interest in Table 27 are the measures of dispersion for the income distributions. The semi-interquartile ranges appear much larger for the private practitioners than for other providers.

To gain further perspective on the relative remunerativeness of a variety of alternative work settings, and to examine pay differences according to gender and ethnicity, Tables 28 through 30 present annual (12-month) *salary* information. The distinction between salary and total earned income is that salary refers to pay from one's principal employment and total earned income includes income from such additional sources as consulting fees or additional part-time work.

Table 28 shows information about salary distributions for master's and doctoral providers according to the service setting of their primary

Table 22: *Time Spent by 1976 Health Service Providers in the Independent Provision of Services for a Fee by Degree*

Hours per week	Postbaccalaureate degree (%)			
	None	Other	Master's	Doctoral
41 or more	.0	6.6	1.7	4.6
31–40	.0	2.6	2.0	8.1
21–30	7.1	2.2	3.2	7.8
11–20	8.2	4.5	7.9	12.0
Up to 10	47.8	25.8	18.0	35.3
None	34.5	55.4	64.8	30.3
No response	2.4	2.9	2.4	1.9
Weighted *n*	47	342	2,820	13.734

Note. Each entry represents a percentage of the weighted *n* for each respective column.

employment (persons not employed in service settings, e.g., colleges or university psychology departments, are not shown in this table). These results reinforce the earlier evidence that doctoral workers are substantially higher paid than master's workers. In addition, doctoral workers show substantial salary differences according to work setting. Independent doctoral practitioners make more than others, with a median salary of $36,100; and doctoral psychologists working in counseling centers, mental hospitals, CMHCs,

Table 23: *Weekly Client Visits Made to Health Service Providers by Degree Level of Provider*

Clients per week	Postbaccalaureate degree (%)			
	None	Other	Master's	Doctoral
None	.0	.7	2.1	1.0
1–20	78.1	52.5	56.0	54.2
21–40	14.1	26.1	23.8	27.4
41–60	.0	7.4	6.8	10.1
61–80	.0	1.4	2.6	1.6
81–100	2.4	1.1	1.1	1.0
101–120	.0	.0	.2	.3
121–140	.0	1.1	.1	.2
141–160	.0	.7	.5	.2
161–180	.0	.8	.0	.1
181–200	.0	.0	.1	.0
201–220	.0	.0	.0	.2
221–240	.0	.0	.0	.1
241–260	.0	.0	.0	.0
261–280	2.4	.0	.6	.0
281–300	.0	1.1	.2	.2
Unknown	3.0	7.2	5.7	3.5
Weighted *n*	47	342	2,820	13,734

Note. Each entry represents a percentage of the weighted *n* for each respective column.

Table 24: *Usual Hourly Fee for Individual Clients by Degree—1976 Health Service Providers*

Hourly fee	Postbaccalaureate degree (%)			
	None	Other	Master's	Doctoral
$50 or more	12.9	2.4	1.8	7.2
$45–$49	.0	9.0	2.3	7.6
$40–$44	.0	10.2	9.9	22.0
$35–$39	19.4	3.6	13.9	21.5
$30–$34	3.2	21.0	19.5	17.6
$25–$29	3.2	25.2	20.4	14.6
$20–$24	41.9	7.8	11.9	5.5
$15–$19	16.1	12.0	8.7	2.3
$10–$14	3.2	6.0	4.1	.9
$9 or less	.0	3.6	7.7	.8
No response (weighted *n*)	(16)	(175)	(1,686)	(3,993)
Total (weighted *n*)	47	342	2,820	13,734

Note. Each entry represents a percentage of the weighted *n* for each respective column. Percentages exclude nonrespondents.

"other human service settings," and the criminal justice system all have median salaries below $25,000. Results for groups with weighed *n*s smaller than 25 are not shown in order to preserve confidentiality. Note that some of the remaining sample sizes are still so small that the estimates are unreliable.

Table 29 contrasts the salaries of men and women doctoral psychologists working in various service settings. In every case, the median salary for women is lower than the corresponding salary for men. Note that some of the sample sizes are extremely small, making the salary estimates unreliable. Nevertheless, the pattern of salary differences is consistent, lending credibility to the generalization that women typically earn less than men.

Table 25: *Adjustment of Fees According to Client's Ability to Pay—1976 Health Service Providers*

Degree	Yes (%)	No (%)	No response (%)	Weighted *n*
Doctoral	57.5	15.4	27.1	13,734
Master's	30.5	12.2	57.3	2,820
Other	40.4	11.4	48.2	342
No postbaccalaureate	63.3	2.1	34.5	47

Note. Each entry represents a percentage of the weighted *n* for each respective row. The "no response" category includes many service providers who do not provide services in exchange for a fee.

Table 26: *Earned Income for 1976 Health Service Providers by Degree Level*

Postbaccalaureate degree	Percentile			Semi-interquartile range	Weighted n		
	25th	50th	75th		Responding	No response	Total
Doctoral	$21,154	$27,375	$34,768	$6,807	12,262	1,471	13,734
Master's	12,936	18,262	23,712	5,388	2,415	405	2,820
Other	13,222	19,745	28,695	7,736	288	55	342
None	9,000	16,428	25,000	8,000	28	18	47

Finally, Table 30 shows median salaries according to ethnicity for doctoral-level psychologists. Because of the very small ns, salaries by employment setting cannot be shown. These results suggest that whites and Asian-Americans may earn slightly more than the other groups. Naturally, the extent to which race or gender differences in salary may be due to age, experience, or other variables is unclear from these simple tabulations.

Discussion

Limitations

The major limitations of the present attempt to describe psychologists currently providing health services seem to be the following:

1. The membership list of the American Psychological Association was used to specify the sample. Naturally, not all psychologists who provide health services are members of the Association. Mills and Wellner (Note 2) reported that about 84% of licensed and certified

psychologists in their 1976 survey were APA members. Although one might expect health service providers to be members somewhat more often than psychologists in general, no clear evidence exists. Mills and Wellner did report, however, that 88% of private practitioners in their survey were members of the APA. This accords closely with Boneau and Cuca's (1974) estimate that 90% of doctoral psychologists are members. The exclusion of nonmembers from the present survey may introduce some unknown bias when the results are used to characterize health service psychologists in general.

2. The response rate of 74%, although gratifying, may also introduce bias. It is about the same as for other surveys of this type. Wellner and Mills (Note 2) had a 73% response rate to their 1976 survey; Boneau and Cuca (1974) obtained a 77% response rate from the APA members in their 1972 survey; the American Psychiatric Association (Arnhoff & Kumbar, 1973) had a 68% response rate to its 1970 survey.

One way of evaluating the effect of non-

Table 27: *Total Earned Income for Psychologists Providing Services Primarily in Independent Private Practice Versus Other Settings by Degree*

Setting and degree	Percentile			Semi-interquartile range	Weighted n		
	25th	50th	75th		Responding	No response	Total
Independent private practice							
Doctoral	$23,027	$31,521	$41,629	$ 9,301	5,058	653	5,711
Master's	8,621	21,041	29,112	10,246	417	55	472
Other than private practice							
Doctoral	20,296	25,566	31,125	5,414	6,941	766	7,709
Master's	15,940	18,062	22,910	3,485	1,966	340	2,306
All service settings[a]							
Doctoral	21,154	27,375	34,768	6,807	12,262	1,471	13,734
Master's	12,936	18,262	23,712	5,388	2,415	405	2,820

[a] Includes health service providers who did not report the primary setting in which they provide services.

Table 28: *Full-Time Salaries (in Hundreds of Dollars) of Health Service Psychologists Employed in Selected Settings—1976*

Setting	Master's				Doctoral			
	Q1	Mdn	Q3	n	Q1	Mdn	Q3	n
University counseling center	—	—	—	11	164	194	257	85
General hospital	135	166	191	32	226	269	301	564
Mental hospital	150	175	200	123	228	242	280	891
Independent or group practice	226	276	325	116	261	361	487	1,781
Medical/psychological group practice	—	—	—	10	228	308	478	183
Outpatient clinic	155	179	207	84	221	267	303	342
Community mental health center or mental health center	131	163	192	317	193	227	272	1,052
Counseling/guidance center (noneducational)	135	170	198	70	177	209	235	134
Special health services (retardation or other)	147	171	194	135	203	240	295	232
Other human service	126	161	205	88	182	225	276	272
Criminal justice system	165	192	200	57	204	226	248	132

Note. Table shows weighted *n*s.

response on the representativeness of the results is to compare estimates of membership composition made using the survey data with known characteristics of the membership. The APA *Membership Register* (American Psychological Association, 1977c) shows that 73% of Association members are men; this is close to the weighted estimate of 74% men obtained from the present survey.[5] Similarly, assuming that fellows and members, but not associates, hold a PhD, ScD, EdD, or PsyD, a total of 81% of APA members have this level of education. This matches the weighted estimate of 81% with these degrees obtained from the survey. Although the close correspondence of these estimates is reassuring, it does not guarantee a lack of bias.

The postcard follow-up of those who failed to respond to the two mailings of the full questionnaire provides some clues to the likely nature of response bias. A higher proportion of postcard respondents (69%) than respondents to the full survey (56%) reported providing services. This implies that the estimates of the number of service providers made in the text by assuming that non-respondents resemble respondents to the survey may be conservative.

3. Definitions of health service providers in

psychology differ, and none is clearly preferable. Jone's (1969) report, based on analyses of the National Science Foundation's 1966 National Register of Psychologists, included only respondents who indicated that their principal employment was "related to the field of mental health." Cuca's (Note 8) report on a 1972 APA survey was limited to respondents who spent some of their professional time in at least one of the following work activities: application or practice, clinical service, counseling service, consultant or advisory service, or test administration and evaluation. The 1976 survey conducted by the Council for the National Register of Health Service Providers in Psychology (Wellner & Mills, Note 6) defined a health service provider in psychology as

a psychologist, certified/licensed at the independent practice level in his/her state, who is duly trained and experienced in the delivery of direct, preventive, assessment, and therapeutic intervention services to individuals whose growth, adjustment, or functioning is actually impaired or is demonstrably at high risk of impairment.

Each of the recent definitions has virtues and defects. The present definition (an APA member who reports providing "psychotherapy, counseling, assessment, or other *health services*") has the weakness of excluding those who are not APA members, but it includes self-designated health service providers who may not be licensed. It respects the reality of the current

---

[5] These estimates refer to all members, not just health service workers, because membership figures for health service providers cannot be obtained.

Table 29: *Full-Time Salaries (in Hundreds of Dollars) of Doctoral Health Service Psychologists Employed in Selected Settings by Gender—1976*

Setting	Men				Women			
	Q1	Mdn	Q3	n	Q1	Mdn	Q3	n
University counseling center	177	199	312	43	152	188	236	43
General hospital	237	275	313	456	204	239	274	108
Mental hospital	214	249	285	691	200	225	250	200
Independent or group practice	277	378	496	1,452	222	292	384	328
Medical/psychological group practice	245	352	504	148	173	197	268	35
Outpatient clinic	238	274	308	268	172	216	277	74
Community mental health center or mental health center	201	232	280	802	176	208	247	250
Counseling and guidance center (noneducational)	183	213	234	96	169	191	404	37
Special health service (retardation or other)	215	255	325	182	158	200	231	50
Other human service	194	230	288	205	170	206	241	67
Criminal justice system	206	229	254	118	—	—	—	14

Note. Table shows weighted *n*s.

situation, in which all providers are not licensed and in which licensing laws differ greatly across states. The Council for the National Register's definition is fairly narrow and excludes unlicensed service providers. The Council's definition does include providers who are not APA members.

4. The report primarily provides information about the characteristics of service providers, with little detail about the characteristics of those receiving services or the nature of the services provided.

Despite these limitations, the present report extends or complements existing information about health service providers in important ways, and it provides new information in other areas. The following sections discuss some of

Table 30: *Full-Time Salaries (in Hundreds of Dollars) of Doctoral Health Service Psychologists by Ethnicity—1976*

Ethnicity	Q1	Mdn	Q3	n
White	210	258	334	6,041
Black	204	240	323	49
Spanish-speaking/surnamed	183	227	284	26
Asian	215	254	285	48
Native American	—	—	—	5
Other citizen	185	221	357	61
Noncitizen	201	233	267	48

Note Table shows weighted *n*s. Because minorities were sampled at 100%, however, weighted *n*s roughly equal actual *n*s. Salary results for native Americans were deleted to preserve confidentiality.

these contributions and compare the results with those from other surveys.

Numbers and Characteristics of Providers

The 1966 National Science Foundation Register (Jones, 1969) included 7,743 doctoral-level psychologists and 3,737 master's-level workers who indicated that their principal employment was related to *mental health*. The estimates from the present survey imply that over 13,700 doctoral-level members and over 2,800 master's-level APA members provide health services. Although the definitions used in the two surveys differ, it appears that the number of doctoral-level health workers has greatly increased over this time interval. The change in numbers of master's-level workers is difficult to interpret because it is relatively rare for people trained at the master's level in psychology to seek associate member status in the APA.

The proportion of doctoral-level health service psychologists who are women appears to have increased. About 17.9% of the "mental health" psychologists in 1966 were women (Jones, 1969); about 18.3% of the "psychological service" providers in 1972 were women (Cuca, Note 8); and about 23.9% of the 1976 health service providers were women. Naturally, some of this difference may be due to a change in the way the samples are defined, but the trend does appear to be in accord with other evidence (Simon & Frankel, 1976) that increasing proportions of psychology degrees are being earned by women.

No readily interpretable evidence about the level of training of workers who provide psychology-related health service is available. The major reason for this problem is that the definition and sampling of appropriate populations is difficult to accomplish. The present results imply that 81% of APA-member health service providers hold the doctorate. This estimate is inappropriate if generalized to all providers of psychological services, however, because the doctorate is generally required for membership in the Association. The Mills and Wellner (Note 4) estimates that 84% of active and 76% of inactive health service providers hold the doctorate is also inappropriate if generalized to all providers of psychological services, because only licensed psychologists were included in their survey and the doctorate is a requirement for licensing in most states. Unfortunately, the available current information (collected by NIMH's Biometry Branch) on the staffing patterns of mental health facilities (e.g., Witkin, 1976) does not provide separate information on doctoral versus nondoctoral providers of psychological services. Although such data are not now collected by NIMH, they were collected in 1972. Witkin (1974) shows results of the 1972 survey of mental health facilities which indicate that 50% of full-time "psychologists" held the doctorate, 39% were master's-level workers, and 11% held only lower degrees. Although evidence implies that people with master's-level training do provide extensive services to the public (Dimond, Havens, Rathnow, & Colliver, 1977; Whiting, Note 9), no evidence now available allows an assessment of the relative extent of services provided by doctoral versus subdoctoral providers of psychological services.

Licensure. Because information on licensure or certification was not solicited in the National Science Foundation's *National Register* or NIMH surveys, long-term trends in licensure are impossible to assess. The available evidence, however, suggests a striking recent change in licensure status. According to APA's 1972 survey (Cuca, Note 8), about 65% of doctoral APA members who provided services were licensed or certified. This compares with 81% of doctoral-level providers in the present survey. In contrast, whereas about 53% of master's-level respondents to the 1972 survey reported being licensed, only about 40% of master's-level respondents to the present survey are licensed. One speculation is that the recent emphasis on licensure has led to an increase in the proportion of doctoral-level psychologists who seek licensure. At the same time, the requirement of a doctoral degree for licensure in most states, and the expiration of "grandfathering" provisions, has excluded new master's-level providers from licensure.

The emphasis on licensure is related to concern for the welfare of potential users of psychological services (APA Committee on Legislation, 1967) and for clear identification of providers eligible for third-party reimbursement for services. In recent years, licensed psychologists have been recognized as independent providers in the Civilian Health and Medical Program of the Uniformed Services (CHAMPUS), the Federal Employees Health Benefits Plan, Civilian Health and Medical Program of the Veterans Administration, Aetna insurance programs, Medicaid (in 17 states), some Blue Cross/Blue Shield plans, and other programs. It appears reasonable to speculate that this increasing recognition of licensed psychologists as independent practitioners under third-party reimbursement plans may have stimulated some psychologists to become licensed. The trend toward licensure is apparent even among psychologists who provide services for a fee. In Cuca's (Note 8) report, 83% of fee-for-service therapists were licensed, in contrast with the 90% of independent practitioners licensed in the present survey.

Related to the issue of third-party payment is the recent development of the *National Register of Health Service Providers in Psychology,* first published in 1975. One purpose of the *Register* is to serve as a reference guide to help third-party payment organizations identify providers who meet certain training, licensure, and experience criteria. About 41% of the doctoral-level health service providers in the present survey are listed in this register. Calculations made by using Wellner and Mills's (Note 6) tables imply that slightly higher percentages of licensed psychologists (48%) and of doctoral-level licensed psychologists (51%) are included in the *Register*. The voluntary registration of such a large proportion of health service providers (for a listing fee that is currently $50) suggests that identification as a "qualified" practitioner is now an important consideration for many psychologists.

The official policy of the American Psychological Association is that a person who represents himself or herself to the public as a psychologist, and offers services to the public for a fee, should be licensed (APA Committee on Legislation, 1967; adopted as policy by the Council of Representatives, September 1967). In addition, licensing requirements appear to be in accord with the spirit of the *Ethical Standards for Psychologists* (American Psychological Association, 1977a). In a more recent policy statement relating to the provision of psychological services (American Psychological Association, 1977b), the Association has endorsed a single standard for licensure so that the current exemptions for psychologists working in some organized settings would be eliminated:

> There should be a uniform set of standards governing the quality of services to all users of psychological services in both the private and public sectors. There is no justification for maintaining the double standard presently embedded in most state legislation whereby providers of private fee-based psychological services are subject to statutory regulation, while those providing similar psychological services under governmental auspices are usually exempt from such regulations. This circumstance tends to afford greater protection under the law for those receiving privately delivered psychological services. On the other hand, those receiving privately delivered psychological services currently lack many of the safeguards that are available in government settings; these include peer review, consultation, record review, and staff supervision. (p. 3)

Some of the results are interesting in the light of these policies. First, although 90% of independent practitioners are licensed, and although this percentage has increased in recent years, one would expect *all* of this group to be licensed. One interpretation of the result that about 10% of those reporting independent practice did not report licensure is that some respondents may have misunderstood the question. Some individuals who are licensed as marriage and family counselors, for example, may engage in therapy but not consider that they are licensed as psy-

chologists or hold themselves out to the public as psychologists. An alternative possibility is that some individuals working primarily in exempt settings may work part-time in independent practice and be unaware of APA policy (and usually also state law) with regard to licensure.

A second interesting result is the large variation across settings, with licensure less prevalent in exempt settings than in independent practice. One might expect the APA's (1977b) recent policy statement with regard to a single standard for providers of psychological services to eventually contribute to higher licensure rates in currently exempt settings, particularly if state laws change in accord with the Association's recommendation.

Practice Locations

Service settings. Using data from a variety of surveys, it is possible to construct a crude composite of the settings in which psychologists provide services. The most common primary setting for the provision of health services is independent *or* group private practice; this setting was reported by nearly 42% of doctoral-level psychologists (Table 9). Independent practice or group practice are, however, the primary employment settings of only 21% of these psychologists (Table 8). Private practice for psychologists contrasts with the extent of involvement in private practice for psychiatrists. According to Arnhoff and Kumbar (1973), 35% of psychiatrists derive their professional income primarily from private practice.

A comparison of the evidence about primary employment settings of psychologists from a number of surveys may be of interest. Boneau and Cuca (1974) reported that 7.3% of the doctoral-level APA members in their 1972 survey were primarily employed in independent or group private practice. A more detailed examination of doctoral-level providers of psychological services from the same survey (Cuca, Note 8) revealed that 10.2% of this group were primarily independent or group private practitioners. The present report's large percentage (20.7%) of doctoral providers of psychological services whose primary employment is independent or group practice may be the result of (a) a substantial increase in psychologists providing services via this route, (b) differences in the definition of the population, or (c) both. At the same time, an independent report by Wellner and Mills (Note 6) estimates that 24.8% of health service providers are full-time private practioners, and Garfield and Kurtz's (1976) report of a 1974 survey of 855 clinical psychologists showed 23.3% of their sample primarily working in private practice. Taken together, then, the evidence suggests a substantial increase in private practice as a primary activity of psychologists. At the same time, it should be noted that few recent graduates of psychology training programs enter private practice immediately after completion of their training. Schneider (Note 11) reported information on the first job of graduates of NIMH-supported training programs in clinical, counseling, community, and school psychology which implies that only 2.7% of these graduates go directly into individual or group private practice.

Independent practice of the provision of health services is largely a part-time enterprise. Although 34% of doctoral-level psychologists providing services did so primarily via independent practice (Table 9), only 20% of doctoral service providers spent more than half-time (20 hours) in the independent provision of services for a fee (Table 22). The mean time spent per week in fee-for-service independent practice was 15.9 hours for doctoral psychologists who provided any services in that setting.[6]

This characterization of private practice as a part-time activity engaged in by a large fraction of service providers is in rough accord with other characterizations. According to a Mills and Wellner (Note 3) report of their 1976 survey of licensed psychologists, approximately 70% of private practitioners have part-time practices. Because data were not reported separately by degree level, this percentage applies to all degree levels combined. If full-time practice is defined as more than 30 hours of service per week, the present results imply that 81% of doctoral-level independent practitioners engage in private practice only as part-time workers. Nevertheless, using Tables 20 and 22 to account for hours spent providing services in inde-

pendent practice and for all settings, it can be estimated that 54.7% of the *hours* spent providing health services by doctoral psychologists are spent by private practioners.[7] This exceeds Dörken and Whiting's (1976) estimate that those in primary independent practice provide 30% of the health services delivered by psychologists. In other words, despite its generally part-time nature and because of the large number of individuals involved, more than half of the hours of health services delivered by doctoral-level psychologists appear to be delivered in private-practice settings.

Geographic distribution. The geographic distribution of health workers is currently a major concern of Congress[8] and executive-branch agencies (Public Health Service, 1976). In general terms, the concern is that highly trained health workers are unavailable in some locations. Based on observations that locations lacking in physicians often have psychologists present, and that the number of psychologists across geographical units correlates highly with total population in these units, some authors have suggested that geographic maldistribution of psychologists is not a serious problem (Dörken, 1976; Webb, 1974). Other research, however, implies that when rates per 100,000 population are examined, the correlates of service provider location are very similar for psychologists, physicians, psychiatrists, social workers, and school guidance workers (Richards & Gottfredson, 1978; Gottfredson, Note 12, Note 13). All groups appear concentrated in affluent, urban locations. The absolute numbers of members of the professions do vary, of course, and representatives of the more numerous professions will often be found in localities lacking in representatives of the less numerous professions. The numbers and rates for health service providers for the present report resemble results for psychological service providers in 1972 (Gottfredson, Note 12) and for licensed psychologists in 1976 (Wellner & Mills, Note 5).

To provide some perspective on the geographical distribution of psychologists across

---

[6] This was calculated from Table 22, assuming that the midpoint of the top category is 45.5 hours. Master's-level providers spent less time—13.8 hours per week.

[7] (147,750.5 hours in independent practice per week)/ (270,037.0 hours total per week).

[8] Health Professions Educational Assistance Act of 1976, PL 94-484, Stat. 2243.

time, information from several sources is assembled in Table 31. The table shows rates of psychologists per 100,000 state population for 1960-1976. Unfortunately, in earlier surveys psychologists were not directly asked if they provided health services. Consequently, an effort has been made to bring together information about the subgroups of psychologists believed to most closely approximate the group of service providers. The following descriptions of the columns in Table 31 may aid in its interpretation:

1. *Clinical psychologists in 1960* was calculated from unpublished tabulations (Computer Usage Company, Note 14) for clinical psychologists in the 1960 National Science Foundation's (1962) *National Register of Scientific and Technical Personnel* and information about state population in 1960 (U.S. Bureau of the Census, 1969).

2. *Psychologists in mental health in 1966* was calculated using 1966 state population (U.S. Bureau of the Census, 1969) and tabulations (Jones, 1969) for psychologists who reported in the 1966 *National Register of Scientific and Technical Personnel* (National Science Foundation, 1968) that their primary employment was related to mental health.

3. *Doctoral psychological service providers in 1972* is based on 1970 census data and information about APA members who reported that they spent some of their professional time in application or practice, clinical, counseling, consultant, or advisory services, or test administration and evaluation. This column is transcribed from a table presented by Gottfredson (Note 12).

4. *Licensed psychologists in 1976* is based on information about licensed psychologists (Wellner & Mills, Note 5) and Census Bureau estimates (U.S. Bureau of the Census, 1976) of 1975 population.

5. *Doctoral APA service providers in 1976* is based on data from the present survey and estimates of 1975 state population.

Although the groups represented in Table 31 are not strictly comparable, taken together they present a picture that suggests an increasing pool of personnel who were, and continue to be, located primarily in the more populous and affluent states. The rates per 100,000 population in all states (including those with relatively low rates) have increased. One interesting anomaly in Table 31 is the rate per 100,000 population in South Dakota. In the 1976 APA data this state jumped to fifth in rank. This may be the result of several possibilities including (a) sampling error, (b) the small absolute number of doctoral psychologists and state population in South Dakota, or (c) recent developments in the state's liberal licensing law that may have encouraged migration to the state. Even a small change in the number of psychologists would have a large effect on the rate for this state because of its small total population.

For comparison, Table 32 shows information about the number of psychiatrists per 100,000 in various years. These rates were calculated using the following sources: Albee (1959), Whiting (1969), Arnhoff and Kumbar (1973), and the U.S. Bureau of the Census (1969, 1976). The trends in Table 32 for psychiatrists generally resemble those in Table 31 for psychologists.

Kinds of Services Provided

Individual therapy is the primary service provided by almost 60% of the doctoral-level providers. Except for assessment and evaluation services (16%), other services are the primary activity of relatively few doctoral-level providers. Although individual therapy and assessment are also the primary services provided by most master's-level providers, the mix is different: 39% therapy and 36% assessment. This implies that some differentiation in function exists between workers with these two levels of training. One speculation is that assessment or evaluation may more often be an ancillary or supporting function, because it is disproportionately the primary service of the less highly trained personnel.

It is important not to misinterpret the percentages for primary activities as percentages of time spent in these activities. Garfield and Kurtz (1976) reported that only 25% of the time of their sample of clinical psychologists was spent in individual psychotherapy, and that large percentages of time were spent in teaching and administration (14% and 13%, respectively).

Table 31: *Psychologists per 100,000 State Population, 1960–1976*

State	Clinical psychologists: 1960	Psychologists in mental health: 1966	Doctoral psychological service providers: 1972	Licensed psychologists: 1976	Doctoral APA service providers: 1976	All APA service providers: 1976
Alabama	1.0	1.6	2.8	4.3	3.4	3.8
Alaska	1.3	2.3	3.3	8.5	4.8	6.2
Arizona	1.4	6.6	8.1	14.3	10.8	12.1
Arkansas	1.3	2.0	3.0	7.7	4.0	4.6
California	5.3	8.2	8.2	15.2	8.8	10.3
Colorado	4.9	9.4	9.8	12.6	7.5	8.9
Connecticut	4.0	7.0	8.5	13.0	8.3	10.2
Delaware	4.2	7.8	6.0	10.0	3.4	4.8
District of Columbia	12.1	27.7	34.8	56.3	26.8	33.7
Florida	3.0	4.7	5.2	7.4	6.2	7.0
Georgia	1.3	3.0	4.0	6.4	4.4	4.9
Hawaii	3.4	4.6	6.8	9.5	8.6	8.7
Idaho	1.3	5.6	2.8	8.5	6.7	7.3
Illinois	3.2	6.6	5.8	10.1	5.0	6.9
Indiana	2.0	4.2	4.6	10.0	3.5	4.4
Iowa	2.6	7.5	4.8	4.7	5.0	6.7
Kansas	5.3	8.9	7.0	10.9	5.9	7.4
Kentucky	1.1	2.8	2.8	9.2	3.1	4.0
Louisiana	1.8	2.3	2.5	4.5	2.3	3.1
Maine	2.9	4.3	4.6	14.8	5.2	6.4
Maryland	4.1	7.6	8.8	13.5	7.8	9.2
Massachussetts	4.3	9.2	9.7	26.1	9.8	11.8
Michigan	2.8	5.7	5.3	5.8	5.6	7.3
Minnesota	2.9	7.0	6.5	17.8	5.4	7.2
Mississippi	.7	1.7	2.7	4.4	2.4	2.9
Missouri	2.0	3.3	4.5	4.7	3.0	4.9
Montana	1.2	3.0	4.0	9.9	8.4	11.0
Nebraska	2.7	5.3	4.8	10.2	6.7	7.9
Nevada	3.4	3.4	5.7	8.6	7.4	8.1
New Hampshire	1.6	3.6	4.3	11.1	7.2	8.6
New Jersey	3.9	6.0	6.3	12.0	6.5	9.2
New Mexico	1.3	4.5	5.9	7.8	3.8	4.3
New York	6.9	10.8	10.6	19.1	11.2	13.9
North Carolina	1.5	2.9	4.2	5.4	5.4	5.9
North Dakota	2.8	3.4	4.5	7.7	5.2	5.2
Ohio	2.7	4.6	4.8	16.8	5.4	6.7
Oklahoma	2.0	3.4	4.2	5.9	3.4	3.9
Oregon	3.4	6.6	7.3	9.1	7.0	7.3
Pennsylvania	3.2	5.9	6.2	18.0	5.6	8.1
Rhode Island	2.6	5.1	3.4	13.0	5.9	7.4
South Carolina	.6	1.6	3.1	5.7	5.8	6.4
South Dakota	1.5	4.8	3.4	3.7	9.1	9.2
Tennessee	2.1	3.5	4.4	10.2	5.3	6.0
Texas	1.5	2.9	4.8	8.5	5.1	6.2
Utah	3.3	6.7	6.7	11.3	6.1	7.0
Vermont	3.1	5.4	6.5	12.3	5.7	11.5
Virginia	2.1	3.1	4.4	9.9	6.0	7.6
Washington	3.2	7.2	5.7	7.8	8.0	8.8
West Virginia	1.4	1.9	3.4	6.0	3.5	4.9
Wisconsin	2.2	5.8	6.0	10.4	5.7	7.2
Wyoming	.0	8.1	7.8	13.6	4.3	4.8
U.S. total	3.3	6.0	6.2	11.9	6.4	8.0

Table 32: *Psychiatrists per 100,000 State Population, 1957–1970*

State	1957	1967	1970
		Year	
Alabama	1.5	1.8	3.1
Alaska	.5	3.0	6.0
Arizona	2.7	4.7	7.1
Arkansas	3.3	3.2	5.7
California	7.9	9.5	16.0
Colorado	5.0	9.6	14.8
Connecticut	11.3	10.7	19.1
Delaware	6.2	5.7	10.4
District of Columbia	24.1	36.8	58.2
Florida	3.5	5.0	8.4
Georgia	2.0	3.1	6.9
Hawaii	3.4	5.1	10.2
Idaho	1.8	1.0	2.5
Illinois	4.9	5.7	9.4
Indiana	2.5	2.4	4.4
Iowa	2.4	3.5	6.4
Kansas	6.7	7.6	13.0
Kentucky	2.9	3.3	5.1
Louisiana	3.1	3.4	7.0
Maine	2.6	3.7	5.8
Maryland	10.3	12.2	21.8
Massachusetts	10.5	12.9	21.0
Michigan	4.6	5.4	9.3
Minnesota	3.8	4.0	6.3
Mississippi	1.5	1.8	3.6
Missouri	3.5	4.9	10.5
Montana	1.7	1.4	3.3
Nebraska	3.7	4.5	6.2
Nevada	2.0	2.7	4.7
New Hampshire	3.6	5.6	9.9
New Jersey	4.8	5.5	9.8
New Mexico	1.6	3.0	6.1
New York	13.2	14.8	25.6
North Carolina	2.7	4.1	7.0
North Dakota	1.4	2.7	3.9
Ohio	3.8	4.1	7.4
Oklahoma	2.1	3.6	5.6
Oregon	3.1	4.4	7.3
Pennsylvania	5.4	7.0	11.8
Rhode Island	5.0	6.6	11.0
South Carolina	1.5	2.5	4.6
South Dakota	1.6	2.4	3.9
Tennessee	1.8	2.7	5.0
Texas	2.6	3.8	7.1
Utah	4.8	4.2	6.5
Vermont	4.9	6.9	13.4
Virginia	3.8	4.1	8.5
Washington	4.2	6.3	10.1
West Virginia	1.5	1.3	3.0
Wisconsin	3.1	4.6	7.5
Wyoming	2.8	4.4	2.7
U.S. total	5.3	6.6	12.5

Extent of Services

Although difficult, it seems appropriate to use information from the present survey, together with pieces of information from other sources, in an attempt to describe the amount of psychological health services delivered to clients. We estimated earlier that about 366,000 hours are spent by doctoral-level APA members in the provision of services each week. A more interesting question, however, pertains to the number of individuals seen each year by psychologists. One way of estimating this number is to use information on the number of clients seen each week from the present survey, together with informed guesses about the number of times individual clients are seen. A recent report by Dörken (1977) provides information on the average number of visits in the CHAMPUS experience. Average visits regardless of type of provider (psychologist, psychiatrist, physician) range from 6.7 to 21.1, depending on the diagnosis, with a mean of 14.0. When a provider serves many people not included under a third-party payment plan, the number of visits may be smaller. One might guess that 5–8 visits may be within the range of reasonable estimates. Table 33 shows estimates of the number of people seen by APA-member psychologists, given several different assumptions about the number of visits per client. These estimates may be inflated

Table 33: *Estimates of the Number of Individuals Served in One Year by Doctoral-Level APA Members*

Assuming how many visits per client?	People served yearly	
	By the average provider	By all APA providers
5.0	244	4,544,988
6.7	182	3,390,114
8.0	152	2,831,304
14.0	87	1,620,549
21.1	58	1,080,366

Note. Estimates of the number of people served by a typical provider are made by multiplying the average number of visits per week (24.4) by 50 weeks and dividing by the assumed number of visits per client. Estimates for the population of APA members assume that 18,627 doctoral-level members provide services.

somewhat if many people are seen by more than one psychologist in a year. Nevertheless, Table 33 suggests that somewhere between 2 and 4 million people annually receive health services from a doctoral-level APA member. In short, these crude estimates imply that recipients of psychological services number well into the millions each year.

Income and Fees

The results of the income analyses have two strong but not surprising implications. First, the higher incomes and salaries of doctoral-level health service psychologists compared to those of master's-level providers make it reasonable to speculate that many employers may choose to employ master's-level workers rather than to pay the higher salaries required to obtain the services of doctoral-level workers. Second, the salaries and total incomes of psychologists who provide services primarily via private practice are so much higher than those of other service providers that it seems reasonable to assume that the demand for services in private offices is sufficiently high that the provision of these services is a financially attractive undertaking. Despite the wider variation in incomes of private practitioners versus those primarily employed in other ways, even those doctoral-level private practitioners at the 25th percentile in total income make over $23,000 per year. This contrasts with a 25th-percentile total income of about $20,250 for other doctoral service providers.

Hourly fees typically charged for individual psychotherapy appear to have increased about 8% per year in recent years. According to Peck (1969), the median hourly fee was about $20 in a 1967 survey, and fees were higher in larger population centers. Cuca's (Note 8) report implied that the median hourly fee was about $25 for doctoral service providers in 1972. In contrast, the median hourly fee in the present survey was $36 for doctoral-level providers. *Mean* hourly fees for individual psychotherapy in the Kling and Davis (1977) survey of Florida psychologists ranged from $37 to $49 depending on the city. Similarly, the hourly fee charged by psychologists in the CHAMPUS experience (Dörken, 1977) has grown about 8% per year.

Based on this scattered evidence, hourly fees appear to be just slightly outpacing inflation and to be somewhat higher in large cities.

Summary and Conclusion

The provision of health services is a growing and changing enterprise for psychologists. About 18,500 doctoral-level APA members provide health services at least part time, for a total of nearly one-third million hours of services per week. Service providers still tend to be located, like other professionals, primarily in affluent urban states, but some positive trends are evident. For example, although presently only about 1% of health service providers are black, the number of black doctorate holders in clinical psychology is increasing. A total of 3.4% of the 1976 graduating class of clinical psychologists were black (National Research Council, Note 15). Similarly, 24% of today's health service providers are women, compared with 18% in 1972; and 31% of clinical psychologists earning their doctoral degrees in 1976 were women. Progress is also being made in licensure, with 81% of doctoral health service providers now licensed.

Sustaining this progress will require continued effort. Fostering minority and women graduate students will require continuing commitment of federal funds to high-quality training programs. Equalizing licensure across health service delivery settings will require efforts to improve state laws. Improving the access of all segments of the country's population to the health services psychologists can provide may require efforts to tie training support to service payback provisions and increased third-party payment for services for those who may not now be able to pay for them. In short, sustaining progress will depend not only on the flexibility of the profession but also on national training policy and national health delivery structures. Much of the information in this report can be used to form baselines against which to evaluate future national programs.

Reference Notes

1. Mills, D. H., & Wellner, A. M. *An analysis of the private practitioner whose clientele is predominantly in*

one age group (Register Research Report No. 6). Unpublished manuscript, Council for the National Register of Health Service Providers in Psychology, 1977.

2. Mills, D. H., & Wellner, A. M. *Organizational membership and the professional psychologist* (Register Research Report No. 4). Unpublished manuscript, Council for the National Register of Health Service Providers in Psychology, 1977.

3. Mills, D. H., & Wellner, A. M. *Some professional issues relating to private practice* (Register Research Report No. 5). Unpublished manuscript, Council for the National Register of Health Service Providers in Psychology, 1977.

4. Mills, D. H., & Wellner, A. M. *The highest academic degree of the licensed/certified psychologist* (Register Research Report No. 3). Unpublished manuscript, Council for the National Register of Health Service Providers in Psychology, 1977.

5. Wellner, A. M., & Mills, D. H. *An unduplicated count of licensed/certified psychologists in the United States* (Register Research Report No. 2). Unpublished manuscript, Council for the National Register of Health Service Providers in Psychology, 1977.

6. Wellner, A. M., & Mills, D. H. *How many health service providers in psychology? Finally an answer* (Register Research Report No. 1). Unpublished manuscript, Council for the National Register of Health Service Providers in Psychology, 1977.

7. Wellner, A. M., & Mills, D. H. *The highest academic degree and ABPP diplomate status of psychologists in private practice and listed in the National Register* (Register Research Report No. 7). Unpublished manuscript, Council for the National Register of Health Service Providers in Psychology, 1977.

8. Cuca, J. M. *1970 survey of psychologists in the U.S. and Canada: Responses of APA-member respondents who provide psychological services (n = 17,210), and responses of APA-member respondents who perform psychotherapy or counseling on a fee-for-service basis (n = 7541)*. Unpublished manuscript, American Psychological Association, undated.

9. Whiting, J. F. *Psychology's human resources for service provision: The empirical data base for standards development*. Paper presented at the meeting of the American Psychological Association, Montreal, August 1973.

10. Dyer, S. E. *The early labor market experiences of 1975 doctoral recipients in psychology* (Office of Programs and Planning Report No. 1). Washington, D.C.: American Psychological Association, 1977.

11. Schneider, S. *A survey of first positions of graduates of NIMH supported psychology training programs, 1968–1975*. Unpublished manuscript, Psychology Education Branch, National Institute of Mental Health, January 1976.

12. Gottfredson, G. D. *The distribution of psychologists, psychiatrists, and physicians*. Unpublished manuscript, American Psychological Association, 1976.

13. Gottfredson, G. D. *A county-level examination of the geographical distribution of licensed psychologists, psychiatrists, and physicians*. Unpublished manuscript, American Psychological Association, 1977.

14. Computer Usage Company. Tables for clinical psychologists. Unpublished tabulations prepared for NIH under Contract No. PH 43-63-64, Washington, D.C., 1962.

15. National Research Council. Unpublished tabulations from the 1976 survey of doctoral degree recipients. Washington, D.C., 1977.

References

Albee, G. W. *Mental health manpower trends* (Monograph Series No. 3, Joint Commission on Mental Illness and Health). New York: Basic Books, 1959.

American Psychological Association. *Ethical standards of psychologists*. Washington, D.C.: Author, 1977. (a)

American Psychological Association. *Standards for providers of psychological services*. Washington, D.C.: Author, 1977. (b)

American Psychological Association. *1977 membership register*. Washington, D.C.: Author, 1977. (c)

APA Committee on Legislation. A model for state legislation affecting the practice of psychology 1967. *American Psychologist*, 1967, *22*, 1095–1103.

Arnhoff, F. N., & Kumbar, A. H. *The nation's psychiatrists—1970 survey*. Washington, D.C.: American Psychiatric Association, 1973.

Boneau, C. A., & Cuca, J. M. An overview of psychology's human resources: Characteristics and salaries from the 1972 APA survey. *American Psychologist*, 1974, *29*, 821–840.

Clark, K. E. *America's psychologists: A survey of a growing profession*. Washington, D.C.: American Psychological Association, 1957.

Council for the National Register of Health Service Providers in Psychology. *National register of health service providers in psychology*. Washington, D.C.: Author, 1976.

Dimond, R. E., Havens, R. A., Rathnow, S. J., & Colliver, J. A. Employment characteristics of subdoctoral clinical psychologists. *Professional Psychology*, 1977, *8*, 116–121.

Dörken, H. CHAMPUS ten-state claim experience for mental disorder: Fiscal year 1975. *American Psychologist*, 1977, *32*, 697–710.

Dörken, H., & Whiting, J. F. Psychologists as health service providers. In H. Dörken & Associates, *The professional psychologist today: New developments in law, health insurance, and health practice*. San Francisco: Jossey-Bass, 1976.

Garfield, S. L., & Kurtz, R. Clinical psychologists in the 1970s. *American Psychologist*, 1976, *31*, 1–9.

Jones, D. R. *Psychologists in mental health based on the 1964 National Register of the National Science Foundation* (PHS 1557). Washington, D.C.: U.S. Government Printing Office, 1966.

Jones, D. R. *Psychologists in mental health—1966: An analysis of the 1966 National Register of Psychologists of the National Science Foundation* (PHS 1984). Washington, D.C.: U.S. Government Printing Office, 1969.

Kling, J. S., & Davis, J. C. 1976–1977 salary survey for psychologists. *Florida Psychologist*, 1977, *28*, 41–44.

National Science Foundation. *American science manpower 1960: A report of the National Register of Scientific and Technical Personnel* (NSF 62-43). Washington, D.C.: U.S. Government Printing Office, 1962.

National Science Foundation. *American science manpower 1966: A report of the National Register of Scientific and Technical Personnel* (NSF 68-7). Washington, D.C.: U.S. Government Printing Office, 1968.

Peck, C. P. Fee practices of psychologists. *Professional Psychology*, 1969, *1*, 14–19, 154.

Public Health Service. Proposed rules: Health manpower programs. *Federal Register,* 1976, *42,* 15433–15438.

Richards, J. M., Jr., & Gottfredson, G. D. Geographic distribution of U.S. psychologists: A human ecological analysis. *American Psychologist,* 1978, *33,* 1–9.

Simon, K. A., & Frankel, M. M. *Projections of education statistics to 1984–85* (NCES 76-210). Washington, D.C.: U.S. Government Printing Office, 1976.

U.S. Bureau of the Census. *Statistical abstract of the United States: 1969* (90th ed.). Washington, D.C.: U.S. Government Printing Office, 1969.

U.S. Bureau of the Census. *Statistical abstract of the United States: 1976* (97th ed.). Washington, D.C.: U.S. Government Printing Office, 1976.

Webb, J. T. Distribution of psychologists and psychiatrists by zip code areas in Ohio. *Ohio Psychologist,* 1974, *20,* 5–12.

Whiting, J. F. *Psychiatric services, systems analysis, and manpower utilization.* Washington, D.C.: American Psychiatric Association, 1969.

Witkin, M. J. *Staffing of mental health facilities: United States 1972* (ADM 74-28). Washington, D.C.: U.S. Government Printing Office, 1974.

Witkin, M. J. *Staffing of mental health facilities: United States 1974* (ADM 76-308). Washington, D.C.: U.S. Government Printing Office, 1976.

At the time of original publication of this article, *Gary D. Gottfredson* was Administrative Officer for Special Projects and directed Human Resources Research efforts for the American Psychological Association. He is now at Johns Hopkins University. *Sharon E. Dyer* was Administrative Associate in the Human Resources Research Office of the American Psychological Association.

The authors are grateful to Thomas Willette and Bruce Roth, who prepared the questionnaires for optical scanning, oversaw the fielding of the survey, and prepared the initial data tape for use in this research. Others who contributed to this report by helping to design the survey instrument, by giving advice on a draft of this report, or by providing clerical assistance include C. Alan Boneau, Arthur Centor, Linda S. Gottfredson, Joann Horai, Ruth Leggin, Robert Lowman, David H. Mills, Stephen D. Nelson, Ralph Nemir, Dalmas Taylor, Marlene Wicherski, Jan B. Woodring, and Joan Zaro.

The National Register Survey:
The First Comprehensive Study of
All Licensed/Certified Psychologists

David H. Mills, Alfred M. Wellner, and Gary R. VandenBos

This article reports a 1977 survey conducted by the Council for the National Register of Health Service Providers. The first complete, unduplicated list of licensed/certified psychologists in the United States was developed. The entire population was surveyed, and a response rate of 74% was obtained. The survey found that 88.5% (N = 22,588) of licensed/certified psychologists reported being trained as health service providers. Almost 19,000 report being active in the delivery of health care services. Of these, 15,422 report involvement in private practice; however, only 4,683 are in private practice on a full-time basis. Information is also presented on hourly fees, specialization by age populations, type of independent practice, consultation practices, office location, professional liability coverage, highest academic degree, and professional association membership.

For many years it has been difficult to estimate the number of psychologists who provide health services. Questions have been raised with regard to the potential professional resources in psychology available for the implementation of a national health insurance program. Data on the provision of psychological services in full-time and part-time independent practice, as well as in public settings, have been lacking.

While it might be expected that comprehensive data would be available from the National Institute of Mental Health (NIMH) or the National Center for Health Statistics (NCHS), such is not the case. The Biometry Branch of NIMH conducts a biannual survey of the staffing patterns of mental health facilities. However, that survey does not currently collect data on psychologists in a manner that allows either the determination of the number of doctoral psychological providers employed in such organized settings or the identification of the amount of service provided by doctoral psychologists in organized public and private institutions and clinics (e.g., Witkin, 1976). Moreover, sole practitioners are not included.

The problem of the adequacy of data on professional personnel is not unique to psychology or the mental health field. A committee report (National Center for Health Statistics, 1972) evaluating the National Center for Health Statistics reported: "Health manpower data today are generally limited . . . definitions even of the persons to be included in a total count are far from precise." The overall situation has not improved since that time, particularly in the mental health field. An NIMH task force (National Institute of Mental Health, 1977) reported: "At present there is no satisfactory mental health manpower data system. Instead we have information from several sources which lacks uniformity, overlaps, and is seldom complementary." The Alcohol, Drug Abuse, and Mental Health Administration's Manpower Policy Analysis Task Force (ADAMHA, 1978) more recently has called for increased governmental efforts to collect comprehensive and comparable professional personal data on the core mental health professions. The Task Force detailed the importance of such information for policy analysis, human resources program management, and program/system evaluation. NIMH plans to incorporate some changes (including a differentiation between doctoral psychologists and subdoctoral providers with limited training in psychology) in their 1980 facilities survey. The National Center on Health Statistics is currently developing procedures for routinely collecting data on all licensed/certified psychologists. However, those procedures will probably not go into effect until 1981, and the NCHS's data collection system will probably not be complete until 1983. Hence, the availability of comprehensive, federally collected data on psychologists is still three to five years away.

A need for information regarding psychology's resources for providing health services has existed for several years. To meet this need, the Council for the National Register of Health Service Providers in Psychology was established by the American Board of Professional Psychology (ABPP) in 1974 at the request of the Board of Directors of the American Psychological Association. The stimulus for the development of the *National Register* was the press for data from federal agencies, regulatory groups, and others regarding psychology as an independent health profession. A system and data were needed to make possible the identification and listing of health service providers in psychology.

The Council for the National Register of Health Service Providers in Psychology

The Council for the National Register of Health Service Providers in Psychology was actually formed in 1974 when ABPP brought together a group of psychologists familiar with the many issues involved (Zimet & Wellner, 1977). The Council for the National Register, an independent organization, was established to develop a mechanism that would facilitate the identification of health service providers in psychology from among all licensed/certified psychologists. The *National Register* was designed as a vehicle for identifying psychologists who meet the criteria and voluntarily apply for inclusion. The criteria for listing are based on the state statutes and the standards of the profession.

As of January 1, 1978, the criteria for listing in the *National Register* include (a) current licensure/certification by the State Board of

Examiners of Psychology at the independent practice level, (b) a doctoral degree in psychology from a regionally accredited educational institution, and (c) two years of supervised experience in health service, of which at least one year is postdoctoral and one year is in an organized health service training program. During the first three years of the development of the *National Register,* persons with other than a doctoral degree were considered for listing if they had at least six years experience in the field, had earned the advanced degree prior to January 1, 1969, and had been certified/licensed at the independent practice level prior to January 1, 1975. The "grandfather" period was intended to recognize those licensed/certified psychologists whose credentials and experience were obtained prior to the current standards for practice. The first *National Register* was published in 1975, and it has grown substantially since that time. Presently, approximately 12,000 psychologists are listed. This number is estimated to represent over 60% of the psychologists eligible to be listed.

The *National Register* has become a major resource in the field. Psychologists listed in the *National Register* have been recognized as qualified providers of health care by a number of insurance carriers and government programs. The *National Register* is frequently mentioned in state legislation dealing with psychology's position as an independent profession.

One of the first tasks in compiling the *National Register* was the identification of all known licensed/certified psychologists in the country. As of 1977, all 50 states and the District of Columbia had statutes covering the title of psychologist and the practice of psychology, so current listings were requested from each state's licensing/certification board.

Such listings were immediately available from a large number of states. Each State Board of Examiners and each state agency responsible for the State Board of Examiners manage their regulatory functions in different ways. Some organizations make lists of licensed professionals readily available to the public. Others have no resources to make such lists available. Some boards have computer printouts of all the licensed/certified psychologists at any point in time; others make lists on an annual or semiannual basis. However, there are some boards and some state agencies that do not make available lists of licensed psychologists. If a consumer wishes to know if a particular psychologist is licensed, such information is made available. That is, for some states, verification of the license of an *individual* psychologist is made, but lists of all licensed psychologists or the rosters of such groups are not made readily available to the public. Other states have policies varying between the free distribution of lists to the restricted distribution of information based on those lists. These differing policies obviously present some critical problems in compiling an unduplicated list of licensed/certified psychologists.

Moreover, because licensing or certification is a continuing process, there is no ideal date or time for establishing an accurate number of all licensed/certified psychologists in the country. At any time, boards are reviewing new applicants and credentialing additional psychologists. Moreover, some psychologists who may only be delinquent in their renewal of dues for their licenses may officially not be identified as licensed at that point in time. These problems make it clear that a listing of the licensed/certified psychologists at any time is a best estimate and that the number listed will change because of the continuing nature of credentialing.

Development of the Unduplicated List

Rosters of licensed/certified psychologists were continually received, and as new psychologists were licensed or certified, the information was added to the data base. New rosters were checked so that updated information could be included in the data base. Addresses were updated on the basis of information received through the membership rosters of the American Psychological Association, data from the National Register of Health Service Providers in Psychology, and information received from the state boards directly. An alphabetically arranged computer printout of all psychologists was then developed, based on the rosters. Many psychologists are licensed in more than one state and, therefore, appeared several times on the national printout. Names on the printout were checked for the most recent state roster listing or the most recent known address. Names that appeared more than once were checked and listed only once in order to maintain an unduplicated file. If an individual was licensed in several states, that information was noted, but for roster tabulation purposes, only the most recent or preferred address was used.

This unduplicated list of all licensed/certified psychologists was developed, in part, to facilitate the implementation of the national survey of all licensed/certified psychologists, conducted by the *National Register,* which is reported here. The data presented here, therefore, represent state rosters received in 1975 and 1976, APA membership data as of the fall of 1976, *National Register* data as of November 1976, and address updates and changes as of December 1976.

Initial Information

On the basis of the procedures outlined above, there were an estimated 25,510 licensed or certified psychologists in the country in early 1977. Table 1 presents a tally of identified licensed/certified psychologists in each of the 50 states and the District of Columbia. This number includes 243 psychologists whose addresses were not in a zip code format permitting state identification. This is the first unduplicated count of licensed psychologists ever compiled.

It must be noted that the state totals reflect persons who are licensed/certified *and* who gave that state as a state of preferred address. A simple count of the number of names on any individual state roster would be greater than those identified in Table 1 because of the substantial number of people licensed in more than one state. Consequently the total listed for a particular state is smaller than that state's roster.

The list is not a compilation of any special type of psychologist and reflects only the total of all identified psychologists of all specialties licensed or certified by the 51 Boards of Examiners of Psychology. Psychology licensing/certification statutes, similar to medical and other professional licensure statutes, are typically generic and cover all specialties—clinical, counseling, industrial, physiological, developmental, human engineering, etc. The balance of this report presents data on those

Table 1: *Unduplicated Number of All Identified Licensed/Certified Psychologists by State*

No.	State	No.	State
157	Alabama	74	Montana
30	Alaska	157	Nebraska
318	Arizona	51	Nevada
162	Arkansas	91	New Hampshire
3213	California	880	New Jersey
318	Colorado	89	New Mexico
402	Connecticut	3463	New York
58	Delaware	297	North Carolina
403	District of Columbia	49	North Dakota
614	Florida	1803	Ohio
314	Georgia	159	Oklahoma
82	Hawaii	209	Oregon
70	Idaho	2132	Pennsylvania
1122	Illinois	121	Rhode Island
530	Indiana	160	South Carolina
136	Iowa	25	South Dakota
247	Kansas	427	Tennessee
313	Kentucky	1039	Texas
172	Louisiana	136	Utah
156	Maine	58	Vermont
553	Maryland	491	Virginia
1520	Massachusetts	276	Washington
529	Michigan	109	West Virginia
697	Minnesota	479	Wisconsin
103	Mississippi	51	Wyoming
222	Missouri	243	Inadequate address or out of country

Note. $N = 25,510$.

licensed/certified psychologists who specialize in the provision of health services.

The National Register Survey

The *National Register* survey consisted of 35 questionnaire items and was designed to provide basic information on psychology as an independent health profession. It represents the first survey undertaken of the licensed/certified psychologists in the country. The questionnaire items are presented in Table 2.

The survey forms were mailed in late 1976 to the most recent addresses of all psychologists ($N = 25,510$) on the unduplicated roster. The response rate was 73.4%, an excellent response rate for survey research and comparable to the 73.7% response rate obtained by Gottfredson and Dyer (1978) in their stratified random sample survey of 10,000 members of the American Psychological Association regarding somewhat similar issues. A total of 18,766 individuals returned the *National Register* survey questionnaire. The data presented in the balance of this chapter are thus based on a very substantial portion of the licensed/certified psychologists in the United States. In view of the health service focus, it may be expected that a larger percentage of health service providers responded than non-health-service providers. Consequently, although the total number identified (25,510) may be conservative because of the ongoing licensing process, the response rate of health service providers probably allows a very good estimate of that group.

Number of Health Service Providers

Not all licensed/certified psychologists, as noted earlier, are health service providers. Hence, one of the first questions addressed by the survey concerned whether or not the psychologist was identified as a health service provider. Further information was also sought regarding whether or not the individual was currently active in the provision of psychological services.

The definition of a health service provider used in the survey was as follows: "A Health Service Provider in Psychology is defined as a psychologist, certified/licensed at the independent practice level in his/her state, who is duly trained and experienced in the delivery of direct, preventive, assessment, and therapeutic intervention services to individuals whose growth, adjustment, or functioning is actually impaired or is demonstrably at high risk of impairment." The item provided for three possible responses: (a) I am a Health Service Provider and provide such services now; (b) I am a Health Service Provider but am not providing such services now; or (c) I am *not* a Health Service Provider.

The data on the number of licensed/certified health service provider psychologists, as of early 1977, are presented in Table 3. Of those responding to the survey questionnaire, 16,577 indicated that they were trained and licensed/certified as health service providers. Assuming that the survey respondents were representative of the entire population, this suggests that a total of 22,588 of all licensed/certified psychologists have such training and experience. However, not all psychologists trained,

Table 2: *Form used in the Survey of Provision of Health Services in Psychology*

COUNCIL FOR THE NATIONAL REGISTER
OF HEALTH SERVICE PROVIDERS IN PSYCHOLOGY
1200 Seventeenth Street, N.W., Suite 403
Washington, D. C. 20036 • 202/833-7568

SURVEY OF PROVISION OF HEALTH SERVICES IN PSYCHOLOGY

───────── ADDRESS CORRECTION ─────────

NAME _____

First   M.I.   Last

Street

City   State   Zip

DIRECTIONS: Your responses will be read by an optical mark reader. Your careful observance of these few simple rules will be most appreciated.

● Use only a black pencil.
● Make heavy black marks that fill the circle.
● Erase cleanly any answer you wish to change.
● Make no stray markings of any kind.
● Where write-in responses are necessary, please confine your writing to the limits of the lines provided.
● For the questions that require you to write in and code your response, please complete by entering the numbers in the boxes provided and by darkening the corresponding circle below each box.

EXAMPLE A:

In what year did you begin your private practice? . . . . 19- [5][4]

EXAMPLE B:

Will marks made with ball pen or fountain pen be properly read?
○ Yes
● No

1. If the address shown above is not your correct mailing address, please PRINT that address in the space provided to the right of the address shown.

2. What is your age? . . . .

3. What is your sex?
○ Male
○ Female

4. Are you an APA: (Mark one)
○ Associate member
○ Member
○ Fellow
○ None of the above

5. Do you belong to your state's psychological association?
○ Yes
○ No

6. Highest Degree earned in psychology: (Mark one)
○ Ph.D. or Psy.D.
○ Ed.D. or D.Ed.
○ Masters
○ Bachelors
○ Other; Specify_____

7. In what year did you earn your highest degree?. 19-

8. Are you a diplomate of the American Board of Professional Psychology? (Mark one)
○ No
○ Yes(Clinical)
○ Yes(Counseling)
○ Yes(Industrial/Organizational)
○ Yes(School)

Table 2 (*continued*)

9. What one specialty within psychology are you primarily identified with? (Mark one)

○ Experimental Psychology
○ Physiological Psychology
○ Developmental Psychology (life span)
○ Personality Psychology
○ Social Psychology
○ Clinical Psychology
○ Community Psychology
○ Counseling Psychology
○ School Psychology
○ Educational Psychology
○ Engineering Psychology
○ Industrial Psychology
○ Other; Please specify _____

10. Using the following definition, are you a Health Service Provider in Psychology?

"A Health Service Provider in Psychology is defined as a psychologist, certified/licensed at the independent practice level in his/her state, who is duly trained and experienced in the delivery of direct, preventive, assessment, and therapeutic intervention services to individuals whose growth, adjustment, or functioning is actually impaired or is demonstrably at high risk of impairment."
(Mark one)

○ I am a Health Service Provider and provide such services now.
○ I am a Health Service Provider but am not providing such services now.
○ I am not a Health Service Provider. **(If you marked this response, please return this questionnaire to us in the postage-paid envelope provided. You need not complete the remainder of the questionnaire.)**

11. Are you listed in the <u>1976 National Register of Health Service Providers in Psychology?</u>

○ No
○ Yes (If Yes, please skip to Item 13)

12. Why have you opted not to apply for listing in the National Register? (Mark one)

○ Don't know about the National Register
○ Don't think it is important to me to be listed
○ Have reservations about the concept of the Register
○ Have intended to but have not yet done so
○ Have applied and application is pending
○ Have applied and not been approved for listing in the Register
○ Have not applied because don't meet criteria.

13. How did you first hear about the National Register? (Mark one)

○ APA publications
○ Attendance at conventions/meetings
○ Word of mouth
○ State or local associations/newsletters
○ Boards of Examiners of Psychology
○ Direct mailing from the Register
○ No source; didn't know about it prior to this survey.

14. Are you: (Mark one)

○ In full-time private practice
○ In part-time private practice
○ Not in private practice now but have definite plans to be by Jan. 1, 1978
○ Not in private practice but possibly will be so in the future
○ Not in private practice and do not intend to be so.

15. What is the nature of your private practice? (Mark one)

○ Individual practice—self-employed
○ Group practice
○ Partnership
○ Employed by another mental health professional
○ Employed by a pre-paid health plan
○ Employed by a professional corporation
○ Other; Please specify_____

16. <u>Where do you get referrals</u> for your private practice? (Mark one answer for each source)

	Never Refer To Me	Occasionally Refer To Me	Regularly Refer To Me
Other psychologists	○	○	○
Psychiatrists	○	○	○
Social workers	○	○	○
Non-psychiatric physicians	○	○	○
School system	○	○	○
Court system	○	○	○
Attorneys	○	○	○
Former patients	○	○	○
Self referred	○	○	○
Community agencies; Please specify:_____	○	○	○
_____	○	○	○
Other; Please specify: _____	○	○	○
_____	○	○	○

17. Specify the County and State in which your private practice is located:

_____ _____
County   State

Location of practice is primarily:
○ Urban
○ Suburban
○ Rural

Table 2 (*continued*)

18. Estimate the number of billable <u>hours</u> per week for your private practice for an average week for the past year. (Mark one)

   ○ 5 or less   ○ 21 to 30
   ○ 6 to 10   ○ 31 to 40
   ○ 11 to 15   ○ 41 and over
   ○ 16 to 20

19. How many more billable hours per week would you be able and willing to accept in your private practice? (Mark one)

   ○ None
   ○ 1 to 5
   ○ 6 to 10
   ○ 11 to 15
   ○ 16 to 20
   ○ Over 20

20. As differentiated from billable hours, estimate how many <u>individuals</u> (different persons) you have seen in an average week for the past year. (Mark one)

   ○ 5 or less
   ○ 6 to 10
   ○ 11 to 15
   ○ 16 to 20
   ○ 21 to 30
   ○ 31 to 40
   ○ 41 and over

21. What office arrangement do you have for your private practice? (Mark one)

   ○ Own or rent a separate practice
   ○ Have office in my home
   ○ Have access to office space through my salaried position
   ○ Have arranged for use of office space from another professional
   ○ Other; Please specify_____
   _____

22. In what year did you begin your private practice?......................19-

23. What is your hourly rate for individual patient hours?

   This Year   Last Year
   $ [ ][ ] /hour $ [ ][ ] /hour

24. What services do you provide in your private practice? (Mark all that apply)

   ○ Individual therapy
   ○ Group therapy
   ○ Marital or conjoint therapy
   ○ Family therapy
   ○ Assessment/evaluations
   ○ Consultation (case, agency, etc.)
   ○ Other; Please specify_____

25. Please estimate the percentages of your patients who fall in the following age ranges. (Mark one for each age group)

	Up to 25%	26-50%	51-75%	76% and over
Less than age 12 (Children)	○	○	○	○
Age 12-17 (Adolescents)	○	○	○	○
Age 18-64 (Adults)	○	○	○	○
Over age 65 (Senior Citizens)	○	○	○	○

26. What percentage of your patients are:

   Male [ ][ ] %   Female [ ][ ] %

Table 2 (*continued*)

27. Please estimate the average number of sessions you see a typical patient for therapy.

(If the number is less than 10, please use a leading zero for the first digit)

28. What percentage of your private cases are supported fully or in part by third party payments (e.g., Blue Shield, CHAMPUS, Aetna, Medicaid, etc.)? (Mark one)

O None
O Less than 25%
O 26% to 50%
O 51% to 75%
O Over 75%

29. Do you have Professional Liability (Malpractice) Insurance?

O No
O Yes; If yes, what is the carrier?_____

30. Do you have regular (e.g., weekly, biweekly) formal case related consultation for your private practice?

O No
O Yes; If Yes, with whom? (Mark all that apply)
  O Psychologist
  O Psychiatrist
  O Non-psychiatric physician
  O Social worker
  O Other; Please specify_____

31. Do you see yourself possibly leaving a salaried position for private practice? (Mark one)
O No
O Yes
O Am in full-time private practice now

32. What is your primary job setting? (Mark one)

O Academic
O Public agency (federal, state, local)
O Private for-profit agency/organization
O Private not-for-profit agency/organization
O Private practice
O Other; Please specify_____

33. Is the location of your primary job setting predominately:

O Urban
O Suburban
O Rural

34. Do you provide health services in your primary job setting?
O Yes
O No

35. Of the APA Divisions of which you are a member, what Division do you feel primary affiliation with? (Mark one)

O Not an APA member
O APA, but no Divisional membership

O Division 12 (Clinical)
O Division 13 (Consulting)
O Division 14 (Industrial)
O Division 15 (Educational)
O Division 16 (School)
O Division 17 (Counseling)
O Division 18 (Public Service)
O Division 22 (Rehabilitation)
O Division 25 (Experimental Analysis of Behavior)
O Division 27 (Community)
O Division 29 (Psychotherapy)
O Division 33 (Retardation)
O Division 35 (Women)
O Other; Please specify_____
_____

36. In order to facilitate future data gathering on additional issues relating to health services, we would like to establish a representative (stratified) sample of psychologists engaged in such services. Possible topics might include career patterns, characteristics of patients, and income (which would be gathered anonymously). If selected, would you be willing to be part of that sample?
O Yes
O No

37. Comments:

Table 3. *Number of Licensed/Certified Health Service Providers in Psychology*

Health service provision	Survey responses		Population projection
	No.	%	
Trained as health service provider	16,577	88.3	22,588
Not trained as health service provider	2,189	11.7	2,983
Not a health service provider (n = 2,073)			
No response (n = 116)			
Total	18,766	100.	25,571

Table 4: *Number of Currently Active Health Service Providers in Psychology*

Health service provision	Survey responses		Population projection
	No.	%	
Active health service provider	13,857	83.6	18,882
Not active in health service provision	2,720	16.4	3,706
Total	16,577	100.	22,588

qualified, and licensed/certified as health service providers are currently active in the provision of such services. They may be solely occupied in research, teaching, or administration or may be retired. The data on the number of licensed/certified psychologists active in the provision of psychological services, in early 1977, is presented in Table 4. Of the survey respondents, 13,857 were currently active in the delivery of health care services. This figure leads to a projected 18,882 currently active, licensed/certified health service provider psychologists.

In summary, there were 25,510 licensed/certified psychologists at the time of the survey. It is estimated that 22,588 (or 88.5%) were trained and experienced as health service providers in psychology but that only 18,882 (or 74%) were actively providing such service. And as noted below, an even smaller percentage are involved in independent fee-for-service practice.

Degree Level of Licensed/Certified Psychologists

For some time the profession has identified a doctoral degree as the requisite academic preparation for the independent practice of psychology. Most state statutes require the doctorate for such independent psychological practice. In view of the fairly recent advent of licensing and certification, however, consideration (in the form of grandfather clause provisions) has generally been granted to psychologists with other academic degrees if they have been providing services prior to the enactment of licensing/certification legislation. Hence, some state licensing/certification statutes include master's-level psychologists as independent practitioners. The *National Register* established the doctoral degree as a criterion for listing but accepted (until January of 1978) applications from psychologists without such a degree if they had been licensed/certified prior to January 1975.

Because of the difference between the state statutes on this issue and because of the grandfather clauses that allow licensing/certification for practitioners who may not meet current (typically doctorate) state standards, the actual number of practitioners with various graduate degrees has not been known. The *National Register* survey asked the respondents to list their highest degree in psychology (Item 6), and to report whether they were "health service providers" (Item 10). The results of a cross-tabulation of these two items are reported in Table 5.

Fully 82% of all licensed/certified psychologists possess a doctoral degree. The highest percentage (84%) of licensed/certified psychologists possessing a doctorate are active health service providers. Non-health-service providers constitute the lowest percentage (72%) of individuals possessing a doctorate, while inactive health service providers are intermediate. The doctorate is the predominant degree held among all three groups. It is reasonable to assume that the proportion of doctorates among licensed/certified health service providers will continue to increase, since the doctorate is essentially the "entrance degree" under most state laws and most master's-level providers were licensed under grandfather clause provi-

Table 5: *Academic Degrees of Licensed/Certified Psychologists by Health Service Provision*

	Active health service provider		Inactive health service provider		Not a health service provider		All licensed/ certified psychologists	
Highest degree in psychology	No.	%	No.	%	No.	%	No.	%
Doctoral								
PhD or PsyD	11,609	84.1	2,055	76.1	1,472	71.7	15,136	81.6
EdD or DEd	10,439	75.6	1,699	62.9	1,327	64.5	13,465	72.6
Master's	1,952	14.1	584	21.6	531	25.8	3,067	16.5
Bachelor's	51	.4	8	.3	9	.4	68	.4
Other	188	1.4	55	2.0	44	2.1	287	1.5
Total	13,800	100.	2,702	100.	2,056	100.	18,558	100.

sions. The *National Register* survey data thus suggest that in early 1977, there were about 19,000 active, licensed/certified, health service provider psychologists and that the vast majority of these were doctorally trained.

Data on Private Practice

The survey also sought information regarding the setting (public or private) of the respondent's practice. The number of providers involved in the private practice of psychology in 1977 is presented in Table 6. The data are further differentiated between full-time private practice and part-time practice.

Of the 18,766 survey respondents, 2,189 were not trained as health service providers (see Table 3). Of the 16,577 respondents trained as health service providers, 2,720 were not actively providing services (see Table 4). In Table 6, it can be seen that of the active health service pro-

Table 6: *Number of Current Psychologist Providers Involved in the Private-Practice Delivery of Health Services*

	Active health service providers		
Type of private practice	No.	%	Population projection
Full-time private practice	3,437	24.8	4,683
Part-time private practice	7,881	56.9	10,739
Health service provider but not in private practice	2,539	18.3	3,460
Total	13,857	100.	18,882

viders, 2,539 were *not* engaged in the private practice of psychology. Thus, of the total survey respondents ($N = 18,766$), only slightly over 60% ($n = 11,318$) were actively involved in the independent or private practice of psychology. Projecting from the sample suggests that slightly over 15,400 psychologists were involved in either the full- or part-time private practice of psychology in early 1977.

Table 6 also reveals that only 3,437 health service providers were engaged in the independent practice of psychology on a full-time basis. This represents 24.8% of the active health service providers in psychology (and 18.3% of the survey respondents). This suggests that of the total population of licensed/certified psychologists ($N = 25,510$), about 4,700 psychologists, in early 1977, were involved on a full-time basis in the private practice of psychology. This figure is highly consistent with the data of Gottfredson and Dyer (1978); their data, based on APA membership, suggested that about 4,450 (21% of an N of 22,980) psychologists were in full-time private practice. When their data are adjusted in light of our data (see Table 17) on the percentage of licensed/certified active health service providers who belong to APA, a figure in the range of from 4,700 to 4,800 is obtained. The percentage of psychologists involved in full-time private practice is less than half of the percentage of psychiatrists (61%) in such practice (Marmor, Scheidemandel, & Kanno, 1975).

The majority of psychologists in private practice were involved on a part-time basis. Almost 57% of the active health service providers (and 42% of all respondents) reported this type of practice. Psychologists involved in part-time practice outnumbered full-time private practitioners 2.3 to 1. Almost 20% of active health service providers reported not being involved in private practice. In general, the data support earlier impressions that psychologists tend to be employed full-time in public settings but provide additional services in private practice on a part-time basis. Some data (Gottfredson & Dyer, 1978) indicate that more than 50% of *all* service hours provided by health service provider psychologists are provided in private practice. This suggests that in public settings, health service provider psychologists play a major role in the supervision of lesser trained therapists, in administration, and in other indirect activity and that their direct clinical practice in public settings only slightly exceeds the amount of direct clinical hours they provide in "overtime" private practice.

Systematic data on the hourly fees charged by psychologists, both in terms of national averages and state averages, have also been lacking. The hourly fee charged by private-practice health service provider psychologists has been of marked interest to policymakers and professionals for some time. As more psychologists enter the arena of private practice, fee information has become more important. Third-party payers (both government and insurance carriers) have increasingly sought information on psychologist fee practices, and now health human resources planning officials are also requesting such data.

The *National Register* survey asked respondents to report their "hourly rate for individual hours" for "this year (1976–1977)" and for "last year (1975–1976)." More than 10,000 of the over 11,000 psychologists who reported involvement in private practice provided information on their hourly fees. These data on the national averages of hourly fees charged by private-practice health service provider psychologists for individual treatment are summarized in Table 7. It should be noted that the fee data combine part-time and full-time practitioners.

The average nationwide fee for an individual hourly session charged by private practice health service provider psychologists in 1975–1976 was $32.69. This increased to $35.69 in

Table 7: *National Data on Hourly Fees for Individual Treatment*

Statistic	Fees	
	1975–1976	1976–1977
Mean	$32.69	$35.69
Mode	35.00	40.00
Median	35.00	35.00
Range	1.00–$100.00	2.00–$100.00

Note. For 1975–1976, n = 10,309; for 1976–1977, n = 10,719.

1976–1977, an increase of slightly over 9%. It seems reasonable to assume that the private-practice rates of health service provider psychologists are lower than and consistent with the current inflation rate and clearly lower than the general rate increases (from 14.6% to 17.8%) in the health care field (Cohen, 1977).

Table 8 presents the statewide average hourly fee charged by private-practice health service provider psychologists for individual services in 1976–1977. The statewide averages ranged from a low of $27.22 for Vermont to a

Table 8: *Mean Hourly Fee by State for 1976–1977*

State	No.	Mean fee	State	No.	Mean fee
Alabama	64	$34.00	Missouri	95	$34.68
Alaska	12	52.67	Montana	27	33.85
Arizona	150	36.07	Nebraska	70	28.83
Arkansas	46	32.15	Nevada	14	40.00
California	1408	39.26	New Hampshire	36	31.61
Colorado	174	33.95	New Jersey	461	35.79
Connecticut	182	36.72	New Mexico	37	41.43
Delaware	17	35.59	New York	1701	35.49
D.C.	170	38.14	North Carolina	122	31.04
Florida	289	39.73	North Dakota	11	33.91
Georgia	166	39.52	Ohio	601	33.06
Hawaii	46	42.39	Oklahoma	79	40.65
Idaho	30	30.23	Oregon	113	36.46
Illinois	515	34.24	Pennsylvania	791	29.21
Indiana	179	30.88	Rhode Island	60	31.92
Iowa	65	31.60	South Carolina	84	34.58
Kansas	97	37.71	South Dakota	6	35.00
Kentucky	71	30.86	Tennessee	131	36.54
Louisiana	81	35.59	Texas	452	38.40
Maine	70	31.21	Utah	64	30.84
Maryland	269	37.10	Vermont	18	27.22
Massachusetts	672	34.03	Virginia	172	37.04
Michigan	282	37.00	Washington	110	34.20
Minnesota	206	35.83	West Virginia	29	29.07
Mississippi	49	33.96	Wisconsin	209	35.86
			Wyoming	8	34.75

high of $52.67 for Alaska. The majority of state averages were between $30 and $40 at that time, with only four states (Nebraska, Pennsylvania, Vermont, and West Virginia) averaging below that range and five states (Alaska, Hawaii, Nevada, New Mexico, and Oklahoma) averaging above it. Thus, while the model fee charged by individual providers in 1976–1977 was $40.00, the average statewide hourly fee charged by private-practice health service provider psychologists rarely exceeded that figure.

Of considerable interest are practitioners who "specialize" in particular age groups. These populations are now often referred to as "underserved" populations (President's Commission on Mental Health, 1978). The *National Register* survey collected data related to this topic. Respondents were asked what proportion of their practice was made up of persons in each of four age groups: under age 12, between the ages of 12 and 17, between ages 18 and 64, and age 65 and over. For purposes of data analysis, a "specialist practitioner" was operationally defined as a psychologist in private practice 76% (or more) of whose clients fell in one age group. These data on "age-specialty" practice are presented in Table 9. The survey identified 5,280 such practitioners (46.7% of active health service providers in psychology): 225 predominantly saw children, 80 saw adolescents, 28 exclusively saw elderly patients, and 4,947 primarily saw adults. Over half of the active health service provider respondents do not appear in this analysis because they reported a "general practice" in which they saw patients in several age groups with no one age group exceeding the 76% criterion level.

It must be noted that this criteria of a "specialist" focuses on current practice, not on training or experience. Moreover, the "76% or more" criterion is a rigorous definition of specialty. It provides a reasonable estimate of the number of providers who *restrict* their practice to a particular age group, but it does not permit the estimation of the availability of service to those age groups. Few professionals treat one population exclusively. A larger percentage are trained, experienced, and active in providing service to the underrepresented specialty populations but are not exclusively (e.g., less than 75%) serving these groups. The operational definition adopted in this survey thus underestimates the number of individuals active in the provision of services to "atypical" populations such as children, youth, and the elderly and underestimates the services actually available to such populations.

The most frequent "specialty" population was working-age adults (ages 18 to 64). Psychologists working with this specialty group

Table 9: *A Comparison Among the Four Types of "Age Specialty" Practices*

Practitioner characteristic	% total sample ($N = 5,280$)	"Age specialty" practice			
		% child ($n = 225$)	% adolescent ($n = 80$)	% adult ($n = 4,947$)	% elderly ($n = 28$)
Age of practitioner					
45 years old and under	53.3	55.6	48.8	53.5	35.7
46 years old and over	46.7	44.4	51.3	46.6	64.3
Sex of practitioner					
Male	77.0	57.5	76.9	77.9	63.0
Female	23.0	42.5	23.1	22.1	37.0
Highest degree in psychology					
Doctoral	88.0	75.0	68.8	89.0	75.0
Master's	10.3	22.8	31.2	9.3	17.9
Other	1.7	2.2	0	1.6	7.1
Listed in *National Register*					
Yes	55.3	37.2	38.2	56.3	61.5
No	44.7	62.8	61.8	43.7	38.5
Amount of practice					
Part-time	70.5	92.4	89.9	69.1	85.2
Full-time	29.5	7.6	10.1	30.9	14.8

seem to mirror the total sample, because there are few "specialists" (by the above criteria) who treat the "atypical" populations (children, adolescents, and the elderly). However, such a differentiation points up some interesting differences between those who specialize in underserved "age-specific" patient populations and those who seem exclusively to see "working-age adults."

The child practice. This group of practitioners is somewhat younger than the total sample and includes a relatively high number of women and of master's-level persons. These practitioners are almost exclusively in part-time practice.

The adolescent practice. Two characteristics of this group are of note—almost one-third of them are predoctoral (the highest such percentage of any of the groups) and, like the child practitioners, 90% are in part-time practice.

Practice with the elderly. This very small group of providers are significantly older than the other groups and the most likely to be in the *National Register.* Presumably because of their age, slightly over 7% of them have an "unusual" degree (i.e., neither a doctorate nor a master's degree) but, from further examination of the responses, a graduate degree nonetheless.

The adult practice. The predominant "age specialty practice" is adult practice. This group tends, more than the others, to consist of males with doctoral degrees who are in the *National Register.*

A comparison of these four categories of psychologists who practice almost exclusively with a specific age population (children, adolescents, adults, and the elderly) suggests a direct (although nondramatic) relationship between the age of the practitioner and the age of his or her clientele. There are relatively more female psychologists working with children and the elderly. The three "pure practice" groups concentrating on "underserved" populations include a higher percentage of nondoctoral providers and more part-time practitioners.

As noted earlier, the extremely small numbers of providers who specialize in services to children, adolescents, and the elderly do not necessarily mean that services are not provided to these groups. Indeed, the fact that over 6,000 of the active health service providers could not be classified as limiting their practice to a particular age group attests that service is being provided to the other than working-age populations although on a less extensive basis than that provided by the pure practitioners. It may well be that the data represent the impact of the reimbursement policies of government programs and insurance carriers. Medicare provides very limited mental health benefits, and psychologists do not have independent provider status under Medicare. Hence, it is not at all surprising that only 28 active health service providers report specializing in practice with the elderly. The underlying cause of many apparent "professional personnel shortages" may be the lack of adequate financial resources or administration procedures to support such needed services. Professionals cannot specialize in services to a particular "underserved" age population if there are no funds available to pay for such services or if administrative regulations forbid coverage of services by a particular provider group. The Manpower Policy Analysis Task Force of the Alcohol, Drug Abuse, and Mental Health Administration (ADAMHA, 1978) found support for this view.

The *National Register* survey also sought to establish the nature or type of practice that psychologists engaged in and to examine the differences between full-time and part-time private practitioners. Data on the nature of the private practice of full- or part-time psychologist health service providers are presented in Table 10.

Table 10: *Type of Independent Practice of Psychologist Health Service Providers*

	Full-time		Part-time		Total	
	No.	%	No.	%	No.	%
Individual (self-employed)	2,571	76.2	6,346	82.0	8,917	80.3
Group	282	8.4	450	5.8	732	6.6
Partnership	182	5.4	316	4.1	498	4.5
Professional corporation	260	7.7	249	3.2	509	4.6
Employed by other mental health professional	29	.9	116	1.5	145	1.3
Prepaid health plan	4	.1	6	.1	10	.1
Other	47	1.4	253	3.3	300	2.7
Total	3,375		7,736		11,111	

Table 11: *Data on Routine Case Consultation Practices of Private Practitioners*

Case consultation on a routine basis	Full-time practice		Part-time practice		Total	
	No.	%	No.	%	No.	%
Yes	1,301	38.8	1,984	25.7	3,285	29.7
No	2,050	61.2	5,722	74.3	7,772	70.3
Total	3,351		7,706		11,057	

The most typical type of practice of private-practice health service psychologists is the solo-practitioner model. Approximately 80% of psychologists in private practice operate in this manner, regardless of whether in full-time or part-time private practice. However, there is a slight tendency for full-time health service providers to be involved in "other-than-individual" practices. Those reporting such other-than-individual practices as group, partnership, and professional corporation constitute 21.5% of full-time health service provider psychologists compared to only 13.1% of part-time health service provider psychologists.

The survey also addressed the consultation practices of private-practice health service provider psychologists. The questionnaire item asked whether or not case consultation was sought on a *routine* basis. This is quite different from a broader question that might have been asked such as "Do you seek case-specific consultation on troublesome or unusual cases at least once a month?" The more conservative form of the survey item thus probably underestimates the number of private-practice health service provider psychologists who obtain consultation.

Data on the use of routine case consultation is presented in Table 11.

Approximately one-third of health service provider private-practice psychologists routinely obtain case consultation. Full-time health service providers are somewhat more likely to regularly seek consultation than are part-time providers (38.8% versus 25.7%). In this regard, the solo aspect of private practice appears quite substantial.

The survey also sought data on office-space utilization and professional liability coverage. The data on the type of office space utilized by private-practice health service provider psychologists are presented in Table 12; the data on professional practice liability insurance coverage are presented in Table 13.

Full-time psychologist health service providers are 2½ times as likely as part-time psychologist health service providers to own or rent their own offices (68% versus 25%). Part-time practitioners are more likely to use their homes as offices (34% versus 17%), to have salaried office space (21% versus 6%), or to have arrangements with other professionals (16% versus 5%) than are full-time practitioners. From an eco-

Table 12: *Office Locations of Private-Practice Health Service Provider Psychologists*

Type of office	Full-time practice		Part-time practice		Total	
	No.	%	No.	%	No.	%
Own or rent office	2,244	67.7	1,861	24.8	4,105	37.9
Home as office	576	17.4	2,544	33.8	3,120	28.8
Salaried position space	190	5.7	1,563	20.8	1,753	16.2
Arrangement with another professional	149	4.5	1,177	15.7	1,326	12.2
Other	158	4.8	373	5.0	531	4.9
Total	3,317		7,518		10,835	

Table 13: *Data on the Professional Liability Coverage of Private-Practice Health Service Providers in Psychology*

Have professional liability coverage	Full-time practice		Part-time practice		Total	
	No.	%	No.	%	No.	%
Yes	3,057	90.1	5,566	71.5	8,623	77.1
No	336	9.9	2,219	28.5	2,555	22.9
Total	3,393		7,785		11,178	

nomic perspective, such findings are understandable and to be expected.

Almost 80% of private-practice health service provider psychologists carry professional liability insurance. The frequency of such coverage is higher among full-time practitioners (90%) than among part-time providers (71%). These data underestimate the extent to which part-time, private-practice health service providers in psychology are covered by professional practice liability insurance. It is not uncommon for a public agency (e.g., a community mental health center) to have a malpractice policy covering its professional staff in both public and private settings; hence, separate professional liability insurance is not needed for practitioners working in such agencies.

National Register *as a Standard for Health Service Providers in Psychology*

The *National Register* survey sought comparative data on those listed or not listed in the *National Register* on several dimensions: highest degree, ABPP diplomate status, and membership in professional associations. These data

place the *National Register* in perspective as a standard for identifying qualified providers.

Table 14 presents the data regarding the highest academic degrees earned by psychologists listed in the *National Register* and by psychologist health service providers not listed in the *National Register*. In addition, the same data are given for private-practice versus non-private-practice health service providers.

A higher percentage of psychologists listed in the *National Register* have attained doctoral degrees than those not listed (88% versus 79%). Moreover, those listed in the *National Register* are more likely to possess a PhD or PsyD rather than another type of doctoral degree. Those not listed in the *National Register* are more likely to possess a master's or other degree (22% versus 12%) than those listed.

Likewise, psychologists involved in private practice are more likely than those not involved in private practice to hold a doctoral degree (86% versus 75%). Private practitioners, whether listed in the *National Register* or not, have generally attained higher degrees than those not involved in private practice. The data suggest both greater academic training and

Table 14: *Highest Academic Degree by* National Register *Listing and Private Practice*

Highest degree in psychology	Listed in National Register		Not listed in National Register		In private practice		Not in private practice	
	No.	%	No.	%	No.	%	No.	%
Doctoral	6,792	87.9	6,561	78.3	9,736	86.3	3,893	75.0
PhD or PsyD	6,152	79.6	5,714	68.2	8,730	77.4	3,380	65.1
EdD or DEd	640	8.3	847	10.1	1,006	8.9	513	9.9
Master's	847	11.0	1,610	19.2	1,348	12.0	1,180	22.7
Bachelor's	12	.2	45	.5	35	.3	24	.5
Other	73	.9	164	2.0	154	1.4	91	1.8
Total	7,724		8,380		11,273		5,188	

Table 15: *ABPP Diplomate Status by Category of Psychologist*

Category	With diplomate		Without diplomate	
	No.	%	No.	%
All licensed/certified psychologists (ñ = 17,969)	1,676	9.3	16,293	90.7
Health service providers (n = 13,301)	1,253	9.4	12,048	90.6
Private-practice psychologists (n = 10,853)	1,104	10.2	9,749	89.8
Psychologists listed in the *National Register* (n = 7,465)	962	12.9	6,503	87.1

Note. ABPP = American Board of Professional Psychology.

greater willingness to demonstrate competence and relevant training and experience among those listed in the *National Register* and involved in private practice.

Table 15 presents the data regarding those with ABPP diplomate status at various levels of licensure, practice, and professional listing. The data reflect a progressive increase in the percentage of psychologists possessing an ABPP diploma as progression is made through licensure/certification (9.3%), health service provider (9.4%), private practitioner (10.2%), and *National Register* listing (12.9%).

As supplemental information, Table 16 presents data on diplomate status by the traditionally recognized "specialty" areas of clinical, counseling, industrial/organizational, and school psychology. Clinical psychologists predominate at all levels (licensed/certified, health

service provider, private practice, and *National Register* listing). Industrial/organizational psychologists are likely to be licensed/certified but not qualified as health service providers or listed in the *National Register*.

Information on the pattern of professional membership in the APA and state psychological associations of licensed/certified psychologists, private practitioners, and psychologists listed in the *National Register* is presented in Table 17. Of licensed/certified psychologists, 84% are members of the American Psychological Association and 64% belong to their state psychological association. When the data for psychologists involved in private practice are considered, the percentage of APA membership increases to 88% and the rate of membership in state psychological associations increases to 72%. In a similar manner, when those listed in the *National Register* are considered, the percentage of APA membership further increases to a 94% rate and membership in state psychological associations increases to 79%. In general, the vast majority of licensed/certified psychologists belong to the national psychological association and a clear majority belong to their respective state psychological associations. As involvement in private practice and *National Register* listing are considered, both membership rates increase further.

The more actively involved professional groups tend much more to hold membership in APA (94% for persons listed in the *National Register* and 88% of private practitioners) and in state associations (79% of registrants and 72% of private practitioners) than do nonregistrants

Table 16: *ABPP Diplomate Status by Specialty Area of Diplomate Holder*

Diplomate holders	Clinical		Counseling		Industrial/ organizational		School	
	No.	%	No.	%	No.	%	No.	%
All licensed/certified diplomates (n = 1,676)	1,178	70.3	133	7.9	108	6.4	257	15.3
Health service provider diplomates (n = 1,253)	996	79.5	75	6.0	12	1.0	170	13.6
National Register diplomates (n = 962)	871	78.9	66	6.0	18	1.6	149	13.5
Total number of diplomates (N = 2,374)	1,605	67.6	232	9.8	208	8.8	329	13.9

Note. ABPP = American Board of Professional Psychology. *N*s of diplomate holders derived from listings in the *1977 APA Membership Register*.

Table 17: *Membership in APA and State Psychological Associations by Licensed/Certified Status and Listing in* National Register

Organization membership	Licensed/ certified No.	%	In private practice No.	%	Not in private practice No.	%	Listed in *National Register* No.	%	Not listed in *National Register* No.	%
Membership in APA										
Fellows	15,744	84	9,952	88	4,070	78	7,625	94	6,472	77
Members	1,349		609		408		502		475	
Associates	13,100		8,621		3,261		6,269		5,400	
No membership in APA	3,022	16	1,336	12	1,135	22	471	6	1,925	23
Membership in state association	12,014	64	8,069	72	2,924	57	6,045	79	4,763	57
No membership in state association	6,752	36	3,163	28	2,241	43	1,648	21	3,588	43
Total	18,766		11,232		5,165		7,693		8,351	

or nonpractitioners. Nonetheless, the majority of licensed/certified psychologists belong to the national psychological association (84%) and to a state psychological association (64%).

Summary

This report summarizes the result of the 1977 survey conducted by the Council for the National Register of the (then) 25,510 licensed or certified psychologists in the United States. It describes the evolution of the first comprehensive and unduplicated listing of such psychologists as well as the development of the survey (the response rate for which was 73.4%, representing 18,766 respondents). Projections were made to the entire population of licensed/certified psychologists from the data obtained from the respondents.

The report includes the number of health service provider psychologists (full-time and part-time), the number currently providing such services, demographic data such as the highest academic degree earned by various categories of respondents, the number of respondents in each state (with the average fee for services provided in each state), and the differential characteristics of the psychologists providing services to different patient populations (i.e., children, adolescents, adults, and the elderly).

Contained in this report, therefore, are an overall description, as of 1977, of the health service provider psychologists in the country, the type of practice in which they are engaged, and the nature of their clientele. These data are of interest to and can be of use for not only the profession but also health policymakers at the federal and state levels. This study also represents base rate data for later studies of the profession of psychology and its health service activities.

References

Alcohol, Drug Abuse, and Mental Health Administration. *Report of the ADAMHA Manpower Policy Analysis Task Force.* Washington, D.C.: U.S. Department of Health, Education, and Welfare, Public Health Service, Alcohol, Drug Abuse, and Mental Health Administration, 1978.

Cohen, H. A. The Maryland Health Services Cost Review Commission. *Viewpoint,* January 1977. (New York: Health Insurance Association of America).

Gottfredson, G. D., & Dyer, S. E. Health service providers in psychology. *American Psychologist,* 1978, *33,* 314–338.

Marmor, J., Scheidemandel, P. L., & Kanno, C. K. *Psychiatrists and their patients.* Washington, D.C.: American Psychiatric Association, 1975.

National Center for Health Statistics. *Report of the Committee to Evaluate the National Center for Health Statistics: Health statistics today and tomorrow.* Washington, D.C.: U.S. Department of Health, Education, and Welfare, Public Health Service, Health Resources Administration, National Center for Health Statistics, 1972.

National Institute of Mental Health. *Draft report of the Task Force for a Uniform Data Set for Manpower Data.* Rockville, Md.: National Institute of Mental Health, 1977.

President's Commission on Mental Health. *Report to the*

President from the President's Commission on Mental Health (vol. 1). Washington, D.C.: U.S. Government Printing Office, 1978.

Witkin, M. J. *Staffing of mental health facilities: United States, 1974* (ADM 76-308). Washington, D.C.: U.S. Government Printing Office, 1976.

Zimet, C. N., & Wellner, A. The Council for the National Register of Health Service Providers in Psychology. *International Encyclopedia of Neurology, Psychiatry, Psychoanalysis, & Psychology,* 1977, *5,* 329–332.

David H. Mills is a professor at the University of Maryland. *Alfred M. Wellner* is Executive Director, the Council for the National Register of Health Service Providers in Psychology. *Gary R. VandenBos* is Administrative Officer for Mental Health Policy, the American Psychological Association.

David H. Mills and Alfred M. Wellner were co-investigators in the *National Register* survey, which occurred during Mills's sabbatical leave from the University of Maryland. Some of the survey data were previously reported in the *National Register* Research Reports and at a symposium held at the annual meeting of the American Psychological Association in San Francisco, August 1977.

Licensed Psychologists in Health Care: A Survey of Their Practices

Herbert Dörken and James T. Webb

In 1977 a survey of health service practice by licensed/certified psychologists was sent to licensed psychologists in 10 states, a sample comprising about half of the licensed psychologists in the nation. About half responded to the highly detailed 57-section questionnaire. Data were obtained on (a) health service practitioner psychologists' education, public training support, mobility, and distribution; (b) the scope and dimensions of psychologists' fee-for-service practices; (c) the extent of psychologists' practices in hospital settings; (d) psychologists' fees and incomes; (e) insurance reimbursement experience; (f) experience with professional standards review committees; and (g) a cross-section description of clients seen by fee-for-service psychologists. This article contrasts these survey results with those of several previous comparable surveys. The results clearly show that the practicing psychologist has an active and growing, but recent, presence in health care, particularly in fee-for-service modes of practice. However, hospital practice and health insurance reimbursement procedures have not yet fully integrated clinical psychologists into the generic health care system.

Information on the resources and roles of professional psychologists who provide health care services is essential for policy and planning purposes. While some information concerning psychological services in government facilities has been available, very few data have been reported on psychologists engaged in private practice either on a fee-for-service or a salaried basis (Gottfredson & Dyer, 1977; Wellner & Mills, 1977). Also, only recently has the practice of psychology in private and nonprofit hospitals become an issue (Dörken & Morrison, 1976; Matarazzo, Lubin, & Nathan, 1977). Some relevant data on these matters can now be reported.

During the spring and summer of 1977, a survey of health service practice by licensed psychologists was mailed to a current unduplicated roster of all licensed psychologists in 10 states (Alabama, California, District of Columbia, Florida, Illinois, New York, Ohio, Rhode Island, South Carolina, and Texas). Previously, the utilization of mental health services under the Civilian Health and Medical Program of the Uniformed Services (CHAMPUS) had been studied in these 10 states; these studies were conducted both for fiscal year 1974 (Dörken,

1976) and for fiscal year 1975 (Dörken, 1977a). In anticipation that health service practice data from the present survey might be combined with CHAMPUS utilization data for fiscal year 1976, the same 10 states were chosen for the present survey. Since the present survey, however, the CHAMPUS data for fiscal year 1976 have proven inaccessible in usable form for such comparisons. Thus the present survey data are presented without such cross-analyses.

The roster utilized in the present survey, according to the *National Register of Health Service Providers in Psychology*, listed 12,095 licensed psychologists in the 10 states, or 47% of the 25,510 psychologists licensed in the United States at that time (Mills, Wellner, & VandenBos, 1979; Wellner & Mills, 1977). In these 10 states resided 42% of the U.S. population at that time.

The survey particularly sought information concerning (a) characteristics of health service practitioners, including their education, public training support, mobility, and distribution; (b) the scope and dimensions of fee-for-service practice; (c) the extent of, and limitations on, psychologists' practices in hospital settings; (d) insurance reimbursement experience; and (e) a cross-section description of characteristics of patients seen by fee-for-service practitioners. Heretofore little has been known about these areas.

Of the 12,095 questionnaires mailed, an initial return rate of approximately 39% was attained, with an additional 13% return obtained following a second mailing. Between the first and second mailings the nonrespondents were individually called via WATS phone service to encourage their response. However, this direct contact did not noticeably increase the return rate. The postal authorities returned 540 questionnaires as "undeliverable." Of the remaining 11,555 questionnaires, 6,044 (52%) were returned, though only 5,865 (51%) were usable due to the manner in which they were completed.

The 52% response rate was substantially lower than the 73% response rate reported by Wellner and Mills (1977) or the 74% response rate reported by Gottfredson and Dyer (1978). The discrepancy in response rate between the present study and these two previous studies is likely due to several reasons. First, the present survey was mailed to psychologists less than 6 months after these two earlier surveys, and thus there may have been resistance to completing yet another questionnaire. Second, the present survey, in contrast to the others, was not sponsored by a widely known and prestigious organization. Third, the present survey was longer (57 items) than the other two surveys (36

items and 47 items, respectively). Finally, the instructions with the present survey openly stated the intent to gather data on health practitioners and on fee-for-service practice; thus the present survey may have been relatively unappealing for psychologists not engaged in health practice, particularly on a fee-for-service basis. In retrospect, it would have been desirable to have sent a postcard to the nonrespondents (as done by Gottfredson & Dyer, 1978) to attempt to gain at least minimal information about the nonrespondents. Without such data it is not possible to know the extent of any sampling biases that might have been present. Sample representativeness can only be assumed.

Even with the above limitations, the present report is based on replies from about one quarter of the licensed/certified psychologists in the country. Although the number of licensed psychologists on the roster in particular states differed greatly (ranging from 121 in Rhode Island to 3,463 in New York), the proportionate contribution to the total usable sample was essentially equal across states (see Table 1).

The sample data were tabulated separately for several subgroups in order to provide a clearer picture of the characteristics of these subgroups. The survey results, then, are presented for these subgroups in the following order: (a) licensed psychologists in general, referred to as the general sample, (b) health service provider

Table 1: *Distribution of Psychologists Across the States Surveyed*

State	No. of APA members[a]	No. of licensed psychologists	No. of licensed psychologists responding	No. of HSP psychologists responding	No. of HSP psychologists in FFS practice responding	No. of HSP psychologists in FFS 30+ hrs/wk responding	No. of HSP psychologists in FFS ≤10 hrs/wk responding
Alabama	402	157	79	62	40	25	11
California	5,804	3,213	1,600	1,132	957	596	201
District of Columbia	853	403	195	139	122	69	25
Florida	1,342	614	328	263	204	134	37
Illinois	2,312	1,122	586	420	345	211	96
New York	6,667	3,463	1,565	1,230	1,076	611	208
Ohio	1,723	1,803	855	498	384	266	90
Rhode Island	185	121	42	24	22	11	8
South Carolina	311	160	94	75	61	42	14
Texas	1,965	1,039	521	339	283	200	62
Total	21,564	12,095	5,865	4,182	3,494	2,165	752

Note. Abbreviations: HSP = health service provider; FSS = fee for service.
[a] Approximately 23% of these are associate members.

(HSP) psychologists, (c) psychologists in health service practice on a fee-for-service (FFS) basis, (d) psychologists engaged in health service practice on a full-time, fee-for-service basis (FT-FFS), and (e) psychologists engaged in health service fee-for-service practice on a very part-time basis (VPT-FFS).

In addition to examining these subgroups of licensed psychologists, results are presented concerning (f) the fees charged by psychologists, (g) the incomes of HSP psychologists, (h) a cross-section description of the clients of FFS psychologists, (i) the experiences of psychologists in submitting reimbursement claims for third-party payment, and (j) their experiences with professional standards review committees concerning fees charged for services. Finally, for clarity it should be noted that the number of usable responses varied across each of the above categories, largely because the survey questionnaire instructed respondents to "Stop here and return the survey questionnaire" at different points depending on whether the respondent (a) was licensed but not a health service provider, or (b) was licensed and a health service provider but was salaried only and not engaging in any fee-for-service practice. This variation of usable responses across items implies that the respondents did not just discard the questionnaire at the first difficult question but rather that they seriously attempted to answer the questions relevant to them.

Licensed Psychologists

Of the general sample of all licensed psychologists, 74% were male, similar to the proportion

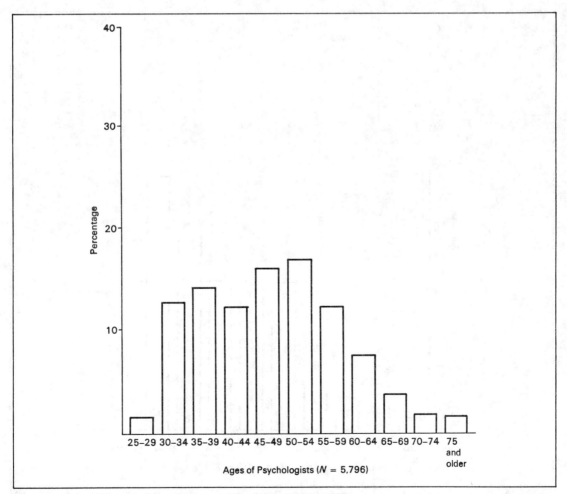

Figure 1: *Age Distributions of Licensed Psychologists in 1977*

among APA members who are male (75%). Eighty-five percent of the licensed psychologists had doctoral degrees (78% PhD/PsyD; 7% EdD). The age distribution showed both a median and a mean age of 47 years ($X = 47.43$, $sd = 10.76$). The youth of the profession of psychology is readily apparent from an examination of Figure 1.

The licensed psychologist clearly is a recent phenomenon, even more than the youthful age distribution would suggest. As shown in Figures 2 and 3, 75% of the licensed psychologists received their highest degrees since 1955, and 75% have been licensed only since 1962. The median licensed psychologist received his or her highest degree in 1964 and was licensed in 1969.

The basic demographic data of age, sex, and percentage of doctoral degrees reported above closely parallel the findings of a survey carried out in the winter of 1976 by the Council for the National Register of Health Service Providers in Psychology (Wellner & Mills, 1977). That survey contacted all licensed psychologists in the United States but focused on broad rather than specific issues. The similarity of the basic demographic data is not surprising (since the two surveys utilized as their mailing lists the same unduplicated roster of licensed/certified psychologists) and suggests that the respondent samples are similar on some dimensions.

Low mobility is typical of licensed psychologists; 51% of the licensed psychologists had been awarded their psychology degree in the state where they currently were employed. Half have resided in their present state for at least 24 years and have been employed there for 11 or

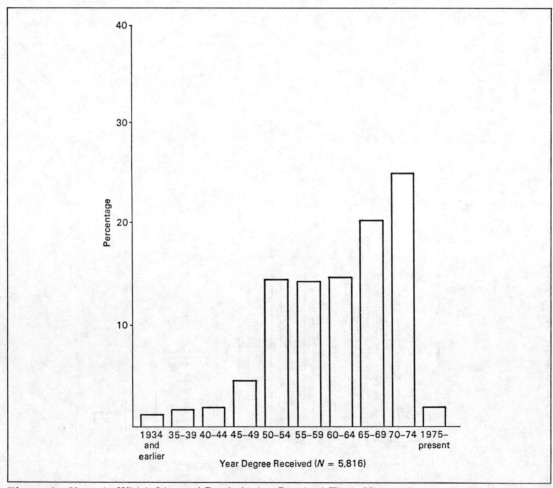

Figure 2: *Years in Which Licensed Psychologists Received Their Highest Degrees in Psychology*

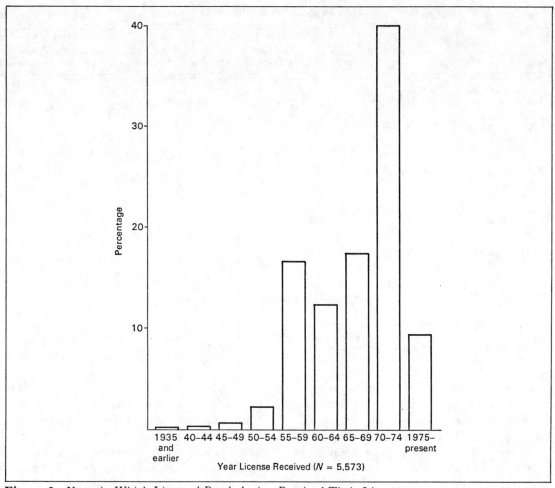

Figure 3: *Years in Which Licensed Psychologists Received Their Licenses*

more years. Less than 1.2% of licensed psychologists have migrated within the last year into the state in which they are currently employed. Only 1.6% of these psychologists had been trained outside of the United States.

The majority (72%) of licensed psychologists listed clinical (63%) or counseling (9%) as their current specialty. However, as shown in Table 2, only 69% were originally trained in these specialty areas (53% in clinical, 14% in counseling). Clinical psychology, with its 10% "specialty crossover" (i.e., 63% minus 53%), was the only specialty area that showed more than the 4% crossover "gain" of the industrial/engineering specialty.

The amount of specialty crossover becomes dramatically apparent within the subgroup of licensed psychologists who are health service providers; the formal definition of HSP psychol-

ogists is presented below. Among HSP psychologists, the shift to clinical practice is high (15.5%), and it is even higher (18%) among HSP psychologists who are in full-time, fee-for-service practice. In addition to confirming the interest in the practice of clinical psychology by large numbers of psychologists, these specialty crossover figures strongly confirm the need for development of formal, postdoctoral specialty retraining in clinical psychology.

When the data are examined from a different perspective, it appears that the specialty retraining is only one issue; current specialty training in clinical psychology appears necessary also. Table 3 presents relevant data on HSP psychologists of different ages.

As shown in Table 3, the specialty crossover appears as great, if not greater, for HSP psychologists below the age of 40 as for

Table 2: *Percentage of Psychologists Changing Postgraduate Specialties*

Subgroup	Clinical	Counseling	School/ educational	Industrial/ engineering	Community	Rehabili- tation	Personality/ social/ developmental	Experimental/ physiological
Licensed psychologists ($N = 5,867$)								
Current specialty	62.9	9.0	11.3	7.3	2.2	1.6	3.7	1.9
Specialty trained in	53.1	13.4	14.7	3.5	.3	.8	7.8	6.5
Gain/loss	+9.8	−4.4	−3.4	+3.8	+1.9	+.8	−4.1	−4.6
Health service providers ($N = 4,184$)								
Current specialty	77.9	8.3	6.5	1.5	2.0	1.4	1.8	.6
Specialty trained in	62.4	13.3	11.7	.8	.4	.7	6.4	4.2
Gain/loss	+15.5	−5.0	−5.2	+.7	+1.6	+.7	−4.6	−3.6
Health service providers, fee-for-service, full-time ($N = 2,167$)								
Current specialty	82.3[a]	7.5	4.1	1.6	1.5	1.0	1.4	.6
Specialty trained in	64.2	13.4	9.7	.8	.3	.9	6.4	4.2
Gain/loss	+18.1	−5.9	−5.6	+.8	+1.2	+.1	−5.0	−3.6

[a] For the occasional (very part-time) fee-for-service psychologist, 65.5% listed clinical as their current specialty, although only 54.7% had originally been trained in clinical, a difference of 10.8%.

older psychologists. It is of note that the percentage of HSP psychologists with doctoral degrees has risen steadily each decade. Apparently these HSP psychologists are receiving a great deal of formal training, but a substantial portion of it is in areas other than clinical psychology even though these persons soon thereafter cross over into the practice of clinical psychology. The extent of this shift to clinical practice supports the frequent contention that substantial numbers of psychologists have found that they must wait to complete their graduate training before they can pursue their clinical interests.

The 16% specialty crossover among HSP psychologists in general is, on the one hand, substantial and has clear implications for training. On the other hand, and as a matter of perspective regarding human resources issues in the delivery of mental health services, it should be borne in mind that clinical psychology is not unique in such crossover. For example, only 48% of U.S. psychiatrists have completed their specialty training (Manson, 1972). Further, the implications of the percentages of specialty crossover into clinical psychology are difficult to evaluate in this regard owing to the recency of entrance of these licensed psychologists into the

Table 3: *Characteristics of Health Service Provider (HSP) Psychologists of Different Ages*

Age of HSP psychologist	N[a]	% male	% having PhD/EdD or PsyD	Current specialty in clinical psychology	Originally trained in clinical psychology	Mean year became an HSP	Mean professional hours/week
≤29	51	69	96.1	92.2	60.8	1,974.4	45.7
30–39	1,294	78	94.1	80.1	63.8	1,971.7	41.7
40–49	1,240	77	89.8	76.8	61.3	1,965.7	41.2
50–59	1,123	74	85.1	76.6	64.6	1,958.9	40.4
60–69	382	64	82.8	76.4	58.3	1,954.4	34.9
≥70	55	56	70.9	79.6	54.7	1,950.8	19.0

[a] The total N of HSP psychologists only sums to 4,145 owing to 37 respondents who omitted this question.

HSP area. As shown in Table 3, the average year in which psychologists entered HSP practice was over a quite brief and recent time span of approximately 20 years, even though their training in psychology occurred over a rather extensive time span. Further investigation into the specialty crossover issue appears needed, particularly regarding implications for delivery of health and mental health services.

Health Service Provider Psychologists

Health service providers are those licensed psychologists who provide direct health care services. As a subset of the present general sample, they were defined with a slightly different emphasis than in the definition[1] used in the 1976 survey conducted by the Council for the National Register of Health Service Providers in Psychology (Mills, Wellner, & VandenBos, 1979; Wellner & Mills, 1977). The present definition also required health service providers to have greater clinical experience than the definition used by the American Psychological Association in its survey of a stratified random sample of APA members in November 1976.[2] The present definition was drawn from the Model Psychologist Direct Recognition Bill:[3] "a psychologist *certified/licensed at the independent practice level* in his/her state who has a doctorate degree in psychology and has had at least two years clinical experience in a recognized health setting, or who has met the standards of the *National Register in Psychology*."

Although 83% of the general sample of licensed psychologists identified themselves as health service providers by the above definition, 13% of these were at the time otherwise engaged and were not currently providing health care services.[4] Only 1.6% indicated they were retired, and .5% stated that they were unemployed (whether voluntarily or not is unknown). Thus, about 70% of licensed psychologists in the present survey are active health service providers, a figure somewhat lower than the 74% of licensed psychologists found by Wellner and Mills (1977) in their national survey and substantially lower than the 83% and 79% (doctoral and nondoctoral, respectively) of licensed psychologists who reported being health service providers in the 1977 survey of members and associate members of the American Psychological Association (Gottfredson, Note 1). The latter study sought the identity of those members providing "psychotherapy . . . or other health services." Thus the higher figures are to be expected.

The median age of the HSP psychologist was 45, significantly younger ($p < .001$) than the median age of 51 for the non-HSP licensed psychologist in the general sample as well as significantly younger ($p < .01$) than the mean age reported for psychiatrists in 1973 (Marmor, 1975). The present data thus indicate that the HSP psychologist is a young entrant into the health care field as well as being a recent entrant (as noted earlier in Table 3).

The influx of psychologists in recent years into health care areas, including private practice, may be attributed not only to their training and preparation (Wolberg, 1967) but also in part to recent licensing, insurance reimbursement, and other laws (see *Directory of the American Psychological Association*, 1978, pp. xlii–xlvi), in part to increased awareness of psychologists' services, and perhaps in part to the reduced opportunity for academic employment. Parenthetically, Gottfredson and Dyer (1977, 1978) found the HSP psychologists, according to their definition, to be even younger, having a median age of 42; this again replicates the find-

---

[1] "A psychologist certified/licensed at the independent practice level of his/her state, who is duly trained and experienced in the delivery of direct, preventive, assessment, and therapeutic intervention services to individuals whose growth, adjustment, or functioning is actually impaired or is demonstrably at high risk of impairment."

[2] A member of the American Psychological Association who reports providing "psychotherapy, counseling, assessment, or other *health services*," including providers who were not licensed.

[3] This model bill for state "freedom-of-choice" legislation, developed jointly by the American Psychological Association's Committee on Health Insurance (COHI) and the staff of the Health Insurance Association of America (HIAA) was approved by the Government Relations Committee of HIAA on May 18, 1976 and by the APA's Council of Representatives on September 2, 1976.

---

[4] Using the less rigorous definition of health service provider psychologist noted earlier, Wellner and Mills (1977) found that 88% of licensed psychologists identified themselves as health service providers, though 14.5% were not providing such services at that time.

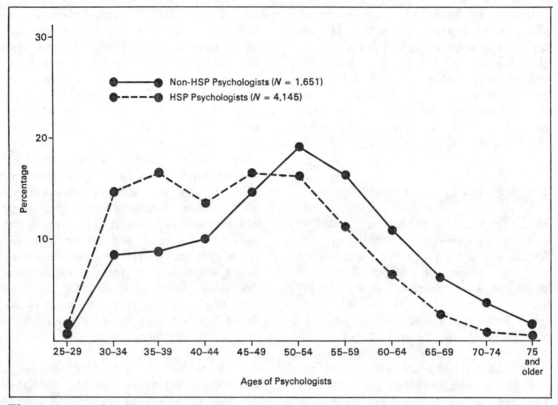

Figure 4: *Age Distributions of Health Service Provider (HSP) and Non-Health Service Provider (Non-HSP) Licensed Psychologists in 1977*

ing of youth of HSP psychologists. The age differences of HSP psychologists as compared with non-HSP psychologists in the present study are presented graphically in Figure 4.

In keeping with this younger age, the median HSP psychologist received his or her highest degree in psychology in 1965, began engaging in health service practice in 1967, but was not licensed until 1970. Thus HSP psychologists received their degrees and their licenses more recently ($p < .01$) than did non-HSP licensed psychologists in the general sample. This can be seen by comparing the mean values presented in Table 4. The finding that the median HSP psychologist received his or her license, on the average, 3.1 years after becoming a health service provider reflects both the postdoctoral experience requirements of licensure and the recency of passage of licensing statutes in state legislatures. In fact, 50% of U.S. licensing laws were effected in the last 12 years (i.e., since 1966), and for 5 of the 10 states in the

present survey, statutes were adopted as recently as from 1968 (South Carolina) to 1972 (Ohio).[5]

Fully 89% of the HSP psychologists possessed the doctoral degree, significantly (χ^2 (1) = 212, $p < .001$) more than licensed non-HSP psychologists (see Table 4). The HSP psychologists were more likely to be male (χ^2 (1) = 12, $p < .01$). The percentages of the HSP and non-HSP groups whose degrees were awarded in their state of current employment and in a foreign country were highly similar.

Even though the HSP psychologists were approximately 5½ years younger than their non-HSP counterparts, this age or time difference was not mirrored or magnified in the duration of state residency in the two groups (see Table 4). The median HSP psychologist had resided in

---

[5] The first psychology certification act was passed in Connecticut in 1945. It was not until 1977, 32 years later, with passage of the Missouri law, that the practice of psychology was regulated by statute in all 50 states and the District of Columbia.

Table 4: *Age, Gender, Educational, and Mobility Characteristics of HSP and Non-HSP Licensed Psychologists*

Characteristic	Non-HSP		HSP	
	No.	%	No.	%
Age (median)	51.4		45.9	
Gender (male)	1,157	70.5	3,088	75.0
Education				
PhD/EdD/PsyD	1,221	73.9	3,704	89.1
Less than doctoral degree	432	26.1	454	10.9
Degree awarded				
In state where currently employed	831	50.1	2,130	51.1
In another state	806	48.6	1,966	47.2
In a foreign country	21	1.3	72	1.7
Year of receiving highest degree (mean)	1,958.1		1,963.2	
Year of receiving license (mean)	1,965.8		1,967.6	
Mobility				
Years employed in present state (median)	14.1		10.1	
Years resident in present state (median)	26.6		22.9	

Note. HSP = health service provider.

his or her present state of employment for 23 years (only 3.7 years less than the median non-HSP psychologist). The median HSP psychologist had been employed in that state for 10 years (only 4 years less than the median non-HSP psychologist).

As can be seen in Table 5, 40% of the HSP psychologists reported receiving *no* publicly funded support (either federal or state) for their graduate training, excluding internships, and in the aggregate. Only 32% of the total years of training of HSP psychologists was subsidized through public funds (6,658 of 20,800 years). The support received probably was in large part through the Veterans Administration and the National Institute of Mental Health. Thus, the recent and substantial growth of professional health service psychology has been largely inde-

pendent of public financial support of psychology trainees. Rather, the existence of the growing national health care resources that professional psychology represents probably has occurred mainly owing to widespread graduate student interest in the subject, along with the growth of career opportunities for psychologists (Dörken & Cummings, 1977).

Seventy-five percent of the HSP psychologists worked over 35 hours per week in direct professional hours per week for HSP psychol-the HSP psychologists worked more than 49 hours per week (median, 42 hours). The mean professsional hours per week for HSP psychologists at different ages is shown in Table 3. The present data are consistent with those of Vetter (1973), who found that "of psychologists who were APA members, 74% spent more than 40 hours per week in direct and indirect work activities." The median HSP psychologist saw 15 patients per week on a salaried basis and 12 patients per week on a fee-for-service basis. In addition, a median of about 7 hours per week was devoted collectively to health consultation, teaching, research, and administration.

Table 5: *Years of Publicly Funded Support Received During Graduate Training (Excluding Internship) of Health Service Provider Psychologists*

Years of support	Frequency	Percentage	Cumulative percentage
0	1,653	39.7	39.7
1	494	11.9	51.6
2	668	16.1	67.7
3	714	17.2	84.8
4	469	11.3	96.1
5	162	3.9	100.0

Involvement of HSP Psychologists in Health Care

Although it is frequently assumed that psychologists are mental health (rather than *health*) practitioners, the survey data suggest a developing broader perspective. As can be seen in Table 6, well over two thirds of the HSP psychologists are involved in seeing clients during the course of a year who are seen *primarily* due to psychological aspects of physical problems. The data in Table 6 suggest further, however, that few HSP psychologists at this time specialize exclusively in psychological aspects of physical problems. Nevertheless, when the percentage categories are collapsed into a weighted average, the data indicate that approximately 10% of the clients of the average HSP psychologist in 1977 were seen primarily for psychological aspects of organic illness, disease, dying, or surgery, and an additional 8% were seen primarily for psychological aspects of physical accident, injury, or dismemberment. These percentages of the clientele of HSP psychologists clearly are not negligible. The weighted average indicates that approximately 12% of clients were seen primarily because of mental retardation or developmental disabilities. Clients with such problems often are also considered to be experiencing psychological difficulties stemming primarily from physical anomalies. Thus, the data indicate that HSP psychologists quite frequently see clients for health reasons that go far beyond traditional mental health notions.

HSP Psychologists' Relations With Other Professionals

Health service practitioner psychologists appear to be serving a clientele frequently referred to them by a variety of other health care profes-sionals and agencies. Nevertheless, the majority (57%) of these practitioners indicated that they primarily (i.e., "often" or "very often") get their referrals from former patients. Whereas 28% indicated that their patients primarily were referred from nonpsychiatric physicians, psychiatrists were primary referral sources for 17% of the psychologists, and other psychologists were primary referral sources for 22%. Of interest are that 19% of the health service providers indicated community or government agencies to be a primary referral source and that 24% listed self-referral as a primary source.

Thus the sources of the practicing psychologists' clientele are varied and quite extensive, and no one profession or type of agency accounts for a majority of psychologists' referrals. Moreover, the data suggest that psychologists are serving a clientele separate from and not typically referred to them by psychiatrists and that psychologists have more interaction in their practices with nonpsychiatric physicians than with psychiatrists.

Of related interest are data from other studies of patients of psychologists and psychiatrists showing varying results concerning the similarity of patients or the degree of severity of conditions for which these patients are being seen. Dörken (1977a), in a study primarily of outpatients being seen under CHAMPUS, found that psychologists see somewhat fewer of the "severe" conditions, at least as defined according to the diagnosis given the patient by the psychologist or psychiatrist, respectively. In contrast, Webb (Note 2) examined the Minnesota Multiphasic Personality Inventory (MMPI) test profiles and demographic characteristics of 12,174 patients of 1,197 psychiatrists and 218

Table 6: *Percentages of Clients of Health Service Provider Psychologists Who Were Seen Primarily Due to Health Disorders*

Primary reason for seeing client	Percentages of such clients seen in last year						Base N
	0	1%–20%	21%–40%	41%–60%	61%–80%	81%+	
Mental retardation or developmental disability	36	50	7	3	2	2	3,232
Psychological aspects of organic illness, disease, dying, or surgery	31	59	7	2	.4	.6	3,062
Psychological aspects of physical accident, injury, or dismemberment	41	50	6	2	.6	.4	2,949
Other emotional, mental, or behavioral disorders	1	5	6	11	21	56	3,860

psychologists in private practice in a nationwide sample and found that the patients of psychiatrists were not more "severe" than those of private-practice psychologists. Such slight differences as did exist in the patients as measured by the MMPI could be accounted for by the differences in demographic characteristics of the patients. Both studies, nevertheless, clearly indicate that there is at least a large degree of overlap in the characteristics of patients seen by psychiatrists and by psychologists (see also below).

The referral patterns described above are of interest in light of previous findings that from one fourth to one third of psychiatrists' patients were referred to the psychiatrists by the patients' family physicians (Avnet, 1962; Fink et al., 1967). Even in the context of a prepaid medical group practice, only one half of the persons seeing psychiatrists had been referred by physicians (Fink, Goldensohn, & Shapiro, 1970). It is of note that all of these studies indicated that from between one fourth and one third of psychiatrists' patients were self-referred or were referred by former patients, a finding similar to the present results regarding psychologists' clients.

The data of the present survey also suggest that psychologists frequently refer patients to other professionals. Of the health service providers, 25% refer patients "often" or "very often" to other psychologists, 22% to nonpsychiatric physicians, 16% to psychiatrists, and 17% to community/governmental agencies.

The high level of referral and consultation between psychologists and other health professionals may seem surprising in light of the recency of psychology's professional resources, on the one hand, and the resistance on the part of other professions to "market penetration," on the other hand (Dörken & Morrison, 1976). Relatedly, since psychologists are seeing clients largely independent of psychiatry and yet are serving a generally similar population, then the services of psychologists to this extent offset those of psychiatrists and thus are not an added cost but instead introduce economic competition. It would also hold that any report on the extent of private-sector mental health delivery that does not include the services of practicing psychologists seriously underrepresents the total of the services provided.

HSP Psychologists and Hospital Practice

The involvement by psychologists in the broad sphere of health care notwithstanding, health care sometimes is narrowly defined as "medical" care (and sometimes defined even more narrowly as "hospital" care). Hospitals and their affiliated medical staffs do typically serve as centers for promoting interaction, communication, and cross-referral among health care providers. Of paramount importance in such an informational/referral system is acceptance as a colleague, with membership in the hospital medical staff and the possession of clinical privileges. In nongovernmental hospitals, hospital staff membership typically is limited to medical or osteopathic physicians and dentists who are in independent practice on a fee-for-service basis in offices separate from the hospital. It is not uncommon for such professionals to hold membership on the staffs of two or more hospitals. With the exceptions of health maintenance organizations (HMOs) or some physicians retained on contract, these professionals are not salaried employees of the hospital. Hospital staff membership has numerous categories (e.g., active, associate, consulting, courtesy), and although these categories generally correspond to the "privileges" one has within the hospital, there is some variation within each category as the specific privileges are delineated, subject to determination locally by the hospital staff. Even so, membership on the active hospital staff (and sometimes in other categories of membership) virtually always carries with it the privilege to admit, and discharge, private patients under the primary care of the professional holding such staff membership. The specific services or procedures that the practitioner can provide will vary depending upon his or her privileges. Because of these variations, and because of some variations in customs in different parts of the country, the present survey called for information in some detail about "hospital staff membership" and "clinical privileges" separately. (For a more extended discussion, see Dörken & Webb, 1979.)

The present data indicate that only a minor proportion of HSP psychologists have been accepted for membership on hospital medical staffs or have designated clinical privileges, a finding consistent with that of Matarazzo, Lubin, and

Nathan (1977). Thus it is not surprising that the data also reveal that of the HSP psychologists, 70% do not provide any direct service to hospital inpatients (general, psychiatric, or day/night care) either on a salaried or on a fee-for-service basis. Undoubtedly, this limited involvement in inpatient care is a reflection of the lack of full acceptance of psychologists into organized health care settings, as demonstrated by the findings of extremely low rates of inclusion of psychologists on hospital staffs and/or with clinical privileges.

Since psychologists may have "clinical privileges" (i.e., be able to provide direct professional services to patients) but may or may not hold "hospital staff membership" (particularly membership with vote in the medical/dental/professional staff), the questionnaire surveyed these two areas separately. The data clearly revealed that clinical privileges (particularly "informal" nondesignated ones) are much more frequent than formal memberships on the hospital staff. Further, the data showed that these psychologists themselves often were unclear about their formal status and privileges within hospitals.

Of the HSP psychologists in the current survey, 13% provided no information regarding hospital staff membership, and 57% noted that they did not have such status. Thus, only 30% held some type of hospital staff membership. Since very few hospitals have distinct sections of psychology practitioners designated as such within the "medical/dental/professional" staff, it is highly probable that this item was misunderstood by some psychologists who are employed by hospitals but who are not members of the hospital's organized staff.

Only 18% of the HSP psychologists held membership in the "medical/dental/professional staff," while 2% held "allied health professional" staff membership, and less than 1% had "HMO-type setting" staff membership. Of the 18% holding membership on the "medical/dental/professional staff," only 4.6% were members of the active medical staff; membership on associate, consulting, affiliate, or courtesy staffs was held by 13.6%.

The reasons that HSP psychologists did not hold some kind of membership on the "medical/dental/professional staff" were explored. No information was provided by 47% of the HSP psychologists, and 21% stated that they had no interest in such membership. However, slightly over 3% had either applied and been denied or had been advised by the medical staff/administration not to apply. An additional 29% indicated that although they had not applied, they currently were interested in obtaining membership.

When examined from the viewpoint of designated clinical privileges (rather than medical staff membership), the results are similar, although the involvement of HSP psychologists is slightly higher. Only 36% of the HSP psychologists held designated hospital clinical privileges that allowed them to see patients either "hospitalwide" (20%) or just in providing specific services in departments (16%). However, the data indicate that these privileges are not uniformly broad. Although 36% of the HSP psychologists had clinical privileges of some kind, only 28% of the HSP psychologists had privileges allowing them to practice psychotherapy within the hospital. Further, of those psychologists claiming privileges (36% of HSP psychologists), one third have their privileges on the basis of informal, rather than formal, arrangements—noblesse oblige.

Hospital privileges enabling the psychologist to function independently as a practitioner were not common, with 65% reporting no such privileges. Though 35% held privileges, only 12% could provide inpatient clinical treatment independently as the attending therapist, while 12% could do so only with medical referral and 10% only under medical direction. Of the HSP psychologists, 18% could write orders on their patients in the medical records in their own name (10% are not permitted to write such orders), and another 7% are permitted to only if the orders are countersigned by a physician.

Admission and discharge privileges appear even more restricted. Only 3% of the HSP psychologists could arrange for the admission of a patient on their own signature. An additional 21% could do so only on physician signature or cosignature. The proportions having discharge authority are fewer still; 2% could arrange for discharge under their own signature, while 19% could do so only on a physician's signature or cosignature.

That the hospital is but a limited-practice setting for the 4,182 HSP psychologists surveyed is highlighted by specific examination of the involvement of the 2,165 full-time, fee-for-service (FT-FFS) practitioners. Such examination reveals even this subgroup to be involved only peripherally. Only 4% of these practitioners reported membership on the active medical staff, with 22% holding membership on the associate, consulting, affiliate, or allied health staffs. Further, only 8% held staff membership with voting privileges, though 12% could vote in specific committees. In contrast to medical staff membership, the clinical privileges of these FT-FFS practitioners were as follows: 22% held clinical privileges that were hospitalwide, with an additional 15% indicating that they held clinical privileges in specific departments within a hospital. Thus, 37% of these FT-FFS psychologists held privileges, scarcely more than the HSP psychologists in general. The HSP and the FT-FFS psychologist were also similar with respect to the "clinical privileges" that were held more frequently than "hospital staff membership," particularly on the "active" staff. Fully 40% of these FT-FFS practitioners holding "clinical privileges" reported that their privileges are on the basis of "informal arrangements" and thus are not formally sanctioned by the hospital or by their health professional peers. Further examination of the types of privileges held by the FT-FFS group showed that 29% held privileges allowing them to provide psychotherapy and 29% to provide consultation. Writing treatment orders in their own name was limited to 17.5%, admitting clients on their own signature to 3.3%, and discharge to 2.2%.

In short, the large majority of these licensed/certified HSP psychologist practitioners, even those in full-time, fee-for-service practice, have no recognized access to direct hospital practice of their profession. The contrast between the situation in hospital practice and the participation of psychologists in ambulatory health care is striking!

HSP Psychologists in Fee-for-Service Practice

Although HSP psychologists are not heavily involved in hospital practice, they clearly are involved in fee-for-service practice. As seen from the data below, the overwhelming proportion of psychologists who engage in fee-for-service practice do so either full-time or do so on a very occasional basis, resulting in a rather surprising bimodal distribution.

Seventy-five percent of HSP psychologists (53% of licensed psychologists in general) engaged in some direct services to clients in private-office practice on a fee-for-service basis, with a median of 10 hours per week spent in this health service mode. In looking at private practice beyond the office, note that 84% of HSP psychologists (60% of licensed psychologists in general, or an estimated 16,800 licensed psychologists in the United States in 1978) are engaged in fee-for-service health practice in one setting or another. In keeping with the data presented earlier on HSP psychologists, only 4,370 of these 16,800 FFS psychologists (26%) hold any type of facility "staff" membership. This contrasts sharply with the obvious growth of psychological practice in outpatient fee-for-service office health care discussed below.

That 84% of HSP psychologists (60% of licensed psychologists) were engaged in at least part-time, fee-for-service practice is generally in keeping with the survey results of Gottfredson and Dyer (1978), who found that 76% of licensed HSP psychologists, according to their definition, engaged in at least some provision of health services for a fee. Similarly, Wellner and Mills (1977) found that 82% of the health service providers (60% of licensed psychologists) surveyed by them were currently in "private practice."

The findings of Gottfredson and Dyer (1978) and Wellner and Mills (1977) are, however, sharply discrepant with the present data concerning the percentage of HSP psychologists in full-time, fee-for-service practice. The former study found that only 15% of "doctoral level licensed providers" reported 31 or more hours each week in providing health services for a fee (Gottfredson & Dyer, 1978). Wellner and Mills (1977) reported that 25% of their licensed health service providers were engaged in full-time private practice. In the present study, however, fully 52% of the HSP psychologists (37% of licensed psychologists in general) reported engaging in fee-for-service health practice essentially full-time (i.e., for 31 or more hours per week).

The sharp differences in estimates of FT-FFS psychologists require comment. The differences appear to stem largely from the way in which the questionnaires sought the information leading to classifying HSP psychologists as FT-FFS, although they may, in part, also reflect one of the differences in the respondent sample.

The survey by Wellner and Mills asked directly "Are you in full-time private practice?" The Gottfredson and Dyer survey first asked whether the psychologist provided "psychotherapy, counseling, assessment or other *health* services" and subsequently asked "Do you independently provide fee-for-service health services, i.e., in individual or group practice?". The

present survey used a more detailed approach, utilizing the question format shown in Table 7. By summing the fee-for-service hours indicated for the various health categories, it was possible to include not only the usual direct in-office practice but also such areas as regular (but part-time) health consultation on a fee-for-service basis. Undoubtedly this careful questioning led, in large part, to the higher FT-FFS figures found in the present study, along with the corollary finding in the present study (discussed below) of fewer part-time FFS psychologists.

With "at least 28,000 psychologists" currently licensed (Stigall, Note 3), the present data would suggest there are about 10,360 (or 37% of) HSP licensed psychologist practitioners in full-time, fee-for-service clinical practice. Of the

Table 7: *Survey Question Used to Ascertain Salaried Versus Fee-for-Service Professional Activities*

12. For each category below, enter the *average hours per week* where you currently perform your psychological services. Please indicate which hours are salaried and which are fee-for-service hours. (Write the number of hours in each box and mark the corresponding circle to the right.)

(*Please include part-time work*)		No. of hrs./wk.	None	1–5 hrs.	6–10 hrs.	11–20 hrs.	21–30 hrs.	31–40 hrs.	Over 40 hrs.
Direct services to clients in private office practice	Salaried hours .... / Fee-for-service		○ ○	○ ○	○ ○	○ ○	○ ○	○ ○	○ ○
Direct services to clients in clinic or center	Salaried hours .... / Fee-for-service		○ ○	○ ○	○ ○	○ ○	○ ○	○ ○	○ ○
Direct services to clients in university health service	Salaried hours .... / Fee-for-service		○ ○	○ ○	○ ○	○ ○	○ ○	○ ○	○ ○
Direct services to hospital inpatients (general, psychiatric, or day/night care)	Salaried hours .... / Fee-for-service		○ ○	○ ○	○ ○	○ ○	○ ○	○ ○	○ ○
Health consultation (including mental health)	Salaried hours .... / Fee-for-service		○ ○	○ ○	○ ○	○ ○	○ ○	○ ○	○ ○
Health teaching (including mental health)	Salaried hours .... / Fee-for-service		○ ○	○ ○	○ ○	○ ○	○ ○	○ ○	○ ○
Health research/evaluation (including mental health)	Salaried hours .... / Fee-for-service		○ ○	○ ○	○ ○	○ ○	○ ○	○ ○	○ ○
Health program administration (including mental health)	Salaried hours .... / Fee-for-service		○ ○	○ ○	○ ○	○ ○	○ ○	○ ○	○ ○
Non-health professional, scientific or teaching services	Salaried hours .... / Fee-for-service		○ ○	○ ○	○ ○	○ ○	○ ○	○ ○	○ ○

PLEASE TOTAL YOUR ACTUAL PROFESSIONAL HOURS PER WEEK (i.e., sum the hours in column #1) and enter the total in the boxes and circles to the right ....

⓪ ① ② ③ ④ ⑤ ⑥ ⑦ ⑧ ⑨
⓪ ① ② ③ ④ ⑤ ⑥ ⑦ ⑧ ⑨

IF YOU ARE NOT INVOLVED IN *ANY* HEALTH/CLINICAL PRACTICE (EITHER SALARIED OR FEE-FOR-SERVICE) AND DO NOT PLAN TO ENGAGE IN SUCH PROFESSIONAL SERVICES IN 1977, PLEASE STOP HERE AND RETURN THIS QUESTIONNAIRE TO US IN THE POSTAGE PAID ENVELOPE.

HSP psychologists, 18% (13% of licensed psychologists) saw fee-for-service patients on a very part-time (VPT) basis (i.e., from 1 to 10 hours per week). The remaining 14% of HSP psychologists (10% of licensed psychologists) saw fee-for-service patients an aggregate of between 11 and 30 hours per week. Conversion of these data to full-time equivalents (FTE) reveals that there are approximately 12,850 FTE-HSP licensed psychologists in fee-for-service practice. This FTE estimate is only somewhat less than the number of FTE psychiatrists (excluding "psychiatrists in training") currently providing direct patient care on a fee-for-service or salaried basis (Reed, Myers, & Scheidemandel, 1972) but is 16% less than the 15,250 FTE health care psychologists reported in the Task Panel Report on Mental Health Personnel by the President's Commission on Mental Health (1978, Vol. 2, p. 484). Note also that most fee-for-service psychologists, even those classified as "full-time," also provided services other than fee-for-service practice. These services were primarily on a salaried basis, providing direct services to clients in clinics, or were in health-related professional, scientific, or teaching services.

Assuming that there are 12,850 FTE-HSP licensed psychologists in fee-for-service practice in the United States, and given that the median HSP psychologist in the present survey saw 12 patients per week on a fee-for-service basis (as well as seeing others on a salaried basis), these figures indicate that 154,200 patients are being seen each week by licensed FFS psychologists. Assuming that these psychologists engage in such FFS activities for 48 weeks per year and that the average patient is seen for seven visits, the data would further indicate that approximately 1,057,370 persons are seen (on a fee-for-service basis alone) by licensed psychologists each year. This number approximately doubles the estimate of the number of patients being seen by "private practice psychologists" in 1975 as estimated in the Task Panel Report on the Nature and Scope of the Problems in the *Report of the President's Commission on Mental Health* (1978, Vol. 2, p. 92).

The striking finding that 37% of all licensed psychologists were in full-time, fee-for-service health practice in mid-1977 warrants reference to other reported indexes of practice.

Peck, in 1969, found only 10% of licensed psychologists to be engaged in full-time, fee-for-service practice, while Garfield and Kurtz (1974) found in 1974 that 23% of their sample of "clinical psychologists" were in full-time, fee-for-service practice. Dörken (1977b), based on an earlier pilot study of a national sample, had reported that 7% of all psychologists (licensed or unlicensed) in 1975 were in full-time practice, a number equivalent to about 16% of all licensed psychologists. Then Wellner and Mills (1977), in the first national survey of licensed psychologists, found that 81.7% of health service providers were in private practice at least some of the time, with 25% of health service providers engaging in full-time practice. Of course, the Wellner and Mills percentages are reduced when discussed in terms of licensed psychologists rather than health service providers, so that only 18.4% of all licensed psychologists in 1976 were engaged in the full-time practice of psychology. Even so, the finding in the present 10-state study that 37% of licensed psychologists were in full-time, fee-for-service practice represents an estimate double that of Wellner and Mills (18.4%) and approximately 2½ times greater than the estimate of Gottfredson and Dyer (15.1%). Even if these three estimates (all of which were made during 1976–1977) are averaged, the resulting average indicates that 23.5% of all licensed psychologists are engaged in FT-FFS health care practice. This is a notable increase over the figures reported for earlier surveys.

The striking level of FT-FFS practice found in the present study is, then, probably due in part to the detailed nature of the questions but is also probably due to two synergistic factors: (a) the recent adoption of legislation that recognizes the practice of psychology and facilitates it, and (b) the heightened professionalization of psychology (Dörken & Cummings, 1978) and consequent interest in practice. This heightened interest in practice is likewise apparent in the number of recent licenses issued to psychologists across the United States.

Of the 10 states surveyed, only four had freedom-of-choice (i.e., direct recognition) legislation fully effective at the time of the present survey (New York, 1969; California, 1969,

1974; Ohio, 1974; and the District of Columbia, 1976). These four states accounted for about 24% of the U.S. population. Of the remaining states in the survey, Texas enacted direct-recognition legislation in May 1977, while the Illinois law became effective in July 1977. Thirty-five percent of the U.S. population resides in these six states. It is likely that such direct-recognition legislation will increase the numbers of HSP psychologists who engage in full-time, fee-for-service practice (Dörken & Webb, in press), although the effects of this legislation probably will not be apparent for a few more years.

In contrast to psychologists, 35% of psychiatrists derive their primary professional income from private practice (Arnhoff & Kumbar, 1973), with private practice accounting overall for 42% of psychiatric time (Whiting, 1969). It seems clear that the progressively increasing fee-for-service activity by psychologists reflects the growth and increased recognition of psychologists as health care practitioners, at least in ambulatory health care, (Dörken, 1976). The results of the present study show this increased involvement even more clearly than previous studies because of the more rigorous definition of health provider used in the present study and as a result of the more detailed questioning about specific fee-for-service activities.

In order to obtain a more detailed description of the current FFS practitioners, characteristics of these practitioners were tabulated separately from those of the other HSP psychologists who were salaried only. These data are presented in Table 8 and show the FFS practitioners, particularly those in full-time practice, to be significantly younger than HSP psychologists who are salaried only. Although the salaried HSP psychologists received their degrees and licenses at about the same time as their FFS colleagues, the salaried psychologists appear to be slightly more mobile. Significantly more FFS psychologists received their degrees in the state in which they currently are employed, and they have resided in their present states significantly more years. FFS psychologists, except those in very part-time practice, more often possessed the doctoral degree than did their salaried counterparts, and the FFS psychologists more often were male, particularly those in FT-FFS practice.

When viewed in terms of the types of services or procedures provided by fee-for-service practitioners, there is a broad general similarity in their practice emphasis by group, whether the practitioners are engaged in fee-for-service practice full-time, some of the time, or on a very part-time basis. As shown in Table 9, about two fifths of professional time is occupied in indi-

Table 8: *Comparisons of Salaried and Fee-for-Service Licensed Health Service Provider Psychologists*

Characteristic	HSP-salaried		VPT-FFS		HSP-FFS		FT-FFS	
	No.	%	No.	%	No.	%	No.	%
Age (median)	47.3		47.6		45.6		44.4	
Gender (male)	487	71.9	532	72.3	2,601	75.5	1,682	78.5
Education								
PhD/EdD/PsyD	593	86.3	640	86.0	3,111	89.6	1,956	90.5
Less than doctoral degree	94	13.7	104	13.4	360	10.4	204	9.5
Degree awarded								
In state currently employed	274	40.1	403	53.8	1,856	53.2	1,122	51.9
In another state	392	57.4	332	44.3	1,574	45.2	1,011	46.7
In foreign country	17	2.5	14	1.9	55	1.6	31	1.4
Year of highest degree (mean)	1,962.6		1,963.0		1,963.3		1,963.4	
Year received licensed (mean)	1,967.8		1,967.4		1,967.7		1,967.8	
Mobility								
Years employed in present state (median)	9.9		10.0		10.1		10.0	
Years resident in present state (median)	16.8		24.3		24.3		23.2	

Note. Abbreviations: HSP = health service provider; VPT = very part time; FFS = fee for service; FT = full time.

Table 9: *Mean Percentage of Fee-for-Service Practice by Procedure*

Procedure	FT-FFS	FFS	VPT-FFS
Individual therapy	42	41	36
Group therapy	7	7	6
Marriage family therapy	13	13	13
Behavior therapy	8	8	8
Biofeedback	2	2	2
Hypnosis	4	4	4
Assessment	15	16	18
Consultation	6	6	7
Other	4	4	6

Note. Abbreviations: FT = full time; FFS = fee for service; VPT = very part time.

vidual psychotherapy and one sixth of the time in assessment. On only these two procedures was any trend toward a difference reported. Emphasis on individual psychotherapy seems somewhat greater the greater the involvement in practice, but the converse may hold, to an extent, for assessment. The more recently developed procedures of behavior therapy and biofeedback account for only one tenth of FFS time.

Psychologists Engaged in Part-Time, Fee-for-Service Practice

Eighteen percent of licensed HSP psychologists in the present study engaged in fee-for-service practice on a very part-time, or occasional, basis (i.e., 10 or fewer hours per week). This was notably fewer than the 40% of licensed HSP psychologists whom Gottfredson and Dyer (1978) found to be in "private practice" 10 or fewer hours per week. The primary reason for this difference probably is the same as that discussed above regarding full-time FFS practitioners (Gottfredson and Dyer found fewer FT-FFS practitioners than the present study did). That is, the present survey question (see Table 7) was more detailed and elicited more information about FFS practice, perhaps causing more HSP psychologists to be categorized as engaging in FT-FFS practice.

The very part-time (VPT) FFS practitioners in the present study were notably different from the FT-FSS practitioners. These occa-

sional, or VPT-FSS practitioners were older, more likely to be female, and less likely to possess the doctoral degree. However, they did not differ in terms of the year in which they received their highest degrees in psychology or the year in which they received their licenses (see Table 8). As noted below, the VPT-FFS practitioner typically charges lower fees. Further, the clients of these VPT-FSS practitioners are on the average significantly ($p < .01$) more often in the age ranges from 12 to 17 or less than 12 and are significantly more likely to have been seen by the psychologist because of mental retardation and/or developmental disabilities.

The implications of these findings are of some concern. It appears that a disproportionate percentage of children, particularly those suffering mental retardation and/or developmental disabilities, are being seen by psychologists who, as a group, are somewhat less well trained and likely to be less well-equipped in their office practice to follow through with their clients. In fact, this group of psychologists spends a significantly greater percentage of its time (27%) in psychodiagnostic assessment functions than FT-FFS practitioners (20%) do, suggesting that these VPT-FFS practitioners are more likely to receive cases from others only for assessment. This notion is supported by the finding that the median number of client visits to the VPT-FFS practitioner is significantly less both for the under 18 age group (5 vs. 7 visits) and for clients 18 and over (12 vs. 17 visits).

Fees of Psychologists

The survey asked about fees charged in 1976 and in 1977. The median hourly fee in 1977 charged by the FFS psychologist for psychotherapy was $40 (see Table 10), with the middle 50% charging from $34 to $44 (the middle 80% charged from $25 to $49). This represents a $5 increase over 1976, at which time the median fee was $35, with the middle 50% charging from $29 to $40. This compares to the mean hourly fee of $36 for outpatient psychotherapy paid to psychologists under CHAMPUS in 1975 (Dörken, 1977). For 90-minute group therapy,

Table 10: *Fees of Health Service Provider Psychologists for Individual and Group Psychotherapy in 1976 and 1977*

Type of therapy and year	FT-FFS	FFS (total)	VPT
Individual therapy			
1977			
Mean hourly fee	39.65	38.44	34.95
Median hourly fee	39.88	39.71	35.03
Modal hourly fee	40	40	40
1976			
Mean hourly fee	36.52	35.45	32.27
Median hourly fee	35.31	35.11	30.50
Modal hourly fee	35	35	35
Group therapy (90′)			
1977			
Mean fee	21.46	21.32	20.18
Median fee	19.76	19.66	15.25
Modal fee	20	15	15
1976			
Mean fee	19.87	19.93	18.68
Median fee	15.46	15.41	15.06
Modal fee	15	15	10

Note. Abbreviations: FT = full time; FFS = fee for service; VPT = very part time.

the median per-person fee in the present study for 1977 was $20 (the middle 50% fees being from $15 to $25). In 1976 the median fee was $15 (the middle 50% charged from $15 to $20).

As shown in Table 10, the fees charged in 1977 by FT-FFS health care psychologists were significantly higher than fees charged by psychologists who engaged in 10 or fewer hours of fee-for-service practice per week (VPT-FFS group). This finding applied to median per-person group therapy fees ($20 vs. $15) as well as median fees for individual psychotherapy ($40 vs. $35). In terms of mean fees charged in 1977 on an hourly basis for individual psychotherapy, the fees were significantly higher the more the psychologist was involved in practice. A mean fee comparison of VPT-FFS to FFS to FT-FFS psychologists is illustrative: $34.95 to $38.44 to $39.65. Even the increase in mean fee from 1976 to 1977 was more—$2.68 to $2.99 to $3.13—and ranged from an 8.3% to an 8.6% increase.

By way of perspective, the fees of HSP psychologists compare favorably with those of psychiatrists, who in 1973 charged a median hourly fee of $35 (Owens, 1974); psychologists' median hourly fee did not reach $35 until 1976. It is of

further interest that in 1974 the actual cost per hour of service delivered at a community mental health center was found to be $40 (Van Buskirk, 1974), a figure that represents the median fee charged in 1977 by psychologists for fee-for-service practice. While there are some differences between states and for certain procedures, overall it appears that the fees of psychologists are somewhat less than those of psychiatrists (Dörken, 1977b). The median fee for individual psychotherapy by a psychiatrist in the spring of 1978 has been reported as $51, with a mean of $53 (Kirchner, 1978; Mattera, 1979).

Incomes of HSP Psychologists

The incomes of licensed psychologists engaged in health care may be viewed along several dimensions. As seen in Figure 5, total gross professional income at the 25th, 50th (median), and 75th percentiles, respectively, appears to increase progressively as one moves from salaried-only psychologists ($N = 576$; $Q_1 = $21,306; $Q_2 = $25,476; $Q_3 = $30,585) to salaried psychologists who also have some part-time fee income ($N = 1,207$; $Q_1 = $23,810; $Q_2 = $30,532; $Q_3 = $38,719) to psychologists in full-time, fee-for-service practice ($N = 1,900$; $Q_1 = $25,691; $Q_2 = $34,097; $Q_3 = $43,253). Combining these categories (see Figure 6) revealed that for HSP psychologists in general ($N = 3,683$), the incomes were $Q_1 = $23,886; $Q_2 = $31,049; $Q_3 = $40,366. Note that the incomes for FT-FFS psychologists reported here are just slightly higher than those of doctoral level psychologists in private practice as found by Gottfredson and Dyer (1978): $Q_1 = $23,027; $Q_2 = $31,521; $Q_3 = $41,629.

The data also revealed a modest but clear relationship between annual income and the age of the HSP psychologist. The data in Table 8 show that annual gross income increases until age 60, at which time income declines. However, the difference in average gross income between ages 35 and 55 is only about $6,500. Expressed differently, when this $6,500 is considered over a 20-year time span (i.e., age 35 to 55), the average yearly increase is only about $325, or 1%.

Whereas the fees charged by psychologist

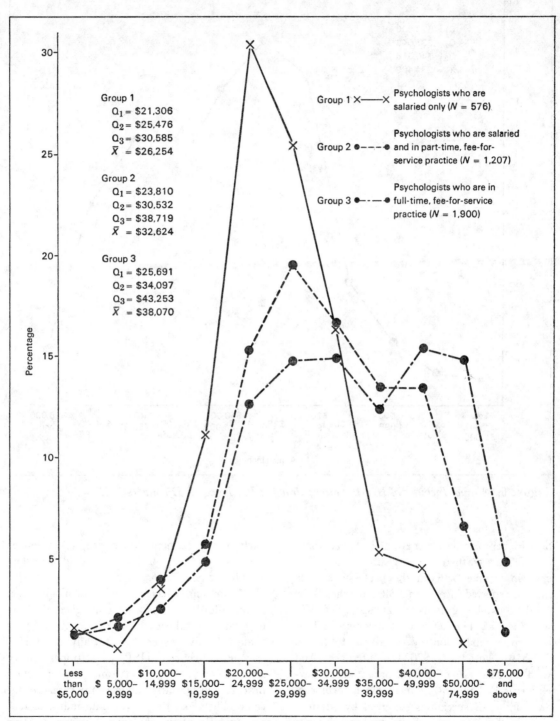

Figure 5: *Annual Incomes of Salaried and Fee-for-Service Health Service Provider Psychologists During 1977*

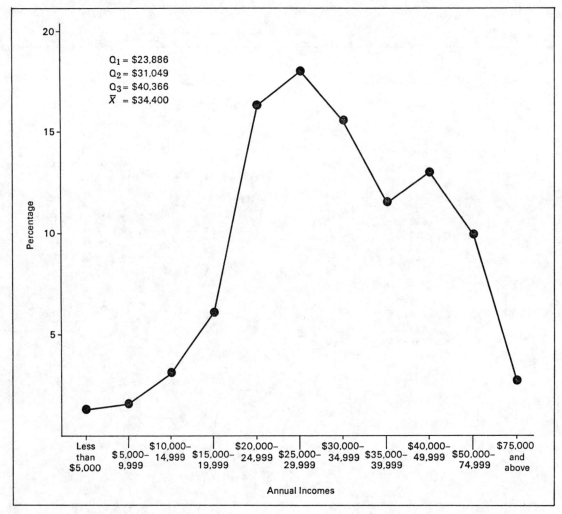

$Q_1 = \$23,886$
$Q_2 = \$31,049$
$Q_3 = \$40,366$
$\bar{X} = \$34,400$

Figure 6: *Annual Incomes of Health Service Provider Psychologists During 1977 (N = 3,683)*

practitioners are only somewhat less than those of psychiatrists, there is a very substantial difference in income between the professions. The median reported income (net after overhead) for FT-FFS psychologists in the late spring of 1977 was $34,097. The net median income of office-based psychiatrists for 1977 was $53,790 (mean $55,510), close to a $20,000 difference. And with the exception of general practitioners, psychiatrists had the lowest median net income of any of the 12 specialties surveyed by Mattera (1979): "The typical office-based psychiatrist has only 48 patient visits during a 58-hour work week." Thus, the income difference seems attributable to four conditions: (a) somewhat higher fees, (b) probably more satisfactory third-

party reimbursement experience, (c) a longer work week (48 vs. 42 hours), and (d) a better-established hospital practice.

Apparently, few licensed psychologists are, or can afford to be, salaried only, given the narrow range of salaried income (see Figure 5) for "salaried only" psychologists. Only about 16% of these licensed HSP practitioners were salaried only. Even part-time, fee-for-service practice substantially enhances the spread of income. Then too, the survey data indicated that among FT-FFS psychologists, at least a major proportion of them have income from sources other than fee-for-service practice. While 88% of these FT-FFS practitioners reported their total income and 93% reported their fee-for-service income, 49% also reported that they received additional income from salary, and 40% reported some further professional income from still other sources.

Nevertheless, assuming that FT-FFS practitioners must provide for their own "fringe benefits," it is apparent that even with allowing 22% of total net income (*Report of the National Commission on State Workmen's Compensation Laws*, 1972) for such fringe benefits (office expenses had already been deducted from the total net income reported), the net total income of FT-FFS practitioners still was somewhat higher than the net total income of "salaried only" psychologists. However, it should be noted that the net total income of FT-FFS practitioners was (a) functionally less than that of HSP psychologists who were salaried but also had some part-time practice, and (b) functionally less than the incomes of HSP psychologists in general. Thus, although increased and growing involvement by psychologists in private practice appears evident, the net income of full-time practitioner psychologists apparently is not higher than that of the majority of their HSP colleagues in mid-1977. There also is an evident "floor" (approximately $20,000) and an upper "ceiling" on the incomes of HSP psychologists. Only .5% of HSP psychologists reported an annual salary at or above $50,000, and only 12.9% reported a total annual gross income at this level. Among FT-FFS practitioners, this annual income level is achieved by 19.6%.

A hypothetical projection will set FT-FFS practice in further perspective. Assume that the "average" FT-FFS practitioners saw 35 clients per week for 48 weeks, that they charged the 1977 median fee of $40, and that all of the 35 client-hours per week were booked and paid for during the year (an unlikely occurrence). Such a set of assumptions would yield a *gross* annual income of $67,200. When this figure is reduced by, say, 23% ($15,456) for office expense overhead (Mattera, 1979) and is also reduced by 22% ($14,784) for fringe benefits (*Report of the National Commission on State Workmen's Compensation Laws*, 1972), our hypothetical FT-FFS practitioner will have earned a net equivalent of $36,960 for providing 1,680 hourly clinical visits. It should be noted that even a highly efficient organization such as the

Kaiser Permanente Medical Group of Northern California projects only 1,200 hours annually of direct clinical service by its psychologists. A further benchmark for psychologists' income is the salary of a GS-13-level Veterans Administration (VA) psychologist ($26,022–$33,825). The VA is the single largest employer of psychologists in the country, and more than one half of their psychologists are classified at the GS-13 level.

Clients of Fee-for-Service Health Providers: A Cross Section

Psychotherapy clients have been described as typically YAVIS (young, attractive, verbal, intelligent, and successful) by Schofield (1967) and predominantly from the middle and upper classes of society (Albee, 1977), even though several recent studies (Sharfstein, Taube, & Goldberg, 1977; Stern, 1977) have shown little or no relation between such variables and acceptance as psychotherapy clients. Information exists about the YAVIS and social class characteristics of clients in community mental health centers and other publicly funded facilities (e.g., Sharfstein et al., 1977; Stern, 1977), but little is known about the characteristics of clients of FFS psychologists, although Marmor (1975) did conduct a similar survey for clients of psychiatrists. Though the present study could not measure all of the YAVIS characteristics (e.g., verbalness or attractiveness) of the respondents' patients, some estimates of the other dimensions were obtained. Some notable differences from middle- or upper-class YAVIS characteristics are apparent and clearly indicate that the clients of FFS psychologists are *not* limited to the upper or middle classes.

The present survey sought information on the characteristics of the last fee-for-service patient seen by each FFS psychologist prior to filling out the survey questionnaire. Thus, each FFS psychologist contributed one case to the sample, providing a cross section of 3,319 patients. This cross-sectional approach is similar to that used by Marmor (1975) with clients of psychiatrists, and although such an approach has certain advantages, potential biases nevertheless result from using this "last patient" approach. These have been discussed at length by Albee (1976).

Age

The median age for these clients of FFS practitioners was 31, slightly older than the 1977 U.S. median age of 29 (U.S. Bureau of the Census, 1978c).

As shown in Table 11, 50% of the cases in the combined sample were in the age range from 24 to 38, with a clear concentration of cases apparent in the 20 to 44 age group (see Figure 7). This age-range pattern for clients of FFS psychologists replicates exactly (a) the pattern in the report of the Social and Rehabilitation Services of the U.S. Department of Health, Education, and Welfare concerning the ages of mentally ill clients being rehabilitated in 1969 (Wiggins, 1976), and (b) the age clustering of patients of private-practice psychiatrists in 1973 (Marmor, 1975).

Although the distribution of client ages is reasonably widespread, as can be seen in Figure 7, there clearly were age groups within the U.S. population that were not involved with the FFS practitioners. Only 2.8% of the patients in the present survey were age 55 or older, and only .6% were age 65 or older. In contrast, 11% of the population in these 10 states in 1977 was age 65 or older (U.S. Bureau of the Census, 1978c). Similarly, 16% of the clients were younger than age 18, compared to 29% within the 10 states surveyed.

For further analyses, the present sample was divided into adults (age 18 or older) and children (age 17 or younger). The means, medians, quartiles (Q_1 and Q_3) and modes of ages for the adult and child groups are reported in Table 11. The median age of the adult sample was 33 ($\overline{X}$ = 34.48, sd = 9.90); 25% were between the ages of 18 and 28, and 25% were age 40 or older.

Gender

The adult sample contained fewer males (43%) than females. This finding was significantly reversed for the child sample, which, as shown in Table 11, had 64% males.

Table 11: *Gender, Age, Marital, Ethnic, and Educational Characteristics of Clients of Fee-for-Service Psychologists*

Characteristic	Adult (age 18 or over)		Child (age 17 or under)		Combined	
	No.	%	No.	%	No.	%
Gender (male)	1,143	43	325	64	1,470	46
Age						
Mean	34.5		12.2		31.2	
Q_1	27.6		9.3		24.3	
Median	32.5		12.8		30.7	
Q_3	40.1		15.4		38.2	
Mode	30		16		30	
Marital status						
Single	847	31	466	94	1,313	41
Married	1,340	50	22	4	1,392	43
Separated/Divorced	490	18	9	2	499	15
Widowed	36	1	0	0	36	1
Ethnic groups						
Caucasian	2,543	93	461	90	3,004	93
Negro	90	3	34	7	124	4
Other	90	3	20	3	110	3
Education						
Grade 8 or under	40	1	273	52	314	10
Grades 9–12	583	21	208	40	791	24
Some college	689	25	12	2	700	21
College graduate	1,475	53	3	6	1,507	45

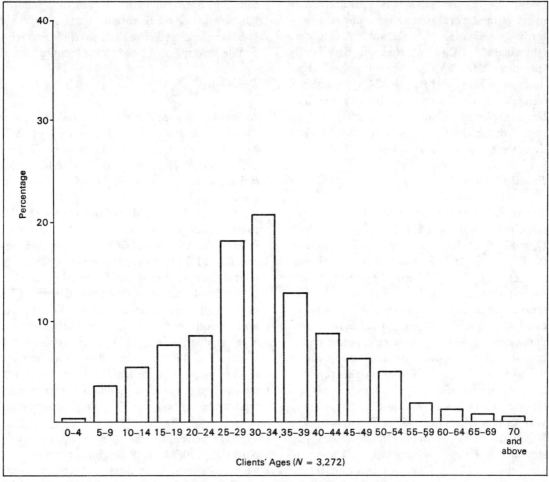

Figure 7: *Distribution of Ages of Clients Seen by Fee-for-Service Psychologists in 1977*

Marital Status

Fifty percent of the adult clients of FFS psychologists were married, 31% were single, 18% were separated or divorced, and 1% were widowed (Table 11). In the child grouping, 6% of these clients, although "children," were either married, separated, or divorced.

Ethnic Groups

Ethnic minority representation among fee-for-service patients clearly is below that within the general population (approximately 15%) of the 10 states surveyed in the present study (U.S. Bureau of the Census, 1978a). The vast majority (93%) of clients were white/Caucasian, and the remaining total were composed of black (4%) and Chicano-Spanish, Asian-American,

and other ethnic minorities (3%) (see Table 11). Within the child sample, ethnic representation was slightly more widespread, with approximately 10% being nonwhite.

Education

The median adult client of the FFS psychologist had graduated from college, although fully 22% of these clients had a high school education or less (Table 11), compared with 35% of the U.S. population in 1977 (U.S. Bureau of the Census, 1978b). For the child patients, the median education was seventh grade.

Employment

In the adult sample, a surprisingly large percentage (approximately 24%) were unemployed (see Table 12). Although it is not known how many of these persons were unemployed voluntarily, examination of the family income data (showing 6% of the adult clients to have family incomes under $5,000) would suggest that perhaps as many as 18% (i.e., 24% unemployed minus 6% having incomes less than $5,000) may be unemployed voluntarily. Of interest with regard to the child patients is that fully 14% of them were reported to be employed.

Family Income

The median family gross annual income for the combined sample was $20,259 ($Q_1$ = $12,937, Q_3 = $29,859). In comparison, the U.S. median family income in 1977 was $16,010 (U.S. Bureau of the Census, 1978d). The present results suggest that although most patients of fee-for-service psychologists are relatively well-educated, these patients do not appear to be as economically successful as might be expected on the basis of their education. Approximately 2% of the patients of these FFS psychologists reported a family income of zero, and approximately 5% reported a family income of less than $5,000 per year (Table 12). This total of 7% compares to 9% of the U.S. population in 1977 who had similarly low family incomes (U.S. Bureau of the Census, 1978d). Thus, in terms of client income, FFS psychologists are serving families who are better off financially than the average U.S. family; nonetheless these psychologists see a sizable percentage of low-income families.

Residence

As can be seen in Table 12, the percentages of clients (both adult and child) of FFS psychologists who live in the inner city or in rural areas are, respectively, 3% and 5%. The residence locations were overwhelmingly urban (49%) or suburban (43%).

The above data describing clients of FFS psychologists suggest some notable differences from the YAVIS mode but at the same time suggest that FFS psychologists are not yet as active with the unserved or the underserved of the U.S. population as might be desirable. Even so, FFS psychologists clearly have not limited their practices exclusively to YAVIS, middle-class clients. The age distribution, while overly concentrated in the 20 to 45 age range, shows a median age of the patients significantly older than the median age of the U.S. population, even though the population over age 50 is highly underrepresented.

The present findings may reflect, at least in part, the youthfulness of psychology health service practitioners. In support of this notion is the

Table 12: *Employment, Family Income, and Residential Characteristics of Clients of Fee-for-Service Psychologists*

Characteristic	Adult (age 18 or over)		Child (age 17 or under)		Combined	
	No.	%	No.	%	No.	%
Employed	2,104	76.2	68	14	2,173	67
Family income						
Under $5,000	176	6	37	7	213	7
$5,000–$9,999	258	9	35	7	293	9
$10,000–$14,999	437	16	81	16	519	16
$15,000–$19,999	502	18	68	14	571	18
$20,000–$24,999	439	16	61	12	500	15
$25,000–$29,999	301	11	47	9	348	11
$30,000–$39,999	258	9	77	15	335	10
$40,000–$49,999	149	6	37	8	187	6
$50,000 and above	217	8	60	12	277	8
Residence						
Urban	1,385	50	211	41	1,597	49
Inner city	99	4	15	3	114	3
Suburban	1,136	41	257	50	1,394	43
Rural	133	5	36	7	169	5

finding of Wellner and Mills (1977) and of the present study that HSP psychologists engaged in practice with the elderly were themselves significantly older than other HSP psychologists. Another factor is the lack of legislative recognition of HSP fee-for-service psychologists as qualified, independent practitioners under Medicare programs, thus essentially eliminating FFS psychological services for the elderly except when the patient can pay from personal resources. Even so, Eisdorfer and Lawton (1973) found a severe and generalized underutilization of various mental health services by the elderly, even when available. The data, then, suggest that future training of psychologists could benefit from increased emphasis on services to the elderly.

Financing of Service

The financing of psychological health services by the patient or family in this cross section appears to be a major problem. One half of the patients of fee-for-service providers had *no* third-party coverage, either public or private, to reimburse them for the services being provided (see Table 13). This lack of coverage was as true for children as for adults. Of those patients who did have such third-party coverage, however, the median percentage of charges covered for the combined sample was 65%, with children having slightly better coverage (70%) than adults (65%). The family income figures reported above point up even more keenly the need to provide in some systematic fashion for the anticipation of expenses for psychological health services. Although the need for additional third-party reimbursement clearly is great, recognition also should be given to the apparent improvement in the amount of coverage in the last decade. Myers (1970) reported that in 1967 only 26% of patients had insurance coverage for outpatient care. Of those covered, 44% received coverage of 50% of the costs, with 20% having less than 50% covered by third-party payment.

Although psychotherapy is alleged to be very expensive, the median bills of the clients of FFS psychologists compare favorably with bills charged for various medical, surgical, dental, or other health care procedures such as orthodonture, hysterectomies, or treatment of chronic diabetes or hypertension. The data indicate the median adult patient to have acquired a bill of approximately $665, while the median bill for child patients was approximately $290. These estimates are figured by multiplying the median

Table 13: *Number of Visits, Visit Frequency, and Percentage of Fee Covered by Third Party for Clients of Fee-for-Service Psychologists*

Item	Adult (age 18 or over)		Child (age 17 or under)		Combined	
	No.	%	No.	%	No.	%
Number of visits						
Mean	52.7		26.2		48.5	
Q_1	5.7		2.7		5.0	
Median	16.6		7.2		15.0	
Q_3	49.9		20.0		40.0	
Mode	1		2		1	
Visit frequency						
Daily	16	1	2	1	18	1
Several times weekly	423	15	49	10	473	15
Weekly	1,752	65	276	57	2,028	63
Every second week	255	9	59	12	314	10
Monthly/intermittently	262	10	96	20	359	11
Percentage of fee covered by third party						
None	1,374	50	259	50	1,633	50
1%–20%	97	4	11	2	108	3
21%–40%	149	5	20	4	169	5
41%–60%	359	13	61	12	421	13
61%–80%	450	16	75	14	526	16
81% or more	341	12	91	18	432	13

hourly fee ($40) by the median number of visits (see Table 13) for adults (16.64 visits) and children (7.18 visits), respectively. The median number of client visits revealed in the present study was higher than past studies have reported for psychologists; most past studies have shown the median number of client visits to be between 6 and 9 (Bent, 1976). Dörken (1977a) found an average of 13.9 outpatient visits under the CHAMPUS plan. However, because the present study sampled the last client seen by each practitioner, the likelihood of sampling a longer term case may have been increased.

The modal frequency of visits is weekly, both for children (57%) and for adults (65%). However, 32% of the children and 19% of the adults were being seen on a less frequent basis than once per week. Of particular note is the finding that 18% of the children and 8% of the adults were being seen on an intermittent basis less frequently than once per month.

Client Variables and Age of the Fee-for-Service Psychologist

In an attempt to ascertain whether the clients of FFS psychologists differed depending on the age of the practitioner, the basic data on the clients were tabulated for subgroups of FFS psychologists of differing ages. These results are presented in Table 14. No trends are noticeable for the variables of ethnic group, employment, or gender of the client. However, the data show that FFS psychologists age 50 and over see, on the average, patients who are several years older ($p < .01$) than those of psychologists below the age of 50. It is also notable that approximately two thirds (64%) of the FFS psychologists are younger than age 50.

Perhaps the most striking finding in this regard was the continuous decrease in the number of visits, the younger the psychologist. It seems clear that the younger psychologists are

Table 14: *Differences in Fee-for-Service Clients as a Function of the Age of Fee-for-Service Psychologists*

Client characteristic	Ages of Psychologists					
	<29	30–39	40–49	50–59	60–69	70+
Age of client						
$\overline{X}$	30.78	29.86	30.85	32.77	32.50	34.63
Standard error	2.00	.35	.39	.42	.78	2.45
N	40	1,056	976	854	288	35
Median	30.50	29.66	30.41	32.39	32.19	39.00
% of clients >50	10	6.2	7.4	10.7	11.8	8.6
% clients >65 (estimated)	6.5	5.6	6.5	7.1	7.1	9.4
Education of client[a]						
$\overline{X}$	5.18	5.01	5.04	5.22	5.06	5.15
Standard error	.31	.05	.06	.06	.11	.34
N	40	1,072	989	861	292	34
Family income						
$\overline{X}$	19,875	21,219	22,782	24,740	24,560	18,676
Standard error	1,160	392	450	494	871	2,036
N	40	1,050	976	835	284	34
% of fee paid by third party						
$\overline{X}$	37.74	33.21	33.48	28.09	28.10	27.06
Standard error	5.47	1.10	1.14	1.16	2.12	6.29
N	39	1,061	984	857	288	35
No. of visits by client						
$\overline{X}$	29.36	36.29	48.52	57.43	66.22	66.39
Standard error	8.46	2.21	3.25	4.25	8.34	20.06
N	39	1,063	971·	846	285	36
Median	6.75	12.46	15.14	16.10	19.86	10.50

Note. No trends were evident for frequency of visits, sex, ethnic group, or employment.
[a] The code "5" represents "some college."

seeing clients for significantly fewer visits, on the average, than are older psychologists. This likely reflects the increased training of younger psychologists in short-term intervention techniques (and de-emphasis on long-term psychoanalytic approaches) or possibly shows that the older FFS psychologists have acquired in their practices a disproportionate percentage of severely disabled persons as clients, who thus need supportive or longer term care. Clearly, more study of this finding is indicated.

The percentage of the psychologist's fee that was covered by third-party reimbursement decreased as the age of the FFS psychologist increased. This likely is a function of the above finding regarding the increased number of visits for patients of older psychologists. That is, the client may have used up his or her benefits over the course of the relatively high number of visits.

Third-Party Reimbursement

The average HSP psychologist engaged in fee-for-service practice (FFS = 3,494) reported 34% of the clients during 1976 to have "private or employer health disability insurance" from which they were reimbursed. Another 14% of the clients of FFS psychologists were covered by public assistance programs for third-party reimbursement. Fully 46% of the clients, however,

were *not* covered by any third-party reimbursement (a figure in keeping with the 49.7% reported above for the "last client seen"). In part, this lack of insurance for outpatient psychological care is due to subscribers' more commonly having hospital insurance than comprehensive health insurance. Also, as noted previously, at the time of the survey six states (Alabama, Florida, Illinois, Rhode Island, South Carolina, and Texas) were without freedom-of-choice legislation enabling direct access to, and reimbursement for, insured health care services provided by psychologists.

In the survey, specific and detailed information was requested from the health practitioner psychologists about their fee-for-service experiences in third-party reimbursement. Particularly, information was sought concerning experiences of the FFS psychologists with individual carriers. Since the FT-FFS psychologists (N = 2,165) have the most active private-practice involvement, only the experiences of these practitioners rather than the entire group of FFS psychologists are reported, since the FT-FFS psychologists have broader experience with the various carriers.

The proportion of the 2,165 FT-FFS psychologists billing specific carriers/plans for total visits in 1976 is summarized in the tabulation of their claim experiences in Table 15. At a

Table 15: *Claim Experiences of Full-Time, Fee-for-Service Psychologists: Claims Year 1976*

Third party	% psychologists billing	% no visits	No. visits billed	% all visits	Average no. visits to psychologist	% favorable claim experience	No. claims to PSRC
Medicare	11.4	84.2	6,540	1.4	26	40	103
Medicaid	20.0	73.5	34,571	7.6	80	60	235
Rehabilitation	29.9	59.8	49,203	10.8	76	85	129
Worker's Compensation	12.5	82.7	7,470	1.6	28	79	31
CHAMPUS	34.5	56.7	48,500	10.6	65	82	117
Foundations	8.3	87.9	12,428	2.7	70	86	53
Blue Cross/Blue Shield	57.1	28.9	111,028	24.3	90	66	157
Aetna	44.8	41.0	40,499	8.8	42	87	71
Metropolitan	32.6	54.7	29,544	6.5	42	82	34
Occidental	17.8	74.1	12,033	2.6	31	89	30
Prudential	38.5	48.3	38,342	8.4	46	90	31
Travelers	36.3	50.5	30,978	6.8	39	85	38
Other 1	20.0	38.1	27,831	6.1	64	84	56
Other 2	6.5	66.4	8,424	1.8	61	86	—
Total			457,391	100.0			1,085

Note. Base N = 2,165. PSRC = Professional Standards Review Committee.

median fee of $35 in 1976, and an average of 211 visits for each FT-FFS psychologist, these visits carried an average reimbursement value of $7,385 per practitioner.

Reimbursement experience varied markedly by type of third-party payer. The present survey sought information about selected private carriers as well as about major governmental plans. Of the private carriers, Aetna, Travelers, Metropolitan, and Prudential were selected because they reported the highest dollar volume of health premiums paid in 1976; Occidental was chosen because of its particularly high health insurance volume in California (U.S. Department of Health, Education, and Welfare, 1976). In 1976 only two states recognized psychologists by statute under Worker's Compensation programs (Montana and Ohio; such law did not become effective in California until 1978). Foundations for Medical Care are a western, largely California, phenomenon, and Occidental Life is headquartered in California. Thus it is not surprising that the 10-state data show a high proportion of all psychologists (83%, 88%, and 77%) billing no visits to these programs. Otherwise, it is only in the Social Security programs of Medicare and Medicaid that the percentage of non-billings reached 84% and 73%, respectively. Medicare, of course, only accepts psychological assessment and only upon medical referral. Most states have not elected to include psychological services in their state Medicaid plans (only California, Ohio, and New York, except New York City, of these 10 states).

Between 82% and 90% of the psychologists reported favorable experience with such major commercial carriers as Aetna, Travelers, Prudential, and Occidental. But only 66% reported a similar favorable experience with Blue Cross/Blue Shield (the "Blues"), very significantly lower ($\chi^2 = 441$, $p < .001$) than for the commercial carriers. That these psychologists billed the highest proportion of claims to the "Blues" highlights the magnitude of the problem. In dollar terms, therefore, for the FT-FFS practitioners in these 10 states, over $1.3 million worth of claims to Blue Cross/Blue Shield were often or regularly reduced, rejected, or questioned. When prorated to include the 12,850 FTE psychologists in FFS practice in the United States, this dollar amount in 1976 exceeded $7.84 million (111,028 × 34% × $35 × 12,850 ÷ 2,165). By figuring more conservatively using only the 10,050 FTE psychologists found by Wellner and Mills (1977), this formula yields a dollar amount of $6.13 million.

Favorable experience was reported by from 82% to 85% of these FT-FFS practitioners for such government programs as CHAMPUS and Rehabilitation, but only for 60% and 40%, respectively, under Medicaid and Medicare (see Table 15). The Foundation for Medical Care (FMCs), a new and growing type of Individual Practice Association recognized under the HMO Development Act (PL 93-222) (Dörken, 1978), though medically controlled and billed by few psychologists to date (8.3%), accorded a favorable (86%) experience to psychologists serving as FMC providers. Only one eighth of the HSP-FFS psychologists were engaged in Worker's Compensation services. However, this is a major market, and one for which quite favorable experience (79%) was reported despite the limited formal recognition of psychologists under law for such services at this time. A comparison between states having and not having freedom-of-choice legislation, which recognizes the practicing psychologist for direct reimbursement under health insurance, is reported separately (Dörken & Webb, in press).

Professional Standards Review Committees

As coverage by insurance companies of psychological services has increased, both psychologists and insurance companies have been concerned about keeping appropriate controls on the rising cost of health care. For several years most state psychological associations have had professional standards review committees (PSRCs) to review specific cases upon request and to provide the public, the third-party payer, and the psychologists with an accessible avenue of redress should a question arise over the nature of any fee or service rendered by a psychologist. The present survey elicited information on the frequency during 1976 that psychologists' bills had been referred to PSRCs either by the third-party payers or by consumers (see Table 15). Eighty-seven percent of the psychologists had not had *any* of their bills referred to PSRCs during the entire year. Less than 10% of the FFS psychologists had more than one bill referred to PSRCs for peer review.

If one uses the data presented earlier that the average FFS psychologist had 39 patient visits per week (either on a salaried or fee-for-service basis) and if one assumes that each FFS psychologist saw patients for 48 weeks per year and that these 3,490 FFS practitioners were involved in about 6.5 million visits to psychologists, the data then suggest that of the approximately 6.5 million visits in 1976, only 479 were referred to PSRCs, a ratio of 1 to 13,500. This rather striking lack of referrals to PSRCs is consistent with the reports of several major insurance companies (Dörken, 1976) that they have experienced no untoward utilization experience upon recognizing psychological services in group health plans. This reflects positively on the soundness of psychological practice. Indeed, Wolberg (1967, p. 324) concluded that "taking into consideration the total graduate education, specialty, training, and supervision, it would seem doubtful that psychologists are exceeded by any other mental health profession in the extensiveness of preparation for the private practice of psychotherapy."

Discussion

It is apparent that major changes are under way in the practice of psychology. This is due, in part to the expanding science base of psychological practice; in part to the increasing application of psychological procedures to health as distinct from mental health problems; in part to the broadening array of laws that recognize the practice of psychology; and in part to the increased productivity of graduate programs and professional schools of psychology and the now more common orientation of graduates to clinical practice. All of these aspects of the changes have been reported on previously. It is when they are viewed in the aggregate, however, that one becomes aware not only of the extent of the shift to clinical practice but of the potential for even further development.

Psychology, as a young profession, has yet to experience the replacement turnover of substantial numbers leaving the work force through death, disability, or retirement. This, coupled with recently expanded doctoral-level production, brings a time-limited added accumulation of psychologists to the profession's human resources pool. The fact that many more psychologists are licensed than practice full time is another aspect of the potential of this profession for a rapidly heightened involvement in practice (Dörken, 1977b). It is in the age range from 50 to 54 that we find 17% of these psychologists. Some 900 annually will be needed in 10 years to offset the natural attrition in existing positions through age retirement (Table 1), less than one third of the current doctoral-level production. Thus, the profession of psychology can be particularly responsive to an expanded need for health care and to supply the competition that can stimulate both innovation and cost control.

While they have an equally high level of professional training, licensed health service practitioner psychologists are less mobile geographically than their salaried colleagues. To that extent, the former are a more stable factor for local health service planning. Moreover, McGuire (Note 4) estimates that with a 20-visit limit for mental disorder under national health insurance, the cost would escalate 52% without psychologists but only 11% with their inclusion. Also, the current fees of psychologists ($40 median, 1977) appear to be competitive with those of psychiatrists and also with the per-patient-hour costs of seeing patients in community mental health centers.

There is ample indication that psychologists are increasingly engaged in health care (Wright, 1976) and are continuing to pioneer in the development of procedures effective in resolving specific health problems ("Biofeedback in Action," 1973; Fordyce, 1973). Further, since "54% of the mentally disordered receive mental health services primarily from the general health care system" rather than from practitioners specifically trained for these services (President's Commission on Mental Health, 1978), the growing availability of psychological services should lead to improved health care.

The extent to which psychologists provide health services, as described throughout this survey, and the extent to which they receive referrals from and make referrals to other practitioners and community resources, suggests that they are a needed and involved component of local health care services. Inasmuch as health practitioners are usually major decision makers regarding care beyond the first visit and decisions that materially affect treatment/health objectives, potential benefits, utilization, and cost, it appears that practicing psychologists should be systematically recognized and involved in health planning, health resource management, and health legislation.

The referral linkage deserves further comment. While some psychiatrists emphasize the need of psychiatry to serve a "gatekeeper" role in which the psychiatrist determines whether and when to refer to a psychologist, such an adjunct role is hardly consistent with the public expectations of a licensed, independent health profession. According to this survey, rather few of the psychologists' clients overall were actually referred by psychiatrists. Indeed, somewhat more were referred by nonpsychiatric physicians. Similarly, psychologists in turn refer somewhat more patients to physicians other than psychiatrists.

In addition to current practitioners, it is the current trainees in the "pipeline" who offer some indication of what can be expected in terms of future services. The most common procedure of either psychiatrists or psychologists (Dörken, 1977b) is psychotherapy. Apart from training in behavioral science and personal sensitivity, effectiveness hinges on the ability to communicate through language and knowledge of the culture. Only 1.6% of the licensed psychologists responding were not trained in the United States (see also Garfield & Kurtz, 1974, 2%; Cuca, 1975, 1.5%). This low percentage represents a striking difference when compared to psychiatry (Jenkins & Witkin, 1976). Well over 20% of psychiatrists are foreign trained (Torrey & Taylor, 1973), with 50% of all psychiatrists employed in the public sector being foreign medical graduates (Finke & Field, 1978). Almost 48% of current psychiatric residents are foreign medical graduates, which suggests that the trend appears to be continuing (Brown, 1977; Finke & Field, 1978).

While the extent to which graduates in specialties other than clinical psychology have subsequently shifted to clinical practice was noted above (+18% for FT-FFS), the main sources of this shift deserve some mention. It is from the allied counseling and school psychologist specialties, human service specialties, that the bulk of the shift (11.5%, Table 2) has occurred. To a large extent, then, this increased involvement in clinical psychology represents more of a reorientation than a change.

This increased involvement in clinical practice has apparently been achieved without major public support of professional training. Psychologists increasingly are becoming licensed, and of the licensees, apparently, a higher proportion are in full-time practice. Moreover, none of the support for psychological training derives from the Health Professions Educational Assistance Act. Though comparable to or greater in its health personnel than veterinary medicine, optometry, or podiatry, psychology is not included among the MODVOPPP professions (medicine, osteopathic medicine, dentistry, veterinary medicine, optometry, podiatry, pharmacy, and public health administration). To the extent that there is training support in the future for schools of the health professions, clearly it is about time that some support become available for the professional schools of psychology.

The number of psychologists in organized health facilities appears to be growing. In public mental health facilities, psychology (all levels) experienced the largest relative increase in number of full-time equivalent staff positions of any discipline (21%) during the period 1974–1976, and their numbers increased 75% in private psychiatric hospitals at the same time (National Institute of Mental Health, 1976). However, the data reported here on hospital staff membership and clinical privilege indicate that practicing psychologists have a long way to go to be generally recognized as colleagues in hospital practice. Perhaps there is a growing edge here, too. Of the privileges reported, about 40% were on an informal basis. With the exception of the federal Medicare law, it is not statutes but state health facility licensing regulations and established policies that serve as barriers to change. These state regulations and policies quite commonly mirror the accreditation standards of the Joint Commission on Accreditation of Hospitals. One can question, then, whether these standards are standards of accreditation or of restraint and monopoly.

Historically, the practice of psychology has very largely been conducted on an outpatient basis. The direct-recognition laws among 29 states now cover 76% of the U.S. population. Despite the fact that the majority of health insurance coverage is hospital based, there is reason to believe that these new laws have influenced the recent rapid increase in the private practice of psychology. Whereas the commercial carriers underwrite only slightly more health insurance nationally than Blue Cross/Blue Shield 41% of all psychologists' visits were billed to the commercial carriers, in contrast to 24% to the "Blues." In part, this reflects greater acceptance by the industry than among the Blue Shield plans, which are derivatives of the county medical societies.

In summary, the data of the present study answer many questions that have been raised concerning health care provider psychologists, particularly those in fee-for-service practice. The independent practice of clinical psychology on a fee-for-service basis is widespread and growing. Psychologists, however, must make a serious effort to achieve more integration of their services as collegial practitioners in organized health care facilities and systems, including hospitals and multidisciplinary-ambulatory care group practice. Clinical psychologists represent a major health-personnel resource that warrants systematic inclusion in health planning, health professions training, professional standards review, and national health insurance and similar legislation.

Reference Notes

1. Gottfredson, G. Personal communication, January 3, 1979.
2. Webb, J. *Differences in patient populations of private practice psychologists.* Paper presented at the meeting of the Southeastern Psychological Association, Louisville, Kentucky, April 25, 1970.
3. Stigall, T. Personal communication in his capacity as President of the American Association of State Psychology Boards in a letter to Mrs. S. Galli, Office of the Actuary, Social Services Administration, April 21, 1978.
4. McGuire, T. *Some simple projections of the cost of national health insurance for the private practice of psychiatry.* Paper presented at the meeting of the Washington Business Group on Health, Employee Mental Wellness Programs, Washington, D.C., December 1–2, 1978.

References

Albee, G. Into the valley of therapy rode the six thousand (Review of *Psychiatrists and their patients: A national study of private office practice* by J. Marmor). *Contemporary Psychology,* 1976, *21,* 525–527.

Albee, G. Does including psychology in health insurance represent a subsidy to the rich from the poor? *American Psychologist,* 1977, *32,* 719–721.

Arnhoff, F. N., & Kumbar, A. H. *The nation's psychiatrists—1970 survey.* Washington, D.C.: American Psychiatric Association, 1973.

Avnet, H. H. *Psychiatric insurance: Financing short-term ambulatory treatment.* New York: Group Health Insurance, 1962.

Bent, R. J. Impact of peer review on future health practice. In H. Dörken and Associates, *The professional psychologist today.* San Francisco: Jossey-Bass, 1976.

Biofeedback in action. *World Medical News,* March 9, 1973, pp. 47–60.

Brown, B. S. The federal government and psychiatric education: Progress, problems, and prospects (DHEW Publication No. (ADM) 77–511). Washington, D.C.: U.S. Government Printing Office, June 1977.

Cuca, J., Clinicians comprise thirty-six percent of APA. *APA Monitor,* June 1975, p. 4.

Directory of the American Psychological Association. Washington, D.C.: American Psychological Association, 1978.

Dörken, H. Forms of health insurance. In H. Dörken and Associates, *The professional psychologist today: New developments in law, health insurance, and health practice.* San Francisco: Jossey-Bass, 1976.

Dörken, H. CHAMPUS ten-state claim experience for mental disorder: Fiscal year 1975. *American Psychologist,* 1977, *31,* 697–710. (a)

Dörken, H. The practicing psychologist: A growing force in private sector health care delivery. *Professional Psychology,* 1977, *8,* 269–274. (b)

Dörken, H. Foundations for medical care. *Professional psychology,* 1978, *19,* 175–177.

Dörken, H., & Cummings, N. A school of psychology as innovation in professional education: The California School of Professional Psychology, *Professional Psychology,* 1977, *8,* 129–148.

Dörken, H., & Cummings, N. More on professional schools. *Professional Psychology,* 1978, *9,* 528–530.

Dörken, H., & Morrison, D. JCAH standards for accreditation of psychiatric facilities. *American Psychologist,* 1976, *31,* 774–784.

Dörken, H., & Webb, J. The hospital practice of psychology: An interstate comparison. *Professional Psychology,* 1979, *10,* 619–630.

Dörken, H., & Webb, J. 1976 third-party reimbursement experience: An interstate comparison by carrier. *American Psychologist,* in press.

Eisdorfer, C., & Lawton, M. P. (Eds.). *The Psychology of adult development and aging.* Washington, D.C.: American Psychological Association, 1973.

Fink, R., et al. Treatment of patients designated by family doctors as having emotional problems. *American Journal of Public Health,* 1967, *57,* 1550–1564.

Fink, R., Goldensohn, S., & Shapiro, S. Family physician referrals for psychiatric consultation and patient initiative in seeking care. *Social Sciences and Medicine,* 1970, *4,* 273–291.

Finke, P. J., & Field, H. L. Residency training: A changing scenario. *Psychiatric Opinion,* 1978, *15*(4), 13–16.

Fordyce, W. An operant conditioning method for managing chronic pain. *Postgraduate Medicine,* 1973, *53,* 123–128.

Garfield, S. L., & Kurtz, R. A survey of clinical psychologists: Characteristics, activities, and orientations. *The Clinical Psychologist,* 1974, *28,* 7–10.

Gottfredson, G. P., & Dyer, S. F. *Health service providers in psychology: 1976* (Report No. 2, Office of Programs and Planning). Washington, D.C.: American Psychological Association. October 1977.

Gottfredson, G. P., & Dyer, S. F. Health service providers in psychology. *American Psychologist,* 1978, *33,* 314–338.

Jenkins, J., & Witkin, M. Foreign medical graduates employed in state and county mental hospitals. In *Mental Health Statistical Note No. 131.* Washington, D.C.: U.S. Department of Health, Education, and Welfare, July 1976.

Kirchner, M. Fees: Are they getting out of hand? *Medical Economics,* October 16, 1978, pp. 167–192.

Manson, H. Manpower needs by specialty. *Journal of the American Medical Association,* 1972, *219,* 1621–1626.

Marmor, J. *Psychiatrists and their patients: A national study of private office practice.* Washington, D.C.: American Psychiatric Association, 1975.

Matarazzo, J., Lubin, B., & Nathan, R. Psychologists' membership in the medical staffs of university teaching hospitals. *American Psychologist,* 1977, *31,* 23–29.

Mattera, M. Why psychiatrists are behind the economical eightball. *Medical Economics,* February 5, 1979, pp. 158–167.

Mills, D. H., Wellner, A. M., & VandenBos, G. R. The *National Register* survey: The first comprehensive study of all licensed/certified psychologists. In C. A. Kiesler, N. A. Cummings, and G. R. VandenBos, (Eds.), *Psychology and national health insurance: A sourcebook.* Washington, D.C.: American Psychological Association, 1979.

Myers, E. Insurance coverage for mental illness: Present status and future prospects. *American Journal of Public Health,* 1970, *60,* 1921–1930.

National Institute of Mental Health. *Staffing of mental health facilities: United States 1976* (Series B, No. 14, DHEW Publication No. (ADM) 76–308). Washington, D.C. U.S. Government Printing Office, 1976.

Owens, A. Which fees should rise this year? *Medical Economics,* 1974, *51,* 162–169.

Peck, C. Fee practices of psychologists. *Professional Psychology,* 1969, *1,* 14–19; 154.

President's Commission on Mental Health. Task panel reports, Appendix. In *Report to the President from the President's Commission on Mental Health* (Vol. 2). Washington, D.C.: U.S. Government Printing Office, 1978.

Reed, L. S., Myers, E. S., & Scheidemandel, P. L. *Health insurance and psychiatric care: Utilization and cost.* Washington, D.C.: American Psychiatric Association, 1972.

Report of the National Commission on State Workmen's Compensation Laws (0-477-053). Washington, D.C.: U.S. Government Printing Office, 1972.

Schofield, W. *Psychotherapy: The purchase of friendship.* Englewood Cliffs, N.J.: Prentice-Hall, 1967.

Sharfstein, S., Taube, C., & Goldberg, I. Problems in analyzing the comparative costs of private versus public psychiatric care. *American Journal of Psychiatry,* 1977, *134,* 29–32.

Stern, M. Social class and psychiatric treatment of adults in the mental health center. *Journal of Health and Social Behavior,* 1977, *18,* 317–325.

Torrey, F. F., & Taylor, R. Cheap labor from poor nations. *American Journal of Psychiatry,* 1973, *130,* 428–433.

U.S. Bureau of the Census. *Statistical abstract of the U.S.: 1975* (96th ed.). Washington, D.C.: U.S. Government Printing Office, 1975.

U.S. Bureau of the Census. *Current population reports* (Series P-23, No. 67). Washington, D.C.: U.S. Government Printing Office, 1978. (a)

U.S. Bureau of the Census. *Current population reports* (Series P-23, No. 75). Washington, D.C.: U.S. Government Printing Office, 1978. (b)

U.S. Bureau of the Census. *Current population reports* (Series P-25, No. 734). Washington, D.C.: U.S. Government Printing Office, 1978. (c)

U.S. Bureau of the Census. *Current population reports* (Series P-60, No. 116). Washington, D.C.: U.S. Government Printing Office, 1978. (d)

U.S. Department of Health, Education, And Welfare, Social Security Administration, Office of Research and Statistics. *Health insurance administrative costs* (Staff Paper No. 21, DHEW Publication No. (SSA) 76-11856). Washington, D.C.: U.S. Government Printing Office, 1976.

Van Buskirk, D. Training and treatment costs in a community mental health center. *Administration in Mental Health,* 1974 (Summer), 28–36.

Vetter, B. Survey points fiction of psychology manpower. *APA Monitor,* April 1973, pp. 3; 7.

Wellner A. M., & Mills, D. H. *National Register research reports Nos. 1 through 9.* Washington, D.C.: Council for the National Register of Health Service Providers in Psychology, 1977.

Whiting, F. *Psychiatric services, systems analysis, and manpower utilization.* Washington, D.C.: American Psychiatric Association, 1969.

Wiggins, J. G. Disability and rehabilitation services. In H. Dörken and Associates, *The professional psychologist today.* San Francisco: Jossey-Bass, 1976.

Wolberg, L. R. *The technique of psychotherapy* (Vol. 2). New York: Grune & Stratton, 1967.

Wright L. Psychology as a health profession. *The Clinical Psychologist,* 1976, *29,* 16–19.

Herbert Dörken is an Adjunct Professor and Research Psychologist, Department of Psychiatry, Langley Porter Institute, University of California, San Francisco; *James T. Webb* is with the School of Professional Psychology, Wright State University, Dayton, Ohio.

Acquisition of the data upon which this report is based was made possible by Grant MH-26852 from the Mental Health Services Development Branch, National Institute of Mental Health, and with the cooperation of the Council for the National Register of Health Service Providers in Psychology. This article was presented in part at the annual conventions of the Southeastern Psychological Association (Atlanta, March 17, 1978) and the American Psychological Association (Toronto, August 29 and 30, 1978).

The authors wish to express appreciation to Jack Wiggins for his helpful review of an early draft and to Michael Munger for his assistance with the data analysis. We are particularly indebted to Gary Gottfredson and Gary VandenBos for their thorough review and many suggestions that have led to the improved organization and clarity of this manuscript.

The Practicing Psychologist: A Growing Force in Private Sector Health Care Delivery

Herbert Dörken

Psychology may well be unique among the major health professions in its current rate of growth and in the number of licensed, qualified personnel practicing part-time who could shift the extent of their involvement in fee-service or salaried practice given a significant change in incentives, such as a national health insurance plan. Recent major legislation at the federal and state levels has served to establish psychology as a health profession. When contrasted to professions engaged in similar work, social work and psychiatry, the training standards in psychology appear clearly higher and more uniform.

The private clinical practice of psychology can be seen from various perspectives. Its numbers, as full-time practitioners, can correctly be represented as accounting for about 7% of all psychologists, even though they render 30% of all direct clinical services. Yet, it is also known that some 40% of all psychologists are involved in fee-service health practice some of the time. Of this part-time practice component, one third of all psychologists, approximately half are employed in academic settings. Thus, the clearly visible private practitioners are but the tip of the iceberg of psychological practice (Dörken & Whiting, 1974). There is probably no other health profession with the same magnitude of working professionals and proportion of professional time whose activities are potentially available for redirection into increased health care delivery, given the necessary fiscal and social incentives.

What are psychology's human resources? Membership in the American Psychological Association (APA) has increased dramatically in recent years from 35,000 in 1973 to an expected level of 41,500 at the beginning of 1976 (Little, 1975) and a projected budget membership of 44,710 in 1977. Not all psychologists, of course, belong to APA, as was evident through the consolidated roster of psychologists, which showed a 1972 U.S. resident total of 43,461 in contrast to the 33,930 APA members (APA, 1973). If the same 78% proportion holds today, then the total number of U.S. psychologists now exceeds 57,320. From the private practice standpoint, however, it is necessary to restrict consideration to those psychologists who are licensed/certified. Psychology has, with no little difficulty, reached a functional definition of health service providers and has compiled an initial voluntary *National Register of Health Service Providers in Psychology* (Council, 1975). Only 8,500 are now listed (Editor's note: In 1979, almost 12,000 psychologists are listed.), but with its adoption as a reference by Blue Shield for the Federal Employees Plan and by CHAMPUS (Civilian Health and Medical Program of the Uniformed Services) and growing perception within the profession of its value for public relations, the current expectation is that this directory will double in size in the next few years. With the exception of Missouri (Editor's note: Missouri passed a psychology licensing law in 1977.), psychologists are licensed or certified by statute in all states in the country and in the

Reprinted from *Professional Psychology*, 1977, 8, 269–274.

District of Columbia. The first attempt to derive an unduplicated listing of state resident licensed/certified psychologists, based on directories of 1973–1974, yielded a total of just over 18,000, which when corrected for the three states with statues from which information was not then available, yielded a figure of 19,000. The 30% proportionate increase since that time suggests that there are now some 25,300 psychologists (Dörken & Whiting, 1976; 25,510 tallied, see Wellner & Mills, Note 2) recognized for practice under state statutes.

Psychologists have been engaged in clinical services in this country at least since the turn of the century. A small, though increasing, number was evident prior to World War II. In retrospect, however, the massive infusion of Veterans' Administration funds can be said to have created clinical psychology. Later, extensive funding was added through the National Institute of Mental Health, not only in training fellowships but also in direct support of university graduate programs, to effect a further major expansion of clinical psychology.

The development of professional schools of psychology is a quite recent and new phenomenon (Dörken, 1975). Their history has recently been reviewed (Dörken & Cummings, 1977). The inclusion of professional schools of psychology in the Health Manpower Training Act would quickly maximize a third stage in the development of professional psychology. Indeed, the Health Professions Education Assistance Act of 1976 would enable project grants to schools of psychology under Title VIII, Special Projects Section 788(d)(13) of PL 94-484, a far cry from capitation funding, but perhaps a constructive beginning.

Although psychology has been one of the most popular undergraduate majors in universities across the country, it expanded recently through a marked increase in graduate study enrollment (Cuca, 1974). Admission to graduate studies in psychology is now even more competitive than admission to medical school (Nyman, 1973). There are now some 40,000 doctoral candidates in psychology throughout the country, and by 1978, instead of graduating some 2,612 PhDs, as occurred in 1973, we may soon be approaching 5,000 (Albee, Note 1). The APA projects the number of PhD recipients in psychology from 1975 to 1980 to be about 16,500 (Cuca, 1976). Moreover, clinicians compose 36% of the APA (Cuca, 1975) and this proportion might increase. This represents another unique situation in terms of psychology's potential to contribute to health service delivery. An increase in the number of professionals graduated is in process and could be further accelerated. Thus, although the future is not entirely predictable, the prospects for growth are very much at hand.

How many clinical psychologists does the country really need for direct health care delivery? Is the clinical psychologist a specialist or primary health care professional? A rough staffing rule of thumb in health maintenance organizations is at least one specialist per 10,000 subscribers and not less than one primary practitioner per 1,000 subscribers—a tenfold difference. Will future health care delivery be affected through health maintenance organizations or individual practice associations, in which the emphasis is on ambulatory care, or will the majority of services be under isolated fee-service practice and public services, with their penchant for hospital use? Projections to a national level based on Kaiser versus CHAMPUS (Dörken, 1976, p. 274) experience would indicate a need for 62,000 versus 110,000 mental health practitioners. We might have the former, albeit maldistributed, but nowhere near the latter figure (Dörken & Rodgers, 1976). Will clinical psychology be viewed essentially as a mental health profession, or will it merge into the mainstream of health care delivery? For both patients and significant others, there are very substantial psychological aspects to terminal illness and death; disability, dismemberment, and disfigurement; major surgery and chronic illness; as well as the sudden loss of significant others. Psychological factors are often the main impediments to productive community living and to occupational rehabilitation (Medical Care, 1972). Wright (1976) illustrated the importance of psychology's role in treating people who are physically ill. Given such a broad perspective and the often reported fact that the majority of persons under a doctor's care have a primary or secondary psychological disability, a case can be made for considering psychologists (and psychiatrists) primary care personnel rather than specialists.

A comparison of clinical psychology to its closest professional rival, psychiatry, is favorable. The number of clinical psychologists qualified and available for practice is beginning to approach that of psychiatry (Dörken & Whiting, 1976). Moreover, the distribution of psychologists apparently more closely parallels the general population, thus facilitating access outside major metropolitan areas (Dörken & Whiting, 1976). Further, there are insufficient psychiatrists upon which to effectively sustain a gatekeeper model. When training standards are considered, they are clearly higher and more uniform in psychology.

Now that the statutory base to the practice of psychology is substantial—it is not in the case of social work—the profession's self-definition and its training standards become the bottom line. What is a social worker? Although protested by the clinical (psychiatric) social worker, the National Association of Social Workers in July 1974 shifted from the master's in social work to the bachelor's in social work as its (journeyman) standard of professional preparation (Spingarn, 1974). Moreover, this profession is only licensed for practice with a master's in social work and 2 years of experience in nine states (California, Colorado, Idaho, Kansas, Kentucky, Maryland, South Dakota, Vermont, and Virginia), although there are other licensure provisions (Louisiana and Puerto Rico) and registration by statute in eight states.

Well then, what is a psychiatrist? Is a psychiatrist a foreign medical graduate with only recent exposure to U.S. culture and limited facility with the English language, perhaps yet unlicensed, but working in a psychiatric facility (Torrey & Taylor, 1973)? (Only 1.5% of psychologists are foreign trained [Cuca, 1976].) Or, is a psychiatrist a U.S.-trained, licensed physician who has chosen to limit his/her practice to psychiatry but who has had little if any formal training in psychiatry during medical school and anything ranging from a full residency with noncompletion of specialty board exams to no apprenticeship in psychiatry at all. Or, is a psy-chiatrist a board-certified medical specialist? Only 48% of the physicians limiting their practice to psychiatry and listed in the 1971 *Directory of Medical Specialists* were board certified, and fewer than 10,000 of them at that.[1]

Contrast the situation in social work and psychiatry to the extensive formal training and high standards for doctoral training in clinical psychology at the 100 APA-accredited programs. Then, recognizing that generic licensure does not convey any assurance of specialty competence, psychologists developed the *National Register of Health Service Providers in Psychology,* for which listing is based on credential review by peers.

The 93rd Congress brought very substantial formal recognition to clinical psychology. The Rehabilitation Act of 1973, PL 93-112, affords parity to "licensed psychologists or physicians" in both assessment and restorative services. Then, regulations implementing the Health Maintenance Organization Development Act of 1973, PL 93-222, named "clinical psychologists" among the health providers. Under PL 93-363, the Federal Employee Health Benefits Act was revised to ensure federal employees and their dependents access to and free choice of qualified "clinical psychologists" for covered services. Later, the United States Code was amended to include *clinical psychologists* within the definition of *physician* and among the "medical, surgical, and hospital services and supplies," so that they are among the providers for this Federal Work Injuries Compensation Program, PL 93-461. The Department of Defense Appropriation Act, 1976, PL 94-212, is most explicit under Section 751 by excluding from funding under the CHAMPUS "any other service or supply which is not medically or *psychologically necessary* to diagnose and treat a

---

[1] The Director of the National Institute of Mental Health, at the 1977 meeting of the American Psychiatric Association, noted that "Over the past four years, the number of American medical graduates in psychiatric residency has dropped by almost 400 . . .". This is in the face of a rise in medical school enrollment and coupled with a report (DHEW-ADM-76-158) based on a 1975 survey of state and county mental hospitals that "60 percent of all residents" (physicians in psychiatric training) are foreign medical graduates, only 13% of whom were licensed, reflects on prospective psychiatric manpower and training standards on the one hand, while implying some systemic problem on the other.

mental or physical illness, injury, or bodily malfunction as diagnosed by a physician, dentist, or a clinical psychologist" (italics added).[2] Other pertinent laws and regulations have been adopted at the state level. For example, under disability, health insurance, and medical service plans, 24 states and the District of Columbia (including California, New York, Ohio, Michigan, and New Jersey), covering 60% of the population, had by December 1976 enacted statutes providing for direct access to and free choice of licensed/certified psychologists for covered benefits (Dörken, 1976).[3] The Health Insurance Association of America on May 18, 1976 approved a Model Psychologist Direct Recognition Bill intended as a model to assist the remaining 26 states in securing comparable legislation.[4]

Major legislative proposals are before the 95th Congress and many states to (a) amend clinical psychologists into Medicare and Medicaid, (b) implement national/state standards for workers' compensation laws that would recognize clinical psychologists, and (c) establish a national/state mandatory health insurance program including mental health benefits. The extent and nature of psychology's recognition in such major federal/state legislation will very materially affect not only the demand for the services of psychologist practitioners in the immediate future but will also serve as an incentive to their future supply through training.

Reference Notes

1. Albee, G. *The uncertain future of American psychology.* Unpublished paper submitted to the American

---

[2] The 1978 DOD Appropriation Act not only contains this language, but also, the Conference Committee in its report to H.R. 7933 intends that whether the psychological services are on an in- or out-patient basis, that ". . . clinical psychologists shall be employed to review the (appropriateness of) services of their own peers."

[3] By the end of 1978, 29 states (which includes the District of Columbia) had such legislation. More than 75% of the U.S. population is now covered by freedom of choice legislation.

[4] It was later approved by the Council of Representatives of the American Psychological Association on September 2, 1976.

Psychological Association Policy and Planning Board, November 1972. (Mimeo)

2. Wellner, A., & Mills, D. *An unduplicated count of licensed/certified psychologists in the United States* (Research Rep. No. 2). Washington, D.C.: Council for the National Register of Health Service Providers in Psychology, March 4, 1977. (Mimeo)

References

American Psychological Association. *The consolidated roster for psychology.* Washington, D.C.: Author, 1973.

Council for the National Register of Health Service Providers in Psychology. *National Register of Health Service Providers in Psychology.* Washington, D.C.: Author, 1975.

Cuca, J. Graduate enrollments leveling off. *APA Monitor,* November 1974, pp. 16–19.

Cuca, J. Clinicians compose 36 percent of APA. *APA Monitor,* January 1975, p. 4.

Cuca, J. PhDs in psychology: Supply and demand. In P. J. Woods (Ed.), *Career opportunities for psychologists.* Washington, D.C.: American Psychological Association, 1976.

Dörken, H. Private professional sector innovation in higher education: The California School for Professional Psychology. *Journal of Community Psychology,* 1975, *3,* 15–21.

Dörken, H. Laws, regulations and psychological practice. In H. Dörken and Associates, *The professional psychologist today: New developments in law, health insurance and health practice.* San Francisco: Jossey-Bass, 1976.

Dörken, H., & Cummings, N. A. A school of psychology as innovation in professional education: The California School of Professional Psychology. *Professional Psychology,* 1977, *8,* 129–148.

Dörken, H., & Rodgers, D. Issues facing professional psychology. In H. Dörken and Associates, *The professional psychologist today: New developments in law, health insurance and health practice.* San Francisco: Jossey-Bass, 1976.

Dörken, H., & Whiting, J. F. Psychologists as health service providers. *Professional Psychology,* 1974, *5,* 309–319.

Dörken, H., & Whiting, J. F. Psychologists as health service providers. In H. Dörken and Associates, *The professional psychologist today: New developments in law, health insurance and health practice.* San Francisco: Jossey-Bass, 1976.

Little, K. Editorial, *APA Monitor,* March 1975, p. 2.

Medical Care and Rehabilitation Objective. In, *National Commission Report on State Workmen's Compensation Laws.* Washington, D.C.: U.S. Government Printing Office, 1972.

Nyman, L. Some odds on getting into PhD programs in clinical and counseling psychology. *American Psychologist,* 1973, *28,* 934–935.

Spingarn, N. Social work as a profession confounded by contradictions. *Chronicle of Higher Education,* 1974, *8,* 8.

Torrey, F., & Taylor, R. Cheap labor from poor nations. *American Journal of Psychiatry,* 1973, *130,* 428–433.

Wright, L. Psychology as a health profession. *The Clinical Psychologist,* 1976, *29,* 16–19.

At the time of the original publication of this article, *Herbert Dörken* was an Adjunct Professor and Research Psychologist in the Department of Psychiatry, Langley Porter Institute, University of California, San Francisco.

Geographic Distribution of U.S. Psychologists

A Human Ecological Analysis

James M. Richards, Jr., and Gary D. Gottfredson

Characteristics of cities and states were correlated with measures of the geographic distribution of U.S. psychologists. Correlations for psychologists providing mental health services were compared with correlations for psychiatrists, clinical social workers, and school guidance personnel. Population size is the strongest correlate of the absolute number of psychologists in various states and cities. When number relative to population is considered, psychologists are concentrated in affluent urban states and in university towns. The same pattern was obtained for all the groups providing mental health services. No evidence was obtained that any of these groups is distributed in a way offering special advantages for serving groups such as poor, black, or rural people, who appear to need better access to mental health services.

Psychological studies of occupations and professions usually emphasize characteristics of individuals, paying much less attention to aggregate characteristics of occupational groups. But aggregate characteristics, such as geographic distribution, may be critically important to questions of social policy, especially in the case of health care, where access by all is a widely shared goal. Moreover, funding decisions that could strongly affect the future of psychology, scientific as well as professional (Cuca, 1975a; Perloff, 1972), are being proposed or made partly on the basis of distributional data. An apparent maldistribution of mental health specialists seems to have influenced the Alcohol, Drug Abuse, and Mental Health Administration's (Note 1; National Institute of Mental Health, Note 2) effort to phase out the training of such specialists in favor of providing more mental health training for "generic" care providers—general practitioners, nurses, and others who deliver primary health care. Similarly, a concern with geographic distribution underlies the 1976 Health Professions Educational Assistance Act (PL No. 94-484, Stat. 2243). Questions of geographic distribution have also

influenced the testimony of psychologists about national health insurance (APA, CAPPS, & AAP, Note 3) and debates about the training of psychologists and other professionals (Moore, 1976).

These considerations imply a need for comprehensive information about the distribution of psychologists and other mental health specialists. The importance of geographical distribution has been implicitly recognized in the occasional practice of listing the number of various kinds of psychologists by states (e.g., Boneau & Cuca, 1974; Cates, 1970), and a few investigators (Webb, 1974) have made explicit but limited comparisons of the distributions of psychologists and other mental health professionals. Unfortunately, the data have usually been examined only descriptively, so the present study aims to treat the geographic distribution of psychologists and members of other health professions more analytically by applying some of the techniques of human ecology.

Human ecology can be defined as the study of the relationships between human populations and their environments (Bailey & Mulcahy, 1972; Duncan & Schnore, 1959; Hawley,

Reprinted from *American Psychologist*, 1978, *33*, 1–9.

1950). Its basic approach is to study population aggregates not just as collections of individuals, nor as simple distributions of personal traits, but as organized wholes that can be characterized by their patterns of activities. Although human ecology has been more influential in sociology[1] than in psychology, Michaels (1974) has presented a persuasive integration of human ecology with approaches that apply the principles of operant conditioning to the analysis of social process and organization. The present study assumes that human ecology is a useful perspective not only for sociology but also for psychology, especially social and vocational psychology.

A general paradigm has evolved for ecological investigations of the geographic distributions of professionals. This paradigm involves measuring the characteristics of some convenient units of analysis, such as states, cities, or Standard Metropolitan Statistical Areas (SMSAs), and correlating those characteristics with measures of the distribution of professionals among the same units (Marden, 1960; Reskin & Campbell, 1974; Richards, 1977). The present study applies these procedures to the distribution of psychologists and other mental health professionals.

Method

The design of this study is basically correlational, and a number of variables were skewed or had other undesirable properties. Therefore, all measures of geographic distribution were transformed to normalized standard scores (Angoff, 1971, pp. 515–519). That is, scores within each distribution were converted to percentile ranks, and normal deviate values corresponding to these percentile ranks were taken from the table of the normal curve. Such normalizing transformations are relatively common in geographical investigations such as the present study (e.g., Harries, 1976; Meyer, 1972). The main properties of distributions that are invariant under this transformation are ordinal relationships, so using such a transformation is equivalent to following Rummel's (1970) recommendation that investigators use Kendall's tau coefficient to measure the association between ecological variables when those variables are not normally distributed or when it is suspected that systematic error may be present.

Choice of appropriate units of analysis is a difficult problem in human ecological studies, but researchers, of necessity, usually must use units for which data are available from government surveys. Studies using such units are complicated further by the large mass of data typically reported in government surveys, so factor analysis has been used to organize data for nations (Sawyer, 1967), for states (Richards, in press), and for cities, counties, and SMSAs (Bonjean, 1971). Two units of analysis were used in this study. The first such units were the 51 states, treating the District of Columbia as a state. The second units of analysis were the 916 cities and unincorporated places that had populations of 25,000 or more in the 1970 census (U.S. Bureau of the Census, 1973).

State characteristics were measured by factor scores on five (orthogonal) factors obtained in an earlier investigation (Richards, in press). These factor scores were computed from normalized variables but were not themselves normalized. These five factors are identified and described briefly below:

Emphasis on Large-Scale Agriculture. High-scoring states have large land areas, much of their land in farms, and relatively high incomes per farm from field crops and livestock.

Population Size. High-scoring states had relatively many inhabitants at the 1970 census. They also have large numbers of institutions providing education in health fields and relatively low male-female ratios. The chosen title is Population Size rather than just Size because land area does not load on this factor.

Affluence-Urbanization. The high-scoring state has a high median family income and a large proportion of its population living in cities.

White Predominance. The most outstanding characteristic of the high-scoring state is that a large proportion of its population is white.

Emphasis on Specialized Agriculture. High-scoring states have relatively high incomes

---

[1] In sociology, the emergence of human ecology as a major subdiscipline is usually dated from Hawley's 1950 book and thus predates the current, somewhat faddish concern with "ecology" by more than a decade.

per farm from poultry, dairy products, and "horticulture other than field crops." They also have high incomes relative to their labor force from manufacturing.

The three nonagricultural factors resemble factors obtained in each of the studies of cities, counties, and SMSAs reviewed by Bonjean (1971). Size and Affluence factors also were obtained when nations (Sawyer, 1967) and colleges and universities (Astin, 1962; Richards, 1973a) were used as the units of analysis. These findings suggest that ecological dimensions with considerable generality can be identified. The two agricultural factors tap human activities (a) on which states vary widely, (b) that are critically important to the future of humanity (Hutchinson, 1969), and (c) that have been almost completely ignored by psychologists (Richards, 1973b).

The measures of city characteristics were chosen on the basis of Bonjean's (1971) integration of several factor-analytic studies. It was not feasible to compute factor scores, however, so each factor was estimated by a single (normalized) variable, taken from standard reference sources (U.S. Bureau of the Census, 1973), that seemed representative of that factor. Several factors also were retitled to make their interpretation clearer and more comparable to the state factors or to reduce possible confusion between individual-level and aggregate-level concepts (Robinson, 1950). The factor called Urbanism by Bonjean was retitled Population Size and estimated by 1970 population. Bonjean's Socio-Economic Status was retitled Affluence and estimated by median family income. Residential Mobility was estimated by the percentage of occupants of housing units who moved into those units during the 5 years preceding the 1970 census. White Predominance (Bonjean's Nonwhite) was estimated by the percentage of the 1970 population classified as white.

Although Bonjean did not include it in his summary list, he pointed out that cities also seem to vary on a factor which he called Educational Center. A major characteristic measured by this factor appears to be the extent to which a given city is a college or university town, and a city's being a university town also appeared to have potential relevance to the distribution of psychologists. Accordingly, a measure devised to assess this characteristic directly was titled Emphasis on Higher Education. Specifically, the total number of students enrolled in colleges and universities in each city (U.S. Office of Education, 1972) was divided by the total population of that city. As intended, cities such as Ithaca, New York; Chapel Hill, North Carolina; and Iowa City, Iowa, had relatively high scores on this variable.

The major source of data about the geographic distribution of psychologists was the geographical-directory section of the 1973 APA *Biographical Directory* (American Psychological Association, 1973a). This procedure treats being an APA member and being a (U.S.) psychologist as equivalent and is more appropriate if one defines *psychologist* in terms of professional self-identification than if one defines it in terms of, say, eligibility for APA membership. By "committing *petit legerdemain,*" Boneau and Cuca (1974) estimated that about 90% of doctoral psychologists are members of APA but that only one fourth of the eligible persons holding master's degrees in psychology are members. The proportion of membership among eligible persons holding degrees in other fields is unknown but presumably still smaller. Therefore, data from an APA *Directory* probably should be interpreted as roughly representative of doctoral-level psychologists in the United States.

The first measures of geographic distribution used in this study were the total number, and the number relative to the population (as enumerated in the 1970 census), of psychologists in each state and city. As a check on the generality and stability of the results based on the 1973 *Directory,* two additional sets of data were analyzed at the state level. The first set was taken from the *Consolidated Roster* of psychologists (American Psychological Association, 1973b). This roster attempts to include all psychologists, not just APA members, but probably is also most complete for doctoral-level psychologists. Second, state-level data were taken from the 1975 APA *Directory* (American Psychological Association, 1975), which was issued just as the main data analyses for this study were being completed.

A primary focus of this study is on psychologists who provide mental health services. Therefore, three measures of the distribution of such psychologists were analyzed. The first was the number of psychologists listed in the 1973 APA *Directory* who reported that they had a private or group practice. The second was the number of psychologists listed (by primary site of practice) in the *National Register*[2] (Council for the National Register of Health Service Providers in Psychology, 1976). The third measure, which was available for states only, was the number of psychologists who reported that they were providing psychological services in the 1972 APA survey of members (Cuca, Note 4).

The geographic distributions of three comparison groups also were analyzed. First, data for psychiatrists were obtained from their 1970 *Membership Directory* (American Psychiatric Association, 1970). Second, data for clinical social workers were obtained from their *Register*[3] (National Association of Social Workers, 1976). Lastly, data (state level only) for school guidance workers were obtained from a standard reference source (U.S. Office of Education, 1974). In four states it was necessary to estimate the number of such workers from the number of teachers by assuming that the guidance-worker-teacher ratio in those states was the same as the ratio for all other states combined. A fairly large proportion of these guidance workers might be eligible for a master's-level Associate memberhip in the APA.

Finally, it appeared desirable to study the possibility of a differential distribution of psychologists by types. Adkins (1954, 1973) has used factor analyses to identify types of psychologists from the divisional structure of APA, so specific divisions that appeared representative of each of Adkins's most recent (1973) factors were chosen and the number of psychologists in each state holding membership in those divisions determined. The small size of some divisions

precluded an analysis at the city level. A psychologist may be a member of any number of divisions, so these data are not inherently ipsative. The specific divisions chosen were Psychotherapy, Personality and Social, Physiological and Comparative, History, Engineering, Industrial and Organizational, and Educational.

Results

Table 1 summarizes the zero-order and multiple correlations between state characteristics and the various measures of the total number of psychologists in the states. These and other correlations obtained in this study are population values, so tests of significance were not applied. State characteristics were measured by scores on orthogonally rotated factors (for the same units of analysis used in performing the factor analysis), so the zero-order correlations are equal within rounding error to the beta weights. Because the measures of geographical distribution were transformed to normalized standard scores, the appropriate measures of raw-score central tendency and dispersion appeared to be, respectively, the median and the semi-interquartile range.

The ecological variables account for approximately 90% of the variance among states in numbers of psychologists and for approximately 60% of the variance in relative numbers of psychologists. These results are comparable to those obtained in studies of other health professions (Richards, 1977). Results for all three measures of the number of psychologists are highly similar, an indication that these ecological relationships are stable, at least in the short run. Population Size, of course, is the major correlate of the absolute number of psychologists. When number relative to population is considered, psychologists are concentrated in affluent, urban states.

Table 2 summarizes the correlations for the various measures of the number of psychologists who provide health services and for the three comparison professions. These results are basically similar to the results shown in Table 1. Population Size is the strongest correlate of the total number of each of these groups, and when number relative to population is con-

---

[2] The considerations that motivate psychologists to list themselves in the *National Register* are somewhat obscure at the present time but may be related both to regulations concerning third-party reimbursement for health services and to laws regulating the practice of psychology. Unpublished tabulations from a 1976 APA survey imply that about 40% of doctoral-level APA members who provide health services are listed in the *National Register*.

[3] The considerations that motivate social workers to list themselves in this *Register* presumably are similar to the considerations that motivate psychologists to list themselves in the *National Register*.

Table 1: *Zero-Order and Multiple Correlations Between State Characteristics and the Overall Distribution of Psychologists*

State characteristic	Number			Number per 100,000 population		
	1973 APA Directory	1973 Consolidated Roster	1975 APA Directory	1973 APA Directory	1973 Consolidated Roster	1975 APA Directory
Emphasis on Large-Scale Agriculture	−.13	−.11	−.14	−.22	−.17	−.23
Population Size	.86	.86	.86	.20	.17	.20
Affluence–Urbanization	.27	.27	.27	.69	.69	.71
White Predominance	−.11	−.10	−.13	.16	.23	.15
Emphasis on Specialized Agriculture	.25	.27	.25	.07	.04	.08
R	.95	.95	.95	.77	.77	.79
Median	323.0	458.0	353.0	13.8	17.6	15.2
Semi-interquartile range	312.6	391.3	351.1	4.2	5.4	4.3

Note. Since the District of Columbia was treated as a state, $N = 51$. All ratio measures are expressed relative to population as enumerated in the 1970 census.

sidered, all of these groups are concentrated in affluent, urban states. There is some variation in the absolute magnitudes of the correlations, but the overall pattern is highly consistent. Moreover, there appears to be as much variation in absolute magnitudes among the different measures of the number of psychologists providing health services as there is between psychologists and the three comparison professions. Therefore, these correlations provide no evidence that any one of the groups is distributed in a way that offers special advantages for serv-

ing poor people, black people, rural people, or other groups who appear to need improved access to mental health services.

Table 3 summarizes the relationships between state characteristics and the distributions of members of APA divisions representing Adkins's (1973) factors. Because Population Size was the strongest correlate of the absolute number of all groups analyzed previously, Table 3 is limited to results for numbers relative to population. Membership in the Division of Psychotherapy could be viewed as still another

Table 2: *Correlations of State Characteristics with the Distribution of Professional Psychologists and of Members of Comparison Professions*

State characteristic	Psychologists			Comparison professions		
	With private or group practice	Providing professional services	Listed in the *National Register*	Psychiatrists	School guidance personnel	Clinical social workers
Number						
Emphasis on Large-Scale Agriculture	−.06	−.12	−.05	−.18	−.03	−.15
Population Size	.79	.87	.83	.82	.88	.78
Affluence–Urbanization	.40	.23	.27	.30	.16	.36
White Predominance	−.16	−.11	−.15	−.17	−.11	−.04
Emphasis on Specialized Agriculture	.28	.24	.24	.27	.31	.28
R	.94	.95	.92	.94	.95	.91
Median	35.0	173.0	67.3	131.0	724.0	70.0
Semi-interquartile range	39.9	146.3	66.5	172.8	475.6	64.5
Number per 100,000 population						
Emphasis on Large-Scale Agriculture	−.06	−.14	−.04	−.32	−.07	−.28
Population Size	.18	.21	.10	.29	−.19	.16
Affluence–Urbanization	.82	.65	.56	.60	.54	.67
White Predominance	−.05	.24	.07	−.04	.16	.14
Emphasis on Specialized Agriculture	.10	.01	.01	.18	−.16	.00
R	.85	.74	.57	.76	.62	.76
Median	1.4	6.5	3.2	5.1	25.9	2.7
Semi-interquartile range	.6	1.8	1.3	2.0	4.4	1.7

Table 3: *State Characteristics and the Distribution of Various Types of Psychologist*

State characteristic	Members per 100,000 state population of division						
	Division 29 (Psychotherapy)	Division 8 (Personality and Social)	Division 6 (Physiological and Comparative)	Division 26 (Historical)	Division 21 (Engineering)	Division 14 (Industrial and Organizational)	Division 15 (Educational)
Emphasis on Large-Scale Agriculture	−.26	−.33	−.33	−.29	−.16	−.25	−.17
Population Size	.18	.17	.30	.14	.39	.46	.24
Affluence–Urbanization	.71	.61	.49	.40	.44	.39	.61
White Predominance	.05	.09	.09	.25	−.15	−.13	−.03
Emphasis on Specialized Agriculture	.00	.15	.16	−.04	.06	.21	.06
R	.78	.74	.68	.57	.63	.70	.68
Median	.76	1.55	.19	.17	.09	.39	1.43
Semi-interquartile range	.38	.68	.11	.09	.10	.29	.53

measure of the number of psychologists providing mental health services, and the pattern of correlations for this division is quite similar to the patterns shown in Table 2. That is, members of this division are also relatively concentrated in affluent, urban states. Results for the Division of Educational Psychology and the Division of Personality and Social Psychology also follow this pattern fairly closely. The tendency to be concentrated in affluent, urban states is considerably weaker, but still present, for the other divisions, an outcome that may result from the relatively small size of some of these divisions (i.e., some states have zero members of such divisions). Except for these differences, there is little indication of large variations in the distribution of different types of psychologists.

Finally, Table 4 summarizes the relation of city characteristics to (a) the total number of psychologists, (b) two measures of the number of psychologists providing health services, and (c) the number of members of two comparison professions. The measures of city characteristics, unlike the ecological measures in the state analyses, are not completely independent. For this reason, beta weights, or, more exactly, standardized partial regression coefficients, are shown in this table. Because measures of virtually all of the known city characteristics are included, it appears meaningful to interpret these coefficients as the correlations between given city characteristics and the distribution of

psychologists when other city characteristics are held constant.

Both the zero-order and the multiple correlations for cities are somewhat lower than the corresponding correlations for states, a pattern to be expected from the lower level of aggregation involved in the city correlations (Robinson, 1950). Two thirds to three fourths of all these mental health professionals are located in these cities, compared to about 45% of the general population and about 65% of the physicians. (It is commonly reported that more than 65% of the general U.S. population now live in urban areas, so a significant proportion of that population must live in cities or suburban areas with fewer than 25,000 inhabitants.)

Once again, Population Size tends to be the strongest correlate of the total number of members of all these professional groups. When number relative to population is considered, all of these groups appear concentrated in college and university towns. Psychologists constitute a significant proportion of university faculties, so this finding is not very surprising for the total APA group (and indeed the relationship appears notably stronger for this group). The extent to which all of the professional groups are also concentrated in university towns was less expected but is consistent with earlier studies indicating that when health professionals choose practice sites, they consider the quality of the social and cultural environment, the availability of colleagues, and the quality of educational

Table 4: *Correlations, Beta Weights, and Multiple Correlations Between City Characteristics and the Distributions of Psychologists and of Members of Comparison Professions*

| | Psychologists | | | | | | Comparison professions | | | |
| | Listed in 1973 APA *Directory* | | With a private practice | | Listed in *National Register* | | Psychiatrists | | Clinical social workers | |
City characteristic	r	β	r	β	r	β	r	β	r	β
Number										
Population Size	.58	.455	.57	.483	.55	.474	.61	.515	.58	.515
Affluence	−.01	.225	.06	.268	.06	.252	−.03	.200	.17	.367
Residential Mobility	.14	−.005	.13	.021	.12	.017	.09	−.027	.05	−.038
White Predominance	−.25	−.152	−.22	−.155	−.18	−.108	−.31	−.227	−.18	−.180
Emphasis on Higher Education	.60	.526	.41	.340	.44	.372	.38	.279	.32	.273
R	.78		.68		.68		.69		.69	
Median	6.0		.9		1.6		2.4		1.6	
Semi-interquartile range	8.8		1.3		2.5		3.7		2.3	
Number per 100,000 population										
Population Size	.22	.079	.21	.128	.16	.080	.27	.169	.17	.108
Affluence	.05	.274	.17	.331	.17	.321	.05	.261	.30	.460
Residential Mobility	.14	.010	.11	.035	.11	.033	.06	−.035	.01	−.039
White Predominance	−.14	−.131	−.06	−.105	−.02	−.064	−.21	−.236	−.02	−.172
Emphasis on Higher Education	.65	.669	.41	.428	.43	.470	.36	.349	.28	.332
R	.70		.52		.53		.48		.50	
Median	11.7		1.9		3.5		4.9		3.5	
Semi-interquartile range	11.3		2.1		3.8		5.3		3.2	
Percentage of total group in cities	73		76		67		74		66	

Note. Based on the 916 cities and unincorporated places with populations of 25,000 or more in the 1970 census.

facilities for children (U.S. Department of Health, Education, and Welfare, 1974). The standardized partial regression weights indicate that if other city characteristics are held constant, all of these groups tend to be concentrated in relatively wealthy cities. Most importantly, again there is no evidence that any of these groups are distributed in a way that offers special advantages for meeting the needs of black people, poor people, etc., for mental health services.

Discussion

Viewed strictly as an ecological investigation, or as a first try at a more analytic treatment of the geographic distribution of psychologists, this study appears successful. The characteristics of states and cities are correlated substantially and meaningfully with measures of the geographic distribution of psychologists and other mental health professionals. Equally important, the pattern of correlations for psychologists is sufficiently different from the pattern obtained in an earlier study of veterinarians (Richards, 1977) to provide considerable support for the differential validity of the ecological measures and approach. (Many veterinarians are located in states with large-scale agriculture.) At the same time, these correlations must be interpreted with caution. Such aggregate correlations cannot be interpreted as applying to individuals (Robinson, 1950). For example, the fact that many psychologists are located in affluent states does not necessarily mean that psychologists chose those states *because* the states were relatively rich. Such issues could be clarified by surveying psychologists (or members of other professions) to obtain their own reports of reasons for their choice of location. Then it would be possible to investigate whether individual explanations of choice or location covary systematically with ecological characteristics.

If the study is viewed in terms of implications for social policy, a number of limitations should be mentioned. First, membership directories differ in the extent to which they provide comprehensive lists of the members of the professions, are obsolete as soon as they are compiled, and are subject to error of an unknown magnitude from such sources as whether professionals list their place of practice or their place of residence as their address. Also, none of the measures of number of psychologists providing health services was designed specifically to provide data on the proportion of time spent providing services, type of client served, or nature of services provided. Indeed, in some cases it is unclear whether or not a given psychologist really is a health service provider. Possible differences in the specialties and activities of the comparison professionals are a further source of possible ambiguity in the present results. For these reasons, it would be highly desirable to base future analyses on surveys designed specifically to yield data about the distribution and specific activities of professionals who provide mental health services. Ideally, such surveys also should identify practice location in a way that permits maximum flexibility in choice of units of analysis. For example, in addition to cities and states, it should be possible to use counties, SMSAs, community mental health center catchment areas, or zip-code areas as the units of analysis.

Also, the use of rates of service providers per 100,000 population is questionable as a measure of equity in access to services, and there is no clear way to determine an optimal ratio of providers to population. In the case of physicians, interpreting such ratios as measures of the adequacy of health care is controversial (Confrey, 1973; Fuchs, 1974; Senior & Smith, 1972). Despite this controversy, low practitioner-to-population ratios usually are viewed as evidence that the area in question is underserved, and policies intended to equalize practitioner-to-population ratios, such as the Health Professions Educational Assistance Act of 1976, usually are viewed as desirable.

In the context of these limitations and controversies, the results of this study that are most relevant to social policy are probably the findings that psychologists, psychiatrists, and social workers are distributed in strikingly similar ways and that none of these groups can claim to be distributed in special, desirable ways for meeting the needs of all segments of the population. These outcomes, of course, pertain to overall distributions. There will be specific areas that have members of some one of these professions but not the others,[4] and such specific instances have been used to support third-party reimbursement for the mental health services of psychologists (Webb, 1974). But this study indicates that none of these professions is in a position to assert that its *overall* distribution provides an especially compelling argument for third-party reimbursement. Therefore, professions like psychology that are seeking to obtain such reimbursement should make their case mainly on grounds other than overall geographic distribution.

The results also suggest the desirability of efforts to produce a more equal distribution of psychologists. It is true that the number of graduate students in psychology is large relative to the number of practicing psychologists (Cuca, 1975b), and simple market mechanisms may lead to a somewhat more equal distribution. For example, over the next 10 to 20 years, new psychologists probably will be less able to locate in university towns than current psychologists have been. It seems likely, however, that significant "improvement" in the distribution of psychologists will require policies deliberately aimed at producing such improvement. Some of these policies might take the form of specific incentives, such as broadening the National Health Service Corps Scholarship program to include psychologists in its provisions for support of training and subsequent payback through services in shortage areas. Other policies might involve recruiting, selecting, and supporting the training of psychology graduate students who appear relatively likely to locate in areas with low psychologist-to-population ratios. Results from studies of the practice locations of physicians (Bible, 1970; Taylor, Dickman, & Kane, 1973; U.S. Department of

---

[4] In general, the more numerous professions will be able to demonstrate more such specific instances.

Health, Education, and Welfare, 1974) suggest that such students will be those who *come* from low-ratio areas. These policies would contrast with repeated attempts in recent Administration budgets to eliminate federal funds for the training of mental health specialists (Moore, 1976) and probably would contrast with many current practices in the recruitment and selection of psychology graduate students. It would be surprising, for example, to find many clinical programs deliberately favoring students from nonurban areas in recruitment and selection.

Reference Notes

1. Alcohol, Drug Abuse, and Mental Health Administration. *ADAMHA clinical manpower plan for FY 1978–82* (draft). Unpublished manuscript, June 21, 1976.
2. National Institute of Mental Health. *1978–1982 Forward Plan: Mental health services manpower.* Unpublished manuscript, June 7, 1976.
3. American Psychological Association, Council for the Advancement of the Psychological Professions and Sciences, and Association for the Advancement of Psychology. Testimony on the subject of national health insurance, before the Subcommittee on Health, Committee on Ways and Means, U.S. House of Representatives, November 14, 1975.
4. Cuca, J. *1972 survey of psychologists in the U.S. and Canada: Responses of APA members who provide psychological services.* Unpublished tabulations, American Psychological Association, undated.

References

Adkins, D. C. The simple structure of the American Psychological Association. *American Psychologist,* 1954, *9,* 175–180.
Adkins, D. C. A simpler structure of the American Psychological Association. *American Psychologist,* 1973, *28,* 47–54.
American Psychiatric Association. *Membership directory of the American Psychiatric Association.* Washington, D.C.: Author, 1970.
American Psychological Association. *Biographical directory of the American Psychological Association* (1973 ed.). Washington, D.C.: Author, 1973. (a)
American Psychological Association. *Consolidated roster for psychology.* Washington, D.C.: Author, 1973. (b)
American Psychological Association. *Biographical directory of the American Psychological Association* (1975 ed.). Washington, D.C.: Author, 1975.
Angoff, W. H. Scales, norms and equivalent scores. In R. L. Thorndike (Ed.), *Educational measurement* (2nd ed.). Washington, D.C.: American Council on Education, 1971.
Astin, A. W. An empirical classification of higher educational institutions. *Journal of Educational Psychology,* 1962, *53,* 224–235.
Bailey, K. D., & Mulcahy, P. Sociocultural versus neoclassical ecology: A contribution to the problem of scope in sociology. *Sociological Quarterly,* 1972, *13,* 37–48.
Bible, B. L. Physicians' views of medical practice in nonmetropolitan communities. *Public Health Reports,* 1970, *85,* 11–17.
Boneau, C. A., & Cuca, J. M. An overview of psychology's human resources: Characteristics and salaries from the 1972 APA survey. *American Psychologist,* 1974, *29,* 821–840.
Bonjean, C. M. The community as a research site and object of inquiry. In C. M. Bonjean, T. N. Clark, & R. L. Lineberry (Eds.), *Community politics: A behavioral approach.* New York: Free Press, 1971.
Cates, J. Psychology's manpower: Report on the 1968 national register of scientific and technical personnel. *American Psychologist,* 1970, *25,* 254–263.
Confrey, E. A. The logic of a "shortage" of health manpower. *International Journal of Health Services,* 1973, *3,* 253–259.
Council for the National Register of Health Service Providers in Psychology. *National register of health service providers in psychology.* Washington, D.C.: Author, 1976.
Cuca, J. Job crunch hits scientists harder than professionals. *APA Monitor,* June 1975, p. 10. (a)
Cuca, J. Psychology Ph.D.s climb as others succumb to "new depression." *APA Monitor,* August 1975, pp. 5; 8. (b)
Duncan, O. D., & Schnore, L. F. Cultural, behavioral, and ecological perspectives in the study of social organization. *American Journal of Sociology,* 1959, *65,* 132–146.
Fuchs, V. R. *Who shall live?* New York: Basic Books, 1974.
Harries, K. D. Cities and crime: A geographic model. *Criminology,* 1976, *14,* 369–386.
Hawley, A. H. *Human ecology: A theory of community structure.* New York: Ronald Press, 1950.
Hutchinson, J. (Ed.). *Population and food supply.* Cambridge, England: Cambridge University Press, 1969.
Marden, P. G. A demographic and ecological analysis of the distribution of physicians in metropolitan America. *American Journal of Sociology,* 1960, *72,* 290–300.
Meyer, D. R. Classification of U.S. metropolitan areas by the characteristics of their nonwhite populations. In B. J. L. Berry (Ed.), *City classification handbook: Method and applications.* New York: Wiley, 1972.
Michaels, J. W. On the relation between human ecology and behavioral social psychology. *Social Forces,* 1974, *52,* 313–321.
Moore, P. Turnaround slated for mental health training: Providers wonder, bombshell or shellgame? *APA Monitor,* August 1976, pp. 10–11.
National Association of Social Workers. *N.A.S.W. register of clinical social workers.* Washington, D.C.: Author, 1976.
Perloff, R. (Ed.). Psychology's manpower: The education of psychologists. *American Psychologist,* 1972, *27,* 355–506.
Reskin, B., & Campbell, F. L. Physician distribution across metropolitan areas. *American Journal of Sociology,* 1974, *79,* 981–998.
Richards, J. M., Jr. A study of the "environments" of Japanese universities. *Research in Higher Education,* 1973, *1,* 87–99. (a)

Richards, J. M., Jr. The psychology of farming: A review of twenty-five years of research. *Journal of Vocational Behavior*, 1973, *3*, 485–501. (b)

Richards, J. M., Jr. An ecological analysis of the geographic distribution of veterinarians in the United States. *Journal of Vocational Behavior*, 1977, *7*, 216–231.

Richards, J. M., Jr. An ecological analysis of the impact of the U.S. Supreme Court's 1973 abortion decision. *Journal of Applied Social Psychology,* in press.

Robinson, W. S. Ecological correlations and the behavior of individuals. *American Sociological Review*, 1950, *15*, 351–357.

Rummel, R. J. *Applied factor analysis.* Evanston, Ill.: Northwestern University Press, 1970.

Sawyer, J. Dimensions of nations: Size, wealth, and politics. *American Journal of Sociology*, 1967, *73*, 145–172.

Senior, B., & Smith, B. A. The number of physicians as a constraint on the delivery of health care. *Journal of the American Medical Association*, 1972, *222*, 178–183.

Taylor, M., Dickman, W., & Kane, R. Medical students' attitudes toward rural practice. *Journal of Medical Education*, 1973, *48*, 885–895.

U.S. Bureau of the Census. *County and city data book 1972.* Washington, D.C.: U.S. Government Printing Office, 1973.

U.S. Department of Health, Education, and Welfare. *Factors influencing location of professional health manpower: A review of the literature* (Report No. HRA 75-3). Washington, D.C.: Author, 1974.

U.S. Office of Education. *Education directory 1972–73: Higher education.* Washington, D.C.: U.S. Government Printing Office, 1972.

U.S. Office of Education. *Digest of educational statistics, 1973.* Washington, D.C.: U.S. Government Printing Office, 1974.

Webb, J. T. Distribution of psychologists and psychiatrists by zip code areas in Ohio. *Ohio Psychologist*, 1974, *20*, 5–12.

At the time of original publication of this article, *James M. Richards, Jr.,* was on staff with the School of Health Sciences, The Johns Hopkins University. *Gary R. Gottfredson* was Administrative Officer for Special Projects, the American Psychological Association.

This study was conducted as part of the overall research program of the Office of Health Manpower Studies, School of Health Services, The Johns Hopkins University. This office is supported in part by a grant from the Robert Wood Johnson Foundation.

3

Current Legal and Legislative Status of Professional Psychology

The majority of the statutory and regulatory recognition of professional psychologists has occurred in the last 20 years, despite the fact that psychologists as providers of health services have a long history. Psychologists are now licensed or certified by statute in all 50 states and the District of Columbia. A national standardized examination has been developed for use as one component in the licensing process. A *National Register of Health Service Providers in Psychology* has been established to identify psychologists who are licensed/certified and are health service providers. The *Register* has been adopted as a reference source of qualified practitioners by many insurance carriers and government programs. In addition, an increasing number of federal and state laws and programs recognize psychologists as independent and autonomous providers of mental health assessment and treatment. In the first article in this section, Dörken reviews the range and degree of recognition that psychology has achieved.

The second article in this section, also by Dörken, provides an excellent overview of the legislative and regulatory process and demonstrates that the development of the rules and procedures influencing a profession is not a single-stage event. Rather, it is a process extending over time and influenced by many different parties with differing perspectives. Dörken details the various steps in the passage and implementation of a law—initiation of a bill, hearings, passage, regulation development, and administrative enforcement—and argues that psychologists are often overly idealistic in their beliefs about legislative efforts. Merely presenting the facts and a logical analysis of them one time will not result in appropriate and realistic laws being passed and meaningfully implemented. Multiple factors influence legislation and regulations, and Dörken underscores the need to monitor and participate in every stage of the process to ensure legislative success.

Patrick DeLeon, a psychologist and Senate staff member, presents the cross-pressure the Carter administration has placed on itself regarding national health insurance and encourages psychologists' continued involvement in helping to shape any legislation. He believes that organized psychology is in excellent political shape. While psychology may only be a small force in the shaping of national health policy, DeLeon feels it is an important one. He argues that it is essential to strive for the inclusion of psychological services under any national health insurance plan, for the best interest of both the nation and our profession.

Laws, Regulations, and Psychological Practice

Herbert Dörken

The recognition of psychologists as independent health care providers is traced through national laws and regulations (CHAMPUS, HMO legislation, federal employee health benefits, IRS regulations, etc.), the licensure/certification movement, the adoption of freedom-of-choice legislation, and judicial recognition.

In years to come, psychology may well look back upon the 93rd Congress as the turning point in its formal recognition as a health profession. Since the late 1960s, some major insurance carriers (see Chapter Six) have recognized psychological services in their coverage; CHAMPUS (see Chapter Nine) was directed to consider the profession as a primary provider of health services in June 1970. The first federal law recognizing psychology as an independent profession entitled to engage in health practice, however, was the District of Columbia Licensing Law. Passed in 1971 by the Congress and signed into law, it helped to set the stage for later events. It remained for the 93rd Congress to pass a series of laws broadening the statutory base of psychology as a health profession.

The Veterans Health Care Expansion Act of 1973, PL 93-82, in recognizing the services of psychologists for the dependents of totally disabled veterans, opened a new area for psychologists in health services. Then, after two prior vetoes, the Rehabilitation Act of 1973 was passed. This legislation, PL 93-112, in delineating the scope of services, recognizes the services of physicians *or* licensed psychologists for both assessment and restorative services, and for physical or mental disability, within the scope of practice of these two professions. This law has a broad impact in setting standards and guidelines for all state rehabilitation programs. Extended restorative services (up to eighteen months) can be authorized when these services carry the prospect of employability or improving employment.[1] Mental disorder is the single largest disability category and, together with mental retardation, comprised over half (50.7%) the clients receiving rehabilitation services nationally according to 1972 reports from the Social and Rehabilitation Services (see Chapter Four).

Following extended consideration of models to improve health care delivery, Congress passed PL 93-222, the Health Maintenance Organization (HMO) Act of 1973. Basic health care services are to include "short-term (not to exceed twenty visits) out-patient evaluative and crisis intervention mental health services." Services are also to include treatment and referral services for the abuse of or addiction to alcohol or drugs. Supplemental health services could extend these mental health services. The HMO model includes both "medical groups" and "individual practice associations." The regulations implementing this act explicitly enumerate "clinical psychologists" among the recognized health professionals (Title 42—Public Health, Subchapter J, Part 110, Section 110.101 [h] [1]). The Disaster Relief Act of 1974, PL 93-288, also provided for professional counseling for mental health problems caused or aggravated by a disaster. So that health services will be more equitably available, attention is being given to critical manpower shortage areas and to

---

[1] Psychologists were first recognized by CHAMPUS in 1970 by directive. In the 1977 Appropriation Act, the phrase "medically or psychologically necessary" was added. These words were omitted in 1978 and reincorporated in the 1979 Appropriation Act (PL-95-111).

the potential role of the National Health Service Corps established pursuant to PL 92-585. Proposed rules were issued in the Federal Register on January 6, 1975. Included within the definition of "assigned personnel" are such professions as "physicians, dentists, *psychologists,* nurses [italics added]." Guidelines for implementing the Head Start Performance Standards were published in July 1975. The resources that may be contracted include "Private Practitioners of . . . Psychology . . ." (HEW, OCD, 1975, p. 27). Further, this manual defines a "mental health professional" as including "a licensed psychologist."

Psychology, together with optometry (much of whose technology derives from the experimental findings and methods of sensory psychology), sought recognition as primary providers in Federal Employee Health Benefit Plans through HR 9440 (Jerome Waldie, California) and S 2618 (Gayle McGee, Wyoming) such that the employee would have free choice of and direct access to such licensed providers. The bills drew opposition from the Civil Service Commission, from the National Association of Blue Shield Plans, and from the American Psychiatric Association. As amended to licensed clinical psychologists and optometrists, S 2619 was approved unanimously by the full committee and signed into law as PL 93-363 on July 30, 1974. This law amended Title 5, U.S. Code, Chapter 89—Health Insurance, Section 8902 (j), by providing that "an employee, annuitant, or family member . . . shall be free to select, and shall have direct access to, such a clinical psychologist . . . without supervision or referral by another health practitioner." Parity for clinical psychology with other health practitioners was thus established in a nationwide program covering about 8.5 million federal employees and dependents or retirees. Eighteen states had already enacted similar freedom-of-choice statutes, since increased to twenty-three as of July 1975.

Psychological services are also recognized in tax laws. Beginning with the 1973 Federal Income Tax Form instructions for Standard Form 1040, Schedule A, itemized deductions for medical and dental expenses have included, "payments to . . . psychiatrists, *psychologists,* and psychoanalysts" ([italics added] page 10, Column 1, 1974 IRS Form 1040 instructions).

This change on clarification was agreed to by the Internal Revenue Service upon request of the author.

Congress also paid attention to the problems of handicapped children. PL 93-380 amended the Elementary and Secondary Education Act, Title VI, Education of the Handicapped.[2] This legislation includes the mentally retarded and emotionally disturbed among those handicapped who are "health impaired." The conference report clearly intends that the services for these children whose health is handicapped will include psychological processes.

Employability is a matter of concern to Congress and federal agencies. The U.S. Department of Labor regulations implementing PL 93-203, the Comprehensive Manpower Program, define psychological services within health care, ". . . to the extent any such treatment or services are necessary to enable a participant to obtain or retain employment. . . ." (Title 29, Part 94, Section 94.4 [x]). In a similar vein, the Department of Labor has adopted and published regulations in the *Federal Register* (September 18, 1974, p. 43174) to implement the work incentive program (WIN) for recipients of Aid to the Families of Dependent Children (AFDC) under Title IV of the Social Security Act. Section 56.20 (b)(4) requires that the AFDC recipient shall register unless "Incapacitated, when verified by the IMU [Income Maintenance Unit] that a physical or mental impairment, determined by a physician *or licensed or certified psychologist* . . . prevents the individual from engaging in employment or training under WIN [emphasis supplied]." Supportive services include selected vocational rehabilitation services as defined by the Rehabilitation Act of 1973. Looking to the field of workers' compensation and to federal employees, PL 93-416 was signed September 7, 1974, amending Chapter 81 of Subpart G of Title V of the U.S. Code relating to work injuries compensation under the Federal Employee Compensation Act (FECA). Among other things, this law broadened the definition of both "physician" and "medical, surgical, and hospital services and supplies," to include "clinical psychologists." What may be of special sig-

---

[2] This has been substantially superseded by PL 94-142.

nificance is that, in contrast to the Rehabilitation Act, the law amending the Federal Employee Health Benefit Act (FEHBA), and the regulations implementing the HMO Act, in which cases psychology had exerted a concerted effort to secure its inclusion in these signed pieces of health legislation, the inclusion of "clinical psychologist" in PL 93-416 was accomplished essentially by "referencing in." Perhaps psychology *has* turned the corner as a health profession.

Just as in the CHAMPUS directive, federal agency decisions can have a very substantial impact. Thus, in the early 1960s National Institute of Mental Health (NIMH) regulations provided that psychologists could serve as directors of community mental health centers—after they were faced with such a fact in a number of states. More recently, the Veterans Administration has issued regulations providing that psychologists and other health professionals licensed or certified by the state may provide services on a fee basis to outpatients through VA clinics and that psychologists, among others, may be appointed to direct such facilities. The United States Department of Defense now includes psychologists in its policy, which provides that "any qualified health professional may command or exercise administrative direction of a military health care facility . . . without regard to the officer's basic health profession" (Memorandum from Secretary of Defense to the Secretaries of the Military on subject of Staff and Command Assignments of Health Professionals, May 1, 1973).

During the 93rd Congress, the national health insurance bill with the most sponsors was the Vance Hartke-Clifford Hansen (Indiana and Wyoming) S 444 bill, generally referred to as the AMA (American Medical Association) Medicredit Bill. Without any evident subsequent objection from the AMA, Senator Hartke introduced a series of amendments to this bill early in 1974, amendments that, essentially, throughout changed *medical* to *health, illness* to *disability, medical and dental services* to *professional health care services, doctor* to *licensed practitioner,* and *psychiatric* to *mental health.* And in the enumeration of professions these amendments added psychology, optometry, and podiatry. The Hugh Scott-Charles Percy bill (Pennsylvania and Illinois) S 2756, would have recognized licensed psychologists as independent providers from the outset. In 1974 the insurance industry amended its Omar Burleson-Thomas McIntyre bill (Texas and New Hampshire), S 1100, to include licensed doctors of clinical psychology. Senator Daniel Inouye (Hawaii) then introduced S 3645 to recognize psychologists as primary providers under Part B of Medicare. This move was followed on November 26 with HR 17520 by Representative James Corman (California), intended to so recognize clinical psychologists.

By the end of January 1975 both the Inouye and Corman bills had been reintroduced in the 94th Congress, with strong supporting statements. This time, however, the language of both was identical (*clinical psychologist*), and as of March, S 123 and HR 2270 had already accumulated substantial cosponsorship. Representative Patsy Mink (Hawaii) had also introduced HR 3980, a separate bill with identical language. Soon after, Representative Spark Matsunaga (Hawaii) introduced HR 3674, amending the Edward Kennedy-James Corman Health Security Act (Massachusetts and California) to recognize the services of clinical psychologists and to increase the extent of ambulatory mental health services. In March, Senator Phillip Hart (Michigan) concerned that the national health insurance proposals being submitted did not provide for adequate mental health care, introduced S 1332, the Mental Health Act of 1975. This bill seeks "to end the discrimination between mental health care and other forms of health care." In the process it delineates a more realistic range of benefits and includes psychologists as fully recognized providers in all phases. Then, by May, the insurance industry's National Health Care Act of 1975 had been introduced, including qualified clinical psychologists as physicians (HR 5990 Burleson [Texas]; S 1438 McIntyre [New Hampshire]).

Obviously, future events are not predictable with certainty. The country's economic crisis appears likely at this time to delay implementation of National Health Insurance, perhaps for a few years. Consequently, potential changes in Medicare take on added importance, as do the establishment of national guidelines or standards for the National Workers' Compensation

Act of 1975 (S 2018 Harrison Williams [New Jersey]). This bill recognizes clinical psychologists as primary providers within the definition of *physician*. Malpractice has emerged as a major problem in health care delivery by physicians and S 215 (Inouye), the National Medical Injury Compensation Insurance Act of 1975, would introduce a "no-fault" method of claim settlement. It would also include "clinical psychologists" among the designated "health professionals."

Lay organizations such as the National Association for Mental Health (NAMH) have become increasingly active, fighting impoundment of federal funds for community mental health center training, and research. NAMH has been equally vocal in its demands that national health insurance include realistic coverage for nervous and mental disorders and that all the major mental health professions meeting national standards of training be recognized as providers, whether in private practice or in organized settings.

The past few years have shown that if psychology is to be recognized as a health profession more will be needed than a distinguished record in the field of health research. More will be needed than the significant supply of competent professionals in positions of administrative responsibility in health, rehabilitation, mental health, and mental retardation services. Recognition will require effective advocacy. The Council for the Advancement of Psychological Professions and Sciences (CAPPS), formed in 1972, has been joined by the Association for the Advancement of Psychology (AAP), established in 1974. Both advocacy organizations are now working in cooperative "common cause"— indeed, are in the process of merging into a single organization (AAP). And psychologists— or at least more of them—have become alerted to public policy issues and the legislative process.

Licensure and Certification

In 1945, Connecticut became the first state to *certify* psychologists. In 1946, Virginia passed the first law that *licensed* those who might practice psychology. By 1972, a quarter century later, forty-six states, the District of Columbia,

and six Canadian provinces had laws governing the title of psychologist or the practice of psychology. Since then, Iowa has passed such legislation, leaving only Missouri, South Dakota, and Vermont without such statutes.[3]

The distinction between licensing and certifying is important. A licensing law is intended to define the practice of psychology and to restrict such function to qualified persons, who may be psychologists or members of other professions using psychological techniques. By contrast, a certification law limits the use of the title *psychologist* to qualified persons and may or may not include a definition of practice (APA, 1967). Twenty-six states have licensure, the remainder certification. All provincial laws (Canadian) are of the certification type. Currently, in many states psychologists are taking steps, where necessary, to secure a "practice" law, one in which the practice of psychology is properly defined.

The APA Committee on State Legislation (COSL) has monitored and provided guidance in these developments. Model conditions were outlined in the COSL report (1967). For example, using illustrative language, the report recommended that these statutes provide for privileged communication between therapist and client. As of January 1973, thirty-seven of the U.S. laws (including that passed by the District of Columbia) had such a provision for confidentiality. Then, to not unduly restrict professional mobility, reciprocity was encouraged between states with equivalent standards. Only the Arizona law fails in this respect. For licensing or certification as a "psychologist," the doctorate has consistently been recommended as the minimum standard, a standard that has vigorously been reaffirmed by key committees of APA, such as COHI (Committee on Health Insurance) and COSL, by the Board of Professional Affairs, and by the Council itself, as recently as January 1975. Iowa, Pennsylvania, and West Virginia, in enabling the licensure (quite apart from a grandfathering clause) of master's-level training, with additional experience to compensate for the lack of training, are thus in

---

[3] In 1977, Missouri became the last state to enact a psychology licensing law. The process of gaining licensure in all fifty states and the District of Columbia took 32 years.

conflict with the national standards. Subsequent progress and changing conditions, however, now are leading to serious reconsideration of many "standard" provisions. Whereas exemptions from the law had typically included salaried employees of state and federal agencies—of public service—the Standards for Providers of Psychological Services adopted as APA policy by the Council of Representatives, September 2, 1974, when implemented, would require elimination of this dual standard. In effect, it is now the national policy of organized psychology that all psychologist service providers must be licensed or certified.

The statutory base of practice should be consistent with psychology's claim that it is a health profession. Critical in this regard is the definition of practice. As of January 1973, whereas forty-three statutes contained a definition of practice, psychotherapy was explicitly included in twenty-four states and in the District of Columbia. The guideline definition, however, seems overly focused on mental disorder and to be without a key word, *treatment* (included in the California law). Thus, serious consideration should be given to securing practice legislation that ". . . includes, but is not restricted to: diagnosis, prevention, *treatment* and amelioration of adjustment problems and emotional and mental disorders of individuals and groups *and of the psychological concomitants of disease, illness, injury or disability*" [italics added]. Moreover, since psychology has provided the major impetus and leadership in the development of the behavior therapies and of biofeedback technology, it would also seem advisable to broaden the definition of *practice* so that these modes of treatment are explicitly included.

The primary purpose of this legislation has always been protection of the public and assurance of improved quality by demanding sound standards for qualification. Originally that public was more narrowly seen in the perspective of private practice. Hence, licensing was a requirement when psychological services were to be offered for a fee, monetary or otherwise. The rapid growth of health insurance and of service contracting, points to the need for a broader definition of *fee,* to include third-party reimbursement and services prepaid by premium or contract.

Psychologists, just as physicians and some other professions, have been licensed generically, with the expectation, built into the profession's code of ethics, that the licensee will limit practice to his or her area of competence. But now there is a growing public recognition that no one can be truly competent in all the specialties of a broad profession and that the recipient of services should be protected by the addition of specialty certification to the licensing process. Specialty certification should not simply be a voluntary limitation of one's practice to a specialty area—whether or not one has completed the required training or passed professional exams. Specialty certification should be issued by the regulatory state agency, with this certification and the basic license subject to conditions of continuing education for reissue. The state of Oregon, in fact, recently passed new legislation giving the Board of Psychologist Examiners the authority to require continuing education of psychologists. The first of its kind in psychology, this legislation is seen as a forerunner of general provisions to come. The current climate would suggest that clear delineation of clinical training and experience in organized health settings may become essential for continued recognition of psychologists as health service providers.

The insurance industry has shown a willingness to recognize psychologists as health practitioners, but it increasingly wants assurance that the practitioner has the requisite training and experience in health care delivery and that the services being provided are health services. A collegial relationship among health professions requires that the professions involved be health providers, not education specialists, specialized counselors, or management or vocational specialists. With such concerns in mind, the National Register of Health Service Providers in Psychology has been established. Its first directory became available in the summer of 1975, with listing made on the basis of a credentials review. Not only will this directory help to delineate the current available health manpower resources of psychology but it is also expected to facilitate claim processing and reimbursement for those listed. Indeed, the directory could well be "referenced in" as a criterion guideline by insurance carriers and agencies contracting for health services.

No unduplicated roster of state licensed or certified psychologists yet exists, not even an exact count, though estimates have been attempted (see Chapter One) (before the *National Register* survey). Three states do not have statutory regulation of psychology—Missouri, South Dakota, and Vermont.[4] The Iowa law is too recent (1974) to have yet provided sufficient time for the processing of those to be "grandfathered in." And, by local policy, Hawaii will advise whether a specific person is licensed there or not, but will not release a directory of its state licensed psychologists. Despite passage of the Pennsylvania law in 1972, funding uncertainties and other problems have delayed availability of a directory. Rhode Island simply does not respond to requests for such information.

Summary detail is provided in Table 1, with licensing and certification figures for forty-four states and the District of Columbia. The most current directories ranged from January 1973 to February 1975. In each instance, out-of-state residents were dropped from the count, so that the tabulation presented is unduplicated. For example, 218 residents of Maryland and Virginia, since licensed in their resident state, are not included in the District of Columbia count, which as a result totals only 73. In the seven states (Arkansas, Indiana, Maine, Michigan, Minnesota, North Carolina, and Tennessee) where licensing or certification is multilevel, only the top level, the level recognized for independent practice, was counted. Thus, by this conservative count, there were 18,058 psychologists licensed or certified for independent practice in 45 jurisdictions, a ratio of .959 such psychologists per 10,000 of population. Following the same ratio for the other three states with statutory regulation from which no information was available, the overall count would be increased to 19,508. When contrasted to the 1972 APA membership or the *Consolidated Roster for Psychology* (American Psychological Association, 1972) in the country, it is apparent that the number of psychologists qualified for independent practice by statute are but 57.5% of APA members and 45% of all

known psychologists in the country. These figures are of course already outdated. By 1974, total APA membership had grown to just over 37,000; had exceeded 39,000 by mid-1975; and is projected to reach 41,500 in 1976. It may well be, then, that the number of practitioners qualified by statute is at this writing some 20% larger than the above derived total—say, 23,000.

Freedom of Choice

Although the APA Council of Representatives in September 1962 adopted official policy recognizing properly qualified professional psychologists as independent practitioners, it should be noted in historical perspective that the adoption was in reaction to a storm of protest from practitioners over policy adopted in 1960. In May 1960 the APA Board of Professional Affairs had recommended gaining federal acceptance of provisions for covering psychological services when deemed necessary by those having medical responsibility for the treatment of the claimant. In other words, the APA had recommended supervision by *another* profession. When that policy was adopted, the association's governance heard clearly from its clinical membership. The insurance problem became a cause célèbre.

In the mid-1960s the APA Committee on Health Insurance (COHI) encouraged state psychological associations to introduce legislation that would, by state, entitle health insurance subscribers to freedom of choice (FOC) and direct access to qualified psychologist practitioners for covered benefits without the need for referral or supervision by another profession. Twenty-three states (Editor's note: In 1979, twenty-nine states) now have such legislation, six of these statutes having passed in 1974, five in the first half of 1975. The addition of Connecticut by Public Act 75-286 on June 5th seems particularly significant, in view of the state's prominence in the insurance industry. Moreover, both the Connecticut and the new Minnesota laws mandate minimum levels of coverage for mental and nervous conditions or disorders. As already noted, comparable FOC law was passed by Congress for federal employee health plans—over considerable opposi-

---

[4] As of 1977, all fifty states and the District of Columbia have legislation licensing or certifying the practice of psychology.

Table 1: *U.S. State Resident Psychologists Qualified for Practice*

States	Population 1973 Census Estimates; in Thousands	Licensed or Certified Psychologists (State Residents)	Registry Date Month/ Year	Licensed/ Certified	Ratio Licensed Psychologists per 10,000 Population	1973 APA Member Directory	1972 Consolidated Roster Psychologists
Alabama	3,539	112	9/74	L	.316	235	298
Alaska	330	21	74	L	.636	29	37
Arizona	2,058	318	2/75	C	1.545	323	441
Arkansas	2,037	62	1/74	L	.304	113	151
California	20,601	2,953	5/73	L	1.433	4,426	5,655
Colorado	2,437	253	1/75	L	1.021	507	763
Connecticut	3,076	293	11/73	L	.953	740	955
Delaware	576	57	4/74	L	.990	110	141
District of Columbia	746	73	73	L	.979	720	830
Florida	7,678	396	10/74	L	.516	916	1,124
Georgia	4,786	196	73	L	.410	455	581
Hawaii	832	Individual confirmation only		L	—	143	184
Idaho	770	50	74	L	.649	51	93
Illinois	11,236	1,414	8/74	L	1.258	1,879	2,448
Indiana	5,316	350	1/74	C	.658	604	782
Iowa	2,904	Directory under development		—	—	333	493
Kansas	2,279	199	11/73	C	.873	364	520
Kentucky	3,342	107	8/73	L	.320	273	374
Louisiana	3,764	161	11/73	L	.428	223	297
Maine	1,028	74	74	L	.720	120	160
Maryland	4,070	420	6/73	C	1.032	970	1,160
Massachusetts	5,818	1,212	1/75	L	2.083	1,372	1,705
Michigan	9,044	405	7/73	C	.448	1,324	1,795
Minnesota	3,897	215	3/73	L	.552	594	884
Mississippi	2,281	91	7/74	L	.399	119	156
Missouri	4,757	Nonstatutory	—	—	—	532	667
Montana	721	43	8/73	L	.600	61	92
Nebraska	1,542	124	4/74	L	.804	173	237
Nevada	548	26	2/74	C	.474	68	80
New Hampshire	791	62	7/74	C	.784	110	153
New Jersey	7,361	732	2/75	L	.994	1,393	1,703
New Mexico	1,106	62	12/73	C	.561	144	179
New York	18,265	3,192	6/74	L	1.748	5,415	6,509
North Carolina	5,273	283	7/73	L	.537	537	710
North Dakota	640	40	74	C	.625	54	67
Ohio	10,731	1,342	1/74	L	1.251	1,361	1,709
Oklahoma	2,663	119	73	L	.447	247	348
Oregon	2,225	169	7/74	L	.760	318	458
Pennsylvania	11,905	(2,056) licenses issued by 5/75		L	—	2,081	2,556
Rhode Island	973	110	9/74	C	1.131	131	182
South Carolina	2,726	129	1/74	L	.473	191	267
South Dakota	685	Nonstatutory	—	—	—	41	65
Tennessee	4,126	224	11/73	L	.543	421	579
Texas	11,794	845	4/74	L	.716	1,330	1,738
Utah	1,157	157	4/74	L	1.357	181	267
Vermont	464	Nonstatutory	—	—	—	92	112
Virginia	4,811	172	73	L	.358	746	883
Washington	3,429	241	1/73	L	.703	497	733
West Virginia	1,794	84	3/74	L	.468	147	172
Wisconsin	4,569	424	4/74	L	.928	668	893
Wyoming	353	46	1/74	L	1.303	48	73
44 States and the District of Columbia	188,304	18,058	—	—	.959	30,254	38,761
U.S. Total[a]	209,851	—	—	—	—	30,930	43,461

[a] Author's note: In 1977, all states had psychology licensing laws. More current data on the number of psychologists per state is found in Mills, Wellner, and VandenBos (1979) which appears in Section 2.

tion. The current status of these statutes is summarized in Table 2.

New Jersey, in 1968, was the first state to adopt FOC legislation. The present twenty-three states cover over half the U.S. population and 12,853, or 66% of the 19,508 estimated total of psychologists with statutory authorization for independent practice. The 12% differential suggests that FOC legislation may have an effect on (or be due to) the manpower supply of psychologist practitioners. Both Illinois and Hawaii do not have FOC legislation, though they report reasonable recognition by insurance carriers and by Blue Cross and Blue Shield.

Illinois, however, now has a bill active in the current legislative sessions. Similar informal local "understandings" may exist in other parts of the country. For example, the Washington law covers disability policies. A bill to extend it to all types of plans several years ago was vetoed by the governor on the assurance of local medical cooperation. Nearly two years passed, however, before all county health plans put this assurance into effect. In some states, the office of the commissioner of insurance will actively pursue delivery of coverage for insured citizens. Thus, while the Michigan FOC law does not include health service plans, the Michigan In-

Table 2: *Freedom-of-Choice Legislation Recognizing Psychology*

State	Passed	1973 Census (1,000)	1972 APA Members	Licensed or Certified Psychologists[a]	Directory Date	Licensed or Certified Psychologists per 10,000 Population	Explanatory Note[b]		
1. Massachusetts	12/73	5,818	1,372	1,212	1/75	2.083	M	B	OS
2. New York	6/69	18,265	5,415	3,192	6/74	1.748		B	OS
3. New Jersey	68, 12/73	7,361	1,393	732	2/75	.994		B	OS
4. Utah	3/69, 75	1,157	181	157	4/74	1.357		B	OS
5. Maryland	7/72	4,070	970	420	6/73	1.032		B	OS
6. California	69, 8/74	20,601	4,426	2,953	5/73	1.433	(M)	B	
7. Virginia	9/73	4,811	746	172	73	.358		B	
8. Oklahoma	6/71	2,663	247	119	73	.447		B	OS
9. Kansas	3/74	2,279	364	199	11/73	.873		B	
10. Nebraska	4/74	1,542	173	124	4/74	.804		B	
11. Tennessee	2/74	4,126	421	224	11/73	.543		B	
12. Louisiana	74, 7/75	3,764	223	161	11/73	.428	(M)	B	
13. Mississippi	7/74	2,281	119	91	7/74	.399		B	
14. Montana	3/71	721	61	43	8/73	.600	WC		
15. Colorado	7/71	2,437	507	253	1/75	1.021		(B)	
16. Washington	71	3,429	487	241	1/73	.703		(B) on 12/74	
17. Michigan	6/68	9,044	1,324	405	7/73	.448			
18. Ohio	1/74	10,731	1,361	1,342	1/74	1.251	WC	(B*) on 5/74	
19. Arkansas	3/75	2,037	113	62	1/74	.304		B	
20. Minnesota	5/75	3,897	594	215	3/73	.552	M	B	
21. Oregon	5/75	2,225	318	169	7/74	.760		B	
22. Connecticut	6/75	3,076	740	293	11/73	.953	M	B	
23. Maine	6/75	1,028	120	74	74	.720		B	
FEHBA (Federal Employee Health Benefit Act)	1/74	(8,500)	—	—	—	—	F	B	OS
Total[c]	—	113,713 54.2% of 209,851	21,675 63.9% of 33,930	12,853		1.130			
National				23,000 estimated					

[a] Unduplicated, state resident, licensed or certified for independent practice.
[b] Unless otherwise specified, statute applies only to disability (health) insurance policies under the Insurance Code.
M—Mental health coverage mandatory; (M)—must be provided if requested by the insured group.
B—Specific language providing for coverage of Blue Shield contracts; (B)—included by negotiation; (B*)—governed by insurance law.
OS—Specific language requiring recognition of psychological services whether the policy issued within or outside of the state but applies to state residents.
WC—Specific language providing for coverage under Workers' Compensation Plans; (WC)—negotiated inclusion in state fund.
F—PL 93-363; applies to all federal employee plans.
[c] Author's note: Six additional states have passed legislation as of this printing: District of Columbia (1975), Illinois (1976), New Mexico (1977), North Carolina (1977), Texas (1977), and Pennsylvania.

surance Bureau, in advising Blue Cross and Blue Shield of its 1975 program initiatives, noted that certified consulting psychologists in practice were not being reimbursed:

> Based on the nature and extent of the education received by the various specialists, the Insurance Bureau staff is of the opinion that trained certified consulting psychologists may, in almost all cases, be more qualified to provide mental health services than are most D.O.s and M.D.s not specializing in psychiatry. Blue Cross and Blue Shield's denial of coverage for mental health benefits rendered by certified consulting psychologists in solo practice appears to be based on a strict interpretation of their legal mandate to provide medical services . . . this issue seems to be centered around the acceptability to Blue Cross and Blue Shield of the professional discipline providing the service.

Such initiatives and local understandings notwithstanding, the law is a more certain vehicle. Thus, Michigan HB 5078, introduced this year, would extend recognition from simple disability policies to nonprofit medical care corporations as well.

While state insurance codes typically regulate the disability (health) policies of the insurance carriers, disability is but one major segment of the market. To assure that a freedom-of-choice statute will be broadly applicable, it is necessary to also cover self-insured employee welfare benefit funds, hospital corporation plans, and health service plans (see Chapter Six; also, Table 2), which, depending on the state, may fall under the labor, health and welfare, government, or other code. Moreover, it is not sufficient simply to cover policies or plans issued, amended, or renewed in the state, but also policies, wherever issued, that are delivered within the state or apply to residents or employees of a state. The "out-of-state" problem applies principally to the disability policies and to health service plans that are designed for national coverage of a particular group.

The "corrective" potential of this type of legislation is well illustrated by the New York Court of Appeals decision (*Moore* v. *Metropolitan,* 1973). As one outcome of that judicial decision, the state insurance commissioner instructed the home office of Travelers to pay all claims of New York psychologists treating New York patients, retroactive to 1969 (the date the law was enacted). In November 1973, Travelers issued a circular memorandum (S. A. Maher,

Vice President, Group Policies) to all group health insurance policyholders, which stated, in part: "For purposes of compliance with these statutes, effective immediately, medical care and treatment under medical, comprehensive medical and major medical expense insurance coverages will be considered to include the services of a licensed or certified clinical psychologist when acting within the legal scope of his practice . . . for psychological testing and for psychotherapy in connection with a mental or nervous illness or disorder to the extent benefits would have been paid if the psychotherapy had been performed by a psychiatrist." Then, faced with a class action suit by the California State Psychological Association, Metropolitan Life decided to reimburse psychologists, effective August 1973, for services covered by one of the largest single health insurance plans in California, namely the North American Rockwell Health Plan (Rockwell International). These were important breakthroughs, but more was to come.

The nature of contract insurance law is such that the conditions in the state of issue are to apply wherever delivered unless there are explicit provisos to the contrary. Thus, for example, a master policy issued in New Jersey, which has an all-encompassing, strong freedom-of-choice law, should recognize the services of licensed psychologists in another state, whether or not that state has FOC legislation. Counsel for the New Jersey Psychological Association recently put this question to the Equitable Life Assurance Society and received a January 22, 1975 reply, which stated, in part: "Under this law recognition of psychologists will be provided in all States unless in a particular State a psychologist is not recognized under State law, that is, there is no certification or licensing act for a psychologist."

Even prior to PL 93-363, this matter was discussed with the U.S. Civil Service Commission whose director of the Bureau of Retirement, Insurance and Occupational Health, Thomas A. Tinsley, on March 12, 1974, noted that Commission policy is that its insurance carriers must comply with applicable state law. "We have advised our carriers that they should not rely on their contracts with us to avoid a state law and that if they pay benefits to comply with a state law, such payment would be an allowable charge to our contract." The Group Health Association in the District of Columbia had confirmed that Blue Cross and Blue Shield was paying psychologists on a par with psychiatrists as of January 1, 1974, under FEHBA (Federal Employee Health Benefit Act) contracts.

Some consideration has been given to mandating the inclusion of coverage for mental disorder in all health insurance policies issued or renewed within or outside a state. The Massachusetts law (SB 1985, Daniel Foley) appears to cover all types of policies from January 1974 and includes, "consultations or diagnostic or treatment sessions, provided that such services under this clause are rendered by a psychotherapist (physician, practicing psychiatry) or by a psychologist licensed (in Massachusetts)." At the close of 1973, AB 49 (Frank Lanterman, California) became law and now requires that every group health insurance plan (all types) "shall offer to every member of the plan coverage for mental and nervous disorders in such coverages and limits as the member/insured/employee may select." Thus, if requested by the insured group, such coverage must be offered in California. The provider component was then made explicit in 1975 by passage of AB 991 (Walter Ingalls, California): "Each prepaid health plan shall provide the services of a psychologist and psychiatrist when the . . . contract requires the provision of mental health services." Moreover, it is later specified that the "enrollee may be seen initially by either a physician or a psychologist." The Connecticut law that had mandated certain minimum mental health benefits in group plans was revised in 1975 to recognize the services of licensed psychologists. The new mandatory Minnesota law of 1975 requires that where in-hospital mental disorder coverage is provided, a group contract must henceforth provide for ambulatory mental health benefits. There is no distinction in level of benefits whether the services are rendered by a qualified practitioner or by an organized health facility.

Specialized or limited freedom-of-choice provisions may also apply to various states. It is reported that in Illinois, state employee plans must recognize the services of psychologists.

California, effective September 1974, adopted a pilot program for its state employees extending a broad range of services for the care and treatment of alcoholism. This program provides for outpatient care "up to 45 visits" as well as inpatient and day or night controlled residential care. The licensed psychologist is one of the designated providers with fees at parity.

Program Direction

It is one thing to be qualified for or licensed to practice. It is quite another to have the authority for policy and program determination or program direction. In the public sector psychologists and some other nonmedical health professions have moved into positions of program responsibility. A 1970 national survey (Dörken) reported that psychologists held or could hold high-level positions within a state agency or department—such as director, commissioner, deputy director, or assistant commissioner—in ten states. According to informal data, such positions were held by psychologists in an additional five states by 1975: Illinois, Massachusetts, Colorado, Minnesota, and Nevada. Posts of a statewide divisional level such as community mental health or mental retardation programs were actually held by psychologists in half the states in 1970. Further positive change has since occurred here too. The past five years have also seen an increase in the number of states where psychologists are or can be directors or superintendents of state mental hospitals or retardation facilites; from four to at least seven and from twenty-three to at least twenty-five, respectively. For example, in 1975 Virginia dropped the physician requirement for head of its state hospitals. However, the class specifications for positions of program leadership— whether exempt, under civil service, or set by regulation—still warrant close review and potential revision.

Psychologists were actually directors of community mental health centers in a majority of the states in 1970, while a current estimate exceeds the 80% mark. Such developments have been strongly resisted in some states such as California, where it has taken no less than four successive laws since 1971 to make the conditions explicit. Thus, while the 1971 law (Petris SB 725) called for regulations enabling the director of local (county) mental health services, when not the local health officer or medical administrator of the county hospitals, to be a psychiatrist, psychologist, or clinical social worker and also called for the adoption of standards for these three professions employed as program chiefs, further legislation became necessary. SB 542 (Nicholas Petris, California) of 1972 was explicit in stating that, "No regulations shall be adopted which prohibit a psychiatrist, psychologist or clinical social worker from employment in a local mental health program in any professional, administrative or technical positions in mental health services." Further statutory clarification was passed in 1973 and 1974, but as of this writing the complete set of implementing regulations had still not been presented for hearing by the department of health and counties continued to advertise vacancies for director and program chief as restricted to psychiatrist, in direct and open violation of the law—even when the violation was brought to their attention.

In recent years, there has been a shift from disciplinary to programmatic organization of services in public mental institutions. This shift has brought with it a reorganization of hospital services where specific competence and experience rather than discipline in itself become the requisites for appointment as program or service director (Dörken, 1973). This shift has occurred not only throughout many major state services but in facilities of the Veterans Administration as well. When given the opportunity, members of clinical disciplines appear to be equally competent in administration—a skill for which few are rarely trained.

Because of the shortage of competent, clinically trained administrators—especially in circumstances that foreclose the possibility for all but physicians and given the notion that the clinician should be saved for direct patient service—an anomaly appears to be developing in public service. On the one hand, there is little incentive in terms of higher status or pay to reward demonstrated clinical expertise. On the other, there seems to be an increased receptivity to program managers having business administration or comparable training, even though they do not have the experiential background really to understand, from the delivery standpoint, the services they administer. Such prospects appear self-defeating. It is not enough that the trained health professional may be allowed to make the clinical decisions and be responsible for the treatment program. Ultimately, whoever controls the dollar controls the program.

Competency Determination

There are further marks of recognition which the psychologist claims. Pacht and others (1973) have reviewed the status of the psychologist as an expert witness. *United States* v. *Jenkins* (307 F 2d 637, U.S. App. D.C., 1962), in which the appellate court for the District of Columbia established the acceptance of the psychologist as an expert witness, is generally considered to be a landmark case. By 1971, eighteen states (including New York, Florida, Texas, Illinois, Michigan, and California) and the District of Columbia clearly accepted the testimony of a psychologist as an expert witness. It would appear that this acceptance will extend to other states, particularly where the profession is recognized through licensing or certification. Examples of recent case law recognizing psychologists as independent experts for diagnosis or treatment include *United States* v. *Brawner* (471 F 2d 1190, 4th Cir., 1969); *Hogan* v. *Texas* (496 SW 2d 594., Crim. App. Texas, 1973); and *United States* v. *Green* (373 F Supp., 149 ED Pa, 1974).

Congress is currently considering a reform of the federal criminal law code to clarify the distinction between those responsible for their behavior and those who lack the capacity to appreciate their conduct, the so-called distinction between the "mad" or "bad." The M'Naghten rule held that a defendant is criminally responsible unless it can be proven that because of mental illness he did not know the nature and quality of his acts. The Durham decision of 1954 held that the defendant is not criminally responsible if his unlawful act was the product of mental disease or defect. This ruling facilitated the introduction of expert testimony by psychiatrists and, later, clinical psychologists. The history of this development is succinctly reviewed by Miller (1975).

During the time that the 700-page Criminal Justice Codification, Revision and Reform Act is under consideration by the 94th Congress (S 1) it is likely to be mirrored by similar considerations in state legislatures. As an illustration, after extended staff and committee consideration, the California legislature passed a bill (AB 1529, Frank Murphy) amending the Penal Code and the Welfare and Institutions Code. The intent of this law was to change various procedures relating to a person's "sanity" in a criminal proceeding to a person's "mental competence." It changed the definition of "gravely disabled" for purposes of hospitalization to include one who is deemed mentally incompetent, who is named in an indictment charging certain felonies, and who, as a result of mental disorder, is unable to understand the nature and purpose of the proceedings. Such a person cannot be tried or adjudged to punishment while mentally incompetent. During the deliberation on provision for expert testimony, it was possible, due to the definition of practice in the Psychology Licensing Act and to prevailing recognition of the profession, to gain the inclusion of psychologists. Thus, in a trial by court or jury on the question of mental competence, Section 1369 of the Penal Code as of September 1974 now states, in part: ". . . the court shall appoint two psychiatrists, licensed psychologists, or a combination thereof. . . ." This inclusion provides for a major entry into criminal law for the profession of psychology in California. The 1974 Hawaiian penal code amendments enabled even broader use of certified psychologists or physicians as consultants to the state court system for examinations with respect to "physical or mental disease, disorder or defect"; acquittal or such grounds; application for discharge or conditional release; or "pre-sentence psychiatric or medical examination."

Civil commitment has also been the subject of recent consideration, even though many states have passed a "Bill of Rights" for the mentally disordered (Baynes, 1971). Baynes points out that the majority of states do not have a statutory definition of mental disorder nor is there mention of "medical or psychological terminology" (p. 491). In effect, the statutes for the most part refer to "behavioral aspects, that is, personal acts or characteristics" (p. 492) as the paramount mode of definition. Thus, the determining factors are nonmedical, for such terms as mental illness and mental disease are defined by "behavioral characteristics in a perpetual statutory circus" (p. 492). Baynes concludes from his review of fifty-one statutes that they are really not criteria or guidelines but, rather, "conflicting labels that are the social excuse for incarcerating the gauche" (p. 495). Give such a situation, the determination of either insanity or mental competence hardly falls within the exclusive province of psychiatry or medicine—or of psychology, for that matter.

It is not surprising, then, that the laws relating to the commitment of mentally disordered or mentally retarded persons are gradually broadening to enable the participation of a recognized psychologist in this legal process. In 1970 (Dörken) the involvement of a qualified psychologist was required in the commitment process of the mentally retarded in twelve states and accepted in another fifteen.[5] Minnesota, in 1967, was the first state to adopt such a statute. With regard to mental disorder, such participation was possible in only four states at the time. Generally two signatories are required. Over the past five years five additional states have adopted laws enabling a psychologist to be one of the signatories in involuntary commitment (Colorado, Nevada, Oregon, South Carolina, and Washington). This subject clearly warrants consideration by psychology in those states where the profession is a nonparticipant. With passage of SB 349 in Colorado in 1975 licensed physicians or psychologists can commit mental patients to hospital. Also in 1975 Nevada legislation enables emergency and temporary commitment by a licensed psychologist.

The classic *Wyatt* v. *Stickney* case in Alabama (1972) is likely to have widespread repercussions on the right to treatment, institutional conditions, minimal staffing requirements, and related matters. Of special interest to psychology is the fact that the doctoral psychologist, among several other disciplines, was recognized as a "Qualified Mental Health Professional."

---

[5] This review was updated by Dörken in 1978, in *The Clinical Psychologist.*

Other State Laws

Other areas of state law have an effect on the practice of psychology. These areas have not been approached in a systematic fashion comparable to that attention given licensure and freedom of choice. With limited resources, priorities do have an effect. The next several years are likely to see significant change in state Medicaid programs, workers' compensation laws, and prepaid health plans—among the areas of vital concern to clinical psychologists. It is also probable that there will be an increase in consumer-oriented legislation. In California, AB 3250 (Henry Waxman, now Congressman for California), the Health Insurance Disclosure Act of 1974, which becomes effective January, 1976, is one such example. This law requires the development of a standard disclosure form to include the exceptions, reductions, and limitations of the policy.

There is also a need for law facilitating collegial relations among the various health professions rather than fostering isolation. Practitioners must, of course, be licensed. They may also incorporate individually. And a group of practitioners may form a professional corporation. At that point, given current state law, the enterprise must ordinarily be unidisciplinary. Professional corporation law, then, prevents professionals of several disciplines from having membership and owning stock in such a corporation. In 1974, Hawaii Revised Statutes amended Section 416-146 to read in part: "Shares of capital in a professional corporation may be issued only to a licensed person . . . provided, that notwithstanding . . . any psychologist certified under the provisions of chapter 465 may own stock in a medical corporation as long as . . . the sum of all shares not held by a physician in a medical corporation does not exceed forty-nine % of the total number of shares . . . ." A broader model has been extant in the state of Washington since 1969. There, professional service corporations may be composed of shareholders or professional employees all licensed "to render the same professional services

as the corporation" (Chapter 18.100). To the extent that the same services are rendered, more than one discipline may be involved. These are models for private-sector corporate health practice, but they require enabling state legislation. Entitlement of qualified psychologists to hospital staff privileges is another area overdue for closer attention by organized psychology and, possibly, remedial legislation. In California, for example, AB 1570 (Paul Carpenter—a California psychologist), if enacted, would require recognition (under certain criteria) of psychologists as members of the hospital's professional staff, in accord with criteria of the Joint Commission on Accreditation of Hospitals.

To be effective in the legislative process will require a substantial investment of time and talent by state psychological associations. Since the law is a basic determinant of the scope and nature of practice, however, such an involvement in state legislative activities should be accepted as a fact of life. Moreover, sound recognition in state law is generally given consideration in the formulation of federal law. A "grass-roots" network is vitally important to effectiveness at the national level.

References

American Psychological Association. *The consolidated roster for psychology.* Washington, D.C.: American Psychological Association, 1973.

Baynes, T., Jr. Continuing conjectural concepts concerning civil commitment criteria. *American Psychologist,* 1971, *26,* 489–495.

Committee on Legislation, American Psychological Association. A model for state legislation affecting the practice of psychology 1967. *American Psychologist,* 1967, *22,* 1095–1103.

Dörken, H. Reorganization of California state hospitals: Impact on the allied health professions. *Administration in Mental Health,* 1973, Fall, 42–51.

Dörken, H. Utilization of psychologists in positions of responsibility in public mental health programs. *American Psychologist,* 1970, *25,* 953–958.

Miller, J. Insanity defense: Mad or bad? Congress considers reforms. *APA Monitor,* 1975, June, 4, 6.

Pacht, A. et al. The current status of the psychologist as an expert witness. *Professional Psychology,* 1973, *4,* 409–413.

Herbert Dörken, former Chair of APA's Committee on Health, is an Adjunct Professor and Research Psychologist in the Department of Psychiatry, Langley Porter Institute, University of California, San Francisco. He is also Special Health Services Consultant to the Division of Psychologists in Clinical and Independent Practice of the California State Psychological Association, and was Advisor in Program Development to the California School of Professional Psychology.

Avenues to Legislative Success

Herbert Dörken

The legislative process in its various stages is described, with illustrative examples. Its broad context goes well beyond the direct passage of law and includes the interactive effect of federal upon state law, law upon regulation, administrative posture upon regulation, and the resolution of internal inconsistencies within and between codes to advantage. Success on any comprehensive basis is dependent upon organization, the delineation of achievable objectives, knowledge of the system, and a willingness to work with it.

As psychologists, we have perhaps been over-idealistic in depending for legislative success on the consumer advantage of our services, on social pertinence, and on the relevance of our concerns—that is, on the public interest—and above all, on our integrity as a profession and science, on the prevailing facts, the accuracy with which we address the issues, and logic. This parsimonious approach, while sound, is in the long run naive. Legislative success requires more than just being "good"; we have to learn the system and work with it.

By the fall of 1976, the American Medical Association (AMA) was reported to have contributed over $936,000 to 1976 Congressional candidates—about 50% more than the AFL-CIO. The November-December 1976 issue of *Frontline,* published by Common Cause, noted that by October 1, the AMA was the leading single-interest contributor at over $1.5 million. Our profession is simply not prepared to make the fiscal commitments that are apparently a fact of life for other health service professions such as medicine, chiropractic, optometry, and podiatry. In its heyday, CAPPS (the Council for the Advancement of Psychological Professions and Sciences) had a 1974 annual budget of only $126,000 for all its activities. Today, the Association for the Advancement of Psychology (AAP) has a 1977 budget of but $175,000. Clearly, psychology ought to have a deeper commitment not only to the issues but also in the legislative process (Shapiro, Dörken, Rodgers, & Wiggins, 1976).

Direct Passage of Law

The direct approach to health legislation calls for identifying an issue or objective, acquiring a legislative sponsor (author) committed to the issue, and supporting it through the various approval process levels. While there are many potential bills of interest to psychology, priorities must be weighted by considerations such as the following: What are the issues most in need of resolution? What issues have the greatest likelihood of passage? What alliances are available? Most, if not all, psychology licensing and certification laws were passed by this approach, as well as most of the 28 direct-recognition, or so-called insurance "freedom-of-choice," laws. On the federal level, this approach is illustrated by our success in passing PL 93-363, which revised the Federal Employees Health Benefits Act to enable federal employees to have direct consumer access to clinical psychologists for covered benefits within the practice of psychology, effective January 1975. It was authored originally as a House bill (H.R. 9440) by Representative Waldie (California), who was interested in further establishing that the medical dominance of Blue Shield added certain unnecessary costs, such as the featherbedding costs of mandating physician referral to a psychologist. The Senate (S. 2619, McGee, Wyoming) came to similar conclusions, so that despite Civil Service Commission, Blue Shield, and American Psychiatric Association's opposition, the bill passed the final Senate committee unanimously. This process

Reprinted from *American Psychologist,* 1977, *32,* 738–745.

and the necessary supportive organizational effort have been previously described (Dörken & Associates, 1976, pp. 35, 112, and 254).

But there are many other issues of concern to psychologists that may effectively be resolved by one or more approaches, often requiring less visibility, less effort, and above all, less direct intervention in changing the statutory base of health care delivery.

Influencing State Programs by Federal Laws

The Rehabilitation Act of 1973, PL 93-112, provides that within the scope of services (Section 103) for both assessment and restorative services for both the mentally and physically disabled, "physicians or licensed psychologists" are delineated as qualified practitioners. This law was the first major Congressional act recognizing psychology as a health profession. All state rehabilitation programs must meet federal standards to qualify for 80% federal subvention. It should be obvious to psychological associations at the state level that they should review their state plans to see that licensed psychologists are, indeed, appropriately involved in the rehabilitation services according to law.

In a similar vein, in the regulations pursuant to the Health Maintenance Organization (HMO) Development Act of 1974, clinical psychologists are enumerated among the recognized professions. Thus, when any Health Maintenance Organization or Individual Practice Association is being assisted in its development or operation with federal funding, it becomes appropriate for psychologists to inquire of the role of clinical psychology in these health care service plans.

Several other laws, while not requiring psychological participation, do certainly allow for such local option. Title XIX of the Social Security Act (Medicaid) includes psychological services not among the mandated, but among the permissive, services. Thus, if a state program includes psychological services, the usual 50% federal matching will be available. Psychological services, on a direct-access basis, are embraced in varying degrees in some 12 state plans at this time (Editor's note: In 18

state plans in 1979), a fact that reflects the lack of political and organizational sophistication among state psychological associations (Wiggins, Dörken, Dworin, & Shapiro, 1976).

Potential legislation that could be of great consequence to psychology would be the setting of national minimum standards for all state workers' compensation laws. Such a bill was proposed (S. 2018, The National Workers' Compensation Act of 1975 [Williams, New Jersey]) and, as reintroduced, would specifically recognize the services of clinical psychologists. Obviously, if enacted, it would greatly facilitate the involvement of psychology in disability evaluation and restorative services for job-injured employees in all states. At present, only two states,[1] Montana and Ohio, formally recognize psychology under their workers' compensation laws, while five states explicitly exclude psychological services (Alabama, Louisiana, New York, South Dakota, and Vermont). Passage of the Williams bill would resolve a matter nationally that has been quite resistant to resolution at the state level.[2]

Departmental Regulation

Basic statutes often have an explicit provision whereby responsible departments, federal or state as the case may be, promulgate in-depth regulations in order to carry out and implement the services required and under their direction. After an extended procedure that includes publication of proposed regulations, opportunity for public comment, and then formal adoption, the regulations have the force of law. Perhaps it

---

[1] In 1977, a third state, California, joined this list.

[2] The process can work in the reverse! A number of state "freedom of choice" laws included self-insured employee benefit plans. The number of union and certainly industry health programs is growing. Passage of the Employee Retirement Income Security Act (ERISA), PL 93-406, included pre-emption of state by federal law. Since this aspect of the federal law is silent on psychology, industries and unions may choose not to recognize psychologists, a state FOC law regardless. This jurisdictional authority has been made clear by case law (Hewlett-Packard v. Barnes (Commissioner of Corporations, CA), No. C-76-160-CBR). If the industry is truly self-insured, that is, pays its own costs of health care, then ERISA prevails. But if, for example, the union's welfare benefit fund contracts with Blue Shield then that contract is subject to state codes.

may be surprising, but it is not unusual to find that a regulation exceeds legislative intent or that, in fact, it is in conflict with other law. For example, key phrases in California's Short-Doyle (Community Mental Health Services) Act such as "professional person in charge" and "mental disorder" have been narrowly interpreted by regulation to mean "psychiatrist" and "mental/psychiatric illness," and subsequent mandating of psychiatric direction for all services and programs has resulted, contrary to the initial legislative intent. In this case, it actually required successive and increasingly explicit legislation to finally break the psychiatric monopoly behind these regulations, and now, with the exception of one particularly resistant county where the state psychological association has begun legal proceedings, psychologists, among others, are generally appointed on the basis of competence to direct any service or program that comes under this Community Mental Health Act (California Administrative Code, Note 1). Similarly, essentially psychological services are no longer, according to law, subject to medical discretion or supervision. It actually took three new laws and then 6 years of close attention to resolve these issues. The point of note, however, is that since the intent of a key legislator had been violated, he pursued the principle and other legislators were sympathetic to the introduction of remedial legislation. Ordinarily, the principle at issue must be refocused. Last year's concurrences are by no means this year's agreements, but precedence can often assist in securing conforming amendments.

Medicine is a long-established profession, and the "medical model" is widely equated in the public's mind with health care, an extensive scientific and professional literature documenting the capability of other health professions notwithstanding. This prevalent attitude can also be the orientation of rule makers. Thus, if you study various state regulations, you will find that some are not congenial to psychological practice yet may have no explicit statutory base. Many states, for example, have "borrowed" quite liberally from the Joint Commission on Accreditation of Hospitals (JCAH) for state facility licensing standards—standards that are highly restrictive in terms of psychological practice and the appointment of psychologists even

as affiliates of the medical staff. The Health and Safety Code in California—that is, the actual statute or law—is essentially silent regarding psychology. It does not appear to give the Department of Health such powers over a recognized health profession; yet the regulations do. This could be the case in your state. In such instances, silence, however, can be an obstruction. *Expressio unius est exclusio alterius,* a principle of statutory construction, holds that what is not expressly included is excluded. We are working with a historical mass. Within that history may lie a "turnkey." If that approach, too, is void, the permissive approach of declaratory intent may be the legislatively achievable resolution. In this approach, a hospital may recognize psychologists but it need not; however, no hospital that does is exposed to sanction since such legislation would declare the option permissible and would overturn or offset prior precluding regulations (without seeking to undo them directly).

Most state legislatures retain an Office of Legislative Counsel, which is available only to or through legislators for their confidential assistance, not only in drafting legislation but also in gaining legal opinions on specific questions. A sympathetic legislator may be willing to obtain such legal advice for you on a matter of mutual interest. If the opinion obtained is one desired, your legislator ally may then decide to formally address the issue to the Attorney General, requesting a legal opinion that would then become binding upon the state officials. As a practical matter, if it appears that the opinion will be against the department, there will be considerable internal pressure to resolve the matter. This process was used successfully in California to make clear that psychotherapy was within the province of the practice of psychology and to gain a recision of a Medicaid regulation that placed psychological services under physician prescription and supervision even though the law recognized psychological services as among the basic services to which the Medicaid beneficiary was entitled.[3]

---

[3] Later, to avoid loss of federal financial participation, based on Medicaid regulations requiring that inpatient services be under physician direction (Federal Register: June 4, 1970, Sec. 249.10 [b] [1]; January 17, 1974, Sec. 405.1123; and March 24, 1975, Sec. 249.10 [b] [16], the Department

As described earlier, it is frequently simply an administrative attitude or a prevailing belief that has a "governing" quality. For example, the notion of "medical responsibility" is often referred to as a legal requirement, obliging medical control and supervision of all health services. Paradoxically, the Medical Practices Act in California nowhere includes, let alone defines, this phrase. Certain procedures are clearly reserved for physicians: cutting, severing, penetrating tissue, injecting substances, and prescribing medications—functions not within the practice of psychology, a profession legally regarded in California as a *drugless practitioner*. Nonetheless, for years the concept carried an intrusive and constraining effect upon the practice of psychology. Clearly, this situation held an opportunity for psychology to again differentiate its services, and in 1973, a regulation was adopted that defined medical responsibility in the following terms: "A physician meeting the qualifications of 620 (a) [a Board-eligible or Board-certified psychiatrist] shall assume responsibility for all those acts of diagnosis, treatment, or prescribing or ordering of drugs which may *only* be performed by a licensed physician" (explanation and emphasis supplied). This same language was embodied in 1976 into legislation relating to state hospital services (A.B. 4146, chapter 962).[4]

Resolving Regulatory Conflict

Obviously, different state departments have jurisdiction over different though often complementary programs and tend to draft regulations from their own perspective. The basic legislation for the different programs and services may also

---

issued clarification that the removal of the prescription and supervision requirement applied only to outpatient services. Back to GO! Either the state must be granted a waiver, or the federal regulations must be revised. This, however, illustrates the interactive effect of federal upon state regulations.

[4] The proceeding shows how the administration can drag its feet on not only drafting regulations but in implementing them. When regulations fail to implement legislative intent and the bureaucracy is resistant, the legislature will usually support a new directive law. For example, SB-1560 (Petris), amended 1978, made very explicit that the conditions of appointment of psychiatrists and psychologists and social workers have to be equal. It is explicitly stated.

have been passed by different legislative committees with different compositions and priorities. It is not surprising, then, that the regulations relating to health services in state hospitals, community mental health services, facility licensing, Medicaid, rehabilitation, or workers' compensation are not always entirely consistent. It may be that certain more recent and favorable laws or regulations can be held to take precedence, thereby presenting an opportunity to "piggyback" more favorable regulations onto programs that have been less responsive. It is not unusual for psychologists to be accorded considerable administrative and program responsibilities in public services such as state hospitals and community mental health centers. These facilities typically must be licensed by the state and by the same department that licenses private and nursing facilities, in which regulations typically more in keeping with those of JCAH prevail. If the variance appears favorable, it may be worth pursuing. The legislative intent, the theme, or the objective reflected in bill hearings should properly have a determining effect upon the regulations. Of course, there may well be exceptions that were intended by the Legislature. More often, the more recent law reflects more recent views.

Enforcement

At times it is not sufficient merely to have sound laws or regulations on the books. Law, as we know, is not universally heeded. Some 26 states and the District of Columbia now have direct-recognition laws, or so-called "freedom-of-choice" laws, (Editor's note: In 1979, such legislation exists in 29 states), that in varying degrees are intended to assure the consumer direct access to and free choice of a qualified psychologist for covered benefits under various types of health insurance policies. Typically, the responsible state department, such as the Department of Insurance, is not an enforcement department designed to protect the provider or force provider status, but rather is there to protect the citizen or consumer. Hence, if claim reimbursement difficulties occur, appeals by the provider may not bring the desired action from the State Department of Insurance. Appeals from an aggrieved consumer, however, must be addressed; after all, it is the consumer who is insured, not the provider. The decision in *Moore v. Metropolitan Life Insurance Co.* in New York State illustrates this well ("Insurance Law Upheld," 1973). Not only was Mr. Moore's claim settled, but also, settlement was directed to all similar claims against this and another company.

In disputes of smaller fiscal magnitude, there is an expeditious route, typically available at the county seat. If reimbursement is being denied the consumer (or provider) and the law is clearly on the side of reimbursement, prompt relief is usually obtainable through Small Claims Courts (Clark, 1973). This approach can, of course, be pursued systematically on a statewide basis for fuller impact.

Sometimes states have regulations on the books that are advantageous yet neither known to psychologists nor enforced. For example, some of us in California have had a long-standing concern for the elimination of dual standards between public and private services. To this end, when the State Psychology Class Specifications were revised in 1965, an attempt was made to require licensing, but it was denied by the Personnel Board. Then, in 1974, legislation was introduced that would have required the licensing of psychologists in any health facility, public or private, that charged for its services. Though it cleared the Senate, the bill failed in the Assembly on the arguments that the state agencies are sovereign and exercise necessary standards, and that licensure, if desirable, should be required of all human services agencies whether they charge for their services or not (e.g., the Department of Corrections). More recently, however, in reviewing facility licensing regulations, we have discovered that whether in an acute-care general hospital, a psychiatric facility, a skilled nursing facility, or an intermediate-care facility, these regulations (California Administrative Code, Note 2) define psychologists as licensed. All state mental hospitals and all county and community residential health facilities are licensed under these regulations. Yet, of course, a number of psychologists in the state hospital system and in the community mental health programs are not licensed. It will be interesting to see what happens now

that a complaint has been filed with the State Department of Health requesting enforcement of this regulation.[5]

Statutory Referencing

Once there is a major precedent in the law as new, related legislation is adopted, unless there is contrary legislative intent, the new statutes will usually be rendered compatible, generally by the action of committee or legislative staff. Thus, when the Government Code relating to work-injuries compensation for federal employees was under consideration in mid-1974—it was passed in September (PL 93-416)—it included "clinical psychologists" within the definitions of "physician" and "medical, surgical and hospital services and supplies." This positive development was not sought by organized psychology and, indeed, we only learned of it after the fact. However, major hearings had been held on the Federal Employees Health Benefits Act, finally adopted in July 1974 (see above), which recognized the clinical psychologist. That precedent was incorporated into this federal-employee equivalent of Workers' Compensation.

Consistency may also be requested. The HMO Development Act, PL 93-222, enumerates a number of professions and then adds, "and such other individuals engaged in the delivery of health services as the Secretary may by regulation designate." Given recent Congressional recognition of "clinical psychology" and its increasing recognition at the state level in statute, the Secretary of the Department of Health, Education and Welfare and many key members of his staff were asked in writing and in person to designate clinical psychology within the regulations to be promulgated for this Act. And it was done (*Federal Register,* October 18, 1974, Vol. 39, No. 203, p. 37312, Section 101.101 [h]).

The California Legislature, in 1974 after extended study, decided to amend its Penal Code and certain related codes so that there would be a determination of "mental competence" rather

---

[5] The Department did not enforce this regulation. The Psychology Licensing Act exempts psychologists on the staff of government facilities from licensure. Law is held to supersede regulation.

than "sanity" in criminal proceedings. Psychologists had not been included in the insanity determination, but matters of mental competence clearly fell within the scope of their practice. Thus, A.B. 1529 (chapter 1511), passed in 1974, states, among other things, "The Court shall appoint two psychiatrists, licensed psychologists, or a combination thereof." It had been understood that as related laws were revised over the next several years, they would be amended to be consistent. Thus in 1976, when the Legislature revised the code for mentally disordered sex offenders, the Court was given the latitude to appoint two or three psychiatrists or licensed psychologists or a combination thereof. Some aspects of the California Code have not yet been brought into consistency. Those points that may have escaped staff or legislative attention should simply require follow-up by the profession of psychology for "clean-up" language.[6]

Generalizing Established Intent

At times in the adoption of legislation, specific language or amendments are agreed to which can serve as a reference for future legislation. So it was in the passage of California's freedom-of-choice law in 1974 (S.B. 2002, chapter 958). It was passed with a "friendly amendment" that protected the staffing integrity of the HMOs like that at Kaiser Permanente: "Nothing in this Section shall be construed to allow a member to select and obtain mental health services from a certificate holder who is not directly affiliated with or under contract to the health care service plan to which the member belongs." Passage depended not simply on overcoming the opposition but on achieving an accommodation with friends. In the next year, 1975, when the state was addressing the reorganization of prepaid health plans under its Welfare and Institutions Code, legislation was passed (A.B. 991, chapter 913), which states quite clearly, "Each prepaid health plan shall provide the services of a psychologist and psychiatrist when the prepaid health plan contract requires the provision of

mental health services. Mental health services shall be provided so that an enrollee may be seen initially by either a physician or a psychologist."

Thus, the "friendly amendment" had both direct and supplementary beneficial outcome. But in the press of the legislative process, a full appreciation of "new" language cannot always be forecast. Thus, the language, "a certificate holder who is not directly affiliated with or under contract to the health care service plan," while designed for the Kaiser HMO situation, is now being used by some Blue Shield plans to deny reimbursement, for, in fact, Blue Shield does not have psychologists who are "directly affiliated" or "under contract." Catch 22. And this posture can be taken even when they reimburse member (participating) and nonmember physicians. Back to remedial legislation. The introduction of S.B. 1204 would have closed this loophole. Shortly following its introduction in 1977, Blue Shield agreed, in writing, to reimburse psychologists for covered benefits, and the bill was accordingly withdrawn.

Greater specificity or new delineation in one section of law can have a generalizing positive (or negative, for that matter) effect on legislative attitude and public acceptance. Thus, though the Waldie-McGee bills were originally introduced to include psychologists and optometrists within the Federal Employees Health Benefits Act, when the legislation came out of its final Conference Committee, the focus was sharpened to "clinical psychologists" (PL 93-363) and it was passed July 30, 1974. The term *clinical psychologist* was adopted for work injuries under the Federal Employees' Compensation Act (PL 93-416) and for regulations for the Health Maintenance Organization Development Act (PL 93-222), both of which were adopted in September 1974.

Definitional Clarity

Generic licensure and membership in professional associations do not carry sufficient precision to define who psychologists really are. The clinical psychologist designation was an early attempt to delimit that group of psychologists who were trained and deemed qualified by the rest of

---

[6] Most of this "clean-up" has been achieved AB-3665 (Berman).

their colleagues to render health services. Until 1975, however, psychology had not agreed on a precise definition, but it was under pressure to do so before others defined "clinical psychology" for them.

The proposed Burleson-McIntyre National Health Care Act of 1975 (H.R. 5990, S. 1438), the insurance industry's bill, recognized clinical psychologists with one definition; the Civilian Health and Medical Program of the Uniformed Services (CHAMPUS) issued directives which, by another but similar definition of "clinical psychologist," limited the group to which beneficiaries could have direct access without medical referral; and Blue Shield in its federal employee program evolved yet another equivalent definition. The *National Register of Health Service Providers in Psychology* (1976) was established in 1975, and its definition of clinical psychologist, while explicit, was not so unworkably narrow as those promulgated by others. By now, there are over 8,500 psychologists listed in the *Register,* and it has been officially recognized by CHAMPUS and by Blue Shield for its federal employee program. In the recent New Hampshire law mandating mental health coverage in health insurance, the *Register* is cited as qualifying for psychological providers.

In the spring of 1976, discussions which had begun some years ago with the Health Insurance Association of America (HIAA) were brought to a conclusion. On May 18, the Government Relations Committee of HIAA approved the Model Psychologist Direct Recognition Bill, developed jointly by HIAA and APA's Committee on Health Insurance. On September 2, 1976, it was also approved by the APA's Council of Representatives. Not only has the Model Bill been sent to all State Insurance Commissioners and to all of the 320-odd member insurance companies, but also, counsel for HIAA has offered to assist any state without such freedom-of-choice legislation to draft a bill compatible with the laws of that state. While the Model Bill clarifies several aspects of psychology's involvement in insured health services, particular note should be taken of what, in effect, is specialty certification. The Model Bill defines the psychologist as "duly licensed or certified in the state where the service is rendered and has a doctorate degree in psy-

chology and has had at least 2 years of clinical experience in a recognized health setting or has met the standards of the *National Register of Health Service Providers in Psychology.*" As such freedom-of-choice legislation or regulations are adopted in any state, they will have the effect of adding specialty certification for such health services onto the generic psychology license. Similarly, such a definition can be added onto any subsequent legislation or regulations in the health field where it is necessary or desirable to define psychology. Thus, for certain purposes, such as hospital staff privilege or recognition under workers' compensation acts, present law might simply be broadened to include "licensed psychologists who meet the following qualifications:"—and then the Model Bill definition quoted above could be inserted.[7]

Planning Ahead

At times, legislation is introduced to signal the direction of one's intent, to serve as a vehicle for broader understanding of the issue through the "hearings" process, or to achieve a measure of accommodation. Psychology made a serious effort to gain inclusion as a recognized provider in the Medicare program under the Social Security Amendments of 1972, PL 92-603. The opposition could not be surmounted and, indeed, has not been even 5 years later. During conference between the House and Senate, there was indication of a willingness to recognize psychological services but only under medical referral. On psychology's objection, this was withdrawn. The law, however, authorized the Secretary of Health, Education and Welfare, within 2 years, "to determine whether the services of clinical psychologists may be more

---

[7] Indeed, S.B. 311 (P. Carpenter and Wilson) became effective in California in January 1978, Chapter 1168. It amended the definition of "physician" in the Labor Code for purposes of Workers' Compensation by adding psychologists to this definition. Section 3209.3 (b) then states: "'Psychologist' means a licensed psychologist with a doctorate degree in psychology and who either has at least two years clinical experience in a recognized health setting, or has met the standards of the National Register of Health Service Providers in Psychology." The same was done in amending SB-259 (P. Carpenter) regarding the health and safety codes. In essence, the model bill definition was incorporated into statutes. The difference between the California law and the model law, though, is that the California law only involves doctoral level providers.

generally available to persons . . . under . . . this Act in a manner consistent with quality of care and equitable and efficient administration."

This authority from the 92nd Congress lay dormant for the 2 years of the 93rd Session. By the 94th Congress, however, in recognition of Medicare's probable direct relationship to national health insurance, Senator Inouye (Hawaii) and Representative Corman (California) introduced legislation to again provide for the independent recognition of clinical psychology under Medicare. After 2 years, nearly one third of both Congressional bodies had co-sponsored S. 123 and H.R. 2270. The support was quite bipartisan and included both Vice-Presidential candidates in 1976. It appears that this gathering support prompted the development and initiation of the Social Security Administration's Expanded Clinical Psychology and Mental Health Benefits Experiment in Colorado. The design provides for direct consumer access to clinical psychologists and increases dollar coverage for outpatient mental health services by both psychologists and psychiatrists. Before the expanded benefits became available to designated segments of the statewide Medicare population on October 1, 1976, it was first necessary to set a definition of "clinical psychologist," to establish a means for selection of qualified providers by proficiency review, to designate the psychological services (procedures) to be covered and to be excluded, to set limits on services, to organize a method of peer review, and to establish a rational basis for provider reimbursement through a third party. Done, but far easier said than done. This first phase, or process, will be evaluated by the contractor (Stanford Research Institute) by July 1, 1977, with the expectation that their report will be accepted by the Social Security Administration (SSA) within several months. On acceptance, it becomes a public document. Meanwhile, it must be noted that SSA has committed about $1 million to this pilot study.[8]

Both Senator Inouye and Representative Corman have reintroduced their bills in the 95th

Congress, and they expect to schedule hearings in the summer of 1977 in a more encouraging climate. Passage, however, depends upon developing the necessary base of support and on psychologists' actively promoting sponsorship of these bills by their senators and representatives. It will not happen by wishing or by the efforts of others.

As we know, national health insurance was one issue on which the two recent candidates for the presidency of the United States differed. Mr. Carter consistently advocated the implementation of a comprehensive national health insurance program that would include mental health coverage. It is of special significance for psychology that in a letter of September 11, 1976, to Mr. Clarence Martin of the Association for the Advancement of Psychology, our President stated in part:

> As you are aware, I have proposed National Health Insurance on a phased-in basis, as revenues permit, with the phasing to depend upon need and feasibility. I believe that mental health should be considered as a service covered by national health insurance and that the public should have free choice and direct access to those psychologists who will qualify as health care providers under a national health insurance program. Sincerely, Jimmy.

He also noted in this letter that he had been aware of the contributions of psychologists while he was Governor of Georgia and was supportive of their recognition as independent providers of service. Such a note is a promising one for psychologists in the 4 years ahead.

Discussion

Obviously, the legislative process is complex in itself. Further, many roads can lead to Rome. Success is seldom quick, easy, or achieved in one shot. Careful monitoring is required of related legislation as it is introduced, of regulations under development, and of changes in administrative policies. Existing regulations and statutes need careful review. One-year terms of a small legislative committee or legislative advocate alone hardly provide the necessary continuity or resources even in calm times. Long-run success is dependent on systematic knowledge of the field, determination of desired priorities, and feasible actions. The establishment of a grass-roots legislative network whereby constituents establish a personal relationship with their

---

[8] Details are in "Evaluation of the Colorado Clinical Psychology/Expanded Mental Health Benefits Experiment: Process Evaluation Report." United States Department of Health, Education, and Welfare, Social Security Administration, Publication Number (SSA) 77-11722.

legislator and alert the legislator to situations where support is desired, greatly facilitates the entire process. This is the model used by the New Jersey Psychological Association (Shapiro et al., 1976). Its effectiveness is illustrated by the fact that both New Jersey Senators and *all* 15 Representatives cosponsored the S. 123 and H.R. 2270 bills in the 94th Congress, bills that proposed amending Medicare to include psychological services. If state psychologists seriously review their collective contacts, they will be amazed at the personal-contact resource-base they have (Milgram, 1967).

Each year in the preparation of one's tax return, one is guided by the IRS instructions to Form 1040. On page 13 of the instructions for Schedule A (itemized deductions), medical and dental expenses, explicitly enumerates "psychologists." Psychologists were inserted in the instructions back in 1974 in response to a direct written request of mine. In the ensuing dialogue, it turned out that the official then responsible for writing the revision of that section was married—to a psychologist! Small world, indeed.

Sometimes you can do everything right, or so it seems, and then circumstances will change during the course of an action. In 1973, then Senator Moscone (now Mayor, San Francisco) authored psychology's bill to amend California's Labor Code to recognize psychological services for job-injured employees under Workers' Compensation. That bill, in contrast to its predecessor and two successors, was passed by the Legislature. But at about that time, the Senator declared himself a candidate for Governor in 1974. Nearly all of his bills were then vetoed by the incumbent Governor.

At times, when proper recognition is not accorded psychology, it may be tempting to give vent to frustration and "sue the bleeps." Unless the pertinent statutes and regulations are clearly in favor of psychology, however, this can be a very costly, slow, and generally unsatisfactory approach. Before filing suit, it is prudent to pursue the "exhaustion of administrative remedies," a doctrine of law. If all reasonable avenues of resolution have been tried and/or considered to no avail, a court will likely be more sympathetic, and, in any event, your case, if not already otherwise resolved, will be strengthened in the process.

Time, patience, and an appreciation of current realities are necessary ingredients for legislative success. Just as others will accommodate the interests, presence, and services of psychologists when these come to be viewed positively in the legislative process, so too must psychologists come to understand what is possible at a given time and how to convert sought objectives into "ideas whose time has come." Politics is "the art of the possible." Possibilities are dependent on voted support.

Reference Notes

1. California Administrative Code, Title 9, Subchapter 3. *Community mental health services under the Short-Doyle Act,* Register 75, No. 5. Sacramento, Calif.: Documents Section, January 31, 1976.
2. California Administrative Code, Title 22, Division 5. *Licensing and certification of health facilities and referral agencies,* Chapters 1–5, Register 75, No. 24. Sacramento, Calif.: Documents Section, June 14, 1975.

References

Clark, C. Courts of first resort. *Money,* 1973, *2,* 32–35.

Council for the National Register of Health Service Providers in Psychology. *National register of health service providers in psychology.* Washington, D.C.: Author, 1976.

Dörken, H., & Associates. *The professional psychologist today: New developments in law, health insurance, and health practice.* San Francisco: Jossey-Bass, 1976.

Milgram, S. The small world problem. *Psychology Today,* 1967, *1,* 61–67.

"Insurance law upheld." *New York State Psychologist,* 1973, *25*(1 & 2).

Shapiro, A. E., Dörken, H., Rodgers, D. A., & Wiggins, J. G. The legislative process. In H. Dörken & Associates, *The professional psychologist today: New developments in law, health insurance, and health practice.* San Francisco: Jossey-Bass, 1976.

Wiggins, J. G., Dörken, H., Dworin, J., & Shapiro, A. E. Major social security programs. In H. Dörken & Associates, *The professional psychologist today: New developments in law, health insurance, and health practice.* San Francisco: Jossey-Bass, 1976.

Herbert Dörken is an Adjunct Professor and Research Psychologist in the Department of Psychiatry, Langley Porter Institute, University of California, San Francisco.

This article was presented, in part, at the symposium "The Psychologist and the Legislative Process" at the meeting of the American Psychological Association, Washington, D.C., September 1976. For their reviews and helpful critiques, special thanks are due to colleagues: A. Eugene Shapiro, Lewis G. Carpenter, Jr., and Patrick H. DeLeon.

Psychology and the Carter Administration

Patrick H. DeLeon

Due to the spiraling costs of health care, it is extremely likely that a comprehensive program of national health insurance will be enacted under the Carter Administration. Mental health services will be included as a primary health benefit. Psychologists should spend their considerable energies not arguing whether psychotherapy is a health service, but instead insuring that psychology is independently recognized under national health insurance. Otherwise, we should expect that all training support will soon be phased out and that the profession will cease to exist.

President Carter recently announced that his Administration would strive aggressively to contain the escalating costs of our nation's hospital care. Citing figures indicating that since 1950 the cost of a day's stay in a hospital has increased by over 1,000%, or more than eight times the rise in the Consumer Price Index, and that today the average hospital stay costs over $1,300, whereas just 12 years ago, a slightly shorter stay cost less than $300, the President went on to emphasize that although this relentless increase places a severe burden on all of us, it strikes hardest at the poor and the elderly.

At the same time, the President also indicated that his Administration would be placing a high priority on improving the health services provided to our nation's children. At the President's request, Senator Abraham Ribicoff recently introduced the Child Health Assessment Act (S. 1392), which the President described as a "crucial first step." This legislation will expand and improve the existing Early Periodic Screening, Diagnosis and Treatment program (EPSDT). Currently, it is estimated that only about 2 million of the 12 million children who are eligible for Medicaid are appropriately screened and that 22% of those who are found to be in need of treatment do not in fact receive it. Further, there are approximately 700,000 children under the age of six who come from poor families that do not meet all of the current Medicaid eligibility requirements. The Administration's bill would seek to fill these gaps and to insure that quality services are provided through comprehensive health care centers or primary-care physicians capable of providing the necessary follow-up diagnosis and treatment. To accomplish these lofty ends, the Administration proposes that the federal government should increase its percentage matching rate under EPSDT from the current average of 55% to a projected average of over 75%. It is especially noteworthy for the psychological community that the President expressly indicated that "treatment for all conditions found in the assessment would have to be provided, with limitations only on mental illness, mental retardation, developmental disabilities, and dental care."

The real significance for psychology in these first two major health proposals presented by the Administration is not so much in their specific content, nor the explicit limitation on mental health services, but in the underlying notion that the Carter Administration is firmly committed to containing the spiraling cost of our nation's health care. This year health care will cost an average of over $700 for every man, woman, and child. Each worker's share of our nation's health bill will require more than a month's work. The federal government's expenditure for health now comprises approximately 11.3% of the entire federal budget; only national defense, interest on the national debt, and income security programs command a larger share. It is estimated that unless major

Reprinted from *American Psychologist,* 1977, *32,* 750–751.

corrective legislation is rapidly enacted, our nation's health care costs will double within 5
years. Such a state of affairs is clearly intolera-
ble and without doubt would wreak havoc with
our standard of living.

There is no doubt in my mind that under
the leadership of the Carter Administration,
Congress will enact a comprehensive national
health insurance program. It would be reassuring to think that such a major restructuring of
our nation's health delivery system would evolve
naturally from our public officials' sincere interest in assuring high-quality health services to all
citizens, and not primarily as a reaction to
rapidly escalating costs. However, for both
reasons, there is no question that a major reorganization and establishment of national health
care priorities must be instituted. Mental health
services will be included, but most likely will
continue to be considered as an optional, or
second-class, benefit. With the ever-increasing
evidence that from 60% to 70% of all physician
office visits are for primarily psychological
rather than organic reasons (Dörken, 1976),
such a de-emphasis on mental health services
suggests that our profession has not done a very
creditable job in selling itself to our nation.

Although I personally believe that "mental
illness" is a rather tragic coping mechanism in
response to one's social-psychological environment, and thus not a medical disease or sickness
per se, I am distressed to see distinguished
members of our profession debating publicly
whether or not psychotherapy should be included under national health insurance (Albee
& Derner, 1977). The pros and cons of this
argument are admittedly most intriguing and intellectually challenging. Our didactic training
prepares us well for engaging in such a heated
encounter. However, the decision of whether or
not to include mental health services under national health insurance, and under what conditions, will not be made by psychologists, or even
by psychiatrists, but instead by politicians, by
the elected officials who establish our nation's
health policy. There appears to be very little
doubt that mental health services will be included; however, the status of psychologists as
potentially independent providers is very much
up in the air.

The 380,000 members of the medical

profession form an imposing political opponent,
especially when one realizes that the *National
Register of Health Service Providers* estimates
that there are only 22,588 psychology health
care providers. The president of the American
Psychiatric Association has publicly advocated
before the Congress that only psychiatrists
should be considered qualified to receive reimbursement under national health insurance
(Kiesler, 1977). If psychology will not stand up
and defend itself, we can be sure that no one else
will defend our right to practice for us.

Our profession is at a major crossroads. If
we are able to obtain independent inclusion
under national health insurance, then we will be
assured of continuous training funds, financial
security, professional challenges, etc. If not, I
am afraid that our training institutions will soon
be phased out, and we will find ourselves as
very expensive specialists for whom no one
wants to pay the bill. The first step in insuring
our inclusion would be to obtain independent
status under Medicare, and accordingly, Senator
Inouye (S. 123) and Representative Corman
(H.R. 2270) have introduced appropriate legislation. However, to succeed, our profession must
now convince our elected officials that such
legislation is socially meaningful. As psychologists, we know that our services are important; unfortunately, few elected officials even
know that we exist, much less are willing to pay
for our services.

Yet, I am personally convinced that our
profession is in the best political shape that it
has ever been. Our profession's governance
structure is clearly alerted and concerned about
the long-range implications for national health
insurance; our academic, scientific, and professional communities seem to be working together.
The *National Register* is viable and visible—for
the politician there is finally an objective means
of determining who is a psychologist. Our
political action arm, the Association for the
Advancement of Psychology, according to one
high-ranking Carter official, "has real clout."
But more importantly, individual psychologists
are becoming aware of the importance of national health insurance to *their* profession and
are willing to get involved. In the last session,
the whole Congressional delegations from New
Jersey and Hawaii supported, through cospon-

sorship of the relevant bills, inclusion of psychologists under Medicare; this support was largely a response to urgings from constituents, especially psychologists. I hope that in the current session of Congress, more states will demonstrate this support.

In short, psychology has a voice, albeit a small voice, in shaping national health policy. I believe we can have very little influence on whether there is national health insurance or whether mental health services are included in national health insurance. The political forces pushing for these are simply stronger than psychology. However, we can influence the decision of whether psychologists are to be considered health service providers under national health insurance, and it is essential that we do so.

References

Albee, G. W., & Derner, G. F. Should psychology strive to be included in national health insurance? *The Clinical Psychologist,* 1977, *30*(3), 3–13.

Dörken, H., & Associates. *The professional psychologist today: New developments in law, health insurance, and health practice.* San Francisco: Jossey-Bass, 1976.

Kiesler, C. A. Editorial: The training of psychiatrists and psychologists. *American Psychologist,* 1977, *32*, 107–108.

At the time of original publication of this article, *Patrick H. DeLeon* was Legislative Assistant to U.S. Senator Daniel K. Inouye, member of the APA Board of Professional Affairs, and a Consulting Editor to *Professional Psychology.*

4

Experience with Systems of Delivery of Services

It is rare in discussions of possible national health insurance benefits that anyone asks what benefit package would best fit the mental health needs of the nation or even how national health insurance can benefit the most individuals most effectively at the least cost. The foremost concern about the inclusion of a mental health component in national health insurance is cost. Fear and apprehension abound regarding overutilization, inappropriate utilization, and runaway costs. It is falsely argued that utilization rates cannot be predicted and, hence, that mental health is "uninsurable." Costs and cost containment are important, but they are not the only issue. Moreover, all of this speculation goes on as if there were no data on and/or experience with the delivery of mental health services within large organized systems of care.

In fact, considerable data addressing these issues exist. We know a great deal about how to deliver mental health services in a cost-efficient and clinically effective manner. The HMO model discussed in several of the papers in this section meets these criteria. Considerable data exist concerning the length of mental health treatment and the utilization rate of mental health benefits. Several articles in this section report utilization rates consistently under 2% among HMOs, insurance plans, and government programs. Length of outpatient psychotherapy is repeatedly found to average between 6 and 12 sessions, with 80% of treatment being completed in less than 20 sessions.

Experience with different forms of mental health coverage does provide suggestions about how *not* to structure mental health coverage under national health insurance. The most costly and inhumane coverage would be a narrow benefit covering only catastrophic mental illness requiring hospitalization. Such a narrow benefit encourages costly and inappropriate hospitalization and places unnecessary pressures on both patient and therapist. The practitioner wants to be helpful to the patient (as well as to realize income) and may unwarrantedly hospitalize patients to activate insurance coverage. Stricter criteria for hospitalization in a limited-benefit situation only increase the frustration and sense of helplessness of the patient. Symptoms and functioning then intensify to justify hospitalization. This is of no benefit to the patient and only serves to drive costs higher. Under national health insurance, the emphasis should be on less costly outpatient services for the benefit of the consumer and the taxpayer.

Separate mental health deductibles and mental health coinsurance rates higher than physical health coinsurance rates pose significant barriers to access to mental health services, particularly for the poor. Deductibles, copayments, and arbitrary limitations on services are cost-control devices developed by accountants that are of little relevance to the service needs of the patient. These artificial cost-control techniques encourage delays in seeking treatment, which in turn increase the severity of the difficulties as well as the length and cost of treatment. Moreover, such arbitrary and discriminatory disincentives also encourage somatization, the translation of emotional distress into physical symptoms, which leads to costly utilization of inappropriate and unavoidably ineffective general medical tests and services. National health insurance should include easy direct access to mental health services without separate deductibles and without initial copayments. For example, the first 20 sessions per year might be available at no cost to the patient, and a coinsurance could begin with the 21st session and increase progressively thereafter.

The most clinically responsible method of cost control is to develop organizations that deliver comprehensive services with maximum cost-therapeutic effectiveness. This demands attention to the outcome of treatment, broadly defined, and systematic evaluation of programs and providers. So far, the most successful demonstration of an accessible, clinically effective, and cost-effective organizational structure is the Health Maintenance Organization (HMO) as conceived and pioneered by Kaiser-Permanente Health Care Systems. Other organizational structures that can deliver comprehensive care with maximum cost-therapeutic effectiveness need to be developed and implemented. The HMO is only one such concept. The development of further innovation in delivery systems is the greatest challenge confronting the health field today. Rather than etching into any proposed national health insurance system the present inadequate, artificial, and unresponsive methods of controlling costs, it would be beneficial to establish a transition period in which costs would be temporarily controlled by traditional means while the government stimulates, through categorical aid, experimentation with new organizational structures.

The papers in this section provide a sample of the research and data existing on the delivery of mental health services within organized systems of care. These articles focus on mental health service delivery within HMOs and under government programs. These settings and this research have been selected for two reasons. First, the programs studied tend to be organized, describable in terms of organizational structure and population served, and readily available for public review. Second, psychologists are involved in the provision of mental health services within these programs as well as in the evaluation of clinical effectiveness and cost/benefit efficiency.

The first three articles report a series of investigations into the relationship between utilization of psychological services and subsequent medical utilization in a prepaid health-plan setting. Twenty years of experience at Kaiser-Permanente, the original health maintenance organization, has demonstrated not only that a comprehensive mental health package can be financed but that the cost of providing the mental health benefit is more than offset by the savings in medical costs of patients who previously overutilized medical facilities due to somaticized emotional problems. In the first study, Follette and Cummings found that persons with identifiable emotional distress, although not necessarily diagnosed as having "psychiatric problems," made significantly higher than average use of both inpatient and outpatient medical facilities. When these emotionally distressed individuals received psychotherapy, their medical utilization declined significantly compared to that of a control group of matched emotionally distressed health-plan members who did not receive psychotherapy. Significant declines in medical utilization were seen in the period following the completion of the psychological intervention (i.e., the year after the initiation of mental health contact). These declines remained constant following the termination of psychotherapy, and no additional psychotherapy was required to maintain the lowered level of utilization.

In the second study, Cummings and Follette instituted intensive efforts to increase referrals to psychotherapy. This was done as part of a routine early-detection program. Attending physicians were alerted to possible emotional problems through the use of in-service training and computerized psychological screening procedures. The researchers found that the number of subscribers seeking psychotherapy reached an optimal level and did not increase thereafter, despite attempts to induce an increase. In the third study in the series, Cummings and Follette conducted an 8-year follow-up on patients who had had contact with the psychological service. The results suggested that the reduction in medical utilization was a consequence of resolving emotional distress that had been reflected in physical symptoms and had necessitated medical visits. Cummings and Follette found that the actual problem existing in the patient's life at the time, rather than the "physical" symptom, was recalled as the reason for the "psychiatric" visit.

It is interesting to note that Kaiser-Permanente mental health costs have not been subject to the same magnitude of inflation as general health costs. In 1959, the Kaiser-Permanente rate to subscribers for mental health services (including both inpatient and outpatient) was 75 cents per person per month. In 1979, the rate was $1.28. In 20 years, the rates had increased only 71%—an annual increase of only 3.5%. During the same time span, increases in general medical costs often ranged between 12% to 20% *per year* according to reports of the Health Insurance Association of America. In the last 10 years, average, per day, inpatient costs have more than tripled. Regardless of whether medical utilization is appropriate or inappropriate, medical care costs more than mental health care. As the Kaiser-Permanente studies demonstrate, mental health service represents a cost-containment mechanism for the physical health system.

Another study that assessed the impact of mental health benefits on the utilization of general medical services within an HMO is presented in the article by Goldberg, Krantz, and Locke. The medical utilization rates of 256 patients who were referred for outpatient psychotherapy were examined for the 12-month period before the referral and the 12 months after treatment (a 3-month treatment period was excluded). There was a marked reduction in medical utilization during the follow-up period: approximately a 15% reduction in total number of visits and a 30% reduction in X-ray and laboratory services. These studies on the impact of mental health services on medical utilization within HMOs are illustrative. Similar studies with similar findings have been conducted under traditional insurance plans (i.e., Jameson, Shuman, & Young, 1976).

The Willens article presents the history of the Colorado Medicare study. This study, running from 1976 through 1978, was designed to examine issues of cost and utilization related to two "experimental" Medicare benefits: (a) including psychologists as independent providers, and (b) increasing the dollar limit on mental health coverage under Medicare while decreasing the coinsurance. While the data on this study will not be fully available until 1980, the project has already demonstrated two important facts: (a) psychologists can agree on a definition of a psychologist qualified to deliver services on an autonomous basis, and (b) psychology can assure quality control over services delivered on an independent basis.

The Civilian Health and Medical Program of the Uniformed Services (CHAMPUS) is a quite comprehensive health care program that supplements the direct medical care system of the uniformed services. The beneficiaries are dependents of active-duty military personnel, the dependents of deceased military personnel, and retired military personnel and their dependents. Dörken reports on the 1975 mental health claim experience of CHAMPUS for a 10-state region. He found that psychologists provided 30% of reimbursed outpatient services. Psychologists were found to be more involved in meeting the mental health needs of children and adolescents than were psychiatrists or physicians. The CHAMPUS data suggest a mental health utilization rate of less than 2% of all beneficiaries, ranging from .7% to 3.9% for various states. This rate was stable over three separate years. The average utilization of mental health services per actual user was 13.9 visits, and 83.7% of such treatment was completed in 24 or fewer sessions. Dörken makes the important point of the need to analyze utilization data on the basis of service actually delivered, not simply on the patient's diagnosis. When tabulation by diagnostic code is utilized, the data can reflect as much as a 50% exaggeration in utilization rates because of routine physical health visits by patients who happen to also have mental health problems.

The last article in this section is an NIMH report on federal employees' health benefits. It presents utilization data similar to that reported by Dörken. Again, fear and apprehension about long-term intensive psychotherapy leading to uncontrollable costs is not based on fact. The utilization rate for intensive psychotherapy is miniscule, even when such treatment is available through the joint decision of patient and therapist, as under the federal program at that time. Once again, almost 80% of all patients utilizing mental health benefits were seen for 20 or fewer sessions. The average monthly cost of mental health benefits per covered person was approximately $1 when averaged over the entire country and about $2 when only metropolitan Washington, D.C., beneficiaries are considered.

There are almost no data to support the oft-stated fears of overutilization and runaway costs related to the inclusion of mental health benefits in health care packages. There is a growing mass of positive data supporting the inclusion of mental health benefits from both a total-health-care-system cost perspective and from a humanitarian perspective. Experience in the delivery of mental health services within an organized system of care has demonstrated that mental benefits are "insurable," that the rate of utilization and length of utilization are predictable and stable, and that the inclusion of mental health services has an "offsetting" advantage in that it lowers inappropriate medical utilization. The failure to include mental health benefits in national health insurance would have disastrous consequences for the health of the citizens of our nation and for the economic base of the health care financing system.

Reference

Jameson, J., Shuman, L., & Young, L. *The effects of outpatient psychiatric utilization on the costs of providing third party coverage* (Research Services Report 118). Blue Cross of Western Pennsylvania, December 1976.

Psychiatric Services and Medical Utilization in a Prepaid Health Plan Setting

William T. Follette and Nicholas A. Cummings

This article reports the first Kaiser-Permanente study comparing medical services utilized before and after short-and long-term psychotherapy. Findings indicate that persons in emotional distress were significantly higher users of medical facilities, that medical care utilization by individuals seen in psychotherapy declined, and that this decline continued and remained constant during the 5 years after termination of psychotherapy.

In two previous studies (Cummings, Kahn, & Sparkman, 1964; Follette & Cummings, 1962) the psychiatric practitioner's contention that emotionally disturbed patients do not seek organic treatment for their complaints following the intervention of psychotherapy has been investigated. Although it has long been recognized that a large number of the physical complaints seen by the physician are emotionally, rather than organically, determined, the more precise relationship between problems in living and their possible expression through apparent physical symptomatology has been difficult to test experimentally. As noted in the previous study, the GHI Project (Avnet, 1957) demonstrated that users of psychiatric services were also significantly frequent users of medical services, but the Project was not able to answer the question of whether there is a reduction in the use of medical services following psychotherapy.

Because the facilities and structure of the Kaiser Foundation Health Plan accord an experimental milieu not available to Avnet, the original pilot project in San Francisco was able to demonstrate a significant reduction in medical utilization between the year prior to psychotherapy, and the two years following its intervention. Certain methodologic problems inherent to the pilot study indicated caution and the need for refinement and replication to avoid arriving at premature conclusions. The lack of a control group of what might be termed psychologically-disturbed high-utilizers who did not receive psychotherapy was a serious omission in the first experiment.[1] Furthermore, an error in the tabulation of inpatient utilization was discovered after the experiment had been concluded.[2] In addition, the question was raised whether the patients studied might, subsequent to the two years following psychotherapy, revert to previous patterns of somatization or, as a new pattern, merely substitute protracted and costly psychotherapy for previous medical treatment.

The Problem

This study investigated the question of whether there is a change in patients' utilization of outpatient and inpatient medical facilities after psychotherapy, comparing the patients studied to a matched group who did not receive psychotherapy.

Psychotherapy was defined as any contact

---

[1] The authors acknowledge their debt to Dr. M. F. Collen for this and other suggestions, and to Mr. Arthur Weissman, Medical Economist, Kaiser Foundation Medical care entities, for his expert consultation.

[2] At that time days of hospitalization per patient and by year were tabulated from each patient's outpatient medical records. Subsequent investigation has revealed that only about a third of the outpatient charts reviewed contained summaries of hospital admissions, and that tabulation of inpatient utilization must be made directly through the separately-kept inpatient records.

Reprinted from MEDICAL CARE © J. B. Lippincott Company, 1967, 5, 25–35, by permission.

with the Department of Psychiatry, even if the patient was seen for an initial interview only. The year prior to the initial contact was compared with the five subsequent years in both groups.

The problem can be stated simply: Is the provision of psychiatric services associated with a reduction of medical services utilization (defined as visits to other medical clinics, outpatient laboratory and x-ray procedures, and days of hospitalization)?

Methodology

The setting: The Kaiser Foundation Health Plan in the Northern California Region is a group-practice prepayment plan offering comprehensive hospital and professional services on a direct service basis. Professional services are provided by the Permanente Medical Group—a partnership of physicians. The Medical Group has a contract to provide comprehensive medical care to the subscribers, of whom there were more than a half million at the time of this study. The composition of the Health Plan subscribers is diverse, encompassing most socio-economic groups. The Permanente Medical Group comprises all major medical specialties; referral from one specialty clinic to another is facilitated by the organizational features of group practice, geographical proximity and use of common medical records. During the years of this study (1959–1964); psychiatry was essentially not covered by the Northern California Health Plan on a prepaid basis, but in some areas of the Northern California region psychiatric services were available to Health Plan Subscribers at reduced rates. During the six years of the study, the psychiatric clinic staff in San Francisco consisted of psychiatrists, clinical psychologists, psychiatric social workers, resident psychiatrists at the third- or fourth-year level, and psychology interns, all full-time. The clinic operates primarily as an outpatient service for adults (age eighteen or older), for the evaluation and treatment of emotional disorders, but it also provides consultation for non-psychiatric physicians and consultation in the general hospital and the emergency room. There is no formal "intake" procedure,

the first visit with any staff member being considered potentially therapeutic as well as evaluative and dispositional. Regardless of professional discipline, the person who sees the patient initially becomes that patient's therapist unless there is a reason for transfer to some other staff member, and he continues to see the patient for the duration of the therapy. An attempt is made to schedule the first interview as soon as possible after the patient calls for an appointment. There is also a "drop-in" or non-appointment service for emergencies so that patients in urgent need of psychiatric help usually can be seen immediately or at least within an hour or two of arrival at the clinic.

One of the unique aspects of this kind of associated health plan and medical group is that it tends to put a premium on health rather than on illness, i.e., it makes preventive medicine economically rewarding, thereby stimulating a constant search for the most effective and specific methods of treatment. The question of how psychiatry fits into comprehensive prepaid medical care is largely unexplored; there are not many settings in which it can be answered. Another feature of group practice in this setting is that all medical records for each patient are retained within the organization.

Subjects: The experimental subjects for this investigation were selected systematically by including every fifth psychiatric patient whose initial interview took place between January 1 and December 31, 1960. Of the 152 patients thus selected, 80 were seen for one interview only, 41 were seen for two to eight interviews (mean of 6.2) and were defined as "brief therapy," and 31 were seen for nine or more interviews (mean of 33.9) and were defined as "long-term therapy."

To provide a control group, the medical records of high medical utilizers who had never presented themselves to the Department of Psychiatry were reviewed until a group was selected which matched the psychotherapy sample in age, sex, socio-economic status, medical utilization in the year 1959, Health Plan membership including at least the years 1959 through 1962, and criteria of psychological distress. Thus, each experimental patient was matched with a control patient in the criteria above, but without reference to any other variable. Both samples ranged in age from 24 to 62, with a mean of 38.1. Of these, 52% were women and 63% were blue-collar workers or their dependents. The satisfaction of so many criteria in choosing a matched control group proved to be a tedious and time-consuming procedure.

Review of the medical records of the psychiatric sample disclosed consistent and conceptually useful notations in the year prior to the patients' coming to psychotherapy, which could be considered as *criteria of psychological distress*. These consisted of recordings, made by the physicians on the dates of the patients' visits, which were indicative of those patients' emotional distress, whether or not the physicians recognized this when they made the notations. These (38) criteria were assigned weights from

one to three in accordance with the frequency of their appearance in medical records and in accordance with clinical experience about the significance of the criteria when encountered in psychotherapeutic practice. The criteria, with weights assigned, are presented in Table 1. In comparing the charts of the psychiatric patients with those of Health Plan patients randomly drawn, it was determined that although some criteria were occasionally present in the medical records of the latter, a weighted score of three within one year clearly differentiated the psychiatric from the non-psychiatric groups. Accordingly, therefore, in matching the control (non-psychotherapy) group to the experimental (psychotherapy) group, the patients selected had records which indicated scores of three or more points for the year 1959. The mean weights of

Table 1: *Criteria of Psychological Distress with Assigned Weights*

One point	Two points	Three points
1. Tranquilizer or sedative requested.	23. Fear of cancer, brain tumor, venereal disease, heart disease, leukemia, diabetes, etc.	34. Unsubstantiated complaint there is something wrong with genitals.
2. Doctor's statement pt. is tense, chronically tired, was reassured, etc.	24. Health Questionnaire: yes on 3 or more psych. questions.[a]	35. Psychiatric referral made or requested.
3. Patient's statement as in no. 2.	25. Two or more accidents (bone fractures, etc.) within 1 yr. Pt. may be alcoholic.	36. Suicidal attempt, threat, or preoccupation.
4. Lump in throat.		37. Fear of homosexuals or of homosexuality.
5. Health Questionnaire: yes on 1 or 2 psych. questions.[a]	26. Alcoholism or its complications: delirium tremens, peripheral neuropathy, cirrhosis.	38. Non-organic delusions and/or hallucinations; paranoid ideation; psychotic thinking or psychotic behavior.
6. Alopecia areata.	27. Spouse is angry at doctor and demands different treatment for patient.	
7. Vague, unsubstantiated pain.		
8. Tranquilizer or sedative given.	28. Seen by hypnotist or seeks referral to hypnotist.	
9. Vitamin B_{12} shots (except for pernicious anemia).	29. Requests surgery which is refused.	
10. Negative EEG.	30. Vasectomy: requested or performed.	
11. Migraine or psychogenic headache.	31. Hyperventilation syndrome.	
12. More than 4 upper respiratory infections per year.	32. Repetitive movements noted by doctor: tics, grimaces, mannerisms, torticollis, hysterical seizures.	
13. Menstrual or premenstrual tension; menopausal sx.		
14. Consults doctor about difficulty in child rearing.	33. Weight-lifting and/or health faddism.	
15. Chronic allergic state.		
16. Compulsive eating (or overeating).		
17. Chronic gastrointestinal upset; aereophagia.		
18. Chronic skin disease.		
19. Anal pruritus.		
20. Excessive scratching.		
21. Use of emergency room: 2 or more per year.		
22. Brings written list of symptoms or complaints to doctor.		

[a] Refers to the last 4 questions (relating to emotional distress) on a Modified Cornell Medical Index—a general medical questionnaire given to patients undergoing the Multiphasic Health Check in the years concerned (1959–62).

Table 2: *Scores for Criteria of Psychological Distress, for the Experimental Groups and the Control Group during the Year Prior to Psychotherapy (1959)*

Group	Total score	No. of patients	Average score
One session only	264	80	3.30
Brief therapy	134	41	3.27
Long-term therapy	246	31	7.94
All experimental (psychotherapy) groups	644	152	4.24
Control (non-psychotherapy) group	629	152	4.13

the three experimental groups and the control group in terms of the 38 criteria of psychological distress are presented in Table 2: note that there was no significant difference between this dimension of the two groups in 1959.

In order to facilitate comparison of the experimental (psychotherapy) and control (non-psychotherapy) groups, one last criterion for inclusion in the matched group was employed. Each subject in the control group had to be a Health Plan member for the first three consecutive years under investigation inasmuch as the experimental group, though demonstrating attrition in continued membership after that time, remained intact for those years.

Dependent variable: Each psychiatric patient's utilization of health facilities was investigated first for the full year preceding the day of his initial interview, then for each of the succeeding five years beginning with the day after his initial interview.

The corresponding years were investigated for the control group which, of course, was not seen in the Department of Psychiatry. This investigation consisted of a straightforward tabulation of each contact with any outpatient facility, each laboratory report and x-ray report.[3] In addition a tabulation of number of days of hospitalization was made without regard to the type or quantity of service provided. Each patient's

utilization scores consisted of the total number of separate outpatient and inpatient tabulations.

Results

The results of this study are summarized in Table 3, which shows the differences by group in utilization of outpatient medical facilities in the year before and the five years after the initial interview for the psychiatric sample, and the utilization of outpatient medical services for the corresponding six years for the non-psychotherapy sample.

The data of Table 3 are summarized as percentages in Table 4, which indicates a decline in outpatient medical (not including psychiatric) utilization for all three psychotherapy groups for the years following the initial interview, while there is a tendency for the non-psychotherapy patients to increase medical utilization during the corresponding years. Applying t-tests of the significance of the standard error of the difference between the means of the "year before" and the means of each of the five "years after" (as compared to the year before), the following results obtain. The declines in outpatient (non-psychiatric) utilization for the "one session only" and the "long-term therapy" groups are not significant for the first year following the initial interview while the declines are significant at either the .05 or .01 levels for the remaining four years. In the "brief therapy" group, there are statistically significant declines in all five of the years following the initial interview. As further indicated in Table 4, there is a tendency for the control group to *increase* its utilization of medical services, but this proved significant for the "fourth year after" only.

The question was raised as to whether the patients demonstrating declines in medical utilization have done so because they have merely substituted protracted psychotherapy visits for their previous medical visits.

As shown in Table 5, the number of patients in the one-session-only group who return in the third to fifth years for additional visits is negligible. Comparable results are seen in the brief-therapy group. In contrast, the long-term-therapy group reduces its psychiatric utilization by more than half in the "second year after,"

---

[3] These procedures were counted as one even if there were more than one laboratory or x-ray procedure per report in the chart.

Table 3: *Utilization of Outpatient Medical Services (Excluding Psychiatry) by Psychotherapy Groups for the Year Before (1-B) and the Five Years After (1-A, 2-A, 3-A, 4-A, 5-A) the Initial Interview, and the Corresponding Years for the Non-psychiatric Group*

Group	1-B	1-A	2-A	3-A	4-A	5-A
One session only, unit score	911	815	612	372	321	217
No. of pts.	80	80	80	57	53	49
Average	11.4	10.2	7.7	6.5	6.1	4.4
Brief therapy, unit score	778	471	354	202	215	155
No. of pts.	41	41	41	32	30	27
Average	19.0	11.5	8.6	6.3	7.2	5.7
Long-term therapy, unit score	359	323	279	236	151	108
No. of pts.	31	31	31	27	24	19
Average	11.6	10.4	9.0	8.7	6.5	5.7
All experimental (psychotherapy) groups, unit score	2048	1609	1245	810	687	480
No. of pts.	152	152	152	116	107	95
Average	13.5	10.6	8.2	6.4	6.4	5.1
Control (non-psychotherapy) group, unit score	1726	1743	1718	1577	1611	1264
No. of pts.	152	152	152	127	111	98
Average	11.4	11.5	11.3	12.4	14.5	12.9

but maintains this level in the succeeding three years. By adding the outpatient medical visits to the psychiatric visits, it becomes clear that whereas the first two psychotherapy groups have not substituted psychotherapy for medical visits, this does seem to be the case in the long-term psychotherapy group. These results are shown in Table 6, and indicate that the *combined* outpatient utilization remains about the same from the "year before" to the "fifth year after" for the third psychotherapy group, while declines are evident for the first two psychotherapy groups. As regards the combined (medical plus psychiatric) utilization, the long-term psychotherapy group is not appreciably different from the control (non-psychiatric) group.

Investigation of inpatient utilization reveals a steady decline in utilization in the three psychotherapy groups from the "year before" to the "second year after," with the three remaining "years after" maintaining the level of utilization attained in the "second year after." In contrast, the control sample demonstrated a constant level in number of hospital days throughout the six years studied. These results are shown in Table

Table 4: *Comparison of the Year Prior to the Initial Interview with each Succeeding Year, Indicating Per Cent Decline or Per Cent Increase (Latter Shown in Parentheses) in Outpatient Medical (Non-psychiatric) Utilization by Psychotherapy Grouping, and Corresponding Comparisons for the Control Group, with Levels of Significance*

	1-A		2-A		3-A		4-A		5-A	
Group	% change	*Signif.*	% change	*Signif.*	% change	*Signif.*	% change	*Signif.*	% change	*Signif.*
One session only	10.5	NS	32.8	.05	44.75	.05	46.5	.05	61.4	.01
Brief therapy	39.5	.05	53.2	.05	66.8	.01	62.1	.01	70.0	.01
Long-term therapy	10.0	NS	22.3	.05	25.0	.05	43.0	.05	50.9	.05
All experimental (psychotherapy) groups,	21.4	.05	39.2	.01	48.2	.01	52.3	.01	62.5	.01
Control (non-psychotherapy) group	None	—	None	—	(8.8)	NS	(27.2)	.05	(13.2)	NS

Table 5: *Average Number of Psychotherapy Sessions per Year for Five Years by Experimental Group*

Group	1-A	2-A	3-A	4-A	5-A
One session only	1.00	0.00	0.00	0.02	0.06
Brief therapy	6.22	0.00	0.09	0.57	0.52
Long-term therapy	12.33	5.08	5.56	5.88	5.05

7, which indicates that the approximately 60% decline in number of days of hospitalization between the "year before" and the "second year after" for the first two psychotherapy groups is maintained to the "fifth year after"; this decline is significant at the .01 level. The inpatient utilization for the "long-term therapy" group in the "year before" was over twice that of the non-psychiatric sample, and about three times that of the first two psychotherapy groups. The significant (.01 level) decline of 88% from the "year before" to the "second year after" is maintained through the "fifth year after," rendering the inpatient utilization of the third psychotherapy group comparable to that of the first two psychotherapy groups.

In terms of decline in use of inpatient services (days of hospitalization), however, the long-term psychotherapy group and the control group are different, in that the former patients significantly reduce their inpatient utilization from the "year before" to the "fifth year after." However, the small size of the samples limits the conclusions that can be drawn.

Table 6: *Combined Averages (Outpatient Medical plus Psychotherapy Visits) of Utilization by Years Before and After Psychotherapy for the Experimental Groups, and Total Outpatient Utilization by Corresponding Years for the Control (Non-psychiatric) Group*

Group	1-B	1-A	2-A	3-A	4-A	5-A
One session only	11.4	11.2	7.7	6.5	6.1	4.5
Brief therapy	19.0	17.7	8.6	6.4	7.7	6.2
Long-term therapy	11.6	22.7	14.1	14.3	12.4	10.8
All experimental (psychotherapy) groups	13.5	15.3	9.2	8.3	7.9	6.2
Control group	11.4	11.5	11.3	12.4	14.5	12.9

Discussion

The original pilot study of which this project is an outgrowth was proposed by the senior author as an aid in planning for psychiatric care as part of comprehensive prepaid health-plan coverage. It had long been observed that some of this psychiatric clinic's patients, as well as many patients in the hospital for whom a psychiatric consultation was requested, had very thick medical charts. It was also repeatedly noted that when these patients were treated from a psychiatric point of reference, i.e., as a person who might have primarily emotional distress which was expressed in physical symptoms, they often abandoned their physical complaints. It seemed reasonable to expect that for many of these people, psychiatrically-oriented help was a more specific and relevant kind of treatment than the usual medical treatments.

This would be especially true if the effects of psychiatric help were relatively long-lasting, or if a change in the patient affected others in his immediate environment. In the long run, the interruption of the transmission of sick ways of living to succeeding generations would be the most fundamental and efficient kind of preventive medicine. It therefore seemed imperative to test the intuitive impressions that this kind of patient could be treated more effectively by an unstructured psychiatric interview technique than by the more traditional medical routine with its directed history.

The Balints (Balint, 1957; Balint & Balint, 1961) have published many valuable case reports which describe the change in quantity and quality in patients' appeals to the general practitioner after the latter learns to listen and understand his patients as people in distress because of current and past life experiences. It would be difficult, however, to design a statistical study of those patients and of a matched control group treated for similar complaints in a more conventional manner.

Psychiatry has been in an ambivalent position in relation to the rest of medicine: welcomed by some, resented by others, often, however, with considerable politeness which serves to cover up deep-seated fears of and prejudices against "something different." In a medical group associated with a prepaid health

Table 7: *Number of Days of Hospitalization and Averages by Psychotherapy Group for the Year Before and the Five Years After Psychotherapy, and the Corresponding Period for the Non-psychotherapy Group* (Note: Health Plan average is .8 per year for patients 20 years old or older.)

Group	1-B	1-A	2-A	3-A	4-A	5-A
One session only, days/year	117	78	52	32	33	31
No. of pts.	80	80	80	57	53	49
Average	1.46	0.98	0.65	0.56	0.62	0.63
Brief therapy, days/year	66	44	31	24	23	23
No. of pts.	41	41	41	32	30	27
Average	1.61	1.07	0.76	0.75	0.77	0.85
Long-term therapy, days/year	153	37	19	18	16	13
No. of pts.	31	31	31	27	24	19
Average	4.94	1.09	0.61	0.67	0.67	0.68
All experimental (psychotherapy) groups, days/year	336	159	102	74	72	67
No. of pts.	152	152	152	116	107	95
Average	2.21	1.05	0.68	0.64	0.67	0.71
Significance		.05	.02	.05	.05	.05
Control (non-psychotherapy) group, days/year	324	307	477	255	208	197
No. of pts.	152	152	152	127	111	98
Average	2.13	2.02	3.07	2.02	1.87	2.01
Significance		*NS*	.05	*NS*	*NS*	*NS*

plan, conditions are favorable for integrating psychiatry into the medical fraternity as a welcomed and familiar (therefore unthreatening) member specialty. The inherent ease of referral and communication within such a setting would be much further enhanced by the factor of prepayment, which eliminates the financial barrier for all those who can afford health insurance. For many reasons, then, this setting provides both the impetus and the opportunity to attempt an integration of psychiatry into general medical practice and to observe the outcome. In the past two decades, medicine has been changing in many significant ways, among which are prepaid health insurance, group practice, increasing specialization, automation, and a focus on the "whole person" rather than on the "pathology."

Forsham (Forsham, 1959) and others have suggested that at some not-too-distant date the patient will go through a highly automated process of history, laboratory procedures and physical tests, with the doctor at the end of the line doing a physical examination but occupying mainly the position of a medical psychologist. He will have all the results of the previously completed examinations which he will interpret

for the patient, and he will have time for listening to the patient, if he wishes to do so. The "Multiphasic Health Check" (Collen, Rubin, et al., 1964), which has been used for many years in the Northern California Region in the Kaiser Foundation Medical Clinics and which is constantly being expanded, is just such an automated health survey, and Medical Group doctors are in the process of becoming continually better psychologists. Eventually many more of the patients who are now seen in the psychiatric clinic will be expertly treated in the general medical clinics by more "compleat physicians."

A study such as this raises more questions than it provides answers. One question alluded to above is whether, with an ongoing training program such as Balint has conducted for general practitioners at Tavistock Clinic, internists might not be just as effective as psychiatric personnel in helping a greater percentage of their patients. A training seminar such as this has been conducted by Dr. Edna Fitch in the department of Pediatrics of Permanente Medical Group in San Francisco for many years and has been effective in helping pediatricians to treat, with more insight and comfort, emotional problems of children and their families and physical disorders which are an expression of emotional distress.

Using a broader perspective than the focus on the clinical pathology, one can wonder what social, economic or cultural factors are related to choice of symptoms, attitudes toward being "sick" (mentally or physically), attitudes toward and expectations of the doctor, traditions of family illness, superstitions relating to bodily damage, child raising practices, etc. How often is the understanding of such factors of crucial importance for effective and efficient treatment for the patient? Of special interest in general medical practice and overlooked almost routinely by physicians (and by many in the psychological field) are the "anniversary reactions" in which symptoms appear at an age at which a relative had similar symptoms and/or died.

Health Plan statistics indicate an increase in medical utilization with increasing age in adults. This is consistent with the relatively flat curve seen in the "medical utilization" of the control sample over the six year period and is in marked contrast to that of the experimental sample. There is the implication in this that some of the increasing symptoms and disability of advancing years are psychogenic and that psychotherapeutic intervention may in some cases function as preventive medical care for the problems associated with aging as well as preventive medicine in children.

A certain percentage of the long-term psychotherapy group seems to continue without diminution of number of visits to the psychiatric clinic: these patients appear from the data to be interminable or life-long psychiatric utilizers just as they had been consistently high utilizers of non-psychiatric medical care before. They seem merely to substitute psychiatric visits for some of their medical clinic visits. A further breakdown of the long-term group into three parts, e.g., less than 50, 50 to 150, and more than 150 visits, would probably help to sort this population's utilization into several patterns. More precise data on these groups would suggest modifications in classifications and methods of therapy or might suggest alternatives to either traditional medical or traditional psychiatric treatment in favor of some attempt to promote beneficial social changes in the environments of these chronically disturbed people.

Sources of Criticism

(1) One problem in providing a control group comparable to an experimental group in this kind of study is that, although undoubtedly having emotional distress, and in a similar "quantity" according to our yardstick, the control group did *not* get to the psychiatric clinic by either self- or physician referral. The fact that the control patients had not sought psychiatric help may reflect a more profound difference between this group and the experimental group than is superficially apparent. One cannot assume that the medical utilization of this control group would change if they were seen in the Psychiatry Clinic. (This objection will be minimized in the "prospective" part of this study, which will be reported in another paper). Although the average inpatient utilization for the three combined psychotherapy groups is the same as that of the control group in the year before (1959), the inpatient utilization of the long-term psychotherapy group is two and a half times that of the control group. If the study were extended to several years before, rather than just one year, it would become evident whether this was just a year of crisis for the long-term group or whether this had been a longer pattern of high inpatient utilization.

(2) Patients who visit the psychiatric clinic may, for one reason or another, seek medical help from a physician not associated with the Medical Group so that his medical utilization is not recorded in the clinic record, the source of information about utilization. In the long-term-therapy group the therapist is usually aware if his patient is visiting an outside physician, and although it is an almost negligible factor in that group, there can be no information in this regard for the one-session-only and brief-therapy groups without follow-up investigation.

(3) There is no justification in assuming that decreased utilization means better medical care, necessarily. Criteria of improvement would have to be developed and applied to a significantly large sample to try to answer this important question.

(4) Patients may substitute for physical or emotional symptoms behavioral disturbances which do not bring them to a doctor but may be just as distressing to them or to other people.

(5) The "unit" of utilization cannot be used as a guide in estimating costs, standing as it does for such diverse items. In itself the units are not an exact indicator of severity of illness nor of costs. A person with a minor problem may visit the clinic many times, while a much more severely ill person may visit the clinic infrequently. Even more striking is the variation in the cost of a unit, varying from about a dollar for certain laboratory procedures to well over a hundred dollars for certain hospital days (with admissions procedures, laboratory tests, x-rays, consultations, etc.) each worth one "unit." To arrive at an approximation of costs, the units have to be retabulated in cost-weighted form.

Suggested Further Studies

(1) The question of treatment of patients by non-medical professional clinicians has been argued for more than a half century. It is generally recognized that there are not enough psychiatrists now and that there will not be enough in the foreseeable future to treat all those persons who have disabling emotional disorders. In the late President Kennedy's program for Mental Health this lack was recognized; the recommendation for professional staff for community Mental Health Centers included clinical psychologists, psychiatric social workers and other trained personnel. Having little distinction in our psychiatric clinic between the various disciplines as far as their functions are concerned, it would be feasible and interesting to compare therapeutic results of the disciplines as well as individuals with various types of patients and various types of psychotherapy.

(2) Is length of treatment correlated with diagnostic category, original prognosis by therapist, socio-economic level of patient, discipline and orientation of therapist, or "severity of pathology"?

(3) What happens to the spouse, parents, and children of the patients who are seen in psychiatry?

(4) Are there distinguishing patterns of complaints in the three psychotherapy groups?

(5) How do blue-collar patients differ from white-collar or professional patients in number of interviews, diagnostic label, use of medication, recommendation of hospitalization, and type of complaints?

(6) What is the nature of the illness that resulted in hospitalization before the patient came to psychiatry—and after? How often was this a diagnostic work-up because the internist could not find "anything wrong" in the clinic?

Summary

The outpatient and inpatient medical utilization for the year prior to the initial interview in the Department of Psychiatry as well as for the five years following were studied for three groups of psychotherapy patients (one interview only, brief therapy with a mean of 6.2 interviews, and long-term therapy with a mean of 33.9 interviews) and a control group of matched patients demonstrating similar criteria of distress but not, in the six years under study, seen in psychotherapy. The three psychotherapy groups as well as the control (non-psychotherapy) group were high utilizers of medical facilities, with an average utilization significantly higher than that of the Health Plan average. Results of the study indicated significant declines in medical utilization in the psychotherapy groups when compared to the control group, whose inpatient and outpatient utilization remained relatively constant throughout the six years. The most significant declines occurred in the second year after the initial interview, and the one-interview-only and brief-therapy groups did not require additional psychotherapy to maintain the lower utilization level for five years. On the other hand, after two years the long-term-psychotherapy group attained a level of psychiatric utilization which remained constant through the remaining three years of study.

The combined psychiatric and medical utilization of the long-term-therapy group indicated that for this small group there was no over-all decline in outpatient utilization inasmuch as psychotherapy visits seemed to supplant medical visits. On the other hand, there was a significant decline in inpatient utilization, especially in the long-term-therapy group from an initial utilization of several times that of the Health Plan average, to a level comparable to that of the general adult Health Plan population. This decline in hospitalization rate tended to occur within the first year after the initial interview and remained generally comparable to the Health Plan average for the five years.

References

Avnet, H. H. *Psychiatric Insurance: Financing Short Term Ambulatory Treatment.* New York, Group Health Insurance, Inc., 1962.

Balint, Michael. *The Doctor, His Patient and the Illness.* New York, International Universities Press, 1957.

Balint, M. & Balint, E. *Psychotherapeutic Techniques in Medicine.* London, Tavistock Publications Limited, 1961.

Collen, M. F., Rubin, L., Neyman, J., Dantzig, G. B., Baer, R. M., & Siegelaub, A. B.: Automated multiphasic screening and diagnosis. *Am. J. Pub. Health* 1964, *54.*

Cummings, N. A., Kahn, B. I., & Sparkman, B. Psychotherapy and Medical Utilization. As cited in Greenfield, Margaret: Providing for Mental Illness. Berkeley, Calif., Berkeley Institute of Governmental Studies, University of California, 1964.

Follette, W. T., & Cummings, N. A. Psychiatry and Medical Utilization. An unpublished pilot project, 1962.

Forsham, P. H. Lecture before the Permanente Medical Group. San Francisco, 1959.

At the time of original publication of this article, *William T. Follette* was Chief Psychiatrist and *Nicholas A. Cummings* was Chief Psychologist at the Kaiser Foundation Hospital and the Permanente Medical Group, San Francisco.

Presented at one of the Contributed Papers Sessions sponsored by the Medical Care Section at the 94th Annual Meeting of the American Public Health Association, San Francisco, Cal., October 31-November 4, 1966.

This study was primarily financed by Grant PH 108-64-100 (P), U.S. Public Health Service. The authors gratefully acknowledge the assistance and cooperation of Mr. Royal Crystal, Deputy Chief, Health Economics Branch. Secondary financial support for this study was through Grant No. 131-7241, Kaiser Foundation Research Institute.

This paper is a report of the first of two investigations seeking to develop and test methods of assessing the effect of psychiatric services on medical utilization in a comprehensive medical program. Part II deals with prospective, rather than retrospective, methodology, and will be reported later.

Psychiatric Services and Medical Utilization in a Prepaid Health Plan Setting: Part II

Nicholas A. Cummings and William T. Follette

From physicians' notes and medical charts, a "criterion of psychological distress" was developed and used as part of the computerized screening of general medical patients to provide psychotherapy referral recommendations to physicians. In spite of intense efforts to increase referrals to psychotherapy, the number of HMO subscribers seeking psychotherapy reached an optimal level and remained fairly constant thereafter. The study demonstrated that in spite of increased demand, providing psychological services lowers overall health care costs.

Does psychotherapy alter the pattern of medical care? Can emotionally distressed patients who might benefit from psychotherapy be identified by screening a group of patients taking a health checkup? Will an automated psychological test be useful in such a screening process? These are the questions we set out to answer in this study.

The first question has been studied and the results reported by the authors (Follette & Cummings, 1967). It was found that psychotherapy patients initially were high "utilizers," but that after psychotherapy their utilization declined significantly. On the other hand, the utilization of the matched "control" group (not receiving psychotherapy) did not decline. The brief therapy and one-session-only psychotherapy groups had the largest decline in outpatient utilization, which theoretically helped to offset the cost of providing the psychotherapy. The decline in outpatient utilization of the long-term psychotherapy group was not enough to offset the cost of psychiatric and non-psychiatric treatment, being greater than the cost of prior medical utilization alone. However, this group showed considerable decline in days of hospitalization, which helped to make their psychiatric care financially less costly in this setting.

A major criticism of Part I (Follette & Cummings, 1967) was that, although the psychotherapy and "control" groups were matched socioeconomically and demographically, in medical utilization and in degree of emotional distress, the groups remained different in one crucial respect: the psychotherapy sample, whether self- or physician-referred, voluntarily presented themselves to the psychiatric clinic. In contrast, the matched group did not come to the psychiatric clinic even if referred by their physicians. The nature of the difference between the two groups made conclusions tentative. The question is crucial, because it may be that the group which did not come to the psychiatric clinic is *unable* to make use of psychiatric services in a meaningful manner, and that psychotherapy would not decrease the medical utilization of this group. The most obvious way to provide a valid control group would be to choose a large sample by uniform criteria and randomly divide it into two parts, then treat the two parts differently and observe the results. The present paper is a report on such a prospective study.

Method

The setting: The Kaiser Foundation Health Plan of Northern California is a group-practice prepayment plan offering comprehensive hospital and professional services on a direct-service basis. Professional services are provided by the Permanente Medical Group—a partnership of physicians. The Medical Group has a contract to provide comprehensive medical care to the members of the Plan, of whom there were

Reprinted from MEDICAL CARE © J. B. Lippincott Company, 1968, *6*, 31–41, by permission.

three-quarters of a million at the time of this study. The composition of the Health Plan membership is diverse, encompassing most socioeconomic groups. The Permanente Medical Group comprises all major medical specialties; referral from one specialty clinic to another is facilitated by the organizational features of group practice, geographical proximity and the use of common medical records. During the years of this study (1965–1966), only 17% of Health Plan members were eligible for psychiatric benefits on a prepaid basis, but in most areas of the Northern California region psychiatric services were available to Health Plan Subscribers at reduced rates. The psychiatric staff in the San Francisco Clinic, where the present study took place, consists of psychiatrists, clinical psychologists, psychiatric social workers, and psychology and social work interns. The clinic operates primarily as an outpatient service for adults and children for the evaluation and treatment of emotional disorders, but it also provides consultation for non-psychiatric physicians and consultation in the general hospital and the emergency room. There is no formal "intake" procedure, the first visit with any staff member being considered potentially therapeutic as well as evaluative and dispositional. Regardless of professional discipline, the persons who sees the patient initially becomes that patient's therapist unless there is reason for transfer to some other staff member, and he continues to see the patient for the duration of the therapy. An attempt is made to schedule the first interview as soon as possible after the patient calls for an appointment. There is also a "drop-in" or non-appointment service for emergencies so that patients in urgent need of psychiatric help usually can be seen immediately or at least within an hour or two after arrival at the clinic.

One of the unique aspects of this kind of associated health plan and medical group is that it tends to put a premium on health rather than on illness, i.e., it makes preventive medicine economically rewarding, thereby stimulating a constant search for the most effective and specific methods of treatment. Another feature of group practice in this setting is that all medical records for each patient are maintained within the organization.

The subjects: The source of the population for this study was 10,667 patients who voluntarily presented themselves in a six-month period to the San Francisco Kaiser-Permanente Automated Multiphasic Clinic for a health check, part of which includes 19 computerized procedures, ranging from simply body measurements to complex laboratory tests (Collen, 1964). A routine part of the three-hour series of examinations is the administration of a psychological test known as the Neuro-Mental Questionnaire, or NMQ (Cummings, Siegelaub, Follette, & Collen, in preparation). This consists of 155 dichotomous questions which (eventually, when the test is fully developed) will identify approximately 60 psychological categories. Each question is printed on a separate pre-punched card, which the patient must deposit in either the "true" or the "false" section of a divided box. For this study only the six major psychological categories were used: depression, hysteria, obsessional, panic and anxiety attacks, passive-aggressive, and schizophrenia. (This probably would identify most of the patients who could be identified by the full test, because 87% of the patients seen in the Department of Psychiatry fall into one or more of these six categories.)

The NMQ was computer-scored, and results were sent to the investigators within 24 hours of the time the patient had the questionnaire. The medical charts of the patients identified by the test were reviewed for evidences of psychological distress in the 12-month period prior to the Multiphasic examination.

"Criteria of psychological distress" (developed in Part I [Follette & Cummings, 1967] and presented in Table 1) refer to physicians' notes in the patients' medical charts which indicated emotional distress, whether or not the physicians recognized them as such. These 38 criteria have assigned weights from one to three, a weighted score of three within one year being accepted as an indication that a patient is in psychological distress. Accordingly, patients for the present study had 1) a "positive NMQ," and 2) a score of three or more points in "Criteria of Psychological Distress," for the 12 months prior to taking the Multiphasic examination.

Of the 10,667 patients who took the NMQ, 3,682, or 36.4%, yielded a positive score in one or more of the six NMQ categories (depression, hysteria, obsessional, panic-anxiety, passive-aggressive, schizophrenic). Of this group, 822 (7.7%) also scored three points or more in "criteria of distress." Of the 6,985 patients who did not score positively on the NMQ, only 56 (0.8%) scored three or more points on the "criteria of distress." Thus the use of scales in only six categories of the NMQ proved to be a useful method of eliminating two-thirds of the Multiphasic population in our search for a group of experimental subjects.

The psychological, socioeconomic and demographic characteristics of the 822-patient sample are given in Table 2. It will be noted that the mean age of 45.1 years is higher than the mean age of 38.1 years for patients generally seen in the Department of Psychiatry. Because

the NMQ was administered to only the first 100 patients taking the Multiphasic examination each day, rather than the full 130, appreciably more women were tested than men, because the men tend to make evening appointments. Consequently, 71.0% of the sample is composed of women. It will be noted further that in the 822-patient sample 43% were categorized as neurotic, 32% as having character disorders and 25% as psychotic. There was no difference between the percentages of blue-collar patients and white-collar patients diagnosed "psychotic."

Experimental condition: All patients with both positive NMQ's and three or more "distress" points were alternately assigned to either the referred or non-referred ("control") groups. For the referred patients the computer printed out

Table 1: *Criteria of Psychological Distress with Assigned Weights*

One point	Two points	Three points
1. Tranquilizer or sedative requested.	23. Fear of cancer, brain tumor, venereal disease, heart disease, leukemia, diabetes, etc.	34. Unsubstantiated complaint there is something wrong with genitals.
2. Doctor's statement pt. is tense, chronically tired, was reassured, etc.	24. Health Questionnaire: yes on 3 or more psych. questions.[a]	35. Psychiatric referral made or requested.
3. Patient's statement as in no. 2.	25. Two or more accidents (bone fractures, etc.) within 1 yr. Pt. may be alcoholic.	36. Suicidal attempt, threat, or preoccupation.
4. Lump in throat.		37. Fear of homosexuals or of homosexuality.
*5. Health Questionnaire: yes on 1 or 2 psych. questions.	26. Alcoholism or its complications: delirium tremens, peripheral neuropathy, cirrhosis.	38. Non-organic delusions and/or hallucinations; paranoid ideation; psychotic thinking or psychotic behavior.
6. Alopecia areata.		
7. Vague, unsubstantiated pain.	27. Spouse is angry at doctor and demands different treatment for patient.	
8. Tranquilizer or sedative given.		
9. Vitamin B_{12} shots (except for pernicious anemia).	28. Seen by hypnotist or seeks referral to hypnotist.	
10. Negative EEG.	29. Requests surgery which is refused.	
11. Migraine or psychogenic headache.	30. Vasectomy: requested or performed.	
12. More than 4 upper respiratory infections per year.	31. Hyperventilation syndrome.	
13. Menstrual or premenstrual tension; menopausal sx.	32. Repetitive movements noted by doctor: tics, grimaces, mannerisms, torticollis, hysterical seizures.	
14. Consults doctor about difficulty in child rearing.		
15. Chronic allergic state.	33. Weight-lifting and/or health faddism.	
16. Compulsive eating (or overeating).		
17. Chronic gastrointestinal upset; aereophagia.		
18. Chronic skin disease.		
19. Anal pruritus.		
20. Excessive scratching.		
21. Use of emergency room: 2 or more per year.		
22. Brings written list of symptoms or complaints to doctor.		

[a] Refers to the last 4 questions (relating to emotional distress) on a Modified Cornell Medical Index—a general medical questionnaire given to patients undergoing the Multiphasic Health Check in the years concerned (1959–62).

the following "consider-rule": *Consider referral to psychiatry for emotional problems.* The 411 patients assigned to the control group did not, of course, have such a consider-rule on their print-outs.

The physician participants: A few weeks after the Multiphasic screening, every patient has a routine follow-up office visit with one of 32 internists. At this time the physician interviews the patient, completes the physical examination, reviews the clinical information from all sources, and provides appropriate treatment or referral. Prior to conducting the present experiment, the physician co-author of this paper met with the internists, explained the nature of the study and solicited their individual cooperation. They were informed that they would be seeing patients whose Multiphasic printouts would contain the consider-rule suggesting referral to psychiatry. This was to be regarded as one more item of information to the physician, who would weigh it along with his total knowledge of the patient and make the ultimate decision whether to make such a referral. The internists also were advised that other patients would comprise the control group of the study, would not have the consider-rule in their print-outs, and would be undistin-

guishable from the other Multiphasic patients they would see routinely on follow-up visits.

Thus, "referred" patients (consider-rule) might or might not be referred to psychiatry, and, if referred, might or might not choose to come; or, if not referred by the internist, they might come to the psychiatric clinic through other channels. On the other hand, control patients (no consider-rule) might be referred to psychiatry as the result of the routine practice of medicine in this setting and without regard to the experiment, and, again, might choose to come or not to come to the psychiatric clinic. The various possibilities are shown in Figure 1.

Results

No Experimental Generation of a Psychiatric Population

Six months after the last experimental subject consulted with his internist on his Multiphasic follow-up visit, only five of the 411 patients given the consider-rule had made and kept appointments in the psychiatric clinic! This figure is exactly the same as the number of patients

Table 2: *Psychological, Socioeconomic and Demographic Characteristics of 822-patient Sample with Positive NMQ and Plus-3 or More on Criteria of Distress*

NMQ categories (with category number)		Blue collar			White collar			Totals	
		Urban	Suburban	Rural	Urban	Suburban	Rural		
Neurotic								352 (42.8%)	
Depressive	30	37	11	2	43	2	1	96	*Mean age:* 45.1 yrs.
Hysteric	16	12	5	1	2	4	2	26	*No. women:* 70.1%
Obsessional	25	23	6		35	6		70	*Blue collar:* 53.2%
Obs. hysteric	16, 25	10	3	2	12	3		30	*Urban:* 71.8%
Panic/anxiety	22	25	11		13	7	1	57	*Suburban:* 25.0%
Phobic	24	28	9	2	19	15		73	*Rural:* 3.2%
Character disorders								261 (31.8%)	*Neurotic:* 42.8%
Anal char.	13, 25	4	2		3	2		11	*Char. dis.:* 31.8%
Depressive	25, 30 (13)	26	7	2	18	3		56	*Psychotic:* 25.4%
Hysterical	13, 16	15	8	1	14	2	1	41	
Phobic	16, 24	21	12	1	20	7	1	62	
Passive/aggr.	13	27	5	1	25	13		71	
Sado-masoch.	13, 16, 30	6	3	1	8	2		20	
Psychotic								209 (25.4%)	
Schizophrenic	37	55	19	3	44	20	1	142	
Pseudo-neur. Schiz.	37, 25, 30 (plus 1 more)	21	8	2	24	11	1	67	
		310	109	18	280	97	8		

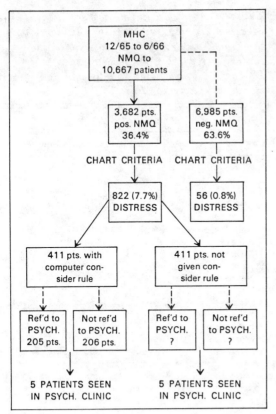

```
            MHC
         12/65 to 6/66
            NMQ to
        10,667 patients

      ┌──────────────┐   ┌──────────────┐
      │ 3,682 pts.   │   │ 6,985 pts.   │
      │ pos. NMQ     │   │ neg. NMQ     │
      │ 36.4%        │   │ 63.6%        │
      └──────────────┘   └──────────────┘
      CHART CRITERIA     CHART CRITERIA

      ┌──────────────┐   ┌──────────────┐
      │ 822 (7.7%)   │   │ 56 (0.8%)    │
      │ DISTRESS     │   │ DISTRESS     │
      └──────────────┘   └──────────────┘

   ┌───────────────┐         ┌───────────────┐
   │ 411 pts. with │         │ 411 pts. not  │
   │ computer con- │         │ given con-    │
   │ sider rule    │         │ sider rule    │
   └───────────────┘         └───────────────┘

 ┌────────┐ ┌────────┐    ┌────────┐ ┌────────┐
 │Ref'd to│ │Not ref'd│   │Ref'd to│ │Not ref'd│
 │PSYCH.  │ │to PSYCH.│   │PSYCH.  │ │to PSYCH.│
 │205 pts.│ │206 pts. │   │  ?     │ │   ?    │
 └────────┘ └────────┘    └────────┘ └────────┘

 5 PATIENTS SEEN          5 PATIENTS SEEN
 IN PSYCH. CLINIC         IN PSYCH. CLINIC
```

Figure 1.

from the control group who made and kept appointments in the psychiatric clinic. Thus, the experimental conditions failed to generate a psychiatric population, and were in no way superior in obtaining early referral to psychiatry than the usual, routine medical practice in this setting (see Figure 1).

Within the referred group there were found to be 40 patients who had previously been seen in the psychiatric clinic, and in the control group there were 42. None of the 82 patients previously seen in psychotherapy returned during the course of the experiment.

Usefulness of Automated Screening

The NMQ, as part of an automated multiphasic screening, proved to be a useful instrument in identifying a population within which the patients in emotional distress would be found. As seen in Figure 1, 36.4% of the patients with positive NMQ's also were in emotional distress, while less than one percent of the patients who did not have positive NMQ's were found to be in emotional distress.

Degree of Internists' Participation

At the conclusion of the primary phase of this study, and after the last patient had undergone his follow-up visit, 30 of the 32 participating internists were interviewed individually to determine their reactions to the computerized procedure and why they did or did not refer to psychiatry. As noted in Figure 1, about half the patients given the consider-rule in their computer printouts actually were referred to psychiatry by their internists according to notations to that effect in the patients' charts.

a. Ten (33%) of the internists did not even recall seeing a consider-rule for referral to psychiatry; 20 (67%) stated they saw instances of such a consider-rule, but the number seen varied from one to 15.

b. Of the 20 internists who saw the consider-rule, eight made no referrals, four referred all such patients, and eight referred half or more.

c. Reasons given for reluctance to refer centered mostly about the physician's feelings regarding having to deal with an emotional problem when his time with the patient was limited. He felt he would open a "Pandora's box" that could not appropriately be handled in the fifteen minutes allotted for the initial return visit. The second most-mentioned reason for not referring was the physician's knowledge of the patient and his circumstances. Typical of this was the reply: "I know this patient well. I referred him before and he wouldn't go. I had no reason to believe he would go this time." Or, "I know this patient has emotional problems, but we have been handling them here because she is reluctant to see a psychiatrist." A third type of response by the physician was one of antagonism to the procedure. A few internists complained that it was "cold" or "impersonal."

d. Internists who made referrals remarked that it made their job somewhat easier. They were startled by the accuracy of the consider-rule, for after opening up the issue of emotional problems, they found their patients eager to discuss them. One physician stated he felt more comfortable referring a patient to psychiatry when the patient could blame the computer and not the doctor.

e. Ultimately, the internist's individual procedure regarding referral to psychiatry seemed little affected by the consider-rule. Physicians who routinely and easily refer to psychiatry continued to do so in the experiment, while physicians who usually do not refer to psychiatry essentially ignored the consider-rule. For the most part, it was the individual physician's mode of practice that mattered.

Degree of Outpatient and Inpatient Medical Utilization

Each referred and control patient's utilization of health facilities was investigated for the full year prior to the patient's having taken the Multiphasic screening. This investigation consisted of a straightforward tabulation of each contact with any outpatient facility, each laboratory report and x-ray report. In addition, a tabulation of number of days of hospitalization was made without regard to the type or quantity of service provided. Each patient's utilization scores consisted of the total number of separate

Table 3: *Average Utilization of Outpatient Medical Services for the Year Prior to the Multiphasic Screening for Both Referred and Control Groups by Diagnosis, Socioeconomic Status, and Residence (Excluding Rural)*

| | Blue collar | | White collar | | |
	Urban	Suburban	Urban	Suburban	Totals
Neurotic					
No. patients	135	45	124	37	341
Score	2538	886	2505	673	6602
Mean	18.8	19.6	20.2	18.4	19.4
Character disorder					
No. patients	99	37	88	29	253
Score	1168	396	994	336	2894
Mean	11.8	10.7	11.3	11.6	11.4
Psychotic					
No. patients	55	19	44	20	138
Score	677	217	480	234	1608
Mean	12.3	11.4	10.9	11.7	11.6
Pseudo-neurotic					
No. patients	21	8	24	11	64
Score	452	158	571	289	1470
Mean	21.5	19.7	23.8	26.3	22.9

Table 4: *Average Utilization of Inpatient Medical Services (Days of Hospitalization) for the Year Prior to the Multiphasic Screening for Both Referred and Control Groups by Diagnosis, Socioeconomic Status, and Residence, Excluding Rural[a]*

| | Blue collar | | White collar | | |
	Urban	Suburban	Urban	Suburban	Totals
Neurotic					
No. patients	135	45	124	37	341
Score	170	60	165	48	443
Mean	1.26	1.34	1.33	1.29	1.30
Character disorder					
No. patients	99	37	88	29	253
Score	285	93	239	84	701
Mean	2.88	2.51	2.72	2.91	2.77
Psychotic					
No. patients	55	19	44	20	138
Score	235	94	200	79	608
Mean	4.27	4.95	4.54	3.95	4.41
Pseudo-neurotic					
No. patients	21	8	24	11	64
Score	105	39	122	58	324
Mean	5.00	4.88	5.08	5.27	5.03

[a] Note: Health Plan Average is 0.8 per year for patients 20 years old or older.

outpatient tabulations. These results are summarized in Table 3 (outpatient) and Table 4 (inpatient). The rural patients were excluded, inasmuch as their number was too small to contribute significantly to the results. As expected, no significant differences were found between the experimental and control groups, and both groups are combined (with rural patients excluded) in Tables 3 and 4.

All 796 patients (26 rural patients excluded) were significantly high utilizers of both outpatient and inpatient medical services.

A $2 \times 3 \times 4$ analysis of variance of the 796 patients indicated no significant difference in terms of blue versus white collar, or urban versus suburban conditions, as regards the utilization of both outpatient and inpatient medical services.

There was a significant difference in the degree of utilization of both outpatient and inpatient medical services in terms of diagnostic category. The neurotic patients had the highest outpatient utilization, whereas the psychotic patients had the highest inpatient utilization.

The outpatient utilization of the pseudoneurotic schizophrenic resembled that of the neurotic, while the inpatient utilization of the pseudoneurotic schizophrenic is not significantly different than that of the psychotic.

Patients with character disorders utilize outpatient services at the same rate as psychotics, but their inpatient rate is approximately half-way between neurotic and psychotic inpatient rates.

Discussion

Research in human behavior is easy to do, but difficult to do well. A research design may look fine on paper, but may not be feasible in fact. Such was the case with the present experiment: no experimental population was generated. This result can be instructive, however, and we will proceed to search for serendipitous results. Human subjects cannot be manipulated for experimental or therapeutic purposes in the same way that animals or machines can. This applies to the doctors in this experiment as well as the patients.

This observation may be timely and relevant now when vast sums of money are being spent in developing mental health programs, many of which are designed on paper from an armchair and have never been proven to be clinically effective.

A recent paper from the University of California at Los Angeles Alcoholism Research Clinic (Ditman, Crawford, Forgy, Moskowitz, & MacAndrew, 1967) found the results to be the same in a group of alcoholics randomly assigned by court probation to one of three treatment conditions: (1) a psychiatrically-oriented outpatient alcoholic clinic, (2) Alcoholics Anonymous, (3) no treatment. One might conclude that the answer to the problem of alcoholism *may not* be the provision of a multitude of "alcoholic clinics" across the country. Similarly, it has never been demonstrated that a "suicide prevention center" has lowered the incidence of suicide in any community. We might, on the other hand, expect that such a center would be likely to increase (1) preoccupation with suicide in the community, (2) the number of suicidal threats, and (3) the number of suicidal gestures. In other words, if people volunteer to play dramatic life-saver, we can confidently expect others to volunteer to threaten self-destruction. Nevertheless, we have suicide prevention centers popping up all over the land.

The question is to what extent psychiatric patients can be "found" in the community and then successfully treated. Is is possible and worthwhile to induce an ever-greater percentage of the population to get some treatment to improve mental health? Are the patients who come to a psychiatric clinic via the common traditional channels (referral by self, relative, friend, family doctor) more or less treatable than those produced by newer "case finding" methods in the community?

The setting in which this study was done is unusual in having had a psychiatric clinic as part of comprehensive health services for about 15 years. For this reason there was no large reservoir of patients needing and wanting psychiatric services which they could not afford. Note that 10% of the patients identified as emotionally disturbed and in acute distress already had been seen in the psychiatric clinic. Many of the others in this group undoubtedly have been referred but will never be seen in psychiatry for a number of reasons, among which may be the following: (1) they have too much invested in their roles of being (physically) sick; (2) they have major physical illnesses which they and their doctors use to ignore the emotional illness; (3) they are terrified by the idea of mental illness ("craziness"); (4) there is often a payoff for "real," i.e. physical, illness, but not for emotional disturbance from family, friends, doctors, insurance companies. The fact that 90% of these patients have never gotten to the psychiatric clinic demonstrates that non-psychiatric physicians have been treating and will continue to treat the bulk of the emotionally-disturbed people in the population.

While we have demonstrated that emotionally-disturbed patients who are seen in psychiatry reduce their use of the other medical services, we are still unable to determine whether this would hold true for all those patients identified by our double-screening technique as likely candidates for psychotherapy.

One should be cautious in using statistics from mental health clinics when they deviate from the averages reported by most other clinics.

It has often been reported that about one per cent of a population will seek psychiatric services per year. The Group Health Insurance study (Avnet, 1962) showed the pattern of response that is usually seen when a population is offered low-cost psychiatric services for the first time: increased utilization for the first few months due to an accumulation of need for such services. After that, the demand stabilizes. Active "promotion" of psychiatric benefits did not increase the utilization of psychiatric services in their population.

It is possible to report a much higher rate of utilization, e.g., 5%/year, if one organizes his psychiatric clinic in the following manner: (1) "crisis" orientation; (2) very brief therapy and counseling; (3) representing the psychiatric staff member as "your friendly family counselor"; (4) fostering dependency relationship by encouraging patients to return frequently—whenever they have to make decisions, feel anxious or depressed, etc.; (5) counting each family member as a separate patient when a family is seen together; (6) most of all—by counting each return to the clinic a "new patient." Unfortunately, the higher the percentage, the more effective the service.

Antes muerto que mudado (death rather than change), a Spanish proverb quoted by Lichtenstein (1961) in his classic monograph on identity, dramatizes the tremendous dynamic force behind the human being's need to maintain his identity—a force that has priority over all forces motivating a person's behavior and life style. Many otherwise baffling aspects of the behavior of individuals, groups and nations become clear if this force is recognized. Patients do not want to change, in fact resist change, even though their lives are full of misery and pain. A psychotherapist, then, is relatively helpless unless the patient is highly motivated, i.e., in a great deal of "pain." Getting a patient to the office of a psychotherapist is likely to be a waste of everybody's time unless the patient is "ready" or motivated for some kind of change. It is, of course, the psychotherapist's job to foster and capitalize on every shred of motivation he can find. Many emotionally-disturbed people in the community may seem to "need help" but are not at all interested in change. This is certainly true of a high percentage of alcoholics, "hip-

pies," addicts, "psychopaths," criminals and many other types whom the community at large thinks "need help."

The assessment of the effectiveness of psychotherapy has always presented great difficulties, conclusions varying from "psychotherapy is worthless" (Eysenck, 1966) to the behavior therapists' claim of as high as 86–95% effectiveness in 30 interviews or fewer. (Wolpe & Lazarus, 1966) By far the best investigation of brief psychotherapy was done by the Tavistock group, reported by Malan. (Malan, 1963) We need much more high-quality research of this kind in assessing the value of mental health programs.

It is interesting to note the few differences between blue-collar and white-collar workers (Table 2). The blue-collar patients are more apt to be in only three (of 14) categories: hysteric; panic and anxiety attacks; and depressive character; and less likely to be obsessional. Otherwise, the two groups are comparable in percentages in the other neurotic and character-disorder categories and in all the psychotic categories. The "pseudoneurotic schizophrenic" category defines a group of patients who have a wealth of symptoms of many kinds. These patients are the ones that seek professional help constantly, who "never get well" and may make up a large percentage of those long-term patients in the office of every physician, psychotherapist and psychoanalyst.

The similar percentages of incidence of psychoses in blue-collar and white-collar groups may reflect the greater impartiality of the computer than the clinician, if we accept the contention of Hollingshead and Redlich, (1958) that middle-class psychotherapists tend to over-diagnose psychosis in patients of lower socioeconomic classes as compared with those of middle or upper classes.

Summary

During a six-month period, 10,667 patients taking the Automated Multiphasic Screening Examination (Kaiser-Permanente Medical Center, San Francisco) were given a computerized psychological test as a routine part of that screening. The tests revealed that 3,682 patients, or one third, had evidence of neurosis, personality disorder, or psychosis. Of these, 822 (or 7.7% of the total Multiphasic patients tested) also had high degrees of "emotional distress." The 32 internists conducting the Multiphasic follow-up examinations received computer-printed "consider-rules" suggesting referral to psychiatry for half (411) of these patients, while the other half served as a control group and did not have such a "consider-rule."

It was found that attempts at early detection of emotional problems did not generate more psychiatric clinic patients than those generated through routine medical practice in this setting. There was considerable resistance on the part of physicians to the "artificiality" of referral by automated procedures, and there was a comparable rejection by patients of a referral made as a result of such procedures.

The population selected by this automated psychological screening method were high utilizers of medical services. Where neurotics tend to use outpatient medical services, psychotic patients tend to use inpatient medical services. Patients with personality disorders seem to use both. No differences in utilization rates were found in terms of blue collar versus white collar, or urban versus suburban.

The implications of these findings are: (1) attempts at early detection of psychiatric problems will not create as great a demand for psychiatric services as might be expected; (2) whereas many patients seeking outpatient medical treatment may be reflecting neurotic problems, psychotic patients often manifest symptoms which so simulate a variety of baffling problems that they are hospitalized for medical diagnostic workups. Patients with personality disorders seem to require both outpatient and inpatient attention in above-average amounts.

References

Avnet, H. H. Psychiatric Insurance: Financing Short Term Ambulatory Treatment. New York, Group Health Insurance, Inc., 1962.

Collen, M. F. Periodic health examinations using an automated multitest laboratory. 1966, *J.A.M.A., 195,* 830.

Collen, M. F., Rubin, L., Neyman, J., Dantzig, G. B., Baer, R. M., & Siegelaub, A. B.: Automated multiphasic screening and diagnosis. *Am. J. Pub. Health,* 1964, *54,* 741.

Cummings, N. A., Siegelaub, A., Follette, W., and Collen, M. F. An automated psychological screening test as part of an automated multi-phasic screening. In preparation.

Ditman, K. S., Crawford, G. G., Forgy, E. W., Moskowitz, H., & MacAndrew, C. A controlled experiment on the use of court probation for drunk arrests. *Amer. J. Psychiat.,* 1967, *124,* 160.

Eysenck, H. J. The Effects of Psychotherapy. New York, International Science Press, Inc., 1966.

Follette, W., and Cummings, N. A.: Psychiatric services and medical utilization in a prepaid health plan setting. *Medical Care,* 1967, *5,* 25.

Hollingshead, A. B., and Redlich, F. C.: Social Class and Mental Illness. New York, John Wiley, 1958.

Lichtenstein, H.: Identity and Sexuality. *J. Amer. Psychoanal. Assn.* 1961, *9,* 179.

Malan, D. H.: A Study of Brief Psychotherapy. Springfield, Ill., Charles C Thomas, 1963.

Wolpe, J., and Lazarus, A. A.: Behavior Therapy Techniques. London, Pergamon Press, 1966.

At the time of original publication of this article, *Nicholas A. Cummings* was Chief Psychologist and *William T. Follette* was Chief Psychiatrist at the Kaiser Foundation Hospital and the Permanente Medical Group, San Francisco.

Presented at a session sponsored by the Group Health Association of America at the 95th Annual Meeting of the American Public Health Association, Miami Beach, Florida, October 23–27, 1967.

This study was financed by Contract PH 108-66-235, U.S. Public Health Service. The authors gratefully acknowledge the cooperation and assistance of Mrs. Agnes Brewster, Chief, Health Economics Branch, and Mr. Royal Crystal, Chief, Medical Care Data and Resources Center. The authors also acknowledge their debt to Dr. M. F. Collen, who research design is reflected in this study, and whose Automated Multiphasic Health Clinic made possible the field tests employed.

This paper is Part II of a two-part series seeking to develop and test methods of assessing the effects of psychiatric services in a comprehensive medical program. Part I involved retrospective methodology, while the present paper reports a prospective study.

Brief Psychotherapy
and Medical Utilization

Nicholas A. Cummings and William T. Follette

The way in which psychotherapy services are delivered, rather than the number of patients served, determines the cost-effectiveness of service. Immediate intervention that avoids lengthy waits for appointments and evaluative sessions often relieves emotional distress. An 8-year follow-up of patients' recollections of their symptoms and treatment is reported.

It has been suggested that hospital overutilization is caused partly by the very nature of hospital insurance benefits—services are reimbursable if done in hospital, but not in the practitioner's office. Pacific Mutual's five years of experience with a health maintenance plan in Southern California (Gamlin, 1975), administered through the Orange County Medical Foundation (see Chapter Six) clearly supports this view by demonstrating that when the traditional benefits are reversed, there is an actual decrease in dollars paid out. Contrary to common practice, the foundation placed a $100 deductible on hospital stays while offering first-dollar coverage for outpatient physician's services. Claims increased 30% but dollars paid out decreased. This refutation of traditional fears has been demonstrated by the Kaiser Health Plan for years as illustrated in the eight-year follow-up study reported in this chapter.

In the first of a series of investigations into the relationship between psychological services and medical utilization in a prepaid health plan setting, the authors (Follette and Cummings, 1967) found that (1) persons in emotional distress were significantly higher users of both inpatient and outpatient medical facilities as compared to the health plan average; (2) medical utilization declined significantly in those emotionally distressed individuals who received psychotherapy as compared to a control group of matched emotionally distressed health plan members who were not accorded psychotherapy; (3) these declines remained constant during the five years following the termination of psychotherapy; (4) the most significant declines occurred in the second year after the initial interview, and those patients receiving one session only or brief psychotherapy (two to eight sessions) did not require additional psychotherapy to maintain the lower level of utilization for five years; and (5) patients seen for two years or more in regular psychotherapy demonstrated no overall decline in total outpatient utilization, since psychotherapy visits tended to supplant medical visits. However, there was significant decline in inpatient utilization in this long-term therapy group from an initial hospitalization rate several times that of the health plan average, to a level comparable to that of the general adult health plan population. In a subsequent study the same authors (Cummings and Follette, 1968) found that intensive efforts to increase the number of referrals to psychotherapy by computerized psychological screening with early detection and alerting of the attending physicians did not increase significantly the number of patients seeking psychotherapy. The authors concluded that in a prepaid health plan setting already maximally employing educational techniques for both patients and physicians, and already providing a range of prepaid psychological services, the number of health plan subscribers seeking psychotherapy reached an optimal level and remained fairly constant. During the entire period of the study, as well as in the insured years before and after the eight years of this study, the utilization of mental health services was consistently .5 per 1,000 insureds for inpatient (hospitalization), and 9 per 1,000 insureds for outpatient services. The average length of hospitalization remained under eight days, and the average outpatient psychotherapy series remained at 6.6 visits.

Sixteen years of prepayment experience demonstrates that there is no basis for the fear that an increased demand for psychotherapy will financially endanger the system. It is not the number of referrals received, but the manner in which psychotherapy services are delivered, that determines optimal cost-therapeutic effectiveness. The finding that one session only, with no repeat psychological visits, could reduce medical utilization by 60% over the following five years, was surprising and totally unexpected. Equally surprising was the 75% reduction in medical utilization over a five-year period in those patients initially receiving two to eight psychotherapy sessions (brief therapy). The data offered no conclusive reason as to how and why this early, brief psychotherapeutic intervention resulted in a persistent reduction in medical utilization throughout the following half decade. The authors speculated that the results obtained demonstrated a psychotherapeutic effect, inasmuch as the clinic procedure was to offer early and incisive intervention into the patient's crisis problem, to get beneath the manifest symptoms to his or her real concerns, and to offer understanding and therapy in the very first session. Such a hypothesis would suggest that a patient's understanding or appreciation of his or her problem and its relationship to symptoms would diminish the somaticizing of emotions, and consequently reduce medical visits. This speculation is in keeping with the experiences of providing psychotherapy under national health care in Great Britain (Balint, 1957). Perhaps a less satisfactory, but an equally plausible hypothesis might be that the patient attained no mastery over his problems and that after the psychological visit he found ways other than visiting the doctor to express emotional distress. The

present eight-year follow-up tried to clarify the effect of brief psychotherapy previously reported.

It is important to describe the setting in which the past and present studies were conducted. The Kaiser Foundation Health Plan of Northern California is a group-practice prepayment plan offering comprehensive hospital and professional services on a direct-service basis to 1,250,000 subscribers in the greater San Francisco Bay Area. Professional services are provided by the Permanente Medical Group, a partnership of physicians that uniquely and effectively utilizes an impressive number of nonmedical doctors (such as clinical psychologists and optometrists) as primary health service providers. The San Francisco Kaiser-Permanente Medical Center, where the studies were conducted, is one of ten centers in the San Francisco Bay Area offering direct and indirect mental health services. Its staff of six clinical psychologists, four psychiatrists, and two psychiatric social workers reflects the fact that throughout the Northern California facilities it is typically the nonmedical, and particularly the psychological personnel that provide the bulk of the psychotherapy and consultation. Working on an equal patient-responsibility level with their psychiatric colleagues, clinical psychologists and psychiatric social workers assume full responsibility for their patients; admit and discharge from the hospital; provide consultation for nonpsychiatric physicians and consultation in the general hospital; participate in twenty-four hour "on call" duty; and make determinations of mental health emergencies (such as suicidal attempts and acute psychotic episodes) appearing at night in the emergency room of the general hospital. The ability of a psychologist or social worker to function effectively as a primary health service provider with full patient responsibility is a condition of employment at Kaiser-Permanente, San Francisco.

As the original health maintenance organization (HMO), one of the heretofore unique aspects of this setting is that it tends to put a premium on health rather than on illness, by making preventative medicine economically rewarding. The same principle holds true for the delivery of mental health services where there is a constant search for the most effective and specific methods of treatment. Consequently, effective cost-therapeutic techniques have been developed for the treatment of alcoholism, suicidal activity, drug abuse, heroin addiction, and a variety of other conditions often excluded from insurance coverage. To deny psychotherapeutic intervention in these problems merely results in having to medically and surgically treat their expensive physical consequences. On the other hand, traditional intake procedures, waiting lists, and protracted therapies have been eliminated in favor of rapid, immediate intervention with individual and group psychotherapy, which is most often relatively brief, but which occurs in programs specifically designed to promote maximum patient recovery to his effective state. All therapists perform long-term psychotherapy when indicated, but other dynamic modalities are most often the treatment of choice.

The present study investigated the question of whether the reduction in outpatient and inpatient medical utilization following brief psychotherapeutic intervention reflects a positive, or therapeutically defined change in the patients' behavior. The hypothesis can be stated simply: if the reduction in medical utilization is the result of the patient's having coped more effectively with emotional distress, then the presenting symptom (called the "manifest problem") should disappear, and the patient should have an awareness of the real or underlying concern that produced his or her symptom.

The psychotherapy charts of the eighty patients seen for one session only and the 41 patients seen for brief therapy (a total of 121 patients seen eight years previously) were drawn and reviewed for the following information obtained from the psychotherapists' notes:

1. What is presenting symptom, problem, or "manifest" reason why patient was referred or is here?
2. What is underlying psychological reason for patient's symptom, problem, or complaint?
3. Did the therapist suggest that patient return, or did he or she ask patient to return? Did patient express an interest in returning? Did patient make return appointment?
4. From the therapist's notes, did you get the feeling anything was dealt with by the patient that would be of value? Was patient un-

duly resistive, angry; or was patient friendly, impressed?

This information was necessary as background orientation for a telephone questionnaire conducted by a masters-level psychology assistant. Whenever possible each patient, when located, was individually interviewed. It was not possible to locate all patients after eight years, as over 50% of each group were no longer members of the health plan, a typical situation in the highly mobile California labor force. Meticulous tracing, often out of state and sometimes as far away as the East Coast, resulted in telephone contact with 56 of the 80 one-session-only group, and 31 of the 41 brief-psychotherapy group. The telephone interviewers employed the following questionnaire as a guide:

Telephone Call to Patient
(Try to record extensively patient's exact words.)

I am _____, a psychologist at Kaiser-Permanente. We are following up on some of the people we saw sometime back, and would like to know how you are getting along.

1. Do you remember your appointment or visit with a psychotherapist? How long ago was it?
2. Do you remember whom you saw?
3. How did you know of our service? Did a doctor refer you, or did you ask for a referral?
4. What was the reason you consulted a psychotherapist? (If patient says something to the effect that "my doctor wanted me to go," try to elicit the reason [such as symptom, complaint, problem] why the doctor thought the referral a good idea. We are interested here in what the patient remembers, whether he focuses on the manifest problem or the psychological problem.)
5. What do you recall was discussed with your psychotherapist? (If this has not been spelled-out in No. 4 above.)
6. Do you feel the visit with a psychotherapist was of any benefit to you? If so, how? If not, why not?
7. How have you been getting along? (Here if the patient has not recalled the

manifest symptom or complaint, remind him and ask about it. If he has not recalled the psychological problem which was discussed, remind him and ask about it.)

In the telephone interviews the researchers were interested in whether the patient recalled the presenting symptom (manifest problem) as the reason for having consulted a psychotherapist, or whether, instead, he or she remembered the actual focus and direction taken by the therapist in bringing to awareness the patient's real concern as the reason for the consultation. Of importance, also, was the patient's own perception of the degree of help derived from the single consultation or brief series of sessions. Of the 87 patients located and interviewed, only two refused to cooperate. A third who initially refused cooperation changed her mind after verifying the legitimate nature of the research project.

All 85 patients contacted and who were diagnosed in terms of anxieties, phobias, somaticization, depression, and psychosis in their presenting problems could readily be categorized in terms of the actual problem that was creating the symptom, and on the basis of even one interview. They could be classified as marital difficulties, problems with children or pregnancy, alcohol or drugs, job problems, and so forth, and all cut across psychodiagnostic categories. The therapist was quick in eliciting the patient's immediate life problem, but it must be emphasized that often he was also able to formulate for the patient the immediate crisis in terms of his dominant psychological dynamics and life-style. This formulation was made without fostering long-term dependency or plans for a complete personality overhaul, and within the context of immediate, brief, incisive therapeutic intervention.

The telephone interviews found that although all but one of the 85 persons responding remembered seeing a psychotherapist, only two could recall the therapist's name. There was a tendency to underestimate the eight years elapsed since the last session, with "two or three years ago" being the response in almost 60% of the cases. The patients were nearly equally divided between those who recalled being referred by a physician (44) and those who were self-referred, or by the spouse, a relative or a friend (41).

The crucial question was whether the patient remembered the manifest or the actual problem in recalling the interview. The results are unequivocal, for 78 patients, or 92%, recalled the problem discussed (marital, familial, job, and so forth) rather than the presenting symptom as the reason for the referral. In fact, when these 78 patients were asked directly about the presenting symptom (such as, "Did you ever have severe headaches?"), all but five denied ever having consulted a doctor for such a complaint. Thus the patient seems to have understood that the problem was more "real" than the symptom.

In view of the latter finding, it is somewhat surprising that the patients generally felt their psychotherapeutic contact had not been helpful. This trend existed in spite of the response that they were getting along well and had either resolved the psychological conflict or were coping with the problem. The responses elicited were as follows:

		Yes	No
1.	Do you feel the visit with the "psychiatrist" was of any benefit to you?	9	76
		Well	Not Well
2.	How have you been getting along (in regard to the psychological problem)?	83	2

The patients tended to attribute their coping with the problem to their own, rather than the therapist's solution, with "I just worked it out" being the frequent answer. On further consideration, this finding need not be surprising, as real insight becomes part of the patient's own belief system.

In several instances the patient reported being very angry with the psychotherapist, but in each case the patient added that, "He made me so mad I realized I had to solve this myself." Two illustrative cases might be helpful.

Case 1

Mrs. W., age 39, married 16 years, with three children, was referred by her internist for severe headaches that had become less and less responsive to medication for the past ten months. She was seen by a psychologist three times, during which time her anger at her husband (whom she reluctantly said was seeing his secretary) was discussed, along with her feelings of being old at 39 and unattractive. Between the second and third sessions she blew up at her husband, put her foot down regarding his staying out at night, and was surprised to find he was remorseful and eager to make amends. On telephone interview eight years later she denied ever having suffered from severe headaches, and recalled clearly that she consulted a psychotherapist for a marital problem. She did not find the sessions helpful, and stated flatly that she and husband worked it all out and they have been happier than ever.

Case 2

Mrs. S., age 54, office worker, divorced after one year of marriage at age 47, has no children, and lives alone. She was diagnosed as an involutional psychotic after being referred by her internist for delusions in which her neighbor was wiring her house to kill her with electricity. She saw the psychiatrist only once and left in a rage when, after discussing her lifelong loneliness, isolation and feelings of uselessness, he suggested she was envious of a neighbor woman's happy marriage, her four older children, and her new baby. On telephone interview eight years later she expressed frank hostility toward her psychiatrist and was outspoken in stating he made her worse. On the other hand, she recalls discussing her loneliness, denied ever having had her delusion, and insisted the neighbor had always been her best friend. In fact, the patient was the neighbor's frequent and only babysitter and had become "like a member of the family." At the conclusion of the interview she could not resist adding heatedly that "psychiatry is bunk; they try to make lonely people think they're crazy."

The results suggest that the reduction in medical utilization was the consequence of resolving the emotional distress being reflected in symptoms and doctors' visits. The modal patient in this eighth-year follow-up may be described as follows: "He denies ever having

consulted a physician for the symptoms for which he had been originally referred. Rather, he recalls the actual problem discussed as the reason for the "psychiatric" visit, and although he reports the problem is resolved, he attributes this to his own efforts and does not give credit to his psychotherapist." This description reaffirms the contention that the reduced medical utilization reflected the diminished emotional distress expressed in symptoms presented to the doctor.

The findings suggest that the expectations of the therapist influence the outcome of psychotherapy, for if the first interview is merely "evaluation" or "intake," not much of therapeutic value is likely to occur in the first interview. If the therapist's attitude is that no real help is forthcoming from less than prolonged "intensive" psychotherapy, he may be right (for his own patients). Malan (1963), in his classic study of brief psychotherapy, was able to examine honestly the prejudices of his group of psychiatrists about brief therapy and the kinds of benefit possible, the kinds of patients who could utilize it, the permanency of the results, and so forth. He concluded that traditional attitudes about very brief therapy were mostly in the nature of unjustified prejudices. It would appear that therapeutic effects of brief therapy that can be labeled "transference cure," "flight into health," "intellectualization," and other derogatory terms can often be long-lasting and result in a major change in the person's symptoms, relationships, and even lifestyle. Many of the patients in this study would undoubtedly be called "poorly motivated for treatment" or "dropouts from therapy" in many psychotherapy clinics.

Immediacy of availability and treatment is probably a very important aspect of this study. The results tend to support the crisis-clinic thesis that a great deal more can be done in less time during a time of emotional disturbance than during a period when a patient is relatively comfortable (such as often occurs after being on a waiting list for several months). The lack of "intake procedure" and the beginning of psychotherapeutic intervention in the first interview—sometimes even in the waiting room before the first interview—are probably crucial in obtaining psychotherapeutic results in a minimum amount of time and maintaining cost-effectiveness as well.

References

Balint, M. *The doctor, his patient, and the illness.* New York: International Universities Press, 1957.

Cummings, N. A., & Follette, W. Psychiatric services and medical utilization in a prepaid health plan setting (Part II). *Medical Care,* 1968, *6,* 31–41.

Follette, W., & Cummings, N. A., Psychiatric services and medical utilization in a prepaid health plan setting. *Medical Care,* 1967, *5,* 25–35.

Gamlin, J. Claims are up, but payments are down for insurer's health maintenance plan. *Business Insurance,* 1975, April 21, 56.

Malan, D. H. A study of brief psychotherapy. *Mind and Medicine Monographs.* Springfield Illinois: Charles C. Thomas, 1963.

At the time of original publication of this article, *Nicholas A. Cummings* was Chief Psychologist and *William T. Follette* was Chief Psychiatrist at the Kaiser Foundation Hospital and the Permanente Medical Group, San Francisco.

Effect of a Short-term Outpatient Psychiatric Therapy Benefit on the Utilization of Medical Services in a Prepaid Group Practice Medical Program

Irving D. Goldberg, Goldie Krantz, and Ben Z. Locke

A pilot study was conducted to measure the effect of a short-term outpatient psychiatric therapy benefit on the utilization of general medical services at Group Health Association of Washington, D.C. (GHA), a prepaid group practice medical program. The study group consisted of 256 patients who were referred for such outpatient therapy and who were GHA members for a full 12-month period both before and after the psychiatric referral. Study patients experienced a marked reduction during the year after referral as compared with the prior year in the utilization of GHA nonpsychiatric physician services and laboratory or x-ray procedures. The reduction in number of patients seen was 13.6 per cent for nonpsychiatric physician services, and 15.7 per cent for laboratory or x-ray procedures. In terms of visits made, reduction was approximately 30 per cent for each of these services. Basic finding of reduced utilization was still obtained when factors of age, race, sex, psychiatric diagnosis, and number of therapy sessions attended under benefit were taken into account. Results support findings of reduced utilization in other studies and suggest more efficient utilization of appropriate medical services as a result of short-term outpatient mental health benefits in prepaid health plan settings.

Only in the past decade have significant increases in mental health benefits been included in the rapid growth in health insurance protection through private voluntary insuring organizations. Since 1963, the National Institute of Mental Health (NIMH) has actively stimulated this development by encouraging the expansion of private voluntary health insurance coverage for mental health (Public Information Section, 1965). In a collaborative effort with the NIMH, the United States Civil Service Commission, which administers the Federal Employees Health Benefits program,[1] requested insurance carriers and health plans participating in that program to incorporate new or improved mental health benefits, particularly coverage for outpa-

tient services, into their existing benefit structures.

A total of some four million people are enrolled in community prepaid group practice health plans which are essentially comprehensive in their health coverage (Reed, 1969). Prior to 1960, when the federal employees program went into effect, these plans in the main were without prepaid mental health benefits. However, all federal employees enrolled in these plans now have some mental health coverage, including outpatient benefits; and similar coverage is also available to other members and contractor groups in these plans.

With the adoption of mental health benefits in prepaid group practice plans, it has become possible to evaluate to some extent the effects that these benefits might have on patient utilization of nonpsychiatric medical services covered by the plans (Health Insurance Plan of Greater New York, 1969; Follette & Cummings, 1967).

---

[1] The Federal Employees Health Benefits program, which became effective in 1960 under an Act of Congress, is the largest employer-sponsored contributing health insurance program in the world covering more than seven million persons, including employees, annuitants, and dependents.

Reprinted from MEDICAL CARE © J. B. Lippincott Company, 1970, *8*, 419–428, by permission.

Group Health Association of Washington, D.C. (GHA) cooperated with the Biometry Branch of the NIMH in conducting a small pilot study directed towards this question. This paper reports on the results of that study which is based on the first year's experience with a mental health benefit at GHA before benefits were expanded and before the total population of GHA was included.

Setting and Nature of Short-Term Mental Health Benefit

The Group Health Association of Washington, D.C. is a comprehensive prepaid group practice program whose participating population resides almost entirely in the metropolitan Washington, D.C. area and is comprised of three groups: federal government employees, D.C. transit workers, and general members. In November 1964, GHA included a limited outpatient mental health benefit in its structure of benefits for its government employee group who then comprised 66% of the GHA participant population of approximately 54,000. In January 1965, this benefit was extended to the general members who accounted for 18% of the participant population. Thus, 84% of the GHA population had some coverage for short-term outpatient psychiatric care at the inception of the partially prepaid benefit. Acute short-term hospital care had previously been part of the benefit structure.

At its initiation, the GHA mental health benefit offered under prepayment was essentially as follows: GHA paid up to 15 dollars for each of 10 therapy sessions in a membership-year for outpatient treatment of acute mental illness and emotional disorders subject to significant improvement through short-term outpatient therapy.[2] A GHA screening psychiatrist determined eligibility for referral on benefits. When the patient was referred by a GHA non-psychiatric physician to the GHA screening psychiatrist for evaluation purposes as to eligibility for benefits, there was no charge to the patient for that visit or visits. During the study period, a patient could also self-refer to the screening psychiatrist. An evaluation of the patient's psychiatric condition was made by the screening psychiatrist and, on the basis of his diagnostic impression, he recommended appropriate psychiatric care where indicated, and he determined whether GHA coverage for benefits could be approved. If short-term therapy was authorized under the benefit, the patient was referred to psychiatrists or other mental health disciplines. If the condition was chronic, and hence not covered by the benefit, referral could still be made to another agency or psychiatrist, but no payment would be made by GHA for such care.

Study Design

The basic study plan was to compare, for the case group under study, the utilization of GHA medical services before and after each patient was referred on benefits for short-term outpatient psychiatric therapy. The "before" period was the 12-month interval immediately preceding the date of referral by the screening psychiatrist. It was considered likely that virtually all of the patients undergoing therapy would have completed such care during the first three months immediately following referral. Since such therapy was apt to affect the utilization of GHA services during this period, and to allow sufficient time for completion of the therapy on benefits, the "after" period of 12 months' duration was taken to begin three months following the referral date. Thus, the records for each study patient were reviewed for a 27-month exposure period, although the three-month "psychiatric therapy interval" was not to be included in the "before-after" analysis of medical services utilization.

For purposes of the study, it was desirable that the study group be confined to persons who were covered by the same mental health benefit. It was, therefore, decided to limit the study group to all patients enrolled under the "high option" or "premium" plan who were referred on benefits for psychiatric therapy during the

[2] The limit of 10 therapy sessions was a renewable benefit each membership-year (i.e., year beginning with each anniversary date of joining the plan). Thus, if therapy was initiated towards the end of one membership-year and carried into the next, the patient could actually have as many as 19 sessions for the same referral.

first year the benefit structure was in effect.[3] Thus, as a by-product, the results of the study could provide a baseline for any future studies based on a revised benefit structure. (After the first year, the GHA mental health benefit was substantially increased and broadened.) (United States Civil Service Commission, 1966)

Since the GHA mental health benefit during the study period applied only to the federal employee and general member groups (including covered family members), they comprised the study population. The GHA medical records for these enrollees were reviewed by GHA staff to identify all patients who were referred to, and seen by, the screening psychiatrist during the period November 1, 1964 through October 31, 1965, the first full year in which the psychiatric benefit was in effect. To protect the confidentiality of the patient, individuals were not identified by name to the study staff. Also, it should be noted that the confidential psychiatric notes are not part of the medical record and were not made accessible for this study.

A total of 726 patients (excluding GHA staff and dependents) were referred to the screening psychiatrist. Of this total, 409 patients were excluded from the study because they were judged ineligible for coverage under this benefit or because they overtly refused psychiatric care. Specifically, 161 were judged not to be in need and hence not referred for outpatient psychiatric care; 197 were referred for psychiatric care but not on benefits; referral was deferred for 45 patients; and 6 patients who would have been referred on benefits overtly refused to accept such care.

The records for the remaining 317 patients seen by the screening psychiatrist were reviewed for the 27-month period referred to earlier. From this total, 61 were eliminated from the study as follows: 57 cases were not available for the full 27-month period (35 began membership less than one year prior to the date seen by the screening psychiatrist, and 22 terminated their membership within the 15-month period following that date); for four patients the files were not available. This left 256 patients who com-

prised the study group. Of the final study group, 197 were enrolled in the federal employee program and 59 were general members—approximately in the same ratio to one another that these two groups comprised in the total GHA population.

As a point of interest, the age distributions were examined for the 409 patients ineligible for benefits and the 61 eligibles who did not otherwise meet the study criteria. The age distribution for the former group was found to be very similar to that of the 256 study patients; however, the latter group of 61 patients had a somewhat younger age distribution than the final study group.

Data extracted from the medical records were counts of all visits to GHA physicians for medical care, all visits for x-ray and laboratory procedures, as well as the number of visits made for psychiatric therapy under the mental health benefit. Other data abstracted for each patient, where available, were age, race, sex, and psychiatric diagnostic impression. Information on psychiatric and nonpsychiatric hospitalizations recorded in the medical record was also extracted. However, study data on hospitalizations were incomplete because such information was not generally recorded on patients who were hospitalized outside of GHA auspices. Also, during the period of study, the GHA hospitalization information was not consistently available in the progress notes which formed the primary source of data for this pilot study.

Results

The distribution of the study population by age, sex, and race is shown in Table 1. Approximately 70% of the study group were from 25 to 64 years of age at time of referral on psychiatric benefits. In contrast, only 50% of the total GHA participant population (in the federal employee and general groups) were in this age group during the study period (Group Health Association, 1965). About 60% of the study group were female, which was slightly higher than the proportion of females in the total GHA membership. With respect to race, about 83% of the study group were Caucasian. Although no precise data on race are available

---

[3] Under the "low option" or "standard" plan, GHA paid up to 10 dollars (as compared with 15 dollars under "high option") per therapy session. Only about 10 percent of the GHA members are enrolled in the "low option" plan.

Table 1: *Distribution of Study Group by Age, Race, Sex, and Psychiatric Diagnostic Impression*

Patient characteristics	Number	Percent[a]
Total study group	256	100.0
Age group (years)		
0–14	22	8.6
15–24	49	19.1
25–44	97	37.9
45–64	82	32.0
65+	6	2.4
Race		
Caucasian	210	82.7
Other	44	17.3
Unknown	2	
Sex		
Male	100	39.1
Female	156	60.9
Psychiatric impression		
Psychosis	40	20.7
Psychoneurosis	106	54.9
Personality disorder	21	10.9
Transient situational personality disorder	22	11.4
Other	4	2.1
Unknown	63	

[a] Based on total patients for whom characteristics were known.

for the total GHA membership, the proportion of Caucasians in the total membership is estimated to have been appreciably less than that in the study group. Specific psychiatric diagnosis for each patient was not uniformly recorded in the medical records. However, from information which was recorded, based on the evaluation of the screening psychiatrist or the psychiatrist providing therapy, it was possible to classify the psychiatric diagnostic impression into broad categories for three fourths of the study group. Among those for whom the diagnostic impression was determined, 21% were classified psychotic, 55% psychoneurotic, 11% with personality disorders, 11% as having a transient situational personality disorder, and 2% were considered to have some other psychiatric problem.

Initially, the data were analyzed separately according to the specific medical department or ancillary service in which the patients were seen (i.e., internal medicine, other nonpsychiatric medical department, laboratory, x-ray). Almost 95% of the visits by the study patients for physician services were made to the department of internal medicine. However, since the study findings for visits to internal medicine were similar to those for other nonpsychiatric medical departments, the data for all medical departments were combined in the analysis presented here. Similarly, with respect to ancillary services, the findings on visits for laboratory procedures were essentially the same as those for x-ray visits, so the data for laboratory and x-ray services were also combined.

Study findings presented below compare separately the physician and ancillary (laboratory or x-ray) services received by the study group during the 12-month periods before and after referral on psychiatric benefits, by age, race, sex, diagnosis, and number of psychiatric therapy sessions attended on benefit. It was not possible to conduct a "before-after" analysis with respect to utilization of psychiatric services. Although some psychiatric counseling was provided on a fee-for-service basis prior to the initation of the mental health benefit, there was no psychiatry department as such at GHA at that time and, therefore, no comparable or meaningful basis for comparison. Thus, the "before-after" analysis was limited to utilization of nonpsychiatric medical services.

Table 2 shows the number of study patients who received care from the various GHA departments, except psychiatry, and the number of visits made to these departments during the "before" and "after" periods. Also shown is the percent decrease from the "before" period to the "after" period with respect to number of patients seen and number of visits made. Each visit for laboratory or x-ray services was counted only once regardless of the number of procedures performed at each visit.

It is clearly evident from these data, in terms of persons seen and visits made, that medical and ancillary services were each provided to more of these patients and more frequently before psychiatric referral than after. Thus, the reduction in the number of patients seen by the nonpsychiatric medical departments was 13.6%, and for laboratory or x-ray procedures, 15.7%. Similarly, in terms of number of visits made, the reduction was approximately 30% both for physician services and for laboratory or x-ray procedures.

Viewing the reduction in utilization

Table 2: *Comparison of Number of Patients Seen and Visits Made During Year Before and Year After Psychiatric Referral by Type of Service*

Type of Service (nonpsychiatric)	Patients Seen (N = 256)			Visits Made*		
	Year before referral	Year after referral	Percent change	Year before referral	Year after referral	Percent change
Physician services	243	210	−13.6	1264	876	−30.7
Laboratory or x-ray	210	177	−15.7	795	558	−29.8

> * Each visit for laboratory or x-ray services was counted only once regardless of the number of procedures performed at each visit.

another way, the average (mean) number of visits made by the 256 study patients, during the "before" and "after" periods, respectively, were 4.94 and 3.42 for physician services, and 3.11 and 2.18 for laboratory or x-ray procedures.

Overall, the study group experienced a total reduction of some 30% in the number of visits made for physician and ancillary services. The difference between the periods before and after referral with respect to the number of patients seen was statistically significant (P < .001)[4] for physician services as well as for laboratory or x-ray procedures. Similarly, for each of these services, the reduction in the mean number of visits was also statistically significant (P < .001).[5]

The study data were analyzed further to determine whether the observed decreases after psychiatric referral held for various subgroups of the study population. Thus, for both physician services and ancillary services, the "before" and "after" periods were compared with respect to the percent change in number of persons served and total visits made according to age, race, sex, psychiatric diagnostic impressions and number of psychiatric therapy sessions attended under benefit.

The findings presented in Table 3 clearly show the overall consistency of reduction in utilization of the physician and ancillary services by the study group. Although some variation existed in the extent of decrease (partly due to small numbers in some cells), the pattern of reduced utilization of these services held

throughout each of the distributions.[6] There was particularly little variation in the percent change by age. It is also of interest to note that patients who did not avail themselves of the short-term outpatient therapy benefit generally showed as great a relative reduction in utilization of medical services as did those who received the full benefit of at least 10 sessions.

Another indication of the consistency of reduced utilization of physician and ancillary services after psychiatric referral is evident in the data in Table 4. Here, a determination was made as to whether each patient made fewer, more, or the same number of visits during the 12-month period after psychiatric referral as he or she made during the prior year for physician services or for laboratory or x-ray procedures. Only about one fourth of the study patients made more visits for physician services after referral than before in contrast with the almost 60% who made fewer visits after referral. Similarly, only 28% of the patients made more visits for laboratory or x-ray procedures after referral than before, while 52% made fewer such visits.

---

[4] McNemar's chi-square test for correlated samples was used.

[5] The two-tailed t-test of paired (before-after) differences was used.

[6] For both of the service categories, statistical tests of significance were performed comparing the various age groups, Caucasians with those of other races, males with females, the various diagnostic categories, and those who had no psychiatric therapy sessions under benefit with those who had 10 or more sessions. With respect to persons seen, each patient was classified as to whether or not he showed a "before-after" reduction in number of visits made, and a chi-square test was used to compare the dichotomous distributions for the various comparison groups. None of these comparisons was significant at the .05 level. With respect to visits made, either an analysis of variance or a two-tailed t-test was made of the difference between the comparison groups in the mean "before-after" reduction in number of visits. In only one instance (the greater reduction observed among males than females in average number of laboratory or x-ray visits, P < .02) was the observed difference statistically significant at the .05 level.

Table 3: *Percent Decrease During Year After Referral as Compared with Prior Year in Utilization of Nonpsychiatric Physician Services and Laboratory or X-ray Procedures, According to Patient Characteristics and Psychiatric Therapy on Benefits*

Patient characteristics and therapy received	Number in study	Percent decrease after referral[a]			
		Patients seen		Visits made	
		Physician services	Lab or X-ray	Physician services	Lab or X-ray
Total Study Group	256	13.6	15.7	30.7	29.8
Age (years):					
0–14	22	4.5	21.1	23.8	35.6
15–24	49	17.4	15.8	36.1	33.0
25–44	97	16.5	17.9	29.7	27.4
45–64	82	11.5	13.0	31.7	30.8
65 & over	6			20.6	20.0
Race:					
Caucasian	210	13.1	15.9	26.1	30.5
Other	44	14.0	14.7	49.0	25.6
Unknown	2				
Sex:					
Male	100	16.1	23.5	37.8	47.6
Female	156	12.0	10.9	26.0	18.0
Psychiatric impression:					
Psychosis	40	25.0	28.6	35.0	29.0
Psychoneurosis	106	10.0	6.7	23.4	23.3
Other	47	4.4	12.2	46.9	32.2
Unknown	63	19.0	26.7	24.7	41.5
Psychiatric therapy sessions:					
None	70	16.9	24.1	39.2	22.6
1–9	75	12.7	18.5	30.4	23.8
10 or more	104	11.0	6.0	23.3	35.3
Unknown	7			50.0	44.4

[a] Percent not shown in any cell where base (number before referral) was less than 10.

Table 4: *Number and Percent of Persons with Fewer, Same, or More Visits in Year After Referral Compared with Year Preceding Referral, by Type of Service*

Visits before and after referral	Physician Services		Laboratory or X-ray	
	Number	Percent	Number	Percent
Total study group	256	100	256	100
Fewer visits in year after referral	152	59.4	134	52.3
Same number of visits both years	42	16.4	50	19.5
More visits in year after referral	62	24.2	72	28.1

Both of these differences were statistically significant (P < .001).[7] When the patients were grouped according to the actual number of visits made in the year preceding referral, this pattern of fewer visits held for virtually all groups of patients who had at least two visits in the prior year for physician or ancillary services. The greatest relative reductions occurred among those who made the most visits during the prior year. Thus, of the 81 patients who made more than five visits for physician services during the year preceding referral, 64 (79%) made fewer visits in the post-referral year than they did in the prior year.

Discussion

The consistent results of this pilot study clearly indicate that the short-term outpatient psychiatric benefit at GHA was associated with a decrease in the utilization of physician and ancillary services under the plan. Not only was there a decreased utilization following psychiatric referral for the study group as a whole, both with respect to the number of persons seen and the number of visits made, but this decreased utilization held—to a greater or lesser degree—for all subsegments of the population studied.

Of some interest in this regard is the relationship between utilization of physician and ancillary services at GHA and the number of therapy sessions attended under the short-term psychiatric benefit. Note has been made of the fact that the study patients who did not attend any outpatient therapy sessions under benefits (although referred by the screening psychiatrist for such care) showed as great a relative reduction of medical services utilization as did those who received all or part of their authorized therapy. This finding would seem to imply that the visit to the screening psychiatrist alone may have had a beneficial effect on the patient, at least to the extent that the patient apparently had reduced need or desire for physician or ancillary services following the screening. However, it should be noted that some patients

referred on benefits may have elected to obtain their psychiatric therapy outside the GHA benefit structure at their own expense. Unfortunately, the GHA records do not ordinarily reflect such outside care. In any event, it is clear that whether or not the referred patients as a group actually availed themselves of the benefit provisions, they showed a reduced subsequent utilization of general medical services provided by the group practice plan.

It is reasonable to assume that the observed reduction in utilization of physician and ancillary services at GHA to a large extent reflects a reduced need or desire for such services, rather than a shift by the patients to other sources for their medical attention at additional cost to themselves (although, undoubtedly, some such shifting did occur). This assumption is based upon the fact that these patients continued to maintain their GHA membership throughout the 27-month study period, and that the very great majority did return to GHA for at least some medical attention during the "after" period.

When viewed in terms of the effect on the provider of services, the reduction in use of physician and ancillary services at GHA would seem to imply a reduction in cost which would otherwise occur in the provision of such services and, theoretically, a more efficient utilization of appropriate services. There was no attempt to do any cost-benefit analysis in this study, the primary purpose of which was directed at utilization without regard to costs. However, an inference could be made that the cost savings due to reduced utilization would be reflected in the entire benefit structure without setting forth dollar amounts.

Comment should be made about the possible effect of hospitalization on the study findings, since a question might be raised as to whether or not there was appreciably more hospitalization in the period after psychiatric referral than in the prior-referral year. As mentioned previously, during the period of study, the GHA hospital records were not totally coordinated with the medical record, which was the principal data source for this study. Therefore, the effect of episodes of hospitalization on the study findings could not be evaluated. With respect to psychiatric hospitalization, however, since the

---

[7] The chi-square test was employed to test the equality of the number of patients showing a decrease in number of visits with those showing an increase.

study group excluded all patients whom the screening psychiatrist considered to have a chronic condition requiring inpatient or long-term outpatient psychiatric care, it is very unlikely that more than a handful of study patients would have required such hospitalization. In any event, the study findings were of such magnitude and consistency that they are unlikely to be materially affected by the factor of hospitalization.

Another consideration relates to the study design whereby each patient was used as his own control in the "before-after" comparison. The absence of a suitable control group in this pilot study, against whom the "before-after" findings of the case group could be compared, limits the conclusions which can be drawn at this time; however, efforts are underway in a broader study to obtain similar data for such a comparison group. The question which arises here is whether the study patients, having already received medical attention one year, would be likely to require more or less care in the following year. If need for less care were to be expected, this might account, at least in part, for the reduction in utilization observed among the study group. However, the GHA experience in the past indicates that patients using the plan, with its emphasis on preventive services and early detection of chronic disease, tend to use the services increasingly in subsequent years. This is supported by the following data for the total GHA experience around the study period, which show a level or rising per capita utilization in contrast to the observed finding of markedly reduced utilization by the study group (Group Health Association, 1965; 1967).

Year ending September 30	GHA Per Capita Utilization		
	Office Consultations	Laboratory	Radiology
1963	3.65	3.88	1.08
1964	3.77	4.43	1.08
1965	3.77	5.06	1.14
1966	3.71	5.25	1.12

Follette and Cummings (1967) also studied medical utilization before and after psychiatric therapy in a prepaid health plan setting, namely the Kaiser Foundation Health Plan in the Northern California Region. Their case group consisted of persons who received psychotherapy defined as any contact with the plan's department of psychiatry. The medical utilization for the year prior to the initial contact with that department was compared with the utilization for each of five subsequent years, both for the case group and a matched control group who did not receive psychotherapy. The oupatient medical services in that study included visits to outpatient medical (nonpsychiatric) clinics and contacts for outpatient laboratory and x-ray procedures; however, these three types of service were lumped together in the analysis. Despite differences in the setting, benefit structure, mental health disciplines utilized, and study design from those of the GHA study, Follette and Cummings also found a significant decline in utilization of medical services following psychotherapy.

A further, although limited, indication of reduced utilization of general medical services following outpatient psychotherapy is contained in an unpublished report of another study. In 1965, the Health Insurance Plan of Greater New York (H.I.P.) instituted, as a demonstration project, a mental health service which, upon referral by a group physician, provided an outpatient psychiatric treatment benefit in one of its medical groups. One section of the final report of that project (Health Insurance Plan of Greater New York, 1969) submitted by H.I.P. to the National Institute of Mental Health, which partly supported the demonstration project, contains an analysis of the relationship between psychiatric treatment and the use of medical services including family physician office visits, specialist office visits, and x-ray and laboratory services. Due to sample size limitations and other considerations, the results of this analysis were viewed in the report as exploratory only. The "treatment" group (those seen in the mental health service for consultation or treatment) and three comparison groups were employed in a "before-after" analysis of medical utilization for periods covering one year before the appropriate "study" or "consultation" date and each of two years after. Although the report notes that the analysis did not demonstrate a consistent pattern across all comparison groups, it also states that the analysis indicated ". . .

some tendencies pointing to lower medical utilization in the group to whom psychotherapy was available."

The supporting evidence of the Kaiser, H.I.P., and GHA studies strengthens the hypothesis of reduced utilization of medical services, and more efficient utilization of appropriate services, as a result of short-term outpatient mental health benefit in prepaid health plan settings.

On the basis of the findings of the GHA study presented in this paper, the authors are now initiating a broader study which will include a "before-after" evaluation of the utilization of GHA medical and hospital services by all family members of patients referred on psychiatric benefit and will also employ one or more comparison groups.

References

Department of Research and Statistics, Health Insurance Plan of Greater New York. Psychiatric Treatment and Patterns of Medical Care. Unpublished final report to the National Institute of Mental Health, Project MH 02321, July 1969.

Follette, W., and Cummings, N. A.: Psychiatric services and medical utilization in a prepaid health plan setting. *Medical Care,* 1967, *5*(25).

Group Health Association. GHA News—Annual Report Issue, 1965, *28,* (1).

Group Health Association. GHA News—Annual Report Issue, 1967, *30,* (2).

Public Information Section, National Institute of Mental Health. Improving Mental Health Insurance Coverage. Washington, D.C., U.S. Department of Health, Education, and Welfare. PHS Publication No. 1253, August 1965.

Reed, L. S.: Private health insurance, 1968: Enrollment, coverage, and financial experience. U.S. Department of Health, Education, and Welfare, *Social Security Bulletin,* 1969, *32,* No. 12, 19.

United States Civil Service Commission. Summary of Benefits—Group Health Association. BRI 41-41, January 1966.

At the time of original publication of this article, *Irving D. Goldberg* was Chief, Evaluation Studies Section, Biometry Branch, and *Ben Z. Locke* was Assistant Chief, Center for Epidemiologic Studies, at the National Institute of Mental Health, Chevy Chase, Maryland. *Goldie Krantz* was a program analyst, Group Health Association, Inc., Washington, D.C.

The authors wish to thank Josephine Tate (GHA) for her assistance in abstracting the study data; Robert F. Woolson and Warnilla Cook (both of the Biometry Branch, NIMH) for their assistance in the analysis; and Mildred Arrill (Division of Mental Health Service Programs, NIMH) for her consultation.

Colorado Medicare Study

A History

Joan G. Willens

A demonstration project in Colorado from October 1976 to December 1978 will study what effect the availability of two new benefits under Medicare, the inclusion of the services of independent psychologists and the expansion of existing mental health coverage, will have both on the use and cost of total mental health services and of other medical and hospital services. Questions that express the concerns of legislators also will be evaluated: namely, (a) Can psychology agree upon the definition of a psychologist who can deliver services on an autonomous basis, and (b) can psychology assure quality service on an independent basis? Procedures to define provider status, to provide peer review, and to identify reimbursable services have been instituted to address these questions and should prove to be precedent setting in future national health legislation.

Early in 1975, conversations initiated by myself with the staff of the Senate Finance Committee led to a proposal for a demonstration project to determine the advisability of covering the services of independently practicing clinical psychologists in Medicare. Although an earlier report from the Department of Health, Education, and Welfare had recommended against such inclusion (Cohen, 1968), we had by this time accumulated enough new evidence and support to warrant a new look at the issue. In July 1975 a formal meeting was held with members of the Senate Finance Committee staff, the Social Security Administration, and the office of the Assistant Secretary for Health, Education, and Welfare. Subsequently, in a conference call with officers and directors of CAPPS (Council for the Advancement of the Psychological Professions and Sciences) and AAP (Association for the Advancement of Psychology) and the acting Executive Officer of APA, it was agreed to participate, under certain conditions, in the proposed study. The primary condition was that a Psychology Advisory Committee be involved throughout the development and evaluation of the demonstration project. The consultants for the project were selected to represent the interested organizations: Joan Willens, Herbert

Dörken, Russell Bent, and Lee Sechrest. Pat DeLeon, a psychologist and legislative assistant to Senator Daniel Inouye (D-Hawaii) became an ex officio member.

The site, approved by the Social Security Administration and agreed to by the consultants, with some reservations, was Colorado. The reservations arose from information that there was considerable hostility existing between the psychology and psychiatric communities, and from the fact that Colorado has a fairly small population, both of psychologists and Medicare eligibles. The Social Security Administration was responsible for developing the project by virtue of the 1972 Social Security Amendment Section 222B (Hartke) to "determine whether the services of clinical psychologists may be made more generally available . . ." under Medicare (Wiggins, Dörken, Dworin, & Shapiro, 1976, p. 91).

From September 1975 to April 1976, the consultants and members of the Program Experimentation Branch, Office of Research and Statistics, of the Social Security Administration, headed by the director, James Kaple, met seven times to develop the project. The project began officially in October 1976 and will continue until December 1978. The demonstration has

Reprinted from *American Psychologist*, 1977, *32*, 746–749.

been expanded to include a second part, namely, to determine the feasibility of expanding all mental health coverage in Medicare from the existing $250 limit with 50% co-insurance per year, to $500 with 20% co-insurance. The design of the experiment is a 2 × 2 factorial design, randomly assigning Medicare beneficiaries to control and experimental groups. The first factor, clinical psychology coverage, divides into Level I, current Medicare coverage, and Level II, coverage of clinical psychologists as independent practitioners. The second factor, outpatient mental health coverage, divides into Level I, current Medicare coverage, and Level II, expanded coverage ($500 maximum, 20% co-insurance).

The primary purpose of the study has developed, then, into determining what effect the availability of both new benefits—the inclusion of independently practicing psychologists and the expanded availability of mental health services—has on the use and cost of total mental health services and of other medical and hospital services. The concern by legislators and government agencies has been that both changes will lead to an "induced demand" effect, that is, that as services become more available, individuals, will make greater use of them. Inclusion of psychologists has consistently been related to a general concern about the escalating costs of mental health services in Medicare. However, during the initial phases of the study, the consultants discovered that the fiscal intermediaries for Medicare have never tabulated the use and cost of outpatient mental health services, so that no actual figures of such costs have ever been available. While limited data calling into question the existence of any induced demand are available to some extent by determining the effect on general medical costs (Follette & Cummings, 1967), we may for the first time be able to estimate what level of availability of mental health services will prove to be a cost-effective factor in total health care.

Some of the questions involved in the present investigation are being studied for the first time. Though some will be answered, there will also be limitations to the experiment, notably that the generalizability from Colorado to the whole nation is not known, nor is the generalizability from the Medicare population to the general population.

In addition to the issues to be dealt with analytically, of more immediate political significance to psychologists are the "process" questions which will be evaluated in the first 6 months of the study. These are questions of great concern to legislators and are areas where psychologists have received the most criticism. They are: (1) Can psychology identify and agree upon the definition of a psychologist who can deliver mental health services on an autonomous basis? (2) Can psychology assure quality service on an independent basis? (3) In order to accomplish quality assurance, can psychology set up both prospective and concurrent peer-review procedures for therapy, assessment, and consultation which are functional? (4) And further, can psychology establish criteria for identifiable therapeutic services that should and should not be covered?

For the purposes of this experiment, the first question has been resolved by developing procedures acceptable to the Social Security Administration, to the staff of the Senate Finance Committee, and to Colorado psychologists for the purpose of identifying eligible providers of service. A Proficiency Review Committee, consisting of psychologists, reviews applicants and selects those whose quality of work experience and professional judgment meet certain standards; and only then does the psychologist become a designated provider. One significant factor in the process has been the charge of the Committee to require each potential provider of service to furnish the name of a professional colleague who is familiar with the psychologist's work. Another has been that the Committee reviews the work experience of both doctoral- and master's-level licensed psychologists who have been practicing independently for a certain number of years. The Committee itself exists under the aegis of the State Department of Health of Colorado.

The criteria for inclusion in the study as providers of service closely resemble criteria developed by the Council for the National Register (1975). The decision was made, however, to introduce some differences which were responsive to the uniqueness of the Colorado situation, where there is a group of long-practicing master's-level psychologists, and at the same time are responsive to the concerns of legislators who have questioned the inclusion of subdoctoral psychologists in Medicare or any subsequent national health insurance legislation. The definitions of *psychologist* developed for the study are as follows:

A. Licensed/certified as a psychologist at the independent practice level with an earned doctoral degree in psychology from a regionally accredited university, college, or professional school; have not less than two years of full-time-equivalent supervised health service experience as a psychologist in an organized health program or in a group practice professional health corporation;

or, alternately,

B. Until 1 October 1976, be' licensed/certified as a psychologist in the state in which they practice wherein the standard for obtaining full entry into the profession at the independent practice level is the doctoral degree; hold an earned graduate degree in psychology and have more than ten years of full-time-equivalent postgraduate health service experience as a psychologist in the delivery of health and/or mental health services, not less than four years of which has been supervised by a licensed/certified mental health practitioner.

Experience such as that had by a school or education psychologist, a personnel or industrial psychologist, or a vocational psychometrist will not be considered qualifying.

The other question, assuring quality service, enabled psychologists to expose and deal with some very important problems. While one of the reasons for selecting Colorado as the experimental site was the fact of an existing, functioning Professional Standards Review Organization (PSRO), it rapidly became clear that the psychiatric community, an integral part of the PSRO, was strongly opposed both to psychology's participating in the PSRO, and in fact to the existence of the demonstration project. Contacts between the President of the American Psychiatric Association and the Commissioner of Social Security revealed psychiatry's concern about the advisability of the study. It was noted, however, that there had been ample opportunity for psychiatry to raise objections earlier and to include a psychiatric consultant in the developmental phases of the project had they so desired. Attempts by Colorado psychologists to integrate their already actively functioning peer review committee with the PSRO have continued to be unsuccessful. Several factors appear to be contributing to this impasse. One is the extremely competitive economics of Colorado, where there is an unusually large number of mental health

practitioners per capita. A second factor is a licensing law in Colorado, which includes a medical collaboration clause, until recently interpreted only to mean that psychologists should seek consultation or collaboration from a physician when needed. Colorado psychologists perceive the law as now being interpreted by some psychiatrists as prohibiting psychologists from practicing independently. The demonstration project takes care of this issue by a peer review procedure which requires that there be adequate collaboration with a primary-care physician to assess the patient's physical state.

An organized peer review plan has been developed by Colorado psychology that will function independently of the Colorado PSRO, although the hope of some later collaboration still exists (APA, 1975). Colorado psychologists already had a functioning peer review committee which was expanded for the purpose of the experiment (Bent, 1976). The plan to be used by the Colorado Psychology Peer Review Committee (PRC) has two general levels of authorization to control utilization. The first requires no prior authorization by the PRC for the carrier to reimburse the provider—up to 6 hours of therapy or 3 hours of assessment or consultation at the discretion of the provider. However, a service plan must be submitted to the PRC in order to evaluate provider profiles on a quarterly basis. A prior authorization is required for extended treatment, assessment, or consultation that exceeds these limits; and a more detailed description of objectives, concurrence of the patient, and the time and type of service must be submitted by the provider. After the services are completed, a follow-up plan is submitted, and with reasonable congruence between the two plans, the carrier reimburses the provider. The PRC handles any questions of denial of reimbursement that may arise or questions about the decision making of the psychologist.

In dealing with the issue of identifying covered and not-covered services, the consultants proposed to Blue Shield, the carrier, and its Medical Advisory Committee that psychologists should be the ones to determine which techniques and procedures were considered generally acceptable to the profession at large. In very general terms, the covered procedures include individual psychotherapy, group therapy, behavior therapy, psychological assessment, group assessment, and consultation of varying time limits or by report. Certain services were excluded either on the basis of lack of general acceptance or on the basis of their irrelevance to a Medicare population. These services include vocational assessment and counseling; education testing and assessment; marathon therapy and retreats; sexual competency training; sensitivity training, encounter groups, and personal growth services; primal scream therapy, Z-therapy, and other "exotic" therapies; and co-therapy or multiple-therapist methods. The method of reimbursement made use of the California State Psychological Association's Relative Value Guideline wherein services are generally measured in units of time. The basis on which the maximum reimbursement limit for other services was established was $35 for 1 hour of psychotherapy. Through use of the California Relative Value Guidelines, this schedule provides some incentive toward the use of less costly group therapy procedures, just as within the Peer Review system there is an emphasis on shorter term therapy by exempting it from prior authorization by the PRC. Reimbursement for services is made at the lower of (a) the psychologist's actual charge or (b) the maximum amount established through the Relative Value Scale.

The Colorado Demonstration Project has been developed up to the actual starting point in a genuine spirit of cooperation between members of the Social Security Administration, members of the Colorado psychology community, and the psychology consultants.

In August 1976 the Social Security Administration selected as the independent evaluator of the study on a competitive basis the Stanford Research Institute. The selection of the evaluator has been of important significance for this experiment. All participants recognized the necessity of choosing an evaluator whose independence from any connection with the American Psychological Association was clearly ascertained. In addition, the position of the American Psychological Association throughout has been solely as an interested observer with no participation in either the development or evaluation phases of the demonstration.

While the actual outcome of the study may answer important cost and utilization questions regarding the inclusion of psychologists in Medicare, and by extension potentially in national health insurance, the "process" questions may in fact have far greater significance. We have in this study already determined that psychology can address the issues that have historically plagued us politically, although we must wait for the study to get further under way to assess these as functioning processes. Perhaps of greater importance to mental health in general is the impact of expanding mental health services to give beneficiaries at least as much service as is available to them for physical disorders. Should it prove that costs do not increase in the magnitude that has been the fear of legislators, or should it prove that medical costs are offset by greater and more effective use of mental health services, then the study will have made a very important contribution to national health legislation at a time when innovative approaches are sorely needed.

References

American Psychological Association, Committee on Professional Standards Review of the Board of Professional Affairs. *Procedures manual for Professional Standards Review Committees of state psychological associations.* Washington, D.C.: Author, August 1975.

Bent, R. J. Impact of peer review on future health practice. In H. Dörken & Associates, *The professional psychologist today.* San Francisco: Jossey-Bass, 1976.

Cohen, W. *Independent practitioners under Medicare: A report to the Congress.* Washington, D.C.: U.S. Department of Health, Education, and Welfare, December 1968.

Council for the National Register of Health Service Providers in Psychology. *National register of health service providers in psychology.* Washington, D.C.: Author, 1975.

Follette, W., & Cummings, N. A. Psychiatric services and medical utilization in a prepaid health plan setting. *Medical Care,* 1967, *5,* 25–35.

Wiggins, J. G., Dörken, H., Dworin, J., & Shapiro, A. E. Major social security programs. In H. Dörken & Associates, *The professional psychologist today.* San Francisco: Jossey-Bass, 1976.

At the time of original publication of this article, *Joan G. Willens* was a clinical psychologist in Beverly Hills, California. The article represents the viewpoint of the author and not that of the Social Security Administration.

CHAMPUS Ten-State Claim Experience for Mental Disorder: Fiscal Year 1975

Herbert Dörken

The utilization of mental health services by beneficiaries under the Civilian Health and Medical Program of the Uniformed Services (CHAMPUS) for fiscal year 1975 is described in detail, including tabular presentation by treatment procedure, diagnosis, profession, state, and average fees. Some interpretative comments are offered, as well as trend comparisons with utilization in the 2 prior years. Since qualified psychologists are now recognized by federal law as independent providers in this program, the data are of special significance to the profession of psychology.

Broad and comprehensive utilization data on insured mental health services are rare indeed. Frequency of utilization and proportion of total cost are basic parameters for which few reports are available (see chaps. 10 and 11, Dörken & Associates, 1976). What makes the CHAMPUS data truly unique is not only the indices of visit frequency by type of mental disorder and whether inpatient or outpatient service, but basic data by procedure, by provider, and by state (for 10 states) together with fee information.

The Civilian Health and Medical Program of the Uniformed Services (CHAMPUS), with an estimated 6.31 million beneficiaries in the 50 states and the Washington, D.C., area in calendar year 1974, is the single largest group health plan in the nation. Although similar in structure in many respects, CHAMPUS is *not* an insurance program because there is no contract guaranteeing indemnification of specified loss in return for a premium paid. Moreover, the program is not subject to state regulatory bodies which control the insurance business. The basic program is essentially a supplemental program to the uniformed services direct medical care system.

Although the Federal Employees Health Benefits Act (FEHBA) plans have a greater total number of lives insured, about 8.8 million,

the subscribers are distributed over some 40 plans, with the two largest, Blue Cross-Blue Shield (The Blues) and Aetna, covering about 5.5 and 1.5 million lives, respectively, or 80% of federal employees and beneficiaries. In the majority of regions in the country, the Blues serve as the fiscal intermediary for CHAMPUS. During the 1975 fiscal year, Blue Cross processed claims for hospital services in 33 states and the District of Columbia, while Mutual of Omaha served as the fiscal intermediary for 17 states. For professional services, the claims were processed by Blue Shield in 37 states and the District of Columbia and by Mutual of Omaha in 6 states. The balance was handled by medical society plans in 4 states, with Continental Life, Connecticut General, and Blue Cross serving 1 state each. CHAMPUS benefits were set by Congress in 1966 to be not less than that of the largest FEHBA plan (Blues, high option). Recent testimony before Congress (U.S. House Armed Services Committee, 1974) notes the rapid increase in the size of the retired community (retirees and dependents) from 2.4 million in 1964 to 3.2 million in 1974, though the active-duty personnel are decreasing. For a summary outline of the CHAMPUS program, its objectives, and recent changes, see Penner (1975).

CHAMPUS experience with benefits for

Reprinted from *American Psychologist*, 1977, *32*, 697–710. The appendix to this article was prepared in 1979 to update the original article.

nervous and mental disorder in terms of professional services (procedures) rendered, providers involved, ages of beneficiaries served, diagnoses reported, and fee rate variance by region and provider takes on special significance in terms of future benefit planning and probable imminence of national health insurance. The report to follow is based on CHAMPUS 1975 fiscal year (July 1974 to June 1975) claim experience in 10 states (processed through December 1975), estimated to be 97.2% complete for inpatient and 93.9% complete for outpatient services. In the initial tabulation, there were 79,458 unduplicated users who received some mental health service under a psychiatric diagnosis charged to CHAMPUS. A revised computation method of unduplicated beneficiaries in the Department of Defense Psychiatric Report to be used in future reports, however, yielded a substantial reduction to 51,217 as of the end of December for the 10 reporting states. An analysis of the 1974 fiscal year experience appeared in Dörken and Associates (1976, chap. 9), while that for 1973 was submitted in congressional testimony (Dörken, Note 1).[1]

I am especially appreciative of the courtesy and cooperation of the Denver Office of CHAMPUS for providing a copy of their computer printout claim experience for this period, and in clarifying certain policy controls on cost, and to Warren Shaw and Richard Barnett of the Statistics Division for checking all tables and data. Any interpretation and conclusions reached are those of the author and should not be construed to reflect official procedure or policy of CHAMPUS. Not only did the Denver Office provide helpful clarification on claim processing, fees, and co-insurance, but they also ran the state data on practitioners by procedure code rather than by diagnostic code so that provider charges would be better illustrated. The fees listed are the fees paid, but the co-insurance has *not* been deducted; therefore, the government cost is less to the extent of the co-insurance and deductibles.

Large as it is, CHAMPUS is, of course, a select group as derivatives of uniformed personnel. The dependents of active-duty personnel

(nationally, 44.8% of beneficiaries) had a 20% outpatient co-payment, whereas all others (nationally, 55.2%), the retired military personnel and their dependents and the dependents of deceased military personnel, had a 25% co-payment (all services) during calendar year 1974. The proportion varies somewhat with the age ranges of the beneficiaries, the state, and the diagnosis.

For several reasons, the utilization reported here is not necessarily the total mental health service utilization of the beneficiaries. Some beneficiaries, such as retired military personnel now employed by the federal government, have other additional coverage by virtue of their current employment. Regulations call for a "coordination of benefits" whereby this coverage must be used first before claims are accepted by CHAMPUS. The intent is to avoid any duplication of benefits. Also, acute (only) psychiatric care may be available to military dependents at some installations. Such utilization would not appear in the CHAMPUS claim experience. Finally, it is possible that even though coverage is available, some beneficiaries, for personal reasons, may choose to seek care without submitting any claims to CHAMPUS. Thus, the utilization, in this respect, is underreported to an unknown but probably modest degree.

Benefits

The mental disorder benefits available in fiscal year 1975 were extensive relative to most group health programs. Inpatient benefits could run 120 days and could be extended by prior authorization. The dependents of active-duty personnel paid $25 per hospital admission or, from July through December 1974, $3.50 per diem, and from January through June 1975, $3.70 per diem, when the per diem co-payment was greater. The original professional fees, where necessary, were brought into line with usual, customary, and reasonable (UCR) rates, and not in excess of the 90th percentile for the area. The outpatient services 30 days prior and up to 120 days following hospitalization since August 1974 are no longer merged for the same spell of disability, reducing somewhat the proportion of reported inpatient visits from the previous year

---

[1] Fee data reported were adjusted for co-payment. That advice was in error. Actual fiscal year 1973 average fees are those reported, divided by 1.2.

(27.4% versus 33%). That the dependents of active-duty personnel do not pay the 20% co-insurance when hospitalized may, of course, add somewhat to inpatient utilization. Apart from a $50-per-insured per-year deductible (all health services, maximum $100 a family) for outpatient services (this cost not included in the data) and the co-payment, the mental health benfits could extend to 60 outpatient visits in a year and longer on prior authorization.

These utilization limits relate to the Senate hearings of the summer of 1974, when there were cries of alarm that the costs of psychotherapy had reached nearly 20% of total mental expenditures (all 50-minute outpatient psychotherapy was 21.2% of such costs in fiscal year 1975). A 1972 study (Penner, 1975) had reported that the cost of inpatient psychiatric care represented 24% of the total funds spent for inpatient care, involved 48% of all inpatient days covered, yet only 9% of the beneficiaries were involved. The cost of outpatient mental health care came to 47% of total expenditures for all outpatient care. As will be discussed later (see Tables 1 and 3), when visits are limited to "psychiatric" procedures rather than "psychiatric" diagnostic codes, there are substantially fewer total visits (644,650 versus 941,755).

It is in the interests of all concerned for the major professions to assist CHAMPUS in establishing peer review and other quality controls over providers, utilization, and procedure effectiveness. Since September 1974, a psychiatric panel determines whether further inpatient treatment would be beneficial. Outpatient mental health benefits are also now subject to checkpoint review after 24, 48, and 60 visits (U.S. House Armed Services Committee, 1974), "with provision for recommendations for care in excess of these amounts to be professionally evaluated." Marriage, child, and pastoral counseling services were terminated as a benefit on February 27, 1975, but later restored under court order. Further changes were announced on March 7, 1975, in an effort to bring program costs into line with the available appropriation. Psychologists continue to be recognized as independent providers; however, reimbursement for their services on a "fee for service" basis is now restricted to licensed psychologists with a PhD in clinical psychology and with two years of supervised experience in an organized health setting *or* listing in the *National Register of Health Service Providers in Psychology* (with about 8,500 listed as of February 1977). The CHAMPUS definition is essentially similar to the one in the insurance industry's proposed National Health Care Act of 1977 (H.R. 5-Burleson, Texas; S. 5-McIntyre, New Hampshire). Other psychologists and all other non-medical therapists are subject to a physician's prescription for their services, with a physician's review and recertification every 30 days. The Department of Defense Appropriation Act for 1976 (H.R. 9861) sought again to eliminate the services of family, marital, and child counselors and pastoral counselors, or "any other service or supply which is not medically necessary . . . as diagnosed by a physician." However, when enacted as PL 94-212, counseling services were not eliminated and the status of psychologists was clarified (Sec. 751 [e]: "any other service or supply which is not medically or psychologically necessary to diagnose and treat a mental or physical illness, injury, or bodily malfunction as diagnosed by a physician, dentist, or a clinical psychologist"). Additional controls implemented by CHAMPUS include the requirement that residential facilities for children or adolescent services be accredited by the Joint Commission on Accreditation of Hospitals (JCAH).

It should be noted here that where the number of visits to any provider did not equal at least 1% of the services rendered and 1% of the beneficiaries, or the N was less than 100, the claim costs are not cited.

Procedures

The Schedule of Procedures, with some additions, closely follows that for psychiatric services developed by the California Medical Association (1969) in its Relative Value Studies. Individual outpatient psychotherapy, the 50-minute "hour," was by far the most common procedure, accounting for 57% of all mental health visits (see Table 1). Note also that this one procedure accounted for 80.8% of all outpatient visits to all providers. The data presented in Table 1 derive from an analysis of procedure visits by provider by state, and yield a visit total 32%

Table 1: *Visits and Average Fees Paid to Major Providers by Mental Health Procedure*

Procedure	Site	No. visits	% site total	Attending physician % visits	Attending physician Average fee	Psychiatrist % visits	Psychiatrist Average fee	Psychologist % visits	Psychologist Average fee
Psychotherapy									
50 minutes #90800	in	42,456	22.6	8.7	32.18	86.0	31.80	2.0	34.47
	out	368,769	80.8	4.4	37.83	63.7	37.59	29.9	36.04
25 minutes #90801	in	57,486	30.6	22.6	19.20	74.8	20.36	—	—
	out	33,879	7.4	12.3	20.49	75.5	22.25	7.8	19.46
15 minutes #90802	in	14,923	7.9	25.3	15.66	68.6	15.87	—	—
Group therapy									
90 minutes #90810	in	10,644	5.7	10.3	16.67	81.3	18.44	1.3	19.04
	out	35,387	7.7	4.2	19.66	61.2	20.23	29.9	19.57
60 minutes #90811	in	4,142	2.2	16.9	11.99	78.2	12.92	1.3	17.19
Convulsive therapy									
#90820	in	7,620	4.1	19.5	32.04	67.1	34.44	—	—
Milieu and case conference									
50 minutes #90850	in	33,782	18.0	5.0	38.70	92.4	38.31	—	—
25 minutes #90851	in	11,239	6.0	4.3	19.76	94.6	23.00	—	—
15 minutes #90852	in	3,051	1.6	4.3	13.53	94.7	13.53	—	—
Total visits	in	188,009[a]	—	13.9	22.24	81.4	26.82	1.2	39.61
	out	456,641	—	5.1	32.36	63.7	34.58	28.5	34.68
Grand total		644,650							

Note. In nine states and D.C. area, from special run through December 31, 1975, for fiscal year 1975.
[a] Totals greater than visits listed because some codes are omitted.

less than visits tabulated by mental diagnostic codes. Stated otherwise, tabulation by diagnostic code showed about a 46% higher visit rate because these added visits were for other than mental health procedures. The briefer forms of psychotherapy (25 minutes and 15 minutes) were more commonly on an inpatient basis. Psychiatrists provided 86%, 75%, and 69% of all inpatient psychotherapy visits of 50, 25, and 15 minutes' duration, respectively. The only other provider delivering more than 10% of the inpatient psychotherapy was the attending physician (commonly, the family doctor) for the shorter visits. On an outpatient basis, the psychiatrist was again the major psychotherapy provider, participating in 64% and 75% of visits with a duration of 50 and 25 minutes, respectively. It appears that psychologists, while providing 30% of this "hourly" outpatient therapy (attending physicians, 4%), are rarely engaged in brief therapy (15 minutes) and collectively provide only 8% of the short (25 minutes) outpatient visits. Psychologists and clinics each provided, however, more than 10% of their hourly outpatient psychotherapy to those under 10 years of age, while psychologists provided 33% of their

hours to those aged 10–19 years (clinics, 40%), reflecting their proportionately rather greater involvement with children and adolescents in ambulatory mental health care than the psychiatrist or physician (5% and 5%, 21% and 23%, respectively).

Much has been written of the cost-benefit effectiveness of group therapy. However, it is apparently more often read about than practiced. Only 7.7% of all outpatient visits were for 90-minute group therapy (5.7% on an inpatient basis). Psychiatrists provided 81% and 61% of the inpatient and outpatient 90-minute group therapy, while psychologists provided 30% of such therapy on an outpatient basis.

Psychologists may be surprised to learn that they provided only 62% and 76% of the psychological testing on an inpatient and outpatient basis, at least insofar as billing was concerned. Psychiatrists are shown as providing 32% of inpatient testing and 19% of such outpatient testing. More likely, much of such testing is at their request or direction either by salaried personnel or on a unit cost basis, or they billed for the services provided on referral. In any event, psychological testing accounted for fewer than 1% of either the inpatient or outpatient visits (only .97% of all outpatient visits in contrast to 1.3% in fiscal year 1974).

In comparison to prior years, it appears that the diversity of reported procedures is shrinking. "Not otherwise classified psychotherapy" accounted for about .8% of all outpatient visits (.4% in 1974), while no visits are now reported for psychoanalysis and hypnosis. Indeed a recommendation to CHAMPUS that behavior therapy and biofeedback be assigned procedure codes distinct from verbal psychotherapy received the response that since such procedures are regarded as "experimental by the practicing medical community, it is the intent of the Program to not pay for either procedure in the future," in 1977 presumably. In fiscal year 1974, not otherwise classified psychotherapy (#90849) accounted for 10.7% of all outpatient visits to psychologists, and psychologists provided 72.5% of such outpatient services. Apparently, the future was being signaled, perhaps by the third-party intermediaries, for in fiscal year 1975 this procedure accounted for only 1.4% of outpatient visits to psychologists and they rendered 48.5% of these visits. Will the behavior therapy and biofeedback procedures go the way of psychoanalysis by psychiatrists? Be no longer delivered? Or be no longer reported as such? Probably the answer lies in the axiom, "The program follows the dollar." Such continuing trends will, of course, weaken the value of future data when reported in progressively narrowing confines. In a similar vein, with visits tallied by mental health procedure, social workers no longer accounted for 1% of the visits in any cell.

Of the inpatient mental health visits, 4.1% were for convulsive therapy (electro- or drug-induced). Milieu supervision, however, accounted for more than a quarter of all inpatient visits, well over 90% of them to psychiatrists. In fact, 81.4% of all inpatient visits were to psychiatrists, only 1.2% to psychologists. On the other hand, 28.5% of all outpatient visits were to psychologists. Why the sharp differential? In part it is probably attributable to psychiatrists treating a greater proportion of psychotic conditions. The fact that psychologists are generally precluded from having hospital staff privileges or from being members of the active professional staff by accreditation criteria, such as those of the Joint Commission on Accreditation of Hospitals (JCAH), may serve to restrict practice and patient access, and likely accounts for a significant part of this differential.

As with hourly psychotherapy on an outpatient basis, psychologists provided almost 30% of this 90-minute group therapy. Psychologists' fees for this procedure, when compared to psychiatrists', were slightly higher ($.60) on an inpatient basis, slightly less ($.66) on an outpatient basis. The outpatient services of psychiatrists and psychologists appear mainly to follow the time involved. Thus, double the average cost of a 25-minute visit is 118% and 108% of the average 50-minute visit cost, respectively. On an inpatient basis, however, doubling and tripling the 25-minute and 15-minute visit of a psychiatrist yield returns that are 128% and 150%,

Table 2: *Average Fees Paid for Outpatient 50-Minute Psychotherapy by Provider and State*

State	No. visits	Attending physician		Psychiatrist		Psychologist	
		% visits	Average fee	% visits	Average fee	% visits	Average fee
California	185,089	1.3	34.62	64.4	36.73	33.2	37.32
District of Columbia	75,510	—	—	78.7	37.79	20.1	34.57
Florida	37,921	8.2	41.86	62.9	41.60	26.1	35.87
Illinois	4,840	13.9	34.00	42.3	33.28	16.5	30.58
Ohio	6,182	11.8	34.47	36.5	36.65	48.5	30.99
South Carolina	9,435	15.7	36.89	54.2	36.96	26.6	33.08
Texas	44,241	14.8	38.10	45.6	38.11	37.5	34.57
Total	363,218[a]	4.4	37.83	63.7	37.59	29.9	36.04

[a] Including Alabama, New York, and Rhode Island, the total number of visits was 368,769. The data for these states were omitted because fewer than 1% of the total visits were made in any of these states.

respectively, of the hourly (50-minute) rate. The fees of attending physicians closely follow this pattern. The "head in the door" and short visit at the hospital reflect an economic attraction of hospital practice.

Generally, the average visit costs (fee paid) to attending physicians, psychiatrists, or psychologists are more notable for their similarity than differences. Psychologists, seldom delivering inpatient service, apparently charge a higher average cost ($39.61 versus $26.82 for psychiatrists), perhaps because of involvement on referral for expert opinion. On an outpatient basis, the average fee of psychiatrists was about $2 higher than that of attending physicians per visit. For the predominant procedure, "hourly" psychotherapy, the psychologist received an average of $1.55 a visit less than the psychiatrist. The cry for parity on *rate* can be dropped!

Table 2 reports on the main outpatient procedure of hourly psychotherapy. Psychiatrists provided as many as 79% of such visits in Washington, D.C., as few as 36% in Ohio. Psychologists provided as many as 48% of these visits in Ohio, as few as 16% in Illinois. There

is thus substantial variation among the states, and in average fees as well. The average psychiatric fee for this procedure ranged from $33.28 in Illinois to $41.60 in Florida. For psychologists the range was from $30.58 in Illinois to $37.32 in California. It was only in California, however, that the average psychologist's fee exceeded that of a psychiatrist.

The degree to which specific clients received more than one form of therapy (procedure), the extent of services by client, and the index of their effectiveness per spell of disability cannot be determined from the data.

Diagnosis, Hospitalization, and Visits

That there were 67,381 diagnosed beneficiaries, accounting for 55,862 admissions among 51,217 unduplicated users, indicates that multiple diagnoses/admissions are common (see Table 3); stated otherwise, 32% of the diagnoses were additional to the unduplicated user. The neuroses accounted for 50% of hospital admissions, schizophrenia for 16%. Personality

Table 3: *Hospital Admissions and Professional Visits by Diagnosis*

	Hospital admissions				Professional visits				
Diagnosis	No. admissions	Average stay[a]	Average per diem cost	Average hospital cost per admission	No. inpatient visits	No. outpatient visits	Total visits	Users	Average visits per user
Schizophrenia	9,007	12.1	74.52	904	60,322	53,947	114,269	5,422	21.1
Affective psychoses	1,171	8.9	89.23	790	5,479	7,275	12,754	1,326	9.6
Neuroses	27,688	4.8	83.92	402	113,842	341,514	455,356	29,132	15.6
Personality disorder	2,059	20.4	62.63	1,280	12,191	39,325	51,516	3,868	13.3
Alcoholism	6,432	4.1	74.12	303	11,420	5,622	17,042	2,246	7.6
Drug dependence	1,283	2.9	72.82	208	1,830	1,239	3,069	457	6.7
Physical disorder Psychogenic origin	611	1.9	102.89	196	1,031	5,274	6,305	833	7.6
Transient situational disturbance	2,996	18.6	65.93	1,227	17,265	90,149	107,414	9,922	10.8
Behavior disorder Childhood	1,479	47.4	62.16	2,946	20,977	118,128	139,105	9,460	14.7
Mental disorder Physical condition	1,096	10.6	61.25	650	3,016	6,389	9,384	1,226	7.7
Subtotal	53,819	—	—	—	248,311	668,609	—	63,892	—
Total	55,862	8.6	73.27	630	257,189	684,586	941,775	67,381	14.0

Note. Total *hospitalization* cost = $35,199,875 (correct to 100% from 97.2% claims complete = $36,213,860). Professional *inpatient* visits (257,189) × $25.09 average fee = $6,452,872 (corrected to 100% from 97.2% claims complete = $6,638,757). Therefore, the total inpatient cost = $41,652,747 (corrected to 100% from 97.2% claims complete = $42,852,617). Professional *outpatient* visits (684,586) × $33.11 average fee = $22,666,642 (corrected to 100% from 93.9% claims complete = $24,139,128). Therefore, total *program* costs, both government and private = $64,319,389 (corrected to 100% from 93.9% claims complete = $66,991,745).
[a] In days.

disorders, transient situational disturbances, and childhood behavior disorders accounted for an additional 12% of the admissions, while alcoholism and drug dependence combined were 14% of the admissions. Diagnoses more common among the aged are not evident because CHAMPUS benefits are rarely provided to persons over 64. The law restricts such provision to only those not eligible for Medicare.

The average duration of hospital stay was 8.6 days. This average, however, reflects the longer average duration of stay of those with childhood behavior disorders, personality disorders, and transient situational disturbances at 47.4, 20.4, and 18.6 days, respectively, a sharp reduction, however, from the averages of the year prior (96.6, 48.2, and 36.5), probably reflecting the effect of utilization controls which require residential facilities to be JCAH accredited (July 1974) and authorization for stays over 120 days (August 1974). Young clients contributed heavily to long-term hospital utilization. For example, those diagnosed schizophrenic and aged 1–14 years, while 4% of all admissions for this diagnosis, accounted for 18% of the hospital days, with an average stay of 58 days in contrast to the overall average stay of 12.1 days for this diagnosis. Similarly, 12% of personality disorder admissions (ages 5–14) accounted for 31% of all such hospital days, with an average stay of 53 days in contrast to this disorder average of 20.4 days. Behavior disorders of childhood, largely admitted in the 10–19-year-old range, had the longest average duration of stay when aged 5–14 years. The overall average of 47.4 days was the longest for any diagnostic category. Of shortest duration were the average stays of those with neurosis at 4.8 days; alcoholism at 4.1; drug dependence, 2.9; and physical disorders presumed psychogenic, 1.9.

The total of 67,381 users averaged 14.0 visits, inpatient and outpatient visits combined, ranging from 6.7 for the drug dependent to 21.1 for the schizophrenic and 15.6 for the neurotic, the latter diagnosis comprising 43% of the beneficiaries. Since users were counted but once for a specific diagnostic code and there were but 51,217 unduplicated users, obviously multiple diagnoses were common. The data do not permit separation by user of outpatient from inpatient visits. That some users might seek professional assistance more than once a year seems reasonable. That users would average 1.32 diagnoses *each* does not. More probably, different therapists frequently cited a different diagnosis for the same patient, perhaps viewing the condition differently. More probably, the "overlap" can in part be attributed to the unreliability (Tarter, Templer, & Hardy, 1975) of the diagnostic system (American Psychiatric Association, 1968). On an unduplicated basis (all procedures, all therapists, all locations), each user averaged 18.4 visits, or when reduced 32% for non-mental-health procedures (visits), see above, the average was 12.5 visits.

In terms of the proportional distribution of provider visits, perhaps most striking was that 59% of inpatient alcoholism visits were to attending physicians. In the case of personality disorders, transient situational disturbances, and behavior disorders of childhood, the total outpatient visits to psychologists approached those to psychiatrists, accounting for about 31% of all such visits; otherwise, the psychiatrist was the predominant provider. Even so, 17%, 9%, and 6%, respectively, of outpatient visits to psychologists were clients with neuroses, schizophrenias, or affective psychoses, respectively.

Utilization

The total fees of all providers for all mental health services (to December 31, 1975, billings) were $6.45 million for inpatient services, $22.67 million for outpatient services (the $50 deductible per person not included), or $29.12 million in professional services fees. Hospital service costs (patient and government) were $35.2 million, or 55% of the total cost of mental health services provided; outpatient professional services accounted for 35%, just over one third of the cost.

Of the national total of 6.31 million eligible beneficiaries, 46% or 2.9 million resided in the 10 reporting states of this study (see Table 4). These states account for 42% of the national population. The beneficiaries, incidentally, were 3.2% of the population of the 10 reporting states, somewhat over 5% of the population of Florida, South Carolina, and Texas, and 4.7%

Table 4: *Claim Experience by State and User for Health Services*

State	Eligible bene-ficiaries[a]	Health users[b]	Mental health users[b]	Eligible % health users	Bene-ficiaries % mental health users	$ paid health[b]	$ paid mental health[b]	Mental health as % health paid	Average $ paid mental health/ eligible	Average $ paid mental health/ users
Alabama	123.2	17.92	1.13	14.5	.9	13,626.9	1,048.3	7.7	8.51	927.70
California	988.1	162.53	21.81	16.4	2.2	121,047.3	23,655.5	19.5	23.94	1,084.62
District of Columbia	143.0	19.67	5.55	13.8	3.9	16,048.0	6,704.5	41.8	46.88	1,208.02
Florida	433.4	80.14	7.79	18.5	1.8	56,283.7	8,417.5	15.0	19.42	1,080.55
Illinois	144.3	13.67	1.03	9.5	.7	10,626.2	1,245.4	11.7	8.63	1,209.13
New York	159.3	24.15	1.65	15.2	1.0	16,610.5	2,199.3	13.2	13.81	1,332.91
Ohio	108.5	17.03	1.19	15.7	1.1	11,976.8	1,109.6	9.3	10.23	932.44
Rhode Island	24.5	2.85	.49	11.6	2.0	2,768.1	690.6	24.9	28.19	1,409.39
South Carolina	152.5	13.74	1.74	9.0	1.1	9,283.5	1,357.5	14.6	8.90	780.17
Texas	619.0	72.62	8.85	11.7	1.4	59,851.9	14,084.1	23.5	22.75	1,591.42
Subtotal	2,895.8	424.33	51.23	14.7	1.8	318,122.9	60,512.3	19.0	20.90	1,181.42
National total	6,307.4	935.97	96.72	14.8	1.5	654,429.6	115,995.5	17.7	18.39	1,199.29

Note. $ paid includes in- and outpatient care, government and patient costs.
[a] Calendar year 1974, latest data available by state; this study, 51,217 unduplicated users.
[b] In thousands.

of the metropolitan area of Washington, D.C., while only 1% of Ohio, and .9% of New York. Nationally, CHAMPUS beneficiaries comprised 2.9% of the population.

The proportion using any health service ranged from a low of but 9% of those eligible in South Carolina to a high of 18.5% in Florida. Overall, somewhat less than 15%, about only one in seven eligible persons, used any health service under CHAMPUS. This seems a remarkably low utilization rate; however, the capacity of the direct military medical corps for general health care is substantial. It provides a major proportion of the general health services for the care of beneficiaries residing within 40 miles of a base health service. The systems' ability to provide mental health services beyond the needs of active duty personnel, on the other hand, is apparently quite limited. This appears to account for the fact that CHAMPUS mental health service utilization falls within the range to be expected from other utilization reports. This utilization ranged from a low of .7% in Illinois to a high of 3.9% in Washington, D.C.

In both the 10 reporting states and nationally, mental health services were used by fewer than 2% of the beneficiaries. It merits special note that the annual mental health utilization rate per thousand insureds in these 10 states only varied from 18.95 to 19.89 to 18.20

for fiscal years 1973, 1974, and 1975 (Table 7), respectively. Such a stable pattern of utilization in a program of this size should put to rest concerns that utilization is spiraling or that the utilization of mental health services is at unreasonable levels.

In separate tabulation (Table 4), the 51,217 users received mental health services at a total cost of $60.51 million, an average of $1,181 per user per year in these 10 states. The CHAMPUS (government) costs were lessened by the deductibles and co-payment. On this per capita basis, the mental health services had an average-per-person-covered annual cost of $20.90, just under $1.75 per month. Mental health costs as a proportion of total health costs did, though, vary widely among the states from a low of 7.7% in Alabama to 41.8% in the District of Columbia area. The average cost per mental health user was lowest in South Carolina, but half that of the highest, Texas. With a total program cost of about $654 million, the CHAMPUS cost for mental health services at around $116 million absorbed 17.7% of the total health benefit funds.

Plaut (1976) has reported that for 1975, the total national direct costs for the care of the mentally disordered were in excess of $16 billion, or 13.9% of national health expenditures. Other reports on comparative utilization have been previously summarized (Dörken & Associates, 1976, chap. 9).

Interstate Variance

The location of CHAMPUS beneficiaries does not follow state civilian population but rather the location of uniformed personnel and retirees. This is evident by contrasting the number of insured in California, New York, Washington, D.C., and Illinois to state population.

Detail on the four major providers is listed in Table 5. There is wide variance in the proportion of visits (services) provided by any one profession among the 10 states. Whether the services were on an inpatient or an outpatient basis had an effect on the professions involved. Thus, while attending physicians and psychiatrists accounted for 91% of inpatient services and psychologists and social workers together provided only 2.3% of such services (7.6% by all other providers), the psychiatrists provided just less than half (48.8%) of the outpatient services. Psychologists and social workers delivered 29.7% of such services, with all other providers delivering the 21.5% balance.

Whereas the proportion of inpatient services provided by psychologists in these states ranged from less than 1% to only 1.7%, their delivery of CHAMPUS outpatient services ranged from 6.5% to 29.3% (overall averages 1.2% and 21.4%). This would appear to underscore the importance to psychology of acquiring hospital staff privileges. Interestingly, when psychologists are engaged in inpatient services, their average fees are higher than those of psychiatrists ($47.84 versus $26.37). This suggests, as previously noted, that their inpatient involvement may be more in the nature of special consultation or for particular expertise. Overall, the ratio of psychiatrist to psychologist outpatient services is 5:2, but it is 4:1 in Washington, D.C., while approaching 1:1 in Ohio. The

Table 5: *Visits to Major Providers by State by Diagnosis, All Procedures*

Site	No. visits	Attending physician % visits	Attending physician Average fee	Psychiatrist % visits	Psychiatrist Average fee	Psychologist % visits	Psychologist Average fee	Social worker % visits	Social worker Average fee	All others[a] % visits	All others[a] Average fee
Alabama in	9,725	42.3	17.24	44.2	20.28	—	—	—	—	13.2	34.40
out	7,812	26.7	16.39	29.6	26.19	15.9	33.23	4.5	48.46	23.3	30.13
California in	65,132	7.1	27.81	85.6	33.58	1.7	38.57	—	—	5.1	27.68
out	321,290	2.7	17.57	46.1	34.39	21.6	35.84	8.2	26.98	21.4	28.56
District of Columbia in	13,690	1.5	28.91	91.4	26.79	—	—	5.2	18.75	1.3	33.34
out	112,470	—	—	64.6	36.27	18.2	34.13	9.9	26.49	6.4	29.35
Florida in	47,151	12.7	23.98	78.2	25.55	1.1	49.32	2.3	21.33	5.6	22.91
out	65,038	8.8	33.89	55.3	35.44	20.05	34.55	8.9	20.89	6.5	22.47
Illinois in	6,161	35.6	22.62	58.1	32.60	—	—	—	—	5.5	21.51
out	11,132	19.1	23.53	39.5	31.00	9.2	31.19	4.1	27.29	28.2	33.37
New York in	3,172	5.5	24.40	84.5	32.67	—	—	—	—	9.6	27.40
out	25,332	1.4	27.89	71.8	39.58	16.1	34.45	2.4	31.98	8.4	26.39
Ohio in	7,170	36.8	17.61	55.4	19.90	—	—	—	—	7.5	13.49
out	12,054	23.1	20.20	33.2	31.59	29.3	31.73	8.9	31.49	5.5	25.96
Rhode Island in	1,436	31.5	27.21	67.8	32.35	—	—	—	—		
out	6,802	13.1	34.05	27.3	36.63	6.5	40.85	2.6	26.38	50.6	37.21
South Carolina in	10,548	30.8	15.35	64.5	17.08	1.4	32.26	—	—	2.6	29.56
out	18,075	19.1	24.58	44.3	33.60	21.9	35.58	7.5	26.67	7.2	28.15
Texas in	93,017	30.8	18.52	55.9	20.90	1.3	56.51	—	—	11.4	21.92
out	104,594	18.0	26.45	36.6	33.90	27.5	37.80	9.2	36.48	8.7	39.54
Total[b] in	257,200	20.4	19.92	69.7	26.50	1.2	47.84	1.1	23.99	7.6	23.84
out	684,599	6.7	24.94	48.8	35.00	21.4	35.79	8.3	28.13	14.8	29.52
	941,799										

Note. Claims paid through December 31, 1975; where $N < 100$ or 1%, data are omitted.
[a] But not psychologist or social worker when not tabulated for low frequency.
[b] Inpatient claims estimated as 97.2% complete; outpatient, 93.9%.

highest proportions of visits to psychiatrists are evident in D.C. and New York, areas with the highest concentration of psychiatrists. There was also wide variance among the states in overall utilization, particularly of outpatient mental health services, ranging from a low of 64 such visits (all disorders, all providers) per thousands insured in Alabama, to 786 in the District of Columbia. The overall 10-state ratio was 236 outpatient visits per thousand beneficiaries (325 in California, almost half the 10-state reported visits). The national ratio was 108.

Outpatient visits are nearly three times as frequent (73%) as inpatient visits overall in these 10 states. No certain explanation can be offered for the greater frequency of inpatient versus outpatient visits in Alabama—surely not Southern hospitality! Inpatient visits are 47% of all visits in Texas and 42% in Florida. Perhaps the licensing standards for residential facilities in these states may be a factor. Such utilization hardly seems compatible with the current emphasis on need for ambulatory care.

The average fees reported in Table 5 are for all procedures and therefore differ somewhat from the 10-state averages for "hourly" psychotherapy listed in Table 1. The fees do, however, reflect actual provider fees, but only those prevailing from July 1974 to June 1975. When the average outpatient fees of psychiatrists and psychologists are contrasted by state, one notes that overall the psychologist was paid $.80 more per visit, but the differential ran to $7.04 in Alabama, $1.51 in California, while in Washington, D.C., and New York, psychological fees were somewhat lower.

Social workers provide only 8.3% of the outpatient services (range from 2.4% to 9.9% among these states)—perhaps a reflection of the fact that they are only licensed/certified in 13 states. When their average outpatient fees are compared to those of psychiatrists, they are found to be generally lower ($28.14 versus $35.00), but the differential ranged from +$22.27 (Alabama) to −$14.54 (Florida).

It should be emphasized that the fees, while showing substantial variation between states and professions, do so on an average, even though they have been adjusted by CHAMPUS to UCR (usual, customary, and reasonable) rates. Local economy, custom, licensure laws, and pro-vider availability and involvement undoubtedly are factors leading to intra- and interprofession and interstate variance. Within the 10 states, 5,858 attending physicians, 6,533 psychiatrists, 1,916 psychologists, and 920 social workers were paid providers in fiscal year 1975. Thus, the average earnings by provider from CHAMPUS for the major disciplines were, respectively, $374, $2,515, $2,809, and $1,817. In terms of gross professional services revenue, the program brought earnings to these professions, respectively, of $2.2, $16.4, $5.4, and $1.7 million in the reporting states. Projected nationally in the same proportions (professional visits 45.3% of program costs, with 7.5%, 56.4%, 18.5%, and 5.7% to these professions, respectively), the economic significance of CHAMPUS mental health services to these professions was $3.9, $29.6, $9.7, and $3.0 million. CHAMPUS provider psychologists as a proportion of all licensed psychologists varied widely among the states, with as few as 4% of the licensed psychologists in Illinois and Ohio rendering services to CHAMPUS beneficiaries in contrast to 50% of psychologists in the Washington, D.C., area (see Table 6). Of the 25,510 licensed psychologists in the United States (Wellner & Mills, Note 2), 14% were CHAMPUS providers. Average earnings of provider psychologists appeared substantially higher in the five states where more than 25% of licensed psychologists were involved in this program, $3,213; as contrasted to the five states where fewer than 15% were involved, $1,331. In Washington, D.C., where psychiatrists were relatively their most heavily involved, their average CHAMPUS participant earnings were $3,974. For social workers, too, Washington, D.C., was the area of their greatest activity with average participant earnings of $2,653. Perhaps this says something for involvement? Or for life in the Capital?

Three-Year Trends

The trends reported are based on claims submitted through September following the close of each fiscal year. Despite some internal changes in tabulation of data, this point in time provided the best basis of comparison from data available

Table 6: *Psychologist Distribution and CHAMPUS Earnings*

State	No. licensed psychologists[a]	CHAMPUS psychologist providers	Psychologist provider as % licensed	Average CHAMPUS earnings/ psychologist providers
Alabama	157	22	14	1,924
California	3,213	839	26	3,015
District of Columbia	403	201	50	3,507
Florida	614	216	35	2,253
Illinois	1,122	46	4	712
New York	3,463	160	5	880
Ohio	1,803	76	4	1,485
Rhode Island	121	11	9	1,654
South Carolina	160	46	29	3,427
Texas	1,039	299	29	3,864
Subtotal	12,095	1,916	16	2,809
National total	25,510	3,533	14	NA

Note. NA = not applicable.
[a] From an unduplicated national roster, current to December 1976 (Wellner & Mills, Note 2).

to the author. Table 7 shows that despite a slight decline in eligible beneficiaries, the number of hospital admissions for mental disorder showed a progressive increase. Average length of stay declined progressively and dramatically by 57% in this three-year period (19.9 to 8.5 days), however, so that despite rising per diem costs, the average cost per admission dropped 35% from fiscal year 1973 to 1975 ($952 to $612). Professional fees, as might be expected, were on the rise. Averaged for all providers, all procedures, all diagnoses, all users, the inpatient fee increased 8% from $23.12 to $25.07, a 4% per

year rise. Outpatient fees, higher in each year, showed a sharper rate of increase from $26.99 to $33.26, or 23%, an 11.6% per year rise.

CHAMPUS has recently changed its selection criteria to agree with the method used in its other data programs. The result is a significant reduction in the number of unduplicated users: 51,217 as of December 31, 1975. Utilization then is but 17.69 per thousand for this period and is estimated at 18.20 for the entire period; in other words, fewer than 2% of the eligible beneficiaries in this 10-state study used any mental health services under the CHAMPUS

Table 7: *Professional Mental Health and Hospital Services: All Diagnoses, All Procedures, All Providers*

	1973	1974	1975
No. admissions	36,603	46,592	51,986
Average length of stay	19.9	14.1	8.5
Average per diem cost (in $)	47.77	56.76	72.16
Average cost per admission (in $)	952	800	612
No. inpatient visits	254,793	316,996	242,894
Average inpatient fee (in $)	23.12	24.06	25.07
No. outpatient visits	618,036	643,638	645,051
Average outpatient fee (in $)	26.99	30.67	33.26
Unduplicated users (in $)	52,709[a]	56,837[b]	51,217[b]
Beneficiaries[c]	3,017,200	2,965,235	2,895,839
Utilization per thousand	17.47	19.17	17.69
% claims complete	92.2	96.4[b]	97.2[b]
Utilization adjusted to 100%	18.95	19.89	18.20

[a] Claims through September 30 following fiscal year end.
[b] Newly adjusted count, through December 30.
[c] By calendar year.

Table 8: *Fee Trends by Provider: Predominant Procedures*

Procedure	Year	Total visits	Average fees in $				
			Attending physician	Psy-chiatrist	Psy-chologist	Social worker	Clinic
50-minute psychotherapy #90800							
Outpatients	1973	362,107	34.93	33.57	31.65	24.09	29.66
	1974	400,535	34.94	35.79	33.41	25.98	29.27
	1975	352,309	37.94	37.63	36.05	—	32.87
Inpatients	1973	63,901	32.65	30.08	30.55	—	33.77
	1974	83,281	32.45	31.57	33.28	—	30.19
	1975	40,220	32.10	31.83	34.42	—	—
25-minute psychotherapy #90801							
Outpatients	1973	21,681	19.72	18.64	17.44	13.74	15.93
	1974	24,167	19.34	20.24	18.11	14.69	16.00
	1975	31,303	20.52	22.21	19.54	—	22.20
Inpatients	1973	47,400	16.82	16.44	—	—	17.89
	1974	59,131	17.88	17.78	—	—	18.34
	1975	54,132	19.14	20.29	—	—	19.76
15-minute psychotherapy #90802							
Inpatients	1973	11,432	13.63	12.75	—	—	12.63
	1974	14,368	14.99	14.42	—	—	11.08
	1975	13,768	15.59	15.85	—	—	15.48
90-minute group therapy #90810							
Outpatients	1973	37,968	15.19	17.52	15.62	15.22	15.56
	1974	42,319	15.94	17.85	16.62	15.08	13.12
	1975	32,900	19.76	20.19	19.58	—	15.38
Inpatients	1973	12,536	14.14	16.53	14.68	13.49	13.30
	1974	14,857	14.52	16.18	15.15	14.84	14.86
	1975	10,147	16.73	18.46	19.19	—	22.15
Milieu and case conference, 50 minutes							
Inpatients	1973	26,294	35.92	35.15	—	—	46.08
	1974	26,186	36.96	36.64	—	—	—
	1975	32,151	38.41	38.36	—	—	—

Note. Claims processed through September 30 following each fiscal year.

program in 1974–1975. The frequency of utilization in this program is apparently quite stable, as previously noted.

Recent years have seen an increase in the fees of all providers for essentially all procedures (see Table 8). Only a few points will be commented upon.

From 1973 to 1975, the fees of psychiatrists increased 12% in the two-year period for outpatient "hourly" psychotherapy, and 19% for 25-minute sessions. On an inpatient basis, their increase was 6%, 23%, and 25% for visits of 50, 25, and 15 minutes, respectively. Clearly, the shorter the visit the steeper the rate of increase. Viewed soley from a time perspective, two 25-minute and three 15-minute inpatient visits would "equal" the 50-minute fee but, in fact,

they were in 1975, 127% and 149% greater. Back in 1973, the gradient was less steep: 109% and 127%. The short and brief inpatient sessions are preponderantly rendered by physicians, very largely psychiatrists. Ward team supervision and milieu therapy are also essentially the exclusive province of the physician. Given the widespread positive evidence of the effectiveness of psychologists and others in program direction, ward management, and team supervision in public mental health services, it seems probable that medical control of the hospital environment accounts for the near absence of other than physicians in rendering milieu and short/brief therapy.

From 1973 to 1975, the fees of psychologists increased 14% in this two-year period for outpatient 50-minute psychotherapy and 12% for 25-minute sessions. Given recent increases, it would appear that the average rate for both psychologists and psychiatrists for outpatient hourly psychotherapy is likely to be $40 in fiscal year 1976 and higher in 1977. Psychologist charges for hourly psychotherapy with inpatients were in each year slightly more than that of psychiatrists (8% more in 1975) and only very slightly less and more closely parallel to their outpatient charge for this procedure (5% less in 1975). The higher average inpatient fees of psychologists previously noted for "all procedures" reflect the higher charges for assessment and special procedures.

Outpatient Visit Frequency

Table 9 summarizes the outpatient mental health visits by unduplicated beneficiary to all providers for all procedures. While the national average number of visits by user was 13.9, the *average* ranged from a high of 22.0 visits in the District of Columbia to a low of 7.9 in Alabama. This variation appears to bear some relation to provider density.

The visit-frequency clusters are those adopted by CHAMPUS for utilization and peer review. Overall, about half of all users have fewer than 8 outpatient mental health visits in a year, somewhat less than one eighth the overall

cost of such services. By contrast, only one sixth of the users had more than 24 visits, but they accounted for more than half the cost of such services. Reviewing the number of visits in such a frequency distribution illustrates that cost control can most efficiently be accomplished by progressively closer review of practitioners/clients claiming for higher levels of utilization. In fact, the smaller proportion of clients having weekly or more frequent visits in California, the District, and New York account for well over one third the cost of outpatient service in these states.

Conclusion

Though limited to the 10 sample states and to this select group of beneficiaries, and granting some underreporting, these CHAMPUS data nonetheless provide an unusual perspective on the utilization of fee-for-service practice in the treatment of mental disorder. The mental disorder benefits, apart from a minimal deductible and moderate co-payment, were broader than generally available in group health plans. Utilization rates appear consistent with national user reporting and within the upper limits of experience of other significant group health insurance plans with broad benefits. To the extent that any further controls may be necessary, it is suggested that they be directed to provider

Table 9: *Outpatient Mental Health Care by State: All Providers, All Procedures*

State	No. beneficiaries	Frequency of visits										Average no. visits/ beneficiary
		0-7		8-24		25-48		49-60		60+		
		B	G	B	G	B	G	B	G	B	G	
Alabama	645	66.4	26.1	27.1	45.0	5.6	18.9	.8	9.1	—	.9	7.9
California	20,014	43.0	8.2	35.1	29.8	15.9	34.5	3.1	10.7	2.8	16.8	16.4
District of Columbia	5,262	33.9	5.7	36.1	24.4	19.6	31.9	4.3	10.4	6.1	27.5	22.0
Florida	6,071	56.0	16.2	31.8	38.9	9.6	30.1	1.2	5.8	1.4	9.0	11.2
Illinois	643	49.9	14.0	35.8	38.0	11.5	33.8	1.9	8.4	.9	5.8	12.1
New York	1,492	44.8	7.4	31.9	23.6	14.9	27.4	3.5	10.3	4.9	31.2	18.3
Ohio	767	51.0	13.6	36.8	44.2	10.2	30.1	1.2	5.8	.9	6.3	11.5
Rhode Island	318	53.1	15.0	34.0	39.0	9.7	30.3	1.9	9.4	1.3	6.4	11.8
South Carolina	1,268	52.0	15.9	37.1	45.0	9.3	30.4	1.0	5.3	.6	3.3	11.1
Texas	6,070	52.5	14.5	32.4	34.2	11.4	30.7	2.1	9.2	1.7	11.4	12.8
National	73,582	49.3	11.6	34.0	33.2	12.4	31.6	2.2	9.0	2.1	14.6	13.9

Note. B = % of beneficiaries; G = % of government cost based on claims estimated as 98.7% complete.

profile review, proficiency review for relicensure with designation of practice area, and rate negotiation.

Reference Notes

1. Dörken, H. CHAMPUS ten state claim experience for mental disorder: FY 1973. Testimony to Subcommittee No. 2, Committee on Armed Services, House of Representatives, 93rd Congress, October 11, 1974.
2. Wellner, A., & Mills, D. *Research report #2: An unduplicated count of licensed/certified psychologists in the United States.* Washington, D.C.: Council for the National Register of Health Service Providers in Psychology, March 4, 1977. (Mimeo)

References

American Psychiatric Association. *Diagnostic and statistical manual of mental disorders* (2nd ed.). Washington, D.C.: Author, 1968.

California Medical Association. *California relative value studies* (5th ed.). San Francisco: Author, 1969.

Council for the National Register of Health Service Providers in Psychology. *National register of health service providers in psychology.* Washington, D.C.: Author, 1975, with supplement.

Dörken, H., and Associates. *The professional psychologist today: New developments in law, health insurance, and health practice.* San Francisco: Jossey-Bass, 1976.

Penner, N. The CHAMPUS issue. *Journal of the National Association of Private Psychiatric Hospitals,* 1975, *6*, 17–24.

Plaut, T. Some perspectives on national health insurance. *APA Monitor,* January 1976, p. 2.

Tarter, R., Templer, D., & Hardy, C. Reliability of psychiatric diagnosis. *Diseases of the Nervous System,* 1975, *36*, 30–31.

U.S. House Armed Services Committee. *CHAMPUS and military health care* (HASC No. 93-78). Washington, D.C.: U.S. Government Printing Office, December 20, 1974.

Appendix: Services to Children and Adolescents

Additional analyses of the CHAMPUS data were conducted focusing on the age of the patient. In the CHAMPUS data, "children" refers to those under the age of 15, while "adolescents" refers to individuals aged 15 to 19 years. The services provided these age groups were compared with services provide to "adults" (persons aged 20 years or more). The summary of these data are presented in Table 10.

Overall, children and adolescents represented 35.9% of the persons served but accounted for 52.2% of the hospital costs. This was due essentially to their longer duration of stay. Children received proportionately fewer individual professional visits while in the hospital compared to their percentage of users (e.g., 12.4% compared to 19.7%). Adolescents underutilized outpatient professional services relative to their numbers, but were high utilizers of inpatient professional services. Of the overall program costs, almost 65% of the $64 million expenditures were attributable to hospital costs and inpatient services, without consideration of age.

Length of hospitalization appears related to patient age in the analyses; age of patient was inversely correlated with length of stay. Children were hospitalized longer than adolescents; adolescents were hospitalized longer than adults. For all diagnoses combined, the ratio of average length of stay across age groups was approximately 8 : 4 : 1. Children

Table 10: *Hospitalization and Professional Service Costs[a] by Age Group*

Age	Users #	%	$ Costs Hospital	%	$ Costs Professional Services[b] Inpatient	%	Outpatient	%	%
<15	17,785	19.7	7,629,743	21.7	803,674	12.4	5,146,983	22.7	
15–19	14,689	16.2	10,730,752	30.5	1,628,515	25.1	3,096,081	13.7	
20+	57,998	64.1	16,789,339	47.8	4,044,192	62.4	14,415,101	63.6	
Total	90,472[c]	100.0	35,149,834	100.0	6,476,381	100.0	22,658,165	100.0	35.2
							6,476,381		10.1
							35,149,834		54.7
							$64,284,380		100.0

[a] Fiscal year 1975 claims through 12/31/75.
[b] Claim experience estimated to be 97.2% complete for in-patient and 93.9% complete for out-patient services.
[c] Unduplicated users, 51,217.

averaged 38.9 days hospitalized, while adolescents and adults averaged 18.4 and 4.6 days, respectively. The one exception to this general pattern was diagnoses of alcoholism and drug dependence; these diagnoses generally had short average durations of hospitalization.

Analyses considering the diagnoses of children in relation to length of hospitalization revealed that children with behavior disorders of childhood had the longest average stay. This was followed by personality disorders and transient situational disturbances. These diagnoses are ordinarily viewed as less serious than, for instance, schizophrenia. Thus, adolescents with "milder" diagnoses were hospitalized longer than their peers diagnosed as schizophrenic. This suggests either a problem with diagnosis or the need for closer review of hospitalization practices as well as the facilities involved.

When professional visits are contrasted to days hospitalized, children appear to receive substantially less attention, particularly in cases of schizophrenia, neurosis, and personality disorder. Adolescents with a diagnosis of drug dependence, however, received close attention. Overall, there were only 258,126 service visits during 480,387 days of hospitalization. When the professional visits are restricted to mental health procedures by the major professions, it is evident that there was only the equivalent of one visit (187,744) for 39% of the days hospitalized. Comparing the percent of days of hospitalization to percent of inpatient visits shows an approximate ratio of 2 days: 1 visit for children and 3:2 for adolescents, but 2:3 for adults. Hardly active treatment, especially for the children. The impression of protracted hospitalization with infrequent treatment for this age group suggests that the appropriateness of their hospitalization should be reviewed from the outset, if not a priori.

When the services of the four tabulated provider groups are considered by patient age, it is clearly a differential pattern by service setting and age group. Twenty-nine percent, 54% and 41%, respectively, of outpatient hourly psychotherapy, short-term psychotherapy, and group psychotherapy provided by psychologists was with children. This contrasts with 15%, 8%, and 11% of such outpatient services provided by psychiatrists. Services of psychologists accounted for 28.5% of all mental health service visits, but only 1.2% of inpatient visits. Nonetheless, when they provided inpatient service, more than half of it was to children and adolescents. The near absolute monopoly of medicine over hospital practice has been commented upon elsewhere (see Dörken & Morrison, Section 6).

Herbert Dörken, former Chair of APA's Committee on Health, is an Adjunct Professor and Research Psychologist in the Department of Psychiatry, Langley Porter Institute, University of California, San Francisco. He is also Special Health Services Consultant to the Division of Psychologists in Clinical and Independent Practice of the California State Psychological Association, and was Advisor in Program Development to the California School of Professional Psychology.

Preparation of this report was assisted by Grant MH 26852 from the Mental Health Services Development Branch, National Institute of Mental Health.

Federal Employees Health Benefits (FEHB)

National Institute of Mental Health

This article reports an analysis of the Federal Employees Health Benefits (FEHB) plans in terms of demographic and user data. Analyses consider inpatient and outpatient care, utilization by age and family status, and utilization rates.

Trends in Utilization and Cost— Outpatient and Inpatient Care

Table 1 presents data showing higher utilization and cost in the Washington, D.C. area relative to the population as a whole. Utilization and cost is nearly double in the Washington area compared to the country as a whole, reflecting in part the high concentration of providers in this area. Especially significant is the data from the Aetna plan which led to a cut-back in this plan's benefits in 1974 from unlimited outpatient visits to twenty visits per year. Combining Blue Cross and Aetna, the resulting monthly cost per covered person of just over one dollar for the United States and two dollars for the Washington, D.C. area is very reasonable considering the scope of the benefit.

Figure 1 shows for the U.S. as a whole that for inpatient care a small percentage of patients account for a larger percentage of costs. The ten percent who are the highest utilizers account for 37% of the costs. Figure 2 breaks this out in greater detail and Table 2 shows a similar distributive pattern in the Washington, D.C. area, Ohio, California and for the nation as a whole. There is reason to believe that a similar pattern holds for health care as well, with a small portion of the covered population accumulating "catastrophic" expenses.

A major facet of the mental health coverage debate is apprehension regarding long-term intensive psychotherapies. It is feared that covering this costly mode of treatment (under national health insurance, for example) would threaten the fiscal integrity of the entire system. The data in Table 3 however, indicate a minuscule utilization rate for intensive psychotherapy and one that remained stable over the three-year period, 1971–1973.

The standard treatment regimen for intensive psychotherapies involves a minimum of 3 therapy sessions a week. At approximately $40 per visit, the cost for such intensive therapy would be a minimum of $6,000 per year. Table 3 shows that the number of people receiving treatment in the $6,000-$9,000 category, or greater, ranged from 0.9% of all psychiatric outpatients treated in 1971 to 1.1% in 1973. The cost of treatment for this population during the same time period ranged from 8.7% to 10.3% of the total cost for physician's treatment of mental disorders. Thus the availability of unlimited coverage for intensive psychotherapy during the three years did not seem to cause any appreciable increase in the number of people utilizing this form of treatment.

The majority of patients in fact, tend to limit themselves to short-term treatments. The $0–$999 category in Table 3 covers up to approximately 25 visits a year, and the $1,000–$1,999 category covers 50 visits a year or the equivalent of 1 therapy session a week. In each of the three years for which data are presented,

From National Institute of Mental Health, *Draft Report: The Financing, Utilization, and Quality of Mental Health Care in the United States.* Rockville, Md.: Office of Program Development and Analysis, National Institute of Mental Health, April 1976.

Table 1: *Federal Employee Health Benefit Program: Blue Cross-Blue Shield and Aetna Mental and Nervous Benefits Paid Compared with Total Health Benefits Paid for All Covered Persons, District of Columbia Area* and Total United States, by Type of Plan, 1969 and 1973*

Geographical Area, Type and Cost of Benefit, and Covered Population	Blue Cross-Blue Shield Plan		Aetna Plan	Both Plans Combined
	1969	1973	1973	1973
Total Health Benefits (Millions of Dollars):				
D.C. Area*	$102.9	$196.5	$ 35.6	$ 232.1
United States	$480.9	$848.2	$193.0	$1041.2
% D.C. Area of U.S.	21.4%	23.2%	18.4%	22.3%
Mental and Nervous Benefits (Millions of Dollars):				
D.C. Area*	$ 11.0	$ 20.1	$ 11.4	$ 31.5
United States	$ 30.4	$ 61.6	$ 23.2	$ 85.0
% D.C. Area of U.S.	36.2%	32.6%	49.1%	37.1%
Covered Persons:				
D.C. Area*	907,737	1,078,910	205,525	1,284,435
United States	4,671,990	5,394,570	1,329,975	6,724,545
% D.C. Area of U.S.	19.4%	20.0%	15.5%	19.1%
Percent Mental Benefit of Total Health Benefits:				
D.C. Area*	10.7%	10.2%	32.0%	13.6%
United States	6.3%	7.3%	12.0%	8.2%
Annual Mental Benefits Paid per Covered Person:				
D.C. Area*	$ 12.12	$ 18.63	$ 55.47	$ 24.52
United States	$ 6.51	$ 11.42	$ 17.44	$ 12.64
Monthly Mental Benefits Paid per Covered Person:				
D.C. Area*	$ 1.01	$ 1.55	$ 4.62	$ 2.04
United States	$ .54	$ .95	$ 1.45	$ 1.05

* District of Columbia, Virginia, Maryland.
Source: Office of the Actuary, U.S. Civil Service Commission

at least 78% of people in psychotherapy limited their treatment to 25 visits a year, and 90% restricted themselves, on a yearly basis, to 1 visit or less a week.

A trend that is obvious in Table 3 and Figure 3 is the great disparity between the numbers of people in each category and the amount of the costs for which they are responsible. Thus, at least 78% of the patients in each of the three years incurred costs of less than $1,000 each or as a group only 30% of the total expenditures for mental health services. The remaining 20% of the patients incurred 70% of the total costs. Approximately 90% of the patients (those with expenses from $0-$1,999) incurred only about 53% of the costs. Again this distribution of patients and costs holds true for medical illnesses that tend to be chronic, such as diabetes, kidney disease, or cardiovascular disease.

Table 4 presents the national aggregate data for 1971–1973. It is interesting to compare these figures with data from three separate geographic localities. In 1971–1973, the Washington, D.C., metropolitan area (which includes the Maryland and Virginia suburbs) not only had a very large percentage of the total national membership in the high option plan but also had a disproportionate share of patients receiving mental health benefits and intensive psychotherapy.

Utilization by Age and Family Status

Table 5 compares benefits paid by age and family status for non-mental and mental illness with the total covered population.

While under age 19 dependents are 45% of

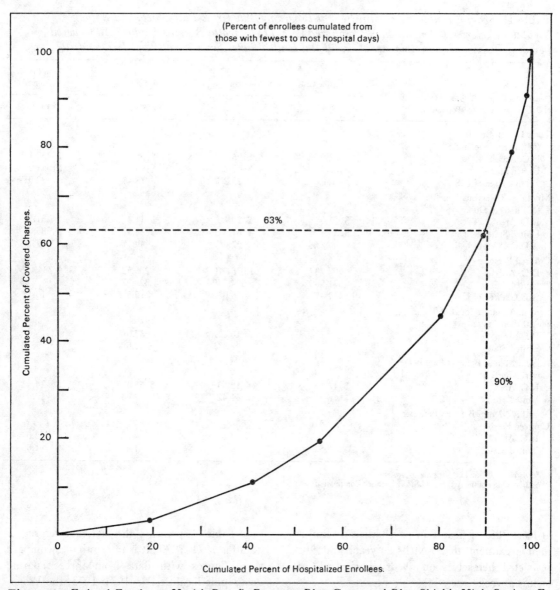

Figure 1: *Federal Employee Health Benefit Program Blue Cross and Blue Shield: High Option. Enrollees Hospitalized for Nervous and Mental Disorders: Percent of All Covered Hospitalization Charges for Mental Disorder Incurred by Indicated Percent of Hospitalized Enrollees, United States, 1973. Source: Blue Cross and Blue Shield: Federal Employee Health Benefit Program.*

the Blues coverage, they only received 13.5% of total benefits and 17.6% of mental illness benefits. Conversely, adults in almost every age group received a larger proportion of total and mental illness benefits than they represent of the population. Blues enrollees aged 19 to 34 represent 8.0% of the total enrollment but received only 7.2% of total benefits which included 13.1% of total mental illness benefits. Dependents age 19 to 34 received 19.1% of mental

illness benefits, over three times their share of enrollment. On the other hand, enrollees and dependents age 55 to 64 received twice their share of enrollment in total benefits but roughly equivalent to the enrollment percentage in mental illness benefits. Over age 65 claims data are distorted by the impact of Medicare.

Patterns for Aetna enrollees are similar to the Blues by age. Spouses' age information is not available for either enrollment or total

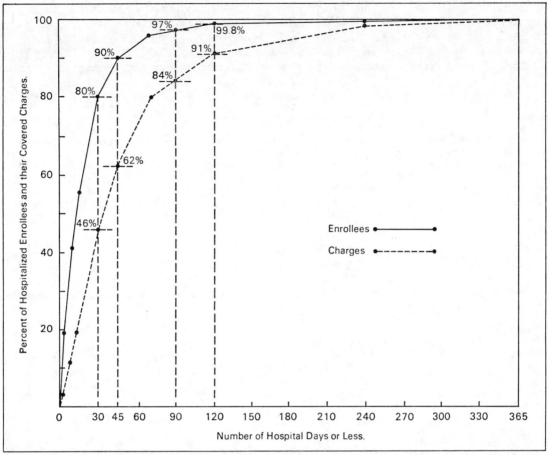

Figure 2: *Federal Employee Health Benefit Program Blue Cross and Blue Shield: Basic, High Option. Enrollees Hospitalized for Nervous and Mental Disorders: Percent Who Were Hospitalized for Indicated Number of Days or Less, and Percent of All Covered Charges for Such Hospitalizations Accounted for by Those Enrollees, United States, 1973.*
Source: Blue Cross and Blue Shield: Federal Employee Health Benefit Program.

benefits, so comparison by age group cannot be made. Children claimed 27% of the Aetna expenses and were 31% of the covered population, a much closer relative portion than in the Blues program but dependent children over age 19 were included in the Aetna data. The number of children covered by both the Blues and Aetna are estimates since actual data on dependents covered are not maintained.

In 1973, all covered children incurred 29.9% of mental illness claims as compared to the 17.6% shown in Table 5 for children under age 19. This is close to the 26.8% in mental illness benefits paid to all children in the Aetna sample.

The implication from these data (paid by age group and incurred by family status) is that children over age 19 receive about 10% of all mental health benefits. Spouses and enrollees age 19–34 receive over 20% of these benefits. In total, therefore, those age 19 to 34 receive 30% to 40% of mental illness benefits but represent only about 15% of the covered population.

Table 6 shows the distribution of type of benefit between hospital and professional services by age and family status. For all claimants, 55% of benefits were hospital charges and 42% were charges for professional services. These percents varied significantly by age and family status.

The percent of benefits paid for hospitalization increased by age group for adults rep-

Table 2: *Federal Employee Health Benefit Program—Blue Cross and Blue Shield: Basic, High Option: Enrollees Hospitalized for Nervous and Mental Disorders: Percent Who Were Hospitalized for Indicated Number of Days or Less, and Percent of All Covered Charges for Such Hospitalizations Accounted for by Those Enrollees, by Selected Areas of Residence and Year of Payment, 1971–1973*

Area of Residence	Number of Hospital Days	Percent of all Enrollees Hospitalized for Mental Disorder			Percent of all Covered Hospitalization Charges for Mental Disorder		
		1971	1972	1973	1971	1972	1973
D.C., Md., Va.	30 or less	76	79	77	41	45	41
	45 or less	88	89	87	58	61	57
	90 or less	96	96	96	79	81	80
	120 or less	98	98	99	87	90	89
Ohio	30 or less	76	76	71	46	42	37
	45 or less	88	90	88	64	66	63
	90 or less	99	97	97	96	84	89
	120 or less	100	99	99	100	91	95
California	30 or less	82	87	86	45	57	56
	45 or less	90	94	92	62	73	68
	90 or less	97	98	97	83	89	87
	120 or less	99	99.5	99	90	98	93
U.S. Total	30 or less	80	81	80	46	46	46
	45 or less	90	90	90	64	62	62
	90 or less	97	97	97	85	83	84
	120 or less	99	99.8	99.8	92	91	91

Source: Blue Cross and Blue Shield: Federal Employee Health Benefit Program

Table 3: *Federal Employee Health Benefit Program—Blue Cross and Blue Shield: High Option Covered Persons with Physicians Charges for Outpatient Care of Mental Disorders under Supplemental Benefits: Distribution of Persons and Their Covered Charges by Expenses Incurred and Year, United States, 1971–1973*

Expenses (Dollars)	1971				1972				1973			
	Persons		Covered Charges		Persons		Covered Charges		Persons		Covered Charges	
	Number	Percent	Amount	Percent	Number	Percent	Amount	Percent	Number	Percent	Amount	Percent
Under 1,000	20,520	78.8	$ 6,171,501	32.3	21,614	78.8	$ 6,504,867	32.1	22,634	78.1	$ 6,685,580	30.8
1,000–1,999	3,198	12.3	4,433,431	23.2	3,385	12.3	4,700,189	23.2	3,694	12.8	5,161,024	23.8
2,000–3,999	1,545	5.9	4,242,583	22.2	1,634	6.0	4,547,043	22.4	1,772	6.1	4,946,042	22.8
4,000–5,999	528	2.0	2,576,115	13.5	544	2.0	2,654,982	13.1	547	1.9	2,668,491	12.3
6,000–9,999	238	0.9	1,642,127	8.6	264	1.0	1,830,541	9.0	315	1.1	2,212,239	10.2
10,000–14,999	1	0.0	12,427	0.1	3	0.0	32,908	0.2	2	0.0	21,159	0.1
15,000–19,999	—	—	—	—	—	—	—	—	—	—	—	—
20,000 or over	—	—	—	—	—	—	—	—	—	—	—	—
Total	26,030	100	$19,078,184	100	27,444	100	$20,270,530	100	28,964	100	$21,694,536	100

Source: Blue Cross and Blue Shield: Federal Employee Health Benefit Program

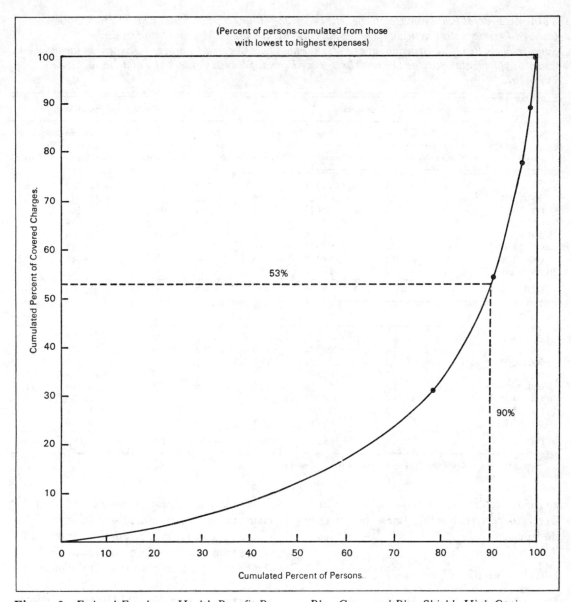

Figure 3: *Federal Employee Health Benefit Program Blue Cross and Blue Shield: High Option. Persons with Covered Physician Charges for Outpatient Care of Mental Disorders under Supplemental Benefits: Percent of Covered Persons Accounting for Indicated Percent of all Such Charges, United States, 1973.*
Source: Blue Cross and Blue Shield: Federal Employee Health Benefit Program

resenting around 70% of the total benefits after age 55. The highest percents for supplemental hospital benefits were for children and those over age 65. Children are more likely to be in nonmember hospitals specializing in mental illness rather than in the psychiatric units of member Blue Cross hospitals. The over age 65 data are distorted by Medicare.

Over half of the expenditures for the younger enrollees were for physicians and other professionals and most of this was for supplemental benefits (i.e., treatment outside of a hospital).

Benefits for younger enrollees and their spouses are primarily for therapy sessions with psychiatrists and other professionals. Children

Table 4: *Federal Employee Health Benefit Program—Blue Cross and Blue Shield: High Option. Covered Persons with Physician Charges for Outpatient Care of Mental Disorders under Supplemental Benefits: Distribution of Persons and Their Covered Charges, by Expenses Incurred under Supplemental Benefits Over a Three-Year Period, Selected Areas and Total United States, 1971–1973*

Expenses (Dollars)	United States				District of Columbia, Maryland, Virginia			
	Persons		Covered Charges		Persons		Covered Charges	
	Number	Percent	Amount	Percent	Number	Percent	Amount	Percent
Under 1,000	43,664	75.3	$13,010,191	21.0	14,112	65.4	$ 4,647,202	14.1
1,000–1,999	6,507	11.2	9,196,426	14.9	3,023	14.0	4,324,554	13.1
2,000–3,999	4,349	7.5	12,151,026	19.6	2,315	10.7	6,524,801	19.8
4,000–5,999	1,466	2.5	7,079,409	11.4	906	4.2	4,373,944	13.3
6,000–9,999	1,188	2.1	9,204,136	14.9	732	3.4	5,689,906	17.3
10,000–14,999	489	0.8	5,952,526	9.6	294	1.4	3,574,409	10.8
15,000–19,999	224	0.4	3,869,619	6.3	157	0.7	2,712,711	8.2
20,000 or over	63	0.1	1,417,106	2.3	50	0.2	1,115,383	3.4
Total	57,950	100	$61,880,439	100	21,589	100	$32,962,910	100

Expenses (Dollars)	Ohio				California			
Under 1,000	1,785	85.7	$ 444,256	28.0	3,236	76.0	$1,035,709	24.2
1,000–1,999	148	7.1	206,124	13.0	502	11.8	708,324	16.5
2,000–3,999	81	3.9	221,334	13.9	301	7.1	844,849	19.7
4,000–5,999	14	0.7	69,974	4.4	98	2.3	472,704	11.0
6,000–9,999	26	1.2	205,150	12.9	78	1.8	597,409	13.9
10,000–14,999	20	1.0	258,783	16.3	28	0.7	339,556	7.9
15,000–19,999	7	0.3	113,508	7.1	14	0.3	242,196	5.6
20,000 or over	3	0.1	69,081	4.3	2	0.0	47,140	1.1
Total	2,084	100	$1,588,210	100	4,259	100	$4,287,887	100

Source: Blue Cross and Blue Shield: Federal Employee Health Benefit Program

and older adults, on the other hand, are more likely to receive mental illness benefits for therapy.

Hospital Inpatient Expenses

One last comment on inpatient care:

Table 7 shows the number of claimants with a basic or supplemental hospital inpatient claim during 1973 by the size of the annual hospital claim. Of particular interest in this table is the number and type of person with very large hospital claims. As might be expected, these claims are more skewed toward the larger amounts than the physician expenses. An individual in psychoanalysis, for instance, might incur total annual expenses of as much as $8,000 (200 visits at $40 each) but a patient under continued hospitalization will have total bills of well over $30,000.

Although more skewed than the physicians'

expenses, a significant proportion (58%) of the claimants had less than $1,000 in insured expenses. These patients, accounting for only 13% of the total hospital expenses, probably were in the hospital for a week or less. At the upper extreme, only 1.8% of the claimants had total hospital expenses over $10,000 but they accounted for 18.6% of the total expenses.

Overall, children were only 22.5% of the total hospital patients but they included 266 of the 400 claimants with expenses of over $10,000 in 1973. Further, the 60 children incurring claims of $20,000 or more were over 81% of the total in this category.

Assuming that the proportions in Table 5 are applicable to all hospital admissions, about 4,900 of the 21,669 total Blues admissions in 1973 stayed in the hospital for more than 30 days. About 450 of these admissions were hospitalized for 120 or more days and over two thirds were children.

Table 5: *Distribution of Population, Total Benefits, and Mental Illness Benefits by Age and Family Status*

	Blue Cross/Blue Shield—1973 High Option Benefits Paid					
	Enrollees			Dependents		
Age	Mental Illness Benefits	Total Benefits	Covered Population	Mental Illness Benefits	Total Benefits	Covered Population
Under 19*	—	—	—	17.6%	13.5%	44.8%
19 to 34	13.1%	7.2%	8.0%	19.1	12.2	6.1
35 to 44	8.8	6.4	5.8	9.4	7.9	5.3
45 to 55	10.2	13.6	8.7	9.4	10.7	6.0
55 to 64	6.5	14.5	7.0	4.0	6.9	3.6
65 & over	1.4	5.5	3.4	.5	1.6	1.3
Total	40.0%	47.2%	32.9%	60.0%	52.8%	67.1%

	Aetna—1973					
	Enrollees			Dependents		
Age	Mental Illness Expenses	Total Non-Maternity Expenses	Covered Population	Mental Illness Expenses	Non-Maternity Expenses	Covered Population
Children*	—	—	—	26.8%	11.7%	31.3%
19 to 34	13.5%	4.0%	6.0%	11.4		
35 to 44	9.3	5.1	6.2	8.6		
45 to 54	8.2	10.8	10.1	12.2	33.4	27.9
55 to 64	4.6	17.4	10.5	3.3		
65 & over	1.3	17.6	8.0	.8		
Total	36.9%	54.9%	40.8%	63.1%	45.1%	59.2%

* All children, including disabled over 22, for Aetna but only children under 19 for Blue Shield.
Source: Office of the Actuary, U.S. Civil Service Commission.

Table 6: *Distribution of Mental Illness Benefits by Category of Treatment, Age and Family Status, Paid Under Blue Cross/Blue Shield High Option in 1973*

| Family Status and Age | Hospital | | | Professional | | | | | |
| | Basic | Supple-mental | Total | Basic | Supplemental | | Total | Drugs | Total |
					Physician	Other*			
Dependents:									
Under 19	48.7%	12.8%	61.5%	9.5%	20.1%	8.2%	37.8%	.7%	100.0
19–34	46.3	10.9	57.2	9.9	26.9	4.3	41.1	1.7	100.0
35–44	48.3	5.1	53.4	11.5	27.6	3.1	42.2	4.4	100.0
45–54	56.1	6.9	63.0	13.2	16.7	1.8	31.6	5.4	100.0
55–64	62.6	7.6	70.2	13.2	11.0	1.0	25.2	4.6	100.0
65 & over	40.2	26.0	66.2	14.3	9.1	.4	23.8	10.0	100.0
Total	49.9%	9.8%	59.7%	10.8%	22.2%	4.6%	37.6%	2.7%	100.0
Enrollees:									
19–34	27.2%	3.0%	30.2%	5.5%	56.5%	6.6%	68.6%	1.2%	100.0
35–44	36.3	3.8	40.1	8.6	44.5	4.0	57.1	2.8	100.0
45–54	54.2	5.9	60.1	11.4	23.0	2.0	36.4	3.5	100.0
55–64	63.3	7.3	70.6	12.3	12.7	1.0	26.0	3.4	100.0
65 & over	56.7	18.8	75.5	10.9	6.9	.8	18.6	5.9	100.0
Total	43.0%	5.2%	48.2%	9.0%	36.4%	3.7%	49.1%	2.7%	100.0
Grand Total	47.1%	8.0%	55.1%	10.1%	27.8%	4.3%	42.2%	2.7%	100.0

* Other Professional includes psychologists, psychiatric nurse, social worker.
Source: Office of the Actuary, U.S. Civil Service Commission.

Table 7: *Persons Hospitalized for Mental Illness By Size of Hospital Expenses Incurred and Family Status*
Blue Cross/Blue Shield—1973 High Option Expenses Incurred (Dollar amounts in thousands)

| Hospital Expenses Incurred | Number of Beneficiaries | | | | Cumulative Percent of Total | Total Expenses | |
	Enrollee	Spouse	Child	Total		Amount	Cumula-tive Percent
0–$999	5,097	4,938	2,491	12,526	57.8%	$ 4,449	13.0%
$ 1,000–1,999	1,675	1,583	742	4,000	76.3	5,500	29.0
2,000–3,999	1,171	1,099	728	2,998	90.1	7,948	52.1
4,000–5,999	358	360	345	1,063	95.0	4,949	66.5
6,000–9,999	187	184	311	682	98.2	5,102	81.4
10,000–14,999	48	44	137	229	99.3	2,747	89.4
15,000–19,999	17	11	69	97	99.7	1,790	94.6
20,000 & over	8	6	60	74	100.0	1,823	100.0
Total	8,561	8,225	4,883	21,669	100.0%	$34,306	100.0%

Source: Office of the Actuary, U.S. Civil Service Commission.

5

Evaluation and Accountability

Although there has been a great deal of talk in the government, both in Congress and in the executive branch, about accountability and evaluation in health service provision, there is little evidence of sympathy or interest in actually developing such mechanisms, incorporating them, and utilizing the findings. It is rare that a federal program is initiated with appropriate and comprehensive evaluation components designed as an integral aspect of the program. What typically happens is that a program is conceived, authorized, and funded and only after several years are questions raised about the efficiency, effectiveness, and value of the program. Evaluation mechanisms tacked onto programs after the fact tend to be inefficient, narrow in focus, and dominated by individuals not knowledgeable about or responsive to the "products" of the program and perceived as enemies by those in the program. When federal programs do include provisions for evaluation, two features stand out. First, evaluation is funded at a very low level. Second, the so-called evaluation is really only management-information "counting" (i.e., how many people served, how many hours of service were delivered, etc.) or compliance assessment (i.e., are services provided only to those authorized by legislation, are the implementing regulations being followed). These two types of information are needed, but they constitute program evaluation in its narrowest definition only. High-quality program evaluation involves utilization data, direct program cost data, clinical effectiveness data, unintended total government system expenses, as well as broad analyses of the impact on those citizens supposedly served.

Evaluation is complex in both definition and process. It can mean a report of services provided or a description of who utilized them. It may be a report of expenditures. It may mean a peer review of whether the service was needed or whether or not it was provided in a reasonable and appropriate manner. It may mean the evaluation of the outcome of service, narrowly or broadly defined, or it may mean estimating the economic and/or human costsavings achieved by providing the service. It is not that the definition of evaluation is ambiguous. Rather, evaluation is many different things, an encompassing process with many uses.

271

When Charles Kiesler first approached a senior official of the National Institute of Mental Health (NIMH) regarding the need to develop a plan for accountability and evaluation in national health insurance, he was informed that the whole issue was a "political football" and that NIMH could have nothing to do with it. Contacts with other professional associations produced no more definitive response. Ultimately Kiesler proposed that the APA Board of Directors establish a special task force to develop such a plan, reasoning that the combined scientific and professional backgrounds of psychologists put them in the best position of the mental health professions for developing such a plan. Since other mental health professions and the executive branch of government seemed uninterested in cooperating, he reasoned that psychology had a special obligation to continue on its own. The APA Board of Directors agreed to fund such a task force.

The outcome of that effort is reproduced here as the first article in this section. The "Principles for Continuing Evaluation and Accountability Controls for a National Health Insurance Program" is an interesting and provocative effort. The uses for continuing evaluation in national health insurance are emphasized, so that only those programs and services that work are paid for and to encourage continuing improvement in standards of care. The plan could easily be adapted to assess medical health care as well as mental health care.

The interests of Congress, the executive branch, providers, and consumers coincide in the need for a mechanism to assure appropriate, high-quality service at the lowest reasonable cost. Well-designed and appropriately utilized evaluation programs should be the core of vital cost-containment and quality assurance measures. National health insurance must provide for the best currently available treatment, yet it must be designed to facilitate innovation and incorporate change. This can best be accomplished by a system that emphasizes a range of alternative services and modes of delivery, assesses their intended and unintended outcomes in a comparative manner, and uses the feedback to produce new change in the system itself. If consideration of a full range of such factors is not built into the system, important information will never be discovered and knowledge will be lost.

First, an evaluation/accountability component must be an integral part of any national health insurance structure. Second, such an evaluation unit must be relatively autonomous. Third, the director of the evaluation section must have an influential position within the health system and the ability to help modify the system. Fourth, the priorities and goals of the national health insurance system must be prospectively articulated. Fifth, the goals of the system must be stated in measurable clinical and behavioral outcome terms. Sixth, such program evaluation, health services research, and clinical research must be a continuous process. Seventh, the results must be publicly discussed and when appropriate, the health system changed.

The advantages from the inclusion of an integral evaluation component in national health insurance are many. The availability of public information on service priorities and actual service delivery would facilitate meaningful input by consumers. Society will support services that realistically and effectively address societal problems. Congress would have the information necessary to determine whether or not funds were being utilized as authorized or mandated and whether services were being provided in a cost-efficient manner. Federal policymakers would have a firm and valid data base on which to make intelligent, informed decisions for rationally modifying the health system. In addition, a properly designed and funded evaluation component would pay off in dollars by continuing the funding only of those services that are demonstrably effective and provided in a cost-efficient manner. Moreover, meaningful program evaluation would minimize interprofessional rivalries by focusing on the service provided, its effectiveness, and its costs, rather than on who provides it. At the base of such rivalries is, in most cases, professional pride. The knowledge that such expertise is shared and used effectively by a variety of disciplines would serve as a reassurance to professionals and as a cost-saving device to the public.

Issues of confidentiality will need careful attention in the design of an evaluation component within national health insurance. Confidentiality standards must not be so severe as to prevent us from learning how we provide services, to whom, at what cost, and with what benefit (or detriment). Legitimate researchers must have access to "identifiable" health care information and other data. What needs to be protected is an individual's right not to be harassed, abused, or discriminated against because of particular knowledge. This does not require that at the earliest possible moment the linkage between individuals and their health care data (and other information) be severed. Researchers need to be able to link separate data base systems. To do this, they must be able to identify individuals. The protection needed is to insure that researchers do not abuse the access to such information and that research is reported in a manner that does not allow identification of individuals.

An example of cost-benefit analysis of mental health care that considers both service costs and clinical effectiveness is provided by Karon and VandenBos in the second article in this section. They compare the cost-effectiveness of the treatment of schizophrenics by psychologists to that provided by psychiatrists. Psychotherapy provided by psychologists was less expensive and slightly more effective than services provided by psychiatrists, primarily because of differences in the nature of the psychotherapy provided and differential reliance on medication. Karon and VandenBos found that reliance on medication led to less attention to therapeutically changing the underlying thought disorder in schizophrenics. Hence, schizophrenic patients of psychiatrists manifested earlier, though temporary, behavioral improvement but less long-term fundamental improvement.

In an earlier study by Karon and VandenBos (1975), a similar cost-benefit analysis compared the treatment of schizophrenics with psychotherapy to treatment with medication. Patients were randomly assigned to treatments. In spite of the high initial cost of providing psychotherapy, the total treatment cost of psychotherapy-treated schizophrenics was from 22% to 36% lower than that for patients treated by medication. That study illustrates the importance of longer-term evaluation of effectiveness and cost. If a short time-frame (for example, from 3 to 6 months) had been used, medication would appear to be more cost-efficient. However, with a longer-term perspective, the real cost-benefit pattern was demonstrated to be the reverse. Moreover, the study illustrates how different patterns of care or treatment plans have differential consequences in other governmental subsystems. While Karon and VandenBos were not able to obtain detailed information concerning other nontreatment government costs (i.e., welfare benefits) because of confidentiality restrictions, even a cursory scrutiny of the data reveals that 75% of the patients treated by medication alone received welfare benefits during the study, compared to only 33% of those who received psychotherapy. Evaluation that only addressed minimal care standards and only considered costs within the mental health subsystem would not have uncovered this information.

The third article in this section, by Nicholas Cummings, provides another example of program evaluation or systems research. This report illustrates how the occasionally conflicting goals of cost control and improvement of services can be considered simultaneously. The Cummings article and the remainder of the articles reprinted in this section originally appeared in a special issue of *Professional Psychology,* edited by Robert and Evelyn Perloff, on the evaluation of psychological service delivery systems. The Perloffs' comments on the state-of-the-art in mental health program evaluation are reprinted here. In the next paper, Stewart argues that it is important for psychologists to become involved in program evaluation and cost-effectiveness analysis because of their unique training in research and practice. Sussna discusses the importance of both inter- and intraprogram comparisons, with particular reference to community mental health centers. Liptzin, Stockdill, and Brown present the NIMH point of view on the evaluation of community mental health centers. Hadley and Strupp briefly present their tripartite evaluation model. Schulberg compares the experimental model of evaluation and the legal model of program evaluation. Finally, Cohen discusses the utilization of program evaluation and research findings.

Reference

Karon, B. P., & VandenBos, G. R. Treatment costs of psychotherapy versus medication for schizophrenics. *Professional Psychology,* 1975, *6,* 293–298.

Continuing Evaluation and Accountability Controls for a National Health Insurance Program

APA Task Force on Continuing Evaluation in National Health Insurance

In order to promote the evolution of an effective program of national health insurance, a system of continuing evaluation must be made an integral part of the development, delivery, and management of services. The objectives of an evaluation system would be to help (a) specify the goals of the national health insurance system in measurable terms so that progress toward those goals can be assessed, and effective components of programs can be identified; (b) provide a mechanism for effective cost management; (c) promote the provision of effective and safe services; (d) further the accountability of providers and system administration for the conduct of the insurance plan; (e) foster equal access to needed services by all segments of the population; (f) facilitate the development and efficient functioning of the service provision system; (g) promote the communication of information about the nature, extent, and costs of services to the public, to providers, and to Congress; and (h) assess the unintended or alternative outcomes of national health insurance. Sixteen characteristics that an evaluation and accountability system should possess in order to meet these goals are discussed, as are a number of practical difficulties in implementing such a system.

Some form of comprehensive health insurance system will almost surely be legislated into existence within the next few years, whether as a national health insurance (NHI) system or as an extension and elaboration of the present system. As the legislation is written, Congress will be under great pressure to establish a system of organized health care accessible to all Americans. Public demand for accountability will require a clear sense of priorities, determination of program effectiveness, the containment of cost, and assurance of the availability of responsive, quality health services. Existing federal programs such as Medicare and Medicaid are thought to be inadequate in coverage for mental health services, and they exclude from participation a number of provider groups that could contribute substantially to the nation's health.

The probable advent of NHI provides psychology and the other health professions with a remarkable opportunity to display professional maturity and leadership in also urging Congress to build into the NHI provisions for systematic evaluation of covered services and reimbursement only for effective treatments and programs. In the vast majority of cases, the only really ethical position lies in providing the public with effective services or services whose effectiveness is under systematic evaluation. It is unlikely that any health profession would in the long run lose by affirming its confidence in its ability to provide effective services, and the public could only gain.

Evaluation is activity carried out to determine the consequences of implementing a treatment or program.[1] Applied to NHI, evaluation is activity carried out to help determine the worth of programs for improving health, preventing illness and disability, or providing necessary support. It pertains to a wide range of research activities extending from testing the ef-

---

[1] For the sake of simplicity, the term *program* will be used henceforth to refer generically to treatments, interventions, and other related concepts.

Reprinted from *American Psychologist*, 1978, *32*, 305–313.

fectiveness of a specific drug or medical procedure to examining a program of national scope. There are many ways in which evaluation could be accomplished, for example, reliance on expert opinion, obtaining of consensus judgments of consumers, logical analysis, etc.; but within the context of this paper, evaluation may be taken to refer to careful and systematic research for determining the extent to which a program is effective. The results of evaluation provide objective evidence of the effectiveness of a program for use by those who will decide what NHI should pay for. Good evaluation research is also directed toward considerations of cost, and cost control must be a powerful restraint within NHI if the system is to be viable. Evaluation research can be useful not only in the determination of whether a program works and in the provision of careful and reasonable measures of its benefits but also to provide comparative data on alternative programs so that cost-effectiveness may be judged. If NHI is to be economically sound and reasonably priced, all programs will have to be carefully evaluated to determine that their benefits are being achieved in a cost-effective way.

It is unrealistic to suppose that a national health insurance system would begin with coverage limited to those services with well-established effectiveness. Many of the health care procedures now considered standard have never been demonstrated in careful experimentation to be effective. Consequently, one realistic suggestion would be the convening of study groups to determine which treatments and other health services have been shown to be effective and then to set priorities for study among those that have not. Reimbursement under NHI might continue for all treatments and services currently judged reasonable; but on a gradual basis, currently accepted practices should be examined and dropped if proven ineffective. No new programs should be added without empirical test.

Decision making in most areas of human services is complex, and considerations other than the worth of a service often properly enter into the decisions. Regardless of the existence of evidence for or against a particular decision, political considerations will be especially likely to contribute heavily to decisions about what services are delivered and how. Nevertheless, in decisions about the delivery of health services within the context of NHI, those involved in the political process should be maximally informed about the effectiveness of the programs in question.

Principles

There are many ways in which the problem of explicating a position about evaluation of and accountability for professional services might be approached. We have here elected to state some general principles that we strongly believe should guide the development of legislation when its time comes.

Principle 1. *Legislation should provide for implementing programs in ways that facilitate rigorous evaluation.*

The history of social and health programs in this country is replete with instances of programs brought into being hastily and nationwide before any evidence of effectiveness could be accumulated. In many other instances, interventions have been introduced so haphazardly that no persuasive evidence of effectiveness could be gathered. It is of the greatest importance that the various features of NHI be introduced systematically, in such a way as to foster rather than retard or frustrate evaluative efforts. The key to linking service delivery to evaluation is the dual recognition that no program or service can actually and effectively be implemented on a national basis instantaneously and that when we do not know precisely what to do about a problem, delay is not disastrous but prudent. What is needed is a set of deliberate strategies for introducing new programs in such ways that data can be collected to assess program effectiveness.

Ideally, evaluation should involve a true experiment, with sampling units, whether persons, hospitals, or HSAs (health services areas), being assigned randomly to various treatment and control conditions. For new interventions especially, such designs are often feasible, and where feasible they should be insisted upon as the most likely to produce high-quality, clear-cut findings. Many current interventions, however, cannot be evaluated against no-treatment control groups because of ethical considerations. Current programs will in most instances have to be tested against innovations that might replace them. Even so, data occasionally come to light that cast such serious doubts on the efficacy of currently accepted practices that a randomized experiment with an untreated control group is acceptable on ethical as well as scientific grounds.

Since the testing and demonstration of effectiveness of many programs is an iterative process, it is probable that the course of evaluating many programs will begin with small-scale demonstration projects and laboratory-type experiments, to be followed by larger scale tests. For many of the larger scale tests, true experiments may not be feasible. Nonetheless, services and programs can be implemented in ways that will facilitate their evaluation without needlessly depriving any group of services of known value.

By phasing in programs systematically at different places or at different times, data of an unusually valuable nature can often be obtained. Programs might, for example, be phased in by geographic regions or by political units so that one could determine whether there were systematic changes within regions or units associated uniquely with the implementation of the program. If a preponderance of the units changed after the intervention, and only after the intervention, and if the intervention began at different times for different units, the case for a causal effect of the program would be strong. Treatments might also be phased in by populations served or by naturally occurring units such as different military units, universities, hospitals, or service clubs.

Although there are limits on the interpretability of many natural variations in health programs because these variations are usually confounded with other variables such as the populations served, opportunities to study normal variations should nevertheless be capitalized upon. For example, in the early days of tranquilizing drugs, the doses of chlorpromazine given in different institutions varied greatly, and only gradually did evidence become available that the very high doses were not needed and

probably were harmful. The same conclusion would have been suggested earlier had easily available information about the practices and experiences of different institutions been used.

Program evaluation is still a new area of endeavor, and the expected development over the coming years of new research designs, better statistical techniques, and other methodological improvements will make the task of evaluating health care interventions easier and, in that respect, all the more mandatory.

Principle 2. *The autonomy of the evaluation components should be guaranteed.*

Our definition of evaluation implies that evaluation should be objective—free of inappropriate political pressures, of the biases of narrow professional interests, of expectancies about what ought to be, and of any other prejudicial factors. In order to achieve that objectivity, it seems essential that any evaluation component established under NHI legislation should be autonomous in virtually every respect. Personnel should be recruited on the basis of scientific competence and personal integrity. The guarantee should be absolute that the evaluation component, although subject to oversight and review, control its own budget, plan its own studies, have authority to collect, analyze, and interpret its own data, and issue its own reports. The evaluation component should be established and operated in such a way that suspicions of either bias or insufficient courage would not be sustainable. There are unfortunate examples in the federal government of evaluative activities that lack credibility because of political and other influence.

There are three important points of contact between an evaluation component and the larger system of which it is a part. First, a variety of interest groups should have a role in the setting of priorities for study and in developing plans to accomplish research. Second, an evaluation component should enter into the decision-making process, but only to the extent of providing the best evidence possible. Third, provision should be made for review of the activities of the evaluation component to ensure that they contribute effectively and efficiently to the overall aims of the NHI system. Evaluation procedures and data should be open to public scrutiny by the time any reports using those data are issued.

Principle 3. *The national health legislation should provide for adequate funding of evaluation.*

Evaluation of health care activities will entail costs of considerable magnitude. We propose that any NHI system have built into it a substantial and continuing mandate and capacity to fund research into the effectiveness of all types of health care. Otherwise, evaluation is not likely to be funded adequately through alternative sources to achieve optimal cost-effectiveness, cost-containment, and health-enhancement goals. In recent decades, enormously costly federal programs have been funded and have proven disappointing in light of the original, perhaps overly idealistic, goals. We believe that the lack of provisions for evaluating these programs from the time of their origin contributed to their failure. The consequence of this failure was the unavailability of a rational basis for modifying the programs as evidence of their ineffectiveness began to appear. The belated addition, often under crisis conditions, of a research and evaluation component proved uniformly unsatisfactory as a way of salvaging programs showing clear signs of incipient failure. Billions of dollars have been wasted, the hopes and aspirations of large portions of the populace have been frustrated, and the federal government has suffered losses in public confidence and trust.

The financing of evaluation studies of the kind we are proposing will involve large sums of money and complex decisions. It is our opinion that research needed to support and improve the effectiveness of a national health insurance system should come from within the system itself, that is, should be paid for out of "premium dollars." Only in that way can the research enterprise be protected from the vagaries of funding decisions. Moreover, it seems only just that research meant to improve a system should be funded out of that system, but in a way that preserves autonomy. The level of funding that should be available cannot be specified in other than an arbitrary way, but it probably should be set at some percentage of the total NHI expendi-

tures, should be a constant and dependable percentage over a period of years, and should be reviewed periodically to determine whether benefits being achieved from the research are outweighing costs. Annual health expenditures of a fairly direct nature amount to something over $150 billion per year and justify effort to develop empirical support for the efficacy of those expenditures. Even a small percentage increase in the efficiency of the system would justify a substantial research budget.

Although good evaluation research can sometimes be done with minimal financial outlay, it is often expensive; sometimes it is *very* expensive. Nevertheless, the justification for these costs is that the costs associated with not doing good evaluation research may be even greater. To begin with, there is a potentially great human cost, both individual and societal, in employing ineffective programs. Bloodletting, a primary medical procedure of the last century, and prolonged confinement in bed following surgery, a practice in the first half of this century, are two examples. Radical mastectomy for a single breast lesion may be a current example. Scarce resources are wasted when they are invested in ineffective programs. Moreover, there is danger in the belief that some condition is being treated when the treatment is in fact of little or no value. Attention is diverted from the problem, and it will persist and perhaps worsen. In addition, poor research is expensive. It is expensive because in the long run much money is spent on series of weak studies that even in the aggregate will rarely be persuasive. High-quality research is likely to be more persuasive and ultimately to involve a lower final dollar cost. Poor research may also be costly in a human sense because it can be misleading and either support the case for an ineffective treatment or steer decision makers aways from a good one.

As with any other activity involving expenditure of public monies, evaluation research itself should be evaluated. The potential benefits should, however, be calculated from the proper base. It may well be a bargain to spend more on a good evaluation of an intervention than the intervention itself costs, if the intervention is likely to be regarded as a prototype for a national program. Account should also be taken of the likelihood that the benefits from many proven interventions will extend for years into the future, although the costs of the evaluation are incurred immediately. Determining whether an evaluation study is worth doing at the proposed cost will not always be simple, but the effort should be made.

Very often the best bargain in research is sound basic research on human processes and problems. Although the emphasis of research within NIH should, we believe, be on evaluating the effectiveness of programs, a strong case can be made for allocating at least some portion of the research dollar to more basic studies, particularly if areas can be identified which may have a high probability of later application.

Principle 4. *The system should have articulated procedures for encouraging new and innovative programs with rigorous evaluation designs.*

The requirement that the effectiveness of a new program be demonstrated prior to its reimbursement under NHI might seem unduly to retard innovation or to make change almost tortuously slow. That need not be the case. Much of the slow pace of development that now exists comes from artificial barriers, professional jealousies, and lack of funds for research. None of these problems is inherent to an empirically based system. Some portion of NHI funds should be invested—perhaps through the National Institutes of Health, or an evaluation component within NHI—in demonstration projects, large-scale clinical trials, and other research activities. Undoubtedly, a large number of important health questions could be resolved within a very few years. Nevertheless, nothing should become routine in the system until tested and proven efficacious and safe. We have more than enough experience of the rapid acceptance of ineffective and even dangerous treatments to justify an insistence on the slightly more deliberate pace that an outcome-based system would follow.

The needs of an NHI system for information will require a type and level of research not now characteristic of that in most of the National Institutes of Health, although other federal agencies such as the National Center for Health Services Research and the National Institute of Mental Health do support some research of the sort envisioned here. With a fully operating NHI system, wide participation in health research will be required.

Nothing here should be taken as implying that development of new programs should be slighted. Special procedures should be established so that individual practitioners, clinics, or other provider units could be reimbursed for nonstandard but innovative services. Those procedures would probably involve prospective peer review focused on the prior research support for the innovation, the logic of the innovation, and the plan by which the innovation would be evaluated. The initial evaluation might be clinical and relatively informal, but with subsequent extension of the innovation, more rigorous evaluation designs could be demanded.

Principle 5. *The system should provide for the evaluation of the relationship of program characteristics to outcomes, with primary focus on how programs affect recipients.*

Desired outcomes should be specified for every health service delivered or for every program to be implemented. Outcomes should be specified in ways that are conceptually clear and in forms that are measurable. It is also necessary to specify the time span during which outcomes should be detectable, for not every program will produce either immediate or permanent effects. Ideally, the set of outcomes expected from an intervention or a program should form a coherent body of related effects with clear linkages to the treatments employed. The outcomes to be assessed should be evident in the characteristics or behavior of the units to which services are delivered, so that, for example, when families are served, effects on families should be detectable, and when communities are served, community effects should be observable.

The focus of all programs under NHI, and thus of all evaluations of them too, should be on the recipient rather than on the provider or the system itself. Every effort should be expended to determine the actual health needs of persons insured by the system and how those health needs might best be met. The NHI and health care systems should then be structured so as to meet those needs. What providers might prefer to do, what might be easy or convenient, or what would be pleasant should be secondary considerations except when such factors pose obstacles to delivery of effective service. Nor should efficiency become such a preeminent criterion that it results in the impersonal or demeaning management of people.

At some point, the effectiveness of the entire health care delivery system must be examined. It will not suffice to evaluate health care treatment by treatment and service by service. The effectiveness of the system will be evident only in terms of system goals. Those goals will have to be stated objectively, and relevant data will have to be collected. The system will be judged deficient and will have to be corrected if system goals are not met. For example, one goal of the health care system might be that no more than .5% of pregnant women should go without prenatal care beyond the fourth month of pregnancy—the small allowance being for exceptional cases of women hiding their pregnancies or refusing care. If 10% of pregnant women are not receiving prenatal care, then the system is failing, no matter how good the care when it is given. Obviously, any single index or even any set of absolute goals must be applied with caution, and progress toward them must be viewed in context.

Principle 6. *Guidelines on which accountability is based should be made explicit and generally understood in advance.*

The interests of the health care system, of providers of services, and of recipients of services coincide with respect to the need for mechanisms to control the delivery of services in such a way that quality and appropriateness are assured and that costs are minimized. Without doubt, a variety of control mechanisms will be required, because the problem is multifaceted and involves a number of different levels of analysis. At one level, provision must be made for determining what services will be covered under NHI, and that determination will involve complex issues having to do with costs to the system, needs of recipients, equity across social class lines, and national priorities. At another level, specifications for quality services will have to be devised and permissible variations stated. At still another level, some sort of review for com-

pliance with specifications of quality will have to take place. It is important to all concerned that the process involved in control of health services delivery be open and comprehensible. Almost surely, mechanisms of control will have to include a system of peer review for providers of services.

Both providers and recipients of services will want the guidelines by which appropriateness, quality, and cost of services will be evaluated to be explicit and understood in advance of any interventions undertaken. Both providers and recipients should know at every step whether a specific treatment plan or procedure would be regarded as appropriate, of good quality, and as a covered service for which reimbursement would be forthcoming from NHI. In general, guidelines should be as simple as is consonant with the assurance of quality of care. In particular, the guidelines for controlling costs should be straightforward, with as few special provisions as possible concerning such matters as proportion of costs covered, deductibles, copayments, and the like.

Principle 7. *Criteria examined via evaluation programs should be explicit and should represent the concerns of diverse constituencies.*

If the goals of accountability and quality of care are to be met, it will be necessary to specify treatment and case management criteria by which judgments can be made. The criteria must be stated in an explicit form; reliance on implicit judgments, even if made by peers, will not be sufficient. As with general guidelines, criteria should be available to all parties involved in the process. Patients and clients no less than peers should be aware of what is considered standard or quality treatment. Explicit criteria do not unnaturally limit decision making by provider and consumer, individually or jointly. Mechanisms for exception should be a part of the system. All that is required in most cases is that the reason for the exception be as explicit and reasonable as the criterion itself.

Consumer satisfaction with health services should be studied as carefully and routinely as with the most successful commercial products. If consumers are dissatisfied with the health services they receive, they may not continue to use those they need and may disuade others from using them. Problems with consumer satisfaction are especially troublesome when health deficits are chronic and when consumer freedom to choose among services is limited. When health problems are chronic, dissatisfaction may lead to poor compliance with a treatment regimen that requires patient cooperation. A case in point is the poor compliance of some males with a hypotensive drug treatment that as a side effect produces impotence. When patients have little freedom of choice in selecting health services, dissatisfaction may lead to a failure to get treatment at all. Humane considerations demand that services be provided in ways that are satisfactory to clients if that is at all possible.

Ours is a large country with a diverse and pluralistic society. Consequently, any satisfactory health care system will have to be both complex and flexible. People of diverse backgrounds will require different types of services. Similarly, people living under some conditions will often require special services, although they will also have to recognize that they may incur some unusual risks by their choice of residence or way of life. Even within a given group or geographic area, people will have different needs or will respond differently to the same services. Neither the complexity of the task of providing diverse services nor the necessity of responding to complex needs should be underestimated. Flexibility and complexity in an adequate health care system will, of course, add to the problems involved in evaluating the system and its components, because a service may be differentially effective across geographic locations or ethnic and socioeconomic groups. Although demonstrating differential effectiveness and building provisions for different services into a national health program with effective quality-assurance mechanisms will be difficult, this effort will be required in an adequate overall health system.

Even though the focus of health program development and evaluation should be on the recipient, the needs of providers and of society more generally should not be ignored. Providers need a health care system within which they can work effectively and which will reward them financially and in other ways commensurate with their contributions to individual and societal welfare. To work effectively, providers need a health care system that not only sets forth clear expectations for behavior but also permits the exercise of individual judgment in the particular case. Providers need a system that is reasonably stable and predictable, and one that yields ample feedback about adequacy of performance. They also need a system that is not capricious but is forgiving of errors that will inevitably be made, without being at all tolerant of errors in the long run or of professional incompetence. In addition, providers should participate in the planning and development of the health care system, while at the same time sharing this responsibility with other interests so that they are not burdened with complete and final responsibility for everything that happens—or does not happen.

Other interests also have a legitimate stake in the way criteria are developed for accountability and assessing quality. Legislators need to be assured that their intentions in approving and funding a health insurance system are represented in the working of the system and in what it achieves. Administrators of the system need workable and efficient mechanisms so that they can perform the tasks with which they are entrusted, know that the system is functioning properly, and modify it appropriately. Taxpayers need to be confident that they are getting good value for their money and that the system is realistic and fair. All of these interests will benefit from an open, explicit system.

Principle 8. *Evaluation and accountability mechanisms should make it possible to assess the degree to which the objectives of individualized treatment plans are achieved.*

Virtually every case seen within a health care system is in some respects unique and represents a fresh challenge to those involved in planning care. Because there are few health conditions that are not influenced by a wide variety of patient characteristics, specifications of treatment and outcomes by general prescriptions can serve only as general guidelines. In the individual case, it will often be necessary to tailor treatments or to modify expectations in light of the characteristics of that case. Since goals have to be set for the individual, some provision must be made for determining whether those individual goals are met.

A review system will have to be devised which will permit review of individual cases and determine the degree to which individual goals are met. The review process might well need the flexibility that would make possible a review of no more than a small percentage of some types of cases and a review of every single case of other types. It will be necessary for clinicians and case managers to be explicit about individualized treatment plans, how they will be evaluated, and procedures for reconciling any persistent differences between providers and those doing the review. It is to be expected that the assessment of the individual being treated will be an important part of the evaluation. Evaluation at the system level would then include aggregating data on outcomes across individual cases. A system might be judged effective if most treatment goals were being met in most cases, however diverse those goals.

Principle 9. *Claims of special competency to perform services by any professional group should be evaluated.*

It is common for various professional groups to claim a special competency in service delivery achieved by special training or selection of members of those groups. Along with the claim of special competence very often goes pressure for licensure of the professional group as a certified, and often the only, provider of a type of service to the public. When any individual, profession, or institution claims special competence to perform some service on behalf of the public, the actuality of that competence should be demonstrated. In that demonstration lies much of what is meant by accountability. In some instances, a virtual monopoly may exist, and a potential client may have no basis for judging quality of service provided, nor have any choice in where to seek it. Under those conditions, a firm and dependable procedure for demonstrating exclusive competence is mandatory.

Through the existing system of statutory certification and licensure, a group of health service providers are identified whose members meet minimum levels of training and experience. This is a point from which systematic study of the various health professions can begin. Just as it seems reasonable to initiate health insurance coverage for currently accepted treatments and services, initial recognition should be accorded to present systems of licensure as entry levels for health service providers. The legal definition of practice under licensure laws will determine the professional's scope of practice. However, any claims made by professional groups that would result in an exclusive position in the health care system should be examined empirically, and status as a provider of a service should be based on evidence of the same nature as would be required for program effectiveness. As provider groups not now commonly recognized make claims on the health insurance system, evidence for effectiveness should be the basis for their inclusion as covered professions. The system should provide workable mechanisms for demonstrating such effectiveness.

Principle 10. *The evaluation system should utilize the judgment and leadership of service providers to help promote both the functioning of service delivery and the cooperation of service providers throughout the evaluation process.*

Bringing about changes in our health care system will not be easy. Despite current efforts to require that the services offered be of demonstrated value, that idea is still considered radical by many. There are no ready and simple answers to questions about how changes of large magnitude might be brought about. Strong leadership exercised by the large and prestigious groups involved in the provision of health care service could be a powerful force for change if those groups displayed a unity of determination and commitment. Each of the individual health professions may have to take some degree of risk in order to demonstrate a persuasive level of unselfish interest. In the long run, none of the health professions stands to lose by insisting on empirical tests of its claims and services.

Every effort must be made to enlist the support of providers of services if evaluation efforts are to succeed. Providers should be prominently represented in those groups established to fix guidelines and define criteria for quality and appropriateness of services. The counsel of providers should be sought in developing review systems so that review will have a maximum effect on quality of care but will produce minimal administrative burden and disruption. Quality-assurance systems should be an integral part of the delivery of services. They should not and need not be onerous and limiting, but the help of providers in designing them will be required if their potentially undesirable features are to be avoided.

Principle 11. *Provision should be made for the systematic collection of information compatible with the needs of program evaluation. Confidentiality must be protected, but at the same time, access to the information required for evaluation must be provided.*

No adequate and systematic program evaluation effort can succeed without an appropriate information system, and the existing health information system is not suited to the task. The need for evaluation of health services is so great that it justifies the development of an information system devised specifically to meet the requirements of evaluation of NHI programs. Such an information system would provide systematic, relevant, accurate, and timely information in a form that could be analyzed efficiently. An information system should be established which would provide for collection of comparable information across political units and geographical and time boundaries.

The problem of maintaining confidentiality of information cannot be ignored. Even apart from evaluation, absolute confidentiality of health records cannot exist under any feasible insurance system because some records must be reviewed by the payer. Currently, medical claims are reviewed in insurance companies by clerks at the very first level. A systematic evaluation plan would not represent a greater threat to confidentiality than the current forms of insurance review. For many evaluation purposes, however, individual-identifying information would be unnecessary because the research questions would require only data aggregated by categories, types of treatments, etc. For these research purposes, then, confidentiality concerning individual records would be preserved. Confidentiality might be more difficult to promise for individual providers, since there are often very few of them involved in any one study, particularly in the case of specialists. To a certain

degree, those who exact the special and favorable position afforded by licensure probably forfeit any rights to absolute confidentiality involving their own behavior. Nonetheless, confidentiality is an important issue, and an evaluation system should not abuse it.

Principle 12. *Special attention should be paid to changes in the functioning or effects of programs as they evolve. Both long- and short-term effects should be examined, and consideration should be given to the unintended as well as intended program consequences.*

Programs always change over time. Some of the changes may represent improvements, others may represent degradations. As programs come into being and reach operational stages, staff members may become more skillful, but they may also become blasé. Clients may become more faithful, but they may also come to take more for granted. Particularly when programs devised in one setting are copied elsewhere, some of the essential features that made the original program successful may be distorted or lost. It is essential that evaluation be regarded as a continuing process rather than as a discrete, point-in-time event.

Attending to the possibility of long-term program effects that are discrepant with more immediate effects is also important. It is possible that a program appearing to have little in the way of immediate effects might have long-term effects that would make the program worthwhile, or that a program appearing immediately effective might have long-term effects of an undesirable nature. Naturally, health program decisions cannot be postponed until all the evidence is in, but provisions should be made for insuring that necessary evidence eventually becomes available.

Efforts should be expended to consider the broad ranges of possible consequences of a program in order to narrow the range of potentially surprising outcomes. During early planning stages for an evaluation, potential clients and experts from various fields relevant to the program might be asked to think about possible side effects. Once a program is in operation it should be monitored carefully to determine the unanticipated side effects. A time lag between the trial of a program and widespread program implementation may be necessary to detect delayed effects.

Principle 13. *Procedures for controls on and reviews of the scientific quality of evaluation should be established.*

How is an evaluation to be evaluated? Some procedures and criteria will have to be established to review evaluations to determine whether they have been properly conducted and whether the conclusions are properly drawn. If the results of evaluation studies are really going to be the basis for policy setting within NHI, then it is essential that the evaluations be of the highest quality. The most efficient way to accomplish this review of evaluations will probably be to convene panels of experts. These panels would use such criteria as adequacy of problem definition, fidelity of adherence to program or treatment standards, appropriateness of the sample studied, soundness of the original research design and effects of any deviations from it, adequacy of data quality-control procedures, adequacy of statistical analysis, and overall legitimacy of the conclusions. Evaluation researchers within NHI must be held to exceptionally high standards. Ultimately, making the nonconfidential data, research design, evaluation, and results a part of the public record open to review by any interested citizen would probably be the most effective control on the process.

Principle 14. *Procedures for disseminating the results of evaluation should be established.*

An overall strategy for disseminating the results of evaluation studies should be developed and implemented. Because of the diverse constituencies represented among those interested in health services and their delivery, no one mechanism for dissemination will be adequate. One tactic that might make research findings easier to disseminate would be, whenever possible, to make the existence of studies known from the beginning and to keep various interested groups informed of progress during the course of the work. The final report on the work would then be anticipated with interest. The important thing, however, is that there be designated responsibility for disseminating the results of every study by all the appropriate channels. Those channels should be well established and provided for within the health insurance system and its evaluation component.

Principle 15. *The national health insurance program should contain a formal mechanism for change incorporating the results of evaluation.*

Problems in achieving appropriate utilization of evaluation results can be anticipated. Findings may not be used and have the desired effect on policy even when they are available. One very important factor having to do with the utilization of research findings is centralized decision making; centralization facilitates the adoption of programs of demonstrated value. That NHI would be characterized by much centralized decision making seems beyond question, and many interventions can be implemented by the fairly simple expedient of announcing that reimbursement for them will begin at a certain time and that reimbursement for alternatives will have to be justified. Still, because the possibilities of nonutilization and misutilization will not be negligible, a panel will be needed to sift through research findings and evaluation studies in order to facilitate the appropriate utilization of results. One additional activity that could have considerable impact would be the conducting of regular, carefully planned workshops and other training activities to help administrators understand and use research findings. Scientists may also want to know more about how to conduct research that is persuasive and usable so that where decisions involving trade-offs must be made, they will be made in the direction of enhancing the impact of the research.

An effective plan for dissemination of information and support for its utilization would probably do much to promote the acceptance of evaluation efforts in the entire health field, including acceptance by providers, consumers, and legislators. One of the persistent criticisms of federally funded research is that so many of its results are never translated into practical programs.

Principle 16. *A program should be developed to inform the public about the process of evaluation and its results.*

Acceptance of evaluation findings by the public, including those with direct or vested interests in health programs, will require general public understanding of evaluation as a process and of the links between evaluation and program decision making. If evaluation as an enterprise is not understood by any segment of the public, then there will probably continue to be resistance within that segment to the idea of evaluation and to conclusions stemming from it, particularly when those conclusions contravene popular beliefs or what many people would prefer to believe. The controversies about Laetrile and saccharin, for example, may be exacerbated by a general lack of understanding about the processes by which they have been evaluated and the reasoning that has gone into the conclusions about them. Some efforts have been made in the public media to explain the research on both substances. Such dissemination channels should be utilized routinely. It would also be desirable to devise longer term, systematic ways of increasing the general sophistication of the public about research on drugs and other substances. A continuing effort to inform the public about the process of health program evaluation, the results of evaluation activities, and the way it operates in the public interest is needed.

Conclusion

Many of the evaluation and accountability principles outlined here will be difficult to implement. Naturally, no system of evaluation can instantly produce widespread improvements on current practice that has grown out of years of experience. Fully developing the potential of evaluation to contribute to the long-term improvement of the health system will require a recognition of the value of continuing evaluation, improvements in evaluation technology, development of a cadre of skilled personnel, and the cooperation and participation of health providers. Containing the cost of a national health insurance program will be extremely difficult without a first-rate accountability and evaluation system. Because evaluation and improved accountability have so much to contribute to the efficiency, safety, and effectiveness of our health system, we cannot afford to forgo their contribution.

The Task Force on Continuing Evaluation in National Health Insurance was established by the APA Board of Directors in May 1976. Members of the task force are *Asher R. Pacht* (Chair), *Russell Bent, Thomas D. Cook, Lewis B. Klebanoff, David A. Rodgers, Lee Sechrest, Hans Strupp,* and *Milton Theaman.* *Gary D. Gottfredson* and *Stephen D. Nelson* were the staff liaison members. This resport represents the views of the task force, and is not necessarily policy of the American Psychological Association, which can only be made by the Council of Representatives.

Cost/Benefit Analysis: Psychologist Versus Psychiatrist for Schizophrenics

Bertram P. Karon and Gary R. VandenBos

This article shows that psychologist-provided psychotherapy is less expensive than that provided by psychiatrists, primarily because of the long-term consequences of relying less on adjunctive medication.

The cost effectiveness data (Karon & VandenBos, 1975a) from the Michigan State Psychotherapy Project (Karon & VandenBos, 1972) have been reported only in terms of the economic consequences of providing psychotherapy to patients as opposed to costs incurred when using medication, without discussing the relative costs and the effectiveness of psychologists and psychiatrists. The data clearly indicate that relevant training and experience in conducting psychotherapy with schizophrenics are the determinants of effectiveness, not whether the therapist has a PhD or an MD.

It may be worthwhile to further detail the cost effectiveness by profession. Psychologists tend to cost less, everything else being approximately equal. Experienced psychiatrist therapists of the calibre of those used in the project could be hired for $35/hour, and experienced psychologist therapists, for $25/hour. Trainees (residents in psychiatry and graduate students in clinical psychology) could be hired for $8/hour and $6/hour, respectively.

A more precise cost comparison can be determined by specifically assessing the actual cost of treatment for each patient in our project. The treatment costs have been updated to a 1971–1972 cost base; the hospitalization cost was $70/day.[1]

Two determinations of cost are presented here. The only difference lies in the initial hospitalization data and the resulting figures for the cost of initial hospitalization. Both the "raw," that is, actual hospitalization data and the statistically "corrected" hospitalization data are presented. We believe that the latter data (Karon & VandenBos, 1975c), are the most appropriate to consider.

While the patients were randomly assigned to treatment groups, they were not precisely matched. Thus, some differences occurred between the groups on patient background variables known to be related to improvement. Therefore, 16 background factors were examined statistically to determine what effect, if any, they had on treatment outcome. The hospitalization data were then examined by analysis of covariance, which allows one to correct for the effects of covariates meaningfully related to the dependent variables. The corrected hospitalization data, which represent the statistical approximation of what the hospitalization data would have been had the groups been precisely matched, are presented. The procedure is detailed by Karon and VandenBos (1972).

The hospitalization and cost data are summarized in Table 1. These figures include only the direct cost of treatment and not the cost of welfare and/or retraining services, nor the economic gain in productivity, earnings, and, consequently, in taxes paid—all of which would make the advantages of providing psychotherapy more impressive.

The cost of additional psychotherapy is included as a separate and additional item because it is not currently being provided at most hos-

[1] In a previous article (Karon & VandenBos, 1975) comparing the cost of psychotherapy versus medication, the hospitalization cost figure of $28.30/day per patient was used. This figure was furnished to us by the State Department of Mental Health; the Auditor General has since determined that the true cost at the Detroit Psychiatric Institute was $70/day during those years. This figure does *not* reflect the subsequent rise in costs; it only corrects previous mistakes in accounting.

Reprinted from *Professional Psychology*, 1976, 7, 107–111.

Table 1: *Length of Hospitalization and Treatment Costs for Controls and for the Psychologist- and Psychiatrist-Treated Groups*

Group	Days hospitalized (0–20 months)	Initial hospitalization cost	Additional psychotherapy cost	Initial cost (Treatment phase)	Days subsequently hospitalized (20–40 months)	Later hospitalization cost	Total treatment cost	Training cost	Treatment cost plus training
Controls[a]									
Raw	113.5	7,945	—	7,945	99.8	6,986	14,931	—	14,931
Corrected	146.4	10,248	—	10,248	99.8	6,986	17,234	—	17,234
Psychologists (pooled)[b]									
Raw	118.4	8,288	863	9,151	7.2	504	9,655	300	9,955
Corrected	87.8	6,146	863	7,009	7.2	504	7,513	300	7,813
Psychiatrists (pooled)[a]									
Raw	62.9	4,403	1,190	5,593	93.5	6,545	12,138	300	12,438
Corrected	59.8	4,186	1,190	5,376	93.5	6,545	11,921	300	12,221

Note. Costs are given in dollars.
[a] n = 12.
[b] n = 9.

pitals. However, knowledgeable staff members have indicated their belief that such treatment could be provided with only minimal funding increases and by a more efficient and different use of current staff time. Our figures are based on the conservative assumption that additional psychotherapy would require proportionate additional funding.

Lower Treatment Costs of Psychologist Psychotherapists

It is clear that not only is the total treatment cost considerably less when psychotherapy is provided (Karon & VandenBos, 1975a) but also that savings are considerably greater when psychologists provide the psychotherapy with the same or better treatment outcome. Compare Table 2, which reports data on improvement in the schizophrenic thought disorder, the most central symptom in schizophrenia (Bleuler, 1950; Cancro, 1968, 1969; Lidz, 1973). Table 2 reports the Drasgow-Feldman Visual-Verbal test findings, which proved to be the most sensitive of the measures of the schizophrenic thought disorder used in the Michigan State Psychotherapy Project (Karon & VandenBos, 1974).

Using the corrected data, total costs of treatment were $17,234 per patient for the medicated control group, $12,221 for those receiving psychotherapy from a psychiatrist, and $7,813 for those receiving psychotherapy from a psychologist. Thus, the direct treatment cost is 29% less when psychotherapy is given by psychiatrists and 55% less when given by psychologists. (The raw data comparisons are equally striking when comparing the professions: a 17% savings gained when using psychiatrists as psychotherapists and a 33% savings gained when using psychologists.)

If these figures seem surprising, the apparent discrepancy with other published data disappears if one examines the detailed information in Table 1. Regarding the short-term effects of the use of medication, our data for hospi-

Table 2: *Comparison of Improvement in Patient Ability to Think Logically for Controls and for the Psychologist- and Psychiatrist-Treated Groups*

Group	n	Test errors[a]
Controls	12	17.5
Psychologist treated (pooled)	9	11.0
Psychiatrist treated (pooled)	12	14.7

[a] Data are for test (Drasgow-Feldman Visual-Verbal) errors at end of treatment phase (corrected for initial performance). Lower values indicate greater improvement.

talization are very similar to the usual findings. If one only considers the short-term data (i.e., up to 20 months), the patients treated by psychiatrists in our project cost less. Indeed, using the raw data, the patients treated by psychologists actually cost more than medication alone because of the shorter initial hospitalizations for the patients of psychiatrists in our project. Psychiatrists produced an early discharge of patients by a greater reliance on medication (prescribing continuing adjunctive medication to 10 of their 12 patients), whereas psychologists seemed to concentrate on producing fundamental changes in the thought disorder of patients (prescribing continuing adjunctive medication to only 2 of 9 patients).

One of the major findings of the Michigan State Psychotherapy Project was that adjunctive medication with psychotherapy produces behavioral control that allows for early discharge but slows fundamental change in the thought disorder (Karon & VandenBos, 1972). It may be that the behavior change diverts the therapist's attention from more fundamental processes. (The control group, of course, by definition, was treated by medication.)

However, if one continues a follow-up of the patients, long-term hospitalization is more closely related to change in the thought disorder (see Table 2) then to length of initial hospitalization (see Table 1); such longer term follow-ups are rarely reported, or even carried out systematically.

The patients treated by psychologists via psychotherapy were only hospitalized an average of 7.2 days in the 2-year follow-up, as compared to 99.8 days for the medicated control group and 93.5 days for patients of psychiatrist psychotherapists. When viewed from a longer term perspective, the total treatment cost comparisons therefore alter radically. Such a perspective has always been the justification for psychotherapy, although systematic data have rarely been available (Karon & VandenBos, 1975b).

Because inexperienced therapists require training and supervision, it is perhaps reasonable to add training costs to the cost of treatment for their patients. We estimate the training costs to be $450 per patient treated by inexperienced therapists (in Table 1, the cost is averaged over all project patients). While the salaries of inexperienced therapists are lower, they are less effective, especially without meaningful supervision. In fact, as previously reported (Karon & VandenBos, 1975a), the more highly paid experienced therapists are actually cheaper. The difference is true for both professions, assuming that the experienced therapist has relevant training and experience in doing psychotherapy with schizophrenics and is truly motivated to do the work.

Role of Training, Experience, and Motivation

All "experienced" psychologists and psychiatrists are not the same. They do not have the same education, clinical training, experience, interests, and/or motivation. These factors relating to the therapist are critical to the effectiveness of treatment and the cost of treatment.

Therapists must have a real interest and commitment in trying to help very disturbed, and disturbing, people by helping them to understand both themselves and the outside world. Our finding, that psychotherapy is effective with schizophrenics, would only generalize to such therapists interested in understanding the total human condition, including seemingly bizarre behavior and so-called irrational thoughts.

We have used the word *relevant* throughout this article as it relates to training and experience. By *relevant*, we mean training, experience, and knowledge about (a) psychotherapy, (b) schizophrenics, and (c) the specific socioeconomic class and/or ethnic group. Experience with and knowledge of socioeconomic class and ethnic group of the patient is as important as knowledge of psychopathology. Training in psychodynamics is important! The therapist should be comfortable with his/her own feelings and fantasies.

Our results, that psychotherapy is effective with schizophrenics and costs less than medication, generalize to experienced therapists who are well-motivated, relevantly trained, and relevantly experienced, or to inexperienced therapists who are well motivated and supervised by experienced therapists such as those we have described.

References

Bleuler, E. *Dementia praecox* (J. Zinkin, trans.). New York: International Universities Press, 1950.

Cancro, R. Thought disorder and schizophrenia. *Diseases of the Nervous System,* 1968, *29,* 846–849.

Cancro, R. Clinical prediction of outcome in schizophrenia. *Comprehensive Psychiatry,* 1969, *10,* 349–354.

Karon, B. P., & VandenBos, G. R. The consequences of psychotherapy for schizophrenics. *Psychotherapy: Theory, Research, and Practice,* 1972, *9,* 111–119.

Karon, B. P., & VandenBos, G. R. Thought disorder, length of hospitalization, and clinical status ratings in schizophrenia. *Journal of Clinical Psychology,* 1974, *30,* 264–266.

Karon, B. P., & VandenBos, G. R. Treatment costs of psychotherapy as compared to medication for schizophrenia. *Professional Psychology,* 1975, *6,* 293–298. (a)

Karon, B. P., & VandenBos, G. R. Medication and/or psychotherapy with schizophrenics: Which part of the elephant have you touched? *International Mental Health Research Newsletter,* 1975, 17(3), 1–13. (b)

Karon, B. P., & VandenBos, G. R. Issues in psychotherapy vs. medication in the treatment of schizophrenics: A reply to Tuma and May. *Psychotherapy: Theory, Research, and Practice,* 1975, *12,* 143–148.(c)

Lidz, T. *The origin and treatment of schizophrenic disorders.* New York: Basic Books, 1973.

At the time of original publication of this article, *Bertram P. Karon* was a professor of clinical psychology, Michigan State University. *Gary R. VandenBos* was Director of Howell-Area Community Mental Health Center, Howell, Michigan, a psychological consultant at the Drug Education Center, East Lansing, Michigan, a crisis intervention therapist for Livingston Crisis Center, and maintained a private practice. VandenBos is now Administrative Officer for Mental Health Policy, the American Psychological Association.

Prolonged (Ideal) Versus Short-Term (Realistic) Psychotherapy

Nicholas A. Cummings

It is argued that not only can psychotherapy be included economically in a prepaid insurance plan such as national health insurance, but also that the failure to include psychotherapy in prepaid insurance schemes would deprive a substantial proportion of patients (with emotional as opposed to organic etiology) of the benefits they might enjoy under such plans. A series of studies examining the outcomes of therapy of varying durations showed that the cost of the psychotherapy was more than offset by the savings in medical visits. A cost-therapeutic-effectiveness index shows that it is not the provision of a mental health component that determines optimal cost-therapeutic effectiveness but the manner in which psychotherapeutic services are delivered. It is shown also that for the vast majority of patients studied, innovative short-term psychotherapy is more effective than long-term psychotherapy.

As we approach the inevitable enactment of national health care in the United States, there is occurring within the larger context of the pros and cons of national health insurance itself a heated debate as to whether any national health scheme can feasibly include a mental health component. The dubious experiences of Medicaid, Medicare, and the Civilian Health and Medical Program of the Uniformed Services (CHAMPUS) have left some members of the Congress with the conclusion that the inclusion of mental health would disproportionately overinflate what is already expected to become a staggering price tag for providing even the basics of a national health system. Several prominent psychologists who themselves have never been engaged in the direct delivery of human services, Albee, Campbell (see Trotter, 1976), and Humphreys (1973) have thrown their persuasiveness solidly against the inclusion of psychotherapy in a national health insurance program. They argue that such a service cannot be financed or monitored, that it is a "subsidy of the rich by the poor," or that the insurance benefit would be of doubtful value in the overall health of the American people. Others, principally the author and his colleague (Cummings, 1975; Cummings & Follette, 1976), have taken the opposite stance, based on 20 years of providing mental health services within a comprehensive, prepaid health plan. They have found that not only can psychotherapy be economically included as a prepaid insurance benefit but also failure to provide such a benefit jeopardizes the effective functioning of the basic medical services, because 60% or more visits to physicians are by patients who demonstrate an emotional, rather than an organic, etiology for their physical symptoms.

To summarize the above-mentioned series of articles by the author and his colleague, it was found that providing psychotherapy was not only economically feasible, in that the cost of the psychotherapy was more than offset by the savings in medical visits, but also through an 8-year follow-up it was demonstrated that the service was therapeutically effective in maintaining the emotional well-being of the patient for years after the psychotherapy had been provided. A cost-therapeutic-effectiveness index emerges, with the inescapable conclusion that it is not the provision of a mental health component that determines optimal cost-therapeutic effectiveness, but the manner in which psychotherapeutic services are delivered. Unfortunately, proponents of the inclusion of psycho-

Reprinted from *Professional Psychology*, 1977, *8*, 491–501.

therapy in a national health insurance program have often misread the so-called "Cummings-Follette effect" to be valid even when psychotherapy is delivered in strictly traditional ways, which is definitely not the case. And even more unfortunately, very little attention has been paid to the actual delivery modalities that would render a mental health benefit cost-effective and therapeutically effective, not only within a national health insurance program but within any comprehensive, prepaid health system, whether public or private.

In the brief space allotted, this article attempts to tantalize the reader with the following conclusions, which have emerged from 20 years of experience in providing psychotherapy within a prepaid, comprehensive health plan of several million subscribers: (a) All persons presenting themselves with emotional complaints and problems in living can be treated immediately with psychotherapy without preselection criteria; (b) for 85% of these unselected persons, active, innovative short-term psychotherapy is more effective than long-term psychotherapy; (c) for 5%–6% of these patients, long-term psychotherapy will actually be deleterious; and (d) by providing short-term therapy as the treatment of choice for 85% of all patients seen, long-term psychotherapy becomes economically feasible for the 10% of the patients for whom long-term psychotherapy is necessary and most effective.

Other Modalities

Before proceeding to the topic of short-term psychotherapy, it is important to touch on two other modalities under serious consideration by various proponents. The first of these is the ominous plan by some segments of organized psychiatry to "remedicalize" psychotherapy. Under such a proposal, a national health insurance program or any health system, public or private, would insure only the organic brain syndromes and functional psychoses, excluding the psychoneuroses and character disorders as being outside the definition of insurable illness. This proposal would reduce the cost of providing psychotherapy by drastically reducing the number of persons eligible. It would further guarantee income to psychiatrists who, as medi-

cal practitioners, would be the only persons eligible to provide what is then defined as a medical service. This obviously leaves psychology in a vulnerable position, but even more important, it deprives the majority of Americans suffering from emotional distress access to treatment.

Of demonstrated effectiveness are the community mental health centers, whose primary limitation is that of cost. Various audits have revealed the cost per unit of service to range from about $60 to a staggering $345 in one center, with a modal cost per unit of service of around $75 to $80 as representative of most centers. Despite the potentially inordinate cost, the National Institute of Mental Health (NIMH) continues to champion the community mental health center concept as the mainstay of the mental health delivery system under a national health insurance program. This is understandable, since NIMH spawned the community mental health center movement; but most authorities have retrenched from the overly ambitious goal of the original Kennedy plan that there eventually be a mental health center in every community. The present author believes that because of their relative effectiveness, the inordinate cost of the centers can still be justified in underserved areas of the nation under a national health insurance program.

A Brief History of Short-Term Psychotherapy

The concept of brief psychotherapy is not new and may be said to date back to Alexander and French (1946). Unfortunately, these authors conceived of the process as a short form of orthodox psychoanalysis, and they touched off such a furor that short-term psychotherapy was plunged into general disrepute. It was not until the classic study of Malan (1963) that brief psychotherapy received unbiased research attention. Perhaps prompted by the necessity to provide mental health services under Britain's national health system, Malan examined the traditional attitudes of psychotherapists toward brief psychotherapy and found them to be mostly in the nature of unjustified prejudices. He found that properly selected patients could achieve long-lasting benefit from brief psychotherapy and that short-term treatment often resulted in major changes in the person's symptoms, relationships, and even life-style.

In the United States the work of Malan (1963) was essentially ignored. Clinics continued the attempt to provide long-term psychotherapy for everyone, and waiting lists of 6 months were standard and 1 year, frequent. The dropout rate was high, but this was accepted as inevitable. The emergence of crisis centers, partly as an effort to provide immediate, brief care to cases regarded as emergencies, did little to alter the prejudice for long-term psychotherapy. It was only conceded that brief therapy might be useful in crisis situations, but it was superficial, supportive, and lacked the dynamic elements that could only take place within the context of long-term treatment. In his most recent studies, Malan (1976) demonstrates what some clinicians have known for some time: Brief psychotherapy can be active and have all the elements of depth attributed to long-term therapy, including the resolution of unconscious conflicts and the analysis of resistance and transference. Unfortunately, Malan (1976) still employed selection criteria for those patients undergoing brief, rather than long-term, therapy. Such selection criteria have been dubbed by Sue (in press) "exclusion criteria," in that they serve as an adverse selection for ethnic minorities, the underprivileged, and the aged.

The Kaiser-Permanente Studies

Before the first Malan report (1963), and between that and the second report (1976), the work at Kaiser-Permanente was demonstrating that psychotherapy could be provided as an insurance benefit to everyone, without preselection criteria. Kaiser-Permanente experimented with a number of attempts to provide long-term therapy for all its members who manifested emotional distress. This effort began with an initial bias that short-term psychotherapy is not as effective as long-term psychotherapy. It was additionally burdened with the discovery that providing easily available comprehensive health services as part of a prepaid plan fostered the somatization of emotional problems, with the consequent overutilization of medical facilities by patients who had no physical illness. The Kaiser-Permanente effort caused a number of problems (which were present in most traditional clinics of the time); these problems included a long waiting list, a high dropout rate, and an only partially successful attempt to reduce the ever-growing waiting list by providing crisis intervention. It was not until a series of evaluative studies were begun, spanning 15 years, that an efficient, cost-therapeutically effective treatment system emerged. The following is a brief summary of this research.

In the first of a series of investigations into the relationship between psychological services and medical utilization in a prepaid health plan setting, Follette and Cummings (1967) compared the number and type of medical services sought before and after the intervention of psychotherapy in a large group of randomly selected patients. The outpatient and inpatient medical utilization for the year prior to the initial interview in the Department of Psychotherapy as well as for the 5 years following was studied for three groups of psychotherapy patients (those who had one interview only, those who underwent brief therapy with a mean of 6.2 interviews, and those who received long-term therapy with a mean of 33.9 interviews) and a control group of matched patients demonstrating similar criteria of distress but not seen in psychotherapy in the 6 years under study. The findings indicated that (a) persons in emotional distress were significantly higher users of both inpatient and outpatient medical facilities as compared to the health plan average; (b) there were significant declines in medical utilization in those emotionally distressed individuals who received psychotherapy as compared to a control group of matched emotionally distressed health plan members who were not accorded psychotherapy; (c) these declines remained constant during the 5 years following the termination of psychotherapy; (d) the most significant declines occurred in the second year after the initial interview, and those patients receiving one session only or brief psychotherapy (two to eight sessions) did not require additional psychotherapy to maintain the lower level of utilization for 5 years; and (e) patients seen 2 years or more in regular psychotherapy demonstrated no overall decline in total outpatient utilization, inasmuch as psychotherapy visits tended to supplant medical visits. However, there was a significant decline in inpatient utilization in the long-term therapy group, from an initial hospitalization rate several times that of the health plan average to a level comparable to that of the general adult health plan population.

In a subsequent study, Cummings and Follette (1968) found that intensive efforts to increase the number of referrals to psychotherapy by computerizing psychological screening, with early detection and alerting of the attending physicians, did not increase significantly the number of patients seeking psychotherapy. The authors concluded that in a prepaid health plan setting already maximally employing educative techniques for both patients and physicians and already providing a range of prepaid psychological services, the number of health plan subscribers seeking psychotherapy reaches an optimal level and remains fairly constant thereafter.

In summarizing 16 years of prepaid experience, Cummings and Follette (1968) demonstrated that there is no basis for the fear that an increased demand for psychotherapy will financially endanger the system, for it is not the number of referrals received that will drive costs up but the manner in which psychotherapy services are delivered that determines optimal cost-therapeutic effectiveness. The finding that one session only, with no repeat psychological visits, can reduce medical utilization by 60% over the following 5 years was surprising and totally unexpected. Equally surprising was the 75% reduction in medical utilization over a 5-year period in those patients initially receiving two to eight psychotherapy sessions (brief therapy).

In a further study, Cummings and Follette (1976) sought to determine in an 8-year telephone follow-up whether the results described previously were a therapeutic effect, the consequence of extraneous factors, or a deleterious effect. It was hypothesized that if better understanding of his or her problem had occurred in the psychotherapeutic sessions, the patient would recall the actual problem rather than the presenting symptom and would have both lost the presenting symptom and coped more effectively with the real problem.

The results suggest that the reduction in medical utilization was the consequence of resolving the emotional distress that was being reflected in physical symptoms and visits to the doctor. The modal patient in this 8-year follow-up may be described as follows: He or she denies ever having consulted a physician for the physical symptoms for which he or she had been originally referred. Rather, the actual problem discussed with the psychotherapist is recalled as the reason for the "psychiatric" visit, and although the problem is resolved, this resolution is attributed to the patient's own efforts and no credit is given the psychotherapist. This affirms the contention that the reduction in medical utilization reflected the diminution in the emotional distress which had been expressed in symptoms that were presented to the physician.

Cost-Therapeutic-Effectiveness Ratio

Demonstrating that savings in medical services offset the cost of providing psychotherapy answers the question of cost effectiveness, but the services provided must also be therapeutic, that is, they must reduce the patient's emotional distress. That both cost *and* therapeutic effectiveness were demonstrated in the Kaiser-Permanente studies was attributed by the investigators to the therapist's expectation that emotional distress could be alleviated by brief, active psychotherapy that involved the analysis of transference and resistance and the uncovering of unconscious conflicts, and had all the characteristics of long-term therapy except length. Given this orientation, it was found over a 5-year period that 84.6% of the patients seen in psychotherapy chose to come 15 sessions or less, with a mean of 8.6, and rather than regarding these as "dropouts" from treatment, it was found on follow-up that they had achieved a satisfactory state of emotional well-being that continued to the 8-year follow-up. This finding is in total agreement with Malan's (1976) Tavistock studies, with the exception that Kaiser-Permanente used no preselection criteria but saw every patient who presented him/herself for treatment without regard to such factors as age, motivation, or duration and severity of symptoms.

The serendipitous finding that therapeutic outcome correlates highly with reduction in medical utilization is understandable in view of the earlier findings that in a prepaid, comprehensive health system the physician's lack of empathy for symptoms of emotional distress encourages the patient to somatize the distress, for which the reward is the physician's interest and attention. Complaining to one's physician that "my boss is on my back" usually elicits impatience from the medical doctor, whereas a low back pain results in X-rays, laboratory visits, consultations with specialists, and return visits. But in addition, this finding yields a reliable, quantifiable index of therapeutic effectiveness that does not suffer from the subjectivity of most criteria. By dividing the medical utilization for the full year prior to psychotherapy (as calculated by Follette and Cummings in their 1967 study) by the medical utilization for the full year following the initial psychotherapy visit *plus* the year's number of such visits yields this ratio of cost-therapeutic effectiveness:

$$\frac{\text{Medical utilization for year before}}{\text{Medical utilization for year after} + \text{Number of psychotherapy visits}} = \begin{array}{c}\text{Ratio of}\\ \text{cost-therapeutic}\\ \text{effectiveness}\end{array}$$

The higher the ratio, the greater is the effectiveness of therapy. Separate ratios can be calculated for inpatient (hospital) and outpatient utilization, or they can be combined by using a cost-weighting factor for the days of hospitalization.

When Is Long-Term Therapy Deleterious?

At Kaiser-Permanente the cost-therapeutic-effectiveness ratios for various populations are these: (a) very brief psychotherapy, comprising 56% of all patients (1 to 4 sessions, with a mean of 3.8), 2.59; (b) brief psychotherapy, comprising 84.6% of all patients (1 to 15 sessions, with a mean of 8.6), 2.11; (c) long-term psychotherapy, comprising 10.1% of all patients (more than 16 sessions, with a mean of 19.2), 1.14; (d) "interminable" psychotherapy, comprising 5.3% of all patients (with special characteristics described below and with a mean of 47.9 sessions per year), .91; and (e) a matched control sample of patients in distress not receiving psychotherapy, .88. The "interminable" patient, though reducing inpatient utilization from several times that of the health plan average to average, merely supplanted frequent outpatient medical visits

Table 1: *Averages of Outpatient Medical Visits Only, Psychotherapy Visits Only, and Combined Averages (Outpatient Medical plus Physcotherapy Visits) for the "Interminable" Subgroup Under Three Conditions of Psychotherapeutic Frequency for the Year Before and the 2 Years After the Initial Psychotherapy Visit*

Condition	No. of Patients	1-B[a]	1-A[b]	2-A[c]
Outpatient medical visits				
One time a week	8	11.2	6.5	7.2
Two times a week	6	12.4	15.1	15.6
Three times a week	7	11.8	18.2	17.4
Psychotherapy visits				
One time a week	8	—	39.3	41.7
Two times a week	6	—	77.2	78.6
Three times a week	7	—	117.9	114.3
Combined outpatient medical and psychotherapy visits				
One time a week	8	11.2	45.8	48.9
Two times a week	6	12.4	92.3	94.2
Three times a week	7	11.8	136.1	131.7

[a] 1-B = One year before initial psychotherapy visit.
[b] 1-A = One year after initial psychotherapy visit.
[c] 2-A = Two years after initial psychotherapy visit.

with weekly psychotherapy, resulting in a cost-therapeutic-effectiveness ratio not significantly better than that of the control group. This population became a concern of the researchers that was the basis for further investigation. In studying the clinical characteristics of these patients, it was found that they manifested a pan-anxiety and closely fitted the diagnostic entity of pseudoneurotic schizophrenia. Once this population and its characteristics were identified, the researchers undertook the broader problem of how to provide a cost-therapeutically effective treatment.

Beginning with an understandable but unwarranted preconception, it was postulated that increasing the intensity (frequency) of the treatment would bring the psychotherapy of these "interminable" patients to an early and successful conclusion. Further defined, the problem seemed to be one of finding the optimal increase in intensity that would prove cost-therapeutically effective. Therefore, a new group of patients presenting themselves for psychotherapy, who demonstrated all of the characteristics of the "interminable" subgroup, were divided into once-a-week, twice-a-week, and three-times-a-week psychotherapy. All had the same diagnosis, and there was an attempt to match them on demographic characteristics. The outpatient and inpatient medical utilization of these patients was studied for the year before and each of the two years following the initial psychotherapy visit. There were 23 patients; 2 withdrew from the clinic prior to the conclusion of the research, leaving 21 experimental patients. This was the sum total of such patients who presented themselves for psychotherapy during a 6-month period. None were excluded, except the 2 aforementioned patients who left the clinic. Since that time a replication with a larger sample was begun, and preliminary results are comparable to those reported here.

Although the investigators anticipated a dramatic initial rise in combined utilization (medical plus psychotherapy visits) because of the doubling and tripling of the frequency of psychotherapy visits, they were not prepared for (a) a concomitant rise in outpatient medical utilization with (b) a failure to rapidly conclude psychotherapy, even within the 2 years of the study. Further, the largest concomitant increase

in outpatient medical utilization was demonstrated by the three-times-a-week psychotherapy patients, with the lowest outpatient medical utilization being found in the one-time-a-week psychotherapy patients. As can be seen in Table 1, the combined (outpatient medical plus psychotherapy) utilization strongly suggests that a different method of managing and treating these patients may be indicated.

In studying the data it was observed that 2 patients, one each in the two-times-a-week and three-times-a-week psychotherapy groups, had failed to keep a majority of their appointments, and this resulted in an average number of psychotherapy visits even below the average for the one-time-a-week psychotherapy group. Surprisingly, these 2 patients had the lowest outpatient medical utilization. The question remained whether these 2 patients just generally did not seek physician visits or whether the planned reduced frequency of psychotherapy visits resulted in the reduction in outpatient medical utilization (all doctors' visits other than psychotherapy).

The investigators decided to initiate drastically curtailed frequencies of psychother-

Table 2: *Averages of Outpatient Medical Visits Only, Psychotherapy Visits Only, and Combined Averages (Outpatient Medical plus Psychotherapy Visits) for the "Interminable" Subgroup in its Third Year After Initiation of Psychotherapy Under Four Conditions of Frequency of Psychotherapy Visits*

Condition	No. of Patients	3-A[a]
Outpatient medical visits		
1–3 times a week	11	13.7
Monthly	3	5.6
Bimonthly	3	5.0
Quarterly	4	5.8
Psychotherapy visits		
1–3 times a week	11	64.8
Monthly	3	10.2
Bimonthly	3	5.1
Quarterly	4	3.6
Combined outpatient medical and psychotherapy visits		
1–3 times a week	11	78.5
Monthly	3	15.8
Bimonthly	3	10.1
Quarterly	4	9.4

3-A = Third year after initiation of psychotherapy.

apy visits in the same patients who had been seen once, twice, and three times a week. Beginning in the third year *after* the initial psychotherapy visit, and with the cooperation of the psychotherapists, the patients were seen at 30-, 60-, and 90-day intervals. Because of therapists' resistance, less than half of the patients were placed in the new spacing, leaving the remainder to serve as a contrasting group. Again, to the surprise of the investigators, the drastically reduced frequency of psychotherapy visits resulted in significantly reduced outpatient medical utilization (all doctor visits excluding psychotherapy), with the 30-, 60-, and 90-day frequencies being equally effective, perhaps because the patients were essentially permitted to self-select the exact curtailed frequency. These results are shown in Table 2.

Summary

A decade and a half of clinical experience and research at Kaiser-Permanente has demonstrated that not only can psychotherapy be economically provided in a comprehensive, prepaid health system but failure to do so places a cost burden on medical facilities by the 60% of the physican visits made by patients who demonstrate emotional rather than organic symptoms. Reduction in medical utilization by such patients correlates with effective therapy, rendering a quantifiable measure of therapeutic outcome. Effective treatment must demonstrate both economic feasibility and therapeutic success, and a method of eliciting a cost-therapeutic-effectiveness ratio is described.

When active, dynamic brief therapy is provided, it is the treatment of choice for 84.6% of the psychotherapy patients. It not only yields a high cost-therapeutic-effectiveness ratio but it is satisfactory to both the patient, in increased emotional well-being, and to the patient's physician, in dramatic reduction of somatization and overutilization of medical facilities. Further, providing such brief therapy makes it economically feasible to provide long-term psychotherapy to the 10.1% of the patients who require it.

With the 5.3% of the psychotherapy patients termed "interminable" for lack of a better word, long-term psychotherapy was found to be ineffective, increased frequency was deleterious, and the spacing of sessions to once every 30, 60, or 90 days yielded optimal cost-therapeutic effectiveness.

To the extent that the Kaiser-Permanente findings are applicable to prepaid, comprehensive health settings generally, there would be implications as to how the delivery of mental health services under a national health insurance program would be fashioned. The inescapable conclusion is that cost-therapeutic effectiveness must be the result of constant evaluation and monitoring, but within such a context, a mental health benefit with an emphasis on brief psychotherapy is a feasible and necessary component of a successful comprehensive health plan.

References

Alexander, F., & French, T. M. *Psychoanalytic therapy.* New York: Ronald Press, 1946.

Cummings, N. A. The health model as entree to the human services model in psychotherapy. *The Clinical Psychologist, 29,* 1975, 19–22.

Cummings, N. A., & Follette, W. T. Psychiatric services and medical utilization in a prepaid health plan setting. Part II. *Medical Care, 5,* 1968, 31–41.

Cummings, N. A., & Follette, W. T. Brief psychotherapy and medical utilization: An eight-year follow-up. In H. Dorken & Associates. *The professional psychologist today: New developments in law, health insurance and health practice.* San Francisco: Jossey-Bass, 1976.

Follette, W. T., & Cummings, N. A. Psychiatric services and medical utilization in a prepaid health plan setting. *Medical Care, 5,* 1967, 25–35.

Humphreys, L. Should psychotherapy be included in national health insurance: The con argument. *APA Monitor,* September-October, 1973.

Malan, D. H. *A study of brief psychotherapy.* New York: Plenum Press, 1963.

Malan, D. H. *The frontier of brief psychotherapy.* New York: Plenum Press, 1976.

Sue, S. Community mental health services to minority groups: Some optimism, some pessimism. *American Psychologist,* 1977, *32,* 616–624.

Trotter, Sharland. Insuring psychotherapy: A subsidy to the rich? *APA Monitor,* November 1976, pp. 1; 16.

At the time of original publication of this article, *Nicholas A. Cummings* was Chief Psychologist at the Kaiser Foundation Hospital and the Permanente Medical Group, San Francisco.

Evaluation of Psychological Service Delivery Programs: The State of the Art

Robert Perloff and Evelyn Perloff

This article highlights the current state of knowledge on the evaluation of psychological service delivery programs. It also features some of the challenges of evaluation research. Additionally, it summarizes the salient features of 21 substantive articles comprising this Special Issue (November 1977) of Professional Psychology. *These articles are concerned with evaluation research methodology; selected evaluation considerations indigenous to psychological service delivery systems; and the support, evaluation, and findings of designated service delivery programs. These service delivery programs focus upon community mental health centers, children's treatment facilities, alcoholism, drug abuse, vocational rehabilitation, the psychology department clinic, and the evaluation of training in organizational settings.*

In our view, the two principal phenomena spearheading the growth and importance of evaluation research are rooted solidly in America's humanitarian and democratic traditions and values.

The Humanitarian Root of Program Evaluation

The first phenomenon is the nation's concern—and some would lament that we are not concerned enough—for the plight of the poor, the handicapped, and the economically and socially neglected and abused, as well as the nation's concern for spreading the benefits of technology and social inventions to the people at large. Translated into concrete, action programs, the foregoing abstractions are identified as a variety of welfare, job training, reading disability, mental health, housing, and other programs intended to help our people increase their economic and educational opportunities, decrease illness and environmental blight, and to make people happier, healthier, and more hopeful about their futures. These desirable outcomes would, for the most part, derive from legislation authorizing massive federal programs.

If it were not for the huge outlays of money, time, and energy needed to achieve these ends, there clearly would be no need to evaluate programs in order to decide how best to invest money and other resources or to determine the feasibility of supporting programs that, on the face of it, would appear to be equally important.

The Consumerism Root

The second phenomenon responsible, we believe, for the prominence of program evaluation and evaluation research is equally rooted in democractic values: the consumer movement. The consumer movement implies in a very real sense the centrality of the consumer in educational, economic, or social program decision making. For example, in higher education a conspicuous illustration of evaluation research is in the evaluation of teaching effectiveness. Make no mistake about it, it was the *consumer* of education, the student, who began to agitate for evaluation, *not* the manufacturer or seller of the information, not the university or the professor. If the dissatisfied student had not begun to raise all kinds of hell about the quality of instruction, you can rest assured that the complacent teacher

Reprinted from *Professional Psychology*, 1977, *8*, 379–388.

would not have insisted on evaluating his or her teaching.

This may sound chauvinistic, but we believe that it was predictable in our democratic society, where inputs from all constituencies are sanctioned, that the consumers of services—education, health services, you name it—would eventually insist on having a critical say in how those services are packaged, delivered, and evaluated.

We make the point that these twin phenomena—(a) sympathy for the human condition and the quest to improve it and (b) consumer or program beneficiary involvement in program modification or even survival—are responsible for the fact that program evaluation may be a growth industry for two reasons. Not only may this hypothesis be of interest in its own right, but, more practically, we believe it is essential to remember the role of the consumer in evaluation research. When we forget these antecedents of evaluation research, we are failing to fully understand the nature of the programs we are called upon to evaluate, the underlying objectives of these programs, and that among the cast of players staging an evaluation performance, perhaps the consumer is the one who must be given star billing.

We believe that a rigorous content analysis of most of the articles in this Special Issue would show that the problems, failures, challenges, or needed research in evaluation may have their origins in humanitarianism and consumer solicitude, and in the accountability implied by these objectives.

Objectives of this Special Issue

Although there is much recent literature in the field of evaluation research (Bernstein, 1975; Cooley & Lohnes, 1976; Dolbeare, 1975; Dressel, 1976; Glass, 1976; Guttentag & Struening, 1975; Perloff, Perloff, & Sussna, 1976; Struening & Guttentag, 1975; Hammer, Landsberg, & Neigher, Note 1; Landsberg & Hammer, Note 2; Neigher, Hammer, & Landsberg, Note 3), our peregrinations in program evaluation suggest strongly that a most useful purpose would be served if articles were developed explictly to focus upon special features

of evaluation technology applicable for special fields. The field with which we are concerned herein is the delivery of psychological services. The evaluation literature reveals that a great deal has been written about evaluating educational programs and about economic and social welfare programs. We do not claim that the evaluation literature has failed to take note of the evaluation of psychological services including mental health, but we do assert that less concerted attention has been given to psychological services—especially in the sense of the needs and interests of the reader of this journal. Therefore, we undertook to compile a series of articles, written by leaders in psychological services and evaluation research, that would highlight the techniques, issues, and unfulfilled needs vis-à-vis the evaluation of psychological services.

Organization of this Special Issue

This issue is organized into three major categories: (a) selected processes for evaluating service delivery programs, (b) considerations indigenous to the evaluation of service delivery programs, and (c) the support, evaluation, and findings of selected service delivery programs. (These three major sections are exclusive of the editor's introductory comments and of the present article.) Each of these sections is introduced by an overview that summarizes and highlights the section's contents. These overviews not only provide some measure of perspective and integration of the substantive articles contained in each section, but they also include cautions to the reader about the omission of articles that may have been appropriate for the section or about conceptual issues not covered by the authors of the substantive articles.

The First Section—Selected Evaluation Processes

The first section, Selected Processes for Evaluating Service Delivery Programs, contains six articles. These articles aggregate for the reader methodologies, concepts, and needs more or less basic to evaluation research as a field and not necessarily uniquely salient for the evaluation of psychological service delivery. They present some of the basic notions for conducting evaluation research, measuring program benefits, undertaking a zero-base budgeting system, and reducing resistance to change.

The Second Section—Indigenous Considerations

The second section, Considerations Indigenous to the Evaluation of Service Delivery Programs, offers five substantive articles whose evaluation concepts begin to move closer to problems and needs central to the services of primary interest. However, these five articles do not really (at least not explicitly) deal with particular service delivery systems per se. For example, one article in this section addresses the fundamental issue of whether one should even engage in the task of evaluating psychotherapy, whereas another considers the utilization of mental health evaluation research findings. (We have occasion later in the present article to offer some information complementing the article on utilization.)

The Third Section—Selected Service Delivery Programs

The final section, The Support, Evaluation, and Findings of Selected Service Delivery Programs, is a sampling of quite specific and explicitly designated service delivery programs, including the funding, the evaluation, and a rather richer array of actual findings than we had initially anticipated.

The specific delivery programs sampled are those in community mental health centers; facilities providing treatment for children, alcoholism, and drug abuse and providing vocational rehabilitation; the psychology department clinic; and the evaluation of training in organizational settings.

Ethics and Confidentiality

Earlier in this article we opined that the support and interest of modern evaluation research in part stem from the solicitude we have in our democratic society for helping people, rehabilitating them, elevating skill levels, overcoming deficiencies, and otherwise bettering the human condition. Missing from the foregoing litany of ways in which the person's condition might be enhanced are such variables as self-concept and self-esteem. Frequently overlooked by the evaluation research community—in its noble aspiration to achieve improvements for *groups* of people—is the fact that the process of evaluation may have a dehumanizing effect on the person. We report that the overall findings of an evaluation research study may have a salutary effect on a stratum or on people as a group, but it is likely that the price of this group benefit is that some individuals, in the process of an evaluation, are told directly or indirectly that they are inadequate in one way or another.

Thus, in an article on accountability and humanism, Splittgerber and Trueblood (1975) list three aspects of the evaluation process in the educational arena that lack humanism. They first point out that teacher accountability (at least in the opinions of teachers) places major responsibility for success or failure in the classroom squarely on the teachers themselves. They feel that they are neither trusted nor trustworthy, since accountability is so emphasized by school administrators and school boards. A second point offered by Splittgerber and Trueblood speaks to the objectives themselves. Humanists object to the predetermination of educational objectives but neglect to encourage an initial evaluation of the "worth" of the objectives. The objectives (frequently administratively determined) are most likely to be group oriented, with the result that attention to individual differences, and hence to the real needs of students, is minimized. The third and last criticism of accountability that these authors attribute to humanists is that the very process of evaluating requires "the kind of superior-subordinate relationship which produces power struggles, poor communication and institutional paranoia" (Splittgerber & Trueblood, 1975, p. 23).

For us, these three criticisms of accountability are very real. We cannot easily dismiss this demeaning of the individual. Like Splittgerber and Trueblood, however, we must also censure humanists for not accepting their responsibility (a) for helping to improve program evaluation by seeking to be more objective, explicit, and operational in what they wish to promote in education and (b) for not developing instruments appropriate for measuring the affective variables they consider so basic for developing and reinforcing meaningful understanding among individuals and groups in our society. Because humanistic values are of the highest order, they cannot be dismissed in educational program evaluation, and they are even more important in psychological services evaluations.

We suspect that other ethical and/or confidentiality issues also fail to consider this dehumanizing factor in accountability procedures. Thus, concern for treatment of participants in evaluation research studies is a very recent consideration. Past researchers were not required to obtain permission from school, agency, or hospital review committees before undertaking evaluation research. The project director was in charge, and all signals were "go." But this is not so today. Many weeks must be allotted for obtaining initial permission to conduct a study to determine that participants will not be psychologically and/or physically harmed. In addition, of course, there must be guarantees that the privacy of participating individuals—students, employees, clients—has been protected. Again, a number of creative and carefully conceived techniques (Astin & Boruch, 1970; Boruch, 1972; Boruch, Note 4) can be followed to assure privacy and confidentiality for each and every participant. Although some additional costs may accrue in this regard, we believe that there can be no justification for failure to consider these essential ethical and confidentiality issues. In fact, we can think of almost no conditions that we would tolerate in evaluation research studies that permitted negative (harmful) intrusion and/or invasion of the human condition. That is, the ends do not always justify the means: We envision that the cost of breaching confidentiality and ignoring client rights and feelings would exceed any benefit. Insensitivity to client rights is simply not cost effective.

Evaluation Research Utilization

Some of the articles in this issue refer to the need to do a better job of promoting the utilization of evaluation research findings. Cohen (1977) speaks directly to this need. Comple-menting Cohen's discussion of communication channels for optimizing the utilization of evaluation research findings, Ball and Anderson (1977) view the utilization process as one that is more explicitly understood, and hence capable of being successful, if particularly detailed attention is given to two essential consequences of evaluation: dissemination and communication.

Three special considerations of dissemination are discussed by Ball and Anderson (1977). The process of dissemination needs to start much earlier in the evaluation process than it does. Typically, dissemination is tacked on at the conclusion of an evaluation, a tactic that Ball and Anderson say may well lead to ineffective communication and hence poor utilization. Rather, dissemination is a process that should occur *during* the evaluation study, helping program personnel make program modification *formatively* (affecting the ongoing evaluation) and not only summatively (affecting the end results of the study).

These authors distinguish between dissemination and communication by identifying communication as the generic context of dissemination. They provide an intriguing table that matches communication forms with potential audiences. Among their 10 communication forms are a technical report, a popular article, and a public meeting. Anderson and Ball list 14 potential audiences, 3 of which are program administrators, interested community groups, and national media. According to their scheme, the best communication forms for disseminating evaluation results to funding agencies are the technical report and an executive summary, whereas the best way to disseminate results to national media is by news releases and press conferences.

In addition to faulty dissemination strategies and inappropriate communication forms, utilization of evaluation results is frequently moribund because the original program evaluation research budget simply does not include enough money to meaningfully undertake a utilization effort. Utilization may all too often be viewed as something beyond evaluation and not quite the province of anyone. Hence, with no one clearly responsible for undertaking utilization, it is not surprising that utilization is frequently not undertaken in the first instance.

Concluding Remarks

When we included the phrase "state of the art" in our article title, we intended that the present article would serve as a synoptic perspective to the 21 articles comprising this issue. The three sections of this Special Issue are discussed in greater detail in the introductory overviews. There is, however, more to be said about the current status of evaluation research. We feel that some useful purpose can be served by pinpointing the more salient characteristics of where we are today in evaluating psychological service delivery programs and by identifying some of the gaps that need to be filled.

Current Status

Our strengths in evaluation research technology are many. First, there are numerous models extant for conducting evaluations systematically and, in many cases, rigorously. Probably, as Riecken (1977) and Schulberg (1977) suggest, the most scientific methods—and those most accepted by the scientific community—are experimental design and quasi-experimental design. There are, of course, other methods for making evaluation inquiries and conducting evaluation research (Perloff et al., 1976).

Regardless of the approach that the investigator employs to conduct an evaluation study, a number of common auxiliaries to research may be used that transcend the kind of design or other approach guiding an evaluation. Most of these have been worked out fairly thoroughly and are at a stage of sophistication that enables us to use these accessories to research confidently and competently. These accessories include sophisticated laboratory procedures, methods of observing behavior, interviewing techniques, analytical tools such as statistics and computer programs, and a rather sophisticated knowledge of the ways to measure and interpret individual differences.

A comparatively new analytic tool that shows great promise and, indeed, has already paid off handsomely in several studies, is what is known as *Secondary analysis.* Secondary analysis involves a consideration of the validity of the original program for which a primary or initial analysis was conducted, a reconceptualization or

redesign of the original program, and a reanalysis of emerging evaluation data in light of this new design. A recent illustration of secondary analysis is offered by Wortman and St. Pierre (1977).

Some Voids In Evaluation Research

Although psychologists deserve a great deal of credit for the giant strides they have taken in developing measurement as a rigorous and sophisticated technology, Boruch and Gomez (1977) point out some critical needs in the measurement area, particularly with respect to treatment measurements and to the individual's response to treatments.

Needed also, we believe, is a taxonomy and a listing of instruments that are or could be used in evaluation studies. When all is said and done, the instrument is the cornerstone of an evaluation. By instrument we mean tests of ability, achievement, and of whatever skills are central to a treatment strategy; scales for measuring attitudes, values, and personality characteristics; and perhaps most important of all, checklists and questionnaires recording client and agency characteristics, which are probably used more often in evaluation research than any other kind of instrument. Many instruments have been tailor-made for specific evaluation studies, but we suspect that many of these same instruments, with but slight changes, could be used in other evaluation studies. If there were a taxonomy and listing of these questionnaires and other instruments, would presently planned studies benefit—not to mention save money—by using already developed instruments and forms that might have normative data and even some indications of reliability and validity? Unfortunately, we suspect that, for the most part, many instruments currently used in evaluation studies possess little validity or reliability, thus making the generalization and utilization of evaluation results difficult.

Another void in evaluation research, which has been suggested by others, is how better to take into account in evaluation studies the political nature of social and psychological service delivery programs, all of which have constituencies and pressure groups favoring this or that objective or client population.

Similarly, the problem facing all evaluators when they encounter anxiety and distrust on the part of program personnel is one that demands thoughtful attention for two reasons. First, individuals so threatened are inclined to conceal data or to provide incorrect or distorted information, which would affect seriously the accuracy of an evaluation. Next, as we suggested earlier in our discussion of ethics and confidentiality, we would hope that efforts are made to anticipate how an evaluation might create anxieties or stress for the people involved in an evaluation. We should not dismiss lightly this kind of harm that is sustained by the participants in an evaluation study.

We realize that the state of the art sketched here, along with the 21 substantive articles that follow, requires a considerable investment of readers' time, both in learning about evaluation research and in putting it into practice. If the payoff from this collective effort is even a quite modest increase in our profession's capacity to deliver services and to make individual clients a bit less wretched or, put positively, somewhat more fulfilled, then we believe the time will have been worthwhile. It is this optimistic expectation that motivated us in our role as guest co-editors of this Special Issue.

Reference Notes

1. Hammer, R., Landsberg, G., & Neigher, W. (Eds.). *Program evaluation in community mental health centers.* New York: Program Analysis & Evaluation Section, Maimonides Community Mental Health Center, 1977. (Available from Maimonides CMHC, Program Analysis & Evaluation Section, 4802 10th Avenue, Brooklyn, New York 11219.)
2. Landsberg, G., & Hammer, R. J. *Measuring the community impact of mental health services: A preliminary workbook.* New York: Program Analysis & Evaluation Section, Maimonides Community Mental Health Center, 1977. (Available from Maimonides CMHC, Program Analysis & Evaluation Section, 4802 10th Avenue, Brooklyn, New York 11219.)
3. Neigher, W., Hammer, R., & Landsberg, G. *Emerging developments in mental health program evaluation.* New York: Program Analysis & Evaluation Section, Maimonides Community Mental Health Center, 1977. (Available from Maimonides CMHC, Program Analysis & Evaluation Section, 4802 10th Avenue, Brooklyn, New York 11219.)
4. Boruch, R. F. *Costs, benefits, and legal implications of methods for assuring confidentiality in social research.* Evanston, Ill.: Northwestern University, Evaluation Research Program, Project on Secondary Analysis, August 1974.

References

Astin, A. W., & Boruch, R. F. A "link" system for assuring confidentiality of research data in longitudinal studies. *American Educational Research Journal,* 1970, *7.* 615–624.
Ball, S., & Anderson, S. B. Dissemination, communication, and utilization. *Education & Urban Society,* 1977, *IX,* 451–470.
Bernstein, I. N. (Ed.). *Validity issues in evaluative research.* Beverly Hills, Calif.: Sage, 1975.
Boruch, R. F. Strategies for eliciting and merging confidential social research data. *Policy Sciences,* 1972, *3,* 275–297.
Boruch, R. F., & Gomez, H. Sensitivity, bias, and theory in impact evaluations. *Professional Psychology,* 1977, *8,* 411–434.
Cohen, L. H. Factors affecting the utilization of mental health evaluation research findings. *Professional Psychology,* 1977, *8,* 526–534.
Cooley, W. W., & Lohnes, P. R. *Evaluation research in education.* New York: Irvington, 1976.
Dolbeare, K. M. (Ed.). *Public policy evaluation* (Vol. 2). Beverly Hills, Calif.: Sage, 1975.
Dressel, P. L. *Handbook of academic evaluation.* San Francisco: Jossey-Bass, 1976.
Glass, G. V. (Ed.). *Evaluation studies* (Vol. 1). Beverly Hills. Calif.: Sage, 1976.
Guttentag, M., & Struening, E. L. *Handbook of evaluation research* (Vol. 2). Beverly Hills, Calif.: Sage, 1975.
Perloff, R., Perloff, E., & Sussna, E. Program evaluation. *Annual Review of Psychology,* 1976, *27,* 569–574.
Riecken, H. W. Principal components of the evaluation process. *Professional Psychology,* 1977, *8,* 392–410.
Schulberg, H. C. Issues in the evaluation of community mental health programs. *Professional Psychology,* 1977, *8,* 560–572.
Splittgerber, F., & Trueblood, R. Accountability and humanism. *Educational Technology,* 1975, *15*(2), 22–26.
Struening, E. L., & Guttentag, M. *Handbook of evaluation research* (Vol. 1). Beverly Hills, Calif.: Sage, 1975.
Wortman, P. M., & St. Pierre, R. G. The educational voucher demonstration: A secondary analysis. *Education & Urban Society,* 1977, *IX,* 471–492.

At the time of original publication of this article, *Robert Perloff* was a professor with the Graduate School of Business, and *Evelyn Perloff* was an associate professor, School of Nursing, at the University of Pittsburgh, Pittsburgh.

Psychology and Accounting: An Interface or a Red Face

The need for the involvement of the psychologist in cost accounting, cost-effectiveness analysis, and program evaluation is emphasized. The psychologist's unique training in the fields of measurement and research provide the necessary skills for involvement in cost-effectiveness and evaluation research. It is argued that in the area of human services, in which benefits and effectiveness are frequently assessed in terms of social costs and benefits rather than dollars and cents, the psychologist is the most qualified professional for undertaking such studies. The implications of psychologists' noninvolvement in cost-effectiveness analysis are discussed, as well as the training and research implications of psychologists' involvement.

Today more and more emphasis is being placed on accountability. The existing energy crisis clearly demonstrates that limits on resources do exist. As our economy has slowed and fewer and fewer resources have been available for the establishment of new programs and the expansion of existing activities, American society has turned to a reassessment of its priorities, the costs and returns of various programs, and the effectiveness and efficiency of a multitude of operations. Nowhere has this emphasis on assessment been more evident than in the myriad of social intervention programs that currently permeate our society. Educational, welfare, medical, and mental health programs have all been subjected to increasing scrutiny. This article focuses on the issue of accountability in the mental health field.

Iscoe (1974) has recently addressed the need for program evaluation and has warned that the criteria for the evaluation of mental health programs may well be developed by individuals who are trained and experienced in the accounting discipline. Nelson (1975) has amplified this concern and delineated the dangers associated with allowing accountants to develop evaluation criteria without substantial input from psychologists. Unfortunately, the evaluative systems presently being developed by

management scientists are both highly marketable to administrators and legislators and somewhat naive. Generally these evaluative criteria involve some sort of cost-effort ratio, in which cost is measured in dollars and cents and effort is measured in time spent in an activity. Such indexes as cost per patient per day or cost per patient per week, staff-patient ratios, length of stay in a residential facility, or number of contacts per patient in an outpatient setting become the standards by which resources are allocated and personnel assigned. Indeed, these are the very indexes used to justify expenditures within most mental health settings today. However, Mechanic (1969) has warned that these indexes are particularly vulnerable to administrative manipulation and therefore of questionable validity when taken alone.

Nelson (1975) has enunciated the results of examining mental health activities from a cost-effort standpoint. Long-term, low intensive care involving minimal individual psychotherapy and maximal paraprofessional and nonprofessional personnel is considerably less expensive than intensive care by professional mental health workers. Research is also a highly expensive activity, with relatively little payoff for treatment. Although some professionals, notably those of the medical profession, may be able to

Reprinted from *Professional Psychology,* 1977, *8,* 178–184.

justify the costs of at least some of their services (after all, relatively few persons will argue costs where saving a life or treating a serious physical disease are involved), psychologists find themselves in the embarrassing circumstance of being rather costly and largely unable to cite clear evidence of the efficacy of their work. The ambiguity within our own clinical literature attests to our lack of reasonably conclusive evidence in support of our endeavors. In fairness to the discipline, however, it should be noted that there is no reasonably conclusive evidence to indicate that we are ineffective. Psychologists have simply neglected the entire area of evaluation until quite recently, with some notable exceptions, and are now faced with proving the effectiveness of their involvement in a multitude of services. The consumer movement, government agencies, and insurance companies are demanding evidence of effectiveness as never before. This neglect of evaluation has been most evident in publicly financed applied settings, in which accountability is perhaps most essential.

The purpose of this article is not to argue that evaluation research should be done. The call for such research is already evident in psychological literature, along with an enumeration of the needs that motivate such research (Campbell, 1969; Iscoe, 1974; Nelson, 1975; Wortman, 1975). And evaluative research will be done regardless of whether psychologists become involved; accountants, systems analysts, public health administrators, and others are already involved. My purpose is to motivate psychologists and to point to some avenues of involvement.

Defining Costs and Benefits

The area of evaluative research to which psychologists have already made a most significant contribution is that of defining and measuring the benefits of the psychotherapeutic endeavor. The number of psychometric instruments on the market and reported in the literature readily attests to this contribution. Nearly all clinicians have relatively specific goals for individual clients and some criterion, at least at an intuitive level, for judging the improvement of a particular case. In many cases there are also likely to

be instruments or procedures available for assessing improvement, though they may not be used. I do not wish to understate the need for further work or disregard the problems in this area, but psychologists are generally familiar with this level of analysis. The average psychologist is unlikely to be equipped to handle the area of defining costs, but, I must argue, no less so than other individuals, including accountants and management scientists.

The term *cost* generally brings to mind the dollar sign or related quantities, such as man-hours or resources expended, that can be readily converted to money spent. However, in mental health services, as in all social intervention activities, there are costs that are not so readily converted to dollar signs.

Arnhoff (1975) has recently addressed the issue of social costs accruing from the present nationwide emphasis on community treatment. Pointing to the potential long-term undesirable effects of the shift from residential care to community treatment of the severely psychotic individual, Arnhoff argued that these undesirable effects must be considered when evaluating the costs and effectiveness of any intervention procedure. Persons with managerial backgrounds are unlikely to be cognizant of potential social costs and are generally ill-prepared to measure such costs. Psychologists and sociologists are, in fact, better prepared to deal with these issues, and Smith (1961) has forcefully argued that psychologists can make a significant contribution to this area.

It therefore behooves the psychologist to demand a role in the development of a cost analysis framework. As was noted earlier, the cost-effort criterion often used by systems analysts is subject to misuse and may misrepresent actual events within the mental health setting. A more appropriate criterion for analysis is the cost-benefits ratio, in which costs now include not only fiscal expenditures and man-hours but also social costs, and benefits reflect the effectiveness of the intervention procedure for both the individual client and the larger community. Unfortunately, this frame of reference can become exceedingly complex, particularly for the legislator, administrator, or policymaker. To deal with this complexity, we must take two simultaneous tacks. We must make legislators and administrators aware of the complexity and the reasons for it, and we must attempt to simplify wherever possible.

Emphasizing and Simplifying Complexity

David (1975) has recently reacted to a call from a prominent federal legislator for "one-armed" scientists. The call was occasioned by testimony of scientists who insisted upon saying, "On the one hand, the evidence is this, but on the other hand. . . ." David argued that scientists must be willing to be equivocal when equivocality is called for, without being pressured into lending premature scientific credence to the decisions of policymakers and by so doing relieving the decision maker of the responsibility for the decision. As behavioral scientists we have an obligation to emphasize the complexity of human behavior. We must educate administrators, legislators, and the public at large so that they understand the assumptions, limitations, and implications of our discipline. The responsible approach requires proper qualification of empirical findings and theoretical constructs.

It is tempting to merely write off the work of systems analysts and accountants as naive and simplistic. However, we cannot fault individuals in other disciplines for effectively applying their skills. Management scientists have not only succeeded in providing quick, low-cost, and useful summations of large amounts of data but they have also succeeded in selling their systems to administrators. The kind of information provided by such systems—for example, how much it costs to treat x number of individuals, with y number of staff members, over time period z—is both valuable and necessary. However, I would argue that it is not sufficient, as would most psychologists. Unfortunately, not only have we not become involved in cost accounting research but we have done relatively little evaluative research. All this means is that it will now be more difficult and time consuming to develop and sell our own evaluative systems to decision makers.

One reason for the success of systems analysts has been their ability to provide a rapid description of large amounts of data in readily understood language. Accountants have been able to simplify complex relationships for the policymaker by providing a substantial amount of information in a compact form. If we as psychologists are to succeed in selling our evaluative programs, we cannot be content to merely escape into complexity. We must begin to understand that complexity and simplify it where possible. We must also be prepared to develop evaluative systems that provide almost immediate feedback. Administrators and legislators are unlikely to be willing to wait several years for the results of an evaluative study. Beyond the mere impatience of policymakers, we must also recognize that such a complex organization as a treatment facility will not be the same organization after the passage of several years. Our evaluative work must take this into account; our present efforts largely do not.

It has been argued elsewhere (Glass, Wilson, & Gottman, 1972; Nelson, 1975; Wortman, 1975) that the present methodology used in evaluating treatment procedures is not appropriate and may be misleading. However, the methodology does exist, at least in part, for use in large-scale evaluative programs. It is the same methodology used by the systems analysts and applied throughout much of industry. It is to that methodology that I now turn.

Operations Research

The loosely defined area known as operations research has perhaps the greatest potential applicability to evaluative and cost-accounting research in the mental health setting. Variously called quantitative methods, management science, or systems analysis, operations research is an interdisciplinary science drawing on applied mathematics, physics, biology, psychology, sociology, economics, and a variety of other disciplines for its base. This discipline provides the techniques necessary for summarizing large amounts of data. It sets up an explicit representative model of a given situation by means of formal mathematical models. The model is then used to make predictions of future events given certain parameters. These parameters may be based on existing historical data, hypothesized relationships, or a generated representation of some population distribution.

Many psychologists are already familiar with some of the procedures that fall into the realm of operations research. The time series designs, perhaps first introduced to psychologists by Campbell and Stanley (1963), have been receiving attention in our literature. Monte Carlo techniques have long been used by the methods specialists for examining properties of various statistics. The optimization, maximization, and minimization techniques of operations research bear strong similarities to the procedures employed in arriving at factor-analytic and other multivariate solutions, and in some cases, use the same mathematical operations. Markov chaining and other stochastic models have been applied to the development of learning theories. Computer simulations have been used to develop models of personality, decision making, and client-therapist interaction, to mention a few. Thus, the particular operations and procedures employed by the operations research specialist are not altogether unknown to psychologists. However, these procedures have not been widely applied to evaluative research in the clinical setting.

One reason for the limited application of operations research in the discipline of psychology has been the general lack of even an introduction to the area in most of our training programs. Even our industrial-organizational curriculums fail to provide a substantial amount of training in the area. We need to encourage some of our students to pursue courses and applied experience in the area of operations research. This encouragement might not only be given to our applied students but to our experimental students as well. With the present dearth of academic positions, just such skills might well qualify the more experimentally inclined student for a position in an applied setting. Indeed, Wortman (1975) has already suggested evaluative research as a potential market for our recent PhD recipients.

But obviously it is not necessary for every psychologist to be a methodologist to make substantial contributions to evaluation and accounting. Every operations research procedure, indeed every research problem, is based upon some model. Psychologists can and must contribute to mental health models. This is not easy. We must spend considerable time determining important parameters and then must sell the importance of those parameters to policymakers and legislators. We must also work closely with the management scientists as they develop their own models. We must be aware of what the accountants are doing. As a measurement-oriented specialty, we may be able to make substantial contributions to the quantification of many variables and help build evaluative research into cost-accounting research. It is possible to do effectiveness analysis and cost analysis independently. However, to do so may result in considerable embarrassment, and as Nelson stated (1975), we may find ourselves moving backwards in time.

References

Arnhoff, F. N. Social consequences of policy toward mental illness. *Science,* 1975, *188,* 1277–1281.

Campbell, D. T. Reforms as experiments. *American Psychologist,* 1969, *24,* 409–429.

Campbell, D. T., & Stanley, J. C. *Experimental and quasi-experimental designs for research.* Chicago: Rand-McNally, 1963.

David, E. E. One-armed scientists? *Science,* 1975, *189,* 679.

Glass, G. V., Wilson, V. L., & Gottman, J. M. *Design and analysis of time-series experiments.* Boulder, Colo.: Laboratory of Educational Research, 1972.

Iscoe, I. Community psychology and competent community. *American Psychologist,* 1974, *29,* 607–613.

Mechanic, D. *Public expectations and health care.* New York: Wiley-Interscience, 1969.

Nelson, R. H. Psychologists in administrative evaluation. *American Psychologist,* 1975, *30,* 707–708.

Smith, M. B. Mental health reconsidered: A special case of the problem of values in psychology. *American Psychologist,* 1961, *16,* 299–306.

Wortman, P. M. Evaluation research: A psychological perspective. *American Psychologist,* 1975, *30,* 562–575.

At the time of original publication of this article, *David W. Stewart* was a member of the Research Department of Needham, Harper, and Steers, Inc., Chicago.

An earlier version of this paper was presented to the Louisiana Psychological Association, October 24, 1975. The present version was completed while the author was a research psychologist at Central Louisiana State Hospital and was partially supported by U.S. Department of Health, Education, and Welfare Grant MH 22215.

Measuring Mental Health Program Benefits: Efficiency or Justice?

Edward Sussna

The conceptual issues in evaluating program benefits—where the example used is a community mental health center—are identified, illustrated, and discussed. The position is taken that the use of a monetary measure as a means for calibrating program benefits permits an assessment of intraprogram effects over time and makes possible interprogram comparisons. Examples are provided of economic benefits to individuals and communities, which appear to be reasonable conceptually and practically, as yardsticks against which program costs may be assessed. The expression of benefits in monetary terms also allows a program administrator to make comparisons among, and decisions relating to, specific program features. Considerations of income redistribution, equity, and consumer freedom of choice are also discussed.

It is hard enough to be a scientist; it is worse to be a moral philosopher. Consider the difficulties of measuring and evaluating variables of interest to behavioral scientists; consider also how much more complex is the treatment of such non- or perhaps antiscientific notions as ethics and justice. Yet evaluation of public programs generally leads to a shotgun marriage between science and social values.

It is proposed here to examine the evaluation of program benefits in the context of community mental health centers. The reasons are twofold. First, many of this journal's readers will find such a setting of greater professional interest than other public programs, and second, this author can cite direct experience in the evaluation of a community mental health center (Birnberg, Perloff, & Sussna, Note 1). The purpose of this article is to identify the conceptual issues of such evaluation. Program analysis is usually couched in monetary terms because the standard question to be answered is: How much public funding should be allocated to Program A versus other programs? In short we need to identify the costs that are reasonably allocable to a given program and weigh them against the related benefits. More specifically, we ought to extend public investment in a program until its

marginal costs and marginal benefits are equal. That is the efficiency criterion.

But efficiency is not the only goal of public programs. Equity may be as important a motivating consideration in the mix of publicly supported programs. And the fact is that the twin goals of efficiency and fairness are likely to be incompatible. Moreover, they are generally interwoven in ways that defy direct measurement. Nevertheless, we can attempt partial analysis of these dimensions and hope thereby to explicate some of the less obvious aspects of the determination of benefits.

Let us first examine the process of measuring the benefits of a community mental health center, questions of an ethical nature aside. A major justification for such centers (hereafter referred to as CMHC) is that mental illness generally inflicts pain and possibly economic hardships upon persons and institutions besides the afflicted individual. These "third party" effects, called "externalities," or "spillovers," by economists, might be felt by the patient's friends and family or employer or the community at large. At the extreme, we can conceive of the community benefit enjoyed in reducing acts of violence or other antisocial acts. If, for example, we are able to reasonably impute a reduction in

Reprinted from *Professional Psychology*, 1977, *8*, 435–441.

violent crimes to the existence of a CMHC, we can list that reduction as a benefit of the center. But, likely as not, crisis intervention or the heading off of violent crimes against the community represents a small portion of the output of a CMHC. In fact, much of the CMHC's work may be in much less dramatic dimensions, for example, therapy for children judged as being unruly in school, for individuals seeking assistance in correcting sexual dysfunctions, for alcoholics who cannot meet the obligations of their paid or unpaid positions, or for that matter for anyone who seeks help.

National Benefits of Mental Health Centers

A starting point in assessing the potential benefits of mental health programs is to take a "national income" view. Here we estimate in dollars, for a given year, the costs and losses to society resulting from mental illness. To the extent that treatment reduces the losses in productive economic activity, society has benefited. For example, if we update a set of seemingly conservative estimates, made originally in 1966, to 1976 figures, we get (Conley, Conwell, & Arrill, 1967):

Losses of productive activity:	
Reduced output by the labor force	$28.60 billion
Loss of homemaking services of women	1.94
Reduction in unpaid activities (volunteer work, recreation, etc.)	.48
Total	$31.02 billion

The use of a monetary measure of benefits inevitably raises the hackles of some well-intentioned social critics who are likely to complain that health matters are too important to be left to the accountants and economists. Let me offer at least a partial defense for the use of a monetary measure. Such a measure is reasonably objective and allows year-to-year comparisons within a given social program and, at any point in time, among competing social pro-

grams (not one of which feels it has an adequate budget to meet its objectives). Another advantage, and not the least, is that by attempting to place a monetary value on benefits, we can compare them with the corresponding set of program costs. Ultimately, the measuring device can be arbitrarily set as apples, oranges, or any other unit, provided we are consistent and do not evaluate program costs, expressed in lemons, with program benefits, expressed in cucumbers. We can use dollars without necessarily adopting the personal value orientations of economists and accountants or, for that matter, of psychologists.

The $31 billion cited above is an undoubtedly conservative estimate of the production lost and hence of the potential social benefits of improved mental health. The values of homemaking services of women (or of men in an increasingly liberated society) and of not-for-pay services are likely to be understated.

We can move easily, albeit briefly, from this early evaluation of benefits to a consideration of costs. For we can argue that there is social justification for extending outlays on mental health programs to the point where they equal costs. Again, updating Conley's 1966 figures, we can estimate costs of treatment and prevention in 1977 to be:

Inpatient care	$5.00 billion
Outpatient facilities	2.20
Training, research, and development	.66
Total	$7.86 billion

That number is probably too low and should certainly include the costs of pertinent law enforcement activities. Nevertheless, there is a substantial "surplus" of social benefits over costs in the mental health area, suggesting that increased investment by individuals and the community is sensible.

A Disaggregated View of Benefits

Given, as indicated previously, the substantial national benefits of mental health programs, how might we view these benefits at the community or individual level? Some of these benefits are dramatic. For example, crisis intervention by a CMHC may reduce the number of suicides, acts of vandalism and violence directed against other parties, and the duration of stay in mental institutions. Other benefits may be less dramatic but are important nevertheless. Healthier persons are more likely to be more productive workers, better students, or better housepersons. More productive workers imply lower absentee rates, fewer conflicts on the job, a more positive attitude toward occupational responsibilities, and so forth. All of this should reflect itself in lower unit labor cost, a more profitable enterprise, and increased employment in the community. Similar arguments can be made for students and homemakers.

At the individual level, there are the economic gains cited previously. Beyond those benefits, we may be hard pressed to place objective values on the broad array of outputs of a CMHC. How much is it worth to an individual to be happier, where some of this happiness is manifested in better social relations, improved self-worth, more satisfying sex, and so on? In principle, the problem is not different from that of assessing the benefits of education or of owning a Mercedes-Benz. We could get out of this quandary of putting an objective value on the full benefits of mental health treatment if each patient paid the full cost of treatment. We would then be able to say that rational consumers have indicated how much, at given prices, they were willing to buy of this service called mental health. The fact is that CMHC patients pay substantially less than the full cost of their treatment, a point to be discussed later on.

Another perspective in setting values on the benefits of mental health treatment is that of the administration of CMHCs. For example, the administrator must set a mix, and regularly adjust it, of patient services to be provided by his or her center. How, for example, will the center's capacity be allocated to the treatment of alcoholics, mentally retarded persons, geriatric cases, or patients requiring lengthy hospitalization? An administrator might very well take a "cost-effective" view, although that begs the ultimate problem of determining the benefits of each program. The basic approach in cost effec-

tiveness would be to establish objectives, for example, the treatment of 75 alcoholics, 100 youngsters, and so on, within a given budget period. A judgment would then have to be made as to how those targets could be met within the CMHC's budget. Clearly, treatment costs per patient and judgments of the value of treatment are critical considerations. For example, if we determine that the treatment of an alcoholic requires 18 hours at $29 per hour, and of a teenager 12 hours at $17 per hour, we can at least say that for each $1,000 available to us, we can treat two alcoholics (18 hours × $29 per hour = $522) or five teenagers (12 hours × $17 per hour = $204). If administration of a CMHC is not to become inane, one has to be careful that the center's value does not hinge upon numbers of patients treated. As a reductio ad absurdum, the most cost-effective level of treatment is zero patients. Not much less absurd is a treatment policy that maximizes something called "patient throughput."

The argument is not against measuring the costs of different levels and types of treatment. We should have information on how much of the CMHC's resources go into alternative treatment methods, such as chemotherapy, counseling of various forms, and so on. We would want also to know how costs vary with intensity of treatment. It may be that reducing the number of treatments by 25% adds rather little to the likelihood that an illness will recur. In such cases, the CMHC would be well advised to shift some of its resources to other programs or even to add to the number of patients undergoing treatment.

In recent years there has been a move under way to reduce the number of long-term patients in state mental institutions. This trend coincides with the dramatic expansion of CMHCs. Treatment costs in state institutions are extremely high (more than $12,000 per patient per year in Pennsylvania in 1974, for example; Note 1) and certainly so in comparison with CMHCs (perhaps $400 per patient per year in the CMHC we studied). In fact, there was a spectacular decline from 600 to 100 patients in a nearby state institution during a period of great growth of a local CMHC. It is tempting to attribute some of that benefit, in reduced institutionalizations and public expenditures, to the CMHC. How well the CMHC has served to facilitate the shift from hospitalization to outpatient care needs to be evaluated carefully (Blumenthal, Note 2).

CMHCs and Private and Public Interests

The area in which public support for mental health services is most compelling is where there is clear danger of violence committed against the community. In a crude sense, by supporting preventive treatment in such extreme cases, the community is buying a form of protection. And this protection will be bought whether or not the potentially violent person is willing or able to pay for treatment. In fact, such a person is not likely to consider the matter rationally and place any value or benefit on treatment, and the financial burden falls on the community. How much is the reduction of violence by mentally ill persons worth to the community? This question is not much different from that of determining the proper level of support for national defense, and the answers are equally vexing. There is no reasonable outlay that will insure complete protection. Further, whatever level of protection is decided on by the community is enjoyed by all its members, regardless of how much each has contributed to the protection fund. Given that exclusion from this particular form of community benefit is impossible, a rational citizen might well decide to pay nothing or less than what is regarded as his or her fair share of the cost. But notice that we are now talking about fairness and, by implication at least, about the vast array of individual value orientations of which the community is comprised. We meet these issues with a system of taxes and government regulations that we hope are designed to advance the public interest.

There seems to be little argument against the funding of public mental health services described above, despite an uneasiness about setting an equitable system of raising the needed funds (to say nothing of this layman's concern with operating definitions of *dangerous psychotic behavior*). But the vast majority of persons seeking mental health services do not fall into the extreme category presented previously. They are seeking relief from such problems as alcoholism, depression, and sexual dysfunction. These ailments are neither trivial nor therefore bereft of potential benefits to cured patients. But the case for public funds for such treatment rests mainly on affording to poor persons the same services available to the community at large. The facts are that disproportionate numbers of CMHC patients are from low-income families, and they pay nothing or much less than the cost of treatment.

The arrangement by which the patients (beneficiaries) of a CMHC pay less than the cost of service is in effect a subsidy of a very specified type to poor persons. This form of income redistribution is hardly unusual in our society; witness, for example, food stamps and hospital clinics. Nor is it intended here to go into the deeper issues of how income redistribution, private wants, and social welfare are related—a topic well presented elsewhere (Okun, 1975). But at the least we can sort out some of the implications of publicly funded CMHCs. By providing assistance to poor people in specified ways, the community dictates the forms of income redistribution. The CMHC, acting for the public, reserves for itself the decision on the makeup of the services to be offered to its patients. The latter have very limited options and certainly not the power to decline the service and transfer the money saved thereby to some other use. Who knows? The poor person might have latent middle-class values and prefer better liquor and a newer car.

An egalitarian might argue that if the community wants to reduce poverty, it should use its powers to transfer money from the rich to the poor, no strings attached. The money can then be budgeted by the poor among mental and other health services, food, shelter, and so forth, in ways that are considered most beneficial by the individual. After all, we do not tell the middle or upper classes how much they must spend on mental health. Given money and free choice, the once-poor would undoubtedly use less of the fully priced services of a CMHC. One result would be that the CMHC, which enjoys a captive clientele, would have to educate and convince the public that its services are as beneficial as its price suggests.

Social equity might well be defined to include (a) the highest degree of personal freedom to all members of the community and (b) a minimum income to insure a fair distribution of social benefits. Exceptions should be taken very deliberately. If we cannot quite put our money where our egalitarianism lies, we might consider a compromise, health vouchers, which would give low-income recipients some choice in an area where they otherwise have none.

Reference Notes

1. Birnberg, J. G., Perloff, R., & Sussna, E. *1974 utilization review of selected services of the County of Butler MH/MR program.* Unpublished manuscript, 1974. (Available from Robert Perloff, Graduate School of Business, University of Pittsburgh, Pittsburgh, Pa. 15260.)
2. Blumenthal, M. D. *A proposed exploration of cost effectiveness in mental health programs.* Unpublished manuscript, University of Pittsburgh, 1974.

References

Conley, R. W., Conwell, M., & Arrill, M. B. An approach to measuring the cost of mental illness. *American Journal of Psychiatry,* 1967, *124,* 755–762.
Okun, A. M. *Equality and efficiency, the big tradeoff.* Washington, D. C.: Brookings Institution, 1975.

Most of this article was written while *Edward Sussna* was a visiting professor at the École Superieure des Sciences Économiques et Commerciales, Cergy, France. At the time of original publication, he was a professor, Graduate School of Business, University of Pittsburgh, Pittsburgh.

A Federal View of Mental Health Program Evaluation

Benjamin Liptzin, James W. Stockdill, and Bertram S. Brown

This article discusses the current thinking at the National Institute of Mental Health on what evaluation is, who it is directed to, how it can be used, and what other activities relate to it. The article discusses the sections of the Community Mental Health Centers Amendments of 1975 that relate to program evaluation, quality assurance, and standards. The relationship of quality assurance activities to private office practice is also addressed. Evaluation is discussed in relation to decision making from two points of view: political and management.

Program evaluation is a rather new field, though a rapidly developing one. Much of the early federal impetus to program evaluation in mental health came from Section 262 of the Community Mental Health Centers Amendments of 1969 (PL 90-174), which authorized evaluation studies of the community mental health centers program. This authority was later expanded by a 1970 amendment to Section 513 of the Public Health Service Act, which authorized the Secretary of the Department of Health, Education, and Welfare to spend up to 1% of any appropriation to evaluate any program under the act. A Congressional committee report made clear the purpose of this section. It reads, "If judicious decisions are to be made in regard to the future directions of health programs, we must learn which programs are successful, which are not, and why" (House Committee, 1973).

Since July 1969, the National Institute of Mental Health (NIMH) has contracted for approximately 70 program evaluation studies. Earlier articles have reported on the results and impact of many of these mental health evaluation studies (Feldman & Windle, 1973; Windle, Bass, & Taube, 1974). This article describes our current thinking on what evaluation is, who it is directed to, how it can be used, and what other activities relate to it.

Definition of Evaluation

Weiss (1975) has defined *evaluation* as an enterprise which

> examines the effects of policies and programs on their targets (individuals, groups, institutions, communities) in terms of the goals they are meant to achieve. By objective and systematic methods, evaluation research assesses the extent to which goals are realized and looks at the factors associated with successful or unsuccessful outcomes. The assumption is that by providing "the facts," evaluation assists decision-makers to make wise choices among future courses of action. Careful and unbiased data on the consequences of programs should improve decision making. (p. 13)

The focus on decision making suggests that the evaluator must clearly identify the decision makers he is trying to influence and the nature of the decision-making process. It must be recognized that evaluation results may assist but are only one factor in decision making. It has also been pointed out that there is

> a growing trend to romanticize evaluation as a scientific process; preferably uncontaminated by political compromise and based on some intellectual power. This trend can serve to weaken the influence of the evaluator on the policies and decisions of administrators and politicians. (Stockdill & Sharfstein, 1976, p. 652)

It is important to recognize that decisions involve the allocation of resources, including personnel and the authority to carry out pro-

Reprinted from *Professional Psychology,* 1977, *8,* 543–552.

grams. To the extent that evaluation results attempt to influence the power relationships involved in such decisions, evaluation becomes a political activity.

Some Practical Considerations

One issue in evaluation research is timing. An example may illustrate some aspects of timing related to the usefulness of evaluation results. Several years ago, we funded a major study on the impact of the Part F grants to community mental health centers and noncommunity mental health centers to develop children's mental health services (Lieberman, Claiborn, & Sowder, 1975). The study found that the grants had significantly increased the availability of services to children and that the increase was even greater at noncommunity than at community mental health centers. A major finding of the study was that categorical children's grants are essential to ensure that children's services are allotted an adequate share of program resources. The findings of the study came too late to affect the Community Mental Health Centers Amendments of 1975, which eliminated the categorical grants for children and made children's services 1 of 12 services that must be provided under the basic grant. In addition, the new law required Part F grantees that were not part of a community mental health center to convert to a full community mental health center in 2 years or lose all support. Although on the surface this seems like an example of an evaluation study that was of little value, it is important to recognize several redeeming points. First, the findings were helpful in developing regulations and guidelines for the new community mental health centers legislation. Second, it provides a basis for raising areas of possible revision when renewal of the legislation takes place. Finally, it developed a methodology and a data base that can be used in the future to test hypotheses about what happens to children's services when they have to compete for funds.

An example of the relationship between legislation and program evaluation is the new requirement in Section 206(c)(4) of the Com-

munity Mental Health Centers Amendments of 1975:

> In each fiscal year for which a CMHC [community mental health center] receives a grant . . . such center shall obligate for a program of continuing evaluation of the effectiveness of its programs in serving the needs of the residents of its catchment area and for a review of the quality of the services provided by the center not less than an amount equal to 2 per centum of the amount obligated by the center in the preceding fiscal year for its operating expenses.

This new requirement raises two fundamental questions for implementation to be successful. First, are there methodologies available to do the evaluation required by this section and also to meet the requirements of Section 206(c)(1)(A)(ii), which calls for

> an effective procedure for developing, compiling, evaluating, and reporting to the Secretary statistics and other information (which the Secretary shall publish and disseminate on a periodic basis and which the center shall disclose at least annually to the general public) relating to (I) the cost of the center's operation, (II) the patterns of use of its services, (III) the availability, accessibility, and acceptability of its services, (IV) the impact of its services upon the mental health of the residents of the catchment area, and (V) such other matters as the Secretary may require. (PL 94–63)

Second, is there adequate personnel available to carry out such studies in all centers?

As a partial answer to the first question, NIMH has made a significant investment in the development of evaluation methodology for such areas as cost accounting, cost-effectiveness, goal attainment scaling, patient care evaluation, and the like. In addition, written descriptions of many program evaluation techniques have been published under NIMH contracts and are available (Hagedorn, Beck, Neubert, & Werlin, 1976; Hargreaves, Attkisson, Siegel, McIntyre, & Sorenson, 1977). An NIMH contract also funded regional workshops for teaching evaluation methodologies to center staff. Other new technical assistance approaches are also being developed. The second question, on the availability of personnel, has not been answered. We expect to review a sample of community mental health centers as they try to implement the new program evaluation requirements over the next year to see how much activity is actually going on, who is doing it, and what further training would be useful. Clinical psychologists are obvious candidates for program evaluation positions because of their unique combination of clinical and research skills.

Two other major areas related to mental health program evaluation were raised by the 1975 amendments. The first relates to standards for the centers and the second to quality assurance programs.

Standards

Section 304(b), Title III (PL 94-63) requires that

> not later than eighteen months after the date of the enactment of this Act the Secretary of HEW shall submit to the Committee on Interstate and Foreign Commerce of the House of Representatives and the Committee on Labor and Public Welfare of the Senate, a report setting forth (1) national standards for care provided by CMHCs, and (2) criteria for evaluation of CMHCs and the quality of the services provided by the centers.

In response to this requirement, NIMH has prepared and submitted a report (Note 2) organized into three sections. Part 1 presents a historical sketch of the evolution of various approaches to assessing the quality of health and mental health care. Part 2 presents standards related to program administration and to services, along with criteria to assist in evaluating performance. Because the Community Mental Health Centers Amendments of 1975 did not specify how such standards were to be used, Part 3 discusses various uses that could be made of the standards once they have been validated by field testing. The uses discussed in the report include a guide to the field, a guide to the development of state and local standards, validating eligibility for health insurance reimbursements, monitoring federally funded centers, program development, and a reference point for other center standards as a way to reduce overlapping and conflicting review procedures.

The standards presented in this report to Congress draw heavily on accreditation standards for community mental health centers developed by the Joint Commission on Accreditation of Hospitals (JCAH) with some NIMH funding. Compared to the JCAH standards, the NIMH standards are organized differently, have a different format, and use terms and concepts that are more common to the field. During

1977 the JCAH standards will be field tested, and significant revisions are expected.

There are two major areas of concern related to standards as evaluation tools. The first includes the technical problems involved in any standards process, such as insuring that the measures used to evaluate compliance are reliable (between observers or at different points in time) and valid (i.e., measure the concept involved). A further problem is whether national standards that are necessarily primarily structural assessments of the capacity of a program to deliver high-quality care relate in any way to clinical judgments of what constitutes quality care in terms of therapeutic process or to measures of patient outcome. These issues are complex and beyond the scope of this article, but it is important to maintain a healthy skepticism of whether such standards efforts actually improve the quality of care or the health status of the population treated (O'Donoghue, 1974). Such standards may be helpful in assessing compliance with agreed upon levels of performance and may be tied to incentives to promote positive changes in programs.

A second major concern about community mental health center standards is that programs are subject to overlapping and, at times, to conflicting requirements from various agencies and organizations. To quote from a report on standards prepared by the Southern Regional Education Board (Note 1) under an NIMH contract:

> Standards of the various agencies often apply to the same program components (i.e., facilities, records, or support services), but the criteria are often different or the procedures and interpretations are different. Sometimes criteria are actually in conflict with each other, but more often the conflicts are in the procedures and interpretations rather than in the standards themselves. The programs are then put in the difficult position of deciding which set of standards to follow.

The report went on to state:

> Frequent changes in the standards themselves or in the monitoring procedures can be very disruptive to programs that are trying to stay in compliance. There is need for a considerable measure of stability in standards programs as well as need for their periodic review and revision.

The board furthermore reported:

> The costs of preparing for survey visits and the cost in hosting the survey teams are also a problem. Some programs estimate that it requires as much as 247

mandays a year to fill out survey forms, host survey teams, and prepare plans of correction for various sets of standards. This is the equivalent of one full-time professional person. This is expensive and non-productive particularly when so much of it is repetition or duplication of what has already been done for other standards agencies.

The national standards, which have general acceptance and have been validated through field testing, can serve as the reference point for other standards. Where identical information is required for different purposes by different agencies, attempts should be made to collect the information only once from the service program and to make it available to all the agencies that need it.

Quality Assurance

In addition to the sections of PL 94-63 that deal with program evaluation and standards, Section 201(d)(1) requires that community mental health centers "establish an ongoing quality assurance program (including utilization and peer review systems) respecting the center's services" (House Committee, 1973). That general requirement has been interpreted in regulations to include a written description of the program and the composition of the responsible committee, the review procedures to be used, the criteria and standards to be used in the reviews, and the procedures to ensure dissemination of the findings of the committee.

As with the program evaluation requirements, we expect to follow up centers to see how much and what kinds of quality assurance activities are actually taking place. Such a review will identify needs for technical assistance, as well as help us to rethink the appropriateness of the requirements. The latter is especially important in light of a recent study that questioned the effectiveness and costs of all currently used quality assurance methodologies (Institute of Medicine, 1976). It is particularly important to assess whether positive changes have occurred as a result of quality assurance programs.

The relationship of program evaluation to quality assurance programs is often confusing. At times program evaluation is thought of as an activity to ensure quality, whereas at other times a quality assurance program is thought of as a way to evaluate a program. Both are correct interpretations because both approaches aim at promoting constructive system change. It is important that both approaches continue and be coordinated with each other within a given program. The distinction that we generally use is that quality assurance programs involve activities that have previously been called "utilization review," "medical audit," or "peer review." These examine the activities of clinical providers in delivering care and, to an extent, the results of that care. At times deficiencies may be identified that require administrative or organizational change, but often corrective action is directed toward individuals or groups of practitioners and involves an educational process. In contrast, program evaluation activities tend to look at system variables and to ask such questions as, Are the program's services accessible or acceptable to the entire population of potential users? At the present time, such questions are only being asked about organized systems of care, such as community mental health centers. As health systems agencies develop their abilities to assess community needs, they are likely to identify gaps or inequities in the private office sector as well as in organized systems. Although to date there has been strong resistance to any suggestion that individual practitioners be subject to regulation by health planning agencies, it is not inconceivable that at some future time controls or incentives could be instituted. As an example, in the province of Ontario, Canada, concern about rising health care costs led to restrictions on the immigration of physicians, except for practice in underserved areas. Such restrictive licensing is one way to affect the distribution of professionals in the private sector.

Just as program evaluation is more difficult in the unorganized private sector because there is often no "program" to evaluate, so also the effectiveness of quality assurance programs is questionable with respect to private office practice. Two models of outpatient mental health peer review that were supported by NIMH were both done in organized care settings (Newman & Luft, 1974; Riedel, Tischler, & Myers, 1974). In both of these there were administrative structures with responsibility for the quality of care and for allocating resources given a limited budget. Peer review was a way to monitor the care given and to assist in deciding how much and what kinds of care individuals would receive. There was clear authority and group pressure to modify the behavior of individual practitioners. The same pressures do not operate in an insurance system that will pay for any needed care if it is judged to be appropriate.

There are a number of problems in peer review of mental health care (Liptzin, 1974). Given the wide variability in what is currently considered "appropriate" mental health care and the limited data that are available in patient records, outpatient peer review groups may be reluctant to question anything but the most clearly deviant care. Some more information may be provided by a major research initiative planned by NIMH in psychosocial treatment assessment research. This effort should help define what patients are best helped by what treatment approaches from what providers under what conditions. This may be of help in peer review of psychosocial treatments, although experience in peer review of pharmacologic treatments suggests that it is often some time before research findings reach the mainstream of clinical practice. Attempts are being made to develop effective peer review models in two large federal insurance programs: the Civilian Health and Medical Program of the Uniformed Services (CHAMPUS), for military dependents, and the Federal Employees Program of Blue Cross/Blue Shield, for civil service subscribers. NIMH is assisting the Department of Defense and the Civil Service Commission, which have responsibility for those two programs, respectively, to work with local provider groups and local fiscal agents to develop effective peer review. This includes negotiations among provider groups representing psychiatry, psychology, psychiatric social work, and psychiatric nursing for ways to cooperate in multidisciplinary review, and between providers and insurance representatives to establish a climate of mutual trust and a sense that despite different perspectives, there are areas of mutual interest.

In a number of areas of the country, local professional associations have established peer review groups to assist insurance carriers in determining if claims should be paid. In most areas of the country, peer review of acute hospital care is being conducted under the auspices of professional standards review organizations. As these organizations begin to review outpatient care, it will be important for psychologists and their professional associations to get involved even though by law only physicians can be members.

Further Thoughts on Program Evaluation

Earlier in this article we discussed the relationship of program evaluation to decision making. Another way to consider evaluation is as a basic function of management in an organization or system. As part of the control function, it serves to gather intelligence that feeds back into other management functions, such as planning, organizing, directing, and staffing (Koontz & O'Donnell, 1974). Evaluation assists managers in knowing whether current activities are meeting current program objectives, what program changes may be needed to better meet current objectives, whether changing needs or environments dictate new objectives, and what program changes will be required to meet future objectives. This management view of evaluation was difficult to apply at NIMH during the period from 1969 to 1977 because there were diametrically opposed views of NIMH program objectives in the executive and legislative branches of the government. The executive branch sometimes used evaluation results to recommend termination of programs. In the case of the community mental health centers program, the argument used at one point was that it was a demonstration program, evaluations had shown it to be successful, and therefore, continued federal support was unnecessary. Even the basic management tool of budgeting was compromised be vetoes, impoundments, and rescissions. Such a highly charged atmosphere of confrontation is not very conducive to the appropriate use of evaluation. With the executive and legislative branches controlled by the same political party, there may be agreed upon program objectives, and evaluation may become a more effective management tool as part of an open decision-making process.

One problem in considering the management view of evaluation for mental health programs is that traditionally programs have been managed by clinicians who have generally been promoted into management positions because of clinical rather than managerial skills and experience. Negative attitudes toward "management" by clinicians and researchers has also inhibited the development of good management systems in research and training programs even more than in service programs. Those in service programs and even more clinicians may still feel that the task of management is to hire well-trained and properly certified clinicians and then to leave them alone to "do their own thing." Two current pressures make this unrealistic. The first is the strong, public pressure for accountability, particularly when tax dollars pay part of the costs of programs. The second is the recognition that resources are limited and that programs must make maximum use of available resources to meet program goals and objectives.

Given the new pressures, evaluation takes on a potentially much more important role in service programs. That potential will only be realized if useful tools are available and if program managers are interested and know how to use them. Program directors who have functioned with no management information system or evaluation unit are unlikely to make use of such information even if it is forced on them. Even worse, in a budgetary crunch, such activities are likely to be the first to be cut back. By contrast, program directors who understand how evaluation feedback can be vital to their organizations don't need a federal regulation to build evaluation into their programs.

Our approach over the next several years will be to improve our own capability to conduct evaluations and to make use of the findings in policy development and program management. In addition, it is essential that we seek to improve the internal evaluation capability of NIMH-supported programs. We plan to do this by developing and disseminating program evaluation, quality assurance, and other manage-

ment techniques while educating and training responsible individuals as to why and how these techniques should be used.

Reference Notes

1. Southern Regional Education Board. *Developing and using mental health standards* (NIMH Contract No. ADM-42-74-90). Unpublished manuscript, 1976.
2. National Institute of Mental Health. *National standards for community mental health centers: A report to Congress.* Unpublished manuscript, 1977.

References

Feldman, S., & Windle, C. The NIMH approach to evaluation of the community mental health centers program. *Health Services Reports,* 1973, *88,* 174–180.

Hagedorn, H. J., Beck, K. J., Neubert, S. F., & Werlin, S. H. *A working manual of simple program evaluation techniques for community mental health centers* (Arthur D. Little, Inc., Contract No. 278-75-0031). Washington, D.C.: U.S. Government Printing Office, 1976.

Hargreaves, W. A., Attkisson, C. C., Siegel, L. M., McIntyre, M. M., & Sorenson, J. E. (Eds.). *Resource materials for community mental health program evaluation* (DHEW Publication No. [ADM] 75-222). Washington, D.C.: U.S. Government Printing Office, 1977. (Stock No. 017-024-00554-1).

House Committee on Interstate and Foreign Commerce. *Compilation of selected public health laws, 93rd Congress, 1st Session* (Vol. 1). Washington, D.C.: U.S. Government Printing Office, March 1973.

Institute of Medicine. *Assessing quality in health care: An evaluation.* Washington, D.C.: National Academy of Sciences, 1976.

Koontz, H., & O'Donnell, C. *Principles of management* (5th ed.). New York: McGraw-Hill, 1974.

Lieberman, E. J., Claiborn, W. L., & Sowder, B. J. Assessment of child mental health needs and programs (General Research Corp., Contract No. HSM-42-73-78 [OP]). Rockville, Md.: National Institute of Mental Health, 1975. (NTIS No. PB-249-786).

Liptzin, B. Quality assurance and psychiatric practice: A review. *American Journal of Psychiatry,* 1974, *131,* 1374–1377.

Newman, D. E., & Luft, L. L. The peer review process: Education versus control. *American Journal of Psychiatry,* 1974, *131,* 1363–1366.

O'Donoghue, P. *Evidence about the effects of health care regulations: An evaluation synthesis of policy-relevant research.* Denver, Col.: Spectrum Research, 1974.

Riedel, D. C., Tischler, G. L., & Myers, J. K. *Patient care evaluation in mental health programs.* Cambridge, Mass.: Ballinger, 1974.

Stockdill, J. W., & Sharfstein, S. S. The politics of program evaluation. *Hospital and Community Psychiatry,* 1976, *27,* 650–653.

Weiss, C. H. Evaluation research in the political context. In E. L. Struening & M. Guttentag (Eds.), *Handbook of evaluation research* (Vol. 1). Beverly Hills, Calif.: Sage, 1975.

Windle, C., Bass, R. D., & Taube, C. S. PR aside: Initial results from NIMH's service program evaluation studies. *American Journal of Community Psychology,* 1974, *2,* 311–327.

At the time of original publication of this article, *Benjamin Liptzin* and *James W. Stockdill* were part of the staff of the Program Analysis and Evaluation Branch, Office of Program Development and Analysis, National Institute of Mental Health, Rockville, Maryland. *Bertram Brown* was Director of the National Institute of Mental Health.

Evaluations of Treatment in Psychotherapy: Naiveté or Necessity?

Suzanne W. Hadley and Hans H. Strupp

Although a number of problems continue to hinder the empirical evaluation of psychotherapy, the need for evaluation is more urgent than at any previous time. Conceptual deficiencies in evaluation are described and a remedy proposed in the form of a tripartite model of mental health and psychotherapy outcome that subsumes the judgmental perspective of three major "interested parties" to psychotherapy evaluation. Application of the model to clinical practitioners and researchers demonstrates its value in providing the basis for comprehensive assessments of treatment. The pitfalls of inadvertent value judgments in psychotherapy evaluation are noted, and the advantages of a strictly empirical approach based on the tripartite model are described.

Is the evaluation of psychotherapy an urgent necessity or merely a manifestation of well-intentioned, but hopeless naiveté? Discussions of this topic subsume two major questions: (a) Why should we, or more accurately, why *must* we evaluate psychotherapy? and (b) Realistically, *can* we evaluate psychotherapy? It is our view that we can and must evaluate psychotherapy, but that in order to do so meaningfully, it is imperative that we make conceptual and methodological innovations in our approach to the problem. We shall examine both the necessity and the limitations of current psychotherapy evaluations and then describe a model that we believe provides the basis for the most meaningful conceptual and practical approach to evaluation.

Why Must We Evaluate Psychotherapy?

Ideally, the evaluation of therapy within the context of a single case should be considered intrinsic to the therapy itself—a "critical step" in the therapy (Urban & Ford, 1971)—for it is this evaluation that provides the basis for corrections of the therapy in process and for decisions concerning the termination of therapy at the most auspicious time. Behavior therapy has always given prominence to evaluation, but the same principles that apply to behavior therapy argue for the critical importance of evaluation in all therapeutic modalities.

Beyond the clinical assessment of individual cases, the scientific study of psychotherapy outcome has shown substantial quantitative increases, together with technical and methodological advances, over the past 15 years. Moreover within the last few years, the need for the evaluation of therapy outcomes has received additional impetus from developments within the field as well as within the broader social and political context.

Negative Effects in Psychotherapy

Within the field, psychotherapists have recently begun to openly acknowledge the possibility of at least occasional negative effects resulting from attempted therapeutic interventions. Previously, the view prevailed that therapy, often of benefit to a number of patients, is at worst an innocuous experience. If such were the case, evaluation would clearly be less than urgent. However, in 1971 Bergin alerted the field to the possibility of deterioration in psychotherapy; and more recently an in-depth analysis of negative effects by Strupp, Hadley, and Gomes-

Reprinted from *Professional Psychology,* 1977, *8,* 478–490.

Schwartz (in press) demonstrated clearly that psychotherapy's potency in general is now given far greater credence, that is, that psychotherapy does have measurable effects, both for good and for ill. Because of this growing awareness of the possibility of negative effects, it is clear that, more than ever, evaluations of the outcome of psychotherapy are essential.

As Strupp et al. (in press) have documented, the need for evaluation generated by our cognizance of the reality of potential negative effects has clinical, political, and social implications. Particularly urgent is the development of procedures for evaluating the competence of aspiring and practicing clinicians. Bergin (Note 1), for example, has called for evaluations of therapy skills in vivo as a requirement for screening of trainees and licensure of clinicians.

Greater Availability and Variety of Therapy

Greater respect for therapy's potency and the heightened awareness of negative effects in particular have resulted in large part from the rapid growth in the number of persons seeking help and the great variety of "therapies" continuing to emerge. For a variety of reasons, psychotherapy services have become accessible to a greater number and variety of persons than ever before. To illustrate, community mental health centers, many of which engage in advertising and outreach programs, have increased the availability of therapy to the public, and tax dollars and insurance programs are funding therapy for low- and middle-income persons. Thus psychotherapy is no longer restricted to a socially, educationally, and financially privileged few but is becoming available to a far greater variety of persons, many of whom do not possess the social and verbal skills usually associated with positive outcomes in the "traditional" therapies. The net result is that traditional therapy techniques designed for a fairly select segment of the population are often indiscriminately applied to patients with widely varying conceptions of therapy and commitments to the therapeutic task as well as divergent therapeutic goals. The need for evaluations of what psychotherapy "does" to such individuals is readily apparent.

Not only has the number of patients vastly increased, but these patients are entering into a greatly expanded arena of therapies and quasi-therapies. For example, Parloff (1976) noted that there are now more than 130 different approaches to psychotherapy "in the marketplace"; Harper (1975) gives a similar figure. Many of these are novel approaches to the solution of human problems that depart from more tried, traditional therapies. Some of these innovations smack of sensationalism, promising substantial results in brief periods of time. A recent issue of *The Village Voice,* for example, carried 40–45 advertisements (the number depending on the definition used) for counseling or therapy. These ads offer the reader personal growth, heightened awareness, and an end to anxiety and depression. Such claims are often predicated upon intense emotionally charged experiences patients are expected to undergo. Do these therapies deliver what they promise, and if so, at what cost? Despite the increased potential for negative effects related to such interventions, there has been remarkably little research into the outcomes of these therapies, and often what little research has been done represents work carried out by proponents of the therapy under study (Hartley, Roback, & Abramowitz, 1976). Holtzman (1975) summarized the situation vis-à-vis the new therapy techniques as follows:

> A major challenge for all workers in this field is to develop more adequate methods for evaluating therapeutic techniques and to apply them on a large enough scale so that the more useful methods can be sustained while the ineffectual or misguided approaches can be abandoned. (p. x)

Even within the province of the more traditional therapeutic approaches, there is a trend toward the greater use of brief, focused, and "product-oriented" interventions. As a result, many outcome evaluations are based on a narrow range of criteria or "target complaints" that fail to provide a complete assessment of the treatment's impact on the totality of the patient's life. This deficiency is particularly serious when we are dealing with focused, confrontative, or short-term therapies.

Increased Patient and "Third-Party" Awareness of Therapy Outcome

The press for evaluation derives from the desire of clinicians or researchers to improve the quality of therapeutic services; additional developments extrinsic to the field render evaluation an absolute necessity for therapists' self-protection, if no other reason. In the broader social context, there has been a recent marked intensification of the consumer advocacy movement and an increase in consumer awareness of product quality. In the mental health field, this development has led many patients to scrutinize the process and outcome of their own therapy. Consumer guides for selecting therapists and therapies and the new concept of therapist-patient contracts attest to increased consumer consciousness. More ominous are the lawsuits based on allegations of therapist malpractice, reflecting patients' attention to the outcome of their therapy and their right to evaluate that outcome.

Nor are patients the only new arrivals to therapy evaluation. In recent years we have seen a substantial increase in the interest· of "third parties" as insurance companies have increased coverage for mental health care and as more tax dollars have been allocated to mental health facilities and services. Therapists themselves have fought for these developments, yet with third-party funding has come the demand for accountability. Thus society, through insurance executives, public administrators, and legislators, is demanding that psychotherapy be accountable—that we as mental health professionals show what we can do, for whom, and under what circumstances.

Third parties interested in the evaluation of psychotherapy also include significant others in the patient's life—spouse, children, friends, employer. Substantial changes in a patient's adjustment of course have implications for relationships with these individuals, and society typically focuses on the interpersonal implications of therapy-induced change. Thus, society's heightened interest in therapy evaluation has induced therapists themselves to become increasingly sensitized to the necessity of evaluating psychotherapy in this broader context.

Can We Evaluate Psychotherapy?

In sum, it is clear that the evaluation of psychotherapy is not merely desirable, it is an absolute necessity; yet this conclusion is more easily derived than implemented. For a variety of reasons, definitive evaluations of psychotherapy continue to elude us. This brings us to our second major area of inquiry: *Can* we evaluate psychotherapy? Is there a "product" in psychotherapy? Is it amenable to scientific evaluation, and if so, have we developed adequate means to do the job?

Part of the problem to date is that evaluation has not been unanimously regarded as crucial by psychotherapists. There have always been many therapists who regard evaluation with suspicion, if not downright hostility. Freud, and to an even greater extent, certain of his followers, tended to dismiss questions concerning therapy's effectiveness as evidence of "resistance" to psychotherapy. Even clinicians who value research question whether it is possible to evaluate "effectiveness" if the purpose of therapy is seen not as a "cure" of some dysfunction but as a search for answers to existential dilemmas or as a "growth" experience. Indeed, many clinicians as well as philosophers of science continue to believe that psychotherapy is more an art than a science, thus ultimately defying scientific study.

The foregoing dictum probably reduces to a value judgment. As a working assumption for an individual therapist, it may be as valid as any other. But there are at least two problems with the view that "psychotherapy is primarily an art." First, it may serve partisans as a convenient excuse when research fails to demonstrate psychotherapy's unique effectiveness. Thus, the lack of significant results is ascribed to shortcomings in the evaluation process, such as failure to tap subtle, elusive, and almost mysterious dimensions of impact on the patient's life. Second, the view that psychotherapy is an art will not suffice as an answer to contemporary demands for demonstrations of psychotherapy's effectiveness. If we accept as a given that we must evaluate psychotherapy—and we believe it is essential that we do—we must commit ourselves to the assumption that the changes resulting from therapy can be measured and begin doing it in the most logical and precise manner possible.

It is here that we encounter the major obstacle to evaluation, for even among those clinicians and researchers firmly committed to the principle of evaluation, a variety of problems continue to confound the search for conclusive findings. The fundamental question being asked is, What can psychotherapy do and how does it do it? The amount of research carried out in pursuit of the answer continues to proliferate, and the sophistication and rigor of research have steadily improved (Strupp, 1976). Yet, notwithstanding this progress, it remains possible to argue that psychotherapy on the whole or in general is either highly effective, moderately effective, or ineffective (Strupp et al., in press).

Many of the persisting problems in the research involve faulty conceptions and deficiencies in methodology or design. Kiesler (1966) and Gross and Miller (1975) are among those researchers who have identified the issues and proposed improvements. The fact that many of the deficiencies identified over a decade earlier persist in current studies documents a regrettable neglect on the part of researchers to heed important lessons.

Conceptual Deficiencies in Psychotherapy Evaluation

Our present concern is with an even more fundamental deficiency in the research literature, namely, the lack of conceptual uniformity and precision. Psychotherapy in general is a technique designed to assist the patient in self-improvement—to potentiate the achievement of some ideal of mental health. The simple fact is that there is no consensus in the research literature, or anywhere else, on what that ideal may be. Thus one researcher reports therapy to be successful for those patients with shorter hospital stays; another describes as effective those interventions that lead to improvements in ego functioning; still another reports successes based on patients' expressions of satisfaction with the experience. Do these assessments have anything in common? It is possible to draw conclusions about the effectiveness of psychotherapy in general based on such diverse criteria of success?

We believe that it is not possible to draw such conclusions. Instead, we contend that profound discrepancies in evaluative criteria are continuing to confound our best efforts at evaluating the outcomes of psychotherapy. The tripartite model briefly described below and presented at greater length elsewhere (Strupp & Hadley, 1977) comprises three major perspectives on mental health and psychotherapy evaluation. It is our view that all three of these perspectives must be considered simultaneously in order to develop comprehensive definitions of mental health and meaningful evaluations of psychotherapy outcome. Similar models have been developed and applied previously, most notably by Parloff, Kelman, and Frank (1954) and Kelman and Parloff (1957). The following elaboration of our own model is considered useful for highlighting the conceptual and definitional problems inherent in evaluations of therapy outcomes and for indicating how such evaluations can be substantially improved. In the process it will also become clear that certain questions can profitably be addressed by researchers, whereas others cannot.

A Tripartite Model for Psychotherapy Evaluation

Our earlier discussion of recent developments related to the need for evaluating psychotherapy outcomes highlighted the growing need of attending to the views of individual patients and agents of society. Thus, there are three major "interested parties" in mental health and outcome evaluations: *the individual patient, society* (including significant persons in the patient's life), and *the mental health professional*. Each interested party approaches questions of evaluation from a unique perspective, for each defines an individual's mental health in terms of unique purposes it seeks to fulfill. Consequently, each interested party focuses on specific aspects of an individual's functioning in determining his state of mental health and the outcome of therapy.

1. The individual client evaluating his own mental health relies on the most accessible and significant data base for him—his own subjective feelings of well-being. The individual wishes first and foremost to be happy, to feel content. If he is happy, he perceives himself as well. When he is unhappy, he feels something is amiss. A wide variety of social, cognitive, and emotional factors enter into one's sense of contentment; thus, in many instances, an individual's judgment of his own mental health based on well-being will coincide with societal expectations or the mental health professional's opinion. However, it is important to realize that agreement in such instances results from independent evaluations based on different pieces of

data. Thus it is possible that an individual's judgment of his mental health may be at odds with the views of society and/or those of a mental health professional. In any case, the point to be made is that an individual's sense of well-being is a unique source of data with a validity all its own and, therefore, that the individual's judgment of his own mental health must be accorded due weight by clinicians and researchers. This is true because of the implications for what has traditionally been called the patient's "motivation for therapy" and because a *complete* evaluation of therapy is impossible without the patient's perspective.

2. Society is primarily concerned with the maintenance of social relations, institutions, and prevailing standards of conduct. Agents of society do not have access to the data bases from which the individual and the mental health professional judge mental health, and in any case, as agents of society, they seek to fulfill their own unique aims. Society and its agents thus tend to define an individual's mental health in terms of behavioral stability, predictability, and conformity to the prevailing social code. Accordingly, the mentally healthy individual is one who is productive, or who at least "pays his own way" in society. The mentally unsound are those who threaten society in any of a variety of ways, ranging from the commitment of criminal acts, to incapacitation requiring hospitalization, to threatening the family structure, for example, by seeking divorce, abandoning their spouses, children, etc.

The reaction of many mental health professionals to the prospect of acknowledging society as a bona fide evaluative agent of mental health and psychotherapy outcome is often less than enthusiastic. In part, this response arises from therapists' rejections of the noxious image of psychotherapy as an instrument of social control (Kittrie, 1971; Szasz, 1970) and the implication that its practitioners are either the agents of, or are accountable to, social and political authorities. In part, the response may arise from therapists' concerns that agents of society are not sufficiently knowledgeable about and sensitive to the intricacies of the individual. But as we described earlier, it is clear that—like it or not—society has become increasingly involved in assessments of mental health and psychother-

apy. Thus, just as is true of the patient's perspective, society's perspective must be considered if one seeks a comprehensive evaluation of the effects of psychotherapy.

3. Most mental health professionals tend to view an individual's functioning within the framework of some theory of personality structure that transcends social adaptation and subjective well-being (although clinical judgments of a person's mental health are often significantly influenced by the latter two criteria). The professional thus defines mental health largely with reference to some theoretical model of a "healthy" personality structure and functioning. Numerous models of psychological structure and functioning have been proposed, with considerable variation as to content and degree of inference involved in observations and assessments deriving from a particular model. What all models have in common, however, is the assumption that there is more involved in good mental health than subjective well-being or adaptive behavior and, therefore, that the evaluation of psychotherapy involves more than changes in the individual's feeling state or behavior.

Evaluations of an individual's functioning are often made from only one of the three perspectives—and in some circumstances, for specific, narrowly defined purposes, such evaluations are adequate. However, there are at least two serious problems associated with evaluations based on a single perspective. In the first place, the discrepant perspectives set the stage for discrepancies in judgments of mental health and therapy outcome. Such discrepancies have, unfortunately, occurred often in psychotherapy research and have contributed substantially to the confused state of the field, that is, researchers' inabilities to provide relatively straightforward answers to the question of what psychotherapy *does*. The notorious lack of correlation among outcome criteria, that is, information based on data deriving from different perspectives, illustrates the point.

An equally serious problem stems from the fact that single-perspective evaluations of mental health and psychotherapy may do a great injustice to the totality of an individual's functioning; thus they fail to provide adequate answers to questions concerning the effects of therapy. Change, or the lack of change, in one component of an individual's functioning frequently affects other aspects. Thus, whenever one seeks comprehensive assessments of an individual's functioning—and surely the evaluation of psychotherapy is such an instance—all three major dimensions of functioning must be assessed.

Implications for the Therapist

For the clinician, comprehensive assessment requires an awareness of the breadth and scope of outcome extending beyond the traditional perspective of the mental health professional. Therapists must look to the patient—to his perceptions and reactions to therapy—as one valid index of outcome (cf. Strupp, Fox, & Lessler, 1969, for a study of patients' self-reports). Therapists who rely on the interpretation of behavior as an integral part of therapy may have particular difficulty in accepting a patient's behavior at face value. Yet, as Malan (in press) observed, apparent improvement is not always a "flight into health," and even when it is, "a patient is sometimes able to make use of it as point of growth." Conversely, a patient's dissatisfaction with therapy or the therapist is not always a sign of "resistance" but may be indicative of one or another of the pernicious sources of negative effects of psychotherapy identified by Strupp et al. (in press).

A fundamental aspect of the therapist's unique skill and training is his ability to look beyond the patient's immediately observable behavior and to work with the underlying cognitions and emotions. Of course, we intend in no way to denigrate this vital function, nor do we advocate its abandonment. We simply wish to emphasize the necessity for therapists to recognize and acknowledge the patient's perspective on therapy, both in the interest of comprehensive assessment and because the patient's perspective invariably has imporat implications for his desire to enter therapy and his commitment to work in therapy.

By the same token, therapists must also be sensitive to psychotherapy outcome from society's perspective, which may include the interests of significant others in the patient's life as well as those of society as a whole. Pragmatically, this awareness is necessitated by the multiplicity of "interested parties" to therapy evaluation, a reality that cannot be ignored despite the fact that most therapists rightly construe their primary obligation to be the patient's well-being. The point is that sensitivity to the social context of therapy outcome and concern for the individual patient are not antithetical or mutually exclusive. Indeed, a therapist's concern with the social manifestations of therapy-induced change in a patient accrues substantially to the good of that patient because an individual's mental health is strongly influenced by the feedback he receives from others about his behavior. This is not to argue that therapists should encourage only socially sanctioned changes in their patients. Rather, we argue that therapists should increase their awareness of the social repercussions of changes sought by the patient and that therapists use their awareness to facilitate the patient's awareness of, and preparation for, the reactions of others.

In addition, the increasing importance of the patient's and society's evaluations of therapy has important theoretical implications for clinicians whose approaches to therapy are based on a structural theory of personality functioning, for it seems likely that clinicians will increasingly be called upon to demonstrate the relevance of these theories to measurable changes in the patient's sense of well-being and social adjustment. As noted above, psychotherapy evaluations based on theories of inferred structure and functioning may be at odds with evaluations from other perspectives. Only to the extent that therapists can demonstrate the relevance of sound psychological structure to long-lasting effective behavior and subjective well-being will there be a consensus on judgments of mental health and psychotherapy outcome. As a practical reality, the existence of a consensus makes it much more likely that psychotherapists will have highly motivated patients and adequate support from society.

Implications for Research

For psychotherapy researchers, perhaps even more than for practicing clinicians, it is essential to adopt the comprehensive approach to assessment embodied in the tripartite model. Thus, in order to obtain a full and accurate picture of therapy's effects on a patient, researchers must attempt to tap simultaneously all three major areas of functioning.

Another point of particular importance to researchers is the assessment of a patient's functioning on at least three occasions: before therapy, immediately following therapy, and again some months or a year later. The assessment of the patient on two occasions following therapy must, as always, be comprehensive (i.e., tap all three perspectives) in order to provide information on the implications of change in one area of functioning for change in other areas. Such information has tremendous practical value in that it provides researchers with data on the relative "cost effectiveness" of various therapies in terms of the time, money, and effort invested. It may be true, for example, that patients in some therapies manifest substantial improvement in a relatively brief time. But if such changes are not sustained over time, or if some changes are accomplished only at the expense of other aspects of the patient's functioning, the apparent superiority of these methods becomes questionable.

Questions of cost effectiveness will undoubtedly increase as the involvement of consumers and society in therapy evaluation expands. Researchers whose designs provide for the kind of comprehensive and long-term evaluation described here will be prepared with better data to confront those issues.

Finally, an essential first step in bringing order into a confused area of study is for researchers to initiate the development and adoption of standardized measurement instruments and techniques to be applied in many settings to a variety of patients and a variety of therapies. This is clearly a difficult recommendation to implement. It will require considerable time and effort, not to mention *willingness* on the part of researchers to identify common dimensions of assessment (for a beginning, see Waskow & Parloff, 1976), but it is not an impossible task. Rapprochement among diverse theoretical orientations (Wachtel, 1977) is growing. As our knowledge has increased, even behavior therapists and psychoanalysts have found that some of their differences may be more illusory than real (Birk & Brinkley-Birk, 1974).

Standardized assessment is not only highly desirable, it is essential. The present situation, characterized by individual researchers developing their own measurement devices, provides no basis for comparisons among studies nor for solid conclusions regarding the relative effectiveness of various therapies, and even less of a basis for conclusions about the effectiveness of psychotherapy in general.

A final issue remains to be noted; we refer to the matter of value judgments and the potential pitfalls associated with them. In the first place, it is important that we recognize value judgments and learn to distinguish them from objective statements of fact. Statements that "psychotherapy was successful" or a "failure" are judgments based on standards of which psychotherapy-related effects are important and which are unimportant, and of which changes are "good" and which are changes for the worse. Researchers cannot, or more accurately must not, fall into the trap of making value judgments. Inevitably, therapists, patients, and agents of society will make value judgments, each from their own unique perspectives and based on their own values. What researchers can and should do is to provide the data—comprehensive data bearing on all major aspects of patients' functioning—upon which sound value judgments can be based. Decisions concerning the integration of the dimensions of functioning into a composite, specifically the importance and weight assigned to each dimension, are significant aspects of such value judgments. Because value judgments of psychotherapy's effects are made from various perspectives and because they are based on divergent values, differing weights often will be assigned to observed effects. Thus, the likelihood of high agreement among "interested parties" that a given outcome is positive or negative is predictably slim. Nonetheless, objective and comprehensive statements of psychotherapy's effectiveness that are maximally value free are a necessity for researchers and for the future respectability of psychotherapy research. Persisting disagreements among judgments of outcome will then clearly be based upon discrepancies of values, rather than upon ignorance of what psychotherapy *does*.

Psychotherapy *must* be evaluated and it *can* be evaluated, although we have no illusions about the difficulties of the undertaking. Many problems in therapy research have been created by investigators themselves. By the same token, researchers have it within their power, by organizing and delimiting their efforts, to refine substantially the quality of available knowledge.

Reference Note

1. Bergin, A. E. Identifying the pseudoshrink. In H. H. Strupp (Chair), *Psychonoxious therapy: Clinical, theoretical, and research perspectives.* Symposium presented at the meeting of the American Psychological Association, Washingtion, D.C., September 1976.

References

Bergin, A. E. The evaluation of therapeutic outcomes. In A. E. Bergin & S. L. Garfield (Eds.), *Handbook of psychotherapy and behavior change.* New York: Wiley, 1971.

Birk, L., & Brinkley-Birk, A. W. Psychoanalysis and behavior therapy. *American Journal of Psychiatry,* 1974, *131,* 499–510.

Gross, S. J., & Miller, J. O. A research strategy for evaluating the effectiveness of psychotherapy. *Psychological Reports,* 1975, *37,* 1011–1021.

Harper, R. A. *The new psychotherapies.* Englewood Cliffs, N.J.: Prentice-Hall, 1975.

Hartley, D., Roback, H. B., & Abramowitz, S. I. Deterioration effects in encounter groups. *American Psychologist,* 1976, *31,* 247–255.

Holtzman, W. N. Foreword, In R. M. Suinn & R. G. Weigel (Eds.), *The innovative psychological therapies: Critical and creative contributions.* New York: Harper & Row, 1975.

Kelman, H. C., & Parloff, M. B. Interrelations among three criteria of improvement in group therapy: Comfort, effectiveness, and self-awareness. *Journal of Abnormal and Social Psychology,* 1957, *54,* 281–288.

Kiesler, D. J. Some myths of psychotherapy research and the search for a paradigm. *Psychological Bulletin,* 1966, *65,* 110–136.

Kittrie, N. N. *The right to be different: Deviance and enforced therapy.* Baltimore, Md.: Johns Hopkins University Press, 1971.

Malan, D. H . Personal communication. In H. H. Strupp, S. W. Hadley, and B. Gomes-Schwartz, *Psychotherapy for better or worse: An analysis of the problem of negative effects.* New York: Jason Aronson, in press.

Parloff, M. B. Shopping for the right therapy. *Saturday Review,* February 21, 1976, 14–20.

Parloff, M. B., Kelman, H. C., & Frank, J. D. Comfort, effectiveness, and self-awareness as criteria of improvement in psychotherapy. *American Journal of Psychiatry,* 1954, *3,* 343–351.

Strupp, H. H. Themes in psychotherapy research. In J. L. Claghorn (Ed.), *Successful psychotherapy.* New York: Brunner/Mazel, 1976.

Strupp, H. H, Fox, R. E., & Lessler, K. *Patients view their psychotherapy.* Baltimore, Md.: Johns Hopkins University Press, 1969.

Strupp, H. H., & Hadley, S. W. A tripartite model of mental health and therapeutic outcomes: With special reference to negative effects in psychotherapy. *American Psychologist,* 1977, *32,* 187–196.

Strupp, H. H., Hadley, S. W., & Gomes-Schwartz, B. *Psychotherapy for better or worse: An analysis of the problem of negative effects.* New York: Jason Aronson, in press.

Szasz, T. S. *The manufacture of madness: A comparative study of the inquisition and the mental health movement.* New York: Harper & Row, 1970.

Urban, H. B., & Ford, D. H. Some historical and conceptual perspectives on psychotherapy and behavior change. In A. E. Bergin & S. L. Garfield (Eds.), *Handbook of psychotherapy and behavior change.* New York: Wiley, 1971.

Wachtel, P. L. *Psychoanalysis and behavior therapy.* New York: Basic Books, 1977.

Waskow, I. E., & Parloff, M. B. (Eds.). *Psychotherapy change measures.* (DHEW Publication No. [ADM] 74-120). Washington, D.C.: U.S. Government Printing Office, 1975.

At the time of original publication of this article, *Suzanne W. Hadley* and *Hans H. Strupp* were at the Department of Psychology, Vanderbilt University, Nashville, Tennessee.

Issues in the Evaluation of Community Mental Health Programs

Herbert C. Schulberg

The new federal emphasis on program effectiveness mandates that a new perspective be developed for evaluating community mental health programs. In discussing data collection designs for evaluation studies, the pros and cons of the experimental method are considered, along with a legal model for evaluating programs. Accepting task-oriented adversarial relationships, the legal model considers societal laws and administrative regulations. Included among evaluation techniques and indexes used in program assessment are management information systems and a number of considerations relating to the measurement of client change and of client outcomes. Priorities must be established among the various evaluation foci, and the values of those urging specific analyses over others will have to be explicated.

Community mental health programs have been central elements in the delivery of psychiatric care for over 10 years. Much attention has focused on the shortcomings of the more than 600 federally funded centers (Chu & Trotter, 1974; U.S. General, 1974); these programs, nevertheless, provide a substantial volume of services and have demonstrated a capacity to remain fiscally viable. Approximately 23% of all patient care episodes in the United States occurred in such facilities during 1973, an increase from close to 0% only 10 years earlier. The annual budgets for these programs, now over $600 million, have swelled at similarly rapid rates since passage by Congress of the initial Community Mental Health Centers Act in 1964. Additional data could be cited on staffing patterns, physical facilities, training programs, citizen involvement, and the like, to demonstrate the burgeoning scope of community mental health programs, but friend and foe alike would agree that these service delivery systems have evolved into "big businesses."

In light of these developments, it may be surprising, even disturbing, to note that the evaluation of community mental health programs has only recently become a formal statutory requirement. After functioning for years on the informal honor system and being permitted to submit any evidence of success that seemed relevant or practical, the Community Mental Health Centers Amendments of 1975 (PL 94-63) required for the first time that community mental health centers establish ongoing quality assurance programs.

Before detailing the act's requirements and their implications for evaluating community mental health programs, it should be emphasized that this and similar statutory thrusts are not aimed at mental health practitioners alone. Rather, they are part of a continuing, major societal effort to hold professionals accountable for the services they provide clients. Schulberg (1976) noted that recent incursions upon the mental health professional's traditional ability to function in splendid, unobserved isolation stem from certain developments.

1. Judicial decisions have established standards of clinical care. The *Wyatt v. Stickney* ruling in Alabama detailed minimal treatment patterns for state hospital patients, and the *O'Connor v. Donaldson* decision in Florida limited the hospitalization of nondangerous patients.
2. The general public is disillusioned with the classic premise that professionals are fundamentally humanitarian helpers who do no

Reprinted from *Professional Psychology*, 1977, *8*, 560–572.

harm. The recent rash of malpractice suits attests to the intensity of present consumer wrath.

3. The federal government has enlarged its role in paying for medical care. This has led Congress to require that physicians audit fiscal expenditures and the clinical results of treatment. Professional standards review organizations now review inpatient psychiatric services and will undoubtedly extend their authority to other essential mental health services as well.

Instead of taking the initiative, mental health professionals have traditionally responded negatively to pressures for greater quality control. More stringent standards have been adopted only after dubious practices evoked adverse publicity (e.g., defining guidelines for the use of electroconvulsive therapy; Frankel, 1973). To some degree, this reactive pattern is evident with regard to community mental health programs as well; it is quite conceivable that federally prescribed rather than center-selected evaluative procedures will serve as the framework for future quality control assessment.

The Community Mental Health Centers Amendments of 1975

As part of its commitment to the continued federal funding of community mental health programs, Congress required that recipients of such grants obligate at least 2% of the preceding year's operating budget for the evaluation of program quality and effectiveness (Windle & Ochberg, 1975). The National Institute of Mental Health (NIMH) has devoted considerable effort during the past year to translating the act into policy and procedural guidelines. Recent drafts of the guidelines make it appear likely that evaluation will focus on the following content areas: (a) cost of a center's operation by type of service, (b) service utilization rates for catchment area residents, (c) service availability in relation to population size, (d) residents' awareness of services, (e) service acceptability to community residents and caregivers, (f) service accessibility in terms of time, geography, costs, and psychological comfort, (g) impact of indirect services on attaining program goals, (h) effectiveness in reducing inappropriate institutionalization, and (i) impact of services on the mental health and related problems of catchment area residents.

It will be evident to even a novice that these evaluative categories range considerably in conceptual and methodological complexity. Some analyses are forthright and easily performed (e.g., calculating service utilization rates and service availability); other analyses require resource capabilities and technical sophistication far beyond that of most centers (e.g., determining the impact of direct and indirect services on a catchment area's residents). Nevertheless, the intent of PL 94-63 is clearly one of shifting evaluative procedures from their traditional focus on input and process to the more significant realm of output. Thus, it is likely that with the passage of time, data of the type now provided by each center on NIMH's annual "Inventory of Comprehensive Community Mental Health Centers," (i.e., primarily client counts and measures of how staff spend their time) will recede in significance. In their place, or as a corollary to them, centers will be required to present data regarding the degree to which defined outcome goals have been achieved under given conditions of resource allocation and service delivery procedures. This new federal emphasis on program effectiveness will create major dilemmas for those administrators and clinicians long accustomed to justifying programmatic growth on the basis of body counts and sheer volume of staff effort. A new perspective will be needed and the elements of this fresh outlook are considered next.

The Purposes of Program Evaluation

Most organizations evaluate policies and programs only periodically, if at all. Human services organizations, in particular, tend to maintain established practices with only minimal concern about their effectiveness and/or propriety; funding usually continues regardless of whether client improvement can be demonstrated. Mental health centers, however, are under increasing pressure to function as self-evaluating organizations that carefully link planning, service delivery, and assessment. These three functions have often been erroneously perceived as discrete rather than related components in an ongoing cycle of program operation, but such arbitrary distinctions are fading. Administrators and researchers are struggling to frame answerable questions that address basic concerns, and as this process unfolds, choices must be made regarding which of the following evaluative categories are most relevant to a given community mental health program's development.

1. Assessment of effort: How are staff utilized and how do these patterns compare with local or national standards?
2. Assessment of performance: What outcomes have the program's efforts produced?
3. Assessment of adequacy: To what extent has the community's problem been solved by this program?
4. Assessment of efficiency: Can the same outcome be achieved at lower cost?

Each type of question is answered with a different type of data. Administrators, therefore, must specify their information needs with some precision if the evaluator's contribution is to be relevant. A review of present mental health evaluation activities leads to the encouraging conclusion that indeed data needs are being expressed in more refined and researchable ways. For example, most administrators now recognize, at least superficially, that they cannot pose global inquiries about their program's worth to evaluators. The repeated admonition in the evaluation literature that program objectives must be specified before assessment can be initiated seems to be paying off! It is particularly significant that in present times of fiscal austerity, increased attention is being paid to assessments of efficiency and cost-benefit (Rosenthal, 1975). Although mental health practitioners have long viewed the economic perspective as irrelevant and even dehumanizing, their resistance is crumbling under the combined weight of legislative demands for fiscal data and improved management information system capabilities. Thus, in addition to growing demands for the assessment of performance or effectiveness, administrators are simultaneously being required to justify fiscal support in the light of criteria more familiar to the world of business than human services.

Given the diverse types of assessment possible within a community mental health program, how are choices made among them? Gaver (1976) highlighted this dilemma by noting that the administrator of a publicly funded program must consider his/her accountability to the patient, clinical staff working with the patient, the center's administrative staff, executive staff within government, appropriate legislative bodies, and the general public. Surely the concerns, even the basic value orientations, of these bodies vary, and the administrator-evaluator must judge how responsive the program can be to each. Priority has often been assigned to the clinical concerns of staff associated with the center (Spivack, St. Clair, Siegel, and Platt, 1975), but, as was previously noted, the economic interests of governmental administrators and legislators are now also rising to the top of the evaluation list.

The Community Mental Health Centers Amendments of 1975 have added a further complexity to the priority selection process by requiring that each center annually prepare an evaluation report, involving the center's board to the extent that this public body is able to participate meaningfully. Although such participation will likely be minimal during the next few years, citizen bodies are increasingly being trained to determine whether mental health programs effectively solve the problems that the community considers most important (MacMurray, Cunningham, Cater, Swenson, & Bellin, 1976). One clearly envisioned consequence of this trend is that assessments of program adequacy (i.e., the degree to which a program not only is effective but also meets a community need) will become much more frequent.

Reference has been made to the implicit, if not explicit, role played by value orientations in people's choices of evaluative priorities and criteria. Studies of organizational effectiveness are not performed in pristine experimental laboratories but rather within a community's sociopolitical framework. Krause and Howard (1976) asserted that evaluative criteria are determined by the values of those participating in action-research programs and through the essentially political and educative process whereby consensus is reached among differing perspectives. It is therefore vital that evaluators explicate the differing values of all parties concerned with a program's purposes and the specific linkages between services and outcome criteria. Community mental health programs usually have multiple goals related to differing value structures (e.g., modifying societal ills and/or clients' acute distress); if evaluative procedures are to be meaningful, they must reconcile the conflicting values of the multiple groups concerned with particular program goals.

Edwards, Guttentag, and Snapper (1975) suggested that "multi-attribute utilities theory" is an appropriate conceptual framework for dealing with such situations; it locates outcomes of concern on relevant value dimensions through such techniques as experimentation, observation, and/or subjective judgment. By weighting each location to reflect its importance relative to the others, it becomes possible to construct a scale of weighted values, reflecting the significance assigned by each interest group to each programmatic outcome criterion. Thus, choices among services and assessment procedures become objective and open to scrutiny.

Data Collection Designs

Evaluation can legitimately be directed toward a variety of purposes whose data needs differ considerably. Nevertheless, controversy continues on the appropriate model of data collection and analysis. Advancing the scientific model as if it were the single yardstick of methodological propriety, some contend that the use of anything less than experimental design relegates evaluation to the domain of art rather than science. Conversely, opponents of the experimental model cite its lack of applicability to their assessment purposes and are quite comfortable with more "artistic" approaches to evaluation. The experimental model is particularly useless for those who view evaluation as "program evaluation," an administrative function geared to management decisions, in contrast to "evaluative research," which produces new knowledge.

However, even those who assess programs without full scientific rigor too often naively disregard the limited internal validity of nonexperimental studies in deriving conclusions and utilizing them for programmatic purposes. What, then, are the key characteristics of data collection models, and which factors need to be considered when selecting from among them?

A fundamental purpose of evaluating community mental health programs is to determine effectiveness (i.e., whether a given service produced a hypothesized outcome on preselected criteria). Because this purpose fits readily within the classical experimental paradigm that seeks to verify causal linkages, much effectiveness assessment is pursued within the experimental model. It adheres to well-accepted scientific principles for ensuring the validity of conclusions and eliminating rival explanations of observed findings. The experimental model requires that the investigator (a) isolate dependent variables and manipulate independent ones and (b) maximize the influence of independent variables while minimizing sources of variance.

An assumption vital to the use of the experimental model in evaluating community mental health programs is that the service to be assessed employs theory to predict the specific consequences of clinical interventions. In the absence of guiding theory, assessment can be directed only at immediately observable and randomly selected processes. Theory-based evaluation employing the experimental model has the advantages of (a) potentially contributing to knowledge about the problem area, (b) exposing assumptions guiding services and choices of variables for study, and (c) permitting interprogram comparisons.

Despite the methodological rigor of the experimental model, its relevance for evaluating community mental health programs is increasingly being questioned (Wells & Fishman, Note 1). Critics assert that the model's key requirements can rarely be met—for example, patients often cannot be assigned randomly among groups, intervention and outcome commonly have only tenuous theoretic linkages, many programs simultaneously employ multiple clinical interventions, and key sources of variance cannot be controlled. Warren (Note 2) is particularly concerned that evaluators seeking to ob viate these practical problems through highly refined research designs so fragment the program being studied that ultimate findings, either positive or negative, are irrelevant to programmatic decision making. If indeed most psychiatric problems have multiple causations, preconditions for the experimental model usually cannot be met. Warren argued that in such instances, evaluators should not confine themselves to designing technically elegant but essentially useless research.

If the experimental model has little usefulness within community mental health program settings, what alternative models are available to those assessing program effectiveness? A closely related approach that has gained considerable acceptance is the quasi-experimental model (Campbell & Stanley, 1963). In has many advantages over the experimental model and is more readily adaptable to operational programs (e.g., it does not require that patients be randomly assigned to experimental and control groups). Nevertheless, both models share a fundamental assumption, that is, "scientific" assessment requires data based upon quantifiable criterion measures gathered in "experimental-type" situations. Although this premise about the conditions necessary for reaching conclusions enjoys wide support among researchers and mental health practitioners, it has little support among those who derive conclusions using different premises.

Meehl (1971) contrasted the differing conceptual frameworks of psychologists and lawyers, and noted the advantages and pitfalls inherent in each group's general approach to information analysis. The relevance of the legal model to program evaluation was described by Levine and Rosenberg (in press). Among its several advantages is the substitution of a common frame of reference for the implicit, possibly contradictory, values and criteria often plaguing experimental studies. By using applicable societal laws and administrative regulations, the legal model makes available explicit criteria against which programmatic performance can be scrutinized and departures tested.

A fundamental characteristic of the legal model is its acceptance of task-oriented adversarial relationships. This contrasts sharply with the scientific model, which usually blurs or minimizes such relationships. With regard to the conclusions to be drawn from presented evidence, Levine and Rosenberg suggested that a cross-disciplinary team classify types of evidence and the inferences to be drawn from each type. Furthermore, decisions regarding the weight of needed evidence should relate to the social costs of Type I and Type II errors, rather than the arbitrary .05 level of probability, which has inherent limitations and misuses. The legal model's usefulness for evaluating health programs remains largely untested, but its principles and rules of evidence must be viewed as potential rivals to those of the experimental and quasi-experimental models.

Evaluation Techniques and Indexes

Evaluators have long recognized that in choosing a program assessment model, they are also selecting the techniques and indexes applicable to a given study. Schulberg, Sheldon, and Baker (1969) reviewed, for example, the variety of techniques and indexes appropriate to the goal attainment model and the systems model. Although Schulberg et al.'s analysis remains largely pertinent at the present time, sophisticated computer technologies for assembling relevant data have been refined in recent years, and advances are also evident in new applications of traditional indexes. Finally, new measures are being developed to fill existing gaps in process and outcome criteria. Given these developments, what indexes can be used to assess community mental health programs, and how can evaluators assemble data relevant to these criterion measures?

The ability to collect and analyze data on clients, staff, funds, and services delivered is basic not only to program evaluation but to the administration of a community mental health program as well. Nevertheless, most observers would agree that despite considerable recent progress in the design of information systems capable of generating needed data (Crawford, Morgan, & Gianturco, 1974), their use is still exceptional rather than routine. A bright spot in this picture is that the Community Mental Health Centers Amendments of 1975 will consider the development or substantial modification of basic data systems part of a center's program evaluation effort for purposes of the requirement that it obligate 2% of operating funds to assessment. Although an information system per se is not considered program evaluation, the data that it produces can be used for various assessment purposes. Broskowski (in press) suggests that management information systems are generally most relevant for measuring organizational effort; they are relatively less ueful for effectiveness studies unless routine, valid measures of client status at intake and discharge are available.

As the capability of management information systems to assemble, store, and analyze countless pieces of data is increasingly refined, it becomes all the more important that clinicians, administrators, and evaluators capitalize on these technological advances. Assessment indexes relate to the evaluatyve purpose on which a center focuses, and they cannot all be enumerated here. However, because indexes of service outcome are of particular salience at this point in the evolution of program evaluation, they warrant a brief review.

If service outcome is to be assessed on meaningful criteria, agreement is needed among the program's key participants about (a) which domain of client change is the target of clinical intervention and (b) whose vantage points are to be considered in determining the meaning of client change on relevant indexes. With regard to the first issue, reduction of symptomatology and psychopathology are the primary outcomes that mental health professionals have traditionally viewed as the goals of treatment. Thus, psychoactive drugs are prescribed in relation to target symptoms; their efficacy is measured in terms of symptom reduction. Similarly, the purpose of psychotherapy is often conceived as reducing psychopathology; measures of psychiatric status are then employed to determine outcome (Waskow & Parloff, 1975).

Community mental health programs are concerned with these criterion measures, but they also place considerable emphasis upon their clients' social functioning and ability to fulfill familial and vocational roles. In fact, one of community mental health ideology's conceptual principles is that clinical services should be directed at improving the client's social functioning rather than reconstructing his/her personality (Baker & Schulberg, 1967). Community mental health programs pursuing socially oriented client goals would employ measures of personal adjustment and role skills, and deemphasize client symptomatology in assessing service outcome.

Regardless of which domain of client change is the program's focus, evaluators must decide whether outcome is to be assessed on existing or newly constructed instruments. There are obvious advantages in using the former; scales with established psychometric properties are more efficient and readily interpreted. A wide array of pertinent tests and rating scales, together with validity, reliability, and normative data, are described by Buros (1972), Comrey, Backer, and Glaser (1973), Chun, Cobb, and French (1973), and Hargreaves, Attkisson, Siegel, McIntyre, and Sorenson (1975).

In contrast to the nomothetic approach underlying standardized measures of change, the idiographic approach is viewed by many evaluators as much more pertinent to the study of client outcome. Kiresuk's (1976) work is the most prominent recent effort to develop unique outcome indexes for each client, and variations of his goal attainment scaling are now employed to assess virtually all types of human services. The technique's fundamental premise—that personalized goal statements should be designed for each client—is operationalized by constructing follow-up scales on which measures of posttreatment functioning are arrayed on a 5-point continuum ranging from least to most favorable outcome. Each scale, covering a different problem area, can be weighted according to its relative importance; the aggregate of individual scale scores produces a total goal attainment scaling score. Although this evaluative procedure is less technically refined than standardized psychometric instruments, it has the distinct advantages of focusing client energies on specific goals and assessing outcome on meaningful indicators.

The rapidly expanding use of goal attainment scaling has also focused fresh concern on the other issue pertinent to evaluating service outcome, that is, whose perspectives are to be considered in analyzing client change. This article has repeatedly suggested that present trends are in the direction of expanding rather than restricting judgmental viewpoints. For example, areas of treatment and outcome criteria may be jointly determined by psychotherapist and client rather than by the former alone; the views of both have equal credence in judging progress toward explicit goals. The views of families are also receiving consideration in formulating therapeutic objectives, particularly in those instances in which relatives resume community living after long-term hospital care. Finally, the views of concerned citizens are now also deemed pertinent. The requirement of the Community Mental Health Centers Amendments of 1975 that citizen boards participate in developing annual evaluation plans will lend further impetus to the inclusion of their outlook on the appropriateness and significance of outcome indexes.

This brief overview of the relationship between evaluative purposes and assessment indexes must also cite the growing concern about a mental health program's cost-efficiency and/or cost-benefit ratio, and the selection of measures suitable to such analyses. The economic perspective generally asserts that public funds should be expended when benefits exceed costs, that they shouldn't be expended when costs exceed benefits, and that when benefits equal costs, the decision can be based on other grounds. Programmatic costs are relatively easy to estimate, but rarely is this true with regard to the benefits of mental health care. Halpern and Binner (1972), Sharfstein and Nafziger (1976), and Murphy and Datel (1976) have generated estimates of the fiscal benefits accruing to clients and society from intensive and/or community-based care, but such analyses require further refinements if economists are to consider their data seriously.

Given the greater feasibility of determining cost per unit of service, particularly when management information systems accurately document the use of staff time, cost-efficiency is assessed by determining the least expensive treatment needed to produce a specified clinical objective. Perhaps the most sophisticated of recent such studies are May's (1971) analyses of the cost to discharge acute schizophrenics from inpatient care. In comparing the length of time needed before patients in each of five treatment modalities could leave the hospital, "drug

alone" was found to be the most cost efficient—a finding with major implications for operating psychiatric inpatient units.

Summary

The evaluation of community mental health programs presents many of the same challenges inherent in the assessment of any human services program. Recent community mental health legislation has created the additional burden, however, of mandating comprehensive evaluations that will exceed local capabilities unless data collection is routinized. Thus, the use of management information systems is imperative, but even with this foundation, long-avoided dilemmas still await administrators and evaluators. Priorities must be established among the various possible evaluative foci, and the values of those urging specific analyses over others will have to be explicated. Of particular concern at this point in time is whether fiscally oriented cost-effectiveness studies will displace other perspectives, a dismaying prospect for clinicians concerned with outcome regardless of cost. Choices among diverse evaluative techniques and indexes similarly remain ambiguous, and this will continue to be the case until clinicians specify the relationship of outcome criteria to theory-based interventions. Finally, data collection designs continue as the subject of controversy between those espousing scientific rigor in program evaluation and those confronting the hard realities of operating clinical services. The experimental and quasi-experimental models are most commonly used for generating valid conclusions, but the legal model, with its unique conceptual framework and rules of evidence, warrants increased attention.

Reference Notes

1. Wells, K. S., & Fishman, D. B. *Classical experimental design: Its usefulness in program evaluation.* Paper presented at the meeting of the American Psychological Association, Chicago, August 31, 1975.
2. Warren, R. *The social context of program evaluation research.* Paper presented at the Ohio State University symposium entitled "Evaluation in Human Services Programs," June 1973.

References

Baker, F., & Schulberg, H. Development of a community mental health ideology scale. *Community Mental Health Journal,* 1967, *3,* 216–225.

Broskowski, A. Management information systems for planning and evaluation in human services. In H. Schulberg & F. Baker (Eds.). *Program evaluation in the health fields* (Vol. 2). New York: Human Sciences Press, in press.

Buros, O. *The seventh mental measurements yearbook.* Highland Park, N.J.: Gryphon Press, 1972.

Campbell, D., & Stanley, J. *Experimental and quasi-experimental designs for research.* Chicago: Rand McNally, 1963.

Chu, F., & Trotter, S. *The madness establishment.* New York: Grossman, 1974.

Chun, K., Cobb, S., & French, J. *Measures for psychological assessment.* Ann Arbor: University of Michigan Institute for Social Research, 1973.

Comrey, A., Backer, T., & Glaser, E. *A sourcebook for mental health measures.* Los Angeles, Calif.: Human Interaction Research Institute, 1973.

Crawford, J., Morgan, D., & Gianturco, D. *Progress in mental health information systems.* Cambridge, Mass.: Ballinger, 1974.

Edwards, W., Guttentag, M., & Snapper, K. A decision-theoretic approach to evaluation research. In E. L. Struening & M. Guttentag (Eds.), *Handbook of evaluation research* (Vol. 1). Beverly Hills, Calif.: Sage, 1975.

Frankel, F. Electro-convulsive therapy in Massachusetts: A task force report. *Massachusetts Journal of Mental Health,* 1973, *3,* 3–29.

Gaver, K. Perspectives of accountability in mental health and retardation services. *Hospital & Community Psychiatry,* 1976, *27,* 635–641.

Halpern, J., & Binner, P. A model for an output value analysis of mental health programs. *Administration in Mental Health,* 1972, Winter, 40–51.

Hargreaves, W. A., Attkisson, C. C., Siegel, L. M., McIntyre, M. H., & Sorenson, J. E. (Eds.). *Resource materials for community mental health program evaluation. Part IV. Evaluating the effectiveness of services* (DHEW Pub. No. [ADM] 75-222). Rockville, Md.: National Institute of Mental Health, 1975.

Kiresuk, T. Goal attainment scaling at a county mental health service. In E. Markson & D. Allen (Eds.), *Trends in mental health evaluation.* Lexington, Mass.: D.C. Heath, 1976.

Krause, M., & Howard, K. Program evaluation in the public interest: A new research methodology. *Community Mental Health Journal,* 1976, *12,* 291–300.

Levine, M., & Rosenberg, N. An adversary model of fact finding and decision making for program evaluation: Theoretical considerations. In H. Schulberg & F. Baker (Eds.), *Program evaluation in the health fields* (Vol. 2). New York: Human Sciences Press, in press.

MacMurray, V., Cunningham, P., Cater, P., Swenson, N., & Bellin, S. *Citizen evaluation of mental health services.* New York: Human Sciences Press, 1976.

May, P. Cost-efficiency of mental health care. III. Treatment method as a parameter of cost in the treatment of schizophrenia. *American Journal of Public Health,* 1971, *61,* 127–129.

Meehl, P. Law and the fireside inductions: Some reflections of a clinical psychologist. *Social Issues,* 1971, *27,* 65–100.

Murphy, J., & Datel, W. A cost benefit analysis of community versus institutional living. *Hospital & Community Psychiatry,* 1976, *27,* 165–170.

Rosenthal, G. The economics of human services. In H. Schulberg & F. Baker (Eds.), *Developments in human services* (Vol. 2). New York: Behavioral Publications, 1975.

Schulberg, H. Quality-of-care standards and professional norms. *American Journal of Psychiatry,* 1976, *133,* 1047–1051.

Schulberg, H., Sheldon, A., & Baker, F. (Eds.). *Program evaluation in the health fields.* New York: Behavioral Publications, 1969.

Sharfstein, S., & Nafziger, J. Community care: Costs and benefits for a chronic patient. *Hospital & Community Psychiatry,* 1976, *27,* 170–173.

Spivack, G., St. Clair, C., Siegel, J., & Platt, J. Differing perspectives on mental health evaluation. *American Journal of Psychiatry,* 1975, *132,* 1295–1299.

U.S. General Accounting Office. *Need for more effective management of community mental health centers program* (Report to the Congress, B-164031 [5]). Washington, D.C.: U.S. Government Printing Office, August 1974.

Waskow, I., & Parloff, M. (Eds.). *Psychotherapy change measures* (DHEW Publication No. [ADM] 74-120). Rockville, Md.: National Institute of Mental Health, 1975.

Windle, C., & Ochberg, F. Enhancing program evaluation in the community mental health centers program. *Evaluation,* 1975, *2,* 31–36.

At the time of original publication of this article, *Herbert C. Schulberg* was a professor of clinical psychiatry and psychology, Regional Programming, Western Psychiatric Institute and Clinic, University of Pittsburgh, Pittsburgh.

Factors Affecting the Utilization of Mental Health Evaluation Research Findings

Lawrence H. Cohen

This article provides an overview of the factors that seem to affect the use of mental health evaluation research findings. Relevant variables are divided into four major categories: characteristics of (a) the evaluation research, (b) the participants, (c) the organization, and (d) the communication channels. A discussion of research characteristics includes coverage of negative findings, methodology, type of evaluation, and site at which it was conducted. The section on the participant contains an analysis of the administrator, the clinical staff, and the evaluator. Research in the area of innovation diffusion is described in the organization section; and finally, the examination of communication channels includes a discussion of techniques designed to enhance utilization as well as an emphasis on the importance of interpersonal communication channels.

It has been assumed over the years that when scientific information exists, it will influence social policy in some manner proportional to its objective value. That assumption now seems oversimplified and probably inaccurate. It is quite evident that mental health program evaluation has had relatively little impact on mental health program policy. Rossman, Hober, and Ciarlo (Note 1), for example, found that in a community mental health center with a strong research department, evaluation data were rated by management and staff as the least relevant input for program decision making among a choice of nine input sources.

The purpose of this article is to provide a brief overview of the factors that seem to affect the use of mental health evaluation research findings. It must be understood at the outset that the broad area of research utilization is a most complex subject, about which few discursive articles have been written, and on which even fewer empirical studies have been conducted.

There is, first of all, a serious problem of definition. The literature is replete with inconsistent and often vague definitions of *research utilization*. Although some writers have stated that awareness of research findings constitutes their utilization, others have claimed that utilization entails the consideration of findings when making decisions. Still others have contended that *utilization* means the implementation of findings, or at least the recommendation of some policy that is consistent with the findings. Finally, many others have equated, at least implicitly, the process of innovation diffusion with research utilization (Cohen, 1976).

In this article, *research utilization* means the consideration of evaluation research as one of several information inputs examined during a decision-making process. A decision maker who decides to pursue some course of action that is inconsistent with evaluation findings may still be employing the research if it provided some input for his/her decision. Preference for this definition of *utilization* is based on the fact that there are multitudinous factors in addition to evaluation research affecting mental health program policy, including political circumstances, legal, ethical, and cultural restraints, and financial limitations. Given the salience of these other factors, it seems unrealistic for an evaluator to expect his/her findings to be automatically converted into program policy (i.e., implemented). However, it does not seem unrealistic to expect evaluation research findings to

Reprinted from *Professional Psychology*, 1977, 8, 526–534.

337

have some bearing on mental health policy decisions.

Four broad classes of variables that seem to affect evaluation research utilization are the characteristics of (a) the evaluation research, (b) the participants (administrator, staff, and program evaluator), (c) the organization, and (d) the communication channels. Such a division is admittedly simplistic, but given the limited space allotment, this division should expedite a brief discussion.

Mental Health Evaluation Research

It is widely known that evaluations of mental health programs often produce negative findings, thus raising serious doubts concerning the efficacy of their respective treatments. However, negative findings are especially difficult to interpret and use. Because few evaluations compare alternative programs or assess the various components of a program, negative findings often do not provide clear information as to what treatment would be effective. Furthermore, few evaluations provide an explication of the theoretical premises underlying the program. Without a specification of the process model of linkages that lead from program input to output, it is difficult to interpret negative findings in terms of the weak links in the program.

Many mental health program evaluations are characterized by methodological inadequacies, which is not surprising given the difficulties associated with conducting true experiments in field settings and operationalizing mental health program goals. Hetherington, Greathouse, O'Brien, Matthias, and Wilner (1974) documented these inadequacies. They surveyed published evaluation research in mental health via their DOPE (Databank of Program Evaluations) computerized library and found that the research was generally characterized by poor experimental design and a lack of reliable information about the programs and their clientele. Some writers, in fact, have claimed that evaluation research should not be used to any great extent because sufficiently sophisticated methodology is not yet extant to warrant confidence in interpreting evaluation findings (Mushkin, 1973).

From a logical standpoint, it would seem that utilization would be affected by the quality of evaluation research. However, it appears that methodology has only a slight effect on the judged usefulness of evaluation research (Patton, Grimes, Guthrie, Brennan, French, & Blyth, Note 2; Sechrest, Note 3). In any case, methodological adequacy is probably not evaluated in an unbiased fashion; when findings confirm management's expectations, design flaws may be overlooked, but when findings are controversial, these same flaws may be highlighted.

One other point related to methodology concerns the measurement of multiple criteria. Because most mental health evaluations assess several goals, agreement between evaluators and program personnel on the program objectives and their relative importance must be reached before an evaluation is conducted. Otherwise, selective or premature use of the findings may result.

Two other factors that seem to be significant determinants of utilization are the type of evaluation and the site at which it was conducted. Formative evaluation findings are probably used more easily than those obtained from a summative project. In addition, because many program administrators are wary of considering evaluations of other programs, offsite evaluations seem rarely to have a significant impact on program policy. This is an unfortunate state of affairs because many programs do share important similarities, and clearly the findings of some evaluations are generalizable to other programs. Of course, caution is warranted; inappropriate use of offsite evaluations may result in specious generalization of the findings to irrelevant treatments and patient populations.

The Participants

The Administrator

Clearly, the role of program administrator is a central one in the utilization process, but there has been literally no scientific investigation of the relationship between the use of scientific information and the characteristics of decision makers. Although the personality and social psychological literature contains a sizable number of investigations examining the general area of decision making and information utilization, these studies have only peripheral relevance to a discussion of research utilization.

Two general points do seem worthy of note. First, it would appear that evaluation research utilization is facilitated by a centralized program administration. The more centralized the administration, the less likely it is that irrelevant input will compete with evaluation findings. Second, administrators vary in the degree to which they value and understand scientific information. Sechrest (Note 3), for example, found that a sizable percentage of health care administrators have virtually no research training and little comprehension of even the basic principles of experimental design.

The Clinical Staff

An evaluator and administrator may agree on what, if any, program changes are necessary, but without the cooperation of the clinical staff, these changes may never even be seriously considered, or if they actually reach fruition, they may be rendered impotent by a threatened and resistant staff.

Clinicians' use of evaluation findings may be hindered by differences, either veridical or perceived, between practitioners and researchers. A lack of understanding between the two groups could lead to practitioners' resistance to the application of research findings. This lack of understanding may be the result of basic differences between the two groups, and several writers have articulated these hypothetical differences: researchers ask why, practitioners ask how; researchers doubt, practitioners believe; researchers are logical, practitioners are intuitive; researchers seek the general, practitioners seek the unique; researchers can tolerate tentativeness, practitioners require certainty (Loevinger, 1963).

Evaluation research may not be used by clinicians because it can be too threatening to the established and already learned theoretical frameworks and practices. Because in most cases they are the treatment agents, mental health service providers have a significant investment in the efficacy of treatment, and resistance to evaluation findings, which are often negative, is

understandable. Furthermore, negative findings may have serious implications for staff job security and status.

Essential to a discussion of clinicians' use of evaluation research is an examination of their attitudes toward applied research in general. It is common knowledge that many clinicians are quite skeptical of research. In a survey of mental health innovators, Larsen and Nichols (1972) found that 38% believed that no research existed that was relevant to their work. Unfortunately, no study to date has used psychometric techniques to measure clinicians' attitudes toward research, and therefore these attitudes must be inferred from other behaviors. One such inference can be made from studies which found that the process of conducting research in clinical settings was viewed by practioners with disfavor (Mitchell & Mudd, 1957; Rosenfeld & Orlinsky, 1961).

Another indication of clinicians' attitudes toward research may be their willingness to participate in research projects. When asked to volunteer even very brief periods of time for psychotherapy research, psychotherapists, as a whole, refuse (Bednar & Shapiro, 1970). One suggestion put forth by Sechrest (1975) and others to improve clinicians' participation in research projects is that researchers should enlist their help at the planning stage of a research project.

The Program Evaluator

It is unclear exactly how evaluation research utilization is affected by the role of the program evaluator. In general, it would seem that the more integrally involved he/she is in the program administration and the higher up he/she is in the administrative hierarchy, the more likely evaluation data will be used and implemented. Outside evaluators, affiliated with an academic or research institution, are often viewed with mistrust, and program personnel may feel that they are unable to adequately assess their program because they do not really comprehend its rationale and objectives. On the other hand, outside evaluators may also be seen as possessing more expertise and objectivity than internal evaluators, and their findings may then be accepted as more valid and objective.

An evaluator who is perceived as a program consultant may be in the position to expedite evaluation research utilization. Several writers in the field of evaluation have begun to view the evaluation process from a planned-change perspective, emphasizing the role of the evaluator as a combination of researcher-organizational change consultant. Discussed in the last section is the importance of effective interpersonal communication of research findings, and it would seem that unless evaluators assume major responsibility for communicating their findings via the interpersonal mode, utilization may be negligible.

As a final point, the personality of the evaluator would also seem to influence utilization. A researcher who views the program as his/her laboratory and the program staff as his/her underlings will generally have a deleterious effect not only on the process of data collection but also on that of research utilization.

The Organization

Despite the fact that utilization would seem to be greatly influenced by organizational features, there exists no discrete body of knowledge explicating the relationship between organizational characteristics and research utilization and implementation. A related field of research has examined those organizational features that are associated with innovation adoption, but the findings are less than persuasive. In a study of innovation diffusion among community mental health centers, the examination of such variables as staff size, number of clients, size of budget, region of the country, distance from the nearest university, and professional disciplines of the staff has failed to produce significant findings (Larsen, Note 4). Similarly, Fairweather, Sanders, Tornatsky, and Harris (1974), in their classic study of innovation diffusion among state and federal mental hospitals, were unable to uncover any organizational characteristics related to the adoption of their community lodge program for chronic mental patients.

Attkisson, McIntyre, Hargreaves, Harris, and Ochberg (1974) developed a conceptual model of the internal evaluative capability of mental health programs. This model integrates essential components of an evaluation process that has potential value for management decision making. Their model specifies one dimension that warrants mention here. Mental health programs vary along a continuum of information capability ranging from unplanned and uncoordinated natural data banks to planned access data systems supported by allocated resources. It would seem that in general, the more a program falls toward the latter end of this continuum, the more capable it is of utilizing evaluation findings.

The Communication Channels

The manner in which mental health evaluation findings are communicated would seem to be a significant determinant of the degree to which they are used by administrators and clinical staff. The following guidelines, gleaned from the research utilization literature, represent important means for facilitating the use of evaluation findings.

1. Interim reports should be provided. Regular research reports, specifying the progress made on the project and the nature of the data obtained, might encourage a feeling of community ownership of the research.

2. A timely final report should be submitted. If evaluation findings are disseminated after program decisions have been reached, they will not constitute an important information input.

3. The findings should be disseminated to significant decision makers. Rossman et al. (Note 1) found that it was critical that community mental health evaluation findings find their way directly to top management personnel.

4. The interpretation of the findings should emphasize the theory underlying the program, rather than the program per se. This could help reduce the threatening nature of negative findings and provide an objective perspective from which the findings may be evaluated.

5. A candid discussion of the limitations of the research is necessary so that it can be objectively scrutinized.

6. Written reports distributed to all program staff should be nontechnical, bereft of jargon, and clearly written. The highly technical and erudite vocabulary of researchers often confuses administrators and practitioners and hence discourages research utilization.

7. It is extremely important that evaluation findings be effectively communicated interpersonally. Researchers have known for many years that interpersonal communication is a great facilitator of change. One study found that the most important factor affecting the impact of health care evaluation on program participants was the interpersonal one, that is, the degree to which the findings were effectively communicated interpersonally to appropriate decision makers (Patton et al., Note 2). In the mental health field specifically, it appears that practitioners value and use interpersonal channels more than formal written channels in their practice (Larsen & Nichols, 1972). Finally, Fairweather et al. (1974) and Larsen, Arutunian, and Finley (Note 5), in their study of innovation diffusion among mental hospitals and community mental health centers, respectively, found that interpersonal communication (i.e., consultation and site visitation) in conjunction with written communication was a more effective diffusion strategy than the mere provision of written descriptions of the innovations.

It should also be pointed out that unlike other fields, such as vocational rehabilitation, mental health has not yet developed professional linkage roles designed to foster the application of research findings to clinical programs. In 1969 the Research Utilization Branch of the Social and Rehabilitation Service of the U.S. Department of Health, Education, and Welfare began granting funds to nine states to support vocational rehabilitation research utilization specialists, who serve as liaisons among the state agency, regional office, and research programs. The role of the specialist is to persuade administrators and practitioners to adopt innovations coming from research. Evaluation of this role has shown that it is an effective linkage innovation, and the creation of a similar position in mental health might help to bridge the research-practice gap characterizing the field.

Conclusion

The use of mental health evaluation findings seems to be affected by the characteristics of the research, the program participants, the organization, and the communication channels. Specific recommendations for enhancing evaluation research utilization are, for the most part, conspicuously absent from this article because the fund of knowledge in this area is quite scarce. Unfortunately, mental health evaluation research has itself not been extensively evaluated in terms of its impact on mental health program policy. From a broader perspective, it should be pointed out that the amount of scientific information produced in Western society is growing at an exponential rate, perhaps doubling every 15 years (Price, 1962), and evaluation research is but one form of scientific investigation that apparently has had only a trivial societal impact relative to its potential.

Reference Notes

1. Rossman, B., Hober, D., & Ciarlo, J. *Awareness, use, and consequences of evaluation data in a community mental health center.* Unpublished manuscript, 1976. (Available from James Ciarlo, Department of Psychology, University of Denver, Denver, Colo.)
2. Patton, M., Grimes, P., Guthrie, K., Brennan, N., French, B., & Blyth, D. *In search of impact: An analysis of the utilization of federal health evaluation research.* Unpublished manuscript, 1975. (Available from M. Patton, Minnesota Center for Social Research, University of Minnesota, Minneapolis, Minn.)
3. Sechrest, L. *The use of research in policy decisions.* Final report on Grant HS 01628, 1976. (Available from author, Department of Psychology, Florida State University, Tallahassee, Fla.)
4. Larsen, J. Personal communication, February 17, 1976.
5. Larsen, J., Arutunian, C., & Finley, C. *Diffusion of innovations among community mental health centers.* Final report on Grant MH 21215, 1974. (Available from J. Larsen, American Institutes for Research, Palo Alto, Calif.)

References

Attkisson, C., McIntyre, M., Hargreaves, W., Harris, M., & Ochberg, F. A working model for mental health program evaluation. *American Journal of Orthopsychiatry,* 1974, *44,* 741–753.
Bednar, R., & Shapiro, J. Professional research commitment: A symptom or a syndrome. *Journal of Consulting and Clinical Psychology,* 1970, *34,* 323–326.

Cohen, L. Clinicians' utilization of research findings. *JSAS Catalog of Selected Documents in Psychology*, 1976, *6*, 116. (Ms. No. 1376)

Fairweather, G., Sanders, D., Tornatsky, L., & Harris, R. *Creating change in mental health organizations.* New York: Pergamon Press, 1974.

Hetherington, R., Greathouse, V., O'Brien, W., Matthias, R., & Wilner, D. Inside DOPE: The nature of program evaluation in mental health. *Evaluation*, 1974, *2*, 78–82.

Larsen, J., & Nichols, D. If nobody knows you've done it, have you? *Evaluation*, 1972, *1*, 39–44.

Loevinger, J. Conflict on commitment in clinical research. *American Psychologist*, 1963, *18*, 241–251.

Mitchell, H., & Mudd, E. Anxieties associated with the conduct of research in a clinical setting. *American Journal of Orthopsychiatry*, 1957, *27*, 310–323.

Mushkin, S. Evaluations: Use with caution. *Evaluation*, 1973, *1*, 31–35.

Price, D. The exponential curve of science. In B. Barber & W. Hirsch (Eds.), *The sociology of science.* New York: Free Press of Glencoe, 1962.

Rosenfeld, J., & Orlinsky, N. The effect of research on practice. *Archives of General Psychiatry*, 1961, *5*, 176–182.

Sechrest, L. Research contributions of practicing clinical psychologists. *Professional Psychology*, 1975, *6*, 413–419.

At the time of original publication of this article, *Lawrence H. Cohen* was at the Department of Psychology, Ohio Wesleyan University, Delaware, Ohio.

6

Other Review Mechanisms

There are a number of mechanisms for assuring quality services and accountability in addition to the program evaluation strategies discussed in the previous section. This section considers the advantages and disadvantages of such mechanisms as minimum care standards and retrospective review of services. The methods presented in these two sections differ in perspective, cost, and benefits. Program evaluation is a continuing process that examines the actual outcomes of all services and all providers (or repeated random samples thereof). It is often costly, but it also provides valuable comparative information for improving the system and/or the services of individual providers. Obviously, it is also very threatening. On the other hand, the development of training standards, facility standards, and service delivery standards is less costly. It needs to be performed less frequently and consumes less time. It is also more subjective and less frequently based on empirical data. The purpose of developing such standards is to eliminate those gross and obviously inadequate providers or services, but little additional information is obtained in the process.

While these two general strategies of quality assurance are different, they are not true alternatives. Program evaluation, facility and provider standards, and peer review of service should be complementary components of a comprehensive quality assurance process. Too often these various mechanisms are seen as separate alternatives for assuring quality rather than as parts of a complete accountability system. Moreover, when the two strategies are combined within one review system, a genuine merger of the two strategies often fails to occur, particularly if the system is dominated by professionals with a single perspective, as in the case of Professional Standards Review Organizations (PSROs).

The medical profession and the psychological profession differ in their orientations toward quality assurance. The medical profession's model of quality assurance most frequently addresses whether or not a minimum level of acceptability has been reached. Any mature profession can and should do this. (Examples of such efforts by organized psychology include the *Standards for Providers of Psychological Services,* which we have reprinted in this volume, the APA Accreditation Standards, the APA Ethical Code, and the Model Guidelines for State Legislation Affecting the Practice of Psychology.) Psychology tends to seek proof, not just expert opinion. Prospective statements of outcomes are emphasized over intentions. As such, qualifying examinations in specialty areas require both work samples and task performance under observation. The psychology-developed CHAMPUS claims-review process includes the requirement of prospective statements of expected improvements and assessment of the degree of achievement of the goals.

Minimal care or qualification standards improve the profession and protect the public when a long-term perspective is taken. They assure minimum training standards and minimum facility standards that serve to eliminate the most obviously inadequate or nonhelpful treatments. This is valuable, but it is also slow. Of necessity, such a review system disapproves only a miniscule number of cases, rejecting only the most grossly harmful procedures or providers. If this system rejected even 5% of those reviewed, those threatened with disenfranchisement would likely move to end or limit the review process. In addition, such a system of review provides no further differentiation in the quality of care beyond the minimal level.

The medical model of quality assurance is similar to the medical model of treatment. Administrators bring their review problems to the assumed expert who renders a decision on the "appropriateness" of the particular procedure. A pronouncement is made with minimal explanation or rationale. It is based on the limited local opinion of "acceptable practice," not on empirical data. The advice is to be followed, not questioned. Medical input and opinion is obviously useful in the treatment process and the review; however, it offers only one perspective and not always the best or most appropriate one. Moreover, the medical model of quality assurance is a procedure that limits the expansion of ability to judge and ignores the issue of whether or not another treatment procedure would have been clinically "better" and/or more cost-efficient. The basic orientation of the medical model of quality assurance constitutes a disincentive to the production of knowledge and an impediment to change. Such quality-of-care processes look at each individual incident of treatment, office visit, or clinical procedure in an isolated manner and consider whether or not in that situation a reasonable course of action was followed. Thus a system-wide perspective focused on the ultimate outcome of treatment is not taken. It is this limited model of quality assurance that allows our nation to simultaneously have a high overall quality-of-care rating and a high rate of infant mortality.

The orientation of psychology to quality of care is more systematically comparative than that of the medical profession. It addresses the final outcome and total impact of the intervention on the patient and is more likely to compare two different treatment procedures (or a treatment with no treatment) in order to state outcomes in relative or comparative terms. This approach considers intended as well as unintended outcomes, facilitates more rapid improvement in clinical practice, and encourages rigorous systematic research to determine the specific conditions under which one clinical procedure is better than another. As noted earlier, psychology attempts to incorporate such empirical and outcome criteria within its minimal care or minimal qualification standards as well.

In this section we present a variety of articles related to the current state-of-the-art of quality assurance in mental health care. First, we present the *Standards for Providers of Psychological Services,* a policy statement of the American Psychological Association passed by its Council of Representatives. The *Standards* represent psychologists' efforts at self-regulation in the public interest. Next, Claiborn and Zaro's article illustrates how psychology attempts to bring outcome evaluation into treatment planning and, later, peer review and claims review. (Nonpsychologists might be interested in reading the *Ethical Standards of Psychologists,* available from the American Psychological Association.)

Professional Standards Review Organizations (PSROs) were created as a quality assurance and cost containment mechanism by Public Law 92-603, an amendment to the Social Security Act. PSRO review components are intended to include concurrent "necessary to use" utilization review, retrospective peer review of quality of care, and retrospective "profile analyses" or patterns-of-care analyses. PSROs have functionally excluded nonphysicians. Psychologists have always had difficulty with the narrow definition of health care used by PSROs and with PSROs' almost sole emphasis on medicine. Many of these criticisms are included in the reprinted 1977 APA testimony on PSROs to the House Ways and Means Subcommittee on Health.

In addition, we have included the summary of a comprehensive Institute of Medicine study of health care quality assurance. This study was requested by Congress (as part of the Health Maintenance Organization Act of 1973—Public Law 93-222). The emphasis is on medical treatment, not health care. Little attention is given to mental health care and its quality assurance. Next are included a few pages from a 1976 study by the National Institute of Mental Health on the financing, utilization, and quality of mental health care, in which mental health care seems to be equated with care provided by psychiatrists.

Medical/psychiatric control in the mental health field is explored in the Dörken and Morrison article. Dörken and Morrison describe the problems psychologists have had with the Standards for Accreditation of Psychiatric Facilities utilized by the Joint Commission for the Accreditation of Hospitals. These problems are still unresolved. Schacht and Nathan discuss some of the difficulties they find with DSM-III (the *Diag-*

nostic and Statistical Manual of Mental Disorders promulgated by the American Psychiatric Association). They present DSM-III not only as a conceptualization of diagnostic practice but also as a document of considerable legal and economic consequence. Heck criticizes public mental health programs in general and urges the development of new service delivery systems. Albee and Kessler urge psychologists to develop their own mechanisms of quality assurance lest inappropriate procedures be developed by others and forced on the profession. Finally, Morrison describes how he attempted to entice consumers into the evaluation of services by setting up a consumer advisory board for his clinic.

Standards for Providers of Psychological Services

American Psychological Association

The Standards for Providers of Psychological Services are organized psychology's code for regulating itself and protecting the public interest. The Standards specify minimum acceptable levels for providers, programs, professional accountability, and service environments. The Standards cover psychological functions, not classes of practitioners.

In January 1975, the APA Council of Representatives created the original Committee on Standards for Providers of Psychological Services. The Committee was charged with updating and revising the Standards adopted in September 1974. Members of the Committee were Jacqueline C. Bouhoutsos, Leon Hall, Marian D. Hall, Mary Henle, Durand F. Jacobs (Chair), Abel Ossorio, and Wayne Sorenson. Task force liaison was Jerry H. Clark, and Central Office liaison was Arthur Centor.

In January 1976, Council further charged the Committee to review the *Standards* and recommend revisions needed to reflect the varying needs of only those psychologists engaged in the activities of clinical, counseling, industrial-organizational, and school psychology. The Committee was reconstituted with one member representing each of the four applied activities, plus one member representing institutional practice and one representing the public interest.

Members were Jules Barron, clinical; Barbara A. Kirk, counseling; Frank Friedlander, industrial-organizational (replacing Virginia Schein); Durand F. Jacobs (Chair), institutional practice; M. Brewster Smith, public interest; Marian D. Hall, school; Arthur Centor was Central Office liaison.

The Standards that follow are the first revision of the national Standards for Providers of Psychological Services originally adopted by the American Psychological Association (APA) on September 4, 1974.[1] (Note: Footnotes 2-24 appear at the end of the Standards. See pp. 502–505.) The intent of these Standards is to improve the quality, effectiveness, and accessibility of psychological services to all who require them.[2]

These Standards represent the attainment of a goal for which the Association has striven for over 20 years, namely, to codify a uniform set of standards for psychological practice that would serve the respective needs of users, providers, and third-party purchasers and sanctioners of psychological services. In addition, the Association has established a standing committee charged with keeping the Standards responsive to the needs of these groups and with upgrading and extending them progressively as the profession and science of psychology continue to develop new knowledge, improved methods, and additional modes of psychological service. These Standards have been established by organized psychology as a means of self-regulation to protect the public interest.

While these revised Standards contain a

---

[1] Members of the Task Force on Standards for Service Facilities that submitted the original Standards in September 1974 were Milton L. Blum, Jacqueline C. Bouhoutsos, Jerry H. Clark, Harold A. Edgerton, Marian D. Hall, Durand F. Jacobs (Chair, 1972–1974), Floyd H. Martinez, John E. Muthard, Asher R. Pacht, William D. Pierce, Sue A. Warren, and Alfred M. Wellner (Chair, 1970–71). Staff liaisons from the APA Office of Professional Affairs were John J. McMillan (1970–1971), Gottlieb C. Simon (1971–1973), and Arthur Centor (1973–1974).

Reprinted from *American Psychologist,* 1977, *42,* 495–505.

number of important changes, they differ from the original Standards in two major respects:

1. They uniformly specify the *minimally acceptable levels* of quality assurance and performance that providers of those psychological services covered by the Standards must reach or exceed. Care has been taken to assure that each standard is clearly stated, readily measurable, realistic, and implementable.

2. The revised Standards apply to a more limited range of services than the original Standards. The present Standards have been restricted to applications in "human services" with the goal of facilitating more effective human functioning. The kinds of psychological services covered by the present Standards are those ordinarily involved in the practice of specialists in clinical, counseling, industrial-organization, and school psychology. However, it is important to note that these Standards cover psychological *functions* and not classes of practitioners.

Any persons representing themselves as psychologists, when providing any of the covered psychological service functions at any time and in any setting, whether public or private, profit or nonprofit, are required to observe these standards of practice in order to promote the best interests and welfare of the users of such services. It is to be understood that fulfillment of the requirements to meet these Standards shall be judged by peers in relation to the capabilities for evaluation and the circumstances that prevail in the setting at the time the program or service is evaluated.

Standards covering other psychological service functions may be added from time to time to those already listed. However, functions and activities related to the teaching of psychology, the writing or editing of scholarly or scientific manuscripts, and the conduct of scientific research do not fall within the purview of the present Standards.

Historical Background

Early in 1970, acting at the direction of the Association's Council of Representatives, the Board of Professional Affairs appointed a Task Force composed of practicing psychologists with specialized knowledge in at least one of every major class of human service facility and with experience relevant to the setting of standards. Its charge was to develop a set of standards for psychological practice. Soon thereafter, partial support for this activity was obtained through a grant from the National Institute of Mental Health.[3]

First, the Task Force established liaison with national groups already active in standard setting and accreditation. It was therefore able to influence the adoption of certain basic principles and wording contained in standards for psychological services published by the Joint Commission of Accreditation of Hospitals (JCAH) Accreditation Council for Facilities for the Mentally Retarded (1971) and by the Accreditation Council for Psychiatric Facilities (JCAH, 1972). It also contributed substantially to the "constitutionally required minimum standards for adequate treatment of the mentally ill" ordered by the U.S. District Court in Alabama (*Wyatt* v. *Stickney,* 1972). In concert with other APA committees, the Task Force also represented the Association in national-level deliberations with governmental groups and insurance carriers that defined the qualifications necessary for psychologists involved in providing health services.

These interim outcomes involved influence by the Association on actions by groups of nonpsychologists that directly affected the manner in which psychological services were employed, particularly in health and rehabilitation settings. However, these measures did not relieve the Association from exercising its responsibility to speak out directly and authoritatively on what standards for psychological practice should be throughout a broad range of human service settings. It was also the responsibility of the Association to determine how psychologists would be held accountable should their practice fail to meet quality standards.

In September 1974, after more than 4 years of study and broad consultations, the Task Force proposed a set of standards, which the Association's Council of Representatives adopted and voted to publish in order to meet urgent needs of the public and the profession. Members of Council had various reservations about the scope and wording of the Standards as initially adopted. By establishing a continuing Committee on Standards, Council took the first step in what would be an ongoing process of review and revision.

The task of collecting, analyzing, and synthesizing reactions to the original Standards fell to two successive committees. They were charged similarly to review and revise the Standards and to suggest means to implement them, including their acceptance by relevant governmental and private accreditation groups. The dedicated work of the psychologists who served on both those committees is gratefully acknowledged. Also recognized with thanks are the several hundred comments received from scores of interested persons representing professional, academic, and scientific psychology, consumer groups, administrators of facilities, and others. This input from those directly affected by the original Standards provided the major stimulus and much of the content for the changes that appear in this revision.

Principles and Implications of the Standards

A few basic principles have guided the development of these Standards:

1. There should be a single set of standards that governs psychological service functions offered by psychologists, regardless of their specialty, setting, or form of remuneration. All psychologists in professional practice should be guided by a uniform set of standards just as they are guided by a common code of ethics.

2. Standards should clearly establish minimally acceptable levels of quality for covered psychological service functions, regardless of the character of the users, purchasers, or sanctioners of such covered services.

3. All persons providing psychological services shall meet minimally acceptable levels of training and experience, which are consistent and appropriate with the functions they perform. However, final responsibility and accountability for services provided must rest with psychologists who have earned a doctoral degree in a program that is primarily psychological at a regionally accredited university or professional school. Those providing psychological services who have lesser (or other) levels of training shall be supervised by a psychologist with the above training. This level of qualification is necessary to assure that the public receives services of high quality.

4. There should be a uniform set of standards governing the quality of services to all users of psychological services in both the private and public sectors. There is no justification for maintaining the double standard presently embedded in most state legislation whereby providers of private fee-based psychological services are subject to statutory regulation, while those providing similar psychological services under governmental auspices are usually exempt from such regulations. This circumstance tends to afford greater protection under the law for those receiving privately delivered psychological services. On the other hand, those receiving privately delivered psychological services currently lack many of the safeguards that are available in governmental settings; these include peer review, consultation, record review, and staff supervision.

5. While assuring the user of the psychologist's accountability for the nature and quality of services rendered, standards must not constrain the psychologist from employing new methods or making flexible use of support personnel in staffing the delivery of services.

The Standards here presented have broad implications both for the public who use psychological services and for providers of such services:

1. Standards provide a firmer basis for a mutual understanding between provider and user and facilitate more effective evaluation of services provided and outcomes achieved.

2. Standards are an important step toward greater uniformity in legislative and regulatory actions involving providers of psychological services, and Standards provide the basis for the development of accreditation procedures for service facilities.

3. Standards give specific content to the profession's concept of ethical practice.

4. Standards have significant impact on tomorrow's training models for both professional and support personnel in psychology.

5. Standards for the provision of psychological services in human service facilities influence what is considered acceptable structure, budgeting, and staffing patterns in these facilities.

6. Standards are living documents that require continual review and revision.

The Standards illuminate weaknesses in the delivery of psychological services and point to their correction. Some settings are known to require additional and/or higher standards for specific areas of service delivery than those herein proposed. There is no intent to diminish the scope or quality of psychological services that exceed these Standards.

Systematically applied, these Standards serve to establish uniformly the *minimally acceptable levels* of psychological services. They serve to establish a more effective and consistent basis for evaluating the performance of individual service providers, and they serve to guide the organizing of psychological service units in human service settings.

Definitions

Providers of psychological services refers to the following persons:

A. Professional psychologists.[4] Professional psychologists have a doctoral degree from a regionally accredited university or professional school in a program that is primarily psychological[5] and have appropriate training and experience in the area of service offered.[6]

B. All other persons who offer psychological services under the supervision of a professional psychologist.

Psychological services refers to one or more of the following:[7]

A. Evaluation, diagnosis, and assessment of the functioning of individuals and groups in a variety of settings and activities.

B. Interventions to facilitate the functioning of individuals and groups. Such interventions may include psychological counseling, psychotherapy, and process consultation.

C. Consultation relating to A and B above.

D. Program development services in the areas of A, B, and C above.[8]

E. Supervision of psychological services.

A *psychological service unit* is the functional unit through which psychological services are provided:

A. A psychological service unit is a unit that provides predominantly psychological services and is composed of one or more professional psychologists and supporting staff.

B. A psychological service unit may operate as a professional service or as a functional or geographic component of a larger governmental, educational, correction, health, training, industrial, or commercial organizational unit.[9]

C. A psychologist proving professional services in a multioccupational setting is regarded as a psychological service unit.

D. A psychological service unit also may be an individual or group of individuals in a private practice or a psychological consulting firm.

User includes:

A. Direct users or recipients of psychological services.

B. Public and private institutions, facilities, or organizations receiving psychological services.

C. Third-party purchasers—those who pay for the delivery of services but who are not the recipients of services.

Sanctioners refers to those users and nonusers who have a legitimate concern with the accessibility, timeliness, efficacy, and standards of quality attending the provision of psychological services. In addition to the users, sanctioners may include members of the user's family, the court, the probation officer, the school administrator, the employer, the union representative, the facility director, etc. Another class of sanctioners is represented by various governmental, peer review, and accreditation bodies concerned with the assurance of quality.

Standard 1. Providers

1.1 *Each psychological service unit offering psychological services shall have available at least one professional psychologist and as many more professional psychologists as are necessary to assure the quality of services offered.*

INTERPRETATION: The intent of this Standard is that one or more providers of psychological services in any psychological service unit shall meet the levels of training and experience of the professional psychologist as specified in the preceding definitions.[10]

When a professional psychologist is not available on a full-time basis, the facility shall retain the services of one or more professional psychologists on a regular part-time basis to supervise the psychological services provided. The psychologist(s) so retained shall have authority and participate sufficiently to enable him or her to assess the needs for services, review the content of services provided, and assume professional responsibility and accountability for them.

1.2 *Providers of psychological services who do not meet the requirements for the professional psychologist shall be supervised by a professional psychologist who shall assume professional responsibility and accountability for the services provided. The level and extent of supervision may vary from task to task so long as the supervising psychologist retains a sufficiently close supervisory relationship to meet this standard.*

1.3 *Wherever a psychological service unit exists, a professional psychologist shall be responsible for planning, directing, and reviewing the provision of psychological services.*

INTERPRETATION: This psychologist shall coordinate the activities of the psychological service unit with other professional, administrative, and technical groups, both within and outside the facility. This psychologist, who may be the director, chief, or coordinator of the psychological service unit, has related responsibilities including, but not limited to, recruiting qualified staff, directing training and research activities of the service, maintaining a high level of professional and ethical practice, and assuring that staff members function only within the areas of their competency.

In order to facilitate the effectiveness of services by increasing the level of staff sensitivity and professional skills, the psychologist

designated as director shall be responsible for participating in the selection of the staff and supporting personnel whose qualifications and skills (e.g., language, cultural and experiential background, race, and sex) are directly relevant to the needs and characteristics of the users served.

1.4 *When functioning as part of an organizational setting, professional psychologists shall bring their background and skills to bear whenever appropriate upon the goals of the organization by participating in the planning and development of overall services.*[11]

INTERPRETATION: Professional psychologists shall participate in the maintenance of high professional standards by representation on committees concerned with service delivery.

As appropriate to the setting, these activities may include active participation, as voting and as office-holding members on the facility's executive, planning, and evaluation boards and committees.

1.5 *Psychologists shall maintain current knowledge of scientific and professional developments that are directly related to the services they render.*

INTERPRETATION: Methods through which knowledge of scientific and professional development may be gained include, but are not limited to, continuing education, attendance at workshops, participation in staff development, and reading scientific publications.[12]

The psychologist shall have ready access to reference material related to the provision of psychological services.

Psychologists must be prepared to show evidence periodically that they are staying abreast of current knowledge and practices through continuing education.

1.6 *Psychologists shall limit their practice to their demonstrated areas of professional competence.*

INTERPRETATION: Psychological services will be offered in accordance with the provider's areas of competence as defined by verifiable training and experience. When extending services beyond the range of their usual practice, psychologists shall obtain pertinent training or appropriate professional supervision.

1.7 *Psychologists who wish to change their service specialty or to add an additional area of applied specialization must meet the same requirements with respect to subject matter and professional skills that apply to doctoral training in the new specialty.*[13]

INTERPRETATION: Training of doctoral-level psychologists to qualify them for change in specialty will be under the auspices of accredited university departments or professional schools that offer the doctoral degree in that specialty. Such training should be individualized, due credit being given for relevant coursework or requirements that have previously been satisfied. Merely taking an internship or acquiring experience in a practicum setting is not considered adequate preparation for becoming a clinical, counseling, industrial-organizational, or school psychologist when prior training has not been in the relevant area. Fulfillment of such an individualized training program is attested to by the award of a certificate by the supervising department or professional school indicating the successful completion of preparation in the particular specialty.

Standard 2.   Programs

2.1 *Composition and organization of a psychological service unit:*

2.1.1 *The composition and programs of a psychological service unit shall be responsive to the needs of the persons or settings served.*

INTERPRETATION: A psychological service unit shall be so structured as to facilitate effective and economical delivery of services. For example, a psychological service unit serving a predominantly low-income, ethnic, or racial minority group should have a staffing pattern and service program that is adapted to the linguistic, experiential, and attitudinal characteristics of the users.

2.1.2 *A description of the organization of the psychological service unit and its lines of responsibility and account-ability for the delivery of psychological services shall be available in written form to staff of the unit and to users and sanctioners upon request.*

INTERPRETATION: The description should include lines of responsibility, supervisory relationships, and the level and extent of accountability for each person who provides psychological services.

2.1.3 *A psychological service unit shall include sufficient numbers of professional and support personnel to achieve its goals, objectives, and purposes.*

INTERPRETATION: The workload and diversity of psychological services required and the specific goals and objectives of the setting will determine the numbers and qualifications of professional and support personnel in the psychological service unit. Where shortages in personnel exist so that psychological services cannot be rendered in a professional manner, the director of the psychological service unit shall initiate action to modify appropriately the specific goals and objectives of the service.

2.2 *Policies:*

2.2.1 *When the psychological service unit is composed of more than one person wherein a supervisory relationship exists or is a component of a larger organization, a written statement of its objectives and scope of services shall be developed and maintained.*

INTERPRETATION: The psychological service unit shall review its objectives and scope of services annually and revise them as necessary to insure that the psychological services offered are consistent with staff competencies and current psychological knowledge and practice. This statement should be distributed to staff and, where appropriate, to users and sanctioners upon request.

2.2.2 *All providers within a psychological service unit shall support the legal and civil rights of the user.*[14]

INTERPRETATION: Providers of psychological services shall safeguard the interests of the user with regard to personal, legal, and civil rights. They shall continually be sensitive to the issue of confidentiality of information, the short-term and long-term impact of their decisions and recommendations, and other matters pertaining to individual, legal, and civil rights. Concerns regarding the safeguarding of individual rights of users include, but are not limited to, problems of self-incrimination in judicial proceedings, involuntary commitment to hospitals, protection of minors or legal incompetents, discriminatory practices in employment selection procedures, recommendations for special education provisions, information relative to adverse personnel actions in the armed services, and the adjudication of domestic relations disputes in divorce and custodial proceedings. Providers of psychological services should take affirmative action by making themselves available for local committees, review boards, and similar advisory groups established to safeguard the human, civil, and legal rights of service users.

2.2.3 *All providers within a psychological service unit shall be familiar with and adhere to the American Psychological Association's* Ethical Standards for Psychologists, Psychology as a Profession, Standards for Educational and Psychological Tests, *and other official policy statements relevant to standards for professional services issued by the Association.*

INTERPRETATION: Providers of psychological services, users, and sanctioners may order copies of these documents from the American Psychological Association.

2.2.4 *All providers within a psychological service unit shall conform to relevant statutes established by federal, state, and local governments.*

INTERPRETATION: All providers of psychological services shall be familiar with appropriate statutes regulating the practice of psychology. They shall also be informed about agency regulations that have the force of law and that relate to the delivery of psychological services (e.g., evaluation for disability retirement and special education placements). In addition, all providers shall be cognizant that federal agencies such as the Veterans Administration and the Department of Health, Education, and Welfare have policy statements regarding psychological services. Providers of psychological services shall be familiar with other statutes and regulations, including those addressed to the civil and legal rights of users (e.g., those promulgated by the federal Equal Employment Opportunity Commission) that are pertinent to their scope of practice.

It shall be the responsibility of the American Psychological Association to publish periodically those federal policies, statutes, and regulations relating to this section. The state psychological associations are similarly urged to publish and distribute periodically appropriate state statutes and regulations.

2.2.5 *All providers within a psychological service unit shall, where appropriate, inform themselves about and use the network of human services in their communities in order to link users with relevant services and resources.*

INTERPRETATION: It is incumbent upon psychologists and supporting staff to be sensitive to the broader context of human needs. In recognizing the matrix of personal and societal problems, providers shall, where appropriate, make available information regarding human services such as legal aid societies, social services, employment agencies, health resources, and educational and recreational facilities. The provider of psychological services shall refer to such community resources and, when indicated, actively intervene on behalf of the user.

2.2.6 *In the delivery of psychological services, the providers shall maintain a continuing cooperative relationship with colleagues and co-workers whenever in the best interest of the user.*[15]

INTERPRETATION: It shall be the responsibility of the psychologist to recognize the areas of special competence of other psychologists and of other professionals for either consultation or referral purposes. Providers of psychological services shall make appropriate use of other professional, technical, and administrative resources whenever these serve the best interests of the user, and shall establish and maintain cooperative arrangements with such other resources as required to meet the needs of users.

2.3 *Procedures:*

> 2.3.1 *Where appropriate, each psychological service unit shall be guided by a set of procedural guidelines for the delivery of psychological services. If appropriate to the setting, these guidelines shall be in written form.*

INTERPRETATION: Depending on the nature of the setting, and whenever feasible, providers should be prepared to provide a statement of procedural guidelines in either oral or written form that can be understood by users as well as sanctioners. This statement may describe the current methods, forms, procedures, and techniques being used to achieve the objectives and goals for psychological services.

This statement shall be communicated to staff and, when appropriate, to users and sanctioners. The psychological service unit shall provide for the annual review of its procedures for the delivery of psychological services.

> 2.3.2 *Providers shall develop a plan appropriate to the provider's professional strategy of practice and to the problems presented by the user.*

INTERPRETATION: Whenever appropriate or mandated in the setting, this plan shall be in written form as a means of providing a basis for establishing accountability, obtaining informed consent, and providing a mechanism for subsequent peer review. Regardless of the type of setting or users involved, it is desirable that a plan be developed that describes the psychological services indicated and the manner in which they will be provided.[16]

A psychologist who provides services as one member of a collaborative effort shall participate in the development and implementation of the overall service plan and provide for its periodic review.

> 2.3.3 *There shall be a mutually acceptable understanding between the provider and user or responsible agent regarding the delivery of service.*

INTERPRETATION: Varying service settings call for understandings differing in explicitness and formality. For instance, a psychologist providing services within a user organization may operate within a broad framework of understanding with this organization as a condition of employment. As another example, psychologists providing professional services to individuals in clinical, counseling, or school settings require an open-ended agreement, which specifies procedures and their known risks (if any), costs, and respective responsibilities of provider and user for achieving the agreed-upon objectives.

> 2.3.4 *Accurate, current, and pertinent documentation shall be made of essential psychological services provided.*

INTERPRETATION: Records kept of psychological services may include, but not be limited to, identifying data, dates of services, types of services, and significant actions taken. Providers of psychological services shall insure that essential information concerning services rendered is appropriately recorded with a reasonable time for their completion.

> 2.3.5 *Providers of psychological services shall establish a system to protect confidentiality of their records.*[17]

INTERPRETATION: Psychologists are responsible for maintaining the confidentiality of information about users of services whether obtained by themselves or by those they supervise. All persons supervised by psychologists, including nonprofessional personnel and students, who have access to records of psychological services shall be required to maintain this confidentiality as a condition of employment.

The psychologist shall not release confidential information, except with the written consent of the user directly involved or his or her legal representative. Even after the consent has been obtained for release, the psychologist should clearly identify such information as confidential to the recipient of the information.[18] If directed otherwise by statute or regulations with the force of law or by court order, the psychologist shall seek a resolution to the conflict that is both ethically and legally feasible and appropriate.

Users shall be informed in advance of any limits in the setting for maintenance of confidentiality of psychological information. For instance, psychologists in hospital settings shall inform their patients that psychological information in a patient's clinical record may be available without the patient's written consent to other members of the professional staff associated with the patient's treatment or rehabilitation. Similar limitations on confidentiality of psychological information may be present in certain school, industrial, or military settings, or in instances where the user has waived confidentiality for purposes of third-party payment.

When the user intends to waive confidentiality, the psychologist should discuss the implications of releasing psychological information, and assist the user in limiting disclosure only to information required by the present circumstance.

Raw psychological data (e.g., test protocols, therapy or interview notes, or questionnaire returns) in which a user is identified shall be released only with the written consent of the user or legal representative and only to a person recognized by the psychologist as competent to use the data.

Any use made of psychological reports, records, or data for research or training purposes shall be consistent with this Standard. Additionally, providers of psychological services shall comply with statutory confidentiality requirements and those embodied in the American Psychological Association's *Ethical Standards of Psychologists* (APA, 1977).

Providers of psychological services should remain sensitive to both the benefits and the possible misuse of information regarding individuals that is stored in large computerized data banks. Providers should use their influence to ensure that such information is used in a socially responsible manner.

Standard 3.   Accountability

3.1 *Psychologists' professional activity shall be primarily guided by the principle of promoting human welfare.*

INTERPRETATION: Psychologists shall provide services to users in a manner that is considerate, effective, and economical.

Psychologists are responsible for making their services readily accessible to users in a manner that facilitates the user's freedom of choice.

Psychologists shall be mindful of their accountability to the sanctioners of psychological services and to the general public, provided that appropriate steps are taken to protect the confidentiality of the service relationship. In the pursuit of their professional activities they shall aid in the conservation of human, material, and financial resources.

The psychological service unit will not withhold services to a potential client on the basis of that user's race, color, religion, sex, age, or national origin. Recognition is given, however, to the following considerations: the professional right of psychologists to limit their practice to a specific category of user (e.g., children, adolescents, women); the right and responsibility of psychologists to withhold an assessment procedure when not validly applicable; the right and responsibility of psychologists to withhold evaluative, psychotherapeutic, counseling, or other services in specific instances where considerations of race, religion, color, sex, or any other difference between psychologist and client might impair the effectiveness of the relationship.[19]

Psychologists who find that psychological services are being provided in a manner that is discriminatory or exploitative to users and/or contrary to these Standards or to state or federal statutes shall take appropriate corrective action, which may include the refusal to provide services. When conflicts of interest arise, the psychologist shall be guided in the resolution of differences by the principles set forth in the *Ethical Standards of Psychologists* of the American Psychological Association and by the Guidelines for Conditions of Employment of Psychologists (1972).[20]

3.2 *Psychologists shall pursue their activities as members of an independent, autonomous profession.*[21]

INTERPRETATION: Psychologists shall be aware of the implications of their activities for the profession as a whole. They shall seek to eliminate discriminatory practices instituted for self-serving purposes that are not in the interest of the user (e.g., arbitrary requirements for referral and supervision by another profession). They shall be cognizant of their responsibilities for the development of the profession, participate where possible in the training and career development of students and other providers, participate as appropriate in the training of paraprofessionals, and integrate and supervise their contributions within the structure established for delivering psychological services. Where appropriate, they shall facilitate the development of, and participate in, professional standards review mechanisms.[22]

Psychologists shall seek to work with other professionals in a cooperative manner for the good of the user and the benefit of the general public. Psychologists associated with multidisciplinary settings shall support the principle that members of each participating profession shall have equal rights and opportunities to share all privileges and responsibilities of full membership in the human service facility, and to administer service programs in their respective areas of competence.

3.3 *There shall be periodic, systematic, and effective evaluations of psychological services.*[23]

INTERPRETATION: When the psychological service unit is a component of a larger organization, regular assessment of progress in achieving goals shall be provided in the service delivery plan, including consideration of the effectiveness of psychological services relative to costs in terms of time, money, and the availability of professional and support personnel.

Evaluation of the efficiency and effectiveness of the psychological service delivery system should be conducted internally and, when possible, under independent auspices.

It is highly desirable that there be a periodic re-examination of review mechanisms to ensure that these attempts at public safeguards are effective and cost efficient and do not place unnecessary encumbrances on the provider or unnecessary additional expense to users or sanctioners for services rendered.

3.4 *Psychologists are accountable for all aspects of the services they provide and shall be responsive to those concerned with these services.*[24]

INTERPRETATION: In recognizing their responsibilities to users, sanctioners, third-party purchasers, and other providers, wherever appropriate and consistent with the user's legal rights and privileged communications, psychologists shall make available information about, and opportunity to participate in, decisions concerning such issues as initiation, termination, continuation, modification, and evaluation of psychological services. Additional copies of these *Standards for Providers of Psychological Services* can be ordered from the American Psychological Association.

Depending upon the settings, accurate and full information shall be made available to prospective individual or organization users regarding the qualifications of providers, the nature and extent of services offered, and, where appropriate, financial and social costs.

Where appropriate, psychologists shall inform users of their payment policies and their willingness to assist in obtaining reimbursement. Those who accept reimbursement from a third party should be acquainted with the appropriate statutes and regulations and should instruct their users on proper procedures for submitting claims and limits on confidentiality of claims information, in accordance with pertinent statutes.

Standard 4. Environment

4.1 *Providers of psychological services shall promote the development in the service setting of a physical, organizational, and social environment that facilitates optimal human functioning.*

INTERPRETATION: Federal, state, and local requirements for safety, health, and sanitation must be observed. Attention shall be given to the comfort and, where relevant, to the privacy of providers and users.

As providers of services, psychologists have the responsibility to be concerned with the environment of their service unit, especially as it affects the quality of service, but also as it impinges on human functioning in the larger unit or organization when the service unit is included in such a larger context. Physical arrangements and organizational policies and procedures should be conducive to the human dignity, self-respect, and optimal functioning of users, and to the effective delivery of service. The atmosphere in which psychological services are rendered should be appropriate to the service and to the users, whether in office, clinic, school, or industrial organization.

Notes

[2] The footnotes appended to these Standards represent an attempt to provide a coherent context of other policy statements of the Association regarding professional practice. The Standards extend these previous policy statements where necessary to reflect current concerns of the public and the profession.

[3] NIMH Grant MH 21696.

[4] For the purpose of transition, persons who met the following criteria on or before the data of adoption of the original Standards on September 4, 1974, shall also be considered professional psychologists: (a) a master's degree from a program primarily psychological in content from a regionally accredited university or professional school; (b) appropriate education, training, and experience in the area of service offered; (c) a license or certificate in the state in which they practice, conferred by a state board of psychological examiners, or the endorsement of the state psychological association through voluntary certification, or, for practice in primary and secondary schools, a state department of education certificate as a school psychologist provided that the certificate required at least two graduate years.

[5] Minutes of the Board of Professional Affairs Meeting, Washington, D.C., March 8–9, 1974.

[6] This definition is less restrictive than Recommendation 4 of the APA (1967) policy statement setting forth model state legislation affecting the practice of psychology (hereinafter referred to as State Guidelines), proposing one level for state license or certificate and "requiring the doctoral degree from an accredited university or college in a program that is primarily psychological, and no less than 2 years of supervised experience, one of which is subsequent to the granting of the doctoral degree. This level should be designated by the title of 'psychologist'." (p. 1099)

The 1972 APA "Guidelines for Conditions of Employment of Psychologists" (hereinafter referred to as CEP Guidelines) introduces slightly different shadings of meaning in its section on "Standards for Entry into the Profession" as follows:

Persons are properly identified as psychologists when they have completed the training and experience recognized as necessary to perform functions consistent with one of the several levels in a career in psychology. This training includes possession of a degree earned in a program primarily psychological in content. In the case of psychological practice, it involves services for a fee, appropriate registration, certification, or licensing as provided by laws of the state in which the practices will apply. (APA, 1972, p. 331)

In some situations, specialty designations and standards

may be relevant. *The National Register of Health Service Providers in Psychology,* which based its criteria on this standard, identifies qualified psychologists in the health services field.

[7] As noted in the opening section of these Standards, functions and activities of psychologists relating to the teaching of psychology, the writing or editing of scholarly or scientific manuscripts, and the conduct of scientific research do not fall within the purview of these Standards.

[8] These definitions should be compared to the State Guidelines, which include definitions of *psychologist* and the *practice of psychology* as follows:

A person represents himself to be a psychologist when he holds himself out to the public by any title or description of services incorporating the words "psychology," "psychological," "psychologist," and/or offers to render or renders services as defined below to individuals, groups, organizations, or the public for a fee, monetary or otherwise.

The practice of psychology within the meaning of this act is defined as rendering to individuals, groups or organizations, or the public any psychological service involving the application of principles, methods, and procedures of understanding, predicting, and influencing behavior, such as the principles pertaining to learning, perception, motivation, thinking, emotions, and interpersonal relationships; the methods and procedures of interviewing, counseling, and psychotherapy; of constructing, administering, and interpreting tests of mental abilities, aptitudes, interests, attitudes, personality characteristics, emotions, and motivation; and of assessing public opinion.

The application of said principles and methods includes but is not restricted to: diagnosis, prevention, and amelioration of adjustment problems and emotional and mental disorders of individuals and groups; hypnosis; educational and vocational counseling; personnel selection and management; the evaluation and planning for effective work and learning situations; advertising and market research; and the resolution of interpersonal and social conflicts.

Psychotherapy within the meaning of this act means the use of learning, conditioning methods, and emotional reactions, in a professional relationship, to assist a person or persons to modify feelings, attitudes, and behavior which are intellectually, socially, or emotionally maladjustive or ineffectual.

The practice of psychology shall be as defined above, any existing statute in the state of _____ to the contrary notwithstanding. (APA, 1967, pp. 1098–1099)

[9] The relation of a psychological service unit to a larger facility or institution is also addressed indirectly in the CEP Guidelines, which emphasize the roles, responsibilities, and prerogatives of the psychologist when he or she is employed by or provides services for another agency, institution, or business.

[10] This Standard replaces earlier recommendations in the 1967 State Guidelines concerning exemption of psychologists from licensure. Recommendations 8 and 9 of those Guidelines read as follows:

8. Persons employed as psychologists by accredited academic institutions, governmental agencies, research laboratories, and business corporations should be exempted, provided such employees are performing those duties for which they are employed by such organizations, and within the confines of such organizations.

9. Persons employed as psychologists by accredited academic institutions, governmental agencies, research laboratories, and business corporations consulting or offering their research findings or providing scientific information to like organizations for a fee should be exempted. (APA, 1967, p. 1100)

On the other hand, the 1967 State Guidelines specifically denied exemptions under certain conditions, as noted in Recommendations 10 and 11:

10. Persons employed as psychologists who offer or provide psychological services to the public for a fee, over and above the salary that they receive for the performance of their regular duties, should not be exempted.

11. Persons employed as psychologists by organizations that sell psychological services to the public should not be exempted. (APA, 1967, pp. 1100–1101)

The present APA policy, as reflected in this Standard, establishes a single code of practice for psychologists providing covered services to users in any setting. The present minimum requirement is that a psychologist providing any covered service must meet local statutory requirements for licensure or certification. See the section Principles and Implications of the Standards for an elaboration of this position.

[11] A closely related principle is found in the APA (1972) CEP Guidelines:

It is the policy of APA that psychology as an independent profession is entitled to parity with other health and human service professions in institutional practices and before the law. Psychologists in interdisciplinary settings such as colleges and universities, medical schools, clinics, private practice groups, and other agencies expect parity with other professions in such matters as academic rank, board status, salaries, fringe benefits, fees, participation in administrative decisions, and all other conditions of employment, private contractual arrangements, and status before the law and legal institutions. (APA, 1972, p. 333)

[12] See CEP Guidelines (section entitled "Career Development") for a closely related statement:

Psychologists are expected to encourage institutions and agencies which employ them to sponsor or conduct career development programs. The purpose of these programs would be to enable psychologists to engage in study for professional advancement and to keep abreast of developments in their field. (APA, 1972, p. 332)

[13] This Standard follows closely the statement regarding "Policy on Training for Psychologists Wishing to Change Their Specialty" adopted by the APA Council of Representatives in January 1976. Included therein was the implementing provision that "this policy statement shall be incorporated in the guidelines of the Committee on Accreditation so that appropriate sanctions can be brought to bear on university and internship training programs which violate [it]."

[14] See also APA's (1977) Ethical Standards of Psychologists, especially Principles 5 (Confidentiality), 6 (Welfare of the Consumer), and 9 (Pursuit of Research Activities); and see Ethical Principles in the Conduct of Research with Human Participants. (APA, 1973a)

[15] Support for this position is found in the section in Psychology as a Profession on relations with other professions:

Professional persons have an obligation to know and take into account the traditions and practices of other professional groups with whom they work and to cooperate fully with members of such groups with whom research, service, and other functions are shared. (APA, 1968, p. 5)

[16] One example of a specific application of this principle is found in Guideline 2 in APA's (1973b) "Guidelines for Psychologists Conducting Growth Groups":

The following information should be made available in writing [italics added] to all prospective participants:

(a) An explicit statement of the purpose of the group;

(b) Types of techniques that may be employed;

(c) The education, training, and experience of the leader or leaders;

(d) The fee and any additional expense that may be incurred;

(e) A statement as to whether or not a follow-up service is included in the fee;

(f) Goals of the group experience and techniques to be used;

(g) Amounts and kinds of responsibility to be assumed by the leader and by the participants. For example, (i) the degree to which a participant is free not to follow suggestions and prescriptions of the group leader and other group members; (ii) any restrictions on a participant's freedom to leave the group at any time; and,

(h) Issues of confidentiality. (p. 933)

[17] See again Principle 5 (Confidentiality) in Ethical Standards of Psychologists (APA, 1977).

[18] Support for the principle of privileged communication is found in at least two policy statements of the Association:

In the interest of both the public and the client and in accordance with the requirements of good professional practice, the profession of psychology seeks recognition of the privileged nature of confidential communications with clients, preferably through statutory enactment or by administrative policy where more appropriate. (APA, 1968, p. 8)

25. Wherever possible, a clause protecting the privileged nature of the psychologist-client relationship be included.

26. When appropriate, psychologists assist in obtaining general "across the board" legislation for such privileged communications. (APA, 1967, p. 1103)

[19] This paragraph is drawn directly from the CEP Guidelines. (APA, 1972, p. 333)

[20] "It is recognized that under certain circumstances, the interests and goals of a particular community or segment of interest in the population may be in conflict with the general welfare. Under such circumstances, the psychologist's professional activity must be primarily guided by the principle for promoting human welfare." (APA, 1972, p. 334)

[21] Support for the principle of the independence of psychology as a profession is found in the following:

As a member of an autonomous profession, a psychologist rejects limitations upon his freedom of thought and action other than those imposed by his moral, legal, and social responsibilities. The Association is always prepared to provide appropriate assistance to any responsible member who becomes subjected to unreasonable limitations upon his opportunity to function as a practitioner, teacher, researcher, administrator, or consultant. The Association is always prepared to cooperate with any responsible professional organization in opposing any unreasonable limitations on the professional functions of the members of that organization.

This insistence upon professional autonomy has been upheld over the years by the affirmative actions of the courts and other public and private bodies in support of the right of the psychologist—and other professionals—to pursue those functions for which he is trained and qualified to perform. (APA, 1968, p. 9)

Organized psychology has the responsibility to define and develop its own profession, consistent with the general canons of science and with the public welfare.

Psychologists recognize that other professions and other groups will, from time to time, seek to define the roles and responsibilities of psychologists. The APA opposes such developments on the same principles that it is opposed to the psychological profession taking positions which would define the work and scope of responsibility of other duly recognized professions. . . . (APA, 1972, p. 333)

[22] APA support for peer review is detailed in the following excerpt from the APA (1971) statement entitled "Psychology and National Health Care":

All professions participating in a national health plan should be directed to established review mechanisms (or performance evaluations) that include not only peer review but active participation by persons representing the consumer. In situations where there are fiscal agents, they should also have representation when appropriate. (p. 1026)

[23] This standard on program evaluation is based directly on the following excerpts of two APA position papers:

The quality and availability of health services should be evaluated continuously by both consumers and health professionals. Research into the efficiency and effectiveness of the system should be conducted both internally and under independent auspices. (APA, 1971, p. 1025)

The comprehensive community mental health center should devote an explicit portion of its budget to program evaluation. All centers should inculcate in their staff attention to and respect for research findings; the larger centers have an obligation to set a high priority on basic research and to give formal recognition to research as a legitimate part of the duties of staff members.

. . . Only through explicit appraisal of program effects can worthy approaches be retained and refined, ineffective ones dropped. Evaluative monitoring of program achievements may vary, of course, from the relatively informal to the systematic and quantitative, depending on the importance of the issue, the availability of resources, and the willingness of those responsible to take the risks of substituting informed judgment for evidence. (Smith & Hobbs, 1966, pp. 21–22)

[24] See also CEP Guidelines for the following statement: "A psychologist recognizes that . . . he alone is accountable for the consequences and effects of his services, whether as teacher, researcher, or practitioner. This responsibility cannot be shared, delegated, or reduced." (APA, 1972, p. 334)

References

Accreditation Council for Facilities for the Mentally Retarded. *Standards for residential facilities for the mentally retarded.* Chicago, Ill.: Joint Commission on Accreditation of Hospitals, 1971.

American Psychological Association, Committee on legislation. A model for state legislation affecting the practice of psychology 1967. *American Psychologist,* 1967, *22,* 1095–1103.

American Psychological Association. *Psychology as a profession.* Washington, D.C.: Author, 1968.

American Psychological Association. Psychology and national health care. *American Psychologist,* 1971, *26,* 1025–1026.

American Psychological Association. Guidelines for conditions of employment of psychologists. *American Psychologist,* 1972, *27,* 331–334.

American Psychological Association. *Ethical principles in the conduct of research with human participants.* Washington, D.C.: Author, 1973. (a)

American Psychological Association. Guidelines for psychologists conducting growth groups. *American Psychologist,* 1973, *28,* 933. (b)

American Psychological Association. *Standards for educational and psychological tests.* Washington, D.C.: Author, 1974.

American Psychological Association. *Ethical standards of psychologists* (Rev. ed.). Washington, D.C.: Author, 1977.

Joint Commission on Accreditation of Hospitals. *Accreditation manual for psychiatric facilities 1972.* Chicago, Ill.: Author, 1972.

Smith, M. B., & Hobbs, N. *The community and the community mental health center.* Washington, D.C.: American Psychological Association, 1966.

The Development of a Peer Review System: The APA/CHAMPUS Contract

William L. Claiborn and Joan S. Zaro

The American Psychological Association, under contract with the U.S. Department of Defense, is developing an independent psychology review system for the Civilian Health and Medical Program of the Uniformed Services (CHAMPUS) that will utilize psychologists to review reports of clinical services provided by their peers in order to assess necessity and quality of care. This article describes development and form of the project and discusses (a) retrospective review, (b) quality-assurance efforts, (c) limitations of benefit, and (d) cost containment. The project represents a study of the ability of the profession to create a self-monitoring system acceptable both to the profession and to third-party health benefits agents that should result in improved quality of services, reduced abuse, and improved cost containment. If successful, the CHAMPUS psychological peer review process may provide a model for use in other national insurance plans and may play a role in the evolution of a national health insurance plan.

Brief History

American psychology has made considerable progress in its professional development since 1945 when Connecticut passed the first statutory psychology certification law. At the present time, all states and the District of Columbia have enacted either certification or licensing laws regulating the use of the title "psychologist" and/or the practice of psychology.

In the intervening years, professional psychology has become increasingly visible to the public, the government, other professions, and the health industry as an independent health care provider group. Particularly noteworthy is the increased recognition of psychologists as independent providers of mental health services reimbursed through third-party payers.

As a consequence of the profession's development as a provider of health care reimbursable by third-party payers, psychologists have become more involved in developing review and other quality-control mechanisms.

In 1970 the American Psychological Association (APA) initiated its first systematic approach to self-regulation. The APA appointed individuals to serve as coordinators for each HEW-designated region to set up psychology peer review committees nationwide. The charge of the committees was to determine (a) the reasonableness of fees and utilization of services, and (b) the customary and usual procedures for treating particular psychological problems. These committees were formed to assist the consumers and sanctioners of psychological services in assuring the adequacy of treatment and to collect data about the extent and nature of services being provided by psychologists.

At a slightly later point, APA established a formal group at the national level, the Committee on Professional Standards Review (COPSR), to create a system of such groups in every state. The Committee on Professional Standards Review was also requested to provide guidance to and monitor the state review committees in their operation. In that context, COPSR has facilitated the development of a *PSRC Procedures Manual* and criteria for short-term inpatient review.

State Professional Standards Review Committees (PSRCs) are now established and functioning in all 50 states and the District of Columbia. They are typically appointed by the state psychological association and are composed of psychologists representing a variety of treatment orientations in various settings who serve without pay. The committees publish their availability as a resource to consumers, other professionals, and third-party payers who have questions or complaints about the costs or quality of psychological services. PSRCs typically attempt to resolve conflict informally by educational means but are available to make a formal judgment if one is called for. At this time, PSRCs are infrequently utilized because (a) most paying agents have internal utilization review mechanisms, and (b) PSRCs suffer from low public visibility.

CHAMPUS's Recognition of Psychological Services

CHAMPUS (Civilian Health and Medical Program of the Uniformed Services, covering approximately 6.9 million beneficiaries), one of the largest health programs in the country, was early (1966) in recognizing psychologists as independent providers and in reimbursing psychologists directly for services.

The most dramatic documented abuses both with regard to inadequate care and unreasonable costs occurred within CHAMPUS-supported residential treatment programs. Consequently, the U.S. Department of Defense collaborated with the National Institute of Mental Health (NIMH) authorities to set and enforce standards for quality care through the Select Committees on Psychiatric Care Evaluation (SCOPCE).

After establishing control of costs and utilization in residential treatment settings, CHAMPUS officials turned their attention to inpatient and outpatient care. Early in 1977, the Department of Defense's Office of CHAMPUS (OCHAMPUS), proposed a contract with the American Psychological Association whereby the Association would develop and implement a peer-review and quality-assurance system for outpatient psychological services provided under the CHAMPUS program. OCHAMPUS also proposed a similar contract with the American Psychiatric Association for the development of parallel but independent outpatient review capabilities. In addition, the American Psychiatric Association was asked to develop a review system for inpatient psychiatric care, while the

American Psychological Association was asked to study the feasibility of developing inpatient criteria. Both contracts were signed in July of 1977.

The Philosophy Behind Peer Review

The development of an effective peer review system by psychologists can provide an important measure of service to the consumer, to the profession of psychology, and to society as a whole. A peer review system can result in reduction and control of costs associated with unnecessary or poor-quality care. If the profession demonstrates that it is capable of effectively monitoring the practices of its own members, it becomes politically and economically easier to defend a generous mental health benefit. With effective peer review, third-party administrators are given an alternative to restriction of services. This alternative can serve to diminish the antagonism between third-party payers and members of the profession by acknowledging the legitimate professional role in determining necessity and quality of care, while still providing effective control over services reimbursed under the third-party coverage. The development of a model system on a national basis takes advantage of the resources of the national psychological organization in securing legitimacy for the system and avoiding the consequences of idiosyncratic, regional, peer review procedures. Development on a national scale can also permit uniform monitoring of the peer review in order to insure that it works effectively.

There are two major overlapping purposes for the review of health care. The first, often primary, concern of health plan administrators is the containment of costs. The second purpose is to protect the beneficiary from unnecessary, inappropriate, or poor-quality care.

From the simplest perspective, control of costs can be easily accomplished by successive restrictions of the service covered. This strategy of limiting services, increasing deductibles, and building in co-payments has been a traditional device used by third-party payers to maintain control over utilization and program costs. However, this strategy can result in unintended effects. For example, allowing payment for inpatient but not outpatient services has the effect of forcing patients into inpatient settings when a less costly alternative may be more appropriate. In mental health care, the most common limitations of benefit have been either those that set "total dollar" limits or that specify that payment will be made for a limited number of services (such as outpatient sessions or inpatient days). It should be obvious that such limitations may not allow for the most appropriate, or even least costly, treatment.

Third-party payers have also attempted to control the mental health benefit through restriction in the categories of eligible providers. Typically, insurance plans have restricted mental health benefits to physicians. Only in recent years, coincident with the development of freedom-of-choice legislation mandating direct payment to licensed psychologists, has the limitation of eligible providers begun to disappear. In the absence of an alternative, insurance plan managers have argued that they are able to control costs only through setting limitations in benefit. A workable review system that permits a dynamic form of control over the mental health benefit (by tailoring the allowed services to the needs of the individual patient) offers an opportunity to avoid the "limit of benefit" strategy while still controlling utilization and costs.

Assuring quality (necessity, appropriateness, effectiveness, and adequacy) requires the judgment of trained professionals. It is dependent upon the ability of a profession to agree upon definitions of quality and to make a commitment to enforce these standards within its membership. Definitions of quality can be based upon information of several types. Experimental and quasi-experimental studies can indicate forms of treatment that are more or less effective for particular types of patients with certain kinds of problems. These studies can be used in the development of guidelines for practice and applied in the review of cases. Lacking experimental evidence, standards for quality of care can be derived from surveys of standard practice and from the opinion of experts. While experimental determination of quality has obvious advantages, in many cases the latter two strategies may represent the highest level of evidence available.

The application of quality control procedures to the delivery of mental health care will have cost consequences. The cost of review will add to the cost of mental health services, while the restriction or limitation of unnecessary, poor-quality, or inappropriate care will result in cost savings. Whether a net increase or a net decrease results is determined in part by the nature of the review system and the context of the underlying mental health benefit. For example, if the goal of a quality assurance program is to allow only the highest possible quality of care, then it will require review of large numbers of cases and involve the rejection of a large number of claims. Such a system, which results in wholesale rejection in claims, is likely to be unacceptable to both the patient and the psychologist as well as unrealistic in terms of the costs of review.

A more realistic approach is to focus on the *exception* to typical care, the 5%–10% of care that is the poorest, the least necessary, or the most inappropriate. In order to keep the costs of review at a minimum, it is desirable to develop a set of procedures that minimize unnecessary review, restrict review to the most critical cases, and permit the making of review decisions at the earliest possible point. Where criteria for quality care can be clearly articulated, these criteria may be applied by the staff of a claims processor at a lower cost. Where the specification of quality criteria is less precise, or impossible, full peer review should be employed.

The final review process should reflect a careful balance of appropriate benefit, levels of review, selected review criteria, and targeted information requests. Since gathering of patient information is costly and because it creates a risk of inappropriate disclosure, only that information that is necessary and relevant to the decision process should be obtained. If all elements of the system match, the result will be a review system that, in a cost-efficient manner, permits review of only those cases representing the most deviant (inappropriate, ineffective, unnecessary, poor-quality care), with review decisions occurring at the earliest point and based upon minimally sufficient information. Such a review system should be acceptable to the provider, the patient, and the third-party payer because it offers maximum protection of all three interests. A review system meeting these characteristics would be a benefit to the profession and reflect on a high level of responsibility of its members.

The APA/CHAMPUS Contract

Overview

In entering into this contract, the APA agreed to complete several tasks that would result in the creation of a peer review system to review the claims made by psychologists for services rendered to CHAMPUS beneficiaries. The contract required the development of an independent set of criteria that would apply to services provided by psychologists and designated as "psychologically necessary." The establishment of a unique review process and unique standards for psychological providers acknowledges, for the first time, the full recognition of psychologists as independent providers.

The major tasks of the project included the creation of a National Advisory Panel of psychologists to advise the project staff, the development of criteria that would lead to peer review, the identification and education of qualified peer reviewers, the implementation of the peer review system, and the monitoring of the new peer review system.

National Advisory Panel Selection

A CHAMPUS National Advisory Panel was appointed by the Board of Directors of the APA to oversee contract activities and to provide consultation to OCHAMPUS. Seven senior psychologists were selected on the basis of their experience and knowledge of clinical practice, review activities, health care delivery systems, treatment modalities, and program evaluation. The Panel is made up of individuals with recognized stature in the profession who represent a spectrum of theoretical orientations, treatment approaches, and geographical regions and who have had extensive involvement in

governance and committee work at national and local levels of professional psychology. They and the project staff are responsible for the development and implementation of the review mechanism and the criteria to be used therein.[1]

APA/CHAMPUS Project Approach to Standards

The peer review system developed by the project provides for assessment of psychological necessity and quality of care by review of a treatment plan containing a statement of the patient's problems, goals for treatment, intervention strategies, and progress toward goals. The treatment plans are developed sequentially so that review of continuing care will include examination of series of formulations of the patient's problems, goals, treatments, and progress. A basic assumption underlying the developing of the peer review system was that a "document-based" review system can be effective and that examination of written reports of treatment can result in reliable determinations of the necessity and adequacy of care.

The treatment plan is the central document in the review process. The treatment plan requires involvement by the patient so that there is a shared understanding about the nature of the problem, goals of treatment, and the means to reach the goals. In subsequent treatment reports, there should be agreement on continuing progress and joint provider-client predictions on the likely conclusion of treatment services.

The National Advisory Panel developed criteria that permit their comparison to the contents of the treatment report submitted by the provider. This basic examination results in an initial recommendation (and generally a decision) for the approval or disapproval of benefits.

---

[1] Panel members are George Stricker (Chair—Great Neck, New York), Russell Bent (Vice-Chair—Dayton, Ohio), William L. Claiborn (Project Director—Washington, D.C.), Melvin Gravitz (Washington, D.C.), Anna Rosenberg (Randallstown, Maryland), Lee Sechrest (Tallahassee, Florida), Joan Willens (Beverly Hills, California), and Harl Young (Evergreen, Colorado).

Melvin Gravitz resigned from the Panel after more than one year of service. William Claiborn replaced Daniel Alevy as Project Director early in the project.

The criteria define the elements necessary for an adequate treatment plan, including that the treatment normally must be having a positive effect on the patient. Most of the criteria are stated in terms of the presence of specific elements within the treatment plan, rather than in terms of specific words or phrases. Thus, the criteria are not simply "semantic" and cannot be met simply by learning the correct vocabulary.

The peer review system outlined here is unique in that it is not related to traditional diagnostic categories, and it does not simply define the conditions under which treatment may occur. Instead, it creates a vehicle for examining the dynamic process of treatment in the context of the overall situation. Reviewers examine documentation of the "thought process" of the provider as reflected in the development and revision of treatment plans. The system requires the production of a report that should be directly useful to the patient and provider as well as the reviewer. The format of the treatment report permits wide latitude to the provider in completing the form and is not bound to one theoretical orientation. The treatment report bears a familiar and conceptual resemblance to the problem-oriented record now in use in many mental health settings, though the peer review treatment report is less structured and less formal.

In addition to the criteria defining the adequacy of the treatment plan, the peer review system includes a number of criteria that set limitations on certain patterns of practice. These are based upon the clinical judgment of the National Advisory Panel members, as well as on the results of surveys of providers and of the project's peer reviewers. "Normal limits" have been established for the frequency and length of psychotherapy sessions and on the occurrence and extent of psychological assessment. If care reported exceeds such "normal limits," the review process will lead to the determination of whether or not the treatment will be recommended for reimbursement. It is expected that these limitations of benefit, as part of the peer review criteria, will provide a means to control benefits for services that are of questionable quality and permit review of reasonable exceptions to the criteria. It is expected that these criteria will curtail apparent excesses in long-term care such as multiple services to the same patient or to the same patient's family by one or more providers. These patterns of practice, while relatively rare, may constitute some of the most significant causes of abuse in care and are highly visible to third-party payers.

Following are some examples of criteria relating to an adequate treatment plan:

1. At least one statement must be present evidencing either significant functional impairment or significant personal distress.

2. Description of problem must be sufficiently specific to indicate that the patient is unable to function effectively in at least one of the following spheres: home/family, job/school, interpersonal relationships (neighbors, friends, colleagues), bodily function, protection of self and/or others, personal comfort.

3. Goals must be specific, concrete, and expressed in terms of change expected by the next review point.

4. The treatment procedure must be directly related to major goals and problems.

Examples of criteria defining "exceptions" to quality care that would lead to disapproval of benefits or to peer review include (a) a patient with a physical illness not being evaluated by an appropriate health care provider, (b) group psychotherapy sessions lasting less than 60 minutes, (c) a patient receiving psychotherapeutic services from two mental health providers, and (d) psychological assessment requiring more than 6 hours.

A treatment report submitted by a psychologist covering, for example, 24 sessions of individual psychotherapy, would make a statement of the progress since the last review (at the eighth session) in terms of the goals indicated in the earlier report. It would include the current problems of the patient, the goals to be reached by the next review point (40 sessions), and the planned treatments. The patient and provider would have discussed the treatment report and indicated the amount of agreement between them. When received by the claims processor, the treatment report is examined against the criteria as discussed above. If possible, a decision is made by the staff reviewers, but in some specified instances the case is prepared for peer review.

Peer reviewers, in contrast to the staff reviewers, apply their own professional judgment to the case. Peer reviewers examine the materials and make recommendations, and the recommendations are used in a final determination of the claim.

Generally, it is expected that providers and patients will receive CHAMPUS reimbursement for services rendered professionally. While treatment rendered in some cases may not meet all the specified criteria, the professional peer judgments should reflect a realistic appraisal of the overall quality and psychological necessity of treatment rendered. Providers who anticipate services that deviate from the criteria are encouraged to submit additional explanation and documentation so as to facilitate the consideration of the unique features of the case. In addition, the CHAMPUS system allows for appeals and reconsideration of adverse benefit decisions. The peer review system developed under this project does not restrict the practice of psychologists, nor does it define an orthodoxy of quality care—it is strictly a mechanism for the review of claims for payment. Patients can, irrespective of CHAMPUS coverage, participate in treatment of their own choosing at their own expense.

The use of the treatment form as the basic mechanism for conducting this "document-based" review of care is founded upon the assumption that the ability to formulate a case reasonably is a requisite to delivering quality care. Further, it is assumed that in most cases, a discussion between the patient and psychologist and an agreement upon goals of treatment and anticipated length of treatment will facilitate quality care.

The CHAMPUS review system is retrospective in that it results in approval or denial of payment for previously provided services. The patient could, under this system, suddenly discover, perhaps months after treatment, that he or she has a major financial obligation to the provider that will not be covered by CHAMPUS; there is no reliable means for the patient to know *in advance* that denial is likely. The results of a retrospective system are highly undesirable from the perspective of the patient and provider because of the delays and the potential of "after the fact" denial of claims.

Prospective or concurrent review provide for authorization prior to the rendering of services. These forms of review can give guidance to the provider, shaping practice directly and yielding the opportunity for the patient and provider to make informed decisions about care based upon a full knowledge of the cost consequences.

Awareness of the problem of retrospective review has led to the development of mechanisms to reduce the impact of this form of review through utilizing prospective review for long-term cases (greater than 60 sessions) and through encouraging expression of negative review findings by enabling reviewers to recommend immediate or near-future termination of coverage as well as retrospective denial.

Peer Reviewers Selection

Under the conditions of the APA/CHAMPUS contract, the Association was required to generate a list of psychologists to serve as reviewers for the peer review system. The project's National Advisory Panel solicited nominations for peer reviewers from the state association presidents and from the chairs of the state PSRCs. The total number of nominees solicited from each state varied as a function of the volume of CHAMPUS claims experience in that state. States with large volumes of CHAMPUS claims (such as California, Texas, and North Carolina) were permitted 48 nominations; the remaining states were permitted somewhat fewer.

The Panel and staff developed guidelines to use in the final selection, including (a) number of years of postdoctoral experience, (b) amount and nature of ongoing clinical work, (c) experience with peer review, (d) areas of applicant's self-identified professional competencies, and (e) state certification or licensure. Generally, psychologists selected as reviewers are several years postdoctorate, have heavy involvement in direct clinical work, and reflect a diversity of treatment orientation. All are licensed or certified.

The Panel attempted to group applicants by the practice specialties of adult and adolescent, child, marriage and family, and psychological assessment. The characteristics of the selected reviewers are summarized in Table 1. The final list of reviewers reflects a mixture of treatment orientations. Depending upon claims experience, specialized teams may be established to review exceptional cases that fall outside the expertise of the regular panels.

Under the terms of the contract, each of the reviewers is to be paid at the hourly rate of $40 for claims reviewed. This represents a departure from practices of the PSRCs. In their short history, PSRC activities have been performed through the voluntary efforts of the Association membership. Third-party payers have traditionally used paid consultants, usually general-practice physicians or psychiatrists, to review mental health claims "in house." The decision by OCHAMPUS to pay for the psychiatry and psychology review systems marks an evolu-

tionary step, signifying both the formal recognition of the review process and the acceptance that systematic use of review adds to the cost of processing mental health claims. The cost of the review can become a signficant component of the costs of the total system and should be weighed against value of review in terms of cost containment and/or quality assurance.

Peer Reviewer Education and Training

The project has developed three major methods to communicate with and educate reviewers. The first means of educating peer reviewers is through the *APA/CHAMPUS Outpatient Psychological Peer Reviewer Manual*. This document outlines the criteria applied by second-level reviewers in the CHAMPUS

Table 1: *Summary of Selected Peer Reviewers' Characteristics*

Characteristic	Percentage of peer reviewers	Characteristic	Percentage of peer reviewers
Sex		Average hours of private practice/week	
Male	83	None	3
Female	17	1–10 hours	26
Degree		11–20 hours	22
PhD	94	21–30 hours	19
EdD	4	31–40 hours	21
MA	2	41 or more	9
Year degree received		Average hours of organizational	
Prior to 1950	3	practice/week	
From 1950–1959	32	None	15
From 1960–1969	47	1–10 hours	32
From 1970–1974	17	11–20 hours	29
1975 or later	1	21–30 hours	14
Specialty area		31–40 hours	9
Clinical	78	41 or more	1
Counseling	7	Private practice with CHAMPUS clients	
Other psychology	10	None	41
Other profession	1	Less than 25%	59
More than one	4	Professional orientation	
Major postdoctoral training	37	Psychodynamic	45
Listed in *National Register*	84	Behavioral	18
Membership in American Board of	29	Humanistic	12
Professional Psychology		Other	19
Membership in APA	98	More than 1	6
Membership in state psychological	98	Self-identified areas of expertise	
association		Child	47
Year private practice began		Adolescent	56
Prior to 1950	2	Adult	87
From 1950–1959	19	Marriage and family	64
From 1960–1969	36	Group	32
From 1970–1974	31	Testing	74
1975 or later	12	Carry malpractice insurance	90
		Have significant peer review experience	32

claims processors and contains a set of specific procedural instructions for completing the review. Supplements to the *Manual* will provide summaries of key review issues in order to assist reviewers' analyses of cases. These supplements will include relevant literature reviews, results of empirical surveys, expert opinion, and other information that could improve the quality of reviewer recommendations.

The second means of training reviewers and nonreviewers in peer review is through symposium/workshop presentations in conjunction with all of the major regional association meetings. These presentations have permitted face-to-face contact with reviewers and other interested psychologists and have encouraged discussion of potential problems and concerns. The workshops have utilized sample case materials, thus providing "hands on" training for reviewers.

Third, the project produces and distributes a quarterly newsletter, *APA/CHAMPUS Update*, which contains current project news, recent procedural changes, discussion of conceptual issues, and guidelines for reviewers. This three-pronged approach (*Manual*, symposium/workshop, and newsletter) is intended to create and maintain a unified and consistent, smoothly functioning review process. The project staff plans to develop more complete training materials that can be used by reviewers and others to develop review skills.

The CHAMPUS Mental Health Claims Review System[2]

The major steps of the claims review/peer review process are as follows:

1. Providers of services to CHAMPUS beneficiaries are given instructions outlining requirements for reimbursement under CHAMPUS. These instructions include specification of the information required for second-level and peer review of claims for outpatient services. Providers are required to complete the treatment report at each of the review points prior to the review and approval of the claims (i.e., 8th, 24th, 40th, and 60th visits).

2. An initial review to insure the presence of all necessary information is made when the form arrives at the claims office.

3. Reviewers in the claims processing office (called Level II Reviewers) review the submitted documents for compliance with the formal requirements of the CHAMPUS program and evaluate the claim against the standards developed by the project. The Level II reviewer takes one of four actions: (a) authorization for full payment, (b) authorization for partial payment, (c) denial of benefit, or (d) referral to peer review. The decision is the result of the application of the APA/CHAMPUS criteria. For example, if the treatment report and other information meet all of the criteria, the claim is processed for payment. If, however, the case documentation fails to meet one or more of the criteria, then the action indicated in the decision rule associated with each criterion is taken. That action may be to deny the claim or to refer it to peer review. The decision to deny is attached to those criteria that, if not met, are, in the judgment of the National Advisory Panel, examples of inadequately justified or inappropriate care. The decision to refer to peer review occurs when the application of the criteria results in the detection of treatment that is of questionable quality. In these cases, it is believed that professional consideration of the entire treatment report is warranted before a judgment can be made. If the case is to go to peer review, the Level II reviewer selects three authorized reviewers from the geographic region of the claim's origin. A copy of the treatment report (without provider-, beneficiary-, and patient-identifying information) is combined with previous reports and sent to each of the three psychologist reviewers and to the project office.

4. Upon receipt of the material and within 5 working days, the three reviewers make independent recommendations regarding the case. The peer reviewers provide advisory opinions as to disposition of the claim, based on whether the care reported constitutes good psychological practice, whether the treatment was psychologically necessary, and whether treatment represents a high standard of quality. The peer

---

[2] At the time of this writing, peer review was only in its early stages. Experience with the system may result in modifications to the plans for implementation.

reviewers make recommendations, not decisions, acting as agents of CHAMPUS. Reviewers may recommend that claims be approved or denied, or that preconditions be imposed on claims for continuing treatment.

5. The project staff monitors the review documents by examining the criteria leading to review, reviewer recommendations, and characteristics of the practice under review. These data form the basis for the study and analysis of the peer review system.

6. The CHAMPUS claims processor Level II reviewer evaluates the recommendations of the peer reviewers and makes a final determination for benefit approval or denial. Should the beneficiary or the provider be dissatisfied with the decision, the CHAMPUS regulations provide for appeal. In addition, providers who have knowingly submitted claims for treatment that exceed the limits of benefit as defined by the criteria are invited to submit special justification of their pattern of practice for peer review. In such cases, reviewers may recommend approval for individual cases or may recommend a "blanket" approval for the pattern of practice of an individual provider. This provision permits an important amount of flexibility within the system by allowing for unique and individual practice, while maintaining routine standards of practice within which the majority of good practice occurs.

System Operations

In order to participate in the CHAMPUS system or to assist patients who are CHAMPUS beneficiaries, psychologist providers will routinely have to complete these treatment reports on care that extends beyond 8 sessions. Providers who refuse to submit treatment reports or who are unable or unwilling to provide the detail required can expect to have claims for reimbursement denied.

The proposed peer review system phases in peer review over a several-month period. Initially, only cases that have reached the 100th session are to be sent to peer review. Providers of these long-term cases are asked to submit a treatment report that details their progress to date and that outlines their treatment plans for the coming sessions. These treatment plans (without identifying information) are sent to

three separate peer reviewers. Subsequent changes in the review system will result in cases reaching 60 sessions being sent for review.

Ultimately, all cases reaching one of the review points (8, 24, 40 sessions) will receive a Level II review to determine if peer review is required or if the care should be approved or denied by the Level II reviewer. Under the proposed system, all claims for testing and assessment receive a Level II review; the review is based upon an examination of the treatment report submitted by the provider. It is expected that most claims for assessment will be resolved at the Level II review. Typically, it is expected that the kinds of treatment cases receiving peer review will be those that are for care that is outside the "normal limits," or that appears unusual or unorthodox, or that does not seem to be based upon a reasonable formulation of the problem, goals, and planned treatments.

The degree of impairment that justifies a short-term treatment is less than that required for longer term care. Thus, progressively more difficult standards face the provider as care continues, and it is expected that most care ending within 8 sessions will receive routine payment, whereas care reaching 60 sessions and beyond will be subject to more stringent review. An advantage of examining cases at later points in the treatment process is that the treatment history has been developed in the previously submitted treatment reports. It should be possible, then, to examine the care over the entire course of treatment, based upon the documentation supplied by the providers.

Evaluation of the Peer Review Process

The evaluation of the peer reviewers' performance was designed in the overall review system to provide information related to the following issues: how long the claims process takes, how long the average reviewer requires to complete his or her review, what the specific document flow problems are, what the net cost of review is, whether the fiscal intermediaries find the recommendations useful in the determination of claims action, what effect the review process has on appeals, what volume of reviews are generated, what kinds of cases are being reviewed, what criteria lead to referrals for peer review, what factors determine which reviewed cases receive recommendations for approval, and what kinds of cases result in lack of agreement among reviewers.

The questions raised above, answered in the context of interactions with other variables, should provide a means of improving, modifying, and adjusting the review system. Ultimately, such data may have an impact on education within the profession as key problems in patterns of practice are identified that would improve the quality of care. For example, if providers are shown to be unable to articulate treatment goals, it could be possible to develop training programs focused on goal-setting that could be offered as continuing education to providers. From a more indirect perspective, detection of weakness in practice could lead to suggested changes in graduate curricula and internship training, or in licensing/certification standards.

Evaluation of the peer review process will show whether the peer review process has shaped the practice of psychology. Examination of the nature of treatment rendered may show changes over time, reflecting both the impact of peer review on individual providers and also the effects of provider education resulting from the project. The National Advisory Panel members expect that many providers will begin to reconsider aspects of their own practices as a result of the requirements of the peer review system. The effects will likely result from the effort required to prepare treatment reports or as the result of discussions of treatment plans with patients, rather than as the direct result of peer-reviewer recommendations. It is expected that while only a few psychologists will be subject to adverse peer-reviewer recommendations, the majority of providers will be affected by the review process in more subtle ways.

Examination of the changes in the CHAMPUS approval and denial rates or the "causes" of these actions will yield information about the nature of practice and changes that occur as a result of the review system. Subsequently, the cost of these changes can be measured directly and in comparison with prior expenditure rates. The test of the peer review program from the perspective of CHAMPUS officials lies in determining whether the project has significantly improved the quality of care

bought by the mental health benefit dollar. The desire of the OCHAMPUS officials to achieve the best benefit together with the exclusion of the least useful and most inefficient treatment is accomplished through a professionally determined set of standards that act as a *triage* (allocation of limited treatment resources). The project plans to develop additional procedures to evaluate the impact of the process on the peer reviewers and to assess attitudes, acceptance, and other aspects of the peer review experience. It is likely that the preliminary answers to some questions will lead to the formulation of other questions that can be answered with a quasi-experimental study in subsequent years of the project.

Finally, the results of the evaluation of the CHAMPUS peer review system will be useful in determining whether a nationally developed, regionally administered psychological peer review system produces improvement in the quality of care in a cost-effective manner and whether it contributes to the belief that mental health benefits can be reasonably managed by members of the profession in the interests of the patient, the consumer, the provider, the third-party payer, and the profession.

Special Issues

Will Peer Reviewers Review Critically?

Some evidence from PSRO and other review projects suggests that peer reviewers are reluctant to enforce standards on their peers. This tendency to resist making adverse judgments works against an effective peer review system. It is important that CHAMPUS peer reviewers be willing to render negative judgments; their inability to do so would suggest that the profession cannot regulate itself through peer review and may lead to agents outside the profession doing so, principally through limitations of benefit.

Confidentiality

The personal nature of psychotherapy requires that special efforts be undertaken to protect the privacy of the individual patient while at the same time permitting an adequate review of care. Any "document-based" review system depends upon the written description of treatment for a determination of the adequacy of care and requires disclosure of information sufficient to allow peers to understand the nature and severity of the problems, the goals and strategies for treatment, and the progress already achieved. At one level, confidentiality can be protected by careful choice of descriptive terms used by the provider in the narrative in order to convey the strategy of the treatment without revealing the most intimate details. On a system-wide basis, it is necessary to have procedures for document holding and control that provide the maximum feasible limitation in the distribution of documents and reduce the likelihood of inadvertent or advertent disclosure of documents and reduce the likelihood of inadvertent or advertent disclosure of the private information.

CHAMPUS, which is covered by the Privacy Act, has strict limitations on the disclosure of patient information and requires that the beneficiary consent to the use of the claims information for purposes of claims adjudication and, where indicated, certain other defined uses. Procedures followed by OCHAMPUS and its contractors require segregation of detailed treatment-report information and the elimination of identifying information on those treatment reports that are distributed to peer reviewers. If, for example, a careless peer reviewer lost a treatment report sent in for review, confidentiality would not be jeopardized, since the treatment report would not identify the patient, the provider, the beneficiary, or even the state in which the treatment occurred. Peer reviewers serving the CHAMPUS program have been reminded of their ethical obligation to protect confidentiality. Everyone who handles these documents is subject to legal redress for violations of the Privacy Act.

Success and acceptance of the peer review system will depend, to a significant degree, on the ability of the system to maintain confidentiality and to convince the patient and the provider that confidentiality is protected.

Acceptability

The project acknowledges and accepts the legitimacy of claims review and the fact that review of claims requires providers to generate information for review by the paying agent and by peers. However, acceptance and full willing participation by members of the profession is a critical variable in the viability and success of any review program. Many assumptions implicit in this project are relatively new to the profession, and considerable effort is being expended to sensitize psychologists to the issues involved.

Limitations of Data

While the project staff and National Advisory Panel members have been excited by the possibilities of generating factual information about the practice of psychology and observing changes in that practice over time, there are limitations of the data that restrict the generalizability of the findings. First, the project plan does not represent a true experimental design but instead is, at best, quasi-experimental. The data obtained from pre- and post-standards periods may permit time-line comparisons; however, baseline data is limited and other factors will be intervening. Similarly, individual provider data may be more important than overall population data in determining effects of review. Current restrictions on availability of data may preclude analysis of individual provider profiles.

Implications of the Project and Future Prospects

As has been indicated earlier, this project represents the first time that psychology has had a major role in defining its own standards of quality practice. The opportunity is also a challenge—to develop a consensus that allows the profession to agree and support such a system. The APA, by participating in the project, has acknowledged the legitimacy of placing self-defined restrictions on the nature of practice. The resulting *triage*, having an impact on provider and patient, is no longer an academic exercise but a serious attempt to set and enforce reasonable standards of practice. The assertion of standards tests the limits of psychological theory and experimental research.

If the project is effective, it will change the practices of the profession and will affect the livelihood of many of the profession's members. Whether the Association and the project can withstand the likely pressures will reflect the quality of the project effort, the success in sharing the responsibility for standards and procedures, and the ability of the Association and its members to reach consensus about some very complicated issues.

The CHAMPUS project may become a model for other plans, such as the Federal Employees Health Benefits Plan, or for other of the major private insurance plans. Informal reactions of insurance officials have suggested that if the project is successful, these groups would be interested in applying a similar model to their own plans.

At present, there are factors that work against adoption of these CHAMPUS-derived standards, including (a) that review is retrospective, (b) that fees are paid for review, and (c) that competitive conditions make the adoption of a review plan by any one company disadvantageous. (Unless all plans use similar criteria, the plan that uses more restrictive procedures could be at a competitive disadvantage from the perspective of the patient and provider, possibly resulting in a lowered provider participation and consequent loss of business.)

Within the project itself, there are several possible future directions: (a) continuation of peer review, (b) evaluation of peer review, (c) development of criteria for use by peer reviewers, (d) development of specialized continuing and graduate education programs based upon findings of the project, (e) development of empirical standards for quality of care, (f) development of a prospective review system, and (g) development of an inpatient review system.

Recapitulation

The APA/CHAMPUS project is a unique experiment within one of the major national health benefit systems in which the psychological profession has the challenge and the opportunity to develop quality-of-care standards and to affect the practice of the profession through the implementation of a national peer review system. Success, in terms of demonstrably improving the quality of care or demonstrably containing costs, can help move this pilot project from the confines of CHAMPUS to other national and regional programs as a model for peer review of psychologist providers. Its failure, likewise, could lead to the diminished opportunity for psychology to achieve and maintain recognition or to monitor itself as an independent profession. The challenge to the project lies in creating a workable plan that imposes minimally on the provider and patient and that makes useful and valid judgments about practice—judgments that will shape the broad middle range of practice toward improving care, limiting abuses, and making the most effective utilization of limited dollar resources. The project requires the mature participation of the profession and widespread acceptance and should meet the political test of appearing to be "the right thing at the right time at the right place."

Most of the issues raised in debates about national health insurance are faced in the CHAMPUS plan. The efforts of the APA/CHAMPUS project represent a potential answer to some of the questions within the CHAMPUS system—a good field test that may help to shape the future.

William L. Claiborn is Director, CHAMPUS project, and *Joan J. Zaro* is Administrative Officer for Professional Affairs, American Psychological Association.

Statement on the PSRO Program (PL 92-603) of the Social Security Act Amendments Submitted to the House Ways and Means Subcommittee on Health

William Buklad

Representatives from the "other-than-physician" health specialties are essentially excluded from PSRO panels, to the detriment of patients and contrary to Congressional intent. These health professionals should be members of primary panels rather than of poorly utilized advisory groups. Quality assurance programs now suffer from their absence.

The legislation which in 1973 amended the Social Security Act to establish the Professional Standards Review Organization (PSRO) Program must be regarded as a landmark in the development of the health sciences. In entrusting the responsibility for health care quality assurance to the professions involved in the actual delivery of health services to the patient, the Congress has underscored its willingness to work with the health care community in developing uniform standards of health care for all Americans.

The vehicle that the Congress has selected to guarantee quality care is, of course, peer review. To a very great extent, the success or failure of the PSRO program will depend upon the professionals who will constitute the review system itself. Since the program confers so much authority to PSROs at the local level, we would encourage the Congress to monitor the progress of the program on an ongoing basis. The possibility will always be great that if left unattended, the program might end up becoming something much different than the peer-based review system that the Congress originally had in mind.

After careful observation of the progress that has been made by the PSRO program to date, the American Psychological Association would like to point out several areas that are of great concern not only to our membership involved in health care delivery but also to their patients and to the other health specialties as well. First among our concerns is the overall thrust of the review program itself. Time and time again, we have seen terms such as *medical care* and *medically necessary* appear in the Department of Health, Education, and Welfare's implementational guidelines for PSRO. We have seen the focus of PSRO review shift from the totality of the health services delivered to the patient, to the purely medical aspects of the health package alone. The consequence of this shift is clear. By failing to take a broad perspective on health services delivered to a patient, the PSRO program will find it difficult to fulfill its quality-assurance mandate. By stressing the medical necessity for health services, the review process will overlook the many other nonmedical health services that can have a dramatic impact on a patient's well-being. Should the program continue to focus solely upon the medical aspect of health service, PSRO will do a disservice to Medicare, Medicaid, and Maternal and Child Health Program patients.

Section 730153 of the *PSRO Program Manual* stresses the necessity for multidisciplinary review of the broad range of health services provided to a patient. In reality, the program is straying from this principle, to the extent that true multidisciplinary review does not take place at all. At present, PSRO membership is limited to physicians and osteopaths. Physicians and osteopaths are likewise guaranteed a majority of the available seats on the PSRO's governing board. A wide range of independent health professions recognized by state law are presently excluded from the local PSRO structure. Among the recognized health professions left out are dentistry, oral surgery, optometry, podiatry, and psychology. In theory, these professions may work on multidisciplinary review methodology as part of the "other than physician" Advisory Council to the local PSRO or statewide PSRO council. Unfortunately, Advisory Councils are either meeting regularly or being called upon by the PSRO to begin work on multidisciplinary review structure in only a handful of districts.

The number of seats available to recognized independent health professional representatives on the Advisory Councils is inadequate. In the field of mental health alone, several established "other than physician" professional representatives will find themselves competing for the few available seats on the Advisory Councils. An adequate number of seats should be available for qualified professional representatives. In order for peer review to work, the professionals involved simply must have a voice in the process through which review procedures are promulgated. Failing that, much stronger encouragement from the Department of Health, Education, and Welfare will be needed before individual PSROs seriously begin to form their Advisory Councils and to give the Councils a meaningful role in the multidisciplinary review process.

We call the Congress's attention to the fact that legislation has already been proposed which would either confer PSRO membership privileges or establish a separate review status for several of the "other than physician" health specialties, including those mentioned above. We would encourage the Congress to treat this problem as one issue. We feel that the criteria for membership in a PSRO should be uniform and based upon whether or not the particular health specialty representative is either licensed or certified by the state government in which state their practice is located, and that the health specialist recognized for membership adheres to an established code of professional conduct. We also recommend that a fixed number of PSRO governance structure seats be allocated to the recognized independent health specialties, particularly in the mental health field.

While Advisory Councils may be established at the individual PSRO and PSRO statewide council levels, no parallel mechanism exists at the national level. Consequently, the National Professional Standards Review Council, which meets quarterly in Washington, has the sole authority to influence both the tone and the content of federal policy on PSRO peer review. The independent health professions other than physicians and osteopaths have no representation on the Council, and no systematic channels of communication currently exist for them to make their concerns known to the Council.

During 1976, the Bureau of Quality Assurance did assist in the development of a liaison network for the nonrepresented independent health specialties. While a good deal of Bureau of Quality Assurance staff time was allocated to the project, no federal funds were directly involved in the operation of the liaison network that was subsequently established. The project relied solely upon the voluntarism of the health professional organizations interested in the goals of PSRO. After a promising start, and only one formal meeting, the Liaison Network was disbanded. The reason that was given at the time was that the network was a federal advisory group de facto, operating without a charter approved by the federal government. Work on the required charter was slowed because it was said that then Secretary of Health, Education, and Welfare David Mathews was observing a Nixon/Ford administration moratorium on the formation of federal advisory groups, pending "imminent" governmental reorganization.

This year, the Bureau of Quality Assurance has completed a draft charter for an advisory group to the National Professional Standards Review Council, and the document has gained the approval of the Assistant Secretary for Health. It was only within the last few days that we have learned that the draft charter is once again delayed, this time at the level of the

Secretary of Health, Education, and Welfare. The reason being given is that a moratorium on the formation of advisory groups is again being observed while federal reorganization progresses. The creation of an Advisory Council to the National Professional Standards Review Council would be an essential first step in reorienting the PSRO program toward the track of true patient-oriented, multidisciplinary peer review. The role of "other than physician" independent health specialties in Medicare, Medicaid, and Maternal and Child Health Care is vastly underestimated. The involvement of these professions in the review process cannot be ignored without doing substantial damage to the quality assurance program itself.

As psychology is one of the involved independent health professions, a review of psychology's status in regard to Medicare, Medicaid, and the Maternal and Child Health Program is in order. Seventeen states, representing over 40% of the U.S. population, have opted to recognize psychological services provided independently of physician supervision for reimbursement purposes, under the terms of their Medicaid (Title XIX) plans. At present, the Department of Health, Education, and Welfare and the Social Security Administration are evaluating the quality and cost performance of psychological services provided and reviewed independently under the Medicare program in the State of Colorado. Preliminary information gained from the Colorado Clinical Psychology Experiment can be expected to greatly enhance the chances for the passage of Senate Bill 123 and its House counterpart, HR 2270. Both of these pieces of legislation would extend the principle of direct recognition for psychological services to the entire Medicare system. It is interesting to note that psychological services are held to be reimbursable independently of physician supervision under the Federal Employees Program (over 3 million individuals covered) and under the Civilian Health and Medical Program for the Uniformed Services (CHAMPUS) (over 6 million covered).

Federal health planners with a special interest in peer review as a cost and quality oriented management approach will want to know that the Department of Defense has entered into a contract with the American Psychological Association to develop an *independent* peer review system to evaluate the delivery of psychological services provided through the CHAMPUS program. The Champus program is the largest organized health plan in America, and many see it as one of several working prototypes for national health care. The Department of Defense has entered into a similar contract with the American Psychiatric Association. The review systems for psychological and psychiatric services will be separate and independent, in recognition of the unique and special skills of each profession. We would hope that the PSRO program would follow this model in recognizing the independent status of the other-than-physician health specialties in the review process. We believe that it will be counterproductive and harmful for physical and osteopathic medicine to assume the review responsibilities for services about which they are uninformed and which lie outside their professional expertise.

Legislation recognizing psychological services for reimbursement purposes provided independently of physician supervision has been enacted in 27 states and the District of Columbia. These laws, which are frequently known as "freedom of choice" laws, cover nearly 70% of the U.S. population. Psychological services provided independently of physician supervision are also recognized in a substantial number of other federal programs and their administrative regulations.

As extensively as psychology is currently recognized as an independent health specialty, its future growth prospects are even more interesting. Human behavior, which can be studied and influenced through well-established scientific techniques, represents possibly the most underestimated factor in health care prevention and maintenance today. As a profession and a science, psychology is eager to contribute its skills and techniques to the general problems of health care. Psychology has pioneered in the development of specific techniques such as program evaluation, which could play a major role in the management of a comprehensive health care plan.

While psychological services have traditionally been associated with ambulatory (outpatient) care, professional psychology aspires to a greater role in inpatient hospital care delivery. Already, two separate but related actions on the subject of inpatient care privileges are being undertaken. While the Joint Commission on the Accreditation of Hospitals (JCAH) and the American Psychological Association are engaged in an ongoing discussion on hospital privileges and facility accreditation, the Association for the Advancement of Psychology (AAP) has filed a memorandum of complaint with the Federal Trade Commission regarding those JCAH policies which the AAP sees as constituting restraint of trade. In essence, the issue is that psychologists in a significant number of inpatient teaching and care facilities are fighting to preserve those health care responsibilities that they have earned as individuals over the years from various facilities. Due to a shift in JCAH accreditation policies, the important and often pioneering work that these psychologists have been doing in these inpatient facilities is now threatened. Some of our colleagues have actually lost their jobs, and their patients have been denied continued access to their care. While psychologists view this occurrence as a great professional indignity, we are even more concerned about the thousands of patients who are being and will be denied the benefits of psychological services because of the policies of the Joint Commission. For several years now, organized psychology's initiative to gain membership on the Joint Commission has been thwarted, even though the profession's status as an independent health specialty is well recognized in law and administrative precedent.

Our hope is that the PSRO program can become a tool for identifying the actual health needs of patients. Data from the PSRO program could be of inestimable value in restructuring our health care delivery system to meet the real as opposed to the perceived needs of our citizens. PSRO can fulfill its mission if it focuses upon the totality of health care delivered to patients, and if the review system itself is given the flexibility to embrace new approaches to health care prevention and maintenance as they are proven and developed. We commend the Congress for undertaking a review of the progress made by PSRO to date.

William Buklad heads the State Associations Office of the American Psychological Association.

Assessing Quality in Health Care:
An Evaluation

Summary and Recommendations

Institute of Medicine, National Academy of Sciences

This report suggests that quality assurance programs themselves need improvement, particularly as they relate to services not provided by physicians. The cost-effectiveness of such audits has yet to be demonstrated, in part because of methodological difficulties and the absence of valid and reliable information (e.g., the nonempirical orientation of most reviews).

The concept of quality in medical care historically has been a part of the ethos of the medical profession. In recent years, public interest in health care quality and cost has been heightened by the increase in public expenditures for health care. One congressional reflection of that interest was the enactment in 1972 of legislation that authorized the establishment of Professional Standards Review Organizations (PSROs) (House of Representatives, 1972) to monitor the appropriateness of health services financed by the Medicare, Medicaid, and Maternal and Child Health programs. The following year, Congress requested a major study of alternative mechanisms for health care quality assurance, a request that was included in the Health Maintenance Organization Act of 1973 (Senate, 1973).

A limited version of that study was contracted to the Institute of Medicine by the Department of Health, Education, and Welfare. The study, reported in this document, had the following objectives:

- The description and assessment of the effect of operational quality review programs, based on existing written information and supplemented by observations and data obtained in selected site visits;
- A detailed literature review of several topics, designated as "priority areas" because of their importance in determining the effec-

tiveness of quality assurance programs and the absence of reviews that integrate and analyze relevant information;

- A delineation of areas in which additional research and evaluation are required.

The purpose of the study was not to evaluate the PSRO program—a relatively recent, large-scale undertaking not yet organizationally complete. Nevertheless, some quality assessment programs reviewed were PSROs, and some recommendations refer specifically to the PSRO program.

In limiting the scope of the study, the steering committee established criteria for selecting quality assurance programs for detailed review. Because the concept of quality is multidimensional and complex, a single definition of quality was not used. Instead, components of quality that have been identified and emphasized by existing programs were accepted within the focus of this study. Particular attention was given to programs with the stated purpose of improving the health status and satisfaction of patients. The committee did specify characteristics of an ideal quality assurance system: the existence of an organizational entity for assessing quality; the establishment of standards or criteria against which quality is assessed; a routine system for gathering information; assurance that such information is based on a representative sample of the total population of patients or potential pa-

From Institute of Medicine, *Assessing Quality in Health Care: An Evaluation: Final Report, November 1976.* Washington, D.C.: National Academy of Sciences, 1976.

tients; a process for providing the results of review to patients, the public, providers, and sponsoring organizations; and methods for instituting corrective actions.

A survey of existing programs, including many of those reviewed in detail in this study, makes apparent the fact that most programs do not meet all of the characteristics of an ideal system specified above. Most concentrate on the assessment of the medical care process, rather than the assurance of improved quality of health care. Few programs routinely provide review information to patients and providers, impose corrective actions, or determine through reassessment whether the quality of care has improved. Thus, one might more realistically describe the programs as quality assessment activities, rather than quality assurance. However, the term "quality assurance" is so prevalent that it is unlikely to be obliterated because of this distinction. Both terms are used in this report.

Several timely health policy issues that influence the quality of care were excluded from this report. For example, malpractice and the existence of fraud in federally financed health programs were not considered. Existing quality assessment programs do not emphasize the detection of fraudulent practices and may not be capable of doing so. Other mechanisms are being developed to deal with malpractice. Similarly, many factors in the financing and delivery of health care that influence quality were not studied in detail. These include the organizational arrangements through which care is provided, insurance or reimbursement programs that specify reimbursable methods of treatments, health professional education, the numbers and distribution of physicians and non-physicians geographically and among specialties, provisions for licensing and certification of individual health care providers and facilities, and the recording, storage, and retrieval of information about patients.

Thus, the study is not an exhaustive review of all factors in the health care sector that influence the quality of care. Rather, it is an examination of existing quality review programs. The primary purpose is to describe the manner in which they function and their reported effectiveness in improving health status or patient satisfaction and conserving resources. Additional

issues relating to quality assurance are reviewed in the priority areas: outcome-oriented approaches to quality assurance, quality assurance for ambulatory care, quality assurance for long-term care, methods for changing behavior patterns of health care providers, and patient and consumer involvement in quality assurance programs.

Determining the effectiveness of quality review programs is particularly difficult—in part because of methodological problems, but also because of the absence of valid and reliable information. The effect of review on quality of care usually is described anecdotally because of limitations in current measures of health status or outcome. Although improvements in quality attributed by program officials to review may be impressive, there is no current method for relating the individual anecdotes to the total review effort in a manner which would facilitate the determination of cost effectivness. Because of the close link between quality and utilization of services, the relative ease of measuring utilization, and its associated relationship to cost control, effectiveness is frequently measured in terms of utilization, as expressed in costs. However, the measures customarily used are frequently inadequate and difficult to interpret. This is discussed in detail in the body of the report. Variations among review programs limit one's ability to compare program effectiveness. The relative effect of different types of review mechanisms might be assessed by comparing programs according to the magnitude of changes within them, assuming all other influences could be held constant. However, adequate baseline data are not available to permit before-and-after measurements. A period of time must be allowed for program development and refinement before effectiveness can realistically be expected.

Description of Quality Assessment Programs

The 18 quality assessment programs reviewed in detail represent what have been regarded as the "better" programs. Most have benefitted from considerable financial support and extensive experience, as compared with programs not included in the study. The programs reviewed cannot be regarded as a representative national sample. Many of them were pioneers in the field of quality assurance and have created models that have been adopted elsewhere. Their accomplishments, however, were not made without difficulties, and these may be equally instructive. To draw conclusions from the experiences of these programs perhaps would be to pass judgment prematurely on programs that have had insufficient time to work on a very complex problem. The information presented here, therefore, is intended to assist in re-examining and, possibly, redirecting current efforts before they become so established in custom as to make modification difficult.

A majority of the programs visited can be characterized as follows:

- The stated goals are to ensure high quality medical care at a reasonable cost. But the goals are not expressed in terms that permit measurement of the degree to which they are achieved. The margin by which quality might be improved is not known. Even rough estimates of the magnitude of currently inappropriate care were unavailable. Without such measures, it becomes difficult to determine whether a program is achieving its objectives and whether the resultant improvement is sufficient to justify program expenditures.

- Programs are oriented toward users of health services, rather than people who do not use services, and with a few exceptions, do not consider access to care and under-utilization of services.

- Compliance with PSRO review requirements is the major concern of most hospital programs. PSRO review components include: concurrent review—intended to assure that individual hospital admissions and continued stays are medically necessary; medical care evaluations (MCEs) or medical audits—a detailed, frequently retrospective review of the quality of care given to groups of patients; and profile analysis—a retrospective analysis of patterns of care that may concentrate on particular diagnoses, patients, or physicians and identify areas for special attention by either concurrent review or MCEs.

- Most hospital review programs place primary emphasis on concurrent review activities.

There is considerable variation among programs in the timing, depth, and frequency of review. Similarly, the degree to which review coordinators and physician advisors are trained and supervised varies by program.

- Less emphasis is placed on medical care evaluation studies. Common problems have been encountered in conducting MCEs: the incompatibility between requirements of the Joint Commission on Accreditation of Hospitals (JCAH) and PSRO; the difficulty of selecting audit topics which result in the identification of significant problems so that improvements can be made; the difficulty of developing criteria that are relevant for all patients without becoming too general; and the difficulty of achieving change, once deficiencies in patient care have been identified. Innovative efforts which address these problems are underway.

- Profile analysis, the third component of PSRO review, is the least developed.

- Integration of the three review components is seldom achieved within hospitals or within PSRO administrative staffs.

- The most common type of quality assessment for ambulatory care is based on a review of claim forms submitted by physicians to fiscal intermediaries for reimbursement purposes. Alternatives to claims review should permit greater emphasis on quality by reviewing the provision of medical care over time and assessing access to care and health outcomes. However, they require further refinement and evaluation before being widely implemented.

- There is difficulty in achieving improvements after deficiencies in patient care have been documented. Most programs rely on educational methods for encouraging improved performance. Some internal appraisals of the effects of review have been made, but no program has established a formal mechanism for self-assessment. Some have been evaluated by external groups, however.

Effectiveness of Quality Assessment Programs

The steering committee believes that the widespread interest in quality assurance activities and the intellectual stimulation and professional re-examination that occur as programs are initiated and standards for care are established should eventually improve the general quality of medical practice. The committee found impressive examples of stated improvements in quality and changes in utilization of health care services in the programs reviewed. Assessing the broader impact, however, requires consideration of the total magnitude of the effort, not merely isolated examples.

The difficulty of measuring the quality of care and the effectiveness of quality review systems was noted at the outset. Information on cost and effectiveness, in particular, covers a relatively short time span and reflects whatever information was readily available rather than what could be collected in a carefully designed effort at evaluation. These limitations notwithstanding, the steering committee was able to reach some preliminary conclusions about the current effectiveness of programs visited:

- Existing information does not substantiate the effectiveness of MCEs. MCEs or medical audits have been required for accreditation and reimbursement purposes for several years. Yet, there is no reliable source of data to reflect the numbers, topics, and associated costs of currently performed MCEs, the identified deficiencies in patient care, the remedial actions proposed and taken, or the extent and duration of improvement in patient care. MCEs may have caused improvements in quality, but reliable, generalizable assessments are not available.

- Evidence is not yet available for a conclusion that hospital concurrent review programs are effective. Although changes in utilization patterns have been noted, the reasons are not adequately understood. The costs of conducting concurrent review vary widely. Assertions of cost savings are exaggerated, because they assume that total per diem cost will be saved for each day of care denied and do not adequately take into account fixed hospital costs or the cost of alternative care.

- Most ambulatory care claims review programs considered in this study yield dollar reductions in submitted claims that are more than adequate to pay the costs of review, and

some improvements in quality have been noted. At least for the fiscal intermediary, claims review is cost effective. A claim denied or reduced, however, is not necessarily a claim unpaid—some providers are persistent in recovering some portion of their fee, which may be eventually paid by the patient, other fiscal intermediaries, or society. Furthermore, most savings come from administration reviews of patient eligibility for insurance coverage, the range of reimbursable benefits, or the amount of reimbursement claimed. These savings would be realized under most claims review systems and generally are unrelated to considerations of either quality or appropriateness of care. The additional benefits from the medical peer review component of claims review are not well documented.

The reasons for lack of demonstrated effectiveness of quality review programs are difficult to isolate. Whether they are due to faulty conceptualization of the nature of quality or to defects in program design is not clear. At the very least, it is evident that the objectives of current programs are not well specified and include a mixture of goals: cost control alone, utilization control (a desire to increase the potential benefits of care by controlling the types and quality of resources used, which also generate costs), and increased effectiveness of medical care (improved quality in terms of greater patient satisfaction and better health outcome). Though these objectives may be conceptually interrelated, it is not clear that a single review program can address these and possibly other objectives simultaneously.

These uncertainties notwithstanding, the steering committee believes that some monitoring, perhaps on a sample basis, of the quality of medical care provided to all patients—not just those for whom the federal government has financial responsibility—is essential. At the level of quality assurance expenditures anticipated for FY 1977, the total cost for hospital and ambulatory review could exceed $1,250,000,000 annually if extrapolated for the entire U.S. population. There is a need for less expensive methods to achieve better results. It should be possible to increase the efficiency of existing quality assessment techniques while also developing new strategies for areas which do not now receive adequate attention.

The steering committee identified a number of actions that could be taken to achieve these goals. The committee's recommendations are divided into two sections. General recommendations stem primarily from the site visits and are not confined to any specific priority area. They are mainly actions which should be taken by national policymakers, although other national policy recommendations in the priority areas are properly cited under those headings, which follow the general recommendations.

Both general and priority area recommendations are categorized into those which should be implemented immediately and long-term recommendations which require further research and evaluation. Many of the long-term recommendations emphasize the need to develop more refined techniques for conducting quality assurance activities, with particular concentration in two areas: research to develop more reliable and valid assessment tools to measure the levels of quality; and research to foster the improvement or assurance of quality, which involves the development of better methods for altering the behavior of both health care providers and consumers. Thus, many of the recommendations for the priority areas constitute a long-range research agenda.

General Policy Recommendations

Immediate

1. Review techniques should be refined to facilitate a more concentrated (targeted) examination of diagnoses, patients, or providers associated with questionable patterns of care, as an alternative to the current practice of reviewing all cases. A targeted review should enable more frequent identification of truly inappropriate care and less frequent review of appropriate care, which should increase the efficiency of review. Cases excepted from routine review should be monitored periodically to assure that more frequent review is not warranted. Profile analysis must be further developed to provide the information to identify patients or providers who require more concentrated review.

2. Criteria for excepting cases from review should be clearly specified. The new Medicare and Medicaid utilization review regulations, which permit each hospital independently to specify cases that will not be routinely reviewed and do not include adequate provisions for monitoring, may reduce the likelihood of identifying inappropriate care.

3. Within PSROs, a conscious effort is needed to integrate the three types of review. The common practice of delegating responsibility to hospitals for conducting MCEs independent of concurrent review should be discontinued because it encourages fragmentation. Within hospitals, PSRO review activities should be better integrated with prior utilization review and other quality assurance activities.

4. Intensified efforts should begin immediately to evaluate both federal and privately sponsored health care quality assurance systems by comparing the quality of care in geographic areas with and without quality review programs, or in areas of otherwise similar characteristics but different types of review. This should have been accomplished before a uniform national quality assurance program was required by the PSRO legislation. Nevertheless, the committee believes that planned experimentation should still be possible in order to determine the relative effects of alternative review mechanisms on health status, utilization and cost of services, and other measures of quality.

5. There should be fewer, better designed, and better evaluated MCEs. The JCAH and PSRO requirements for MCEs should be compatible in content, as well as numerical requirements. Hospitals should be permitted to count re-audits of completed audits in fulfilling MCE numerical requirements.

6. Criteria should be developed for categorizing successful and unsuccessful MCEs and isolating factors associated with success, so that more effective MCEs may evolve. Data bases must be developed to describe current MCEs, so that a more definitive, future assessment of effectiveness can be made. Since there currently is no "good" model of a MCE, a wide range of innovation and evaluation should be encouraged. The effectiveness of concurrent and prospective MCEs, that permit direct intervention in the process of care where warranted, should be

tested. The relative merits of areawide MCEs, as opposed to individual hospital MCEs, should be assessed.

7. Uniform data elements, but not necessarily data formats, should be required in all health care settings to facilitate quality assurance activities, as well as program management, planning, and evaluation. Requirements for the Uniform Hospital Discharge Data Set as modified for PSROs should be enforced. The Minimum Ambulatory and Long-Term Care Data Sets should be implemented. Methods for linking information from the Medicare Part B supplementary insurance program with Part A hospital information should be devised. More general methods are needed to integrate hospital and ambulatory patient care information using a common identification number. Better "denominator" data must be generated to define the population eligible for care and to provide the basis for monitoring utilization of services. Important confidentiality issues must be resolved to protect individual privacy and the public right to information.

8. Both nationally and locally, PSROs and Health Systems Agencies (HSAs) should establish mutually beneficial working relationships, beginning with an exchange of data. HSAs have information on the population eligible for care, which is needed by PSROs. PSROs can document variations in the use of services, which may suggest problems in access and under-utilization that should be addressed by both HSAs and PSROs.

9. Quality assurance programs should further specify their objectives and establish internal self-assessment units for program evaluation. The Department of Health, Education, and Welfare should provide technical assistance involving both trained researchers and persons experienced in peer review. Appropriate links with health services research centers should be established. Additional support is required for research training programs to develop the necessary cadre of skilled personnel.

10. Policy mandates for quality assurance should impose comparable levels of stringency on all health care delivery arrangements, even though the manner in which requirements are met may vary. The greater ease of conducting quality assessment activities in larger, formally organized health care programs, such as Health Maintenance Organizations, should not lead to the imposition of more rigorous requirements on such organizations.

Long-Term

1. Better evaluative measures are needed to identify and aggregate the effects on health status that result from the provision of medical care, and to assess the impact of quality assurance programs, continuing education, and other activities designed to improve the quality of care.

2. Better techniques are needed to determine the effect of quality assurance programs on utilization and cost of medical care. Data should be adjusted to enable comparisons among facilities with different patient and provider characteristics. Measures should assess the effect of review on the total community, rather than individual facilities, and should take into account the costs of alternative care. Additional research is needed to determine the conditions under which hospital costs vary according to occupancy rate in both short and long-term situations. Adjustments for fixed costs and the cost of alternative care should be included in estimates of cost savings resulting from utilization review.

3. The assumption that hospitals have incentives to conduct meaningful utilization review programs should be examined. Current reimbursement mechanisms provide little incentive for hospital administrators to reduce variable costs associated with lower hospital utilization. Therefore, actual savings may be minimal.

4. The indices of quality currently used by quality assurance programs should be expanded. Access to care and potential under-utilization should be assessed. This requires attention to the availability of health care providers and facilities, appropriate links between levels of care, and policies (such as on-call arrangements) to assure that services are easily accessible. Benefit packages and reimbursement policies should be examined to determine their impact on the quality of care, particularly with respect to coverage of long-term care, both institutional and non-institutional. Greater efforts should be made to link the separate programs, which currently address only care provided to specific pa-

tients by specific providers or facilities, into an integrated program which assesses the quality of care provided by the total health system.

5. A systematic accumulation of data is needed to describe current patterns of medical care in all settings. Special attention should be given to unusual departures from customary practice, the extremes of under- and over-utilization, and the reasons for such variation. This information should provide a better estimate of the margin by which quality and utilization of services might be improved, which in turn, would help to determine the magnitude of the required quality assurance effort and identify areas of achievable gain for special attention.

6. The curricula for health professionals should include courses in health care evaluation and assessment designed to be relevant in routine practice and implemented throughout one's professional career. Quality assurance activities should be applied in facilities where physicians-in-training provide care.

Recommendations for Assessing Health Outcomes

Immediate

1. Additional research is needed to develop substitute or short-term outcome measures which occur closer in time to the provision of care than final end-result measures. The relationship between such measures and process and final outcome measures should be established.

Long-Term

1. The steering committee believes that health care should be assessed on the basis of health outcome, despite the limitations of current measures and uncertainties about the contribution of medical care to health status. Patient satisfaction must be recognized as one indicator of outcome. Research is needed to develop better measures of patient satisfaction and health status. In addition to the use of short-term outcome measures, greater reliance should be placed on existing instruments for assessing functional status and the growing body of

knowledge of the natural history of disease—particularly for assessing the progress of the chronically ill.

2. In the same sense that process measures of quality are currently required of PSROs, limited post-discharge outcome information should be gathered. The cost and utility of outcome studies should be carefully monitored. Outcome data should assist in identifying patients and providers for whom the process of care should be more thoroughly assessed and in isolating areas in which efficacy studies are required. The accumulated data should lead to a better understanding of the natural course of illness. Over time, sufficient knowledge should be accumulated so that if patients of a particular provider have not progressed as expected, the provider's treatment methods could be questioned or the patient referred elsewhere for evaluation and consultation.

3. Individual practitioners should be encouraged to join with their patients in establishing outcome objectives for patient care and examining reasons for failure to meet them.

4. Additional research is needed to establish the natural history of diseases and the efficacy of medical procedures and therapies. For research findings to be useful in assessing the quality of care, determinations of efficacy should be made under average as well as ideal treatment situations at various points in time and should include a broad range of outcome measures. The Department of Health, Education, and Welfare should further specify the responsibilities of its component agencies in this area and increase the level of funding.

Recommendations for Ambulatory Quality Assurance

Immediate

1. Ambulatory claims review should be more widely implemented in an experimental manner while more appropriate ambulatory quality assurance techniques are being developed. Despite the limitations of claims review, it will permit the detection of the most serious deficiencies. Governmental agencies and other purchasers of health care should be en-

couraged to require more stringent claims review by their fiscal intermediaries. Careful evaluation of these programs should be required.

2. Closer monitoring should begin immediately of pharmacy services, small clinical laboratories, and free-standing radiological units. Monitoring techniques using pre-identified specimens should be more widely applied to determine the accuracy of judgments within labs and radiology services.

Long-Term

1. Intensified research and development is needed for ambulatory quality assessment methods. Primary ambulatory care is different from secondary and tertiary care and requires different quality assessment techniques. Many ambulatory review programs rely on a diagnostic-specific review of the medical record, but the bulk of primary ambulatory care consists of signs and symptoms that cannot readily be assigned to diagnostic categories. Classification schemes to record patient-reported symptoms are being developed and could form the basis of an experimental quality assurance project. Another approach might focus on the basic skills or tasks which constitute primary ambulatory care, such as the elicitation of signs and symptoms and their history, performance of a physical exam, the synthesis of this information into recommendations for care, and determination of the appropriate point for referral. Much of the success of primary care depends on the extent to which the practitioner coordinates care provided over a relatively long period of time. Very little of this information is found in the medical record, and other recording and assessment methods must be devised.

2. Additional work is needed to devise means for supplementing information recorded on the claim form. The Minimum Ambulatory Care Data Set should be the basis on which such work proceeds. In addition, the value of diagnostic, patient, and laboratory registries to facilitate problem identification and provide information over time should be explored. Probability sampling techniques must be developed for claims review to focus on patients and providers who fall at the extremes of dis-

tributions of care patterns and at the same time give estimates of the broader spectrum of care provided to the total population.

3. A single approach to quality assurance will not accommodate the diversity of functions and personnel included within the ambulatory care sector; further research is required before a range of proved alternative methods can emerge. The widest possible range of review techniques should be included in the ambulatory demonstration projects to be funded by the Bureau of Quality Assurance. Recipients of awards should not necessarily be limited to PSROs. The budget for these activities should be increased.

Recommendations for Long-Term Care

Immediate

1. Existing standards to protect residents of long-term care facilities should be enforced, while more appropriate quality assurance mechanisms for long-term care are being developed.

2. The certification and licensure process for long-term care providers should be reconsidered. The Department of Health, Education, and Welfare study, scheduled to begin in April of 1977, should go beyond a review of existing structural standards to address more fundamental issues of quality and analyze the financial and other ramifications of forced compliance with standards.

Long-Term

1. Quality assurance programs for long-term care should be designed to address the unique needs of the chronically ill. The etiology of many chronic conditions remains obscure; many individuals, particularly the aged, have several chronic conditions. Thus, an assessment of quality based on diagnostic-specific criteria is often inappropriate, and functional status is a more relevant measure. Furthermore, because of the long-term nature of the patient's condition and frequent fluctuations in physical and mental states, treatment requirements vary. Patients may require differing levels of care within a relatively short time period, ranging from intensive hospital care, skilled nursing services, cus-

todial care, or home health services, to periodic office visits. Methods for assessing the quality of care should include all sources of care and should consider the impact of care on the patient's expected and actual ability to function in daily life.

2. The responsibility for quality assurance in long-term care belongs at the community level so that an integrated review of the total range of services can occur. Anything less will be based on evaluation of care from the fragmented view of individual facilities or programs and will perpetuate the inefficient and costly services which currently exist. Steps should be taken to develop community-level organizations to include a broad range of providers, facilities, professional groups, consumers, and representatives from planning and certifying agencies. The community organization should consider such issues as access to care, appropriateness of placement, scope of available services, and the accumulation of uniform data. Assessment of the technical components of care could be delegated to PSROs and other groups of health care providers. Demonstrations should be initiated to test the feasibility of such an approach in terms of both cost and effectiveness. Evaluation should occur after prototype organizations have passed the developmental phase.

3. State and federal reimbursement policies for long-term care should be reformed. State and federal regulations for reimbursement and accounting should be made compatible and redesigned to enhance their influence on the quality of care. The levels of reimbursement should not be so inadequate as to lead to poor quality. Experimental reimbursement projects should examine the effect of capitation, which would permit the individual to move from one level of care to another without being penalized. Similarly, experimentation with facility reimbursement rates based on the customary mix of patients, rather than specific patients, might permit patients to be moved from one level of care to another, depending on their conditions.

4. Support of existing programs to train personnel for work in long-term care should be continued and expanded. Program content should focus on the unique characteristics of long-term care, the multiplicity of skills which are required to meet patient needs, and the necessity of a team approach.

5. The long-term care quality assurance demonstration projects to be funded by the Bureau of Quality Assurance should represent a wide variety of alternative approaches to review and should not be limited to PSROs. The budget for these activities should be protected and expanded.

Recommendations for Improving Provider Performance

Immediate

1. There should be no mandated provisions for any specific technique for improving provider performance in the immediate future, including continuing medical education. Existing evidence of effectiveness is inadequate.

2. Because of the limitations of education in improving individual provider performance, alternative methods should be explored. In particular, the influence of the organization of health care resources on quality needs immediate attention.

Long-Term

1. Research is needed to devise methods for encouraging improvements in patient care, once deficiencies are identified. Relevant literature from the social sciences, as well as from medical education, should be utilized. Existing quality deficiencies should be categorized to assist in determining the reasons for their occurrence and the design of appropriate corrective actions. All methods for improvement should be carefully evaluated to determine the extent to which they result in lasting behavior change.

2. Studies are needed of the effectiveness of various methods for informing a physician that he is providing inadequate care, including presentation of information describing his practice patterns compared with his peers, structuring the information to emphasize particular deficiencies, or providing incentives for review and change. Reasons for failure to change should be explored.

3. For instances in which clearly inappropriate care is identified and behavior does not change, sanctions which are less drastic than permanent loss of licensure may be more readily applied. Experimentation is needed with intermediate sanctions, including curtailment of privileges, licensing with restrictions on specified areas of practice, mandatory supervision of medical practice, or remedial education. Demonstrations should test the effectiveness of equipping PSROs with a wider range of sanctions for clearly inappropriate behavior, including more direct links with licensing bodies or authorizing the PSRO to remove a license with due cause. State legislative bodies should waive or amend existing statutes, if necessary, to permit such experimentation.

4. The feasibility and effectiveness of publicizing instances of persistently poor quality care by individual practitioners in public media should be explored.

Recommendations for Consumer Involvement

Immediate

1. Health care consumers, both individually and collectively, should be educated to accept greater responsibility for their own health and should be involved in decisions regarding the provision and evaluation of health care. One immediate step for furthering this concept would be the inclusion of representatives of the public as members of the National Professional Standards Review Council. This may require a legislative amendment.

Long-Term

1. The steering committee believes that consumer involvement in the planning, management, and evaluation of health care programs should be encouraged and expanded. A better public understanding of the determinants of health, the limitations of health care, the resources required to provide it, and the necessity to work in partnership with professionals to create a system of health care should

result in improvements in the quality and appropriateness of health services and a healthier public. The objective is clear, but the methods for achieving it are not. Research and experimentation are required.

2. More information is needed to identify aspects of health care that are important to the consumer, which can then be incorporated into valid and reliable instruments for assessing patient expectations and satisfaction. Additional information also is needed to relate expectations and satisfaction to compliance with medical instructions and to health outcome. Once the measures are adequate, the feasibility of implementing them in formal quality assurance programs can be better tested.

3. Although some health education programs have been effective in changing patient behavior, additional research is needed to identify factors associated with effectiveness. Attention should be given to the effect of alternative media, differing levels of patient and family involvement, the duration of behavior change and whether reinforcement is needed, the potential contribution of motivational research, and patient factors which may influence effectiveness, such as emotional state, demographic characteristics, and health status. Different approaches may be required for different patient conditions, ranging from preventive care to acute illnesses and chronic conditions.

4. When patient education is known to be essential, quality assessment criteria should require that education activities be performed. To the extent that process-oriented criteria are used to monitor care, current efforts to include educational components (such as dietary instruction for diabetics) should be encouraged. If changes in the process of care or delivery setting are anticipated, the acceptance of such changes will be increased if information is provided to patients in advance.

5. On an experimental basis, quality assurance programs should include consumer or patient boards to hear patient complaints and evaluate their validity. The use of patient questionnaires in assessing quality should be tested, as well as the effect of asking patients to review their own medical records. Patient expectations upon seeking care might be determined and used

as the basis for providing patient education and instituting treatment; the influence of expectations on compliance and outcome could then be determined. A more direct involvement of consumers with providers in assessing the quality of care should be tested; each group may learn from the other.

6. Existing laws should be exploited whenever possible to further health education. Informed consent requirements, for instance, provide a unique opportunity to educate the patient, rather than simply to obtain an unthinking agreement to treatment.

7. The consumer's role in governance and policymaking requires careful documentation and analysis to facilitate more responsible, comfortable, and effective relationships with health care professionals.

References

House of Representatives, U.S. Congress, *Social Security Amendments of 1972,* Pub. L. 92-603, 92d Cong., 2d sess., 1972, H.R.1.

Senate, U.S. Congress, *Health Maintenance Organization Act of 1973,* Pub. L. 93-222, 93d Cong., 1st sess., 1973, S. 14.

Quality Assurance for Mental Health Care

National Institute of Mental Health

This article reviews the growing interest in quality assurance for mental health care. Insurance companies, government agencies, and consumers seek such information. Various attempts at assessing provider credentials, treatment outcome, and review procedures are described.

In recent years there has been increasing pressure for public accountability of health care since most of it is financed through third-party payors. This general concern was part of the rationale for the PSRO Program. Specific concerns about mental health care were voiced in Congressional hearings on the CHAMPUS Program. In a speech given at the Butler Hospital Symposium in June 1975, Dr. Robert Laur of Federal Employees Program, Blue Cross said "... compared to other types of services, there is less clarity and uniformity of terminology concerning mental diagnoses, treatment modalities and types of facilities providing care...." He went on to say: "If subscribers and providers want coverages which are not arbitrarily limited, or which do not require high cost-sharing, it is necessary that creditable, reliable and uniform utilization review processes be established. For mental health services, such processes are not widely available today. I believe their absence constitutes the single most important barrier to the extension of mental health coverage by third-party payors."

This chapter will discuss the status of quality assurance activities for mental health care and put them in the context of general health care. The first part of the chapter will provide some background and the second part will discuss specific review mechanisms.

Background

Donabedian (1968) divided quality assessment into structure, outcome and process measures. How does mental health compare to other areas of health care with respect to these three types of measures of quality?

Structure

Structural review examines the tools necessary to provide care—facilities, services and manpower. For a facility this is reflected in licensure and accreditation. Mental hospitals and clinics are all subject to state laws on licensure. Accreditation is a voluntary process and is generally associated with the Joint Commission on Accreditation of Hospitals. In addition to psychiatric units in general hospitals which are surveyed in the same way as the rest of a general hospital, there are separate standards for accreditation of psychiatric facilities. Standards are presently being written or tested for accreditation of Community Mental Health Centers, alcohol treatment centers, and drug treatment centers. Up until the last few years, many psychiatric facilities, particularly large public mental hospitals, were not accredited. At the present time that is no longer true as mental hospitals have worked toward accreditation in order to qualify for third-party reimbursement.

Structural appraisal applied to the individual practitioner is reflected in licensure and certification. Psychiatrists are fully licensed medical practitioners in every state and must pass the same licensure examinations as all other physicians. Many public mental hospitals have employed general physicians, often foreign-trained, who have not passed licensure exams.

From National Institute of Mental Health, *Draft Report: The Financing, Utilization, and Quality of Mental Health Care in the United States.* Rockville, Md.: Office of Program Development and Analysis, National Institute of Mental Health, April 1976.

That practice has been criticized and many states are now requiring physicians in mental hospitals to be licensed. Clinical psychologists must also be licensed in most states. Registered nurses are licensed in all states with no special requirements for psychiatric nurses. At the present time, there are licensure requirements for social workers in 8 states.

With respect to specialty certification, psychiatrists may take certification examinations given by the American Board of Psychiatry and Neurology. The ABPN is a specialty board which functions in essentially the same way as other medical and surgical specialty boards such as the American College of Surgeons. One difference between psychiatrists and other specialists is that many fewer psychiatrists take the examinations (58% compared with 96%, 91% and 85% for surgery, pediatrics and internal medicine). The statistics for actual board certification are even more disturbing: 34% of practicing psychiatrists have been certified, compared with 89% for pediatrics and 61% for internal medicine (Levit, 1974). These figures need to be seen in context. Board Certification has not been a condition of payment and therefore there was little incentive to take the exams. This is particularly true for psychiatrists specializing in psychotherapy who make little use of neurology or even psychopharmacology in their practice. Furthermore, any licensed physician can practice and be paid for psychotherapy without organized formal training much less board certification. In Canada, specialty certification is required in order to receive a higher fee and under those conditions, almost all psychiatrists do get certified. On the other hand, being recognized and certified as a psychoanalyst by the American Psychoanalytic Association is a long and arduous process which is separate from the ABPN certification process. This certification is required in order to be a full fledged psychoanalyst.

Credentialing is progressively less formalized for psychologists, nurses, social workers, marital and family counselors, pastoral counselors, group therapists, psychiatric technicians, and the myriad of other mental health workers. Each field will need to define its areas of competence and training requirements. At the present time, psychiatrists as medical practitioners are the only mental health professionals whose services have been legitimized by all health insurance programs.

Psychologists are increasingly being accepted as individual practitioners as are psychiatric social workers. Licensure and certification are usually prerequisites to health insurance reimbursement. Careful consideration needs to be given to the implications of conferring individual practitioner status. In addition to the question of whether physician referral is necessary, allowing private practice may pull psychologists and social workers out of organized care settings.

Outcome

Large scale outcome studies in mental health have been done for drug therapy and electroshock therapy. There are fewer convincing outcome studies of psychosocial treatments although some recent reports do support the effectiveness of psychotherapy (Malan, 1973; Bordin, 1974). The latter author states: "As I have shown, there is respectable evidence of short or long-term effects of various aspects of the psychotherapeutic situation."

Compared to other medical care evaluation, evaluation in mental health has been more multidimensional and looked at multiple aspects of an individual's functioning (Linn & Linn, 1975). Some mental health programs have set explicit objectives for treatment which allow for evaluation of the degree to which the goals for an individual patient have been met (Kiresuk & Sherman, 1968) The goals set for mental health care are more likely than for medical care to be comprehensive and include measures of patient satisfaction, patient compliance and subjective relief of symptoms.

Process

There tends to be wider variation in mental health than in general medical care on what are acceptable modes of treatment. As an example, an early attempt by the American Psychiatric Association at developing model review criteria seemed to indicate that few specific treatments are required but that almost any treatment is "consistent with diagnosis." Except for detecting potentially flagrant abuses, individual case analysis using process criteria is probably of less value than reviewing whether the particular treatment goals have been achieved as described in the section on outcome. Process review is of limited value in the review of medical care as well as mental health care.

Review Mechanisms

Various review mechanisms are presently being used to assure the necessity, appropriateness and quality of care received by patients. Utilization review committees have been required in institutions under Medicare and Medicaid since their inception. Psychiatric units in general hospitals use the same utilization review plan as all other units in a hospital. Mental hospitals are subject to additional review requirements by both Medicare and Medicaid. Institutional review programs will gradually be coordinated and supervised by Professional Standards Review Organizations which were mandated by PL 92-603 and are being set up all around the country. Psychiatrists have been active participants in most of the PSROs established to date. The American Psychiatric Association has also been a full participant in an HEW contract with the American Medical Association to develop criteria for use in PSRO review (American Medical Association, 1975). Just like their medical colleagues, psychiatrists will be designing medical care evaluation studies for groups of patients and performing concurrent review on individual patients. In terms of claims review for payment purposes, most fiscal intermediaries and carriers have a psychiatric consultant to assist them in deciding if a claim for psychiatric services should be paid. If cases are questioned, they are usually referred to a Peer Review Committee of the local psychiatric society. This is used for other medical specialties as well. There is no evidence that psychiatrists are more or less likely to overcharge for services or submit fraudulent claims.

In addition to the above activities in institutional utilization review and ordinary claims review, there have been some innovative quality assurance activities in the field of mental health. The Peninsula Community Mental Health Center in Burlingame, California, has set up a peer review system to assist clinical decision making on the appropriate treatment for individual patients given a limited budget with which to provide services (Newman & Luft, 1974). A comprehensive program of patient care evaluation in a community mental health center has been in progress at the Connecticut Mental Health Center since 1969 (Riedel, 1974). In another project, under the auspices of NIMH and the Department of Defense, a Select Committee on Psychiatric Care and Evaluation made up of nonfederal mental health professionals has provided since October, 1974, an independent assessment of the care and treatment of children and adolescents whose care in residential treatment centers was being paid for by CHAMPUS. As of December, 1975, 832 cases had been reviewed and 146 were still in the process of review. In addition, 51 cases were re-reviewed following appeals of the initial review. This peer review process is now being tested by comparing the results of record review with those of on-site clinical assessment of the same children. Another Select Committee is now carrying out review of quality of care of hospitalized adult schizophrenics whose care is being paid for by CHAMPUS. Through this project, payment for care will be continued only if the hospital meets specific standards in each case. A similar effort is now being considered for all other psychiatric diagnosis under the CHAMPUS program. A cost analysis of the CHAMPUS review system found that at a review cost of $100,000, the program was able to save $5.0 million.

In addition to peer review activities which investigate the care given to groups of patients or to individuals, the Community Mental Health Center Program has fostered the development of program evaluation activities. Methodologies have been developed to measure specific program goals such as accessibility of services and continuity of care (Abt Associates, 1972; Bass & Windle, 1972). Techniques have been developed to assist program managers in allocating resources through cost-finding and cost effectiveness studies (Sorensen & Phipps, 1972; Fishman, 1973). Organized care settings like CMHC make it possible to study broad program goals, and to make policy decisions among various options for providing care. Program evaluation is given additional emphasis in PL 94-63 which extends the CMHC program and provides for greater public accountability. These activities are much harder to require from the private sector or from individual practitioners. However, the Health Systems Agencies to be set up under PL 93-641 will also be expected to assess community health needs in relation to available resources and should benefit from the experience of the CMHC program.

References

Abt Associates: A Study on the Accessibility of Community Mental Health Centers. Report to NIMH on Contract HSM-42-70-92.

American Medical Association. Model screening criteria to assist PSROs. May 1975.

Bass, R. D., and Windle, C. Continuity of Care: An Approach to Measurement. *American Journal of Psychiatry*, 1972, *129*, 196–201.

Bordin, E. S. Research Strategies in Psychotherapy. John Wiley and Sons, New York, 1974.

Donabedian, A. Promoting Quality Through Evaluating the Process of Patient Care: *Medical Care*, 1968, *6*, 181–202.

Fishman, D. C. *Development and Test of a Cost-Effectiveness Methodology for CMHCs*. Report to NIMH on Contract HSM-42-73-162.

Kiresuk, T. J., & Sherman, R. E. Goal Attainment Scaling: A General Method for Evaluating Comprehensive Community Mental Health Programs. *Community Mental Health Journal*, 1968, *4*, 443.

Levit, E. J., et al. Trends in Graduate Medical Education and Specialty Certification. *New England Journal of Medicine*, 1974, *290*, 545–549.

Linn, M. W., & Linn, B. S. Narrowing the Gap Between Medical and Mental Health Evaluation. *Medical Care*, 1975, *13*, 607–614.

Malan, D. H. The Outcome Problem in Psychotherapy Research. *Archives of General Psychiatry*, 1973, *29*, 719–729.

Newman, D. E., and Luft, L. L. The Peer Review Process: Education Versus Control. *American Journal of Psychiatry*, 1974, *131*, 1363–1366.

Riedel, D. C., et al. *Patient Care Evaluation in Mental Health Programs*. Ballinger Publishing Co., Cambridge, Mass., 1974.

Sorensen, J. E., and Phipps, D. W. *Cost-finding and Rate Setting for Community Mental Health Centers*. DHEW Publication No. HSM-72-9138.

JCAH Standards for Accreditation of Psychiatric Facilities

Implications for the Practice of Clinical Psychology

Herbert Dörken and Delmont Morrison

The Joint Commission for the Accreditation of Hospitals has recently developed standards for the accreditation for psychiatric facilities. The standards will have major implications for the practice and training of clinical psychologists. Although the Joint Commission endorses the need for the services of clinical psychologists, it maintains the position that patient care is the ultimate responsibility of the psychiatrist. The standards for accreditation were developed with minimum contributions from organizations and individuals representing the views of the profession of clinical psychology. A review of the standards adopted by the Joint Commission indicates that a good many of them are objectionable to the profession of clinical psychology, contrary to current state and federal regulations and laws, and antithetical to good patient care.

Prior to 1972, the Joint Commission on Accreditation of Hospitals (JCAH) accommodated within its hospital accreditation procedures (JCAH, 1973) facilities that were primarily designed for the diagnosis and treatment of psychiatric disorders. During this time the accreditation program was geared primarily to the general hospital, and its surveyors were trained principally in the complexities of medical–surgical hospitals. At times, JCAH recruited psychiatrically oriented physician surveyors, who might use the American Psychiatric Association's (1969) Standards for Psychiatric Facilities in interpreting the medical–surgical hospital standards for application to psychiatric hospitals. In 1970, the Joint Commission and a group of organizations concerned with psychiatric services agreed to establish an Accreditation Council for Psychiatric Facilities (AC/PF) to develop standards and accreditation programs for psychiatric hospitals and other kinds of psychiatric facilities. AC/PF first annotated the JCAH hospital standards for application to psychiatric hospitals, then developed separate standards for psychiatric facilities (JCAH, 1972). The American Psychiatric Association's

1969 standards served as the basic resource for both endeavors. Subsequently, AC/PF developed separate accreditation standards for psychiatric facilities (inpatient, outpatient, and partial hospitalization) serving children and adolescents (JCAH, 1974). The Council is currently developing standards for community mental health centers and alcoholism and drug abuse programs. The original 1972 standards are applied to public and private adult psychiatric hospitals, including inpatient, outpatient, and partial hospitalization services; pending the development of specialized standards, they are also applied to community mental health centers. AC/PF's specialized standards are applied to programs within a psychiatric facility (e.g., a children's program in a psychiatric hospital), a medical–surgical hospital (e.g., an alcoholism program), or another kind of facility surveyed by a JCAH accreditation program (e.g., a psychiatric treatment unit within a residential facility for the mentally retarded).

A review of the current listing of clinical training programs approved by the American Psychological Association (APA, 1975) and/or

Reprinted from *American Psychologist*, 1976, *31*, 774–784.

the several hundred listed by the Association of Psychology Internship Centers (1975) reveals that most training programs in clinical psychology are also found in facilities that may be reviewed for accreditation by the AC/PF. The standards of the AC/PF thus impact not only on clinical psychologists but also on the professions' interns. It becomes cogent, therefore, to review these accreditation standards as they relate both to the practice of clinical psychology and to the training of clinical psychologists.

Joint Commission Structure and Policies

JCAH was established in 1951 by the American College of Physicians, the American College of Surgeons, the American Hospital Association, and the American Medical Association, to carry on the hospital accreditation program begun in 1918 by the College of Surgeons. In 1966, JCAH began an accreditation program for long-term care facilities, responsibility for which was assumed by the Accreditation Council for Long Term Care Facilities (AC/LTC) organized in 1971. An Accreditation Council for Facilities for the Mentally Retarded (AC/FMR) was established in 1969 (the American Psychological Association became a member of this council in 1973), an Accreditation Council for Psychiatric Facilities was established in 1970, and an Accreditation Council for Ambulatory Health Care was created in 1975. Each accreditation council is composed of organizations concerned with facilities or services within the council's purview. Each member organization appoints councillors who constitute the council's Board of Directors and govern its affairs. Some organizations belong to more than one council. The original program for hospital accreditation is now called the JCAH Hospital Accreditation Program and is governed directly by the Board of Commissioners, consisting of representatives appointed by the four corporate members of JCAH. All actions of an accreditation council concerning standards, survey procedures, and accreditation decisions must also be approved by the Board of Commissioners.

Interestingly, the JCAH Board of Commissioners in 1975 considered a statement subsequently withdrawn: "JCAH owes its first allegiance and responsibility to those health professions and institutions which have created it and give it sustenance . . . " (Porterfield, Note 1). The Accreditation Manual for Hospitals makes clear that the enhancement and protection of quality with respect to medical care and supportive medical services are primarily the responsibility of the medical staff. This professional bias hardly promotes a collegial recognition of the other health professions.[1]

When the AC/PF was formed as a categorical council of the Joint Commission, it was composed of seven member organizations: the American Association on Mental Deficiency, the American Hospital Association, the American Psychiatric Association, the National Association of Private Psychiatric Hospitals, the National Association of State Mental Health Program Directors, the National Council of Community Mental Health Centers, and the American Academy of Child Psychiatry. The American Association of Psychiatric Services for Children, the Association of Mental Health Administrators, and the Coalition for Alcoholism Program Accreditation were subsequently admitted to council membership. Supported by contributions from the member organizations and the National Institute of Mental Health, the council developed the current accreditation standards. Various organizations and individuals with recognized expertise in the areas of mental health participated in the establishment of these accreditation standards. However, the key officers and the majority of the 10-member organizations are medically dominated. The American Psychological Association did on invitation contribute to the chapter on psychological services. Otherwise, the minimal input by psychology is highlighted by the fact that the APA was not a member organization of the AC/PF during its formative

---

[1] However, in an update of its accreditation criteria on April 1977, the JCAH now holds that "Medical Staff membership shall be limited, *unless otherwise provided by law* to individuals . . . licensed to practice medicine and . . . to . . . dentists." (emphasis added) This accords some recognition to state determinism. Very recently, the American Medical Association's House of Delegates (*AMA News*, December 12, 1977) concluded for local determinism. "The determination of which physicians and other classes of health care practitioners shall be granted clinical privileges in the hospital shall be established at each particular hospital in accordance with community needs and applicable state laws and regulations."

period. Indeed, after several years of expressing its interest, the APA formally applied for one seat on this council in September 1974, and a second in February 1975. Apart from notice that this council is reviewing its criteria for membership, the applications have gone without a substantive reply. On July 28, 1975, Alan Boneau, as Acting Executive Officer of APA, notified the AC/PF that "standards . . . written without . . . full and active participation [of psychology] are neither representative nor comprehensive and thereby unacceptable." In February 1975, APA also applied for membership, one seat, in the Accreditation Council on Long Term Care Facilities (AC/LTC), and in January 1976, the APA Council of Representatives, "without dissent," approved application for membership in the JCAH proper. The AC/LTC was separately notified on July 28, 1975, that an "associate membership" would not be acceptable since the APA looks to being "a full peer in all deliberations and decisions." As a further indication of psychology's disquiet about this impasse, Charles A. Kiesler, Executive Officer of APA, wrote on April 6, 1976, to the recently established Accreditation Council for Ambulatory Health Care, objecting to exclusion from this Council and to several of its bylaws.

Application for accreditation is voluntary, and survey fees are paid by the facility. Surveyors of psychiatric facilities are selected and trained by AC/PF. Psychologists are not included as survey team members. The maximum period of accreditation resulting from the survey is two years, but a facility found to be in substantial compliance with the standards, although manifesting certain shortcomings, can be granted one-year accreditation. A facility granted two years' accreditation shall perform a self-survey during the interim year, using procedures and submitting reports as required by the AC/PF. The AC/PF thereby attempts to ensure that a facility will maintain a constant review of its operations to maintain accreditation. A certification of accreditation is provided by the JCAH which specifies all the categories of services surveyed, each facility accredited, and the year in which accreditation is granted. The Joint Commission also periodically publishes and distributes lists of accredited facilities.

Failure to obtain accreditation not only can result in the facility obtaining an undesirable professional reputation but also can result in the loss of funds from third-party payees. For example, JCAH accreditation is currently recognized in federal law or regulation as follows:

Title XVIII of the Social Security Act, as amended in 1972, provides that a hospital accredited by JCAH is deemed to meet the Conditions for Participation as a provider under Federal Health Insurance for the Aged (Medicare), subject [as a result of the 1972 amendment] to inspection by the state agency for HEW's Bureau of Health Insurance. Such inspection may be initiated either by BHI's receipt of a "substantial complaint" regarding the hospital or by the hospital's inclusion in the sample for which HEW must conduct "validation" surveys [to validate that a hospital deemed certifiable by virtue of accreditation is actually certifiable]. Except as noted below, a hospital is not required to be accredited in order to participate in Medicare; a nonaccredited hospital may be certified by the state inspection agency [and many are].

HEW's regulations to implement the application of Title XVIII to psychiatric and tuberculosis hospitals require such hospitals to be accredited by JCAH, except that a distinct part of an institution may qualify for participation if it meets requirements equivalent to those of JCAH, even though the entire institution is not accredited. [Such a distinct part is considered to meet requirements equivalent to JCAH accreditation if it is in substantial compliance with the Conditions of Participation for Hospitals. All psychiatric and tuberculosis hospitals must, in addition, meet special Conditions for Participation concerning records and staff.]

Facilities providing Inpatient Psychiatric Hospital Services for Individuals Under Age 21, under Title XIX (Medical Assistance Program, or Medicaid) of the Social Security Act must be accredited by JCAH. There is no alternative method of certification.

To qualify for payments under its so-called Basic Program, the Office for the Civilian Health and Medical Program of the Uniformed Services (CHAMPUS), since the summer of 1975, has required the following types of facilities, other than those that are owned and operated by states, to be accredited by JCAH: (a) residential facilities that provide therapeutic programs only or primarily for children and adolescents; (b) facilities such as mental health centers, child guidance centers, psychiatric and psychological clinics, day centers, institutions, schools, and similar programs that provide nonresidential day care and/or partial hospitalization programs only or primarily for children and adolescents; (c) all other psychiatric hospitals. Such facilities are accredited by the JCAH Accreditation Council for Psychiatric Facilities as psychiatric facilities or as psychiatric facilities serving children and adolescents. Accreditation is not required for facilities serving mentally retarded or other handicapped persons under the CHAMPUS Program for the Handicapped.

These requirements are having a pronounced effect on facilities that want to be eligible for CHAMPUS reimbursement. In the case of a treatment facility for behaviorally disordered children, this often means increasing psychiatric input, supervision, and control, and adopting a psychodynamic, as distinguished from a behavioral, treatment orientation, without regard to any effect on the program's effectiveness. Because there are demonstrably effective treatment programs (including behaviorally oriented programs) that do not meet AC/PF's requirements for medical direction, it is possible to question whether those requirements are for the benefit of the individuals served or for the benefit of the medical and psychiatric professions. It is also possible to question the legitimacy of the CHAMPUS accreditation requirements, since its effect is to force treatment facilities for behaviorally disordered children (specifically including "psychological clinics") to become psychiatric facilities as defined by AC/PF (PL 92-603, Section 1865).

Lack of accreditation can also place training programs in jeopardy. These descriptive parameters of the accreditation process lead to an anticipation of quality assurance, thorough review, and careful monitoring. Operationally, however, the inspection process appears to be a "club" operation; AC/PF accredits about 90% of the adult psychiatric hospitals and children's facilities that it surveys. AC/FMR has accredited 36% of the residential facilities and 56% of the community agencies surveyed.

The Accreditation Manual for Psychiatric Facilities (JCAH, 1972) outlines the accreditation standards to be used by surveyors. Its main purpose is to delineate the standards that should be implemented by facilities. A broad range of administrative, service, and research functions are covered. Particular emphasis is placed on the administrative organization of the governing body and the medical staff. These two components are listed first, and the remaining services are listed in alphabetical order. Excerpts from this manual place matters in perspective for psychologists. To be eligible for survey, the psychiatric facility shall be one

> in which the medical responsibility for patients rests with a psychiatrist or other physician. (p. 1)

In psychiatric hospitals, the diagnosis and treatment of psychiatric disorders are the ultimate responsibility of psychiatrists. . . . In psychiatric facilities other than hospitals . . . other mental health professionals including but not limited to psychologists . . . may serve as administrative officer, providing the ultimate responsibility for the treatment and care of patients shall rest with a psychiatrist who is responsible to the governing body. (pp. 21–22)

The bylaws are to require a medical staff. Membership is limited to physicians and dentists. Moreover,

> the bylaws . . . shall . . . delineate clinical privileges of non-medical professionals as well as responsibilities of the physician members of the medical staff in relation to nonmedical professionals. (p. 30)
>
> It is recommended that the medical staff delineate in its bylaws . . . the qualifications, status, clinical duties and responsibilities of those members of the allied health professions whose patient care activities require . . . their appointment . . . for specified services . . . processed through . . . medical staff channels. . . . They exercise judgment within their areas of competence, provided that a physician member of the medical staff shall have the ultimate responsibility for patient care; they participate directly in the management of patients under the supervision or direction of a member of the medical staff. (p. 31)

A psychiatric facility is not eligible for accreditation unless ultimate patient responsibility rests with a physician. Indeed, in some instances where psychologists were directors of programs or had been accorded staff privileges, the AC/PF on review in 1975 began to challenge such appointments ("Professional Advertising," 1976). Medical staff membership of other than physicians and dentists is held to be a very serious deficiency and not in compliance with standards.

Of major concern to clinical psychologists is the requirement that the medical staff must assess the competence of nonmedical staff and delineate their privileges accordingly. This theme of ultimate responsibility for patient care and program direction being held by the medical staff runs consistently throughout the Accreditation Manual for Psychiatric Facilities. Bylaws are established by the medical staff, and only members of the "medical staff" may hold office. Therefore, the practice of clinical psychologists is essentially defined by the medical staff of each psychiatric facility. At the same time, psychologists may not be a member or hold office in this regulatory body. Psychology as an established health profession (Schofield, 1969, 1975) finds such subordination neither appropriate nor acceptable (Bent, 1972, 1976).[2]

In general hospitals, the conditions for the practice of psychology are, if anything, placed under narrower restraint. Policies stated in the Accreditation Manual for Hospitals (JCAH, 1970/1973) accord psychologists an affiliate status, whether their services are in association with psychiatry or other service. Thus, the

> General Administrative Policies . . . shall ensure that only a member of the medical staff shall admit a patient to the hospital. . . . (p. 8)

The medical staff bylaws are to delineate

> the qualifications, status, clinical duties and responsibilities of those members of the allied health professions, such as doctoral scientists and others, whose patient care activities require that their appointment and authority for specified services be processed through the usual medical staff channels. . . . They exercise judgment within their areas of competence, provided that a physician member of the medical staff shall have the ultimate responsibility for patient care; they participate directly in the management of patients under the supervision or direction of a member of the medical staff; . . . members of allied health professions shall be individually assigned to an appropriate clinical department as staff affiliates. . . . (p. 48)

Nor does the situation differ in hospital outpatient services:

> Clinical privileges in the outpatient service may be granted to other practitioners on the same basis as would apply to inpatient services. . . . (p. 121)

Accreditation Standards Versus the Law

There is some acknowledgement that prevailing law is to be recognized.

---

[2] All this prevails, mind you, despite the fact that in the Staffing of Mental Health Facilities (NIMH, 1976) the number of full-time equivalent psychologists had the largest increase of any discipline (21%) between 1974–76 and that psychologists had increased to a 10.7% proportion of total professional patient care positions, the same as psychiatry, which has decreased to this level. Moreover, the increase of psychologists is not restricted to public services as their increase in private mental hospitals was 74.6% from 1974 to 1976. Nor do the AC/PF survey teams regularly include a psychologist member despite the extent of the reliance of psychiatric facilities on the services of psychologists and their widely acknowledged contribution to improved patient care. Ironically, the new staff Director, Accreditation Program for Psychiatric Facilities, appointed in 1977, is a Ph.D. psychologist.

> Psychological Services . . . should be consistent with professionally recognized standards of psychology, and shall be in accord with the legal requirements governing the practice of psychology in the state. (JCAH, 1972, p. 142)

Moreover,

> the psychiatric facility shall comply with the pertinent federal, state, and local laws. In the event that such laws place requirements above those contained herein, *the facility shall comply with the law.* (p. 18; emphasis added)

The law, in fact, casts quite a different perspective, recognizing the licensed clinical psychologist as an autonomous health professional. The following summary of California and federal laws and regulations are illustrative of the statutory basis of psychological practice.

California

1. *Psychological Licensing Law,* Chapter 6.6, Business and Professions Code, as amended in 1974. In Section 2903,

> the practice of psychology is defined as rendering . . . any psychological service involving the . . . procedures of interviewing, counseling, *psychotherapy,* behavior modification and hypnosis. . . . The application of such . . . methods includes, but is not restricted to: *diagnosis,* prevention, *treatment,* and amelioration of psychological problems and *emotional and mental disorders.* . . . (Emphasis added)

This law imposes *no* special limits or distinctions upon practice in a hospital setting as distinct from ambulatory care.[3]

2a. *Health and Disability Insurance.* In 1974, Chapter 958 added to and amended the Government Code and the Insurance Code. Section 12531.5 of the Government Code now reads:

> A health care service plan may provide for coverage of . . . professional mental health services. . . . No plan shall prohibit the member from selecting any psychologist who is the holder of a certificate . . . to perform the particular services covered under the terms of the plan, such certificate holder being ex-

---

[3] In 1977, the Business and Professions Code and the Corporations Code were amended to enable the formation of mixed psychological-medical corporations, wherein a psychologist could practice psychology in a medical corporation and a physician practice medicine in a psychological corporation (Chapter 1126). Clearly, the relationship between these two health professions in such a corporation would be collegial.

pressly authorized by law to perform such services. . . .

Section 10176 of the Insurance Code carries comparable language relative to disability (health) insurance policies, likewise Section 10177 for self-insured employee welfare benefit plans, and Section 11512.8, also of the Insurance Code for hospital service contracts. The intent of this law is not only to recognize licensed psychologists as health practitioners but also to assure consumer choice and direct access to their services under all forms of health insurance. This law makes *no* distinction in the locus of care. Most group and individual health insurance policies, however, provide for more extensive benefits/coverage for care on an in-hospital basis.

2b. In 1975, Chapter 913, Section 14302.6 was added to the Welfare and Institutions Code to read:

> Each prepaid health plan shall provide the services of a psychologist and psychiatrist when the prepaid health plan contract requires the provision of mental health services. Mental Health services shall be provided so that an enrollee may be seen initially by either a physician or a psychologist.

This law complements and reinforces the objectives of 2a.[4]

3a. *Community Mental Health Services,* Title 9, California Administrative Code, Subchapter 3, Section 620:

> Director of Local Mental Health Services. Where the Local Director is other than the local health officer or medical administrator of the county hospital, he shall be one of the following: . . . (b) A psychologist who shall be licensed in the State of California and shall possess a doctorate degree . . . at least three years of . . . clinical psychology experience, two years of which shall be administrative experience.

There are comparable qualifications in Subsections (a), (c), and (d) for psychiatrist, clinical social worker, and hospital administrator, respectively.

3b. Section 5751 of the Welfare and Institutions Code was amended in 1972 and restated in 1974, to add:

---

[4] In 1977, Chapter 1168 amended the definition of "physician" to include "psychologists" in Section 3209.3 of the Labor Code for purposes of Workman's Compensation (and, because of cross-referencing, into the Unemployment Insurance Code).

> No regulations shall be adopted which prohibit a . . . psychologist . . . from employment in a local mental health program in any professional, administrative, or technical positions in mental health services.

The intent is that psychologists may be among the professions directing an overall countywide mental health program or any service within the program. There are psychologists now holding program director and service chief positions.

3c. Implementing regulations, including those filed January 31, 1976, in Register 76, No. 5, brought change to Title 9, Subchapters 3 and 4 of the California Administrative Code, Community Mental Health Services under the Short-Doyle Act. Thus a psychologist may now be the "Professional Person in Charge of a Facility" (see 822), be a member of the "Attending Staff" (see 823), and serve as the director and/or as a member of the professional staff without apparent restriction on ability to admit (accept), treat, and discharge patients, all without a medical referral or supervision requirement on inpatient services (see 663); outpatient services (see 680); partial hospitalization services (see 690); consultation, education, and information services (see 716); and rehabilitative services (see 740).

4. *Medical Responsibility,* Title 9, California Administrative Code, Subchapter 3, Regulation 522.

> A physician meeting the qualifications of [Board eligibility in psychiatry] shall assume responsibility for all those acts of diagnosis, treatment, or prescribing or ordering of drugs which may *only* be performed by a licensed physician. (Emphasis added)

The phrase "medical responsibility" is neither included nor defined in the Medical Practices Act in California. Nor for that matter is it defined in the AC/PF Manual (JCAH, 1972) even though called for throughout the text.

5. *State Hospital Program Director.* In 1969, the Welfare and Institutions Code, Section 4300, was amended to enable program directors to be appointed on the basis of competence, regardless of discipline. A job requirement now is that the background of the program director be "relevant to the nature of the treatment." Each program director (a Civil Service class) has full responsibility for the plan-

ning, development, coordination, and direction of a major treatment service involving 50–100 staff members, including medical and other professional staff, and some 150–250 patients. By July 1972, half of the program directors and the large majority of assistant program directors were nomedical.[5]

Federal

1a. *Group Health Plans.* By directive of the Deputy Assistant Secretary, Department of Defense, on June 23, 1970, the Civilian Health and Medical Program of the Uniformed Services (CHAMPUS) has recognized the independent practice of qualified psychologists in all states. In 1974, an estimated 6.3 million persons were insured under this program. Both inpatient and outpatient visits are covered. Psychologists are similarly recognized in a program for the dependents of totally disabled veterans (CHAMPVA), established in the Veterans Health Care Expansion Act of 1973 (PL 93-82). The Department of Defense's Appropriation Act, PL 94-212, now directs in Section 751 that none of the funds shall be available for CHAMPUS for

any other service or supply which is not medically or psychologically necessary to diagnose and treat a

mental or physical illness, injury, or bodily malfunction as diagnosed by a physician, dentist, or clinical psychologist.[6]

1b. PL 93-363, signed July 30, 1974, established parity between clinical psychologists and other providers of health services for some 8.5 million *federal employees* nationwide. (Twenty-nine states covering 75% of the population, including California, New York, Ohio, Michigan, and New Jersey, have enacted similar direct recognition of "freedom of choice" of psychologist practitioner status. The District of Columbia passed a similar enactment, and the Health Insurance Association of America adopted a Model Psychologist Direct Recognition Bill on May 18, 1976, formally supporting the introduction of such legislation in any state). Although there is some variance among the 20-plus employee health plans, they all, with the exception of group practice prepayment plans, from January 1, 1975, recognize the services of psychologists for covered benefits. In-hospital coverage tends to be more extensive in most plans. Neither this federal nor these state direct recognition laws impose any special limits or distinctions upon hospital practice in contrast to office practice.

1c. Regulations implementing the Health Maintenance Organization's Development Act of 1973, PL 93-222, explicitly enumerate "clinical psychologist" among the health practitioners in such group practice prepayment health services. Indeed, these regulations require a "health professional" to coordinate the patient's overall health care, thereby *not* imposing medical referral and supervision upon health care.

1d. Beginning with the 1973 Federal Income Tax Forms, instructions for the Standard Form 1040, Schedule A, itemized deductions for Medical and Dental Expenses have included "payments to . . . psychiatrists, *psychologists,* and psychoanalysts . . ." (emphasis added; see p. 10, column 1, 1974 IRS Form 1040 instructions).

---

[5] At this time, a sixth section entitled *Practice in Health Facilities* should be added. On January 1, 1979, SB 259 enabled any licensed health facility, on local determination, to appoint psychologists, under such terms and conditions as are agreeable, to staff and committee membership, and to grant clinical privileges. This law defines clinical psychologists and this definition applies to general acute care hospitals, acute psychiatric hospitals, skilled nursing facilities, and intermediate care facilities. Later, SB 1496 (Gregorio) was passed creating a new class of "psychiatric health facility" which is a 24-hour residential acute care non-hospital. Basic services mandated include services of clinical psychologists. Regulations are under development at the time of writing with psychology represented, under law, on the ad hoc committee to draft the regulations. Meanwhile, the Attorney General issued an opinion in April, 1979, that clinical psychologists may admit patients to a hospital and treat them there without physician supervision or direction. In the same legislative session, AB 3665 (Berman) was passed which defines psychologists for purposes of court proceedings, among which psychologists may be the primary and/or the secondary signatory on certification for involuntary commitment of patients to hospitals. These amplify on the presence of clinical psychologists in licensed health facilities, i.e. hospitals and nursing homes.

[6] Not only was the "psychologically necessary" concept retained in the DOD Appropriation Act for 1978, PL 95-111, Section 844, but whether on an in- or out-patient basis, the psychological necessity and appropriateness of the services provided by clinical psychologists shall be reviewed by their own peers.

2a. *Restorative Services.* The Rehabilitation Act of 1973, PL 93-112, recognizes the services of licensed psychologists or physicians for both assessment and/or restorative services in cases of mental disability.

2b. PL 93-416, signed September 7, 1974, amended Chapter 81 of Subpart G of Title 5, United States Code, relating to *work injuries compensation* of federal employees under the Federal Employees Compensation Act (FECA) by broadening the definitions of both "physician" and "medical, surgical, and hospital services and supplies" to include "clinical psychologists." Clearly, office and hospital visits are covered.

2c. The Department of Labor's regulations of June 1974, implementing PL 93-203, the Comprehensive Manpower Program, define psychological services within health care to the extent that this treatment or services are necessary to retain or obtain employment (Section 94.4[x].

3. *Program Direction.* Psychologists have been active in the leadership of community mental health centers. The NIMH/CMHC Policy and Standards Manual, Part 1, pages 2–26 (g)A, entitles a psychologist to be a director of a community mental health program (U.S. DHEW, 1971). Similarly, regulations of the Veterans Administration allow psychologists to direct mental hygiene clinics, day treatment services, and other specialized programs.[7]

Thus, the statutory basis of psychological practice appears to be clearly established in both the public and private sectors of health/mental health services in California (and with some variation in almost all other states). Licensed psychologists are explicitly authorized to render diagnostic and treatment services within the scope of their practice and, when so appointed, to direct clinical services and programs. These statutes are silent about the roles of attending therapist or about admitting patients to or discharging them from licensed psychiatric facilities

and hospitals in California; but they do not appear to circumscribe psychological practice by type of setting, nor does the regulatory delineation of "medical responsibility" encroach upon or narrow the practice of psychology. Since the referenced state and federal statutes make no distinction between ambulatory and inpatient care, it is assumed that they apply equally to both.

Unless the Joint Commission, in implementing its standards, clearly reconciles or accedes to federal and state law and Civil Service specification, there is a direct conflict. This is an issue having national implications. The essence of the matter is whether the Joint Commission will abide by its own fundamental principle that "the psychiatric facility shall comply with pertinent Federal, state, and local laws. In the event that such laws place requirements above those contained herein, the facility shall comply with the law" (JCAH, 1972, p. 18).

The prevailing codes, both California and federal, invite a number of questions:[8]

1. Cannot licensed and otherwise properly qualified psychologists, as members of a psychiatric facility's professional staff, be entitled to hold privileges on the clinical units with which they are associated; these privileges to include treatment and diagnosis as attending therapists, and writing appropriate orders?

2. Cannot licensed psychologists meeting credential review be granted staff privileges to enable their practice in private and community health facilities?

3. Cannot psychologists as members of the professional staff be entitled to representative participation in the governance of the facility as voting members of an executive professional board on all matters relating to health manpower use, health care program planning, administrative policy, and resource allocation, development, and coordination?

4. Cannot qualified psychologists hold positions of responsibility for the direction of programs/services involving a multidisciplinary staff?

---

[7] Also, the United States Department of Defense now includes psychologists in its policy, which provides that "any qualified health professional may command or exercise administrative direction of a military health care facility . . . without regard to the officer's basic health profession" (Staff and Command Assignments of Health Professionals, May 1, 1973).

[8] These questions were developed by a staff privilege committee of psychology faculty at the University of California, San Francisco (H. Dörken, Chair; C. Attkisson, E. Burke, J. Steinhelber, and G. Stone, Committee Members; February 1975).

A major role of some facilities is the training of psychologists, psychiatrists, and other mental health professionals. The Accreditation Manual (JCAH, 1972) states

> when residents and other mental health trainees are involved in patient care, sufficient evidence should be documented in the medical record to substantiate the active participation of a senior psychiatrist in the supervision of the patient's care. (p. 77)

For clinical psychology trainees, in view of the use of the verb "should," which by definition allows the "use of effective alternates" (JCAH, 1972, p. 12), there is a specific question:

5. Would it not suffice to show active participation of a senior clinical psychologist rather than a psychiatrist in the supervision of the patient's care, assuming proper review for medical problems by a licensed physician and active participation of a physician member of the medical staff in any medical problem that may be present?

6. On the same basis, cannot psychiatric residents receive clinical training from psychologists supervising the patient's mental health care?

Whether for credential review or the evaluation of clinical competence or performance, it would seem that review by peers is the most appropriate basic process. This method of professional accountability seems best suited to maintaining uniform excellence of practice. It does, however, require a parity of professional responsibility among the licensed disciplines providing mental health care. Accordingly,

7. Cannot psychologists have a voting participation in the review and approval of clinical and staff privileges for psychologists?

Under current AC/PF standards, the answer to Questions 1 and 2 is "Yes," only if granted and supervised by the medical staff; the answers to Questions 4 and 6 are "Yes," provided ultimate responsibility for care of a patient rests with a physician; and the answers to 3, 5, and 7 are "No." These seem among the questions to bear in mind as one revises a facility's bylaws or seeks change in these accreditation standards per se.

Although the constant theme of medical responsibility and supervision recurrent throughout the AC/PF Accreditation Manual is certainly a negative aspect, the AC/PF is very clear on the need for clinical psychology services in a psychiatric facility. The Accreditation Manual for Psychiatric Facilities states that psychological services *shall* be available to meet the needs of patients of all psychiatric facilities. The services of a clinical psychologist must be available, and if such service is not available within the facility, outside resources should be employed. Clinical psychologists are to have a broad range of patient responsibilities, such as diagnostic testing and therapy with individuals and groups, and their services should include research, consultation on research design, and dissemination of research findings. The psychological services are to be clearly stated in the treatment plan for each patient, and all psychological services provided by psychological associates, technicians, assistants, or clerks shall be under the direct supervision of a qualified psychologist or psychiatrist. The recognition by the Accreditation Council of the necessity for adequate clinical psychology services is obviously of major importance for clinical psychology. Again, in keeping with the stress on interdisciplinary treatment and communication of research findings, it holds the potential of an open and liberal approach to the treatment of patients.

Professional Training

Training is scarcely dealt with by the AC/PF. Rather, the emphasis is on patient care as the most important function of a psychiatric facility. Yet, in many facilities, trainees carry the bulk of treatment responsibilities. Their services should be under the close supervision of qualified professional staff. Of the internship programs for doctoral training in psychology, 118 are fully approved by the APA (1975) Committee on Accreditation. Standards in other settings can vary widely. The standards for residency training in psychiatry have been illustrated and described by Taylor and Torrey (1972) as pseudo-regulations. The extensive involvement of foreign-trained professionals in U.S. psychiatric training (Torrey & Taylor, 1973)—with all the inherent communication and quality problems—is, however, not one shared by psychology. Fewer than

2% of U.S. clinical psychologists are foreign trained (Garfield & Kurtz, 1974). The National Academy of Sciences' 1973 Profile of Doctoral Scientists documents that 1.5% of those employed in psychology have foreign doctorates (Cuca, 1976). Nonetheless, the theme of psychiatric responsibility and supervision again permeates this area. Again, supervision is not defined in the glossary of the AC/PF Manual. Any requirement that psychiatrists essentially have the supervisory responsibility for the psychotherapy training of clinical psychology interns is not acceptable. Supremacy notions are compatible neither with a collegial relation among health professions nor with the facts of psychology's contribution to knowledge in this field (Dörken & Associates, 1976).

The AC/PF makes a positive contribution to training as well as to patient care by its clearly defined statements regarding the necessity for adequate health records. Entries into medical records shall be made by persons given this right under the facility's policy, and the entry should be identified by author and specialty. The stress on adequate records should be an integral aspect of the training of clinical psychologists. Frequently, clinical psychology trainees enter internship programs with little knowledge of the importance of health record keeping and grudgingly participate in the documentation of treatment. Record keeping and documentation are important aspects of the patient's care. Also, as there is more insurance coverage for mental health problems, there will be a need for clearcut documentation to secure reimbursement for these services.

A forward-looking aspect of the Accreditation Manual for Psychiatric Facilities is a statement that psychiatric facilities shall have research programs when consistent with their goals and resources. This would certainly be applicable to university-based facilities such as medical schools. The manual is quite clear that the research programs should be intricately involved with ongoing psychiatric services and under the leadership of trained staff. This could be an endorsement for an open evaluation of treatment techniques that goes beyond the narrow idea that the best treatment is limited to a particular kind of professional training.

Discussion

The fundamental issues of concern to psychology—and the general public as well—are (a) essential control of the accreditation program by a single profession; (b) defining facilities by the discipline in charge, rather than by the kinds of persons served, the problems they present, and the services they need; (c) requiring physician control of each treatment program in the absence of evidence that such control is always necessary for effective treatment; (d) requiring an organized staff in which only physicians and dentists (!) may hold membership and vote; and (e) requiring physicians to determine the competence of psychologists and other professionals, to delineate their practice, and to supervise their work.

These AC/PF standards are sharply in conflict with the policy of the American Psychological Association in its Standard for Providers of Psychological Services (APA Task Force, 1976). The situation is such that it is entirely possible in an adult psychiatric hospital for a well-qualified psychologist to be supervised by a physician who lacks any formal qualification in psychiatry. The medical orientation of the AC/PF standards probably stems from the composition of that council. All the more reason for an early revision to properly accommodate the involved professions. The AC/FMR standards, for instance, developed by a multidisciplinary council on which psychology is represented, do *not* reflect a medical orientation.

Too often, psychology's potential and contribution to health care are viewed as limited to mental health/retardation services. Yet, psychology has a major role to play in rehabilitation (Wright, 1959); in the psychological aspects of chronic and terminal illness, dismemberment, and disfigurement; and in the preparation for and recovery from major surgery. Increasingly, major disabilities are being shown to have psychological components (APA Task Force on Health Research, 1976). Wright (1976) illustrated very clearly the importance of psychology's role in treating people who are physically ill, describing the effectiveness of psychological techniques in treating encopresis, bruxism, the battered child, tracheotomy addiction, refusal of medication or food necessary to sustain life, the dying child, and the behavioral residuals of various medical disorders, such as congenital heart defects, not to mention the emotional problems caused by hospitalization itself. Indeed, the extent of psychological factors in general health care seems sufficient to argue that psychologists should be among the primary providers. Recent testimony by a psychiatrist on National Health Insurance (Kelly, Note 2) highlighted the extent to which emotional problems are a fact of health care.

> Indeed, it is conservatively estimated that well over 50% of all patients seeking care for physical ailments are suffering from symptoms primarily caused by emotional problems. The Kaiser-Permanente prepaid group practice plans found, for example, that 68% of its doctor visits made by 36% of its 1.3 million members were for complaints for which *no organic cause* could be found. (Emphasis added; later reported by Garfield et al., 1976)

An increasing number of states, 23 as of June 1975 (Dörken & Associates, 1976), have passed "freedom of choice" legislation, such that consumers are to be assured direct access to and free choice among licensed psychologist practitioners for covered services. Indeed, on May 18, 1976, the Health Insurance Association of America adopted a Model Psychologist Direct Recognition Act, including an offer to assist states in drafting such a bill. Even given the access of a direct recognition law, the nature of health insurance today is that, generally, most policies provide more extensive coverage under hospital than under ambulatory care. The Joint Commission's policies definitely limit the availability of a psychologist in a hospital setting and have an exclusionary effect upon psychological practice, a restraint in trade as it were. Comparable supraordinate views apparently prevail in medicine: "the AMA believes that the diagnosis and *selection of treatment for any* disease is best performed by a physician" (Sammons, 1975, p. 745; emphasis added). A practice privilege is not an incidental issue among clinical psychologists, however. Karon and VandenBos (1976) in a cost/benefit analysis have shown that psychologists compare favorably with psychiatrists in the treatment of hospitalized schizophrenics.

Late in 1973, Garfield and Kurtz (1976)

found by survey that 23% of the psychologists in Division 12 (Clinical) of APA listed private practice as their main occupational setting, an increase of 6% over a survey conducted in 1961. Another 47% were engaged in some part-time private practice. Thus, a total of 70% of these psychologists were in private practice some of the time. Perhaps the best utilization data available, which show the extent of services rendered by psychologists and other practitioners, are those derived from the CHAMPUS program (Dörken, 1976). In the 10 reporting states, psychologists provided 19%, 23.1%, and 28.5% of the outpatient visits in fiscal years 1973, 1974, and 1975, respectively, but only 2%, 2.5%, and 1.2% of the inpatient visits. The 456,641 outpatient visits in 1975 were 70.8% of all visits. Psychiatrists and attending physicians provided 68.8% of the outpatient, but 95.3% of all inpatient, visits. One factor in the scant involvement of psychologists in hospital practice is their limited access to clinical privilege. The higher average fee of psychologists for inpatient versus outpatient visits ($39.61 versus $34.68) suggests that their hospital involvement is largely restricted to services as special consultants.

For some inpatient psychiatric services, treatment techniques, such as drugs and shock (convulsive) therapy, may be the interventions of choice and are within the professional training and competence of psychiatrists. However, it should be obvious that such treatment is not required for many patients with mental disorder whether in inpatient psychiatric facilities or in other settings, such as community mental health centers. The AC/PF focuses on professional competence and peer review of this competence as major criteria for clinical privilege. If the basis for rendering services to patients is on well-documented competence, rather than on professional affiliation, the skills and competencies of various therapists from divergent backgrounds will be available to patients. Under this situation, patient care will be of the highest caliber. However, if the AC/PF Manual is interpreted as meaning that only psychiatrists are competent enough to take the responsibility for patient care, then it is less likely that competent care represented in a full range of recognized treatment techniques will be rendered, and more than likely that only limited services will be available to the patient.

One of the unique aspects of mental health care is that it need not be under the domain of one particular profession and, indeed, is enhanced by multidisciplinary participation. Psychologists for their part have pioneered and led in the development of assessment techniques (Buros, 1972) and in the introduction of behavior therapies (Bandura, 1969) and use of biofeedback ("Biofeedback in Action," 1973) in developing new and improved methods of care, as well as contributing to the development of the more traditional psychotherapies.

Summary

Briefly, the areas of conflict between clinical psychology and the psychiatric facility and hospital accreditation standards of the Joint Commission on Accreditation of Hospitals center on law, status, and economics:

1. Despite the fact that these standards are voluntary rather than statutory, they conflict with much of the formal code (law, regulations, Civil Service specifications) supporting the practice of psychology.

2. Psychology regards itself as an independent autonomous health profession, willing to establish collegial relations with other health professions in which the status of any individual practitioner will be according to competence; it does not accept in principle or operational fact that its services must be subservient to and under the supervision and direction of another profession.

3. The economics of health care, particularly under third-party reimbursement, are such that health insurance benefits/coverage are typically more extensive for hospitalization than for ambulatory care; the incentives should be toward improved quality of multidisciplinary care and to less costly nonresidential alternatives rather than to curtailment of psychological practice in hospital settings.

Reference Notes

1. Porterfield, L. *JCAH-government relations* (Position paper). JCAH Board of Commissioners' Meeting, April 26, 1975, Agenda Item III A, p. 7.
2. Kelly, A. Testimony as President of the Washington Psychiatric Society, to the Committee on Ways and Means, Subcommittee on Health, Washington, D.C., November 14, 1975.

References

American Psychiatric Association. *Standards for psychiatric facilities*. Washington, D.C.: Author, 1969.

American Psychological Association. APA-approved internships for doctoral training in clinical and counseling psychology: 1975. *American Psychologist*, 1975, *30*, 1089–1091.

APA Task Force on Health Research. Contributions of psychology to health research: Patterns, problems, and potentials. *American Psychologist*, 1976, *31*, 263–274.

APA Task Force on Standards for Service Facilities. Standards for providers of psychological services. *American Psychologist*, 1976, *30*, 685–694.

Association of Psychology Internship Centers. *Directory of internship programs in clinical psychology*. Columbus, Ohio: Author, 1975.

Bandura, A. *Principles of behavior modification*. New York: Holt, Rinehart & Winston, 1969.

Bent, R. J. A professional issue—the psychologist supervised by medical doctors. *Professional Psychology*, 1972, *3*, 351–356.

Bent, R. J. Professional autonomy and medical supervision. In H. Dörken & Associates (Eds.), *The professional psychologist today: New developments in law, health insurance and health practice*. San Francisco, Calif.: Jossey-Bass, 1976.

Biofeedback in action. *World Medical News*, March 1973, pp. 47–58.

Buros, O. *The seventh mental measurements yearbook* (2 vols.). Highland Park, N.J.: Gryphon Press, 1972.

Cuca, J. M. PhDs in psychology: Supply and demand. In P. J. Woods (Ed.), *Career opportunities for psychologists: Expanding and emerging areas*. Washington, D.C.: American Psychological Association, 1976.

Dörken, H. CHAMPUS ten-state claim experience for mental disorder. In H. Dörken & Associates (Eds.), *The professional psychologist today: New developments in law, health insurance and health practice*. San Francisco, Calif.: Jossey-Bass, 1976.

Dörken, H., & Associates (Eds.). *The professional psychologist today: New developments in law, health insurance and health practice*. San Francisco, Calif.: Jossey-Bass, 1976.

Garfield, S. L., & Kurtz, R. A survey of clinical psychologists: Characteristics, activities and orientations. *The Clinical Psychologist*, 1974, *28*, 7–10.

Garfield, S. L., & Kurtz, R. Clinical psychologists in the 1970s. *American Psychologist*, 1976, *31*, 1–9.

Garfield, S. L., et al. Evaluation of an ambulatory medical-care delivery system. *New England Journal of Medicine*, 1976, *294*, 426–431.

Joint Commission on Accreditation of Hospitals. *Accreditation manual for hospitals.* Chicago, Ill.: Author, 1970, updated 1973.

Joint Commission on Accreditation of Hospitals. *Accreditation manual for psychiatric facilities.* Chicago, Ill.: Author, 1972.

Joint Commission on Accreditation of Hospitals. *Standards for residential facilities for the mentally retarded.* Chicago, Ill.: Author, 1973.

Joint Commission on Accreditation of Hospitals. *Accreditation manual for psychiatric facilities serving children and adolescents.* Chicago, Ill.: Author, 1974.

Karon, B. P., & VandenBos, G. R. Cost/benefit analysis: Psychologist versus psychiatrist for schizophrenics. *Professional Psychology,* 1976, *7,* 107–111.

Professional advertising: It may be sooner than you think! *Advance,* 1976, *3*(1), 3.

Sammons, J. Cooperation, not competition, in the health professions (Editorial). *Journal of the American Medical Association,* 1975, *234,* 745.

Schofield, W. The role of psychology in the delivery of health services. *American Psychologist,* 1969, *24,* 565–584.

Schofield, W. The psychologist as a health care professional: Medicine and health. *Intellect Magazine,* January 1975, pp. 255–258.

Taylor, R. L., & Torrey, E. F. The pseudo-regulation of American psychiatry. *American Journal of Psychiatry,* 1972, *129,* 34–39.

Torrey, E. F., & Taylor, R. L. Cheap labor from poor nations. *American Journal of Psychiatry,* 1973, *130,* 428–434.

Wright, B. (Ed.). *Psychology and rehabilitation.* Washington, D.C.: American Psychological Association, 1959.

Wright, L. Psychology as a health profession. *The Clinical Psychologist,* 1976, *29,* 16–19.

At the time of original publication of this article, *Herbert Dörken* and *Delmont Morrison* were faculty members of the Department of Psychiatry, Langley Porter Institute, University of California, San Francisco.

But Is It Good for the Psychologists?

Appraisal and Status of DSM-III

Thomas Schacht and Peter E. Nathan

As the American Psychiatric Association's most recent effort at orchestrating the conceptual cacophony of mental disorders, the DSM-III is both a major advance and a document that leaves much to be desired. DSM-III displays its flaws brazenly, sometimes mistaking them for virtues. There are many exceptional advances over DSM-II to be found here, but difficulties with larger issues overshadow these positive features. Many of the new features of DSM-III were created in apparent reaction to criticisms of DSM-II, rather than as positive expressions of a unifying basic conception. The resulting document, then, may be likened to a symphony written by a committee—the notes are all there, but the way they are put together reflects the mediocrity inherent in such a process rather than integrated purpose and understanding. Issues of multiaxial diagnosis and of operationalization of diagnostic criteria are basically technical ones which further research and refinement will undoubtedly solve. The problem of the medical model and of social, political, and professional influences on diagnosis is another matter, however, which will likely be with us until the mental health professions experience their own equivalent of the Copernican revolution.

Most cases are mixed cases, and we should not treat our classifications with too much respect.

> William James, *Varieties of Religious Experience*
> (1902, p. 148)

William James's sentiments at the turn of the century are still a good foundation for a critical appraisal of the art and science of diagnosis. It was with his caveat in mind that we approached the task of evaluating current draft versions of the third edition of the *Diagnostic and Statistical Manual of Mental Disorders* (DSM-III), which is currently under active development. The DSM-III (Task Force on Nomenclature and Statistics, Note 1), successor to the DSM-II (American Psychiatric Association, 1968) now in use, is sure to be of intense interest to professional psychologists, both as a reconceptualization of diagnostic practice and as a document of considerable legal and economic consequence. Although it may seem premature to direct criticism at an as-yet unfinished work or to do more than simply describe the current status of

a monumental task, there is a countervailing interest to psychologists and others to have both a glimpse of things to come and a sense of how what is to come will affect them—for good and for ill. Many of the issues raised by DSM-III are substantive ones that can be properly approached only through empirical investigation. Other issues, however, derive from fundamental philosophical and conceptual positions held by the authors of DSM-III in their anticipation of the document's impact on the academic community, the helping professions, government, business, and, ultimately, the consumer of mental health services. It is to these latter issues that we have focused the evaluative portions of this paper.

A Brief History

Work began on DSM-III in September 1973 with the creation of a new Task Force on Nomenclature and Statistics by the American Psychiatric Association. Robert L. Spitzer, a prominent and well-respected research psychia-

Reprinted from *American Psychologist*, 1977, *32*, 1017–1025.

trist with a long history of productive research on diagnostic decision making, was named Chair of this group. The task force came into being in response to general agreement among members of all the mental health professions that DSM-II was both relatively unreliable and rarely as useful as it might be. Various advisory committees were formed to prepare and review initial drafts of sections of the new document; an initial report on the activities of these groups was given at a special session of the American Psychiatric Association's annual meeting held in May 1975. At additional national conferences in May and June of 1976, additional comment was invited from experts in nosology as well as from representatives of many national organizations interested in the development of DSM-III (including the American Psychological Association). These meetings resulted in the addition of many new diagnostic categories as well as a commitment to the new "multiaxial" approach to diagnosis, which is described as one of DSM-III's major advances over DSM-II.

In October 1976, an invitation was issued by the American Psychiatric Association to the American Psychological Association and other like professional groups, inviting the appointment of liaison committees to the Task Force on Nomenclature and Statistics. The resultant American Psychological Association committee, appointed by its Board of Directors, consists of Maurice Lorr (Chair), Leonard Krasner, and Peter E. Nathan. That group has met once with Robert Spitzer and plans additional meetings with him in the future.

In January 1977, pilot field trials of DSM-III were begun in order to test the adequacy of the major classifications (e.g., schizophrenia, effective disorders, organic mental disorders). Almost simultaneously, the American Psychiatric Association was invited to join the Council on Clinical Classification to contribute to the ICD-9 (International Classification of Diseases) under development by the World Health Organization. The net effect of this participation will be to increase the likelihood that DSM-III and ICD-9 are relatively compatible, while providing for differences in the direction of greater specificity by DSM-III.

In April 1977, additional field trials of DSM-III began at over 100 facilities across the country; at the same time, copies of the DSM-III draft were made available to the public at a cost of $10. Although the final version of DSM-III will not appear until 1979 or 1980, it is not expected that the draft version described and appraised below—the first public product of the task force's efforts—will be significantly different from the final product. It is this draft, dated April 1977, and its accompanying "Guiding Principles" (Spitzer, Sheehy, & Endicott, in press) which are reviewed here, along with a conceptual paper by Spitzer and Endicott (in press) which, while not now officially part of DSM-III, was included with earlier drafts as an encapsulation of much of the philosophy and rationale that went into its creation.

DSM-III: Status and Appraisal

DSM-III is both larger and more comprehensive than its predecessor, encompassing half again as many separate diagnostic descriptions as does DSM-II. This change in scope may be attributed in part to the policy stated in the prefatory "Guiding Principles" of the draft (Spitzer et al., in press): that DSM-III has chosen to be inclusive rather than exclusive, that "whenever a clinical condition can be described with clarity and relative distinctness it is considered for inclusion." This policy of inclusiveness is perhaps best viewed in the light of the overall goal of DSM-III: to "develop a classification system that will reflect our current state of knowledge regarding mental disorders." This is to be achieved by (a) clear and brief professional communication facilitating professional inquiry, (b) providing a guide to current differentiated treatments, (c) providing information concerning likely outcomes with and without treatment, (d) reflecting current knowledge of etiology/pathophysiology, (e) meeting needs of practitioners and administrators in a variety of settings.

Ideally, critical appraisal of DSM-III would start out by testing the consistency of the document against these stated goals and purposes. However, the draft document available to us fails to specify criteria for determining how these goals are to be achieved and how success or failure to reach them will be assessed. In the absence of empirically derived criteria, we must base our reactions to DSM-III on other criteria necessarily more personal and less objective. We believe, nonetheless, that the larger conceptual issues to which this paper is addressed form a context in which the goals of DSM-III can be appraised meaningfully in the absence of more empirical evaluation criteria. Our selection of issues, while not meant to be comprehensive (although we do not believe that it distorts), is nonetheless organized around what seems central and fundamental.

Multiaxial Diagnoses

In what the authors describe as a major innovation, diagnoses in DSM-III take a multiaxial form. That is, each diagnosis contains information on at least five predetermined dimensions—axes—which are designed to be of value in planning treatment and predicting outcome, as well as in categorizing and classifying. Ideally, of course, all of the relevant diagnostic information about a patient would be communicated in a single diagnostic statement. Understandably failing this ideal, however, the authors of DSM-III have selected the following five areas of special significance:

Axis I: Formal psychiatric syndrome
Axis II: Personality disorders (adults) and specific developmental disorders (children)
Axis III: Nonmental medical disorders
Axis IV: Severity of psychosocial stressors one year preceding disorder (Range: 1–7)
Axis V: Highest level of adaptive behavior one year preceding disorder (range: 1–7)

The multiaxial system confronts the central problem of DSM-II, categorizing from symptoms alone, by including information which—unlike most symptoms—is demonstrably more relevant to treatment and prognosis; Axes III, IV, and V are especially important here. Multiaxial diagnosis also eases the problem of multiple diagnosis; the format requires frank psychiatric conditions to be listed and described first (Axis I), followed by less disabling characterological problems or tran-

sient disorders of childhood, followed by medical disorders that may or may not play a role in the disorder(s) already listed. The following includes an example of each axis as they might appear for a single patient:

Axis I: 296.80 Atypical Depressive Disorder
Axis II: 301.81 Narcissistic Personality Disorder
Axis III: Diabetes, Hypertension
Axis IV: *Psychosocial stressors:* 5, severe (business failure)
Axis V: *Highest adaptive behavior past year:* 3, good.

Accompanying this interesting new approach to diagnosis, however, are some unaddressed assumptions about multiaxial classifications that ought to be considered. Above all, the apparent simplicity of multiple diagnosis belies the enormous complexity of the process of classification and categorization; categories may exist at numerous levels of abstraction and within diverse structures of meaning. For purposes of enhanced reliability, the categories chosen for DSM-III are relatively uncomplex. As a result, multiaxial diagnoses for complex cases may be likened to the concretistic thinking of the child who must enumerate all of the edible items in a bowl because he or she has not yet achieved the abstraction of *fruit* to encompass them all. We do not wish to fault the levels of abstraction selected for the axes of DSM-III, for they merely reflect our current crude knowledge. What is unfortunate, however, is the implicit suggestion that the multiaxial approach is more than the modest increment in diagnostic method it appears to be.

Further, the reliability of judgments required within the two nondiagnostic axes must be questioned. To complete Axis IV, for example, one is told,

> The rating of severity of stress should be based on the clinician's assessment of the stress or change in life patterns that an average person would experience from the event(s). [Specifically], the patient's idiosyncratic vulnerability or reaction should not influence the rating. (Task Force on Nomenclature and Statistics, Note 1, p.2)

These instructions imply a consensus among clinicians in rating "stress" that almost certainly does not exist, as well as a presumed ability on their part to assess its effect on an "average" individual that may be just as uncommon.

Axis V (level of adaptive functioning) permits the clinician to indicate the highest level of adaptive functioning exhibited by the client during the past year. Of great potential value for prognostic purposes, the 7-point scale is, unfortunately, unaccompanied in the present draft of DSM-III by criteria for objectively applying the scale. Further, although adaptability can only be defined in relation to its environmental context, DSM-III does not address the issue of which environment is to be chosen. This issue, at the heart of current controversies over culture-fair assessment, is an unfortunate one for the authors of DSM-III to have failed to consider, since variables like socioeconomic status, ethnicity, and cultural milieu are clearly germane to considerations of level of adaptive functioning.

The authors of DSM-III acknowledge that although an infinite number of axes could be coded for a given patient, the number chosen—five—was selected as a compromise between workability and comprehensiveness. In our judgment, an additional axis, coding *response to treatment,* merits serious consideration for inclusion in the multiaxial system. To this end, clinicians often depend upon response to treatment as a diagnostic aid, especially in doubtful or complex diagnostic situations. A suspected manic-depressive patient may be given a trial on lithium in order to help confirm or disconfirm the initial diagnostic impression, while the patient who shows signs of schizophrenic disorganization might be given phenothiazine for the same purpose. An axis for coding response to treatment could include both the treatment offered and the patient's response to it—for example, "phenothiazine-positive psychosis" or "tricyclic-negative depression."

Operational Criteria

The "operational" nature of the diagnostic criteria offered by DSM-III is also open to question. The criteria used in DSM-III are adapted from research criteria generated by Feighner et

Table 1: *Criteria for Diagnosis of Simple Phobia, DSM-III 300.24 (All Should Be Present)*

A. Avoidance of the irrationally feared object or situation. If there is any element of danger in these objects or situations, it is reacted to in a fashion out of proportion to reality.
B. The avoidance has a significant effect on the patient's life adjustment.
C. The patient has complete insight into the irrational nature of his fear.
D. The phobic symptoms do not coincide with an episode of Depressive Disorder, Obsessive Compulsive Disorder, or Schizophrenia, nor are they limited to a period of two months prior to, or two months after, such an episode.

Note. From the draft version of the third edition of the *Diagnostic and Statistical Manual of Mental Disorders* (Task Force on Nomenclature and Statistics, Note 1, pp. G-6, G-7).

al. (1972) and Spitzer, Endicott, and Robins (1975). An example of the form in which these criteria are requested is given in Table 1, which lists the requirements for the diagnosis of simple phobia (300.24). This diagnostic label was chosen for illustration because of its simplicity. Other DSM-III labels describing conditions with more varied symptomatology understandably call for far more extensive and complicated diagnostic criteria.

The drafters of DSM-III claim that use of criteria of this degree of specificity in this format increases interrater reliability, although figures from ongoing reliability studies are not yet available. However, the DSM-III criteria differ crucially from the research criteria from which they derive; unlike the research criteria, the DSM-III criteria are to be employed even when the clinician does not have sufficient information to satisfy all criteria for a diagnosis. In that case, the diagnosis is still to be made—on the basis of criteria perceived as "clinically probable."

Recognizing that it is unrealistic to expect all patients to fit all of any set of operational criteria, it nonetheless appears risky to throw the entire weight of diagnostic responsibility back upon the unfettered clinical judgment of the clinician. Ironically, Spitzer himself, as have many others, has questioned the reliability and validity of unguided clinical judgment, even by very experienced clinicians (e.g., Spitzer, Cohen, Fleiss, & Endicott, 1967). As a consequence, we suggest that additional DSM-III decision rules be drafted to account for decisions that must be made when criteria for those decisions are only partially fulfilled. One such approach might be development of an empirically validated system for assigning weights to the various component criteria for each diagnosis so that the importance of missing data to the diagnosis could be known and taken into account.

While DSM-III does not make exaggerated claims for the reliability of its operational criteria, it does seem imprudent, in view of the status of DSM-III as a quasi-official document, to delay research on the reliability of these criteria until after their adoption with publication of the document. Since a major portion of the current DSM-III developmental project involves field trials at selected institutions, reliability data could be gathered as part of this field research without major overhaul of the overall project. Each agency might simply be expected to provide multiple diagnoses of the same patient rather than the single diagnosis currently sought. Examination of the consistency of these diagnoses would generate important information on the reliability and internal consistency of DSM-III criteria as they are now written.

Conceptual Problems of the Medical Model

As expressed by Spitzer and Endicott (in press), a central purpose of DSM-III is "designation of mental disorders as a *subset of medical disorders* . . . with primarily behavioral manifestations" (emphasis added). It is most unfortunate that this statement is not accompanied by an effort to define "behavior" or "behavioral manifestations." As we learn more and more about ourselves, the range of bodily events that have come to be considered "behavioral" on some level has steadily increased. Through concepts developed from biofeedback research, for example, we now almost routinely think of internal events like changes in blood pressure or skin temperature as behavioral. At a semantic extreme, chemists speak of the "behavior" of molecules, and physicists of the "behavior" of atomic particles. Is a change in a blood chemistry value to be considered behavior if it

precipitates a reactive hypoglycemia that is, in turn, associated with anxiety attacks? The point is that the limits and conditions of the general concept of behavior are too vague to be used as fundamental boundaries for a diagnostic classification system without some additional clarification of precisely what is and what is not included in the definition.

Rather than defining behavior per se, DSM-III backs into the issue by specifying what it is that behaves—the "organism." The concept of "organism," in turn, is central to Spitzer and Endicott's definition of *medical disorder,* of which mental disorder is a subset. According to Spitzer and Endicott, a medical disorder involves all of the following: (1) negative consequences of the condition, (2) inferred or identified organismic dysfunction, and (3) an implicit call for action. Of these three criteria, the first and third are as true of any of life's obstacles in general as they are for problems distinctly medical; as a result, they would apply equally well to a malfunctioning automobile engine or an obstinate computer program as to an aching bunion. In short, only the second criterion for judging a medical disorder, "organismic dysfunction," seems unique to these disorders; it is this decision on the part of Spitzer and Endicott, then, that is crucial to the ensuing discussion.

Particularly important to the concept of organismic dysfunction in DSM-III is the relationship between organism and environment postulated in the "Guiding Principles." The essence of this relationship is expressed in the following quotes from these principles (Spitzer et al., in press):

> The controlling variables (in a disorder) tend to be attributed to being largely *within the organism* with regard to either initiating or maintaining the condition. . . .
>   Frequently individuals come to the attention of mental health professionals with a problem which appears to be *primarily related to environmental factors* so that *no inference of organismic dysfunction can be made.* (Emphasis added)

As Spitzer et al. imply in both excerpts, we are referring to *inferences* which we make about a *process* when we talk about "organismic dysfunction" and not to anything that is concretely observable. Indeed, an organism is a system, a process, a set of ordered relations—it is not a concrete thing but an idea, a conceptual entity. And, as the second quote also indicates, Spitzer et al. agree with most of the rest of us that there are problems that come to the attention of mental health professionals that are wholly attributable to the environment "so that no inference of organismic dysfunction can be made." It makes sense, then, to conclude from these two quotes that "environment" is not within the "organism" and that organism and environment are separate entities that are physically complementary. However, if the defining characteristic of a system is that it represents an ordered set of *relations,* then to be outside of the system is to be unrelated or irrelevant to it. Thus, Spitzer et al.'s dichotomy between organism and environment seems to lead us to the unacceptable conclusion that environment is irrelevant to the organism.

This problem arises because of Spitzer et al.'s decision to define "organism" in two mutually incompatible ways, giving rise to an unavoidable conceptual inconsistency. To them, "organism" refers both to a systematic set of relations—to a system—as well as to the concrete observables which the relations place in conceptual order. In DSM-III, these semantic levels meet in one word, so that "organism" means both a system and a concrete observable (with boundaries at the skin). Although Spitzer and Endicott (in press) explicitly aver that DSM-III does not presume that all "organismic dysfunctions" are "physical," in fact the usage of the term confounds its physical referents with its conceptual ones. In this way, DSM-III's exclusive focus on the concrete "operational" data from which we infer process leads to reifications by which processes (inferences) become physical entities (organismic disorders).

A better conceptualization—one more truly reflective of our contemporary usage of these terms—is to view both organism and environment as *ideas* that do not have fixed or concrete referents, but rather have logical roles that permit flexible interchange of observables. Organism and environment are both conceptual rather than physical, and the concrete referents of these ideas are able to switch roles. Thus, we may talk of the "inner environment" of the neuron in terms of the blood and tissues which surround it and nourish it, even though the

blood and tissues are—in the traditional medical view—assigned to the organism and not to the environment. Analogously, a modern family therapist may see an aggregate of people together as an "organism" when approaching diagnosis from a family-systems point of view. It is instructive to view the ideas of organism and environment as parallel to the notion of independent and dependent variables: Just as an independent variable in one situation becomes a dependent variable in another, so do organism and environment switch logical roles depending on the level and focus of our interest in them.

Practical Problems of the Medical Model

Beyond the conceptual problems which derive from Spitzer and Endicott's (in press) designation of the mental disorders categorized by DSM-III as medical disorders, there are practical ones with that designation as well. Of the more than 230 behaviors included in DSM-III, more than half are certainly or almost certainly not attributable to known or presumed organic causes, a more conventional definition of "organismic dysfunction." The inappropriateness of considering these behaviors as medical disorders can be illustrated in compelling fashion. Seventeen major headings encompass the broadest level of diagnostic grouping in DSM-III; these headings are reproduced in Table 2. The table also shows that of these 17 groupings, 3 subsume disorders that are likely of organic or physical etiology and 4 others categorize disorders for which organic etiology has been implicated. This leaves 10 groups of disorders that have not been shown to share (and, very likely, do not share) such etiologic factors. To lump these 3 distinct and very different groups of disorders together by calling all of them "medical disorders" seems to us to make little sense.

On a molecular level and by example, consider the illogic of including alcohol abuse as a medical disorder. This disorder was chosen to be representative of many others categorized by DSM-III. Etiologic theories of alcoholism run the gamut from psychoanalytic, behavioral, and sociocultural to genetic and biochemical; treatment, from Alcoholics Anonymous to Antabuse.

Table 2: *Major Diagnostic Headings in DSM-III Draft Version*

Organic Mental Disorders (senile and presenile dementias; drug-induced disorders)[a]
Drug Use Disorders[b]
Schizophrenic Disorders[b]
Paranoid Disorders
Affective Disorders (episodic, intermittent, atypical)[b]
Psychoses Not Elsewhere Classified
Anxiety Disorders
Factitious Disorders
Somatoform Disorders
Dissociative Disorders
Personality Disorders
Psychosexual Disorders (gender identity, paraphilias, psychosexual dysfunctions, other disorders)
Disorders Usually Arising in Childhood or Adolescence (mental retardation, pervasive developmental disorders, attention-deficit disorders, specific development disorders, stereotyped movement disorders, speech disorders, conduct disorders, eating disorders, anxiety disorders of childhood or adolescence, disorders characteristic of late adolescence, other disorders of childhood or adolescence)[b]
Reactive Disorders Not Elsewhere Classified (adjustment disorders)
Disorders of Impulse Control Not Elsewhere Classified
Sleep Disorders (nonorganic, organic)[a]
Other Disorders and Conditions (unspecified mental disorder—nonpsychotic, psychic factors in physical conditions, no mental disorder, conditions not attributable to known mental disorder, administrative categories)[b]

Note. From the draft version of the third edition of the *Diagnostic and Statistical Manual of Mental Disorders* (Task Force on Nomenclature and Statistics, Note 1).
[a] Signifies known organic etiology.
[b] Signifies strongly implicated organic etiology for some (or all) subcategories of major heading.

Yet throughout virtually every informed consideration of those who suffer from the condition is the conviction that, though plagued by a host of physical and psychological sequelae of excessive drinking, the alcoholic's behavior stems from a single *behavioral lesion:* the inability to drink alcohol in a controlled fashion. A variety of studies (reviewed in Nathan & Briddell, 1977) show that the key to modification of this maladaptive behavior pattern is not a vaccine or an injection designed to prevent or eliminate a metabolic insufficiency or dysfunction because, almost certainly, there is not one for most alcoholics. Instead, these same data suggest, systematic modification of environmental maintainers of excessive drinking and systematic alteration of the drinker's own orientation to drinking and the consequences of his or her drinking can modify that drinking—not for every alcoholic but for enough to suggest that if

there is a demonstrable lesion responsible for alcoholism, the lesion is modifiable by environmental, not physical, means. Much the same logic could be employed to reject the unfortunate "medical disorder" designation of many other behaviors categorized by DSM-III.

A Definition of Health

The question of environmental versus organismic preeminence in psychodiagnosis would lose much of its urgency if we had a definition of psychological health against which to assess deviance. The limiting factor in diagnosis in that case would not be our ability to make inferences but rather the resolving power of our criteria and the instruments of our observation—that is, the point at which we become unable to say *"this* is not *that."*

Furthermore, if we worked from a concept of health, we could then diagnose individuals in terms of problems and needs rather than in illness-modeled nosological entities. Problems and needs may or may not be localized in the individual; indeed, to determine where they are localized for any given individual case is one of the tasks of diagnosis (cf. Mischel's 1968 concept of behavioral assessment). DSM-III, however, makes a priori assumptions regarding the locus of problems as within the skin. This is the essence of the medical model—and what makes it inappropriate, in our judgment, for contemporary understanding.

Spitzer and Endicott (in press) acknowledge that a definition of health would radically alter DSM-III and the structure of our nosology, but they despair of attaining such a goal. The World Health Organization's definition of health as a "state of complete physical, mental, and social well being and not merely the absence of disease or infirmity" is criticized by Spitzer and Endicott as "virtually worthless . . . as a guide towards the development of a classification of mental disorders." We believe, however, that the mental health professions already employ unstated, inchoate definitions of healthy process—at the roots of the value judgments which determine what is to be labeled as a disorder. The reason that a definition of health is "virtually worthless" to Spitzer and

Endicott is that it diminishes the claim the medical profession makes on society for primacy in treating organismic dysfunction. While it may be possible to define disorders narrowly as having only intra-skin correlates, a contemporary definition of health must be broader, inclusive of an ecological systems perspective. If we operate from a narrow concept of organismic disorder, then it is reasonable to think of mental disorders as a subset of medical disorders. If, on the other hand, we operate from a broad concept of health, then the domain of mental disorders is not wholly a subset of medical disorders but rather an *intersecting* set, in which the traditional elements of organismic dysfunction are but part of the whole system.

Defining the Profession

We contend that the real distinction between mental and medical disorders lies in the different tools required for their diagnosis and treatment (our professional epistemology, so to speak), not merely in the intra- versus extraorganismic processes involved in their development. Use of these diagnostic and treatment tools is regulated by society and, in that way, serves as an important institutional basis for claiming professional status. Spitzer and Endicott (in press) have created a definition of medical disorders which subsumes mental disorders as a subset. Why? What makes it so important that mental disorders be a subset of medical disorders?

Spitzer and Endicott answer:

> The ultimate issue in judging the proposed definition and criteria for medical and mental disorder is simply—is it *useful*? As eminent a nosologist as Feinstein has asserted that "the only workable definition of disease is that it represents whatever doctors of a particular era have defined as disease." We disagree. We believe that whether we like it or not, the issue of defining the boundaries of mental and medical disorder cannot be ignored. *Increasingly there is pressure for the medical profession and psychiatry in particular to define its area of prime responsibility.* (Emphasis added)

The last sentence, which answers the question of how DSM-III is to be useful to psychiatry, underscores the significance of making mental disorders a subset of medical disorders. *There is pressure on physicians and DSM-III is designed to relieve it.* By its own criteria, then, DSM-III may itself be diagnosed as an adjustment reaction: In this case, the "organism" is psychiatry and the "dysfunction" results from incapacitating intraprofessional conflicts!

A related example of how professional identity interacts with definitions of disorders in DSM-III is provided by instructions to formally diagnose a condition according to DSM-III "if it is not reversible by simple educational or nontechnical means." In essence, this criterion defines a disorder relationally, in respect to the profession's tools for treatment; the disorder appears only as a figure against the changing ground of our intervention capabilities. If this principle is followed with consistency, disorders may disappear from the official classification as our relative capacity to intervene increases.

Another agenda item for the creators of DSM-III, then, was to define the profession of psychiatry. Unhappily, however, the definition chosen by Spitzer, Endicott, and their coworkers also *enlarges* the domain of psychiatry and, correspondingly, *diminishes* the domain of other mental health professionals, including psychologists. In a marvelous circularity, the professional domain of psychiatry is defined as treatment of organismic dysfunction—and organismic dysfunctions are defined to fit the special areas of existing expertise claimed by the profession of psychiatry. While we, with Spitzer and Endicott, do not yet have the data needed to assess the usefulness of DSM-III for the mental health professions, to imply, as they do, that DSM-III was influenced only by professional concerns rather than professional territorialism suggests to us an exceptional lack of candor.

In much the same vein, Spitzer and Endicott (in press) maintain that "the classification of a condition as a medical disorder and the response of society to manifestations of that condition are separate issues which should not be confused." It is true that this conclusion deduces ineluctably from the medical version of the premise that mental disorders are intra-organismic and that only medically trained experts have the requisite skills to diagnose and treat them. If, however, we view these problems from an ecological perspective, then we cannot ignore their social context—the sociopolitical impact of diagnosis.

One such impact, of course, derives from the potentially stigmatizing, coercive aspects of diagnostic labeling well-known to most clinicians. Less widely acknowledged is that the diagnostic process may also itself affect what we see as normal. The specificity of DSM-III's diagnostic criteria, helpful for purposes of reliability, contributes to this iatrogenic impact of diagnosis. Perhaps the greatest potential for such a process in DSM-III is its handling of Briquet's syndrome (similar to DSM-II's hysterical neurosis). Among the diagnostic criteria specified for the disorder, DSM-III specifies different behavioral criteria depending upon the sex of the patient. The effect of these differential criteria is to make it easier to label a woman than a man with this diagnosis, in that way "proving" the widespread assumption that women are more often diagnosed hysteric than men.

Another example of a similar effect has to do with DSM-III's inclusion of guilt and shame over homosexuality ("Dyshomophilia") as a mental disorder. Many homosexuals have claimed that they experience more distress from being labeled "sick" than from the consequences of their sexual orientation. Spitzer and Endicott (in press) believe, however, that "the more prudent approach is to recognize the condition as a disorder *so as to legitimize the patient role for those who desire treatment. . . .*" If, indeed, "legitimization" is to become an accepted function of diagnosis, then let us also recognize that the role of the professional as *provider* of treatment is equally legitimized by official recognition of a condition as a disorder.

But Is It Good for the Psychologists?

We have been critical of DSM-III, but we have also recognized its strengths. Overall, then, is the document good for psychologists or bad for them?

In our judgment, DSM-III has the potential to be very bad for the psychologists, despite the real and potential advances in scope, diagnostic reliability, and diagnostic logic it represents. Notwithstanding its clarification of important aspects of the diagnostic process, the extensive pilot testing which is planned for it, and the inclusive nature of the diagnostic categories it includes, DSM-III has sufficiently important shortcomings that organized psychology, in our judgment, ought to be most concerned at its possible adoption. Its professional and legal significance for psychology appear to be especially troublesome. It is entirely possible, for example, that promulgation of DSM-III as an official action of the American Psychiatric Association will carry sufficient weight to call it to the attention of insurors and legislators who will see in it quasi-official recognition of the primacy of physicians in the diagnosis and treatment of the disorders categorized by DSM-III. Since these disorders are inclusive of virtually every psychological ill to which men and women are heir, little will be left for psychologists and other mental health professionals to work with. Even less will be left if legislators and third-party payers conclude that, since these conditions are all "medical disorders," they must first be evaluated by physicians, who will then decide whether they or ancillary mental health professionals (e.g., the psychologists) will treat the disorder.

While it would be unkind to conclude that this predictable turn of events was envisaged by the drafters of DSM-III, it would be worse than that to ignore that possibility and fail to anticipate its consequences.

Reference Note

1. Task Force on Nomenclature and Statistics, American Psychiatric Association. *Diagnostic and statistical manual of mental disorders* (3rd ed., draft version of April 15, 1977). (Available from Task Force on Nomenclature and Statistics, American Psychiatric Association, 722 West 168 Street, New York, New York.)

References

American Psychiatric Association. *Diagnostic and statistical manual of mental disorders* (2nd ed.). Washington, D.C.: Author, 1968.

Feighner, J. P., Robins, E., Guze, S. B., et al. Diagnostic criteria for use in psychiatric research. *Archives of General Psychiatry*, 1972, *26*, 57–63.

James, W. *Varieties of religious experience.* New York: Macmillan, 1902.

Mischel, W. *Personality and assessment.* New York: Wiley, 1968.

Nathan, P. E., & Briddell, D. W. Behavioral assessment and treatment of alcoholism. In B. Kissin & H. Begleiter (Eds.), *The biology of alcoholism* (Vol. 5). New York: Plenum Press, 1977.

Spitzer, R. L., Cohen, J., Fleiss, J. L., & Endicott, J. Quantification of agreement in psychiatric diagnosis. *Archives of General Psychiatry*, 1967, *17*, 83–87.

Spitzer, R. L., & Endicott, J. E. Medical and mental disorder: Proposed definition and criteria. In R. L.

Spitzer & D. Klein (Eds.), *Critical issues in psychiatric diagnosis*. New York: Raven Press, in press.

Spitzer, R. L., Endicott, J. E., & Robins, E. Clinical criteria for psychiatric diagnosis and DSM-III. *American Journal of Psychiatry*, 1975, *132*, 1187–1192.

Spitzer, R. L., Sheehy, M., & Endicott, J. E. DSM-III: Guiding principles. In V. Rakoff (Ed.), *Psychiatric diagnosis*. New York: Brunner/Mazel, in press.

At the time of original publication of this article, *Thomas Schacht* and *Peter E. Nathan* were faculty members of the Department of Clinical Psychology, Graduate School of Applied and Professional Psychology, Rutgers University.

The authors would like to express their gratitude to the other members of the DSM-III liaison committee of the American Psychological Association, Maurice Lorr and Leonard Krasner, for a critical reading of this manuscript and for the benefit of discussions with them about DSM-III. At the same time, it should be made clear that the opinions expressed in this paper are solely those of its authors and do not reflect in any way the position either of the liaison committee or the American Psychological Association.

Professional Psychology and Public Programs: A Critique

Edward T. Heck

The relationship between public mental health programs and professional psychology is discussed from a systems point of view, and possible relationships between professional psychology and future health care delivery are explored.

In this article I argue that public mental health programs are chronically ineffective and unstable human service systems because they are, and have always been, out of context with the main body of American human service systems. I contend that if professional psychology is to realize its full potential for bettering the human condition in contemporary American society, it must be aware of these areas of dysjunction and address them wisely and decisively.

For purposes of this article, I define public mental health programs as organizations whose primary purpose is the delivery of mental health services to a population within specific geographic boundaries, and whose funding comes mainly from grants or allocations rather than from fees for individual services. Examples of public mental health programs are state mental institutions and comprehensive community mental health centers.

There are three major areas of organizational life in which public mental health programs are discordant with the values and practices of contemporary American human service systems: (a) public policy, (b) program administration, and (c) professional roles and responsibilities.

Public Policy

Public mental health programs are discordant with most other contemporary professional human service systems because they are islands of program-oriented, subsidized service in a sea of individually arranged, fee-for-service contracts. Most, if not all, noncoercive professional human services in our society are provided by practitioners of the consumer's choice in return for a monetary consideration negotiated between the consumer and the service provider. These direct service contracts are reciprocal transactions and approximate behavioral contracts (Heck, Gomez, & Adams, 1973). In actual practice, course, these contracts are influenced by forces beyond the consumer-provider relationship. Typically, this influence involves licensure or regulation of the qualifications of the service provider, a situation that allows the consumer to choose between qualified providers.

Private medical practice is an example of this type of reciprocal, contractual relationship for professional services. Such contracts are consonant with the values and practices of contemporary society because they do not, in principle, usurp the basic right of the consumer to be the ultimate evaluator of the services received; the consumer can terminate unsatisfactory relationships and seek more satisfactory services elsewhere.

Although clients of public mental health programs have the right to terminate unsatisfactory service contracts, they do not have easy access to comparable services outside of their assigned catchment areas. When service eligibility is arbitrarily determined and coercively enforced, the consumer's prerogative to seek out the services he or she considers best suited to his or her needs is seriously impaired. No service

Reprinted from *Professional Psychology*, 1976, 7, 420–427.

eligibility restriction is more destructive of the consumer's rights in this respect than the *catchment area* concept, the very cornerstone of public community mental health program organization and funding.

The catchment area concept violates the rights of consumers in ways other than geographically restricting shopping for services. One such constraint of the consumer's prerogatives involves the service programs that are offered to clients in the first place. When services are provided *through* programs rather than *to* individuals, the consumer finds him- or herself at a serious disadvantage relative to the providers of services. In such a circumstance, the service outcomes desired by individual people tend to be preempted by services developed and supported by program developers and funders. Classic examples of this are mental health consultation and the prevention of mental health problems.

The nonlocal program funding patterns that characterize public mental health programs make it possible for funding agencies to dictate which service programs will be offered locally by virtue of their abiility to selectively support (or stimulate the development of) programs that fit current concepts or political agendas or the funding agencies. The fact that public programs may or may not meet local needs and priorities is important, but it is not the essential public policy issue at the root of the consumer's dilemma when he or she is forced to deal with them.

The basic public policy problem is, in my opinion, the practice by funding agencies of simultaneously funding and regulating and providing program service. It is obvious that a government cannot simultaneously perform all these functions without invalidating at least one of them. No organization can impartially regulate services that it provides, regardless of the purity of its intentions in doing so. Neither can an organization be expected to efficiently deliver services that it funds in the absence of competition. The result is again the erosion of the rights of the consumer because funding, regulating, and providing organizations are permitted to usurp the consumer's right to reinforce appropriately and directly the adequacy or inadequacy of services available to him or her.

I contend that professional psychology has accepted the current public mental health program system whole-heartedly and virtually without question. The system has, after all, been a major source of support for many of us over the years, and judging from our reaction to threats of program cutbacks, I believe we will part with it reluctantly. But we will be forced to part with it in the near future, and at the same time we must broadly reassess ourselves and our competencies—our clients and their needs—and the service delivery system upon which we both depend.

Program Management

As a prerequisite to effective functioning, public mental health programs must enable one to distinguish mental health problems from non-mental-health problems. This discrimination can be made at the program level by requiring that both program orientation and staffing be comprehensive in the broadest sense. From a systems point of view, however, most comprehensive mental health programs are anything but comprehensive. The comprehensive range of services appears comprehensive only with respect to currently acceptable concepts of what mental health services are supposed to be from the point of view of the program funding agencies. These concepts have become increasingly parochial as programmatic mental health funding patterns have widened the chasm between program-oriented mental health systems and the rest of the human service system.

Similarly, the so-called multidisciplinary approach currently in vogue is in reality multidisciplinary only with respect to currently acceptable concepts of what mental health disciplines are supposed to be from the point of view of mental health program funders. As a result, under the influence and active support of public mental health programs and their funders, the mental health professions have grown closer together, but further apart from the main body of human service professions.

Such situations can exist only when public mental health programs are essentially out of touch with the life circumstances of the people they are supposed to serve. An example of these systematic factors in action follows. Alan

Gruber and I (Heck & Gruber, 1976a) recently completed a study of 564 children in private residential treatment centers under the auspices of the Massachusetts Department of Public Welfare, Division of Family and Children Services. These children were identified early in life as suffering serious mental disturbances and were thus clearly within the area of concern of their respective public mental health programs. The residential treatment services ultimately provided to these children, it should be noted, were provided exclusively by the nonpublic sector. We made this amazing discovery: Fewer than 20% of these children had any contact with the Massachusetts public mental health system when entering residential treatment! And we defined *contact* to include diagnosis, referral, and treatment. In this context, it is astounding to note that Massachusetts has one of the most highly developed public mental health systems in the nation, with more than 50 state-supported mental health clinics, several community mental health centers and major institutions, more than 18,000 employees, and an annual budget of well above $200 million!

We studied this group and other groups of children in residential treatment extensively over the past few years, and we were repeatedly surprised by similar discoveries. We have demonstrated that many of these children could be treated within their communities (Heck & Gruber, 1976b), yet their families appeared unable to provide them with adequate care and protection. This is not a mental health problem; it is a legal problem. But there was virtually no legal input into the decisions to send these children to residential treatment. In another study (Heck & Gruber, Note 1), we found that more than 30% of the children referred to residential treatment exhibited signs of neurological impairment; yet there was virtually no neurological consultation or input when these children's problems were being defined or when residential treatment was being prescribed for them. In my opinion, the services provided to these children cannot be described as comprehensive or multidisciplinary. And I do not believe that this situation is confined exclusively to Massachusetts.

To be really comprehensive, mental health services must be both sensitive and responsive to the life circumstances of the people who use (or might use) them. This, of course, implies a continuous process of communication between consumers and providers of mental health services. From a systems or program point of view, the process is perhaps best illustrated by outcome-oriented, periodic review and evaluation of the client's experience in treatment. Although periodic review and evaluation are mandated by law in several public mental health program jurisdictions, they are not widely used or implemented.

Psychologists associated with public mental health programs have historically expressed an interest in service accountability; but rather than accounting to the consumers of mental health services through processes such as periodic review and evaluation, we have concentrated our efforts on accounting to the funders of programs through processes such as program evaluation. That adequate program evaluation is the exception rather than the rule in public mental health programs does not alter the fact that our efforts in this respect have served to reinforce the notion that the most important service contract as well as accountability for mental health services is between the funders and the providers of these services.

Program evaluation is necessarily episodic and therefore disproportionately influenced by program funding schedules instead of the life dilemmas of individual clients. Program evaluation in the absence of comprehensive periodic review and evaluation is a travesty that could exist only in an environment in which there is little or no meaningful communication between providers and consumers of mental health services.

The relationships between professionals in public mental health programs exhibit the same lack of communication as do those between service providers and consumers. Human service professionals in the main have not, in my experience, extensively sought or accepted mental health consultation from public mental health programs. Nor is their consultation sought by public mental health programs in proportion to their concern, expertise, or direct involvement with mental health problems. When these professionals require mental health consultation, they usually seek it in order to solve a particular problem of one of their patients or clients. They contract for it with a mental health professional in whom they have confidence, and they judge its effectiveness on the basis of its utility in solving the specific problem experienced by the patient or client.

Public mental health programs have lost touch with the lives of consumers because outcome-oriented direct services have been deemphasized or ignored. A direct service orientation requires capable, purposeful, clinical practice and sound program management. This kind of orientation keeps the relationship between consumers and programs in balance by ensuring that indirect services, such as consultation, are related to direct service outcomes. It is admittedly difficult to develop this orientation in public mental health programs when program funders are reinforcing the polar orientation. Fortunately, this situation will change in the near future, and that change will present a major opportunity for professional psychology to create, manage, and serve. If we are to seize that opportunity, we must reconceptualize the programs with which we have associated and their relationships to the people they are intended to serve.

Professional Roles and Responsibilities

I believe that American psychiatry has historically been the single most dominant influence in defining the roles and responsibilities of professional psychology and other mental health professions. It has also been the dominant force in defining the relationships *between* the various mental health professions. Thus, professional psychology, particularly in public mental health programs, reflects the history, organization, and current problems of organized American psychiatry. How those problems are ultimately resolved and how we relate to and participate in the solution of these problems will, in my opinion, determine the future of professional psychology.

Since the days of the child guidance movement, American psychiatry has been the only American medical specialty that has claimed for itself both specific clinical competencies and exclusive administrative prerogatives. These clinical competencies have not been well defined or well accepted by the rest or organized medicine or, for that matter, by the general public. I belive this credibility, or perceived utility gap, is the result of two factors that have influenced organized American psychiatry over the years. The first is the long-standing dominance of American psychiatric thinking and practice by psychoanalytic theory, making the treatment of choice unavailable to most people in need of mental health services. The second, and more important, factor has been the wholesale commitment of American psychiatry to public mental health programs as the vehicle of organizational choice for the delivery of mental health services to the populus.

While these developments were shaping the course of mental health practice, the main body of organized medicine continued to dispense direct services to an accepting public—one individual at a time. From the point of view of the consumer, dissatisfaction with medical practice is mainly directed at its availability and cost, not at its accomplishments. In contrast, public dissatisfaction with mental health practice is directed at its utility and credibility; cost has not been a major source of public dissatisfaction with it.

And although the clinical competencies claimed by American psychiatry became less credible and relevant from the point of view of the consumer, the administrative prerogatives claimed by it began to be challenged by other mental health professionals and also by organized medicine. Until now, such challenges were feeble because over the years the administrative prerogatives claimed by organized psychiatry have been translated into statutes, regulations, and policies that made meaningful changes unlikely and the process of seeking them tedious. Thus defined, they were perpetuated by the funding practices of public mental health programs.

As public mental health programs grew larger, increasing numbers of nonmedical mental health professionals, including psychologists, became associated with them. And as this happened, we began to clamor for more responsible roles in the operation and management of these programs. In my view, organized psychiatry has negotiated a kind of détente with us and other groups by gradually conceding its questionable clinical competencies on the condition that its ensured administrative prerogatives be left intact. That was, after all, the most economical and conservative strategy to use under the circumstances.

Although professional psychologists rejoiced in the victory of being grudgingly acknowledged as psychotherapists, the real issues of the relationships between psychology and psychiatry and medicine have gone virtually unnoticed. Consequently, psychologists have given tacit approval to the proposition that because no mental health profession can clearly demonstrate unique clinical competence in any area of practice, all professionals are competent to perform all mental health service functions. On the sidelines, of course, the service-consuming public had expanded the proposition to include its reciprocal: Because no mental health profession is competent to deliver any service, all of them are equally incompetent. Among ourselves, professional roles have become blurred when they should have become more defined. In this atmosphere, professional roles and responsibilities, including our own, have been increasingly determined by reliance upon organizational affiliation and administrative prerogatives rather than upon demonstrable clinical competence. Understandably, this situation has confused both the providers and the consumers of mental health services.

In this context, currently fashionable attacks on the medical model of mental health services are, in reality, misdirected complaints against the administrative prerogatives claimed by organized psychiatry in public mental health programs. In that respect, they are not useful because they contribute little to defining relationships between professionals or to conceptualizing differing professional roles and responsibilities relative to consumers.

Future Prospects for Professional Psychology

The future of both professional psychology and public mental health programs will be profoundly influenced by the implementation of a national health insurance plan. It is only a mat-

ter of time until this becomes a reality. Such a plan will probably shift the focus of mental health service funding to the individual service consumers and away from arbitrarily defined service programs. This realignment from programmatic to individual funding is consistent with current practices and values of contemporary society and with procedures shared by most human service consumers and providers. Recent important developments at the state level, such as the mandatory inclusion of mental health benefits in group health insurance policies (Massachusetts General Laws, 1974, chaps. 1174 and 1221), demonstrate that the first wave of this change is already upon us.

In the near future, professional mental health services provided to individuals and funded by third-party payers, such as Blue Shield, will be defined as to content, duration, outcome, cost, and qualifications of providers by regulatory agencies traditionally uninvolved with and unsympathetic toward public mental health programs. And their influence over our practice will prevail because they will control the funding power to implement these changes.

The major vehicle by which mental health services (and all health services) will be regulated is the exclusively medical Professional Service Review Organization (PSRO). The PSROs are based on the organizational unit of the County Medical Society, although the extent of their national organizational network and funding support is formidable.

In the short range, PSRO activities involve neither professional psychologists nor consumers of any health services. In the long range, their activities will almost certainly become the precedents and/or framework for any plan of national health insurance. At this point, professional psychology is barely aware of PSROs, much less dealing with them effectively. We will have to deal decisively with the present reality of PSROs if we are to have any future at all in the delivery of mental health services. My view of the struggle of organized psychiatry to reconcile itself to the main body of medicine via PSROs has convinced me that vaguely defined clinical competencies and program-dependent administrative prerogatives will no longer be sufficient to distinguish or perpetuate an area of professional practice.

If professional psychology is to participate in the delivery of mental health services to the large numbers of people who require those services, it must, by definition, participate in the organizational systems through which those services will be delivered in the future. It seems clear that public mental health programs are not the organizational vehicle by which this goal can be accomplished. We must, therefore, participate in the development of new service delivery systems and practices and diminish our dependence upon public mental health programs. To accomplish this, we must define our areas of competence independently and offer them with confidence to a wider range of health care professionals and consumers than we have done previously. In this respect, the current decline of public mental health programs should provide a major opportunity for the growth and development of professional psychology.

Reference Note

1. Heck, E. T., & Gruber, A. R. *Neuropsychological assessment of children referred to residential treatment.* Manuscript submitted for publication, 1975.

References

Heck, E. T., Gomez, A. G., & Adams, G. L. *A guide to mental health services.* Pittsburgh, Pa.: University of Pittsburgh Press, 1973.

Heck, E. T., & Gruber, A. R. *Children in residential treatment* (TAP Technical Document No. 2). Boston: Boston Children's Service Association, 1976. (a)

Heck, E. T., & Gruber, A. R. *Treatment alternatives project: Final report* (TAP Technical Document No. 3). Boston: Boston Children's Service Association, 1976. (b)

Massachusetts General Laws, Acts of 1974.

At the time of original publication of this article, *Edward T. Heck* was Associate Director of Research, Boston Children's Service Association, Boston, Massachusetts, and a clinical instructor in pediatrics, Tufts Medical School.

Evaluating Individual Deliverers: Private Practice and Professional Standards Review Organizations

George W. Albee and Marc Kessler

As independent practitioners in psychology are increasingly reimbursed with public funds or through third-party payments, demands will rise for controls on costs and on cost-benefit analysis. Traditionally the processes of guaranteeing competency have included careful selection of neophytes, evaluation and accreditation of training programs, licensing, and specialty examinations. New demands are appearing for continuing education and for peer review. If psychology is to move into service delivery systems where evaluation criteria and procedures are essential, we had better develop our own mechanisms and procedures, or they will be developed for us by others.

In the not too distant past psychologists in independent practice were relatively unencumbered by bureaucratic extraprofessional controls and restrictions. It is true we had to contend with the relatively uninspired opposition of psychiatrists who, with varying temporary successes, managed to delay or block for a time the passage of certification or licensing laws regulating the practice of psychology. But eventually most states have accorded psychology legal recognition and until recently those psychologists in full-time independent practice (about 7% of the membership) or part-time independent practice (about 25%) could operate according to the rugged individualism that has characterized professions in America for most of the 20th century. But things are changing fast. As more and more professional services are extended by government supported and funded programs to those who cannot afford to pay for traditional private interventions, more and more governmental controls and demands for accountability are moving to center stage.

What have been, and are, the quality controls that affect the current practice of professional psychology? We will deal only with clinical psychology, but the reader will recognize

that most of what follows also applies to industrial and other professional settings.

The first control of professional quality has been the selection criteria used for admission of students to programs of professional study. As the popularity of careers in professional psychology has increased, the growing pool of applicants has resulted in the careful selection of neophytes with excellent undergraduate records, high test scores on such measures as the Graduate Record Examination and the Miller Analogies Test, and with positive personal recommendations. While there may be some danger that we are selecting obsessive high achievers (Albee, 1977), instead of "creative" individuals, in general our neophytes are highly competent intellectually and high achievers academically.

Once our fledgling professional students are accepted, they are led through a carefully structured graduate program with usually well-planned courses and experience requirements. They have been required to master a core of basic general psychology as well as to participate in practicum and internship experiences, to pass preliminary examinations, and to master research techniques culminating in a disserta-

Reprinted from *Professional Psychology*, 1977, *8*, 502–515.

tion based on data collection and hypothesis testing. While the establishment of new professional schools has introduced some loosening of some of these requirements, the content of professional training follows roughly the same pattern, with changes largely in emphasis rather than in content.

For many years doctoral programs in clinical, counseling, and more recently school and professional psychology have been accredited by the American Psychological Association's (APA) Committee on Accreditation of the Education and Training Board. Most state licensing boards require that applicants for licensing be graduates of such accredited programs (or programs with equivalent training). The APA does not consider programs until the educational institution is accredited by a regional branch of the National Commission on Accrediting.

Following completion of doctoral training, most state licensing laws require 1 or 2 years of postdoctoral supervised experience before a psychologist can be licensed for independent practice, that is, sale of services to the public for a fee (APA, 1967). Many state licensing boards, after review of the applicant's education and experience, require that the applicant take a test developed by the American Association of State Psychology Boards. This examination covers a broad range of basic psychology, methodology, and professional practice. It contains 150–200 objective items (see Terris, 1973). Upon receipt of a license the individual practicing psychologist is expected (and usually has agreed, as part of the licensing process) to adhere to the APA's Ethical Standards of Psychologists (APA, 1977).

Recently the *National Register of Health Service Providers in Psychology* has been established. It publishes an annual directory of qualified psychologists licensed by their states and meeting other educational and experience requirements for independent practice (see Council for the National Register of Health Service Providers in Psychology, 1976). Many states now suggest or require that the practicing psychologist be engaged in regular continuing educational activities in order to obtain license renewal periodically (APA's Continuing Education Task Force, Note 1). Some practitioners after 5 or more years of experience take

the examination of the American Board of Professional Psychology, widely (but not universally) recognized as a measure of professional competence (Ross, 1970).

It might be argued that this entire process—selection, education, supervision, assessment, and licensing—is sufficient to produce competent practitioners. It is interesting to observe that scientists, in academia especially, are rarely required to be licensed and are often excluded by licensing laws regulating the practice of psychology. Scientists themselves strongly oppose any attempt at formal legal evaluation of their competence. In sharp contrast, professionals usually seek licensing or certification laws to identify those competent to practice. The reason advanced by the profession for legal recognition is protection of the public, but clearly our motives also include the status accorded a member of a licensed profession, the control of (unqualified) competition, and the assurance of at least minimum competence among those using the title of the profession (Albee & Loeffler, 1971).

It is instructive to examine other differences between the scientist and the professional because of the light it casts on the problems of competence measurement in the latter. Albee and Loeffler (1971) have discussed this issue in great detail. The activities of the scientist are open to constant scrutiny, while the activities of the professional are much more likely to be closed and secret. Scientists specify as clearly as possible each step in their procedures and each finding of their observations and experiments. Science thrives on replication, controversy, open argument, dispute, and mutual criticism. A profession, on the other hand, derives a significant measure of its power and effectiveness from its mystique, from the secrets of practice that it imparts with caution to carefully selected neophytes and apprentices. Science develops an open operational language, while the profession develops a secret language. Because professions are appliers of knowledge to the relief and solution of human problems, the professional never has all the knowledge he or she requires and so must deal with incomplete and inadequate knowledge while retaining the confidence of the client. It is interesting to note that scientific training programs are almost never accredited while professional training programs nearly always seek accreditation. The content of scientific training at the graduate level is rarely specified in any detail. The fledgling scientist takes whatever courses are appropriate to his or her research interests, while the fledgling professional is marching lock step through a series of required courses designed to insure that all significant areas of useful knowledge are covered during training. Graduate training in scientific psychology neither asks for nor receives any formal accreditation; rather, each program is uniformly evaluated by the scientific peer group. The quality of a scientifically oriented psychology department is determined primarily by the quality of the research generated and published by the departmental faculty. Thus a small department with a very few high-quality scientists may surpass in reputed excellence a large department that produces little research. Similar observations can be made about the reputed competence of the individual scientist. It seems reasonable to say that in science no one is competent until judged so by his or her peers. Among professionals, on the other hand, everyone is judged competent until it is fairly clearly established that a particular individual falls below the competence threshold. Both groups, of course, are bound by the same ethical codes (APA, 1973, 1977).

Because the professional psychologist commonly deals with his or her client privately and because any observation of this interaction, whether through a one-way vision window or through tape recordings, changes the essential nature of the relationship, evaluation of this intimate interaction is difficult. The relatively modest reliability of clinical assessment procedures and the uncertain validity of therapeutic interventions also pose serious problems in evaluating effectiveness. This literature is so vast, and so well reviewed elsewhere, that we will not attempt to document a statement we regard as widely accepted on the evidence.

Measuring professional competence is easy, or difficult, or impossible, depending primarily on the reliability and the specificity of the criterion. The more easily defined and objectively measured the criterion, the fewer the problems. Thus for certain occupations it is not difficult to devise criterion measures with a high degree of validity and reliability. If a plumber sweats joints that leak or if an engineer is unable to design a heating system that works efficiently, we are justified in questioning her or his competence. Even in more highly professional occupations there may be fairly exact criteria available. Thus hospitals have tissue committees that examine the organs and other tissues removed by the surgeon. If a surgeon frequently removes healthy tissue, the tissue committee may question his or her competence in diagnosis or his or her honesty in recommending surgery. The competence of architects, engineers, accountants, or dentists may be easier to judge because of reliable and objective criteria, than the competence of artists, poets, or psychotherapists where there is less agreement about what constitutes success. In the case of psychotherapy there is some evidence that problems that bring the client to the therapist are increasingly less specific and less subject to simple treatments such as diminution or elimination of specific behaviors (Wheelis, 1958).

Williamson (Note 2) has reviewed a number of validation studies of performance measures in medicine. Because medicine is a much older profession than psychology and because many more studies have been done attempting to assess the competence of the physician in diagnosis, treatment, and prognosis, we may learn much from our sister discipline. The results are far from encouraging. Williamson (Note 2) concludes, "Unless we have a practical and effective means for establishing the efficacy of therapeutic interventions and the validity of our diagnostic interventions in terms of sensitivity and specificity, it will continue to be difficult to establish standards for quality assessment or certification" (p. 27).

Williamson was driven to this discouraging conclusion on the basis of a number of specific studies he reviewed. Without attempting to summarize these studies in detail, we might well note that a frequent medical and surgical error was "giving symptomatic treatment without attempting to obtain a diagnosis" (Williamson, Note 2, p. 22). In general, quality of performance of physicians in teaching hospitals by both house staff and certified physicians was superior to the work done in nonteaching hospitals, even though it was the performance of certified physicians that was evaluated in the latter. In another study, no significant differences were found among general practitioners, noncertified specialists, and certified specialists in dealing with heart patient management problems. In another study that may be instructive to psychologists, physicians did well on written examinations but "shockingly poor" in actual practice (Williamson, Note 2, p. 22).

Further, there appears to be no clear relationship between grades in professional school and later performance as physicians. Ironically, one major study found a slightly negative correlation that did not reach statistical significance. In another study done in Hawaii, the physicians who did better than average were in group practice at the Kaiser Hospital. In a major study of 21 different conditions, the "performance of the certified and noncertified physicians was the same" (Williamson, Note 2, p. 23).

Considering all these and a number of related studies, Williamson (Note 2) concludes:

> In summary, an intensive search of available information sources involving validation of certification procedures by performance measures was conducted. Although definitive data were not identified, a growing series of independent studies seemed significant in the similarity of their findings. Based on correlational evidence, certification results, whether measured by professional undergraduate grades or medical speciality certification examinations, seemed to have very little relationship to quality of subsequent professional performance. On the other hand, the type and length of formal postgraduate professional training have consistently been shown to have a strong correlation with the quality of medical practice. (pp. 24–25).

In major studies using the critical incidence (sic) method, Sanazaro and Williamson (1968, 1970) found consistent correlations between quality performance and the length of actual formal postgraduate training. It is tempting to conclude that postgraduate training may lead to more extensive knowledge and experience that is later reflected in better professional practice. But this conclusion might be a confusion of correlation with causation. It is also possible that the more conscientious and responsible professionals are the ones who seek postdoctoral training, while those with more crass financial motives are the ones who rush into practice. This would make an interesting research study.

If the medical profession, with its long history of board certification and its relatively more objective criteria for successful performance, has such discouraging evidence of performance effectiveness based on evaluations of undergraduate education and on speciality certification, psychologists had better proceed with care.

Our review of a very large number of studies of physician competence—where good and objective criteria are available—is not really directly relevant to our purpose in this paper. The easy availability of these studies, however, and the current critical issues of malpractice insurance escalation and health cost escalation led us to read more than we intended in this area. As a fringe benefit to our readers we feel impelled to sound a series of serious warnings: (a) General practitioners, especially those in rural areas, may be dangerous to your health, (b) municipal nonteaching hospitals are not the best places to have an illness or a baby, (c) small hospitals are more likely to give unsatisfactory care than large hospitals, (d) nonteaching hospitals are not as good for all illnesses studied as teaching hospitals, (e) surgery by a certified surgeon is safer than by a surgical resident, but while you are asleep it may be the resident who does the surgery even though the bill may come from the surgeon, (f) emergency room treatment for nonemergency gastrointestinal symptoms is to be avoided, and (g) an appendectomy in a hospital with an active tissue committee is safer than one without. Frankly, we have been moved to reassess our perhaps too facile rejection of our peasant grandparents' advice about the dangers of medical care, hospitals, and drugs. Many of the benefits of medical care seem more clearly limited to the physician entrepreneur than to the recipient of "care." The best strategy is to remain symptom free; the second is to find a certified board specialist who is a personal friend working in a university affiliated teaching hospital and who will agree in advance to give the minimal treatment she deems necessary.

Using knowledge tests to evaluate the competence of the individual practitioners is to make the assumption that there is a significant correlation between the individual's factual knowledge and his or her competence in practice. While this assumption is often questioned, it is not inconsistent with the usual definition of the professional as a person who applies knowledge to the solution of human problems. Clearly, if one accepts this definition, then knowledge is a necessary, if not sufficient, criterion for practice as a professional. This means that knowledge tests are often found at different stages in the training of the professional and as a requirement for licensure and/or certification. The American Association of State Psychology Boards makes available an objective examination for use by state licensing boards in assessing the knowledge base of persons seeking a license (Terris, 1973). Similar examinations are given by medical and accounting licensing boards and by other practice-regulatory agencies.

At the most advanced level of competence in professional psychology is the American Board of Professional Psychology (ABPP), which, since 1947, has been issuing a diploma widely recognized as indicating superior competence at an advanced level (Ross, 1970). The nature of the ABPP examination has varied somewhat over the years and is revised and reexamined frequently. Basically, however, ABPP asks for evidence of appropriate advanced education, competent supervision of postdoctoral practice, reputation among one's peers, and the submission of a sample of the candidate's work in the form of interviews, therapy transcriptions, assessment, protocols, etc. The candidate then undergoes a relatively lengthy oral examination by a group of senior professionals in his or her field. Currently the ABPP is working on a fairly complex new examining procedure including a standardized interview and the use of videotape interviews with a series of different clients where the candidate is asked to make judgments about such things as the nature of a problem, probable therapeutic outcome, and appropriate forms of intervention.

Most psychologists would agree that a practitioner could not make the most effective use of standardized psychological tests in assessing a client without a sophisticated understanding of such concepts as reliability and validity, the standard error of measurement, standard scores, and the properties of the normal curve. While understanding these concepts does not guarantee effectiveness in the practitioner, without such understanding it is difficult to imagine that a psychologist would be effective. Similarly,

it might be argued that to be effective in psychotherapy the therapist ought to be knowledgeable about the basic research concepts in the field. While no one would insist on a particular theoretical orientation in a therapist, he or she ought to know the essentials of classical and instrumental conditioning and the basic concepts of psychodynamic theory. Again, such knowledge is no guarantee of effectiveness, but its absence is clearly a sign of potential ineffectiveness. Persons in independent practice may also be called on, from time to time, to work with or advise about individuals with developmental disabilities, suspected (or unsuspected) neurological involvement, sensory or perceptual problems associated with aging, or cerebral conflicts of lateral dominance. Even those psychologists who restrict their practice to psychotherapy or to some special group of clients may need to be sensitive to these and other possible problems. As a result, examinations for certification or licensing should cover the broad range of topics offered in the core areas of psychology, at least according to the philosophy of the developers of the test of the American Association of State Psychology Boards. Passing the test does not guarantee competence, but failing it strongly suggests insufficient knowledge for practice.

Another source of competence in a profession is sophistication in the use of tools and the quality of the tools or instruments available for use in performing specific professional functions. The invention of the plethysmograph greatly increased the reliability of the diagnosis of high blood pressure. Most clinicians are familiar with Meehl's (1954) discussion of the relative merits of global clinical judgment as opposed to the use of objective measuring instruments in clinical practice. In general, cookbook approaches using objective measures are often superior to global judgments based on interviews and clinical observations. Therefore, assessment of competence often involves measures of sophistication in the use of psychological measuring instruments.

Psychotherapeutic skills are more difficult to specify and measure. There is simply little agreement, and little data, on the relative importance of therapist variables, client variables, and theoretical approaches. Phillips (1967) proposed that the vague criterion "therapeutic success" should be replaced with "enhancement of competence" in the clients of mental health programs. It is not a long inductive leap to interpret his proposal as one that would assess the competence of the practitioner as a function of measured competence improvement in clients. The appeal of his proposal lies in the more reliable measures of social competence available. Phillips (1967) argues, "Program efficiency may be defined in terms of the cost of a given unit of successful achievement, for example, an increase in earning power measured in terms of additional dollars of income per year" (p. 76).

For data-oriented psychologists it is tempting to find measurable, quantitative, countable variables to plug into formulas for evaluating practitioner competency. But there is a serious problem with this approach. If formal procedures involving such indices as "cure rate," "rate of improvement," or "number of visits to criterion" were introduced as measures of individual competency, we could expect to generate an unfortunate phenomenon that Campbell (1975) has called "the corrupting effect of quantitative indicators." He points to a wide variety of illustrations of this phenomenon. For example, pressure on police departments to raise "clearance rates" (the proportions of crimes solved) led to all sorts of distortions and failures to record citizen complaints and to plea bargaining where sentences were reduced according to the number of previously unsolved burglaries the accused was willing to say he committed. Where the number of cases seen or helped was the criterion, "creaming" occurred—easier cases were handled and more difficult and needy cases were neglected. Soviet studies Campbell discussed showed that quantitative criteria in manufacturing—number, weight, total value— each seriously distorted output. Body count as a criterion measure in Viet Nam led to all sorts of corrupting and tragic consequences. The point is clear. The focusing on quantitative indicators— in psychological services as in continuing education—in evaluating competence is a dangerous procedure where quality of service is the goal.

We have been unable to find relevant, data-based studies of competency beyond those sketched above. Clearly there is a widespread sense of need for the development of measures in this area. A group at George Peabody College for Teachers has embarked recently on a long-term investigation to gather all available written competency statements for psychological specialties and to develop ways for graduate students and professionals alike to be able to judge their own competencies. On the basis of responses to a widely distributed request for help in defining and measuring professional competencies, the group has elicited statements of encouragement for its efforts but little in the way of real measures (Solomon, Note 3).

The *Revised Standards for Providers of Psychological Services*, developed in 1977 by the APA Committee on Standards for Providers of Psychological Services and submitted to the APA Council of Representatives in January 1977, is directed toward the codification of standards for psychological practice as a means of self-regulation in the public interest. In a real sense they are aimed at promoting and maintaining competence in service delivery by stressing accountability. Their effects have not been assessed, of course.

One of the most recent and direct confrontations of the problems of education and credentialing in psychology took place in June 1976 at a meeting jointly sponsored by the APA Education and Training Board and the APA Board of Professional Affairs. The report of the meeting (Wellner, Note 4) is essential reading for persons interested in this area. Among the recommendations presented for consideration by relevant groups within the APA were (a) the establishment of a thorough review of the whole credentialing system in psychology and the possible establishment of a national commission on accreditation and credentialing in psychology, (b) the urgent need for the identification of the substantive core of psychology required as a foundation for practice, and (c) the need for psychology to demand more responsibility from training programs that prepare people who claim to be psychologists. These programs should be in departments of psychology or in integrated programs that meet APA standards.

Related to this is psychology's vulnerability to lawsuits and "legislative infringements" on the practice of psychology as a result of the increasingly wide range of graduate programs and of varied criteria for legal recognition. Because of the heterogeneity of both education and credentials, it is difficult for psychology to mount an effective defense. One solution is to establish a national set of minimal educational standards for certification or licensure.

In the second half of the decade of the seventies continuing educational activities for psychologists have assumed major importance. The growing interest is reflected in the activity of APA Division 12's (Clinical Psychology) Section II, which has its own Newsletter, *Continuing Professional Development,* and the activity of the new Continuing Education Task Force of the APA Education and Training Board (Note 1). In a working draft (APA, Note 1), the latter group calls on the profession for a commitment to "the development of competency assessment techniques" (p. 6). Psychologists would have the option of "documenting continuing education as one track and competency assessment as the second track" (APA, Note 1, p. 6). The purposes are laudatory—the ways to realize them are not identified.

The Committee on Continuing Education of the American Association of State Psychology Boards (Note 5) argues that licensure or certification is not enough to ensure the continuing competence of the professional psychologist to perform professional duties at the highest possible level. The committee further argues that these laws only set minimum standards for initial credentialing very largely based on the study of subject matter. Only with continuing education in psychology can competence be maintained. It has developed a model law for continuing education in psychology. Increasingly states have required documented evidence of continuing education in order to renew or maintain the license of the practitioner. Efforts of other state psychological associations to encourage their members to engage in continuing education are reported in the American Association of State Psychology Board's publication.

Persons who have examined the continuing education requirements of various professions generally agree that these provide only the structure for learning and cannot guarantee content. A requirement that psychologists show evidence of various kinds of continuing education cannot guarantee that new knowledge and improved competence results. This leads, of course, to the need to develop procedures for evaluating continuing education programs and their effects.

After a psychologist has obtained a license from a state psychology licensing board, has attended continuing education programs, and in some cases has obtained an ABPP specialty diploma, a process that may take many years, there is still need for continuing review of the quality of the person's individual practice.

The question of whether to establish a review process has been made academic by recent history. As a result of the need to control costs, both private insurers and the federal government (who pay for much of the health care in the country and who may soon pay for psychological services) have established ways of reviewing services provided by medicine. Psychology cannot be far behind. The mechanism at first was a voluntary system of peer review in medicine. Subsequently in 1972, the federal government mandated the development of peer review organizations. Prior to 1972 traditional evaluation of medical services included ethical practices boards, utilization review committees, tissue review committees in hospitals, etc.

The federal government obviously concluded that these mechanisms were not sufficient to provide adequate review, especially for services to the large number of poor and elderly who were newly covered under Medicare and Medicaid programs. In 1972, over the opposition of the American Medical Association (AMA), the U.S. Congress passed amendments to the Social Security Act (the amendments were contained in Public Law 92-603) calling for the establishment of Professional Standards Review Organizations (PSROs). The PSROs were to be designed to insure that (a) services conform to appropriate professional standards, (b) payment is made only when the service is necessary, and (c) inpatient services are used only when outpatient treatment will not accomplish the desired purpose (Langsley, 1973).

This government "intrusion" into the practice of medicine was met with anger and opposition. The AMA tried to delete the PSRO provisions from the legislation, but it was unable to accomplish this; it was able to get some revisions into the bill including the requirement that only physicians may operate PSROs during the first two years of the program and including a provision that limited PSRO review of inpatient services. However, the bill stated that if physicians could not develop and approve PSROs by January 1976, other interested parties (i.e., nonphysicians) could apply for designation as the local PSRO (Sullivan, 1974). The AMA reluctantly decided to cooperate while at the same time mounting an ongoing effort to try to get the law changed.

We have cited this brief legislative history to make the point that if professions are unwilling to take responsibility for monitoring their own practices, others are going to be asked to do it for them. In fact, even if professions do monitor performance, unless the monitoring system is effective, they will be subject to outside control. Obviously one way to avoid this kind of outside interference is not to accept insurance payments from the federal government.

Where has psychology been while all this has been going on? Not far behind, and some say in front of, the bandwagon. In 1968 guidelines for the establishment of insurance review committees were drawn up by the APA Committee on Health Insurance (COHI) in consultation with the Health Insurance Council, and by 1971, 10 regional review committees for psychology had been established. In 1972 there was a special meeting jointly sponsored by the Board of Professional Affairs, the Regional Review Committees and COHI that dealt with two topics—problems arising during the use of the regional review committees and issues emerging from the participation of psychologists in AETNA's insurance plan for federal employees. (See McMillan (1974) for a discussion of this meeting and a history of the review committees.) Two recommendations emerged from the meeting: (a) that the Board of Professional Affairs establish a task force on peer review committees, and (b) that a national network of review committees, sponsored by state and local organizations, be established.

The Board of Professional Affairs did indeed establish a task force on review committees, which became, in due course, the Committee on Professional Standards Review. This task force promulgated guidelines for review committees and produced, in 1975, the *Procedures Manual for Professional Standards Review Committees* of state psychological associations (APA, 1975). To quote from the manual, "The Professional Standards Review Committee (PSRC) is a mechanism by which the consumer or third-party payer (private insurance carriers, governmental agencies, etc.) can have questionable claims or practices investigated" (APA, 1975, p. 2).

The PSRCs, established by the state psychological organizations, are to provide service to psychologists, clients, and third-party payers. "Typically (PSRCs) are asked to render opinions as to whether a practice or procedure in question is 'usual, customary, or reasonable'" (APA, 1975, p. 2). And they are expected to render opinions about whether the services were needed, were of professional quality, were appropriate and whether the charges were usual, customary, or reasonable.

While APA has established other guidelines for professional practice (e.g., the Code of Ethics and the Standards for Providers of Psychological Services), the PSRC is the single organization (if it functions appropriately and if the insurance carriers use it) that will monitor on a regular basis psychological practice. While some psychologists may object to such a review, they should remember that self-regulation is preferable to imposition of external controls. The manual tries to delineate procedures that will be fair to all types of psychological practice and to all theoretical positions.

Another question that arises inevitably is, How will the PSRCs relate to the PSROs? The PSROs are supposed to establish peer review committees for health care providers other than physicians. APA hopes, naturally, that the PSROs will adopt the already established PSRCs as the peer review committee for psychological services. As Congress accepted that PSROs should be controlled by physicians (for a while anyway), psychology once again finds itself in the position of supplicant to the medical profession. Perhaps in those Department of Health, Education, and Welfare areas in which none exists, the PSRC can be designated the PSRO.

Before people start overreacting about the negative effects of peer review, we would like them to have the benefit of reading some of the reactions within the psychiatric community to the establishment of the PSROs. The *American Journal of Psychiatry* had a special section on the PSROs (December, 1974, pp. 1354–1388). We also refer interested psychologists to the 1974 issue of *Psychiatric Opinion*. Surprisingly, there have even been some articles favorable to peer review systems. For example, Newman and Luft (1974) present the experience of a privately practicing group of psychiatrists, psychologists, and social workers in establishing a review procedure for a system that was fiscally out of control. Their control system rapidly became a quality control system—something they say is bound to happen with peer review and a desirable outcome.

In spite of licensing and specialty certification (McNamara, 1975), for the near future peer review seems to be how psychological practice will be evaluated. At first only contested fees are going to be reviewed, but as experience develops, more stringent intervention requirements will be established. And as the government moves into this payment for services arena we can be sure of increased regulation. For example, the PSROs are supposed to develop patient and physician profiles and norms of care as well as diagnosis and treatment based on regional practices. Medical practitioners will be required to obtain prior approval for those patients who are to receive care beyond the 50th percentile of length of stay for patients in the same age group and with a similar diagnosis. We can look for similar restrictions on psychological practice.

As with most government regulations, things are not working quite as planned and adjustments will have to be made. But one thing is for sure, if psychologists get coverage under national health insurance they will also get peer review.

Reference Notes

1. American Psychological Association, Continuing Education Task Force. *Continuing education guidelines for the psychological profession.* Unpublished manuscript, 1976.
2. Williamson, J. W. *Validation by performance measures* (Conference report: Extending the validation certifica-

tion). Chicago: American Board of Medical Specialties, 1976.
3. Solomon, S. T. Personal communication, February 1977.
4. Wellner, A. *Education and credentialing in psychology.* (Preliminary report of a meeting, June 16–17, 1976). Washington, D.C.: American Psychological Association, 1976.
5. American Association of State Psychology Boards, Committee on Continuing Education. *Guidelines for accrediting continuing education in psychology.* Unpublished manuscript, 1976.

References

Albee, G. W. The protestant ethic, sex, and psychotherapy. *American Psychologist,* 1977, *32,* 150–161.

Albee, G. W., & Loeffler, E. Role conflicts in psychology and their implications for a reevaluation of training models. *Canadian Psychologist,* 1971, *12,* 465–481.

American Psychological Association. Procedures manual for professional standards review committees of state psychological associations. Washington, D.C.: Author, 1975.

American Psychological Association. Revised ethical standards of psychologists. *APA Monitor,* March 1977, pp. 22–23.

American Psychological Association, Committee on Ethical Standards in Psychological Research. *Ethical principles in the conduct of research with human participants.* Washington, D.C.: Author, 1973.

American Psychological Association, Committee on Legislation. A model for state legislation affecting the practice of psychology 1967. *American Psychologist,* 1967, *22,* 1095–1103.

American Psychological Association, Committee on Standards for Providers of Psychological Services. *Revised standards for providers of psychological services.* Washington, D.C.: Author, 1977.

Campbell, D. T. Assessing the impact of planned social change. In G. Lyons (Ed.), *Social research and public policy.* Hanover, N.H.: The Public Affairs Center of Dartmouth University and the University Press of New England, 1975.

Council for the National Register of Health Service Providers in Psychology. *National register of health service providers in psychology.* Washington, D.C.: Author, 1976.

Langsley, D. G. Peer review: Prospects and problems. *American Journal of Psychiatry,* 1973, *130,* 301–304.

McMillan, J. Peer review and professional standards for psychologists rendering personal health services. *Professional Psychology,* 1974, *5,* 51–58.

McNamara, J. R. An assessment proposal for determining the competence of professional psychologists. *Professional Psychology,* 1975, *6,* 135–139.

Meehl, P. E. *Clinical versus statistical prediction.* Minneapolis: University of Minnesota Press, 1954.

Newman, D. E., & Luft, L. L. The peer review process: Education versus control. *American Journal of Psychiatry,* 1974, *131,* 1363–1366.

Phillips, L. The competence criterion for mental health programs. *Community Mental Health Journal,* 1967, *3,* 73–76.

Ross, A. O. ABPP: In pursuit of excellence. *The Clinical Psychologist,* 1970, *23*(3), 1–3.

Sanazaro, P. J., & Williamson, J. W. The end result of patient care: A provisional classification based on reports by internists. *Medical Care,* 1968, *6,* 123–130.

Sanazaro, P. J., & Williamson, J. W. Physician performance and its effects on patients: A classification based on reports by internists, surgeons, pediatricians, and obstetricians. *Medical Care,* 1970, *8,* 299–308.

Sullivan, F. W. Professional standards review organizations: The current scene. *American Journal of Psychiatry,* 1974, *131,* 1354–1358.

Terris, L. D. The national licensing examination. *Professional Psychology,* 1973, *4,* 386–391.

Wheelis, A. *The quest for identity.* New York: Norton, 1958.

At the time of original publication of this article, *George W. Albee* and *Marc Kessler* were members of the faculty of the Department of Psychology, University of Vermont, Burlington.

An Argument for Mental Patient Advisory Boards

James K. Morrison

It is suggested that psychologists and psychologist administrators in the field of community mental health can no longer dismiss the importance and the need for consumer evaluations of their services.

Although cogent arguments have been presented for the creation of citizen community mental health boards (Robins & Blackburn, 1974; Rooney, 1968; National Association of Social Workers, Note 1), no one has yet advocated advisory boards composed of the actual consumers, that is, the psychiatric clients. Perhaps this parochialism in thinking derives in part from the traditional construing of the mental patient as somewhat bizarre and ineffectual (Arieti, 1959; Bellak, 1958; Joint Commission on Mental Illness and Health, 1961; Schooler & Parkel, 1966; Searles, 1965). In fact, according to Sarbin (1969), the mental patient, especially the "psychotic," is often viewed as a "non-person." If this perception of the mental patient is common in the field of mental health, it is not surprising that professionals in the field have not seriously considered establishing advisory boards composed of such patients.

It is the contention of proponents of a radical psychosocial model (Braginsky, Braginsky, & Ring, 1969; Laing, 1972; Sarbin & Mancuso, 1970; Szasz, 1961, 1970a, 1970b) that mental patients are persons with "problems in living," who, despite the stigma attached to the patient "sick role" (Parsons, 1951; Petroni, 1972), are capable of social sensitivity in their intelligent use of impression management to attain desired goals. Patients' perception of and evaluation of others are at times surprisingly more accurate than that of psychiatric professionals (cf. Rosenhan, 1973). The disenfranchisement of mental patients from society is often based on the false assumption that they are incompetent in all areas of human activity. However, studies such as the one by Klein and Grossman (1968) indicate that patients are competent in at least certain areas (e.g., voting) of functioning.

If mental patients are actually quite capable persons, why are they so seldom consulted? It is true that therapeutic communities (Daniels & Rubin, 1968; Mardikian & Glick, 1969) have informally solicited patients' opinions at community meetings. However, in such settings clients have no clear authority to formally evaluate treatment programs, the staff, or the clinic setting in general. In spite of the hypothesized risks involved in giving patients more control over their treatment, Darley (1974) and Weitz (1972) have argued that this type of patient involvement would foster the kind of independent role functioning that mental health professionals hope to encourage in clients. The case for client advisory boards is actually a logical extension of this type of reasoning.

But if patients are to become advisory board members and if they are then to act more maturely and more responsibly, they must be viewed and treated as reasonably intelligent persons capable of such behavior. If being a mental patient is, at least in part, a learned role (Becker, 1962; Erikson, 1957; Goffman, 1961; Lemert, 1962; Scheff, 1966; Szasz, 1970a, 1970b), then such a negatively valued role can be unlearned (Morrison, 1974; Morrison, Fasano, Becker, & Nevid, Note 2) and more

Reprinted from *Professional Psychology*, 1976, 7, 127–131.

positively valued roles (e.g., an evaluator of treatment, a spokesman for fellow clients, etc.) learned. But such learning will not take place in an atmosphere in which the expectations of behavior change are minimal. And certainly, client boards will not be effective in facilities in which the staff have not begun to view clients as capable of higher level functioning.

It has already been argued that one of the obstacles to the establishment of client advisory boards is the outmoded traditional view of the client as incompetent, strange, and irresponsible. Another obstacle to the creation of such boards is the fear on the part of many mental health professionals that patients would unilaterally evaluate a facility's programs in a very negative fashion if given the opportunity to evaluate those programs. However, a study by Mayer and Rosenblatt (1974) suggests that when given the opportunity, mental patients express a more positive view of a mental health facility's programs than do the mental health professionals who work there. Other professionals may fear that clients will attempt to take over the running of the clinic. But one study (Fanning, Deloughery, & Gebbie, 1972) of patient attitudes has suggested that patients have no real desire to take over the control of mental health facilities.

The following suggestions for the establishment of a client advisory board derive from the author's experience in establishing such a board. Because the specific structure of this board was designed for its appropriateness to a relatively small community mental health team (8 staff members, 70 psychiatric after-care patients), the suggestions that follow are general so as not to exclude their application to a variety of settings.[1]

Preliminary Meetings

Before establishing a client board, it is useful to call five or six preliminary meetings of staff and clients in order to solicit the opinions of staff, and especially of clients, about the optimal structure and composition of such a board. Both staff and clients can be rotated through such meetings until all of the staff and a representative sample of patients have had the opportunity to voice their opinions. These preliminary meetings will introduce many clients to the concept of client responsibility for treatment. For many patients it will be the first time they have been asked for their opinions about the services they receive. This kind of experience offers clients a better idea of what an advisory board will be like and thus should facilitate a decision on the part of patients as to whether they should become involved in such a board in the future.

Initial Proposal for an Advisory Board

After soliciting ideas from at least 15% of the client population, a proposal for the structure and composition of the board can be drawn up. This document should represent the mainstream of client and staff opinion. The following are some of the specific variables that should be considered in the general proposal for the client board: (a) the number of clients composing the board; (b) the type of board members (e.g., "regular" or "rotating"); (c) the length of term for each member; (d) the authority, tasks, and responsibilities of the client board, and of each specific member (e.g., various officers); (e) procedures for electing members to the board; (f) procedures for substitutions because of sickness, discharge, etc.; (g) training of board members related to tasks and responsibilities; (h) frequency, time, and place of meetings; (i) the number and type of staff to meet with the client board; and (j) evaluation of the effectiveness of the board.

This proposal should be agreed upon, in some form, by both the staff and the elected client board as its first order of business. One should expect that the original proposal will undergo at least one revision before it is accepted by both clients and staff.

Election of Board Members

It would seem reasonable to make eligible for election to board membership only those clients who are actually willing to serve on the board. To have all the clients in a facility elect the most popular or most vocal client accomplishes noth-

---

[1] Specific details related to the client advisory board created by the author and his staff can be obtained from the author upon request.

ing if that client does not want to become a board member. And if in many community settings it is almost impossible to hold a general election by all clients, one may opt for an alternative. That is, one could announce an informal get-together or party for all clients willing to serve in any capacity on such a board. During this get-together, the volunteers for the board could become better acquainted and thus vote more meaningfully for those volunteers who can most adequately represent them. At this party-election, clients can express in "campaign speeches" why the board would be important for them and what they would do for clients if elected. Volunteers for the board can be originally ascertained by soliciting the total client population by letter, telephone, or both.

Conclusion

In spite of the obstacles to creating a client advisory board, I believe that such boards can be successfully established and that their advantages far outweigh the disadvantages. It makes sense for the actual consumers of services to have more say about the quantity, quality, and delivery of those services. It also seems eminently reasonable for these consumers to have a forum in which to evaluate staff effectiveness. And with some training, the client board members will be able to devise methods of evaluating services and programs. If as I have argued, the mental patient is a much more responsible and capable person than we have traditionally construed him or her to be, then psychologists and psychologist administrators in the field of mental health can no longer ethically postpone involving the consumer client in further responsibility related to his or her treatment. From the author's personal experience with a client board, there are few better methods of inducing a client toward independent responsibility, self-confidence, and a secure feeling for once of some control over his or her life.

Reference Notes

1. National Association of Social Workers. *Position statement on community mental health.* Washington, D.C.: Author, 1968. (Mimeo)

2. Morrison, J. K., Fasano, B. L., Becker, R. E., & Nevid, J. S. *Changing the "manipulative-dependent" role performance of psychiatric patients in the community.* Manuscript submitted for publication, 1975.

References

Arieti, S. *American handbook of psychiatry.* New York: Basic Books, 1959.

Becker, E. Socialization, command of performance and mental illness. *American Journal of Sociology,* 1962, *67,* 494–501.

Bellak, L. *Schizophrenia: A review of the syndrome.* New York: Logos Press, 1958.

Braginsky, B., Braginsky, D., & Ring, K. *Methods of madness.* New York: Holt, Rinehart & Winston, 1969.

Daniels, D., & Rubin, R. S. The community meetings: An analytical study and a theoretical statement. *Archives of General Psychiatry,* 1968, *18,* 60–75.

Darley, P. J. Who shall hold the conch? Some thoughts on community control of mental health programs. *Community Mental Health Journal,* 1974, *10,* 185–191.

Erikson, K. T. Patient roles and social uncertainty—a dilemma of the mentally ill. *Psychiatry,* 1957, *20,* 263–272.

Fanning, V. L., Deloughery, G. L., & Gebbie, K. M. Patient involvement in planning own care: Staff and patient attitudes. *Journal of Psychiatric Nursing and Mental Health Services,* 1972, *10,* 5–8.

Goffman, E. *Asylums: Essays on the social situation of mental patients and other inmates.* Garden City, N.Y.: Doubleday, 1961.

Joint Commission on Mental Illness and Health. *Action for mental health.* New York: Basic Books, 1961.

Klein, M. M., & Grossman, S. A. Voting competence and mental illness. *Proceedings of the 76th Annual Convention of the American Psychological Association,* 1968, *3,* 701–702. (Summary)

Laing, R. D. *The politics of the family and other essays.* New York: Vintage Books, 1972.

Lemert, E. M. Paranoia and the dynamics of exclusion. *Sociometry,* 1962, *25,* 2–20.

Mardikian, B., & Glick, I. D. Patient-staff meetings: A study of some aspects of content, tone, and speakers. *Mental Hygiene,* 1969, *53,* 303–305.

Mayer, J. E., & Rosenblatt, A. Clash in perspective between mental patients and staff. *American Journal of Orthopsychiatry,* 1974, *44,* 432–441.

Morrison, J. K. Labeling: A study of an "autistic" child. *Journal of Family Counseling,* 1974, *2,* 71–80.

Parsons, T. *The social system.* Glencoe, Ill.: Free Press, 1951.

Petroni, F. A. Correlates of the psychiatric sick role. *Journal of Health and Social Behavior,* 1972, *13,* 47–54.

Robins, A. J., & Blackburn, C. Governing boards in mental health: Roles and training needs. *Administration in Mental Health,* 1974, *3,* 37–45.

Rooney, H. L. Roles and functions of the advisory board. *North Carolina Journal of Mental Health,* 1968, *3,* 33–43.

Rosenhan, D. L. On being sane in insane places. *Science,* 1973, *179,* 250–258.

Sarbin, T. The scientific status of the mental illness metaphor. In S. C. Plog & R. B. Edgerton (Eds.), *Changing perspectives in mental illness.* New York: Holt, Rinehart & Winston, 1969.

Sarbin, T., & Mancuso, J. C. The failure of a moral enterprise: Attitudes of the public toward mental illness. *Journal of Consulting and Clinical Psychology,* 1970, *35,* 159–173.

Scheff, T. J. *Being mentally ill: A sociological theory.* Chicago: Aldine, 1966.

Schooler, C., & Parkel, D. The overt behavior of chronic schizophrenics and the relationship to their internal state and personal history. *Psychiatry,* 1966, *29,* 67–77.

Searles, H. *Collected papers on schizophrenia and related subjects.* New York: International Universities Press, 1965.

Szasz, T. *The myth of mental illness.* New York: Hoeber-Harper, 1961.

Szasz, T. *Ideology and insanity.* New York: Doubleday, 1970. (a)

Szasz, T. *The manufacture of madness.* New York: Delta, 1970. (b)

Weitz, W. A. Experiencing the role of a hospitalized psychiatric patient: A professional's view from the other side. *Professional Psychology,* 1972, *3,* 151–154.

At the time of original publication of this article, *James K. Morrison* was a team leader with the Capital District Psychiatric Center, Cohoes, New York.

The author would like to express his appreciation to the staff and clients of his clinic for their support of the client advisory board.

7

Issues in Professional Training

There has been continuing debate during the last 30 years over the "best" model for training professional psychologists. In 1949, the Conference on Graduate Education in Clinical Psychology was held in Boulder, Colorado, to establish a basic model of professional training. It produced a model that put central emphasis on the scientific aspect of the scientist-professional model. Training in research was stressed, and an emphasis on theory was intended to provide the means by which students would organize their study and evaluate their techniques. The "Boulder" Conference also gave added impetus to the development of ethical principles and standardized accreditation criteria.

A series of conferences on professional training in psychology took place over the next 24 years. In 1973, the National Conference on Levels and Patterns of Professional Training in Psychology was held in Vail, Colorado. This conference explicitly endorsed the professional model of training for health service psychologists, without abandoning comprehensive psychological science as the substantive and methodological base of such training, and without depreciating the value of the scientist training model and the scientist-professional training model for achieving other objectives. The "Vail" model was incorporated as part of the APA accreditation criteria in 1979, although not to the exclusion of the other models.

The scientist-professional training model and the professional training model are very different. The scientist-professional model instills a highly critical attitude. It focuses on methodology, empirical assessment, and statistical analysis of professional practices and theoretical beliefs. It teaches a skeptical attitude toward knowledge—accepting only that which is clearly proven and reserving final judgment on issues that have neither been empirically proven or disproven. In contrast, the professional model focuses on the effective application of technical skills toward a particular outcome. Observation and discussion of the professional efforts of others and observation and review of one's own professional activities are more central to training. It teaches a practical attitude toward knowledge—accepting that which is theoretically and technically reasonable and has not been empirically disproven.

At the present time, it is clear that organized psychology has accepted a de facto two-model system of professional training. Thus, professional psychologists are trained in a variety of settings. These include freestanding professional schools, university-based professional schools, training programs in psychology departments, and training programs in medical schools. Either model could be used in each setting, and, in some cases, both models are used within the same department in parallel training programs. We know both models work. We have bright, innovative, clinically sensitive, and effective health service providers who are products of both of those systems of training.

We doubt that there is a single ideal model for training. We believe that any national policy regarding the training of mental health professionals should explicitly plan for a range of heterogeneous training models. The best way to promote growth and innovation is through the use of a variety of training models within the overall system. A single concept and process of training can only lead to stagnation.

Improvement should be sought, even within a multiple-model system of professional training. This requires continuing evaluation and assessment of the training system and the individuals trained under the different models. Within psychology, many training issues are still unanswered. The recent proliferation of professional schools has been a reaction to the perception that the traditional scientist-professional training programs did not offer enough practical experience. Was it an overreaction? Do professional schools now offer too little theory and too little research training?

What is the right blend of research training, practical clinical training, and theoretical training to produce a professional who is responsive and adaptive to change, and who, in fact, provokes it? What should be the nature of the scientific training provided to health service providers in psychology? Although they conduct research of various types, few psychological service providers publish scientific research articles. In such cases, how critical is it for all professional psychologists to be trained as scientists or research initiators? Perhaps their scientific training should be geared toward making them knowledgeable consumers of scientific information. Would such a change in training alter the career patterns and career flexibility of professional psychologists?

Psychologists trained in each philosophy are clearly needed. We do need more psychologists involved directly in the delivery of human service and with greater pragmatic training in the day-to-day activities of the practicing professional. The national need for services is there, and psychology must play its role in addressing it. We also obviously will continue to need the scientist-practitioner—advancing knowledge, challenging current practices, demanding and producing evidence regarding our collective assumptions of practice.

The intended advantages and obvious disadvantages of each model of training can be stated. The unintended consequences (both positive and negative) of different training circumstances can only be determined by research—by examination of the subsequent clinical effectiveness and career patterns of psychologists with different training backgrounds. For example, does geographic distribution differ for professionals trained in university-based programs and those trained in freestanding professional programs? How do the career patterns of professional psychologists trained within medical schools differ from those trained in psychology department programs? These are just a few of the unanswered questions about our current methods of training professional psychologists.

While organized psychology can play a large role in shaping the training of professional psychologists and assuring the quality of that training, professional training occurs in a real world where many factors affect the nature and quality of training. National health insurance and the specific nature of the mental health benefit package will have considerable impact on future training in psychology. If national health insurance is universal and outpatient mental health benefits are excluded, the number and type of psychologist health service providers trained will be seriously affected. If mental health benefits of a particular nature are included, professional training will undoubtedly be induced to emphasize that type of service.

As discussed in the introduction to Section 2, the federal role in the training of health and mental health providers has been questioned. While the 1978 ADAMHA Manpower Policy Analysis Task Force has recommended continued federal support of mental health training, it also recommended a general redirection of federal policy on human resources. The task force suggested that federal training funds be "targeted" in such a manner as to produce mental health professionals specialized in treating those underserved or inappropriately serviced (i.e., children, youth, elderly, women, minorities) and/or especially trained for service in particular service settings (i.e., rural areas, center-city areas).

How broadly or narrowly "targeted support" is defined will greatly influence training. Federal policy is rapidly losing sight of the critical importance of systematic core-training in mental health. Specialized training or retraining needs to be based on a systematic core of basic professional training. Federal funds for targeted training will be most efficiently utilized and effective in accomplishing their intended goals if they build on a general foundation of professional training. If only specialized and technical clinical training is funded, the professionals developed will soon be of narrow expertise and skill. Moreover, most mental health professionals work in several specialty areas over their career. Narrow training would require costly and time-consuming retraining. It is imperative that the implementation of targeted training not produce second-class professionals to serve those currently underserved or unserved.

If the federal government were to withdraw support for the training of mental health professionals, the nature of professional training and the setting of such training would obviously change. In the absence of support, there would probably be a further acceleration in the growth of professional schools of psychology. The "professional" model of training might well become the only model for training health service providers in psychology. The practice of psychology would become as far removed from its scientific base of research as is psychiatry. The persons applying for training would also undoubtedly change as much as the nature of the training. Tuition would surely escalate. Enrollment of minorities, women, and low-income students would probably decrease. The role of theory and research training would deteriorate. Practical experience and supervision would receive even more emphasis than they currently do in professional schools, and science would likely become more peripheral. How these changes would affect the unmet mental health needs that already exist is unclear, but they would not be expected to lessen them.

The articles in this section describe the current status of the training of professional psychologists as well as some of the current issues. Excerpts from the recommendations of the Vail Conference provide a perspective on the most recent statement regarding training. Hess's article discusses educational preparation in professional psychology and its relation to state licensing laws. Hess also describes the national exam often used as part of the licensing process, the Examination of Professional Practice in Psychology.

Kiesler, in an article originally published as an editorial in the *American Psychologist,* describes some of the strengths and weaknesses in the training of psychiatrists and psychologists and concludes that psychologists have some real strengths that could be better utilized within the mental health field. In a second paper, Kiesler describes some of the needs and problems in the training of professional psychologists and emphasizes the necessity for continued involvement with scientific psychology, more extensive training relative to organized systems of care, experience in a variety of practice settings, and greater knowledge of health care psychology. In a similar vein, Saccuzzo notes the trends in psychotherapy away from the one-to-one model into new roles and new approaches. He highlights advances in social and physiological psychology that have direct implications for therapeutic interventions and implies that the rate of advances in scientific psychology will pose a problem for professional psychologists in keeping abreast of the new techniques.

Wiggins and Schofield both describe how changing practice settings will change the practices of psychologists. Wiggins urges an integration of health and mental health services but stresses that such an integration would need a broadened definition of clinical psychology. He suggests including, "the psychological aspects of all conditions having adverse effects on the health of the individual," and, in support of his thesis, quotes the World Health Organization's definition of health as "a state of physical and mental well-being." Schofield urges psychologists to become more sophisticated regarding problems of physical health/illness and behavioral treatment, in light of the necessity of relating more closely with physicians in a variety of settings, including HMOs.

Training of Professional Psychologists: Excerpts of the Recommendations of the Vail Conference

American Psychological Association

The recommendations regarding training of the Vail Conference on Levels and Patterns of Professional Training in Psychology are presented. The conference endorsed a professional training model for practitioners, with comprehensive psychological science forming the core of such training. The scientist-practitioner model was acknowledged as of continuing value but for different objectives.

The conference made recommendations for all training programs (in medical schools, colleges of education, university departments of psychology, and autonomous professional institutions) regarding setting, doctoral training, curricula, research, accreditation, and continuing education. Specific criteria were also set for provision of services to and by minority populations.

A national conference on the levels and patterns of professional training in psychology was held in July of 1973 in Vail, Colorado. The proceedings of that conference, generally referred to as the Vail Conference, were edited by Maurice Korman, and published in 1975 by the American Psychological Association. This paper consists of excerpts from the recommendations of the conference. These recommendations provide a perspective on the range, quality and relevance of clinical and research training of professional psychologists.

The Vail Conference represented a major reevaluation of the training of professional psychologists. Almost 120 individuals representing a range of interests and expertises were invited to participate. This included 14 trainees in psychology, 36 minority-group members (29 male, 7 female), and 40 women. Administrators, educators, scientists, and practitioners were involved.

The Vail Conference acknowledged that psychology had "come of age." It explicitly endorsed the professional training model as the primary model to guide programs unambiguously defining themselves as training psychological practitioners. This was a landmark decision. It was made *without* abandoning comprehensive psychological science as the substantive and methodological core of such train-

ing, and *without* depreciating the value of the scientist model or scientist-practitioner model for training programs with different objectives. It is the judgment of this task force that the development of psychological science has sufficiently matured to justify creation of explicit professional programs, in addition to programs for training scientists and scientist-professionals.

The task group recognizes the variety of new organizational settings within which professional training programs have begun to develop: for example, medical schools; departments, schools, and colleges of education; free-standing schools of professional psychology, and autonomous professional schools in academic settings in addition to departments of psychology in universities. The task group also recognizes the influence of the administrative and organizational setting upon the quality and effectiveness of the professional training program. Rather than seeking to define the variety of potential new settings for the development of professional training, we chose to set forth the following criteria that any setting should meet in order to plan effectively and conduct professional training in psychology.

These criteria are applicable to any specialty area in the field of psychology involved in professional training, for example, school, clinical, or social.

From Maurice Korman (Ed.), *Levels and Patterns of Professional Training in Psychology* (Vail Conference). Washington, D.C.: American Psychological Association, 1976.

We offer the following recommendations:

A. Settings and Criteria

1. The content of professional practice and training shall be rooted ideologically and theoretically in comprehensive psychological science with regard to both substance and methodology.
2. Principles of affirmative action
   a. Settings for professional training shall include ethnic minorities and women at all levels of the training enterprise, that is, administration, faculty, students, and field experiences.
   b. Persons in adjunct roles or at lower levels of professional training shall have the option and assurance of potentially receiving the training necessary to perform at all levels.
3. Minority client involvement
   a. Services in which professional training and practice are provided shall be congruent with the needs of the full range of clients of the community.
   b. The process of program evaluation shall include ethnic minorities and women clients as equal participants.
4. The value of professional service and training for its own sake shall be reaffirmed by administrators at all levels who are responsible for the operation and financial support of the program.
5. In order to insure a continuing professional emphasis throughout the program, the director and a significant proportion of the voting faculty shall consist of psychologists actively and currently engaged in professional services.
6. The policies governing employment conditions of faculty members shall attach equal weight to performance of professional service and training, theoretical and basic research, and other scholarly activities.
7. Financial support for professional training shall be sufficient in amount and dependably available from the sponsoring institution.
8. The training program shall include a significant proportion of field experience at all training levels, and field experiences shall be integrated with theoretical and didactic education throughout the course of study.
9. Evaluation of the program shall be conducted systematically and regularly (no less than annually) by faculty, students, and client representatives involved in and affected by the program.
10. Institutions involved in professional training have a responsibility to maximize student program completion. Students and faculty need appropriate financial, academic, and psychological support systems. This responsibility and these support systems shall be criteria for all training settings. Examples of such support systems include relevance of curriculum, access to appropriate role models, provision for redress of grievances, and nondiscriminatory treatment.

    In setting forth these criteria for settings within which professional training programs can develop, there is no intent to constrain departments of psychology in universities or other settings from seeking to provide or continuing to provide types of educational preparation or training other than professional, for example, scientist-professional training, research, or other scholarly activities.
11. We further recommend to funding agencies that support of professional training programs be dependent upon fulfillment of these criteria by the settings within which the training programs are located.
12. We also recommend to APA that accreditation criteria for professional training programs be modified and expanded to include these criteria regarding settings.

B. Doctoral Training

In general, we recommend that doctoral training programs broaden the range and nature of core academic courses and professional training requirements. These modifications can and should be accomplished without sacrificing standards for educating students in the fundamentals of behavioral science.

More specifically:

1. We recommend that each graduate program requirement be examined for its functional

relationship to the role of the professional psychologist in light of existing social needs and ethical issues; that nonfunctional requirements be modified or deleted; that these requirements be assessed relative to the assurance that students acquire competence in the performance of professional activities.

2. We recommend that doctoral programs undertake self-studies to insure that basic academic teaching conforms with these recommendations and that specific solutions for existing deficits be developed.

3. We recommend that doctoral students participate in the shaping of their curriculum, possibly through arranging specific academic contracts with faculty advisers.

4. With regard to practicum and internship training, we recommend:

   a. That the content of professional experiences be diversified and broadened to incorporate the development of a variety of specific job skills not traditionally included in doctoral training programs, such as administrative skills, program development and evaluation, and field research.

   b. That professional programs be encouraged to have professional experiences organized in not only traditional but also nontraditional settings. This may be done despite the absence of psychologists on the staff of these institutions, provided the faculty insures that this constitutes a valuable professional experience (e.g., public school systems, Head Start programs, and community drug rehabilitation centers).

   c. That students be exposed to a continuous and varied range of relevant professional experiences beginning in the first year of graduate study. These experiences should be carefully integrated with core academic teaching.

5. We recommend that professional training programs be encouraged to consider the admission of less than full-time students. Such programs must review their offerings in the light of the special needs of part-time students, with a view toward removing constraints that may preclude the acceptance of part-time students into professional training.

6. We recommend that professional training programs develop and/or maintain linkages with service delivery systems extrinsic to the training program itself.

7. We recommend that professional training programs make an effort to provide relevant input to various regulatory agencies insofar as these agencies impinge upon professional training requirements.

8. Recognizing the special skills and preparation necessary for working in the area of child and/or developmental psychology, we recommend:

   a. The endorsement of the principles stated in the Chicago Conference relative to the inclusion of preparation in child and/or developmental psychology in all relevant training programs.

   b. The adoption of the recommendation that all professional training programs heighten the awareness of their graduates that it is unethical to offer professional services for which they are not specifically competent, and that the inclusion of either child, clinical child, school, or developmental psychology be an essential requirement for professional psychologists.

C. Training Programs

The following recommendations are submitted in recognition of the need of training programs for accurate program information, for improved student selection criteria and application procedures, and for the institution of evaluative feedback mechanisms. We recommend:

1. That this Conference go on record as being in full support of the resolution submitted by the Trainee Interest Group regarding the accurate description of graduate programs to prospective students. Furthermore, efforts should be made to ease the transferability of credits and candidacy when geographical changes occur due to family moves or similar events.

2. That alternative life-styles reflecting unpopular political or personal practices not be considered as disqualifying anyone for training or employment in psychology. APA should work to encourage legislation pro-

hibiting discrimination against persons for these reasons.

3. That it be recognized that the usual selection criteria for graduate admission, that is, grades and Graduate Record Examination (GRE) scores, have been inadequate in providing culturally diverse and socially responsive psychologists; that graduate selection committees give more consideration to the applicant's socially relevant experiences; that graduate schools admit a greater percentage of "nontraditional" students, who may not have the highest academic credentials yet may have sufficient academic ability to complete the program and may also have socially relevant experiences and goals.

4. That a unified application procedure be developed for applying to graduate programs in psychology, similar to the procedure now used in dentistry, law, and medicine, thereby making available a great deal of objective and self-report data without overburdening the applicant.

5. That each professional psychology program institute outcome evaluations and five-year follow-up evaluations of the adequacy of its training program in meeting its specified goals for professional training.

D. Human and Cultural Diversity

Recognizing that human and cultural diversity are important factors deserving our increased sensitivity and awareness, this task group submits the following recommendations:

1. That the provision of professional services to persons of culturally diverse backgrounds by persons not competent in understanding and providing professional services to such groups shall be considered unethical. It shall be equally unethical to deny such persons professional services because the present staff is inadequately prepared. It shall therefore be the obligation of all service agencies to employ competent persons or to provide continuing education for the present staff to meet the service needs of the culturally diverse population it serves.

2. That in order to counter both uneducated and educated arrogance regarding cultural diversity, both doctoral and continuing education programs include appropriate content. Seminars or courses on contemporary social issues and their historical perspectives could aid in developing an awareness of value differences in culturally diverse groups, as well as an awareness of the implications and issues these differences present in providing psychological services for such groups.

3. That provisions contained in Recommendations 1 and 2 above are equally applicable to women, children, elderly people, and other groups with special needs.

4. That graduate psychology programs appoint faculty from presently underrepresented groups, not only to meet affirmative action plans but also to benefit from the contributions such faculty can make to the understanding of human diversity.

5. That each graduate program develop a plan for the continuing education of its faculty, with special consideration given to continuing education in the psychological issues and the understanding of human and cultural diversity.

E. Research

Recognizing the need for a more flexible handling of research in graduate psychology programs, the following recommendations are submitted:

1. That all students in professional programs receive explicit education in the evaluation of the effectiveness of professional interventions; that existing courses be modified, or where necessary, new courses be developed to provide appropriate research content and methodology; that supervised experience in such research be provided for all students in professional programs.

2. That graduate psychology programs develop more flexible criteria for defining the appropriateness of dissertation proposals from doctoral students in professional psychology, in order to insure that the student's project be relevant to the professional role for which he or she is preparing.

3. That graduate psychology programs give serious consideration to the inclusion on

dissertation committees of psychologists or other competent persons from agencies and/or other campuses, who may be better qualified than the program faculty in the area of a given student's dissertation; that consideration be given to the appointment of faculty members presently excluded due to existing policies (such as those regarding tenure) as chairpersons of dissertation committees.

F. Quality Control and Accreditation

In the spirit of this redefinition of professionalization, which emphasizes a new or expanded accrediting process (such as a commission on accreditation) should be created to include not only the traditional representation from relevant groups within APA but also representatives from state psychological associations, students, and consumers. The accreditation process should focus on not only the quality of training but also the interrelationship of various settings. The effective practice of professional psychology is of considerable importance to the well-being of our society. The training of professional psychologists is therefore a matter of central concern to our profession.

Accreditation, as a method currently used by organized psychology to appraise professional training, is not able to fully evaluate the efficacy of training, the quality of graduates of such training, the value of the services to the ultimate recipient, or the nature and significance of the impact of training on society.

The proposal that follows rests on several assumptions:

1. Complete evaluation of a training program must include an evaluation not only of the content of the program but also of the graduates when they complete the program and at various points in their later careers.
2. The values underlying evaluative criteria must be determined by the profession as a whole rather than by the evaluators.
3. Although evaluation of a particular program by the profession as a whole is essential, it is only one part of the total evaluation process. Each program should build its own self-evaluation mechanisms.

4. In addition to the more obvious purposes of evaluation, feedback of evaluation results should be designed to benefit the training institution and the individuals evaluated.

G. Continuing Professional Development

This task force recognizes the need for a greater number of relevant experiences in continuing professional development (CPD) for all professional psychologists. The CPD experiences should address themselves to the needs of professional psychologists to update their knowledge and skills as well as to permit career changes for psychologists wishing to prepare themselves for new roles for which they were not specifically trained. In view of the knowledge explosion and emergence of new and socially important professional roles, participation in CPD activities is felt to be vital for all trainers of professional psychologists as well as practitioners.

The task force makes the following specific recommendations:

1. Institutions involved in the training of professional psychologists should be encouraged to establish or cooperate in programs of continuing education. While continuing education programs shall be an explicit function of the institution, CPD programs must encompass much broader resources than are often available within a single department (e.g., psychology). Multidisciplinary content and participation is essential if CPD programs are to be relevant to the role of professional psychology.
2. Formats of training need to be flexible so that CPD offerings can easily be attended by professional psychologists who are not able to become full-time students. Evening sessions, one- or two-day workshops and seminars, short-term apprenticeships, cable TV, and other technical innovations (e.g., tape cassettes) should be included.
3. In planning CPD activities, a distinction should be made between one-time offerings and planned sequences of educational experiences. The former are more suitable for professional psychologists who wish to stay informed about new developments, while the latter are more suitable for professional psy-

chologists who wish to prepare for new professional roles or functions.

4. Educational institutions need to devise ways and means of giving "credit" for participation in CPD activities. The question of the definition of a unit of CPD participation needs to be resolved. The definition of a CPD unit as consisting of 10 hours of participation might tentatively be suggested. The issue of equivalencies between CPD units and regular academic credit hours also needs to be dealt with by the educational institution.

5. Institutions offering CPD programs should have evaluative mechanisms built into their programs so that their effectiveness can be known. The evaluation of CPD programs offered by institutions with approved graduate training programs should be included in the accreditation process of the Education and Training Board, using the same standards and criteria that are applied to other aspects of the program.

6. An often unrecognized potential of CPD programs is that they provide a mechanism for the part-time training of students who may, for a variety of financial and personal reasons, be unable to be full-time students (e.g., members of ethnic groups, women, single parents). Institutions offering CPD programs should give serious consideration to the inclusion of such persons in the program and to the establishment of criteria, so that successful completion of CPD offerings can count toward the completion of degree requirements.

Entry Requirements for Professional Practice of Psychology

Harrie F. Hess

Applicants for licensure as professional psychologists frequently encounter frustration and disappointment caused by failure to pass the requirements for licensure. To avoid difficulties in the licensing process, potential licensees are advised to become thoroughly familiar with the requirements of the law in their jurisdictions, and to seek broad educational experiences equivalent to those available in APA-approved training and internship programs. The content of examinations for licensure is discussed, with particular attention to the Examination of Professional Practice in Psychology, the national examination prepared by the American Association of State Psychology Boards.

The American Association of State Psychology Boards (AASPB) has become increasingly concerned that students preparing for the professional practice of psychology be made aware of the legal requirements for entry into such practice. This article acquaints students with typical requirements for licensure or certification in the various jurisdictions in the United States and Canada. The AASPB hopes that an understanding of these requirements will enable the student to better meet the standards established by law to regulate the practice of psychology in the public interest.

What Is the American Association of State Psychology Boards?

The AASPB was formed in 1961 to serve a number of needs of state psychology boards throughout North America. One primary need fulfilled was the establishment of a standardized, written examination for professional practice in psychology, which could be used by all jurisdictions to examine candidates for licensure or certification. In addition, the AASPB also coordinates efforts of the various boards, facilitates communication among the boards, and acts as a voice for those responsible for the legal regulation of the practice of psychology.

What Is the Purpose of Licensure or Certification of Psychologists?[1]

The practice of professional psychology is now regulated by law in 49 of the 50 states of the United States, as well as in the District of Columbia and eight provinces of Canada.[2] The laws are intended to protect the public by limiting licensure to those persons who are qualified to practice psychology as defined by state law.

The legal basis for licensure lies in the right of the state to enact legislation to protect its citizens. *Caveat emptor,* or "buyer beware," is felt to be an unsound maxim when the "buyer" of services cannot be sufficiently well informed to beware, and therefore states have established regulatory boards to license qualified practitioners. A professional board is a state agency acting to protect the public, not to serve the profession. However, by insuring high standards for those who practice independently, the board is simultaneously serving the best in-

---

[1] When both the title and practice of psychology are regulated, the law is called a *licensing law*; when only the title of psychologist is regulated, the law is called a *certification law.* To avoid redundancy in the remainder of our discussion the word *licensure* will be used to stand for either licensure or certification.

[2] Throughout this text the term *state* will refer to Canada's provinces as well as political subdivisions of the United States.

Reprinted from *American Psychologist*, 1977, *32*, 365–368.

terests of both the public and the profession. The major functions of any professional board are (a) to determine the standards for admission into the profession and to administer appropriate procedures for selection and examination and (b) to regulate practice and to conduct disciplinary proceedings involving violation of standards of professional conduct embodied in the law.

Those who practice the profession of psychology in a research laboratory, in a state or federal institution or agency, or in a college or university are still exempt from the requirements of licensure in some states, although there is a trend toward requiring licensure of agency employees. The psychologist who offers direct services to the public for a fee must be licensed.

What Are Typical Requirements of Psychology Licensing Laws?

Licensing laws in the various jurisdictions differ considerably, yet most have a common core of agreement. Each board is the final authority on all matters of requirements within its jurisdiction and should be contacted for specifics. The typical requirements for licensure in the various jurisdictions are as follows:

1. *Education*: a doctoral degree in psychology from an approved program, or the equivalent as deemed by the board. The definitions of approved programs vary widely but often refer to accreditation of the academic institutions by recognized accrediting bodies. (Some states have two or more levels of licensure, with the lower level requiring less than the doctoral degree and entailing more restrictions on the practitioner.)

2. *Experience*: one or two years supervised experience in a setting approved by the state board. Most, but not all, states require that some of the supervised experience be postdoctoral.

3. *Examination*: demonstration of relevant knowledge by passing an objective written examination. The Examination of Professional Practice in Psychology, constructed by a committee of AASPB in association with the Professional Examination Service, is used in about 48 jurisdictions. The cutoff point for suc-

cessful performance on the examination is determined by the board having authority for the jurisdiction. In some states, successful performance is also required on an oral and/or essay examination conducted by the board or a committee designated by the board. Specialty examinations (e.g., in clinical psychology, industrial psychology, or school psychology) may become common in the near future.

4. *Administrative requirements*: in addition to the foregoing requirements, the various state laws specify different citizenship, age, and residency requirements, as well as requiring evidence of good moral character.

Stated succinctly, the major hurdles that any candidate will meet in the evaluation by the board are (a) the board's review of credentials (transcripts, applications, references) and (b) examination (written and/or oral). Most candidates successfully pass these hurdles, but some fail. Potential sources of difficulty are discussed in the next section.

How Should One Prepare to Successfully Meet the Requirements of Licensure?

Although well-prepared candidates have little or no problem with the licensing process, certain areas can be identified in which difficulties are most likely to occur. These potential problem areas are discussed below:

1. *Knowledge of the law and regulations*: The applicant should examine the law for the jurisdiction in which licensure is sought to assure that there has been full compliance with the law before an application is submitted. The applicant also should be familiar with, and comply with, any regulations of the board with respect to qualifications.

2. *Adequacy of training and/or experience*: The problems subsumed under this heading include a lack of the appropriate degree specified by law (usually a PhD in psychology); failure of the candidate to complete the required number of graduate hours in psychology; failure of the institution from which the degree was granted to meet the criteria for approval by the board; failure of the specific curriculum in which the student was enrolled to meet the re-

quirements of the particular state board. With regard to the last-mentioned criterion, most laws contain a stipulation that the graduate work be predominantly psychological in nature and the doctoral degree be based upon a dissertation that is psychological in content. It should also be noted that some jurisdictions require evidence of continuing education, beyond the PhD, for psychologists to retain their licenses.

In addition to these problems having to do with the nature of the candidate's education, each law specifies the duration of experience required, and each board stipulates the type of setting in which approved experience may be obtained. Typical of such approved settings are the APA-approved internship programs. Each candidate should plan for supervised experience that will satisfy the legal requirements for practice in the jurisdiction in which licensure is desired.

3. *Examination performance*: Successful performance in state licensing examinations usually requires demonstration of knowledge of basic psychology relevant to professional practice, along with knowledge of professional ethics and professional affairs. Although numerous factors are undoubtedly operative, probably the most frequent source of failure is the candidate's lack of sufficient knowledge of basic psychology. Candidates may also be disqualified in oral examinations because of insufficient knowledge about the management of professional problems, particularly ethical problems.

What Is the Content of the Examination of Professional Practice in Psychology?

In order to help the candidate to prepare for the Examination of Professional Practice in Psychology (EPPP), a separate brochure has been prepared by AASPB, and is available from AASPB, the Professional Examination Service, or the board of examiners in those jurisdictions using the exam. In the paragraphs below, the content of that examination is summarized briefly.

1. *Background knowledge*: physiological and comparative psychology, learning, history, theory and systems, sensation and perception, motivation, social psychology, personality, cog-

nitive processes, developmental psychology, psychopharmacology, and individual differences.

2. *Methodology*: research design and interpretation, statistics, test construction and interpretation, and scaling.

3. *Professional practice*: (a) clinical psychology: test usage and interpretation, diagnosis, psychopathology, therapy, judgment in clinical situations, and community health; (b) behavior modification: learning and applications; (c) other specialties: management consulting, industrial and organizational psychology, social psychology, T-groups, counseling and guidance, communications, systems analysis; (d) professional conduct, affairs, and ethics: interdisciplinary relations, and knowledge of professional affairs.

The EPPP is published in various forms, with new forms published periodically. The examination varies from 150 to 200 items in length. The content areas enumerated above are not equally weighted.

The requirements for licensure, delineated above, and the discussion of potential bases for denial suggest that the student who seeks out a broad and sophisticated background in psychology is likely to encounter few problems in the licensing process. The student should especially seek experiences that emphasize the application of psychological knowledge to problems likely to be encountered as a professional psychologist. Narrowly based training, avoiding the complexity of the field of psychology, is probably not in the student's best interest if professional practice is a goal. Cursory or limited supervision, or supervision by other than a qualified psychologist, is also likely to lead to deficiencies. Moreover, since psychologists tend to be mobile, a broad background acceptable to all or most boards is preferable to training narrowly designed to meet the requirements of a single jurisdiction. Students who have sought out educational experiences consistent with APA standards, and have taken training at recognized facilities of quality, rarely experience difficulty in obtaining licensure.

An Interstate Reporting Service has been established by the Professional Examination Service to facilitate mobility by permitting easier endorsement of licenses among states. The reporting service maintains a permanent record of examination scores on the EPPP for those candidates who choose to register. On the candidate's request, the service will report the score, accompanied by appropriate normative data, to the board of another state in which licensure is being sought.

Resources

It cannot be overemphasized that the final and absolute word concerning requirements for licensure in any state must be obtained from the specific board in question. Addresses for state boards are published each calendar year in the June *American Psychologist*. In addition to the individual boards, the following are other sources of information that may be of value to students and faculty:

American Association of State Psychology Boards
  c/o Morton Berger
  New York State Board for Psychology
  99 Washington Avenue, Room 1841
  Albany, New York 12230

American Psychological Association
  Office of Educational Affairs
  1200 Seventeenth Street, N.W.
  Washington, D.C. 20036

American Psychological Association
  Office of Professional Affairs
  1200 Seventeenth Street, N.W.
  Washington, D.C. 20036

Professional Examination Service
475 Riverside Drive
New York, New York 10027

Secretary of the State Board of Examiners, your state (see June *American Psychologist* for addresses).

APA-Approved Doctoral Programs in Clinical, Counseling, and School Psychology (published annually in the December *American Psychologist*).

APA-Approved Internships for Doctoral Training in Clinical and Counseling Psychology (published annually in the December *American Psychologist*).

Ethical Standards of Psychologists. *American Psychologist*, 1963, *18*, 56–60. (Amended 1965, 1972, and 1977.) Published and updated periodically by the American Psychological Association.

A model for state legislation affecting the practice of psychology 1967: Report of the APA Committee on Legislation. *American Psychologist*, 1967, *22*, 1095–1103.

A model for state legislation affecting the practice of psychology 1975. Committee on State Legislation, American Psychological Association, 1975. (Draft)

Standards for Providers of Psychological Services. Washington, D.C.: American Psychological Association, 1977.

Terris, L. D. The National Licensing Examination. *Professional Psychology*, 1973, *4*, 386–391.

At the time of original publication of this article, *Harrie F. Hess* was a member of the Executive Committee of the American Association of State Psychology Boards, and is presently Professor of Psychology at the University of Nevada, Las Vegas.

The information contained in this article is available in brochure form and can be obtained by writing AASPB or any state Board of Psychological Examiners.

The Training of Psychiatrists and Psychologists

Charles A. Kiesler

This editorial considers the nature of the training of psychologists and psychiatrists. The differences and similarities in training and competency are noted, and the importance and value of training in psychology are underscored.

Recently the President of the American Psychiatric Association testified before Congress that only psychiatrists should be considered qualified to receive reimbursement under national health insurance. His testimony is an example of a reentrenchment among many psychiatrists against the freedom of the patient to choose whether to receive treatment from a psychiatrist or a psychologist.

This point of view, not unusual these days among psychiatrists, has potentially very negative implications for psychologists, not only in freedom to practice but also in access to research and training funds. Presumably the argument rests on the assumption that psychiatrists are better trained. But are they? A comparative review of the training of psychiatrists and psychologists should be worthwhile.

Basically, a psychiatrist is a physician who has undergone the standard medical school 3- or 4-year sequence plus a year of internship. Very little psychology is involved in medical school training: The psychiatrist Alan Mariner, for example, described his education in medical school as having essentially no relationship to his subsequent practice. The core of psychiatric training for practice and research is typically a 3-year residency. The amount of formal course work varies considerably across residencies, but the residency experience consists primarily of actual treatment of patients under supervision by a more experienced psychiatrist. About 25% of psychiatrists have had more than a 3-year residency, but about 10% have had less. Three years of residency are necessary to be accepted for full membership in the American Psychiatric Association, but any physician can limit his or her practice to psychiatry without any specialized training in that field.

For most psychiatrists, their knowledge about human behavior and the vast array of theory and data associated with the study of human behavior is transmitted in the context of a 3-year residency. There is typically no training in advanced statistics, mathematics, methodology, research design, or related basic issues of scientific work in human behavior. An additional problem for American psychiatry is the influx of foreign medical graduates: 32% of all psychiatric residents in 1974 and more than 50% of the psychiatrists in practice in many state institutions were graduates of foreign medical schools. In short, psychiatrists have little formal training in the broad study of human behavior, little contact with problems and methods in science (particularly those aspects of science dealing with complex social events, such as social programs and the like), and a fairly high probability of receiving their medical training in some other country.

Psychiatrists are, by and large, practitioners. It has been found that 60% of the full-time-equivalent activities of psychiatrists were accounted for by direct patient contacts. Administration accounted for 15% of total time and consultation 9%. Teaching at 8% and research at 4% were far behind. Indeed, only .1% of psychiatrists stated that they spent all of their time

Reprinted from *American Psychologist*, 1977, *32*, 107–108.

in research, and only 2.4% indicated that they spent as much as 40% of their time in research. The average yearly salary of psychiatrists is in excess of $40,000.

These statistics might be compared with the 1972 APA Manpower Survey of 21,000 doctorate-level members. These members spent 5.4 years registered time (and 6.7 years total elapsed time) in their doctoral training. Their undergraduate grade point average was 3.6 out of a possible 4.0 (the undergraduate grade point average of all medical students was 3.5 out of a possible 4.0). Typical doctorate psychologists have completed at least two extensive research projects, the master's thesis and the doctoral dissertation, and have completed a wide variety of other courses in statistics, methodology, and the basic science of human behavior. Clinical psychologists must also undergo a year of internship training preceded by fairly extensive practicum work under close supervision. The pressure for space in graduate schools in psychology appears to be greater than that in medicine. Medical schools as a whole accept approximately one third of the applicants, while psychology accepts about one sixth.[1] The average yearly salary of psychologists is slightly in excess of $20,000.

The differences in training and competencies between psychiatrists and clinical psychologists seem very clear. Psychiatrists receive

standard medical training, little formal training in the study of human behavior, and practically no experience in research. Clinical psychologists, on the other hand, receive very little training in medicine (although many have strong backgrounds in neuroscience), rather standardized and extensive sets of experiences in research, and are engaged for 5 or more years in a broad study of human behavior.

A person who needs to be treated with drugs should undoubtedly go to a psychiatrist. Certainly there have been some recent advances in the treatment of depression and schizophrenia with drugs. However, if one would like to be treated by someone with broad training in the study of human behavior and with enough research training to maintain some scientific skepticism and open-mindedness, then a psychologist might be preferable.

Dr. Bert Brown, the Director of the National Institute for Mental Health, recently suggested that there are two strong reasons for going to a skilled psychiatrist rather than another "mental health professional." One is to enjoy the status of the MD degree. The other is to benefit from the biological background of the psychiatrist in case there is some biological condition requiring attention. Let me add here that there are a couple of strong reasons for going to a psychologist. One is the more extensive background of the psychologist in the study of human behavior and another is the formal training in science which should both lead the psychologist to be up-to-date on scientific findings and produce a healthy skepticism about current fads.

---

[1] Medical schools have a better handle on the number of people who are applying as opposed to the number of acceptances, and so the psychology figure is probably inflated, although some good programs in clinical psychology are running 100:1 in a ratio of applicants to acceptances.

Charles A. Kiesler is Executive Officer of the American Psychological Association.

Training in Professional Psychology: National Needs

Charles A. Kiesler

This paper, expanding the preceding editorial, considers the current legal and legislative status of professional psychologists, as well as some of the continuing problems in securing such recognition. The need to continually modify professional training and develop innovative models of service delivery is noted.

Last year I published an editorial in the *American Psychologist* comparing the training of psychiatrists and psychologists (Kiesler, 1977). According to Mary Beyda, the Assistant to the Editor, that two-page editorial provoked more mail than any other article in her ten years of experience with the *American Psychologist*. A sample of those comments was ultimately published in the October (1977) issue of the *American Psychologist*. Your editor, Ernst Beier, invited me to discuss some of these issues further.

I would like to discuss some of the issues relevant to the training of professional psychologists, but not exactly in the same vein as in my previous editorial. In that editorial, I essentially said that, compared to other fields, professional psychologists are very well trained to deliver competent services. I believe that, and I think the data support it. However, to say that we are as well trained as other groups is not to say that we are as well trained as we could be (and perhaps should be). In this paper, I will discuss the current status of professional psychology nationally, and my perception of the cutting edge of training issues for the future. In this discussion, I will emphasize national needs, national priorities, and others' perceptions of how the country can support the delivery of effective mental health services.

Current Status of Professional Psychology

Professional psychology has made great progress in becoming established in regulation and legislation. Professional psychologists are now regulated through licensing or certification laws in all fifty states and the District of Columbia, although five states still permit the licensing of non-Ph.D.s as independent providers. Organizers and procedures for the review of professional psychology services now exist in every state. Twenty-eight states, comprising 70 percent of the country's population, now have freedom of choice legislation, allowing the client to choose to obtain services from a psychologist. Psychologists are recognized as independent providers under the CHAMPUS Program, the CHAMPVA Program, in the HMO Development Act of 1973, under Public Law 93-363— 8.5 million member Federal Employees Health Plan—and under the Comprehensive Manpower Program of 1974. The readers of this journal probably know these facts better than anyone in APA, but the sheer variety of legislation and regulations incorporating services by psychologists is sometimes not sufficiently appreciated.

We are also making good progress in further developing our collective efforts on innovative national programs. APA's Committee on

From *Psychotherapy Bulletin*, 1978, *12*(3), 13–16. Copyright 1978 by the Division of Psychotherapy of the American Psychological Association. Reprinted by permission.

Health Insurance has completed model legislation for National Health Insurance, and the Council of Representatives has endorsed it as within an acceptable range for the Association. The Council has also endorsed a collective statement by the Liaison Group for Mental Health on mental health benefits in National Health Insurance as within an acceptable range. An APA Task Force, appointed by the Board of Directors, has recently completed a report outlining proposed evaluation and accountability mechanisms for National Health Insurance (In press, 1978); this report proposes a tough-minded approach to evaluation and accountability which emphasizes outcome of services delivered, yet details procedures to promote innovative new approaches to treatment. APA currently has a half million dollar contract to develop professional service review mechanisms for the CHAMPUS Program. We hope to have this contract renewed for a second year, which would allow our national panel to develop ways of incorporating mental health services into National Health Insurance.

All of these activities—model legislation, evaluation and accountability techniques, and professional service review—are building blocks towards effective national planning of organized delivery of mental health services, particularly under some sort of National Health Insurance. The APA in general, and our professional psychologists in particular, have spent an enormous amount of effort in a conscientious and publicly responsible national plan for the delivery of service.

Let me note parenthetically that at the same time, APA is trying to develop a better data base for assessing what psychologists now do nationally. For example, based on a report by Gottfredson and Dyer (published 1978), we estimate that in 1976 psychologists delivered approximately 18 million hours of mental health services to approximately 4 million people in the United States. These estimates already have provided me with some ammunition in discussing federal policy with agency officials and others. For example, these data quite clearly illustrate that psychologists are oriented toward short-term therapy, a critical point of one is trying to plan effectively and predict the costs of mental health benefits within National Health Insurance.

From all of this, it is obvious that professional psychology is clearly and demonstrably a national resource. It is set in place, to a considerable extent, in legislation and regulation. The field has operated responsibly to develop in its plans, such consumer-oriented issues as evaluation, accountability, and service review mechanisms. Professional psychology already delivers an extraordinary amount of service to a very large number of people, and this clearly requires that we discuss how this national resource should be used. When discussing the potential of professional psychology as a national resource, there are several different problems related to training that are worth mentioning. Some are old problems needing continuing attention, and some are only emerging problems. I will only sample a couple of each type.

Continuing Problems in the Training of Professional Psychologists

There are some problems in the training of professional psychologists that are probably not solvable in any unequivocal way. However, they do need continuing and constant attention, lest they get out of hand. One problem is how to develop an attitude of tough-minded and critical self-assessment on the part of professional psychologists that lasts throughout their professional lives. How can we ensure that the people we train will continue to emphasize the outcome of their services and actively promote such evaluations? Obviously, I personally feel it is important for professional psychologists to maintain continuing contact with the science of psychology. It is critical for the continuing development of our field that our professionals keep abreast of the literature in some manner, and use the literature in developing innovative techniques and services.

Another continuing issue is our public image. All sorts of newspaper reports, magazine articles, and television interviews regarding psychology are brought to my attention. They make very salient the fact that somehow, as a field, we have to develop ways to handle our own self-aggrandizing members. Every month some proponent of the therapeutic-fad-of-the-month-club outlines his or her ideas in an authoritative way in a major newspaper or magazine article.

What could be potentially provocative and interesting new approaches to service are presented as if they had already been tested by both time and trial. Some of these articles, and the comments of some of their proponents, are a serious disservice to the public and to psychology. This problem is so serious that sometimes I think the most salient perception of us by the public comes through such articles.

The intertwining of professional and scientific psychology, and the issue of appropriate public information are not new problems. However, the fact that the problems are old does not mean that they are solved. More importantly, as the training of professional psychologists becomes more systems-oriented, more completely professional in nature, these problems will almost surely get worse, unless we attend to them very forthrightly.

New Needs and Problems in the Training of Professional Psychologists

I suspect that the changes in the training of professional psychologists will be related to the demands of our society on the field to orient its training more specifically in terms of national priorities—not only priorities in terms of the type of problems to handle, but priorities also in terms of the number of people to be treated. Each societal need will produce a training problem for psychology which will have to be solved.

The sheer number of people needing some treatment in the country demands that the people being trained have more direct training and more experience in organized systems of care. The demand for organized systems of care is in part specifically related to the sheer number of people needing care, and we therefore must develop better ways of handling a larger number of people effectively.

At the same time, organized systems of care provide easier access for clients to greater expertise (through specialty training) within a small setting. Therefore, professional psychologists in their training need more and better interaction and experiences with such systems as health maintenance organizations, community mental health centers, neighborhood health clinics, and various state-level organized systems such as those related to rehabilitation services.

In addition, I suspect we should more systematically investigate the possibilities of organized group practice with general medical practitioners. Each of these practice settings will provide new and significant opportunities for professional psychologists in the near future. In many psychology departments, there is little contact with such organizations. The possible exception is community mental health centers where the number of psychologists has been increasing at a rapid rate, but the proportion of total professional psychologists delivering services in community mental health centers is still quite small.

I am assuming here that in national health planning, in National Health Insurance and in other legislation, the Congress and the Executive Branch will continue to emphasize organized systems of care. Private practice will almost surely not be the core of any federally funded effort. Indeed, some people are opposed to private practice having any role in a federally organized effort. There is no question that we need more extensive training and practical experience for our professional psychologists in various settings for care.

I also suspect we need more emphasis in our training on treating somatic problems, specifically those problems in which psychological techniques can play an important and often critical role, such as bruxism, epilepsy, hypertension, tracheotomy addiction, and the like. Sometimes, a psychologist can help more than the medical specialist in question. For example, a psychologist might be of greater assistance with a problem of bruxism than the dentist who diagnosed it. A psychologist could probably be more helpful with a problem of tracheotomy addiction than the surgeon who produced it. These psychological points of contact with overtly medical problems deserve more emphasis in our professional training.

People estimate that between 50 and 80 percent of the patients in a general medical practitioner's office have psychological rather than medical problems. That datum is a national problem of some consequence. In the training of psychologists, we need to address directly the potential of psychologists to provide service close to the initial entry point into organized health care. The lack of good match-ups between expert and problem in our current system of medical care dramatically affects both the cost and the effectiveness of care. Psychologists can and surely will make a substantial contribution to this effort in the future.

Because of the increasingly public nature of what we do, it will probably be important as we go along to put some sharper teeth into our Ethics Code and our standards of professional practice to protect the public. We have a very good Ethics Code in the American Psychological Association, but the costs of violating it are not necessarily severe. The protection of the public will necessitate an increasing amount of time and energy on these issues.

Conclusions

Some people were distressed with the editorial I wrote in the *American Psychologist*. Most people responded very favorably, and I keep hearing of a rather extraordinary network of photocopied reproductions around the country. A few people objected strenuously, but almost as many wrote in to say that they felt the editorial was not extreme enough.

In listening to influential people around Washington and to the problems of my colleagues around the country, I felt it was necessary to get down on paper some statement that said that psychologists have a great deal to be proud of in their graduate professional training. I think that was a useful statement to make, and I do not at all regret making it. There are many facts regarding the training and competence of professional psychologists that we collectively can point to with pride. However, we can distinguish between comparative and absolute levels of competence: that we are as good or better than others, is not to say that we are as good as we can be. With the rapid national progress of professional psychology, we do not need many comparative statements of psychologists with others. What we do need is the maturity and the wisdom to continue to strive towards our ideals.

Reference

Gottfredson, G. D. & Dyer, S. E. Health service providers in psychology. *American Psychologist* 1978, *33*, 314–338.

Charles A. Kiesler is Executive Officer of the American Psychological Association.

The Practice of Psychotherapy in America: Issues and Trends

Dennis P. Saccuzzo

This article presents current issues and trends that are shaping the practice of psychotherapy in America. These trends include movement away from the one-to-one model, changes in the therapist's role and in the delivery of service, and increasing use of nonprofessionals. The most profound trend is the systematic application of the science of psychology to psychotherapy. Such application has resulted in cognitive, learning, social psychological, and psychophysiological methods of treatment.

For more than 2000 years, it was generally believed that abnormal or deviant behavior was caused by demons or supernatural forces. Psychotherapy was therefore limited to forbidding, ordering, confession, exorcism, and torture. Finally, at the turn of the 18th century, enlightened individuals rejected the theory of demonology. People with abnormal behavioral patterns were treated with kindness; psychotherapy was limited to advice, suggestion, catharsis, and hypnosis. It wasn't until early in this century, however, that the revolutionary Freudian movement introduced intellectual interpretation as the first method of psychotherapy based on modern ideas from the science of medicine (e.g., Rogers, 1942). Subsequently there developed numerous schools of psychotherapy, all based in some way or another on Freudian concepts and medical science. In fact, it required nearly a half century after the introduction of Freudian concepts before a truly different approach to psychotherapy was introduced by psychologist Carl Rogers (1942, 1951). Rogers' pioneering work introduced a trend within psychotherapy that continues to be the dominant influence in the field and that, no doubt, will continue to influence and shape the future of psychotherapy. This trend, simply stated, is the application of the basic science of psychology to the art of solving human problems.

The application of psychology's scientific base to psychotherapy has resulted in a flexible, empirical, open-minded approach and continuous innovation. This innovation has produced such current trends as: (a) movement away from the one-to-one model of treatment, (b) a new look at time as a variable in psychotherapy, (c) changes in the conceptualization of the role of the therapist, (d) increasing use of paraprofessional and nonprofessional workers, (e) alternative and expanded conceptions concerning delivery of services, and (f) a proliferation of new models.

Movement Away from the One-to-One Model

The 1965 Chicago conference on clinical training (Hoch, Ross, & Winder, 1966), although stressing the importance of alternative approaches, viewed training in the one-to-one model of psychotherapy as an essential part of the training of all clinical psychologists. Only 12 years later, with unprecedented advances in psychotherapy, this idea is perhaps being questioned. Scientific studies of therapeutic method and outcome (e.g., Barron & Leary, 1955; Frank, Gliedman, Imber, Nash, & Stone, 1959; Gelder, Marks, & Wolff, 1967; Novick, 1965; Paul & Shannon, 1966; Thorley & Craske,

Reprinted from *Professional Psychology,* 1977, *8,* 297–306.

1950) indicated little difference in outcome between group and individual therapy for outpatients, inpatients, children, adults, and across techniques of therapy (Meltzoff & Kornreich, 1970). Perhaps this finding, coupled with an emphasis within the psychological profession on meeting the needs of society, has resulted in the current strong tendency toward the one-to-many model of treatment. Little known in the 1960s, Gestalt, Transactional Analysis, Reality, and other methods of group psychotherapy are growing at an astonishing pace (e.g., Harman, 1974). Another reflection of the movement away from the one-to-one model is the increase in family therapy techniques. Friedman (1974) recently listed 26 types of marital and family therapy alone. Finally, in addition to reflecting a change from the one-to-one model to the one-to-many model, the rapid growth of such special groups as encounter, sensitivity, marathon, and nude reflects still another trend in psychotherapy in America. Less disturbed people are seeking and receiving treatment, and more emphasis is being placed on human effectiveness and positive mental health.

Time in Psychotherapy

Scientific research from the psychological sciences pertaining to average or typical length of psychotherapy has clearly suggested that psychotherapy is a relatively brief procedure. Two comprehensive literature reviews (Garfield, 1971; Meltzoff & Kornreich, 1970) both clearly find that the median length of treatment falls between six and seven interviews. Garfield (1971), for example, found that approximately two thirds of the patients studied between 1948 and 1959 received less than 10 interviews. Less than 9% actually received as many as 25 interviews. The realization that psychotherapy, as it is currently practiced in the United States, is a relatively short-term process has resulted in considerable experimentation and innovation with temporal variables in psychotherapy. Thus, in addition to shifting to a one-to-many mode of treatment, therapists are developing methods whose goals are based on relatively brief patient-therapist contact. Short-term crisis counseling (e.g., Caplan, 1964) and time-limited psychotherapy (e.g., Shlien, Mosak, & Dreikurs, 1962) are becoming more a part of the practice of psychotherapy in America every day. Also interesting are other innovations with temporal variables in psychotherapy, such as varying length of session (e.g., Garetz, 1964) or frequency of sessions (e.g., Ends & Page, 1959; Ramsay, Barends, Breuker, & Kruseman, 1966).

New Roles for Psychotherapists

Two powerful influences, the community mental health movement and the introduction of learning principles into psychotherapy, independently converged to accelerate the ever-expanding role of the professional psychologist. These influences have revolutionized current conceptualizations of the role of the psychotherapist. Both of these models, in response to social consciousness and internal pressures to provide a real service to society, saw that the psychotherapist's role must be expanded. Thus, even while the one-to-one model is being replaced by the one-to-many model, an even more effective use of valuable professional time is becoming a dominant trend. This new model, which puts the therapist into such roles as teacher (e.g., Kanfer & Phillips, 1970), consultant (e.g., Bandura, 1969; Toal, 1970), social change agent (e.g., Spielberger & Iscoe, 1970), and mental health quarterback (e.g., Cowen, 1970), might generally be termed the *one-to-one-to-many* model of treatment.

The one-to-one-to-many model grew out of the recognition of manpower shortages (e.g., Albee, 1968; Caplan, 1964) and the recognition that one doesn't need a PhD or an MD to be a helping person (e.g., Carkhuff 1969, 1973). In the one-to-one-to-many model, the PhD psychotherapist may concentrate on training and supervising a group of helping agents, who in turn each provide direct, one-to-one service, or the therapist may concentrate on training relevant members in the environment of the patient, such as parents, siblings, peers, and the like. As Bandura (1969) noted, this one-to-one-to-many approach is ideally suited to producing enduring and generalized changes in psychological functioning. Obviously the approach multiplies the potential effectiveness of a single therapist.

Given the need for human services, there is little doubt that this model will play an ever-increasing role in American psychology.

Paraprofessional and Nonprofessional Workers

Intricately tied to the development of the one-to-one-to-many model is the increasing use of paraprofessionals and nonprofessionals as psychotherapeutic agents. It is not the purpose of this article to debate the pros and cons of the nonprofessional helping agents. However, despite criticisms suggesting that the effectiveness of nonprofessionals has been oversold and that it is irresponsible to reduce standards of training through overuse of nonprofessionals (Meltzoff & Kornreich, 1970) and that concern is no substitute for competence (Genthner, 1974), the most critical challenge for the future is how we can best integrate this huge manpower source into the mental health delivery system. As Blau (1969) has noted, the challenge for the future is not proving the effectiveness of paraprofessionals. The challenge is providing adequate safeguards, training, supervision, and control of such workers. Thus, it seems clear that paraprofessionals will continue to assert their presence in the delivery of psychotherapeutic services in America. Whether this influence turns out to be a blessing or a disaster, however, is up to the present professional community.

Delivery of Services

Also tied to the expanding role of the psychotherapist and increasing use of nonprofessionals are the profound changes that have taken place in the delivery of mental health services (e.g., Kleinmuntz, 1974). Scientific investigation (e.g., Brown, 1960) indicated the futility of long-term hospitalization. Since findings such as Brown's (1960), three main tendencies have developed in the delivery of psychotherapeutic services: (a) the development of increasing numbers of alternatives to hospitalization, (b) shorter hospitalization, and (c) increased facilities for outpatient care.

The delivery of mental health psychotherapeutic services has become briefer and more decentralized. Halfway houses, day treatment centers, and night hospitals, virtually unknown 15 years ago, are springing up across the country. No doubt this trend will continue until the back ward becomes a thing of the past. Americans of the future will probably see more of such innovations as home treatment and cooperative retreats (e.g., Kleinmuntz, 1974). Paralleling shorter term hospitalization and alternatives to the hospital are increased facilities for outpatient care. Community mental health centers, unknown in the 1950s, now seem as established as psychiatric hospitals. These centers are now complemented by such innovations as crisis intervention centers, free clinics, crisis call, suicide prevention centers, and peer self-help groups. However, these innovations, although encouraging, are still only remedial in function. Although rapid, inexpensive community treatment for the broader spectrum of the population is a desirable trend, it still falls short of our ultimate goal of prevention. Thus, the future must see even greater creativity and expansion of concepts in the delivery of psychotherapeutic services. Prevention clinics, nonexistent today, may soon spread just as rapidly as crisis call centers and become a part of the American mental health delivery system.

Therapeutic Models from the Science of Psychology

One of the most interesting and exciting effects of the application of the science of psychology to the treatment of human problems has been the growth of new therapeutic models. Applications from learning, cognitive, social, and psychophysiology, for example, promise to elevate psychotherapy from a mysterious, undefinable art to a precise science. Thus, an ever-increasing trend in psychotherapy is the development of therapeutic interventions based on scientific psychological principles.

Behavior modification, the application of the science of learning psychology, is now so entrenched that it is no longer a trend but an established part of American psychotherapy. Still, the list of therapeutic interventions based on learning principles continues to grow as the laboratory and the clinic become a two-way street (e.g., Lazarus & Davison, 1971). Techniques such as modeling, shaping, flooding, massing, behavioral contracts, token economies, and so on (e.g., Bandura, 1971; Eysenck & Beech, 1971; Krasner, 1971; Murray & Jacobson, 1971) are now a common part of modern psychotherapy.

Not so traditional are the innovations in social psychology that are being applied to psychotherapy (e.g., Harari, 1971, 1972; Heller, 1971; Storms & Nisbett, 1970). Experiments from social psychology (e.g., Festinger & Carlsmith, 1959), for example, have suggested that behavior change can often lead to and result in attitude change. This finding alone suggests a complete reversal of the older psychodynamic position, in which the goal was attitude change (insight) to produce behavior change. The knowledge from social psychology has taught us that if we can change behavior, the ultimate goal of most if not all psychotherapies, attitude change will often follow. This finding alone has produced a number of innovations and provided a scientific basis for such older techniques as Kelly's (1955) fixed-role therapy. Other innovations from social psychology presently being applied to psychotherapy center around interpersonal attraction and the psychotherapeutic relationship. This has resulted in such techniques as structuring to increase patient attraction to the therapist through positive communication to the patient. Results show that the higher the attraction, the greater the interpersonal influence (e.g., Burdick & Burns, 1958; Sapolsky, 1960). Social psychological experiments have also provided interesting results regarding the importance of therapist status (e.g., Goldstein & Simonson, 1971), degree of effort on the part of the patient, and patient-therapist matching (e.g., Heller, 1971). These encouraging results have contributed to an understanding of the factors involved in interpersonal influence and successful psychotherapy.

Paralleling these innovative applications from social psychology to psychotherapy are exciting applications from psychophysiological psychology. It's almost hard to believe that a mere 10 years ago there was no such thing as biofeedback. It wasn't until the early groundwork of experimental psychologist Joe Kamiya (1968) exploded previous myths concerning human ability to exert conscious control over certain "involuntary" functions that psychophysiology was changed almost over night from an interesting science to a solver of human problems. Psychophysiological applications to psychotherapy, in conjunction with other applications from scientific psychology, have clearly elevated the scientific respectability of psychotherapy. These procedures can be used as diagnostic, treatment, and outcome measures (e.g., Lang, 1971). They have been applied to such diverse areas as treatment of a 9-month-old infant with chronic ruminative vomiting (e.g., Lang & Melamed, 1969), patients with sensory-induced epileptic seizures (e.g., Lang, 1971), cardiac patients (e.g., Engel & Hanson, 1966), and hypertensive patients (e.g., Shapiro, Tursky, Gershon, & Stein, 1969).

The major challenge for psychologists regarding psychophysiology, however, is not how to refine and develop psychophysiological technology for solving human problems. The current challenge involves a much deeper issue: psychology's right to employ techniques and innovations developed by psychologists and based on the psychological sciences. So impressive are the clinical possibilities from this branch of psychology that physicians are trying to convince legislators that psychologists aren't qualified to use them (e.g., Slattery, 1974). This nonfunctional constraint on psychology is repugnant to the American Psychological Association (APA) position paper on relations with other professions (APA, 1954). The APA (1954) position paper on interprofessional relations states, among other things, that as an autonomous profession, psychology cannot accept limitations upon its freedom of thought and action, except those imposed by social responsibility and public welfare. No one is more qualified to use the psychological sciences than psychologists. Taking away our right to employ our own science for the solution of human problems would eventually bring a halt to the trend initiated by Rogers, which has produced such a great technology in psychotherapy. It has been the close association between applied and experimental psychologists and the ability of the applied psychologist to evaluate and employ experimental psychology that has been responsible for the unprecedented breakthroughs of the past 10 years.

Physicians are not trained to use the psychological sciences. Their emphasis and training are in chemistry and biology. It is primarily through the efforts of the applied psychologist that psychological science has been and is being converted to practical use. Take this right away from us and progress will be seriously curtailed and society will suffer. Morally and ethically we must protect our unique professional and scientific methods from being destroyed and exploited by outside influences.

Not so spectacular, but nonetheless important, have been applications from other branches of psychology. Advances in cognitive psychology (e.g., Raimy, 1975) in conjunction with learning techniques have produced such innovations as cognitive control and psychotherapy by imagery. All of these advances are relatively new and no doubt even the next 10 years will see a revolution in the practice of psychotherapy. As more and more professional psychologists abandon the dogma of previous generations and apply the principles of psychology to psychotherapy, psychotherapy will undoubtedly equal, if not surpass, medicine as an art based on science.

Conclusion

The science of psychology has produced a technology for the treatment of human problems unmatched by any other discipline. Yet these developments are nothing compared to future possibilities because psychology as a science is still in its infancy. The therapist of the future will have in his armamentarium a technology that will probably make methods used in the 1930s and 40s (when psychologists didn't dream of doing psychotherapy with adults) seem as archaic to us as methods used 200 years ago seemed to the followers of Freud. The major ingredients in successful psychotherapy will no doubt be isolated and therapists will learn how to use such principles as interpersonal attraction, reinforcement, conditioning, cognitive dissonance, scientific suggestion, and placebo enhancement from the moment he/she begins treatment. These principles will then be employed in conjunction with psychotherapeutic hardware, such as biofeedback devices, that will enable patients to control anxiety and produce the calm, relaxed alpha state in the shortest possible time.

The application of scientific psychology to psychotherapy is providing the thread by which all systems and schools of therapy can be tied. Reproach among the various systems is inevitable as the essential ingredients of psychotherapy are uncovered and the scientific principles governing these ingredients determined. We are living in a world changing many times faster than the world of only 50 years ago. Given the high level of training in psychology programs, the high quality of our graduate students, and our strong commitment to use our science for meeting human needs, anything is possible in the last quarter of this century.

References

Albee, G. W. Conceptual models and manpower requirements in psychology. *American Psychologist,* 1968, *23,* 317–320.

American Psychological Association. *Psychology and its relations with other professions.* Washington, D.C.: Author, 1954.

Bandura, A. *Principles of behavior modification.* New York: Holt, Rinehart & Winston, 1969.

Bandura, A. Psychotherapy based upon modeling principles. In A. E. Bergin & S. L. Garfield (Eds.), *Handbook of psychotherapy and behavior change.* New York: Wiley, 1971.

Barron, F., & Leary, T. F. Changes in psychoneurotic patients with and without psychotherapy. *Journal of Consulting Psychology,* 1955, *19,* 239–245.

Blau, T. The professional in the community views the nonprofessional helper. *Professional Psychology,* 1969, *1,* 25–31.

Brown, G. W. Length of hospital stay in schizophrenia: A review of statistical studies. *Acta Psychiatrica et Neurologica Scandinavica,* 1960, *35,* 414–430.

Burdick, H. A., & Burns, A. J. A test of the "strain toward symmetry" theories. *Journal of Abnormal and Social Psychology,* 1958, *57,* 367–370.

Caplan, G. *Principles of preventive psychiatry.* New York: Basic Books, 1964.

Carkhuff, R. R. *Helping and human relations* (2 vols.). New York: Holt, Rinehart & Winston, 1969.

Carkhuff, R. R. *The art of helping.* Amherst, Mass.: Human Resource Development Press, 1973.

Cowen, E. L. Training clinical psychologists for community mental health functions: Description of a practicum experience. In I. Iscoe & C. D. Spielberger (Eds.), *Community psychology: Perspectives in training and research.* New York: Appleton-Century-Crofts, 1970.

Ends, E. J., & Page, C. W. Group psychotherapy and concomitant psychological change. *Psychological Monographs,* 1959, *73,* (10, Whole No. 480).

Engel, B. T., & Hanson, S. P. Operant conditioning of heart rate slowing. *Psychophysiology,* 1966, *3,* 176–187.

Eysenck, H. J., & Beech, R. Counterconditioning and related methods. In A. E. Bergin & S. L. Garfield (Eds.), *Handbook of psychotherapy and behavior change.* New York: Wiley, 1971.

Festinger, L., & Carlsmith, J. M. Cognitive consequences of forced compliance. *Journal of Abnormal and Social Psychology,* 1959, *58,* 203–210.

Frank, J. D., Gliedman, L. H., Imber, S. D., Nash, E. H., Jr., & Stone, A. R. Why patients leave psychotherapy. *Archives of Neurological Psychiatry,* 1957, *77,* 283–299.

Friedman, P. H. Outline (alphabet) of 26 techniques of family and marital therapy: A through Z. *Psychotherapy: Theory, Research and Practice,* 1974, *11,* 26–30.

Garetz, F. K. A statistical study of treatment oriented behavior. *Archives of General Psychiatry,* 1964, *10,* 306–309.

Garfield, S. G. Research on client variables in psychotherapy. In A. E. Bergin & S. L. Garfield (Eds.), *Handbook of psychotherapy and behavior change.* New York: Wiley, 1971.

Gelder, M. G., Marks, I. M., & Wolff, H. Desensitization and psychotherapy in the treatment of phobic states: A controlled inquiry. *British Journal of Psychiatry,* 1967, *113,* 53–73.

Genthner, R. Evaluating the functioning of community-based hotlines. *Professional Psychology,* 1974, *5,* 409–414.

Goldstein, A. P., & Simonson, N. R. Social psychological approaches to psychotherapy research. In A. E. Bergin & S. L. Garfield (Eds.), *Handbook of psychotherapy and behavior change.* New York: Wiley, 1971.

Harari, H. Interpersonal models in psychotherapy and counseling: A social psychological analysis of a clinical problem. *Journal of Abnormal Psychology,* 1971, *78,* 127–133.

Harari, H. Cognitive manipulations with delinquent adolescents in group therapy. *Psychotherapy: Theory, Research and Practice,* 1972, *9,* 303–307.

Harman, R. L. Techniques of Gestalt therapy. *Professional Psychology,* 1974, *5,* 257–263.

Heller, K. Laboratory interview research as an analogue to treatment. In A. E. Bergin & S. L. Garfield (Eds.), *Handbook of psychotherapy and behavior change.* New York: Wiley, 1971.

Hoch, E. L., Ross, A. O., & Winder, C. L. *Professional preparation of clinical psychologists.* Washington, D.C.: American Psychological Association, 1966.

Kamiya, J. Conscious control of brain waves. *Psychology Today,* January 1968, pp. 57–60.

Kanfer, F. H., & Phillips, J. S. *Learning foundations of behavior therapy.* New York: Wiley, 1970.

Kelly, G. A. *The psychology of personal constructs* (2 vols.). New York: Norton, 1955.

Kleinmuntz, B. *Essentials of abnormal psychology.* New York: Harper & Row, 1974.

Krasner, L. The operant approach in behavior therapy. In A. E. Bergin & S. L. Garfield (Eds.), *Handbook of psychotherapy and behavior change.* New York: Wiley, 1971.

Lang, P. J. The application of psychophysiological methods to the study of psychotherapy and behavior modification.

In A. E. Bergin & S. L. Garfield (Eds.), *Handbook of psychotherapy and behavior change.* New York: Wiley, 1971.

Lang, P. J., & Melamed, B. G. Case report: Avoidance conditioning therapy of an infant with chronic ruminative vomiting. *Journal of Abnormal Psychology,* 1969, *74,* 1–8.

Lazarus, A. A., & Davison, G. C. Clinical innovation in research and practice. In A. E. Bergin & S. L. Garfield (Eds.), *Handbook of psychotherapy and behavior change.* New York: Wiley, 1971.

Meltzoff, J., & Kornreich, M. *Research in psychotherapy.* New York: Atherton Press, 1970.

Murray, E. J., & Jacobson, L. I. The nature of learning in traditional behavioral psychotherapy. In A. E. Bergin & S. L. Garfield (Eds.), *Handbook of psychotherapy and behavior change.* New York: Wiley, 1971.

Novick, J. I. Comparison between short-term group and individual psychotherapy in effecting change in nondesirable behavior in children. *International Journal of Group Psychotherapy,* 1965, *15,* 366–373.

Paul, G. L., & Shannon, D. T. Treatment of anxiety through systematic desensitization in therapy groups. *Journal of Abnormal Psychology,* 1966, *71,* 124–135.

Raimy, V. *Misunderstandings of the self.* San Francisco: Jossey-Bass, 1975.

Ramsay, R. W., Barends, J., Breuker, J., & Kruseman, A. Massed versus spaced desensitization of fear. *Behavior Research and Therapy,* 1966, *4,* 205–207.

Rogers, C. R. *Counseling and psychotherapy.* New York: Houghton Mifflin, 1942.

Rogers, C. R. *Client-centered therapy.* New York: Houghton Mifflin, 1951.

Sapolsky, A. Effect of interpersonal relationships upon verbal conditioning. *Journal of Abnormal and Social Psychology,* 1960, *60,* 241–256.

Shapiro, D., Tursky, B., Gerhson, E., & Stein, M. Effects of feedback and reinforcement on the control of human systolic blood pressure. *Science,* 1969, *163,* 588–590.

Shlien, J. M., Mosak, H. H., & Dreikurs, R. Effect of time limits: A comparison of two psychotherapies. *Journal of Counseling Psychology,* 1962, *9,* 31–34.

Slattery, P. Medical device legislation may hurt biofeedback. *APA Monitor,* April 1974, p. 8.

Spielberger, C. D., & Iscoe, I. The current status of training in community psychology. In I. Iscoe & C. D. Spielberger (Eds.), *Community psychology: Perspectives in training and research.* New York: Appleton-Century-Crofts, 1970.

Storms, M. D., & Nisbett, R. E. Insomnia and the attribution process. *Journal of Personality and Social Psychology,* 1970, *2,* 319–328.

Thorley, A. S., & Craske, N. Comparison and estimate of group and individual methods of treatment. *British Medical Journal,* 1950, *1,* 97–100.

Toal, R. Reflections on the postdoctoral program in community mental health of the laboratory of community psychiatry, Harvard Medical School. In I. Iscoe & C. D. Spielberger (Eds.), *Community psychology: Perspectives in training and research.* New York: Appleton-Century-Crofts, 1970.

At the time of original publication of this article, *Dennis P. Sacuzzo* was an assistant professor of psychology, San Diego State University.

The article is based on a paper presented at the meeting of the Western Psychological Association, Los Angeles, April 1976.

The Psychologist as a Health Professional

William Schofield

If the psychologist is to play a significant role in health maintenance organizations, he or she will need greater sophistication regarding physical health and illness than is required by training in the area of mental health and illness.

To think in appropriately broad terms about the role of the psychologist as a health professional and to perceive the opportunities for new and diverse functions for psychology in health maintenance organizations (HMOs), it is desirable to keep certain definitional emphases in mind. The following remarks pertain to the psychologist as a potential health professional as distinguished from the mental health professional. Similarly, attention is to the potential of the psychologist as a health scientist as distinct from the mental health scientist. The argument has been made elsewhere that psychology is one of the health sciences and that certain patterns of training in the disciplines of psychology can appropriately prepare the psychologist to function as a health professional (Schofield, 1969). That argument, which has been generally accepted, need not be repeated here.

Until now, the health impact of psychology, both as science and profession, has been too restrictively identified with clinical psychology, with psychiatry, and with mental illness. The fact of that restricted identification of psychology with a single segment of health concerns could be illustrated by examination of the allocation of psychological manpower over all clinical settings. An even more telling illustration is found in the distribution of our research efforts. When psychological publications are plotted against a broad spectrum of 22 health-illness topics covering the birth-to-death life span, it is found that half of all studies are accounted for by only three topics: schizophrenia, psychotherapy, and neurosis.

This restricted range of psychological health concerns to date has serious implications for the potential role of the psychologist as a health professional. Our most visible image now, as clinical psychologists in the traditional sense, will either serve doubts as to whether we have a legitimate place in HMOs or favor plans for a restricted role in the mental health department of the HMO, if indeed such a department is contemplated.

We need to encourage the development of a new and broader image of the psychologist as a health professional who can contribute meaningfully to the evaluation and management of health problems beyond those entailing emotional or psychiatric components as usually conceived. We need to develop a new professional identity and new patterns of professional education. Clearly, we need to greatly expand the scope of our research endeavors over the broad spectrum of health-related behavior. Eventually, perhaps very soon, we will need an appropriate name to identify a field of specialization to be practiced, researched, and taught by a new breed of psychologists. But titles can be helpful or can hinder, and the choice of one should be made carefully.[1]

The Rationale of the HMO

The basic goal of the HMO is to provide comprehensive health care. This requires minimally

---

[1] For instance, after these remarks were prepared, the name of the Division of Clinical Psychology, University of Minnesota Health Sciences Center, was changed to Division of Health Care Psychology to reflect the greatly expanded range of functions of the staff since the Division's establishment in 1951.

Reprinted from *Professional Psychology*, 1976, 7, 5–8.

that all components of health service—preventive, diagnostic, therapeutic, consultative, inpatient and outpatient, physical and mental—be conveniently and continuously available to the client. But the availability of a comprehensive collection of care components does not guarantee that the patient will be treated comprehensively.

The subscriber population of any HMO will have a small percentage of patients with significant emotional or psychiatric disorders, without significant medical illness or physical handicap. Another small percentage will be patients whose clearly organic illness is caused by, contributed to, or complicated by serious psychological dimensions. But all patients have significant psychological components associated with any complaint that has brought them to a clinic or hospital. All significant disorders of function are "psychosomatic" in the broad sense. The push for the development of HMOs is due, in part, to a chronic failure on the part of the health establishment to maintain a holistic approach to patients. If HMOs are to achieve significant gains, they must focus equally on comprehensiveness and integration of services.

Contributions of Psychology

How can the psychologist contribute to recognition and provision for the psychological components in all illnesses?

All illnesses are to some degree psychologically stressful. The patient responds to the stress with anxiety, depression, confusion, resentment, or denial. What factors of previous experience or dimensions of personality determine these reaction patterns? Are they differentially associated with types of illness? How do they interact with the patient's response to a particular medical regimen? How can these psychologic reaction patterns, when self-defeating, be most effectively managed? These questions can be answered only by extensive psychologically oriented research.

With prepaid comprehensive health care available to subscribers, there are two obvious types of possible abuse: overuse and underuse. What are the characteristics of persons associated with these deviant patterns of health facility usage? What are the characteristics of persons who avail themselves of cunsultation, diagnosis, and prescription but then fail to properly observe the recommendations they receive? Can they be identified in advance? What patterns of counseling or education will elicit better responsiveness to medical advice? Again, these are basic research questions in the psychological domain.

Prospects

The HMO is a relatively new idea. Some are already operational; many are in planning stages. There is general agreement, but not unanimity of opinion, that HMOs should provide mental health services, and less agreement as to the structure for such services. Where mental health services are envisioned, there is general agreement that the staff should include psychologists, but no consensus as to what the role of the psychologist should be. Proposals range from the traditional role of the clinical psychologist to the innovative role of "educational consultant."

We have an opportunity to develop new and varied roles and to compare the effectiveness of their contribution. Should the HMO psychologist affiliate with a primary medical service or should he or she be an unattached consultant on a clinic- and hospital-wide basis, providing both clinical and research expertise? It would be well, at least in some HMOs, to explore comparatively the role of the psychologist when based in internal medicine or in pediatrics.

Given the current state of our knowledge, it would be well for the psychologist in some HMOs to concentrate his/her research energies (give priority) on, for example, effective and efficient means of screening for emotional disorders as part of multiphasic health screening; determinants of the acceptability of various modes of psychiatric referral; effects of psychological screening before versus after medical examination on rate of response to psychiatric consultation; and the contribution of group therapy to management of patients with chronic disorders.

In the clinical role, the HMO psychologist will find opportunity for the traditional diagnostic and therapeutic contributions to psychiatric problems. Of greater importance will be the opportunity to discover innovative roles in providing for the psychological components of medical problems.

Finally, in an educational role the psychologist should develop opportunities to contribute to staff training with a particular view to enhancing the integration of comprehensive services to the patient. The problem of adequate (meaningful) communication to patients is a likely starting point for such in-service training.

Needs

If the HMO proves to be a viable widely disseminated structure for providing integrated, comprehensive health care and if psychological services are to be an element of such services, there will be a need for an additional complement of psychologists whose training prepares them to function as health professionals. While much of the current training of the scientist-practitioner clinician is appropriate, the education of the health psychologist will require greater emphasis on the biological sciencies, on public health, and health administration. The pattern of internship training must be different, with a deemphasis on psychiatric services and greater time spent in medical, pediatric, and surgical clinics. Of prime importance will be the intern's introduction to the special problems and methodologies for research in the area of health problems.

Certain of the problems, deficiencies, and dissatisfactions that we have come to recognize in the context of the scientist-practitioner model for the training of clinical psychologists could equally plague the development of graduate programs for the education of health professionals. With the advantage of historical perspective, we should be able to do better in laying the foundation of a new psychological profession.

Reference

Schofield, W. The role of psychology in the delivery of health services. *American Psychologist,* 1969, *24,* 565–584.

At the time of original publication of this article, *William Schofield* was a professor at the University of Minnesota, Minneapolis.

This article is based on a paper presented at the symposium "The Roles of Psychologists in Health Maintenance Organizations" held at the meeting of the Western Psychological Association, Portland, Oregon, April 27, 1972.

The Psychologist as a Health Professional in the Health Maintenance Organization

Jack G. Wiggins

The recognition of the clinical psychologist as a health professional underscores the need for a broadened definition of clinical psychology to include the psychological aspects of all health conditions.

The delineation of the role of a psychologist as a health service provider in contrast to a mental health service mentioned by Schofield (1976) in the preceding article in this issue is especially timely because of the recently issued regulations of Pub. L. No. 93-222, the Health Maintenance Organization Act of 1973. The health maintenance organization (HMO) concept offers great promise to new applications in psychology. At the same time, the HMO poses a serious threat to the psychologist as a health and mental health practitioner.

The greatest danger of the HMO to psychology is that of an organizational transplant of the current medical model into the HMO concept. If traditional delivery of medical services merely is marketed as a prepaid capitation payroll plan option for all corporations with 25 or more employees (as required by the HMO law), then the dream of integration of all health services with a view toward the betterment of the patient's condition may be lost. While the HMO law does require comprehensive services including mental health benefits, this alone will not accomplish the benefits of the integration of services Schofield so ably outlines.

In order for the patient to receive the full benefits of an integration of health services, there must be better recognition and more effective use of all health specialists. Modern business management has created and used specialists for greater productivity and quality control. Similarly, medicine has also sought excellence through specialization and the development of health technicians. Now, medicine has been called upon to accept as peers other health and mental health specialists, who, for better or for worse, have not been trained in medical schools. The acceptance of nonmedical health (both physical and mental) specialists is a bitter pill for medicine to swallow but hopefully can be a cathartic to the vested interest of the health establishment and of ultimate benefit to the consumer of health services.

Organized medicine's response to the HMO legislation is likely to be the formation of foundations for medical care by county medical societies. Using this format, each county medical society will organize its own HMO for the delivery of both outpatient and inpatient services by individual practitioners who will bill the foundation at their usual customary and reasonable rates. This foundation concept has been pioneered by the San Joaquin Foundation for Medical Care and fulfills the requirements of an HMO for the purposes of the federal legislation. While the foundation does provide extensive internal review for both the use of services and quality control, it does not necessarily provide either a comprehensive or integrated amalgam of health services. For example, it was only through the extensive negotiations of the Committee on Health Insurance of the APA, spearheaded by Herbert Dorken, that psychologists were eligible for membership in the San Joaquin Foundation as independent health service providers. Thus, it will be necessary for local psychologists to organize themselves into a panel of mental health specialists acceptable to the foundation of their community. While the foundation for medical care concept may not be the ultimate model for health service delivery, it is

Reprinted from *Professional Psychology*, 1976, 7, 9–13.

likely to be the most practical interim service model acceptable to both the public and the social engineers who are planning national health insurance. Of the more than 200 HMOs that are at least partially operational, many are of the medical care foundation type. Most of the state and/or county medical societies already have either incorporated or are planning to incorporate such a foundation.

An example of the new applications of psychological expertise in the health field is the development of biofeedback technology. It is well known and increasingly well documented that the biofeedback technique has tremendous potential for the control of headaches, pain in general, control of blood pressure, epileptic seizures, hyperkinesis, and many other bodily functions. Psychologists have been using behavior modification techniques for the treatment of alcoholism, kidney dialysis, and heart conditions and have been studying the effects of surgical procedures such as vasectomies and vein transplants for heart conditions. But contributions by psychologists are frequently not recognized as contributions by psychologists, because the psychologists are part of an integrated health team and because the results of their research findings are reported in journals other than those typically reviewed by *Psychological Abstracts*. Thus, psychology's sizable contribution to an integrated health delivery system may be lost because of the failure of our current psychological research data retrieval system to include the appropriate ciphers for the Psychological Abstracts Search and Retrieval (PASAR) system for health research.

The creation of new entry ciphers for PASAR may provide additional documentation of psychologists' contributions to health services, but documentation requires proper presentation to legislators so that the comprehensive integrated health concept will be sufficiently flexible to incorporate innovations. A glaring example of health legislation inflexibility with respect to psychologists is the proposed Medical Devices Act, which is now in the Health Subcommittee of Congress chaired by Paul Rogers. The proposed Medical Devices Act would classify biofeedback instrumentation as medical devices and would place unnecessary restrictions on the use of these devices by trained, qualified

psychologists, who are largely responsible for the development of the techniques. Another example of the hazards of some health legislation to the viability of psychologists as health practitioners occurred in the Vocational Rehabilitation Act of 1973 (Pub. L. No. 93-112). While the wording of the legislation clearly established "mental restoration" at parity with "physical restoration" and specifically stated that licensed psychologists were able to provide services on an independent basis without medical referral or supervision, the interim regulations for the administration of the Vocational Rehabilitation Act promulgated by the U.S. Department of Health, Education, and Welfare specifically required medical referral and supervision for mental health benefits provided by the psychologist. The final regulations, however, reflect the independence and parity of mental health services provided by a licensed psychologist but only as a result of the protest against the interim regulations by the Council for the Advancement of the Psychological Professions and Sciences (CAPPS). Thus, the value of a strong legislative advocacy organization for psychology as a health profession (like AAP)[1] can be clearly understood, and its financial support by all segments of psychology is deserved.

The permanent regulations of Pub. L. No. 93-222, the Health Maintenance Organization Act of 1973, are of particular interest to psychology because "clinical psychologists" are listed as one of the providers of service in the Act. Presumably, clinical psychologists are licensed psychologists, but the practice of clinical psychology is not defined in the Act in the same way that social work is. This raises some questions, because social workers are licensed in only 17 states. The HMO regulations are sufficiently broad and vague so that it is possible for an institution to certify unlicensed individuals to perform certain functions, even though licensure to perform these functions is required by the state in which the HMO operates (see U.S. DHEW, 1974) as follows:

(h) (1) *"Health professionals"* means physicians, dentists, nurses, podiatrists, optometrists, physicians' assistants, *clinical psychologists,* social workers, pharmacists, nutritionists, occupational therapists,

---

[1] Association for the Advancement of Psychology.

physical therapists and other professionals engaged in the delivery of health services who are licensed, practice under an institutional license, are certified or practice under authority of the health maintenance organization, a medical group, individual practice association or other authority consistent with State law.

(2) "Physician" means a doctor of medicine or a doctor of osteopathy. (p. 37312; italics added)

Thus, it appears that an HMO also may be a new kind of state licensing board as well as a service delivery organization. This type of certification power by an HMO is likely to be the subject of heated debate and further restrictive legislation. Temporarily, it does provide an opportunity for employment for newly trained master's-level psychology students who do not meet the qualifications for state licensure.

The HMO regulations do not mandate that psychologists be employed by an HMO, but rather allow for permissiveness in hiring psychologists, along with physicians, social workers, and psychiatric nurses. It must also be noted that the Federal Freedom of Choice legislation, Pub. L. No. 93-363, which requires that mental health services provided by psychologists to federal employees must be reimbursed by insurance carriers according to the terms of their contract, specifically excludes HMOs from this requirement. It appears that legislators primarily interested in health legislation are unwilling to be too restrictive of the innovative concept of HMOs.

The efforts of mental health specialists to have the HMO regulations stipulate that mental health programs should be directed by a mental health specialist were defeated. However, as a major concession, the final HMO regulations require a "health professional," instead of a "physician" to coordinate the patients' overall health care. Furthermore, clinical psychologists are included under the definition of health professionals. This discards the old costly medical referral and supervision concept of cost containment.

Another fundamental and progressive change in the delivery of mental health services provided in the HMO law is that 20 outpatient mental health visits are required as part of the basic health sercices rather than being a "suptablishing the preconditions for a truly compre-

hensive and integrated physical and mental health service system. Clinical psychological services are thus permitted at the outset of diagnosis and treatment, rather than being adjunctive to physical health services.

In order to attain the benefits of the integrated physical and psychological health services in HMO, a broadened definition of clinical psychology is required. An expanded definition of mental health beyond "nervous and mental disorders" would include physiological conditions subject to conscious and volitional control and would further include the psychological aspects of all conditions having adverse effects on the health of the individual. This broadened definition of the clinical psychologist as a health specialist is in line with the World Health Organization's definition of health "as a state of physical and mental well being."

But broadening the definition of clinical psychology so that psychological services may be directly provided for all health conditions rather than just nervous and mental disorders will not be gained without a struggle. The struggle will be won first by the provision of effective health services at a reasonable cost by individual practitioners. Verification of the effectiveness of these services by research and the response of psychological training programs to broader issues of health will follow. The HMO concept and regulations provide an exciting challenge to the profession of psychology. It is likely the present HMO regulations will undergo some significant modifications to coincide with the experience of practice, and it is essential that psychology carefully monitor these developments. With strong legislative advocacy to prevent narrow, restrictive legislation or regulation of the practice of psychology, the professional psychologist can come of age as a health science provider, as well as a mental health practitioner in the HMO.

References

Schofield, W. The psychologist as a health professional. *Professional Psychology,* 1976, *7,* 5–8.

U.S. Department of Health, Education, and Welfare, Public Health Service. Health maintenance organizations. *Federal Register,* 1974, *39,* 37308–37323.

At the time of original publication of this article, *Jack G. Wiggins* was President of the Psychology Development Center, Cleveland, Ohio.

8

National Health Insurance Plans

The United States will be among the last of the industrial nations to adopt a comprehensive national plan for the provision and payment of health care. There are many reasons for this delay: historical debate between free enterprise versus government control, fear of power and income loss by the medical lobby, consumer concerns about benefits, and taxpayers' fears about costs. These are important issues worthy of much close attention. Control of the system is also an issue. Government officials, insurers, providers, and consumers debate how policy and benefits will be determined, who will administer the program, and how prompt, equitable access will be combined with cost-efficient quality care.

Discussion of national health insurance has focused on physical health. This is not unexpected. Physical health costs are 10 times greater than mental health costs, and, depending on the perspective, inflation in physical health costs is two to three times greater. Focusing on the physical health issues first, however, may have deleterious effects on the delivery system ultimately developed and on the nature and quality of mental health services. Mental health care is seen as similar but somehow different from medical care, as it should be. The danger is that the same mechanisms used to address physical health problems will simply be transferred to the mental health field without the unique aspects of mental health care being considered.

A mental health delivery mechanism that is merely patterned after the physical health delivery system will be weak and ineffective and probably result in a lower quality of mental health care than that currently provided. The mental health area has unique problems and possibilities, and its delivery system is based on a broader conceptualization than that of physical health care. The overall mental health system is broader and less expensive and could adapt itself more easily to the inclusion of physical health coverage within its system than the physical health system could adapt itself to the delivery of quality mental health care.

Any attempt to integrate the health and mental health delivery systems must be done in a manner that provides mental health with a substantial share of the policy and administrative positions if any serious effort is to be made to make the system truly responsive to mental health needs and issues. The only effective system will be one in which mental health is at least a coequal partner. Any other plan will result in the mental health field's receiving all of the negative features of the physical health care system without the physical health system's receiving any of the positive aspects of the structure of mental health delivery. If we treat mental health as a small part of the health care system, rather than as a coequal and qualitatively different aspect of health, we will get a lower quality of mental health care because we will be retreating to a limited and inappropriate service model—the medical model.

Alain Enthoven of the Stanford School of Business has proposed a unique national health insurance plan that would provide freedom-of-choice provisions and cost-saving incentives for all parties. The plan emphasizes private insurers operating under a competitive framework. Enthoven believes in a minimum of government regulation, with cost control maintained by competitive, organized systems of care that would include HMOs and other health care alliances. The government's role would be to regulate against the exclusion of high-risk populations and to prevent inadequate coverage. The system would be financed by tax credits for workers and a voucher system for the poor. A tax credit sufficient to cover the insurance premium would be allowed working families. An incentive to enroll in the best and most economical plan would be created by allowing the insured to keep any savings. Annual open enrollment would permit the insured to leave an unsatisfactory plan for a better and more economical one. Experience, such as with HMOs, has demonstrated that mental health services become an integral and cost-efficient component in a health care system under such conditions of financing and freedom of choice.

In this section, we present a sample of articles struggling with issues surrounding national health insurance. The first two papers are from an excellent book by Karen Davis, a health economist and currently the Deputy Assistant Secretary for Programs, Planning, and Evaluation in the Department of Health, Education, and Welfare. These chapters provide a perspective on the general context in which the national discussion is occurring. The work of Davis has had impact. Its effectiveness probably lies in its strong emphasis on empirical data as the basis for policy and program recommendations. The Davis recommendations are favorable to the inclusion of mental health benefits in national health insurance, but they do not go far enough. No distinction is made between physical health benefits and mental health benefits; the reasoning and planning follow a simple extension from physical health problems to mental health problems.

The third article is a briefing document submitted to the President in May of 1978 by Joseph Califano, Secretary of Health, Education, and Welfare. It presents a spectrum of plans of varying costs and coverages as

a means of illustrating the options available in planning and implementing national health insurance. The problem with Secretary Califano's
strategy is that it struggles to make the fewest modifications in the current system while still enacting some type of national health insurance.
Such a strategy can only lead to a medicalization of mental health services, with a resulting decrease in effectiveness and increase in cost.

The fourth article is President Carter's statement of 10 principles
for a national health plan. As in Secretary Califano's memo, there is a
clear conflict between issues of accessible comprehensive care, consumer
influence, and freedom of choice on the one hand, and offsetting issues of
inflation, cost-control, and financing on the other.

The fifth article in this section is the report of the National
Health Insurance Subcommittee of the Liaison Group for Mental
Health. The Liaison Group for Mental Health is a Washington-based
coalition of representatives from 19 national mental health associations.
Members include the Mental Health Association, American Psy-
chological Association, American Psychiatric Association, American
Nursing Association, National Association of Social Workers, National
Council of Community Mental Health Centers, American Hospital
Association, American Medical Association, National Association of State
Mental Health Program Directors, and other groups. The Liaison
Group provides a form for discussion of major policy issues in the mental
health area and for determination of specific points of agreement and
disagreement. This 1976 report resulted from such an attempt to identify
shared opinion, during a time when Charles Kiesler served as Chair of
the group. The report was specifically endorsed by several of the organizations involved in drafting it. Among the exceptions were the American
Medical Association and the American Psychiatric Association. In 1977,
the American Psychological Association's Council of Representatives
voted to accept the Liaison Group's statement on national health
insurance as within the latitude of opinion acceptable to the Association
and Council.

The Liaison Group has illustrated that the mental health field is
not in disarray. In fact, there is far more unity and shared opinion than
commonly acknowledged by those outside the field. Items of agreement
include the estimates of the number of persons needing mental health
services, common concerns about quality of care, and shared theories and
clinical techniques. In fact, it is probably safe to say that there is 95%
agreement on most general topics. That the disagreement is seized upon
and publicized is not surprising—disagreement always seems more interesting than agreement. But it would be an error to assume that mental
health groups cannot agree on anything.

The next document, entitled "Consumer-Oriented Health
Insurance (COHI) Proposal," was developed by the APA Committee on

Health Insurance. It is a plan emphasizing consumer involvement and consumer interests: freedom of choice, accessible services, quality of care, and systematic program evaluation. The Council of Representatives of the American Psychological Association has also endorsed this statement.

In the final article, Cummings discusses the ways in which mental health services should be structured under national health insurance. He argues that the medical model would be inappropriate because it encourages "somatization" of emotional distress and hence overburdens medical facilities. Research has demonstrated that over 60% of all visits to physicians and consequent medical diagnostic tests are made by sufferers of emotional distress rather than organic illness. Cummings argues that the exclusion and/or systematic underutilization of psychological services under national health insurance would cause costly, inappropriate, excessive utilization of medical services. He argues further that the provision of psychotherapy would be a cost-saving feature. He cautions, however, that mere across-the-board inclusion of any and all mental health procedures would be clinically ineffective and cost-inefficient and presents a model for the delivery of active outpatient treatment and prevention services utilizing both dynamic and behavioral components.

A National Plan for Financing Health Care

Karen Davis

This paper reviews recent government involvement in the provision of health care and notes the potentially conflicting goals of national health insurance. It suggests that while the goals of national health insurance are clear-cut and agreed upon, the best methods for achieving these goals are less clear.

Unlike most major industrial countries, the United States has never had a comprehensive national plan for the provision of and payment for health care. While public programs at all levels of government affect the provision of health care in a multitude of ways, these programs lack a unifying policy designed to meet the health care needs of all Americans. It is not surprising, therefore, that some Americans fare well under the current mix of public programs and private initiatives while others are unassisted in their efforts to cope with the high cost of medical care.

Since the government has not developed a comprehensive public plan for meeting the costs of medical care, private institutions have assumed much of the responsibility for helping Americans to meet these costs. The private health insurance industry has grown from a $1 billion industry in 1950 to an expected $32 billion in 1975. This growth has been closely linked to the work place. About 80% of all private insurance is sold through employer groups. Thus, families that have an able-bodied, employed worker have been best served by this system—although workers often find that how good their coverage is depends largely on their employers. For those outside the work force, private insurance has been minimal.

In the mid-1960s, the federal government moved to assume responsibility for many of the people who were poorly served by the private system. Medicare and Medicaid were instituted to help the elderly and those on welfare, and more recently the permanently disabled, pay for medical care. In 1975, federal and state governments are expected to spend $25 billion under these programs. The government also provides indirect assistance to workers and their families through tax subsidies for the purchase of private health insurance and the payment of large medical bills. These tax subsidies result in an annual loss of $6 billion in federal tax revenues.

In spite of the phenomenal growth of private insurance and the large outlays by the government, many gaps remain. Over 6 million people below the poverty line are not covered by Medicaid, and few of the working poor have adequate private health insurance, if any. Less than 30% of the workers who lose their jobs and major source of income retain private health insurance coverage to protect them during this period when they are most vulnerable to the high cost of medical care. Even those covered by Medicare, Medicaid, or private health insurance plans often experience severe financial hardships because of restrictions on what is covered and how much will be paid.

Perhaps even more important, this patchwork approach to financing medical care has proved impotent in controlling high costs and has undoubtedly fostered much of the rapid inflation in medical care costs. The 1971–73 Economic Stabilization Program demonstrated that the rapid rise in medical care costs can be curbed—at least temporarily. A permanent solution, however, is likely only if medical care is financed under a single system that effectively uses the power of the purse to control costs.

Goals of National Health Insurance

While it is doubtful that any single plan can cope with *all* the ills of the health care system, it is increasingly recognized that genuine progress can be achieved only through reform of the method of paying for medical care that national health insurance addresses. A revamped payment system would make it possible to pursue programs to reorganize the delivery of health services, to upgrade the quality of care, and to promote the development of the right kinds of medical resources in the right places. National health insurance, however, is primarily concerned not with these important goals, but with those most easily achieved through financial mechanisms. Of these, three are of primary importance: (1) ensuring that all persons have access to medical care, (2) eliminating the financial hardship of medical bills, and (3) limiting the rise in health care costs.

Ensuring Access to Care

All Americans should have access to adequate high-quality medical care provided in a manner that respects their rights and personal dignity. At present, this goal is far from being reached.

While the Medicaid program, implemented in 1966, has helped many poor people obtain adequate medical care, almost 28% of the poor continue to be excluded from coverage. Private insurance has not filled this gap. Less than 40% of the poor in the labor force have even limited private health insurance, and only 11 percent have insurance for nonhospital services. Those poor who are covered by Medicaid have made dramatic gains in obtaining health care, and many now use medical services as extensively as people with higher incomes who have similar health problems, although the type and quality of care may differ. Those who have been excluded from Medicaid and private plans are lagging well behind the others in their use of medical services. The result for these unfortunate people is diminished health, reduced productivity, and needless suffering.

The United States can ill afford a work force that is restricted in productive capacity and a society whose quality of life is impaired because of sicknesses that could easily have been prevented or remedied at an early stage by more equitable application of the nation's medical technology. Meeting the needs of all those who cannot afford adequate medical care without some assistance must be a top priority of any national health insurance plan.

Eliminating Financial Hardship

With the rapid rise in medical care costs, the ability to afford adequate medical care is no longer a problem only for the poor. While public programs and private health insurance mitigate the problems many Americans face in meeting the high cost of medical care, they have failed to protect all people from the consequences of large medical bills. Over a million Americans are denied coverage because the insurance industry regards them as "uninsurable." People who work for small firms, who are self-employed, or who work in low-wage industries are frequently unable to purchase private insurance at group rates and must either go without insurance or pay exorbitant premiums for even limited coverage.

For families with large medical bills, private insurance is markedly inadequate. Only half of the population has any major medical coverage. For those who have major medical policies, limits on the expenditures that will be covered and requirements for sizable patient payments are the rule, not the exception. In a day when the average cost of health care for such conditions as terminal cancer exceeds $20,000, even those with some insurance can face bankrupting medical outlays.

Since the system of private insurance coverage has failed to protect all people from the consequences of large medical bills, the second major goal of national health insurance is to ensure that no family is forced to endure genuine financial hardship in obtaining needed medical care.

Limiting the Rise in Health Care Costs

National health insurance could also be one means of stemming the rising tide of medical care costs that is due in part to the present system, which covers some kinds of expenses but not others. The growth of private insurance and the implementation of Medicare and Medicaid have heightened awareness that the "wrong" kind of insurance—whether public or private— is partially to blame for the rise in medical costs. Historically, insurance policies have emphasized complete coverage for short hospital stays; therefore, patients may prefer to be hospitalized even when outpatient or nursing-home care would be cheaper. Hospitals have taken advantage of assured revenues from insurance plans to provide a wider range of sophisticated services— leading to ever rising costs. Complete coverage for short hospital stays under most insurance plans has also reduced incentives for patients and physicians to "police" the medical care market or to insist that services be efficiently produced and worth the resources devoted to them.

National health insurance could reverse many of these adverse effects. A comprehensive benefit plan with cost sharing,[1] for example, might help reduce the tendency of patients to choose hospital care over less expensive alternatives, curb runaway costs, and promote more efficient organization and delivery of medical services. Alternatively, financial controls and incentives for more efficient practices could be designed to promote these purposes, even without a centralized health insurance plan. However, tying the payment of medical services to cost controls undoubtedly provides the widest range of alternatives for combating high costs and promoting great efficiency.

It should be recognized that, although a national health insurance plan can be the instrument for restructuring the kinds of private insurance currently available and although it might discourage some types of excessive insurance promoted in the private market, it can only achieve its goals of ensuring access to medical care and limiting financial hardship by adding to existing coverage in some cases. These increments in insurance coverage are likely to be inflationary, particularly if they are not offset by reductions in coverage for those expenses that are not a financial hardship. If the plan covers all medical expenses above a certain limit, as it must to provide good protection from financial hardship, excessive use of the most costly medical technology may be encouraged. Clearly, regulatory mechanisms as well as automatic incentives for efficiency in the use of medical resources are essential parts of a good national health insurance plan.

Supplementary Goals

A national health insurance plan meeting each of these three goals is unlikely to be acceptable, however, unless it also (1) can be equitably financed, (2) is easy to understand and administer, and (3) is acceptable to providers of medical services and to the public.

An equitable method of financing is generally regarded as one that does not fall more heavily on lower-income families than on higher-income families. Financing for most national health insurance plans is based on premiums, payroll tax revenues, and federal and state general revenues. Financing by premiums is the most regressive method because it requires a fixed amount from each family, regardless of income. The payroll tax is less regressive because it represents a fixed percentage of earnings, but since it does not affect other sources of income, such as interest, dividends, rent, and capital gains, the tax typically represents a higher share of total income for low-income families than for high-income families.[2] Furthermore, if the payroll tax applies to only a limited portion of earnings, as it does currently, it represents a declining share of income for all families above the taxable base. General federal revenues, which are drawn primarily from personal and corporate income taxes, are the most progressive sources of financing. State general revenues are derived largely from sales and property taxes and fall more heavily on low-income families.

Since the medical care system is inherently complex, it would be unrealistic to expect any national health insurance plan to meet all the

---

[1] "Cost sharing" means any payments required of patients by deductible and coinsurance provisions.

[2] See Joseph A. Pechman and Benjamin A. Okner, *Who Bears the Tax Burden?* (Brookings Institution, 1974), pp. 58, 72, 78.

special needs of the population in a simple fashion. Yet a plan cannot succeed if it is bewildering to those eligible for benefits. Some trade-offs between having a plan that is efficiently designed to achieve its major goals and having a plan that is understandable may be required. A plan that is so administratively complex that it causes long delays in reimbursement for services rendered and misunderstanding regarding what is covered and what is not can lead to disillusionment and disappointment with the system.

A national health insurance plan also must be acceptable to those responsible for its success—physicians, hospitals, and other providers of medical services—as well as patients. If the plan calls for a radical alteration of the relative income position of current providers or for sudden changes in current medical practices, considerable resistance to implementation can be expected. If patients feel that their views are not adequately represented and if there are no established grievance processes for voicing frustration about perceived inequities in the plan, the plan cannot function optimally. Thus, the greatest possible input from a wide range of views is essential in the planning, implementation, and ongoing administration of a national health insurance plan.

National Health Insurance: A Confusing Proliferation of Choices

While the goals of national health insurance are clear-cut and fairly widely agreed upon, the best approach to achieving these goals is much more open to question. More than twenty national health insurance bills were introduced in the Ninety-third Congress—ranging from bills that would provide federal tax subsidies to encourage more people to buy private health insurance to plans that would replace most private health insurance with a public plan. Some plans would cover all of the population, others would exclude certain segments. Some would replace the Medicare program for the elderly, some would modify it, and others would leave it alone. Some plans would be voluntary; others would automatically provide a specified health policy to

everyone. Some would incorporate special plans for different groups; others call for a uniform plan for all persons. Some cover a wide range of medical services, including preventive services, family planning, maternity care, long-term care, and mental health services; others contain only a few of these benefits. A variety of methods for paying hospitals, physicians, and other health providers is to be found in the bills under consideration. Financing of the plans relies on a varied mix of revenues from state governments, employers, patients, and federal payroll taxes and general revenues.

While a broad consensus exists that a national plan should be adopted, the array of choices before the American people is indeed bewildering. Few people can sort out the best choice or even understand clearly how they would be affected by the various plans.

Even with a lawyer to explain the complexities of the bills, many important ramifications of alternative plans are simply not apparent. How much would each plan cost? In particular, how much could any given family expect to have to pay for the plan—either directly, through premium payments, taxes, or payments to hospitals and physicians, or indirectly, through reduced wages or higher prices? How would the plan change their present health insurance coverage for better or for worse? Would employers supplement a national plan if it were inadequate for their needs? Or, even harder to predict, if a community has few physicians or specialized medical facilities, could it expect that a plan would attract more medical resources to the area or would residents of the community wind up paying for medical care that someone else receives?

In spite of the complexity of national health insurance, it is essential to have widespread understanding of the implications of selecting any one approach. National health insurance, of whatever form, promises to have far-reaching effects and high costs. The health services industry is a $100 billion industry. Even without national health insurance, federal and state governments will be paying $25 billion for medical care services under Medicare and Medicaid in 1975. The most modest proposals would raise this to about $35 billion; one would increase it to almost $100 billion. Although some of the plans would not significantly increase government expenditures, they could radically alter the composition of private payments—among employers and workers and among families at various income levels.

This study is an attempt to focus greater attention on the costs, benefits, and consequences of national health insurance and to foster greater understanding of the implications of alternative approaches.

Karen Davis, a health economist, is Deputy Assistant Secretary for Programs, Planning, and Evaluation, Department of Health, Education, and Welfare.

National Health Insurance: Choice Among Alternative Approaches

Karen Davis

This article reviews the range of approaches to national health insurance. It includes consideration of the populations covered, the benefits included, costs, reimbursement mechanisms, and the impact on providers, consumers, and government.

The national health insurance bills that have been introduced in Congress share a commonality of goals. They try to (1) ensure that all persons have financial access to medical care, (2) eliminate the financial hardship of medical bills, and (3) limit the rise in health care costs.

Current Alternatives

In spite of this uniformity of goals, there is a wide variety of approaches from which to choose. The proposal backed by the American Medical Association relies on tax credits to induce greater coverage under private health insurance plans. Senators Russell B. Long and Abraham A. Ribicoff would replace Medicaid with a federal plan for the poor and cover catastrophic expenses for everyone. The administration, the American Hospital Association, and the Health Insurance Association of America have all backed bills that rely heavily on the purchase of basic and catastrophic private health insurance through employer groups, with government contributions for care of the poor and aged. The compromise plan advanced by Senator Edward M. Kennedy and Congressman Wilbur D. Mills relies more heavily on public insurance financed by payroll taxes and federal and state general revenues. The Health Security Act, originally introduced by Senator Kennedy and Congresswoman Martha W. Griffiths and still backed by the AFL-CIO, replaces private insurance with a federal program covering virtually all medical bills for U.S. residents.

These major bills, while quite different in approach, have some similarities. They would provide a wide range of benefits to nearly all of the population. Direct payments by patients are minimal or nonexistent for the lowest-income groups, and all covered persons, regardless of income, would be guaranteed some ceiling on contributions. Working families with annual incomes below about $8,000 to $10,000 would receive at least partial subsidies under most plans.

The major bills differ markedly, however, in the methods of financing, administration, and reimbursement of providers. Because some plans are financed primarily by private insurance premiums through employer groups, they retain a much larger share of expenditures in the private sector. Private health insurance companies stand to benefit considerably by such plans; employers would face much greater obligations for employee benefits; and the cost of the plans would ultimately fall much more heavily on lower-income working families. State governments, in most plans emphasizing private coverage, would have much greater responsibility for administering coverage for the poor and those not covered by employer groups and for regulating and controlling health insurance companies and medical care providers.

The principal similarities of the major national health insurance bills and the different impacts they may have are summarized below.

Population coverage. All the plans would cover most of the population. The Health Security Act calls for universal coverage of all U.S. residents. The Long-Ribicoff bill would provide catastrophic benefits to persons of all ages who are insured or receiving benefits under social security, as well as basic benefits to all low-income people. Other bills would exclude small, but significant, fractions of the population. The Kennedy-Mills plan would not cover 3 million people—mostly young adults who are no longer eligible for their parents' plans and who have not yet had sufficient work experience to qualify for their own coverage. The administration plan would exclude 6.5 million people—mostly families with incomes above $5,000 who are not covered by employer groups, including the long-term unemployed, those newly or temporarily employed, part-time workers, families without an able-bodied worker, and the self-employed. The Health Insurance Association of America plan would not cover 25 million people—mostly those who do not currently have private health insurance, such as poor health risks, workers in small firms, workers in agricultural, construction, and retail trade industries, and the self-employed.

Range of medical benefits. The most striking similarity among the major national health insurance bills before Congress is their emphasis on a comprehensive range of health services. All cover both inhospital and ambulatory services. All would cover skilled nuring-home care, with limits ranging from 30 days under the American Hospital Association plan to 180 days under the Health Insurance Association of America plan. The Kennedy-Mills plan would introduce a new program to provide long-term care for the elderly in a variety of settings. All except the American Medical Association and the Long-Ribicoff plans would cover prescription drugs. The administration and Kennedy-Mills plans emphasize family planning, maternity care, and well-child care. Dental services for children are provided under all plans except the Long-Ribicoff bill and the Health Insurance Association of America; the latter would provide one dental examination annually to adults and children.

Direct patient payments. The Health Security Act would not require patients to contribute toward the cost of medical bills incurred; care would be provided free of charge for virtually all medical services. At the other extreme, the Long-Ribicoff plan would require families (except those with incomes below $4,800 for a family of four and $2,400 for a single individual) to pay for the first sixty days of hospital care, the first $2,000 of medical bills, and at most an additional $1,000 of coinsurance payments. Working families without private insurance to meet these payments would be subject to severe financial hardship in the event of a medical catastrophe.

Other plans incorporate moderate direct patient contributions for all except low-income families. The administration and Kennedy-Mills plans contain deductibles of $150 per person (for three family members in the administration bill and two family members in the Kennedy-Mills bill) and a coinsurance rate of 25% on bills exceeding the deductible. The trade association bills have more moderate patient cost-sharing requirements.

All plans reduce or eliminate cost sharing for low-income families and place a ceiling on family contributions. The maximum ceiling for the highest-income families is set at 10 percent of income under the American Hospital Association and American Medical Association plans, at $1,000 under the Kennedy-Mills and Health Insurance Association of America plans, and at $1,500 under the administration plan. Only the administration plan requires substantial patient payments for families with incomes below $5,000. Maximum ceilings are reduced for families with incomes below $8,000 to $10,000 in most plans.

While these ceilings should protect most families from severe financial hardships, a number of plans permit physicians to charge patients more than the amounts that would be paid by the insurance plan. These excess charges are not included in calculating maximum patient contributions, so that a patient undergoing complex surgery might receive a physician's bill several thousand dollars in excess of amounts that would be paid by the plans.

Cost of the plans. The cost study made in 1974 by the U.S. Department of Health, Education, and Welfare permits a comparison of the major national health insurance plans.[1] This study applies a uniform methodology to all plans to derive estimates of costs by sources of payment. One crucial assumption of this study is that the price controls proposed under Phase IV of the Economic Stabilization Program are in effect regardless of the provisions of a bill for controls on prices. Thus, the rate of price increase is assumed to be the same regardless of which, if any, bill is implemented.

Three concepts of costs are important: (1) real resource costs (total amount spent on medical care in the United States); (2) expenditures under the plan (excluding direct payments by patients and uncovered services); and (3) federal and state government expenditures. (See Tables 6-1 and 6-3 for a summary of cost estimates.) The net incremental impact on federal and state budgets is of course affected by funds that would be expended in any event and any changes in federal revenues that would occur.

The plans differ little in real costs, and those plans with higher costs simply reflect the greater use of medical services that they would generate. In terms of expenditures covered by the plan, the Long-Ribicoff plan would cover about 35% of all medical expenditures, while the Health Security Act would cover 82%. The total expenditure cost of the administration and Kennedy-Mills plans is about the same—$69 billion and $72 billion, respectively. The latter, however, would require $39 billion of added federal financing, while the administration plan, by relying on employer premiums as a major source of financing, would require only $6.3 billion of additional federal financing. State government expenditures (including local government outlays for charity hospital care) would be reduced in most plans.

Impact on employers. Any additional costs of national health insurance for employers are likely eventually to be borne either by consumers, in the form of higher prices, or by employees, in the form of lower wages than would have been earned without the insurance. However, any sudden marked change in the responsi-

bilities of employers can have important short-run effects.

Employer contributions to health insurance coverage are estimated to increase from $20 billion in the absence of a national health insurance plan to $27 billion under the administration plan, and $35 billion in the American Hospital Association plan. Employers would be expected to contribute about $7 billion toward supplementary private insurance plans in the Kennedy-Mills bill; however, any employer facing a reduction in health insurance costs would be required to pay either the employee's share of the payroll tax or compensate employees for the reduction in his obligation.

The administration plan would require all employers to pay $390 per family in the first year. The American Hospital Association plan would set the employer contribution at $758 per family. These amounts greatly exceed current employer contributions, particularly in small firms and in service, finance, retail trade, and agricultural industries. The Health Insurance Association of America and American Medical Association plans would be voluntary for the employer and employee, and do not specify the employer's share of the premium (which would exceed $900 per family).

Limited federal subsidies to employers would be available for five years in the administration plan and for up to ten employees in the American Hospital Association plan. Even so, many firms that do not currently make significant contributions to health insurance plans would face substantial increases in labor costs.

Cost to individuals by income class. The cost of national health insurance, whether nominally paid by federal or state governments or by employers, must ultimately be borne by individuals. Of primary concern in the analysis of the cost of any national health insurance plan, therefore, is the distribution of that cost among persons of different income classes.

When the costs of the two plans are compared with income, the administration plan is seen to be highly regressive over the entire income range. Families with incomes below $3,000 contribute 22% of their income to the plan, compared with 4% of income for families with incomes above $50,000. The cost of the Kennedy-Mills plan is distributed approxi-

[1] HEW, *Estimated Health Expenditures under Selected National Health Insurance Bills,* A Report to the Congress (1974).

mately in proportion to income, with the lowest-income and middle-income groups paying 7 to 8% of their income and the highest-income groups paying 5%.

While both the administration and the Kennedy-Mills plans receive some funds from federal and state general revenues, the principal difference in their sources of financing is the heavy reliance on premiums in the administration plan compared with a payroll tax on the first $20,000 of earnings in the Kennedy-Mills plan. This difference is reflected in the declining proportion of income devoted to national health insurance in the administration plan and the constant proportion of income (up to $20,000) applied to the Kennedy-Mills health insurance plan.

Effect on private insurance companies. The administration bill and the trade association plans would greatly increase sales and administered business (primarily administration of coverage for the poor and elderly) of private insurance companies. Combined sales and administered business would increase from about $55 billion without national health insurance to $80 billion under the administration plan and $90 billion under the American Hospital Association plan. The Health Insurance Association of America and American Medical Association plans would increase sales from $33 billion in 1975 without national health insurance to $62 billion, since under these plans even coverage for the poor would be through the subsidized sale of private health insurance.

The Kennedy-Mills plan and the Health Security Act would greatly reduce the role of private health insurance companies. While the Kennedy-Mills plan, like the administration plan, would result in $80 billion of sales and administered business, only $12 billion of that amount would represent sales, instead of $37 billion as in the administration plan. The Health Security Act would almost completely eliminate the private health insurance business.

Role of state governments. The Long-Ribicoff plan, the Kennedy-Mills bill, and the Health Security Act would all be federally run programs, with the federal government responsible for administration of the plan and establishing methods of paying medical care providers.

State government participation would be limited to some contributions for care of the poor.

The administration and trade association plans would create a much larger role for state governments. They would be charged with the regulation and supervision of private health insurance companies and with the establishment of methods of reimbursing hospitals, physicians, and other providers of medical services. The American Medical Association plan, on the other hand, would reimburse all providers according to usual and customary charges, and no state or federal intervention would be permitted. The states would also be charged with the provision of insurance coverage to the poor (with federal subsidies and regulations) under the administration and Health Insurance Association of America plans.

Methods of payment for hospitals, physicians, and other providers. The methods of reimbursing providers of medical services range from unrestricted methods in the American Medical Association bill to fairly stringent curbs on payments under the Health Security Act. Most bills would favor moderate methods of reimbursement that attempt to leave physicians and hospitals with about the same average level of reimbursement as they currently earn. The administration and the Kennedy-Mills bills would try new methods of reimbursement, while the Long-Ribicoff bill would model reimbursement along the same lines as used in the Medicare program.

While precise methods of reimbursement are not spelled out, the administration and Kennedy-Mills plans would establish prospective methods of reimbursing hospitals and other institutions that would not depend on actual expenses incurred during the year. Physicians would be reimbursed according to a fee schedule that would probably vary by specialty and by geographical location. Any physician electing to do so could charge patients (other than poor and elderly patients in the administration plan) more than the established fee. Physicians electing to accept the established fee would receive some billing and collection advantages, but most physicians would probably opt for the more generous incomes they could derive by setting their own fees.

A Recommended Plan for National Health Insurance

While most of the national health plans contain several good features, none is without flaws. The administration and Kennedy-Mills plans are similar in benefit structure and should both be largely effective in meeting the major goals of national health insurance. The cost of the administration plan, however, falls heavily on lower-income working families, and the plan would be a boon to private health insurance companies and a bane to employers. The Kennedy-Mills plan, while distributing costs much more equitably among income classes, would require substantial increases in federal expenditures. Neither plan would effectively curb cost increases, and some segments of the population would be excluded from coverage under both plans.

Since evaluation of any given approach to national health insurance must carefully weigh the possible advantages and disadvantages, selection of a "best" plan is difficult. The following recommendations, however, outline the principal features of a national health insurance plan that would meet the major goals of ensuring access to care, avoiding financial hardships, and limiting the rise in medical care costs, while at the same time distributing the costs equitably among different income classes.

- *Universal coverage.* The plan should cover all U.S. residents and should not exclude anyone because of family composition, employment status, or social security contribution history.
- *Comprehensive benefits.* The plan should cover both inhospital and ambulatory services, including services of health centers or clinics, prescription drugs, preventive services for children, maternity and family planning services, dental services for children, and at least limited skilled nursing-home and mental health benefits. Services provided by paramedical personnel should be covered if provided under the supervision of a physician—whether the physician is physically present or not. The same broad, comprehensive benefits should be available to all families.
- *Direct patient payments.* Direct payments should not be required for low-income families (those, say, with incomes of less than $5,000 for a family of four). While moderate direct patient payments should be required for middle- and upper-income families (to reduce the cost of the plan and to encourage efficiency), some reduction in these amounts should be made for lower-income families (those, say, between $5,000 and $10,000). Ceilings should be placed on the maximum contributions to health care, required of any family.

One schedule meeting this general recommendation would include no cost sharing below $5,000, a deductible of $150 per person (for three family members), 25% coinsurance, and a ceiling of $1,000 for all families with incomes above $10,000. For families with incomes between $5,000 and $10,000, the ceiling could be set at 20% of income in excess of $5,000. These income classes and deductible and ceiling amounts should be automatically adjusted upward over time as income and medical expenditures increase.

If the Medicare program is retained for the elderly, comparable ceilings on patient payments should be added. The program for the elderly should gradually be modified over time to a structure similar to coverage for other persons.

- *Tax subsidies for supplementary insurance.* Purchase of supplementary insurance to pick up required direct patient payments should not be subsidized by tax provisions. Any contributions by employers to such plans should be counted as taxable income to the employee and a nonlegitimate business expense of employers. No personal income tax deductions for premiums of supplementary insurance should be permitted.
- *Financing.* The plan should be financed in such a way that the burden does not fall disproportionately on low-income families. A combination of general revenues and a tax on payroll and unearned income would be preferable—similar to the financing provided in the Kennedy-Mills plan. If financing instead relies on premiums by employers, a credit should be allowed for any premiums in excess of some percentage of payroll (such as

4%) to convert the impact of the premium from a fixed amount per worker to a fixed percentage of earnings.

- *Administration.* The plan should be administered by the federal government. Reimbursement of claims for segments of the population could be undertaken by private organizations or state governments on the basis of competitive bidding, with federal supervision, provided safeguards on the privacy of income information were installed. If private insurance companies are permitted to sell the standard insurance plan, premiums should not be permitted to exceed 10 percent of benefit expenses.
- *Consumers.* Consumers should be represented on all advisory boards. Grievance processes should be established for patients to file complaints about improper handling of claims or inadequacy of care provided.
- *Minorities and access to care.* Hospitals, physicians, and other providers should be prohibited from discriminating among patients on the basis of race, nationality, or creed. Procedures for enforcement of nondiscriminatory provisions should be incorporated in the plan, including site visits for compliance, administrative procedures for informing patients of rights, and processes of filing complaints of discriminatory treatment. A health resources development fund should be created and funds earmarked for programs that will increase the availability of medical resources in minority neighborhoods.
- *Rural residents and access to care.* Methods of reimbursement should encourage the creation and optimal utilization of medical resources in rural areas, including the establishment of fee schedules for physicians that reward rather than penalize physicians for practicing in underserved areas, and reimbursement for services rendered by paramedical personnel and rural health centers whether a physician is physically present when service is rendered or not. Funds of a health resources development board should be specifically targeted on personnel who desire to locate in rural communities and on the development of innovative approches to health care delivery in rural areas. Supplementary programs to overcome specific barriers to medical care in rural areas—such as transportation services and coordination of medical and other services affecting health—should be developed.
- *Reimbursement of hospitals, physicians, and other providers.* Prospective methods of reimbursement for hospitals and other institutional providers should be developed and tried experimentally. Controls that place limits on per patient costs, similar to those in Phase IV of the Economic Stabilization Program, should also be considered. Limits should be placed on the incomes of such hospital-based specialists as anesthesiologists, radiologists, and pathologists.

Physicians and other noninstitutional providers should be required to accept the allowable charge as full compensation for services. Fees should be established on a basis that encourages a socially appropriate distribution of physicians by location and specialty rather than on the basis of past patterns of physician charges. Adjustments in the fee schedule over time should be established in such a way as to tie increases in total expenditures to an economic index, such as earnings in the economy.

Karen Davis, a health economist, is Deputy Assistant Secretary for Programs, Planning, and Evaluation, Department of Health, Education, and Welfare.

Memorandum for the President on the Basic Decision in Developing a National Health Insurance Plan

Summary of Four Sample Plans

Joseph Califano

This May 1978 memorandum from the Secretary of Health, Education, and Welfare to the President details the range of choices for national health insurance. The options include broad versus targeted population coverage, comprehensive versus catastrophic benefits coverage, and the conflict between accessibility and cost containment.

Memorandum for the President, May 22, 1978

As a result of the Presidential review process to date, discussions within the govt. have highlighted a fundamental policy choice that you must make before further development of the Administration's Natl. Health Insurance plan can occur: Should the Administration adopt

A *targeted approach* that guarantees basic health benefits to the very poor and provides only restricted benefits (such as catastrophic protection) to the rest of the population; *or*

A *broad approach* that ensures everyone in the nation will receive basic health benefits?

Virtually all other decisions in developing an NHI plan turn upon your resolution of this threshold decision, although a targeted approach could be presented as the first step towards broad reform.

The purpose of this memorandum is to highlight the implications and consequences of this decision—particularly for the health care system and for the economy—and to seek your guidance on which of these major forks in the NHI road we should take. This memorandum attempts to synthesize the comments from all the departments and agencies on this crucial question.

On a subject of this magnitude and complexity, virtually any point in this memorandum will seem conclusory. We, of course, stand ready to provide you with more detail, analysis or information on any of the points discussed below.

The Issue in Context

A. The Nature and Extent of Coverage

A program of Natl. Health Insurance should address a number of important problems in the nation's health care system: inflationary costs, a bias towards acute care rather than prevention, and the maldistribution of health resources, to name a few.

But the fundamental problem that a Natl. Health Insurance program will address is the extent to which it covers the millions of Americans who do not presently have either basic health coverage or catastrophic health coverage.

The two approaches differ dramatically regarding the extent of coverage.

1. *Definitions.* In order to gain orientation for the following discussion, it is important to have two basic definitions in mind:

Reprinted from *The Blue Sheet Supplement*, June 14, 1978, S8–S17.

- *Basic Health Coverage.* In judging the adequacy of present health coverage and making cost estimates, an essential concept is basic health coverage. By basic health coverage (or the basic benefit package) we mean: at least 30–60 days of hospitalization; basic laboratory tests; X-rays; and most MD services. It should be noted that we do not—purely for purposes of definition at this point—include most mental health services, dental services or long-term care in our concept of basic health coverage.
- *Catastrophic Coverage.* In essence, catastrophic coverage means coverage of large medical expenses normally associated with prolonged hospital stays. (Lab tests and MD services, even for an extended period of time, would be covered under a basic health package.)

2. *Present Gaps in Coverage.* Currently, public and private insurance is extensive for 220 mil. Americans[1]. But according to relatively crude statistics, the following gaps in health insurance coverage nonetheless exist:

- 24 mil. do not have basic health coverage (9 mil. below the poverty line and 15 mil. above the poverty line);
- 19 mil. have inadequate basic health coverage, that is, their health coverage does not include some of the elements in our definition of basic health coverage (4 mil. below the poverty line, 15 mil. above the poverty line); and
- Roughly 88 mil. do not have catastrophic health coverage.

3. *Coverage: The Target Approach and The Broad Approach*

- The *target approach* increases coverage in two ways (although variants of a target plan might take just one of the two steps). It provides catastrophic health coverage for all Americans, regardless of income level. It provides basic health coverage for all the poor (at present 9 mil. of the poor are not covered by

Medicare or Medicaid) as well as for the non-poor aged and disabled.
- The *broad approach* provides *both* basic health coverage and catastrophic health coverage to *all* Americans.

The basic difference in coverage between the two approaches is that the broad approach provides basic health coverage to an additional 30 mil. Americans above the poverty line who are not adequately covered at present and who would not be covered under the target approach.

The additional coverage includes the following types of individuals:

About 7 mil. Americans with incomes between the poverty line and $10,000 who currently have no health insurance whatsoever; about 8 mil. individuals with incomes between the poverty line and $10,000 who have only individual health insurance policies which in general provide poor coverage; about 15 mil. individuals with incomes above $10,000 who have either no coverage or who have only individual policies generally offering inadequate protection. (The majority of these 15 mil. are in the $10,000 to $15,000 range).

B. Cost

The costs associated with the target approach and the broad approach are strikingly different. To be sure, the costs for each plan have to be expressed in a range of some magnitude at this point. Nonetheless, the differences—because the broad plan will cover at least 30 mil. more persons—are significant. These costs are new dollars over current govt. and employer expenditures, and they are expressed in 1980 dollars (even though the plan would not begin to take effect until 1982).

- *Target Approach.* We presently estimate the cost of the target approach to be in the range of $15–27 bil. in new federal funds: $15–20 bil. to give *all* those below the poverty line basic coverage; and about $7 bil. to give all Americans catastrophic coverage.

It should be noted that the cost to the federal govt. of the targeted plan would be less if catastrophic benefits were not entirely

[1] In FY 78, federal health spending totaled $57 bil., including $26 bil. for Medicare covering 26.6 mil. ($4 mil. below the poverty line) and $11 bil. for Medicaid, covering 21 mil. (15 mil. below the poverty line).

financed by general revenues but in part by mandated private insurance coverage.

- *Broad Approach.* A broad NHI plan will involve, at a *rough minimum,* about $40 bil. in new funds. This could be financed in a number of ways, but one version of the broad approach which relies in part on mandated premiums by employers to finance insurance for workers assumes the following: $30 bil. in new federal expenditures, including $20 bil. in direct expenditures and $10 bil. in subsidies to employers; and $10 bil. in net new payments by employers (employers would pay a total of $20 bil. in new payments but receive $10 bil. in federal subsidies to offset partially these costs).

The rough $40 bil. cost for this version of a broad plan assumes: that the basic benefit package is the one defined above; that there is some cost-sharing by patients; and that certain important services—dental, mental health, preventive and long-term care—are not included (or included in only a minimal fashion).

Obviously, to the extent those variables are altered—and you need not face such issues now—the cost of the broad approach decreases or increases. For example, if cost-sharing by patients were dropped, the cost of the broad approach would increase by $23 bil., or if dental, drug, expanded mental health and preventive benefits were added, the cost would increase by about $28 bil.

It should also be noted that the very rough costs of both the targeted and the broad approaches do *not* include any assumptions about cost-savings from system-wide reforms in the health care industry. To the extent such reforms are instituted and savings from them are realized, then the amount of new money required for NHI—over the projected costs of the present system without either system reforms or additional coverage—will decrease accordingly.

C. Some Preliminary Caveats

1. *Costs*—This memorandum stresses the different costs of the two approaches and provides specific estimates of these costs. But a number of cautions must be underscored.

These estimates are extremely soft and tentative. They do no more than provide the general range in which a plan's cost would fall. They will almost certainly change as we refine them further.

The cost of either approach would obviously increase by adding a variety of benefits. However, costs could be reduced only with difficulty below the bottom range figures we have given you: for example, the basic benefit package is sufficiently "lean" that it would be very hard to cut it back in either a target or broad plan and increasing patient cost-sharing beyond the levels assumed in the broad approach described above will be very controversial.

Savings from system-wide reforms, while not reflected in our present cost estimates, will reduce the amount of new money required for a Natl. Health Insurance Plan.

2. *Phasing*—It is important to recognize that the choice between the two options cannot be entirely resolved by phasing.

Phasing *cannot* erase the difference between the two approaches—particularly the substantial differences in administrative and financing structures that each approach requires. To be sure, a targeted plan could represent the first stages of a broader plan. But, in proposing legislation, we will need to commit on when—or if—a broad plan will go into effect.

Those who support a broad approach would almost certainly criticize any proposal to "phase in" a broad plan over more than a decade.

Regardless of the method of phasing the Administration chooses, the press and those opposed to a broad approach will certainly focus on the cost of such a plan when fully implemented. Phasing in a broad NHI plan only postpones the budgetary impact, but obviously neither eliminates the costs involved nor softens the financial commitment.

Targeted NHI Approach vs. Broad NHI Approach

In this section, we compare the target approach and the broad approach by a number of important criteria. The alternative consequences of adopting the targeted or broad approach are highlighted. We have attempted to reflect the comments we received from the depts. and agencies in response to the Lead Agency Memorandum which was circulated in early April.

The approaches are compared by seven criteria which are organized under three broad headings: Effects on the Health Care System; Budgetary and Economic Considerations; and Administration.

A. Effects on the Health Care System

1. *Access to Services.* As set out above, the basic difference between a targeted NHI approach and a broad NHI approach in terms of affecting changes in the health care system is that a broad plan would extend basic health coverage to 30 mil. additional Americans above the poverty line who are not adequately covered at present.

As noted, this is the critical difference between the two approaches.

2. *Capability to Contain Increases in Health Care Costs.* Any national health insurance plan must control cost inflation. The nation cannot afford to purchase health care if costs continue to rise at current rates. Effective cost restraint must come both from greatly increased competition and from industry-wide regulation.

Some of your advisors believe strongly that effective cost controls can be established independently of any NHI plan through regulatory controls and improved incentives. They stress that effective cost could be realized by a targeted plan.

Others—including HEW—think that leverage to control health costs would be much stronger under a broad NHI plan; and that indeed this is a significant difference between the approaches.

TARGETED APPROACH

Because it does not finance care for all, a targeted approach would give the federal govt. little ability to control costs by limiting the fees paid through the plan to health care providers. Successful cost containment would, therefore, have to rest on authority and initiatives outside the basic financing proposals embodied in this type of plan.

Cost controls theoretically could be put in place independent of an NHI plan:

- The Administration's hospital cost containment legislation represents one example;
- Limits on MD fee increases were put in place under the Economic Stabilization Program—independent of govt. financing of health care although not of a larger wage-price structure.
- Financial incentives could also be created within the private sector to control costs by, for example, hinging tax subsidies for private health insurance coverage on stringent reimbursement provisions.

BROAD PLAN

Supporters of a broad NHI approach argue that it offers much more potential for controlling health care costs. Since the government will be mandating some form of insurance coverage, for *all* Americans, rather than relying on voluntary insurance coverage, its authority to regulate the amounts that health care providers are paid throughout the health sector will be strengthened. This system-wide authority could provide greater leverage to set and enforce fee schedules if such schedules are deemed desirable. Some have urged that this authority also be used to set area-wide budgets.

For example, the authority could be used to place across-the-board limits on the fees paid to health care providers by the govt. and by insurance companies—and then prohibit health care providers from charging patients additional sums. Such a prohibition probably could only occur if it were a condition of participation in a universal natl. health insurance plan, and not externally imposed by law.

3. *System Reform.* The Administration's NHI plan must transform the basic ways the health care delivery system operates: to increase use of HMO's in order to reduce hospitalization and realize other efficiencies; to place medical resources in underserved areas; to promote use of physician assistants and nurse practitioners; to emphasize prevention and early primary care.

Many steps to promote needed change can be taken under either a targeted approach or a broad approach.

- Either a targeted approach or a broad NHI approach could provide grant money to fund needed services in center city and rural underserved areas.
- Any NHI option could continue and expand current federal support for health maintenance organizations to promote more efficient provisions of health care services.
- Any NHI plan could override state laws prohibiting the use of physician assistants and nurse practitioners.

TARGETED PLAN

But since the target approach only provides basic health benefits to the poor, aged, and disabled, it will have only limited capability to structure financial incentives to promote HMO's, or to ensure the equitable geographic distribution of services. Providing additional coverage for the poor, aged, and disabled will undoubtedly funnel additional funds to some in underserved areas—funds which may attract new health care professionals. But our experience with Medicaid suggests it is unrealistic to expect a program limited to providing subsidies to the poor to produce dramatic shifts in the availability of health care services.

BROAD PLAN

A broad plan's authority over reimbursement policy should give it substantial additional leverage to promote reform in the health industry effectively. Such a plan could provide reimbursement incentives to HMOs to seek new members and can build in consumer incentives by reducing premium liabilities for employers and employees if they choose less expensive health maintenance organizations.

Similarly, a broad plan should be able to influence the geographical distribution of health professionals and facilities as well as encourage provision of preventive services through its control of reimbursement policy. For example, geographical distribution of health care providers should improve if reimbursement levels are used to attract providers to underserved inner city and rural areas and to halt the inflation in income levels in areas which are overserved.

4. *Quality of Care for the Poor, Aged, and Disabled.* Many Medicaid beneficiaries too

often receive substandard care largely because Medicaid is separated from the mainstream of private health insurance and pays less for equivalent services than the private market. If an NHI plan permits payments by private insurers or individuals to be higher than the amounts paid by a public insurance plan, public plan beneficiaries are likely to receive second class care.

The ability of an NHI plan to assure that health care providers are paid equally for all patients—thereby eliminating a strong incentive for unequal treatment—will largely determine the potential of an NHI plan to minimize "second-class" care. Both a targeted approach and a broad approach could obtain the needed control over the reimbursement system, if the govt. were given sufficient regulatory authority. But, as noted above, a broad plan has a stronger claim to the authority to regulate the amounts that all health care providers are paid since the govt. will be mandating and regulating all basic health insurance for everyone.

B. Budgetary and Economic Considerations

1. Budgetary Priorities.

TARGETED APPROACH

The targeted approach, providing basic benefits for the poor and catastrophic benefits for all, will add $15–27 bil. to the federal budget, depending on whether catastrophic coverage is financed through federal revenues or mandated through employers.

BROAD APPROACH

As noted, requiring basic medical benefits for everyone would increase federal expenditures and employer payments by at least $40 bil.

Moreover, there will be pressure to adopt an NHI program with even higher costs:

- An NHI plan that included no patient cost-sharing—as proposed by some—could add another $20 to $25 bil. to the costs. In the $40 bil. broad approach, we assumed 25% patient cost-sharing by the non-poor up to $1,500 per year.

- As noted, these cost estimates use a lean benefit package which is smaller than the Medicaid benefits provided currently by many states. It does not cover drugs or dental care, and only limited mental health and preventive services. Expansion of the NHI benefit package to Medicaid levels or beyond would be extremely expensive (in the range of an additional $20 to $40 bil.).

These very high additional costs of a broad plan have raised serious questions. Plainly the very large commitment that a broad NHI plan entails should be made with a recognition of its effort on competing natl. priorities.

During the Presidential campaign, you were careful to exempt natl. health insurance from your overall goal to restrain federal expenditures to 21% to GNP, and further indicated a willingness to increase federal expenditures to finance NHI by 1–2% of GNP—which would be about $25–50 bil.

Nonetheless, adopting a broad NHI approach would have several important economic consequences:

- A broad NHI plan would significantly affect efforts to hold the line on budget totals overall in the 1980's.
- A broad natl. health insurance program could absorb expenditures that would otherwise be available for competing natl. needs in future years.
- Phasing in of NHI postpones the budgetary impact, but obviously does not eliminate the costs involved.

2. *Financing: New Taxes and Increased Employer Payments.* Both NHI approaches will pose the same tough choices in finding funds to finance new federal expenditures to pay for coverage of basic benefits for the poor and for catastrophic coverage for everyone. But a broad NHI plan that requires adequate insurance for everyone poses an additional major fiscal challenge that has no counterpart in the targeted approach; finding the financing required to pay for basic health benefits for workers.

Three potential methods exist: federal general taxes, payroll taxes, or mandated employer premiums. (A decision on the method of financing an NHI plan will be presented to you

in another round of decision-making.) To finance coverage for all workers from increases in federal income taxes or from payroll taxes has not seemed realistic. Substantial attention has, therefore, been devoted to the option of mandated employer premiums.

Under this option, a broad NHI plan would probably *require* employers to pay for a significant percentage (probably 75%) of the premium costs for their employees. HEW projects that employers will pay about $40 bil. in premiums in 1980, in the absence of any NHI plan. Financing NHI by mandating employer premiums would require employers to pay these current costs plus any additional costs from providing new or better coverage to workers.

The decision on the size of the Administration's plan (and ultimately on the method chosen to finance it) must consider three related economic issues: inflation, employment effects, and administrative complexity.

a. *Inflationary Pressures.* The precise effect that any NHI plan will have on inflation will depend on a variety of decisions not yet made: for example, the exact increase in federal expenditures, the kinds of taxes used to raise new federal revenue, the extent of new obligations placed on employers to finance health insurance for their workers, the effectiveness of cost controls in reducing inflation in the health care sector, the phasing-in of NHI, and the monetary policy of the Federal Reserve Board.

But, in general, a natl. health insurance plan could increase prices in three ways:

- Through the increase in public and private expenditures required;
- Through the financing method used; and
- Through the impact of the expenditures on prices in the health care sector.

Expenditure Increase: In general, the inflationary impact of a plan as a result of increased expenditures can be offset by economic policy. The larger the plan and the quicker it is phased in, the more difficult this task will be.

Method of Financing: For plans requiring about a $20–30 bil. increase in federal expenditures, the inflationary impact could be minimized if the new expenditures were financed entirely through the personal income tax. For each $10 bil. financed from employer premiums, from payroll taxes, from sales taxes, from excise taxes or from a value added tax— and the program were put in place immediately—then, it is estimated, that current price levels could increase after two years by 0.5 to 0.6 percentage points. But this would be a one-time effect, after which prices would stabilize at a higher level. Phasing would stretch out—or even reduce—this effect.

Health Sector: Whether increased expenditures from a plan would exacerbate inflation in the health sector would primarily depend on the effectiveness of cost controls. General agreement exists that the level of increased expenditures from a targeted NHI would not outstrip the supply capacity of the health industry. But a targeted plan whose cost controls proved ineffective could fuel an inflation in the health sector similar to the experience after Medicare and Medicaid were enacted.

Economists disagree on the extent to which a broad NHI plan would pose a greater threat of inflation in the health sector than a targeted approach.

• Strong concern does exist that a broad NHI plan will stretch thin the resources of the health sector. To the extent that expenditures in health care increase more than $15 bil., concern has been expressed that serious bottlenecks could arise, sparking marked sectoral inflation problems to an extent that the nation could not afford.

• Other economists believe that a broad NHI plan can effectively control total costs and that adequate supplies of personnel and facilities currently exist to handle the increases in demand anticipated under a broad approach.

b. *Employment Impact.* Especially in the case of larger plans, premium financing would imply a very substantial increase in the cost of hiring workers who earn near the minimum wage. This increase could give employers an incentive to replace low paid workers with more skilled employees and aggravate the structural unemployment problem.

This increase in the relative cost of hiring low wage workers could result in substitution of higher-paid workers for minimum wage workers. In the larger plans, this substitution could result in a loss of 100,000 to 200,000 low wage jobs. This effect could be reduced by providing tax credits or subsidies to employers to help cover the expense of health insurance for low-wage workers.

Another option to reduce the unemployment effects would be to structure payments so that they were not a flat amount per worker but rather were based on the amount of earnings— which would reduce employer payments for low-wage workers. ("Earnings-related premiums" may be so similar, however, to a payroll tax that recent Social Security experience raises questions about this alternative.)

Premium financing also has the potential to affect significantly the incentives to hire part-time workers, secondary workers, and workers holding multiple jobs. If these workers are not required to pay premiums, employers would have an incentive to replace heads of households with secondary workers.

c. *Administration of Financing Mechanism.* Any move to employer-related financing, however, brings with it a quantum jump in administrative complexity. *Premium financing engages the federal govt. in overseeing health insurance transactions between every employer and employee in the country.*

The federal govt. will need to assure the payment of premiums by employers and make complex liability calculations for part-time workers, seasonal workers, workers with two jobs, workers who change jobs, second workers in families, etc.

Moreover, administration of the payments to cushion the potential inflationary and unemployment effects of increased employer premiums will also be complex. HEW has proposed tax credits, but the complexities involved in administering these credits remain to be worked out. Alternatively, direct subsidies and/or gradual phasing in of new obligations on employers could be employed.

C. Administration

1. *Role of the Federal Govt. and of Private Insurance Companies.* A broad NHI plan will present a far more difficult administrative

challenge than a targeted approach. Under a broad NHI approach the federal govt. will become deeply involved in regulating and overseeing the health insurance industry. This of course is in addition to the administrative problems involved in the potential employer based financing of a broad plan.

TARGETED PLAN

Under a targeted plan, the federal govt. would basically federalize Medicaid and operate a unified federal insurance plan to cover the poor, aged and disabled. Administration of a substantially increased federal health insurance plan will entail substantial and complex tasks of income determinations, processing and verifying claims, etc. While complex, Medicare and Medicaid currently perform these tasks. A targeted plan would yield little conflict or overlap with the health insurance industry.

BROAD NHI PLAN

Under a broad plan, the nature of the industry could change substantially. Whether firms continue to operate on a risk-taking basis in which they expect to make a profit, or operate instead as administrative agents for the govt., will depend on subsequent decisions about how a NHI plan should be structured and administered.

A broad NHI plan which requires basic health coverage for everyone could stipulate either that coverage be provided entirely through the private insurance industry, or through a mixed public/private system.

In either case, extensive regulation of the private insurance industry would be necessary. One version of the broad approach favors coverage of the entire population under private plans subject to extensive public regulation of private companies.

At the time of original publication of this memorandum, *Joseph Califano* was Secretary of Health, Education, and Welfare.

Presidential Directive on a National Health Plan

Ten Principles for National Health Insurance

Jimmy Carter

This July 1978 Presidential Directive endorses a "broad-option" national health insurance plan. Carter spells out 10 principles for the implementation of such coverage, which include freedom-of-choice options, accessibility, and cost-effective delivery of service.

Presidential Directive/DPS–3, July 29, 1978

To: The Secretary of Health, Education and Welfare

I have consistently expressed my support for the goal of a universal, comprehensive national health plan to contain skyrocketing health costs and to provide all Americans with coverage for basic health services and with protection from catastrophic expenses.

Such a plan would be the cornerstone of a broader national health policy designed to improve the health of Americans by reducing environmental and occupational hazards and encouraging health enhancing personal behavior, as well as by improving the effectiveness of our medical care system.

The current health care system has significant defects which must be remedied:

- The health care system is highly inflationary. Spending in the health care industry—the nation's third largest industry—has been rising at an annual rate of 12%, with little improvement in the health of Americans. These expenditures cannot be successfully contained under current health delivery and financing methods, which produce unnecessary hospitalization, over-reliance on expensive technology and inadequate preventive care.

- At least 20 million Americans have no health insurance.
- Another 65 million Americans face potential bankruptcy because they lack insurance protecting them against catastrophic medical expenses.
- Health resources are unevenly distributed across the country, resulting in significant gaps in vital medical services for many residents of rural and inner city areas.

In pursuing the goal of a comprehensive national health plan, I also wish to draw on the strengths of the American health care system:

- American health care professionals and hospitals are among the finest in the world and deliver dedicated, high quality medical care.
- A growing number of Americans have private health insurance. American business increasingly is paying for health coverage for its employees.
- Various government programs have provided an opportunity for millions of elderly, poor and geographically isolated Americans to obtain quality health care.

In past months you and other members of my Administration have been exploring the most effective means of fulfilling my commitment to a comprehensive national health plan. You have considered a broad range of options. However,

Reprinted from *The Blue Sheet Supplement*, August 2, 1978, S1–S2.

before I submit legislation to the Congress, I want to be certain that the plan is consistent with our efforts to control inflation in the health care sector and the general economy. Before you send me final recommendations for a national health plan, you should analyze the issues of cost control and health system reform in greater depth. The American people would not accept, and I will not propose, any health care plan which is inflationary.

At the same time, the American people must recognize that if we fail to act, health expenditures will continue to soar. In 1977, health expenditures were $162 billion; they are expected to reach $320 billion by 1983. A comprehensive national health plan will provide a critical opportunity to mount a national effort to bring the system under control.

I am directing you to address these concerns as you proceed to develop in greater detail a national health plan for the American people. The plan must improve the health care system, and combat inflation by controlling spiralling health care costs. To achieve these objectives, the plan, when fully implemented, should conform to the following principles.

(1) The plan should assure that all Americans have comprehensive health care coverage, including protection against catastrophic medical expenses.

(2) The plan should make quality health care available to all Americans. It should seek to eliminate those aspects of the current health system that often cause the poor to receive substandard care.

(3) The plan should assure that all Americans have freedom of choice in the selection of physicians, hospitals, and health delivery systems.

(4) The plan must support our efforts to control inflation in the economy by reducing unnecessary health care spending. The plan should include aggressive cost containment measures and should also strengthen competitive forces in the health care sector.

(5) The plan should be designed so that additional public and private expenditures for improved health benefits and coverage will be substantially offset by savings from greater efficiency in the health care system.

(6) The plan will involve no additional federal spending until FY 1983, because of tight fiscal constraints and the need for careful planning and implementation. Thereafter, the plan should be phased in gradually. As the plan moves from phase to phase, consideration should be given to such factors as the economic and administrative experience under prior phases. The experience of other government programs, in which expenditures far exceeded initial projections, must not be repeated.

(7) The plan should be financed through multiple sources, including government funding and contributions from employers and employees. Careful consideration should be given to the other demands on government budgets, the existing tax burdens on the American people, and the ability of many consumers to share a moderate portion of the cost of their care.

(8) The plan should include a significant role for the private insurance industry, with appropriate government regulation.

(9) The plan should provide resources and develop payment methods to promote such major reforms in delivering health care services as substantially increasing the availability of ambulatory and preventive services, attracting personnel to underserved rural and urban areas, and encouraging the use of prepaid health plans.

(10) The plan should assure consumer representation throughout its operation.

I am directing you to develop a tentative plan as soon as possible which embodies these principles and which will serve as the basis for in-depth consultation with the Congress, state and local officials, interest groups, and consumer representatives. You should then provide me with detailed recommendations so that I can make final decisions on the legislation I will submit to the Congress next year. To respond fully to my economic and budgetary concerns, you should develop alternative methods for phased implementation of the plan.

JIMMY CARTER

As one of his first official acts as President of the United States, *Jimmy Carter* formed the President's Commission on Mental Health. *Rosalynn Carter* serves as Honorary Chair of the Committee.

Report of the National Health Insurance Panel

Liaison Group for Mental Health

This article is a report of the National Health Insurance Panel of the Mental Health Liaison Group. It includes consideration of the organization and administration of national health insurance, benefits, qualifications of providers, program development, and program evaluation/research.

Introduction

The future well-being of this nation is dependent upon a population that is both mentally and physically healthy. A tradition of minimizing the importance of mental health and denigrating the victim of mental illness has been practiced by the population as a whole and even promoted by state and federal policy and statutes. At this time, when serious consideration is being given to a national health insurance policy, the constituents of the mental health community have pledged to halt discrimination against the mentally ill and to contribute to the development of a national health insurance program that would benefit not only the mentally ill and their families but also the general economy and the social fabric of our nation should such a program be developed.

We therefore have identified principles that provide a basis for the inclusion of mental health benefits in a national health insurance plan.

Administration and Organization of National Health Insurance

1. Services delivered under the national health insurance system should be provided for the benefit of the citizens. It is essential that citizens be involved in the development of those services at all levels. Citizens who are accountable to the public should be in the majority on boards and committees involving planning priorities.

Citizens should have representation at policy levels in matters including quality assurance and rate setting, professional standards review organizations, accreditation and certification of organizations, licensure/statutory certification of facilities and practitioners, and the systems by which records are kept. Citizens shall be represented on all governance authorities of service delivery organizations either in an advisory or policymaking capacity.

2. National health insurance should include the development of effective methods and standards for accountability in fiscal, programmatic aspects and impact of the service delivery system.

3. National health insurance should provide benefits that promote an integrated and coordinated system of mental health service delivery that assures easy access and continuity of care. Special efforts should be made to assure that benefits shall facilitate concerted efforts to humanize, upgrade, and expand services in the community for individuals who have had extended inpatient care.

4. In conformance with local health planning requirements, national health insurance benefits should encourage a pluralistic and competitive health care system involving the resources of the private and public sectors and

From *Report of the National Health Insurance Panel*. Washington, D.C.: Liaison Group for Mental Health, 1976.

enabling a choice of provider and provider systems by consumers.

5. There should be a guarantee of privileged communication between practitioners and patients. Confidentiality must be protected within both the mental health delivery system and the national health insurance system. Patients should be aware of the information system and should have access to their service records and information and the opportunity to correct factual errors.

6. There should be no limitation of coverage or discrimination based upon age, sex, race, creed, economic circumstances, or previous mental or physical condition or diagnosis.

7. National health insurance should provide separate funding for consumer health education and preventive services with the intent of maximizing health maintenance and minimizing the utilization of services.

8. National health insurance should provide mental health benefits so as to encourage the use of services in the community and out of the hospital. National health insurance benefits for mental health services should be provided to individuals irrespective of residence or of vocational or institutional settings such as schools or court-designated placements.

9. There should be a full right and easy access to educational services, vocational services, and social services when indicated in the individualized mental health service plan.

Mental Health Benefits for Citizens

Mental health services funded under national health insurance should be responsive to the needs of the population to be served and therefore may vary for geographical areas, age groups, and socioeconomic settings. Any designation of specific mental health services and limits of utilization is arbitrary. Such arbitrary decisions often influence the utilization of mental health services. Inappropriate utilization of such services may impact upon the effectiveness of care and upon the cost of care. Organized peer review, regional planning, and other control mechanisms may be effective in controlling costs and, at the same time, make possible the provision of appropriate mental health services at the local level.

An individualized service plan must be authorized by a mental health practitioner for each patient. Such a plan should stipulate clear service objectives within designated time intervals, indicate procedures to be used to obtain these objectives, and identify the mental health personnel who will carry out these procedures. There must be documentation of progress related to the service plan, a periodic review, and documentation of modifications. Where appropriate, the service plan shall also include a medical evaluation and medical treatment by a physician properly qualified to fulfill legal requirements for physician responsibility where mandated in state or federal law. The plan must be developed with patient involvement and shall require periodic review by both patient and provider related to the objectives.

To assure qualified services, the practitioner, within a system of organized review, will have (a) maximum latitude to provide services during the initial phases of treatment subject to monitoring audit procedures, (b) moderate latitude for more extended treatment subject to provider profile analysis and exception recording, and (c) restrictive latitude over extended treatment and costs through a prospective and concurrent review process under an organized peer review system.

Present concepts of reimbursement tend to emphasize the setting rather than the specific service provided to a patient. The treatment provided to a patient, rather than the setting, should be the more important determinant of reimbursement. The following services should be made appropriately available as determined through each individualized treatment plan.

Diagnostic and Treatment Services

- Ambulatory diagnosis; evaluation; emergency care; outpatient services; inpatient services; partial hospitalization services; medications; crisis intervention; individual, group, and family therapy modalities provided through various approaches and in various settings.

Specialized and Extended Health Services

- Preventive services *and services designed to promote effective individualized growth and development.*

- Skilled nursing, intermediate, or other 24-hour care that includes an organized program of health services.
- Home health care.
- Consultation and education services.
- Outreach or follow-up visits through multidisciplinary health counseling and education, and therapies to patients in their own homes and in various types of community settings.
- Transitional living facilities.

Such services should be reimbursed as long as they can be documented as an integral part of a specific treatment plan and are provided by or under the supervision of a qualified mental health practitioner in accordance with the above-mentioned principles relative to quality and cost control.

Qualifications for Mental Health Practitioners and Organization-Providers

Qualifications for Organization-Providers

In order to qualify for reimbursement, organization-providers must:

1. Be licensed by the state. State licensure shall be directed toward safety, sanitation, and living arrangements.

2. Be accredited by a nationally recognized body. The accreditation process should include representation of the major mental health professions, institutional associations, and citizens. The major emphasis of the accreditation process should be the quality of services and programs with focus on the outcome of services rendered.

3. Have all mental health services delivered under the supervision of qualified mental health practitioners.

4. Be relicensed and accredited at least biennially.

Qualifications for Mental Health Practitioners

Only qualified mental health practitioners would be eligible for direct reimbursement. Psychiatrists, psychologists, social workers, nurses,

and other disciplines as might be designated in a national health insurance plan would qualify as mental health practitioners providing they met the qualifications below:

1. Have an MD or *the appropriate* graduate degree in a mental health specialty from a regionally accredited educational institution as a minimum.

2. Have at least two years of demonstrated, supervised mental health experience following the graduate degree.

3. Be designated as a qualified mental health professional through an approved validation program developed and administered *with the participation* of the appropriate national professional organization.

4. Be licensed/statutorily certified in a state.

5. *Have license or statutory certificate renewed at least biennially. Such renewal must be contingent upon* demonstrated, competent practice and continuing education according to established standards developed *with the participation* of a national professional organization.

Resource Development and Training

Administration, funding, and implementation for resource development and training should be separate from the health insurance program and should provide appropriate education and training to the providers, the administration, and related systems to maximize knowledge and skills to better develop and implement the national health insurance program.

Research, Development, and Information Systems

1. The national health insurance budget shall provide for the development of a standardized, unified, management information system as an aid to quality, coordinated service, cost control, and audit procedures, while maintaining proper confidentiality and privileged communication.

2. There shall be support for program research, development, and evaluation as an integral part of the mental health delivery system.

This support shall be funded at a stipulated amount of the National Health Insurance budget.

3. Basic and clinical research that embraces the physical, psychological, and environmental bases of health should be separate in administration, funding, and implementation from any health insurance program. Support for basic and clinical research of physical, psychological, and environmental bases of health should be in accord with national priorities and related to the identification of high-risk populations and incidences of unresolved health disability.

Members of the Mental Health Liaison Group were *F. Lee Goldberg,* Association of Mental Health Administrators; *Russell Bent,* American Psychological Association; *James Gibbs,* American Academy of Child Psychiatry; *Ruth Lewis,* American Nurses' Association; *Roger Peele,* American Psychiatric Association; *Hilda Robbins,* National Association of Mental Health.

These individuals represented a subcommittee of the Liaison Group of Mental Health. The document was approved by the Council of Representatives of the American Psychological Association.

Consumer Oriented Health Insurance (COHI) Proposal: Criteria for National Health Insurance

APA Task Force on the Consumer Oriented Health Insurance Proposal

This Consumer-Oriented Health Insurance (COHI) proposal, developed by an APA committee and endorsed by the APA Council of Representatives, encourages implementation of multidisciplinary, multimodal, competitive delivery systems of care. Care should be accessible, cost-efficient, flexible, and responsive. The model recommends criteria for benefits, providers, financing, administration, training, and research.

Preamble

The intent of this proposal is to assure the primacy of consumer interests. The consumer is assured choice of practitioner and of plan, is assured representation at policy and governance levels, and is guaranteed personal and human rights. To enhance quality assurance, competitive models of health care in the private and public sectors are to be strengthened. The federal role is focused on determination of minimum standards; state roles are focused on the licensing of facilities and health professionals, again with consumer representation. Standards of accreditation, licensure, and statutory certification are to be established for all health professions and types of health facilities, subject to systematic implementation, consumer participation, and regular review.

The entitlement of the consumer to health care shall assure access to necessary care and continuity, with regional planning to assure adequacy in the distribution of health resources and efficiency in their delivery. The federal role is limited to oversight, standard-setting through regulations, statistical data collection and reporting, protection of privacy, revenue allocation, and setting of conditions and incentives for the rational distribution and most effective use of the full range of qualifying health facilities and professional resources. Coverage is seen as mandatory, with all residents entitled to the full range of services as they are phased in

sequentially. All civilian health care, including the current Medicaid, Medicare, and other health care services provided under the Social Security Act, but with the exception of veterans and occupational injury and disease programs, would be subsumed by this Proposal. The predominant focus in health delivery would be on the effective utilization of competitive health plans, including those of the health insurance industry, the health service plans, individual practice associations, and health maintenance organizations. The intent is to encourage the implementation of multidisciplinary, multimodal, competitive systems of health care delivery. This orientation is based on the conviction that such care will be more accessible, more cost-effective, more flexible, more innovative, more responsive to changing knowledge in the health field and to consumer needs, and of better quality than services delivered solely under government aegis or other monopoly.

General Principles

1. All residents of the United States shall be equally entitled to the full range of quality health services available under the Consumer Oriented Health Insurance proposal.

2. Consumers shall have representation in the implementation and development of health services at all levels. Citizen representatives

shall serve on boards and committees involved in planning, setting priorities, setting rates, and evaluating services. Consumer shall also have representation in setting policies regarding quality assurance, professional standards and accreditation, and certification and licensure of facilities and practitioners.

3. There shall be no discrimination in quality of health care by the practitioner or health facility based upon age, economic circumstances, national origin, pre-existing or current health conditions, race, or sex. This principle does not preclude the availability of additional coverage or services on an optional basis.

4. All health plans (a) shall provide a comprehensive range of services for all health impairment, whether physical and/or psychological, (b) shall provide for preventive services, and (c) shall provide for services designed to promote health maintenance and enhancement. The goal is to promote a healthful life-style and to maximize consumer responsibility for personal health.

5. The consumer shall be assured a choice among health practitioners and health service plans. Consumer choice, with access to those services that are locally available, shall be guaranteed. Competitive health care systems will be developed as needed. Local health systems shall include arrangements for availability of necessary services not locally provided.

6. State planning, reviewed through federal oversight procedures, shall arrange for the funding, staffing, and resources necessary to assure that the health needs of the public are adequately served.

7. An evaluation program for assessing health services and their cost shall be a substantially independent major component of the health system and shall be adequately financed as a cost to each plan. Evaluation shall emphasize cost-effectiveness assessment and shall include the development and utilization of outcome measures.

8. Specific funding shall be provided for research and the training of professional and other health personnel.

9. Quality-assurance and cost-containment controls shall be achieved primarily by monitoring health services. The primary focus of control shall be placed on provider decisions subject to organized review, regional planning, and prospective rate setting.

10. There shall be assurance for the consumer of respect for individual dignity and confidentiality within the health care system. Services shall be delivered on the basis of informed consent.

11. In the provision of direct services, emphasis shall be placed on community-based ambulatory care and on restoration of functional capacity.

Health Benefits

1. Health services shall be responsive to the needs of the population to be served. As appropriate, patterns of service may vary among geographical areas and according to the needs of special groups of consumers.

2. Co-insurance and/or deductibles shall not be applied as utilization controls or financing mechanisms to entry-level, minimal, or moderate use of ambulatory health care.

3. Benefits for both the psychological and physical components of health shall be provided concurrently, with the scope of benefits phased in as revenues permit.

4. Given the emphasis on hospital insurance in much current health insurance, the first priority shall be health planning and the introduction of health education, disability prevention, and health enhancement services. Second shall be the development of comprehensive ambulatory health care. Third shall be coverage for acute hospital care, and fourth shall be the services of extended health and convalescent care. The intent is to reorder the priorities of health care to assure the broadest impact on improving and maintaining the general health of the consumer and consumer groups rather than to emphasize the treatment of illness after it occurs.

5. An individualized service plan must be developed by a health professional for each patient, for each treatment program. These plans shall provide a basis for quality and utilization control. They shall stipulate service objectives within designated time intervals, indicate procedures to be used to attain these objectives, and identify the health personnel who will be in-

volved. Progress related to the service plan must be documented with periodic review and modifications noted. The plan will be developed with the patient's informed consent and its progress review shall be with patient awareness and participation. Provisions shall be made for broad-scale outcome analysis to improve treatment planning.

6. Quality and utilization controls shall allow the professional (a) latitude during the diagnostic and initial phases of service and resource utilization, and (b) moderate latitude for intermediate utilization with a treatment plan but close control over extended or expensive services and costs, which shall be subject to prior authorization and peer review processes.

7. Health services shall be reimbursed, regardless of the site where provided, so long as they follow an individualized service plan and meet the requirements of quality and cost control. Specifically, services, if covered when delivered in the hospital, will also be covered as appropriate if delivered in ambulatory care, including minor surgery and diagnostic evaluations.

8. The program shall cover essential costs of health care, not just services and professional fees. Benefits shall include generic prescription medications, prosthetic and corrective devices, and other equipment considered appropriate and essential to health maintenance.

9. To assure the equitable and accountable delivery of health care, each consumer will be issued a health service entitlement card. Use of the card will enable the development of a health transaction monitoring system capable of providing a service profile for each person.

10. When two or more health care procedures have essentially equivalent expected outcomes, the least intrusive or hazardous and least costly methods will be used.

11. Benefits shall include provision for out-of-area services and transferability upon change in residence.

Health Professionals

Designated independent health professionals qualified to develop service plans and to implement those aspects within the scope of their statutory recognition and competency, shall include: physicians and surgeons, osteopathic physicians and surgeons, dentists, psychologists, podiatrists, optometrists, and other health professions as designated by the Secretary of the Department of Health. The disciplines designated in the Proposal shall meet the following qualifications:

1. Individual providers must have (a) a doctoral degree in a recognized health profession from a regionally accredited educational institution or professional school; (b) not less than 12 months of full-time, approved, supervised clinical experience; (c) statutory recognition in the state where practicing; (d) a license or statutory certificate renewed at least biennially. Such renewal must be contingent upon demonstrated, competent practice and continuing education according to established standards developed with the participation of a national professional organization.

Additionally, each profession shall develop and maintain a national register of its health providers, based upon explicit standards. Listing shall be based on proficiency (credential) review by peers, with areas of specialty competence designated.

2. The relationships among the designated health professions shall be collegial.

3. Financial and tuition incentives shall be provided to acquire an adequate supply of health professionals according to the needs of each geographic area of the country.

4. Except for criminal damages, malpractice claims shall be arbitrated on a no-fault basis.

5. Service by a health professional in the peer review process, when without prejudicial intent, shall be exempt from personal liability.

Health Facilities

1. While the delivery of services in all health facilities shall be the responsibility of qualified health professionals, to quality for reimbursement, health facilities must (a) be licensed by the state (state facility licensure shall be limited to safety, sanitation, and public health standards); (b) be accredited by a nationally recognized body that includes repre-

sentatives of the designated health professions, institutional associations, and consumers (major emphasis of the accreditation process shall be the quality of services and programs, with retrospective review of the outcome of service rendered); (c) have all health services delivered under the supervision of qualified health practitioners; and (d) be reviewed biennially for licensure/certification.

2. No organized health setting or institution may exclude from its staff or governance any of the health professions recognized under this Proposal whose services are appropriate to the mission of the facility.

3. Organized health facilities shall be entitled to subcontract with health practitioners and/or other facilities for specified health services.

Financing

1. Health care shall be financed on a prepaid basis, via premiums for the private sector and advances from general revenue for the public sector.

2. Financing shall be derived from three sources. There shall be direct payment by residents and/or employers, these payments being credited annually against personal and business taxes. The premiums of those consumers not fully covered by these two sources, shall be paid from general tax revenue.

3. The funding sources proposed assume that the majority of health care will not require general tax revenue expenditures. Premiums shall be fully paid by those persons and their families with sufficient income to do so. The temporarily unemployed and their families shall be covered by unemployment insurance. Partial or full premiums for those with insufficient income shall be paid from general tax revenues. Prepayment shall be made directly to the insuror. Worker's Compensation would remain an employer liability.

4. There shall be no restriction of benefits for prior existing conditions. Insurors licensed within a state shall establish a risk reinsurance pool to enable coverage of all persons, including those of high risk for health disability.

5. The organizational goals and balanced

distribution and supply of practitioners and services shall be achieved through necessary financial incentives.

6. Philanthropic support of any aspect of health services shall be protected and encouraged.

7. There shall also be an individual report to each plan member of his or her services received and the amount paid on his or her behalf. There shall be a uniform annual audit and report to the plan administrators of the plan's benefits, benefit coordination, costs, and projected needs.

8. Methods will be established to provide for prospective setting of reasonable fee benefits, by region, for provider procedures and for hospital charges. Fee limits shall be reviewed annually. Participating providers shall agree to assignment with right of appeal.

9. In order to identify patterns of inappropriate or excessive utilization, individual provider services shall be developed and shall be subject to peer review.

10. The continued existence of any service plan or facility is fiscally dependent upon its ability to remain an effective part of the health services under this Proposal.

11. In accord with the particular plan, providers may be reimbursed on a salaried, capitation, contract, or fee-for-service basis.

Administration

1. A Cabinet-level Department of Health shall be established with full responsibility for development and coordination of national health insurance, for assuring implementation of the program through the states, and for advising the President and the Congress on health matters.

2. The federal role should be directed toward determining minimum standards for benefits and establishing standards of quality. The implementation of control mechanisms shall be primarily at the state level, subject to federal oversight.

3. The regulatory role of states shall be limited to review of benefits provided by the plans, determination of competence of participating providers, certification of service need and planning activities, and utilization review

and controls, carried out under appropriate federal guidelines and oversight.

4. The governor of each state shall establish a State Health Service Board, which shall be responsible for policy determination and for review, evaluation, and regulation of all responsibilities assigned to the state under this proposal. The board shall be composed of at least 11 and not more than 21 members with staggered terms of office. Participating health professions shall be eligible for board membership; however, the board shall have a majority of consumer representation. The provider representation shall be distributed among the designated health professions and major health facilities. The consumer representation shall also be diverse and broadly representative.

5. The planning and monitoring of health service delivery, including the psychological and physical components of health, shall be conducted by health systems agencies and professional standards review organizations with the participation of regional health planning staff.

6. To assist in planning and monitoring of health care, there shall be a national standardized, unified, management information system, to facilitate cost control and program audit while assuring proper confidentiality and consumer safeguards.

7. The health plans that meet federal and state requirements shall be eligible to compete for consumer enrollment. Competition may be in terms of premium cost and model of service delivery.

8. It is the intent of this proposal that the role of government in providing direct health care should be limited to those services that are cost- and quality-effective in comparison to private care or for which no private-sector competitive alternative can be generated (e.g., Veterans Administration Hospitals).

Training

1. Financial support for training shall be dependent upon a contractual agreement to serve in areas of need upon completion of training, with individual choice in selection among the designated underserved areas.

2. Support for the training of health professionals and allied personnel (a) shall be in accord with health priorities, (b) shall be related to anticipated staffing needs for psychological and physical health care, (c) shall provide capitation support to accredited schools to provide professional training for all the designated health professions, and (d) shall be funded at a stipulated amount from general revenues.

Research

1. Support for basic and clinical health research shall be in accord with national priorities and related to the incidence of unresolved health disability and identified high-risk populations, and shall be funded at a stipulated amount from general revenues.

2. Basic health research shall be separate in administration and implementation from the health insurance programs and shall embrace both the physical and the psychological bases of health. Research funding shall include a balance of competitively selected, contract, and governmentally managed projects. Cooperative research and development projects across administrative boundaries shall be encouraged.

The members of the Task Force on the Consumer Oriented Health Insurance Proposal of the APA Committee on Health Insurance included Russell J. Bent, David A. Rodgers, Jack G. Wiggins, Herbert Dörken (chair), and Patrick H. DeLeon (consultant).

The Anatomy of Psychotherapy Under National Health Insurance

Nicholas A. Cummings

Experience has demonstrated that when all barriers to medical care are removed, the medical model encourages somatization, and medical facilities become overburdened by the 60% of physician visits that are from sufferers of emotional distress rather than organic illness. When psychotherapy is properly provided within a comprehensive health system, the costs of providing the benefit are more than offset by the savings in medical utilization. Furthermore, it is not the provision of a psychotherapy benefit that can bankrupt a system, as has occurred in a number of programs, but the manner in which the service is delivered that makes the difference for cost-therapeutic effectiveness. Finally, cost-therapeutically effective programs can be developed for problems in living that traditionally have been regarded as too resistant and, therefore, too costly to be insurable. The implications for national health insurance are that the inclusion of an appropriate, realistic psychotherapy benefit is both essential and economically feasible.

As the Carter administration evidences serious concern for the mental and emotional well-being of the American people, there is occurring within the larger context of the pros and cons of national health insurance a heated debate as to whether any national health scheme can feasibly include a mental health component. The dubious experiences of Medicaid, Medicare, and CHAMPUS have left some members of the Congress with the conclusion that the inclusion of a mental health provision in whatever national health system is eventually enacted would overinflate what is already contemplated to be a staggering price tag to provide even the basics of national health insurance. Several prominent psychologists, including two past presidents of the American Psychological Association, who have never been engaged in the direct delivery of human services (Albee, 1977; Campbell, cited in Trotter, 1976; Humphreys, 1973) have thrown their persuasiveness solidly against the inclusion of psychotherapy in national health insurance. They argue that such a service cannot be financed or monitored, that it is a subsidy of the rich by the poor, and that the insurance benefit would be of doubtful value to the overall health of the American people. Others, principally myself and my colleague (Cummings, 1975, in press; Cummings & Follette, 1976), have taken the opposite stance based on two decades of providing mental health services within a comprehensive, prepaid health plan. We have found not only that psychotherapy can be economically included as a prepaid insurance benefit but also that failure to provide such a benefit jeopardizes the effective functioning of the basic medical services, since 60% or more of the physician visits are made by patients who demonstrate an emotional, rather than an organic, etiology for their physical symptoms.

Despite extensive misquotations to the contrary, Follette and I have never advocated mere across-the-board inclusion of traditional delivery modalities of mental health services into public or third-party payment structures. Rather, we have argued that for psychotherapy to be cost-therapeutically effective, considerable clinical research is necessary before abuses are minimized, therapeutic benefits are maximized, traditionally underserved groups are reached, and deleterious effects are eliminated. It is by addressing the problems confronting the delivery of psychother-

Reprinted from *American Psychologist*, 1977, *32*, 711–718.

apy under public and third-party payment that the anatomy of psychotherapy under national health insurance will be developed and accepted as efficacious by the Congress and the consumer. The failure by the mental health professions to take a proactive research stance may result in the elimination of mental health services from national health insurance or, even worse, may result in the provision of an ineffective token benefit that will only underscore the argument that psychotherapy is an unnecessary service. Before proceeding to this basic issue, it is important to examine arguments made by the opponents of psychotherapy's inclusion in national health insurance, inasmuch as they have presented some warnings that have rightfully commanded the attention of consumer groups and the Congress.

Warning: The Reverse Robin Hood Phenomenon

The fact that, traditionally, psychotherapy was sought by the more affluent sectors of our society while the underprivileged tended not to utilize such services has prompted some critics, such as Campbell (cited in Trotter, 1976), to view the inclusion of psychotherapy in national health insurance as regressive taxation or, even more harshly, as a "subsidy of the rich by the poor." Simply stated, this view holds that by taxing all of the American people to provide a benefit applicable to a select segment such as the upper-middle class, the benefit is being paid for by the poor, who are least likely to utilize the service and are least able to afford the subsidy. By itself, this position is not totally persuasive, because, as Campbell would be the first to admit, many of our most valued institutions are financed by regressive taxation. The state university system is a case in point. No one would seriously argue the elimination of the state university, but many are striving to make the university more accessible to eligible persons from groups that have traditionally under-utilized it. The same would hold true for a mental health benefit if, in fact, it were a valuable service to all of the segments of our population who are at risk.

Since medicine in the United States was originally dispensed under the principle that services to the poor are provided by soaking the rich, it is curious to find mental health subject to a reverse Robin Hood phenomenon. Of the recent rash of so-called abuses that have come to light, two may serve as startling examples of the kind of facts that render the Congress uneasy and that ought to serve as warning signs to the profession that restraint and caution are indicated. According to the U.S. Civil Service Commission (Note 1), under the Blue Cross and Blue Shield Federal Employees Health Benefits Program in the Washington, D.C., greater metropolitan area, for the years 1971, 1972, and 1973, 2.3% of those seeking psychotherapy exceeded outpatient costs of $10,000 each per year and accounted for approximately one fourth of the total annual psychotherapy dollar. Furthermore, these same 2.3% of utilizers in the District of Columbia area accounted for 66% of the *national* figure spent by Blue Cross and Blue Shield for the over-$10,000-per-year utilizers in the Federal Employees Health Benefits Program during this same 3-year period. For psychotherapy to cost over $10,000 per year, one must visit a psychotherapist no less than four times a week for an entire year at $50 per session. One may speculate that Washington is a fertile area for the young psychiatrist who wants a job for 2 or 3 years so as to complete a training analysis at taxpayer expense and then leave Washington for an originally intended private practice, but this is only speculation. This experience prompted Aetna in 1974 to severely limit its psychotherapy benefit and resulted in Blue Cross/Blue Shield's initiating a troublesome claims review that threatens the confidentiality of the therapist-client relationship, the latter in the interest of determining the variables in the apparent overutilization.

The second example is from an unpublished study by Elpers (Note 2), available through the Orange County (California) Mental Health Department. As a county health officer, Elpers compared the allocation of Medi-Cal (California's Medicaid program) money to private psychiatrists with a state formula of county needs based on Medi-Cal caseload. He found that the dollars follow not the need but the number of psychiatrists practicing within a county, since Medi-Cal reimburses the practitioner on the basis of number of patients seen. It comes as no surprise that psychiatrists tend to congregate in urban areas; thus Marin County, an affluent bedroom community for San Francisco, received 470% of its "needed" share in 1975, while that same year, rural Lake County, with virtually no psychiatrists, received only 2%. In counties like Marin and San Francisco, the latter having received 271% of its "needed" share in 1975, there is a large supply of psychiatrists, and the competition for patients results in Medi-Cal patients' having no trouble in finding a psychotherapist. In underserved counties, the practitioners tend to shun the Medi-Cal recipient in favor of the higher paying, affluent client.

Such problems notwithstanding, California's Medi-Cal figures reveal that 5% of all recipients utilize psychotherapy. This is two-and-one-half times the national average, thus tending to refute the contention by Campbell (cited in Trotter, 1976) and Albee (1977) that the poor do not seek psychotherapy. In fact, there is reason to believe that the poor are at greater risk and will avail themselves of psychotherapy if it is provided in a manner meaningful to the consumer. Such an example is provided by Kaiser-Permanente in San Francisco, which has over the past decades taken meticulous care to provide a consumer-oriented, comprehensive health plan. There, psychotherapy is not merely an upper- or middle-class white phenomenon, and subscribers seeking psychotherapy do so in direct proportion to their occupational class numbers in the health plan population. Additionally, black and Chicano clients in psychotherapy are rapidly approaching figures proportional to the numbers of these ethnic groups in the total health plan population. Utilization by Asian Americans lags behind the proportional figures because of the large Chinese population in San Francisco and its traditional resistance to psychotherapy, but the last few years have seen rapid erosion of that resistance, especially in young persons who not only seek services for themselves but bring their parents in when the latter hesitate to come themselves.

Minority and feminist leaders, as well as consumer advocates, have enunciated the limitations of white, middle-class, male psychotherapists, but in attempting to remedy this problem care must be exercised not to substitute a mischief of a different sort. In stressing the indigenous mental health counselor as an alternative, these leaders are not truly expressing the attitudes of their constituents, for the underprivileged resent (and rightly so) receiving care from paraprofessionals while the more affluent have access to journey-level practitioners. The possible exception may be among native Americans, where the understandable distrust of the white man's "doctor" is pervasive and deeply rooted. Interestingly, when a group practice retains an appropriate balance of minority and female psychotherapists, the consumer demand for a certain kind of therapist tends to disappear. It is almost as if the client senses the awareness of the institution and is confident that his or her problems will receive the appropriate perspective and proper understanding. The poor, the minorities, and women have an inherent right of access to practitioners who are both aware and experienced, and any proposed national health scheme must take this into account.

Warning: The New Mind-Body Dualism

During the past decade, Albee has demonstrated a propensity to anger clinicians, causing them to overlook his contribution as a critic whose consistent illumination of the flaws and foibles of psychotherapy spurs the serious practitioner to strive to improve the state of the art. Perhaps much of the negative reaction stems from the willingness of the semipopular media to carry Albee's arguments the extra few inches into the realm of absurdity, often beyond his own fondest hopes. Thus, Albee can state that he never advocated suspending all psychotherapy until research can verify the art, that he never pronounced clinical psychology dead, and that he does not believe that all professional societies are conspiracies against the laity, to name only a few excessive positions variously attributed to him in the press. Yet he was the first to point out that psychology does not practice in its own house but in that of medicine. He has tirelessly assailed the medical model and has held steadfastly to the concept that emotional problems are not illnesses but problems in living.

The difficulty with Albee's view is that it

would prevent psychology's participation in the treatment process. Interestingly, the same arguments he employs to arrive at such a conclusion also make the case for the inclusion of psychological services within the health model as opposed to the medical model, a distinction Albee fails to make. Many, if not most, physical illnesses are the result of problems in living. The way we live, eat, drink, smoke, compete, and pollute relate inevitably to strokes, heart attacks, cancer, obesity, malnutrition, paralysis, cirrhosis, migraine, suicide, and asthma, to list only a few. The attempt to clearly demarcate psychological problems from physical illness by calling them problems in living is a curious form of mind-body dualism that would bring an immediate déjà vu were it not cloaked in this new terminology and sanctified with the struggle against medical domination of the health field. Psychological services are more than health, but they must be a part of health, if not the overriding principle, if the medical model is not to continue to encourage the somatization of emotional problems. The way we live influences our bodies; conversely, chronic illness and intractable pain create a problem in living. Psychotherapy is a viable form of intervention that can alleviate problems in living and lessen disease, and it belongs in any comprehensive health system until that utopian moment when preventive techniques render it unnecessary.

Warning: Research May Be Hazardous to Your Health

Historically, studies of the effectiveness of psychotherapy either have suffered from serious experimental flaws or have yielded negative results. A recent and well-executed review by Olbrisch (1977) appears in another section of this issue. If it were taken completely seriously, every practitioner would lock the office and throw away the key. If taken within the perspective that the flawless experimental design is rarely possible in field research with human subjects, it is a valuable document that can motivate clinical researchers to improve and replicate their work.

In making the valid point that clinical researchers demonstrate greater clinical than ex-

perimental sophistication, Olbrisch neglects the fact that the critics of clinical practice and research show a shocking absence of tough clinical experience and a lack of appreciation for the limitations of the clinical method. Needy human beings cannot be denied treatment for the sake of experimental purity, and control groups are seldom more than better or worse approximations. With all of its imperfections, we are dependent upon the clinical method, for in spite of the enormous contributions basic research has rendered, the pure experimental method is often helpless in the face of the most pressing human problems. This is not to imply that perfection in design is not the goal of every researcher, but by and large, the clinical method will continue to be ponderous, inefficient, inaccurate, and vulnerable to severe criticism, but by its sheer persistence and response to pressing demands, the weight of clinical evidence will continue to be the primary vehicle through which the field of health progresses.

So as not to belabor the topic, one example must suffice. To date, the definitive experiment upon which the Surgeon General's warning on each package of cigarettes might be based has not been forthcoming. Rather, the warning is the result of the preponderance of clinical evidence, any *portion* of which can and is being refuted by the tobacco industry. In fact, the tobacco industry has produced flawless research which demonstrates that there is no causal link between smoking and lung cancer in humans. Should the American people, as some have done, ignore the weight of 50 years of increasingly sophisticated clinical evidence in favor of the tobacco industry's excellent but unconvincing experiments, such a decision may well be hazardous to their health.

Some patients who are treated for pneumonia die, while others not treated at all recover. Similarly, the successes and failures of problems in living are not immediately discernible, and clinicians would do well to heed the criticisms of the clinical method and work toward increasing the sophistication of their tools. At no time, however, should a clinician be dismayed that no one research project yields a clear answer, for the clinical method is most persuasive in its preponderance of accumulated evidence, knowledge, and experience.

Proposed Modalities of Delivery Under National Health Insurance

No matter how effective it may be demonstrated to be, it is unlikely that psychoanalysis or any other open-ended psychotherapy benefit will be provided under national health insurance. Where it has been attempted on a large scale, such as in the Federal Employees Health Benefits Program and CHAMPUS as previously noted, the costs have been prohibitive. Aetna responded by severely limiting the benefit, Blue Cross and Blue Shield are looking toward significantly redefining the benefit, and only CHAMPUS has made a conscientious effort to find innovative answers to the problem of cost-therapeutic effectiveness. The experiences with Medicare and Medicaid have only increased uneasiness within the Congress, and as of this point in time, the proponents of the inclusion of psychotherapy in national health insurance will have to demonstrate its effectiveness.

In response, some segments of organized psychiatry are proposing the "remedicalization" of psychotherapy. Under this ominous plan, national health insurance or any other health system, public or private, would insure only the organic brain syndromes and functional psychoses, excluding the psychoneuroses and character disorders as being outside the definition of insurable illness. Under a unique twist to the basic plan, Harrington (Note 3) would refer all persons with emotional distress, but with no organic brain disease or psychosis, to the community colleges for courses in the art of living. This psychiatric proposal may find a not too distant kinship with the concepts of Albee, who may be somewhat embarrassed by his closeness to the new medical model. Such a plan has appeal because it would reduce the cost of providing psychotherapy by drastically restricting the numbers of persons eligible. It would further guarantee income to psychiatrists who, as medical practitioners, would be the only persons eligible to provide what would be defined as a medical service. This obviously leaves psychology in a vulnerable position, but even more important, it deprives the majority of Americans suffering from emotional distress access to treatment.

Of demonstrated effectiveness are the community mental health centers, whose primary limitation is that of cost. Various audits have revealed the cost per unit of service to range from about $60 to a staggering $345 in one center, and a modal cost per unit of service of around $75 to $80 is fairly representative of most centers. Despite the potentially inordinate cost, the National Institute of Mental Health (NIMH) continues to champion the community mental health center concept as the mainstay mental health delivery system under national health insurance. This is understandable, since NIMH spawned the community mental health center movement, but most authorities have retrenched from the overly ambitious goal of the original Kennedy plan that there eventually be a community mental health center in every community. I believe that because of their proven effectiveness, community mental health centers (and their inordinate costs) can still be justified in underserved areas of the nation under national health insurance.

A third delivery approach (Cummings, 1975; Cummings & Follette, 1976) insists that psychological services are a basic ingredient in any truly comprehensive health plan. Such a view holds not only that psychotherapy can be economically included as a prepaid insurance benefit but also that failure to provide such a benefit jeopardizes the effective functioning of the basic medical services by the 60% or more of the physician visits from patients who demonstrate emotional, rather than organic, etiologies for their physical symptoms.

The Comprehensive Health Model

The Kaiser-Permanente Health Plan is recognizable by most readers as the prototype of the modern Health Maintenance Organization (HMO). Founded by Henry J. Kaiser just before World War II as a benefit for his employees, the health plan prospered during the postwar period because it offered the public comprehensive care in its own facilities at moderate cost and without the limitations, deductibles, and co-insurances characteristic of most health plans. At the present time, the health plan serves over eight million subscribers in several semiautonomous regions: Northern and Southern California, Portland (Oregon), Hawaii, Cleveland, and Denver. The San Francisco Kaiser-Permanente Medical Center is one of a dozen such centers in the northern California region. It is here, in a setting where the clinical psychologist has been the mainstay practitioner, that two decades of pioneering research have been conducted in the delivery of psychological services within a comprehensive health plan. As background, only the briefest summary of several research papers follows.

Beginning with the initial bias that short-term psychotherapy is not as effective as long-term, and burdened with the discovery that providing easily available comprehensive health services as part of a prepaid plan fostered the somatization of emotional problems and the consequent overutilization of medical facilities by patients who had no physical illness, Kaiser-Permanente experimented with a number of early attempts to provide long-term therapy for all its subscribers who manifested emotional distress. The problems inherent in most traditional clinics of the time resulted, such as a long waiting list, a high dropout rate, and an only partially successful attempt to reduce the ever-growing waiting list by providing crisis intervention. Following several years on such an unsatisfactory course, a series of evaluative studies were begun that spanned a decade and a half, and during this time an efficient, cost-therapeutically effective treatment system emerged.

In the first of a series of investigations into the relationship between psychological services and medical utilization in a prepaid health plan setting, Follette and Cummings (1967) compared the number and type of medical services sought before and after the intervention of psychotherapy in a large group of randomly selected patients. The outpatient and inpatient medical utilization for the year immediately prior to the initial interview in the Department of Psychotherapy as well as for the 5 years following were studied for three groups of psychotherapy patients (one interview only, brief therapy with a mean of 6.2 interviews, and long-term therapy with a mean of 33.9 interviews) and a "control" group of matched patients demonstrating similar criteria of distress but not, in

the 6 years under study, seen in psychotherapy. The findings indicated that (a) persons in emotional distress were significantly higher users of both inpatient (hospitalization) and outpatient medical facilities as compared to the health plan average; (b) there were significant declines in medical utilization in those emotionally distressed individuals who received psychotherapy, as compared to a "control" group of matched emotionally distressed health plan subscribers who were not accorded psychotherapy; (c) these declines remained constant during the 5 years following the termination of psychotherapy; (d) the most significant declines occurred in the 2nd year after the initial interview, and those patients receiving one session only or brief psychotherapy (two to eight sessions) did not require additional psychotherapy to maintain the lower level of utilization for 5 years; and (e) patients seen 2 years or more in continuous psychotherapy demonstrated no overall decline in total outpatient utilization, inasmuch as psychotherapy visits tended to supplant medical visits. However, there was a significant decline in inpatient utilization (hospitalization) in this long-term therapy group from an initial rate several times that of the health plan average, to a level comparable to that of the general, adult, health plan population. The authors criticized their retrospective design in its lack of a true control group, and after considerable difficulty and with the unfortunate necessity of denying treatment to needy individuals, they are currently engaged in replicating their work in a prospective experimental design that is responsive to the criticisms of the previous research.

In a subsequent study, Cummings and Follette (1968) found that intensive efforts to increase the number of referrals to psychotherapy by computerizing psychological screening with early detection and alerting of the attending physicians did not significantly increase the number of patients seeking psychotherapy. The authors concluded that in a prepaid health plan setting already maximally employing educative techniques to both patients and physicians, and already providing a range of prepaid psychological services, the number of subscribers seeking psychotherapy reached an optimal level and remained constant thereafter.

In summarizing nearly two decades of prepaid health plan experience, Cummings and Follette (1976) demonstrated that there is no basis for the fear that increased demand for psychotherapy will financially endanger the system, for it is not the number of referrals received that will drive costs up, but the manner in which psychotherapy services are delivered that determines optimal cost-therapeutic effectiveness. The finding that one session only, with no repeat psychological visits, can reduce medical utilization by 60% over the following 5 years was surprising and totally unexpected. Equally surprising was the 75% reduction in medical utilization over a 5-year period in those patients initially receiving two to eight psychotherapy visits (brief therapy).

In a further study, Cummings and Follette (1976) sought to answer in an 8th-year telephone follow-up whether the results described previously were a therapeutic effect, were the consequence of extraneous factors, or were a deleterious effect. It was hypothesized that if better understanding of the problem had occurred in the psychotherapeutic sessions, the patient would recall the actual problem rather than the presenting symptom and would have both lost the presenting symptom and coped more effectively with the real problem. The results suggest that the reduction in medical utilization was the consequence of resolving the emotional distress that was being reflected in the symptoms and in the doctor's visits. The modal patient in this 8th-year follow-up may be described as follows: She or he denies ever having consulted a physician for the symptoms for which the referral was originally made. Rather, the actual problem discussed with the psychotherapist is recalled as the reason for the psychotherapy visit, and although the problem is resolved, this resolution is attributed to the patient's own efforts and no credit is given the psychotherapist. This affirms the contention that the reduction in medical utilization reflected the diminution in emotional distress that had been expressed in symptoms presented to the physician.

Demonstrating, as they did in their earlier work, that savings in medical services offset the cost of providing psychotherapy answers the question of cost-effectiveness, but Cummings and Follette insisted that the services provided must also be therapeutic in that they reduce the patient's emotional distress. That both cost *and* therapeutic effectiveness were demonstrated in the Kaiser-Permanente studies was attributed by the authors to the therapists' expectations that emotional distress could be alleviated by brief, active psychotherapy that involves the analysis of transference and resistance and the uncovering of unconscious conflicts, and that has all of the characteristics of long-term therapy except length. Given this orientation, it was found over a 5-year period that 84.6% of the patients seen in psychotherapy chose to come for 15 sessions or less (with a mean of 8.6). Rather than regarding these patients as "dropouts" from treatment, it was found on follow-up that they achieved a satisfactory state of emotional well-being that continued to the 8th year after termination of therapy. Another 10.1% of the patients were in long-term therapy with a mean of 19.2 sessions, a figure that would probably be regarded as short-term in many traditional clinics. Finally, 5.3% of the patients were found to be "interminable," in that once they began psychotherapy they seemingly continued with no indication of termination.

In a recently reported study, Cummings (in press) addressed the problem of the "interminable" patient for whom treatment was neither cost-effective nor therapeutically effective. The concept that some persons may be so emotionally crippled that they may have to be maintained for many years or for life was not satisfactory, for if 5% of the patients entering psychotherapy are in that category, within a few years a program will be hampered by a monolithic case load, which has become a fact in many public clinics where psychotherapy is offered at nominal or no cost. It was hypothesized that these patients required more intensive intervention, and the frequency of psychotherapy visits was doubled for one experimental group, tripled for another experimental group, and held constant for the control group. Surprisingly, the cost-therapeutic effectiveness ratios deteriorated in direct proportion to the increased intensity; that is, medical utilization increased and the patients manifested greater emotional distress. It was only by reversing the process and seeing these patients at spaced intervals of once every 2 or 3 months that the desired cost-therapeutic effect was obtained. These results are surprising in that they are contrary to traditionally held notions in psychotherapy, but they demonstrate the need for ongoing research, program evaluation, and innovation if psychotherapy is going to be made available to everyone.

The Cost-Therapeutic Effectiveness Ratio (Cummings, in press) and the 38 Criteria of Distress (Follette & Cummings, 1967) have proven to be useful evaluation tools at Kaiser-Permanente, enabling the San Francisco center to innovate cost-therapeutically effective programs for alcoholism, drug addiction, the "interminable" patient, chronic psychosis, problems of the elderly, severe character disorders, and other conditions considered by many to be too costly and, therefore, uninsurable.

Implications for National Health Insurance

The experiences at Kaiser-Permanente demonstrate what has also been found elsewhere: When all barriers are removed from access to medical care, the system will become overloaded with the 60% or more of physician visits by patients manifesting somatized emotional distress. There is every reason to believe this would occur under national health insurance, for the medical model inadvertently encourages somatization. If a patient complains to the physician, "My boss is on my back and it's killing me," a perfunctory, unsympathetic response is most likely. But let the patient unconsciously translate this distress to lower back pain and that patient is immediately rewarded by the physician's attention in the form of X rays, laboratory tests, medications, and return visits. And even worse, temporary disability may be offered which removes the patient from the presence of the hated boss and renders unconsciously mandatory the continuation of the chronic pain as the only possible solution to what originally was an interpersonal problem.

When psychotherapy is properly provided within a comprehensive health system, the costs of providing the benefit are more than offset by the savings in medical utlilization. However, this does not mean that traditional delivery modes of mental health services can be parachuted into the system. Such attempts have proven to be near disasters in a number of programs. On the other hand, "the uses of artificial limitations and co-insurance are only partial answers, for while controlling costs, therapeutic effectiveness is often sacrificed. The experiences over two decades at Kaiser-Permanente indicate that it is not the provision of a psychotherapy benefit that can bankrupt a system, but the manner in which it is delivered. When active, dynamic, brief therapy is provided early and by psychotherapists who are enthusiastic and proactive regarding such intervention, it is the treatment of choice for about 85% of the patients seeking psychotherapy. Such intervention not only yields a high cost-therapeutic effectiveness ratio, but it is satisfactory to both the patient—in increased emotional well-being—and the patient's physician—in dramatic reduction of somatization and overutilization of medical facilities. Further, by providing such brief therapy, it makes economically feasible the provision of long-term psychotherapy to the approximately 10% of the patients who require it for their treatment to be therapeutically effective.

Finally, cost-therapeutically effective programs can be developed for problems in living that traditionally have been regarded as too resistant and, therefore, too costly to be insurable. This requires constant research, innovation, and program evaluation, but it is important, because if national health insurance is to meet the emotional needs of all Americans, it is untenable to think of excluding one group or another.

Reference Notes

1. U.S. Civil Service Commission. Unpublished statistics on the Federal Employees Health Benefits Program, Aetna and Blue Cross-Blue Shield. Washington, D.C.: U.S. Civil Service Commission, Office of the Actuary, 1976.
2. Elpers, J. R. Unpublished report of the Program Chief, Orange County Department of Mental Health, Santa Ana, California, 1977.
3. Harrington, R. Unpublished report to the Executive Committee of the Permanente Medical Group. San Jose, Calif.: Kaiser-Permanente Medical Center, 1977.

References

Albee, G. W. Does including psychotherapy in health insurance represent a subsidy to the rich from the poor? *American Psychologist*, 1977, *32*, 719-721.

Cummings, N. A. The health model as entree to the human services model in psychotherapy. *The Clinical Psychologist,* 1975, *29*(1), 19–21.

Cummings, N. A. Prolonged or "ideal" versus short-term or "realistic" psychotherapy. *Professional Psychology,* in press.

Cummings, N. A., & Follette, W. T. Psychiatric services and medical utilization in a prepaid health plan setting: Part II. *Medical Care,* 1968, *6*, 31–41.

Cummings, N. A. & Follette, W. T. Brief psychotherapy and medical utilization: An eight-year follow-up. In H. Dörken & Associates, *The professional psychologist today: New developments in law, health insurance, and health practice.* San Francisco: Jossey-Bass, 1976.

Follette, W. T., & Cummings, N. A. Psychiatric services and medical utilization in a prepaid health plan setting. *Medical Care,* 1967, *5*, 25–35.

Humphreys, L. Should psychotherapy be included in national health insurance? No! *APA Monitor,* September–October, 1973, p. 8.

Olbrisch, M. E. Psychotherapeutic interventions in physical health: Effectiveness and economic efficiency. *American Psychologist,* 1977, *32*, 761–777.

Trotter, S. Insuring psychotherapy: A subsidy to the rich? *APA Monitor,* November 1976, pp. 1; 16.

At the time of original publication of this article, *Nicholas A. Cummings* was Chief Psychologist at the Kaiser Foundation Hospital and the Permanente Medical Group, San Francisco.

9

Psychotherapy Outcomes
and Psychological Interventions
in Physical Health

Increased research concerning health and patterns of behavior related to both health and illness is needed. The contributions of program evaluation and health services research were discussed earlier. However, broader investigation is needed into the range of basic and applied research topics with direct relevance to psychology and health. Discoveries in biology will aid us in developing healthier infants, and medical research will develop new and better agents for inoculating and curing individuals. But the most critical area of research and innovation in health care during the next 20 years will be in the utilization of knowledge on the individual patient level—the behavioral aspects of health and illness.

We need to know more about why people "choose" to risk sickness or damage to their health. Knowledge is badly needed about why individuals persist in behaviors known to have long-term harmful physical consequences, such as smoking, obesity, and alcohol abuse. The psychological and behavioral components appear to be many, but the specific mechanisms need to be articulated and prevention/treatment strategies developed. A range of applied research is warranted because the specific factors probably vary from problem to problem. These behaviors also reflect a general class of human functioning, however, and basic research addressing related psychological and behavioral processes is also needed.

It is clear that people somatize a wide range of stresses, that is, translate emotional tensions into bodily damage or illness. There are individual differences in the frequency, severity, and specific form of somatization. Physical illness seems more "acceptable" than being angry or saying no. Yet we lack sufficient knowledge of the mechanisms through which this transformation of stress occurs. Why is a particular organ system the site of the physical breakdown? Is the process accessible to conscious control? Are such physical symptoms always "bad," or, in some cases, might they be part of a self-signal system, akin to the function of anxiety?

We may be able to teach people how to minimize illness and physical symptoms if we can understand the psychological and behavioral components in the process of becoming ill. People get sick in different ways. During a flu epidemic, four individuals of apparently similar health may respond very differently. One may never get ill. Another may be among the first to become ill. Another individual might suddenly succumb three days before an important work deadline, while another person might work through the deadline, only to succumb to illness upon completion of the task. Interestingly, such patterns can be remarkably stable within individuals and across various stress situations. Knowledge of both the general and specific aspects of such functioning is needed.

Once people are ill, there are many differences in their reactions to that illness and how well they comply with the treatment regime. Some individuals are always having diagnostic tests run, and others wait so long that such testing procedures are no longer necessary to make a diagnosis. There are sizable individual differences in the degree of compliance with treatment procedures and schedules, the most typical pattern being a high degree of initial compliance that tapers off as the symptoms become less evident and less unpleasant. The need and potential for behavioral research in this area is high.

The involvement of psychologists in health research is wide ranging. It varies from the more traditional efforts in psychotherapy research to the development of behavioral alternatives to surgery. The first article in this section is a report by the Task Force on Health Research of the APA Board of Scientific Affairs. It is one of the so-called NEAR reports (Newly Emerging Areas of Research). The report reviews pockets of psychological research relating to health issues ranging from cancer to stroke. In their review, the task force found that in the years 1971–1973, over 14,000 entries in the *Psychological Abstracts* concerned health-related topics. Psychologists have been actively involved in establishing the emerging area of research and clinical practice often referred to as behavioral medicine. The extent of the interest of psychologists with health research and health behavior is illustrated by the fact that 800 APA members recently formed a new division of Health Care Psychology within the American Psychological Association.

Considerable research has been done on the effectiveness of psychotherapy. The question of whether or not psychotherapy has any lasting effect on a patient is an issue that has been much discussed by both psychologists and Congress. Smith and Glass present a meta-analysis of psychotherapy outcome research, reviewing the results of nearly 400 controlled evaluations of psychotherapy. They found convincing evidence of the efficacy of psychotherapy: The typical therapy patient, after therapy, is better off than 75% of untreated individuals. Smith and Glass did not, however, find evidence for differences in effectiveness among various types of psychotherapy or techniques.

In the third article, Strupp and Hadley present their tripartite model of mental health and therapeutic outcome. They make the point that depending on who the "evaluator" of clinical outcome is (the client, the therapist, or society), the patient could be simultaneously judged mentally healthy or disturbed and, correspondingly, the outcome of the therapeutic process could be judged as either positive or negative. They urge caution in assigning weights to outcome studies that emphasize only one perspective in the evaluation scheme.

In the next paper, Olbrisch reviews the research literature on the clinical effectiveness of psychotherapeutic interventions in physical health. She particularly notes the success of psychotherapeutic preparation for surgery and its relationship to increased postoperative improvement rates and decreased medical complications. She draws attention to the exciting and newly emerging area of the psychological treatment of cardiac patients, noting the interesting interventions made and the provocative research findings reported. Olbrisch concludes that the results of research and the effect of psychological interventions on physical health are highly promising but urges caution in the generalization of the findings and calls for additional research into these methods and their effectiveness.

Finally, Logan Wright discusses some of the psychological issues in the physical health of children and related treatment practices. He states that between one-third and one-half of all of the child patients in the Children's Hospital of the University of Oklahoma have a highly significant behavioral concomitant to their physical illness, in addition to the psychological problems caused by the experience of hospitalization itself. He briefly illustrates behavioral interventions into a diverse range of problems including bruxism, child abuse, chronic health problems, and tracheotomy addiction. He provides a fascinating description of the application of psychological techniques to problems previously thought of as purely physical in nature and previously treated only through physical means.

Contributions of Psychology to Health Research:

Patterns, Problems, and Potentials

APA Task Force on Health Research

Recent years have witnessed growing attention by the public, by professionals, and by all levels of government to issues and problems arising from increasing costs and deficiencies in delivery of health care services. National concern has been reflected in the drafting of federal legislation to provide a national health insurance plan. Health professionals have been increasingly concerned with manpower shortages, training and accreditation standards, provision of continuing education, and recently, in response to federal legislation, with establishing peer review systems to assure quality of service. Public concern is reflected in the consumer advocacy movement and increased representation of consumers on the boards and committees of health agencies. The Task Force on Health Research was established by APA's Board of Scientific Affairs to survey the nature and extent of contributions by psychologists to basic and applied research on behavioral factors in physical illness and health maintenance. A survey and analysis of the research literature was made. Psychologists active in health research have been identified, together with their areas of interest. Funding resources for behavioral science research on health and illness have been identified. Areas of neglect have been pointed up, together with the special training needs for the "health care" researcher.

If asked to indicate the thing in life that they value most highly, most Americans, and probably most people anywhere, would surely list "good health" among the top two or three items. This concern for health is not misplaced. One's state of health may be fundamental to most other pleasures or values. Its economic impact is well documented. A recent report from the Carnegie Commission (Juster, 1975) suggests that individuals in poor health earn on the average about $7,000 per year less than those in good health with the same education (Taubman & Wales, 1975). The importance of health and the extent of health-seeking activity by Americans are clearly indicated by the fact that more than $100 billion was expended on health care services in the United States in 1972 (Burns, 1973). During fiscal year 1974, this level of expenditure represented almost 8% of the gross national product; that is, approximately $1 of every $14 for goods and services produced in this country is a health dollar. Thus, health care is the largest single service industry in the United States today. Yet, the health industry seems to be an unmanaged system. Research on the functioning of its component parts has been undertaken by few psychologists.

Health is rapidly emerging as one of the most crucial social problems facing our nation. Access to health care is increasingly recognized as a basic human right; no citizen should be denied such access because of inability to pay. Despite the huge expenditures on health care services in the past few years, it is widely recognized that large segments of our society do not have access to adequate care. Conventional methods of providing and financing health services are nearly exhausted. Our medical schools are so inadequate in terms of the quantity of physicians they produce that a very large proportion of our physicians are now being trained abroad. Approximately 20% of all physicians in this country are being "imported," and 46% of the physicians licensed in 1972 were graduates

Reprinted from *American Psychologist*, 1976, *31*, 263–274.

of foreign medical schools (Association of American Medical Colleges, 1974). Moreover, the shortage of physicians, along with rapidly growing costs of their services, is encouraging more attention to the use of paraprofessionals and to other innovations in the delivery of traditional health care services. Changes in the service delivery system also have been brought about by an evolution over the years in fundamental medical concepts relating to health and illness.

In earlier times, illness was thought to result from the presence of a single pathogenic agent—germ, toxin, neoplasm, endocrine imbalance, vitamin or other nutritional deficiency, etc. New knowledge, however, has increased the recognition that the etiology of poor health is multifactorial. The virulence of infection interacts with the particular susceptibility of the host. Predisposition of the individual to succumb selectively to various assaults on physical integrity not only is related to particular early life experiences but also is associated with economic and social status, especially as reflected in living and working conditions.

The emergence of health as a social issue has been accompanied by a slow but evident shift in responsibility for coping with the problem. Health care delivery is no longer solely within the purview of medicine. The consumer is assuming a major role in shaping programs and policy, the economist rather than the physician is now leading the search for solutions to the problems of funding the delivery of care, and sociologists are conducting applied research focused upon the development and evaluation of health delivery systems. By contrast, psychology as a discipline has been surprisingly slow to recognize and accept research challenges in this problem area. Possibly the historical prominence of mental health as a focus for applied psychology has overshadowed other types of health-oriented psychological research.

It is time for an increased awareness of the research contributions that may be made in the broader fields of health and delivery of health services by organizational, educational, social, and experimental psychologists. It is obvious that the present crisis in health care delivery is not going to be resolved by psychology alone, or any other single discipline. Nevertheless, certain aspects of the problem call rather uniquely upon the body of knowledge and the methods that have been developed within psychology. This article highlights some of the contemporary issues in health care delivery and identifies research challenges for psychologists.

The American Health Care System

Is there a health care system in the United States? Or is there simply available a large and complex set of facilities and services? The term *system* implies organization and dynamic interaction of functional units; such organization and relationship are found only in limited degree in health services today. The lack of coordination of services that characterizes clinical medicine, general hospitals, optometrists, pharmacies, podiatrists, long-term care facilities, drug manufacturers, and the myriad other parts of our health goods-and-services grab bag is difficult to overstate. There is little evidence of an overall plan (Freymann, 1974; Illich, 1975).

Moreover, the dynamic character of the interrelationships is not always apparent. Each of the groups or institutions referred to above makes decisions as if the others did not exist, and in fact the decisions may have little outside impact. We have most of the elements of a system but without the functional interrelationships and the financial coordination of health services needed for a truly systematic endeavor.

In 1973, 182 million Americans had health insurance that covered part, and often nearly all, of their health expenditures (Health Insurance Institute, 1975), and most of those persons had substantial freedom in picking the purveyors of the facilities or services they sought. Some of these insured Americans, a growing number it appears, belonged to "prepaid" health plans that provided them access to preventive services because it was in the interest of the provider to keep them well. Americans in the military services, along with many in other types of organizations, have health services provided as a condition of employment and can scarcely be distinguished from those persons receiving care under "socialized medicine" systems in other countries. There are, of course, Americans who do not have insurance and who pick and pay the physician of their own choice.

Still others receive a medical subsidy under Medicare and Medicaid programs. There are many Americans, however, who lack personal resources and fail to meet requirements for any program of health care; they do not receive health services of any kind on any consistent basis. The services they receive are haphazard and more often than not are in response to some emergency or personal desperation.

We do not wish to gloss over the complexities alluded to above. What follows is an oversimplification to make another point; we realize that there are limitations to the concept of "system" when that concept is applied to health services in the United States.

Health care delivery involves more than the treatment of illness. The goal is to minimize the need for treatment of disease through positive and proactive programs of health maintenance. With the advances that have been made in modern medicine, infant mortality has been greatly reduced, and mass death from epidemics of highly fatal infectious disease has become almost nonexistent in North America. With the reduction in death from controllable disease and the consequent increase in life expectancy, clinical medicine might be characterized as expanding the traditional concern for treating the sick to include increasing emphasis on prevention of illness and the extended treatment and rehabilitation of the chronically ill.

Health maintenance includes, but extends far beyond, the prevention of infectious disease. It includes the early detection and correction of defects, reduction in the severity of chronic disease processes through early diagnosis and treatment, and education in positive health practices that reduce the need for subsequent treatment. Health care delivery begins with the consumer rather than the physician. If the system is to work, the consumer, rather than the medical team, makes the initial decision to participate. Moreover, initiative for sustained participation rests with the consumer. For many individuals, however, initiative rests with other persons who must detect and assess a problem, often of great complexity, and decide whether further help should be obtained. Children, the aged, the mentally incompetent, and the accident victim are dependent on the judgment of others who make the initial diagnosis and treatment deci-

sion. It should be recognized that many individuals, probably most persons potentially in need of a health service, consult at least one other lay person before making the decision to seek professional help (Friedson, 1970). Wives and husbands ask each other, children ask parents, friends ask neighbors, workers ask supervisors, and so on. An important link in the health care chain is the individual consumer and lay "consultant." It should be recognized also that more often than not when troubled by pain or some other symptom or problem, the consumer diagnoses the problem as a minor or familiar one and treats it himself or ignores it (Fry, 1966). For these reasons health education would be expected to have important payoffs.

The consumer plays yet another role in shaping the health care delivery system. The general consumer advocacy movement in the United States has had a profound impact on health care delivery. The consumer movement is playing a large part in bringing about the establishment of minimal quality standards of health care delivery. Lack of access to adequate health care by large segments of the American population, particularly the disadvantaged and minority groups, has stimulated consumer pressures, which in turn are bringing about the development of innovative change and increased government intervention in the financing and delivery of health care. Although all of the above factors have varying degrees of impact on contemporary health care delivery, it is clear that our present system not only is heavily shaped by consumers but also depends on their behavior as participants.

With the consumer as the first element, the second element in the health services delivery enterprise is that of the professional service provider, broadly defined. Many professionals in the health services system other than physicians may deliver primary health care or provide important diagnostic or preventive services. Although pharmacists may not "practice medicine," it is only in a fairly narrow technical sense that they are constrained from doing so. The victim of a toothache may be given a palliative, the sufferer from nasal congestion may be given a decongestant, and the person in pain from stomach cramps may be given a drug or may be referred to a "specialist," a physician.

Optometrists may prescribe glasses for eye defects or may detect dangerous eye disorders (e.g., diabetic retinopathy), for which they will refer the person to a specialist, that is, a physician. Dentists may treat a wide variety of diseases and defects, and they may also detect conditions (e.g., early signs of cancer), for which they will refer the individual to a specialist, again a physician. For many persons, the first health professional to be seen is perhaps a public health or clinic nurse. Again, treatments may be prescribed and administered or referrals may take place. The important point is that the health services delivery system includes at the very first line of professional action many persons of varied training other than physicians.

The physician is, of course, a vital part of health care delivery. Especially at the level of the so-called "primary care" physician there are important issues of access to and cost of medical care. These may not loom large to most people who do not need or want to visit a physician more than once or twice a year, if that. For other persons with more frequent or more chronic illnesses, the availability of a physician at reasonable cost is critical. Clearly, given the central role and the virtual monopoly on certain aspects of medical care that have been granted to physicians, the public has a vital interest in their performance as a part of a total system of health care.

For people lacking access to an individual physician there are alternate subsystems to provide care. The hospital emergency room is important as a part of the system in its own right. It also provides a source of primary care for many persons, especially those lacking access to other parts of the system. It has been estimated that up to 80% of the cases appearing at the emergency room are not in fact medical emergencies at all (Gibson, Burbee, & Anderson, 1970; Knowles, 1973). A great many of them are seeking help from the only source known to them. Hospitals, other outpatient departments, and clinics are also important as places of first professional contact with the health system for many people. Though it may make some people uncomfortable to acknowledge it, there are many equivalents of "native healers" who provide care for persons seeking help. At present, little is known about the structure and delivery of emergency services or about the factors that lead a person to define his or her situation as an emergency in the first place.

If the first professional contact does not prove adequate to deal with the health problem presented, our health resources present a virtually dazzling array of specialized facilities and professionals to carry on diagnostic and treatment efforts. There are renowned diagnostic centers, hospitals, specialized and superspecialized physicians, and ancillary professionals to provide whatever care can be paid for. The system even provides life-sustaining measures, somewhat undependably and arbitrarily, to individuals who, only a few short years ago, would have died; hemodialysis and kidney transplantation are notable examples. At this level of specialized professionals and the zenith of medical technology, expenses mount rapidly and can quickly become ruinous. Only relatively few persons need access to health care at its most advanced levels, but for those who do, the need is likely to be critical. To the extent that we may think of American health care as constituting a system, it is evident that it is highly complicated, that there is no smooth organization and working together of the parts, that it is often adventitious and even arbitrary in the way services are distributed, and that it can be very expensive at its extended best. Causing the system to operate more effectively, more fairly, and at lower cost is an objective worthy of the attention of all Americans, but especially of psychologists, who have a privileged opportunity to contribute to the attainment of that objective.

Psychological Aspects of Health and Disease

Few persons deny the importance of psychological factors in health and well-being. Educated lay persons as well as scientists express both colloquially and formally some of the interrelationships between good health and successful adjustment or between poor health and poor adjustment. There has been a considerable increase in the interest of social scientists in health and illness. One of the more productive branches of sociology is medical sociology; one of the more intriguing branches of anthropology is one that studies the beliefs and practices of our contemporary primitive and not-so-primitive cultures in the areas of illness, its prevention and treatment; economists and epidemiologists have gathered data that show relationships between social class poverty and illness. Simply to list the behaviors that affect health and its maintenance would be a difficult and tedious task.

One of the questions that psychologists, with their skills in educational technology, are beginning to address is why many people do not follow medical advice about their health and its maintenance. What are the determinants of specific but important acts of commission (brushing one's teeth) or omission (refraining from smoking)? When symptoms do appear, why do some persons avoid formal diagnosis and deny illness—a denial that may be self-destructive. Psychologists are investigating factors that motivate such health-related behaviors.

The area of health research is replete with topics suitable for predictive studies. Measurable constitutional factors that predispose to one or another illness may be the domain of anatomy and physiology, and measurable somatotypical factors have been a subject of physical anthropology. The assessment of life-styles and life crises as they affect near-future illness, however, is certainly a proper study for psychology. Similarly, how and why individuals vary in their responses to sickness are questions for psychological investigation. One sailor aboard ship, for instance, may turn up at sick call when medical evidence indicates that he has little physically wrong; another, apparently much sicker by objective tests, continues at his job and carries his work load. One housewife may keep things going when her temperature is high and her strength low; another, with fewer symptoms, may take to her bed. An elementary-school child, faced with scholastic and peer problems, may find health problems worsened, while another, whose social adjustment is proceeding smoothly, experiences fewer sicknesses. How are these response patterns to be understood?

The substantive areas for application of psychological method to the study of health and illness behaviors are many. Their potential yield of insights into psychobiosocial determinants of such behaviors is great and could provide the basis for improved prophylactic and therapeutic efforts. A few questions can illustrate the challenge: How are health care practices related to the amount and quality of the individual's health information? What are the determinants of more and less effective specific health education programs? How should such programs be evaluated? What are the primary sources of persisting health care attitudes? What are the relations of such attitudes to information and to care resources?

While a proportion of the research effort by psychologists interested in health has been directed toward persons who now, or who may in the future, suffer from some specific illnesses, a surprisingly large share has focused on studies of fairly healthy populations (Heath, 1965). In the 1940s there were many studies of background characteristics, personality factors, and life events that might be related to one or another form of illness. Examples include the many studies of how persons with a specific illness, presumed to be psychosomatic, behaved on a standard set of stimuli, like inkblots, or on an omnibus set of questions, like the MMPI or the Maudsley Personality Inventory. These continue today, as exemplified by the Jenkins (1971) questionnaire about Type A or Type B personality in the prediction of heart disease. Studies of this sort test normal populations, for example, members of an urban fire department or employees of a department store, and then attempt to identify those in the population who may succumb to the disability of interest. Other studies, like those of Gunderson and Rahe (1974), inquire about a person's recent life changes, assuming that situational crises can be weighted and cumulated, and then try to identify, in a healthy population, those who may become ill in any way at all. This adds a new dimension to susceptibility, a psychosocial one, that may create a modest but useful amount of unique variance to prediction of illness.

Some recent work deserves mention as a positive example of what can be done in the area of attitude research. In a series of studies, Richard I. Evans and his colleagues at the University of Houston have applied the tools of social psychology to one aspect of health maintenance, dental hygiene (Evans, Rozelle, Noblitt, & Williams, in press). Recent investigation by these workers on the effects of feedback in modifying health maintenance behavior and maintaining the changes has indicated that repeated contacts with the subject may themselves be more important in maintaining change than the particular method of persuasion or feedback involved. There are many areas of health besides dentistry in which attitudes influence behavior and are extremely important either in health maintenance or in treatment programs. Although some valuable work is currently being done, there is need for additional competent researchers to become involved in this area of endeavor.

The processes of rehabilitation provide another potentially major arena for basic and applied psychological research. The patient who has suffered a major debilitating illness or physical handicap is essentially faced with a variety of learning tasks—learning new patterns of activities, relearning lost aptitudes, or acquiring new skills. Basic fields of developmental, cognitive, learning, and motivational psychology have relevance, and their principles can direct research aimed at the discovery of more efficient rehabilitation programs. In the process, there is opportunity for testing hypotheses and discovering new principles.

Both collegiate and military populations participate in the study of the relationship of stress to disease. How humans adjust to unusual challenges, to perils, to isolation, to disappointments has been studied with health and illness as critical outcomes (Levi, 1971). The ergonomist's criterion of efficiency must be supplemented by the broadest criteria of health. A sizable amount of research on the health of the healthy is done on young populations because of their availability. Normative studies in Boston and Chicago (Heath, 1965) of healthy young college students can be matched by a variety of studies carried on by psychologists in the armed forces. Research centers like the Army Research Institute of Environmental Medicine at Natick, Massachusetts, or the Naval Health Research Center at San Diego, which specializes in cohort studies, have followed some service personnel for almost a decade (Gunderson & Rahe, 1974).

The way people cope when struck by ill health or accident is also an important area of study. Response to pain, to persistent discomfort, to physical handicap, and to debilitation can be assessed by a variety of psychological measures. It is not only the individual differences in coping ability that people show when attacked by illness or handicap that is of interest, however. These differences in adaptation need to be related to physical and psychological characteristics.

Illness can be thought of as the product of exposure interacting with resistance. Some germs are so potent that exposure alone can bring about death—no amount of stamina or determination can prevent the outcome. At another extreme, some illnesses seem to result from a minimum of potency of the invading agent and a maximum of stress.

Researchers into health and illness behaviors must attend to the criterion problem. Longevity is too crude a criterion of health. Definitions are beginning to reflect recognition of degrees of quality of life, as shown, for example, in extent of self-sufficiency, satisfaction, and personal fulfillment.

Illness as a research criterion also does not allow simple definition. The synoptic researchers who have reviewed the concept have seen it as including some role playing. Is illness at least partially a self-defined state? It would be helpful to arrange the array of diseases along an acute-chronic continuum and to investigate the degree to which chronicity is correlated with the extent of disturbed psychological factors.

Psychologists and researchers in related health fields have studied psychological correlates of a number of psychosomatic and somatic disease syndromes (entities) as well as illness in general (Gunderson & Rahe, 1974). Early studies were done of asthma, dermatoses, duodenal ulcer, colitis, and other diseases considered "psychosomatic." Later, interests focused on conditions that previously had been considered purely "somatic," such as hypertension, coronary heart disease, and arthritis. The relationship between hostility and repression of hostility and hypertension was outlined (Alexander, 1950), and a specific personality profile, the so-called coronary-prone Type A behavior pattern, was hypothesized for individuals vulnerable to myocardial infarction (Friedman & Rosenman, 1959, 1974; Jenkins, Rosenman, & Zyzansky, 1974; Rosenman et al., 1966). More recently, investigators have begun to study the role of psychological factors in the etiology of cancer.

The etiology of cancer, or more accurately, the cancers, still is not well understood. Hopes have repeatedly been shattered for finding a specific agent (e.g., a virus) that extends the principles of study that were important for the understanding and control of infectious diseases. The failure of the old approaches is probably related to the fact that cancer is a disease involving basic cell behavior apparently responsive to slight changes in the ribonucleic acid (RNA) and deoxyribonucleic acid (DNA) transmission of genetic coding. Within a systems-theoretical approach, RNA and DNA coding, in turn, are responsive not only to genetic conditions but also to changes in the endocrine, hematologic, immunologic, and neurologic systems and thus, indirectly, to behavioral variables. In the area of immune responses it has been shown (Rasmussen, 1969; Solomon, 1969; Solomon, Amkraut, & Kasper, 1974; Bahnson et al., Note 1) that stress and depression may reduce the antibody response and that adult immunologic responsivity may be a function of early infantile experiences. In animal models (Ader & Friedman, 1965; Ader, Friedman, & Glasgow, 1969; Newton, 1964) it has also been demonstrated that early life experiences and environmental manipulation modify responses to later cancer challenges. This and related research are summarized by Bahnson (1969a) and Bahnson and Kissen (1966).

Psychologic and psychosocial research has been concerned with long-term etiologic behavioral factors (e.g., personality, childhood stress) as well as with behavioral correlates to different types of response to cancer and to impending death. Studies of etiology have implicated three different but overlapping problem areas related to cancer: (a) a particular repressive personality pattern that is related to specific childhood experiences, (b) a tendency to respond with hopelessness-helplessness-despair to the loss of a significant person or life situation, and (c) a history of bereavement or loss of significant interpersonal relationships or life contexts. Traditional studies of personality in cancer patients, using control subjects who were both well and sick, have been done by a number of American and European psychologists including Tarlau and Smalheiser (1951), LeShan (1966; LeShan & Reznikoff, 1960; LeShan & Worthington, 1956). Cobb (1952, 1959), Reznikoff (1955), and Bahnson (1969a, 1969b; Bahnson & Bahnson, 1969). Psychiatrists and medical psychologists overseas have added to this research, including Kissen et al. in Britain (Kissen, Brown, & Kissen, 1969; Kissen & Eysenck, 1962; Kissen & Rao, 1969); Baltrusch (1975) in Germany; Oo (Note 2) in Hungary; and many others. A variety of objective and projective questionnaires and tests were used, and these several different groups arrived independently at a consistent description of the cancer patient as a rigid, authoritarian, innerdirected, and religious person, having ample conflict around sexual and hostile impulses, using excessive repression of affect, and having poor emotional outlets. Patients with slow- and fast-growing cancers have been compared. Blumberg, West, and Ellis (1956), using MMPI and Rorschach data, found that cancer patients with fast-developing diseases are more defensive and overcontrolled than patients with slow-developing diseases. Cobb (1959), using interview data, confirmed these impressions. The patient with rapidly progressing cancer shows a lack of ability to decrease anxiety and presents a polite, apologetic, almost painful acquiescence. This is contrasted with the more expressive and sometimes bizarre personalities of those who respond well to therapy with long remission and survival. Klopfer (1954) related investment in ego defense and ego strength to the differential development of fast- and slow-growing cancers. High investment correlated with fast-growing cancers.

Several psychologists have addressed themselves to the problem of adaptation to cancer and to impending death. Eissler (1955), Feifel (1959; Feifel, Freilich, & Hermann, 1973; Feifel, Hanson, Jones, & Edwards, 1967), Shneidman (1967, 1973), Murray (1962), and Shusterman (1973) are among those who have published in this area. Most have emphasized the importance of both interpersonal and intrapersonal communication for successful adaptation to disease. There is agreement that system approaches also are relevant here, because illness produces problem areas between patient and family, patient and medical staff, medical staff and family, and institution and medical staff. Not only the mental health and quality of life of the cancer patient and family but also the actual length of survival and response to treatment are correlated with the resolution of these several complex psychologic interactions.

Research is greatly needed to improve our understanding of psychological factors related to the onset of cancer. Psychologists can make significant contributions to the sophisticated rehabilitation and psychotherapeutic treatment of the complex emotional reactions of the patient to terminal disease and of the patient's family both to the disease and to death. Several studies have indicated that a new disease appears in a family particularly during the first year following an unresolved loss, indicating that prophylactic psychologic management of bereavement problems may yield significant gains for the survivors with regard to both their mental and physical status in the years to come.

Current Patterns of Psychological Research on Health

The focus of the Task Force has been on research contributions by psychologists who are working on health and illness problems lying *outside* the traditional concerns with mental health and mental illness. It has been difficult to arrive at a secure estimate of the extent of such research activities. An appraisal of the general research literature and an examination of the roster of psychologists who have expressed interest in the work of the Task Force suggest that both the size and impact of our research on health-related behaviors are presently anemic, especially when viewed against the matrix of problems having potential for extensive contributions through psychological research.

The number of psychologists who have identified themselves to the Task Force as having definite interests in health research is quite small (fewer than 500), especially when contrasted to the memberships of those APA divisions (such as clinical, physiological and comparative, personality and social, rehabilitation, and psychopharmacology) in which one might expect health researchers to find their APA "home." The likelihood of sizable research contributions on health and illness factors may be further reduced in light of the fact that approximately one half of those who express health research interests have their major employment outside of medical or health settings. More significantly, their research reports frequently are published in non-APA journals, which not only are rarely seen by the average APA member but in some instances are not included in the *Psychological Abstracts* Search and Retrieval (PASAR's) abstracting review process. Thus, the actual extent of research contributions by psychologists working in the general domain of health problems may be larger than is reflected by the more common modes of visibility.

One of the objectives of the Task Force has been to collect, organize, and disseminate information on the status of health behavior research. To accomplish this objective the task force used the PASAR system to identify literature cited in *Psychological Abstracts* on psychological aspects of (a) physical illness, (b) physical disability, or (c) health. In addition, the search included the role of psychologist and of psychological research in the delivery of health services. Mental health services were included only as they were more generally a part of health services.

The broad search resulted in approximately 3,500 abstracts or citations, covering the years 1966–1973. These abstracts were read and sorted into topical categories. The initial sorts were then reread, and those not relevant to the primary interest of the Task Force were eliminated, namely, all articles that were not research studies (i.e., reviews, anecdotal reports) and those that dealt primarily with mental health variables or psychiatric focuses. This second, more restricted categorization led to a disappointingly small literature sample of approximately 350 articles, scarcely more than 40 articles per year.

The literature search encountered some difficulties along the way. Ambiguity coupled with the limited amount of information available from an abstract impaired attempts to develop a useful classification schema. Abstracts often consisted mostly of the author's conclusions and were unclear as to the research methodology involved. Thus, in many cases it was difficult to distinguish anecdotal reports from more rigorous studies. Kahana (1972) experienced similar difficulties in his search for literature in the area of medical psychology, using the Medlars system of the National Library of Medicine. He reported that it was necessary to search under many terms to identify concepts and that the output was enormous. He too, however, reported that of 5,000 references selected from the computer search, 2,500 were judged directly relevant to the topic, and about 25% seemed useful.

In addition to problems in interpreting the abstracts themselves, the 3,500 abstracts retrieved from PASAR represented only a sample of the total literature in this broad interdisciplinary area. *Psychological Abstracts* is not designed to cover every journal in which a health-related article of interest to psychologists occasionally appears. In the interests of economy it is limited to publications that offer higher hit rates. Further, while a number of core journals are completely abstracted, most of the chosen list of journals is selectively scanned for articles judged likely to be of interest to the user of the system. Some loss of article abstracts in peripheral or less traditional areas such as health research may occur in this way. A final reason for the incomplete nature of the data base is that not all health-related research is reported in a journal format. Health researchers frequently work in nonuniversity settings and publish in-house reports, technical and progress reports, or other items not likely to be picked up by an abstracting system.

With these caveats in mind, the categories and current trends in health research revealed by the PASAR search are interesting. Several schema for breaking down the results of the scan were proposed. The abstracts gathered can be subsumed under three general categories: psychobiological aspects of health, health care delivery, and studies of health-related attitudes. Under the psychobiological category, accounting for 66% of the abstracts, fall such topics as the effects of stress, psychosomatics, social and environmental factors, and the effects of physical health and biological cycles on psychology and behavior.

Papers related to health care delivery (56

papers) accounted for 18% of the abstracts. Nearly half of these dealt with relatively specific aspects of treatment and rehabilitation rather than with larger issues or systems research. Needs and resources in health maintenance, health systems, and manpower, improvement of communication (e.g., between doctor and patient), and evaluation studies (including perceptions and impacts of health care) made up the remainder of this category. Studies of attitudes related to health and health care accounted for the remaining 16% of the abstracts. These ranged from surveys of attitudes held by various populations to attitude-change research.

Still another basis exists for the impression that psychology is neglecting the health area as a fertile field for research contributions. This is found in the topical concentration of our research endeavors, especially when appraised against health areas of major economic importance and public concern. Using "armchair" categories of health-related topics, *Psychological Abstracts* yielded a total of 4,719 entries for 1966–1967 (Schofield, 1969) inclusive, and 14,427 entries for 1971–1973 inclusive. This suggests considerable growth, but the absolute figures constitute an increment of only 5% in the proportion of total abstract entries. More significantly, the areas of research interest have not shifted. Topics neglected in the earlier PASAR survey continue to be relatively ignored, for example, population control, accidents, smoking, cancer, and pain. By contrast, the three topics of psychotherapy, mental retardation, and schizophrenia account for over 50% of the abstracts in both survey periods (see APA Task Force, 1974a).

This appraisal of the extent of health research contributions by psychologists may be unduly bleak. The Task Force has learned that many psychologists who are productive health researchers (e.g., in the field of dentistry) do not belong to APA. Some have resigned because they find no divisional affiliation that is effectively compatible with their research interests.[1]

To some extent, the restricted level of activity by psychologists in health and illness research may result from a lack of awareness of

---

[1] A Section of Health Research has now been formed within Division 18.

support funds from agencies other than the National Institute of Mental Health (NIMH). The Task Force has sought to alert psychologists to the behavioral science research programs presently supported by the National Heart and Lung Institute, the National Dental Institute, the National Institute of Neurological Diseases and Stroke, the National Institute of Alcohol Abuse and Alcoholism, and the National Institute of Occupational Safety and Health. Current planning for behavioral research programs is underway at the National Cancer Institute and the National Institute of General Medicine (see APA Task Force, 1974b).

Two conclusions are suggested. Up to the present time, American psychologists have not been attracted in large numbers to the problems of health and illness as fruitful areas for both basic and applied research activity; nor have these psychologists perceived the potentials for their work in effecting important improvements in health maintenance, illness prevention, and health care delivery. Some good work is being done. There is a need, however, for continuing effort of the sort initiated by the Task Force in stimulating and facilitating increased research contributions by psychologists.

Needs and Potentials

There is probably no more widespread deterrent to the achievement of a truly comprehensive system for health care than our dualistic conceptualization of health and illness. The obstruction to meaningful research and to optimal services resulting from a "practical" adherence to the mind-body dichotomy has been appreciated by persons as diverse as a state governor and a philosopher of science. Governor Evans (1975) of Washington observed, "Doctors, who once treated the human body as an entity, are so specialized that none seem to know any more that the head bone is still indirectly connected to the great toe" (p. 136). Theodore Roszak (1975) said it well when he wrote,

> My position is that every such dichotomy is a symptom of disease in us: of fear, rigidity, compulsive distrust. The dichotomy is the problem, and choosing one or the other half of it is not a solution,

because no healthy personality, no healthy culture, no healthy science can be built on less than the full and integrated range of human mentality. (p. 792)

No other discipline is better suited and equipped than psychology to discover, delineate, and demonstrate the organismic nature of humans and to encourage an ever-broadening realization that humanity's total functional health is threatened whenever either side of the interactive mind-body equation is neglected. Any program for health care and illness management can achieve comprehensiveness and integration only as there is respect for the functional unity of the individual. Psychologists can further the adoption of a usefully integrated concept of humans by applying their research methods to uncover the relationships between psychological factors and physical health.

If the current picture of psychological health research is not impressive, it must be recognized that psychology is probably in the earliest stage of a pioneering endeavor. There is no lack of opportunity. Rather, we need an educational endeavor within our profession. In particular, we need to blueprint programs for graduate education of researchers that will provide an early awareness of the needs and opportunities to apply psychological principles and methods to the understanding and improvement of health behaviors.

Psychological inquiry into factors determining health or illness can be pursued at more molecular or more molar levels. The psychophysiologist can track down the subtle physical responses to perception of threat and provide a basis for the physician to understand better the onset and course of illness in a patient. The personality researchers can explore attitudes (behavioral predispositions) that influence the individual toward responses that bring either immediate or later threat to health. The social psychologist can study the influence of group mores on the individual's accessibility or resistance to health education and health practices. The measurement expert can devise instruments to provide quantitative indexes of important qualitative variables, such as the "quality" of health services. The organizational psychologist may assist in bringing about change in health care delivery systems and in enhancing their effectiveness. The experimental psychologist may be of help in designing better monitoring equipment or in improving diagnostic algorithms. The educational psychologist can explore the variables that determine the extent to which health-related information is understood, stored, and acted upon. There is probably no speciality field within psychology that cannot contribute to the discovery of behavioral variables crucial to a full understanding of susceptibility to physical illness, adaptation to such illness, and prophylactically motivated behaviors. The areas open to psychological investigation range from health care practices and health care delivery systems to the management of acute and chronic illness and to the psychology of medication and pain.

If psychology's potentials for vital contributions to our nation's health are to be realized, certain needs must be met. First among these is the need for psychologists to be aware of the opportunity to contribute significantly to both the philosophy and the programs of our health care system. In this respect, psychologists should acknowledge that they are *life* scientists and consequently, no matter how tangentially, health scientists. The encouragement of such awareness has been one of the charges of the Task Force. This endeavor can be facilitated by recognition of and provision for still another need, the need for health researchers in our discipline to be directly aware of each other's work and of the research of health professionals in other disciplines.

With recognition of the new opportunities likely to arise because of the increasing public concern for better health care, with recognition of the presently very small number of psychologists who are health researchers (outside of the mental health area), and with recognition that these few have largely involved and scratched out their own specialized training, there is a need to give serious thought to innovative programs of graduate training that will prepare psychologists to carry their expertise effectively into the general clinic, the hospital, the rehabilitation center, the community health center, and the group medical practice.

Finally, as a corollary to all of these needs, there is a need to find a suitable home within APA for what has now been identified as a core of health researchers, a distinct interest group that is likely to grow and has need for the basic organizational supports afforded by our major scientific and professional society.

Reference Notes

1. Bahnson, C. B., et al. *Relationship between emotion, repression of emotion, and immunity.* Manuscript in preparation.
2. Oo, M. *Personality examinations of cancer patients.* Paper presented at the Fourth International Conference on Psychosomatic Aspects of Neoplastic Disease, Turin, Italy, June 1965.

References

Ader, R., & Friedman, S. B. Social factors affecting emotionality and resistance to disease in animals. V. Early separation from the mother and response to a transplanted tumor in the rat. *Psychosomatic Medicine,* 1965, *27,* 119–122.

Ader, R., Friedman, S., & Glasgow, L. Psychosocial factors modifying host resistance to experimental infections. *Annals of the New York Academy of Sciences,* 1969, *164,* 381–393.

Alexander, F. *Psychosomatic medicine.* New York: Norton, 1950.

American Psychological Association, Task Force on Health Research. Patterns of psychological study in health related areas. *Newsletter,* July 1974, pp. 6–7. (a)

American Psychological Association, Task Force on Health Research. Sources of funding. *Newsletter,* December 1974, pp. 5–10. (b)

Association of American Medical Colleges. Report of the Task Force on Foreign Medical Graduates. *Journal of Medical Education,* 1974, *49,* 811–822.

Bahnson, C. B. (Ed.). Second conference on psychophysiological aspects of cancer. *Annals of the New York Academy of Sciences,* 1969, *164,* 307–634. (a)

Bahnson, C. B. Psychophysiological complementarity in malignancies—Past work and future vistas. *Annals of the New York Academy of Sciences,* 1969, *164,* 319–334. (b)

Bahnson, C. B., & Bahnson, M. B. Role of the ego defenses: Denial and repression in the etiology of malignant neoplasm. *Annals of the New York Academy of Sciences,* 1966, *125,* 827–845.

Bahnson, C. B., & Kissen, D. M. (Eds.). Psychophysiological aspects of cancer. *Annals of the New York Academy of Sciences,* 1966, *125,* 773–1055.

Bahnson, M. B., & Bahnson, C. B. Ego defenses in cancer patients. *Annals of the New York Academy of Sciences,* 1969, *164,* 546–559.

Baltrusch, H. J. F. Ergebnisse Klinisch-Psychosomatischer Krebsforschung. *Psychosomatische Medizin,* 1975, *5,* 175–208.

Blumberg, E. M., West, P. M., & Ellis, F. W. MMPI findings in human cancer. In *Basic readings on the MMPI in psychology and medicine.* Minneapolis: University of Minnesota Press, 1956.

Burns, E. M. *Health services for tomorrow: Trends and issues.* New York: Dunellen, 1973.

Cobb, B. *A socio-psychological study of the cancer patient.* Unpublished doctoral dissertation, University of Texas, Austin, 1952.

Cobb, B. Emotional problems of adult cancer patients. *Journal of the American Geriatrics Society*, 1959, *1*, 274–285.

Eissler, K. R. *The psychiatrist and the dying patient*. New York: International Universities Press, 1955.

Evans, D. J. The role of the state governments in educating the public about health. *Journal of Medical Education*, 1975, *50*, 130–137.

Evans, R. I., Rozelle, R. M., Noblitt, R., & Williams, D. L. Explicit and implicit persuasive communications over time to initiate and maintain behavior change: New perspective utilizing a real life dental hygiene situation. *Journal of Applied Social Psychology*, in press.

Feifel, H. (Ed.). *The meaning of death*. New York: McGraw-Hill, 1959.

Feifel, H., Freilich, J., & Hermann, J. Death fear in dying heart and cancer patients. *Journal of Psychosomatic Research*, 1973, *17*, 161–166.

Feifel, H., Hanson, S., Jones, R., & Edwards, L. Physicians consider death. *Proceedings of the 75th Annual Convention of the American Psychological Association*, 1967, *2*, 201–202. (Summary)

Freymann, J. G. *The American health care system: Its genesis and trajectory*. New York: Medcom, 1974.

Friedman, M., & Rosenman, R. H. Association of a specific overt behavior pattern with blood and cardiovascular findings. *Journal of the American Medical Association*, 1959, *169*, 1286.

Friedman, M., & Rosenman, R. H. *Type 'A' behavior and your heart*. New York: Knopf, 1974.

Friedson, E. *The profession of medicine: A study of the sociology of applied knowledge*. New York: Dodd, Mead, 1970.

Fry, J. *Profiles of disease: A study in the natural history of common disease*. Baltimore, Md.: Williams & Wilkins, 1966.

Gibson, G., Bugbee, G., & Anderson, O. W. *Emergency medical services in the Chicago area*. Chicago, Ill.: Center for Health Administration Studies, University of Chicago, 1970.

Gunderson, E. K. E., & Rahe, R. H. (Eds.). *Life stress and illness*. Springfield, Ill.: Charles C Thomas, 1974.

Health Insurance Institute. *Source book of health insurance data: 1974–75*. New York: Author, 1975.

Heath, D. *Exploration of maturity*. New York: Appleton-Century-Crofts, 1965.

Illich, I. *Medical nemesis: The expropriation of health*. London: Calder & Boyars, 1975.

Jenkins, C. D. Psychologic and social precursors of coronary disease. *New England Journal of Medicine*, 1971, *284*, 244–255; 307–317.

Jenkins, C. D., Rosenman, R. H., & Zyzansky, S. J. Prediction of clinical coronary heart disease by a test for the coronary-prone behavior pattern. *New England Journal of Medicine*, 1974, *290*, 1271–1275.

Juster, F. T. (Ed.). *Education, income and human behavior*. New York: McGraw-Hill, 1975.

Kahana, R. J. Studies in medical psychology: A brief survey. *Psychiatry in Medicine*, 1972, *3*, 1–22.

Kissen, D. M., Brown, R. I. F., & Kissen, M. A further report on personality and psychosocial factors in lung cancer. *Annals of the New York Academy of Sciences*, 1969, *164*, 535–545.

Kissen, D. M., & Eysenck, H. J. Personality in male lung cancer patients. *Journal of Psychosomatic Research*, 1962, *6*, 123.

Kissen, D. M., & Rao, L. G. S. Steroid excretion patterns and personality in lung cancer. *Annals of the New York Academy of Sciences*, 1969, *164*, 476–481.

Klopfer, B. A. Results of psychologic testing in cancer. In J. A. Gengerelli & F. J. Kirkner (Eds.), *The psychological variables in human cancer*. Berkeley & Los Angeles: University of California Press, 1954.

Knowles, J. H. The hospital. *Scientific American*, 1973, *229*(3), 128–137.

LeShan, L. L. An emotional life-history pattern associated with neoplastic disease. *Annals of the New York Academy of Sciences*, 1966, *125*, 780–793.

LeShan, L. L., & Reznikoff, M. A psychological factor apparently associated with neoplastic disease. *Journal of Abnormal and Social Psychology*, 1960, *60*, 439–440.

LeShan, L. L., & Worthington, R. E. Some recurrent life history patterns observed in patients with malignant disease. *Journal of Nervous and Mental Disease*, 1956, *124*, 460–465.

Levi, L. (Ed.). *Society, stress, and disease. I. The psychosocial environment and psychosomatic diseases*. London: Oxford University Press, 1971.

Murray, H. A. The personality and career of Satan. *Journal of Social Issues*, 1962, *18*, 36–54.

Newton, G. Early experience and resistance to tumor growth. In D. M. Kissen & L. L. LeShan (Eds.), *Psychosomatic aspects of neoplastic disease*. London: Pitman, 1964.

Rasmussen, A. J., Jr. Emotions and immunity. *Annals of the New York Academy of Sciences*, 1969, *164*, 458–461.

Reznikoff, M. Psychological factors in breast cancer: A preliminary study of some personality trends in patients with cancer of the breast. *Psychosomatic Medicine*, 1955, *17*, 96–108.

Rosenman, R. H., Friedman, M., Straus, R., Wurm, M., Jenkins, C. D., & Messinger, H. B. Coronary heart disease in the western collaborative group study. *Journal of the American Medical Association*, 1966, *195*, 86–92.

Roszak, T. Gnosis and reductionism (Letter to the editor). *Science*, 1975, *187*, 790; 792.

Schofield, W. The role of psychology in the delivery of health services. *American Psychologist*, 1969, *24*, 565–584.

Shneidman, E. S. (Ed.). *Essays in self-destruction*. New York: Science House, 1967.

Shneidman, E. S. *The deaths of man*. New York: Quadrangle, 1973.

Shusterman, L. R. Death and dying: A critical review of the literature. *Nursing Outlook*, 1973, *21*, 465–471.

Solomon, G. F. Emotion, stress, and the central nervous system, and immunity. *Annals of the New York Academy of Sciences*, 1969, *164*, 335–343.

Solomon, G. F., Amkraut, A. A., & Kasper, P. Immunity, emotions and stress. With special reference to the mechanisms of stress effects on the immune system. In H. Musaph (Ed.), *Mechanisms in symptom formation*. Basel, Switzerland: S. Karger, 1974.

Tarlau, M., & Smalheiser, I. Personality patterns in patients with malignant tumors of the breast and cervix: An exploratory study. *Psychosomatic Medicine*, 1951, *13*, 117–121.

Taubman, P., & Wales, T. Education as an investment and a screening device. In F. T. Juster (Ed.), *Education, income and human behavior*. New York: McGraw-Hill, 1975.

Bibliography

Balitsky, K. P., Kapshuk, A. P., & Tsapenko, V. F. Some electrophysiological peculiarities of the nervous system in malignant growth. *Annals of the New York Academy of Sciences,* 1969, *164,* 520–525.

Coppen, A. J., & Metcalfe, M. Cancer and extraversion. *British Medical Journal,* 1963, *5348,* 18–19.

Greene, W. A. Psychological factors and reticuloendothelial disease. I. Preliminary observations of a group of males with lymphomas and leukemias. *Psychosomatic Medicine,* 1954, *16,* 220–230.

Greene, W. A. The psychological setting of the development of leukemia and lymphoma. *Annals of the New York Academy of Sciences,* 1966, *125,* 794–801.

Greene, W. A., Young, L. E., & Swisher, S. N. Psychological factors and reticuloendothelial disease. II. Observations on a group of women with lymphomas and leukemias. *Psychosomatic Medicine,* 1956, *18,* 284–303.

Hagnell, O. The premorbid personality of persons who develop cancer in a total population investigated in 1947 and 1957. *Annals of the New York Academy of Sciences,* 1966, *125,* 846–855.

Katz, J. L., Gallager, T., Hellman, L., Sachar, E. J., & Weiner, H. Psychoendocrine considerations in cancer of the breast. *Annals of the New York Academy of Sciences,* 1969, *164,* 509–515.

Kavetsky, R. E., Turkevich, N. M., Akimova, R. M., Khayetsky, I. K., & Matveichuk, Y. D. Induced carcinogenesis under various influences of the hypothalamus. *Annals of the New York Academy of Sciences,* 1969, *164,* 517–519.

Kübler-Ross, E. *On death and dying.* New York: Macmillan, 1969.

Marmorston, J., Geller, P. J., & Weiner, J. M. Pre-treatment urinary hormone patterns and survival in patients with breast cancer, prostate cancer, or lung cancer. *Annals of the New York Academy of Sciences,* 1969, *164,* 483–493.

Schmale, A. H., Jr., & Iker, H. P. The effect of hopelessness in the development of cancer. I. The prediction of uterine cervical cancer in women with atypical cytology. *Psychosomatic Medicine,* 1964, *26,* 634–635.

Schmale, A. H., Jr., & Iker, H. P. The psychological setting of uterine cervical cancer. *Annals of the New York Academy of Sciences,* 1966, *125,* 807–813.

The Task Force on Health Research of the Board of Scientific Affairs was established in June 1973 upon the recommendation of the Committee on Newly Emerging Areas of Research (NEAR). Members of the Task Force are Claus B. Bahnson, Edward J. Kelty, Miriam F. Kelty (APA staff liaison), John E. Rasmussen, Willliam Schofield (Chair), Lee B. Sechrest, and Walter W. Wilkins.

Meta-Analysis of Psychotherapy Outcome Studies

Mary L. Smith and Gene V Glass

Results of nearly 400 controlled evaluations of psychotherapy and counseling were coded and integrated statistically. The findings provide convincing evidence of the efficacy of psychotherapy. On the average, the typical therapy client is better off than 75% of untreated individuals. Few important differences in effectiveness could be established among many quite different types of psychotherapy. More generally, virtually no difference in effectiveness was observed between the class of all behavioral therapies (systematic desensitization, behavior modification) and the nonbehavioral therapies (Rogerian, psychodynamic, rational-emotive, transactional analysis, etc.).

Scholars and clinicians have argued bitterly for decades about the efficacy of psychotherapy and counseling. Michael Scriven proposed to the American Psychological Association's Ethics Committee that APA-member clinicians be required to present a card to prospective clients on which it would be explained that the procedure they were about to undergo had never been proven superior to a placebo ("Psychotherapy Caveat," 1974). Most academics have read little more than Eysenck's (1952, 1965) tendentious diatribes in which he claimed to prove that 75% of neurotics got better regardless of whether or not they were in therapy—a conclusion based on the interpretation of six controlled studies. The perception that research shows the inefficacy of psychotherapy has become part of conventional wisdom even within the profession. The following testimony was recently presented before the Colorado State Legislature:

> Are they [the legislators] also aware of the relatively primitive state of the art of treatment outcome evaluation which is still, after fifty years, in kind of a virginal state? About all we've been able to prove is that a third of the people get better, a third of the people stay the same, and a third of the people get worse, irregardless of the treatment to which they are subjected. (Quoted by Ellis, 1977, p. 3)

Only close followers of the issue have read Bergin's (1971) astute dismantling of the Eysenck myth in his review of the findings of 23 controlled evaluations of therapy. Bergin found evidence that therapy is effective. Emrick (1975) reviewed 72 studies of the psychological and psychopharmacological treatment of alcoholism and concluded that evidence existed for the efficacy of therapy. Luborsky, Singer, and Luborsky (1975) reviewed about 40 controlled studies and found more evidence. Although these reviews were reassuring, two sources of doubt remained. First, the number of studies in which the effects of counseling and psychotherapy have been tested is closer to 400 than to 40. How representative the 40 are of the 400 is unknown. Second, in these reviews, the "voting method" was used; that is, the number of studies with statistically significant results in favor of one treatment or another was tallied. This method is too weak to answer many important questions and is biased in favor of large-sample studies.

The purpose of the present research has three parts: (1) to identify and collect all studies that tested the effects of counseling and psychotherapy; (2) to determine the magnitude of effect of the therapy in each study; and (3) to compare the effects of different types of therapy and relate the size of effect to the characteristics of the therapy (e.g., diagnosis of patient, training of therapist) and of the study. Meta-analysis, the integration of research through statistical analysis of the analyses of individual studies (Glass, 1976), was used to investigate the problem.

Reprinted from *American Psychologist*, 1977, *32*, 752–760.

Procedures

Standard search procedures were used to identify 1,000 documents: *Psychological Abstracts, Dissertation Abstracts,* and branching off of bibliographies of the documents themselves. Of those documents located, approximately 500 were selected for inclusion in the study, and 375 were fully analyzed. To be selected, a study had to have at least one therapy treatment group compared to an untreated group or to a different therapy group. The rigor of the research design was not a selection criterion but was one of several features of the individual study to be related to the effect of the treatment in that study. The definition of psychotherapy used to select the studies was presented by Meltzoff and Kornreich (1970):

> Psychotherapy is taken to mean the informed and planful application of techniques derived from established psychological principles, by persons qualified through training and experience to understand these principles and to apply these techniques with the intention of assisting individuals to modify such personal characteristics as feelings, values, attitudes, and behaviors which are judged by the therapist to be maladaptive or maladjustive. (p. 6)

Those studies in which the treatment was labeled "counseling" but whose methods fit the above definition were included. Drug therapies, hypnotherapy, bibliotherapy, occupational therapy, milieu therapy, and peer counseling were excluded. Sensitivity training, marathon encounter groups, consciousness-raising groups, and psychodrama were also excluded. Those studies that Bergin and Luborsky eliminated because they used "analogue" therapy were retained for the present research. Such studies have been designated analogue studies because therapy lasted only a few hours or the therapists were relatively untrained. Rather than arbitrarily eliminating large number of studies and losing potentially valuable information, it was deemed preferable to retain these studies and investigate the relationship between length of therapy, training of therapists, and other characteristics of the study and their measured effects. The arbitrary elimination of such analogue studies was based on an implicit assumption that they differ not only in their methods but also in their effects and how those effects are achieved. Considering methods, analogue studies

fade imperceptibly into "real" therapy, since the latter is often short term, or practiced by relative novices, etc. Furthermore, the magnitude of effects and their relationships with other variables are empirical questions, not to be assumed out of existence. Dissertations and fugitive documents were likewise retained, and the measured effects of the studies compared according to the source of the studies.

The most important feature of an outcome study was the magnitude of the effect of therapy. The definition of the magnitude of effect—or *"effect size"*—was the *mean difference between the treated and control subjects divided by the standard deviation of the control group,* that is, $ES = (\bar{X}_T - \bar{X}_C)/s_C$. Thus, an "effect size" of $+1$ indicates that a person at the mean of the control group would be expected to rise to the 84th percentile of the control group after treatment.

The effect size was calculated on any outcome variable the researcher chose to measure. In many cases, one study yielded more than one effect size, since effects might be measured at more than one time after treatment or on more than one different type of outcome variable. The effect-size measures represent different types of outcomes: self-esteem, anxiety, work/school achievement, physiological stress, etc. Mixing different outcomes together is defensible. First, it is clear that all outcome measures are more or less related to "well-being" and so at a general level are comparable. Second, it is easy to imagine a Senator conducting hearings on the NIMH appropriations or a college president deciding whether to continue funding the counseling center asking, "What kind of effect does therapy produce—on anything?" Third, each primary researcher made value judgments concerning the definition and direction of positive therapeutic effects for the particular clients he or she studied. It is reasonable to adopt these value judgments and aggregate them in the present study. Fourth, since all effect sizes are identified by type of outcome, the magnitude of effect can be compared across type of outcome to determine whether therapy has greater effect on anxiety, for example, than it does on self-esteem.

Calculating effect sizes was straightforward when means and standard deviations were reported. Although this information is thought to be fundamental in reporting research, it was often overlooked by authors and editors. When means and standard deviations were not reported, effect sizes were obtained by the solution of equations from t and F ratios or other inferential test statistics. Probit transformations were used to convert to effect sizes the percentages of patients who improved (Glass, in press). Original data were requested from several authors when effect sizes could not be derived from any reported information. In two instances, effect sizes were impossible to reconstruct: (a) nonparametric statistics irretrievably disguise effect sizes, and (b) the reporting of no data except the alpha level at which a mean difference was significant gives no clue other than that the standardized mean difference must exceed some known value.

Eight hundred thirty-three effect sizes were computed from 375 studies, several studies yielding effects on more than one type of outcome or at more than one time after therapy. Including more than one effect size for each study perhaps introduces dependence in the errors and violates some assumptions of inferential statistics. However, the loss of information that would have resulted from averaging effects across types of outcome or at different follow-up points was too great a price to pay for statistical purity.

The effect sizes of the separate studies became the "dependent variable" in the meta-analysis. The "independent variables" were 16 features of the study described or measured in the following ways:

1. The type of therapy employed, for example, psychodynamic, client centered, rational-emotive, behavior modification, etc. There were 10 types in all; each will be mentioned in the Results section.
2. The duration of therapy in hours.
3. Whether it was group or individual therapy.
4. The number of years' experience of the therapist.
5. Whether clients were neurotics or psychotics.
6. The age of the clients.
7. The IQ of the clients.
8. The source of the subjects—whether solicited for the study, committed to an institution, or sought treatment themselves.
9. Whether the therapists were trained in education, psychology, or psychiatry.
10. The social and ethnic similarity of therapists and clients.
11. The type of outcome measure taken.
12. The number of months after therapy that the outcomes were measured.
13. The reactivity or "fakeability" of the outcome measure.
14. The date of publication of the study.
15. The form of publication.
16. The internal validity of the research design.

Definitions and conventions were developed to increase the reliability of measurement of the features of the studies and to assist the authors in estimating the data when they were not reported. The more important conventions appear in Table 1. Variables not mentioned in Table 1 were measured in fairly obvious ways. The reliability of measurement was determined by comparing the codings of 20 studies by the two authors and four assistants. Agreement exceeded 90% across all categories.[1]

Analysis of the data comprised four parts: (1) descriptive statistics for the body of data as a whole; (2) descriptive statistics for the comparison of therapy types and outcome types; (3) descriptive statistics for a subset of studies in which behavioral and nonbehavioral therapies were compared *in the same study;* and (4) regression analyses in which effect sizes were regressed onto variables descriptive of the study.

Findings

Data From All Experiments

Figure 1 contains the findings at the highest level of aggregation. The two curves depict the average treated and untreated groups of clients across 375 studies, 833 effect-size measures, representing an evaluation of approximately 25,000 control and experimental subjects each. On the average, clients 22 years of age received 17 hours of therapy from therapists with about 3½ years of experience and were measured on the outcome variables about 3¾ months after the therapy.

For ease of representation, the figure is drawn in the form of two normal distributions. No conclusion about the distributions of the

---

[1] The values assigned to the features of the studies, the effect sizes, and all procedures are available in Glass, Smith, and Miller (Note 1).

scores within studies is intended. In most studies, no information was given about the shape of an individual's scores within treated and untreated groups. We suspect that normality has as much justification as any other form.

The average study showed a .68 standard deviation superiority of the treated group over the control group. Thus, the average client receiving therapy was better off than 75% of the untreated controls. Ironically, the 75% figure that Eysenck used repeatedly to embarrass psychotherapy appears in a slightly different context as the most defensible figure on the efficacy

Table 1: *Conventions for Measurement of the Features of Studies*

Study feature	Value	Study feature	Value
Experience of therapist (when not given)	Lay counselor (0 years) MA candidate (1 year) MA counselor (2 years) PhD candidate or psychiatric resident (3 years) PhD therapist (4 years) Well-known PhD or psychiatrist (5 years)	Type of outcome measure (*continued*)	Personality traits: MMPI or other trait inventories, projective test results. Social behavior: dating, classroom discipline, public speaking, information-seeking behavior, sociometrics. Emotional-somatic disorder: frigidity, impotence. Physiological stress: galvanic skin response, Palmer Sweat Index, blood pressure, heart rate.
Diagnosis of client (neurotic or psychotic)	Neurotic unless symptoms or labels clearly indicate otherwise		
IQ of client (low, average, high)	Average unless identified as otherwise by diagnostic labels (e.g., mentally retarded) or institutional affiliation (college attendance).	Reactivity of measurement	1 (low): Physiological measures; grade point average
			2 Projective device (blind); discharge from hospital (blind)
Source of subjects	Clients solicited for purpose of study. Clients committed to institution, hence to therapy. Clients recognized existence of problem and sought treatment.		3 Standardized measures of traits (MMPI, Rotter)
Similarity of therapist and client ("very similar" or "very dissimilar")	College students: very similar Neurotic adults: moderately similar Juveniles, minorities: moderately dissimilar Hospitalized, chronic adults, disturbed children, prisoners: very dissimilar		4 Experimenter-constructed questionnaires; client's self-report to experimenter; discharge (nonblind); behavior in presence of therapist
Type of outcome measure	Fear, anxiety: Spielberger & Cattell anxiety measures, behavioral approach tests. Self-esteem: inventories, self-ideal correlations, ratings by self and others. Adjustment: adjustment scales, improvement ratings, rehospitalization, time out of hospital, sobriety, symptomatic complaints, disruptive behavior. Work/school achievement: grade point average, job supervisor ratings, promotions.	5 (high): Therapist rating; projective device (nonblind)
		Form of publication	Journal Book Thesis Unpublished document
		Internal validity (high, medium, low)	High: Randomization, low mortality Medium: More than one threat to internal validity Low: No matching of pretest information to equate groups

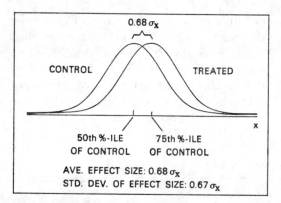

Figure 1. *Effect of therapy on any outcome. (Data based on 375 studies; 833 data points.)*

of therapy: The therapies represented by the available outcome evaluations move the average client from the 50th to the 75th percentile.

The standard deviation of the effect sizes is *.67*. Their skewness is *+.99*. Only 12% of the 833 effect-size measures from the 375 studies were negative. If therapies of any type were ineffective and design and measurement flaws were immaterial, one would expect half the effect-size measures to be negative.

The 833 effect-size measures were classified into 10 categories descriptive of the type of outcome being assessed, for example, fear and anxiety reduction, self-esteem, adjustment (freedom from debilitating symptoms), achievement in school or on the job, social relations, emotional-somatic problems, physiological stress measures, etc. Effect-size measures for four outcome categories are presented in Table 2.

Two hundred sixty-one effect sizes from over 100 studies average about 1 standard deviation on measures of fear and anxiety reduction. Thus, the average treated client is better off than 83% of those untreated with respect to the alleviation of fear and anxiety. The improvement in self-esteem is nearly as large. The effect sizes average .9 of a standard deviation. Improvement on variables in the "adjustment" outcome class averages considerably less, roughly .6 of a standard deviation. These outcome variables are measures of personal functioning and frequently involve indices of hospitalization or incarceration for psychotic, alcoholic, or criminal episodes. The average effect size for school or work achievement—most fre-

quently "grade point average"—is smallest of the four outcome classes.

The studies in the four outcome measure categories are not comparable in terms of type of therapy, duration, experience of therapists, number of months posttherapy at which outcomes were measured, etc. Nonetheless, the findings in Table 2 are fairly consistent with expectations and give the credible impression that fear and self-esteem are more susceptible to change in therapy than are the relatively more serious behaviors grouped under the categories "adjustment" and "achievement."

Table 3 presents the average effect sizes for 10 types of therapy. Nearly 100 effect-size measures arising from evaluations of psychodynamic therapy, that is, Freudianlike therapy but *not* psychoanalysis, average approximately .6 of a standard deviation. Studies of Adlerian therapy show an average of .7 sigma, but only 16 effect sizes were found. Eclectic therapies, that is, verbal, cognitive, nonbehavioral therapies more similar to psychodynamic therapies than any other type, gave a mean effect size of about .5 of a standard deviation. Although the number of controlled evaluations of Berne's transactional analysis was rather small, it gave a respectable average effect size of .6 sigma, the same as psychodynamic therapies. Albert Ellis's rational-emotive therapy, with a mean effect size of nearly .8 of a standard deviation, finished

Table 2: *Effects of Therapy on Four Types of Outcome Measure*

Type of outcome	Average effect size	No. of effect sizes	Standard error of mean effect size[a]	Mdn treated person's percentile status in control group
Fear-anxiety reduction	.97	261	.15	83
Self-esteem	.90	53	.13	82
Adjustment	.56	229	.05	71
School/work achievement	.31	145	.03	62

[a] The standard errors of the mean are calculated by dividing the standard deviation of the effect sizes (not reported) by the square root of the number of them. This method, based on the assumption of independence known to be false, gives a lower bound to the standard errors (Tukey, Note 2). Inferential techniques employing Tukey's jackknife method which take the nonindependence into account are examined in Glass (in press).

Table 3: *Effects of Ten Types of Therapy on Any Outcome Measure*

Type of therapy	Average effect size	No. of effect sizes	Standard error of mean effect size	Mdn treated person's percentile status in control group
Psychodynamic	.59	96	.05	72
Adlerian	.71	16	.19	76
Eclectic	.48	70	.07	68
Transactional analysis	.58	25	.19	72
Rational-emotive	.77	35	.13	78
Gestalt	.26	8	.09	60
Client-centered	.63	94	.08	74
Systematic desensitization	.91	223	.05	82
Implosion	.64	45	.09	74
Behavior modification	.76	132	.06	78

second among all 10 therapy types. The Gestalt therapies were relatively untested, but 8 studies showed 16 effect sizes averaging only .25 of a standard deviation. Rogerian client-centered therapy showed a .6 sigma effect size averaged across about 60 studies. The average of over 200 effect-size measures from approximately 100 studies of systematic desensitization therapy was .9 sigma, the largest average effect size of all therapy types. Implosive therapy showed a mean effect size of .64 of a standard deviation, about equal to that for Rogerian and psychodynamic therapies. Significantly, the average effect size for implosive therapy is markedly lower than that for systematic desensitization, which was usually evaluated in studies using similar kinds of clients with similar problems—principally, simple phobias. The final therapy depicted in Table 3 is Skinnerian behavior modification, which showed a .75 sigma effect size.

Hay's ω^2, which relates the categorical variable "type of therapy" to the quantitative variable "effect size," has the value of .10 for the data in Table 3. Thus, these 10 therapy types account for 10% of the variance in the effect size that studies produce.

The types of therapy depicted in Table 3 were clearly not equated for duration, severity of problem, type of outcome, etc. Nonetheless, the differences in average effect sizes are interesting

and interpretable. There is probably a tendency for researchers to evaluate the therapy they like best and to pick clients, circumstances, and outcome measures which show that therapy in the best light. Even so, major differences among the therapies appear. Implosive therapy is demonstrably inferior to systematic desensitization. Behavior modification shows the same mean effect size as rational-emotive therapy.

Effects of Classes of Therapy

To compare the effect of therapy type after equating for duration of therapy, diagnosis of client, type of outcome, etc., it was necessary to move to a coarser level of analysis in which data could be grouped into more stable composites. The problem was to group the 10 types of therapy into classes, so that effect sizes could be compared among more general types of therapy. Methods of multidimensional scaling were used to derive a structure from the perceptions of similarities among the 10 therapies by a group of 25 clinicians and counselors. All of the judges in this scaling study were enrolled in a graduate-level seminar. For five weeks, the theory and techniques of the 10 therapies were studied and discussed. Then, each judge performed a multidimensional rank ordering of the therapies, judging similarity among them on whatever basis he or she chose, articulated or unarticulated, conscious or unconscious. The results of the Shepard-Kruskal multidimensional scaling analysis appear as Figure 2.

In Figure 2 one clearly sees four classes of therapies: the ego therapies (transactional analysis and rational-emotive therapy) in front; the three dynamic therapies low, in the background; the behavioral triad, upper right; and the pair of "humanistic" therapies, Gestalt and Rogerian. The average effect sizes among the four classes of therapies have been compared, but the findings are not reported here. Instead, a higher level of aggregation of the therapies, called "superclasses," was studied. The first superclass was formed from those therapies above the horizontal plane in Figure 2, with the exception of Gestalt therapy for which there was an inadequate number of studies. This superclass was then identical with the group of behavioral therapies: implosion, systematic desensitization,

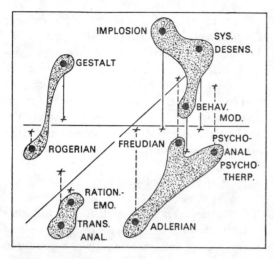

Figure 2. *Multidimensional scaling of 10 therapies by 25 clinicians and counselors.*

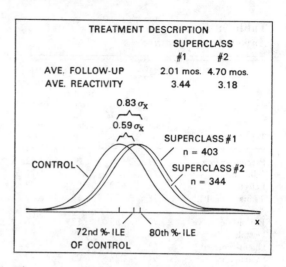

Figure 3. *Effect of Superclass #1 (behavioral) and Superclass # 2 (nonbehavioral).*

and behavior modification. The second super-class comprises the six therapies below the horizontal plane in Figure 2 and is termed the *nonbehavioral superclass,* a composite of psychoanalytic psychotherapy, Adlerian, Rogerian, rational-emotive, eclectic therapy, and transactional analysis.

Figure 3 represents the mean effect sizes for studies classfied by the two superclass. On the average, approximately 200 evaluations of behavioral therapies showed a mean effect of about $.8\sigma_x$, standard error of .03, over the control group. Approximately 170 evaluations of nonbehavioral studies gave a mean effect size of $.6\sigma_x$, standard error of .04. This small difference ($.2\sigma_x$) between the outcomes of behavioral and nonbehavioral therapies must be considered in light of the circumstances under which these studies were conducted. The evaluators of behavioral superclass therapies waited an average of 2 months after the therapy to measure its effects, whereas the postassessment of the nonbehavioral therapies was made in the vicinity of 5 months, on the average. Furthermore, the reactivity or susceptibility to bias of the outcome measures was higher for the behavioral superclass than for the nonbehavioral superclass; that is, the behavioral researchers showed a slightly greater tendency to rely on more subjective outcome measures. These differences lead one to suspect that the $.2\sigma_x$ difference between the behavioral and nonbehavioral superclasses is somewhat exaggerated in favor of the behavioral

superclass. Exactly how much the difference ought to be reduced is a question that can be approached in at least two ways: (a) examine the behavioral versus nonbehavioral difference for only those studies in which one therapy from each superclass was represented, since for those studies the experimental circumstances will be equivalent; (2) regress "effect size" onto variables descriptive of the study and correct statistically for differences in circumstances between behavioral and nonbehavioral studies.

Figure 4 represents 120 effect-size measures derived from those studies, approximately 50 in number, in which a behavioral therapy and nonbehavioral therapy were compared simultaneously with an untreated control.

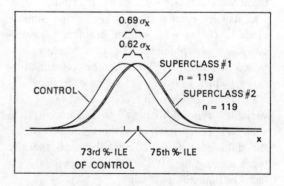

Figure 4. *Effect of Superclass #1 (behavioral) and Superclass #2 (nonbehavioral). (Data drawn only from experiments in which Superclass #1 and Superclass #2 were simultaneously compared with control.)*

Hence, for these studies, the collective behavioral and nonbehavioral therapies are equivalent with respect to all important features of the experimental setting, namely, experience of the therapists, nature of the clients' problems, duration of therapy, type of outcome measure, months after therapy for measuring the outcomes, etc.

The results are provocative. The $.2\sigma_x$ "uncontrolled" difference in Figure 3 has shrunk to a $.07\sigma_x$ difference in average effect size. The standard error of the mean of the 119 different scores (behavioral effect size minus nonbehavioral effect size in each study) is $.66/\sqrt{119} = .06$. The behavioral and nonbehavioral therapies show about the same average effect.

The second approach to correcting for measurable differences between behavioral and nonbehavioral therapies is statistical adjustment by regression analysis. By this method, it is possible to quantify and study the natural covariation among the principal outcome variable of studies and the many variables descriptive of the context of the studies.

Eleven features of each study were correlated with the effect size the study produced (Table 4). For example, the correlation between the duration of the therapy in hours and the effect size of the study is nearly zero, $-.02$. The

Table 4: *Correlations of Several Descriptive Variables with Effect Size*

Variable	Correlation with effect size
Organization (1 = individual; 2 = group)	−.07
Duration of therapy (in hours)	−.02
Years' experience of therapists	−.01
Diagnosis of clients (1 = psychotic; 2 = neurotic)	.02
IQ of clients (1 = low; 2 = medium; 3 = high)	.15[a]
Age of clients	.02
Similarity of therapists and clients (1 = very similar; . . . ; 4 = very dissimilar)	−.19[a]
Internal validity of study (1 = high; 2 = medium; 3 = low)	−.09[b]
Date of publication	.09[b]
"Reactivity" of outcome measure (1 = low; . . . ; 5 = high)	.30[a]
No. of months posttherapy for follow-up	−.10[b]

[a] $p < .01$.
[b] $p < .05$.

correlations are generally low, although several are reliably nonzero. Some of the more interesting correlations show a positive relationship between an estimate of the intelligence of the group of clients and the effect of therapy, and a somewhat larger correlation indicating that therapists who resemble their clients in ethnic group, age, and social level get better results. The effect sizes diminish across time after therapy as shown by the last correlation in Table 4, a correlation of $-.10$ which is closer to $-.20$ when the curvilinearity of the relationship is taken into account. The largest correlation is with the "reactivity" or subjectivity of the outcome measure.

The multiple correlation of these variables with effect size is about .50. Thus, 25% of the variance in the results of studies can be reduced by specification of independent variable values. In several important subsets of the data not reported here, the multiple correlations are over .70, which indicates that in some instances it is possible to reduce more than half of the variability in study findings by regressing the outcome effect onto contextual variables of the study.

The results of three separate multiple regression analyses appear in Table 5. Multiple regressions were performed within each of three types of therapy: psychodynamic, systematic desensitization, and behavior modification. Relatively complex forms of the independent variables were used to account for interactions and nonlinear relationships. For example, years' experience of the therapist bore a slight curvilinear relationship with outcome, probably because more experienced therapists worked with more seriously ill clients. This situation was accommodated by entering, as an independent variable, "therapist experience" in interaction with "diagnosis of the client." Age of client and follow-up date were slightly curvilinearly related to outcome in ways most directly handled by changing exponents. These regression equations allow estimation of the effect size a study shows when undertaken with a certain type of client, with a therapist of a certain level of experience, etc. By setting the independent variables at a particular set of values, one can estimate what a study of that type would reveal under each of the three types of therapy. Thus, a statistically controlled comparison of the effects of psychody-

Table 5: *Regression Analyses Within Therapies*

Independent variable	Unstandardized regression coefficients		
	Psychodynamic ($n = 94$)	Systematic desensitization ($n = 212$)	Behavior modification ($n = 129$)
Diagnosis (1 = psychotic; 2 = neurotic)	.174	−.193	.041
Intelligence (1 = low; . . . ; 3 = high)	−.114	.201	.201
Transformed age[a]	.002	−.002	.002
Experience of Therapist × Neurotic	−.011	−.034	−.018
Experience of Therapist × Psychotic	−.015	.004	−.033
Clients self-presented	−.111	.287	−.015
Clients solicited	.182	.088	−.163
Organization (1 = individual; 2 = group)	.108	−.086	−.276
Transformed months posttherapy[b]	−.031	−.047	.007
Transformed reactivity of measure[c]	.003	.025	.021
Additive constant	.757	.489	.453
Multiple R	.423	.512	.509
σ_e	.173	.386	.340

[a] Transformed age = (Age − 25) ($|$Age − 25$|$)$^{\frac{1}{2}}$.
[b] Transformed months posttherapy = (No. months)$^{\frac{1}{2}}$.
[c] Transformed reactivity of measure = (Reactivity)$^{2.25}$.

namic, systematic desensitization, and behavior modification therapies can be obtained in this case. The three regression equations are clearly not homogeneous; hence, one therapy might be superior under one set of circumstances and a different therapy superior under others. A full description of the nature of this interaction is elusive, though one can illustrate it at various particularly interesting points.

In Figure 5, estimates are made of the effect sizes that would be shown for studies in which simple phobias of high-intelligence subjects, 20 years of age, are treated by a therapist with 2 years' experience and evaluated im-

mediately after therapy with highly subjective outcome measures. This verbal description of circumstances can be translated into quantitative values for the independent variables in Table 5 and substituted into each of the three regression equations. In this instance, the two behavioral therapies show effects superior to the psychodynamic therapy.

In Figure 6, a second prototypical psychotherapy client and situation are captured in the independent variable values, and the effects of the three types of therapy are estimated. For the typical 30-year-old neurotic of average IQ seen in circumstances like those that prevail in men-

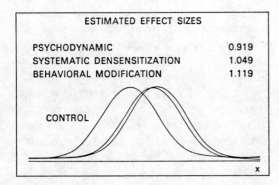

Figure 5. *Three within-therapy regression equations set to describe a prototypic therapy client (phobic) and therapy situation.*

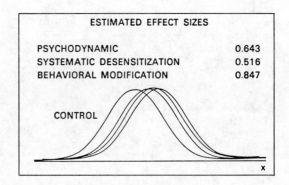

Figure 6. *Three within-therapy regression equations set to describe a prototypic therapy client (neurotic) and therapy situation.*

tal health clinics (individual therapy by a therapist with 5 years' experience), behavior modification is estimated to be superior to psychodynamic therapy, which is in turn superior to systematic desensitization at the 6-month follow-up point.

Besides illuminating the relationships in the data, the quantitative techniques described here can given direction to future research. By fitting regression equations to the relationship between effect size and the independent variables descriptive of the studies and then by placing confidence regions around these hyperplanes, the regions where the input-output relationships are most poorly determined can be identified. By concentrating new studies in these regions, one can avoid the accumulation of redundant studies of convenience that overelaborate small areas.

Conclusions

The results of research demonstrate the beneficial effects of counseling and psychotherapy. Despite volumes devoted to the theoretical differences among different schools of psychotherapy, the results of research demonstrate negligible differences in the effects produced by different therapy types. Unconditional judgments of superiority of one type or another of psychotherapy, and all that these claims imply about treatment and training policy, are unjustified. Scholars and clinicians are in the rather embarrassing position of knowing less than has been proven, because knowledge, atomized and sprayed across a vast landscape of journals, books, and reports, has not been accessible. Extracting knowledge from accumulated studies is a complex and important methodological problem which deserves further attention.

Reference Notes

1. Glass, G. V., Smith, M. L., & Miller, T. I. *The benefits of psychotherapy.* Book in preparation, 1977.
2. Tukey, J. W. Personal communication, November 15, 1976.

References

Bergin, A. E. The evaluation of therapeutic outcomes. In A. E. Bergin & S. L. Garfield (Eds.), *Handbook of psychotherapy and behavior change.* New York: Wiley, 1971.

Ellis, R. H. Letters. *Colorado Psychological Association Newsletter,* April 1977, p. 3.

Emrick, C. D. A review of psychologically oriented treatment of alcoholism. *Journal of Studies on Alcohol,* 1975, *36,* 88–108.

Eysenck, H. J. The effects of psychotherapy: An evaluation. *Journal of Consulting Psychology,* 1952, *16,* 319–324.

Eysenck, H. J. The effects of psychotherapy. *Journal of Psychology,* 1965, *1,* 97–118.

Glass, G. V. Primary, secondary, and meta-analysis of research. *The Educational Researcher,* 1976, *10,* 3–8.

Glass, G. V. Integrating findings: The meta-analysis of research. *Review of Research in Education,* in press.

Luborsky, L., Singer, B., & Luborsky, L. Comparative studies of psychotherapies. *Archives of General Psychiatry,* 1975, *32,* 995–1008.

Meltzoff, J., & Kornreich, M. *Research in psychotherapy.* New York: Atherton, 1970.

Psychotherapy caveat. *APA Monitor,* December 1974, p. 7.

At the time of original publication of this article, *Mary L. Smith* and *Gene V Glass* were at the University of Colorado, Boulder.

The research reported here was supported by a grant from the Spencer Foundation, Chicago, Illinois. This paper draws in part from the presidential address of Gene V Glass to the American Educational Research Association, San Francisco, April 21, 1976.

A Tripartite Model of Mental Health and Therapeutic Outcomes

With Special Reference to Negative Effects in Psychotherapy

Hans H. Strupp and Suzanne W. Hadley

A tripartite conceptual model for the evaluation of mental health and psychotherapy outcomes is presented. The model highlights the values brought to bear by three "interested parties" in these evaluations: society, the individual, and the mental health professional. The model is elaborated in terms of the specific problem of negative effects in psychotherapy, an issue of increasing concern to the public and the mental health profession. Clinical, research, and public policy implications of the model are discussed.

The extensive literature on conceptions of mental health (e.g., see Jahoda, 1958, for a comprehensive discussion) and the voluminous literature on outcome criteria in psychotherapy (cf. Bergin & Garfield, 1971; Strupp & Bergin, 1969) demonstrate the absence of a consensus on what constitutes mental health and, consequently, how changes resulting from psychotherapy are to be evaluated. The reality of this state of affairs vis-à-vis psychotherapy outcomes in general has become clear to us as we have pursued an analysis of the specific problem of negative effects in psychotherapy (Strupp, Hadley, & Gomes-Schwartz, in press).

It may readily be seen that a definition of "worsening" is the fulcrum upon which the problem of negative effects in psychotherapy turns. Because a judgment of "worse" is always made in relation to an implicit or explicit standard, which also presupposes a definition of the meaning of "better," it is clear that *the problem of what constitutes a negative effect is inextricably interwoven with a definition of mental health.* This is the case because any form of psychotherapy or behavior modification is designed to move the patient toward a particular ideal, standard, or norm, and the procedures and tech-

niques used in a given form of therapy are instruments for accomplishing that purpose. Furthermore, we have concluded that only by considering *multiple* perspectives will it be possible to derive a truly comprehensive definition of mental health and meaningful evaluations of psychotherapy outcomes.

Consider the following: Do assessments of change in self-concept have anything in common with observations of overt behaviors, as in the treatment of a snake phobia? If, following psychotherapy, a patient manifests increased self-assertion coupled with abrasiveness, is this a good or a poor therapy outcome? If, as a result of therapy, a patient obtains a divorce, is this to be regarded as a desirable or an undesirable change? A patient may turn from homosexuality to heterosexuality or he may become more accepting of either; an ambitious, striving person may abandon previously valued goals and become more placid (e.g., in primal therapy). How are such changes to be evaluated?

The difficulties inherent in evaluating psychotherapy outcome are exacerbated by the fact that problems in living which bring patients to psychotherapists are no longer necessarily viewed as an "illness" for which psychotherapy

Reprinted from *American Psychologist*, 1977, *32*, 187–196.

is prescribed as a "treatment." In increasing numbers, patients enter psychotherapy not for the cure of traditional "symptoms" but (at least ostensibly) for the purpose of finding meaning in their lives, for actualizing themselves, or for maximizing their potential.

Multiple Perspectives to Be Considered

In our pluralistic society, the term *mental health* has assumed a multiplicity of meanings. If conceptions of mental health are fuzzier than ever, how can we determine whether a particular intervention has led to improvement, deterioration, or no change? Unless we make certain assumptions and develop a generally acceptable set of criteria concerning mental health, it is more or less meaningless to speak of "improvement" or a negative effect from psychotherapy. Further, in deriving these criteria, it is essential that we consider the social and cultural ramifications of therapy-induced change, the patient's place in society, his stage of life, and the general context within which he functions.

In other words, we are commending to practicing psychotherapists and researchers the value of taking into account the *vantage points* of those who judge mental health and therapy-induced change, including the values brought to bear on these judgments. To further the inquiry, we have developed a tripartite model that takes account of three major vantage points from which a person's mental health may be judged. Similar models have been described previously, most notably by Parloff, Kelman, and Frank (1954). The present discussion demonstrates the value of this model for describing changes that may result from psychotherapeutic interventions and for highlighting the difficulties inherent in judgments of these changes.

Three major interested parties are concerned with definitions of mental health: (1) *society* (including significant persons in the patient's life), (2) the *individual patient,* and (3) the *mental health professional.* Each of these parties defines mental health in terms of certain unique purposes or aims it seeks to fulfill, and consequently each focuses on specific aspects of an individual's functioning in determining his mental health.

1. *Society* is primarily concerned with the maintenance of social relations, institutions, and prevailing standards of sanctioned conduct. Society and its agents thus tend to define mental health in terms of behavioral stability, predictability, and conformity to the social code.

Predictably, the reaction of many mental health professionals to the inclusion of society as a bona fide evaluative agent of mental health and psychotherapy outcome is less than enthusiastic. In part, this response arises from therapists' rejection of the noxious image of psychotherapy as an instrument of social control (Kittrie, 1971; Szasz, 1970) and the implication that its practitioners are thus either the agents of or accountable to social and political authorities. In part, the response may arise from therapists' concern that agents of society are not sufficiently knowledgeable and sensitive to the intricacies of the individual. But like it or not, it is clear that society has been and *is* increasingly involved in assessments of mental health and psychotherapy.

The historical involvement of society in mental health evaluations based on its needs to maintain order has increased markedly in recent years with the trend toward third-party payments for mental health care. A patient who pays for his own therapy is certainly at liberty to structure the goals of that therapy to suit his own needs, and he can spend as much time in therapy as his bank account allows. Such an individual is, in a most personal and subjective sense, the ultimate judge of the treatment outcome. But as insurance companies or the taxpaying public have begun to foot the bill, issues of treatment have become translated into issues of accountability. Aldrich (1975) has described the changing scene from the perspective of the practicing psychiatrist:

> As long as Jones paid me for his psychotherapy or friendship, or however he wanted to use the time I sold him, it was none of Smith's business. But when Smith's taxes or insurance premiums began to contribute to my fee, Smith's interest in what I was doing with Jones increased. In other words, Smith now expects me to be accountable—and in terms that he can understand. (p. 509)

The debate over national health insurance is only the most obvious and recent example of the growing interest of society in defining mental health and in developing sound criteria for evaluating psychotherapy outcomes. The issues were squarely joined in a recent meeting of mental health professionals and congressional proponents of the national health insurance package. While the mental health professionals decried simplistic assessments of mental health and psychotherapy outcome, the politicians responded, "We need facts, not messages" ("Quality Psychiatric Care vs. Political Realities," 1976). And thus, at present, an impasse stands.

2. The *individual client* evaluating his own mental health uses a criterion distinctly different from that used by society. The individual wishes first and foremost to be happy, to feel content. He thus defines mental health in terms of highly subjective feelings of well-being—feelings with a validity all their own. Some individuals will experience contentment coincident with behavioral adaptation, and there will thus be agreement by the individual and society that he is mentally sound. But the agreement is, nonetheless, between *independent* evaluations made from different vantage points, and it is thus quite conceivable that an individual may define himself as mentally sound quite independent of society's or the mental health profession's opinion.

3. Most *mental health professionals* tend to view an individual's functioning within the framework of some theory of personality structure which transcends social adaptation and subjective well-being (although clinical judgments of another's mental health are often significantly influenced by these latter two criteria). The professional thus defines mental health largely with reference to some theoretical model of a "healthy" personality structure that may on occasion result in a diagnosis of mental health or pathology at variance with the opinion of society and/or the individual.

The most comprehensive and ambitious model of mental functioning is psychoanalytic theory (e.g., Rapaport, 1960), including prominently such concepts as drives, defenses, and ego structures. For present purposes, we need not concern ourselves with the evolution of the system or its complexities. It is important, however, to note in general the advantages of positing some form of mental structure within which a person's subjective feeling state and behavior

gain meaning. Rapaport (1960) formulated the construct as follows:

> Structures appear as *independent variables* wherever individual differences in behavior, under (relatively) constant motivation and stimulation are studied: for instance, in the comparative study of symptoms in various neuroses, and in the studies of individual differences in perception. . . .
> Structures as *intervening variables* are commonplace in clinical observation. They account for the lack of one-to-one relationship between motivations and behavior. Defensive structures countermand motivations and replace them by derivative motivations (as, for instance, in reaction formation). Controlling structures direct and channel motivations, as in delay- and detour-behavior and in the choice of substitute goals. . . .
> It is less easy to conceive of structures as *dependent* variables, though they appear as such in processes of structural change, including those of learning. Insofar as psychoanalysis as therapy achieves its goals of changing existing structures, in at least some of the observations made in therapy, structures appear as dependent variables. . . . (p. 71)

In concluding his discussion, Rapaport noted that

> Any limitation on the choice of variables seems to result in a limited range of observables and observational methods, and it is the dearth of methods which is probably the major obstacle to bridging the gap between psychoanalysis and academic psychology and between the various schools of psychology. (p. 72)

By introducing the construct of structure—not necessarily the psychoanalytic conception—into the present discussion, we assert that more is involved in assessments of psychotherapy outcome than changes in the person's feeling state and/or behavior. For example, it is one thing to observe that following therapy a previously anxious and shy male asks a girl for a date (overt behavior); one may also inquire whether he is now happier than he was previously (well-being); and it is quite another matter to determine the extent to which any observed behavioral and affective changes have become a part of a generalized disposition to deal differently with women or to determine the *quality* of the experience; for example, whether a rigid defensive structure has been replaced with a more modulated approach in interpersonal relations. Empirical studies of therapy outcomes have rarely dealt with these topics. To be sure, judgments concerning an individual's personality structure are inferential, and they are influenced by reports of his behavior, descriptions of his feeling state, etc. (A possible exception is the evaluation of structure made on the basis of the Rorschach Test, which is assumed to be free from such influences unless the clinician gathers collateral information from the subject, which indeed the clinician often does.)

Models of psychological structure vary considerably both in content and in the degree of inference involved in the observations and assessments derived from them. Indeed, some mental health professionals prefer not to invoke such models at all, but rather focus their attention primarily on observable behaviors and/or feeling states. For many others, however, a model of psychological structure and functioning provides the modus operandi of their therapeutic interventions, and, thus, assessments based on such models comprise a significant aspect of a comprehensive evaluation of each individual.

Implications of Discrepant Vantage Points

It follows from the preceding that the divergent vantage points described may result in different definitions of "mental health" and consequently in discrepant evaluations of a given individual's functioning and performance. Table 1 describes the goals and values pertinent to each of the three perspectives on mental health, as well as the measures related to each frame of reference. It is seen that each person's mental health may

be judged differently, depending on whether society, the individual, or a mental health professional makes the judgment. Concomitantly, a given individual is regarded as being in need of professional help to the extent that he deviates from the standards and values governing each of the vantage points.

No conflict of judgment arises as long as each dimension is considered in isolation. Thus, as long as an individual functions well in society and conforms to its conventions, he is generally not seen by society as suffering from a mental illness or disturbance, and consequently he is not perceived as requiring professional help; similarly, an individual regards himself as mentally healthy as long as he experiences a sense of well-being and happiness; and the mental health professional perceives no problem requiring his attention as long as the individual's personality structure is intact (this leaves out of account such instances as normal grief reactions and other transient conditions for which some form of "supportive psychotherapy" or "counseling" is often undertaken).

Evaluations of an individual's functioning are often made from one of these perspectives. In some cases, for specific, narrowly defined purposes, such evaluations are adequate; however, if one is interested in a *comprehensive* picture of the individual, evaluations based on a single vantage point are inadequate and fail to give necessary consideration to the *totality* of an

Table 1: *Primary Perspectives on Mental Health*

Source	Standards/values	"Measures"
I. Society	Orderly world in which individuals assume responsibility for their assigned social roles (e.g., breadwinner, parent), conform to prevailing mores, and meet situational requirements.	Observations of behavior, extent to which individual fulfills society's expectations and measures up to prevailing standards.
II. Individual	Happiness, gratification of needs.	Subjective perceptions of self-esteem, acceptance, and well-being.
III. Mental health professional	Sound personality structure characterized by growth, development, self-actualization, integration, autonomy, environmental mastery, ability to cope with stress, reality orientation, adaptation.	Clinical judgment, aided by behavioral observations and psychological tests of such variables as self-concept, sense of identity, balance of psychic forces, unified outlook on life, resistance to stress, self-regulation, ability to cope with reality, absence of mental and behavioral symptoms, adequacy in love, work, and play, adequacy in interpersonal relations.

individual's functioning. A single-minded emphasis on performance and conformity to societal expectations is best illustrated by the function of mental health professionals in totalitarian societies, such as the Soviet Union or Communist China, although even our own society is not free from the charge that "mental illness" is at times merely a label by which society attempts to deal with those who deviate from sanctioned behavior. On the other hand, the exclusive concern with the individual's feeling state is a clear-cut example of what has contemporaneously become known as "the new narcissism" (Marin, 1975), characterized by the individual's disregard for societal expectations and the balance of forces (impulse control, ego functioning) that characterize the standpoint of the mental health professional. Finally, the preoccupation with intrapsychic forces and mechanisms to the exclusion of other aspects of a person's functioning is a caricature of the psychoanalyst whose excursions into metapsychology bear little relation to a patient's real life and for whom psychotherapy has become an end in itself, a way of life, rather than a vehicle for change.

Table 2 is designed to call attention to the implications of mental health judgments from the three major perspectives: society, which bases its judgments largely on the adaptive qualities of behavior (B); the individual, who bases his judgments on his sense of well-being (W); and the mental health professional, whose judgments are grounded in the assessment of the soundness of psychological structure (S). Thus,

a comprehensive evaluation of any individual must take account of the BWS configuration. Only in Categories 1 and 8 is there perfect agreement among the three "interested parties" that the person is either mentally healthy or so seriously disturbed as to require the services of a mental health professional. All other categories entail some conflict in mental health judgments, which we consider below.

The tripartite model suggests that the three dimensions of a person's functioning (behavior, sense of well-being, and inferred psychological structure) should be considered *simultaneously* in evaluating his mental health and any changes related to psychotherapy. Of course, in the final analysis, the evaluation of any psychotherapy outcome will be essentially a value judgment. What is highlighted by the tripartite model is the importance of considering fully and simultaneously the *multiple values* that may be brought to bear on such judgments.

Table 3 presents the eight possible combinations of positive and negative poles of the three mental health indicators, along with composite sketches of individuals falling into each of the categories. The eight configurations identified are, for purposes of discussion, the most extreme possible cases. Gradations between the positive and negative poles are certainly possible and, indeed, more likely. Each category is a potential therapy outcome state. The relevant question here is, How shall each of these eight outcomes be judged—as a positive or a negative effect? In the following pages, we turn to a consideration of this question. We deal with the issue at some length because it is the core of the problem under consideration.

Treatment Outcomes Exemplified

We have selected for detailed discussion four of the eight possible outcome states described in Table 3. Categories 1 and 8 are excluded from discussion because, regardless of the evaluative perspective, they are considered clear-cut instances of a positive and negative outcome, respectively. Categories 2 and 6 are excluded for the sake of efficiency inasmuch as they are infrequently encountered as therapy outcome states. The four remaining categories—3, 4, 5, and 7— will be discussed in terms of the most common

Table 2: *Implications of Divergent Perspectives on Mental Health*

Category	Adaptive behavior (society) B	Sense of well-being (individual) W	Personality structure (professional) S	Judgment of "mental health"		
				Society	Individual	Professional
1	+	+	+	HH	HH	HH
2	+	−	+	H	L	H
3	+	+	−	H	H	L
4	+	−	−	H	L	L
5	−	+	+	L	H	H
6	−	−	+	L	L	H
7	−	+	−	L	H	L
8	−	−	−	LL	LL	LL

Note. H = high; HH = very high; L = low; LL = very low.

Table 3: *The Tripartite View of Mental Health and Therapy Outcomes*

Category	Configuration	Mental health status
1	B + W + S +	Well-functioning, adjusted individual, optimal "mental health."
2	B + W − S +	Basically "healthy" person; troubled by dysphoric mood, perhaps due to minor trauma affecting self-esteem, temporary reverses, discouragement, loss, grief reaction.
3	B + W + S −	May have fragile ego (borderline condition, schizoid personality, etc.) but functions well in society and feels content. Underlying psychotic process may be present, but defenses may be reasonably effective.
4	B + W − S −	Similar to 3, but affect may be labile or dysphoric. Has basic ego weakness, but functions adequately in society.
5	B − W + S +	Society judges person's behavior as maladaptive (e.g., unconventional life-style), but his sense of well-being and personality structure are sound.
6	B − W − S +	Similar to 2, except that social performance is considered maladaptive. Example: As part of a grief reaction, person may withdraw, give up job, etc.
7	B − W + S −	Person with ego defects; psychopaths, character disorders, conversion reactions (*la belle indifférence*), individuals who have poor reality testing and poor insight.
8	B − W − S −	Clearly "mentally ill."

Note. B = adaptive behavior (society); W = sense of well-being (individual); S = personality structure (professional).

intake states, for as we have noted, therapy outcome can only be judged as positive or negative relative to a known intake state. While our discussion will be centered on the three aspects of functioning in combination, we shall note particularly those instances in which consideration of only one aspect in isolation (i.e., evaluating an individual from only one perspective) might lead to discrepant opinions of therapy outcome. Finally, we shall offer our judgment as to whether each outcome state represents a positive or negative psychotherapeutic effect.

1. *Outcome Category 3 (B + W + S−).* As noted in Table 3, a person in this category emerges from psychotherapy well-adapted to his social role and feeling comfortable within himself, but he is judged by the mental health professional as suffering from ego defects (e.g., brittle defenses, characterological distortions, deficient impulse control).

Such a person may have entered psychotherapy feeling anxious, depressed, lonely, etc. (W−). Therapeutic interventions may have boosted the individual's morale and perhaps increased his self-esteem, resulting in a self-report of positive outcome. Assuming, however, that there were initially serious ego defects (S−), which would lead most mental health profes-

sionals to diagnose psychopathology of varying degrees, the observed change in feeling state would be seen by them as "symptomatic improvement" without any significant radical or permanent change. Short-term, "supportive," or "relationship" forms of psychotherapy, perhaps administered by an inexperienced therapist, lay counselor, etc., might produce such an outcome. Similarly, participation in a sensitivity training program, encounter weekend, and the like might give rise to changes in the person's feeling state (from W− to W+), but such changes might be short-lived. Whether changes in subjective well-being are seen as consequential or otherwise thus clearly depends on the perspective of the judge. In the present instance, the changes in feeling state, because they were not accompanied by positive structural modifications, would not be regarded by many mental health professionals as having great significance, although the individual might value them highly.

It is also possible that prior to therapy a patient exhibited behavioral deficits (e.g., poor job performance, academic underachievement, phobias that might interfere with his ability to earn a living, etc.). In this case, observations of the person's changed behavior (from B− to B+) would lead to a judgment, particularly by agents of society, of positive therapeutic outcome

With respect to the dimension of inferred structure, one possible situation is that in which the person was found to have marked ego defects prior to entering therapy (S−), and these remained unchanged during therapy. Most mental health professionals would rate such a lack of change as a therapeutic failure. Their judgments of negative outcome would thus be discrepant with judgments of positive outcome made by the individual (based on a greater sense of happiness) and by society (based on more adaptive behavior). Such discrepancies are particularly likely concerning Category 3 outcomes and may contribute to the view of some lay people that therapy is an esoteric luxury that seeks a mythical ideal of psychological integration and functioning. Society wants the individual to function smoothly in his social context; the individual wishes to feel content; and partly because of an inability to assess factors beyond immediately observable behavior or feelings, neither sees the usefulness of therapy beyond the attainment of these goals.

Many mental health professionals, as discussed previously, hold the view that behavioral adjustment and feeling states are not therapeutic ends in themselves, but are reflections of the individual's underlying psychological structure. It would thus be their opinion that any B− to B+ and/or W− to W+ changes observed in Category 3 individuals are likely to be superficial and temporary.

In the event that the Category 3 patient's psychological structure had changed from positive to negative or from mildly to strongly negative, most mental health professionals (including the present authors) would rate a Category 3 outcome patient as having deteriorated, although, as we have seen, from the standpoint of society and the individual himself there would be a judgment of therapeutic improvement. An illustration of this outcome would be a person who entered some form of highly directive therapy aimed at the modification of maladaptive behavior such as nail biting or insomnia. As a result of therapy, the individual might learn to master the problem and concomitantly experience a greater sense of well-being. Such a person would be rated by himself and society as improved. The therapist would likewise consider the therapy a success. However, a more dynamically oriented or otherwise broadly trained mental health professional might judge that the patient had achieved the behavioral changes at the cost of increased rigidity and compulsivity (S+ to S−). This, in turn, might render the patient more susceptible to exacerbations (e.g., depression) at a later period in his life. Such outcomes are by no means uncommon, and they may occur as a function of training programs in assertiveness, self-control, etc.[1]

Again, the implications of such an outcome—society judging the therapy outcome as positive and the mental health profession perceiving it to be a negative effect—are considerable, particularly with reference to public policy and decisions relating to governmental support of mental health programs. Governments are most likely to fund mental health programs and agencies whose goal is restoration of the individual to effective social functioning, as opposed to the goal of long-term psychological restructuring. The individual patient, by the same token, will probably be motivated to continue therapy only as long as he is experiencing some psychic distress. Thus, only to the extent that therapists can demonstrate the relevance of sound psychological structure to *long-lasting* effective behavior and subjective well-being will there be consensus on a definition of mental health and how it may be attained.

2. *Category 4 (B + W − S−)*. Therapeutic outcomes in this category are essentially a variant of those described for Category 3, the only difference being that the patient's self-reported feeling state following therapy is one of unhappiness and discontent. As is true of all the configurations discussed here, the patient may have entered therapy in Category 8—with negative evaluations of his behavior, feeling state, and psychic structure. If so, a Category 4 outcome would be judged a therapeutic success by society (B+) although the individual has remained unhappy (W−) and his psychological structure has remained unchanged (S−). Such

---

[1] In the early days of behavior therapy, it was generally assumed that all patients had adequate ego resources so that modification of the symptom that brought them to therapy was a sufficient criterion of improvement. In recent years, increasing attention is being given to the patient's initial status and prior adjustment as predictors of outcome in behavior therapy (Klerman & Weissman, Note 1).

an outcome is most likely when therapy is overly attentive to society's demands and fails to deal adequately with the patient's personal needs.

It is also possible that at intake the patient was experiencing no feelings of distress and thus manifested a B − W + S− (or less likely, a B − W + S+) configuration. It is highly unlikely that a person would *voluntarily* enter therapy feeling positively about himself (W+), although there are instances in which a behavioral deficiency may be noted by society which the individual does not perceive as a problem. Examples of this kind include a teacher referring a child for therapy because of unruly behavior in the classroom, a psychopath or sexual offender referred by a court of law for treatment, a wife who insists that her husband undergo therapy if their marriage is to continue. In each of the foregoing instances, the patient himself is relatively unmotivated for therapy; that is, he sees no need for change. By contrast, society diagnoses a problem and attempts to force the individual to change against his will. The mental health professional may concur with society that the individual manifests psychopathology (S−), particularly if on closer examination it is inferred that, contrary to his self-defined feeling state (W+), the individual is on a deeper level unhappy and suffering, his self-reported contentment being based on defensive operations, such as denial.

Clearly, if an individual entered therapy with a fairly sound psychological structure and a sense of well-being, although a nonconformist in behavioral terms, and emerged a behavioral conformist with feelings of unhappiness and an impaired psychological structure, we would judge his outcome to be a negative effect. Further, if the person's psychological structure remained unchanged from an originally negative state and if behavioral conformity was achieved at the price of lessened subjective well-being, we would judge this to be a negative effect.

The B + W − S− outcome is particularly likely to occur when behavior is modified without consideration for its adaptive function in the patient's life. If nonconforming behavior meets important defensive needs, and the patient is then deprived of those behaviors, such modifications may have important negative repercussions for his feeling state or psychological structure, which the individual himself and many therapists would consider a negative effect. Examples of such behavior are overeating, which may meet important intrapsychic needs, or self-induced starvation, whereby the refusal to take nourishment may be the manifestation of a deep-seated conflict rather than a "bad habit." Category 4 outcomes may be brought about in such cases by crude or coercive attempts at behavior modification. While the patient's behavior might have become more adaptive and conforming, there may be increases in feelings of negativism, and the patient may feel betrayed by the therapist and indirectly by society. The concomitant resentment may be associated with depression, renewed or exacerbated interpersonal conflicts, and a sense of estrangement and unhappiness.

Another therapy blunder that might lead to outcomes of the B + W − S− type is exemplified by a therapist who encourages the patient to undertake new tasks or roles in life (e.g., marriage or higher education) for which he is insufficiently prepared and which require deployment of nonexistent psychic resources or energies that must be diverted from other areas of life. If he then fails at these tasks, we may anticipate such adverse consequences for his subjective well-being as guilt and depression, which almost certainly have reverberations in his psychological structure.

In summary, a Category 4 outcome is particularly likely when modification of behavior is the primary goal of therapy. Because in our view the psychotherapeutic enterprise should be aimed at helping the individual to achieve an optimal balance between the demands of society, his own desire for contentment, and "professional" conceptions of sound intrapsychic structure, we would regard most outcomes of this type, particularly those that involve W+ to W− and/or S+ to S− changes, as clear-cut negative effects.

3. *Category 5 (B − W + S+)*. Individuals with this configuration emerge from therapy with behavioral deficits (as judged by society), but they perceive themselves as happy and contented, and mental health professionals would rate their psychological makeup as sound. If an individual begins therapy with behavioral, affective, and structural deficits (B − W − S−) and at

termination is found to be happy (W+) and sound in psychological structure (S+), the patient himself and most mental health professionals (including the present authors) would see such a patient as having benefited from psychotherapy, regardless of whether his overt behavior had changed. It is even possible that the patient's behavior might change from B+ to B−, yet because of his W− to W+ and S− to S+ changes, he would still be evaluated from these perspectives as showing overall improvement. Such as assessment, however, would probably be tempered by a *value* judgment concerning the *nature* of the behavioral deficits. Under these circumstances, the therapist's judgment of the patient's status might be equivocal, depending on the degree to which the therapist subscribes to prevailing societal standards.

To illustrate: Suppose a person following therapy decides to dissolve what previously was seen as a functioning marriage (B+) and obtains a divorce (B−). Society would predictably view such an outcome as a negative effect. Similarly, if a latent homosexual came to adopt homosexuality as a life-style, society would enter a similar judgment. Again, a negative judgment would be made by society if as a result of therapy an individual decided to give up a lucrative job and retired to a life of contemplation, abandoning responsibility for his family and beginning to draw welfare checks.

Less drastically, a person might continue his social responsibilities in the areas of vocation and family, but as a result of therapy he might become freer to express himself sexually, which society might judge as promiscuity and thus a negative outcome. This is the kind of situation Freud envisaged when he said that following psychoanalysis, once a person's repressions are resolved (S− to S+), he would accept himself more fully (W− to W+), but he might also become more liberated and expressive sexually. With respect to the latter change, Freud commented that it should be a matter of indifference to the analyst whether the patient's new lifestyle clashed with the standards of society (Freud, of course, was speaking of Vienna in the Victorian era). In this situation, based on the affective and structural components, the patient as well as the analyst would rate the therapy outcome as highly favorable despite the fact that so-

ciety, judging his behavior, might disapprove. Thus, the fact that some therapists view psychotherapy not as a means of making the patient conform to the establishment but as a humane approach for liberating the individual from the shackles of social conventions and his own internalized repressions sets the stage for a clash among judgments of therapy outcome. More recently we have witnessed a similar clash between adherents to conservative mores and standards of conduct that glorify competitiveness and productivity (in an economic sense) and those who strive for liberation, self-actualization, and personality "growth." Thus, the examples of therapy outcome considered here illustrate vividly the potential for such clashes among judgments of outcome, depending on the judge's viewpoint and values.

The issue is drawn most sharply for the mental health professional in public service (e.g., a psychiatrist working in a state mental hospital, a psychologist working in a prison, etc.). Such professionals are generally regarded as agents of society, which has delegated to them the treatment and "cure" of troublesome patients. In practice if not in theory, this frequently means inducing these patients to abandon their deviant ways and become productive members of society. On the other hand, the therapist in private practice may enjoy the luxury of taking a laissez-faire attitude toward his patients' overt behavior. Nonetheless, for most therapists it may prove exceedingly difficult to separate, even in their own minds, society's values, the patient's unique personality, and the therapist's own position both as a mental health professional and as a member of society.

4. *Category 7 (B − W + S−).* An individual entering therapy with deficits in all three aspects of functioning would be considered to be an example of a Category 7 outcome if following therapy he experiences feelings of well-being but is judged by society to have persisting behavioral deficits and by the mental health professional as continuing to manifest psychopathology of varying degrees. These outcomes are typical when the individual's therapy may have dealt with his sense of hopelessness, demoralization, diminished self-esteem, and the like, but when changes in the behavioral realm and more fun-

damental changes in character structure are conspicuous by their absence. As noted earlier, such narrowly defined outcomes are frequent in brief psychotherapy, in supportive psychotherapy, in crisis intervention, or in any of a wider variety of experiences, such as encounter groups or sensitivity training, in which the person experiences increments in well-being and contentment (which are typically short-lived) but where little else has changed.

The patients in many psychotherapy outcome studies in which results are based solely on self-reports, such as Q sorts between "real" and "ideal" self, are typical instances of apparent Category 7 outcomes. In the absence of data on behavioral observations and more penetrating psychodiagnostic studies of these patients, the question of whether changes in behavior and psychological structure have occurred cannot be answered; but it is precisely cases of this kind that lead both society and mental health professionals—albeit for different reasons—to the judgment that supportive or brief psychotherapy is of limited utility and that the changes seen from these two perspectives are unimpressive or trivial. If the individual's well-being and contentment are of paramount concern, improvements in this domain may be seen as quite important; if, on the other hand, concern for the individual's happiness is overriden by an emphasis on adherence to society's standards of performance or to standards of adequate personality functioning, therapeutic interventions resulting in B − W + S− outcomes are by definition inconsequential.

Another likely intake state is the B + W − S− configuration, that is, individuals who meet their social responsibilities but feel anxious and depressed and suffer from neurotic disturbances. This is the case of the typical neurotic patient whose inhibitions and intrapsychic conflicts, coupled with profound unhappiness (often in contrast to a seemingly comfortable set of external circumstances), lead him to seek professional help. If such an individual shows the Category 7 outcome (B − W + S−), he would quite likely be regarded by society as an example of a negative effect of psychotherapy, although he himself, based on his enhanced sense of well-being, would probably judge his therapy to be successful.

Therapist-judged deterioration would most likely be manifested by further decompensation from an S− intake state. Such situations, coupled with an individual's sense of contentment, are probably relatively rare in intensive psychotherapy, but they might result from the patient's wish to escape therapy (in which case the sense of well-being might be self-deceptive or misleading in other respects). Other possibilities include conversion to a new "faith" (meditation, yoga, Christian Science, etc.). In contemporary society, outcomes from many experiences that the individual regards as "therapeutic" or "self-actualizing" are instances of this kind—their value clearly depending on the extent to which they "turn him on." By contrast, both society and most mental health professionals, although for different reasons, tend to reject such experiences as trivial.

Individuals having therapy outcomes of the B − W + S− variety, regardless of their initial status, may be persons with little insight and low motivation for self-exploration and serious work on their characterological problems, such as psychopaths or court-referred criminals. Such individuals may be viewed by society as being in need of psychotherapy or behavior modification (because their performance fails to meet acceptable standards), but, for the stated reasons, they are judged as poor candidates for psychotherapy by mental health professionals.

Conclusions

In summary, the tripartite model analysis of mental health and psychotherapy evaluation points to a number of significant issues with ramifications for clinical, research, and public policy decisions. Of particular note are the following:

(a) The same individual may simultaneously be judged as mentally healthy or mentally ill and, correspondingly, his therapeutic experience may be judged as positive or negative depending on *who* is evaluating the patient.

(b) These differences in evaluation arise from the vested interests each judge brings to the evaluative task. Acknowledging these differences does not necessarily negate the validity of evaluations made from any one perspective, but rather highlights the unique values inherent in each. Furthermore, by acknowledging the reality of the differences, we have highlighted those instances in which a clash of values and thus a clash in evaluations of mental health and psychotherapy outcome are most likely to occur.

(c) One implication of our discussion is that judgments made from a single perspective must clearly be recognized as such and, accordingly, their limited usefulness must be acknowledged. Failure to consider this principle adequately in the past has had extremely unfortunate consequences, particularly in debates concerning the effectiveness of psychotherapeutic interventions. Because psychotherapy outcomes have been judged by a *wide variety* of criteria, the research literature as a whole remains in a seriously confused state, which precludes comprehensive statements or conclusions. Because little or no comparability across studies exists, the urgent question being pressed by the public—Does psychotherapy work?—goes unanswered. (For present purposes we ignore problems of methodology and other deficiencies in published studies, which have received ample attention, e.g., Fiske et al., 1970; Paul, 1969; Strupp & Bergin, 1969).

(d) *A truly adequate, comprehensive picture of an individual's mental health is possible only if the three facets of the tripartite model of functioning—behavior, affect, and inferred psychological structure—are evaluated and integrated.* For psychotherapy researchers, this means that assessments of therapy outcome must be comprehensive, that is, tap *all three* areas of functioning. Equally important, assessments of therapy outcome must be based wherever possible on *standardized*, generally accepted criteria of "good functioning" in each of the three areas. Failure to implement these principles can only mean a continued proliferation of scattered pieces of knowledge that cannot be fitted into an integrated understanding of whether psychotherapy has any effects—either for good or ill—and how these effects are achieved. This article also calls attention to the fact that although researchers must play an important role in evaluating therapy outcomes, they cannot answer the question of how a particular treatment result is to be judged, including how evaluations from the three domains are to be integrated. In the final analysis, this is an issue of human values and public policy, not of empirical research.

Reference Note

1. Klerman, G. L., & Weissman, M. M. Personality as a predictor of outcome of treatment of depression. In A. Beck (Chair), *Current developments in the psychotherapy of depression.* Symposium presented at the meeting of the Eastern Psychological Association, New York, April 1976.

References

Aldrich, C. K. The long and short of psychotherapy. *Psychiatric Annals,* 1975, *5,* 52–58.

Bergin, A. E., & Garfield, S. L. (Eds.). *Handbook of psychotherapy and behavior change.* New York: Wiley, 1971.

Fiske, D. W., Hunt, H. F., Luborsky, L., Orne, M. T., Parloff, M. B., Reiser, M. F., & Tuma, A. H. Planning of research on effectiveness of psychotherapy. *Archives of General Psychiatry,* 1970, *22,* 22–32.

Jahoda, M. *Current concepts of positive mental health.* New York: Basic Books, 1958.

Kittrie, N. N. *The right to be different: Deviance and enforced therapy.* Baltimore, Md.: Johns Hopkins Press, 1971.

Marin, P. The new narcissism. *Harper's,* October 1975, pp. 45–56.

Parloff, M. B., Kelman, H. C., & Frank, J. D. Comfort, effectiveness, and self-awareness as criteria of improvement in psychotherapy. *American Journal of Psychiatry,* 1954, *3,* 343–351.

Paul, G. Behavior modification research: Design and tactics. In C. M. Franks (Ed.), *Behavior therapy: Appraisal and status.* New York: McGraw-Hill, 1969.

Quality psychiatric care vs. political realities. *Behavior Today,* June 1976, pp. 1–2.

Rapaport, D. The structure of psychoanalytic theory: A systematizing attempt. *Psychological Issues,* 1960, *2*(2), 1–158.

Strupp, H. H., & Bergin, A. E. Some empirical and conceptual bases for coordinated research in psychotherapy. *International Journal of Psychiatry,* 1969, *7,* 18–90.

Strupp, H. H., Hadley, S. W., & Gomes-Schwartz, B. *Negative effects in psychotherapy: Clinical, theoretical and research issues.* New York: Jason Aronson, in press.

Szasz, T. *The manufacture of madness; A comparative study of the inquisition and the mental health movement.* New York: Harper & Row, 1970.

At the time of original publication of this article, *Hans H. Strupp* and *Suzanne W. Hadley* were at Vanderbilt University.

The Vanderbilt University Research Team studying negative effects in psychotherapy included Hans H. Strupp, Suzanne W. Hadley, Beverly Gomes–Schwartz, and Stephen H. Armstrong. Support was provided by NIMH Contract 278-75-0036(ER).

Psychotherapeutic Interventions in Physical Health

Effectiveness and Economic Efficiency

Mary E. Olbrisch

Two questions are addressed: (a) Does research support the hypothesis that psychotherapy exerts a favorable influence on physical health? (b) Can psychotherapy be employed to change physical health on a cost-effective basis? Research with overutilizers of medical services, surgical patients, and other groups is discussed in terms of methodological adequacy, and problems faced by researchers in these areas are explored. The effectiveness and economic efficiency of psychotherapeutic preparation for surgery are strongly supported. Studies with overutilizers are promising, but randomized experiments are needed. Implications for inclusion of coverage of psychotherapy under national health insurance are discussed.

National health insurance looms before us as a mass of undetermined shape, size, and content. It will come into being, a nearly certain result of growing recognition that access to adequate health care is an essential human right. Because national health insurance will have far-reaching implications for allocation of resources, quality of life, and changes in the organization of the health care delivery system, the form it will take has become a central issue in the political arena. Psychologists have made a major investment in the battle to mold national health insurance, their principal goals being to win recognition for members of their profession as qualified independent health service providers and to extend the umbrella of health coverage to include services that professional psychologists offer (Dörken, 1976, p. xi). Crucial arguments in psychology's efforts to establish itself in a secure position within the health care delivery system have been the evaporation of distinctions between mental and physical health (Dörken, 1976, p. x) and increasing demands for the application of methods that meet the emotional needs of physically ill patients and consequently decrease demands on traditional medical resources (Schofield, 1975).

The potential for development of new applications of psychology to the field of health care is only beginning to be explored (APA Task Force on Health Research, 1976). While the range of opportunities is impressive, it is likely that the largest number of psychologists who will apply their skills in the restoration and maintenance of physical health will confine their activities to the delivery of traditional psychological services—that is, psychotherapy.

A question of central importance in policy decisions regarding national health insurance is whether it will be economically feasible to cover the cost of psychotherapy. One advocate of such coverage has gone so far as to argue that not only will coverage of psychotherapy be feasible, but that failure to include a psychotherapy component in a comprehensive health system will cause medical services per se to become bogged down in overutilization by persons having no discoverable medical cause for their conditions (Cummings, 1975). Coverage of the cost of psychotherapy under national health insurance is both a political and an economic issue. While there are many other reasons that one could advance for inclusion of psychotherapy coverage under national health insurance, empirical evi-

Reprinted from *American Psychologist*, 1977, *32*, 761–777.

dence that psychotherapy enables the entire health care delivery system to operate on a cost-effective basis would be helpful in winning legislative sanction for this coverage.

This article is addressed to the question of whether, through a critical evaluation of the evidence, the claim that psychotherapy exerts a favorable influence on physical health can be supported. It is further addressed to the question of whether the economic benefits of any such influences would exceed the cost of delivering psychotherapy. Although many factors will be influential in policy decisions regarding coverage of psychotherapy under national health insurance, the answers to these questions may prove to be highly significant for the future of professional psychology.

Should Psychotherapy Affect Physical Health?

The assertion that psychotherapy can cause changes in physical well-being is grounded in centuries of philosophy (Bahnson, 1974) and is supported by theory and research that elucidate the relationships among cultural attitudes, environmental stressors, self-concept, and physical health (Thurlow, 1967). Change in life-style, whether a result of specific behavior change or overall reorganization of the personality, is a psychotherapy outcome that may be related in a number of ways to improved physical health. Removal of a specific psychic conflict thought to be at the root of a particular physical problem is sometimes thought to be curative (Alexander, French, & Pollock, 1968). Crisis intervention is a relatively brief form of psychotherapy used to help a patient cope with a specific stressor, for example, surgery, by enabling the patient to effectively use anxiety in adapting to a stressful situation. Psychotherapy is also thought to be effective in helping people cope with general life stress that at times may become both psychologically and physically demanding, producing lowered resistance to illness (Hinkle & Wolff, 1957; Selye, 1956).

Neither philosophy nor theory nor research has consistently guided investigations of the effects of psychotherapy on physical health. Therefore, the focus of this article is an examination of methodological problems rather than a discussion providing an integrated theoretical perspective.

Review of the Literature

The scope of this review has been determined as much by the literature as by any rules set beforehand. For example, no attempt has been made to define psychotherapy. Health education per se is not considered to be psychotherapy, nor is biofeedback or other mechanical, chemical, and physical treatments. Relaxation training, long considered to be a major psychotherapeutic tool, is included. In some instances, studies are included, even though psychotherapy as the independent variable is only vaguely defined or completely unspecified, because the outcome variables observed are of particular interest.

Outcome Measures

The dependent variables of interest are those indicating some impact on physical health. Thus, reports of psychotherapy with various clinical groups were included only if effects on physical health were directly or indirectly studied. Observations of emotional or attitudinal changes alone were not taken as evidence for change in physical health. Also excluded were volumes of research on life-style and behavior problems such as alcoholism, obesity, and smoking. To the extent that psychotherapy successfully treats these problems it may be considered as exerting a favorable influence on an individual's overall physical functioning.

Measures of physical health cover a large range and their qualities vary extensively. Self-report of symptom frequency and intensity commonly is used, although often little correspondence between self-report and other physiological measures can be observed. To a great extent, the reliability and validity of measures of physical health determine the degree to which one can place confidence in the effectiveness of the independent variable, a problem not limited to psychotherapy research. In most of the studies reported, the criteria for improvement were the same as those that would be used to evaluate the effect of any traditional medical treatment.

Even less adequate as measures of physical health are economic outcome variables such as medical care utilization, employee absenteeism, and health insurance claims. To some extent, of course, these measures are correlated with subjective and objective health status. The correlations are strongest in the case of catastrophic illness; they may be only weak indicators in other cases, tied more to elusive personality variables than to observable physical pathology. Despite their weaknesses, these variables are critical in determining the effectiveness of psychotherapy in an economic analysis. They do not differ from variables used to estimate the economic efficiency of traditional medical treatments. It is difficult to make an objective and independent assessment of a patient's state of health in any situation (Mechanic, 1966), and other problems such as inaccuracy in recording contribute to a situation in which all measures are at best imperfect.

Recurrent Methodological Problems

Psychotherapy research is, unfortunately, beset by many difficult problems. In reviewing the literature on the effects of psychotherapy on physical health, many of the same problems appear that recur in studies of more customary psychotherapy outcome variables. Certain methodological difficulties stand out and are easily identified, as most of the research to be reviewed is at a relatively low level of sophistication. A major reason for this is that a large number of studies in the area were conducted many years ago. Many of them represented significant advances in a field where double-blind studies and randomized trials had not yet been conceived. Nevertheless, the findings from such studies are equivocal in light of present research standards. The problems in interpretation listed below should not be taken as criticisms of the investigators. However, the tendency to accept findings based on studies with such limitations as strong evidence for or against the effectiveness of psychotherapy should be guarded against.

One outstanding problem is that the literature is characterized by a plethora of case studies and minor variations on case studies. Before dismissing this research, one should note that time and again, psychotherapeutic treatments of conditions that have persisted for years and have proven resistant to all forms of medical intervention are reported as successful. For the most part, psychotherapy was employed as a planned intervention—the effect on physical health was fully intended at the outset. On the other hand, the number of similar studies in which psychotherapy proved to be unsuccessful is unknown. Even though psychotherapists may be no less likely to report their failures than any other group of scientists, the favorable outlook based on published case-study material must be balanced against an unknown number of less successful attempts at improving physical health through psychotherapy.

A second design frequently encountered employs a treated group of patients but no control group. Occasionally, experimenters present information about the expected course of an untreated condition, but statements of that sort are rare. While the design permits some estimate of success rates, it has most of the same weaknesses of the case-study approach. Some of the better research of this type involves measurements extended in time both before and after treatment, but since the patients studied are usually selected because of membership in an extreme group, it is seldom that statistical regression can be ruled out as a major plausible, rival hypothesis.

Even when a comparison group is provided, failure to randomize is a major obstacle to clear interpretation in many studies. A number of prospective studies would have benefited from the addition of a wait-list control group to which volunteers for treatment could have been assigned. Often, no mention is made of failure to randomize; in some cases, poor management and lack of cooperation between treatment and research teams are offered as explanations. Retrospective studies present a similar problem: Even the most tedious efforts to choose a control group that matches the treated volunteers can result in comparisons between groups that at the onset differ in motivation, in ability to communicate, or in other important ways. While the uncertainty of success in matching makes it a less desirable procedure than randomization, it is certainly superior to the use of no comparison group at all.

Another important methodological issue that becomes obvious in surveying the research is the question of whether to standardize treatment or to adjust and adapt it to the apparent needs of the patient. In the latter case, it can be argued that the variables responsible for change become obscured; in the former, change will be detected only with a fairly homogeneous population. There is no simple solution to this problem, nor is it limited to psychotherapy research. For example, trials of oral hypoglycemic agents in fixed dosages for the control of diabetes mellitus have been criticized for their lack of sensitivity to critical individual differences (Loubatières, 1972). Eventually, research may enable prediction of the type of psychotherapy to which a particular patient with a particular health problem is likely to be responsive; at the present time, choice of treatment is a difficult issue that requires a great deal of theoretical and empirical study.

The study of economic outcome variables also presents a problem. Attempts to infer cost-effectiveness are often made with no clear demonstration of effectiveness. It is naive to infer that a treatment or program yields monetary return because of decreases in some costs (e.g., insurance claims) when, because of a lack of control groups, there are reasons to doubt its efficacy. In some cases, however, the same variables suggesting that a treatment reduces costs also suggest that it is effective. For example, we usually can assume that patient groups hospitalized for shorter periods of time have less need of medical treatment. Such an inference is possible only when statistics are available from an appropriate control group. Economic analysis, however simple or complex, is only as good as the methodology of the studies from which it draws its inferences.

Another aspect of the relationship between economic analysis and research methodology which raises problems is the difficulty of applying cost analysis to an uncertain magnitude of effect. The advantage of randomized experiments in dealing with this problem is that the effect size—for example, units of improvement or number of lives saved—can be readily determined and translated into a benefit/dollar ratio. Quasi-experimental designs, on the other hand, yield estimates of magnitude of effect that are likely to vary over a wide range, even when it is almost certain that the treatment being evaluated does have some effect (Sechrest, Note 1). Unfortunately, knowing that a treatment costs somewhere between $5 and $100 per unit of effect is not very helpful in decision making, particularly when more than one treatment is available and resources are limited.

Economic studies present a number of additional sticky problems that are beyond the realm of methodological solution. There is a clear tendency to equate the values of good health and even of human life with economic independence and productivity. Carried to absurdity, economic studies might well compare the cost-benefit ratio for treatment with that of preparing massive collective graves. The elderly, the chronically ill and disabled, and any others who draw upon resources but show little promise of repayment through employment, consumption, and payment of taxes are reduced to financial liabilities (Acton, Note 2); at best, psychotherapy might still be employed as a means of minimizing losses.

Along with the problems of research design and economic measurement, one must also give serious consideration to the practical problems that affect psychotherapy research in general and health care research in particular. Few practitioners feel that it is ethical to withhold treatment from persons in need in order to form a wait-list or placebo control group. Even when such groups are formed, strong forces beyond the researcher's control, including help from other professionals, operate to create changes and thus increase the variance not explained by the treatment. Furthermore, individuals generally seek treatment at a point when their problems have become extreme. Statistical regression is an occupational hazard for the psychotherapy researcher. Differential mortality also occurs, although often it is unclear whether the treatment or perhaps lack of treatment is responsible for this.

The psychologist who attempts to conduct research on psychotherapeutic treatment of physical problems or symptoms faces compounded difficulties. Many persons may develop physical symptoms because they are reluctant to define their experiences in terms of difficulties in psychological or social functioning. Another problem is that in many settings, professionals who are not physicians are seriously limited in their access to both patients and data. The age of informed consent has created many new difficulties related to keeping research subjects blind to conditions while providing appropriate reassurance of protection of individual rights. A further difficulty is that with the growth of the field of health care psychology, more communication has fostered a proliferation of research application on the basis of studies still in their formative phases. With increasing acceptance of psychotherapy for medical patients, it becomes increasingly difficult to conduct good research. Some psychologists working in the field report instances of nurses aides and others compensating control group patients who are not getting treatment by paying extra attention to them. Added to this, the dual role of researcher and psychotherapist is undoubtedly a source of much conflict.

In light of the restraints on researchers doing work to advance knowledge in this area, the ingenuity, variety, and complexity of the studies done thus far are laudable. Despite many problems, these researchers have made a valuable contribution to knowledge.

Psychotherapy with Inappropriate Utilizers of Medical Services

A large proportion of persons who seek medical care are under some form of emotional stress; in many cases, no organic cause for physical symptoms can be demonstrated. Conversely, persons suffering from mental disorders and emotional problems tend to be high utilizers of medical services (Avnet, 1962; Cassell, Fraser, & Spellman, 1972). Estimates of the costs of ruling out organic reasons for physical symptoms in cases where psychological reasons are apparent prior to medical diagnosis range from incredible to astronomical.

In his analysis of the records of 36 patients who were admitted to a hospital for diagnostic procedures and whose psychiatric problems were identified at the time of admission, Goshen (1963) found that the cost of negatively confirm-

ing diagnoses already made would have paid for as many as 6 months of psychotherapy for these patients. In actuality, the 36 patients were all subsequently seen and treated on an outpatient basis by the psychiatry department at a low cost, to which was added the high cost of medical diagnostic testing and hospitalization. In a later study of medical tests performed on 66 patients with psychiatric problems, Goshen (1969) noted that the less often some kind of disorder was likely to occur, the more frequently it was investigated. Obviously, the failure to directly deal with the psychological problems of "neurotic" patients places an enormous and expensive burden on the health care delivery system.

A number of early attempts to treat the "emotional habits" of neurotic, inappropriately high utilizers of medical care have been reported (Hadden, 1942; Harris, 1939; Pratt, 1934; Rhoades, 1935; Snowden, 1940). Psychotherapy in these studies consisted of lectures on the relationship between mental distress and physical health delivered to groups of from 6 to 40 patients, testimonials by successful members of the group, and instruction in relaxation. The treatment encouraged suppression of symptoms, rewarded improved patients with attention, and taught relaxation as an essential skill in attaining peace of mind and bodily health.

Unfortunately, little systematic observation was employed with these groups, and no control groups were studied. On the basis of anonymous written reports by 272 patients seen during a 6-month period, Harris (1939) found that 68% experienced improvement ranging from complete freedom from symptoms to alleviation of one or two of the more trying ones. After only one session, 36% of the patients improved to some extent. Of the 32% who did not improve, many failed to attend the therapy sessions because of distance and transportation expenses. Both Hadden (1942) and Harris (1939) reported that 20% of the patients referred for group psychotherapy refused the treatment; Pratt (1934) reported an attrition rate of 45% after one session, noting that many patients compared the treatment to Christian Science.

More dynamic forms of psychotherapy have also been employed with overutilizers of medical services. Schoenberg and Senescu (1966) studied a group of seven female patients who for 4 years prior to psychotherapy had had an average of 12 outpatient visits per year for various somatic complaints. Following nearly 2 years of weekly group therapy meetings, the number of visits decreased to an average of 2.3 per year, remaining low for 7 years. The therapy employed was an analysis of interpersonal dynamics through focus on group process. Somatic complaints were interpreted as avoidance of more basic problems.

It is difficult to estimate whether the group therapies reported on can be considered cost-effective, even if it is assumed that without them medical care utilization would have remained high. When weekly meetings are held for more than a year, the cost of psychotherapy may well exceed the cost of numerous medical visits. It is possible that the same results would have been achieved with a far shorter duration of treatment, as the decline in utilization was sharp during the year treatment was started. The cost of the relatively less frequent medical visits can also be easily underestimated; expensive diagnostic procedures and other variables associated with high utilization can greatly augment the cost of supportive contact with a physician.

Successful treatment of overutilizers through individual psychotherapy has been reported by a number of researchers. Employing very brief psychotherapy in which the therapist interpreted the hostility of three patients, Schüffel and Schonecke (1972) reported complete disappearance of symptoms with only brief relapses. Four patients with back pain were seen in brief psychotherapy in which the therapist (a) provided support through acknowledging the reality of the pain, (b) helped the patients explore emotions, and (c) confronted them with the functional nature of their illnesses (Rosenbaum & Steinhilber, 1973). Three of these patients returned to relatively normal functioning, while one, who had been told by a physician that further surgery would be required, never responded to psychological treatment.

Larger numbers of patients have been treated with individual psychotherapy for physical conditions thought to be related to life stress. There are two reports from a medical clinic at New York Hospital (Berle, Pinsky, Wolf, & Wolff, 1953; Ripley, Wolf, & Wolff, 1948) of

flexible psychotherapy described as including techniques of reassurance and emotional support, advice, and opportunity for free expression of conflict. Of 739 patients seen an average of 15 times over 9 months and followed up after from 1 to 2 years, Berle et al. (1953) rated 34% unimproved, while 24% were rated as experiencing basic improvement and 42% showed symptomatic improvement at discharge. Of 374 patients reevaluated after 1 year, 107 had shifted from one category to another. After 2 years, 28 of 196 patients were found to be in a different category. Most shifts occurred between the symptomatically improved and unimproved groups, although the proportion of patients in each group remained about the same.

In another study of 690 patients seen for an average of 9 hours of individual therapy (Ripley et al., 1948), 19% were rated as basically improved, 38% as symptomatically improved, and 43% as unimproved. Of the 343 unimproved patients, 82 actually received no treatment. Perhaps the most valuable research carried out at this clinic was the development of prognostic scales based on objective data, patients' interpretations, and physicians' interpretations of factors associated with treatment (Berle, Pinsky, Wolf, & Wolff, 1952; Ripley et al., 1948). Considering the availability of superior computer technology and more sophisticated statistical methods, it now should be relatively easier (although by no means simple by any absolute standards) to conduct such research in similar settings and to apply predictions in well-designed cross-validation studies. The hit rate for prediction of patient improvement reported by Berle et al. (1952) looks impressive, but cross-validation was for subsamples of the population studied in forming the prediction equation.

Providing the patient with a sense of control has been emphasized as an important aspect of psychotherapeutic treatment. Of 800 chronic complainers and problem patients referred to an experimental outpatient clinic over a 4-year period, 86% were diagnosed as suffering from masked depression (Lipsitt, 1971). Patients were seen in individual therapy and given freedom to decide the frequency and duration of treatment, freeing them from the necessity of reporting somatic concerns. Patients gradually spaced their visits at intervals of from 2 weeks to a month. The impressions of the clinic staff were that complaints diminished, overall adaptation improved, and utilization of other medical services declined.

In a study of cardiac patients, Cromwell, Butterfield, Brayfield, and Curry (1977) found that patients with an internal locus of control recovered at a faster rate when given free access to various activities designed to promote independent control of physical functioning; external-locus-of-control patients recovered more quickly when encouraged to be passive and dependent on others.

An experimental study specifically testing the effects of control and predictability on the physical and psychological well-being of aged persons living in a retirement home demonstrated that these variables are indeed potent (Schulz, 1976). Individuals who could control or predict visits by a friendly college student over a 2-month period were rated as significantly healthier by the activities director of the home than were those in the randomly visited or no-treatment control groups. The persons able to control visitation frequency also increased their medications by a smaller amount and had a lower increase in number and types of medication taken per day. After termination of the treatment, however, patients in the better groups showed a decline in all measures and were found to be physically worse off than control-group patients (Schulz, Note 3).

One other interesting report of psychotherapy with primarily aged individuals hospitalized for major physical disabilities compared untreated patients with groups receiving from 6 to 12 supportive or problem-solving therapy sessions of 15 minutes' duration (Godbole & Verinis, 1974). Patients in both psychotherapy groups decreased physical complaints and were more likely to become well enough to return home. Although it is not accurate to say that these patients had been overutilizers of medical services, it was still possible to decrease their utilization by employing psychotherapeutic techniques.

Psychotherapy in Prepaid Health Plans

It is difficult to gather accurate, comprehensive data on medical care utilization in the prevailing fee-for-service health care delivery system. Fortunately, this task becomes at least somewhat simplified when records are available through insurance companies or prepaid health plans. Extrapolation from studies conducted in these settings is a particularly difficult issue, but the results are at least suggestive of what might be expected in any health care delivery system.

The earliest research to suggest that psychiatric treatment reduced medical and surgical utilization was Avnet's (1962) observation, a year after initiation of claims for short-term psychiatric treatment, of a slight drop in what had been steadily increasing insurance claims from a group of subscribers. In another study, Cassell, Grunberg, and Fraser (1968) noted that discharged chronic mental patients, presumably treated while institutionalized, were significantly lower in utilization of physician services following return to the community when compared to Saskatchewan Medical Insurance Commission statistics for the general population during a 3-year period. Only a minority of patients exceeded average utilization expenditures. While Cassell et al. (1968) entertained the hypothesis that the study group was healthier after treatment in a sheltered environment, five other explanations, including availability of alternative sources of medical care and patient characteristics such as fear of being rehospitalized and incompetence in seeking medical advice, were considered by the investigators to be equally or perhaps even more plausible. Considering low utilization to be underutilization may be justified on economic as well as humanitarian grounds; the patient who ignores obvious early symptoms of problems requiring medical treatment may eventually develop costly complications (Densen, Shapiro, & Einhorn, 1959).

Formerly hospitalized psychiatric patients are, of course, a rather special group. Similar research with more representative outpatient populations (Follette & Cummings, 1967; Goldberg, Krantz, & Locke, 1970) carried out in Health Maintenance Organizations (HMOs) has provided a broader perspective. In the design employed by Goldberg et al., 256 patients referred for psychotherapy were studied a year prior to and a year after the referral. The majority of these patients decreased their utilization of physician services and laboratory or X-ray procedures. However, patients who saw only the screening psychiatrist and did not avail themselves of the short-term therapy benefit reduced utilization of medical services to the same extent as those receiving the full benefit of at least 10 sessions. This finding suggests that the visit to the screening psychiatrist alone had a beneficial effect on the patient or that factors other than psychotherapy were responsible for reduced medical care utilization.

Follette and Cummings (1967) retrospectively examined the records of patients for up to 5 years after their referral for psychotherapy. Additionally, they studied utilization patterns of matched comparison group never seen for psychological treatment, despite the fact that this group's medical records indicated a need for such help similar to that of the treated group. While outpatient medical care utilization for the comparison group tended to increase in the 5 years observed, there was a significant and persistent decline in utilization for the treated patients. This trend was observed even for patients seen for only one session of psychotherapy. For patients seen in longer-term therapy (more than nine sessions), there was a trend for psychotherapy visits merely to substitute for previous medical visits, but the initially high inpatient utilization by this group decreased significantly.

In a further study designed to cope with the problems of possible initial differences between treated and comparison patients, Cummings and Follette (1968), because of lack of cooperation on the part of both physicians and patients, were unable to effect random assignment of high utilizers with emotional difficulties to psychotherapy and control conditions. Their conclusion that patients who do not take advantage of psychotherapy probably would be unable to benefit from it does not really strengthen the conclusions reached on the basis of their retrospective study. In fact, this finding simply adds weight to the argument that the matched comparison group may have constituted a special group of patients highly refractory to care, given that they seemingly needed but either did not seek or did not accept psychological treatment (Kogan, Thompson, Brown, & Newman, 1975). Since there is evidence that only a small percentage of high utilizers of medical care remain high utilizers over an extended period of time (Densen et al., 1959) and that the group of high utilizers comes from the average utilization population and returns to it after about 5 years (Kogan et al., 1975), statistical regression remains as a plausible rival hypothesis in both of the HMO studies reported.

In the face of these methodological and interpretative problems, all of which were clearly spelled out by the authors in their original articles, Cummings and Follette (1976) recently extended their research to include an 8-year follow-up of the psychotherapy patients who were seen for eight or fewer sessions in their 1967 study. They hypothesized that if the reduction of medical utilization had been the result of the patient's having coped more effectively with emotional distress, then the presenting symptoms should have disappeared and the patient should have an awareness of the underlying concern that produced the symptoms.

Cummings and Follette were successful in conducting telephone interviews with 85 of the 121 patients treated. One patient did not recall being seen for psychological treatment, while only two remembered the name of the therapist. Sixty percent of the patients thought that they had seen the psychotherapist only 2 or 3 years prior to the interview, and 92% recalled the problem discussed with the therapist rather than the presenting symptoms. Of 78 patients questioned directly about the presenting symptoms, only 5 recalled having consulted a doctor for the complaint. Asked if the visits to the psychotherapist had been of benefit to them, 76 patients denied having been helped, and a number reported having become quite angry with the therapist and deciding they would have to cope with their problems alone.

While these findings support the hypothesis proposed by Cummings and Follette and add weight to the conclusions drawn on the basis of their original study, they are not incompatible with the statistical regression hypothesis. Cummings and Follette, aware of these difficulties, have persisted in their efforts to replicate their prospective study (Cummings, Note 4). If such a study can be successfully completed, it will provide a great deal of important information about the effectiveness of psychotherapy with inappropriate utilizers of medical care.

Alcohol Rehabilitation Programs

Persons with alcohol problems constitute a group whose medical costs are very high. In addition to their high utilization of medical services, these individuals cost their employers a great deal in absenteeism and lost production. Some interesting research has been conducted which suggests that active intervention programs not only reduce medical care utilization by troubled persons, but actually result in a profit to the employer funding the intervention program.

The Kennecott Copper Corporation (Note 5) has estimated a return of $5.83 per $1.00 cost per year for its psychotherapy program. Impact is noted in reduced absenteeism, reduced hospital, medical, and surgical costs, and reduced costs of nonoccupational accident and illness. The Kennecott program actually provides services to employees and their families for all types of emotional difficulties. A 24-hour crisis service is available, and many are treated on a short-term basis by the program staff. The Kennecott program also serves as a source of referral to many other community agencies.

Kennecott bases its estimates of reduced costs on two studies. In the first, costs of absenteeism, weekly indemnity, and hospital, medical, and surgical claims over a 12-month period were computed for 30 known alcohol abusers. Of those employees, 12 were referred to the Insight program, while 18 never became involved with it. Referred employees improved, while those who received no treatment became worse. In a second study of 83 employees referred to the program because of absenteeism problems, 77% decreased absenteeism by 44%, while 22% increased their absenteeism by 37%. No comparison group was studied.

It is important to note here that Kennecott's Insight program makes referrals to hundreds of social service agencies. Therefore, not all employees who seek help or are referred to the program necessarily receive psychotherapy. Of those who do receive psychotherapy, some are seen on a short-term basis by the program staff, but many are referred elsewhere. Thus, it is unclear what portion of the cost of psychotherapy is being absorbed by the company.

Another reported success is an alcohol and drug recovery program similar to Kennecott's at Oldsmobile's Lansing, Michigan, plant (Alander & Campbell, 1975). The records of 117 workers who volunteered for treatment were compared with those of 24 workers known to be alcohol and drug abusers who did not seek treatment. The comparison group differed from rehabilitation volunteers in a number of ways. While nonvolunteers worsened in terms of lost man-hours, sickness and accident benefits, leaves of absence, and disciplinary actions, treated employees improved in every category and a large drop in lost wages was noted for the treated group.

A third instance of cost-effective alcohol rehabilitation is an undescribed treatment program for Navy enlisted men (Bucky, Edwards, & Coben, Note 6). Those selected for the study were 161 men whose active duty included at least 2 years of service prior to treatment and 2 years of service after treatment. Date of sobriety was determined to be the date of discharge from the program. A reduction in sick days for all reasons for each man treated and a reduction in both alcohol-related and general medical complaints were observed. While sick days had shown an increase over the 2 years prior to treatment, a decrease began the following year and continued in the 2nd year after treatment. The same pattern occurred for days of hospitalization.

Despite the absence of random assignment to treatment and no-treatment groups, these three studies are particularly impressive because alcoholism is widely regarded as seldom improving on its own. All studies were conducted in settings in which a certain degree of external pressure could be used to motivate troubled people to seek treatment. It would be interesting to make comparisons with similar settings in which no treatment was offered but in which employees were simply informed that behavior change was required, especially since employer supportiveness is considered to be an important variable.

Psychotherapeutic Preparation for Surgery

Observations by Janis (1958) of relationships between personality variables, patient coping style, and reaction to surgery have stimulated a good deal of research on methods of improving patient response to surgery. The unparalleled successes of these interventions in the psychotherapy outcome literature have no doubt contributed to continued investigation. While numerous and diverse psychological interventions have been employed, they share the characteristic of being extremely brief. Randomized experiments have been used more in the area of response to surgery than for any other physical health outcome variable, suggesting that such designs are at least possible to carry out.

Several trials of psychotherapy with patients undergoing cardiac surgery have been conducted, with the intentions of both reducing the high rate of postoperative psychosis and preventing concomitant obstacles to recovery. Three children and five adults trained in systematic muscle relaxation and hypnosis by Marmer (1959) underwent cardiac surgery with reduced anesthesia. All patients were alert at the end of the procedure, had uneventful recoveries, and required minimal or no narcotics postoperatively. Gruen (1972) prepared himself for cardiac surgery with systematic relaxation and suggestion; he required little pain medication and recovered at a better than average rate.

Four controlled studies of presurgical therapy with cardiac patients have yielded favorable results. Lazarus and Hagens (1968) reported that a 1-hour interview conducted 2 to 3 days before surgery and followed up by specific recommendations for postoperative care accounted for a 50% reduction in abnormal responses to surgery. Control patients were studied in a different hospital where recovery room conditions were considered to be more favorable. Data were not reported, however, for patients who did not survive their operations for 1 month. Presumably, the results were not affected by differential mortality. Layne and Yudofsky (1971) also observed a 50% reduction in postoperative psychosis among patients receiving psychological treatment. However, death rates were the same in treatment and control groups. Excellent results have also been found for presurgical training in systematic relaxation for cardiac patients (Aiken & Henrichs, 1971). Nurses trained 15 patients in the technique and provided supportive therapy as well. As compared to a matched control group hospitalized a year prior to initiation of the therapy program, prepared patients required fewer units of blood, experienced a smaller degree and duration of hypothermia, and spent less time in surgery and under anesthetics. Mortality was the same in both groups.

A somewhat troublesome account of surgical preparation with cardiac patients is that of Surman, Hackett, Silverberg, and Behrendt (1974), who accepted the null hypothesis. Forty patients were assigned in alternating fashion to experimental and control groups. All were exposed to a standard educational program on heart surgery given by the nursing staff. In addition, experimental patients were seen for preoperative interviews in which a psychiatrist attempted to provide support, clear up misconceptions about the surgery, and teach the patient an autohypnotic technique. Surman et al. (1974) claimed that this intervention did not influence the incidence of postoperative delirium, anxiety, depression, pain, or medication requirements. It should be noted, however, that randomization was not successful in equating groups on all variables. Experimental patients were more likely to have had prior psychiatric treatment, and on the average they had been ill for 4 years longer than controls. In spite of these unfavorable initial differences, the experimental patients spent 17 hours less in intensive care, had 19 hours less intubation time, and had 3.6 fewer hospital days than controls. That these seemingly important differences were reported as not significant suggests that the experiment lacked adequate statistical power. If anything, this study should certainly spur further research in this very interesting area.

Anesthesiologists have also involved themselves in preparing patients psychologically for other types of surgery. Jackson (1951) interviewed 30 young children the evening before their tonsillectomies in order to build trust and to describe the experiences they would have in the operating room. She did not use any preanesthetic medications, eliminating side effects of physiologic depression. Her impressions were that less anesthetic was used, induction time was shortened, and excitement stages decreased.

Similar techniques have been employed

with adult patients. A special-care group of 46 patients having elective intra-abdominal operations was compared to a group of 51 patients randomly assigned to routine treatment conditions (Egbert, Battit, Welch, & Bartlett, 1964). The special-care patients were seen by their anesthetist prior to surgery. The anesthetist told the patients about the pain that they would experience and instructed them in conscious muscle relaxation through slow, deep breathing. Postoperative visits to provide reassurance and go over instructions in relaxation were also included in the special-care treatment. Although special-care and control patients used an equivalent amount of narcotics on the day of surgery, the special-care patients used less on the next 5 days ($p < .01$). Of 57 patients rated by an independent observer 1 to 2 days following surgery, the 27 special-care patients were rated as experiencing less pain than the 30 controls.

In another look at the effects of brief, supportive therapy, Egbert, Battit, Turndorf, and Beecher (1963) randomly assigned 218 patients undergoing elective surgery to one of four conditions. Control patients received no preparation for surgery; another group was given pentobarbital 1 hour prior to surgery; the third group was visited by the anesthetist up to 18 hours prior to surgery; and the last group received both pentobarbital and the preoperative visit. During the visit, the anesthetist discussed the patient's condition, provided information about the anesthetic and other aspects of the surgery, and questioned the patient about previous experiences with anesthetics. Just prior to administration of the anesthetic, patients were interviewed and rated by an independent observer on drowsiness, nervousness, and adequacy of preparation for surgery. Pentobarbital had an effect on drowsiness, but the strongest effect was that of the preoperative visit on patient nervousness. This preoperative visit also had a stronger effect in terms of judgments about adequacy of preparation. Overall, the combined treatments proved to be most effective.

Hypnosis has been successfully employed in surgical preparation. In one study, 31 patients were given suggestions to ease incisional pain and the discomfort of nasal tubes, catheters, and administration of intravenous fluids (Doberneck,

Griffen, Papermaster, Bonello, & Wagensteen, 1959). Pretreatment with only one or two sessions of hypnosis was successful in reducing narcotic utilization. As compared to a control group, the pretreatment group required an average of 2.4 fewer doses of narcotics and was rated by hospital staff as more cheerful and cooperative and as having far fewer complaints. Kolouch (1964) compared the duration of hospitalization of 190 surgical patients prepared by hypnosis with statistics on patients undergoing the same surgery at Veterans Administration, army, private, and teaching hospitals. Although in all cases the hypnosis patients had shorter hospital stays, the major factor appeared to be the type of hospital. In another study of hypnosis in presurgical care, Kolouch (1962) noted that hypnosis was most effective in simpler surgical procedures, resulting in decreased use of pain-relieving drugs and shorter hospitalization. Costs of hospitalization for patients treated with hypnosis were significantly lower than for control patients. Bonilla, Quigley, and Bowers (1961) prepared nine patients for knee surgery with hypnosis, suggesting that patients would sleep well before surgery, would not bothered by postoperative pain that they would experience, and would be able to exercise the knee immediately after surgery. When compared with 20 patients seen for similar surgery prior to initiation of the hypnosis program, prepared patients used fewer doses of narcotics and were hospitalized an average of 19 fewer days.

Some other interesting outcome variables have been studied in looking at the effects of surgical preparation. Reduced incidence of vomiting in the recovery room was noted for patients given supportive treatment by a nurse prior to gynecological surgery (Dumas, Anderson, & Leonard, 1965). Imaginative use of unobtrusive measures in studies of presurgical psychotherapy with orthopedic surgery patients (Florell, 1971; Ortmeyer, Note 7) and with other elective surgery patients (Davis, 1973) is also noteworthy. Although the patients in Florell's (1971) control group were admitted to the hospital at a period prior to initiation of the therapy program, they were equivalent to the therapy patients on presurgical measures. Following surgery, the control patients stayed 1 to 2 days longer in the hospital, required more pain medication, made more calls for assistance, were written about in more lines of nurses' notes, displayed elevated physiological responses, and experienced more transitory anxiety when compared with patients receiving either supportive or supportive-informational therapy.

Ortmeyer (Note 7) obtained similar but not statistically significant results in a true experiment replicating Florell's study. Unfortunately, Ortmeyer used a simple randomization procedure that resulted in confounding of the treatment with time. It turned out that most of Ortmeyer's control group patients underwent surgery during the summer, and a large proportion of them were athletes who were in better physical condition than patients in the experimental group.

Davis (1973) found that patients who were visited by a pastoral counselor who provided brief, crisis-intervention therapy had a shorter postsurgical stay in the hospital and showed lower physiological responses than patients receiving a nontherapeutic pastoral visit or randomly assigned to a control group. No differences were noted in number of nurses' notes or physicians' ratings of stress, pain, and success of surgery.

Employing several brief social interactions with mothers of tonsillectomy patients, Skipper and Leonard (1968) found that the randomly chosen experimental mothers experienced less stress during and after the operation than mothers in the control group. This in turn was reflected in their children's responses to surgery. Children in the experimental group recovered at a faster rate, seemed to experience, physiologically, less ill effects from the operation, and were lower on physiological stress measures of temperature, blood pressure, and pulse rate.

While there is still much to be learned about the role of psychotherapy in surgical recovery, the problem of causal inference has been handled well in many of the studies done thus far. Further research can proceed from a strong foundation.

Psychotherapy with Specific Health Problems

The remainder of this article briefly summarizes research in which psychotherapy is employed in the treatment of emotional aspects of physical illness. An effort has been made to include any studies with adequate methodological designs, but in the interest of brevity, case studies and other really weak designs have been overlooked. A recent review (Ramsay, Wittkower, & Warnes, 1976) adequately covers much of the material omitted in this section. The issue of cost-effectiveness is not dealt with here, as most researchers in these areas have been particularly concerned with health rather than economics.

Treatment of Cardiac Patients

Newly emerging as an area of special interest is psychological treatment of cardiac patients. Therapy goals include alleviation of anxiety, assistance in returning to an adequate level of functioning, help in adhering to treatment programs, and ultimately improved physical health. Cassem and Hackett (1971) noted that only five patients (3.4%) seen in short-term therapy which emphasized cognitive aspects of coping with stress while in a coronary care unit died, significantly fewer than the expected mortality based on the rate for the total coronary-care-unit population of 12% ($p < .01$).

Group therapy has been employed more frequently with outpatients. Fourteen cardiac patients seen for 10 sessions of group therapy (Mone, 1970) were seen as better adjusted to life and work following treatment. Hypochondriasis and depression scores on the Minnesota Multiphasic Personality Inventory decreased significantly, but no control group was observed. In another study of short-term group therapy (Adsett & Bruhn, 1968), six post-myocardial-infarction patients were seen for 10 sessions, while their wives met in another group on alternate weeks. As compared to matched but not randomly assigned control patients, the therapy patients had higher serum cholesterol levels during and after treatment. After therapy, treated patients also had higher serum uric acid levels. However, no differences in blood pressure, pulse, anxiety, or depression were noted, and no significant changes appeared in electrocardiograms of patients during therapy sessions. These results suggest that psychotherapy does not expose cardiac patients to undue physical stress.

Two controlled trials of group therapy with

post-myocardial-infarction patients (Ibrahim, Feldman, Sultz, Staiman, Young, & Dean, 1974; Rahe, Tuffli, Suchor, & Arthur, 1973) demonstrated that the treatments favorably affected physical health. Rahe et al. (1973) cited a number of benefits, including patient adherence to exercise and weight-control programs, cessation of smoking, and realistic adjustment of work schedules and routines. After 18 months, therapy patients had a lower rate of reinfarction than controls (Rahe, O'Neil, Hagan, & Arthur, 1975). At the time of follow-up, however, randomization had been discontinued owing to diffusion of the treatment. Psychotherapy patients in another study (Ibrahim et al., 1974) were found to have a 10% higher 1-year survival rate. A similar proportion of treated and control patients were hospitalized during the first year of treatment, but therapy patients stayed in the hospital an average of 10 fewer days than controls.

Headache Treatment

Relaxation training is by far considered to be the favored psychotherapy for relieving headache pain. A number of researchers have used the technique successfully with sufferers of both tension (Fichtler & Zimmermann, 1973; Tasto & Hinkle, 1973) and migraine (Lutker, 1971; Mitchell & Mitchell, 1971; Paulley & Haskell, 1975) headaches, and a high percentage of patients report dramatic decreases in frequency and duration of pain. Mitchell and Mitchell (1971) reported that relaxation training alone did not markedly decrease headache pain, while a combined desensitization program involving assertiveness therapy produced greater improvements. To some extent this may be the result of expectations aroused in the introductory session on the psychogenesis of migraine. Mitchell and Mitchell (1971) noted in a second study that patients having received previous pharmacotherapy were less likely to improve with the combined desensitization program. Psychotherapy was seen as highly effective when compared to the moderate successes attained in pharmacotherapy trials.

Hypnosis has also been used in the treatment of migraine headaches (Anderson, Basker, & Dalton, 1975). Comparisons between patients randomly assigned to hypnotherapy or pharmacotherapy showed that the number and the intensity of attacks were significantly lower for hypnotherapy patients. The use of another psychotherapy control group was suggested in order to control better for placebo effects.

Psychotherapy of Asthma

Probably no disorder of physical health has received more attention from psychotherapists than asthma. The belief that asthma is largely a psychogenic problem is held by diverse groups, including analysts and behavior therapists. While it is possible that psychological theories about the causes of asthma have stimulated psychotherapy research, it may be that the relative ease with which respiratory functioning is brought under conscious control has made the problem particularly attractive to therapists. Unlike headache, asthma has been treated by a broad range of psychological interventions, among them dynamic group therapy (Groen, 1953; Groen & Pelser, 1960; Lange-Nielsen & Retterstal, 1959; Mascia & Reiter, 1971; Reckless, 1971; Sclare & Crockett, 1957), hypnosis (British Tuberculosis Association, 1968; Edwards, 1960; Maher-Loughnan, 1970; Maher-Loughnan, MacDonald, Mason, & Fry, 1962; Smith & Burns, 1960; White, 1961), systematic desensitization (Moore, 1965; Yorkston, McHugh, Brady, Serber, & Sergeant, 1974), family therapy (Liebman, Minuchin, & Baker, 1974), and individual psychotherapy (Kleeman, 1967; Miller & Baruch, 1948). In her 1968 review, Sperling concluded that psychotherapy was no more successful than standard medical treatments in the control of asthma. Two controlled studies that have appeared since that time (Maher-Loughnan, 1970; Yorkston et al., 1974) include lengthy follow-ups and show superior results for both hypnosis and systematic desensitization in comparison with simple muscle-relaxation training, even though patients treated with relaxation did improve to some extent. Although Liebman et al. (1974) did not observe a control group, they found significant improvements for seven patients treated with family therapy. The asthma conditions had proven resistant to medical management and individual psychotherapy over a long period of time.

Treatment of Skin Disorders

Various modes of psychotherapy have been reported as successful in the treatment of skin problems. Hypnosis has been found to be useful in the treatment of warts (Sinclair-Gieben & Chalmers, 1959) and other skin conditions (Asher, 1956) when patients were able to achieve a deep trance. Three studies of short-term psychotherapy with patients whose dermatoses failed to respond to usual medical treatments (Schoenberg & Carr, 1963; Seitz, 1953; Walsh & Kierland, 1947) showed significant improvements for approximately one half of the patients. Those not improving tended to be therapy dropouts. In none of these studies was a control group employed to determine whether any spontaneous improvements occurred.

Psychological Interventions in Gastrointestinal Disorders

Just as headache seems to attract therapists skilled in training patients to relax, the gastrointestinal diseases, including peptic ulcer and ulcerative colitis, for some reason are among the favorite problems of psychoanalysts. While analytic psychotherapy has not made a poor showing, the best results reported in the literature were attained through a group-therapy procedure that encouraged suppression of symptoms and anxiety (Chappell, Stefano, Rogerson, & Pike, 1937; Chappell & Stevenson, 1936). All patients were diagnosed as having peptic ulcer and were put on a restricted diet. After 3 weeks, patients also treated with psychotherapy were free of subjective symptoms, and at the end of 6 weeks, most of them were eating anything they wanted. Control-group patients treated only with diet were free of subjective symptoms after 4 weeks, but after expanding their diets, most experienced a recurrence of symptoms. In a 3-year follow-up, most of the psychotherapy patients reported that they were in good health, although 40% were found to have organic pathology without any subjective symptoms.

In contrast to this rather uncomplicated form of therapy, psychoanalytic treatment of peptic ulcer (Orgel, 1958) and ulcerative colitis (Weinstock, 1961, 1962) has been seen as suc-

cessful in proportion to the number of years that the patient remained in therapy. Factors associated with improvement in ulcerative colitis during analytic treatment have been studied (Karusch, Daniels, O'Connor, & Stern, 1968, 1969; O'Connor, Daniels, Flood, Karusch, Moses, & Stern, 1964), but the absence of random assignment to treatment and control groups has been detrimental to demonstrating the effectiveness of psychotherapy, given that many severely disturbed patients who needed psychotherapy were assigned to the therapy groups. These patients, many diagnosed as schizophrenic, displayed a much poorer response to treatment. Results pointing to the effectiveness of supportive therapy (Groen & Bastiaans, 1951) and treatment directed toward alleviation of life stress (Grace, Pinsky, & Wolff, 1954) probably also would have been more persuasive had randomized experiments been used.

Psychotherapy in Other Health Problems

In two studies of psychotherapeutic treatment of hypertension, quite different results were obtained, which on the face of things easily could be attributed to the treatment employed. Using the lecture-class treatment in relaxation described by Pratt (1934), Buck (1937) found that two thirds of the hypertensive patients attending three or more classes experienced a drop in blood pressure. Unfortunately, time of measurement was not reported, but it was noted that patients reported relief of symptoms and a general feeling of well-being. Titchener, Sheldon, and Ross (1959) observed a rise in blood pressure among patients seen in group therapy while participating in a double-blind drug evaluation, but control patients experienced a drop in blood pressure. Patients were not assigned randomly to conditions, although pretherapy groups were rated as equivalent with respect to medical and psychological criteria. Although the type of group therapy was not specified, the authors did state their concern with expression of hostility.

Psychotherapy has also been employed with patients having myofascial pain dysfunction syndrome. Lupton (1969) studied 35 patients randomly assigned to dental treatment or counseling for the condition. Both groups reported symptom relief to about the same extent. Greene and Laskin (1974) reviewed the cases of 135 patients seen over a 10-year period and treated by a number of methods. They concluded that the specific form of therapy does not determine success or failure in treatment of patients and recommended an approach based on good communication in the dentist-patient relationship. Pomp (1974) found that patients who failed to respond to conventional dental treatment improved during the course of brief psychotherapy. Most likely to improve were those patients who recognized the need for psychotherapy.

Finally, some research has been reported on the use of psychotherapy in severe physical illnesses. LeShan and Gassmann (1958) reported on 10 cases in which supportive and in-depth psychotherapy was offered to cancer patients. Three patients experienced improvement to the extent that tumors shrank or disappeared. They also noted, however, that four patients became worse physically when their therapists went on vacation or left the area for a time. Two patients died during their therapists' absences. In a study of group therapy with 12 patients suffering from clinical emphysema, Pattison, Rhodes, and Dudley (1971) observed a strong negative emotional reaction to therapy. Five of the patients died within a year after the conclusion of the experiment, including two of the five patients who seemed to benefit from the treatment emotionally. Although the deaths certainly are not clearly attributable to psychotherapy, there were no physical health benefits to justify the arousal of life-threatening anxiety. Similarly, group therapy with Parkinson's disease patients (Chafetz, Bernstein, Sharpe, & Schwab, 1955) appeared to cause more anxiety than could be justified by the impression that the therapy helped patients adhere to medication schedules. Whatever the advantages of insight therapy, there is no reason to suppose that it can benefit every patient in every situation.

Conclusions

Does psychotherapy influence physical health? In many applications of various psychothera-peutic techniques it would appear that it does, but only in the case of psychotherapeutic preparation for surgery does there appear to be really solid evidence for a beneficial effect on physical health. Research with inappropriately high utilizers of medical services is quite promising, and further evidence, perhaps even generated on the basis of true experiments, will be helpful in making the case for its effectiveness. The quality of evidence for other applications is uneven. Fortunately, recent trends in many areas are toward randomized experiments and research generated by theory. In instances where medical treatment is used to control symptoms of incurable diseases, there seem to be enough reports of poor outcome for insight therapy to encourage caution in further research, especially since there is no clear reason to believe that the treatment will physically benefit the patient and there is an apparent possibility that, through opening up areas of information about which the patient is helpless to do anything, emotional harm will result (Cromwell et al., 1977).

Can psychotherapy for improvement in physical health be delivered on a cost-effective basis? The uncertainty about the magnitude of effects demonstrated thus far puts this question beyond the reach of most of the research. In the case of presurgical therapy, much of the evidence of effectiveness lies in cost savings resulting from decreased use of medications and shorter hospitalizations. Research with overutilizers is suggestive of potentially enormous cost savings, but again the estimated savings may be in part illusory. Continued research in this area is of utmost importance. Experimental research will certainly prove useful in settling this issue. It is also interesting that private industry considers a psychotherapy program to be profitable in treating early alcoholism and associated problems while at the same time reducing medical expenses, but costs to the supporting agencies where employees are referred are not estimated in the cost of delivering psychotherapy. More realistic studies looking at the costs and benefits from a systems viewpoint are needed, and randomized experiments almost certainly will be necessary to determine the economic value of the benefits. While it might even be argued that relatively expensive treatments such as psychoanalysis can be cost-effective, it is unlikely that policymakers will consider it practical to finance such treatments on a large scale.

It should be noted that no research to determine who should deliver psychotherapy has been reported. Successful results have been claimed by physicians, nurses, psychiatrists, psychologists, social workers, and hospital chaplains. It is only reasonable to conclude that if differences in the profession or status of therapists are not found to affect outcome significantly, consumers will be best served by opportunities to freely choose psychotherapists in a competitive marketplace.

Final Comments

The questions posed in the introduction to this article were framed in a tone and context suggesting the necessity of immediate and conclusive answers. Politically, they are questions of major significance. Scientifically, they are also highly relevant and quite amenable to experimental investigation. Unfortunately, scientific progress requires patient effort and almost always entails gradual accumulation of knowledge. Social changes generally will not wait until all the results are in and usually cannot be delayed until perfectly rational decisions are possible.

It can be concluded from this review that the results of research on the effects of psychotherapy on physical health are highly promising. However, statements as to the necessity of including a psychotherapy component within a health care delivery system based solely on its demonstrated effectiveness for physical health problems involve a leap beyond the data and are somewhat premature. Of course, there are many reasons beyond the scope of this discussion that one could put forth in support of covering psychotherapy under national health insurance. But in addition to its contribution in the area of psychotherapy research, psychology has other roles to play in the area of health care delivery.

Psychologists are in a unique position to provide creative leadership in building an equitable health care delivery system. As a profession that has a strong commitment to client welfare, a tradition of providing a broad range of human services, and a history rooted in public service, psychology has an obligation to explore and fairly evaluate alternatives to the traditions and practices that have led to our current health care crisis. Continued creativity, exploration, and service in the face of perplexing human problems will be demanded as stronger attempts to build an equitable health care delivery system are made.

Above all, the interests of consumers who use or pay for health care should guide our efforts in this area. If through research, through delivery of services, through vigorous advocacy of consumer interests, psychology seizes the opportunities to close the gaps between providers and consumers, between consumers who have and consumers who have not, then psychology will surely find its place in an emerging health care delivery system.

Reference Notes

1. Sechrest, L. Personal communication, March 9, 1977.
2. Acton, J. P. *Economic analysis and the evaluation of medical programs.* Paper presented at the Conference on Emergency Medical Services: Research Methodology, September 8–10, 1976. (Available from J. P. Acton, The Rand Corporation, Santa Monica, California 90406).
3. Schulz, R. Personal communication, November 15, 1976.
4. Cummings, N. A. Personal communication, March 3, 1977.
5. Kennecott Copper Corporation. *Insight.* Unpublished report. Utah Copper Division, Salt Lake City, 1975.
6. Bucky, S., Edwards, D., & Coben, P. *Primary and secondary benefits from treatment for alcoholism* (Report No. 75–44). San Diego, Calif.: U.S. Naval Health Research Center, June 3, 1975.
7. Ortmeyer, J. A. Unpublished dissertation in preparation, Pastoral Psychology Department, Garrett-Evangelical Theological Seminary, Northwestern University, 1977.

References

Adsett, C. A., & Bruhn, J. G. Short-term group psychotherapy for post-myocardial infarction patients and their wives. *Canadian Medical Association Journal,* 1968, *99,* 577–584.

Aiken, L. H., & Henrichs, T. F. Systematic relaxation as a nursing intervention technique with open heart surgery patients. *Nursing Research,* 1971, *20,* 212–217.

Alander, R., & Campbell, T. An evaluative study of an alcohol and drug recovery program, a case study of the Oldsmobile experience. *Human Resource Management,* 1975, *14,* 14–18.

Alexander, F., French, T. M., & Pollack, G. H. *Psychosomatic specificity* (Vol. 1). Chicago: University of Chicago Press, 1968.

American Psychological Association, Task Force on Health Research. Contributions of psychology to health research. *American Psychologist*, 1976, *31*, 263–274.

Anderson, J. A. D., Basker, M. A., & Dalton, R. Migraine and hypnotherapy. *International Journal of Clinical and Experimental Hypnosis*, 1975, *23*, 48–58.

Asher, R. Respectable hypnosis. *British Medical Journal*, 1956, *1*, 309–313.

Avnet, H. H. *Psychiatric insurance: Financing short-term ambulatory treatment*. New York: Group Health Insurance Inc., 1962.

Bahnson, C. B. Epistemological perspectives of physical diseases from the psychodynamic point of view. *American Journal of Public Health*, 1974, *64*, 1034–1039.

Berle, B. B., Pinsky, R. H., Wolf, S., & Wolff, H. G. A clinical guide to prognosis in stress disease. *Journal of the American Medical Association*, 1952, *149*, 1624–1628.

Berle, B. B., Pinsky, R. H., Wolf, S., & Wolff, H. G. Appraisal of the results of treatments of stress disorders. *Research Publication of the Association for Research in Nervous and Mental Disease*, 1953, *31*, 167–177.

Bonilla, K. B., Quigley, W. F., & Bowers, W. F. Experiences with hypnosis on a surgical service. *Military Medicine*, 1961, *126*, 364–370.

British Tuberculosis Association, Research Committee. Hypnosis for asthma—A controlled trial. *British Medical Journal*, 1968, *4*, 71–76.

Buck, R. The class method in the treatment of essential hypertension. *Annals of Internal Medicine*, 1937, *11*, 514–518.

Cassell, W. A., Fraser, H. N., & Spellman, M. B. Psychiatric morbidity and utilization of insured health services. *Canadian Psychiatric Association Journal*, 1972, *17*, 417–421.

Cassell, W. A., Grunberg, F., & Fraser, H. N. The discharged chronic patient's utilization of health resources. *Canadian Psychiatric Association Journal*, 1968, *13*, 23–29.

Cassem, N. H., & Hackett, T. P. Psychiatric consultation in a coronary care unit. *Annals of Internal Medicine*, 1971, *75*, 9–14.

Chafetz, M. E., Bernstein, N., Sharpe, W., & Schwab, R. S. Short-term group therapy of patients with Parkinson's disease. *New England Journal of Medicine*, 1955, *253*, 961–964.

Chappell, M. N., Stefano, J. J., Rogerson, J. S., & Pike, F. H. The value of group psychological procedures in the treatment of peptic ulcer. *American Journal of Digestive Diseases and Nutrition*, 1937, *3*, 813–817.

Chappell, M. N., & Stevenson, T. I. Group psychological training in some organic conditions. *Mental Hygiene*, 1936, *20*, 588–597.

Cromwell, R. L., Butterfield, E. C., Brayfield, F. M., & Curry, J. L. *Acute myocardial infarction: Reaction and recovery*. St. Louis, Mo.: Mosby, 1977.

Cummings, N. A. The health model as entree to the human services model in psychotherapy. *The Clinical Psychologist*, 1975, *29*(1), 19–21.

Cummings, N. A., & Follette, W. T. Brief psychotherapy and medical utilization in a prepaid health plan setting: Part II. *Medical Care*, 1968, *6*, 31–41.

Cummings, N. A., & Follette, W. T. Brief psychotherapy and medical utilization: An eight year follow-up. In H. Dörken & Associates, *The professional psychologist today: New developments in law, health insurance, and health practice*. San Francisco: Jossey-Bass, 1976.

Davis, H. S. The role of a crisis intervention treatment in the patient's recovery from elective surgery (Doctoral dissertation, Northwestern University, 1973). *Dissertation Abstracts International*, 1974, *34*, 3490B. (University Microfilms No. 73-30, 570).

Densen, P., Shapiro, S., & Einhorn, M. Concerning high and low utilizers of service in a medical care plan and the persistence of utilization levels over a three year period. *Milbank Medical Fund Quarterly*, 1959, *37*, 217–250.

Doberneck, R. C., Griffen, W. O., Jr., Papermaster, A. A., Bonello, F., & Wagensteen, O. H. Hypnosis as an adjunct to surgical therapy. *Surgery*, 1959, *46*, 299–304.

Dörken, H., & Associates. *The professional psychologist today: New developments in law, health insurance, and health practice*. San Francisco: Jossey-Bass, 1976.

Dumas, R. G., Anderson, B. J., & Leonard, R. C. The importance of the expressive function in preoperative preparation. In J. K. Skipper, Jr., & R. C. Leonard (Eds.), *Social interaction and patient care*. Philadelphia, Pa.: J. B. Lippincott, 1965.

Edwards, G. Hypnotic treatment for asthma: Real and illusory results. *British Medical Journal*, 1960, *2*, 492–497.

Egbert, L. D., Battit, G. E., Turndorf, H., & Beecher, H. K. Value of a preoperative visit by an anesthetist: A study of doctor-patient rapport. *Journal of the American Medical Association*, 1963, *185*, 553–555.

Egbert, L. D., Battit, G. E., Welch, C. E., & Bartlett, M. K. Reduction of postoperative pain by encouragement and instruction of patients: A study of doctor-patient rapport. *New England Journal of Medicine*, 1964, *270*, 825–827.

Fichtler, H., & Zimmerman, R. R. Changes in reported pain from tension headaches. *Perceptual and Motor Skills*, 1973, *36*, 712.

Florell, J. L. Crisis intervention in orthopedic surgery. (Doctoral dissertation, Northwestern University, 1971). *Dissertation Abstracts International*, 1971, *32*, 3633B. (University Microfilms No. 71-30, 799)

Follette, W., & Cummings, N. A. Psychiatric services and medical utilization in a prepaid health plan setting: Part I. *Medical Care*, 1967, *5*, 25–35.

Godbole, A., & Verinis, J. S. Brief psychotherapy in the treatment of emotional disorders in physically ill geriatric patients. *Gerentologist*, 1974, *14*, 143–148.

Goldberg, I. D., Krantz, G., & Locke, B. Z. Effects of a short-term outpatient psychiatric therapy benefit on the utilization of medical services in a prepaid group practice medical program. *Medical Care*, 1970, *8*, 419–428.

Goshen, C. E. The high cost of non-psychiatric care. *GP*, 1963, *27*(4), 227–235.

Goshen, C. E. Functional versus organic diagnostic problems. *New York State Journal of Medicine*, 1969, *69*, 2332–2338.

Grace, W. J., Pinsky, R. H., & Wolff, H. G. The treatment of ulcerative colitis: II. *Gastroenterology*, 1954, *26*, 462–468.

Greene, C. S., & Laskin, D. M. Long-term evaluation of conservative treatment of myofascial pain-dysfunction syndrome. *Journal of the American Dental Association*, 1974, *89*, 1365–1368.

Groen, J. Treatment of bronchial asthma by combination of ACTH and psychotherapy. *Acta Allergologica*, 1953, Supplement 3, 21–48.

Groen, J., & Bastiaans, J. Psychotherapy of ulcerative colitis. *Gastroenterology*, 1951, *17*, 344–352.

Groen, J. J. & Pelser, H. E. Experiences with, and results

of, group psychotherapy in patients with bronchial asthma. *Journal of Psychosomatic Research*, 1960, *5*, 191–205.

Gruen, W. A successful application of systematic self-relaxation and self-suggestions about postoperative reactions in a case of cardiac surgery. *International Journal of Clinical and Experimental Hypnosis*, 1972, *20*, 143–151.

Hadden, S. B. Treatment of the neuroses by class technic. *Annals of Internal Medicine*, 1942, *16*, 33–37.

Harris, H. I. Efficient psychotherapy for the large outpatient clinic. *New England Journal of Medicine*, 1939, *221*, 1–5.

Hinkle, L. E., & Wolff, H. G. The nature of man's adaptation to his total environment and the relation of this to illness. *Archives of Internal Medicine*, 1957, *99*, 442–460.

Ibrahim, M. A., Feldman, J. G., Sultz, H. A., Staiman, M. G., Young, L. J., & Dean, D. Management after myocardial infarction: A controlled trial of the effect of group psychotherapy. *International Journal of Psychiatry in Medicine*, 1974, *5*, 253–268.

Jackson, K. Psychologic preparation as a method of reducing the emotional trauma of anesthesia in children. *Anesthesiology*, 1951, *12*, 293–300.

Janis, I. L. *Psychological stress: Psychoanalytic and behavioral studies of surgical patients.* New York: Wiley, 1958.

Karusch, A., Daniels, G. E., O'Connor, J. G., & Stern, L. O. The response to psychotherapy in chronic ulcerative colitis: Pretreatment factors. *Psychosomatic Medicine*, 1968, *30*, 255–276.

Karusch, A., Daniels, G. E., O'Connor, J. G., & Stern, L. O. The response to psychotherapy in chronic ulcerative colitis: II. Factors arising from the therapeutic situation. *Psychosomatic Medicine*, 1969, *31*, 201–226.

Kleeman, S. T. Psychiatric contributions in the treatment of asthma. *Annals of Allergy*, 1967, *85*, 611–619.

Kogan, W. S., Thompson, D. J., Brown, J. R., & Newman, H. F. Impact of integration of mental health service and comprehensive care. *Medical Care*, 1975, *13*, 934–942.

Kolouch, F. T. Role of suggestion in surgical convalescence. *Archives of Surgery*, 1962, *85*, 304–315.

Kolouch, F. T. Hypnosis and surgical convalescence: A study of subjective factors in postoperative recovery. *American Journal of Clinical Hypnosis*, 1964, *7*, 120–129.

Lange-Nielsen, F., & Retterstal, N. Group psychotherapy in bronchial asthma. *Acta Psychiatrica et Neurologica Scandinavica*, 1959, *34*, Supplement 136, 187–204.

Layne, O. L., Jr., & Yudofsky, S. C. Postoperative psychosis in cardiotomy patients: The role of organic and psychiatric factors. *New England Journal of Medicine*, 1971, *284*, 3518–3520.

Lazarus, H. R. & Hagens, J. H. Prevention of psychosis following open-heart surgery. *American Journal of Psychiatry*, 1968, *124*, 1190–1195.

LeShan, L. L., & Gassmann, M. L. Some observations on psychotherapy with patients suffering from neoplastic disease. *American Journal of Psychotherapy*, 1958, *12*, 723–734.

Liebman, R., Minuchin, S., & Baker, L. The use of structural family therapy in the treatment of intractable asthma. *American Journal of Psychiatry*, 1974, *131*, 535–539.

Lipsitt, D. R. Curing the patient who clings to ill health. *Medical Opinion*, 1971, *7*(4), 46–49.

Loubatières, A. Remarks concerning some recent reports on therapy of diabetes. In E. Shafrir (Ed.), *Impact of insulin on metabolic pathways.* New York: Academic Press, 1972.

Lupton, D. E. Psychological aspects of temporamandibular joint dysfunction. *Journal of the American Dental Association*, 1969, *79*, 131–136.

Lutker, E. R. Treatment of migraine headache by conditioned relaxation: A case study. *Behavior Therapy*, 1971, *2*, 592–593.

Maher-Loughnan, G. P. Hypnosis and autohypnosis for the treatment of asthma. *International Journal of Clinical and Experimental Hypnosis*, 1970, *18*, 1–14.

Maher-Loughnan, G. P., MacDonald, N., Mason, A. A., & Fry, L. Controlled trial of hypnosis in the symptomatic treatment of asthma. *British Medical Journal*, 1962, *2*, 371–376.

Marmer, M. J. Hypnoanalgesia and hypnoanesthesia for cardiac surgery. *Journal of the American Medical Association*, 1959, *171*, 512–517.

Mascia, A. V., & Reiter, S. R. Group therapy in the rehabilitation of the severe chronic asthmatic child. *Journal of Asthma Research*, 1971, *9*, 81–85.

Mechanic, D. Response factors in illness: The study of illness behavior. *Social Psychiatry*, 1966, *1*, 11–20.

Miller, H., & Baruch, D. W. Psychological dynamics in allergic patients as shown in group and individual therapy. *Journal of Consulting Psychology*, 1948, *12*, 111–115.

Mitchell, K. R., & Mitchell, D. M. Migraine: An exploratory treatment application of programmed behavior therapy techniques. *Journal of Psychosomatic Research*, 1971, *15*, 137–157.

Mone, L. Short-term group psychotherapy with postcardiac patients. *International Journal of Group Psychotherapy*, 1970, *20*, 99–108.

Moore, N. Behavior therapy in bronchial asthma: A controlled study. *Journal of Psychosomatic Research*, 1965, *9*, 257–276.

O'Connor, J. G., Daniels, G., Flood, C., Karusch, A., Moses, L., & Stern, L. O. An evaluation of the effectiveness of psychotherapy in the treatment of ulcerative colitis. *Annals of Internal Medicine*, 1964, *60*, 587–602.

Orgei, S. L. Effects of psychoanalysis on the course of peptic ulcer. *Psychosomatic Medicine*, 1958, *60*, 117–125.

Pattison, E. M., Rhodes, R. J., & Dudley, D. L. Response to group treatment in patients with severe chronic lung disease. *International Journal of Group Psychotherapy*, 1971, *21*, 214–225.

Paulley, J. W., & Haskell, D. A. L. The treatment of migraine without drugs. *Journal of Psychosomatic Research*, 1975, *19*, 367–374.

Pomp, A. M. Psychotherapy for the myofascial pain-dysfunction syndrome: A study of factors coinciding with symptom remission. *Journal of the American Dental Association*, 1974, *89*, 629–632.

Pratt, J. H. The influence of emotions in the causation and cure of psychoneuroses. *International Clinics*, 1934, *4*(Series 44), 1–16.

Rahe, R. H., O'Neil, T. Hagan, A., & Arthur, R. J. Brief group therapy following myocardial infarction: Eighteen month follow-up of a controlled trial. *International Journal of Psychiatry in Medicine*, 1975, *6*, 349–358.

Rahe, R. H., Tuffli, C. F., Jr., Suchor, R. J., & Arthur, R. J. Group therapy in the outpatient management of post-myocardial infarction patients. *Psychiatry in Medicine*, 1973, *4*, 77–88.

Ramsay, R. A., Wittkower, E. D., & Warnes, H. Treatment of psychosomatic disorders. In B. B. Wolman (Ed.),

The therapist's handbook: Treatment of mental disorders. New York: Van Nostrand Reinhold, 1976.

Reckless, J. B. A behavioral treatment of asthma in modified group therapy. *Psychosomatics,* 1971, *12,* 168–173.

Rhoades, W. Group training in thought control for relieving nervous disorders. *Mental Hygiene,* 1935, *19,* 373–386.

Ripley, H. S., Wolf, S., & Wolff, H. G. Treatment in a psychosomatic clinic: Preliminary report. *Journal of the American Medical Association,* 1948, *138,* 949–951.

Rosenbaum, A. H., & Steinhilber, R. M. Psychosomatic disorders. Combined therapeutic approach. *Minnesota Medicine,* 1973, *56*(8), 677–679.

Schoenberg, B., & Carr, A. C. An investigation of criteria for brief psychotherapy of neurodermatitis. *Psychosomatic Medicine,* 1963, *25,* 253–263.

Schoenberg, B., & Senescu, R. Group psychotherapy for patients with chronic multiple somatic complaints. *Journal of Chronic Disease,* 1966, *19,* 649–657.

Schofield, W. The psychologist as a health care professional. *Intellect,* January 1975, *103,* 255–258.

Schüffel, W., & Schonecke, O. W. Assessment of hostility in the course of psychosomatic treatment of three patients with functional disorders. *Psychotherapy and Psychosomatics,* 1972, *20,* 282–293.

Schulz, R. Effects of control and predictability on the physical and psychological well-being of the institutionalized aged. *Journal of Personality and Social Psychology,* 1976, *33,* 563–573.

Sclare, A. B., & Crockett, A. J. Group psychotherapy in bronchial asthma. *Journal of Psychosomatic Research,* 1957, *2,* 157–171.

Seitz, P. F. D. Dynamically-oriented brief psychotherapy: Psychocutaneous excoriation syndromes. *Psychosomatic Medicine,* 1953, *15,* 200–213.

Selye, H. *The stress of life.* New York: McGraw-Hill, 1956.

Sinclair-Gieben, A. H. C., & Chalmers, D. Evaluation of treatment of warts by hypnosis. *Lancet,* 1959, *2,* 769–770.

Skipper, J. K., Jr., & Leonard, R. C. Children, stress and hospitalization: A field experiment. *Journal of Health and Social Behavior,* 1968, *9,* 275–287.

Smith, J. M., & Burns, C. L. C. The treatment of asthmatic children by hypnotic suggestion. *British Journal of Diseases of the Chest,* 1960, *54,* 78–81.

Snowden, E. N. Mass psychotherapy. *Lancet,* 1940, *2,* 769–770.

Sperling, M. Asthma in children: An evaluation of concept and therapies. *Journal of the American Academy of Child Psychiatry,* 1968, *7,* 44–58.

Surman, O. S., Hackett, T. P., Silverberg, E. L., & Behrendt, D. M. Usefulness of a psychiatric intervention in patients undergoing cardiac surgery. *Archives of General Psychiatry,* 1974, *30,* 830–835.

Tasto, D. L., & Hinkle, J. E. Muscle relaxation treatment for tension headache. *Behavior Research and Therapy,* 1973, *11,* 347–349.

Thurlow, H. J. General susceptibility to illness: A selective review. *Canadian Medical Association Journal,* 1967, *97,* 1397–1404.

Titchener, J. L., Sheldon, M. B., & Ross, W. D. Changes in blood pressure of hypertensive patients with and without group psychotherapy. *Journal of Psychosomatic Research,* 1959, *4,* 10–12.

Walsh, M. N., & Kierland, R. R. Psychotherapy in the treatment of neurodermatitis. *Proceedings of the Staff Meetings of the Mayo Clinic,* 1947, *22,* 509–512.

Weinstock, H. I. Hospital psychotherapy in severe ulcerative colitis: Its ineffectiveness in preventing surgical measures and recurrences. *Archives of General Psychiatry,* 1961, *22,* 509–512.

Weinstock, H. I. Successful treatment of ulcerative colitis by psychoanalysis: A survey of 28 cases with follow-up. *Journal of Psychosomatic Research,* 1962, *6,* 243–249.

White, H. C. Hypnosis in bronchial asthma. *Journal of Psychosomatic Research,* 1961, *5,* 272–279.

Yorkston, N. H., McHugh, R. B., Brady, R., Serber, M., & Sergeant, H. G. S. Verbal desensitization in bronchial asthma. *Journal of Psychosomatic Research,* 1974, *18,* 371–376.

At the time of original publication of this article, *Mary Ellen Olbrisch* was at Langley Porter Neuropsychiatric Institute, University of California, San Francisco.

This article is based on a manuscript submitted to the Critical Review series of the Florida State University Department of Psychology. Appreciation is expressed to Lee Sechrest and Richard L. Hagen, who assisted in revision of an earlier version of this article.

Psychology as a Health Profession

Logan Wright

This article discusses the contribution of psychology to the treatment of supposed physical health care problems, with particular emphasis on children. A number of behavioral health interventions are described. The author estimates that from one third to one half of all children hospitalized for physical health problems have a highly significant behavioral component to their illnesses independent of the emotional problems caused by the hospitalization itself.

The idea of psychology as a health profession carries different implications depending on how the term "health" is defined, particularly as it relates to *mental* health. Many psychologists object to the concept of mental health since, to them, it condones the so-called medical model for understanding and treating disorders of affect and personality. Unfortunately, however, our disdain for the medical model may have obscured our view of the importance of psychology's role in treating people who are physically ill.

The usual figure for estimating the number of individuals, who at sometime in their life will require professional help for mental or emotional problems, is ten percent. In contrast, everyone is physically ill from time to time. Most individuals maintain some form of chronic physical problem during the middle and latter years of life and finally all life is ended by either an illness or accident. The number of individuals, then, who at sometime will require professional help from a *health* professional, is 100%.

One facet of my job is to attend ward rounds in a children's hospital. After eight years of consistent observation, I can say that somewhere between one-third to one-half of all our children's hospital patients have a highly significant behavioral concomitant to their physical illnesses, aside from the emotional problems caused by the experience of hospitalization itself. Sometimes the illness is psychosomatic, such as in cases of tracheotomy addiction, encopresis, and a variety of dermatologic and gastrointestinal problems. On other occasions, there may be personality factors which hamper recovery as is often the case in hemophilia, diabetes, or burns. Finally, there are the debilitating emotional or developmental sequelae to many diseases which might be avoided with sophisticated behavioral interventions.

I can further illustrate how much disease-related psychopathology exists, by citing a few common physical/behavioral problems. Any psychologist who successfully treats encopresis or fecal soiling is overwhelmed with referrals. Our clinic sees about one new patient per week, verifying the high incidence of this problem. The number of individuals suffering from bruxism or teeth grinding is estimated at between 20 and 30 million (Kennedy, 1975). If this is accurate, they have done over one *billion* dollars of dental destruction through their incessant gnashing. This also figures out to be over 100 bruxists for every applied psychologist in America. My judgment is that over one half of all the psychopathology of children in this world is related to a physical-behavioral symptom of some sort for which help is usually sought first from a dentist or medical doctor; and that *less than* one half of the psychopathology of children falls within the traditional nosological categories of neurosis, psychosis, and character disorder.

Where research is concerned, my examples fall toward the tender-minded end of the relevance vs. rigor continuum. But, in spite of the low prestige status of unrigorous research, it was Einstein who said, "I have little patience with scientists who take a board of wood, look for its thinnest part, and drill a great number of holes where drilling is easy."[1] Having read "extensions" of research knowledge which involve nothing more than the 12th or 13th variation in the reinforcement schedule for the same project, I must admit that I tend to agree with Einstein. Any relatively new field, such as the behavioral aspects of illness, tends to foster exploratory research. It often takes the form of an inductive search for variables which will differentiate between a pathological and a presumably normal sample. Let me cite a study involving the battered child as an example of this embryologic state of research, and to illustrate the kinds of experience which can cause one to begin thinking of psychology as a health profession.

It may surprise some, but is nonetheless true, that in a time of space age technology we must still protect children against medieval cruelty. With this in mind, 13 parents who had been convicted of physically abusing their children, and 13 matched controls, were given a battery of tests as part of an inductive quest for a personality profile of the battering parent. The battering parents appeared *healthier* on the three significant subscales for instruments which had been logically derived, where the items were thus based on content or face validity and where the social desirability of each item was more obvious. They appeared more *disturbed* on the three significant subscales of the instruments which had been empirically derived, where the items were based on concurrent or statistical validity and where the socially desirable response was more ambiguous.

The tendency of battering parents to be significantly disturbed and capable of abusing their children, while being able to convince others

they are neither disturbed nor capable of abuse, was labeled the "sick but slick syndrome." Now, this is a broad and imprecise term which few self-respecting persons of rigor would be willing to employ; yet, it seemed to catch on among the less discriminating professionals who had previously observed these traits in some battering parents, but had no shorthand means for referring to them. A verbal report of these findings was given at the last APA Convention, and *Psychology Today* picked up on the report and ran a short article. As a result, I have received several hundred reprint requests, far more than for any other article I've ever prepared. This is complemented by the fact that somewhere between 30,000 and 50,000 children are abused annually in the U.S. The moral, as it regards the issue of relevance vs. rigor, should be clear enough. Of equal clarity is the fact that battered children have physical health problems, while the forces which produce those problems are just as obviously psychological in nature. A classic illustration of the untapped promise of medical/behavioral research involves the problem of tracheotomy addiction. This disorder had been known to pediatricians and otolaryngologists for decades. It involves the dependency which a young tracheotomy patient can develop on the tube, so that when normal air passageways are again open, s/he still cannot breathe. If the cannula is removed or occluded, s/he will manifest progressively more labored breathing, become cyanotic (blue), have deep substernal retractions (cave ins) when s/he breathes, and eventually pass out and die. The critical period for addiction appears to involve an infant under one year of age who has his trach for more than 100 days before an attempt is made to decannulate him/her. The largest single study of this problem is from England, and covered 12 cases, four of whom died in the fumbling of physicians' not realizing the patient was addicted, performing the usual surgery to close the trach opening, and then not reintroducing the cannula in sufficient time.

I became acquainted with tracheotomy addiction when two infant boys with this problem appeared in our hospital simultaneously during my first year as a medical psychologist. Though the problem was new to me, I was struck by the fact that psychologists had successfully treated

---

[1] Albert Einstein as quoted by Phillip Frank in "Einstein's Philosophy of Science," *Reviews of Modern Physics*, 1949, *21*.

chronic hiccups and sneezing, and therefore should be able to manage this kind of difficulty. A behavior modification program was devised to shape these children toward normal breathing. Their stage of development demanded somewhat unique reinforcers such as: (1) scooting about in a walker, (2) being tossed in the air and generally roughhoused by their fathers, and (3) baths, on the positive side; and taping one child's shoestrings so he couldn't play with them, on the negative. The latter made me about as popular as a hemorrhoid with the nursing staff and the child's grandparents. But the program works and can routinely overcome addiction in three weeks. This is despite the fact that no successful treatment had previously been identified. Different surgical procedures, cannulae made of exotic plastics and metals, and even gradual corking had all proven ineffectual. The treatment of choice at that time was "time." That is, just letting the child grow and develop, then seeing later if he could give up the cannula. (A more detailed description of this technique can be found in Wright, Nunnery, Eichel & Scott, 1968.) Few psychologists ever find a cure for anything. None of our colleagues will ever provide "cures" for schizophrenia or mental retardation as Jonas Salk cured polio. But those "cures" which do eventuate seem most likely to come in the burgeoning field of medical psychology. And that field is rich. One of the reasons is that many physical health problems are really behavioral problems. As evidence I cite the problem of encopresis or fecal soiling.

Thousands of children possess this difficulty, and estimates are that between 80% and 99% of the problems have a psychogenic basis due to holding in of feces à la Freud anal retentive stage. Although the cause is psychological, the result is physical (chronically distended colon and fecal soiling). The soiling, as you might suspect, can lead to a whole array of new psychological difficulties. A treatment program which is economical of professional time, and one offering quantifiable outcome data based on a significant number of patients treated by means of a standardized program was not available, and had to be developed (Wright, 1973a, Wright, in press a).

Another example of health problems which are equally behavioral involves the sequelae to burns and disfigurement. A study by Wright & Fulwiler (1974) investigated the emotional status of 12 burned children and their mothers, an average of 38 months after the injury. The burned children showed no significant differences from their controls. The *mothers* of burned children, however, showed significantly more distress than their controls on 10 of 28 study measures. This work failed to support the hypothesis of preexisting emotional disturbance in the child victim or the notion of a lasting and dramatically negative emotional impact of burns upon the *child*. The finding of numerous differences between experimental and control *mothers* suggests either that the victims' mothers were disturbed to begin with and thus may have somehow contributed to the probability of an accident; or that they may respond to the burning of their offspring with less emotional resiliency than the victims themselves. In any event, the results suggested that behavioral practitioners have an important, health-related role to play with the mothers of such victims, and we may even have a prophylactic role to play with certain accidentogenic parents *prior to* a tragedy.

Another medical problem which is really a behavioral one involves refusal of oral medication which is necessary to sustain life. Wright, Woodcock and Scott (1969) report on the treatment of such difficulties. Most of these cases are children in the two to three year age bracket. Their actions seem to represent a pathologic expression of typical behavior at Erikson's autonomy stage. The patients will refuse pills by turning their heads or locking their mouths shut. If the medicine is forced into their mouths, it is immediately spit out.

Not willing to be outdone, modern medical science has invented the nasogastric tube, which is inserted through the nose into the stomach. Cuffs are placed on the patient's elbows so that they cannot be bent and thus the tube cannot be removed manually. Pills are dissolved in water and gavaged by means of a syringe, through the tube and into the stomach. The only problem is that these patients will then regurgitate any substance so injected. Unless they are conditioned to voluntarily accept oral medication, they will die. Several such patients, including victims of kidney disease and cancer, have been seen in our center. Is their difficulty a health problem? Of course it is. Is it a behavioral problem? Obviously. Surely the team which treats them could benefit from the involvement of psychologists.

About 1% of the total epileptic population has seizures which are precipitated by some form of visual stimulation, sometimes called photoconvulsive cases. Those of you who have observed EEG's have probably seen the stroboscopic light stimulation which is administered to check for this difficulty. There is considerable clinical data which indicate that some patients intentionally induce such seizures. The reason(s) for such induction can only be speculated upon. Parents who react to such self induction by becoming upset or by granting immediate attention may be quite reinforcing. Another possibility is suggested by the extensive body of literature indicating that mild electrical stimulation delivered directly to the brain can be pleasurable for both human and infrahuman subjects. Possibly a mechanism of this type is involved in cases of self-induced seizures. In any event, the problem is obviously one of physical health (the seizures) and just as obviously affected by a behavioral/psychological variable (the self-inducing component). Prior to an aversive conditioning report from our Center (Wright, 1973b) no treatment literature on self-induction (as opposed to the medication-oriented approaches to the seizures themselves) existed.

The work with self-induced seizures has caused a few pediatric neurologists to ask for help in desperate situations where involuntary seizures could not be controlled. One such case involved a 14-year-old boy whose seizures were organic rather than psychogenic, and consisted of fainting states lasting from 15 to 45 seconds. In spite of high average intelligence, he could not attend school because he fainted between 3 and 30 times an hour. Even when the patient was placed in a special education class and tied to his chair, his fainting-seizures were so distracting to the class that he had to be removed. Every feasible medicinal regime, and even seizure control by diet, had been tried unsuccessfully. Here was a boy of high achievement motivation and average intelligence, free of emotional and characterologic symptoms, who couldn't go to school. We were asked to see if aversive conditioning which had proven effective with self induced seizures might provide stimulus control over his *involuntary* seizures.

We found that a loud noise or being required to perform a cognitive task (such as answering the question: What is the capital of the state of New York?) could restore a normal state of consciousness if given during the aura or early phase of a seizure. This stage could be identified clinically by observing dropping eyelids, nodding of the head, slowness of speech, etc. Mild electric shock provided an even more effective means of interrupting the seizures.

We conditioned the patient by administering mild electrical shock as immediately as possible following the initiation of clinically visible seizure-related behavior. After three days, the number of seizure episodes had been reduced by approximately 75%. At that point, the patient was given an EEG, and we discovered that he was having approximately two subclinical seizures for every clinically observable one. We then decided that electrical shock would also be administered upon initiation of subclinical seizure activity as measured by the EEG. Surprisingly, the subclinical seizures could also be interrupted. After two days of such conditioning the patient would begin to seizure for one to two seconds (about the time necessary for us to notice it on the EEG and administer the electrical shock), then the seizure would be aborted. Apparently, the patient had learned to expect the shock and was conditioned *not* to seizure. Our EEG data were examined by three neurologists who were amazed at the counter conditioning for all but the first one to two seconds of the seizure.

Stimulus control over the involuntary seizure activity of cats has been previously demonstrated by Sterman (Sterman and Wyrwicka, 1967). He also reports (Sterman and Friar, 1972) the control of involuntary seizures in a 28-year-old woman via a biofeedback technique for influencing SMR, a 12–14c/sec rhythm (as measured by EEG) appearing over the sensorimeter cortex during voluntary suppression of movement. Stimulus control over the involuntary electrical activity of the human brain brings with it a whole array of almost science fiction-like possibilities which are both psychological as well as physical-health related.

Another area of legitimate psychological concern is the behavioral residual to various medical disorders. The study cited earlier on sequelae to burns is one case in point. Two other studies, one of cognitive and intellectual sequelae to H-Flu meningitis (Wright & Jimmerson, 1971) and one on Rocky Mountain Spotted Fever (Wright, 1972) also fall within this category. The medical literature in both areas suggests that, based on clinical observation, patients seem to emerge intellectually unscathed from a single bout with these diseases. To test this assumption, a battery of cognitive and intellectual measures was administered to victims of both diseases and matched controls. Significant differences favoring controls were found for both diseases on measure of perceptual-motor functioning and abstract thinking ability. The pattern was similar to that seen in children often diagnosed as having learning disabilities. The diseases are physical, but the sequelae are of obvious relevance to behavioral practitioners.

Not all diseases which affect development are "caught"; some are inborn. For instance, the medical literature on congenital heart defects consistently reports delayed performance of these children on measures of both cognitive intellectual and personal/social development. Amazingly, retardation in *these* areas appears more extensive than for *physical* development. No direct link between the physical problem and developmental delay in the other areas has been identified. The mechanism underlying the intellectual and emotional delay might be a tendency of parents to infantilize their cardiac involved children in a way which stifles psychological development. Now, to test this hypothesis, someone needs to develop something like a Kiddy Infantilization SubScale (KISS). Such a measure could also be employed by cardiologists to assess parents' tendencies to infantilize and then to make recommendations, possibly for help from a behavioral consultant.

Indirect psychotherapy for children with chronic health problems is another promising area for both clinical work and research. The problem of battered children cited earlier provides such an opportunity. Techniques for helping these children via psychotherapeutic intervention with their parents are summarized by Kempe & Helfer (1972). Similar research at the University of Oklahoma Health Sciences Center with parents of children possessing a variety of chronic diseases has been generously supported by the vocational rehabilitation program within the U.S. Department of HEW.[2] Much presumably physical disability results from psychological traits such as dependency, external locus of control and tendencies to acquiesce to illness or injury. Skills-oriented group consultation for parents of early adolescents with chronic physical problems can help these parents to relate to their chronically ill children in such a way as to avert *unnecessary* disability (Wright, in press b; in press c).

The dying child may represent the classic medical/behavioral problem in which psychological intervention is a most crucial form of therapy. In spite of the fact that we have sent men to the moon and developed weapons of destruction beyond our wildest imagination, we have not yet learned how to die, or more importantly to be of genuine aid to a child who must do so. Death is life's greatest developmental challenge, but it is often handled more poorly than birth, walking, talking, starting school, puberty and other less pervasive milestones. Most parents of terminally ill children give clear signals to their offspring that they wish to avoid the topic of death. Yet I have never observed a dying child old enough to talk who I didn't feel knew it if he were dying. This combination produces some most destructive circumstances. The child cannot deal with his concerns openly by verbalizing them. S/he must rely exclusively on fantasy, and (even with death) fantasy is always more terrible than reality. The child must avoid talking of death, not for his own sake, but because of those around him. This forces him to spend his failing energies for the protection of others, at a time when his own needs for support are greatest. The psychologists in our Center have attempted to understand these dynamics, and the means of helping parents to cope with them (Wright, 1974; Vore & Wright, 1974; Wright, in press c).

Death is the most obvious and pervasive

[2] This research was supported in part by Grant #15-P-55228 6-02 from the U.S. Social and Rehabilitation Service.

health problem. In this area, if no other, psychology should become a health profession.

There are a variety of other legitimate health problems to which professional psychologists should respond. These include refusal of solid foods or fluids, kidney transplants, pica and lead poisoning, psychogenic vomiting, sleep disturbances, self mutilation, ulcers and gastrointestinal spasms, psychogenic pain, thumbsucking and other dentally deleterious habits such as tongue thrust swallowing and bruxism (teeth grinding), sexual ambiguity, failure to thrive or psychosocial dwarfism, prematurity, phenylketonuria, hypothyroidism, cleft palate, and I could go on. All of these pertain only to the domain of children, and I have not even touched on the multitude of behavioral medical problems of adults including those classified as geratologic and rehabilitation-related.

But, I would hasten to point out the fact that if one suggests that psychology is, or should become, a health profession, s/he does not necessarily support the medical model for conceptualizing and treating disturbances of affect and personality. The medical model is a term which has come to mean more different things to different people than words like "ego," "schizophrenia" and "mind"; or concepts of what really makes America great. In general, it suggests that abnormal behavior derives from internal conditions (anxieties, attitudes, etc.) much as physical illness results from germs, organic conditions, and the like. It discourages the treatment of overt behavior or symptoms, and generally does not focus on the environmental factors which may have produced the disease. The patient must admit his difficulty (implying helplessness) and seek help from others (dependency). In so doing, he may jeopardize both his insurability and future employment opportunities. He is encouraged to convalesce, that is, remain protected from the environment with which he cannot cope. Generally, this "I'm sick" behavior is antagonistic to the well behavior which we refer to as "adaptation," "adjustment," "effectiveness," "competence" or "mental health." Treatment for the problems of (mental) illness according to the medical model must be by a highly trained professional (no teachers or other paraprofessionals, please) and

in a professional location such as a hospital or doctor's office. Some parents are so intimidated by this concept that they are afraid to maintain even the normal controlling relationships necessary for proper execution of their parental role.

The concept of *mental* illness may have served well in the efforts 50 to 100 years ago to humanize society's treatment of individuals whose behavior was deviant. A person who was sick could not be faulted for contracting a disease. S/He could still, however, be isolated, ostracized, pitied, and expected not to exert energy or assume responsibility. Such a concept has obviously outlived its usefulness and must be discarded. But now, while in the process of turning up our noses at the medical model for *mental* illness, we should be careful not to "throw out the baby with the bed pan." The christening of psychology as a new health profession should not direct us backward toward a medical model for conceptualizing and treating emotional problems. An example of such a fallacy is illustrated in the following anecdote.

On March 31–April 1, 1973, a special meeting of APA's Council of Representatives was called to consider the crises created by drastic cutbacks in government support for the training, research, and service programs of psychology. One proposal advanced was for APA to employ a full time central office staff person in charge of Health Related Affairs. At that point, one council person rose to object. He stated that he would oppose any motion which contained the word "health." This action, he said, was based on violent objection to the medical model for conceptualizing and treating emotional disturbance.

The opposition makes for polemic clarity, but such a stance risks disenfranchisement by governmental and private insurance carriers for thousands of colleagues who offer direct services to the public. It would also deal us out of research programs conducted by several of the National Institutes of Health, eliminate funding for trainees in health-related areas and cut off badly needed fiscal transfusions for a profession already suffering from monetary hemophilia due to inflation, and cut by government austerity. After all, more money for any branch of psychology means more jobs for graduates, and that means more money for universities to pay teachers and researchers from all psychological subspecialities.

In January of this year, a former student of mine, who now works in the U.S. Senate, scheduled me to meet with a member of the Health Subcommittee from the Senate Committee on Labor and Public Welfare. This committee member had been appointed by Senator Kennedy and given the responsibility for authoring the language for a bill on national health insurance. My mission, on behalf of psychology's advocacy organizations, once I decided to accept it was to persuade the committee members to include psychologists as eligible for direct payment in the same manner that psychiatrists, optometrists, and podiatrists had already been. Although this inclusion may not be a "mission impossible," should we fail, the public could disavow any knowledge of our discipline and the *practice* of psychology would self destruct. There are times, I must confess, when I think I smell smoke.

In pursuing the above assignment, I applied the most exotic of modern technology in an attempt to free the prisoner (psychology) from a dungeon located in the tropical kingdom of Senatorial Bureaucratica. Only one strategy showed any promise for springing our captive profession! It was a trial in which we contended that psychology is more legitimately a health profession than is psychiatry. The impetus for national health insurance, you see, is primarily from organizations for the disadvantaged and from organized labor. The working classes and the unemployed are not overly concerned about mental health benefits, particularly expensive, long-term psychotherapy. They would rather have the limited amount of available funds spread to as many recipients as possible, for the most basic medical care: i.e. periodic checkups, setting of broken bones, surgery, filling or pulling of teeth, etc. They fear the exploitation of the programs by a recipient who would drain off a large percentage of the funds through expensive treatment that could be avoided, as they see it, if s/he "would just shape up." They also fear exploitation by mental health professionals, some of whose ideas seem a little weird to people of the proponents' socioeconomic and educational points of view. As a result, only the *mental* health benefits of Kennedy's national

health insurance bill have been singled out for the most restrictive utilization.

Now, if psychology can show the bill's supporters that psychiatry is concerned almost exclusively with *mental* health problems falling within the traditional nosological categories of neurosis, psychosis and character disorder; if we can further show the promise of psychologists' efforts in dealing with some of the leading causes of death such as high blood pressure (hypertension) and related strokes (third leading cause of death), alcohol consumption including related traffic deaths (fourth leading cause of death), suicide, the leading cause of death among college students and scores of other behavioral medical problems; this, the committee member stated, could help to produce a favorable verdict from the jury in the psychology vs. psychiatry as a health profession trial, and do much to enhance our inclusion in the Kennedy version of the national health insurance bill. All this represents just one more reason why psychology should "get with it" in becoming a health profession.

In 1968, APA's Board of Professional Affairs requested a study on "the Role of Psychology in the Delivery of Health Services." The product of that effort was an article in the *American Psychologist* (Schofield, 1969). To the question of psychology's being a health profession, the article states "there is no reason why psychology should be generally perceived as a health science any more than geology." (The geologic analogy, I think, is a fortunate one, since if we had studied both it and proctology, then maybe we *would* know our anal orifice from a hole in the ground.) The article continues: "It would be fair to say that psychology (unlike physiology) is not a health science, except that one prominent field of applied psychology addresses itself to the problems of mental health." (Pg. 566) The article cites the testimony of an unnamed distinguished psychologist, who in testifying before the Senate Committee on Governmental Research felt constrained to say: "While I am not a member of the health sciences, I am a member of the life sciences." (Pg. 567)

All of the above claims are supported by a survey of Psychological Abstracts for 1967–1968 which revealed that 1 percent of the articles or less were published on each of the following topics: surgery, smoking, cancer, highway safety, accidents, population control, fertility, and abortion. Fifty-five % of the articles, on the other hand, fell within the three combined categories of psychotherapy, schizophrenia and mental retardation (Pg. 568). The article concludes by saying that "Psychology now occupies a rather restricted position as a health profession, a position manifested primarily by those persons identified as 'clinical psychologists'." How as recently as 1969, we could be so myopic as to disregard the potential contribution of applied, developmental, and physiological psychologists to problems of organic illness is hard to fathom. But the report, of course, didn't create the conditions; it only reported them.

Psychology has developed rapidly of late. We may be at a stage anagolous to adolescence. Problems involving health-related psychopathology are cropping up like ancillary hair. Let's presume, for the sake of illustrative euphemisms, while not implying any sexist tendencies, that psychology is male; and thus the hair is facial. One of three things will happen to it. Some with trichotillomanic tendencies will attempt to excoriate it, casting aside any new product of such development. Others, motivated by a desire to be well-groomed where scientific rigor or traditional nosological areas of psychopathology are concerned, will be more subtle and less harsh, resorting to Nair, shaving or maybe even an "ignore-it-and-maybe-it-will-go-away" attitude. Some, hopefully many, will let it flourish, maybe even apply a growth stimulating tonic or hormone. Let's hear it for a hairy, healthy psychology. Or, better yet, a psychology of health.

References

Kempe, C. H. & Helfer, R. E. *Helping the battered child and his family.* Philadelphia: J. B. Lippincott Co. 1972.

Kennedy, C. Bruxism. *Cosmopolitan,* 1975, 82–88.

Schofield, W. The role of psychology in the delivery of health services. *American Psychologist,* 1969, *24,* 565–584.

Sterman, M. B. & Wyrwicka, W. EEG correlates of sleep: Evidence for separate forebrain substrates. *Brain Research,* 1967, *6,* 143–163.

Sterman, M. B. & Friar, L. Suppression of seizures in an epileptic following sensorimotor EEG feedback training. *Electroencephalography & Clinical Neurophysiology,* 1972, *33,* 89–95.

Task Force on Health Research Newsletter, 1974, *1.*

Task Force on Health Research Newsletter, 1974, *3,* 16–17.

Vore, D. & Wright, L. Psychological management of the family and the dying child. In R. E. Hardy & J. G. Cull (Eds.) Therapeutic needs of the family: *Problems, descriptions and therapeutic approaches.* Illinois: Charles C Thomas, 1974.

Wright, L. Intellectual sequelae of Rocky Mountain Spotted Fever. *Journal of Abnormal Psychology,* 1972, *80,* 315–316.

Wright, L. Handling the encopretic child. *Professional Psychology,* 1973(a), *4,* 137–145.

Wright, L. Aversive conditioning of self-induced seizures. *Behavior Therapy,* 1973(b), *4,* 712–713.

Wright, L. An emotional support program for parents of dying children. *Journal of Clinical Child Psychology,* 1974, *3,* 37–38.

Wright, L. Indirect treatment through principles-oriented parent consultation. *Journal of Consulting and Clinical Psychology,* in press(b).

Wright, L. Outcome of a standardized program for treating psychogenic encopresis. *Professional Psychology,* in press(a).

Wright, L. *The ruling parent.* N. W.: Psychological Dimensions Inc. in press(c).

Wright, L. & Fulwiler, R. Long range emotional sequelae of burns: Effects on children and their mothers. *Pediatric Research,* 1974, *8,* 931–934.

Wright, L. & Jimmerson, S. Intellectual sequelae of hemophilus influenza meningitis. *Journal of Abnormal Psychology,* 1971, *77,* 181–183.

Wright, L., Nunnery, A., Eichel, B., & Scott, R. Application of conditioning principles to problems of tracheostomy addiction in children. *Journal of Consulting and Clinical Psychology,* 1968, *32,* 603–606.

Wright, L., Woodcock, J., & Scott, R. Conditioning children when refusal of oral medication is life threatening. *Pediatrics,* 1969, *44,* 970–972.

At the time of original publication of this article, *Logan Wright* was Associate Professor of Psychology, Children's Hospital, University of Oklahoma, Oklahoma City.

The article was delivered originally as a presidential address to the Southwestern Psychological Association, its style reflecting its initial verbal manner of presentation. The author indicates that while it is appropriate for the thesis of the address to be supported by personal research, this should not suggest that other articles could not also have been cited.

10

Redistributive Aspects of
National Health Insurance

One of the issues surrounding the inclusion or exclusion of mental health benefits in national health insurance has concerned the possibility of reverse redistributive aspects of such coverage. The overall effect of a planned national health insurance program on utilization patterns as a function of race and social class has received serious discussion. It has been argued by some that outpatient psychotherapy would be a benefit disproportionately utilized by the middle class. Moreover, it has been stated that psychotherapy is incompatible with the problems of the poor and that the poor do not utilize such services even when they are available. Hence, psychotherapy benefits under national health insurance are said to represent a subsidy from the poor to the rich.

This has been countered by the argument that the current disproportionate utilization of psychotherapy by the middle class reflects many factors, one of which is that the middle class represents a better-informed consumer group more knowledgeable about psychotherapy and its benefits and that it has sought the inclusion of such services within its health care insurance coverage. Moreover, it is argued that government programs that reimburse health services for the poor do not cover accessible outpatient services for a range of providers and that when such service is covered, the economically poor are often not informed of the coverage. Nonetheless, there is little doubt that the type of problems presented by the average middle-class patient (and the manner in which they are presented and discussed) are easier for middle-class psychotherapists to effectively address than the problems presented by the poor patient.

Obviously, the current redistributive problems are real, but the manner in which national health insurance is structured and the types of mental health services that are covered will influence the general level of utilization and the patterns of utilization by race and social class. Further, specialty training within the context of the entire training system will also influence the availability of appropriate accessible mental health services.

The papers presented in this section concern national health insurance, psychotherapy, and the poor. In the first paper Albee argues that psychotherapy has traditionally been sought out by affluent, female, educated, and suburban clients. He expresses concern that psychotherapy under national health insurance would be a benefit primarily used by similar people and that to the extent that the poor contribute to the financing, it would be a subsidy by the poor to the rich. Albee opposes coverage for any therapy except for genuine organic illness.

McSweeny acknowledges the possibility of a subsidy by the poor to the rich and suggests three approaches to minimize this danger. First, he would disallow certain procedures disproportionately applicable to the rich that probably represent noncritical service. Second, he would emphasize the development of new techniques or approaches to psychotherapy that are more responsive to the needs of the less affluent. Finally, he encourages psychologists to be active in health service research/program evaluation to ensure that psychotherapy coverage under national health insurance provides the genuine and equitable contributions claimed for it.

Crowell suggests that fears of an economically regressive national health insurance program are not unfounded. She concludes, however, that national health insurance is not much different from other national problems. In reviewing a variety of national problems, including Medicare and Medicaid, Crowell suggests that to a considerable extent regressive patterns are evident in all of them, including medical deductions under income tax, payroll taxes for social security, group health insurance through employers, and Medicare and Medicaid. She maintains that the regressive nature of a prospective national health insurance tax depends on the utilization rates by income groups and on other associated factors such as rate and financing mechanisms. She concludes that if cost sharing is tied to both expense and income level, a national health insurance plan may not be as regressive as other taxing plans and methods of financing health care.

In the final article, Edwards, Greene, Abramowitz, and Davidson empirically examine the speculative issues raised in the first three papers. Their research was done in a California community mental health center. Four major hypotheses were examined: (a) that the poor would not utilize mental health services when available, (b) that if services were sought, the poor would receive fewer sessions than more affluent patients, (c) that if services were requested, poor patients would be referred to the less prestigious and/or useful services (e.g., medication clinics rather than psychotherapy) or be treated by the less prestigious staff members, and (d) that poor patients would benefit less from psychotherapy than more affluent patients.

Their data show that the poor do utilize mental health services. There were *no* data, moreover, to suggest that lower-economic-class patients were referred to less prestigious providers. In addition, no differential effectiveness of treatment was revealed as a function of patient income. With respect to length of treatment, there were no significant differences related to income level for those patients receiving individual psychotherapy, group psychotherapy, or medication clinic services. The only service for which there were significant differences in the length of treatment related to income level involved those patients seen in family therapy, a form of treatment rarely offered in this particular clinic. The degree to which one can generalize to other community mental health centers from this one is unclear, but the data suggest that service delivery systems that really intend to serve the poor can be developed and will be utilized.

The structure and financing of the service delivery system, however, must be redesigned to achieve such goals. Easy access, freedom of choice of provider, and reasonable reimbursement rates must be included. Professionals must also be trained and motivated to provide such service to the economically poor. Karon and VandenBos (1977) provide an illuminating description of several key psychological aspects of effective psychotherapy with the economically poor. They cite five areas about which therapists for the poor must have knowledge, technical skill, and/or self-insight. First, the therapist must be aware of, and trained to handle, the special communication problems of the poor in relating to authority, which may prevent psychotherapy from occurring (and even prevent the psychotherapist from being aware of the problem). Second, the "information gap" regarding the process and benefits of psychotherapy must be acknowledged and steps taken within the therapy to illustrate and explain why and how it can be helpful. Third, the therapist must take a therapeutic stance from which all problems are viewed as resulting from an ever-varying blend of reality problems and psychological problems so that the patient can be taught to disentangle them and work at solving both aspects. Fourth, knowledge of and experience with people of the socioeconomic and ethnic groups from which the patients come must be acknowledged to be as important as training in psychodynamics or pharmacology. Finally, the therapist of the economically poor must be able to acknowledge and confront the prototypic countertransference problems elicited while working with a patient from a deprived background. The need for training and experience doing meaningful psychotherapy with the economically poor is one factor in support of continued federal funding of mental health training.

Edwards et al. note the growing literature detailing specific knowledge relevant to the effective psychotherapeutic treatment of the poor. Programs that attract and are sought out by disadvantaged groups have been developed. Research demonstrating the feasibility and effectiveness of verbal psychotherapy with the poor has been reported since 1965. Edwards et al. note that most of the data upon which the fears that poor patients will subsidize the rich are based were collected before 1970— prior to the availability of data on the impact of community mental health centers' programs. They note that more recent data, both from local community mental health clinics and from the National Institute of Mental Health, show that the economically poor have better access to quality mental health services than ever before and that they are utilizing these services. While the situation is by no means ideal, progress has been made, and knowledge is now available to facilitate further improvements.

All of these considerations suggest a number of features that must be explicit in any national health insurance plan. One, not all potential benefits can be included. Two, in order to ensure that services delivered are indeed needed and plausible, some tough-minded review systems will be necessary, such as the APA system developed for CHAMPUS (described in Section 6). Three, to assure that services provided are clearly needed and effective, any health insurance system must include a provision for determining the outcome of service delivery. APA has provided a description of how this might be accomplished through its report on evaluation and accountability in national health insurance. Four, an impeccable national health insurance plan must include mechanisms to make services to the poor and needy more accessible and more specifically and pragmatically tailored to the needs of the client.

Reference

Karon, B. P., & VandenBos, G. R. Psychotherapeutic technique and the economically poor patient. *Psychotherapy: Theory, Research and Practice*, 1977, *14*, 169–180.

Does Including Psychotherapy in Health Insurance Represent a Subsidy to the Rich from the Poor?

George W. Albee

Traditionally, psychotherapy has been sought primarily by the affluent. Surveys have found that psychotherapy users come from the higher social classes, are more often female than male, are college educated and/or in one of the professions, and are drawn from the group labeled neurotic or overcontrolled. For the most part they are suburbanites with moderately serious neurotic problems and capable of paying the high cost of frequent sessions. Clearly, the need for help with emotional problems is not limited to the affluent—every survey reports a higher rate of disturbance among the poor. But psychotherapy, with its traditional emphasis on introspection, verbalization, self-examination, and the development of insight, clearly is not a compatible approach to dealing with the problems of poor people, who do not use it much even when it is available and free. Most psychotherapists are heavily clustered in certain census tracts in certain regions of the country, while other areas are barely supplied. These and other considerations suggest that cost-reimbursed psychotherapy under national health insurance may very well make the therapy available at reduced cost to those affluent persons currently among the heaviest users, while the large numbers of poor people not likely to make increased use of the service would increasingly bear its cost.

Historically, psychotherapy was created for the relief of the emotional problems of affluent clients, and theory and practice in the field reflect this focus on the problems of the affluent. There is no need to recite for this audience the history of the origins of psychoanalysis in Victorian Vienna, but it is instructive to remember that Dr. Freud's first clients were largely middle- and upper-middle-class women suffering from pseudoneurological symptoms that he, as a neurologist, discovered were due to the conversion of unconscious sexual conflicts into mystifying paralyses and anesthesias. In short, the first subjects for psychoanalysis were overcontrolled, neurotic women who were undoubtedly suffering from the sexist, repressive forces characteristic of industrializing societies.

Psychoanalysis has always been prohibitively expensive and therefore available primarily to the rich and especially to the nouveau riche. A recent survey (Marmor, 1975) of the private office practice of psychiatrists in the United States, conducted by the Joint Information Service of the American Psychiatric Association and the National Association for Mental Health, reports as follows:

> The importance of economic factors in access to private psychiatric care is dramatically reflected in figures indicating that, as might be expected, more affluent professional and managerial workers are overrepresented in the private offices of psychiatrists as compared to blue- and white-collar workers. This is particularly true of the more expensive modality of psychoanalytic treatment. A consequence of this fact is that ethnic minorities, and particularly black and Latin American patients, are grossly underrepresented in the private practice of psychiatrists. (p. 39)

But, it will be objected, this is just the purpose of national health insurance—to provide care for everyone and not just for the affluent who now go to private psychiatrists. By extending benefits for coverage to all social class levels, the inability to pay for private care will no longer prevent the poor from getting psychother-

Reprinted from *American Psychologist*, 1977, *32*, 719–721.

apy. This is a naive view. Weihofen has called attention to the double standard of care provided in public tax-supported agencies that, while claiming to be nondiscriminatory, manage to give more attention, to provide better treatment, and to assign more highly qualified therapists to the affleunt clients at the expense of the poor. Weihofen (1967) says:

> Because psychiatrists understandably prefer "good" patients—those who are sensitive and sophisticated with social and intellectual standards similar to their own—the poor who become patients frequently get inferior treatment, even in the public clinics that purport not to make distinctions between paying and non-paying patients. A recent survey revealed that even a public clinic excluding those able to pay for private psychiatric care still distinguished its patients by social class. Not only were patients from upper social classes accepted for treatment more often, but their treatment was more apt to be given by a senior or more experienced member of the staff. (p. 2)

In another recent series of studies discussed in a special paper by Bert Brown, Director of the National Institute of Mental Health, it was found that blue-collar auto workers provided with free psychiatric services by their union contract simply failed to make any significant use of this service. They resisted referral to a "shrink" and did not understand the services available.

Let me be so bold as to suggest that the personality characteristics of professional therapists—psychiatrists and psychologists particularly—make them particularly unqualified to provide one-to-one therapy for the poor and the blue-collar class. And similarly, these latter groups do not want or need psychotherapy. The nature of medical education, with its strict admission requirements, its use of a student peonage system, and its authoritarian hierarchical structure—with residency training in psychiatry nearly always obtained on university hospital wards where the patients have Blue Cross or other hospitalization insurance—in short, the entire system of selection and training that produces psychiatrists selects obsessives for survival whose experiences are very largely limited to patients who are members of the middle and upper classes. While most good psychiatric training programs rotate their residents through the back wards of the state hospital, the rotation is usually swift and is drug-therapy oriented.

The training of clinical psychologists is hardly any better in preparing them to work with the poor. As admission to clinical training programs becomes more and more selective and difficult, the lucky few who are admitted are obsessive high-achievers with outstanding academic records and high test scores. In short, they too are obsessives heavily indoctrinated about the importance of time, inner control, and research. Both groups are selected from the upper-middle class, and few of them speak the language, share the values, or understand the problems of the poor.

As Schofield (1964) has pointed out, psychotherapists prefer people with the YAVIS syndrome (young, attractive, verbal, intelligent, and successful). It may be that the training of psychotherapists makes them unsuited for any kind of intervention except one-to-one psychotherapy with middle-class clients. Psychotherapists are themselves drawn from the middle class, are trained with middle-class patients, and are familar with middle-class problems. Middle-class people tend to be more conscience-laden and guilt-plagued and therefore are more neurotically anxious. The amount of anxiety can often be reduced by individual psychotherapy, and so the process is rewarding and reinforcing to middle-class people. While it may be an oversimplification, there certainly is some epidemiological evidence that neurotic anxiety is less common among the poor. The reality problems of poverty, unemployment, discrimination, poor housing, etc., assume higher levels of urgency than interpersonal relationship problems. Such a formulation would argue that the kind of "mental" outpatient treatment covered in any national health scheme—individual psychotherapy—would be more appropriate and acceptable to the affluent and less utilized by the poor.

Whether the intervention setting is the private office or the community mental health center, the treatment of choice, overwhelmingly, is one-to-one individual psychotherapy. In a study of a group of the nation's best community mental health centers several years ago, Glasscote, Sanders, Forstenzer, and Foley (1964) reported that "psychotherapy is the backbone of treatment." In another study, Rosen, Bahn, Shellow, and Bower (1965) found that adolescents accepted for clinic treatment had to be "preoccupied with self-examination and willing to talk about themselves." This criterion limited service primarily to the middle-class talkers among the teenagers. But because everyone would be paying the bill and only the affluent would have the kind of disturbances for which the treatment was appropriate, once again we see the injustice of everyone paying for help for the few.

In the city with the largest number of psychiatrists, psychologists, and mental health clinics in the nation—Boston—Ryan (1969) found, in a careful survey, that social casework agencies were intervening actively with more emotionally disturbed poor people than were all the psychiatric resources.

Another serious problem involves the geographical distribution of mental health care professionals. Just five states claim the services of more than half of all the psychiatrists in the country. Psychologists are not quite as concentrated as the psychiatrists, but then the majority are not in practice either. There is clearly a significant relationship between the *affluence* of a geographic area or city census tract and the presence of mental health services. At the present time there are few private practitioners in the central city. Even when there are public clinics in the central city, the clientele using them tends to come from the affluent suburbs. Gordon (1965) described the problems involved in getting disturbed poor children through a public-clinic intake process and helping them survive the waiting list. He showed how lower-class children are rejected much more frequently than middle-class children seeking help. One way to accomplish this selection is through the waiting list. Middle-class parents are better able to wait, while poor families are oriented to more urgent, immediate solutions. Also, the higher status agencies have many rigid requirements in defining who will be accepted for treatment. Gordon found that even a child clinic located in the heart of an urban slum attracted most of its clients from suburbia. He found a high correlation between the distance the clients lived from the clinic and the likelihood of their acceptance for treatment!

The distribution of public clinics follows the distribution of mental health personnel. Half of all of the psychiatric clinics in the nation reportedly are in the northeastern states. One survey of more than 2,000 outpatient psychiatric clinics found only 56 of these in rural areas, only 50 of which served children. While one third of all the children in the country live in the rural states, only 4% of the clinics serving children were to be found in these same states.

Senator Edward Kennedy (1975), author of a major national health bill, sounds all of these themes:

> If we were to implement a comprehensive national health insurance program tomorrow, and if we did not change in any way the geographic location of the patient loads of psychiatrists, we would be asking the 86 percent of American families whose earnings are under $20,000 a year to pay the lion's share of the cost of a health care service which is rendered by and large to individuals in families whose incomes are over $20,000 a year. Moreover, we would be asking black families to pay taxes for services only two percent of which go to blacks. And, of course, we would be asking residents of areas of the country which have few psychiatrists available to help pay the bill for other areas of our nation where help can be more easily obtained. (pp. 151–152).

Kennedy sees this public program of mental health care as "contain[ing] the apparent risk of subsidizing services to higher-income citizens directly from tax contributions of middle- and low-income Americans." The really fundamental question, ultimately, is whether persons with the kinds of problems dealt with in outpatient, traditional psychotherapy really are *sick*—whether they truly have illnesses that should be covered by a health insurance plan. Today is not the time to review all of the arguments against a medical or sickness model of emotional disturbance. Let it suffice for me to point out that there is a great deal of evidence to support the position that people have emotional problems in living that are produced by the problems inherent in an industrial civilization and that these problems should not be regarded as illnesses and should not be covered under a national health scheme. I would favor no coverage for any outpatient therapy except in cases of genuine organic illness (Albee, 1975).

References

Albee, G. W. To thine own self be true. Comments on "Insurance reimbursement." *American Psychologist,* 1975, *30,* 1156–1158.
Glasscote, R., Sanders, D., Forstenzer, H. M., & Foley, A. R. (Eds.). *The community mental health center: An analysis of existing models.* Washington, D.C.: American Psychiatric Association, 1964.

Gordon, S. Are we seeing the right patients? Child guidance intake: The sacred cow. *American Journal of Orthopsychiatry,* 1965, *35,* 131–137.

Kennedy, E. M. Commentary. In J. Marmor, *Psychiatrists and their patients.* Washington, D.C.: Joint Information Service of the American Psychiatric Association and the National Association for Mental Health, 1975.

Marmor, J. Commentary. In J. Marmor, *Psychiatrists and their patients.* Washington, D.C.: Joint Information Service of the American Psychiatric Association and the National Association for Mental Health, 1975.

Rosen, B., Bahn, A., Shellow, R., & Bower, E. Adolescent patients served in out-patient psychiatric clinics. *American Journal of Public Health,* 1965, *55,* 1563–1577.

Ryan, W. *Distress in the city.* Cleveland: Case Western Reserve University, 1969.

Schofield, W. *Psychotherapy: The purchase of friendship.* Englewood Cliffs, N.J.: Prentice-Hall, 1964.

Weihofen, H. Psychiatry for the poor. *Psychiatric News,* 967, *2*(10), 2.

At the time of original publication of this article, *George W. Albee* was a member of the faculty in the Department of Psychology, University of Vermont, Burlington.

This article is based on a paper presented at the meeting of the American Psychological Association, Washington, D.C., September 1976.

Including Psychotherapy
in National Health Insurance
Insurance Guidelines and Other Proposed Solutions

A. John McSweeny

Since psychotherapy is best suited to the needs of affluent persons, provisions for psychotherapy in proposed national health insurance plans may benefit the relatively wealthy at the expense of the general public. Short-term solutions to this problem include developing insurance guidelines that disallow reimbursement for unspecified and unproven psychotherapeutic procedures used for educational, recreational, and "personal growth" purposes. Long-term solutions consist of developing new approaches to psychotherapy that meet the needs of less affluent persons. Psychologists should take an active role in developing and testing these solutions to ensure that the inclusion of psychotherapy in national health insurance becomes a genuine asset to our country, rather than a liability.

As the cost of health services has continued to rise, the ability of the working classes and the poor to afford these services had declined. As a result, several responsible legislators have proposed plans of national health insurance to assure that all citizens, including those with limited incomes, will be able to receive quality health care. Several of these plans have provisions for mental health care, including psychotherapy provided by a private practitioner in an outpatient setting. At first glance, a proposal to include insurance reimbursement for psychotherapy appears to be progressive (in an economic sense). The cost of psychotherapy as provided by a private practitioner is beyond the means of many Americans, especially those with limited incomes. In the Chicago area, for example, a 1-hour visit to a psychoanalyst cost, on the average, $35 in 1972 (Johnson & Gittleson, 1976). The current hourly price is $45, which represents an increase of 29% over the 1972 price.

The private clinician, usually but not always a psychiatrist, has continued to be a mental health professional primarily for the middle and upper socioeconomic classes (Scheidemandel, 1972; Rosen, Note 1). In a sample survey of patients being treated by private psychiatrists in the United States in 1970 (Scheide-

mandel, 1972), only 24% of the patients could be considered to have moderate or limited incomes, that is, below $10,000 per year. The majority of patients (56%) reported family incomes between $10,000 and $30,000, and 21% reported incomes over $30,000. On the other hand, the 1970 census (U.S. Bureau of the Census, 1972) indicates that the majority of Americans earned less than $10,000 in that year and, moreover, since the rate of mental disorders is higher among Americans earning less than $10,000 than among those earning greater than $10,000 (Hollingshead & Redlich, 1958; Rosen, Note 1), one can only conclude that the patients of private psychiatrists are the more affluent members of society.

The community mental health centers program, created by the Community Mental Health Centers Act in 1963, was proposed as one way of "bridging the gap" between poor and nonpoor in the accessibility of mental health services, including outpatient psychotherapy. Rosen (Note 1) has presented data indicating that the inauguration of community mental health centers has, in fact, resulted in an increase in the accessibility of outpatient services for the poor. However, many authors now agree that the community mental health centers program has not succeeded in providing quality

Reprinted from *American Psychologist*, 1977, *32*, 722–730.

services for all who need them (Chu & Trotter, 1974; Snow & Newton, 1976). In addition, the persons providing psychotherapy services in a public facility such as a community mental health center are likely to be less well-trained than those providing more lucrative private services (Meltzer, 1975).

In brief, the gap between the poor and the nonpoor concerning the availability of quality psychotherapy is still quite large. Would not a program of national health insurance, with provisions for reimbursement for psychotherapy, make psychotherapy available to the poor and thus help narrow the discrepancy? Certainly supporters of such a program would say *yes*, but opponents have argued that insurance reimbursement in existing private and government insurance plans has produced fewer quality mental health services for the poor and more use of psychotherapy services among members of the middle class (Meltzer, 1975). Still others have argued that including reimbursement for psychotherapy in a national health insurance plan might result in a subsidy for the rich from the nonrich (Albee, 1977; Crowell, 1977). Why might this unwanted result occur? In my opinion, a major reason concerns the nature of traditional psychotherapy itself.

Traditional Psychotherapy as a Middle-Class Activity

Goldstein (1973) and others have argued that traditional psychotherapy is largely a middle-class activity, not only because middle-class patients can afford it, but also because it fits the values, social skills, language, and problems of middle-class patients. Numerous studies have documented the middle-class value bias of the mental health movement in general. For example, Gursslin, Hunt, and Roach (1960), after content-analyzing several publicly distributed mental health pamphlets, noted that the texts of these pamphlets were consistent with typically middle-class values. The pamphlets extolled the virtues of work, controlling one's emotions, planning ahead, and achievement. The authors concluded that "the mental health movement is unwittingly propagating a middle-class ethic under the guise of science" (p. 410).

In a similar vein, Goldstein (1973) noted that traditional psychotherapy requires an orientation toward self-reliance, delay of gratification, and a concern with inner dynamics, feelings, intentions, and motivations. Several investigations of values by Kohn (1969), Miller and Riessman (1969), and others have found these values to be most typical of middle-class individuals. Thus, prospective middle-class psychotherapy clients enter psychotherapy with a useful set of values. They are liable to meet the expectations of the therapist that they take an active role in their therapy, that they examine their feelings, thoughts, and putative motivations in detail, and that they be willing to wait for a significant period of time, sometimes more than a year, for problem resolution.

The lower-class patient's expectations for treatment, on the other hand, are liable to be at odds with those of the psychotherapist. Several investigators (Borghi, 1965; Freedman, Englehardt, & Hankoff, 1958; Goldstein, 1973; Heine & Trosman, 1960; McMahon, 1964; Overall & Anderson, 1963; Sobell & Ingalls, 1964) have confirmed this clash of expectations between middle-class therapists and lower-class patients.

In contrast to their middle-class counterparts, lower-class patients expect the therapist to be "immediately helpful in relieving symptomatic distress . . . [and] that the therapist will act 'on' and 'do' something for [them]" (McMahon, 1964, p. 286). The discrepancies in expectations between middle-class therapists and lower-class patients are likely to lead to mutual disappointment at best and negligible patient change and early termination at worst (Chance, 1959; Goldstein, 1962, 1973; Heine & Trosman, 1960; Lennard & Bernstein, 1960; Overall & Aronson, 1963).

Traditional psychotherapy not only presupposes a particular set of values, it also demands a particular language and a particular set of social skills. Traditional psychotherapy is largely a verbal exercise conducted in an interpersonal setting. Thus, at least a moderate level of verbal skills and the ability to use these skills to examine oneself and one's relations with others are prerequisites for a successful psychotherapeutic experience. Once again, middle-class patients are much more likely than their lower-class counterparts to have the requisite skills.

Bernstein (1961) has described what he calls elaborate and restricted codes. The elaborate code, which according to Bernstein is characteristic of middle-class children, is grammatically complex, emphasizes logical relationships, and contains frequent use of abstract symbols. The restricted code, which is more characteristic of lower-class children, is more descriptive, global, concrete, and less complex than the elaborate code. Goldstein (1973) argues that the elaborate code is much more appropriate for the demands of traditional psychotherapy than the restricted code. Goldstein further asserts that because middle-class therapists and their lower-class patients use different language forms, "much of what is said across this particular social-class gulf goes unheard; . . . in several major and highly consequential ways, therapist and patient are literally not speaking the same language" (p. 40).

The consequences of this language barrier between therapist and lower-class patient are similar to those described earlier for the clash of expectations: mutual frustration, a poor-quality therapeutic relationship, and an eventual lack of therapeutic progress and early termination.

In addition to being suited to middle-class values, psychotherapy may be best suited to middle-class problems. Several studies (e.g., Hollingshead & Redlich, 1958; Overall & Aronson, 1963) have indicated that middle-class and lower-class patients bring different types of problems to clinicians. Middle-class patients are more likely to present interpersonal problems such as marital conflicts, or fairly sophisticated intrapersonal problems such as existential crises. Lower-class patients, on the other hand, are more likely to present somatic problems that are interfering with their ability to carry out their basic roles. Because traditional psychotherapy can be applied most directly to the typical middle-class problems, both therapists and patients may see psychotherapy as irrelevant to typical lower-class problems.

Who Would Use "Free" Psychotherapy?

Clearly, traditional psychotherapy is best suited to middle-class tastes, skills, and problems. It should not be surprising that the primary users of psychotherapy are middle-class persons—the so-called YAVIS (young, attractive, verbal, intelligent, and successful) patients described by Schofield (1964). Likewise, because traditional psychotherapy is clearly not well-suited to the needs of the lower classes, it should come as no surprise that lower-class individuals might not utilize psychotherapy services, even when they are available without charge. Gordon (1965) conducted a study which indicated that this is exactly the case. Gordon's study concerned a child guidance clinic, located in the heart of a Philadelphia slum, which provided free services to its poorest clients. If cost and accessibility were the only barriers to use of psychotherapeutic services, one would expect that the free services would be used most frequently by persons residing close to the center, given the higher rate of psychological disorders among the poor. In fact, the opposite was found. Gordon discovered an inverse relationship between proximity to the center and the probability of using the clinic's services. The poor who lived close to the clinic were less likely to use the services than relatively well-off persons who lived farther away.[1]

What is Psychotherapy Used For?

Up to this point we have assumed that people seek out psychotherapy when they have some sort of psychological problem. However, as London (1974), Meltzer (1975), and Schofield (1964) point out, this is not always the case. Psychotherapy is often used for educational

---

[1] The results of a large-scale research project by Brandon (1975) indicate that the relationship between the proximity to and the utilization of mental health services is quite complex. In a study of the utilization patterns of all public mental health facilities in New York City, Brandon (1975) found that

for low income areas, proximity to a municipal inpatient facility decreases outpatient utilization, while, for middle income areas, proximity to a voluntary hospital increases outpatient utilization [which] suggests that the overall impact of the facility location policy tends to institutionalize low income persons at a disproportionate rate. (p. 420)

Because the relationship between proximity and utilization is complex, Gordon's findings should be viewed with caution.

purposes by trainees in the mental health disciplines. Several schools of psychotherapy, particularly those with psychoanalytic leanings, consider involvement in psychotherapy as an essential part of training for a clinician. Within psychology, this point of view is supported strongly by Shakow (1976, p. 554), who uses the following quote from Browning's "Light Woman" as an instructive illustration:

'Tis an awkward thing to play with souls
And matter enough to save one's own.

The large majority of psychotherapists-in-training are already members of the middle and upper socioeconomic classes, and the remainder are waiting for the day they can join. According to Meltzer (1975), many psychotherapist trainees use whatever insurance funds they have available to support their psychotherapy for training purposes. Given that this pattern has emerged with existing insurance programs, one can expect the pattern to continue and to expand if a national health insurance plan that includes provisions for psychotherapy is adopted.

As London (1974) and Schofield (1964) have pointed out, people often use psychotherapy as a form of recreation or as a means to escape boredom. This use of psychotherapy is exemplified by the resortlike Esalen Institute and by a recent advertisement that I saw for a sea cruise with an "ongoing group experience." Although there are no statistics available for support, one can safely conclude that the recreational use of psychotherapy is restricted to the relatively affluent.

Summary of the Problem

Psychotherapy in its traditional form is a middle- and upper-class activity. Although it has been argued that this is true because the poor and the working classes cannot afford it, there is evidence that they would not avail themselves of psychotherapy even if it were freely available. The problem concerns the basic nature of psychotherapy: It is best suited to the values, social skills, aspirations, and language of the reasonably affluent.

Any national health insurance plan with provisions for psychotherapy would likely support the use of psychotherapy by the financially well-off at the expense of the general public.[2]

Possible Solutions: General Strategies

In the most general sense, three alternatives present themselves when one considers reimbursement for psychotherapy and national health insurance. The first alternative, providing unlimited (or relatively unlimited) reimbursement, is clearly unacceptable for the reasons already discussed. The second alternative, no provision for reimbursement, is also undesirable because it denies help to those persons in all social classes who have a genuine psychological problem that is interfering with their lives and that may be amenable to treatment by some form of psychotherapy. Thus, it becomes reasonable to favor a third alternative—some sort of plan of limited reimbursement for psychotherapy services.

What Guidelines Should Be Used for Reimbursement?

Given that some sort of limited plan of reimbursement appears to be the best alternative, the next question becomes, What limitations or guidelines should be used? Ideally, the guidelines should be structured so as to provide services to those people who have a "real" problem without creating the potential abuse of services by professional trainees or bored but solvent individuals. Drafting such guidelines will by no means be an easy task. However, given their importance in determining whether reimbursement for psychotherapy is an asset or a liability to society, the task cannot be ignored.

An initial step in drafting guidelines should be the definition of what types of client problem would be permitted in the reimbursement plans.

---

[2] This situation would be similar to that which exists with public financing of higher education. Most students in colleges and universities are middle-class individuals. Yet a factory worker who did not attend college and/or whose children do not attend college must pay taxes to support those institutions. Most people feel that public support of colleges and universities is justified since the skills these institutions provide to students are thought to benefit society as a whole. Jencks (1972), on the other hand, has argued that college students alone should finance their educations with the possible assistance of loans.

Problems with obvious class biases, such as existential crises and ennui, should be disallowed in the reimbursement plan. Educational uses of psychotherapy should also be disallowed. The most class-equitable problems appear to be those that interfere with a person's life roles as a breadwinner, parent, or spouse. A problem that disrupts a person's economic productivity seems especially appropriate to include in an insurance reimbursement program. In fact, such problems should be of greatest consequence to those people whose incomes are marginal. There is no doubt that "real" psychological problems exist than can threaten a person's livelihood. The truck driver who develops an intense anxiety reaction to driving after narrowly avoiding an accident has a "real" problem and needs help as much as a person who suffers from a physical disability that threatens his or her job. An insurance reimbursement for a psychotherapy program should permit the truck diver—and others with psychological problems that disrupt their basic role functioning—to seek out and receive aid.

The next step, then, should be to define just what types of psychotherapeutic "aid" should be permitted in an insurance reimbursement program. In my opinion, insurance reimbursement should be limited to the provision of psychotherapeutic procedures for which there exists empirical evidence of efficacy for the amelioration of the client's presenting problems. Insurance reimbursement should not be allowed for unspecified and unproven psychotherapy procedures.

The final steps in formulating guidelines for insurance reimbursement concern implementation issues. First, psychotherapists should provide some proof that they are proficient in the use of empirically established procedures.[3] At present, state licensing and certification requirements for all the mental health professions and for psychologists in particular provide little consumer protection (Meltzer, 1975; Feist, Note 2). Although state licensing and certification boards may be able to certify and catalogue those therapists who have known competency in empirically proven psychotherapy techniques, much of the work may need to be done by respected professional groups. The professional groups that are not bound to a particular discipline but rather are dedicated to an empirical approach to psychotherapy would be most appropriate for this task. The Association for the Advancement of Behavior Therapy (AABT) is an example of such an organization.[4]

A system for monitoring psychotherapists' adherence to the insurance-reimbursement guidelines constitutes the second major implementation issue. Although almost any monitoring system can be corrupted or circumvented, some system must be organized if the proposed guidelines are to have any effect. Whittington (1975) has described a system of monitoring psychotherapist activities in a private network of service providers who were reimbursed by various insurance plans. This system could serve as a model for systems used in a national health insurance plan. The key to the monitoring system was a charting procedure, used by the psychotherapists, which was auditable by a referring supervising clinician and third-party payers. The charting system utilized the goal-attainment scaling procedure (Kiresuk & Sherman, 1968), which allows for the clear specification of treatment goals, expected outcomes, and progress made toward achieving those outcomes. The charts were routinely reviewed by a clinician who screened referred clients to psychotherapists but who was not himself directly involved in treatment. Thus, the clinician could be a relatively objective monitoring agent who reviewed treatment goals, plans, and progress to ensure the appropriate use of financial and psychotherapeutic resources. Although the system described was used in one relatively small treatment system, its essential features—a concrete, goal-oriented record-keeping system and "disinterested" observers—could be integrated with the peer review systems proposed in national health insurance legislation to provide an effective mechanism for ensuring adherence to the reimbursement guidelines.

---

[3] In many cases, "proof" of proficiency in the use of empirically based psychotherapy procedures would consist of training credentials as opposed to actual demonstration. The latter type of "proof" may be more difficult to assess.

[4] Unfortunately, the majority of AABT members surveyed have opposed becoming involved with certification of behavior therapists (Azrin, 1976).

The last implementation issue concerns insurance payment for psychotherapy services. The least complex method would be to provide the same potential benefits to all persons. However, if a goal of national health insurance is to equalize the availability of services to persons in different socioeconomic classes, a graduated benefit plan in which potential benefits varied inversely with personal income would be preferable. A graduated benefit plan would also lessen the probability that insurance reimbursement for psychotherapy would, in fact, become a "subsidy to the rich." The major difficulties of a graduated benefit plan consist of constructing the proper reimbursement formulas and ensuring honest income reporting. If a complicated system is required to overcome these difficulties, a graduated benefit plan would be expensive and impractical. At present, there does not seem to be sufficient justification for favoring a graduated plan over a simple, nongraduated plan.

The Role of Psychologists in Formulating Insurance-Reimbursement Guidelines

Psychologists should become involved in the formulation of psychotherapy cost-reimbursement guidelines, not only for their own benefit, but for the benefit of society and their potential clients as well. Clinical psychologists should be especially well prepared to evaluate the types of problems that would interfere with a client's usual life roles, the types of psychotherapeutic procedures (if any) that would be appropriate, and the evidence that exists for the efficacy of those procedures. The basic problems in formulating reimbursement guidelines are similar to the basic problems in psychotherapy research: "What treatment, by whom, is most effective for this individual, with that specific problem, under what set of circumstances, and how does it come about?" (Paul, 1969, p. 62).

The problem involved in developing a monitoring system should be similar to those encountered in program evaluation. Since psychologists have developed methods for establishing accountability within the program evaluation field, they should be able to provide expertise concerning a system for accountability with insurance reimbursement as well.

The contribution of psychologists to the formulation of insurance guidelines could be given through advocacy organizations such as the Association for the Advancement of Psychology. In any case, the potential for psychologists to make a contribution for the general social good and to enhance the profession exists and should be used.

Beyond Reimbursement Guidelines

As was stressed in an earlier section of this article, one of the reasons that the less affluent people do not utilize traditional psychotherapy is because it is not well-suited to their needs, values, language forms, and problems. Thus, a long-term solution to the difficulty concerns the forms of psychotherapy that are appropriate for the needs, values, and language of the poor. Goldstein (1973) provides detailed descriptions of attempts that he and his colleagues made in this direction in his book *Structured Learning Therapy: Toward a Psychotherapy for the Poor*. Goldstein evaluated combinations of techniques such as instruction, modeling, role playing, and reinforcement that were tailored to the needs and skills of the lower-class client. The initial results of Goldstein's experiments are impressive, although as Goldstein himself freely admits, much more work needs to be done in this area.

A more immediate solution to the problem was developed and evaluated by Hoehn-Saric, Frank, Imber, Nash, Stone, and Battle (1964). These investigators called their technique the *role induction interview*. The role induction interview was designed to reduce discrepancies in therapist and patient role expectations by instructing the patient about the types of therapy behaviors expected in traditional psychotherapy and what outcomes might be expected. Non-YAVIS patients who received this initial interview exhibited more adequate in-therapy behavior, greater commitment to therapy, and greater change than those patients not receiving the interview. The role induction interview differs from *structured learning therapy* in that it is an attempt to modify the patients to make them reachable by psychotherapy rather than an attempt to modify the nature of psychotherapy to make it compatible with the patients it is intended for. For that reason, the role induction interview is a less complete solution than structural learning therapy. Still, it is a positive step toward bringing psychotherapy to the less-affluent patient.

The utilization of lower-class "paraprofessional" psychotherapists represents a third approach to the problem of making psychotherapy compatible with the values and needs of the poor (Allerhand & Lake, 1972; Jacobson, Roman, & Kaplan, 1970; Pearl & Reissman, 1965; Reiff & Reissman, 1965). The paraprofessionals usually provide their services from a community mental health center. Ideally, the paraprofessionals reside in the neighborhood that the center is designed to serve. This policy is designed to ensure that the paraprofessionals are "in tune" with the language, values, mores, problems, and needs of the people in the neighborhood. The paraprofessionals are trained in basic psychotherapy skills by the professional staff in the center and then serve as assistants to the professional clinicians or as relatively independent psychotherapists. Many paraprofessionals are trained for other clinical roles such as psychological testing (Allerhand & Lake, 1972), in addition to the basic counseling-psychotherapy role. Whatever variation of the paraprofessional model is used, the basic idea is to train a person to conduct psychotherapy who is already compatible, in terms of language and values, with the (usually) lower-class client.

Although there are several reports of the successful use of paraprofessionals (Allerhand & Lake, 1972; Kaplan, Boyajian, & Meltzer, 1970; Roen, 1971), there is little empirical evidence of the efficacy of the lower-class paraprofessional in conducting psychotherapy. Most experimental studies of paraprofessionals have involved the use of middle-class paraprofessional psychotherapists and middle-class clients (e.g., Rioch, 1967). The results of these studies have been encouraging, but they need to be extended to lower-class therapists and clients.

My experience with indigenous paraprofessionals has been mixed. The paraprofessionals definitely were more familiar with the language and culture of the community served by the mental health center than were their professional colleagues. Thus, it appeared easier for them to establish an initial working relationship with their clients. On the other hand, the paraprofessionals were usually upwardly mobile individuals who often subscribed to values of self-improvement, striving, delay of gratification, and similar middle-class ideas. As a result, they were often unsympathetic toward their lower-class clients whom they considered to be somewhat unambitious.

Research by Goldstein (1973) confirms a middle-class value bias among many paraprofessionals. His research indicates that this bias may be due to the exposure the paraprofessionals have with middle-class professional models. That is, the paraprofessionals quickly learn to "act like a professional" via observing their professional colleagues in action.

Although empirical data to support their efficacy are lacking at present, the use of paraprofessional psychotherapists represents a promising approach to meeting the psychological needs of the poor. Further experimentation should be conducted in private as well as public settings.

If psychologists wish to lobby for research funds, then the development of psychotherapists and psychotherapy techniques suited to the poor, as exemplified by structured learning therapy and to a lesser extent by the role induction interview and the use of paraprofessionals, should be a primary area represented in those lobbying efforts.

Social Experimentation

At this point in time, the effects of psychotherapy cost-reimbursement in national health insurance remain unknown. One can make a reasoned guess, as I have, that reimbursement will be beneficial only to the affluent unless specific guidelines are implemented. However, this is a hypothesis that requires testing. Thus, it seems advisable to evaluate the effects of various insurance-reimbursement plans in large-scale social experiments. The technology for social experimentation has been refined in the past few years, and the general strategies are described in some depth by Riecken and Boruch (1974). An example of the type of experimenting that can be done with public health insurance plans is provided by the Colorado Medicare Study being conducted by the Social Security Administration (Note 3). Using a classic 2 × 2, randomized, experimental design, this study will attempt to assess the effects of increasing the mental benefits provided and of including clinical psychologists as independent, cost-reimbursable treatment agents on (a) the costs of the Medicare program, (b) the utilization pattern of Medicare beneficiaries, and (c) any possible shifts of clinical psychologists from institutional settings to private practice.[5] Any national health insurance plan that has provisions for psychotherapy should also include funds for experiments to be conducted with various versions of the basic plan. The actual plan adopted for use (if any) should depend upon the outcome of those experiments. Hopefully, social experiments like the Colorado Medicare Study will help us answer the many questions raised in this article and in those of Albee (1977) and Crowell (1977).

Summary and Conclusions

Unless specific actions are taken, the inclusion of psychotherapy in proposed national health insurance plans will benefit only the relatively wealthy at the expense of the general public. Lower-class individuals are not likely to use benefits provided for traditional psychotherapy because it does not suit their values, social skills, language forms, and presenting problems. Middle- and upper-class individuals are likely to use benefits provided for psychotherapy because it does suit their values, social skills, language forms, and presenting problems. In addition, middle- and upper-class persons may use psychotherapy for educational, recreational, or "personal growth" purposes.

A short-term solution to this problem involves developing insurance-reimbursement guidelines that restrict benefits to the amelioration of problems that interfere with a person's ability to perform his or her usual life roles. In addition, insurance reimbursement should be

limited to the provision of psychotherapeutic procedures for which empirical evidence of efficacy exists. Psychotherapists should provide some proof that they are proficient in the use of those procedures. Insurance reimbursement should not be allowed for unspecified and unproven psychotherapy procedures used for educational, recreational, and personal-growth purposes. Certainly such guidelines will be difficult to delineate and implement. However, the difficulty of the task should not deter psychologists and others from attempting to deal with it. It is far too important to ignore.

Long-term solutions to problems presented in this article consist of developing new approaches to psychotherapy that suit the needs of lower-class patients. Structured learning therapy and the use of paraprofessionals represent two promising approaches. All proposed solutions and plans should be tested experimentally. A plan of careful experimentation can confirm or fail to confirm the various hypotheses raised concerning national health insurance and psychotherapy benefits. Thus, any national health insurance program that is adopted should have provisions for experimentation and demonstration projects.

In conclusion, if proper steps are taken, inclusion of psychotherapy in national health insurance could be of benefit to the general public and not just to psychotherapists and their affluent patients. Psychologists should take active roles in setting insurance guidelines, developing new forms of psychotherapy, and conducting social experiments to ensure that the inclusion of psychotherapy in national health insurance becomes an asset to society rather than a liability.

Reference Notes

1. Rosen, B. M. *Mental health and the poor: Have the gaps between the poor and the non-poor narrowed in the past decade?* Paper presented at the Conference on Social Sciences in Health at the 102nd Annual Meeting of the American Public Health Association, New Orleans, October 1974.
2. Feist, J. *Licensing and certification of psychologists in the United States.* Unpublished manuscript, University of Arizona, 1973.
3. Social Security Administration. *Research protocol for section 222. Clinical psychology experiment.* Unpublished document, 1976.

---

[5] Curiously, the American Psychiatric Association has vigorously opposed this research project ("No Peace in Our Time," 1976).

References

Albee, G. W. Does including psychotherapy in health insurance represent a subsidy to the rich from the poor? *American Psychologist*, 1977, *32*, 719–721.

Allerhand, M. E., & Lake, G. New careerists in community psychology and mental health. In S. E. Golann & C. Eisdorfer (Eds.), *Handbook of community mental health*. New York: Appleton-Century-Crofts, 1972.

Azrin, N. H. President's message. *AABT Newsletter,* July 1976, 1–2.

Bernstein, B. Social structure, language and learning. *Educational Research*, 961, *3*, 163–176.

Borghi, J. H. Premature termination of psychotherapy and patient-therapist expectations. *American Journal of Psychotherapy*, 1965, *22*, 460–473.

Brandon, R. N. Differential use of mental health services: Social pathology or class victimization? In M. Guttentag & E. Struening (Eds.), *Handbook of evaluation research*. Beverly Hills, Calif.: Sage, 1975.

Chance, E. *Families in treatment*. New York: Basic Books, 1959.

Chu, F., & Trotter, S. *The madness establishment: Ralph Nader's study group report on the National Institute of Mental Health*. New York: Grossman, 1974.

Crowell, E. Redistributive aspects of psychotherapy's inclusion in national health insurance: A summary. *American Psychologist*, 1977, *32*, 731–737.

Freedman, N., Englehardt, D. M., & Hankoff, L. D. Dropout from outpatient psychiatric treatment. *Archives of Neurology and Psychiatry*, 1958, *80*, 657–666.

Goldstein, A. P. *Therapist-patient expectancies in psychotherapy*. New York: Pergamon, 1962.

Goldstein, A. P. *Structured learning therapy: Toward a psychotherapy for the poor*. New York: Academic Press, 1973.

Gordon, S. Are we seeing the right patients? Child guidance intake: The sacred cow. *American Journal of Orthopsychiatry*, 1965, *35*, 131–137.

Gursslin, O. R., Hunt, R. G., & Roach, J. L. Social class and the mental health movement. *Social Problems,* 1959–1960, *7*, 210–218.

Heine, R. W., & Trosman, H. Initial expectations of the doctor-patient interaction as a factor in the continuance of psychotherapy. *Psychiatry*, 1960, *23*, 275–278.

Hoehn-Saric, R., Frank, J. D., Imber, S. D., Nash, E. H., Stone, A. R., & Battle, C. C. Systematic preparation of patients for psychotherapy. I. Effects on therapy behavior and outcome. *Journal of Psychiatric Research*, 1964, *2*, 267–281.

Hollingshead, A. B., & Redlich, F. C. *Social class and mental illness*. New York: Wiley, 1958.

Jacobson, S. L., Roman, M., & Kaplan, S. R. Training nonprofessional workers. In H. Grunebaum (Ed.), *The practice of community mental health*. Boston: Little, Brown, 1970.

Jencks, C. *Inequality: A reassessment of the effect of family and schooling in America*. New York: Basic Books, 1972.

Johnson, F., & Gittleson, S. Getting by. *Chicago Magazine,* September 1976, pp. 96–103; 218.

Kaplan, S. R., Boyajian, L. Z., & Meltzer, B. The role of the nonprofessional worker. In H. Grunebaum (Ed.), *The practice of community mental health*. Boston: Little, Brown, 1970.

Kiresuk, T. J., & Sherman, R. Goal-attainment scaling: A general method for evaluating community mental health programs. *Community Mental Health Journal*, 1968, *4*, 443–453.

Kohn, M. L., *Class and conformity*. Homewood, Ill.: Dorsey Press, 1969.

Lennard, H. L., & Bernstein, A. *The anatomy of psychotherapy: Systems of communications and expectations*. New York: Columbia University Press, 1960.

London, P. The psychotherapy boom: From the long couch for the sick to the push button for the bored. *Psychology Today*, June 1974, pp. 62–64; 66–68.

McMahon, J. T. The working class psychiatric patient: A clinical view. In F. Riessman, J. Cohen, & A. Pearl (Eds.), *Mental health of the poor*. New York: Free Press, 1964.

Meltzer, M. L. Insurance reimbursement: A mixed blessing. *American Psychologist*, 1975, *30*, 1150–1156.

Miller, S. M., & Riessman, F. The working class subculture: A new view. In A. L. Grey (Ed.), *Class and personality in society*. New York: Atherton, 1969.

No peace in our time. *Advance*, 1976, *3*(4), 1–3.

Overall, B., & Aronson, H. Expectations of psychotherapy in patients of lower socioeconomic class. *American Journal of Orthopsychiatry*, 1963, *33*, 421–430.

Paul, G. L. Behavior modification research: Design and tactics. In C. M. Franks (Ed.), *Behavior therapy: Appraisal and status*. New York: McGraw-Hill, 1969.

Pearl, A., & Reissman, F. *New careers for the poor*. New York: Free Press, 1965.

Reiff, R., & Reissman, F. *The indigenous nonprofessional*. New York: Behavioral Publications, 1965.

Riecken, H. W., & Boruch, R. F. *Social experimentation: A method for planning and evaluating social intervention*. New York: Academic Press, 1974.

Rioch, M. J. Pilot projects in training mental health counselors. In E. L. Cowen, E. A. Gardner, & M. Zax (Eds.), *Emergent approaches to mental health problems*. New York: Appleton-Century-Crofts, 1967.

Roen, S. R. Evaluative research and community mental health. In A. E. Bergin & S. L. Garfield (Eds.), *Handbook of psychotherapy and behavior change*. New York: Wiley, 1971.

Scheidemandel, P. L. Utilization of psychiatric services. *Psychiatric Annals*, 1972, *4*(1), 58–74.

Schofield, W. *Psychotherapy, the purchase of friendship*. Englewood Cliffs, N.J.: Prentice-Hall, 1964.

Shakow, O. What *is* clinical psychology? *American Psychologist*, 1976, *31*, 553–560.

Snow, P. L., & Newton, P. M. Task, social structure and social process in the community mental health center movement. *American Psychologist*, 1976, *31*, 582–594.

Sobell, R., & Ingalls, A. Resistance to treatment: Exploration of a patient's sick role. *American Journal of Psychotherapy*, 1964, *18*, 562–573.

U.S. Bureau of the Census. *Census of population, 1970. General social and economic characteristics* (Final report PC [1]-C1, *United States summary*). Washington, D.C.: U.S. Government Printing Office, 1972.

Whittington, H. G. A case for private enterprise in mental health. *Administration in Mental Health*, 1975, *4*, 23–28.

At the time of original publication of this article, *A. John McSweeny* was a member of the faculty of Northwestern University.

This article is based on a paper supported by Grant MN00180 from the National Institute of Mental Health and presented at the meeting of the American Psychological Association, Washington, D.C., September 1976. The author thanks Richard Bootzin, Donald Campbell, and Paul Wortman for their helpful comments on an earlier draft of this article.

Redistributive Aspects of Psychotherapy's Inclusion in National Health Insurance

A Summary

Elizabeth Crowell

This paper investigates redistributive aspects of national health insurance. Specifically, the charge that the inclusion of noncritical psychotherapy services in national health insurance represents a potential subsidy from the poor to the rich is explored. If universal insurance plans reduce the costs to those currently using these services with no substantial increase in demand by persons with low incomes, then inclusion of "luxury good" psychotherapy may be regressive in effect, thus reducing the program's overall redistributive intent. Recent public finance and health policy literature is reviewed with this question in mind. Notwithstanding the prospective nature of this discussion, the experiences of existing government insurance and health programs such as Medicare and Medicaid suggest that there may be some truth to this charge. A simple impact model is included.

I was asked by a prominent social psychologist to substantiate (or refute) the charge that the inclusion of outpatient psychotherapy within a national health insurance plan would constitute a subsidy from the poor to the rich. Interest in this question was motivated by two items: first, the Weisbrod and Hansen (1969) findings which showed the distribution of benefits of the higher education programs in California to be disproportionate to higher income families (since then, other studies have shown contradictory findings: McGuire, 1976; Pechman, 1970); and second, research findings (Goldstein, 1973; Goldstein & Simonson, 1971; Hollingshead & Redlich, 1958; Schofield, 1964) indicating that therapists are more willing to work with and are more successful with the "young, attractive, verbal, intelligent, and successful" (YAVIS) patient than with the "homely, old, unattractive, nonverbal, and dumb" (HOUND) patient. These findings reinforce the idea that even if the disadvantaged have the financial resources (via national health insurance) to demand mental health care, that care might not be accessible to them. In light of these arguments, I was asked to compile data that would prove or disprove this charge.

Such a task is impossible at this time. First, since the question is prospective, no final answer is possible. Second, information on the current market for noncritical psychotherapy is neither complete nor noncontradictory in terms of the actual composition of high and low families making up the demand side. Third, efforts to obtain a data set of a similar program (e.g., insurance carrier or health maintenance organization's experience with mental health care benefits) have been unsuccessful. Nonetheless, evidence of the redistributive impact of similar government programs can be compiled which at least supports the argument that fears of such a subsidy are not unfounded. This review paper summarizes a larger paper documenting the efforts of the study and the findings with respect to this question (Crowell, Note 1).

National Health Insurance

Of the more than 20 national health insurance bills before Congress, all are directed toward the

Reprinted from *American Psychologist*, 1977, *32*, 731–737.

goal of improving health care for all persons, especially those who cannot afford medical services and adequate insurance protection under the current fragmented and dual health service system. Any plan undertaken must be programmatically sound, each aspect fulfilling policy objectives. The inclusion of a wide range of psychotherapy services in a national health plan may negate to some extent the program's redistributive goals.

This paper summarizes attempts to investigate the charge that the inclusion of psychotherapy services in national insurance represents a subsidy from the poor to the rich. Inclusion of psychotherapy services within a universal, mandatory, and unitary health insurance plan may be regressive in effect, that is, imposing a greater burden on low-income persons even though the method of financing is technically proportional or progressive. Some economists and planners contend that the distributionally regressive nature (inverse relationship of income level and effective tax rates) of taxes such as the payroll (social security) tax is offset by directing the benefits to more low-income than high-income households. The same analysis of distributional regressiveness applies to proposals for national health insurance. The qualifying condition of more benefits to lower income groups may not hold, however, for the case in which psychotherapy services as luxury commodities are consumed primarily by persons with relatively high incomes. If universal insurance plans reduce the costs to those currently using these services, with no substantial increase in demand by persons with lower incomes (i.e., if under federal financing the marginal propensity to consume these services still is greater for the rich than for the poor), then the inclusion of psychotherapy within a national health plan does represent a subsidy to the rich from the poor, resulting in a redistributive effect partially negating the program's overall redistributive goals.

Nature, Scope, and Limitations of Study

Therefore, the objective of my research was to investigate the potential redistributive effects of the inclusion of noncritical outpatient counseling services in national health insurance. This work is based on two premises. One, if the demand for noncritical psychotherapy is, as argued by many psychologists, greater for higher income persons, then the provision and/or financing of such services might well constitute in effect a subsidy from the lower income groups to the higher income groups. Two, in addition to the careful discussion of financing and administrative aspects of national health insurance (or any legislation), care and forethought should be given to specific programmatic considerations and the long-term impact of the program prior to enactment and implementation rather than as an afterthought.

Because no legislation has been passed, the scope of this study was, of necessity, prospective. Notwithstanding this, however, is the fact that past experiences of other insurance programs and indirect government health programs can be used to suggest with some degree of accuracy the possible distributional consequences. This paper (a) suggests that care be taken in determining all programmatic considerations of national health insurance in advance of legislative enactment, (b) presents a model that can be used to determine the redistributional aspects or impact of the inclusion of psychotherapy services within national health insurance, (c) recommends that selective experiments be undertaken by the National Center for Health Service Research prior to passage of a national health insurance program in order to estimate the projected impact of a number of different provisions, and (d) offers provisions that will minimize the potential adverse redistribution of benefits that might be produced or generated by such inclusion.

Several factors limited this study. First, the subject is prospective, seeking to predict the future impact of certain program provisions and to incorporate these findings into the formal legislation. As such, no evidence of the actual effect of the program can be compiled or analyzed, and recommendations based upon such information cannot be made. Instead, this study points out potential inequitable effects of the inclusion of psychotherapy in national health insurance. Much legislation is effected hurriedly. Once all the long-drawn-out political discussion, logrolling, bull, and so on have come to an end, major programmatic considerations and problem areas are decided upon in haste and/or left up to the middle-management bureaucrats of the administrative agency to draw up the formal regulations, the real "guts" of the program. It is imperative that more prospective policy analysis be undertaken in order to insure better program operations.

Second, the subject is extremely controversial and normative in character. There is no right or wrong answer. The problem of a national health plan is beset with differing opinions, normative judgments, and debates over questions as to the proper role of government in providing services and the redistribution of income. Many other questions are debatable. For example, should psychological services be considered reimbursable only on the recommendation of a physician? Which vested-interest groups (psychologists, social workers, carriers), if any, should receive special treatment? This study did not seek to resolve those questions; this study did rest upon the assumption that redistribution of income or program benefits from those with less ability to pay to those with greater resources is contrary to the fiscal rationales of neutrality and vertical inequity.

Third, the data needed to resolve the argument are extremely difficult to obtain. Two major sources of difficulty are the highly sensitive nature of mental illness and counseling in terms of invasion of privacy or potential lack of confidentiality and the fear on the part of some agencies and organizations that such information may be used against them. For these reasons, little data were forthcoming to the researcher. Hence, the evidence presented in this paper is indirect.

Fourth, added to the difficulties in securing data are some very real conceptual difficulties. When is psychotherapy essential and when is it nonessential? How does one differentiate between the demand for psychoanalysis on the basis of need or "fad?" How are tax burdens made equitable?

Fifth, the vast number of proposals before Congress call for far different types of coverage (e.g., comprehensive or catastrophic), financing (tax or premium), and administration (private or public). As such, it is impossible to consider all the variations possible when compromises occur within the arena of legislative decision making.

Despite these limitations, it was felt that some study of these subsidy charges should be conducted because the policy implications are significant. It is in this context that I present the following arguments.

Distributional Impact

There is no question but that the existing health care delivery system (both physical and mental) in this country is dual in nature. In the aggregate, quality and quantity of health care are directly related to the patient's ability to pay. I do not question the need for a national health insurance plan that will provide all persons with adequate care. A comprehensive, mandatory, unitary, and universal health insurance plan should reduce (and ideally eliminate) this duality. *Mandatory* means that both poor and nonpoor are covered. *Unitary* alludes to the fact that one program covers all persons. *Universal* refers to the fact that the risk of loss due to illness will be shared equitably. Under the existing system, many low-income families spend their money on more immediate commodities (rent, food) rather than on insurance premiums of a protective and future (less immediate) nature, risking the chance of having to pay all expenses for health care or doing without care when needed. A person who can afford insurance runs less risk of suffering as great a financial loss from ill health because the insurance reduces the net price the person pays for care. In addition, the program should be comprehensive in terms of services: hospitalization, outpatient treatment, physician visits, laboratory work, and examinations—in other words, preventive as well as ameliorative.

The major beneficiaries of such a national health program would be the lower and middle income groups (Davis, 1975; Mitchell & Schwartz, 1976; "National Health Insurance," 1975). The existing private insurance system is geared to those with the most resources; the greater one's ability to pay premiums, the more protective and extensive the coverage. Those in the lower-middle and middle income brackets, unless covered by extremely good job-related health benefits, cannot afford adequate coverage. Medicare and Medicaid provide health care for the elderly and those with extremely limited means, but questions have been raised about the quality and prices of those services. What about those persons with resources above the minimum need level but below the adequate coverage level? If the financial burden of a national health plan does not fall too heavily on these lower and middle income persons, then the overall redistributive consequences of a national health plan will be desirable.

In this same respect, it is recognized that some mental health coverage is needed and must be included in a comprehensive health plan. Again, the greatest beneficiaries of this coverage would be the poor—if in addition to financing they can be assured of receiving services. The YAVIS-HOUND classifications imply that if community health centers and publicly funded programs are phased out, the poor may be refused treatment by many of those in private practice. Provisions would have to be made to prevent this.

Two areas must be included in program deliberations. National health insurance plans seem desirable in terms of providing more equitable coverage and health services of a more preventive nature. If such a plan encourages overutilization of certain types of services by certain groups (in this case, counseling as a luxury good), then the positive effects of the program are lessened. In addition, other programs have promised redistributive impacts but have not turned out to be as redistributive as promised (Davis & Reynolds, 1975).

The Distributive Impact of Some Existing Taxes and Programs[1]

Much of the present tax system adheres to the concept of distribution of burden by ability to pay. Hence, most tax rates are designed as proportional or progressive in order to allow for differences in payment ability; however, (a) the distributional effect is not always the same as the technical rate-base relationship (tax base may be much smaller than total income), and (b) the burden of a tax can be shifted to others.

---

[1] This discussion is presented in much greater detail in Crowell (Note 1).

This section reviews some taxes and legislative programs that seem to impose tax burdens in a regressive way (harder on those with less ability to pay) or seem to have benefits going to the higher income groups.

Sales and income taxes. The imposition of a proportional sales tax is regressive in effect. Studies have shown that lower income groups spend a greater proportion of their total incomes than do higher income groups, thus paying a higher effective tax rate than those with greater earnings and accumulated wealth (Due, 1957; Pechman & Okner, 1974).

In terms of rate structure, the personal income tax at the federal level is a graduated or progressive tax, but the degree of graduation is not as marked as the tax rates by income brackets suggest. These are marginal rates representing the tax rate for additional increments. The effective tax rate is the total tax payment as a percentage of adjusted gross income (2.5%–18.3% as opposed to a marginal rate range of 14%–70%; Ozawa, 1973). Hence, the federal personal income tax is only moderately progressive.

In addition, the careful use of deductions, exemptions, and special provisions may reduce the taxable income of high-earnings persons to very low tax brackets. Also, the system of deductions favors the higher income groups because the amount of deduction is based on the marginal tax rate.

Ozawa (1973) and Mitchell and Vogel (1975) note that the medical deduction provisions of the federal personal income tax act as an indirect program of national health insurance—indirectly subsidizing via deductions the consumption of health care services. Because this deduction is based on marginal tax rates and income as well as utilization of health services (found to be directly related to income size), benefits are directed more toward the higher income groups.

Payroll tax (social security). The most common example of a regressive tax is the payroll tax used to finance the OASDI (Old Age, Survivors, and Disability Insurance) program. The payroll tax is currently fixed at a flat 5.85% of earnings up to $16,200, beyond which no additional tax is levied. No one questions the regressive effect of this tax—the burden in terms of tax payment relative to total earnings decreases as earnings increase (also, nonearnings income is not taxed). In addition, payments per family depend on the number of wage earners in a family. A couple each earning $16,000 will pay $1,790.10, while a man (with family) earning the same $32,000 will pay only $895.05. Since more low-income families have two wage earners than do high-income families, the burden is felt more by the lower income groups (Ozawa, 1973).

If a national health insurance program is financed by payroll taxes (as some of the plans provide), this same criticism might be applied to it. Therefore, payroll taxes used to finance such a plan must be made more progressive.

Some economists and planners (Pechman, Aaron, & Taussig, 1968) argue that this regressiveness is justified because (a) benefits often exceed the contributions of an individual, and (b) the benefits distributed make up a significantly higher percentage of total income for low-income recipients than for higher income recipients. Progressive transfers offset the regressive financing. Such arguments do not satisfy me. If the ultimate program purpose is redistributive from high- to low-income groups, then the regressiveness of the financing reduces the net redistributive effect.

The taxes cited above are the ones traditionally given as examples of the differences between technical tax structure and distributional impact. More recent studies indicate some additional programs that may be quasi-regressive in the sense that they yield greater benefits to higher income persons than to lower income persons.

Group insurance through employer. Today, the greater share of most persons' health care insurance comes from employer-related health benefits. Part, if not all, of the cost is borne by the employer as part of the total wage package. In addition, these benefits are exempt from the personal income tax. Also, group coverage allows more comprehensive coverage at equivalent, or more often reduced, rates than individual coverage through the same carrier would cost. On the whole, however, rates are distributionally regressive—a flat rate regardless of income.

Medical deduction. The regressive nature of medical deductions has already been discussed. An important factor here, compounding the regressive impact of the medical deduction provision, is the demand for (a) insurance and (b) medical care. Both are positively related to income: the former very strongly, the latter only moderately so, depending on the type of care required. In terms of the demand for health services, the demand for services in response to critical illnesses is similar for all income groups, though the quality of care and the length of convalescence may differ slightly (Holahan, 1975). It is in the area of medical services of a more preventive and more routine nature that the demand is related in a much more significant manner to income levels (highly income elastic). These are the services most needed by the lower income groups. Any national health program put into effect must incorporate provisions that take into account this differential demand for care and also guard against financial arrangements that will have effects similar to the medical deduction in the income tax regulations. Since the demand for mental health care is income elastic, provisions must be made in this regard, too.

Medicare. Directed at persons over 65, Medicare consists of two programs: Part A, hospitalization and related benefits; and Part B, supplemental medical benefits. The first is universal and mandatory; the second, voluntary (Somers & Somers, 1967). The experiences of Medicare, this country's first step to national health insurance, are crucial to this study: first, utilization by income groups; second, the repercussions on the health care market.

Davis and Reynolds (1975) found that income is an important factor in the demand for health care services reimbursable under Medicare. Once health status (the most important demand determinant) is adjusted for, utilization of Medicare services is directly related to income. The dual market existing in the private sector also exists in Medicare, a program designed to counteract this duality and inequity. Persons with higher income have greater ability to purchase supplemental coverage plus additional private coverage. In addition, medical care is more accessible to higher income groups. Davis and Reynolds also found payments to be greater for whites than for blacks.

The uniform financing aspects of Medicare (deductibles, flat-fee premiums, and cost sharing) are regressive in effect. The lower income persons pay a greater proportion of their total income for coverage. Those with greater ability to pay are charged the same as those with lesser ability to pay. When the feature is combined with utilization rates (differential by income) of Medicare services, the higher income groups are found to be receiving more benefits than the poorer ones. That is, the higher incomes seem to be subsidized, if one likes, by the lower income groups.

The Davis and Reynolds study shows that high-income persons (a) receive more eligible services, (b) receive more reimbursements because they are receiving more services, and (c) are charged more for such services (and hence receive a greater total amount of reimbursement).

Medicaid. Similar findings have been made with respect to Medicaid. Holahan (1975) found that utilization of Medicaid services was affected positively by income level. Utilization was directly related to availability and accessibility of physician and income. Within the range of families eligible for income transfers (and hence eligible for Medicaid), Holahan found a significantly positive effect. As incomes increased, both number of services demanded and total amount of expenditures per household increased. Higher incomes make transportation, child care, and other difficulties less burdensome. These types of considerations have to be taken into account before low-income persons can take advantage of national health insurance (relative to higher income persons).

Holahan also found that whites are more likely to use Medicaid than are nonwhites, despite a zero price. This discovery illustrates another facet: limited access to services on a racial basis. Poverty need not be defined solely on the basis of income. Limited services to blacks or other minorities may render the program less effective. This same argument holds true for residents of remote rural regions where there may be a limited number of physicians and few specialists.

The use of Medicaid and Medicare as examples here should not be taken to mean that the programs are not benefiting low-income

groups. Both programs have had the effect of providing needed health services to many who either might not have received such benefits or might have paid more than they could afford for these services. Nonetheless, the main objective of each program is to provide quality health care to those with less ability to pay. Certainly some redistribution of income from those "who have" to those "who have less" has been achieved, but the redistribution aspects of these programs do not seem maximized, because the benefits received (as determined by utilization and reimbursements) are directly related to income.

Recent Experiences and Trends

Mental health coverage is being included in more and more private health insurance plans. At the same time, utilization of those mental health benefits has been greater than carrier expectations (Asher, 1975). Some carriers have had to set limits on numbers of sessions covered, etc. In any case, the experience has been that as insurance coverage reduces the effective price to the individual, some increase in quantity demanded occurs. Unfortunately, data as to utilization of these benefits by income class are not available. It is because of this lack of directly relevant data that the previously mentioned indirect examples of similar health programs were made. If a data set or several sets (especially with different financial arrangements) were made available, it should not be too difficult to estimate the degree to which different income groups utilize noncritical, insured mental health services. With cost and demand information, the distribution of the benefits and the cost by income class could be determined (Mitchell & Vogel, 1975). The following is a very simplistic model of how, given the necessary information, such a distribution might be determined for a straightforward national health plan based on a uniform deduction and co-insurance rate for all subscribers.

Possible Model of Impact

Assuming a very simple national insurance plan which calls for a uniform deductible and co-insurance rate, the following variables for an individual subscriber (household) can be identified:

T = total health expenses for individual household during time period t;

E = portion of health expenses eligible for insurance coverage (total less deductible);

D = deductible paid by individual before claim eligible (flat fee);

M = medical portion of eligible expenses, including inpatient psychological care and critical outpatient care (e.g., autistic child's counseling);

P = psychological portion of eligible expenses—*noncritical*;

r = co-insurance rate representing specific portion of eligible expenses paid by individual after deductible (absolute-premium or income-related rate can be used also);

C = total cost to individual;

G = cost to government of services provided individual ($= T - C$);

C_m, C_p = costs to individual of medical and psychological care, respectively, after deductible;

G_m, G_p = costs to government of medical and psychological care, respectively.

These variables are related in the following way:

$$T = E + D = M + P + D = C + G,$$

where $M + P$ represents the value of the services or expenses incurred after the deductible has been paid, and $C + G$ represents the total payment sources and amounts (private expenses and government subsidy).

The costs of services to an individual household would be divided between the household and the government in the following manner:

Individual: $C = r(E) + D = r(M + P) + D$
[total individual cost including deduction would be $r(E) + D$]
Government: $G = (1 - r)E = (1 - r)(M + P)$.

What is important to the argument presented here, however, is the difference in the use and cost by service type (medical or noncritical psychological). This means determining the cost and expenses incurred by the individual household (not including deductible) for each type, assuming these can be separated (a mammoth record-keeping task).

Two qualifications should be made. First, for simplicity's sake, the model is designed for the individual household. Information on the individual will not be available and aggregation is necessary. Second, this analysis also assumes that information as to the breakdown of services between medical and critical psychological services and noncritical psychological services can be made. This latter represents a heroic assumption.

Because of privacy commitments and sheer record-keeping problems, any forthcoming data would have to be aggregated. Aggregation is not without difficulties. Individuals do not consume services uniformly. Hence, some persons may place no demands on the program during a given time period ($E \leq D$). In addition, to apply this model meaningfully, it is necessary to have the data disaggregated by income levels. This disaggregation should reveal the differences among income groups with respect to total health expenditures, utilization of psychological and medical services and expenses, and private and government payments. In addition, net benefits received (government's share) as a percentage of income should be determined and compared.

Two qualifying statements about possible findings should be made: (1) It is entirely possible that any direct relationship among three variables (P, G_p, and C_p) and income may be offset by much greater transfers of medical services to lower income groups (assuming accessibility and use), and (2) the "regressive" nature depends on the utilization rates by income groups and the financing mechanisms and may not be as regressive if cost sharing is tied to both expenses and income level. The simple model outlined is regressive on two counts. First, the uniform deductible puts a disproportionate burden (as percentage of income) on the low-income groups; second, the uniform co-insurance rate as included here is based on amount of expenses, not income. If, as studies show, the demand for both medical and psychological services is income elastic, then this plan favors those with more expenses (usually those with higher incomes). Therefore, the financing mechanisms are extremely important and should not be decided upon in haste.

Conclusions and Recommendations

The question that this study tried to answer cannot be answered with precision. First, it is impossible to separate accurately noncritical and critical psychotherapy. Second, the question is prospective. Third, little data were forthcoming. Enough indirect evidence was found to suggest that demand conditions of different income groups and the financing provisions of a national health program in its entirety, much less in its noncritical mental health component (if any), might be to some extent regressive, both in financing and in the distribution of benefits. This paper has sought to compile some of that indirect evidence.

This evidence suggests that:

1. Extensive experiments be undertaken by the government to test some of the alternative programs.

2. Safeguards be included in the final legislative program. Such safeguards might take the form of (a) restrictions on coverage and noncritical use, (b) very progressive financing, and (c) provisions encouraging increases in the supply of services and the accessibility of services.

One final note: The initial premise of this study may be "all wet." If so, it should be proved (or disproved). I can only request that those persons with data pertaining to this question allow the data to be studied.

Reference Note

1. Crowell, E. *Redistributive aspects of psychotherapy's inclusion in national health insurance.* Unpublished manuscript, 1976. (Available from E. Crowell, College of Social Professions, University of Kentucky, Lexington, Kentucky 40506.)

References

Asher, J. Soaring medical costs endanger psychologists. *APA Monitor,* December 1975, pp. 1; 12–13.

Davis, K. *National health insurance: Benefits, costs and consequences.* Washington, D.C.: Brookings Institution, 1975.

Davis, K., & Reynolds, R. Medicare and the utilization of health care services by the elderly. *Journal of Human Resources,* 1975, *10,* 361–377.

Due, J. F. *Sales taxation.* Champaign: University of Illinois Press, 1957.

Goldstein, A. P. *Structured learning therapy.* New York: Academic Press, 1973.

Goldstein, A. P., & Simonson, N. E. Social psychological approaches to psychotherapy research. In A. E. Bergin & S. L. Garfield (Eds.), *Handbook of psychotherapy and behavior change.* New York: Wiley, 1971.

Holahan, J. Physician availability, medical care reimbursement, and delivery of physician services: Some evidence from the Medicaid program. *Journal of Human Resources,* 1975, *10,* 378–402.

Hollingshead, A. B., & Redlich, F. C. *Social class and mental illness.* New York: Wiley, 1958.

McGuire, J. W. The distribution of subsidy to students in California public higher education. *Journal of Human Resources,* 1976, *11,* 343–353.

Mitchell, B. M., & Schwartz, W. B. The financing of national health insurance. *Science,* 1976, *192,* 661–628.

Mitchell, B. M., & Vogel, R. J. Health and taxes: An assessment of the medical deduction. *Southern Economic Journal,* 1975, *41,* 660–672.

National health insurance: Which way to go? *Consumer Reports,* 1975, *40,* 118–124.

Ozawa, M. N. Taxation and social welfare. *Social Work,* 1973, *18,* 66–76.

Pechman, J. A. The distributional effects of public higher education in California. *Journal of Human Resources,* 1970, *5,* 361–370.

Pechman, J. A., Aaron, H. G., & Taussig, M. K. *Social security: Perspectives for reform.* Washington, D.C.: Brookings Institution, 1968.

Pechman, J. A., & Okner, B. A. *Who bears the tax burden?* Washington, D.C.: Brookings Institution, 1974.

Schofield, W. *Psychotherapy, the purchase of friendship.* Englewood Cliffs, N.J.: Prentice-Hall, 1964.

Somers, H. M., & Somers, A. R. *Medicare and the hospitals.* Washington, D.C.: Brookings Institution, 1967.

Weisbrod, B. A., & Hansen, W. L. *Benefits, costs and finance of public higher education.* Chicago: Markham, 1969.

At the time of original publication of this article, *Elizabeth Crowell* was a faculty member of the College of Social Professions, University of Kentucky, Lexington.

This paper presents a summary of efforts to investigate the redistributive aspects of the inclusion of noncritical mental health services within a national health insurance program. A more detailed analysis is presented in another paper (Crowell, Note 1).

This work was supported in part by Grant No. 1 T22 MH00180-02 awarded by the National Institute of Mental Health (NIMH). Points of view stated in this document are those of the author and do not necessarily represent the official position or policies of NIMH. The author would like to express her appreciation to NIMH and Donald T. Campbell for the opportunity to work with the Evaluation Research Program, Northwestern University, during the past year.

National Health Insurance, Psychotherapy, and the Poor

Daniel W. Edwards, Les R. Greene, Stephen I. Abramowitz, and Christine V. Davidson

Debate on psychotherapy coverage under national health insurance has centered around perceived inequitable service to different income groups. It has been argued that national health insurance coverage for psychotherapy would represent a subsidy to the affluent by poorer citizens. Four pertinent hypotheses were examined in a series of studies of patients in community mental health centers. It has been maintained that the poor would not seek psychotherapy, would receive fewer sessions, would receive either less prestigious treatments or less trained therapists, and would benefit less than the more affluent. None of these hypotheses were supported. This article discusses the implications of these findings in terms of psychotherapy coverage under national health insurance and the role of psychologists in a national system of service delivery.

Proposals for national health insurance (NHI) have been coming before the U.S. Congress and professional societies for the past 10 years. The major unresolved issues concerning NHI are the kinds of services to be covered, the costs of coverage, the service delivery mechanism (e.g., public, private, or a mix of public and private providers), and ways to ensure equitable distribution.

Psychologists have been actively engaged in these sensitive deliberations, focusing in particular on whether psychotherapeutic services should be included under NHI. Albee (1977), McSweeny (1977), and Crowell (1977) are among those who have recently expressed skepticism about the wisdom of providing coverage for emotional distress, mental dysfunction, and social maladaptation. Concerned about equitable access to services, Albee in essence argued that the poor and minority groups would not seek out psychotherapy under NHI. Even if they did, contended Albee, they would derive meager benefit from it because of the differences in values, expectations, and cognitive styles between them and their predominantly middle-class therapists. He also seemed to assume that NHI would basically support the private sector and concluded that it would represent a subsidy from the underutilizing poor to the overutilizing rich.

McSweeny (1977) was less pessimistic than Albee, although he raised many of the same points. He included a discussion of possible reimbursement schedules to prevent abuse. He also discussed some possible mechanisms for monitoring the provision of services to prevent misuse of psychotherapy coverage by the affluent for purposes of personal growth or recreation. Crowell (1977) likewise stressed the importance of evaluating the distribution of coverage and the financially regressive potential of NHI. Her call for data bearing on use and the potential benefits of psychotherapy coverage furnished an initial impetus to this report.

The viewpoints articulated by Albee, McSweeny, and Crowell suggest four major hypotheses concerning psychotherapeutic treatment of the disadvantaged:

1. *Attraction hypothesis.* Mental health professionals cannot create clinical settings that will attract the poor. Even if they could, the poor would not use them for help with mental or emotional problems.

Reprinted from *American Psychologist*, 1979, *34*, 411–419.

2. *Duration hypothesis.* Even if the poor sought treatment, they would receive fewer sessions than would more affluent groups.

3. *Elitism hypothesis.* Even if the poor were given treatment as extensive as that accorded the affluent, they would (a) receive second-class services such as medication clinics rather than elite services such as individual, group, or family psychotherapy; (b) be treated by nurses and social workers rather than by psychologists and psychiatrists; and (c) be treated by staff rather than by clinicians with faculty appointments.

4. *Effectiveness hypothesis.* Even if the poor sought treatment and were offered the same quantity and quality of treatment as the more affluent, they would profit less.

Review of Literature

A selective review of findings pertaining to each of these hypotheses follows. Although our research was limited to examining the role of patients' income levels on certain parameters of psychotherapeutic service, the literature review also includes social class and education, which are considered to be related to income. Unfortunately, in most of the relevant studies, patient income was not examined independently of the other variables.

Attraction Hypothesis

Most of the data on psychotherapy use and outcome cited by Albee (1977), McSweeny (1977), and Crowell (1977) were collected by 1970—prior to publication of findings concerning the impact of the National Community Mental Health Centers Program. Many of the studies' inferences were consequently based on research in the private sector or with college-affiliated populations. Research from this earlier period that had demonstrated the feasibility of verbal psychotherapy with the poor (Bernard, 1965; Bernstein, 1964; Gardner, 1967; Gould, 1967; Minuchin, 1968; Spiegel, 1964; Yamamoto & Goin, 1965) was seemingly overlooked. Programs that attract and are sought out by disadvantaged groups have been described in

more recent publications (Goldstein, 1973; Lerner, 1972).

Reporting on data from adult outpatients seen in 40 community mental health centers in North Carolina, Stern (1977) found no significant relationship between education level and acceptance for treatment (i.e., more than one visit). Data from the nationwide, federally funded Community Mental Health Centers Program disclose that in 1973 the poor constituted the majority of admissions. Eighty-four percent of persons admitted to such programs had annual incomes of under $10,000 (Sharfstein, Taube, & Goldberg, 1977).

Duration Hypothesis

Outpatient psychotherapy in public mental health clinics is short term, with the median number of sessions varying between 3 and 10 (Brandt, 1965; Rogers, 1960; Rubinstein & Lorr, 1956). In 1966, the National Center for Health Statistics reported an average of 4.7 visits for approximately 1 million patients (Lorion, 1973). Data from the National Institute of Mental Health Biometry Report in 1973 reveal a mean of 5.3 visits per outpatient admission (Sharfstein et al., 1977).

The relationship of socioeconomic status or education to length of treatment has not been empirically resolved. Although Lorion (1974) reported that social class was positively associated with treatment length, Pettit, Pettit, and Welkowitz (1974) failed to find an overall linkage between these two variables. Stern (1977) found no relationship between education and treatment duration in 39 of 40 mental health centers studied. Sue, McKinney, and Allen (1976) reported a weak positive relationship between income and duration which disappeared when ethnicity and education were controlled.

Elitism Hypothesis

Stern (1977) found no connection between level of patient education and type of treatment received in 60% of the centers examined. Again, no studies were uncovered that addressed the relationship of income to certain quality and status parameters of psychotherapeutic service delivery.

Effectiveness Hypothesis

It is clinical lore that lower-class individuals benefit less from psychotherapy than do those from higher socioeconomic strata. The available data, however, are not so clear-cut. Luborsky, Chandler, Auerbach, Cohen, and Bachrach (1971) reviewed 11 studies that dealt with relationships between social status or occupational achievement and psychotherapy outcome. Five investigations reported a positive relationship, five reported none, and one showed a negative association. In none of these studies was income level per se examined in relation to therapy outcome. Lorion (1973) concluded from his review that psychotherapeutic treatment outcome did not differ according to class membership.

Setting for Study

The foregoing hypotheses were tested by data collected from both adult and child outpatients as part of ongoing program evaluation efforts in a consortium of comprehensive community mental health centers administered by a university. Described in detail by Spensley and Langsley (1977) and Tupin, Yarvis, and Edwards (Note 1), this consortium is a collaborative venture between the County of Sacramento and the University of California at Davis.

The consortium provides public mental health services to the general population of Sacramento County, California. The program is a component of California's Short-Doyle System, which is designed to provide community treatment, eliminate unnecessary hospitalization, and offer quality mental health care to those in need. Provision is made to subsidize those who ordinarily could not afford mental health treatment. This setting is intended to serve as a laboratory for the development of progressive public mental health services; we hope to use it to make innovative contributions in mental health service delivery akin to the University's accomplishments in agriculture and veterinary medicine. In addition, this consor-

tium provides unique training opportunities for psychiatrists, clinical psychologists, clinical social workers, psychiatric nurses, and a variety of paraprofessional groups.

Project 1

Data from this project were used to test the attraction hypothesis by examining rates of use (i.e., proportion of a total population receiving services) and penetration (proportion of those individuals in need who receive services) by different income levels.

Method

Subjects. The subject population consisted of 4,786 individuals who registered for services offered by the Division of Mental Health of the University of California at Davis during fiscal year 1976–1977.

Income levels. Based on demographic data routinely collected from all patients at their intake interviews, four categories of gross family income were developed: (1) poor, defined as annual incomes less than $5,000; (2) low income, consisting of incomes between $5,000 and $9,999; (3) low-middle income, comprising incomes between $10,000 and $14,999; and (4) high-middle income, consisting of incomes of $15,000 or more.

Measures of attraction. Use rates for these four income levels were based on recent census data. Population estimates were derived for each census tract in Sacramento County for 1976 by computing the annual growth rate from the 1970 U.S. Census to the 1975 Special Census and then adding the mean annual growth to the 1975 data. Penetration rates were derived from the rates of need or impairment for the various population groups as determined from all known studies of the epidemiology of mental illness with populations in the United States (Yarvis & Edwards, Note 2). A pilot study of mental health epidemiology in a low-income area of Sacramento County (Edwards, Yarvis, Swaback, Mueller, & Wagman, in press) indicated that these rates were generally applicable to our population.

Table 1: *Use and Penetration Rates by Income Level*

Gross family income ($)	Population (persons)	Estimated need (%)	Persons in need	Persons served	Use (% of population served)	Penetration (% of need served)
0–4,999	62,794	35	21,978	2,643	4.2	12.0
5,000–9,999	99,564	25	24,891	1,219	1.2	4.9
10,000–14,999	107,913	20	21,583	498	0.5	2.3
15,000+	173,771	10	17,371	426	0.2	2.5

Results

Table 1 presents the use and penetration rates for all types of admissions (i.e., outpatient, inpatient, day treatment, emergency room) by income level. Fifty-five percent of these admissions had incomes of less than $5,000, with 81% below $10,000. In terms of service to the poor, 4% of those in the lowest income group received services, compared with 1.2% or less for the higher income groups. The rate of penetration into the reservoir of need indicates that 12% of the poor in need were served, compared with approximately 5% of the low-income group and 2% or 3% of the higher income groups. The penetration rates for the poor were 2.4 times that of the low-income group, 5.2 times that of the low-middle income group, and 4.8 times that of the high-middle income group.

These data demonstrate that mental health clinics attractive to the poor can be developed and that use by the poor will occur if that is the intention of the service delivery system.

Project 2

A 3-month cohort of admissions to outpatient services from January through March 1977 provided the data used to test the duration and elitism hypotheses.

Method

Subjects. The subject population comprised a total of 617 adults and 188 children who were offered outpatient services by the professional staff of the Division of Mental Health. Patients who were treated by student therapists were deleted.

Patients are assigned to the professional staff on a rotating basis, with each therapist required to have one or two intakes per week. This assignment process eliminates selective or biasing factors, since each therapist has an equal chance of receiving poor, low-income, or more affluent patients.[1]

Income level. In this and the following project, three categories of patient income level were defined from data collected at intake. As in the first project, the poor were defined as those with a gross family income of less than $5,000, and the low-income group as those with incomes between $5,000 and $9,999. Low-middle and high-middle income groups were combined into a general medium group of those with gross family incomes of $10,000 or more.

Measures. For each patient, the therapist's assessment of impairment at intake, as rated on the Global Assessment Scale (Endicott, Spitzer, Fleiss, & Cohen, 1976), was recorded and retrieved from program evaluation archives. In addition, the modality of treatment (i.e., medication clinic, individual psychotherapy, group psychotherapy, or family psychotherapy) and number of sessions during the 6-month period following intake were tallied. Finally, therapist status parameters, specifically, professional discipline (i.e., nursing, psychiatry, psychology, or social work) and academic appointment (i.e., academic faculty, clinical faculty, or clinical staff), were recorded for each patient.

Analyses. To test the effects of patient income level on duration of treatment, separate one-way analyses of covariance, removing the effect of initial impairment, were performed for each treatment modality. The elitism hypothesis

---

[1] Chi-square analyses revealed no significant relationship between income level and either discipline or academic appointment for assignment of adults or children.

was tested by a series of 3 × 4 (Income × Professional Discipline) and a series of 3 × 3 (Income × Academic Appointment) analyses of covariance.

Results

With respect to the frequency of treatment sessions for adult outpatients, no significant effects of income level were obtained for medication clinic, individual psychotherapy, or group psychotherapy. The data did reveal that the poor received significantly fewer sessions of family psychotherapy, $F(2, 604) = 7.16$, $p < .001$. It should be noted that this form of treatment was rarely offered to any income group and accounted for only 4% of the total service offered to this cohort. Moreover, this one finding, though statistically significant, explains only 3% of the variance in the number of family therapy sessions received.

Similar analyses of covariance were conducted for the 188 children in this 3-month cohort, and results paralleled those for adult outpatients. No significant effects of income level on numbers of medication clinic, individual psychotherapy, or group psychotherapy sessions were obtained. Again, there was a weak but significant effect for the number of family sessions, with the poor receiving fewer sessions, $F(2, 175) = 7.54$, $p < .001$. This statistically significant finding must be viewed with caution. Family psychotherapy constituted only 14% of the mental health services for children, and the effect of income level accounted for only 8% of the variance in the number of family therapy sessions.

The first elitism hypothesis concerns differential modalities of treatment as a function of patient income. The data reported above are directly applicable to this hypothesis. The findings for both adults and children indicate that poor patients, in comparison with the more affluent ones, were not offered less prestigious treatment in terms of more medication clinic visits or fewer individual psychotherapy sessions.

The second elitism hypothesis was tested by examining the effects of patient income and therapist's professional discipline on the number of sessions offered in each treatment modality. If this elitism hypothesis were true, in the absence of a main effect for income, one would expect psychiatrists and psychologists to be offering longer treatment contracts to higher income groups, and social workers and nurses to be providing longer treatment contracts to the poor. With respect to adult outpatients, analyses of covariance controlling for initial impairment showed no significant main effects of therapist discipline on the number of sessions in the four treatment modalities under study. More importantly, there were no significant Income × Professional Discipline interactions on the number of medication clinic, individual psychotherapy, or family therapy sessions. A weak interaction for group psychotherapy sessions was obtained, $F(6, 604) = 2.98$, $p < .05$, but the pattern of means was not in agreement with the elitism hypothesis and was essentially uninterpretable. With respect to the outpatient data for children, neither a significant main effect of therapist discipline nor a significant Income × Discipline interaction was obtained on the number of treatment sessions in any of the four treatment modalities.

The third elitism hypothesis proposes that in a mental health agency affiliated with a university, clinicians with faculty appointments see fewer poor patients than do therapists without faculty appointments. Analysis of covariance yielded no significant main effects of academic status on the amount of therapy offered to adult outpatients. There were also no significant Income × Academic Appointment interactions on the number of sessions of medication clinic, group, or family psychotherapy. A weak interaction was obtained on the number of individual therapy sessions offered to adults, $F(4, 574) = 2.40$, $p < .05$, but it accounted for only 2% of the variance in the number of individual therapy sessions received. Moreover, the cell means were not in the direction predicted by the elitism hypothesis. The data on outpatient services to children disclosed no significant main or interactive effects of the therapist's academic status on the amount of treatment offered.

Project 3

Data on treatment effectiveness (Hypothesis 4) were obtained from three separate studies. In each study, consecutive admissions to psychotherapy were administered selected items from the Davis Outcome Assessment System (Edwards & Yarvis, Note 3) or from the Davis Child Therapy Effectiveness Battery (Zingale, Edwards, & Yarvis, Note 4).

Method: Study 1

Subjects. The subject sample was composed of 90 patients, all of whom had agreed to participate in an outcome study and were receiving some form of verbal psychotherapy. Fifty-five percent of this sample were defined as poor, 29% as low income, and 15% as medium income.

Measures. Therapists completed a revised version of the Multi-State Information System Problem Appraisal Scales (Laska & Bank, 1975) at intake and at the last session. Patients were asked to complete the National Center for Health Statistics General Well-Being Schedule (Dupuy, Note 5) 3 months after termination of psychotherapy; complete data were collected from 70 patients.

Analyses. In this study and the two to follow, raw change scores were derived from pre- and posttherapy ratings by therapists and patients. One-way analyses of variance were performed to test the effects of patient income level on benefits from psychotherapy.

Method: Study 2

Subjects. Outpatient admissions to one clinic in 1976 were asked to participate in this outcome study. Of this sample of 85 patients, 38% were classified as poor, 32% as low income, and 30% as medium income.

Measures. Therapists completed the Global Assessment Scale (Endicott et al., 1976) at intake and at a 3-month follow-up point. At these same two points, patients were asked to complete the Hopkins Symptom Checklist (Derogatis, Lipman, Rickels, Uhlenhuth, & Covi, 1974); 68 patients completed this inventory both times.

Method: Study 3

Subjects. This sample consisted of children under age 18 who were admitted to three outpa-

tient clinics over a 4-month period in 1977. In this sample, 38% of the children were from poor families, 40% were from low-income families, and 22% were from medium-income families. Complete ratings from both therapists and parents were obtained on 221 children; self-ratings were obtained from 128 children over age 8.

Measures. Therapists completed the Children's Symptom Checklist (Guy, 1976) at intake and at a 3-month follow-up. Parents completed the Children's Screening Scale (Langner et al., 1976), and the children completed a 5-item subset of questions from the National Center for Health Statistics General Well-Being Schedule (Dupuy, Note 5) at the same two points.

Results

In Study 1, analyses of variance of both therapist and patient ratings revealed significant symptom reduction over the course of psychotherapy for the total sample. However, neither therapist nor patient ratings revealed differential effectiveness of treatment as a function of patient income level.

In Study 2, the sample as a whole showed significant alleviation of symptoms, as reflected by patients' self-ratings; therapists' ratings revealed improvement just short of statistical significance ($p < .06$). As in the first study, benefit from psychotherapy as assessed by therapist and patient change scores was not linked to patient income level.

With respect to the outcome of psychotherapy for children, the findings from the third study parallel data from the two studies above. Significant improvement for the entire sample was revealed by the ratings of the children, parents, and therapists. Again, however, these three sets of ratings were not significantly related to income level.

Discussion

The foregoing data do not support some major reservations about including coverage for psychotherapy under NHI. The community mental health centers studied were found to be attractive to the poor. They were used more by the poor than by higher income groups and they better met the estimated psychiatric needs of the poor than those of the other groups. Our high rates of use by the poor are consistent with statistics from community mental health centers in North Carolina (Stern, 1977) and Seattle (Sue et al., 1976) and with national data for such programs reported by the National Institute of Mental Health (Sharfstein et al., 1977).

Duration of psychiatric treatment, as measured by number of medication clinic visits, individual psychotherapy sessions, and group psychotherapy sessions, was equivalent across income groups. This finding is in agreement with previous reports of an absence of a relationship between length of treatment and social class in general (Pettit et al., 1974) or education (Stern, 1977). Our data regarding the average number of sessions were, on the whole, similar to those from earlier regional (Brandt, 1965; Lorr, Katz, & Rubinstein, 1958) and national (Lorion, 1974) studies of public mental health clinics. Since the poor used the centers we studied relatively more than did the other income groups, the absence of differential treatment duration according to income suggests that the poor actually received more than their per capita fair share of clinic visits. This differential use is in line with the higher impairment rates found for the less affluent. The implication is that NHI coverage for psychotherapy need not be a subsidy from the poor to the rich. The poor will use mental health services if those services are designed with their needs in mind.

Concerns that the poor would receive second-class treatment were also not substantiated. The poor were not shunted off into medication clinics. Individual psychotherapy proved to be the modal treatment for all income groups, rather than the preserve of the more affluent. Stern (1977) likewise found no relationship between patient education and type of treatment. Moreover, in the present study the poor were as likely as other income groups to be seen by PhD- or MD-level and university-affiliated therapists.

Finally, examination of outcome data did not validate clinical lore about the futility of doing psychotherapy with the poor. In six of seven comparisons using patient self-report or

therapist ratings, significant improvement was noted for the full sample; the seventh comparison was in the same direction but fell just short of the conventional level of statistical significance. Moreover, improvement did not differ according to patient income. The poor benefited as much from psychotherapy as did the other income groups.

As was noted above, our setting has some features that dictate more than the usual caution in generalizing from the present results to other community mental health centers. Our facilities, for example, are organized around an egalitarian team philosophy predicated on a blurring of disciplinary boundaries and on homogenization of work roles. Recent research has shown that interdisciplinary perceptions are in fact strikingly benign in our setting (Folkins, Wieselberg, & Spensley, Note 6). Because of such possibly idiosyncratic elements of our setting, the representativeness of the elitism and effectiveness findings should not be taken for granted; our results clearly demand empirical replication and polemical restraint.

To demonstrate that services attractive and beneficial to the poor can be effectively implemented is, of course, not to claim that many such programs are now available. It does seem, however, that administrators can control access to and use of mental health services. In 1975, site visitors from the National Institute of Mental Health criticized us for providing insufficient services to more affluent citizens in a certain catchment area. The development of a clinic in a middle-class neighborhood resulted in a doubling of the number of individuals served who had annual incomes over $15,000.

The authors are well aware that the formulations we have submitted to empirical arbitration are value sensitive—as much "heartpotheses" (S. I. Abramowitz, 1978) as hypotheses. Some colleagues who have been highly critical of the mental health establishment may be inclined to dismiss our findings by seizing on the unique democratization of our setting or on their disbelief in the disavowal of political motivation implicit in our "empirical approach." Others who have more faith in the mental health establishment may find solace in the findings per se but bemoan our willingness to raise issues regarded as querulous or divisive to the level of scholarly discourse. For our part, we continue to believe that the most responsible social science is conducted and reported in an environment in which political contexts are acknowledged but, to the limits of the investigators' consciousness, are not permitted to overrule the empirical verdict (C. V. Abramowitz & Dokecki, 1977; S. I. Abramowitz, Gomes, & Abramowitz, 1975).

With respect to those concerns and reservations about the financial costs of including psychotherapy coverage under NHI, it is clear from available data (Cummings, 1977a) that such coverage could be disastrous for the taxpayer unless some limitations such as a sliding fee scale, a deductible, or a ceiling on use are imposed. On the other hand, evidence from the Kaiser-Permanente system (Cummings, 1977a, 1977b) indicates that limited psychotherapy coverage is affordable within a prepaid medical plan and that psychotherapeutic services reduce inappropriate use of medical services. We might anticipate this to be the case with a well-designed and well-regulated NHI-supported plan for psychotherapy coverage.

That we have the capacity to create mental health settings that are attractive and offer effective treatment to the poor implies that we also have the ability to create systems that could repel or even stigmatize them. In developing a plan for NHI coverage of psychotherapy, attention needs to be given to ways to ensure that the settings and services covered will be attractive, accessible, and helpful to the poor. Among the likely critical ingredients are (a) location of clinics easily accessible to the poor, (b) commitment on the part of clinicians to psychotherapeutic strategies that may be particularly effective in treating the poor, (c) further development and evaluation of the effectiveness of such strategies, and (d) establishment of fee structures that make NHI-supported psychotherapy financially feasible for both patients and taxpayers. Some of these factors fall within the domains of clinical theory, research, and training. Others will have to be hammered out at the level of public policymaking. Psychologists and other mental health professionals have clearly shown that they are eager to be involved in such deliberations (APA Task Force, 1978).

As a profession we have a responsibility to ensure that equitable, effective, and accountable mental health programs are developed. Data are often readily obtainable concerning the important questions about service delivery with which we are confronted in our day-to-day work. We need not resort to innuendo, inflammatory rhetoric, or political posturing to carve out a respectable niche in a system of national health care. We can use our knowledge of social science and psychotherapy and our skills as clinicians and researchers to ensure that NHI will provide appropriate and effective mental health care to citizens in need.

Reference Notes

1. Tupin, J. P., Yarvis, R. M., & Edwards, D. W. *A CMHC and a university—Under partnership.* Paper presented at the joint meeting of the American Psychiatric Association and the Société Medico Psychologique, Paris, May 1978.
2. Yarvis, R. M., & Edwards, D. W. *Can CMHC's meet the needs of their communities?* Unpublished manuscript, 1976. (Available from Daniel W. Edwards, Sacramento Medical Center, 4430 V Street, Sacramento, California 95817.)
3. Edwards, D. W., & Yarvis, R. M. *The Davis Outcome Assessment System in use in Sacramento County.* Unpublished manuscript, 1978. (Available from Daniel W. Edwards.)
4. Zingale, H. C., Edwards, D. W., & Yarvis, R. M. *Outcome of outpatient child psychotherapy from three different perspectives: Children, parents, and therapists.* Paper presented at the meeting of the Western Psychological Association, San Francisco, April 1978.
5. Dupuy, H. J. *Utility of the National Center for Health Statistics General Well-Being Schedule in the assessment of self-representations of subjective well-being and distress.* Paper presented at the National Conference on Evaluation in Alcohol, Drug Abuse, and Mental Health Programs, Washington, D.C., April 1974.
6. Folkins, C., Wieselberg, N., & Spensley, J. *Discipline stereotyping and evaluative attitudes among community mental health centers staff.* Manuscript submitted for publication, 1979.

References

Abramowitz, C. V., & Dokecki, P. R. The politics of clinical judgment: Early empirical returns. *Psychological Bulletin,* 1977, *84,* 460–476.
Abramowitz, S. I. Splitting data from theory on the black patient-white therapist relationship. *American Psychologist,* 1978, *33,* 957–958. (Comment)
Abramowitz, S. I., Gomes, B., & Abramowitz, C. V. Publish or politic: Referee bias in manuscript review. *Journal of Applied Social Psychology,* 1975, *5,* 187–200.

Albee, G. W. Does including psychotherapy in health insurance represent a subsidy to the rich from the poor? *American Psychologist,* 1977, *32,* 719–721.

APA Task Force on Continuing Evaluation in National Health Insurance. Continuing evaluation and accountability controls for a national health insurance program. *American Psychologist,* 1978, *33,* 305–313.

Bernard, V. W. Some principles of dynamic psychiatry in relation to poverty. *American Journal of Psychiatry,* 1965, *122,* 254–267.

Bernstein, B. Social class, speech systems, and psychotherapy. In F. Reissman, J. Cohen, & A. Pearl (Eds.), *Mental health of the poor.* New York: Free Press of Glencoe, 1964.

Brandt, L. W. Studies of "dropout" patients in psychotherapy: A review of findings. *Psychotherapy,* 1965, *2,* 6–12.

Crowell, E. Redistributive aspects of psychotherapy's inclusion in national health insurance. *American Psychologist,* 1977, *32,* 731–737.

Cummings, N. A. The anatomy of psychotherapy under national health insurance. *American Psychologist,* 1977, *32,* 711–718. (a)

Cummings, N. A. Prolonged (ideal) versus short-term (realistic) psychotherapy. *Professional Psychology,* 1977, *8,* 491–501. (b)

Derogatis, L. R., Lipman, R. S., Rickels, K., Uhlenhuth, E. H., & Covi, L. The Hopkins Symptom Checklist (HSCL). In P. Pichot & R. Olivier-Martin (Eds.). *Psychological measurements in psychopharmacology* (Vol. 7). Basel, Switzerland: Karger, 1974.

Edwards, D. W., Yarvis, R. M., Swaback, D., Mueller, D. P., & Wagman, W. J. Developing comparison groups for community mental health: The utility of community surveys. *American Journal of Community Psychology,* in press.

Endicott, J., Spitzer, R. L., Fleiss, J. L., & Cohen, J. The Global Assessment Scale: A procedure for measuring overall severity of psychiatric disturbance. *Archives of General Psychiatry,* 1976, *33,* 766–771.

Gardner, E. A. Psychological care for the poor: A need for new service patterns with a proposal for meeting this need. In E. L. Cowen, E. A. Gardner, & M. Zax (Eds.), *Emergent approaches to mental health problems.* New York: Appleton-Century-Crofts, 1967.

Goldstein, A. P. *Structured learning therapy.* New York: Academic Press, 1973.

Gould, R. E. Dr. Strangeclass: Or how I stopped worrying about the theory and began treating the blue-collar worker. *American Journal of Orthopsychiatry,* 1967, *37,* 78–86.

Guy, W. *ECDEU assessment manual for psychopharmacology* (DHEW Pub. No. (ADM) 76-338). Washington, D.C.: Department of Health, Education, and Welfare, 1976.

Langner, T. S., Gersten, J. C., McCarthy, E. D., Eisenberg, S. G., Greene, E. L., Herson, J. H., & Jameson, J. D. A screening inventory for assessing psychiatric impairment in children 6 to 18. *Journal of Consulting and Clinical Psychology,* 1976, *44,* 286–296.

Laska, E. M., & Bank, R. *Safeguarding psychiatric privacy.* New York: Wiley, 1975.

Lerner, B. *Therapy in the ghetto.* Baltimore, Md.: Johns Hopkins University Press, 1972.

Lorion, R. P. Socioeconomic status and traditional treatment approaches reconsidered. *Psychological Bulletin,* 1973, *79,* 263–270.

Lorion, R. P. Patient and therapist variables in the treatment of low-income patients. *Psychological Bulletin,* 1974, *81,* 344–354.

Lorr, M., Katz, M. M., & Rubinstein, E. A. The prediction of length of stay in psychotherapy. *Journal of Consulting Psychology,* 1958, *22,* 321–327.

Luborsky, L., Chandler, M., Auerbach, A. H., Cohen, J., & Bachrach, H. M. Factors influencing the outcome of psychotherapy: A review of quantitative research. *Psychological Bulletin,* 1971, *75,* 145–185.

McSweeny, A. J. Including psychotherapy in national health insurance: Insurance guidelines and other proposed solutions. *American Psychologist,* 1977, *32,* 722–730.

Minuchin, S. Psychoanalytic therapies and the low socioeconomic population. In J. Marmor (Ed.), *Modern Psychoanalysis.* New York: Basic Books, 1968.

Pettit, I. B., Pettit, T. F., & Welkowitz, J. Relationship between values, social class, and duration of psychotherapy. *Journal of Consulting and Clinical Psychology,* 1974, *42,* 482–490.

Rogers, L. S. Drop-out rates and results of psychotherapy in government aided mental hygiene clinics. *Journal of Clinical Psychology,* 1960, *16,* 89–92.

Rubinstein, E. A., & Lorr, M. A comparison of terminators and remainers in outpatient psychotherapy. *Journal of Clinical Psychology,* 1956, *12,* 345–349.

Sharfstein, S. S., Taube, C. A., & Goldberg, I. D. Problems in analyzing the comparative costs of private versus public psychiatric care. *American Journal of Psychiatry,* 1977, *134,* 29–32.

Spensley, J., & Langsley, D. G. Interdisciplinary training of mental health professionals. *Journal of Psychiatric Education,* 1977, *1,* 75–84.

Spiegel, J. P. Some cultural aspects of transference and counter-transference. In F. Reissman, J. Cohen, & A. Pearl (Eds.), *Mental health of the poor.* New York: Free Press of Glencoe, 1964.

Stern, M. S. Social class and psychiatric treatment of adults in the mental health center. *Journal of Health and Social Behavior,* 1977, *18,* 317–325.

Sue, S., McKinney, H. L., & Allen, D. B. Predictors of the duration of therapy for clients in the community mental health system. *Community Mental Health Journal,* 1976, *12,* 365–375.

Yamamoto, J., & Goin, M. K. On treatment of the poor. *American Journal of Orthopsychiatry,* 1965, *122,* 267–271.

Daniel W. Edwards, Les R. Greene, Stephen I. Abramowitz, and *Christine V. Davidson* are faculty members of the Department of Psychiatry, University of California, Davis.

11

Primary Prevention

Primary prevention has not been generally discussed as part of the benefit package under proposed national health insurance plans. However, there is no reason why certain aspects of primary prevention can not be handled within the context of national health insurance. In fact, we believe it is critical to include and evaluate prevention services to ensure continuing improvement in the health of all citizens.

The inclusion of readily and directly accessible psychological services has preventive value, both in terms of the prevention of more serious behavior and thought disorders as well as in the prevention of physical illness, as mentioned earlier. But that is early treatment intervention, not primary prevention. A flexible form of national insurance should address special populations and/or problems by actively encouraging utilization of psychological services in certain situations. It is known, for example, that children from terminating marriages and children involved in transient foster homes show a high frequency of emotional disturbance. These two groups of children could easily become special target populations for preventive mental health services under national health insurance. This is just one example of a special population known to be at high risk that could be given easy and encouraged access to services, thereby lowering the number of future instances of mental and physical problems.

Prevention efforts are particularly efficient in that they have a significant "spread of effect." When, for example, children of divorcing parents are seen for prevention services, not only does the child benefit but each of the parents benefit, the family system benefits, and the community benefits. It is not uncommon for a child whose parents are divorcing to struggle with feelings about the divorce and to develop behavior problems. The parents are suddenly in a doubly difficult situation, struggling with feelings about their spouse and the divorce while having to cooperate with the spouse in order to deal with the behavior problem. In addition, the child may manifest learning or behavioral difficulties in school, which cause problems for the school and further aggravation for the parents. With preventive services, all of the parties benefit psychologically, and both personal expenses and overall government expenditures are reduced.

Prevention of illness and dysfunction should be the ultimate goal of all health service providers. Sufficient expertise, research, and knowledge about prevention in mental health now exist to allow prevention efforts to be the immediate goal of some providers. Particularly in high-risk cases, we already know enough to permit us to prevent or minimize mental health problems. To do this, and to encourage growth in this area, national health insurance must reimburse such services and the National Institutes of Health and the National Institute of Mental Health must encourage research and treatment innovation in this area.

To quote from the report to follow, "the term primary prevention refers to a group of approaches that share the common objectives of: 1) lowering the incidence of emotional disorders (i.e., the rate of which new cases occur), and 2) promoting conditions that reinforce positive mental health. Primary prevention, in concentrating its efforts on promotion and maintenance of competence, is distinguished from traditional mental health services designed to identify, treat, or rehabilitate individuals already disturbed." The most up-to-date statement of the state-of-the-art in primary prevention is contained, we believe, in the report of the Task Panel on Primary Prevention to the President's Commission on Mental Health. We reproduce that report as an illustration of what can be done in terms of prevention in the mental health field.

This work is exciting. Enough promise has been demonstrated in the limited efforts undertaken to date to justify substantial increases in research funding to stimulate growth and innovation. However, it has been difficult to get research funding allocated to this promising area. Even after programs have been developed and proven effective, federal funding to ensure widespread dissemination and implementation of such programs has been difficult to secure. Part of the reason for this is that the prevention model is difficult to fit within the conceptualization of mental health derived from the medical model. While organized medicine and psychiatry have generally been responsive to secondary prevention efforts (e.g., early detection and intervention), they have been less responsive to primary prevention efforts—particularly in the mental health field—that do not require a physician or psychiatrist.

Report to the President's Commission on Mental Health

Task Panel on Prevention, President's Commission on Mental Health

This report reviews the current status and potential of prevention efforts in the field of mental health. A rationale for primary mental health prevention is presented, and the barriers to the implementation of such services are described. Prevention priorities are outlined. An extensive review of the research support for prevention is provided.

Summary

Western society's approach to persons with mental disorders has progressed in a series of steps. Each step has been characterized by increasingly humanitarian concern. For thousands of years the insane were reviled, feared, and rejected. Two hundred years ago, in the first mental health "revolution," they were led by Pinel out of the fetid dungeons, up into the light and into more humane treatment. A second revolution, led by Freud, greatly increased our understanding of the continuity between the insane and the sane. Half a century later, a third revolution was dedicated to providing care in a single comprehensive center accessible to all those at high risk. Now, less than a quarter century later, we are on the threshold of a fourth and most exciting mental health revolution. Its goal is to prevent emotional disorders.

Although each revolution has drawn strength from, and built on, earlier ones, we have come more and more to recognize that widespread human distress can never be eliminated by attempts—however sucessful—to treat afflicted individuals. We shall continue to do everything we can for persons in pain. But we are also determined to take action to reduce the identifiable causes of later distress, and thereby decrease the incidence of emotional disturbance and disorder.

Primary prevention means lowering the incidence of emotional disorder (1) by reducing stress and (2) by promoting conditions that increase competence and coping skills. Primary prevention is concerned with populations not yet affected by individual breakdown, especially with groups at high risk. It is proactive—it often seeks to build adaptive strengths through education and reduce stress through social engineering.

We have identified a number of sources of resistance and barriers to primary prevention efforts. We have identified problems in setting priorities where choices must be made among programs of demonstrated effectiveness affecting relatively few people; programs with high (estimated) potential for greater numbers of people based on limited but encouraging research efforts; and programs involving broad social efforts not traditionally associated with the field of mental health but with potentially positive impact for very large numbers of people.

We have reviewed several representative research areas to show that a solid research base exists for primary prevention. As illustrative examples we have focused especially on competence training programs for those at risk by virtue of natural and life crises and the effects of social climate on mental health.

An important "paradigm shift" must be considered in focusing attention on research in

From President's Commission on Mental Health, *Report to the President from the President's Commission on Mental Health* (vol. 4). Washington, D.C.: U.S. Government Printing Office, 1978.

primary prevention. There are good reasons to believe that just as an emotional disorder may result from any of several background factors and life crises, so can any specific intense stressful event precipitate any of a variety of mental and emotional disorders. Different life histories and different patterns of strengths and weaknesses among different individuals can and do lead to different reactions to stress. This new paradigm requires that we recognize the futility of searching for a unique cause for every emotional disorder. It accepts the likelihood that many disorders can come about as a consequence of many of the varieties of causes. This paradigm leads to the acceptance of the argument that successful efforts at the prevention of a wide variety of disorders can occur without a theory of disorder-specific positive causal mechanisms.

Our recommendations include a focus on a coordinated national effort toward the prevention of emotional disorder with a Center for Primary Prevention within the National Institute of Mental Health (NIMH), with primary prevention specialists deployed in each of the 10 U.S. Public Health Service Regional Offices, with the establishment of State-level efforts, and with the creation of field stations and model demonstration centers. Because many other relevant Government agencies can, and should, be concerned with prevention we are recommending the coordination of efforts through the proposed NIMH center that is to have convening authority. We are recommending that first priority in primary prevention be directed toward work with infants and young children (and their social environments). We give a number of illustrations of the kinds of programs we have in mind. We take special note of the urgent need to reduce societal stresses produced by racism, poverty, sexism, ageism, and the decay of our cities. We make certain suggestions about funding and about a broadly competent citizen's committee to have a continuing advisory role.

Preamble

The first revolutionary change in society's approach to the mentally ill and the emotionally disturbed was the humanitarian concern exemplified by Philippe Pinel who, in 1792, removed the chains binding the insane in the fetid dungeons of Paris. He brought those victims up into the sunlight and showed the world that kindness and concern were defensible and appropriate.

The second revolutionary change in our attitudes and values had its origin in Freud's work that stressed the continuities between the sane and the insane, the mind of the child and the mind of the adult, the world of dreams and the world of reality.

The third revolution was the development of intervention and treatment centers serving all persons needing help—comprehensive community mental health centers—where, through a single door, everyone could seek and find skilled help for the whole range of human mental and emotional problems.

Unlike political revolutions, each of these mental health revolutions drew strength and inspiration from the earlier ones.

We believe we now stand on the threshold of a fourth revolution. Like its predecessors, this revolution will not attempt to displace or replace progress already achieved. The new revolution will involve major societal efforts at preventing mental illness and emotional disturbance. It will apply the best available knowledge, derived from research and clinical experience, to prevent needless distress and psychological dysfunction. It will, in the best public health tradition, also seek to build strengths and increase competence and coping skills in populations and thereby reduce the incidence of later disturbance. This fourth revolution, if it happens, will identify our society as a caring society—one that both holds out its hand to its unfortunate members and does all it can to prevent misfortune for those at risk.

In speeches at the 1977 World Federation for Mental Health in Vancouver, both Rosalynn Carter, Honorary Chairperson of the President's Commission on Mental Health, and Bertram Brown, until recently Director of the National Institute of Mental Health, elaborated upon a theme of Margaret Mead about the moral dimensions of mental health services. Dr. Mead has suggested that if we select for first consideration the most vulnerable among us, then our whole culture is humanized (1977). Mrs. Carter believes, as does Dr. Mead, that ". . . our value as individuals, our success as a society, can be measured by our compassion for the vulnerable" (1977). Dr. Brown asserts that "[t]he system that serves the largest collection of this diverse, oppressed, and needful group is mental health. Mental health services . . . increasingly represent the court of last resort for the poor, the ill, the underprivileged, the hungry, and the disenfranchised" (1977, p. 4).

The Task Panel on Prevention applauds the sentiments expressed in these statements and goes further to suggest that an additional template be applied in judging a society: its devotion to the prevention of those tragedies that lead to the creation of society's unfortunate members. Thus the panel takes as its point of departure the conviction that a society must also be measured by the steps it takes to prevent every form of preventable misfortune. Barrington Moore said much the same thing: "Human society ought to be organized in such a way as to eliminate useless suffering" (1970, p. 5).

Increasingly, the ranks of those who seek to emphasize the potential of prevention are growing. President Carter has suggested that "the most important improvement in the quality of health care" would be to make available "additional resources for primary and preventive care, nutritional services, and occupational and environmental health initiatives" (1977). Dr. Julius Richmond, Assistant Secretary for Health in the Department of Health, Education, and Welfare, says "I feel very keenly that we must move to bring our knowledge to the area of prevention" (1977). He stresses the importance of behavioral research in learning how our society "can enlist people in preventive activities for the promotion of their own health." And the Institute of Medicine of the National Academy of Sciences has in process a major document on strategies for promotion of health and prevention of disease in the United States.

The fourth revolution is an idea whose time has come.

Introduction and Rationale

The development and application of primary prevention programs in the field of the emotional disorders is the great unmet mental health challenge of our time. From both a moral and ethical point of view, preventive intervention has the potential for reducing human suffering associated with emotional disorder and the impact of that suffering on family and friends. From an economic point of view, effective primary prevention programs promise to be less expensive in the long run than the direct (fiscal) and indirect (human) costs to society of not providing such services.

The term "primary prevention" refers to a group of approaches that share the common objectives of (1) lowering the incidence of emotional disorders (i.e., the rate at which new cases occur) and (2) promoting conditions that reinforce positive mental health. Primary prevention, in concentrating its efforts on promotion and maintenance of competence, is distinguished from traditional mental health services designed to identify, treat, or rehabilitate persons already disturbed (Kessler and Albee 1975; Albee and Joffe 1977; Cowen 1977; Bloom 1977; Klein and Goldston 1977).

One way in which primary prevention works in the mental health field is to eliminate the causes of disorders of known or discoverable etiologies (e.g., cerebral syphilis). Equally, or perhaps more importantly, primary prevention involves building the strengths, resources, and competencies in individuals, families, and communities that can reduce the flow of a variety of unfortunate outcomes—each characterized by enormous human and societal cost. Because primary prevention approaches can be applied flexibly in a variety of situations they are an especially attractive means for reaching vulnerable, high-risk groups.

Primary prevention activities have two main justifications: (1) the body of evidence supporting the efficacy of these approaches in their own right; and (2) the growing sense of dissatisfaction, as the gap widens between demonstrated need for help and the costly, often unavailable, human resources to meet that need, with mental health's past exclusive reliance on corrective measures.

From a logistical point of view, there can never be a sufficient number of skilled health care providers to meet unchecked intervention needs. And in any case, no major disorder in a population has ever been eliminated by providing one-to-one treatment, however comprehensive.

Historically, the mental health field has always been unswerving in its definition of mandate, i.e., to understand the complexities of psychological aberration and to contain or minimize dysfunction when called on to engage it. However constructive that mandate is, the service systems developed to meet it cannot be expected to resolve society's mental health problems. Thus, today: (1) there are too few resources to deal with mental health problems as defined; (2) distribution of those limited resources is inequitable, following the ironic rule of where help is most needed it is least available; and (3) mental health energies are disproportionately allocated to the exacting and costly task of trying to overcome already rooted, crystallized, "end state" conditions—precisely those that most resist change.

The history of public health in the past century provides ample evidence that programs designed to prevent disease and disorder can be effective and reasonably economical. Infectious diseases that can now be prevented include smallpox, malaria, typhus, cholera, yellow fever, polio, and measles. An equally impressive group of nutritional disorders, including scurvy, pellegra, beri-beri, and kwashiorkor, is now also understood and preventable. Imagine what our health bill would be if those diseases were not preventable and society therefore needed to bear the costs of supporting state malaria hospitals, state pellagra hospitals, and state hospitals for polio victims.

Preventive measures have proved to be a vital extension of health care practices in physical health. The mental health field, however, has yet to use available relevant knowledge to develop systematically comparable efforts. Public health approaches offer a sound conceptual and operating framework for undertaking primary prevention in the mental health field.

Primary prevention approaches, on logical, humanitarian, and empirical grounds, thus offer an attractive, sorely needed extension of existing mental health practices that hold promise for reducing the eventual flow of emotional disorder.

In the history of medicine the response to disease illustrates the relationship between the state of knowledge and what physicians actually do. At a time when few normal physiological processes, let alone the pathological ones, were understood, physicians had to be content with describing what they saw and paltry efforts at palliation. Only with the advance of medical knowledge was it possible to refine descriptions into diagnoses and, with an understanding of etiology, to prescribe disease-specific treatment. As we have become more sophisticated about the nature of illness, efforts to prevent illness have also increased. For diseases with specific etiologies, i.e., in which the pathogenic relationships between causative agent and disease came to be fully understood, prevention efforts were often dramatic. But as most diseases have multiple causes they required more complex strategies for prevention as well.

Most mental conditions lack the single etiology or definitive understanding of pathogenesis needed for dramatic prevention efforts. That very fact has led many people to despair of ever preventing mental disturbance and to continue to advocate an exclusive emphasis on diagnosis and treatment as the only scientifically justifiable approach to mental illness. This broad kind of denial of the possibilities of prevention has led to widespread indifference toward it both by the medical profession and within society at large. We have thus lived through an era of greater and greater expenditures for treatment and rehabilitation without a much needed corresponding attention to existing possibilities for prevention.

Prevention in the field of mental health can properly be seen as an integrating perspective that can fuse our best understanding of the etiology of mental disorder, personal and family relationships, and individual psychodynamics on the one hand with a recognition, on the other, of the salient social forces and pressures that combine to produce the individual and collective disorganization we call emotional illness.

The belief that our thinking must be reoriented away from the past exclusive focus on diagnosis and treatment is not new. More than one hundred years ago Lemuel Shattuck and his coauthors of the 1850 *Report of the Sanitary Commission of Massachusetts* stated:

> We believe that the conditions of perfect health, either public or personal, are seldom or never attained, though attainable:—that the average length

of human life may be very much extended, and its physical power greatly augmented:—that in every year, within this Commonwealth, thousands of lives are lost which might have been saved:—that tens of thousands of cases of sickness occur, which might have been prevented:—that a vast amount of unnecessarily impaired health, and physical debility exists among those not actually confined by sickness:—that these preventable evils require an enormous expenditure and loss of money, and impose upon the people unnumbered and immeasurable calamities, pecuniary, social, physical, mental, and moral, which might be avoided:—that means exist, within our reach, for their mitigation or removal:—and that measures for prevention will effect infinitely more than remedies for the cure of disease. (Quoted by Jonathan E. Fielding, in "Health Promotion—Some Notions In Search of a Constituency," *AJPH* 67:1082, November 1977).

More recently, a major national effort in the field of mental health—the work of the Joint Commission on Mental Illness and Health (JCMIH) (1961)—also acknowledged the need for prevention. However, the JCMIH placed major emphasis on early casefinding and early treatment, i.e., secondary prevention. That emphasis underscored the fact that emotionally disturbed people needed immediate help using resources from their own communities, a recognition that led ultimately to the creation of the community mental health centers system.

Despite its acknowledgement of the need for prevention, the Joint Commission's report and recommendations continued to reflect a powerful emphasis on treatment, with little indication of a concern for the importance of primary prevention. The following statement from the JCMIH's final report, *Action for Mental Health* (1961), clarifies its priorities:

> A national mental health program should recognize that major mental illness is the core problem and unfinished business of the mental health movement, and that the intensive treatment of patients with critical and prolonged mental breakdowns should have first call on fully trained members of the mental health professions.

The President's Commission on Mental Health, established in 1977, set up the Task Panel on Prevention with a charge (see below) to study, report, and recommend efforts at prevention. The purposes of this present Task Panel on Prevention, therefore, are: (1) to identify and develop the conception of primary prevention in mental health; (2) to examine current strategies and program possibilities in this area; and (3) to propose specific recommendations for

primary prevention to the President's Commission on Mental Health.

Charge to the Task Panel on Prevention

In its deliberations the task panel has attended to the following charge from the President's Commission on Mental Health:

> In recent years increasing attention has been paid to methods for reducing needless mental and emotional disorder. The Commission is establishing a Task Panel on Prevention to marshal information demonstrating whether or not prevention is feasible, set forth options for future courses of action, and indicate sources of funding from which programs of prevention can be supported. Specifically, it will be the task of this Panel to:

- Review current definitions of the term "prevention" and, given the state of the art and fiscal and other constraints, develop an operational definition of primary prevention; and, within the confines of that definition, review various services and programs and determine which are or are not successful;
- Identify barriers which interfere with the ability of the consumer to obtain and receive needed preventive services and with the capacity of community institutions to provide these services;
- Assess the national need for prevention services and programs and the manpower and research needs which the effectuation of a national prevention strategy will require; and
- Report to the Commission by January 15, 1978, setting forth materials inventorying what works and in what settings, citing suggested practical models of preventive programs which can be utilized by States, local governments, community mental health centers, and other community institutions.

Definitions: What Primary Prevention "Is" and "Is Not"

Primary prevention in mental health is a network of strategies that differ qualitatively from the field's past dominant approaches. Those strategies are distinguished by several essential characteristics. This brief section highlights primary prevention's essences using the direct contrast style of saying what it is and what it is not.

(1) Most fundamentally, primary prevention is proactive in that it seeks to build adaptive strengths, coping resources, and health in people; not to reduce or contain already manifest deficit.

(2) Primary prevention is concerned about total populations, especially including groups at high risk; it is less oriented to individuals and to the provision of services on a case-by-case basis.

(3) Primary prevention's main tools and models are those of education and social engineering, not therapy or rehabilitation, although some insights for its models and programs grow out of the wisdom derived from clinical experience.

(4) Primary prevention assumes that equipping people with personal and environmental resources for coping is the best of all ways to ward off maladaptive problems, not trying to deal (however skillfully) with problems that have already germinated and flowered.

What Do We Seek to Prevent

We believe there is sufficient evidence to encourage further development of strategies for the prevention of a wide variety of conditions such as the psychoses, especially organic psychoses, neuroses and other social disorders, learning disabilities, child abuse, and other behavioral, emotional, and developmental deviations that fall within the broad range of mental health problems.

One key difference between the human organism and lower animals is the much longer period of time during which the human infant and child must depend on others for survival and support. During that long growth process, successful development can be interfered with by an unusually large number of factors at any point. Thus, under certain unfortunate circumstances, all infants are at risk for subsequent emotional and developmental deviations. Scientific advances have markedly reduced the mortality and morbidity of childbirth. Never before

in our history have infants had as good an opportunity as they now do to be born healthy and to thrive. Unfortunately, however, the delivery of a biologically healthy full-term infant does not guarantee smooth psychosocial development forever after. Precisely because interference with optimal development is known to occur with high frequency, and to exact a heavy toll, it is imperative that programs for primary prevention be developed. It is essential to establish priorities, to select infants and children particularly at high risk, and to develop programs to assure optimal continuing development for such target groups. We firmly believe that efforts directed toward infants and young children will provide maximum return in successful prevention.

The task panel advocates the establishment of programs designed to prevent persistent, destructive, maladaptive behaviors, i.e., those unfortunate "end states" that result from identifiable stresses for which the individual lacks the necessary coping skills and the adaptive competencies. That critical goal suggests the need to identify: (1) agreed upon behavioral conditions that pose a serious threat to others because of the damage they cause; (2) patterns of behavior that are so distasteful for the affected person that he or she cries out for relief; or (3) emotional states that lead to withdrawal from meaningful social participation. Clearly, many such traits or conditions require social value judgments about what is desirable or undesirable behavior, acceptable and unacceptable styles of living. Some of these decisions, in short, may present dangers to liberty and to the freedom of people to follow their own drummers, to be unconventional, and even to be damned fools. There are many historical examples of the tyranny of the majority enforcing patterns of approved behavior and lifestyles, and too many deviants who have been punished, excommunicated, or even killed for nonconformity. Clearly, preventive efforts must be directed toward those end states that cause either genuine harm to others or genuine unwanted suffering in affected individuals.

Attempts to classify mental conditions have turned out to be far more complex than was originally thought. The exciting successes of medicine and biology during the 19th century in classifying physical illnesses were viewed as models that might lead ultimately to successful classfication of mental diseases. Indeed, the discovery of specific physical causes for certain mental conditions—the role of the spirochete, and the relationship of untreated syphilis to the subsequent appearance of a serious mental illness called general paresis; relationships between vitamin deficiency and pellagral psychosis; the serious social and behavioral consequences of oversecretion and undersecretion of certain endocrine glands such as the thyroid and the adrenals—each served to strengthen the belief that eventually all disturbed behavioral states would be found to have an underlying pathological organic cause. That view persists even today. Some experts accept Nobel Laureate Linus Pauling's view that there can be no insanity in a healthy brain (1968). Another world famous chemist, Ralph Gerard, said much the same thing: "There can be no twisted behavior without a twisted molecule." Unfortunately, life is not so simple; indeed many everyday observations contradict that view. For example, soldiers under extreme combat stress often show serious emotional disturbances; children of disturbed parents often exhibit serious emotional problems; many persons undergoing naturally occurring life stresses, such as sudden widowhood or marital disruption, experience extreme personal anguish and depression. Yet each of these conditions is reversible. The critical point to be understood is that while all behavior has an underlying physiological basis, disturbed behavior need not imply an underlying pathological organic process. In short, people react emotionally to stress; they learn to withdraw, to attack, or to distort their relationships with others through normal physical mechanisms.

The Task Panel on Prevention thus advocates a broad-gauged effort in primary prevention directed ultimately to reducing the incidence of the major aberrant conditions and end states that have, for years, occupied the attention, claimed the efforts, and been sources of exasperation to the mental health field: the major childhood behavioral and developmental disabilities, the functional and organic psychoses, symptom and character neuroses, and profound psychosocial disorders such as delinquency and addiction. The task panel advocates a vigorous

national effort to build health and competencies in individuals from birth, so that each person may maximize his or her chances for a productive, effective life.

We note especially that any serious national effort at prevention of mental disorders and promotion of mental health must also be addressed to those social-environmental stressors that significantly contribute to the pathology of prejudice. Racism is a particularly noxious influence. Likewise, bias against ethnic minorities, sexism, and ageism must be recognized as placing significant portions of the populations, merely by membership in these groups and the environmental stress that such membership attracts, at high risk of mental disorder. While outside the direct purview, or immediate special competence, of mental health specialists, elimination of institutionalized and other forms of racism and other biases must continue to be a priority for primary prevention as well as for other aspects of our national interest.

Barriers to Primary Prevention Efforts

However sensible or rational primary prevention is, however critical it is as key future strategy for the mental health fields, it is an approach that must surmount powerful barriers, including the following:

1. Our society is crisis-oriented; we react to here-and-now pain, blood, and visible suffering. Because primary prevention is future-oriented, many see it is postponable—or if not that then certainly as having low priority. Because it is oriented so heavily to strengthening people's resources and coping skills rather than addressing current causality, it lacks a constituency and political "clout."

2. The history, traditions, and past values of the mental health professions have been built on the strategies of repairing existing dysfunction. People are attracted to mental health with that image in mind; moreover, they are trained and they practice in that same mold. That image of self and way of behaving professionally is reinforced because it serves such human needs as the need for status, economic gain, and (understandable) gratifications involved in the

process of being personally helpful to distressed others. The question is whether it serves society equally well.

3. Primary prevention in mental health is threatening to some because its very nature may raise sensitive issues of social and environmental change and/or issues about people's right to be left alone.

4. Existing mechanisms to support certain mental health activities (e.g., funds for third-party reimbursement, treatment staff, hospital beds) are not geared to primary prevention activities. Accordingly, primary prevention proposals are viewed by some not only as threatening to rooted ways and vested interests but also as competing for resource dollars.

5. The past lack of recognition of primary prevention as an accepted way in mental health that differs qualitatively from past approaches leaves a series of "Catch 22" residues:

(a) Fiscal allocations for primary prevention dollars rarely exist, or are at best pitifully small.

(b) We lack appropriate administrative structures charged with the responsibility of promoting the development of primary prevention.

(c) Personnel trained in the ways of primary prevention are in extremely short supply. Moreover, they tend to be the last hired and the first fired.

(d) Few professionals are assigned to primary mental health activities on a sustained, full-time basis.

(e) Activities that are labeled primary prevention often, in fact, are not that at all.

(f) There has been virtually no support for research in primary prevention; yet, ironically, critics argue that the field lacks sufficient evidence to warrant programmatic action. One indication of the difference in attitudes toward treatment and prevention is that treatment efforts are mandated even without adequate effectiveness data, whereas prevention efforts are discouraged because of "lack of evidence." With respect to treatment of already identified cases, the social mandate is to "try to be helpful." No such mandate has existed for prevention efforts.

Problems such as the above cannot be engaged, much less resolved, until primary prevention is accorded a place of visibility and importance, backed by leadership with the mechanisms and resources needed to achieve true viability rather than tokenism.

Priorities

Our task panel was asked to order our priorities among a range of prevention interventions and among the variety of target groups for whom primary prevention efforts are possible. It is not easy to set such priorities; indeed, decisions about them could well vary as a function of the weights given to social value judgments versus scientific criteria.

We can try to illustrate the kinds of choices we considered in setting priorities among the large variety of primary prevention programs the task panel reviewed. We found ourselves considering:

1. Programs with high potential for success that affect relatively few people, e.g.,

(a) Genetic counseling of persons with a family history of Huntington's Disease, PKU, or Down's Syndrome;

(b) Intensive intervention with blind infants (based on the fact that such children are known to be at high risk for psychosis).

2. Programs with significant research effectiveness demonstrated on small samples but with good prospects for reaching large numbers, e.g.,

(a) Competency training in preschool settings and early school grades;

(b) Widow-to-widow self-help counseling groups.

3. Programs with strong theoretical promise for success affecting potentially large numbers of people, e.g.,

(a) Helping groups for people who experience sudden or extreme stresses such as infant death, job loss, or marital disruption.

4. Programs aimed at improving broad social situations with potentially great impact on millions of people. Because such conditions are not usually considered part of mental health's purview, considering them might give the Commission the set that the task panel has too wide a range of things, i.e., "everything" is primary prevention! Candidly, too, such considerations may involve sufficiently controversial social values that it would be politically wiser to avoid them. Examples include the potentially damaging mental health consequences of:

(a) Unemployment, discrimination, and lack of job security;
(b) Boring and/or dangerous work;
(c) The national epidemic of teenage pregnancies, unwanted births, premature parenthood;
(d) Smoking and the use of drugs, including alcohol; their effects on unborn children;
(e) Ethnocentrism—racism, sexism, ageism; the damage wrought, the self-fulfilling prophecy, the damaged self-esteem of the persecutor and the persecuted.

Priority-setting may be premature. One rational, possible approach would be to base priorities on three sources of judgment:

(1) Epidemiological information on prevalence of distress;
(2) Value judgments solicited from affected groups, e.g., minorities, the aged, the impoverished—all at high risk; and
(3) Research and demonstrations of effectiveness.

Strategies Resting on a Research Base

Members of the task panel, pulled between the choice of an overinclusive need to cite every relevant study done on primary prevention and the clear realization that brevity and readability were essential, opted for the latter. Somewhat self-consciously, we regarded ourselves as being among the Nation's experts on primary prevention. We thus hoped that we might have enough credibility with the members of the Commission to be able to say firmly that the existing evidence indeed supports a major shift in emphasis toward primary prevention. For Commission members who already have the vision that mental health's major new thrusts must be toward the prevention of distress and the building of competence in the citizenry, we need cite only enough data to be reassuring that a broad capability for such an effort truly exists.

At the risk of sounding apocalyptic, the task panel believes that a firm, enthusiastic recommendation by the President's Commission for a genuinely accelerated national effort in primary prevention would be a major step forward for humankind. Symbolically, this would mark acceptance of our role as our brothers' and sisters' keepers. It would say that relevant mental health activities must go beyond the here and now and as such would move to center stage a long-term view of benefiting all humankind.

Primary prevention's defining characteristics and mandates necessarily structure its main strategies. With proaction, health and competence building, and a population orientation among its core qualities, it follows, virtually automatically, that primary prevention programs must be heavily oriented to the very young. Although the panel's discussions of programs and strategies have ranged across all developmental stages, we agreed that major primary prevention efforts must be focused on the prenatal, perinatal, infancy, and childhood periods.

The National Association for Mental Health has developed a detailed program of primary prevention that guides efforts from conception through the first months of life. In our recommendations we list a number of other efforts that can be applied at prenatal, perinatal, and subsequent childhood levels. Again, we reemphasize our agreement about the importance of an approach that follows the developmental sequence. In this section, however, we will illustrate the research base with just a few brief programmatic examples.

Let us give a detailed example that involves efforts with children beginning with the preschool years. Such an approach, consistent with the spirit of primary prevention, has yet to be harnessed systematically by the mental health fields. At the same time, a rapidly growing body of evidence demands that it be taken into serious account.

It has been known for some years that performance on an interrelated groups of skills known collectively as interpersonal cognitive problem solving (ICPS) skills consistently discriminates between maladapted clinical or patient groups of children (and adults) and healthy normals (e.g., Spivack and Levine 1963; Platt, Altmann, and Altmann 1973; Spivack, Platt, and Shure 1976; Spivack and Shure 1977). ICPS skills such as the ability to "sense" problems, to identify feelings, to use alternative-solution thinking, means-end thinking, and consequential thinking apparently provide a useful cognitive and emotional technology for engaging interpersonal problems effectively. Those who have and use those skills effectively appear to others in interpersonal relations as well adjusted behaviorally. Those who lack or are deficient in such skills are seen as maladjusted—sometimes even with clinically significant conditions such as neuroses, psychoses, problems of delinquency, antisocial behavior, or addiction. ICPS skills can thus be thought of as mediating effective behavioral adjustment. If that is so, the challenge it presents for primary prevention is to find ways to equip children, as early and effectively as possible, with those skills. The model of ICPS skill training well illustrates primary prevention's defining attributes: it is health building, proactive, mass oriented, and educational. The main theoretical constraint on the ICPS approach is the human organism's limit, developmentally, to profit from such training. Once that developmental point is reached, only the formats and mechanisms of ICPS training, not its goals, need change for different groups who can be exposed to the approach.

Several research teams have implemented ICPS training programs directed to different target groups that are quite diverse in terms of age, prior history, sociocultural and ethnic background. Their findings have been instructive—indeed, exciting.

Spivack and Shure (1974) developed one such program consisting of 46 "lessons" given over a 10-week period for 4-year-old Head Start children. Not only did children in the program

acquire the key ICPS skills, but as that happened their behavioral adjustment was also found to improve. Particularly interesting was the fact that the initially most maladapted youngsters both (1) advanced the most in ICPS skill acquisition and (2) improved the most behaviorally. Spivack and Shure also demonstrated direct linkages between the amount of gain in ICPS skills—particularly in the ability to generate alternative solutions—and improvement in subsequent adjustment. Follow-up of program youngsters a year later, when they had gone on to new class settings, showed that program improvements were maintained over time (Shure and Spivack 1975a). In a closely related project (Shure and Spivack 1975b), it was shown that inner-city mothers given special training in the ICPS method were successful in training their own children in those skills—again with positive radiation to the adjustment sphere. Thus, a potentially powerful primary prevention tool was shown to have coequal applicability in the two settings that most significantly shape a child's early development: home and school.

Several other groups, working with the same general framework, have provided further demonstrations of the applicability and fruitfulness of the ICPS training model as a strategy for primary prevention (Stone, Hinds, and Schmidt 1975; Allen et al. 1976; Gesten et al. 1978; Elardo and Caldwell 1976; Elardo and Cooper 1977). It is beyond the scope of this brief summary to review that body of work in detail. Indeed the main reason for providing the citations is to establish that the efficacy of the approach is not confined to the inputs and wisdom of a single team, working with a particular target group, in a special setting. Rather, it is to say that because the approach has been shown to have generality across diverse settings and age, sex, ethnic, and socioeconomic levels, it stands as an example of a promising generalized strategy for primary prevention.

Findings based on the ICPS approach are in the same research tradition as an earlier set of demonstrations growing out of Ralph Ojemann's pioneering programs (1961, 1969) to train children to think causally. Other workers (Bruce 1958; Muuss 1960; Griggs and Bonney

1970) have shown that successful mastery of causal thinking skills is accompanied by significant gain on measures of (decreased) anxiety, (increased) security and self-concept, and improved overall adjustment status in children.

This broad competence training strategy is limited primarily by its newness and by the minimal investment that has thus far gone into it. Thus, the broad range of its potential has scarcely been explored. By broad range is meant the fact that many other competencies besides those that make up the ICPS group may be clearly shown to contribute significantly to behavior adjustment. Examples might include such qualities as healthy curiosity behavior, altruism, role taking, and the ability to set realistic goals. A promising recent study by Stamps (1975) provides evidence in support of the basic argument. Working with fourth grade inner-city children, Stamps developed a curriculum, based on self-reinforcement techniques, designed to teach realistic goal-setting skills. Program children learned those skills readily. As their goal-setting skills developed, they showed parallel improvements in achievement, in behavioral adjustment, and on personality measures. Teachers, at the end of training, judged them to have fewer behavior problems than demographically comparable nonprogram controls. Moreover, they showed improvement on measures of openness, awareness, and self-acceptance.

The importance of early competence acquisition can be illustrated at a somewhat different level, i.e., in relationship to a rapidly developing body of knowledge about the efficacy of enrichment stimulation programs for young disadvantaged children (Gottfried 1973; Horowitz and Paden 1973; Jason 1975). Among the most impressive program efforts in that area is that of Heber (1976) and his associates in Milwaukee—a 10-year longitudinal program with dramatic and exciting findings. Heber's program, directed to the "high-risk" children of mothers with IQ's of 75 or less, started immediately after the child was born. An intensive, saturated program emphasizing continual skill training was conducted at a day care center where the children spent all day, every day for the first 5 years of life. Each family was also assigned a home teacher who taught mothers child rearing and other life skills.

Careful comparisons of the program children to matched nonprogram controls, over a 10-year period, have uncovered some remarkable findings. For example, this initially high-risk program sample has not only far outpaced controls, cognitively and linguistically (e.g., at age 7 they had a mean IQ of 121 vs. 87 for controls), but they have also run well ahead of expectancies for a normal population of age peers at large. The key message from this impressive demonstration is that systematic, early competence acquisition seems to pave the way for effective later adaptations in key life spheres.

The main sense of the program development and research efforts we are describing here is as follows. We now know that several pivotal competencies, on the surface quite far removed from mental health's classic terrain, can be taught effectively to young children and that their acquisition radiates positively to adaptations and behaviors that are, indeed, of prime concern to mental health. Symptoms and problem behaviors are reduced after acquisition of these skills. Health has been proactively engineered, so to speak, through skill acquisition. This is a message we cannot afford to repress; it is both a paradigmatic example and further mandate for intensified primary prevention efforts.

However promising the competence training approach to date has been, it should be seen as just one model—not as a bible. We urgently need a fuller and clearer understanding of the nature of core competencies in children—how they relate to each other and, even more important, how these may radiate to interpersonal adjustment. We need to understand what changes take place with development in the nature of essential competencies. As competencies that radiate to adjustment are identified, curricula and methods for helping young children acquire them must be developed. The effectiveness of those curricula, as well as their actual behavioral and adjustive consequences, must be carefully evaluated. That is a complex and time-consuming challenge—one that must be met by a concerted effort—not by small, isolated programs or small research grants. The costs will be substantial but so is the potential reward—a healthier, happier, more effective, better adjusted next generation, on the positive side, and cutting down the flow of those types of emotional dysfunctions and behavioral aberrations that are at once socially draining, degrading, costly, and destructive of human beings.

Competence training, though unquestionably a powerful tool for primary prevention, is not the only one. A second strategy, also with high potential, is the analysis and modification of social systems. This second strategy can be applied at multiple levels, from broad to narrow. It rests on the view that people's (especially children's) development, adaptation, and effectiveness are significantly shaped by the qualities of a relatively few high impact environments in which they live (e.g., families and schools and communities). Environments can be many things. One thing they cannot be is neutral. Whether planned or by default, they are factors that either facilitate or impede the growth and adaptation of their inhabitants. The following section illustrates research-based efforts to change environments, including social environments, constructively. The first and most impactful social system is the infant-caregiver relationship.

Broussard (1976) has demonstrated, under careful research conditions, negative later outcomes in first-born children whose mothers perceived them negatively shortly after birth and a month later. In those cases in which the mother reported negative attitudes toward the infant at birth and also a month later, follow-up studies through age 11 have shown a high risk of emotional disturbance in these children. Broussard is now engaged in an intervention study with a sample of these high-risk infants and mothers using family interviews, home visits, and mother-infant groups up to 2 years following birth. Preliminary results show significantly better developmental scores for the intervention children than for intervention-refused and comparison groups. This set of studies again is illustrative. Viewed together with the Klaus and Kennell studies (1976) showing the critical importance of early "bonding" experiences between mother (and/or other caregiver) and infant, certain implications for preventive intervention emerge. Conditions designed to maximize optimal positive social perception of the infant are important to the development of a sense of self-esteem and self-worth.

The demonstration of relationships between characteristics of environments and the emotional well-being of people is not at all limited to the infancy period. Indeed, there are examples of such work involving children of all ages during the school years. Illustratively, Stallings (1975) developed a comprehensive framework for assessing class environments for young school children in Project Follow Through. She reported clear relationships between environmental properties and positive outcomes—academic as well as interpersonal (e.g., cooperativeness, curiosity, persistence). Moos and his colleagues at Stanford (Moos 1973, 1974a, 1974b; Moos and Trickett 1974; Insel and Moos 1974) have pioneered the development of measures of a variety of social environments (e.g., hospital wards, schools, military companies, and work units) and have shown consistent relationships between environmental properties and how people feel and behave in those environments. Environments that score high in relational qualities such as involvement and mutual support, compared to their opposites, appear to have occupants who are less irritable and depressed, more satisfied and comfortable, and have higher self-esteem. Specifically, for high schools, Trickett and Moos (1974) demonstrated that students from classes with high perceived student involvement and close student-teacher relationships reported greater satisfaction and more positive mood states than their opposites.

Although qualities of social environments clearly affect what happens to their occupants, it oversimplifies things to assume that those effects are constant for all people. Several observers have stressed the importance of "ecological-matches," (i.e., environments that are facilitative for one person can strangle another (Hunt 1975))—a point that has been documented empirically in several studies (e.g., Grimes and Allinsmith 1961; Reiss and Dyhdalo 1975). Especially relevant is the extensive work reported by Kelly and his colleagues (Kelly 1968, 1969; Kelly et al. 1971, 1977), who have examined longitudinally the nature of "adaptive" behavior in fluid (high annual pupil turnover) and stable (low annual pupil turnover) high school environments. Their main finding was that what is adaptive in one environment was not in the other. For example, new students integrated much more readily in fluid environments, where personal development was highly valued. By contrast, status and achievement were more important in stable environments. Insel and Moos (1974) bring the "ecological-match" question an important step closer to mental health's prime terrain with the following observation: "A source of distress and ill health is in the situation in which a person attempts to function within an environment with which he is basically incompatible."

The preceding brief summary is simply to establish that there is already a body of data showing that social climate variation relates to person outcomes on variables of central interest to mental health; moreover, such outcomes may differ for different people. Although we still lack a full understanding of those complex relationships, enough is in place to pinpoint future challenges for primary prevention: What *are* the high impact dimensions of the important social environments that shape children? How are they best assessed? What are the relationships between environmental properties and person outcomes (i.e., which qualities facilitate or impede development, and for whom)? Ultimately, the goal for primary prevention is to help to engineer social environments that optimize development for all people.

Research and demonstration strategies based on impactful social systems must rest on prior or concurrent efforts to provide a sound foundation of good health care and nutrition. Good health care before and at the time of birth has preventive impact. Many preventable traumata occur at the time of childbirth, both physiological and psychological, that can affect the later mental health of the child. Prolonged and difficult births often involve anoxia (lack of oxygen) for the infant. Because low birth weight is known to increase the risk of later difficulties, hospital nurseries must be available for premature infants to prevent damage. Psychologically, support from family members and others is important for the woman at the time of childbirth.

Promoting the health of the expectant mother and child during and after pregnancy, together with sound health care to avoid the complications of pregnancy, including prematurity, can materially reduce the incidence of future mental problems.

Clinical observation of many disturbed people documents the important role that identifiable environmental social system stresses play in precipitating emotional breakdown. Situations involving unusual and intense distress often serve as a kind of "natural experiment" establishing this relationship. Thus, children of parents involved in disrupted marriages and children moved from foster home to foster home show a high frequency of emotional disturbance. Adults who lose a job or who experience the loss of a spouse or child often show psychological, physiological, and psychosomatic disturbances. (See Holmes and Rahe 1967; and Dohrenwend and Dohrenwend 1974.)

Although individuals differ in their resistance to environmental pressure, the reduction of environmental stress clearly reduces emotional disturbance. A considerable amount of recent research has related life stresses to subsequent emotional disturbances. The death of a spouse, the loss of a job, going on vacation, marriage, the birth of a child—all are environmental events that may lead to both physical and psychological disturbance.

The individual's social support system is a key factor in determining his or her response to a stressful environmental event (Caplan and Killilea 1976; Collins and Pancoast 1976; Gottlieb 1976). We can point to members of identifiable groups and predict a higher than random chance of their later serious emotional disturbance. Children of adults labeled schizophrenic or alcoholic are more likely to be identified later as emotionally disturbed. Primary grade children who are seen by teachers or peers as having adjustment difficulties have been shown to have higher rates of later emotional problems (Cowen et al. 1973, 1975; Robins 1966; Werner and Smith 1977).

Research on stress reduction is voluminous. Interventions can range from effective sex education for school-age children to "anticipatory guidance" or "emotional inoculation" to "modeling" and/or abreactive approaches before predictable stresses such as elective surgery, all the way through the life cycle to widow-to-widow self-help groups during and following bereavement (Silverman 1976, 1977). Relationships between stress and emotional disturbance are often much less visible or direct than those between environmental toxins and physical illness. But there are exceptions to this rule, one of which is documented more fully in the paragraphs to follow.

Of all social variables that have been studied in relation to the distribution of psychopathology in the population, none has been more consistently and powerfully associated with this distribution than marital status (Bloom 1977). Persons who are divorced or separated have repeatedly been found to be overrepresented among the emotionally disturbed, while persons who are married and living with their spouses have been found to be underrepresented. In a recent review of 11 studies of marital status and the incidence of mental disorder reported during the past 35 years, Crago (1972) found that, without a single exception, admission rates into psychiatric facilities were lowest among the married, intermediate among the widowed and never-married adults, and highest among the divorced and separated. This differential appears to be stable across different age groups (Adler 1953), reasonably stable for each sex separately considered (Thomas and Locke 1963; Malzberg 1964), and as true for Blacks as for Whites (Malzberg 1956). Supportive evidence of these differentials was provided by Bachrach (1975), who noted that "utilization studies [of mental health services] have generally shown that married people have substantially lower utilization rates than nonmarried people and that the highest utilization rates occur among persons whose marriages have been disrupted by separation or divorce."

Not only are highest admission rates to mental hospitals reported for persons with disrupted marriages, but the differential between those rates and similarly calculated rates among the married is substantial. The ratio of admission rates for divorced and separated persons to those for married persons is on the order of 18:1 for males and about 7:1 for females for public inpatient facilities. In the case of admissions into public outpatient clinics, admission rates are again substantially higher for separated or divorced persons than for married persons. Ratios of these admission rates are nearly 7:1 for males and 5:1 for females (Bloom 1977).

Although data documenting the adverse mental health correlates of marital disruption are especially extensive and compelling, that is by no means the only area in which linkages between life stress and emotional upheaval have been shown. Other prominent examples include bereavement, natural disaster, loss of a child, e.g., as in the Sudden Infant Death Syndrome (Goldston 1977), and job loss. It has been said, with good reason, that life stresses and crises involve both danger and opportunity. Such crises are frequent. They menace—often disrupt—the victim's well-being. They have potentially long-term debilitating effects. The challenge for primary prevention is to develop new program models for "at-risk" victims of life stresses—programs that minimize the dangers of stress situations and maximize the opportunities they offer for learning effective new ways of coping.

The task panel reviewed a very large number of studies of social systems and life events that produce high degrees of stress in large numbers of people. It is important, as noted above, to point out that social stress (from child abuse and marital disruption to racism, discrimination, and unemployment) increases the probability of physical and mental breakdown or disturbance. At the same time, because there are no clear-cut cause-specific connections between single identifiable stresses and a subsequent disturbance, the primary prevention strategist cannot always "produce the convincing evidence" of direct linkages of cause and effect so often demanded by research funding agencies.

It should perhaps be stated explicitly that the panel's proposals for program development and research in primary prevention involve what philosophers of science call a major new "paradigm shift" (Kuhn 1970; Rappaport 1977). The area of social stress illustrates the point. The history of efforts to prevent organic disease shows that one particular research paradigm has been remarkably successful in giving us a sound research base for developing preventive methods. That traditional paradigm may be outlined as follows: (1) define a disease or condition that is judged to be in need of prevention and then develop procedures for reliably identifying persons with the condition; (2) study its distribution in terms of time, place, or person characteristics in the population in order to identify factors that appear to be causally related to it; (3) mount and evaluate experimental prevention programs to test the validity of the hypotheses generated by the previous observations.

That paradigm has been enormously successful; it was used, for example, to develop highly effective preventive programs for smallpox and cholera in the 19th century and for rubella and polio in the 20th century. In the case of emotional disorders, general paresis is now preventable, as is psychosis following pellagra—both as a result of this approach.

But there are good reasons to believe that new paradigms are now needed. One such reason is that many emotional disorders do not seem to have a specific biological causal basis; indeed, most result from a multiplicity of interacting factors. Hence, a paradigm that represents a major departure from the earlier model outlined above is now having a much greater impact on our knowledge base. Its steps may be summarized as follows: (1) identify stressful life events or experiences that have undesirable consequences in a significant proportion of the population and develop procedures for reliably identifying persons who have undergone or who are undergoing such events or experiences; (2) study the consequences of those events in a population by contrasting subsequent illness experiences or emotional problems with those of a suitably selected comparison population; (3) mount and evaluate experimental prevention programs aimed at reducing the incidence of such stressful life events and/or at increasing coping skills in managing those events.

This new paradigm assumes that just as a single disorder may come about as a consequence of a variety of stressful life events, any specific stress event may precipitate a variety of disorders, as a result of differing life histories and patterns of strengths and weaknesses in individuals. For example, an unanticipated death, divorce, or a job loss may increase the risk of alcoholism in one person, coronary artery disease in another, depression and suicide in a third,

and a fatal automobile accident in a fourth. That is, this new paradigm begins by recognizing the futility of searching for a unique cause for every disorder. It accepts the likelihood that many disorders can come about as a consequence of any of a variety of causes. With this acceptance comes the realization that successful efforts at the prevention of a vast array of disorders (particularly emotional disorders) can take place without a theory of disorder-specific causative mechanisms.

This section has presented a brief distillation of some of the current knowledge base in three main areas of primary prevention in mental health: (a) competency training emphasizing developmental approaches, (b) the impact of social systems on individual development, and (c) the reduction and management of naturally occurring life development stresses. All three areas already have substantial, promising knowledge bases that not only justify accelerated primary prevention efforts for the future, but that point specifically to areas in which such efforts may be most useful at once.

Recommendations in Primary Prevention

Initiating a significant national effort in primary prevention of mental and emotional disturbances requires that key decisions be made about: (1) the necessary optimizing structures, (2) the needed program emphases, (3) funding mechanisms, and (4) ways of monitoring such efforts to ensure that balance and relevance are maintained.

The task panel's recommendations, though constrained by time pressures, relate to each of the above key components in a national program for primary prevention.

Recommendation 1—Structural

A coordinated national effort is required if significant progress toward the prevention of emotional disorders is to take place. The components of that effort must include:

(a) A Center for Primary Prevention within the National Institute of Mental Health (NIMH).

(b) Primary Prevention Specialists assigned to each of the 10 U.S. Public Health Service (USPHS) Regional Offices.

(c) Offices of Primary Prevention in each State-level mental health agency.

(d) A small number of Primary Prevention Field Stations—"model" centers for training, demonstration, and research-strategically located in representative communities and/or universities.

(e) Legislative authorization for earmarked grants available to local agencies including, but not limited to, community mental health centers on a competitive basis for establishing and evaluating primary prevention programs, perhaps paralleling section 204 (Grants for Consultation and Education Services) of the Community Mental Health Centers Act, as amended (Title III of Public Law 94-63).

(f) Significant expansion of professional training and research opportunities in primary prevention.

DISCUSSION OF RECOMMENDATION 1

A Center for Primary Prevention within NIMH should have the necessary (1) authorizations, (2) monetary resources, and (3) staff to carry out the following functions:

(a) Serve as the "lead agency," with convening authority, to bring together representatives of other Federal departments to discuss, plan, and implement primary prevention activities in which overlapping interests exist;

(b) Prepare and disseminate critical reviews of theory, programs, and research in the area of primary prevention. Such reviews should include periodic surveys of the state of the art and of practitioner needs; the assembling of available knowledge; the preparing of curriculum materials and teaching aids; the identifying of promising areas for applied research and field trials; and promising leads for new research and program development;

(c) Convene conferences and workshops bringing together appropriate persons to discuss,

and review research and practice issues in, primary prevention;

(d) Assist in the development of State-level Offices of Primary Prevention;

(e) Award, with its own review committee mechanism, contracts and grants for research and training in primary prevention. High priority should be given to the allocation of funds for postprofessional, public-health-oriented education for established mental health professionals who can then provide leadership for program development at both State and local levels and who would be in a position to train and supervise others in the field;

(f) Help institutions of higher education to develop curriculum materials for training in primary prevention;

(g) Develop priorities and policy recommendations for program development in primary prevention; and

(h) Publish a professional-level scientific journal in primary prevention.

In order to carry out these objectives the proposed Center for Primary Prevention should establish an advisory group composed of representatives of all relevant agencies and institutions. The advisory group should include, but not be limited to, mental health professionals.

The recommendation that a Center for Primary Prevention be established within NIMH does not preclude establishing similar centers within other appropriate Federal agencies and an interagency mechanism for coordinating Federal efforts by all relevant departments.

Primary prevention specialists in USPHS Regional Offices should provide the impetus for program development within each region and should serve as the major link between State-level Offices of Primary Prevention, local community mental health centers, and other agencies interested in primary prevention program development and training on the one hand and the NIMH Center for Primary Prevention on the other. Such linkages would provide an excellent mechanism for alerting staff within the Center for Primary Prevention about issues of regional concern, needs for specific curriculum materials, and difficulties in implementing programs or research studies.

State-level Offices of Primary Prevention should be responsible for maintaining an overview of each State's governmental structure in order to encourage the development of primary prevention programs. As States have a variety of organizational structures, in terms of relationships of mental health and general health care, public health, welfare, and education, State-level Offices of Primary Prevention should be designed to provide wide-ranging interaction with all of the human service components of State government. State-level Offices of Primary Prevention should seek to provide consultation and financial inducements to local communities interested in developing or expanding primary prevention activities.

It may be necessary, at least initially, to subsidize State-level Offices of Primary Prevention through a Federal funding or matching mechanism.

Primary Prevention Field Stations should function as one key component of the NIMH Center for Primary Prevention's research and demonstration program. they should have clear administrative linkages in the Center.

Field stations should be able to join with the NIMH Center in publishing a professional-level scientific journal in primary prevention. They should provide ongoing training in the practice of primary prevention and in primary prevention research for persons charged with such responsibilities in institutions and agencies across the country.

Field stations should not only conduct basic research on ways to reduce significantly the incidence of emotional disorders, but should also foster long-range field trials to evaluate preventive strategies and to develop feasible dissemination mechanisms for those shown to be effective.

Recommendation 2—Structural

There should be a legislative mandate and Executive Order to the relevant Government agencies (such as the Office of Education, the Office of Child Development, the National Institutes of Health, and other relevant components of the Department of Health, Education,

and Welfare, the Departments of Agriculture, Labor, and Housing and Urban Development) setting up appropriate mechanisms, supported by funding, to develop primary prevention programs. As indicated earlier, the NIMH Center for Primary Prevention should be authorized as the convenor of such groups to coordinate and provide technical assistance for their efforts. There should be an annual reporting to appropriate review agencies of the accomplishments of this effort.

DISCUSSION OF RECOMMENDATION 2

Primary prevention activities often involve agencies other than traditional mental health systems. Preventive intervention is frequently organized to provide assistance to normal children and adults in developmental age-appropriate tasks. Many of these prevention efforts are directed toward ensuring a nurturant environment, physically and psychologically, for the fetus, infant, and child. Many Federal agencies have important and relevant areas of responsibility for such preventive efforts.

Recommendation 3—Emphases

Top priority for program development, training, and research in primary prevention should be directed toward infants and young children and their environments including, particularly, efforts to reduce sources of stress and incapacity and to increase the competence and coping skills in the young.

DISCUSSION OF RECOMMENDATION 3

Both the logic and evidence of primary prevention support the position that "earlier is better." Although serious effective efforts to reduce distress and emotional disorder can, and should, be developed for the entire lifespan, and especially known stress periods, the panel agrees that helping children to develop soundly from the start and to maintain good mental health must be our first priority. Listed below are several proposed program initiatives to promote the mental health of infants, children, and others throughout the lifespan, with a focus on developmental, ongoing processes:

1. *Promoting maternal-infant bonding and facilitating positive maternal perceptions of the newborn child.* Needed strategies in this area include: prenatal parent education; group programs (postdelivery) to enhance the mother's sense of competence and self-esteem in her new role; and adaptation of hospital environments and regulations to create conditions that favor positive mother-child bonding.

2. *Developing systematic educational programs in such preventively oriented areas as:*

(a) Education for marriage and parenthood, beginning in the early school years and continuing through adolescence;

(b) Prenatal parent-education programs, including information on exercise and nutrition during pregnancy, and family planning programs, based on collaboration between mental health and public health workers;

(c) School-based educational programs from kindergarten to sixth grade and beyond to encourage responsible interpersonal relationships, including but not limited to sexual relationships;

(d) Parenting programs that focus on age-appropriate content as children develop;

(e) Genetic counseling, permitting the development of screening programs including amniocentesis and selective (and optional) terminations of pregnancy in cases of clear-cut damage or defect in the fetus.

3. *Utilization of existing program knowledge an development of further programs for building competencies in young children.* Examples of relevant competencies include interpersonal problem solving, realistic goal setting, role taking, and curiosity (question-asking) behaviors.

4. *Analyzing and understanding the nature of social environments,* such as primary grade classrooms, and their effects on young children's educational and personal development, with the ultimate goal of creating environments that maximize the development of all children's potential.

5. *Programs designed to prevent the stressful effects of life crises experienced by high-risk groups such as:*

(a) Parents of premature babies;

(b) Parents who lose a child through death;

(c) Surviving siblings when a child dies;

(d) Parents of malformed children;

(e) Parents who must leave their infants in the hospital beyond the discharge of the mother or those who must rehospitalize an infant. A related example is the development of specific programs to prevent postpartum reactions in parents.

6. *Programs that deal with the mental health needs of children hospitalized for physical conditions.* Approaches must be developed that:

(a) Prepare children for hospitalization by reducing the stress potential of such experiences;

(b) Reduce parents' own anxieties about a child's hospitalization and also provide them with skills to help the child cope successfully with the experience;

(c) Modify hospital procedures so as to reduce the trauma of hospitalization for both children and parents.

7. *Programs designed to reduce stresses associated with major later-life crises such as:*

(a) Bereavement;

(b) Marital disruption (including particularly its negative effects on children);

(c) Job loss;

(d) Natural disaster;

(e) Premature parenthood.

8. *Promoting the development of helping networks and mutual support groups* that deal preventively both with everyday crises and ex-

traordinary crisis situations. Examples of such programs include:

(a) Identifying and working supportively with natural "neighborhood helpers";

(b) Widow-to-widow programs for the recently bereaved.

Closely related is the need to support the naturally occurring everyday help-giving efforts of first-line community "caregivers" who interact continually with inter-personally distressed people (e.g., beauticians, bartenders, divorce attorneys).

9. *Establishing new initiatives and directions in training a wide variety of professionals including those in mental health* as, for example, in:

(a) Public health theory and practice, including epidemiology;

(b) Human growth and development as these relate to prevention efforts.

10. *An increasing focus on the mental health aspects of nutrition.* Nutritional disturbances (e.g., undernutrition and/or overnutrition) are known to relate directly to classical "mental health" conditions such as obesity, school maladjustment, and school failure. We need conjoint nutritional programs and mental health designed to cut down the flow of such adverse end states.

Recommendation 4—Emphases

The national effort to reduce societal stresses produced by racism, poverty, sexism, ageism, and urban blight must be strengthened as an important strategy for primary prevention.

DISCUSSION OF RECOMMENDATION 4

The task panel recognizes that the President's Commission on Mental Health has no magical power to eliminate the above sources of societal stress. That does not, however, deter us from taking leadership in pointing clearly to them as factors capable of producing profound emotional

distress in individuals. Thus, the panel strongly supports efforts to reduce racism and related forms of prejudice as important aspects of a comprehensive national program for primary prevention.

The task panel was often reminded that mental health services are disproportionately available to relatively more affluent, educated, privileged members of the white majority whose first language is English. We are thus compelled to underline the fact that many correlates of emotional distress are economic and cultural. Programs aimed at reducing injustice and discrimination must take into account different linguistic, cultural, and social factors.

Recommendation 5—Funding

If primary prevention is to be a major priority in mental health, funds to support new initiatives in training, program development, and research must be increased at least to $12–$15 million immediately and rise gradually to approximately $20–$25 million by 1985.

DISCUSSION OF RECOMMENDATION 5

According to our best current information the estimated total annual expenditures of NIMH for primary prevention is about $2–$3 million. There is no special NIMH primary prevention program and only one mental health professional is specifically designated as responsible for such work there. Clearly, primary prevention has *not* been a signficant activity at NIMH. Equally clearly, constructive change requires a significant funding increase with specific instructions that such monies be spent to increase program development, training, and research in this field.

Recommendation 6—Monitoring

We recommend that the proposed Federal program in primary prevention be mandated for at least a 10-year period. This new program should be overviewed by a citizens' advisory committee to include experienced persons in the several professions concerned with primary prevention as well as "consumer" and minority group representatives. Such an advisory group should be concerned with both program emphases and management.

DISCUSSION OF RECOMMENDATION 6

Primary prevention efforts are directed toward groups of persons who are not showing individual patterns of distress or disturbance; such efforts often are designed to strengthen competence and coping skills, not to excise weaknesses. The task panel seeks to ensure that primary prevention funding be directed to a wide range of programs. In the past, mental health efforts, because of the health-illness model of individual treatment, have been largely restricted to illness-oriented interventions. We believe, most urgently, that effective primary prevention efforts will be more social and educational than rehabilitative in nature and recommend that a citizens' advisory committee be created to ensure that emphasis.

References

Adler, L. M. The relationship of marital status to incidence of and recovery from mental illness. *Social Forces,* 32, 185–194. 1953.

Albee, George W. and Joffe, Justin M., eds. *Primary Prevention of Psychopathology: The Issues.* Hanover, N.H.: The University Press of New England, 1977.

Allen, G. J., Chinsky, J. M., Larcen, S. W., Lochman, J. E., and Selinger, H. V. *Community Psychology and the Schools: A Behaviorally Oriented Multilevel Preventive Approach.* Hillsdale, N.J.: Lawrence Erlbaum Associates, 1976.

Bachrach, L. L. *Marital Status and Mental Disorder: An Analytical Review.* Washington, D.C.: U.S. Government Printing Office, DHEW Pub. No. (ADM) 75-217, 1975.

Bloom, B. L. *Community Mental Health: A General Introduction.* Monterey: Brooks-Cole, 1977.

Broussard, Elsie. Neonatal prediction and outcome at 10/11 years. *Child Psychiatry and Human Development,* 7 (2), Winter 1976.

Brown, Bertram S. Remarks to the World Federation for Mental Health, Vancouver, British Columbia, August 24, 1977.

Bruce, P. Relationship of self-acceptance to other variables with sixth-grade children oriented in self-understanding. *Journal of Educational Psychology,* 1958, 49, 229–238.

Caplan, G., and Killilea, M., eds. *Support Systems and Mutual Help: Multi-disciplinary explorations.* New York: Grune and Stratton, 1976.

Carter, Jimmy. Hospital cost containment. *National Journal,* 9:964–965, 1977.

Carter, Rosalynn. Remarks to the World Federation for Mental Health, Vancouver, British Columbia, p. 1, August 25, 1977.

Collins, A. H. and Pancoast, D. L. *Natural Helping Networks: A Strategy for Prevention.* Washington, D.C.: National Association of Social Workers, 1976.

Cowen, E. Baby-steps toward primary prevention. *American Journal of Community Psychology,* 1977, 5, 1–22.

Cowen, E. L., Pedersen, A., Babigian, H., Izzo, L. D. and Trost, M. A. Long-term follow-up of early detected vulnerable children. *Journal of Consulting and Clinical Psychology,* 1973, 41, 438–446.

Cowen, E. L., Trost, M. A., Lorion, R. P., Dorr, D., Izzo, L. D., and Isaacson, R. V. *New Ways in School Mental Health: Early Detection and Prevention of School Maladaptation.* New York: Human Sciences Press, Inc., 1975.

Crago, M. A. Psychopathology in married couples. *Psychological Bulletin,* 1972, 77, 114–128.

Dohrenwend, B. S. and Dohrenwend, B. P., eds. *Stressful Life Events.* New York: John Wiley & Sons, 1974.

Elardo, P. T. and Caldwell, B. M. The effects of an experimental social development program on children in the middle childhood period. Unpublished, 1976.

Elardo, P. T. and Cooper, M. *AWARE: Activities for Social Development.* Reading, Mass.: Addison-Wesley, 1977.

Gesten, E. L.; Flores de Apodaca, R.; Rains, M. H.; Weissberg, R. P. and Cowen, E. L. Promoting peer related social competence in young children. In: Kent, M. W. and Rolf, J. E., eds. *Primary Prevention of Psychopathology, Vol. 3. Promoting Social Competence and Coping in Children.* Hanover, N.H.: University Press of New England, 1978.

Goldston, S. E. An overview of primary prevention programming. In: Klein, D. C. and Goldston, S. E., eds. *Primary Prevention: An Idea Whose Time Has Come.* Washington, D.C.: U.S. Government Printing Office, DHEW Pub. No. (ADM) 77-447, 1977, pp. 23–40.

Gottfried, N. W. Effects of early intervention programs. In: Miller, K. S. and Dreger, R. M., eds. *Comparative Studies of Blacks and Whites in the United States: Quantitative Studies in Social Relations.* New York: Seminar Press, 1973.

Gottlieb, B. H. Lay influences on the utilization and provision of health services: A review. *Canadian Psychological Review,* 1976, 17, 126–136.

Griggs, J. W. and Bonney, M. E. Relationship between "causal" orientation and acceptance of others, "self-ideal self" congruence, and mental health changes for fourth- and fifth-grade children. *Journal of Educational Research,* 1970, 63, 471–477.

Grimes, J. W. and Allinsmith, W. Compulsivity, anxiety, and school achievement. *Merrill-Palmer Quarterly,* 1961, 7, 247–261.

Heber, R. "Research in Prevention of Socio-Cultural Mental Retardation." Address presented at the 2nd Vermont Conference on the Primary Prevention of Psychopathology. Burlington, Vt., 1976.

Holmes, T. H. and Rahe, R. H. The social readjustment rating scale. *Journal of Psychosomatic Research,* 1967, 11, 213–218.

Horowitz, F. D. and Paden, L. Y. The effectiveness of environmental intervention programs. In: Caldwell, B. M. and Ricciuti, H., eds. *Review of Child Development Research (Vol. 3).* New York: Russell Sage Foundation, 1973.

Hunt, D. E. Person-environment interaction: A challenge found wanting before it was tried. *Review of Educational Research,* 1975, 45, 209–230.

Insel, P. M. and Moos, R. H. The social environment. In: Insel, P. M. and Moos, R. H., eds. *Health and Social Environment.* Lexington, Mass.: Lexington Books, 1974.

Jason, L. Early secondary prevention with disadvantaged preschool children. *American Journal of Community Psychology,* 1975, 3, 33–46.

Joint Commission on Mental Illness and Health. *Action for Mental Health.* New York: Basic Books, 1961.

Kelly, J. G. Towards an ecological conception of preventive interventions. In: Carter, J. W., ed. *Research Contributions from Psychology to Community Mental Health.* New York: Behavioral Publications, 1968.

Kelly, J. G. Naturalistic observations in contrasting social environments. In: Willems, E. P. and Raush, H. L., eds. *Naturalistic Viewpoints in Psychological Research.* New York: Holt, Rinehart and Winston, 1969.

Kelly, J. G., et al. The coping process in varied high school environments. In: Feldman, M. J., ed. *Studies in Psychotherapy and Behavior Change, No. 2: Theory and Research in Community Mental Health.* Buffalo: State University of New York, 1971.

Kelly, J. G. et al. *The High School: Students and Social Contexts in Two Midwestern Communities.* Community Psychology Series, No. 4. New York: Behavioral Publications, Inc., 1977.

Kessler, M. and Albee, G. W. Primary prevention. *Annual Review of Psychology.* 1975, 26, 557–591.

Klaus, M. H. and Kennell, J. H. *Maternal-Infant Bonding.* St. Louis: C. V. Mosby Co., 1976.

Klein, D. C. and Goldston, S. E. *Primary Prevention: An Idea Whose Time Has Come.* Washington, D.C.: U.S. Government Printing Office, DHEW Pub. No. (ADM) 77-447, 1977.

Kuhn, T. S. *Structure of Scientific Revolutions.* 2nd ed. Chicago: University of Chicago Press, 1970.

Malzberg, B. Marital status and mental disease among Negroes in New York State. *Journal of Nervous and Mental Disease,* 1956, 123, 457–465.

Malzberg, B. Marital status and incidence of mental disease. *International Journal of Social Psychiatry,* 1964, 10, 19–26.

Mead, Margaret. Conversation with Mrs. Rosalynn Carter, The White House, June 28, 1977, as reported by Mrs. Carter in her remarks to the World Federation for Mental Health, p. 1.

Moore, Barrington Jr. *Reflection on the Causes of Human Misery and Upon Certain Proposals to Eliminate Them.* Boston: Beacon Press, 1970.

Moos, R. H. Conceptualizations of human environments. *American Psychologist,* 1973, 28, 652–665.

Moos, R. H. *The Social Climate Scales: An Overview.* Palo Alto: Consulting Psychologists Press, Inc., 1974a.

Moos, R. H. *Evaluating Treatment Environments: A Social Ecological Approach.* New York: John Wiley and Sons, 1974b.

Moos, R. H. and Trickett, E. J. *Manual: Classroom Environment Scale.* Palo Alto: Consulting Psychologists Press, Inc., 1974.

Muuss, R. E. The effects of a one and two year causal learning program. *Journal of Personality,* 1960, 28, 479–491.

National Association for Mental Health. Primary prevention of mental disorders with emphasis on prenatal and perinatal periods. *Action Guidelines.* Mimeographed. Undated.

Ojemann, R. H. Investigations on the effects of teacher understanding and appreciation of behavior dynamics. In:

Caplan, G., ed. *Prevention of Mental Disorders in Children.* New York: Basic Books, 1961.

Ojemann, R. H. Incorporating psychological concepts in the school curriculum. In: Clarizio, H. P., ed. *Mental Health and the Educative Process.* Chicago: Rand-McNally, 1969.

Pauling, Linus. Orthomolecular psychiatry. *Science,* 1968, 160, 265–271.

Platt, J. J., Altmann, N. and Altmann, D. "Dimensions of Real-Life Problem-Solving Thinking in Adolescent Psychiatric Patients." Paper presented at Eastern Psychological Association Meetings, Washington, D.C., 1973.

Rappaport, J. *Community Psychology: Values, Research and Action.* New York: Holt, Rinehart and Winston, 1977.

Reiss, S. and Dyhdalo, N. Persistence, achievement and open-space environments. *Journal of Educational Psychology,* 1975, 67, 506–513.

Richmond, Julius. Remarks made at his swearing-in ceremony as Assistant Secretary of Health, Department of Health, Education, and Welfare, Washington, D.C., July 13, 1977.

Robins, L. *Deviant Children Grown Up.* Baltimore, Md.: Williams & Wilkins Co., 1966.

Shattuck, L. et al. Report of the sanitary commission of Massachusetts, 1850. Quoted by Fielding, Jonathan E. Health promotion—Some notions in search of a constituency. *American Journal of Public Health,* 67:1082, November 1977.

Shure, M. B. and Spivack, G. "A Preventive Mental Health Program for Young 'Inner City' Children: The Second (Kindergarten) Year." Paper presented at the American Psychological Association, Chicago, 1975a.

Shure, M. B. and Spivack, G. Training mothers to help their children solve real-life problems. Paper presented at the Society of Research in Child Development, Denver, 1975b.

Silverman, P. R. The widow as a caregiver in a program of preventive intervention with other widows. In: Caplan, G. and Killilea, M., eds. *Support Systems and Mutual Help: Multidisciplinary Explorations.* New York: Grune and Stratton, 1976, pp. 233–244.

Silverman, P. R. Mutual help groups for the widowed. In: Klein, D. C. and Goldston, S. E., eds. *Primary Prevention: An Idea Whose Time Has Come.* Washington, D.C.: U.S. Government Printing Office, DHEW Pub. No. (ADM) 77-447, 1977, pp. 76–79.

Spivack, G. and Levine, M. *Self-Regulation in Acting-Out and Normal Adolescents.* Report M-4531, National Institutes of Health, 1963.

Spivack, G., Platt, J. J., and Shure, M. B. *The Problem-Solving Approach to Adjustment.* San Francisco: Jossey-Bass, 1976.

Spivack, G. and Shure, M. B. *Social Adjustment of Young Children.* San Francisco: Jossey-Bass, 1974.

Spivack, G. and Shure, M. B. Preventively oriented cognitive education of preschoolers. In: Klein, D. C. and Goldston, S. E., eds. *Primary Prevention: An Idea Whose Time Has Come.* Washington, D.C.: U.S. Government Printing Office, DHEW Pub. No. (ADM) 77-447, 1977.

Stallings, J. Implementation and child effects of teaching practices on Follow Through classrooms. *Monographs of the Society for Research on Child Development,* 1975, 40 (Serial No. 163).

Stamps, L. W. "Enhancing Success in School for Deprived Children by Teaching Realistic Goal Setting." Paper presented at Society for Research in Child Development, Denver, 1975.

Stone, G. L., Hinds, W. C. and Schmidt, G. W. Teaching mental health behaviors to elementary school children. *Professional Psychology,* 1975, 6, 34–40.

Thomas, D. S. and Locke, B. Z. Marital status, education and occupational differentials in mental disease. *Milbank Memorial Fund Quarterly,* 1963, 41, 145–160.

Trickett, E. J. and Moos, R. H. Personal correlates of contrasting environments: Student satisfaction in high school classrooms. *American Journal of Community Psychology,* 1974, 2, 1–12.

Werner, E. E. and Smith, R. S. *Kauai's Children Come of Age.* Honolulu, Hawaii: University of Hawaii Press, 1977.

At the time this report was issued, the members of the Task Panel on Prevention of the President's Commission on Mental Health were *George W. Albee,* University of Vermont; *Bernard L. Bloom,* University of Colorado; *Elsie Broussard,* University of Pittsburgh; *Emory L. Cowen,* University of Rochester; *L. Erlenmeyer-Kimling,* New York State Psychiatric Institute; *Ernesto Gomez,* El Centro Del Barrio, San Antonio, Texas; *Donald C. Klein,* Ellicott City, Maryland; *Roy Menninger,* the Menninger Foundation; *Vera S. Paster,* New York City Board of Education; *John Reilley,* Winston and Shawn, Washington, D.C.; and *Vivian K. Rubinger,* Palm Beach County Comprehensive Community Mental Health Center, Inc., West Palm Beach, Florida.

The Task Panel on Prevention wishes to express special appreciation to Richard A. Millstein, Staff Liaison to the Panel, for his extraordinary contributions to the work of the Panel and his invaluable assistance to Panel members.

The Task Panel also wishes to acknowledge the invaluable assistance of Stephen Goldston, National Institute of Mental Health, Rockville, Maryland.

List of Articles by Author

Albee, G. W., & Kessler, M. Evaluating individual deliverers: Private practice and professional standards review organizations. *Professional Psychology*, 1977, *8*, 502–515.

APA Task Force on the Consumer Oriented Health Insurance Proposal. Consumer oriented health insurance (COHI) proposal: *Criteria for national health insurance*. Washington, D.C.: American Psychological Association, 1978.

American Psychological Association. Standards for providers of psychological services. *American Psychologist*, 1977, *32*, 495–505.

Buklad, W. Statement on the PSRO Program (PL92-603) of the Social Security Act Amendments, submitted to the House Ways and Means Subcommittee on Health, September 30, 1977. Washington, D.C.: American Psychological Association, 1977.

Califano, J. Memorandum for the President on the basic decision in developing a national health insurance plan: A summary of four sample plans, May 22, 1978. *The Blue Sheet*, June 14, 1978, pp. S8–S17.

Carter, J. Presidential directive on a national health plan: Ten principles for national health insurance, White House, July 29, 1978. *The Blue Sheet*, August 2, 1978, pp. S1–S2.

Claiborn, W. J., & Zaro, J. S. The development of a peer review system: The APA/CHAMPUS contract.

Cohen, L. H. Factors affecting the utilization of mental health evaluation research findings. *Professional Psychology*, 1977, *8*, 526–534.

Crowell, E. Redistribution aspects of psychotherapy's inclusion in national health insurance: A summary. *American Psychologist*, 1977, *32*, 731–737.

Cummings, N. A. Mental health and national health insurance: A case history of the struggle for professional autonomy.

Cummings, N. A. Medicare reform: Testimony to the U.S. Senate. *The Clinical Psychologist*, 1976, *30*, 21–23.

Cummings, N. A. Prolonged (ideal) versus short-term (realistic) psychotherapy. *Professional Psychology*, 1977, *8*, 491–501.

Cummings, N. A. The anatomy of psychotherapy under national health insurance. *American Psychologist*, 1977, *32*, 711–718.

Cummings, N. A., & Follette, W. T. Brief psychotherapy and medical utilization. In H. Dörken and Associates (Eds.), *The professional psychologist today*. San Francisco: Jossey-Bass, 1976.

Cummings, N. A., & Follette, W. T. Psychiatric services and medical utilization in a prepaid health plan setting: Part II. *Medical Care*, 1968, *6*, 31–41.

Davis, K. National health insurance: Choice among alternative approaches. In *National health insurance: Benefits, costs, and consequences*. Washington, D.C.: The Brookings Institute, 1975.

Davis, K. A national plan for financing health care. In *National health insurance: Benefits, costs, and consequences*. Washington, D.C.: The Brookings Institute, 1975.

DeLeon, P. H. Implications of national health policies for professional psychology. *Professional Psychology*, 1977, *8*, 263–268.

DeLeon, P. H. Psychology and the Carter administration. *American Psychologist*, 1977, *32*, 750–751.

Dörken, H. Avenues to legislative success. *American Psychologist*, 1977, *32*, 738–745.

Dörken, H. CHAMPUS ten-state claim experience for mental disorder: Fiscal year 1975. *American Psychologist*, 1977, *32*, 697–710.

Dörken, H. Laws, regulations, and psychological practice. In H. Dörken and Associates (Eds.), *The professional psychologist today.* San Francisco: Jossey-Bass, 1976.

Dörken, H. The practicing psychologist: A growing force in private sector health care delivery. *Professional Psychology,* 1977, *8,* 269–274.

Dörken, H., & Morrison, D. JCAH standards for accreditation of psychiatric facilities: Implications for the practice of psychology. *American Psychologist,* 1976, *31,* 774–784.

Dörken, H., & Webb, J. Licensed psychology in health care: A survey of their practices.

Edwards, D. W., Green, L. R., Abramowitz, S. I., & Davidson, C. V. National health insurance psychotherapy, and the poor. *American Psychologist,* 1979, *34,* 411–419.

Follette, W. T., & Cummings, N. A. Psychiatric services and medical utilization in a prepaid health plan setting. *Medical Care,* 1967, *5,* 25–35.

Goldberg, I. D., Krantz, G., & Locke, B. Z. Effect of a short-term outpatient psychiatric therapy benefit on the utilization of medical services in a prepaid group practice medical program. *Medical Care,* 1970, *8,* 419–428.

Gottfredson, G. D., & Dyer, S. E. Health service providers in psychology. *American Psychologist,* 1978, *33,* 314–338.

Hadley, S. W., & Strupp, H. H. Evaluations of treatment in psychotherapy: Naivete or necessity? *Professional Psychology,* 1977, *8,* 478–490.

Heck, E. T. Professional psychology and public programs: A critique. *Professional Psychology,* 1976, *7,* 420–427.

Hess, H. F. Entry requirements for professional practice of psychology. *American Psychologist,* 1977, *32,* 365–368.

Institute of Medicine, National Academy of Sciences. Assessing quality in health care: An evaluation— Summary and recommendations. In *Assessing quality in health care: An evaluation.* Washington, D.C.: National Academy of Sciences, 1976.

Karon, B. P., & VandenBos, G. R. Cost/benefit analysis: Psychologist vs. psychiatrist for schizophrenics. *Professional Psychology,* 1976, *7,* 107–111.

Kiesler, C. A. National health insurance: Testimony to the House of Representatives, November 14, 1975. *The Clinical Psychologist,* 1976, *30,* 18–21.

Kiesler, C. A. The status of psychology as a profession and a science. In T. A. Williams, & J. Johnson (Eds.), *Health in the 21st Century.* Lexington, Massachusetts: Lexington Books. In press.

Kiesler, C. A. Testimony presented at the National Health Insurance Hearing, October 4, 1977, held by the Secretary of Health, Education, and Welfare.

Kiesler, C. A. Training in professional psychology: National needs. *Psychotherapy Bulletin,* 1978, *12,* 13–16.

Kiesler, C. A. The training of psychiatrists and psychologists. *American Psychologist,* 1977, *32,* 107–108.

Korman, M. Recommendations of the conference. *Levels and patterns of professional training in psychology* (The Vail Conference). Washington, D.C.: American Psychological Association, 1976.

Liaison Group for Mental Health. Report of the National Health Insurance Panel. Washington, D.C.: Author, 1976.

Liptzin, B., Stockdill, J. W., & Brown, B. S. A federal view of mental health program evaluation. *Professional Psychology,* 1977, *8,* 543–552.

McSweeny, A. J. Including psychotherapy in national health insurance: Insurance guidelines and other proposed solutions. *American Psychologist,* 1977, *32,* 722–730.

Mills, D. H., Wellner, A. J., & VandenBos, G. R. The *National Register* survey: The first comprehensive study of all licensed/certified psychologists.

Morrison, J. K. An argument for mental patient advisory boards. *Professional Psychology,* 1976, *7,* 127–131.

National Institute of Mental Health, Department of Health, Education, and Welfare. Federal employees health benefits. Appendix II of *Draft report:* The financing, utilization and quality of mental health care in the United States. Rockville, Md.: Office of Program Development and Analysis, National Institute of Mental Health, April 1976.

National Institute of Mental Health, Department of Health, Education, and Welfare. Quality assurance for mental health care. In *Draft report: The financing, utilization, and quality of mental health care in the United States.* Rockville, Md.: Office of Program Development and Analysis, National Institute of Mental Health, April 1976.

National Institute of Mental Health, Department of Health, Education, and Welfare. Utilization and costs of mental health services. In *Draft report: The financing, utilization, and quality of mental health care in the United States.* Rockville, Md.: Office of Program Development and Analysis, National Institute of Mental Health, April 1976.

Olbrisch, M. E. Psychotherapeutic interventions in physical health: Effectiveness and economic efficiency. *American Psychologist,* 1977, *32,* 761–777.

Perloff, R., & Perloff, E. Evaluation of psychological service delivery programs: The state of the art. *Professional Psychology,* 1977, *8,* 379–388.

President's Commission on Mental Health. Report to the President from the President's Commission on Mental Health (Vol. 4), Washington, D.C.: U.S. Government Printing Office, 1978.

Richards, J. M., & Gottfredson, G. D. Geographic distribution of U.S. psychologists: A human ecological analysis. *American Psychologist,* 1978, *33,* 1–9.

Rie, H. E. Psychology, mental health, and the public interest. *American Psychologist,* 1977, *32,* 1–4.

Sacuzzo, D. P. The practice of psychotherapy in America: Issues and trends. *Professional Psychology,* 1977, *8,* 297–306.

Schacht, T., & Nathan, P. R. But is it good for the psychologists? Appraisal and status of DSM-III. *American Psychologist,* 1977, *32,* 1017–1025.

Schofield, W. The psychologist as a health professional. *Professional Psychology,* 1976, *7,* 5–8.

Schulberg, H. C. Issues in the evaluation of community mental health programs. *Professional Psychology,* 1977, *8,* 560–572.

Smith, M. L., & Glass, G. V. Meta-analysis of psychotherapy outcome studies. *American Psychologist,* 1977, *32,* 752–760.

Stewart, D. W. Psychology and accounting: An interface or a red face. *Professional Psychology,* 1977, *8,* 178–184.

Strupp, H. H., & Hadley, S. W. A tripartite model of mental health and therapeutic outcomes: With special reference to negative effects in psychotherapy. *American Psychologist,* 1977, *32,* 187–196.

Sussna, E. Measuring mental health program benefits: Efficiency or justice? *Professional Psychology,* 1977, *8,* 435–441.

Task Force on Continuing Evaluation in National Health Insurance, American Psychological Association. Continuing evaluation and accountability controls for a national health insurance program. *American Psychologist,* 1978, *32,* 305–313.

Task Force on Health Research, American Psychological Association. Contributions of psychology to health research: Patterns, problems, and potentials. *American Psychologist,* 1976, *31,* 263–274.

Task Panel on Prevention. Report to the President's Commission on Mental Health. *President's Commission on Mental Health,* 1978, *4,* 1822–1863.

Wiggins, J. G. The psychologist as a health professional in the health maintenance organization. *Professional Psychology,* 1976, *7,* 9–13.

Willens, J. G. Colorado Medicare study: A history. *American Psychologist,* 1977, *32,* 746–749.

Wright, L. Psychology as a health profession. *The Clinical Psychologist,* 1976, *29,* 16–19.

Index

Page numbers in boldface in individual author entries refer to articles by that author.